stirbt mit der Wahrheit.

David Irving is the son of a Royal Navy commander. Educated at Imperial College of Science & Technology and at University College London, he subsequently spent a year in Germany working in a Ruhr steel mill and perfecting his fluency in the language. Among his thirty books the best-known include Hitler's War, The Trail of the Fox: The Life of Field Marshal Rommel, Accident: The Death of General Sikorski, The Rise and Fall of the Luftwaffe, and Göring: a Biography. He has also translated several books by other authors. He lives in Windsor, and has raised five daughters.

David Irving

Goebbels
Mastermind of the Third Reich

"David Irving is in the first rank of Britain's
historical chroniclers"– THE TIMES

F

In Memory of Michael Sheppard

Who Climbed Too Far

This edition was first published 1996 by Focal Point Publications, Duke Street, London W1M 5DJ

Reprinted December 1997 and September 2013

British Library Cataloguing-in-Publication Data. A catalogue record for this book is available from the British Library.

ISBN 978 1872 197 135

This edition printed and bound in Poland by Drukarnia im. A. Półtawskiego, Kielce

Contents

Acknowledgments

WRITING THIS BIOGRAPHY, I have lived in the evil shadow of Dr Joseph Goebbels for over seven years.

Four years into the ordeal, I had the immense good fortune to become the first – and so far only – person to open the complete microfiche record, made by the Nazis in 1944–45, of Goebbels' entire private diaries and papers from 1923 to 1945; the Red Army had placed these in the Soviet secret state archives in Moscow. There they languished until the ninety or so original Agfa boxes containing the 1,600 glass plates, on which Goebbels had had the diaries filmed for safety, were discovered by the Goebbels diaries expert Dr Elke Fröhlich in March 1992. (On behalf of all historians of the period I place on record here our gratitude for the work she has done on the diaries.)

I was able to use the diaries in June and July of the same year, probably the first person to have untied the original knots on those boxes since 1945. With the support of Dr V. P. Tarasov, chief of the Russian Federation's archives, and Dr V. N. Bondarev, chief of the former Soviet secret state archives, I was able to retrieve or copy some five hundred pages of the most important missing passages of the diary, including Goebbels' first diary begun in 1923, the 1933 Reichstag fire, the 1934 Röhm putsch, the 1938 Kristallnacht, the months before the outbreak of war in 1939 and many other historically significant episodes.

The conditions in these archives in Moscow's Viborg Street were, it must be said, challenging: Soviet archives were designed for keeping things secret, and the very notion of a public research room was alien to Soviet archivists.

This one had no microfilm or microfiche reader. After struggling to read the 1,600 fragile glass microfiches (some 75,000 pages) with a thumbnail-sized 12x magnifier on my first visit, I was able, through the generosity of the London *Sunday Times*, to donate a sophisticated film and fiche reader to the Russians on my second visit; the bulky machine arrived back in London, without explanation, one day after I did in July 1992.

What followed was a less enlightened episode. I provided extracts from these diaries to Times Newspapers Ltd in Britain. The *Sunday Times* published them along with *Der Spiegel* in Germany and other major newspapers around the world. I also donated complete sets to the German federal archives (Bundesarchiv) in Koblenz and to the archives of Goebbels' native city Mönchengladbach. Nevertheless, while the international press celebrated the retrieval of the long-lost diaries many rival historians registered something approaching a cry of pain.

Their injured professional *amour propre* proved infectious. While spending half a million pounds promoting its serialization of the diaries' scoop, the *Sunday Times* mentioned the name of the person who acquired them, myself, in the smallest type-size known to man; *Der Spiegel* printed the series for five weeks without mentioning him at all. A Berlin university historian, whose team has been laboring for years on the other volumes of the diaries, reported at length on the 'new find' to a symposium in the United States, again without reference to either Dr Fröhlich, the discoverer – to whom all real credit is due– or to myself.*

The directors of Piper Verlag, Munich, who a few weeks later published an abridged popular edition of the other Goebbels Diaries,† deplored in a German television news bulletin that 'Mr Irving of all people' should have exclusively obtained these sensational missing diaries – and failed to mention either then or in their publication that without reward I had at the last minute made one hundred pages available with which they had filled aching gaps in their publication.

Even more lamentable have been the actions of the German government's federal archives, the Bundesarchiv, to which I also donated many Goebbels documents, including a set of all the diaries I retrieved in Moscow. On the instructions of the minister of the interior, on July 1, 1993 the archive banished me forever from its halls, without notice, two hours before the conclusion of my seven years of research on this subject. It had earlier provided a hundred photos at my expense – but on the minister's instructions it now refused to supply caption information for them.

When I requested the Transit-Film Corporation, which inherited the copyrights of Third Reich movie productions, to provide still photographs of the leading actors and actresses who play a part in the Goebbels story, the firm cautiously inquired of Professor Friedrich Kahlenberg, head of the Bundesarchiv, whether 'special considerations' might apply against helping me! (A copy of this letter fortuitously came into my hands, but not the pictures I had requested.)

The background can only be surmised. Professor Kahlenberg had hurried to Moscow in July 1992 – too late to prevent the Russians from granting me access to the coveted microfiches of the Goebbels Diaries. (There was no reason why the Russians should have denied me access: Several of my books, including those on Arctic naval operations and on Nazi nuclear research, have been published by Soviet printing houses.) The Bundesarchiv has justified its

---

* Dr Jürgen Michael Schulz, of the Berlin Free University, 'Zur Edition der Goebbels Tage-bücher,' a paper presented to the German Studies Association conference, 1992. See its *Newsletter*, xvii, No. 2, winter 1992, 34ff.

† Dr Ralf Georg Reuth (ed.), *Joseph Goebbels Tagebücher*, five vols. (Munich, Zürich, 1992).

banishment, which is without parallel in any other archives, on the ground that my research might harm the interests of the Federal Republic of Germany.

The ban has prevented me from verifying my colleagues' questionable transcriptions of certain key words in the handwritten diaries. I had a list of twenty such words which I wished to double-check against the original negatives; pleading superior orders, the Bundesarchiv's deputy director, Dr Siegfried Büttner, refused to allow even this brief concluding labor.

As one consequence, evidently unforeseen by the German government, the Bundesarchiv has had to return to England its 'Irving Collection,' half a ton of records which I had deposited in its vaults for researchers over the last thirty years. These include originals of Adolf Eichmann's papers, copies of two missing years of Heinrich Himmler's diary, the diaries of Erwin Rommel, Alfred Jodl, Wilhelm Canaris, and Walther Hewel, and a host of other papers not available elsewhere.

I HASTEN to add that with this one exception every international archive has accorded to me the kindness and unrestricted access to which I have become accustomed in thirty years of historical research. I would particularly mention the efforts of Dr David G. Marwell, director of the American-controlled Berlin Document Center (B.D.C.), in supplying to me 1,446 pages of biographical documents relating to Goebbels' staff. However, these now, like the collections formerly archived in Moscow and in the D.D.R., also come under the arbitrary aegis of the Bundesarchiv. Marwell's predecessor, the late Richard Bauer, provided me with the B.D.C.'s file on Goebbels (my film DI-81).* In the German socialist party's Friedrich Ebert Stiftung in Bonn, deputy archivist Dr Ulrich Cartarius generously granted to me privileged access to the original handwritten diary of Viktor Lutze, chief of staff of the S.A. (1934-43), on which he was currently working. Karl Höffkes of Essen kindly let me use the Julius Streicher diary and papers in his private archives.

The Yivo Institute for Jewish Research in New York also allowed me to exploit their Record Group 215, which houses a magnificent collection of original files of propaganda ministry documents, including Goebbels' own bound volumes of press clippings.

I must also mention my Italian publishers, Arnoldo Mondadori Editore, and their senior editor Dr Andrea Cane, who made available to me for transcription Goebbels' entire handwritten 1938 diary – it was a two-year task, but without that 'head start' in reading Goebbels' formidable script I should have been unable to make the sense of the Moscow cache that I did. This is also the proper place to thank my friend and rival Dr Ralf Georg Reuth, author of an earlier Goebbels biography, for unselfishly transferring to me a copy of Horst Wessel's

---

* I have referred where relevant to my microfilms in the source notes to this work. Most can be ordered, also in digital format, from Microform Academic Publishers Ltd., Main Street, East Ardsley, West Yorkshire WF3 2AT, England (tel. +44 1924 825 700; fax 829 212).

diary and substantial parts of the 1944 Goebbels diary, to which I added from Moscow and other sources.

The attitude of the other German official archives was very different from that of the Bundesarchiv in Koblenz. Dr Holder, president of the German federal statistics agency (Statistisches Bundesamt) in Wiesbaden, provided essential data on Jewish population movements with reference to Berlin. Two staff members (Lamers and Kunert) of the Mönchengladbach archives provided several of the early school photos and snapshots of girlfriends reproduced in this work.

Andre Mieles of the Deutsches Institut für Filmkunde (German Institute of Cinematography) provided many of the original movie stills and other fine photographs of movie stars. I owe thanks to Tadeusz Duda and the Jagielloński Library of the University of Kraków, Poland, for the photographs reproduced from Horst Wessel's diary in their custody. Dr Werner Johe of the Forschungsstelle für die Geschichte des Nationalsozialismus (Research Office for the History of National Socialism) in Hamburg volunteered data from the diary of Gauleiter Albert Krebs. Karl Heinz Roth of the Hamburg Stiftung für Sozialgeschichte des 20. Jahrhunderts (Foundation for the Social History of the Twentieth Century) assisted me in dating certain episodes in 1934.

The state archives of Lower Saxony (Niedersächsisches Staatsarchiv) in Wolfenbüttel let me read Leopold Gutterer's papers and I am glad to have been able to interview Dr Gutterer, now over ninety, on several occasions for this book. I was fortunate to obtain access to the papers of Eugen Hadamovsky as well as those of Joseph and Magda Goebbels and of the propaganda ministry itself at the Zentrales Staatsarchiv in Potsdam while it was still in the communist zone of Germany; most of the files – e.g. vol. 765, Goebbels' letters to his colleagues at the front – had remained untouched since last being used by Dr Helmut Heiber in 1958. In those last dramatic days before November 1989, archivist Dr Kessler gave me unlimited access despite cramped circumstances; those files too have now passed under the less liberal control of the Bundesarchiv.

Although any biographer of Goebbels owes a debt to Dr Helmut Heiber, who first trod the paths to the papers in Potsdam, he will forgive me for not using his otherwise excellent published volumes of Goebbels' speeches; often important phrases – faithfully reported by local British and other diplomats in the audiences – were omitted from the published texts on which Heiber relies; these diplomatic records, as well as other important documents, I have extracted from the holdings of the Public Record Office in London, capably helped by Susanna Scott-Gall as a research assistant. Shortly before its completion Manfred Müller, an expert of the early years of the Goebbels family, generously commented on my manuscript and let me read his own biography of Hans Goebbels, the brother of the Reichsminister.

The Institut für Zeitgeschichte (I.f.Z.) in Munich gave me the run of its library and archives and made available to me its files of press clippings on

Nazi personalities. But here too a possessiveness, an unseemly territorialism came into play as the I.f.Z. contrived to protect its virtual monopoly in unpublished fragments of the Goebbels diaries. Before coming across the Moscow cache, I had asked the I.f.Z., while researching there in 1992, for access to its Goebbels diaries holdings for the two years 1939 and 1944; on May 13 the director of the I.f.Z. refused in writing, stating that it was the institute's strict and invariable practice *not* to make available 'to outsiders' collections that it was still processing. This was why – since I could not conceive of completing the biography properly without those volumes – I travelled to Moscow, where I had learned that the original Nazi microfiches were housed; here I accessed, to the Munich institute's chagrin, not only the volumes for 1939 and 1944 but the entire diaries from 1923 to 1945 – though not before the institute, in an attempt to secure my eviction, had urgently faxed to Moscow on July 3, 1992 the allegation, which it many weeks later honorably withdrew,* that I was stealing from the Soviet archives. Foul play indeed – methods of which Dr Goebbels himself would probably have been proud.

That was not all. A few days later, hearing that the *Sunday Times* intended to publish the diaries which I had found in Moscow, the same institute, with a haste that would have been commendable under other circumstances, furnished to journalists on the *Daily Mail*, a tabloid English newspaper, the diary material which it had denied to me two months earlier: as of course they were entitled to. There was one pleasing denouement. The tabloid newspaper – which had paid out £20,000 in anticipation of its scoop – found that neither it nor its hired historians could read the minister's notoriously indecipherable handwriting. It abandoned its serialization in impotent fury two days later.

OF COURSE this biography is not based on Dr Goebbels' writings alone. In no particular sequence, I must make mention of Andrzej Suchcitz of the Polish Institute and Sikorski Museum in London who provided to me important assistance on the provenance of Goebbels' revealing secret speech about the Final Solution of September 1942; the George Arents library at the university of Syracuse, N.Y., who allowed me to research in the Dorothy Thompson papers; and to Geoffrey Wexler, Reference Archivist of the State Historical Society of Wisconsin, who gave access to Louis P. Lochner's papers, copies of some of which are also housed in the Franklin D. Roosevelt Library at Hyde Park, N.Y. I also owe thanks to the latter library for the use of other collections including William B. Donovan's papers and the 'presidential safe files;' I used more of Donovan's papers at the U.S. Army Military History Institute at Carlisle, Pa.

Dr G. Arlettaz of the Swiss federal archives in Berne, Dr Sven Welander of the League of Nations archives at the United Nations in Geneva, and Didier Grange of the Geneva city archives provided valuable information and photographs on Goebbels' 'diplomatic' visit to Geneva in 1933.

* *Süddeutsche Zeitung*, July 22, 1992.

In Germany I was greatly helped by the officials of the Nuremberg state archive, which houses reports on the postwar interrogations of leading propaganda ministry and other officials (some of which I also read at the National Archives in Washington D.C., where my friends John Taylor and Robert Wolfe provided the same kindly and expert guidance as they have shown for several decades).

Dr Howard B. Gotlieb, director of the Mugar Memorial Library at Boston university, drew my attention to their collection of the papers of the former Berlin journalist Bella Fromm. Archivist Margaret Petersen and assistant archivist Marilyn B. Kann at the Hoover Library at Stanford university, California, allowed me to see their precious trove of original Goebbels diaries as well as the political-warfare papers of Daniel Lerner and Fritz Theodor Epstein. The Seeley Mudd Library of Princeton university let me see their precious Adolf Hitler collection, although they were not, alas, permitted to open to me their Allen Dulles papers, which contain several files on Goebbels and the July 1944 bomb plot. Bernard R. Crystal of the Butler Library of Columbia university, N.Y., found several Goebbels items tucked away in the H. R. Knickerbocker collection. Dr Jay W. Baird, of Miami university, Ohio, volunteered access to his confidential manuscripts on Werner Naumann, whom he had interviewed at length on tape in 1969 and 1970; the manuscripts are currently held at the I.f.Z., which failed to make them available despite authorization from Baird.

The late Marianne Freifrau von Weizsäcker, mother of the later President Richard von Weizsäcker, provided to me access to her husband's then unpublished diaries and letters (later published by Leonidas Hill). The late Freda Rössler, nee Freiin von Fircks, talked to me at length about her murdered husband Karl Hanke, Goebbels' closest colleague and rival in love, and later gauleiter of Breslau, and supplied copies of his letters and other materials.

Major Charles E. Snyder, U.S.A.F. (retired), gave me a set of the precious original proofs of the moving Goebbels family photos reproduced in this work; as in my work Hitler's War (London, 1991) some colour photographs are from the unique collection of unpublished portraits taken by Walter Frentz, Hitler's Headquarters movie cameraman, to whom go my thanks for entrusting the original transparencies to me. Other photographs were supplied by the U.S. National Archives – I scanned around 40,000 prints from its magnificent collection of glass plates taken by Heinrich Hoffmann's cameramen – and by Leif Rosas, Annette Castendyk (daughter of Goebbels' first great love Anka Stalherm), and Irene Pranger, who also entrusted to me Goebbels' early correspondence with Anka.

Among those whom I was fortunate to interview were Hitler's secretary Christa Schroeder, his adjutants Nicolaus von Below, Gerhard Engel, Karl-Jesco von Puttkamer, his press staff officials Helmut Sündermann and Heinz Lorenz, his minister of munitions Albert Speer, and Goebbels' senior aide Immanuel Schäffer, all of whom have since died, as well as Traudl Junge, Otto Günsche, both of Hitler's staff, Gunter d'Alquèn, the leading S.S. journalist attached to the propaganda ministry, movie director Leni Riefenstahl – who privately showed me her productions of the era – and movie star Lida Baarova (now Lida Lundwall). I am grateful to Thomas Harlan for talking to me about his mother the late movie star Hilde Körber, and to Ribbentrop's secretary Reinhard Spitzy and Admiral Raeder's adjutant the late Captain Herbert Friedrichs for anecdotes about Joseph and Magda Goebbels. Gerta von Radinger (widow of Hitler's personal adjutant Alwin Broder Albrecht) reminisced with me and provided copies of Albrecht's letters to her, and of her correspondence with Magda. Richard Tedor provided to me copies of rare volumes of Goebbels' articles and speeches. Dr K. Frank Korf gave me supplemental information about his own papers in the Hoover Library. Fritz Tobias supplied important papers from his archives about the Reichstag fire and trial, and notes on his interviews with witnesses who have since died. Israeli researcher Doron Arazi gave me several useful leads on material in German archives. Ulrich Schlie pointed out to me to key Goebbels papers on foreign policy buried in the German foreign ministry archives. Dr Helge Knudsen corresponded with me in 1975 about the authenticity (or otherwise) of Rudolf Semler's 'diary,' the publication of which he prepared in 1947. I corresponded *inter alia* with Willi Krämer, Goebbels' deputy in the Reichspropagandaleitung; Günter Kaufmann, chief of the Reichspropagandaamt (RPA, Reich Propaganda Agency) in Vienna; and Wilhelm Ohlenbusch, who directed propaganda in occupied Poland. Wolf Rüdiger Hess and his mother Ilse Hess gave me exclusive access to the private papers of his late father, Rudolf Hess, in Hindelang including correspondence with Goebbels. The late Dr Hans-Otto Meissner discussed with me Ello Quandt and other members of Goebbels' entourage, whom he interviewed for his 1950s biography of Magda Goebbels. Peter Hoffmann, William Kingsford Professor of History at McGill University in Montreal, reviewed my chapter on VALKYRIE, as did Lady Diana Mosley those pages relating to her own meetings with Goebbels in the Thirties; Robin Denniston, to whom I owe so much over twenty years, read through the whole manuscript, offered suggestions, and advised me to temper criticism with charity more often than I had.

DAVID IRVING
LONDON 1996

About this new edition:

References in the source notes to Goebbels' 'unpublished diaries' have been left as such, although many have since been published. Professor Sir Ian Kershaw carelessly claimed in an interview with *The New York Times* published on March 19, 2001 that he was the first biographer to exploit the diaries from the Moscow archives. I wrote to Sir Ian mildly reproaching him that I did not see him at my elbow in the KGB archives nine years earlier in 1992, when I untied the knots which had sealed all the dusty boxes of microfiches since 1945.

The original film separations used for the first two editions, are alas no longer used by modern printers. Some of the original photos are no longer available and we have used different ones.

We have reset the entire book in our standard typeface, Minion, and I have taken the opportunity to polish the text slightly and to eliminate where practicable errors which had crept in – here a wrong file number, on which the Lipstadt defence team made some play in court, or there a word misread in German script. For the record, I have not revised my views, particularly about Goebbels as the instigator of the 1938 Kristallnacht and Hitler's ignorance of the plan. On the basis of new material that has accrued, I have added an appendix (pages 696) about Else Janke, Victor Arlosorov, and Richard Friedländer.

The 'Real Insidiousness'

'The real insidiousness of the biography is that its formidable documentation will gain it acceptance as history.' – Review of this book by *Publishers Weekly*, New York

I T SEEMS SOMEHOW FITTING, *writes David Irving*, to preface a biography of the Nazi propaganda chief with a brief history of the concerted and often successful attempts made around the world in 1996 to suppress it.

I began work on this book in 1988. By then I had a twenty-five year record of success with England's leading publishing houses. Macmillan London Ltd had become my regular publishers, and this biography was signed up by Adam Sisman, their editorial director. He told me that they intended to keep all my books in print. In 1989 there was a company reshuffle, and a young female, Felicity Kate Rubinstein, aged just twenty-nine, became CEO. (She was coincidentally the niece of Michael Rubinstein, who was my lawyer for thirty years.) She was not popular, and several members of Macmillan's staff left in dismay, including Sisman. The Hon. Roland Philipps replaced him; he was even younger than Felicity, in fact he was born in the month when I delivered my first best-seller *The Destruction of Dresden* to William Kimber Ltd in 1962.

The Macmillan company's internal papers indicated that Rubinstein, their new chief, soon tried to revoke Sisman's agreements with me. I know this, because I obtained sight of the files during subsequent litigation against authoress Gitta Sereny, who had wrongly accused me of stealing microfiches of the Goebbels diaries from Moscow archives. In July 1991 Miss Rubinstein married Philipps, her somewhat younger editorial chief, and the pieces fell into place. On December 12 of that year an important Jewish body in London held a secret meeting to plot ways of forcing Macmillan to violate its contracts with me and stop publishing my works. Until now their efforts had been rebuffed. With Rubinstein's ascendancy they had the leverage they needed.

On July 6, 1992, two days after I arrived back at Heathrow airport from Moscow with the long-lost diaries of Dr Goebbels, a sensational world scoop, young Philipps signed a secret memo ordering their entire stock of books written by me to be destroyed; there was to be no publicity, he directed, and I was not to be informed. Unaware of the growing antipathy, I meanwhile set about reworking the book to use the new diaries. In September 1992 I wrote to Macmillan's formally withdrawing the book (anxiety about the declining print quality of their finished books was the sole underlying cause, and I told them so). From 1988 until the final typescript was completed on September 7, 1994 the biography went through eight handwritten and typescript drafts. Meanwhile Rubinstein left Macmillan's in 1993 to set up a literary agency.

I confidently planned to issue my own Focal Point edition in November 1994, but that summer Hodder-Headline's managing director Alan Brooke, who had published several books by me over the years, made an offer for *Goebbels*. My diary records that he phoned me at 11:45 a.m. on August 17, 1994, and agreed a purchase price. A week later he cancelled the deal without explanation (something unheard-of in the publishing industry, I am told).

'The project has been vetoed from above,' he said.

'Nothing he can do about it,' I recorded. 'He sounded very upset.'

My agent later said that 'John le Carré,' a thriller writer, had warned Hodder's chairman, Tim Hely Hutchinson, who became group CEO of Britain's biggest publisher Hachette UK, that if they did not cancel the deal, he would pull out as a Hodder author. (In a letter, 'Le Carré' denied it.) We went ahead alone.

I still suspected nothing, but the book soon ran aground in other countries. In Italy my regular publisher Arnoldo Mondadori heaped praise on the biography and bought the rights, and in France Albin Michel signed it up. Both translated the book; neither eventually published, and neither has ever explained why. In retrospect, it can be seen that global forces were at work.

IN THE UNITED STATES my books had been published for thirty years by leading Madison Avenue publishers – among them were The Viking Press, Simon & Schuster, Avon Books, William Morrow, Macmillan, and Little, Brown. They had often hit the bestseller lists – most recently my Rommel biography. But *Goebbels* would run into obstacles here too.

On March 22, 1995 my U.S. literary agent Ed Novak, who controlled the only six advance copies of this book to reach American soil, accepted an offer made by the senior editor of St Martins Press (SMP), Tom Dunne. Dunne had published several other books by me, and for a while things went well. On October 13, 1995 SMP routinely asked what was new in the book. I replied:

What is new: Of course, I am the first and so far *only* historian to have had full use of the 75,000-page Goebbels Diaries that were discovered in the Moscow secret state archives in 1992. I am said to be one of only three historians capable of reading the handwriting. From these diaries we get new insight into the ruthless conduct and planning of Hitler's political conspiracies and military operations; we have fresh evidence about the role of Goebbels (and Albert Speer) in planning and inspiring the Final Solution. On a personal level we learn much about the tortured psyche of the Nazi propaganda minister, from the warped mind created by his physical deformities, through his late sexual development, to his family problems and romantic escapades with Germany's most beautiful film actresses like Lida Baarova. The photographs, most of which have never been published before, also deserve a mention.

Shortly after that the fat really hit the fire. There had already been disconcerting scenes in the London newspaper district when I returned from Moscow carrying the Goebbels diaries in July 1992, with street demonstrations, organised newspaper boycotts, and some intimidation. (*The Sunday Times* editor-in-chief Andrew Neil, who had bought rights from me, told me that he had never experienced anything like it.) Now, echoing these methods, Jewish organisations in the United States started an extraordinary campaign against St Martin's Press, SMP, for having bought the rights, and against Doubleday, Inc., who had proudly announced this work as their Military History Book Club selection for May 1996. None, and I can only repeat it: none, of the hostile organisations had actually seen the book.

The 'Anti-Defamation League of the B'nai Brith,' a wealthy New York based lobby, began the agitation in February 1996. Worried SMP executives phoned me in London to report that they were getting 'hate mail' about my involvement in 'Holocaust controversies.' I had never actually written on the subject. The pressure was increased. Millionaire novelist Elie Wiesel and other Jewish authors threatened the publisher with withdrawal of their services. A seriously nasty smear campaign was beginning. Some writers, notably the late Christopher Hitchens, hastened to my defense. On March 18, American newspapers published a Jewish Telegraph Agency despatch about the horrific 1995 Oklahoma City bombing: it showed pictures of myself and the convicted (and later executed) bomber Timothy McVeigh. Citing the London-based Institute of Jewish Affairs as their source, this disgusting report accused me of supplying McVeigh with the 'trigger mechanism' for his bomb.

Shortly after midnight on March 21, 1996, four days ahead of its publication, Reuters news agency began issuing an advance preview of what the influential New York trade journal *Publishers Weekly* intended to say in an anonymous review about this book. 'British historian David Irving, whom critics have accused of being a Nazi apologist,' it said, was about to get 'blistering prepublication reviews' for the book, which *Publishers Weekly* was calling 'repellent,' and alleging there was 'an agenda to Mr Irving's documentation.' The *Publishers Weekly* reviewer claimed that in this book 'Nazi brutality is almost always retaliation for the plots of international Jewry and the criminality of domestic Jews.' Baffled by the violence of this sudden and totally unjustified broadside, SMP's Tom Dunne told Reuters that both he and his editors were mystified at such suggestions.

The campaign however intensified. The American author Jonathan Kellerman wrote to Dunne: 'David Irving's identity as a neo-Nazi and Holocaust denier is well known. . . Your attempt to elevate him to mainstream status in the U.S. is the single most repugnant act I've witnessed in over a decade of publishing. You should be ashamed of yourself. Don't send me anymore [*sic*] books for blurbs. Anything with the St. Martin's label on it will go straight in the trash.'

A hitherto unknown Atlanta professor, Deborah Lipstadt, was soon exposed as a prime mover; she taught Jewish religious history at a minor university in Georgia. *The Washington Post* quoted her on April 3 as saying: 'In the Passover Hagadah, it says in every generation there are those who rise up to destroy us. David Irving is not physically destroying us, but is trying to destroy the memory of those who have already perished at the hands of tyrants.'

Like all the other critics, of course, she had not read the book. There were only six copies in the United States. The first reviews were already appearing in the British press, and they were brilliant. Thanks to the anonymous critics at *Publishers Weekly* and the Reuters agency however, the rest of the world's press was reverberating to this organized campaign – and in London I was crippled by pneumonia and unable to fight back.

In New York, the newspapers reported that there were street demonstrations against SMP, bomb threats, letter writing, and further orchestrated advance notices in the insider trade journals *Kirkus* and *Library Journal* (which shared offices with *Publishers Weekly* in New York City); somebody published the home addresses of SMP's executives on the Internet. With unconscious irony, *Publishers Weekly* closed its now formally published review with this accusation: 'The real insidiousness of the biography is that its formidable documentation will gain it acceptance as history.'

THE PUBLISHING HOUSE SMP told the press that they would not surrender to intimidation. 'Yes they will,' I told my diary. *Goebbels* now reached New York. *The New York Times* printed Tina Rosenberg's wan admission that it was 'a Rolls-Royce of a book, with costly color photos.' According to my editor Tom Dunne it had been appraised, and praised, by seven different editors. After weeks of assurances to the contrary, Norman Oder of *Publishers Weekly* phoned me late on April 3, 1996 with word that SMP had thrown in the towel.

'If we had known who David Irving was. . ,' stated their CEO Thomas J. McCormack in an extrordinary apologia released to the press (the rest was couched in the same excruciating abject vein). McCormack had dined at my family home in Mayfair, London, more than once, and he had published other books by me and on my recommendation. Now he did the dirty on his own author, releasing the communiqué to the newswires at 6:21 p.m. in New York (without sending a copy to me in London).

I want to emphasize, *continued McCormack*, that we are not canceling under coercion – publishers can often be at their best in resisting pressure – nor was our decision prompted by mere embarrassment. . .

The final decision about whether or not to go forward with Goebbels fell on my desk. Among many other things I did, I at last sat down to examine the page proof myself. I despised it intensively.

There were several reasons for this, but one was sufficient for me: The subtext of Goebbels was in my judgment this: The Jews brought it on themselves. My feeling was that this is at base an effectively anti-Semitic book, an insidious piece of Goebbels-like propaganda that we should have nothing to do with.

I LET McCormack's three-page communiqué pass as being the outpourings of a frightened man. He was married to a Jewess, he reminded the media, and his family was Jewish. It did not save him. He was sacked shortly after.

Of course his less encumbered rivals moved to snap up the now high-profile project. On April 9 Steve Wassermann of Random House Inc., encouraged by Robert Harris, (author of *Fatherland* and a mutual friend), asked to see *Goebbels*. Random House carried the ball for only fifteen days. On April 25, Wassermann sent to me an article from the previous day's *New York Post*: a mole had blown the whistle, and his project was dead.

A literary agent, Keith Korman of Raines & Raines Inc., told trade journals now that my future would be 'floating face down dead in the water.' Two years later, on August 13, 1998, my old editor Don Fehr at Basic Books contacted me having just read the book; his attempts too were killed off at higher levels. When other minor imprints offered to publish *Goebbels*, hoping to capitalize on its notoriety, I rather petulantly told them: 'I may be floating in the water, but I prefer to choose my own stretch of river.'

The loss of the U.S. market was of course very painful, the more so since none of the American edition's mindless killers had actually seen the book.

I turned my attention to Professor Lipstadt, who had been at the center of the campaign. She was author of a heavily subsidized paperback, *Denying the Holocaust: The Growing Assault on Truth and Memory*. It was defamatory and untrue, and largely dead anyway – by 1996 remaindered as unsaleable. Since her publishers had peddled her book in England, within the jurisdiction of our Defamation Act, there was one remedy open to me. I could strike back at her book's dangerous libel, inserted at the last moment at the behest of Yad Vashem in Jerusalem, that I am a 'Holocaust denier.' Discovery and cross examination would reveal who was behind the campaign – and what.

Acting in person – *i.e.*, without lawyers – I had the writ served on Lipstadt in September 1996. The resulting London libel trial in January 2000 lasted over three months. The professor appeared in court flanked by forty expensive lawyers and hired historians, powered by a thirteen-million dollar defence fund created by Hollywood entrepreneur Stephen Spielberg and other donors of less ability and more questionable integrity; she herself did not venture into the witness box or offer herself for cross-examination.

Dazzled perhaps by the wealth displayed in his courtroom, Mr Justice Gray allowed her defence even though he had a copy of this book in front of him. I called his judgment 'perverse,' and others agreed. The late George Carman, QC, one of Britain's leading libel counsel, told his son privately that he felt Gray was wrong. Readers may concur.*

After the negative outcome of the Lipstadt trial, my entire possessions including my research archives, including 40,000 index cards, were seized in May 2002. (The Trustees appointed to do so had informed me four weeks earlier that they were always given 'these high-profile political cases.')

For five years my surviving archives were held in a Sussex warehouse where Lipstadt's experts were allowed to paw over them. At least one, the German historian Tobias Jersak, was caught stealing from them. It took five years of further litigation to force the authorities to return them to me. By then, many files, including all my research on Goebbels and Himmler, were inexplicably missing, for which the Trustees had to pay me substantial damages. Another of Lipstadt's experts, the German professor Peter Longerich, subsequently published at short intervals highly-acclaimed biographies of both Goebbels and Himmler. *Honi soit qui mal y pense.*

I OFFER ONE REDEEMING postscript to what is otherwise a dusky story. On May 6, 1996 *Time* magazine published a letter from Wisconsin, USA:

> I am a Jew whose parents lost their families in the Holocaust. I grew up in Israel among Holocaust survivors. Since I was a child, I have read every book I could find on Nazi Germany. I have tried to understand why and how the Germans came to carry out their plan for exterminating the Jews.
>
> I have read all of Mr Irving's excellent books. He is no 'apologist for Adolf Hitler.' His words record the extermination of the Jews and provide evidence of Hitler's direct involvement. Mr Irving is not an anti-Semite, nor is he a supporter of Hitler or Nazi Germany. His books, more than any others I have read, help explain what happened in Germany.
>
> If we are to prevent future exterminations, we have to eradicate hate. The process must start with free speech and the ability to discuss openly all aspects of history and express all viewpoints. Mr Irving through his writing has made a large contribution toward preventing future Holocausts.

Reprinting this letter, which was signed by Josef Hose, of Madison, Wisconsin, I commented: 'It is comforting to think of six million *Time* magazines around the world containing this prominently displayed letter, from a Jew, vindicating everything I have worked for as an historian.'

DAVID IRVING, *September 2013*

---

* For the whole story see www.fpp.co.uk/StMartinsPress, and /Legal/Penguin. Readers who agree with Sir Charles Gray, QC, no longer a High Court judge, can write him at his chambers, 5 Raymond Buildings, Gray's Inn, London WC1R 5BP; they may wish to draw his attention to passages of this book which he overlooked in court.

Prologue: The Mark of Cain

EVERY MAN HAS SOME SAY in his own fortunes. It is open to each brain's owner to work upon it, to devise by intellectual training the swiftest path between it and the muscles and voice over which it is to be master. From the convolutions in the brain's left frontal lobe springs forth the voice that commands other men to hate, to march, to dance, to die. Moreover, man can condition this controlling instrument. Man is what he eats, that is true. But his brain is more than that – it is what he has seen about him too. The operas, the great works of art and poetry, the ill-defined sensations of national pride and humiliation, all these impressions are encoded and stored away by the neurons of the brain. And thus gradually one man comes to differ from the next.

Since prehistoric times the human brain has remained impenetrable and marvelous. Surgeons have trepanned into the human cranium in the hope of fathoming its secrets. The Greeks, the Romans, and the mediaeval Arabs all opened up their fellow humans' skulls to gaze upon the brain. In 1945 the American army took Benito Mussolini's brain away for examination; they did the same with Dr Robert Ley's brain, and the Russians with Lenin's. But no instrument has yet explained the brain's capacity for evil. *Lenin had syphilis.*

THE BRAIN WHICH indirectly occupies us now has deceased one evening in May 1945. Here it is, punctured by a 6·35-caliber bullet, lying in the ruined garden of a government building in Berlin. Next to its owner are the charred remains of a woman, the metal fastenings tumbling out of her singed, once-blonde hair. Around them both, callously grouped for the photographer, stand a Russian lieutenant-colonel, two majors, and several civilians.

It is May 2, 1945, five P.M., and the building is the late Adolf Hitler's Reich chancellery. The lieutenant-colonel is Ivan Isiavich Klimenko, head of Smersh (a Russian acronym for Soviet Counter-Intelligence) in a rifle corps. He has been led here by the chancellery's cook Wilhelm Lange and its garage manager Karl Schneider. It has begun to pour with rain. Klimenko's men slide the two bodies onto a large red-and-gilt door torn from the building. They scoop up a fire-blackened Walther pistol found beneath the man's body, and another pistol found nearby; a Gold badge; an engraved Gold cigarette case, and other personal effects. All will be needed for identification.[1]

XXI

Driving a Jeep, Klimenko leads the way back to Smersh headquarters set up in the old jail house at Plötzensee. On the following day he returns to the chancellery, still hunting for the Führer. Below ground, inside the bunker, he finds the bodies of six children in pretty blue nightdresses or pajamas. He ships them out to Plötzensee too, together with the corpse of a burly German army officer, a suicide.

The Russians bring all the guests of the five-star Continental hotel out to Plötzensee, including a textiles merchant, a chaplain, and a hospital assistant, and invite them to identify the cadavers.[2] Even if the receding hairline, the Latin profile, the overwide mouth, and the unusually large cranium are not clues enough, then the steel splint with its two ringlike clamps to clutch the calf muscles, and the charred leather straps still tying it to the right leg leave no room for doubt at all. The foot is clenched like a dead chicken's claw: a club foot.

This is all that remains of Dr Joseph Goebbels, the malevolent genius whose oratory once inspired a nation to fight a total war and to hold out to the very end.

The Germans carry all the bodies outside on tarpaulins, and a Red Army truck transports them to a villa some ten kilometers north-northeast of Berlin where the Soviets are equipped to perform autopsies.

Soviet officers bring in Professor Werner Haase, one of Hitler's surgeons, and Hans Fritzsche, one of Goebbels' senior deputies, to view the bodies.[3]

Haase identifies them; Fritzsche hesitates, but the club foot and the orthopedic shoe clinch it for him. 'Check the Gold party badge,' he suggests. The badge is cleaned of soot and dirt, and reveals the number 8762 – Goebbels' membership number in the National Socialist German Workers' Party (the Nazi party). 'It's Dr Goebbels,' Fritzsche confirms.[4]

This is almost the last public appearance of Dr Joseph Goebbels. A few days later the Russians summon Hans Fritzsche out to G.P.U. (secret police) headquarters at Friedrichshagen in south-east Berlin and show him a notebook partly concealed by a metal plate: he recognizes Goebbels' handwriting, and asks to see more. The Soviet officer removes the plate and reveals a diary bound in red leather. 'We found twenty of these, up to about 1941, in the vaults of the Reichsbank,' he says. The Russians arrange one final identification ceremony. In a copse near Friedrichshagen that Whitsun of 1945 they show Goebbels' entire family, now resting in wooden coffins, to his former personal detective, the forty-year-old Feldpolizei officer Wilhelm Eckold. He identifies his former master without hesitation.[5]

AMONG THE PERSONAL EFFECTS was a Gold cigarette case inscribed 'Adolf Hitler,' and dated '29.x.34.' That was Paul Joseph Goebbels' birthday. He had first opened his eyes and uttered his first scream at No. 186 Odenkirchener Strasse in the smoky Lower Rhineland town of Rheydt on October 29, 1897;[6] it was a thousand-year-old textiles centre, set in a landscape of traditionally pious Catholics and hardworking country folk.

'The daily visit to church,' writes Ralf Georg Reuth, Goebbels' most recent biographer, 'confession and family prayers at home and their mother making the sign of the cross on her kneeling children's foreheads with holy water, were as much a part of their life as the daily bread for which their father toiled at Lennartz' gas-mantle factory.[7] Their father Fritz Göbbels – that is the spelling in Paul Joseph's birth certificate – was W. H. Lennartz & Co.'s dependable catholic (though certainly not bigoted) bookkeeper.[8] It is not over-fanciful to suspect that he chose the child's second name in honor of Dr Josef Joseph, a revered local Jewish attorney and close family friend.[9]

He himself had been born here to a tailor's family from Beckrath southwest of Rheydt. He had the same bulbous nose as his father Conrad Göbbels[10] and as his brother Heinrich, a paunchy commercial traveler in textiles with all the ready wit that Fritz so sorely lacked. Fritz's mother Gertrud was a peasant's daughter. From first to last his relations with his youngest son Joseph were strained. Aware that his own career would see little more advancement, he made sacrifices for 'little Jupp' (Jüppche), which were to be most inadequately repaid. As his father, finally a director in the obligatory stovepipe hat, came to the end of his life Joseph would see in him only a 'petty minded, grubby, beer swilling pedant, concerned only with his pathetic bourgeois existence and bereft of any imagination.'[11] Among his effects were found blue cardboard account books in which he had detailed every penny he had spent since marriage.[12] Conceding grudgingly that his father would in all likelihood go to Heaven, Joseph would write: 'I just can't understand why Mother married the old miser.'[13] His sympathies were all with her. 'I owe her all that I am,' he once wrote; and he remained beholden to her all his life.[14]

He had his mother's astute features – the face perceptibly flattened at each side, the nose slightly hooked, the upper front teeth protruding. She had been born Katharina Maria Odenhausen in the village of Uebach-over-Worms in Holland, and occasionally she lapsed into Rhenish Plattdeutsch[15] when speaking with Joseph.[16] Her father was a muscular Dutch blacksmith with a long beard, a man Joseph would look back upon as the dearest of his ancestors. He died of apoplexy in the Alexianer monastery at Mönchen-Gladbach. Her mother had then moved into Germany to serve as housekeeper to a distant relative, a local rector at Rheindahlen; she had spent her youth there with all her brothers and sisters except for Joseph Odenbach, Goebbels' architect godfather, who had stayed at Uebach. It was at Rheindahlen that Katharina had met Fritz Göbbels and married him in 1892.

So much for Goebbels' parents. Two sons had arrived before him, Konrad[17] and Hans.[18] Three sisters followed him: Two, Maria and Elisabeth, died young, a third, also christened Maria, was born twelve years after Joseph. We shall occasionally glimpse Konrad and Hans, struggling through the depression until Joseph's rise to power from which they too profited, being appointed to head Nazi publishing houses and insurance associations respectively. Maria remained the apple of his eye.[19]

Through living frugally, and thanks to a pay rise to 2,100 marks per annum, in 1900 his father was able to purchase outright a modest house at No. 140 Dahlener Strasse in Rheydt (still standing today as No. 156).[20] Young Joseph had his room under the sloping roof, his mansard window's view limited to the skies above. This remained 'home' for him, the fulcrum of his life, long after he left it as a young man.

He remembered his sickly earliest years only dimly. He recalled playing with friends called Hans, Willy,[21] Otto (whom he knew as 'Öttche') and the Maassen brothers, and a bout of pneumonia which he only just survived. He was always a little mite of a fellow. Even in full manhood he would weigh little more than one hundred pounds.

At age six his mother placed him in the primary school (Volksschule) right next to the house. Goebbels was a stubborn and conceited boy. Fifteen or twenty years later he would reveal, in an intimate handwritten note, how his mental turmoil both delighted and tormented him: Each Saturday he would take himself off to church, there to contemplate 'all the good and the bad that the week had brought me, and then I went to the priest and confessed everything that was troubling my soul.'[22]

HIS RIGHT LEG had always hurt. When he was about seven, a medical disaster befell him which would change his life. 'I see before me,' he would reminisce, 'a Sunday walk – we all went over to Geistenbeck. The next day, on the sofa, I had an attack of my old foot pains. Mother was at the washtub. Screams. I was in agony. The masseur, Mr Schiering. Prolonged treatment. Crippled for rest of my life. Examined at Bonn university clinic. Much shrugging of shoulders. My youth from then on,' Goebbels mused piteously, 'somewhat joyless.' So this schoolboy with the large, intelligent cranium, underdeveloped body, and club foot lived out his childhood to a chorus of catcalls, jeers, and ridicule.

In adulthood his right foot was 18 centimeters long – 3·5 centimeters shorter than the left; its heel was drawn up and the sole looked inwards (*equinovarus*). The right leg was correspondingly shorter than the left, and thinner. The indications are that Goebbels' defect was not genetic but was acquired as the result of some disease.[23] It defied all attempts at surgical remedy; had the deformation occurred at birth, when the bones are soft, it would have been relatively easy to manipulate them back into the right alignment. Perhaps it was the product of osteomyelitis (a bone marrow inflammation) or of infantile paralysis. He would hint, at age thirty, that the deformity developed from an accident at age thirteen or fourteen.[24]

When he was ten they operated on his deformed foot. He later recalled the family visiting him one Sunday in the hospital; his eyes flooded with tears as his mother left, and he passed an unforgettably grim half-hour before the anesthetic. The operation left the pain and deformity worse than before. His aunt Christine brought him some fairy tales to read. Thus he discovered in reading a world of silent friends that could not taunt or ridicule.

When he returned to his mansard room he began to devour every book and encyclopedia that he could lay his hands on.

He would show them: The brain, if properly prepared and used, could outwit the brawniest physique.

1: The Hater of Mankind

1: *Eros Awakes*

THE OTHER BOYS at the Gymnasium in Rheydt's Augusta Strasse, which Goebbels entered at Easter 1908, regarded him as a sneak and know-all.[1] He ingratiated himself with teachers, particularly with the scripture teacher Father Johannes Mollen, by telling on his truant comrades. 'My comrades,' he would confess, 'never liked me, except for Richard Flisges.'[2] He would find Flisges in the upper fifth (*Obersekunda*) in 1916. His closest friends were three 'Herberts' – Hompesch, Beines, and Lennartz.[3] Herbert Lennartz, son of his father's boss, died after a minor operation, leaving Goebbels grief-stricken and shocked. It moved him to compose his first poem ('Why did you have to part from me so soon?').[4]

At first he was lazy and apathetic, numbed by the realization of his physical deformity. Then he overcompensated, and later he was never far from the top of the class. His love of Latin came falteringly at first, then in full flood. With biting irony and sarcasm Christian Voss tutored him in German literature – and in sarcasm and irony as well. While his brothers Hans and Konrad had to leave school early, Joseph excelled.[5] With clenched fists and gleaming eyes young Goebbels listened as history teacher Dr Gerhard Bartels taught his class about Germany's checkered past.[6]

His father and mother wanted him to become a priest – not just because the church would then pay for his higher education; they were a deeply religious family. When Joseph's little sister Elisabeth died in 1915 they all knelt around her deathbed and held hands and prayed for her soul.[7] Joseph composed another poem for her, 'Sleep, baby, sleep.'

When the Great War came in August 1914 his friends all rallied excitedly to the Kaiser's colors; he too went to the local recruiting office, but the officer dismissed him with barely a glance. Back at school he wrote a thoughtful essay, 'How can a non-combatant help the fatherland in these times?' He argued in it that 'even those who are denied the right to shed their blood for the honor of the nation' could be of service, 'even if not in such a creditable way.' His teacher marked it 'Good.'[8]

The classroom emptied as the war dragged on. His pals Herbert Hompesch and Willy Zilles, now fusiliers, wrote him exciting letters from the western front.[9] His brother Konrad was a gunner and Hans was soon in French captivity.[10]

3

As author of the best essay, Goebbels, now in the upper sixth (*Oberprima*), had the honor of delivering the valedictory speech when school ended on March 21, 1917. He spoke of Germany's 'global mission' to become 'the political and spiritual leader of the world.'[11] 'Very good,' the headmaster Dr Gruber told him. 'But mark my words, you'll never make a good orator!'[12]

After passing the school-certificate examination at Easter 1917 Goebbels again tried to enlist, but was accepted only for a few weeks' service as a pen-pusher at the Reichsbank. His painful deformity had thus given him at least one advantage, a head-start on his later comrades in the political battle. He would already be at university while Adolf Hitler, Hermann Göring, and Rudolf Hess were fighting under the skies of Flanders.

His intellectual horizon was expanding. In 1909 his father had purchased secondhand a piano, that symbol of the solid middle class; the family and neighbors clustered round as four furniture-men manhandled the piano indoors. Joseph rapidly mastered the instrument. He also developed a talent for play-acting and mime. But what was to become of him now?

The priesthood? Goebbels inclined briefly toward medicine, but Voss, his teacher, persuaded him that his real talents lay in literature. Whichever the subject, the university at Bonn it would be.

JOSEPH GOEBBELS REACHES puberty at about thirteen. But given his later reputation it is worth emphasizing that he will be thirty-three before he first has sexual intercourse with a woman.[13] For the intervening twenty years this brilliant but celibate cripple's life will be a trail of temptations, near-seductions, and sexual rebuffs etched into his memory.

At thirteen he and his pal Herbert Beines have a grubby mudlark of a friend, Herbert Harperscheidt, whose stepmother Therese always wears crisp, clean skirts; so Joseph Goebbels recalls fourteen years later. The sexual arousal that he first detects towards this mature female returns when he is fifteen. He harbors secret crushes on women like Frau Lennartz, the factory owner's wife. All of his pals have girlfriends – Hompesch has one enticingly called Maria Jungbluth. Goebbels however senses only a 'dark yearning' as Eros awakes in him.

'My libido is sick,' he will write aged twenty-six. 'In affairs of the heart we humans are all scandalously selfish. For the phallus we sacrifice hecatombs of immortal souls.'[14] Basking in what he sees as one woman's love he will reflect, 'I am everything to her. . . Or am I allowed to savor life's treasures more intensely because I am doomed to depart it early on? Now and again I have this premonition!'[15]

At age eighteen, in 1915, he begins a three-year infatuation with a local girl, Lene Krage. He calls it love, and will long recall their first chaste kiss in Garten Strasse. But she is capricious and flighty, and his tormented soul drives him to the time-honored refuge of writing a private diary.

At Christmas 1916 he sends her a book of his own poetry. Leaving Rheydt for Bonn university in March 1917 he says farewell to Lene. They find themselves locked in Kaiser Park that night, and he kisses her breast for the first time: Characterizing this milestone event seven years later he writes coyly, 'She becomes a loving woman for the first time.' It will become clear that he means this only in the broadest sense.

HE WAS to study philology, Latin, and history. Desperately lonely, he lodged in a cold bare room. His aspirations were overshadowed by hunger, cold, fatigue, and ill-health. He had made one good friend in the law student Karlheinz Kirsch however and fagged for him as the *Leibfuchs* (freshman valet) in the tradition of all medieval universities. 'Pille' Kölsch, as he was known, remained his foppish, loud-voiced, jovial, staunch friend and rival long after their careers had drifted apart. With his modish headgear and yellow gloves, Kölsch became his first role-model.[16] He roped Goebbels into the tiny Bonn chapter ('Sigfridia') of the catholic fraternity Unitas on May 22, 1917.[17] Its half-dozen members spent the weekly meetings solemnly debating religion and quaffing beer in the local hostelry, the Cockerel. Goebbels had chosen the classical name of Ulex for himself.[18]

His funds ran out, which scarcely mattered as at the end of July 1917 he was briefly inducted into war service, and absolved his obligations by pushing a pen for a few weeks in a home auxiliary service (he wrote an excellent copperplate script).

He was keen to continue at university, but his father could put up only fifty marks per month; Joseph earned a little more by tutoring. He frittered away that summer with Lene on vacation, spending at least one chaste night with her on her sofa at Rheindahlen, and committing to his memory that she 'stayed pure.' He left a number of unpaid bills at Bonn, which his father settled.

The winter semester began on October 1, 1917. He submitted a formal application to the diocese in Cologne, where the Albertus Magnus Society provided aid to promising young Catholics. The documents[19] supporting his application show that his father now earned 3,800 to 4,000 marks per annum, and had no liquid assets. His scripture teacher Mollen testified:

> 'Herr Goebbels comes from decent catholic parents and deserves commendation for his religious fervor and his general moral demeanor.'

Father Mollen would explain years later that he furnished this testimonial with the clearest conscience: 'He was a very promising scholar. For nine years he had taken scripture lessons from me and had always shown much interest, comprehension, and devotion.

He regularly attended school church services and the monthly Communion. His attitude to me was confident, proper, and reverential.' The parish priest at Rheydt seconded him. Backed by these documents, Goebbels humbly submitted on September 5, 1917 his application to the Diocesan Committee of the Albertus Magnus Society for financial support for the winter term 1917–18.

'Because of a lame foot I am exempt from military service,' he wrote, 'and I should dearly like to continue my studies next term.'

Convinced that his was a worthy cause, the society sent him 185 marks as a first interest-free installment of a loan finally totaling 964 marks. His address was now given as No. 18 Post Strasse in Bonn; he would return there in October 1917.

BY THE TIME of his final Ph.D. examination in November 1921 he would have attended five different universities; this was not unusual in Germany. The reasons are obscure: sometimes he was pursuing a particular girl, sometimes a certain professor, sometimes a special course; frequently the lack of lodging space in one city decided that he should study elsewhere that term instead.

His speaking talents were already developed. Hompesch told him he was a born orator.

'Motor mouth!' joked Kölsch's brother Hermann in one letter. 'There you go, shooting it off again. Well, there's nobody can touch you on that score.' 'We really ought to open a stall,' Hermann joked in a letter two weeks later, 'and do the rounds of the church fetes displaying you as the Man with the All-Round Mouth.'[20]

Goebbels stayed on in Bonn after term ended on February 1, and moved into Kölsch's lodgings in Wessel Strasse. The April 1918 issue of the Unitas journal reported that the two friends, by now inseparable, had decided to study next in Berlin.

AT CHRISTMAS Goebbels discovers his pal's sister Agnes Kölsch, and his yearning for Lene turns to aversion. Agnes visits him one day and they exchange one passionless kiss on his sofa.

She foolishly introduces him to her sister Liesel, and an informal triangle develops lasting well into the new year. Agnes visits him in Bonn, and they spend the night together – 'Ulex' kisses her breasts. He often spends weekends at the Kölsch family home at Werl, except once when Liesel comes to Bonn and her sister Agnes is sidelined.[21] On December 5, 1917, after one such weekend, Liesel writes him: 'My lips don't work at all any more, so it won't be possible to use them on Saturday.' Her sister Agnes adds: 'Nor my head neither.' She is soon disillusioned, and writes this jibe on August 15, 1918: 'Do you know, Ulex, that I unfortunately adjudged you as being far too elevated, noble and mature?' Goebbels overlooks the barbed wit; he congratulates himself, with a certain smugness, 'She is all over me.' Mrs Kölsch encourages his relationship with Agnes, although his immaturity is painfully evident.[22]

'She is still a child,' he adds in his own writings. 'We are both children.'

Pille Kölsch meanwhile has dropped Berlin and opted for Freiburg in south-western Germany; Ulex sets off in his comrade's footsteps for the summer term beginning in May 1918.

At Freiburg Pille embraces him, his eyes gleaming. 'Ulex!' he announces, 'I've already found this great girl. Anka Stalherm. She's a student – you've got to meet her.' ('And how deeply and completely I have done just that!' writes Goebbels six years later, still besotted with Anka.)

Female students are in 1918 still rarities at German universities, and Anka is a rarity even among these. She is reading economics. She wears her blonde hair long with a few strands caught up in a knot on top;[23] her ankles are slim, and her legs are rumored to be equally divine. She is twenty-three, two years older than Goebbels. With her Ursuline convent education in Germany and England behind her, she has inherited class, beauty, and wealth as well – her late father owned a distillery and cornmill in the Rhineland.[24]

Kölsch and Goebbels become friendly rivals for Anka's affections. Among her effects will later be found a faded picture postcard showing Goebbels at some student revelry wearing a lampshade on his head.[25] Pille has penned a fond message on the back. And yet – let this be made clear in advance – sexually, Goebbels will get nowhere with her; nor she with him.[26]

Since Anka is a regular at Professor Hermann Thiersch's seminars on classical archeology, Goebbels signs on for them too. Glowing reports reach the charity in Cologne about his interest in these three-hour lectures.

The miracle happens: Anka Stalherm, this goddess of the mysterious gray-green eyes, she who is coveted by half the males at Freiburg university, saves her smiles for when he walks in, or so it seems to him. She is fascinated by this swift intellect. They go out as a threesome for strolls up Freiburg's Castle Hill or into the Black Forest. Kölsch suffers torments of jealousy, which enhances Goebbels' sense of triumph. He serenades Anka on a rented piano, and one precious night he sleeps under the same Black Forest roof as she. The three students tour the sleepy towns along the shores of Lake Constance, with Goebbels dreamy-eyed in blissful anticipation.

Oppressing him despite these carefree moments are his poverty and his own jealousy when she spends days away with Kölsch. His 'uncle' Cohnen, a wealthy insurance-director friend of his father's, twice wires loans to him. The Catholics are less forthcoming. While the Unitas journal reports the unexpected revival of their Freiburg chapter thanks to Ulex and his pal, after August 1918 Goebbels' name vanishes from its pages altogether.

The delicious pursuit of the coquettish Anka continues. Goebbels serenades her on the piano but ascertains that she is, alas, 'chastity itself.' His first letter to her is dated June 15, 1918, a wordy, Latin-garnished, solemn epistle addressing her formally as *Sehr geehrtes Fräulein* Stalherm, embellished with four lines of carefully crafted verse and signing off 'with quite a lot of greetings, yours faithfully, J. Goebbels – Ulex.'[27] Persistence and intellect are rewarded. Up on Castle Hill one afternoon – it is June 28, 1918 – he kisses her for the first time:[28] not on the lips, but on one cheek.[29]

There is a problem: She is of far higher pedigree. There is an unholy row when she does not invite him to meet her visiting brother Willy. And he agonizes over her dalliances with Kölsch: which does she prefer? One evening she pleads with him on bended knee to declare his love for her, and he realizes that women too can suffer.

As she leaves Freiburg at the end of July 1918 after one last night of stifled passion, he visits their old haunts. He sits in the forest hut high above the university city, listening to the rain beating on its roof, and imagines himself all alone on earth. He begins to compose a five-act play, 'Judas Iscariot.'[30]

As the Freiburg term ends he dreams of moving to Munich, but the lack of lodgings there thwarts him and he returns home. During the summer vacation he exchanges scores of letters with Anka, sometimes twice a day. His letters to her reveal a young man still physically frail and lonely; they suggest that he has elected to enter the church.

Romancing Anka occupies every other waking hour. His catchword is *wahnsinnig* – crazy: That is what he is, he confesses, about her. He scrawls that word in the corner of letters, or leaves it unfinished just as *waaa* – . He is untroubled by the wail of rage that comes from Agnes Kölsch: 'I thought far too highly of you, too noble and too mature,' she writes him on August 15, 1918: 'Farewell, it was not meant to be.'[31]

Much ink is expended trying to arrange various trysts with Anka, which Goebbels sometimes prudishly cancels because her worried mother (unimpressed by this parvenu) and her sisters disapprove.[32] Once she gives him a red rose. It graces his desk at Rheydt beneath a carved Black Forest heart she has given him earlier.[33] His soldier brother Konrad, home on leave, jokes to him that he will probably be able to greet him as a cardinal later on; he inquires about the carved heart on the wall. 'A gift from the Archbishop of Freiburg?' he asks ironically. 'From his lady housekeeper,' replies Joseph with a salacious wink.[34]

Joseph beavers away on 'Judas.'[35] Anka incautiously shows it around and in no time the clergy of Rheydt are asking him angry questions about it.[36]

On August 27 he is summoned to his former scripture teacher Father Mollen, who draws his attention to the pernicious nature of such writings. 'I was so furious I would have torn "Judas" into a thousand shreds if I had had it with me,' writes Goebbels.

The priest requires him to undertake to destroy even his own copy of the script. Has all his toil been for nothing? 'What shall I do?' he appeals to Anka. 'I am in despair.'[37] (The play survives among his papers.) It marks his first break with the church. He declines the summons by Unitas to attend their general assembly in Münster to report on the summer semester at Freiburg. Instead, he carouses with his pals in Düsseldorf.

Kölsch has been thrown out of their catholic fraternity. Goebbels supports the ouster, explaining to Anka: 'My best friend turned out to be a scoundrel.' When Anka ironically calls him a puritan he responds that Unitas has principles.[38] By this time he has learned from her that Kölsch has sexually propositioned her.[39]

To seal their friendship, she loyally shows him the letter concerned. Of her solely maternal interest in him there seems no doubt. 'Do you know what I should like now?' she writes to the pint-sized student Goebbels. 'Just to stroke my fingers through your hair and clasp you so tight that you look quite desperate.'[40]

Her widowed mother's disapproval grows. He records in dismay that she regards him as a homo molestissimus and clearly frowns on any notion of them both attending the same university next term. He stiffly asks Anka to inform him where she will be studying, 'so that I can cross that university off my own list.'[41]

ON SEPTEMBER 3, 1918 Konrad Goebbels returns to the western front. He accuses his younger brother Joseph of not taking any interest in the war and finally extracts from him a promise to read at least the daily war communiqués. Konrad declares that he is proud to be fighting for his fatherland. 'As you will realize,' Joseph dryly informs Anka, 'he is Mother's darling. While I claim that privilege, remarkably, more of my father.' But he adds, 'I believe my mother is the best at understanding me.'[42] He advises Anka to read his version of the Last Supper, where Judas – with whom he thus identifies – talks about his mother, how he sulks and does not eat, and she just shakes her head and murmurs, 'Judas, Judas,' and how bitterly he weeps thereafter.[43]

He hopes that Anka's mother will relent and agree to them studying together at Munich. His father prefers Bonn or Münster, both nearer to the parental home. 'The decision is in your mother's hands,' he writes to Anka.[44] A friend tells him that she has boasted to his fiancée about her last evening with Goebbels at Freiburg.[45] Goebbels scolds her for having so rudely dragged in the dust the memory of these, 'the most sacred and beautiful hours of my life.' In the same letter he repents and asks, 'May I today for the first time press a tender kiss upon your rosebud lips?'[46] In her reply, she mocks his stern morals. She has decided to study that winter at Würzburg. He therefore chooses Würzburg too, and finds lodgings on the fourth floor of No. 8 Blumen Strasse – 'A wonderful room right beside the river,' he tells his friend Fritz Prang.[47]

Ecstatic that she is so close, he sends her a note as soon as he settles in, perhaps justifying his lack of physical ardor. 'If love is only in the mind,' he explains, 'it might be called platonic; if only physical, it is frivolous, ugly, unbeautiful. It is the noble union of these two factors that creates the ideal love.'[48]

At Würzburg his studying begins in earnest. He plows through *Crime and Punishment*, he regularly attends the seminars on ancient and modern history and on German literature.

The Armistice of November 1918 makes little mark on him. His father writes pleading with him to come home if things get too dangerous, what with the revolution, in Würzburg.[49] Goebbels notices the returning troops, the popular sense of dismay, the establishment of enemy zones of occupation; he sees Anka weeping, he hears of communist mobs rampaging in Bavaria.

'Don't you also feel,' he asks Prang in a letter on November 13, 'that the time will come again when people will yearn for intellectual and spiritual values rather than brute mob appeal?'

More letters go to Anka. He writes her the kind of letter that romantic females long to receive.[50] In her replies she frets about his frailty, and swears undying love. 'I hope you've gone to bed long ago,' she writes in one, 'and are dreaming that I am pressing the tend'rest kiss upon your forehead to dispel your gloomy thoughts for all eternity.'[51]

For the first time in his life he misses the carol service on Christmas Eve; he spends the hours in Anka's room, and watches entranced as she kneels at her bedside to say her prayers. He sleeps in her chaste embrace – but that is all.[52]

By the time they both leave Würzburg for their respective homes on January 22, 1919, the Belgians have occupied Rheydt. An Allied iron curtain has descended across the Rhineland. Sick and hungry, Goebbels writes her at four-thirty A.M. on a deserted platform, waiting for the slow train to Cologne.[53] At Cologne he has to wait all night – 'the whole station milling with Englishmen, Blacks, and Frenchmen.'[54] Anka writes to him in Rheydt that she misses Freiburg; her sisters, shown Goebbels' photographs, prefer his head to the full figure, she candidly writes.[55]

He looks desperately ill: He is suffering from chronic headaches, for which the university's professor of medicine has found no cure.[56] A ten P.M. curfew is in force. The Belgian censors will not pass letters written in German script; gradually his handwriting deteriorates.

Without a frontier permit, travel to Recklinghausen (Anka's home town) is impossible. Her mother wants their relationship ended anyway; upon her return home, Anka is dragged off to church to confess her sins. She tells Goebbels she has prayed for him. He sets up her three latest photos in his room, including one on a sunlit Castle Hill.[57]

THE POST-REVOLUTIONARY government in Germany ordered elections to be held on January 26, 1919. On the election eve he heard his old teacher Dr Bartels speak for the Democratic Party. 'I was strengthened,' wrote Goebbels, 'in my opposition to the Democrats.'

All his former schoolmates would vote for the catholic Center or the more right-wing German Nationalist party; already, Goebbels inclined toward the latter – 'There are still Germans in the German fatherland, thank God.' He envied those living outside the occupied territories like Anka in Recklinghausen. 'God grant,' he wrote her, his letters displaying political fervor for the first time, 'that our fatherland will once more become the way we knew it as children.'[58]

In the election Joseph and his brother Konrad both voted for the German Nationalists.[59] 'Grim times,' he predicted a few days later, 'lie ahead for us Germans.'[60] A talk with organized workers at Rheydt convinced him that they might have a real case against their capitalist oppressors.[61]

That May of 1919 Anka returns to Freiburg. Kölsch is down there too.

Goebbels hurries to join them. A French Negro soldier lets him through the checkpoint at Ludwigshafen.

Anka seems cooler, and confesses one morning that she has slept with Kölsch. Goebbels forgives her and kisses away the tears of contrition welling in her eyes. For an instant of happiness she is willing to accept an eternity of perdition, he will write in July 1924; a truly divine female, but not one for him to marry, he decides.[62]

They would destroy each other. Yet every time he sees her in the years that follow, his knees knock and his face runs crimson just like the first time.[63]

One afternoon in 1919 there is a knock at his door in Freiburg and Richard Flisges walks in, rain dripping from his demob trenchcoat. An ex-lieutenant, he is back from the wars, decorated and embittered, his arm in a sling.[64] He has failed the university entrance examination and will now turn into a pacifist and agitator against the established order.

Goebbels listens eagerly to this rootless, ill-educated, disillusioned soldier. He has always had a respect for the lower orders. Writing to Willy Zilles in 1915 he has discounted the poet Horace's theme of *odi profanum vulgus et arceo* ('I hate the vulgar mob and keep them at a distance'), preferring instead the romantic poet Wilhelm Raabe's motif: *Hab' acht auf die Gassen!* ('Pay heed to the street!').[65] Flisges introduces him to the socialism of Karl Marx and Friedrich Engels and Walther Rathenau and implants further trace-elements of the anti-bourgeois class struggle in Goebbels.

Thus, while Goebbels attends the seminars on Goethe and on the era of *Sturm und Drang*, he begins to think more about the social and political issues scarring defeated Germany. In the evenings he argues about God; he is beginning to have serious doubts about his religious beliefs.

He and Anka leave Freiburg early in August 1919. He borrows one hundred marks from a friend, and pawns his watch to a waiter to pay for supper. He has to spend the autumn break at Münster as his identity papers will not get him back into the occupied Rhineland.

Anka phones him every day in the local cafe, but he can barely afford the obligatory cup of coffee. He begins to write his own life story as a novel, *Michael*, in which Anka is identifiable as the heroine Hertha Holk. He gets home to Rheydt, crossing the frontier illegally in an overflowing train at Düsseldorf.

On September 19 he posts to the Albertus Magnus Society a fresh application for funds.

Later, heading south to Munich with Anka, he pauses briefly at Frankfurt where he visits Goethe's house. But why tarry in this Jewish city, he asks himself, when Munich beckons from afar? He borrows 1,200 marks from yet another school friend and finds lodgings in Munich on the second floor of Papa Vigier's at No. 2 Roman Strasse, out in Neuhausen.

On October 29, his twenty-second birthday, Anka writes in his diary, 'National Holiday!' He sends two more postcards to the catholic charity; the stamp on one is overprinted with the legend 'People's Republic of Bavaria,' because the communists are now in power.

The charity makes him a final loan of 250 marks. At Munich he studies under the Swiss art historian, Professor Heinrich Wölfflin; he studies music under Professor Hermann Ludwig Baron von der Pfordten and catholic theology under Professor Joseph Schnitzer. But his real intellectual nourishment is from what he takes in at the galleries and museums – the paintings of Arnold Böcklin, of Carl Spitzweg, and of Anselm Feuerbach. He reads voraciously, devouring Sophocles' drama *Antigone*, August Strindberg's *The Red Room*, Thomas Mann's *Death in Venice*, and assorted works by Henrik Ibsen and Leo Tolstoy.

He auctions his suits, sees Anka pawn her own Gold watch, and hocks his own watch for a pittance to – he recalls in 1925 – an 'insolent Jew.' Such stereotyped references are rare in his early letters. On the contrary, he sends Anka a gentle rebuke. 'As you know, I can't stand this exaggerated antisemitism,' he writes, in a reference to their teacher Gerhard Bartels. 'I can't claim that many of my best friends are Jews, but my view is you don't get rid of them by huffing and puffing, let alone by pogroms – and if you could do so that would be both highly ignoble and unworthy.'[66]

There is still little trace of his later murderous antisemitism.

2: *Prodigal Son*

W HILE AT FREIBURG UNIVERSITY in 1919 Joseph Goebbels turned his back on the catholic church. Perhaps the suffocating Catholicism of the diocesan city of Würzburg had contributed to his restlessness. Certainly he was deeply troubled by the nature of God and what he saw as the falsification of the true faith by idolatrous priests. In his novel *Michael* he allowed his hero to brood upon this dilemma. The result was much portentous, empty rhetoric, but there was one proposition of substance: 'It hardly matters what we believe in, so long as we believe in something' – the essence of the later Joseph Goebbels.

In July 1919 the Unitas journal reported that 'Herr Göbbels' had seceded from the fraternity. He continued to waver, and wrote to his father on October 31 about this torment ('But if I should lose my faith . . .'). He spoke of the diligence with which he was persevering in his studies and – be it noted – stressed that he had not compromised his morals. But he added: 'Why don't you tell me that you curse me as the Prodigal Son who has left his parents and gone into the wilderness?'[1]

On November 7, his father sent him an angry reply, followed two days later by a more reasoned epistle setting aside his son's doubts. Many a young man was tormented by doubt, he wrote. He challenged his wayward son to answer this question: 'Do you intend writing books that are not compatible with the catholic religion?' Then he reminded him of how they had prayed together at the deathbed of Elisabeth: 'What was the one consolation in our grief then? It was this: That the dear little soul had been properly provided with the last rites of our Holy Church, and that we could pray for her *together*.'

Scripture teacher Father Johannes Mollen would recall that after leaving university Goebbels continued to speak at catholic conclaves: 'I myself always stayed in touch with him.' Years later, his parish priest would tersely justify his original recommendation to the Albertus Magnus Society: 'None of us could see into the future.'

UNDER the influence of Flisges and his own study of Dostoyevsky Goebbels became politically aware. He was now twenty-two and leaning ideologically to the left. When the student Anton Count von Arco-Valley was sentenced for the

assassination of the extreme left-wing prime minister of Bavaria Kurt Eisner
(alias Isidor Kosmanowski), Goebbels became curious about socialism. Being
as yet more of a literary than a political inclination he explored his ideas in a
drama, scribbled in an exercise book, entitled 'The Working Classes' Struggle.'[2]
Again he pawned his watch and set off, alone, for home. In a few days during the
Easter break he sketched another socio-political drama, *The Seed* (later *Blood-
Seed*).[3] He tried to get employment as a teacher in East Prussia or in Holland
(he had a smattering of maternal Dutch).[4] As the communist revolution swept
across the Ruhr, Goebbels decided to make his home run for that Ph.D. degree;
he chose Heidelberg for the attempt.

   That Christmas he found himself alone in Munich, prevented by the Allied
occupation authorities from joining his family at Rheydt for the festivities.
He stayed in the Bavarian capital, as Richard Wagner's Ring cycle was to be
performed at the National Theater; he found himself strolling through the
cobbled, snowswept streets on Christmas Eve, entirely deserted save for a police
constable wrapped to the ears against the cold. From somewhere came the
sound of children singing; and then of a piano – Franz Schubert, the melodies
borne through the air, he would later write, as though on angels' hands. 'I
know not how long I stood there,' he recorded. 'Only that I sat that evening in
a quiet, dark corner of the church of Our Lady and celebrated Christmas alone,
as though in a dream. On December 29 I went to the Tyrol, going up into the
eternal mountains satiated with the sounds of Wagner.'[5]

HE and Anka have drifted apart since that Christmas of 1919. As recently as
December 19 they have mooched along the shores of Lake Starnberg and Anka
has sketched in his pocket diary a room with two (single) beds. She has given
him a Gold bracelet. He has given her Heinrich Heine's *Book of Ballads* with a
fulsome dedication. But she begins to make possessive scenes; he takes refuge
in Tolstoy's *War and Peace*, he alternately fights with her or forges fantastic
plans of marriage, then sees them shipwrecked on her bourgeois attitudes. He
'runs into' her in Freiburg and finds that she too is making for Heidelberg.
He persuades her to study elsewhere – 'What an idiot I am,' he recalls later,
perhaps rationalizing his own failure to hold on to her. They have entered that
cruel phase in an overlong affair when each partner derives more pleasure
from making the other suffer.

   When he next sees her it will be Whitsun. He reads from *The Seed* to her,
but she, the wealthy miller's daughter, is alienated by its left-wing political
message. The rift widens. She begins to see Theo Geitmann, a close friend of
his.[6] Chagrined, he returns the bracelet. He offers her formal engagement ('If
you don't feel strong enough to say yes,' he writes, 'then we must each go our
separate ways'); she turns him down.[7]

   After one unsatisfactory night, with him on the chaise-longue and her in
bed, he pencils a four-page letter of farewell, a romantic torrent of pleas to
return to his embrace. 'I rest my fortune in your lenient hand,' he concludes.

'Cast the first stone if you must. May it then dash me to pieces, and may you never come to regret it.' Satisfied by this literary effort, he leaves the letter unsent (the four sheets show no folds).[8]

Spending the autumn break at home he reads Dostoyevsky's *The Brothers Karamazov*, and suffers a nervous collapse. He pens a testament, dated October 1, 1920, in which he allocates his books, his alarm clock, his inkwell, and other pathetic chattels to his friends: they are to sell off clothing to repay his debts, to his father, Director Cohnen's wife, a Bonn jeweler, and the Albertus Magnus charity. He wills his poetry and novellas to Flisges and his mother (in that order). 'Miss Anka Stalherm is to be urged to burn my letters ... May she be happy and not brood upon my death.' The final sentences hint unmistakably at suicide: 'I depart gladly from a life which has become just hell for me.'[9] He folds this into a small envelope, but takes no further action.

That autumn of 1920, learning that she is in Munich, he borrows money from his brothers and sends his trusty friend Flisges to find out more. Flisges writes that Anka has been seen escorted by a gentleman in a flashy waistcoat 'with many Gold knobs and pins.'[10]

Distraught, Goebbels hurries from Heidelberg to Munich, to Anka's address in Amalien Strasse; while he waits outside, Flisges stomps upstairs. But she has left for Freiburg the day before, 'with her fiance.'[11] She has fallen for Georg Mumme, a young, stodgy law student five years older, and with better financial prospects, than the crippled aesthete Goebbels.[12] In a daze, Goebbels pens a vile letter to her which gives him brief satisfaction. He writes again in remorse. Her reply is the last for several years.

She is 'very unhappy,' she confesses, as she knows that he is the first and last man who has ever loved her with such intensity. 'I will always be your true Anka,' is her final empty salutation.[13]

To the interloper Mumme – whom she shortly marries – he writes what he calls a 'rather categorical' letter.

In the new year he will ask her to return all his poems and love letters. 'Anka, thou murderess!' he reproaches her memory, and eight years later her betrayal will still fester in his mind. 'Anka walked out on me,' he will write. 'And my entire relationship with women has suffered ever since.'[14]

HE had hoped to study for his degree under the distinguished Friedrich Gundolf, professor of literary history at Heidelberg. Gundolf (Gundolfinger) had written the definitive biography of Goethe. When Goebbels arrived at the university for the summer term of 1920 however Gundolf directed him to Professor Max Baron von Waldberg, a fellow Jew who had authored many a work on the history of literature. Waldberg assigned as his doctoral topic the obscure playwright Wilhelm von Schütz (1776 – 1847). In his competent dissertation Goebbels made perhaps over-frequent use of the first person (as in 'As far as I can see ...') and carefully praised the opinions of Gundolf and Waldberg.[15] Later he would have the university's records doctored to imply that his dissertation was more concerned with the political undercurrents of the Early Romantic Period; and when in 1943 the university ceremonially renewed his degree they tactfully omitted Waldberg's name from the festivities.

He did not ignore the other sex entirely during these last months of his formal studies. He would later refer cryptically to perhaps a score of females. As for Anka, Mumme had now threatened legal sanctions if he did not stop pestering her, so Goebbels took his revenge by rewriting *Michael* to make the heroine suffer as much despair as he.[16]

Back at Heidelberg after Christmas 1920 Professor Waldberg told him to study another term before submitting his dissertation. Goebbels returned to Rheydt in March 1921 to draft and redraft the masterpiece while Flisges kept him company. An unwary comrade loaned him his fiancée, Maria Kamerbeek, to type the dissertation. He dedicated the completed 215-page opus to his parents. Waldberg was impressed and offered a few suggestions for improvement ('But it's already *typed*,' wailed Goebbels in his notes, before submitting it unchanged). He attended the oral examination in the prescribed top hat on November 18, 1921. The four professors included Waldberg himself. At that evening's seminar party Waldberg addressed him with a knowing wink as 'Herr Doctor'.

Thus he had made it. He now had the coveted title which opened doors to class, wealth, and authority.[17] He shared his triumph with his rowdy friend Richard Flisges; they caroused all night long, then traveled tipsily north to Bonn still wearing their top hats. Their friends, also sporting top hats, were waiting on the platform.

Then on to Rheydt: the humble house in Dahlener Strasse was bedecked in flowers as the Prodigal Son returned, haggard but well spoken, educated, and, as always, Latin in his looks. If there had been a fatted calf to hand, old Fritz Goebbels, eyes awash at this visual proof that he was pulling his family through into a better future, would surely have slaughtered it.

3: 'A Wandering Scholar, I'

JOSEPH GOEBBELS CHERISHED that doctor's title. He asked to be called 'Herr Doctor' and used it even when just initialing – 'Dr G.' But for the next four years he remained perforce a nihilist doing nothing. To the quiet despair of his parents he squandered the pittance that he did earn from his meager writings or tutoring. Germany meanwhile slithered into economic chaos. The marching resumed: the Poles into Silesia; new parties in Germany; Mussolini on Rome. And on January 11, 1923 the French marched into the Ruhr. President Friedrich Ebert called for a campaign of passive resistance, and the French put the twenty-nine-year-old Albert Leo Schlageter before a firing squad for sabotage.[1] Later that year a young malcontent called Adolf Hitler, aged thirty-four, staged a *coup d'état* in Munich, was double-crossed by the Bavarian politicians, and ended up in prison at Landsberg. Berlin undertook to pay reparations to the Allies at the rate of 2·5 billion marks a year. Economic ruin faced Germany.

Goebbels neither noticed, nor protested, nor cared. His head was in the clouds. He even laid plans with Flisges to emigrate to India. But that would cost money too, so he stretched out on his bed at home instead and soaked up Oswald Spengler's writings on the decline of the west. The truth about his middle twenties was therefore unedifying, and in later years he would skirt around it in ever-widening circles. Later he allowed legends to circulate about his heroic undercover activity and early commitment to the Nazi party. Clad in what looked like infantry battledress, he was heard beginning one speech in Frankfurt in the winter of 1924–5 with the words, 'Those of us who have our injuries from the war . . .'[2] He later claimed to have attended his first party meeting while at Munich university. (Reworking his drama *Michael*[3] he would elaborate: he had heard an unnamed speaker of extraordinary magnetism speak – 'Hope shines on gray faces . . . A miracle.') He had applied there and then to join the party, he claimed. In 1927 the Goebbels legend would maintain that he had actually advised Hitler in 1919 when the party program was drafted. All of this was quite untrue. He would also suggest that in 1923 Hitler had commanded him to infiltrate into the occupied Ruhr, where under an assumed name he had led a resistance cell not far from the martyr Schlageter himself, until the French had deported him. 'If we had been too refined,' he would brag in 1943, 'none of us would have survived the year 1923.'

17

Goebbels too was behind the 'letter' which would circulate in later years and which he had allegedly sent to Hitler in Landsberg jail ('Like a meteor you soared aloft before our astonished gaze. . . Your address to the court in Munich was the greatest speech in Germany since Bismarck').

These legends endured even in the obituaries printed by his enemies.[4] 'I am not a little astonished,' wrote his fellow Nazi Karl Kaufmann in June 1927, 'that Dr Goebbels portrays things so differently. The rumor I have heard in Berlin, that Dr Goebbels was already advising Adolf Hitler in Munich on the program of the N.S.D.A.P. [Nazi party] in 1919, is also totally untrue.' Dr Goebbels had neither joined the passive resistance in 1923 nor taken any active part in it, said Kaufmann: Goebbels was not even an early party member.[5] True, he would somehow wangle a low number, 8762, for himself, but he did not in fact join until early 1925.

Fortunately Goebbels utilized idle hours in July 1924 to jot down a memoir of his early life. Hitler is mentioned only once, in a passing reference to 1923: 'Bavaria. Hitler.'

Goebbels was rootless, restless, and now friendless too: Richard Flisges had left to work in the mines. Challenged by the Albertus Magnus Society to give due account of his progress, Goebbels replied grandly on January 10, 1922 that he was looking out for a position in the press or theater. After carrying half a dozen of his pieces, the *Westdeutsche Landeszeitung* published no more, although he heard that they had attracted much attention. He worked briefly as the newspaper's art critic but was made redundant just before his birthday in 1922.[6]

A few days later he delivered a public lecture on Oswald Spengler and contemporary literature; he praised Spengler's critical remarks about the Jews, which in his view had gone to the root of the matter and 'must inevitably bring about a spiritual clarification of the Jewish problem.[7] His mother's suitcase would hold clippings of just a dozen newspaper contributions by Dr phil. Joseph Goebbels.[8]

Among the literary products of these otherwise idle years were another drama entitled 'Heinrich Kämpfert'[9] and manuscripts with titles like 'Gypsy Blood,' 'Those Who Adore the Sun,'[10] and 'A Wandering Scholar, I.'[11] One of his poems was called 'At Night.'[12]

> I awoke one night.
>   You lay by my side.
> The pale moon played on your left hand,
>   And it was white as snow.
> But your right lay on your heart,
>   And rose and fell,
> As your breast did rise and fall.

THE HAND, the breast in question belong to a pretty girl in Rheydt. Herbert Hompesch whispers to him that she is Else Janke, a schoolteacher and orphan.

She is well built and motherly, he so slight that, seeing him from the rear once, she thinks him only twelve years old.[13] He will later describe her variously as 'a rare mixture of passion and prudence'[14] and as 'a lovely, sweet-tempered chatterbox.'[15] Interestingly he will write: 'I often think of her as my mother.'[16]

What strikes her most, she relates years later, are his expressive eyes. She and Fritz Prang's girlfriend Alma Kuppe both teach at the Rheydt school attended by Goebbels' young sister Maria. Else teaches needlework and physical instruction. They make up a foursome, go sailing or on excursions together to places like the local Rheydt castle.[17]

He will later recall an evening with her in the summer of 1922: He kisses her, she tries to slap him, he makes as if to leave, she detains him, and they walk out all night long while they talk about their lives. 'I tell her about Anka,' he will write, adding with disappointment, 'She remains demure.' Rebuffed again!

From Baltrum, a Frisian island resort, she wires him not to come: He borrows money and disobeys. Up in her room he swears his love for her. 'I kiss her to my heart's content. She resists no longer.' Inspired by seeing Else nude for the first time ('just as God created her') he will rewrite his long-suffering *Michael* to include a scene where the eponymous hero struggles to conjure up the Muses on a Frisian island. But to his annoyance Else will not admit to their relationship in public.

The crippled Dr Goebbels has much to learn about the mysterious fluids and capillaries that, brought together, make up the female brain.

His girls are bowled over by the literary style and the intensity with which he woos them. He sets Else and Alma to copying out his articles and verses. But his writings are universally rejected by the big Jewish publishers like Mosse and Ullstein in Berlin.

He remarks to Else that you cannot get ahead unless you are 'one of the boys.' Else makes no response.

'My creativity is zero,' he writes. 'Why? Am I a failure?'

Else visits her family's friends in the banking world and finds a clerical job for him at the Dresdner Bank in Cologne. He does not rejoice – indeed his mood seems to darken. In a somber letter to Else at Christmas he lays bare his tortured soul at such length that we must ask where true emotion ends and conscious posturing begins. His letters ramble on, half sermons, half diatribes, acres of blank verse and poetry scattered at the feet of his admiring if tiny audience. Else firmly considers herself engaged to him, and even discusses with Alma whether his deformed foot might be congenital and affect their children. Goebbels has a quarrel with her about his deformity: whereupon she mentions a minor drawback of her own – she is half Jewish. This has not dawned on him until now. The magic goes out of his life, to be replaced by a nagging skepticism about her.

Starting at the bank on January 2, 1923, he sees at first hand the unpalatable side of capitalism, and reacts with repugnance to the 'sacred speculation' by the rich and influential. The country's banks, he finds, are nearly all Jewish.

He begins to ponder upon the relationship between *das Judentum* (roughly, Judaism or the Jewish community) and the Money Problem. The more he looks around the more he perceives the Jews – young Otto Klemperer, whom he hears conducting a Gustav Mahler symphony, turns out to be a Jew; so does Mahler himself. He studies Houston Stewart Chamberlain and he finds himself troubled by the Jewishness of Else.

   He cannot ignore the contrasts. He himself has to set out from Rheydt each morning at five-thirty and gets home at seven or eight each night, while his pay packet shrinks in value through the galloping inflation that has set in. 'Cologne is ad nauseam,' he writes. 'Pay check worthless.' (On March 27 he sends the Albertus Magnus Society a ten-thousand-mark banknote; it is worth less than one Gold mark.) From his grim lodgings in No. 77 Siebengebirgsallee in a southern suburb he writes endless letters to his 'little rosebud' Else. He yearns for her. 'Why have we two, so much in love, been born into so wretched a time?' And yet: 'I am firmly convinced that the time will come for me to use my real strength.'

LYING IN a deckchair on Baltrum island one July afternoon in 1923 trying to avoid Else's tedious sister Gertrud, he received the shattering news that Richard Flisges had been crushed to death down the mines at Schliersee.[18] He would dramatize his grief, wallowing for months in self-pity; and he rewrote the ending of *Michael* to send his hero down the mines to his death despite his landlady's premonition of doom. He has Michael die on January 30: that date is a kind of premonition too.

   Upon his return from Baltrum the bank fired him. Keeping the truth from his parents, he continued to commute to Cologne, but barely troubled to scan the newspapers for vacancies, although he assured Else that he did.[19] During his six weeks away on Baltrum the mark's value had dwindled to almost nothing. The U.S. dollar bought three million marks on August 1 and 142 million eight weeks later.

   Else's savings shrank. From his lodgings in Cologne he wrote to his father pleading illness – a nervous disease which must be congenital, he said – and his father begged him to come home, going so far as to send the fare.[20] Fritz Prang found him a new job as a caller on the floor of Cologne's stock exchange. He wrote an essay about Flisges which the local newspaper published at Christmas.[21] Trapped in his lodgings, Goebbels' brain fevered on. He brought forth a new drama, *Prometheus,* and in September another play, *The Wanderer,* in which a Traveler guides an often despairing Poet across the heights and sloughs surrounding the German people.[22] He witnessed from afar the collapse of passive resistance; he lived sometimes in an alcoholic haze, because one guilder would buy fifty beers.

   The words *Judentum*, *Qual* (anguish), and *Verzweiflung* (despair) whirled kaleidoscopically around his jottings. Else had given him a notebook and on October 17, 1923 he resumed his famous diary.[23] 'I can't stand the anguish any

longer,' he wrote. 'I've got to set down all the bitterness that burdens my heart.'
For Goebbels, writing the diary became something of a fetish, an advance
programming of his brain for great things to come. He was aware of a messianic
sense of mission. In July he asked in its pages: 'Who am I, why am I here, what
is my task and what my purport? Am I a wastrel, or an emissary who is waiting
for God's Word?' And he added: 'Again and again one shining light escapes
the depths of my despair: my belief in my own purity, and my conviction that
some day my hour will come.'

'WHERE ARE YOU now, my dear deceased?' he appealed on the first anniversary
of Flisges' death. 'Why don't you give me some portent of where we must go
and what we must do to obtain deliverance... Leave me not in despair!'[24]
Friendless and jobless, he sank to a low point of mental decline that bordered
sometimes on suicide.[25] As inflation roared out of control his father became
increasingly monosyllabic. 'Why must so many give me up as beyond hope,'
Goebbels had asked Else Janke in a letter in June 1923, 'and consider me lazy
and unreasonable and unmodern?'

Overshadowing their whole relationship is Else's Jewishness, from which
there is no escape: in November 1923 she writes to him, 'Our whole row recently
about the racial problem kept coming back to me. I just couldn't stop thinking
about it and saw it really as an obstacle to our future relationship. In fact I think
you're far too obsessed about the whole thing.'[26] So he stayed at home, whiling
away the hours in the summer house which his parents had built, his powerful
thoughts riding on ahead of his frail frame.[27] He dreamed of launching his
own journal in Elberfeld; but where to raise the capital?[28] He fancied himself
winning the literary prize offered by the *Kölnische Zeitung* with *Michael* and
traveling the continent as a much acclaimed scholar.[29] 'But nobody pays me
anything for what I write,' he moaned in August 1924.[30]

He yearned helplessly for Anka and her glittering green eyes, and spent days
sorting out the letters they had exchanged.[31] 'Just one day together,' he wrote in
his notes, 'and we would understand each other again.'[32] A deep, unremitting
despair had seized him. He bemoaned the God that had created him a crippled
weakling. 'Despair, despair!' he lamented. 'I can't bear to live and see all this
injustice. I must join the fight for Justice and Freedom! Despair! Help me, O
Lord, I am at the end of my strength!!!'[33]

The more the products of his festering intellect were rejected by unseen
editors, the more he saw the Jews behind his torment. He wrote at length on
January 23, 1924 to Mosse's *Berliner Tageblatt*, applying for a job as sub-editor
and boldly asking for 250 marks per month. The curriculum vitæ which he
appended to this application was more than economical with the truth: he
claimed to have studied modern 'theater and press history' from November
1921 to 1922 at Bonn and Berlin – in fact he had never visited Germany's capital;
more recently, he said, he had become familiar with 'broad areas of modern
banking' at the Dresdner Bank. 'In consequence of minor nervous problems

caused by overstrain at work and an accident' – he had been set on in the street a year before – 'I was obliged to give up my employment in Cologne.'[34] Theodor Wolff, Mosse's editor, who turned him down, was Jewish.[35]

The diaries for the next years show him in a painful light – introspective to the point of obsession, scribbling plays, articles, and critiques for a public no larger than himself and, sometimes, the woman in his life. With dwindling hope but dull obstinacy he kept submitting the typescript of *Michael Voorman* to new publishers.[36] Why even get up in the morning? 'Nothing awaits me – no joy, no suffering, no duty, no job.'[37]

HE HAD already tried his hand at public speaking – his notes refer to a November 1922 talk in Rheydt, well received in the local press.[38] Once in June 1924 he and Fritz Prang visited a local communist meeting. Invited to speak, Goebbels was interrupted immediately: 'Capitalist swine!' He rounded on his heckler. 'Here is my purse,' he challenged. 'You show me yours. The one who has the most is the capitalist swine!' The miners and textile workers roared with laughter and allowed him to speak on.[39]

In the wake of the failed Munich putsch the Nazi party had been banned; with Hitler imprisoned, its former members had splintered into factions like the Völkisch-Sozialer Block, a coalition with the former Deutsch-Völkische Freiheitspartei (German Folkish Freedom party) founded by landowner Albert von Graefe.[40] The charismatic leader of the Nazis in northern Germany was Gregor Strasser, a wealthy pharmacist from Landshut in Bavaria. These right-wing groups had fared well in the election of May 4, 1924, attracting 6·5 percent of the votes. On June 29 Goebbels looked in on one pettifogging meeting of Graefe's party at Elberfeld. He was not impressed. 'So these are the leaders of the "folkish" movement in the occupied zone,' he scoffed in his diary. 'You Jews, and you French and Belgian gentlemen, don't have much cause for worry.' He had evidently heard more positive word about the Nazis in Bavaria because he added: 'If only Hitler were free!' The local folkish chieftain was the politician Friedrich Wiegershaus. He was worthy, obliging, and good-natured. 'This notion of a "folkish" Greater Germany isn't bad,' wrote Goebbels, 'but we lack any capable, hardworking, and high-minded leaders.'[41] Germany, he concluded in a typical Goebbels phrase, was crying out for a leader, like the thirst of parched summer earth for rain. 'One man!!! Bismarck *sta up*! My brain and heart reel with despair for my fatherland.'[42]

What were his politics at this time? His reading had vested him with some surprising inspirations. The memoirs of August Bebel (1840–1913), the founder of the Social Democratic party, had taught him not to lose heart.[43] The real workers, Goebbels concluded, were in fact nationalist to the core. The Jews, intellectually head and shoulders above Bebel, had run rings around him. Goebbels for a time even described himself as a German communist; but this was more for the Russian origins of communism than for what it said as a creed. He read the diaries kept by Henri Alexandre de Catt as private secretary to Frederick the Great and three times afterward quoted the monarch's dictum: 'Life becomes a curse, and dying a duty.'

When he plowed through Richard Wagner's autobiography he identified painfully with the maestro's anguished struggle to survive in Paris, and with his physical suffering. He saw Wagner as a wage-slave enchained by the 'filthy Jew' Schlesinger.[44]

Looking around, he scowled at his smug, shallow-minded, pinstriped contemporaries, their lives dominated by the pay packet, football, and sex, and he understood why the communists hated the bourgeoisie.[45] In July 1924 he began holding little political meetings at his house (in his parents' absence), at which he described the great socialist experiment in Russia – 'the glow from the east,' he called it in Latin in his diary: *Ex oriente lux*. Only the Jewish nature of the Bolshevik leadership bothered him. 'Men of Russia!' he wrote. 'Chase the Jews to the devil and put out your hand of friendship to Germany!'[46]

He was not however an *international* socialist. The great Germanic works inspired him. He immersed himself in Johann Sebastian Bach's *Saint Matthew's Passion*, and discovered Wagner's *Meistersinger*.[47]

His antisemitism was reinforced by reading the book *Prozesse* (Trials) by Maximilian Harden – he recorded afterward that Harden was not a German at all but a Polish Jew, Isidor Witkowski.[48] 'What a hypocritical Schweinehund this damn Jew is,' he wrote; and then, broadening his aim: 'Rogues, blackguards, traitors: they suck the blood out of our arteries. Vampires!' Harden, he decided, was a dangerous man precisely because he gave his writing all he had – pungency, a caustic wit, and satire. 'Typical of how the Jews fight,' he assessed.[49] 'Our worst enemies in Germany are the Jews.'[50]

Everywhere he detected their baneful influence. If he, Goebbels, were in power he would pack them all into cattle trucks and ship them out of Germany: so he wrote on July 2, 1924.

However, reading the prison letters of Rosa Luxemburg[51] he was surprised at the idealism and warmth of this militant leftist's letters. He sensed that perhaps he was doing her an injustice. 'You can't change your nature,' he realized guiltily. 'And my nature is now rather biased toward the antisemitic.'

THE RIGHT-WING parties announced a two-day rally to be held at Weimar in mid-August 1924 to agree upon strategy for the next elections, due on December 7.

Weimar! What visions of Goethe and Schiller the name evoked. In the privacy of his diary Goebbels sometimes seriously compared himself with one or the other, particularly Schiller.[52] So when his former schoolfriend Fritz Prang suggested they go to Weimar together he was delighted. It would be his first foray into the heart of Germany.

The Weimar meeting was a milestone in his career.[53] He gained immediate inspiration from the well-attended rally at the National Theater and the shouts of Heil. He saw for the first time the swastika – this sinister four-elbowed symbol – and inked it into his diary. 'All these young people who are fighting alongside me,' he wrote. 'It does my heart good.'

He saw them sporting the same swastika emblem on their helmets – Hitler's elite guard, the Highland League (Bund Oberland) – as they paraded to hear an address by the war hero Erich Ludendorff, patron of the folkish movement. Sizing up the others, he saw Albert von Graefe, a tall gangling ex-major in a black frock-coat, as a man of culture, and Gregor Strasser as a warm human being. He also encountered here the Nuremberg Nazi Julius Streicher, who had founded his own Party for the Struggle against International Jewry: this fanatic with the pinched lips was too intense for his liking, but he reflected that every movement needed the occasional man who went berserk as well.

With Hitler still in prison, the Weimar rally was *Hamlet* without the Prince of Denmark. Ludendorff was no Führer; he was not the messiah that Goebbels was seeking. He spent that Sunday on a quiet pilgrimage through the homes of Goethe and Schiller. Sitting in the former's favorite chair he dashed off a few lines to Else before strolling over to Schiller's large yellow-ochre house. That afternoon, still an outsider, he watched the flags and swastikas parading – some thirty thousand marching men in his estimate.

The tumultuous roars of Heil when Hitler's name was mentioned made a lasting impression. For a while he sat with Fritz Prang in a bar, Chemnitius. Fritz wanted to relax but Goebbels was so keyed up that he talked only about politics, ignoring the come-hither glances directed at him, he claimed in his diary, by girls seated all around him. He had found a new passion. 'I have begun to think *völkisch*,' he wrote. 'It is a *Weltanschauung*, a philosophy of life.'

Pure chance had decreed that he emerge from his hibernation here on the far right, and not on the left. On August 21, 1924, nervous lest the Belgian authorities suddenly show up, he and Prang founded the local (Mönchen-Gladbach) branch of Graefe's movement (the prefix 'National Socialist' was still forbidden). Several friends joined at once. He made a ninety-minute speech and saw how the eyes of one youngster in front began to glow.[54]

These first meetings were held in Batze-Mohn's historic beerhall or at Caumann's in Augustastrasse.[55] At least once in 1924 the Belgian occupation authorities did take him in for questioning. Shown the interrogation record years later he would pride himself on his foresight: 'It's all just as I think today. Nearly fifteen years ago, as a little agitator.'[56]

Shortly after, he moved from Rheydt to Elberfeld. He later put it about that the occupation authorities had expelled him from their zone.[57] He began, despite misgivings, to work for Wiegershaus, who had been subsidizing a political weekly called *Völkische Freiheit* (Folkish Freedom) since March 1924.

Around this time Else returned to his life, arousing God and the Devil in his catholic loins. 'Next to money,' he ruminated, 'Eros is what makes the world go round.'[58]

More usefully, a typewriter also arrived, a machine whose intricacies seemed more easily mastered than those of women.[59] The first contributions signed by 'Dr G.' appeared in issue No. 24 dated September 13, 1924.[60] One was an article examining the concepts of National and Socialist (it concluded: 'We are nothing. Germany is everything!').

It was followed a week later by 'The Führer problem.'[61] On October 4 his name appeared in the imprint for the first time, as 'Dr Paul J. Goebbels' – a clue therein that he disliked the taint of 'Joseph.'

Hitler was still incarcerated in Landsberg prison. Meeting Gregor Strasser, the Nazi leader's burly viceroy, at Elberfeld on September 13 Goebbels asked him whether Hitler would soon be released. 'We are all missing him,' he confessed to his diary. In Hitler, whom he had yet to meet, he saw the unifying concept of the movement – 'The fixed pole around which all national socialist thinking revolves.'[62]

He was flexing his muscles as a public speaker. He recognized in himself the elements of a 'ripe old demagogue' and set about refining his delivery.[63] Over the next year he would deliver no less than 189 speeches, learning to cast off all cant and phony philosophizing, becoming preacher, apostle, and agitator alike.[64] In his hands, he would write, he found that the soul of the German working man was as soft as wax, and he could knead it and mold it as he desired.

He soon fell out with Wiegershaus. His proprietor wanted his little weekly to emphasize German nationalism. Goebbels preferred to put the socialism first. Soon three-quarters of the weekly was being written by Goebbels. By threatening to quit he bluffed Wiegershaus into appointing him managing editor as from October 2, 1924. It was another rung up the ladder. 'Since yesterday,' he wrote the next day, 'I am quite a different person. At home too' – and what measure of relief lies in these words – 'they look at me with quite different eyes.' He had his own mouthpiece. Upward to the stars, onward to freedom for Germany, God be at our side! These were the thrilling phrases that he inscribed in his diary.[65]

Under Dr Paul J. Goebbels the weekly became readable and hard hitting. He was not happy with his writing style, but practice made perfect and his thoughts flowed fast and free. He installed a sub-office in his parental home. As his twenty-seventh birthday came and went his parents were astounded by the change. He still lounged around unshaven, but he had a sense of purpose. He increased his literary intake still more: he digested ten newspapers each day, and dealt with correspondence until two or three A.M. He began a new article, 'The basic problems of Jewry.'[66] His parents stopped nagging. His fame as orator and writer was noised across the Rhineland. True, he was not being paid, but this fame was gratification enough.

4: *The Little Agitator*

I N THE MAY 1924 PARLIAMENTARY elections 1,918,329 people had voted for the right-wing parties' united front, giving them thirty-two of the 472 seats in the Reichstag; but of these only ten, under Gregor Strasser, owed allegiance to Hitler. In the election of December 7 the right wing, now named the National Socialist Freedom movement, attracted only 907,242 votes: Fourteen MPs, with only five representing Hitler.

Writing after this reverse Goebbels encouraged his readers on December 20: 'There is no use denying it: We lost this battle, and the enemy triumphed all along the line.'

He had intuitively perceived the correct propaganda tactic – ruthless depiction of the somberness of the hour. 'The Idea,' he continued, 'is worth any sacrifice, even the sacrifice of lives and property!' And then, in a pale pre-echo of his famous proclamations in the last days of his life, he hinted at the darkness that precedes each dawn: 'Every disaster at Jena is followed by a victory at Leipzig.'

The first rays of the new dawn appeared that same afternoon. Hitler arrived back at his Munich apartment, a free man again. Goebbels acclaimed him in his weekly's Political Diary, published on New Year's Day 1925: 'We greet thee, leader and hero, and there is an enormous joy and anticipation in us knowing that thou art again in our midst.'

Hitler's release from Landsberg threw his party into flux. Goebbels reassessed the conflict between the national and socialist elements of the party's program. He found it impossible to swallow the internationalist aspects of Marxism, but he hoped to steer the nationalist movement toward socialism, rather than see its socialist aspects drenched in mindless nationalism.

In the Ruhr and Rhineland, he found many activists who thought like him – particularly the former members of the paramilitary Free Corps. Among these was Karl Kaufmann. Kaufmann, three years his junior, had organized N.S.D.A.P. *Ortsgruppen* (local groups) in several Ruhr cities until forced by the Prussian police to flee to Bavaria. Now he was back in Elberfeld, raising a political force aligned against the bourgeois, comfortably-off Wiegershaus.

Goebbels too was evidently disillusioned with the folkish movement.

In the final issue of his weekly, an anonymous advertisement appeared on January 17, 1925, announcing under Box R.26: 'Situation wanted. Editor, young, folkish, accustomed to work independently; good leader-writer, organizer, workaholic; unemployed because of political developments; seeks position, possibly in financial firm.' Three days later Wiegershaus invited him to resign, and he cast his lot with Kaufmann instead.

His personal life now was overshadowed by a humiliating lack of funds.[1] He was often unable to pay his rent or buy food, but when Kaufmann needed it desperately Goebbels proudly loaned him his last forty marks.[2] They became firm friends; Kaufmann was one of the very few men he addressed as *du*.[3] But it was hard for him to make true friends, and he found his Alsatian dog more likable than many a human being; indeed, he began to hate the human race, as he often confessed in his diary.[4] While his brother Konrad had now acquired a housemaid and a car, Joseph loathed the trappings of the bourgeoisie.[5]

His romantic escapades left him filled with self-hatred too. Else now rarely wrote to him, having found him juvenile and adolescent. He had started a parallel relationship with another girl, Elisabeth Gensicke, but nothing came of it. 'From year to year,' he reflected, 'I shall be more and more lonely until I end up all alone without love and without a family.'[6] That was his dread.

Comforting afterglows of his expired catholic faith still flickered. That March he dutifully hurried home to celebrate his Saint's Day in the family fold.[7] His brother Hans was no longer welcome there as he had married outside the faith. This brought home to Joseph once more the impossibility of marrying the 'voluminous, chubby, healthy, cheerful' half-Jewess Else, although he did sometimes envisage it: 'I should like her as my wife – if only she were not half-blooded.'[8]

Thus he toyed with Elisabeth's affections. 'The poor child has gone to pieces over me,' he wrote in bemusement. 'She trembles with anguish and joy when she sees me.'[9] He knew that tremor well. On April 20 a farewell letter came from Elisabeth – she could not stand it any longer. He replied with bleeding heart. 'And now,' he noted, 'this beautiful yet oh so ephemeral flowering dream is over. A great loneliness besets me.'[10]

DR GOEBBELS' party membership file is missing, but according to Karl Kaufmann he formally joined soon after Hitler had reconstituted the party in Munich on February 27, 1925.[11] In March Hitler activated a *Gau* (region) covering the North Rhineland. He appointed the middle-aged Baltic German journalist Axel Ripke as gauleiter.

At Kaufmann's instance, Ripke appointed Goebbels his manager (*Geschäftsführer*); among Ripke's other officials were such personalities as the later notorious Erich Koch, one of Leo Schlageter's comrades, and the later commander of the Sturmabteilung (S.A.), the Brownshirts, Viktor Lutze. The Elberfeld police soon took note that 'Goebbels appears as speaker at every function' and directed the evenings organized by the Elberfeld Ortsgruppe of the N.S.D.A.P., whose Führer was identified as 'K. Kaufmann'.[12]

Ripke's gau ran into immediate difficulties. On March 17 the French occupation authorities in Düsseldorf banned the organization and a week later arrested officials of its Elberfeld local.[13]

'We request,' wrote Goebbels to the Reich minister for the occupied territories on April 3, 'that you take appropriate steps to secure the immediate release of our men from custody.'[14] He had founded a local group at Krefeld, and often made speeches to them: One evening three Belgian detectives appeared, blocked the doors, and asked him if 'a Dr Goebbels' was in the hall.

Goebbels replied calmly, 'He's busy right now, I'm speaking on his behalf.' The officials left empty-handed.[15]

His radical views attracted the mistrust of other local officials. Arthur Etterich, who had founded the Hattingen local three years before, likened him to Maximilien de Robespierre; Ripke agreed, and cited Honore Count de Mirabeau's estimation of Robespierre: 'The man is dangerous – he believes what he says.'[16] Neither Goebbels nor Kaufmann felt that their gauleiter, Ripke, was a match for the French. He was too old, too conservative, and too diplomatic.[17]

Suppressing the actual epithet, Goebbels wrote: 'You can't stage a revolution with —s like these.'[18] But Ripke had Hitler's ear, and often traveled to Berlin to deal with Gregor Strasser, Hitler's deputy in all of northern Germany.

Goebbels conceived the idea of a fanatical Freedom League (Freiheitsbund) of thirty members pledged to donate a fixed amount each month – a sort of 'intellectual storm troop' as he put it.[19] Ripke was dismissive, but the first whip round at Hattingen yielded 268 marks.

For hours Goebbels plotted with Kaufmann ways of getting rid of their tedious, bourgeois gauleiter.[20] He had a long talk with Ripke on May 18 which ended, if Goebbels is to be believed, with the gauleiter on his knees pleading for a second chance.

The gauleiter accused him of promoting a new class-struggle. 'Too true!' commented Goebbels: 'With capitalism, you've got to call a spade a spade.'[21] After another five-hour session with Ripke he summed up their differences: 'Socialism means the liberation of the proletariat, not just breaking the Versailles peace treaty. God preserve my passion!'[22]

He was beginning to hate Ripke, and this feeling was mutual. The one wanted bourgeois reform, the other socialist revolution.[23]

In Munich, Hitler had revived the Party newspaper *Völkischer Beobachter*, and Alfred Rosenberg, its editor, invited Goebbels to submit occasional pieces from May.[24] He wrote by day and made speeches by night. He did not flinch from the ugly scenes that often resulted. After he spoke at a flag-dedication ceremony at Remscheid on June 5 there was a battle with communists in the railroad tunnel, and the police arrested 150 of his opponents. 'I was in the thick of it,' he chortled. 'The two factions went berserk and waded into each other. What a way to One Nation!'[25]

WHILE ELSE was away on vacation in the summer of 1925 he made use of her best friend Alma.[26] In mid-August he received a promising postcard from Alma which he described as the first sign after 'that night.' 'This teasing, enchanting Alma,' he mused. 'I rather like this creature.' Such romantic interludes were a cheap opium against the pangs of poverty: His landlord gave him notice to quit his lodgings at No. 122 Gesundheit Strasse (Health Street) in Elberfeld.[27] His parents had sent him 150 marks.[28] 'Damn and blast!' he let fly in his diary, and an unkind Fate, hearing him, responded with a final tax demand for 150 marks.

Once he spoke at Recklinghausen, Anka's hometown, and he half hoped to see her sitting there among his enraptured audience. Those audiences were getting larger. The *Völkischer Beobachter* (*VB*) reported regularly on his speeches. Together with Viktor Lutze, the region's S.A. commander, he spoke to three thousand packing the big concert hall in Essen. A truckload of young right-wingers known as the Falcons drove him home.[29]

Two days later on August 25 the French occupation troops finally pulled out of the Rhineland.

The first volume of Hitler's *Mein Kampf* had just been published, and Goebbels along with twenty thousand others was dipping into it.[30] There was much that he disagreed with.

He learned that on July 12 his gauleiter Ripke had blackened his name to Hitler as a 'bolshevist.' Goebbels fought back, accusing Ripke of embezzling party funds; this was one offense the party would not tolerate. On July 12 Hitler called all the party's gauleiters of northern Germany to Weimar, and it was in a beerhall here that day that he and Goebbels first briefly met.[31] 'Ripke is finished,' Goebbels wrote after an internal committee of inquiry had been set up, with Strasser presiding.[32] Ripke resigned, leaving Kaufmann, Lutze, and Goebbels in charge.

One day in midsummer Strasser came to see him. Strasser had earlier been gauleiter of Lower Bavaria, and in the failed 1923 putsch his stormtroopers had held the Isar bridges. With his rough-hewn features, he was the stereotype Bavarian; but he was shrewd, ambitious, and one of the cleverest in the Nazi hierarchy.

Probably he recognized in Goebbels a useful lieutenant whose politics were similar to his own. He certainly won Goebbels over. 'He has a wonderful sense of humor,' recorded the latter after this meeting. 'Related a lot of sorry things about Munich and about the swine at party headquarters there. Hitler is surrounded by the wrong people; I think Hermann Esser [Hitler's propaganda chief] is his undoing.'[33] Strasser revealed that he was planning to consolidate the party's organization in north-western Germany, and he would want Goebbels to edit a new journal as a weapon against Munich.

This was fighting talk, and Goebbels liked it. Gregor Strasser would become his first real employer: then his sworn rival: and ultimately his mortal enemy.

WHEN STRASSER'S conclave took place, in the grimy Ruhr town of Hagen on

September 10, Gregor himself could not attend as his mother was ill.[34] But those who did were the toughest men the party had in northern Germany, including many former Free Corps officers. Dr Robert Ley, thirty-five, a former aviator and now an industrial chemist, had directed the South Rhineland gau (around Cologne) since mid-July; Professor Theodor Vahlen, fifty-six, was gauleiter of Pomerania; Hinrich Lohse, a businessman, twenty-eight, who headed the northernmost gau, Schleswig-Holstein; Franz von Pfeffer, thirty-seven, who had been condemned to death by the French but had escaped, gauleiter of Westphalia since March; Ludolf Haase, gauleiter of south Hanover; and his deputy Hermann Fobke, who had spent some months in Landsberg with Hitler.

Fobke's report is in party files.[35] He felt that the 'sharp intellect' of Goebbels, whom he called the gau Führer of the north Rhineland, called for thorough analysis, 'as he does not seem all that trustworthy at first sight.'

Goebbels however was delighted at the outcome, telling his diary: 'We pulled everything off.' By that he meant that the regions of northern and western Germany would henceforth operate as a bloc under Strasser's centralized command, with his office at Elberfeld and 'a centralized management (*moi*).' Only Ley had quibbled.

Seventeen days later, on September 27, two hundred men from the Ruhr's local groups met at Düsseldorf to decide who should replace Ripke.[36] Goebbels hoped the choice would fall on him. But Kaufmann was 'unanimously elected' as gauleiter, with Goebbels merely manager as before.[37] It was some consolation that the audience bore him out of the hall on their shoulders. He desperately wanted to be loved.[38]

FOR THE NEXT thirteen months he was Kaufmann's roving agitator. Sometimes he felt ill-used, and cast a jealous, almost womanly eye over all his rivals for the gauleiter's affection. But editing Gregor Strasser's influential new fortnightly journal *National Socialist Letters* more than compensated. It enabled his voice to be heard far from Elberfeld. The journal's masthead proclaimed it as the work of 'leading members of the movement.'[39]

He would edit the first thirty-nine issues. Its four, or eight pages, sometimes carried contributions by Heinrich Himmler, Franz von Pfeffer, and Strasser's bombastic younger brother Otto. But above all Goebbels used it as his platform to argue his own socialist and antisemitic brand of politics. In the second issue he published a letter to 'my friend on the left,' arguing: 'You and I, we fight one another although we are not really enemies at all.'[40]

This was a trenchant theme in all his writings, as was his somewhat ritualized affection for Russia: in the fourth issue he proclaimed, 'we can see the commencement of our own national and socialist survival in an alliance with a truly national and socialist Russia.'[41]

When Gustav Stresemann signed the Locarno pact of nonaggression with France and Belgium (guaranteed by Britain and Italy) Goebbels was therefore appalled. An ugly vision seized him – of Germany's sons dying in the service of western capitalism, 'possibly, even probably, in some "Holy War" against Moscow!'[42] We shall be the mercenaries against Russia,' he repeated gloomily a week later, 'on the battlefields of capitalism. . . We're done for.'[43]

The *Letters* were an undeniable success. Goebbels advertised them in other party publications, calling upon all National Socialists of west and north Germany to pay a 1·50 mark quarterly subscription. 'Thus,' he found, 'we've got our hands on a unique instrument of power.' According to the journal's accountant Paul Schmitz he received 150 marks a month as editor.[44] The *Letters* gave the party a sense of direction. In his sixth issue Goebbels held forth on the N.S.D.A.P.'s need to radicalize socialism. He set this out at greater length in a standard speech, 'Lenin or Hitler,' which he first delivered (according to Prussian police records) in Hanover on September 17, 1925;[45] he delivered it scores of times afterwards, inspiring violent clashes in the 'Red' cities like Altona and Chemnitz, and fervent acclaim in Berlin, Dresden, Plauen, Zwickau, and elsewhere.[46] It was heavy on the theory and history, but still seized the imagination of his listeners, said Albert Krebs, a Party official in Hamburg.[47] 'We Germans,' declared Goebbels, 'are the unluckiest people God's sun shines upon. Sixty millions of us, surrounded by enemies, bleeding from a thousand wounds, the hardest-working nation on earth, and we see our only political exercise as being to tear ourselves limb from limb.' Because their leaders had failed to win over the working classes they had been thrown into the arms of the left; and here the 'systematic underminer of any true workers' movement, the marxist Jew,' had easily led them astray.

'We allowed ourselves to be humiliated at conference after conference,' continued Goebbels, 'in a way we wouldn't have dared humiliate even a nigger nation, and nobody came and thundered the word No! The Ruhr was occupied: the German people hid its bourgeois cowardice behind passive resistance. The Ruhr was lost – and Mr Gustav Stresemann espied a "silver lining" on the horizon. . . Stresemann's fat hand signed everything our grinning enemies laid before him.' 'Then,' he shrieked, 'came Locarno, and Gustav Stresemann trotted off to London and signed that too.' Locarno, he argued, meant not peace but war. He foresaw a gigantic armed struggle against the Soviet Union using German blood. 'And presiding over it all is the Jew, both in the ranks of world capitalism and concealed in Soviet bolshevism, egging on the Russians and Germans against each other. . .in one last orgy of hostilities.'

He introduced Lenin to his by now seething audiences in surprisingly warm terms, as a man who had learned all about social deprivation the hard way. 'Capitalism,' he declared, 'is the immoral distribution of capital.' Nazism made a distinction between creative state capital and a grasping international loan capital. 'Germany will become free,' he promised, 'at that moment when the thirty millions on the left and the thirty millions on the right make common cause.' 'Only one movement is capable of doing this: National Socialism, embodied in one Führer – Adolf Hitler.'

5: *God Disposes Otherwise*

F OR A WHILE KARL KAUFMANN was, after Else, the best friend Goebbels had. But Gregor Strasser was the man he most admired – five years his senior, Strasser was willing to adopt the radical program that Goebbels espoused.[1] He could use Strasser as a battering ram against Munich. They were not of course fighting Hitler himself, but the toadying parasites surrounding him in Munich and in particular the party's propaganda chief Hermann Esser. Munich hinted that Goebbels might like to go down there. The hints fell on deaf ears. Together with Strasser he intended to build his power base between the Rhine and the Ruhr.[2]

It is legitimate to ask whether his proletarian stance was mere posturing. His private writings do show a marked sympathy with the working class. His contempt for the 'bourgeois scum' in the party, toasting their toes on his radicalism as he engagingly put it, was genuine.

'I find it appalling,' he would write, 'that we and the communists are bashing each other's heads in.'[3]

He now drew audiences of two and three thousand with ease. Often there were as many thugs outside, armed with firearms too. At Düsseldorf on October 8, 1925 communists for miles around invaded his meeting, but within minutes he had silenced them and he went on to hold them in his grip for two hours.[4] He drafted in his own hand a cute pamphlet entitled *The Little ABC of National Socialism*, as a catechism for the party. He completed it on October 26 and his friend Director Arnold, a wealthy Hattingen industrialist, put up the capital for a first print of ten thousand.[5]

His personal affairs were in chaos. He was living a gypsy existence, changing trains and lodgings with almost equal frequency.[6] He was driving himself to the limit. His diary entries often end with a motif that remains unchanged for years – of dropping off exhausted to bed, for only a few hours' sleep.

He crisscrossed his tough industrial domain, in painfully slow local trains, setting eyes also on Lübeck, Hamburg ('redolent of ocean and America'), the Ruhr cities smoldering in their infernal polluted semi-darkness, and Hamburg again ('German sweat and German enterprise, exploited by the Jews').[7]

He wished he had hearth, home, and family to greet him at Elberfeld; but he found permanent relations with women difficult to achieve.[8] He placed these remote creatures on a sort of pedestal. He was not averse to exploiting them himself, but was profoundly indignant when he saw Hamburg's red-light district around the Reeperbahn, with the half-naked hookers standing in their doorways. A local party official later recalled that one keen young S.A. man asked, 'Doctor, what'll we do with streets like this after the revolution?', and Goebbels snarled in reply: 'We shall sweep them away like the garbage that they are!'⁹ He saw Germany's blonde girls embracing slit-eyed Chinamen in the street; the police just stood by grinning.¹⁰

He seldom took his women to his meetings, and no longer sent his writings to them either.

After Else wrote him a despairing letter shortly before Christmas he lamented, 'Why can't women be like us? Can they be educated? Or are they by their very nature inferior?'¹¹ 'There is a curse cast over you and women,' he told himself piteously five days later. 'Woe betide those who love you!'¹²

His diaries are still punctuated with wailing references to Anka. But these ululations are surely no more than an affectation. Anka had joined the Undead. Sometimes he journeyed through her town, Weimar, but he made no attempt to visit.

Once he took pen and paper and wrote to all his women friends. He hated himself as soon as he mailed the letter to her.

She did not reply.¹³ His diaries did not resist human nature's tendency to gild the lily: a riot at one meeting left one injured man, who died in hospital, but Goebbels' diary speaks of two dead. Two audiences estimated at fifteen hundred by the *VB* became 'three thousand' in the diary.¹⁴ While the newspapers referred to one shot being fired at an Essen meeting, the diary turned it into 'shooting.'¹⁵ But he was writing for effect.

The early diaries were composed in a lively vernacular, often difficult to convey in translation. Most prevalent in their pages was his sense of loneliness, his happiness when a cheering audience chaired him out onto the street. But one constant in his life was so ever-present that he only rarely referred to it – the pain from his crippled foot, which no doctor seemed able to dispel.

ON OCTOBER 12 a letter came from Gregor Strasser reporting that Hitler mistrusted Goebbels and had even cursed his name. Goebbels wondered if he should quit. He planned to tackle Hitler about the party's program when he came to Dortmund on October 24. In preparation, he finished reading *Mein Kampf*. 'Who is this man?' he exclaimed, strangely impressed: 'Half plebeian, half God. Is he Jesus Christ himself or just Saint John?' But it was not easy arranging an appointment with a messiah; Carl Severing, the Prussian minister of the interior,¹⁶ forbade Hitler to speak anywhere in Prussia, so the violent Dortmund meeting went ahead without him. Hitler attempted to reach Hamm next day, but Severing issued an arrest warrant and he turned back. Strasser spoke instead.¹⁷

When Hitler came to Brunswick, which was outside Prussia, for a regional convention in November, Goebbels saw him again – this was their second meeting.[18] It was November 4, 1925. With Bernhard Rust, he secured a six-thirty P.M. appointment with Hitler.

> He's just having a meal [recorded Goebbels]. At once he jumps to his feet and shakes my hand like an old friend. And those big blue eyes of his! Like stars! He's pleased to see me. I am in transports of delight. After ten minutes he withdraws. Then he has his speech ready in outline.
> Meanwhile I am driven over to the meeting, and speak for two hours. Huge applause, and then shouts of Heil and applause: he is there. He shakes my hand. He is still completely exhausted after his own great speech. Then he speaks here for half an hour too. With wit, irony, humor, and sarcasm, with seriousness, with fervor, with passion. This man's got everything to be a king. The born popular leader! The coming dictator.

Afterwards he waited outside Hitler's door hoping to speak to him, but he was fobbed off with a third handshake.[19] This fell some way short of the heart-to-heart talk he had planned.

At his own meetings the communist violence was getting out of hand. They often ended with riots, with shattered beer mugs and splintered furniture. At Chemnitz on November 18 he put his views on Lenin and Hitler to two thousand communists, who listened in silence. Then a thousand beer glasses were smashed, 150 people were injured and one man (or two) killed.[20]

Two days later he met Hitler again, in Saxony. Hitler invited him to speak first ('How small I feel!'), then presented him with his photograph inscribed with greetings to the Rhineland. The framed portrait would remain on Goebbels' desk until the very hour he died.[21]

ON THURSDAY November 26, 1925 he arrived in Berlin for the first time. His impressions were overwhelming: The vast sea of houses and buildings, the polyglot population, the bustle, the police with their helmets and truncheons. Berlin was a 'sinful Babel' of brick, stone, and concrete. Goebbels addressed that night an audience of thousands – he did not note how many or where. Everybody was there, including both Strasser brothers (he found Otto as 'decent' as Gregor), Gottfried Feder, the party's chief theoretician, and Dr Wilhelm Frick, the lawyer who had connived at Hitler's 1923 putsch from within Munich police headquarters. The Nazi party here in Berlin was weak, probably less than one thousand names. Dr Ernst Schlange, a civil servant, was the local gauleiter. He had lost an arm and half his face in the war.

'They say he's a pacifist,' commented Goebbels laconically.[22] Visiting the Reichstag building he was repelled by the spectacle of these parliamentarians ('Jews and their jackals') in their natural habitat. He dismissed the politicians in his diary with an obscenity and claimed to have felt such nausea that he had to flee.

Afterwards he paid a social visit to Helene Bechstein of the millionaire piano-manufacturing family. The Bechsteins were among Hitler's earliest backers. A few days later the Prussian political police section Ia opened their first dossier on Goebbels.

The Albertus Magnus Society revalued the ancient debt he owed them and on December 7, 1925 mailed a claim for repayment to his old lodgings in Cologne. It was returned marked 'gone away.' It was not that he was lying low. On November 15 he had stage-managed the homecoming of the remains of Ludwig Knickmann, a nationalist shot by Belgian occupation troops at Sterkrade in June 1923; he spoke at the funeral in Knickmann's native town, Buer.[23] Three weeks later he staged an even bigger ceremony in Leo Schlageter's honor.[24] Not for nothing had he read Richard Wagner's *The Art of Directing*.[25] Fifteen hundred (Goebbels wrote two thousand) brown-shirted S.A. men paraded out to the deserted, snowflecked heathland spot where the French had put Schlageter to death. Then, to the throb of muffled drums, the entire force marched down Düsseldorf's most expensive boulevard, the Königsallee.

The public acclaim was in sharp contrast to the frosty silence Goebbels met from his parents. At Rheydt he found that his father had bought a radio set – 'the modern mind-narrowing device,' scoffed his son, oblivious of the role that radio would play in his later life. 'Everything piped in! The philistine's ideal!'[26] But Goebbels had a new father-figure on his horizon. That Christmas Hitler sent him a leather-bound *Mein Kampf* inscribed with a tribute to the 'exemplary manner' of his fight.[27]

At a Hanover conference of the north-western bloc on November 22 Gregor Strasser agreed that Goebbels should draft a new program. Goebbels spent most of December on it, since it had to be ready for their next gauleiters' conference in Hanover. The redrafting was harder than he had anticipated.[28] In its final form it comprised twenty-four basic demands, all of them militantly anti-bourgeois: The party would respect private property, but nationalize all heavy industry and the great estates. Meanwhile Goebbels set about literary projects of his own, including a portrait gallery of political personalities, and a collection of his own political letters, *The Second Revolution*.[29]

To his discomfiture, when he arrived for the Hanover meeting on January 24, 1926 he found that Hitler had sent Gottfried Feder to attend and observe. The debate on Goebbels' 'Elberfeld Guidelines' lasted all next day. There was criticism of his lenient approach to Russia and the communists.[30] He went outside, smoked a cigarette, spoke for an hour, then saw the program adopted. According to Kaufmann, Goebbels was not sparing in his criticism of Hitler and Munich. According to Otto Strasser, he even climbed on a chair and proposed that the 'petit-bourgeois' Hitler be expelled from the party.[31] According to Rosenberg, he shrieked: 'Hitler has betrayed socialism!'[32] Afterwards Strasser pumped his hand – and Feder left to report to Hitler.

Concerned about this ugly trend, Hitler sent for Strasser; Strasser phoned Goebbels afterward, saying that 'Wolf' – Hitler's sobriquet – was 'coming round to their point of view,' but was going to call a conclave of all Germany's

gauleiters at Bamberg, on his own home ground. Totally misreading the
situation, Goebbels was delighted. 'In Bamberg,' he decided, 'we shall act the
coy beauty, and seduce Hitler into our camp.'[33]

At Bamberg on the appointed day, Sunday February 14, he met Gregor
Strasser early and they agreed their plan of action before walking over to the
meeting. Hitler drove grandly past, before halting his chauffeur and offering
Goebbels his hand. The young man took it, but the laugh was on him. Hitler
had packed the audience with loyal local officials: he spoke for four hours about
high politics and diplomacy, and Goebbels thought it prudent, on balance,
to keep his mouth shut. He heard Hitler oppose all thought of dispossessing
the princes and landed aristocracy (they were of course prominent among
his backers). 'For us,' ruled Hitler, 'there are no "princes," only Germans.' He
forbade all further discussion of the party program: It had been sanctified by
the blood of the party's first martyrs.

> I am quite stunned [wrote Goebbels the next day]. What kind of Hitler
> is this? A reactionary? Astonishingly clumsy and unsure of himself. The
> Russian question – he misses the point entirely. Italy and England 'are our
> natural allies.' Awful! 'Our mission is to smash bolshevism. Bolshevism is a
> Jewish sham! We are to disinherit the Russians!' All 180 millions of them!!!

He recorded that Feder, Ley, Streicher, and Esser all nodded approval. Strasser
lost his nerve and spoke only haltingly – 'Good old honest Strasser, *ach Gott,
we are no match at all for these swine down here!*'[34] Goebbels returned to
Elberfeld full of doubts, both about himself and about Adolf Hitler. Strasser in
fact panicked: he circularized all the gauleiters asking them to return to him for
destruction every single copy of the Goebbels guidelines. Goebbels now had the
reputation of a slippery intriguer, an opportunist. People called him the 'chap
with the tiny, cold, monkey's paws.'[35] Behind his back at Bamberg Streicher
called him 'dangerous.'[36] Learning of this from Fobke, Goebbels fired off a
furious handwritten letter to Streicher: 'I am informed that you said . . . that
nobody knew where I come from or what I am really up to in the movement.'
What right, he challenged, had Streicher 'of all people' to cast aspersions on
him?[37] He even wrote to Hitler complaining about Streicher's calumny.

But Bamberg had brought a parting of the ways for Goebbels. He was shifting
his loyalty from Strasser to Hitler, though unconsciously and imperceptibly at
first.

In the next issue of *Letters* he emulated Hitler's condemnation of the demand
by other nationalist organizations for a boycott of Italy for her oppression of
the German community in the South Tyrol.[38]

Returning from a trip to East Prussia to Essen, grimy capital of the Ruhr,
he found it decked out in swastika flags for the party rally on March 6. Four
thousand members filled the concert hall.[39] The delegates agreed to the
proposal that there should be one large Ruhr gau, amalgamating the smaller

Rhineland and Westphalian gaus, with Pfeffer, Kaufmann, and Goebbels jointly in command.[40] Goebbels bulks larger in his own diary version of this meeting than in the official minutes, which mention him only once – when he read out a bland telegram from Hitler. 'The bad,' said Hitler, 'must not be allowed to enslave the good.'[41] This was a precept that both men were to overlook in the years ahead.

A few days later Hitler flattered Kaufmann, Goebbels, and Lutze with invitations to speak in Munich. He pressed lavish treatment on the three: The motor car, that shibboleth of Nazi Germany, played an important part in this softening-up process, for they found Hitler's magnificent Mercedes waiting to drive them to their hotel.

According to Otto Strasser the wealth and power that this vehicle represented clinched it for Goebbels. Hitler loaned it to them with a chauffeur to drive them down to Lake Starnberg for an afternoon. His men had put up posters advertising Goebbels' speech (on 'National Socialism or Communism') at the famous Bürgerbräu beerhall. Hitler embraced him before the audience, amid cheers and tumult, and Goebbels noticed tears in his eyes.[42]

Over dinner he took in the unfamiliar faces around him – Hitler's 'decent, calm, friendly, clever, reserved' private secretary Rudolf Hess; his meticulous treasurer Franz Xaver Schwarz; his diminutive general manager Philipp Bouhler. Hitler showed them over the new party headquarters at No. 50 Schelling Strasse, and again talked of Italy and Britain as future allies and warned of the danger from Russia. On April 9 Hitler signed an Ausweis (certificate) for the three to run the Ruhr gau until further notice.[43]

Goebbels took flowers round to Hitler the next morning and they talked again about foreign policy. 'His case is compelling. But I think he has still not quite sized up the problem of Russia.'

Nonetheless, the two men were finding each other. 'I strongly urge you,' Goebbels wrote to Gregor Strasser on April 19, 'to arrange to talk things over with Hitler as soon as possible.' That day he and Hitler drove up to Stuttgart to speak at two meetings and again Hitler flung his arms around him. 'Adolf Hitler,' the young man wrote mushily in his diary back at Elberfeld, 'I love you: because you are great and simple at the same time – what we call a genius.'[44]

He returned to Munich for the party's annual general meeting at the Bürgerbräu on May 21. The minutes show that 657 party members were present. Goebbels recorded that he was greeted with a 'storm of joy and enthusiasm.' The minutes were less lyrical. They show that Hitler mentioned him only once in his two-hour statement:

'I am glad to say that this year has seen several first-class speakers come to the fore, with our friend Goebbels from Elberfeld out in front [applause] .'[45]

Goebbels put it more vividly. 'He publicly lauded me to the skies,' he recorded.

THE REGIONAL headquarters had moved into a suite of five rooms at No. 8 Auer Schultrasse in Elberfeld.[46] Goebbels was not happy with his own position in the gau however. On June 6 the local party officials (*Bezirk*-leaders) held a meeting to resolve which of the three should be actual gauleiter. The choice fell on Kaufmann. Lutze hinted to Goebbels that Kaufmann had rigged the vote with the help of Koch and Josef Terboven.[47] Disappointed, Goebbels decided to leave the Ruhr. He traveled to Berlin two days later, ostensibly to speak at Spandau and Neukölln, in fact to talk things over with Gauleiter Schlange. Several of Schlange's men asked Goebbels to take over. He declined, unable to decide between Munich and Berlin.

FOR THE TIME being he is still preoccupied with the opposite sex. They are a welcome distraction from work, a habit rather like the cigarette smoking which he now finds impossible to give up.

On June 10, 1926 he receives a letter from Else Janke, the first of several Dear-John letters from her. He asks his diary callously, 'Has the right moment now come?'[48] Dumping this half-Jewess will make way for other less compromising females and for his own possible transfer to Munich away from the political intrigues in Elberfeld.

His roving eye appraises every handsome woman regardless of social or marital standing, and indeed why not? He is young and eligible. 'Opposite me,' he writes one July day in a Berchtesgaden hotel, 'sits a beautiful, beautiful woman.' He spends three days stalking this gorgeous brunette – 'she stays demure, and I am a silly ass. I am chasing her like a schoolboy.'[49]

That same day, as he is visiting the Obersalzberg for the first time, his carriage blocks the narrow mountain lane, immobilized by a broken axle. A blonde country wench is unable to get past until he stands in front of the horses. 'Oh what a beauty you are,' he remarks in his diary. 'She laughs out loud and waves to me long after. We write her a little note – the coachman's lad takes it back to her – asking her to make a signal on the morrow.'[50] That is the last he hears of her.

He accepts defeat, aware of his cruel handicap. 'My foot bothers me a lot,' he writes. 'I can't stop thinking about it.' 'Every woman,' he writes helplessly, 'goes straight to my blood. I chase around like a starving wolf. But I am bashful as a child.'[51]

HE HAD ALL but found his way to Hitler.

Hitler had come north for the first time, spending the third week of June 1926 in the Ruhr and Rhineland, where he addressed private audiences at Elberfeld, Bochum, and Ruhr industrialists at Essen. At Essen he also spoke to two thousand, and met Director Arnold, their local financial backer. Goebbels studied the Nazi leader closely, seeing him alternately as a likable human being, as a towering intellect, and as a wayward, willful character. He studied his talents for gesture, mimicry, and oratory.

'A born agitator,' he concluded. 'One could conquer the world with that man.'[52] Before leaving the Ruhr on the nineteenth Hitler finally ruled that Kaufmann should be the sole gauleiter. Goebbels could ill conceal his chagrin.[53]

It encouraged him therefore that at the party's first annual rally for three years, held at Weimar on July 3–4, 1926, the contingent from Berlin liked him (the capital had sent four companies of S.A. stormtroopers); it provided an added impetus that one of the Berliners, Josephine von Behr, an affectionate girl who had plied him with chocolates in Berlin in February, was there too.[54] His own prepared talk on propaganda had Hitler in stitches.[55] Hitler himself talked on politics, ideologies, and organization. The photographs show Goebbels limping at his side through Weimar's cobbled streets, wearing a jacket buttoned just beneath his tie-knot. He claimed that fifteen thousand men were in the march-past; the party's history would speak of ten thousand. The pictures suggest a smaller turn out.

He willingly accepted Hitler's invitation to the Obersalzberg a few days after Weimar. Emil Maurice, Hitler's chauffeur, drove them out to the idyllic Lake Königssee; Hess and his girlfriend Ilse came too. Up at his still modest mountain villa Hitler dilated on Germany's social and racial questions; Goebbels fell in love with him all over again and decided that here was the creator of the Third Reich: 'Catlike – crafty, clever, skillful, compassionate; but like a lion too, roaring and larger than life.'[56] Infected by this prolonged exposure to his idol, Goebbels saw in the sky a white cloud shaped like a swastika; it could only be a portent of his destiny. 'Now,' wrote Goebbels, hypnotized, leaving him on July 25, 'the last doubts in me have vanished. Germany will live! Heil Hitler!'[57]

HIS BRAIN awhirl with these impressions, he is still nursing Hitler's farewell bouquet of red roses as he boards the overnight train back to the Rhineland. A beautiful woman shares his compartment. She talks engagingly with him, and they arrange to meet in Düsseldorf on the morrow. He limps around the city for two hours searching for her, but without luck.

'God has disposed otherwise,' he writes afterwards, finding the Divinity a useful alibi for his own shortcomings.[58]

II: The Gauleiter of Berlin

6: *The Opium Den*

S HOULD HE ACCEPT the job as the new gauleiter of Berlin? It was no sinecure. With around ten thousand supporters the communist party was aggressively in the ascendant. The N.S.D.A.P.'s Berlin gau had been founded in February 1925 and had attracted only 137 votes in the municipal elections that October. The present gauleiter had lost his stomach for the fight. He was however one of the joint backers of the Strasser brothers' Kampf Verlag publishing house, which had begun issuing a proletarian newspaper, the *Berliner Arbeiterzeitung*, in March 1926; this sold some three thousand copies each week.[1]

Unable to contain the snarling militancy of the Berlin S.A. under Kurt Daluege, Dr Schlange retired on June 20. Deputizing for him, Erich Schmiedicke called a meeting of the district officers in Gregor Strasser's presence and secured a unanimous vote that they should invite Dr Goebbels to come from the Ruhr to take over. The Berlin political police, who had agents planted in the Nazi party, recorded prematurely on July 29 that he had been offered the gau but had turned it down.[2] Goebbels wrote to Otto Strasser on August 3 that he was still undecided: 'Should I, or should I not? Probably not.'

The rumors of his probable defection from Strasser's to Hitler's camp led to rumbles of discontent. Gregor Strasser, who had set the wheels in motion to lure him to Berlin, later remarked ruefully in his Franconian dialect, '*A saublöder Obernarr bin i' g'wesen!*' (What a bloody fool I've been). 'Friend Gregor Strasser is pretty jealous of me,' observed Goebbels. Lying to his own diary, he denied a few days later that he was selling out to Hitler. He blamed Karl Kaufmann's men for starting the 'legend,' and the Strasser brothers for giving it wider currency. 'I'll teach the lot of them!' he added darkly.[3]

He had already acquired a taste for the rough and tumble of radical politics. He led a raiding party on a theater staging an award-winning but anti-German play by Carl Zuckmayer. Goebbels' Nazis hurled stink bombs into the audience and he was disappointed that only five women swooned.[4]

In Berlin, the battles would be uglier. Here the ramshackle and impoverished local party was in crisis. On August 26 there was a rowdy gathering of its officials, around 120 people according to the police. Schmiedicke, standing in as gauleiter, was hooted down by the S.A. The chief of the Berlin S.S. – the Schutzstaffel, an elite emerging within the stormtroopers – shouted that he had just spoken by phone with Hitler in person and been given full powers, which he promptly used to 'dismiss' Schmiedicke.[5] The next day Munich formally asked Goebbels to take over in Berlin, but only as a stop-gap.

He was still in two minds. Playing for time, he sent what he called a 'semi-refusal' to Hitler.[6]

HE SPENDS a weekend at Bayreuth in September 1926. Here he falls briefly in love with Winifred Wagner's young and vivacious daughters, romps around in the hay with the youngest of them ('the sweetest little brat') for an hour and then purples with embarrassment before the others.[7] 'I often wish I had such a darling German female around,' he laments – then remembers young Josephine von Behr in Berlin. The prospect of seeing her excites him, and he returns there in mid-September.[8]

In Berlin he spends an evening alone with Dr Schlange and Schmiedicke. Both men plead with him to take over.[9] In two minds still, he visits the party's primitive headquarters at No. 189 Potsdamer Strasse. It is housed in a gloomy downstairs room at the rear – a windowless vault lit only by a naked bulb, he will later report, in which Schmiedicke sits hunched over his cash ledger struggling to make ends meet.[10]

A cloud of stale air and tobacco smoke hits him as he goes in. Newspapers are stacked around the walls. Out of work party members are loitering around – there are 270,000 unemployed in Berlin alone – chain-smoking and tittle-tattling. They called it the 'opium den.'

He is glad to get out to Potsdam with Josephine that evening. They reverently tread the same sod as Frederick the Great and stroll around Sanssouci park. Goebbels wants to hold her hand, but lacks the courage to try.[11]

The affair with Else is over. They meet one Sunday in Cologne and trade insults, and she writes him another farewell letter. Goebbels sends his sister Maria over to fetch her on Monday morning for one final scene. With tear-streaked face, Else accompanies him in the drizzle to the train. For some reason Goebbels dramatizes their final parting in his diary:

> 'The train draws away. Else turns around and weeps. I close the window. Rain is falling on the coach roof. I have gone out of her life. My heart is broken.'[12]

AMPLIFYING GOEBBELS' own unpublished diaries, the Nazi party's archives acquired a file of vivid monthly résumés on the Berlin gau written by a young activist called Reinhold Muchow, who had joined aged twenty in December 1925.[13] These reports show the methods to which the party resorted, including a barrage of defamatory propaganda, ceaseless rowdy demonstrations, mindless provocations, and violence for its own sake. The party already had three 'martyrs' in Berlin – Willi Dreyer killed in 1924, Werner Doelle in 1925, and now on September 26, 1926 the forty-four year old Harry Anderssen, murdered by a communist gang in Kreuzberg.[14] It was a tragedy for the Berlin gau, recorded Muchow in October 1926, that it had never had a real *leader*. Dr Schlange had made no headway against the internal bickering. Schmiedicke proved even less capable. The opposition – Kurt Daluege and the S.A. – had put forward their own candidate as gauleiter, Oskar Hauenstein. Every top-level meeting ended with a row.[15]

Goebbels began feeling his way into Berlin. October 9 found him speaking at the party's Mark Brandenburg Freedom Rally, a torchlight parade just outside the city in Potsdam. The police file shows that he called for the destruction of the present state. The Berliners roared approval. 'You yourself will have noticed,' wrote Schmiedicke encouragingly, 'how very keenly every member of the party in Berlin wants you as their leader.'[16] His mind already made up, Goebbels told him that the stumbling block was financial: if the terms were right he would accept the job.[17] Schmiedicke bowed to his demands.[18]

While Goebbels even now delayed announcing his decision, the infighting in Berlin increased. Schmiedicke had to reassure officials that Goebbels' salary would be paid by Munich, not Berlin. There were ugly scenes, with Hauenstein thumping Otto Strasser, and Strasser challenging somebody else to a duel. Finally Goebbels took the milestone decision to accept Berlin's offer. Back in Elberfeld on October 17 he broke the news to Lutze and Kaufmann, and noted in his diary, 'Off to Berlin at last on November 1. Berlin is the focal point,' he reasoned, 'for us too.'[19] The formal appointment was dated October 26, and was announced in the *Völkischer Beobachter* two days later. On November 1 the *NS Letters* published his farewell to the Ruhr. 'And now,' he wrote, 'it's full steam ahead into the great asphalt jungle Berlin.'

HE WHO HELD Berlin held Germany. Hitler gave him authority to rule the gau with an iron fist. 'November 5,' recorded Goebbels. 'Hitler. Munich. Signs my terms.'[20]

The Reich capital was like no other city in Europe – over-populated, throbbing with life twenty-four hours a day. It was an international hodgepodge of races, the collision point of western and eastern cultures.

This sprawling heap of bricks and stone was divided into twenty boroughs of varying size and wealth, from Zehlendorf, with 470,000 inhabitants, to the proletarian slum Kreuzberg with 370,000. Politically the city was a red stronghold and Goebbels would find only a few hundred paid-up Nazis there; in the whole Reich there were still only forty-nine thousand. In the March 1925 presidential election 308,591 Berliners had voted for the communist (K.P.D.) candidate Ernst 'Teddy' Thälmann.

In the municipal election that October, 52·2 percent had voted for the Marxist parties, the K.P.D. increasing its vote to 347,382. Its front organizations like the Red League of Combat Veterans (Frontkämpferbund) and the Central Office of Red Aid (Zentralstelle der Roten Hilfe) were funded by the Soviet embassy and trade mission.

Thus Goebbels had a highly visible opponent. Besides, he would be doing battle for the first time with the Jews. 'Berlin,' Muchow observed, 'is Red and Jewish in equal measure.'[21] In 1816 there had been only 3,400 Jews, but this figure had swollen to 36,500 by 1871, and to one hundred thousand at the turn of the century. By the time of Goebbels' arrival, one-third of Germany's half-million Jews were concentrated in the city.[22] They made up 4.3 percent of its population: but they provided over half Berlin's lawyers, 15 percent of the real estate agents, and nearly 11 percent of the doctors; they dominated the wealthy ranks of Berlin's dentists, pharmacists, judges, public prosecutors, and academics, and maintained a near stranglehold on the world of the arts.

While Mosse's Berliner Tageblatt would become one of Goebbels' principal enemies – the newspaper had been founded in 1871 specifically for the protection of Jewish interests in Germany – he would arbitrarily lump all the bourgeois newspapers into the general category of 'Judenpresse.'

When he said that the real power in Berlin was in Jewish hands there was a grain of truth in it. Dr Heinrich Brüning, chancellor of the Reich from 1930 to 1932, could find only one bank not so controlled. After ordering a government inquiry, he directed that its findings be kept secret for fear of provoking antisemitic riots.[23] A series of scandals surrounding Jewish swindlers like Kutisker, Sklarek, and the Barmat brothers paraded through the courts.[24] Many of the public prosecutors in Berlin were Jewish. Goebbels would portray the Berlin police as largely Jewish controlled; in fact of the top officials only the powerful deputy chief (Vize-Polizeipräsident) who directed section Ia, the three-hundred-man political police force, forerunner of the Gestapo, was a Jew.

He was not just any Jew. Forty-six years old, the son of a millionaire grain merchant, Dr Bernhard Weiss had served like his three brothers with distinction in the war, won the Iron Cross, and become the first Jew ever to be accepted for the Prussian higher civil service.[25] His army personnel file speaks of his highly developed sense of honor but also of his over-developed ambition, conceit, and immodesty, and of a 'powerful over-sensitivity tending to cloud his clarity of judgment.'[26] Appointed deputy police chief on March 17, 1927 in the redbrick police headquarters on Alexander Platz, the diminutive (five-foot-four) Bernhard Weiss would become Goebbels' sworn enemy – not just because of the rigor with which he deployed his fourteen thousand truncheon-wielding uniformed police in the struggle for the streets of Berlin, but because he was a Jew and even his best friends said he looked like a caricature of one.[27]

Dr Goebbels would shun no libel to blacken his name. Instinctively carrying on an ancient tradition of name-calling, he seized on Dr Weiss' nickname of 'Isidor' and commissioned a scurrilous Nazi marching song about him.[28] He would highlight every malfeasance of the criminal demimonde and identify it as Jewish. In these closing years of the Weimar republic, he was unfortunately not always wrong. In 1930 Jews would be convicted in forty-two of 210 known narcotics smuggling cases; in 1932 sixty-nine of the 272 known international narcotics dealers were Jewish.

Jews were arrested in over sixty percent of the cases concerning the running of illegal gambling dens; 193 of the 411 pickpockets arrested in 1932 were Jews. In 1932 no fewer than thirty-one thousand cases of fraud, mainly insurance swindles, would be committed by Jews.[29]

Statistical comparisons are of course usually odious, but it was against this background that Goebbels now started his campaign. He would concentrate initially on the western boroughs of Charlottenburg, Wilmersdorf, Schöneberg, and Tiergarten, where over half Berlin's Jews had settled. They had originally populated the disheveled streets around the railroad termini of central and north-western Berlin where they had arrived from the east and from Galicia, but as they had prospered they had descended on the leafier western boroughs. Over 13 percent of Wilmersdorf's 196,000 inhabitants were Jews.[30]

The sheer scale of the battle fought between Dr Goebbels and 'Isidor' Weiss can be judged from the court records. The police targeted the Nazi gauleiter with no fewer than forty court actions; Weiss himself was involved in twenty-three cases; Hitler came only eighth, with sixteen. Goebbels and Weiss would clash head on in four groups of trials, involving ten specific charges against Goebbels and a score more against his editors and journalists. In addition Weiss started nine other court actions, including three against Gregor Strasser, for calling him Isidor. Nearly all of these immensely complex cases were appealed all the way up the German legal system, but Weiss secured sixty convictions (including nineteen against Dr Goebbels). To non-Germans unfamiliar with the stiffness of Prussia, the pomposity of a civil servant like Weiss resorting to such legal sanctions seems breathtakingly pointless and even self-defeating.

His first action, in May 1927, was against a Berlin newsvendor who had displayed on his newsstand a *Völkischer Beobachter* featuring a competent and by no means hostile sketch of Dr Weiss; the unfortunate newsvendor went to jail for a month.[31] 'The mere application of the name Isidor, whereas the police vice-president's first name is in reality Bernhard, was a deliberate and purposeful insult,' argued Weiss's superior, Karl Zörgiebel, on June 1, demanding the prosecution of the *Völkischer Beobachter*'s editor too.[32] In a telling *lapsus linguæ* police chief Zörgiebel's indictment of Goebbels dated March 2, 1928 actually accused him of libeling 'the Polizeipräsident Dr. Weiss' – thus accidentally conceding what all Berlin already knew, that it was his deputy who called the shots, and not he.[33]

Tirelessly and at taxpayers' expense Weiss fought the battles against Goebbels and his newspaper: the court dockets ooze with the cold fury aroused in him by irreverent cartoons (Weiss asking a policeman who demands the arrest of a communist thug: 'Ban them? Why? Did he attack a Jew?'); by caricatures (a bespectacled, big-nosed donkey splay-legged on thin ice),[34] and even by a crossword puzzle.[35]

IT WAS November 7, 1926 before Goebbels actually arrived in Berlin.[36] Dr. Otto Strasser met him at the station.

Goebbels' own legend, written up as *Battle for Berlin*, would have him hurrying straight from the Anhalt station to a packed public meeting. The truth was more prosaic. The Berlin gau was penniless and in disarray. He made his first public speech at a memorial ceremony organized on the ninth, the anniversary of Hitler's failed Munich putsch, by the party's Women's Order (Frauenorden) in the Veterans' Building (Kriegervereinshaus) in Chaussee-Strasse.

When Otto Strasser expressed irritation that Goebbels had arrived late, and had squandered money on a taxi, the new gauleiter replied: 'On the contrary. I would have arrived in two taxis if I could have. The people must see that our firm is up and running.' In his speech he expressed admiration for the men who had gunned down the Jewish politician Dr Walther Rathenau four years earlier. (For this remark he was later summoned to police headquarters; but the resulting prosecution was subsequently abandoned.)[37]

On the same day he issued the famous Circular No. 1 to all gau officials, which began, 'As of today I am taking over the Berlin-Brandenburg gau as gauleiter.' Addressing the unappetizing conditions at the 'opium den' in Potsdamer Strasse, he decreed that gau headquarters was neither a flop-house nor a waiting room; in future party members would need an appointment to speak with him. His circular displayed both realism and clever psychology. While appointing the troublesome and ambitious S.A. commander Kurt Daluege – who was twenty-nine – as his deputy, he simultaneously downgraded the former Greater Berlin gau to the rank of *Ortsgruppe* or local, and downgraded the present locals to sections.[38] This made for a tighter ship and fewer illusions. Defining the role of the militant S.A. he wrote: 'S.A. and S.S. are the instruments whereby we shall attain power,' and he ruled that neither was to appear in public without his prior consent. He ended the circular with the promise: 'Adolf Hitler will visit the gau as soon as we have become a united force and one to be reckoned with.'[39]

The Strasser brothers were aghast at Goebbels' arrival in 'their' capital. But over the coming months he forced a level of activity that Berlin had not seen before; he founded a Nazi speakers' school, he developed a constant, intrusive, drum-beating propaganda campaign, and he provoked clashes with the communists that hit Berlin's newspaper headlines time and again. On Sunday November 14 he led a deliberately provocative propaganda march through the working-class suburb of Neukölln which aroused both fury and consternation among the local communists; the newspapers reported that in the ensuing disorders use was made of 'missiles, knuckle-dusters, clubs, and even pistols.'[40]

Cutting out the dead wood, he threw out half of the gau's members. To secure its finances he founded an elitist Freedom League of three or four hundred Berliners pledged to contribute ten percent of their income in return for promises of later rewards.[41] His first imperative was to finance new premises for the gau in the city center; his second to fund a marching band of forty or fifty musicians with a full-time instructor; his third to purchase motor transport. At the end of December Goebbels moved into new offices at No. 44 Lützow Strasse, four office rooms with all mod cons and two telephone lines.

His tactical object was to capture the communists' pawns, the unemployed hordes of Berlin. Typical of his S.A. foot soldiers was the young law student Horst Wessel, whose handwritten diary we now have. Aged just nineteen, he had joined the party that autumn. 'How I came to the National Socialists?' he asked. 'Out of disillusion really. My nationalist radicalism, or rather my radical nationalism had not found a home. But the Nazis, as they were already called, were radical-radical in every respect.' Wessel had been a member of the Bismarck and then Viking League since 1922, organizations which had just played soldiers. Goebbels' gau was, he soon found, different. The new gauleiter put the accent on socialism. 'The right-wing parties spurned us for our socialist slant,' wrote Wessel, 'and they weren't all that wrong, because National Socialists had more in common with the [communist] R.F.B. [*Roter Frontkämpferbund*] than with the [right-wing] Stahlhelm.'[42]

During December Goebbels reorganized Berlin's S.A. into three regiments (*Standarten*). He tightened discipline, banning smoking and drinking on duty. On November 20 he met district leaders (*Kreisleiter*) and laid down guidelines for the future. Later that month he spoke in the Veterans' Building on 'Germany, Colony or State?' Scores of new members joined that same evening. Two weeks later eighteen hundred people crowded in to hear him speak on 'The Road to Power.' A breathless unanimity replaced the brawling and bickering of previous gau meetings.[43]

Horst Wessel was one of those dedicated to the party. 'No sacrifice in time or money,' he would write, 'no danger of arrest or violence could scare me off. . . The Sturmabteilungen, the S.A., were the stewards, the movement's fist against the police and the Marxists. The structure itself was copied from the communists – sections instead of locals, the cell-system; our press advertising and propaganda clearly betrayed their [communist] inspiration. The vitality of this new movement was vast, best demonstrated by the defections to us from the Marxist camp.'

Goebbels created an atmosphere of constant activity. 'To Dr Göbbels [sic] alone,' wrote Wessel, 'goes the credit for having impinged the movement so rapidly on the Berlin public's consciousness. The man had extraordinary talents for oratory and organization. There was nothing he couldn't turn his hand to. The members were devoted to him. The S.A. would have let itself be torn to pieces for him. Göbbels was like Hitler himself. . . He took care of the injured – he really was a first-class leader, a leader with class.'[44]

At first the 'Judenpresse' ignored Goebbels. Denied the oxygen of publicity, he forced violent confrontations with the communists. After an initial blooding in Spandau on January 25, when two hundred of them infiltrated a meeting intending to disrupt his speech, Goebbels' 'troops' fought three battles, at Cottbus, in Berlin's sleazy Pharus Rooms, and at suburban Lichterfelde.

Goebbels had sent five truckloads of S.A. men to Cottbus to boost the puny local contingent during a two-day Nazi 'freedom rally.' It was an icy January night, and at dawn the men drove into Cottbus, where the local S.A. provided billets. ' We wanted to show them,' wrote Muchow, 'that the Berlin S.A. turned up everywhere we were needed.' The march through Cottbus began: 'Our Doctor [Goebbels] was with Daluege at Kaiser-Wilhelm Platz, taking the salute.'[45] As Goebbels delivered an impromptu speech there were already taunts of 'long live the communist Internationale!'

A pitched battle broke out. The police and soldiers waded in with truncheons and rifle butts. The S.A. had two seriously injured, the police four. But the blood had been shed for naught: 'The entire Berlin "Judenpresse",' lamented Muchow, 'breathed not a word about our Cottbus demonstration.'

The Strassers' *Arbeiterzeitung* (masthead slogan: 'The workers' only newspaper in Berlin not beholden to loan-capital') published Goebbels' appeal for funds for 'our wounded S.A. comrades.' Seven hundred marks flowed in.

Goebbels owed a lot to the Strasser brothers.[46] Otto had also arranged for Hans Steiger, an editor on a bourgeois Berlin newspaper, to provide cheap lodgings in the rooming house run by Frau Steiger at No. 5, Am Karlsbad. No doubt he wanted to keep an eye on Goebbels. Mrs Steiger provided a full-length mirror to enable him to practice public-speaking postures; but her husband erred badly, trespassing on Goebbels' feelings by circulating a ballad that touched upon the gauleiter's private life and using a limping, lop-sided rhythm designed, Goebbels felt sure, to mock his disability.[47] The gauleiter, it turned out, could stand any amount of satire so long as it was not leveled at him.

The second great battle happened in the rundown Pharus Rooms, a traditional communist meeting place behind No. 124 Müller Strasse in Berlin's working-class suburb of Wedding, on February 11. There were two hundred communists among Goebbels' thousand-strong audience. As he spoke on 'The collapse of the bourgeois class state' disturbances broke out and Daluege sent in the S.A. to evict the first troublemakers. The communists retreated, and the Nazis held the high ground, the gallery. In the few minutes before the police could intervene, the S.A. had roughed up eighty-three communists. When Goebbels resumed speaking, the platform was littered with bleeding men on stretchers.[48] One man, Albert Tonak, aged twenty-one, was hospitalized with concussion.[49] In the *VB* report Goebbels described how he had learned that a surgeon called Levy was planning to delve into Tonak's skull; one hundred of his S.A. men, 'unemployed proletarians in brown shirts,' had stormed the hospital and rescued him. Goebbels added an appeal for funds to establish a party clinic of seven or eight rooms to treat their own emergency cases.[50] Tonak became the little Doctor's chauffeur, and later died on Hitler's eastern battlefields.

Goebbels had found the right formula. After this battle the press howled with rage – and more funds flowed in. He got the big car he coveted. He claimed that anonymous benefactors had donated the four-seater Benz motor car to the gau, but 'Isidor' Weiss determined that the vehicle, license tag 26637-LA, had previously belonged to a merchant bank, Grundman & Co., that the two-thousand-marks *purchase* price had come from the Freedom League, and that it was registered in Goebbels' own name.[51] By late February treasurer Franz Wilke could report that the gau now had eight to ten thousand marks in cash and assets.[52] Lecturing the Freedom League, his cash cows, on 'My political awakening' on the fifteenth the gauleiter again claimed to have been plotting clandestinely with Hitler in Munich as early as 1919, and to have fought in the resistance against the French and Belgians occupying the Ruhr.[53]

Just four days after the Pharus Rooms fight, Goebbels and his S.A. hooligans filled all fifteen hundred seats at a hall in Spandau. The left, still reeling, stayed away. Their newspapers uttered dire warnings to the workers to keep their eyes on this unexpected 'fascist menace.' The police watched with mounting fury as control of the streets passed into the hands of the political mobs.

A perverted sense of pride seized the Berlin S.A. Their young chronicler Reinhold Muchow doubted that their brother Brownshirts of Stuttgart, Weimar, or Hamburg could have survived such battles. Now, he observed, the Berlin Jews saw the writing on the wall. More printing ink would flow against the party during February 1927 than in all the preceding three months.

A high-water mark in this carnage came in March, just three days after 'Isidor's' appointment. Goebbels had ordered a night-time function of the Berlin S.A. to be staged at Trebbin, a little town twenty miles away. About seven hundred S.A. men proudly wearing their uniform of jackboots, flat caps, breeches, and brown shirts made their way there: a bonfire blazed on the hillside, the flags and standards foregathered, and Goebbels played organ music to them before speaking. 'These sons of the Brandenburg countryside,' reported Muchow in purple prose, 'hung on every word of this man, their appointed leader in life and death. . .'[54]

The trouble began as the seven hundred Nazis piled into the train back to Berlin. Sitting near the front, they found twenty-three bandsmen of the Red Front's Seventh District (Brandenburg) and a communist member of the provincial parliament, Paul Hoffmann. By the time the train pulled into East Lichterfelde station every window had been shattered. As the Nazis jumped out a shot rang out and one S.A. leader was hit in the stomach. Another S.A. man was grazed on the head by a bullet. The police stormed the platform and arrested several Nazis.

They found the communist bandsmen cowering on the floor surrounded by shattered glass, splintered wood, and rocks; eighteen of them were injured, twelve seriously. Hoffmann was barely recognizable, his face smeared with blood. A thousand more Nazis had meanwhile arrived outside the station to join the S.A. for a march through Berlin's bourgeois western suburbs. The gunfire caused uproar. Goebbels, Daluege, and gau manager Dagobert Dürr arrived in their limousine, to storms of applause. 'Where the road curved,' wrote one S.A. man, 'there stood our Doctor in his car. . . Standing with arm raised he saluted us and looked into our faces.' Goebbels would claim at the resulting court hearings to have called for discipline and calm as his injured comrades were carried out of the station.[55] The owner of a neighboring soap-store testified however that after an injured thirty-five-year old communist had been carried into a taxi two Nazis had torn its door open: one, a thin young man, pulled a pistol out of his pants pocket, and shouted, 'I'm going to shoot the dog dead!' The other, a little man with a right club foot that turned inwards, had dissuaded him.[56] 'The National Socialists,' reported the police, 'charged into the communists with a fusillade of revolver shots and wielding steel flagpoles like lances, leaving nine slightly and five seriously injured on the battlefield.'[57] (Goebbels' version in the *Völkischer Beobachter* differed. 'The first shot fired by the Red assassins,' he claimed, 'hit one of the two police constables in the forearm. He appealed to our S.A. for help, shouting: "Guys, help us, we can't handle it on our own!"')[58]

They marched past Steglitz city hall and on through west Berlin. Wherever Jews were spotted they were set upon and bludgeoned to the ground.[59] At Wittenberg Platz, where eight thousand people had gathered, Goebbels made a speech. 'The Reds have spilled our blood,' he shrieked. 'We're not going to allow ourselves to be treated as second-class citizens any more.' He ended with a transparent hint: 'Now don't all go chasing off massacring those Jews down Kurfürstendamm!'[60] 'Deutschland – awake!' came the response – the battle-cry of the S.A.

Those were his methods. Horst Wessel, soon to become commander of No. 5 Sturm based on the communist-infested Alexander Platz area, was in the thick of it all. 'Gunfight on East Lichterfelde station, three injured but victory. Victory everywhere the S.A. goes into action.' 'We accomplished what no other movement had in Germany,' he wrote with heavy irony in 1929, 'namely to unite the entire people: Because they were all united against us – incredibly united.'[61]

Goebbels now had two more men in the hospital. Eight had been arrested, several would draw prison sentences. 'Isidor' Weiss ordered the Nazis' Charlottenburg and Moabit section headquarterss ransacked for weapons, and for several days the Red Front exacted revenge on any Nazis caught alone in the streets. They had captured the party ID of one Nazi, and splashed its photograph on placards all over Berlin two days later: WANTED – DEAD OR ALIVE.[62] Goebbels however judged only by results: four hundred more Berliners joined the party, bringing its membership to three thousand.

The Strasser brothers despaired, preferring reason and logic to brute force. The 'Judenpresse' seized upon the differences between them and articles appeared in the communist *Welt am Abend*, the *Berliner Tageblatt*, and the equally Jewish *Vossische Zeitung* gloating over a 'feud in the house of Hitler.'[63]

STILL PERFECTING his techniques, Goebbels stood in front of the folding triptych mirror in Mrs Steiger's drawing room practicing each pose and gesture.[64] His oratory drew audiences of thousands. He rode their mood, leading them on a tide of invective to a hysterical, cheering, table-rattling finale. He had instinctively developed the art of ceremonial too, to bring audiences to fever pitch – the flags, the bands, the deliberately delayed arrival. He spoke at locations from Weinheim in the south to Hamburg in the north.[65] Writing in the *Letters* on April 1 he prescribed how to deal with hecklers. 'You don't seem to realize that you're at a National Socialist meeting,' the speaker was to shout at the unfortunate interrupter. 'I'll not be able to guarantee that you won't be made into a useful member of the human race by a suitable head massage.'

When I speak in Essen or in Düsseldorf or in Elberfeld [Goebbels had written once] it's like a holiday for me... We don't have to search for the enemy, he's in our midst, lurking in the audience ready to pounce. When I come into the hall a thousand voices shout Down With Him, there's a hooting and a screeching. Then the struggle begins – two, three hours, sometimes longer... And the miracle happens. What was a wild, howling mob turns into human beings of flesh and blood who think and feel just as we do, only more tormented, more trampled on, with an immense hunger for light and succor... And gradually the people are re-created before my very eyes. I see just fists and eyes, and there is a holy fire in those eyes.[66]

The Ruhr gau held its annual rally on Sunday April 25. Here too the party's ranks were swelling. 'Essen is dominated by the swastika & our flag!' Rudolf Hess boasted to his fiancée Ilse.[67] Goebbels mailed a picture postcard of the huge assembly to Anka Stalherm. While he and Hitler addressed the fourteen thousand invited party members however Goebbels was seething with rage: people had drawn his attention to a scurrilous article published anonymously in the Strassers' newspapers on April 23, entitled 'Results of Race Mixing.' (Its anonymous author was Erich Koch.) *The Koch Brothers, U.S.A.!*

'It is well known [this venomous piece began] that miscegenation results in mental disequilibria... Physical equilibrium is disturbed, either by disease or by the stunted growth of individual limbs or by other physical defects.'

Goebbels took this as a wounding reference to his physical disability. The writer adduced various unflattering examples from history, like the murderous Richard III, who was also 'a dwarf who limped,' and Talleyrand, who 'possessed a club foot... The word "character" could not be applied to him.'[68]

Goebbels complained to Hitler that same afternoon. Hitler agreed that coupled with the Kampf Verlag's other recent irruptions against Goebbels this article was clearly actionable; he warned against litigating, but promised to tackle the Strassers himself. Erich Koch wrote to Goebbels admitting (or claiming) authorship, but could not resist rubbing salt in the wounds by

stating that his article was no more than an exposition of 'the racial theories
our party stands for.'[69]

THE ARTICLE brought the Goebbels–Strasser feud to boiling point. The
Strassers had by now learned that he was raising finance to launch a rival Nazi
tabloid in Berlin called *Angriff* (Attack).[70] Although the Strassers had earlier
provided his gau with every facility in their *Arbeiterzeitung* and the *N.S.
Letters*, of which he was still editor, Goebbels had determined to smash their
monopoly. The *Arbeiterzeitung* was still the official organ of the Berlin gau
and by September 1926 it was already printing a national weekly, the *Nationalsozialist*, for northern Germany (which had also printed the libelous article).
Expanding in 1927, the Strassers had persuaded the tall, flabby twenty-six-year-
old Hans Hinkel, editor of a local southern newspaper, to invest heavily in
their concern; the brothers Gregor, Otto, and Franz Strasser still controlled
51 percent. The firm was thus comparable with the party's Franz Eher Verlag
in the south.[71] But the Strasser publications were less heathen and antisemitic
than the Hitler-Rosenberg newspapers like *Völkischer Beobachter*.

Goebbels undoubtedly nursed an unhealthy complex about the wealthy
Strasser family, although his diaries show that he privately respected Gregor
more than his later public remarks would allow. Gregor was a member of the
Reichstag, which provided him with free first-class travel and immunity from
arrest. But Goebbels could call upon the talents of his gifted caricaturist Hans
Schweitzer ('Mjölnir'), and through him he spread the corrosive rumor that
Otto had Jewish blood. Gregor riposted that both he and Otto had at least
served in the Great War and in the Free Corps after that, 'unlike Dr Goebbels
or Mr Schweitzer,' and there the matter, for the time being, rested.

MAY 1927 brought first triumph, then disaster. On May Day Hitler himself spoke
in Berlin for the first time – before a private audience because the Prussian
minister of the interior Albert Grzesinski had banned him from speaking in
public. The five thousand listeners packing into the Clou, a well-known dance
hall in Mauer Strasse, still made an impressive audience. Unaware that the
police were now just waiting for a pretext to clamp down on him, Goebbels
arranged a further mass meeting at the Veterans' Building for May 4, where he
delivered a poisonous ninety-minute tirade against the press, infuriated by its
spiteful coverage of Hitler's speech at the Clou.[72]

Singling out one journalist, he told his two thousand listeners to note down
the home address of Dr Otto Kriegk of *Lokal-Anzeiger* (who was present) –
a typically Nazi trick – and suggested they find out where others lived and
administer 'a National Socialist head massage' to them too.[73] The olive-
complexioned Goebbels had just recommended his audience to display their
'forceful gratitude' to a journalist on *Germania*, who boasted the suspiciously
Germanic name of Karl-Otto Graetz but was really, he said, a 'swine of a
Jew' (*Judensau*)[74] when Fritz Stucke, an elderly but politically active parson,

exclaimed sarcastically, 'A fine image of Germanic youth you look!'[75] 'I take it,' shouted Goebbels, breaking the pained silence that followed and pointing to the doors, 'that you're keen to get flung out on your ear?'[76] When Stucke taunted Goebbels again, burly young men bundled him downstairs, dragging him the last few yards by his feet.

This time Goebbels had gone too far. By the time his guest, leader of Sweden's Nazis, had also spoken, hundreds of police were cordoning the building. A police major closed the meeting down. He ordered the audience to file out singly and be searched for weapons. The police haul was a veritable arsenal of blackjacks, knuckle-dusters, knives, and revolvers;[77] eighteen Nazis were arrested for resisting the search. The press smelt blood and tasted revenge. Their lurid reports had S.A. thugs battering the parson with beer mugs and kicking him; doctors, they said, marveled that his skull was not fractured.[78]

Twenty-four hours later Dr Bernhard Weiss served a restraining order on Dr Goebbels, banning him from speaking in Berlin, and dissolving his gau.[79] They also charged him with incitement to violence.[80] After just six months in Berlin the unstoppable gauleiter seemed to have run into an immovable object: the police vice-president of Berlin.

7: Fighting the Ugly Dragon

THE BAN WOULD STAY in force for eleven months. It was the work of the Social Democratic politician Albert Grzesinski, the minister of the interior in Prussia. The illegitimate son of a servant girl, Grzesinski was a year older than Dr Weiss and a former metal worker and trade union leader.[1] He had previously been Berlin's police chief himself. The communist *Red Flag* accused him of hating the revolutionary working class; the conservative right wing feared that he would use his power to consolidate the Social Democratic position; the Nazis would fight him tooth and claw. Goebbels would claim that Grzesinski's natural father was not the butcher's boy named in the files but one Ernst Cohn, a Jewish merchant in whose service his mother had been employed. No matter that Cohn was only seventeen at the time in question, the legend persisted – resulting in one of the many libel actions that Goebbels would soon face.

The banning document signed by police chief Karl Zörgiebel on May 5, 1927 alleged a catalogue of misdemeanors – assaults, criminal damage, and firearms offenses – perpetrated by the gau since mid-October. 'In the "Ten Commandments" issued by Goebbels [to the S.A.],' the document read, 'the ninth reads: "Resistance to police and state authority today is always stupid, because you will always come off worse. . . The state will take revenge on you and on us with prison sentences and steep fines. So, if there is no other way, comply with the state authority, but console yourself: we shall square accounts later!"' The ban also quoted from Goebbels' pamphlet *Ways to the Third Reich*:

'Domination of the street is the first step to state power. He who purveys his Weltanschauung with terror and brute force will one day possess the power, and thus the right, to overthrow the state.' 'As such aims of association are incompatible with the criminal law,' Zörgiebel concluded, 'disbandment is justified.'[2]

Goebbels was mortified. He refused to sign a form acknowledging receipt of the ban, stating that it was written in unintelligible German.[3] Writing to Grzesinski, he pointed out that his gau embraced the whole province of Brandenburg, not just Berlin: 'The ban is therefore null and void,' he argued. He also claimed that Berlin's 'gutter press' (*Asphaltpresse*, another invented Goebbels word) had deliberately distorted the Pastor Stucke business. He made no apologies for having publicly identified the journalists who dared to jibe at Hitler, 'a German front-line soldier.' As for Stucke, he said, the clergyman had called out 'du Hund!' (you dog), whereupon members of his audience had 'slowly ushered him out.' He blamed the weapons arsenal on *agents provocateurs* and added that his gau had appealed in writing to Dr Weiss for police protection after individual members had been attacked by 'Red mobs.' 'Your police president,' he lectured Grzesinski, 'is being praised by the entire press of the international money-capital. This proves that it is not the German people, only a clique of international moneybags, who had an interest in seeing the German freedom movement banned.' If Grzesinski still refused to lift the ban, history would prove him wrong since he did not possess the power to kill an idea.

Still smoldering, Goebbels spoke to a provincial Nazi rally in Stuttgart with Hitler on May 7, seizing the opportunity to accuse Weiss, Zörgiebel, and Grzesinski of stage-managing the incident with Pastor Stucke, a parson unfrocked for morals offenses.[4] On his arrival back in Berlin his fans rioted at the Anhalter station, and he was taken off for questioning.[5] He hired a lawyer and appealed, using the gau's headed notepaper; Zörgiebel silkily advised him to refrain from using the banned Nazi notepaper or rubber stamp again.[6] A great silence now overcame the party organization in Berlin.

One fact buoyed Goebbels at this dark hour, the knowledge that he would soon found a weekly newspaper of his own in Berlin, *Angriff.* He announced his plan at a secret meeting in his apartment. But raising the finance was not easy.[7] Gregor Strasser was furious at the plan, and tackled Hitler at his favorite Munich restaurant about rumors that he had agreed to write a regular leading article; Hitler assured him the rumors were not true.[8]

Goebbels had no time for the Strassers since their newspapers had lampooned him and his club foot. A homeopath, Dr Steintel, had told him in a Berlin pub how the Strasser brothers, especially Otto, had plotted to ruin the gauleiter by highlighting his 'racial defect.' There was enough circumstantial detail to make it seem plausible. When Steintel asked the truth about the club foot, Goebbels declared that he had had an accident as a teenager, which ruled out the racially 'otherwise permissible' inference.

Armed with this new information Goebbels dictated a furious letter to Hitler: Neither Jews nor Marxists had, he said, stooped so low to get at him. 'He has to be destroyed,' the Strassers seemed to have said, 'because he is inconvenient for Kampf Verlag, a private enterprise.' Hinting at resignation, he warned Hitler that he would never succeed without 'eradicating' personalities like these.[9] When Hitler, in a quandary, did not reply, Goebbels nagged Hess, Hitler's secretary, to issue a statement backing him.[10] At a private meeting of the Berlin gau's officers on June 10 attended by Steintel he asked for a vote of confidence. He pointed out that Erich Koch, a humble railroad official, could not possibly have authored such a venomously clever article; the club foot, he again insisted, was not congenital but the consequence of a teenage mishap.[11]

The split widened, as Goebbels stepped up the pressure on his rivals. When Gregor Strasser spoke in Berlin he had a member of the audience ask about his lucrative pharmaceutical practice and fat Reichstag paycheck.[12] By mid-June the bickering was so bad that Emil Holtz, the gau's legal arbitrator, appealed to Hitler to settle it in person. Holtz sided with the Strassers, while conceding that Goebbels had succeeded in spurring the Berliners on. 'He has made the movement famous,' he told Hitler. 'But he lacks inner stability and attention to detail.'[13] Since Goebbels was calling on his members to buy only *Angriff* – it was now due to appear on July 4 – Holtz feared irreparable damage to Strasser's publications (which was just what Goebbels desired). Nobody, Holtz pointed out, could tell how long *Angriff* would survive.

Goebbels hurried off to see Hitler in Munich. He wanted both Strassers evicted from the Nazi party. The party's chief arbitrator ruled that the Führer would settle the whole matter at some major Berlin function later on.[14] While still in Munich on the evening of June 20, Goebbels addressed 450 people on his first six months as Berlin's gauleiter – and the ban.

He claimed to have added six hundred new members during April. 'Let the gentlemen in Berlin,' he added, 'take note that the time will come when the National Socialists will pay them back in the same coin and with interest. Nothing will be forgotten.'[15]

The fight against 'Isidor' Weiss went on. 'He who has the police headquarters in Berlin has Prussia,' Goebbels would pronounce. 'He who has Prussia, has the Reich.'[16] Justifying his rowdy methods in a speech on July 10 at Potsdam, just outside Weiss's fief, he said, 'A movement which means to smash the old State cannot march in bedroom slippers. We may not have won the affections of this city of four million, but we have earned its hatred, and hatred can turn to affection.'[17]

Even more seditious in police eyes was Goebbels' now widely disseminated fifteen-page brochure *The Nazi* which clearly spoke of plans to overthrow the state.[18] 'History,' he had written, 'has seen repeatedly how a young, determined minority has overthrown the rule of a corrupt and rotten majority, and then used for a time the state and its means of power in order to bring about by dictatorship . . . and force the conditions necessary to complete the conquest and to impose new ideas.' So too, wrote Goebbels, it would be with the Nazi party. 'And then we, the responsible minority, will enforce our will upon a flabby, lazy, supine, and stupid majority lurking behind which the Jew prosecutes his dark plans.' All of this was noted in Dr Weiss's police files, and more. 'If the German people do not want to be liberated,' Goebbels had written, 'then we shall act without their consent.'

> Then [continued Goebbels] we march against this State, we take one last great risk for Germany; from revolutionaries by word we become revolutionaries by deed.

Then we stage a revolution! . . . The will to power will procure the *means* to power. The others may have the weapons but we have what they do not: the willingness to use force, and this willingness will procure the weapons that we need.[19]

Speaking in Düsseldorf that summer he reiterated: 'Without weapons we'll get nowhere.'[20]

FOR THE MOMENT Goebbels' only weapon was the printed word. During the last days of June 1927 he rained a carefully timed series of blood-red posters on Berlin. The first read simply, 'Attack!' The second, 'Attack is coming.' The third, 'The attack will come on July 4.'

To edit *Angriff* he had picked Dr Julius Lippert; Lippert was imprisoned shortly before the first issue, and Dagobert Dürr, a former meteorologist, stood in for him. But the first edition squibbed. The badly designed, anemic sheet sold only twelve hundred copies, the next only nine hundred. With the newspaper losing money and morale, several of his staff walked out.

Goebbels was no quitter. His street salesmen adopted ruthless tactics. *Angriff*'s circulation staggered upward to around two thousand. Its style was soapbox oratory in print. With a Jesuit's sure instinct for the niceties of the law he defamed without libeling; his pen dipped, thrust, parried, then dipped again. It was more anti-capitalist than Hitler approved of, but the Berlin working classes lapped up the subtle antisemitism of Mjölnir's caricatures. Goebbels contributed a venomous diary column and a weekly leading article ripe with lush verbal raspberries about 'the reader-rabble of the gutter press.' The newspaper would develop a sarcastic, irreverent, scurrilous, mocking style of its own, not unlike the satirical newssheets of later decades: written partly in a well-captured Berlin dialect, its humor was a mixture of sophomoric poetry, puns, innuendoes, and insider-jokes for the entertainment of a very few.

The chief butt of its humor was of course the unfortunate Dr Bernhard Weiss, the self-important, horseback-riding, bespectacled Jewish ex-cavalry officer. Each week *Angriff* carried a regular column mocking the police force, entitled 'Watch that truncheon!' The paper's pages were strewn with puns on the name Weiss, with both blatant and surreptitious antisemitism, with unflattering comments on the deputy chief's riding and driving skills and on the shape of his nose, and with assertions that of course his real name was Bernhard – was it not illegal now to suggest anything else?[21] Soon it was enough for Goebbels to paint a word picture of Him, motoring in a princely limousine down Kurfürstendamm, for every reader to know who was meant.[22]

He seized upon his opponents' more cherished slogans. If enemies called him a Bandit, his next posters announced him as the Arch Bandit of Berlin. A politician of the Weimar republic had spoken of providing Germans with a 'life of beauty and dignity.' Goebbels rode that phrase into the ground over the next six years. He began an article on the mounting suicide rate with the ironic comment, 'The following were unable to endure any longer the happiness of this Life of Beauty and Dignity.'

He recognized that the target must always be an identifiable individual, like 'Isidor,' rather than an idea or group. Humorless, dedicated, and self-important, Dr Weiss made the perfect butt.[23] Goebbels used that 'Isidor' with such a thudding regularity that all Berlin came to assume it was Weiss's real name, as did some of his own officers, whom he then also prosecuted. Weiss had enjoyed a high profile until Goebbels' debut in Berlin: the papers carried many pictures of this diminutive, self-important official at public functions sporting a silk hat, tailcoat, and striped pants. Mounting a campaign brilliantly designed to undermine his authority, Goebbels published no fewer than six leader articles about him.[24]

In every issue of *Angriff* until No. 44 there was an attack on Weiss; its cartoons depicted him as a flatfooted Jew with bow legs, thick-lensed pince-nez, mustache, and jug ears. Undaunted by the laws of libel Goebbels accused Weiss in effect of being a Jew and trying to conceal it.

When Weiss sued, again and again, the courts decided that 'Isidor' alone was not libelous. The supreme court in Leipzig found with Goebbels that to call a Jew a Jew was no more defamatory than to call a catholic a catholic.

AT THE END of the third week in August 1927 the Nazis staged their third national rally, this time in Nuremberg. One hundred thousand people poured into the city: with unemployment rising, curiosity about Hitler's party was increasing. Berlin's forbidden S.A. turned out in force, eager to wear their uniforms; fifty of them had marched all the way to Nuremberg and Goebbels sent hundreds more in chartered trains.

On their return 'Isidor' Weiss ordered the trains stopped at Teltow and his police arrested 435 Nazis.[25] They were detained in police cells all day, and seventy lost their jobs in consequence: Goebbels did not care, because martyrs were more useful to his gau. As Schweitzer's banners for the Nuremberg rally had said, 'Ours is the future.' In northern Germany, in Hamburg and Brunswick, the National Socialists were now winning electoral seats. By the end of the year the party would have 72,590 registered members.

Of these however only some four thousand were in Berlin. Still banned, the gau was not finding the struggle easy.

On October 29, 1927 Goebbels was thirty. At a small party his office staff handed him an envelope containing torn-up notes for the loans used to launch *Angriff* and two thousand marks in cash, and gave him the news that they had collected 2,500 new subscriptions to the weekly.

It was about to break even. In February 1928 it would be selling 31,000 copies each week.[26] Powered by his articles, the newspaper would appear twice weekly from September 30, 1929 and daily from November 1, 1930, increasing its daily circulation from an average 68,600 in 1931 to a peak of 119,000 just after the seizure of power in 1933.[27]

ON HIS BIRTHDAY the Berlin political police lifted the speaking ban on Goebbels; but he was still on probation. The posters announced that he was to speak on Tuesday November 8 in the working-class suburb of Neukölln on 'The German people's dance of death.' Even without the swastika, Goebbels' hand was unmistakable. Addressed to 'Men of the fist and brow, proletarians of the factory bench and study cubicle,' the posters heaped ironic praise on the grandiose achievements of the Social Democrats since 1918. 'Peace, freedom, work, and bread! All of these Social Democracy has given to the German working man, plus' – in large letters – 'A LIFE OF BEAUTY AND DIGNITY.' Tickets were fifty pfennigs (only ten pfennigs for the unemployed). Thus the battlewagon was rolling again, and on November 6 he had the pleasure of seeing his semi-religious play *The Wanderer* premièred in a matinee by the 'National Socialist Experimental Theatere Company' too.

AT THE END of 1927 Dr Joseph Goebbels, agitator, streetfighter, and journalist, received a letter from Cologne, as though from another world: the Catholic charity there was still trying to recover its student loan to him.[28] It had reduced its claim to four hundred marks. Goebbels tossed the letter away.

Permitted to speak but with his party still banned in Berlin, he was careful to flatter Hitler to people with close ties to Munich.[29] He particularly befriended Rudolf Hess, Hitler's private secretary, favored Hess's fiancée Ilse with flowers and wrote to her praising the Führer in the sure knowledge that his words would be passed on. 'I was with the chief in Nuremberg on Sunday and Monday [the 14th and 15th],' he wrote to Ilse on November 16. 'What a guy he is! I could almost envy you for being around him the whole time. We can all be downright proud of him. Now,' he continued, 'I have barricaded myself back into this omnibus-ridden asphalt desert. . . Meanwhile we're back in combat with this magnificent ugly dragon, Berlin. We're at each other's throats again and that's why things are looking up again. Thank God, they've started cursing at us again.'[30]

These Goebbels methods worked.

The propaganda [he explained in a speech] which produces the desired results is good, and all other propaganda is bad. . .Therefore it is meaningless to say your propaganda is too crude, too cruel, too brutal, or too unfair, for none of those terms matter. . . Propaganda is always a means to an end. It is an art which can be taught to the average person like playing the violin. But there comes a point when you say, 'You're on your own now. What remains to be learned can only be accomplished by a genius.'

If people say, 'But you are only propagandists,' then you should answer, 'And what else was Jesus Christ? Did he not make propaganda?. . .Is Mussolini a scribbler or is he a great speaker? When Lenin went from Zürich to Saint Petersburg did he rush from the station into his study to write a book or did he speak before a multitude?'

BY EARLY 1928 Hitler confided in him intimately. In January he told Goebbels he was planning shortly to meet 'Benito.'[31] (Evidently nothing came of it.) In February he promised Goebbels that if the Nazis secured enough seats in the forthcoming Prussian election, Goebbels would be their bloc leader; and that he would also be a Reichstag candidate like Gregor Strasser.[32] A month later Hitler dangled the latter promise over him anew. 'The Chief,' Goebbels recorded smugly, 'used very bitter language about Dr [Otto] Strasser.' Strasser had founded a newspaper in Essen competing with the local gauleiter's. 'Now they all see how right I was in my fight against this loathsome swine,' wrote Goebbels; he would take pleasure in helping the gauleiter, Joseph Terboven, to smash this Strasser brother. 'That's what you get for heaping filth on me month after month,' he remarked in his unpublished diary. 'Revenge is a repast best savored cold' (it was to become one of his favorite aphorisms).[33]

His speeches were now one of Berlin's top attractions. '[Goebbels] spoke on March 23 in the Swiss Gardens at Friedrichshain,' the political police solemnly reported, opening yet another dossier. 'Poked fun at Mr Polizei-Vizepräsident Weiss.'[34] Weiss had twenty-one thousand officials, fourteen thousand uniformed police, three thousand detectives, and four thousand full-blown civil servants; there were forty-seven thousand photos and half a million fingerprints in his Rogues' Gallery; his museum even had the original uniform of the Captain of Köpenick.[35] Yet he could not keep down this poisonous dwarf limping at the head of his Nazis in Berlin. Indeed, in March Goebbels sent off to the printers his 168-page lampoon of Weiss, *The Book of Isidor*, sub-titled 'A Portrait of Our Times, Packed with Laughter and Hate.'[36]

The entertaining public face-off between the pompous police chief and the propagandist continued throughout the year. One beerhall battle on February 23 ended with Goebbels' driver Tonak again injured on this occasion, stabbed three times in the back dangerously close to the heart.[37]

Those were hectic weeks.[38] The next morning Goebbels was arrested at six A.M. That evening he was heading for Cottbus with his S.A. 'lads.' On March 12 he wrote to the courts asking to be excused from testifying in the trial of Nazis involved in the gun battle at Lichterfelde station.[39] But the political police would not brook any delays, and he had to testify.[40] 'He is in fact the leading personality,' they pointed out, 'in the fight against the police headquarters.'[41] Six of his men involved in the gun battle were sentenced to a total of three years and seven months in prison.

On March 24 he was back in court. 'Today I have six hearings,' he recorded. Four were for slandering 'Isidor,' one for high treason, and one for causing bodily harm.[42] The courts fixed April 28 for the case against Goebbels and Dürr for libeling Dr Weiss in *Angriff*. Goebbels did his damnedest to wriggle off the hook, filing several applications for postponements.[43] Weiss's deputy Wündisch, head of the Berlin political police, demanded that Goebbels be arrested if he failed to show up, as they fully expected him to keep spinning things out until he won immunity in the forthcoming election.[44] Midday on the twenty-eighth found the gauleiter duly in court with his editor Dürr. 'Before German judges,' he seethed in his diary. 'A ridiculous farce. Prosecutor demanded two months for Dürr and myself.' The sentence was three weeks. 'I just kept silent,' he added. 'Once I'm immune I will accept full blame to spare Dürr.'[45] The judgment concluded that the newspaper had published wicked and deliberate libels on the worthy Dr Weiss: 'By calling him "Isidor" and publishing the comment, "How dare you kick me with your flat little feet" they were underlining Dr Weiss's Jewish origins.' Revenge in this case was both sweet and cold: in May he received the printer's proofs of *Isidor*.[46] As for the cartoon of the donkey with all four legs splayed on the ice, Goebbels allowed *Angriff* to publish it again with this solemn caption: 'In convicting our editor Dürr the judge stipulated *inter alia*, "This donkey does bear the face of Vice Police President Dr Weiss."'[47]

How he hated that man, and how the Nazis and communists alike laughed when truncheon-wielding police officers accidentally thrashed Weiss as well.[48] The Brownshirts added a new verse to their marching song on 'Isidor' and Goebbels composed an unsympathetic leader for *Angriff* about 'the story of a Jew who didn't want to look like one,' who 'forbade people to call him Isidor because his name was Bernhard – "Bear's Heart,"' and who in broad daylight was 'thrashed by his own police officers with their rubber truncheons because they couldn't believe they could possibly have a chief who looked like that.' The result was yet another prosecution for libeling the humorless Dr Weiss.[49]

THE REICHSTAG dissolved in March 1928. On the last day of the month Dr Weiss lifted the ban on the Nazis, because the elections would be held in May. Goebbels formally relaunched the party in Berlin at a ceremony on April 13, then sent long columns of Brownshirts to march defiantly through the streets again.[50] We marched,' wrote one of his S.A. men, 'and we marched. We marched although people bombarded us with every conceivable projectile and missile.'[51]

The five weeks of electioneering were crippled by lack of funds.[52] Goebbels sat in street cafes with his artist Schweitzer, suggesting poster themes.[53] In the evenings he patrolled the section headquarters at Alexander Platz, Tempelhof, Friedenau, and elsewhere.

Experimenting with propaganda techniques, he dictated one speech onto phonograph discs.[54] He spent his spare time tinkering with *Michael*, inserting new vitriolic lines attacking the Jews, and *Blood Seed*.[55] May Day found him in a grubby Polish international train heading for Düsseldorf; sitting in the audience there he glimpsed his mother, brothers, and little sister Maria; he only rarely saw them nowadays. On May 17 he hobbled at the head of 250 S.A. men marching through Spandau and Tegel and into working-class Wedding, heedless of the screeches and whistles of their baffled enemies – 'chinstraps tightened,' he recorded proudly afterwards, 'With these lads we'll conquer the world.'[56]

In the final weeks before the election he detected signs of unrest among these 'lads.' Munich had appointed Walther Stennes, a former police captain aged thirty-three, to command the S.A. in this part of Germany: 'a regular chap!' Goebbels had written in February, and 'a splendid fellow' in April.[57] But he was soon keeping Stennes at a distance. He was independently wealthy, and had only joined the Party in December when Goebbels insisted. Stennes had found in the Berlin S.A. an undisciplined rabble which goaded the police to no real purpose.[58] He had introduced Prussian discipline, and now he began asking for a larger slice of the cake – more Reichstag candidates should be from the S.A. To Goebbels it was the old story, of 'soldiers' meddling in politics. 'The military should sharpen the sword,' he decided, 'and leave it to us politicians to decide when it has to be used.'[59]

That he was now fighting with the ballot box rather than by revolution seemed a total betrayal of his own teachings. It was expediency. Besides, he intended to raid the Reichstag as the 'arsenal of democracy' and seize its weapons. 'If,' he wrote, 'we succeed in planting in the Reichstag sixty or seventy of our own agitators and organizers, then the state itself will equip and pay for our fighting machine.'

IT WAS STREAMING with rain as Germany went to the polls on May 20. Nationwide, the Nazi party had finished tenth in 1924; it now did rather better, though its share of the vote in Berlin was still unimpressive (only 1·5 percent). Over eight hundred thousand voted for the Hitler movement, but only thirty-nine thousand Berliners. The party increased its representation in the Reichstag from seven to twelve. Goebbels heard the results at a jam-packed election bash at the Victoria Gardens. They shouldered him around the hall with whoops of triumph. He would now be a Reichstag deputy: The other eleven lucky Nazis would include Gregor Strasser, Wilhelm Frick, and Hermann Göring.[60]

As the specter of prison faded, he wrote cynically in *Angriff*; 'I am an I.d.I. and an I.d.F: *Inhaber der Immunität* and *Inhaber der Freifahrkarte*,' possessed of immunity and a free travel pass. 'The I.d.I.,' he continued, 'can call a dungheap a dungheap. He doesn't have to mince his language by calling it a state.' And he added: 'This is but a prelude. You're going to have a lot of fun with us. It's showtime!'

8: *Anka is to Blame*

T HERE WERE DISADVANTAGES in having such a high profile. On June 19, 1928 the catholic charity again wrote to Goebbels from Cologne, suggesting now that he pay off his ten-year-old debt at fifty marks per month. Their letter was returned endorsed 'delivery refused.'

He had resumed the feud with Dr Weiss at once, 'DO YOU BELIEVE THAT ISIDOR IS BEHAVING HIMSELF?' his newspaper headlined. 'Yes, indeed: *Isidor*,' Goebbels repeated. 'I'll defy the ban. Under the cowardly protection of immunity I'll name names. *Isidor*! The *o* must be long drawn out, and the *r* rolled until this name reverberates with inexpressible sweetness and power. The Gift of the East!'[1]

Try as he could, Dr Weiss could not nail him. His prey always dodged in time. More items were clipped into the police dossier: Munich police were charging Goebbels with illegal fund raising; Berlin police heard him announce on May 13, 'The present state is a dunghill and the police president a Jew'; an action was pending for 'incitement to class war'; and there were countless breaches of press regulations.[2] The court hearing of the Pastor Stucke case in June lasted all day. Goebbels spoke for two hours; the six-week sentence was reduced to a fine of six hundred marks. 'A Jew, Löwenstein, sat on the judge's bench,' he observed, 'otherwise we should probably have got off scot free. . . Not a penny shall I pay anyway.'[3] He continued to run rings round the courts; his supporters packing the public galleries hooted and jeered as he and his lawyers made monkeys out of police witnesses, prosecutors, and the bench.[4] The fines were derisory. 'Two hundred marks or twenty days,' he recorded, 'for libeling Ia' – Weiss's political police.[5]

He received his free travel pass. 'Let my voyaging now commence,' he wrote, 'at the Republic's expense!'[6] The new Reichstag opened on June 13. The twelve Nazis marched in wearing uniform. Meeting afterward, the Nazi bloc assigned to him the portfolios of culture and internal affairs.[7] The Strassers blamed him in their publications for the party's poor showing in Berlin.[8] He sensed Gregor's hostility, but decided he could live with it. They were equals now. As he limped down the steps there was a ripple of applause that he recorded for posterity in his diary.

After a month the Reichstag, under joint pressure from its communist and Nazi members, approved an amnesty for all political crimes committed before

1928. Dr Weiss saw his tormentor's slate suddenly wiped all but clean. A year later Berlin police headquarters would endorse his file, 'All judgments and outstanding cases against Dr Göbbels [*sic*] have been quashed or annulled on the basis of the Law of Amnesty passed on July 14, 1928.'

LATE IN June 1928 he transferred the gau headquarters to No. 77 Berliner Strasse in Charlottenburg – fourteen newly furnished rooms on one floor, 'not bad going for eighteen months,' he reflected.[9]

His health, never robust, had suffered in the election campaign.[10] He now felt perpetually tired; overshadowing the head- and backaches, which he attributed to nervous problems, was the permanent agony of his steel-encased lame leg – 'chronic pains and unpleasantness,' he would write that autumn, before a phrase which suggests he was beginning to doubt his own sexuality: 'plus the malicious gossip that I'm a homosexual.'[11] Such gossip was inevitable. Here he was, a young man of thirty, of brains, courage, and notoriety, and yet: a bachelor. Seeking company he was as likely to pick Tonak or Schweitzer for a walk *à deux* around the park at Wannsee or a visit to the lofty new Radio Tower as to scoop up two or three of his female staff for a stroll in Potsdam.[12] 'I am sick in mind and body,' he would confess.[13] Since doctors found nothing wrong, he resorted to that most German of remedies, a *Kur*, that did help him, or so he imagined, which was what mattered.[14] His club foot never ceased hurting – 'for weeks on end now,' he would write early in 1929. 'Sometimes it just blights my whole day.'[15]

His worries had been magnified by the onset of his father's last illness in the late spring of 1928. Laden with filial remorse Joseph Goebbels visited the paternal home as often as he could, sat silently watching the gray-bearded old man, wept as he felt the thin, bony fingers, and romanticized each farewell wave in his diary in case it was the last.

IN JULY 1928 Adolf Hitler came to Berlin. Goebbels wrote that he was fond of him as a son is of his father, and staged a huge private meeting for him at Friedrichshain. 'Although it was the summer silly season,' wrote young Horst Wessel admiringly, 'the hall was packed out. Who else could do that in high summer?' New members flooded in after Hitler's speech.[16] Before Hitler left, Goebbels vented his anger about Dr Otto Strasser, and the Führer waffled reassuringly about winding up the Strassers' publishing house in Berlin. He mentioned that he and his half-sister Angela Raubal would be taking a trip to the island of Heligoland with Angela's daughter 'Geli' – would Dr Goebbels like to join them? Knowing Geli already, Goebbels jumped at the chance.[17]

HE HAS met Geli Raubal, Hitler's barely nineteen-year-old niece, in Munich four months before. Unaware of the nearly forty-year-old Hitler's proprietary interest in her, he has hatched plans to bring her to Berlin.

He is still pining for Anka Stalherm. But married to the humdrum Georg

Mumme she lives in Weimar and he has not seen her for years. 'I must have a good, beautiful woman!' he writes in his unpublished diary at the start of 1928.[18] Göring has come back from Sweden married to a beautiful Swedish countess; Hess is marrying his Ilse.[19]

His *cri de cœur* seems answered by a teenaged girl working at headquarters, a girl of, he writes, almost Asiatic submissiveness.[20] 'I love Tamara von Heede,' he records. 'Wonder if she loves me? Hardly. That's how it always is: what you get, you don't want; and what you want, you don't get.'[21] Tamara puzzles the naïve and sexually innocent gauleiter by being off color at monthly intervals.[22] One evening canoodling with him in the park, she freezes him with a thoughtless remark, perhaps about his foot. She makes up the next day with a basket of fruit and other delights.[23] Their friendship causes the usual tensions at headquarters.[24] Meanwhile Anka abruptly returns to his life: there she is, standing in the doorway of the hotel foyer at Weimar after a renewed staging of his play *The Wanderer*. By his own account Goebbels trembles and stammers with joy at seeing his long-lost love.

For half an hour Anka pours out her heart about her joyless marriage: Mumme has concealed from her until after the marriage that he is infertile from syphilis; her four-month-old son Christian is by another man. Goebbels is under her spell again, it is as though they never parted. 'O, *l'amour!*' his pen exclaims after he has lain awake all night. 'I am like a child.'[25] Tamara is disconsolate that Anka has surfaced again from his past; nevertheless he phones Anka from Berlin and they agree to meet again.[26] A few days later she phones him twice, weeping, in the middle of the night, saying she wants to come to Berlin; divorcing Mumme, he suggests, is her only escape. She arrives at his apartment but receives only coffee and sympathy as she rehearses her entire tragic life once more for him.[27]

'I have kissed her,' he writes afterward, 'and a lucky star has crossed from her to me.' After Anka departs, Tamara phones. 'Poor Tamara!' he writes, and: 'Poor Anka!' – and many a reader of his diary will agree.

He spends another day with his goddess in Weimar soon after. 'I love her, she loves me, neither of us says it but we both know it.'[28] At Easter however there is an awkward scene when her husband shows up. Goebbels capitulates. 'I'm off. Curtly and formally took leave of them both. . . I'm shutting off my heart. For good! Great tasks wait upon me. . . Before me stands a nation! Germany!'[29]

A few days later, great task or no, he phones her Weimar number. Dr Mumme answers and Dr Goebbels hangs up. 'God only helps those,' he writes on a bouquet of flowers for her, 'who help themselves. Farewell. ULEX.'[30]

He is not blind to the rest of the fairer sex. There is a Dora, a 'hysterical lover' who puts a letter through his door threatening to poison herself ('Doesn't know me too good,' he comments callously. 'I've already yielded far too much to this hussy. Let her do it if she really must. I can't say anything but no').[31] 'Since I have set eyes again on Anka,' he sighs, justifying his sexual inactivity, 'all female beauty pales.'[32] It is therefore no surprise to see him shortly alighting from a train at Weimar on the way home from Wiesbaden, embracing Anka on the platform and sharing a compartment for a few minutes until the next halt at Weissenfels. An icy hand may well have clutched at his heart as she chatters away, because she now hints at leaving Mumme for Goebbels in Berlin. The ardent suitor takes refuge in the language of a cheap novel. 'Farewell, farewell!' he writes in the diary. 'She waves until we are out of sight of each other.'[33] He spends the next days in a guilty panic. No word comes from Weimar.[34] Will she really leave her Georg? And what then?

Dr Goebbels appraises the alternatives: there is 'a pretty Miss Böhm' at Schweinfurt; there is Willi Hess's little sister ('a darling thing, unfortunately not good looking'; he will find the same trouble with a Miss Bettge on Borkum island too – 'Pity she's not prettier.'[35]) He has to speak at Weimar late in May, and diffidently phones the Mumme household. A voice tells him that Madam is away.[36] Back in Berlin the next day he bumps into Dora, who has not poisoned herself after all: few girls do nowadays. 'Anka is to blame for all this,' he writes helplessly. 'She's brought me to the point where women are just playthings. The revenge of a creature spurned.'[37]

She is soon forgotten in Berlin. He is overhauling his gau, appointing Reinhold Muchow his chief of organization on July 1, 1928.[38] He has resumed work on *Michael*, rewriting, dictating, proof-reading, and mailing it for Franz Eher Verlag to publish that autumn. He goes on a chaotic gau outing down Brandenburg's waterways, a wasted day were it not for one beautiful girl. 'Without a word,' he romanticizes again, 'we are in love. Neither of us betrays this by the slightest sign, but it is so.'[39] Chemicals are brewing within the crippled, now thirty-year old Dr Joseph Goebbels which he still does not care to test. 'I'll go to pot altogether,' he fears, 'if I can't get together with women.' They are out there, besieging him, but he is searching for a woman that he does not know. Two days later at Bayreuth, as the curtain goes up on the last act of 'Tristan' he finds a stunning beauty next to him: We partake of a little feast of love, without a word between us – just two glances, two sighs. And then she's gone. . . The whole evening I am at my wit's end.'[40]

Matrimony is claiming all his friends. Even Karlheinz Kölsch, 'Pille,' his closest friend and rival from those Freiburg days, gets married this August. Tipsy and reeking of liquor he throws his arms around the little gauleiter and kisses him; Goebbels recoils, fearful that they might be seen. 'Ghastly,' he exclaims in his diary. 'Kölsch always was an asshole.' Together they pen a postcard to Anka at Weimar.[41]

So it goes on: his roving eye feasts on every female, spinster or spoken for, and ravishes or rejects them all – the arrestingly beautiful wife of Dr Robert Ley, and a pompous editor's wife with whom he falls deeply in love for, probably, hours at a time.[42] Each time his train passes through Weimar he peers out, hoping for a glimpse of Anka.[43]

In September the chase is suddenly on again. This time, his quarry is young Hannah Schneider, a true Germanic beauty from Mecklenburg. She is a member of the party's Women's Order. After a hard day's work at his desk, Goebbels begins to look forward to negotiations with the order which he previously hated. He adores Hannah's natural childishness (she is in her late teens). She is pretty and clever, and another virgin. It is surely interesting that he writes of her as this 'glisteningly clean maiden.'[44] Let no careless biographer maintain that he has advanced far with the fairer sex even now: strolling in the Tiergarten after taking her to her first movie, he steals a chaste kiss from Hannah. 'She blushed like a child when I kissed her neck,' he writes, rejoicing in his adventure.[45] He delights in her innocent chatter and writes more than once approvingly of her *Jungfräulichkeit*, her virginity.[46] But he is aware of her limitations. He needs a more mature woman, while Hannah is 'a totally innocent child.'

A little bombshell comes from Weimar. Anka writes that she is indeed divorcing Mumme and coming to work in Berlin.[47] Goebbels reflects how much women have hurt him, and how much they have hurt for him too. 'Is this to be a new tragedy,' he wonders, 'in which I am to be cast in the leading role?' He tells little Hannah none of this. He writes cautiously back to Anka: Perhaps they might meet on Tuesday October 2 in Weimar? The next day, speaking at Hasenheide, he sights Hannah sitting reverently as though in a church pew, smiling with childlike attentiveness. A telegram comes from Anka: yes, Tuesday. In Weimar, they sit up late together. She tells him that she is now in two minds again. Meanwhile, should she come to Berlin for a month or two? 'That might well be ticklish,' senses Goebbels in his diary.

Hannah falls silent. 'She loves me, she loves me not?' wonders Goebbels. 'I'm damned if I can tell.'[48] Shortly a letter comes, spelling out the answer: she does not. Goebbels limps around baffled, groping for an explanation. 'Okay. So I shall have to stay lonely. To be famous or to be loved? That is the question.'[49] On October 12 Hannah reappears at gau headquarters. 'Suddenly the hour is filled with lustrous happiness,' writes Goebbels, extracting much pathos from a scene which must have cruelly punctured his male vanity. 'I kiss her squarely on her full red lips. And then she confesses to me that she loves another. She only came to me because I was so lonely. A terrible discovery. From a thousand heavens I plummet to the depths of a thousand hells.'[50] Innocently twisting her teenaged knife, Hannah writes asking if she can be a good sister to him instead. 'Always the same,' fulminates Goebbels hopefully. 'First these women just want to be your sister. Then whoopee, it's mistress after all.'

'Unhappy love,' he summarizes tersely on October 17, 1928: 'There can be no such thing for a Man with a Mission.'[51]

9: Conjuring up Spirits

THERE WAS A SIDE to Dr Goebbels which few suspected. He half believed in the occult. At the very end of his life he would have horoscopes cast for himself, for Hitler, and for the Third Reich; scattered through the earlier diaries are references to séances at which dark forces were consulted. On leave in Bavaria in 1928 he was to be found conjuring up the spirit of Leo Schlageter. The great martyr of the Ruhr resistance 'appeared' and, when asked Who Shall Save Germany?, replied with a tact that was commendable under the circumstances, 'Vest Your Hopes Only in Hitler.'[1] In 1929 Goebbels and his friends again conjured up the spirits. 'I don't really believe in such frauds,' he noted airily, 'but it's usually quite amusing.'[2] Visiting Princess Wied in August 1930 he found an astrologer there who 'conjured forth from the stars precisely what we would expect to happen anyway.' Goebbels' own apparent cynicism was belied however by the diary passage that followed. Auwi [Prince August-Wilhelm] is very skeptical, but I am flabbergasted.[3] He unquestioningly accepted the mystic powers of graphology. He allowed the party lawyer Ludwig Weissauer to read his hand; Weissauer told him that it betrayed sensitivity and a determination to fight on.

Weissauer found one line to be flawed. That, guessed Goebbels, must be Anka. Since losing her he had had nothing but a sense of loneliness.[4]

AIDED BY YOUNG Horst Wessel, he had spent the summer of 1928 organizing a Hitler Youth detachment and a Nazi student association in Berlin. But those months saw the first problems with the brownshirted S.A. battalions of party stormtroopers. They had believed his earlier talk of revolution; but with Hitler's newfound belief in the legal approach to power they saw the day when they might storm the Reichstag receding. Friction with their commander Captain Stennes grew.[5]

Goebbels was in two minds. Unlike Hitler, he never wholly abandoned the idea of a putsch. He spent much of the summer organizing an S.A. march on Berlin, to culminate in a mass rally in Berlin's largest hall. It would be a show of power. In mid-August Stennes threatened to quit, taking several of his commanders with him.[6] Goebbels told him of the planned 'rally.' 'We can do without a crisis at this moment,' he notified his diary. We must keep the peace. I convince [Stennes], against my own convictions.[7] At the party's

Dr Joseph Goebbels

above: Goebbels in 1908, a first year schoolboy

above: Goebbels, at center, holds hands with a fellow
pupil on their matriculation, 1917

below: cross-legged on the floor, as a member of the
local catholic businessmen's association
(MÖNCHENGLADBACH CITY ARCHIVES)

UNCHANGED TODAY   The Goebbels parental home
Rheydt's Dahlener Strasse. His room beneath the r
overlooks a tombstone merchant's yard
(AUTHOR'S COLLECTION)

above: After student high-jinks at Freiburg university Karlheinz 'Pille' Kölsch, Joseph Goebbels' ultimately successful rival for Anka Stalherm's affections, sends her this picture—it shows Goebbels with a lampshade on his head (STALHERM/IRENE PRANGER COLLECTION)

APPROACHING MATURITY   Goebbels as a young unemployed postgraduate in 1923 (*left*); he keeps the picture as a memento of worse times, gives the snapshots of himself as a well-dressed embryonic agitator at Zwickau in 1925 (*center*), as a suitor in 1925 (*right*) to Anka Stalherm and later to Horst Wessel in 1925 (MÖNCHENGLADBACH CITY ARCHIVES; STALHERM/IRENE PRANGER; HORST WESSEL DIARY)

Agnes Kölsch

Else Janke

Ev. to ~~busse~~. Sportpalast,
S.A.- Appell. Then so busy
worked unt. 2 o'cl.

ILSE STAHL keeps a diary – in English; she
eventually marries another gauleiter, Joseph
Terboven, and blows herself up on the last day of the
war (BOB PITTARD COLLECTION)

... *but always there is Anka*

THE FIRST GIRL Goebbels falls for is Agnes (*above left, in* 1918), a catholic girl with a come-hither look, sister of his best friend 'Pille' Kölsch. Later he discovers Else Janke. All goes well until Else reveals that she has Jewish blood. In Berlin Goebbels starts dating his secretary Ilse Stahl (below *left*).

Ever since the University of Heidelberg however he has had an enduring obsession with his fellow-student Anka Stalherm; her wealthy family (*left*) disapproves of this penniless and clubfooted suitor. After a fruitless midnight visit to his bedroom, when she spends a week with her husband and Goebbels in Weimar in July 1929, Anka receives a snapshot (*top*) as a memento from her 'Ulex'.

Anka Stalherm (sitting at right of middle row)

left: the north-western Nazis parade
through a town in Westphalia in 1926.
Left to right: Joseph Wagner, Gregor
Strasser, Goebbels, and Viktor Lutze

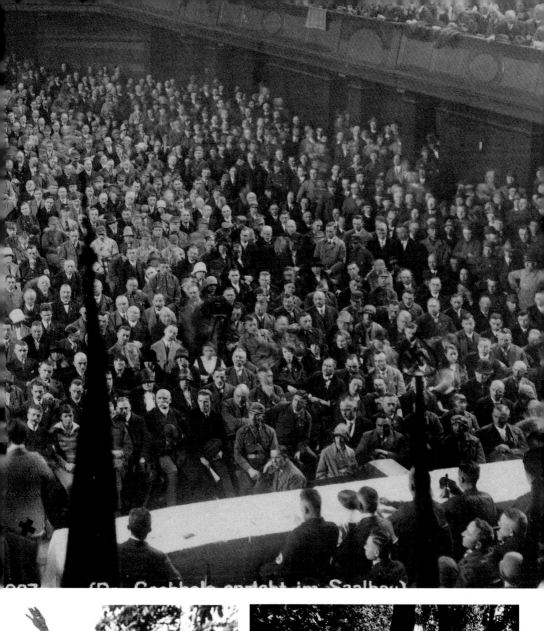

(Der Goebbels spricht im Saalbau)

Hitler and Helga

THE FÜHRER adores Helga, the Goebbels' eldest daughter (seen *above* at Hitler's Berghof in October 1937). He flatters the propaganda minister that if only he were ten years younger, and Helga ten years older, she would make the perfect wife for him.

Immune Again!

THROUGHOUT THE YEARS OF struggle Dr Goebbels is rarely more than one step ahead of the police, whose chiefs Albert Grzesinski (*above*) and 'Isidor' Weiss are determined to lock him away. In 1930 he is re-elected to the Reichstag. On October 13, with every Berlin policeman briefed to arrest him on sight, he reaches the building and makes a dash for the south entrance. Immune again! (BUNDESARCHIV; NATIONAL ARCHIVES, WASHINGTON)

The Struggle for Berlin

IN JUST OVER SIX YEARS, FROM 1926 to 1933, Dr Goebbels wins Berlin for Hitler. Aided by idealistic young Nazis like Horst Wessel – pictured at the extreme right of his Alexander-Platz section in 1927 (*left*) – he stages drum-beating marches by the S.A. Brownshirts through the leafier suburbs of Berlin (*center*). After their prohibition he sends his Berlin S.A. on a propaganda march to Nuremberg for the August 1927 Rally (*below left*)) (HORST WESSEL DIARY, BIBLIOTEKA JAGIELLOŃSKA, UNIVERSITY OF KRAKÓW)

POSTERS ACROSS BERLIN (*below*) announce that Dr Goebbels is to speak on May 4, 1927. The meeting ends in violence – and police chief Grzesinski seizes the opportunity to dissolve the gau (BUNDESARCHIV)

Fussmarsch Berlin-Nürnberg
JULI-AUG.
Trotz Verbot-nicht tot!

above: As the membership of the Berlin gau multiplies Goebbels, wearing the tiepin that Anka gave him, takes on more staff for his headquarters – with an eye particularly for the more comely young females.

below: In the final years of the struggle, every week finds Goebbels speaking at the graveside as another victim of communist violence is buried (BOTH PHOTOS: NATIONAL ARCHIVES, WASHINGTON)

FLANKED BY gau business manager Dagobert Dürr and Martin Bethke ('Orje'), Goebbels addresses a ra[l]
from an open four-seater Mercedes-Benz at Bernau near Berlin, in 1928. Goebbels claims to have been
given the car by anonymous benefactors, but police chief 'Isidor' Weiss determines that the gauleiter has
purchased it for two thousand marks from the merchant bank Grundmann & Co and registered it in his
own name (ALL PHOTOS: NATIONAL ARCHIVES, WASHINGTON)

Nazi Shibboleth

LIMOUSINE More than any other
[poli]tical party in Europe, the Nazis use
[the] car as a brutal demonstration that
[they] have arrived.

[Above?]: In 1929 Goebbels claims that an
[expa]triate German supporter living
[in A]rgentina has donated this blue
[opel] seven-seater landau, license tag
[?]3398, to the gau.

[MER]CEDES-BENZ chief executive Jakob
[Wer]lin (*above*, with Goebbels, Röhm,
[Gör]ing, and Hitler) sees to it that Hitler
[and] Goebbels enjoy a limitless supply of
[the] flashier new limousines.

[Above]: In a shiny new Mercedes-
[Ben]z Goebbels drives up to his new
[pro]paganda ministry building in March
[1933], greeted by house manager Mehlis.

[Belo]w: Driven by chauffeur Albert
[Nas?]ak, Goebbels arrives in style at
[the 1]934 Nuremberg Party Rally, in yet
[ano]ther Mercedes-Benz, license tag
[IA-1]11.

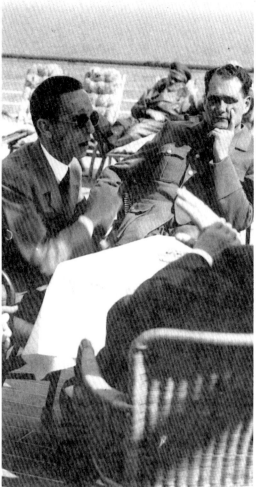

above: Aboard a Strength through Joy (K.d.F.) cruise-ship in the Baltic, Hitler snoozes, leaving Goebbels and Hess to talk party business.

below: The benign face of evil, momentarily softened by the sight of a caged canary in the fall of 1933. Their enemies are now all behind bars.

The Devil an

OPINION IS DIVIDED about Dr Goebbels' relations with Hitler. Which is the evil genius, and which spellbound princeling? Which is the better orator? his diary on April 19, 1926 Goebbels jots, 'I love y because you are great and simple at the same time – w we call a genius.'

above: Hitler and Goebbels, looking somewhat out of place in tails, at a gala function in 1935.

center: Surrounded by their flunkies the two Nazis show themselves to the crowds below.

below: The Führer smiles at his adoring fans through the swing doors at the opera.

is Disciple

irst his loyalty is absolute. Receiving a faked telegram
iouncing Hitler's death, he is close to a nervous
akdown. In unguarded moments, Goebbels muses out
d, 'Now, if I were the Führer . . .' When he hears of the
mpt on Hitler's life in 1944 he is strangely unmoved.

UNLIKE MANY COMRADES, Ernst 'Teddy' Thälmann, the communist party leader, has the courage of his convictions. Sent to a concentration camp after the Reichstag fire, he refuses to work on anti-communist propaganda for Goebbels, and Thälmann is executed at Buchenwald on August 18, 1944 (BUNDESARCHIV)

OPPONENTS POKE FUN at the less than Nordic appearance of 'the Nazi leader Dr Goebbels.' A 1932 election poster for the Bavarian People' Party mobilizes latent anti-Prussian sentimen (SÜDDEUTSCHER VERLAG)

Mjölnir's poster for the 1927 Nuremberg Ra

left: Like many of the top Nazis, Goebbels feels at home with the fading Germany's aristocracy, like 'Auwi,' Prince August-Wilhe of Prussia, son of the Kaiser. Auwi is given hi rank in the Brownshirted S.A. Both are wear the lapel medallion commemorating the 1927 Nuremberg Rally (BUNDESARCHIV)

annual general meeting in Munich at the end of August Hitler directed him to concentrate his efforts now on Berlin, while Brandenburg would be detached to form a separate gau.[8]

Hitherto Goebbels had merely reacted to political events. Now he seized the political initiative. He proclaimed the last week of September 1928 'Dawes Week,' seven days of intense campaigning in Berlin against the pact obliging Germany to pay her war reparations bill regardless of her economic plight. He printed a special issue of *Angriff*, which sold sixty thousand copies.[9] Growing bolder, he risked hiring for the first time the Sport Palace in Potsdamer Strasse for the third Brandenburg Rally (*Märkertag*); to fill the cavernous building, which could seat fifteen thousand people, he placarded the city with lurid posters announcing: 'On Saturday September 30 Adolf Hitler's Brownshirts will march into Berlin.'[10] That day he drove out to Teltow to watch his brown army assemble. Four thousand S.A. men marched into the capital. At Steglitz town hall the immense throng, which Goebbels put at 'tens of thousands,' paused, bared their heads, and roared the national anthem before marching on through the city's frightened, wealthy West End to the Sport Palace building. With thousands of communists massing threateningly outside, a riot began and the police opened fire. Four Nazis were seriously injured. Goebbels left under a barrage of rocks, jeers, and catcalls – 'Hatred and love,' he philosophized. The next day's 'non-Jewish' press was largely sympathetic, the rest less so.[11]

'A day of triumph,' he concluded in his diary: He had Anka sending him telegrams from Weimar; he had young Hannah; he had fifteen thousand Berliners hanging on his every word.[12] A letter of congratulations came from Hitler.[13] A few days later the Führer appeared unannounced at gau headquarters in Berliner Strasse and repeated his congratulations in person. He reiterated that Goebbels alone had his confidence in Berlin, and he spoke harshly about Dr Otto Strasser. The gauleiter could now afford to give his staff, over twenty strong, a substantial pay rise.

DECIDING TO MOVE into larger lodgings, he finds just what he needs in Württembergische Strasse in west Berlin, closer to gau headquarters. His landlady is a Miss Grothe, an elderly spinster, as he is careful to record.[14] The apartment has a pleasant drawing room. He feels entitled to some luxury – 'I have naught else, neither wife nor child, and only seldom a lover.' He uses the word *Geliebte*, although 'girlfriend' would seem more justified. Most are passing fancies, like one Eva Otto – she donates a piano to the new apartment.[15] On October 31, 1928, the day before he moves in, his secretary circulates the new address, requesting it be kept secret 'for obvious reasons.' A copy goes to Anka.[16]

He is still terrified of any hint of homosexuality, a criminal perversion that seems particularly prevalent in the Nazi party. Unable to form lasting relationships with women, he loiters in cafés or haunts movie theaters with his chauffeur Tonak or cartoonist Schweitzer, his only friends.[17] After major events he returns to his empty apartment and mopes. He needs a woman, as 'a starter-motor,' but the malicious gossip will not go away. 'It's too filthy even to think about without being ashamed,' he insists to his diary the day after moving into his new bachelor apartment. 'Decay! Decay! It must be expunged, radically and ruthlessly.'[18]

His reasoning is odd, however – 'Because if the enemy ever learns something like that, we shall be finished.' Is homosexuality for Goebbels, this 'immoral vice,' a crime in the detection rather than in the commission?' It's got to be stamped out radically,' he writes on November 4. 'It's all so dirty' – again, an interesting choice of word – 'It's all so dirty that it would preferable not to hear or see it at all.' Several of his officials are unmasked as homosexuals, and Goebbels does not know whom to trust.[19] 'It's so alien to my own nature,' he writes, 'that I can't work up for them even the vestigial sympathy that I do for any common murderer.'[20]

Over the next months Goebbels, now thirty-one, tries relationships with half a dozen teenage girls but his eye soon roves on. Talking with Josef Terboven his eye lights upon the Essen gauleiter's attractive, 'but unfortunately rather aging,' sister.[21] When Hitler visits Berlin with niece Geli Raubal in mid-November, Goebbels again finds her 'almost lovable' but wisely smites from his mind the horrendous idea of cuckolding the Führer.[22] He visits the party's Women's Order, despite their harridan Elsbeth Zander, and spends an evening watching the healthy young girls dance and sing: surely a sign that he is desperate for female company.

IN 1928 ALONE he spoke at 188 meetings. He seemed not to know fear. On November 3 that year he led the S.A. into one of Berlin's Reddest suburbs. 'A lot of blood will flow,' he accepted. 'But I shall be with them.'[23]

His *Book of Isidor* had sold out and was reprinting. Dr Weiss unsuccessfully canvassed his prosecution for felonious remarks about the Rathenau murder.[24] When the Reichstag reconvened in November there were immediate moves to strip Goebbels of his immunity. He hated the 'rotten' parliamentary system; he behaved outrageously during the debates, and attracted several reprimands.[25]

The ban on Hitler speaking publicly in Prussia had been lifted. On November 16 Goebbels presented him with an overflowing Sport Palace, martial music, and the ceremonial entry of Berlin's Nazi standards as a visible sign of the Party's growing might. As Hitler spoke, eight hundred police protected the hall and its audience.[26] The two men sat far into the night with Hess; Goebbels could not help noticing that Adolf now had his Geli, and Hess his Ilse, while he was still alone.

The next day the body of Hans-Georg Kütemeyer, a Scharführer in No. 15 Sturm of the Berlin S.A., was fished out of the Landwehr canal. What Goebbels called the 'Judenpresse' scoffed that Kütemeyer had killed himself, and there was report of a morose letter to his wife about their poverty. Goebbels was not going to lose his first major martyr that easily ('Never have liars stooped so low!'); he wrote a eulogy in *Angriff* and began a noisy propaganda campaign.[27]

The party buried Kütemeyer with full honors on November 21. Thousands gathered at the graveside. 'Marxists!' Goebbels' street placards challenged. 'Why did you murder the worker Kütemeyer?'[28] The police hefted into their Goebbels dossier a note that he had propagated 'untrue statements' on the case. But the S.A. man's two killers were caught and given suspended sentences of two and four months for manslaughter in June 1929. 'Three Jews as judges,' observed Dr Goebbels, and vowed hatred, vengeance, and retribution against the system.[29]

AS THE APPOINTED 'minister of culture' of the little National Socialist faction he went more often to the theater and the movies, which were still silent. He took Schweitzer to a love movie, only to walk out before the end, but he found the romantic scenes in *Anna Karenina* a delight.[30] Once he went to an all-Negro revue; he sniffed at their 'silly doo-dah'ing and dancing' and was annoyed when the public roared applause.[31] He found Buster Keaton unfunny and incomprehensible. After seeing his first Hollywood movie, again with Schweitzer, he recorded: 'Sheer hell. Jewish kitsch. Virtually all you saw were Hebrews.'[32] The dominance of the Jews in this relatively new industry did not elude him.[33] They were everywhere. He heard Offenbach's opera *The Tales of Hoffmann* on the radio and dismissed it in his diary as Jewish music. 'The Jewish question,' he added intensely, 'is the question of all questions.'[34]

His enthusiasm for the Russian cinema, like much else from Moscow, was undeniable. He viewed Soviet movie director Sergei Eisenstein's silent epic *Ten Days That Shook the World*, and found its crowd scenes good but overburdened with party politics. 'We have a lot to learn from the bolsheviks,' he readily conceded, 'particularly in the fields of agitation and propaganda.'[35] He was thrilled by any movie accompanied by Russian music.[36] Seeing Eisenstein's famous *Battleship Potemkin*, he rejoiced in this spectacle. The sub-titles were so cunningly phrased that they defied contradiction. 'That is what is really dangerous about this movie,' he concluded. 'I wish we had such a film.'[37]

Thus the power of the movie as political propaganda dawned on him. He began to take an interest in the party's own movie production efforts. He supervised the cutting of the movie of his September 1928 rally in the Sport Palace, and helped with a little production called *Fight for Berlin* – his diary shows him driving out to Bernau to direct scenes involving three hundred S.A. men.[38] As the genre got into his blood, he produced a second Nazi movie, *With the Berlin S.A. to Nuremberg*.[39] At its première, he introduced it with a little homily on cinema as a propaganda weapon.[40]

DECEMBER 1928 finds Joseph Goebbels tired but increasingly fulfilled. He spends hours orating to the Reichstag. He has his own newspaper. He has a piano. He has at last perfected his autobiographical drama *Michael* and is about to rewrite his working-class one-act drama *Blood Seed* for the party's Wallner Theater.[41] He will finish it in the Reichstag under the droning voice of some despised democrat. He sends copies to Ilse Hess and all his other friends – but even now Anka's is the only opinion he cares about.[42]

On December 9 we locate him, heart thumping, in a train steaming into Weimar's station. He finds her waiting on the platform, and lends her the first proof copy of *Michael* (in which she is, of course, herself the heroine) to come off the presses. 'We love each other as though but a day separates 1920 from now,' he writes afterwards. 'She buries her head in my chest and weeps.' He misses two trains in his distraction.[43]

A letter comes, returning the play: she is enthusiastic about it. 'She loves me,' swoons Goebbels in his notes, 'and I her.'[44] 'I had awaited your letter with trepidation,' he replies, asking to see her again. He suggests Halle on Wednesday ('at 10:20 A.M.') or Erfurt ('at 11:51'). Something about these deliberately Brief Encounters pleases him: perhaps it is the reassuring knowledge that any demands she makes on him will perforce be limited to the short journey between two stations. 'I would like to talk things over with you,' he writes her alluringly. 'I have got to do something about rearranging my life, now that I have put much of the past behind me with *Michael*.'[45]

No sooner has he lit this fresh candle for Anka in his heart than it is snuffed out by the breezy debut of a young Berlin girl on his staff, Jutta Lehmann. She claims she's eighteen – a slender, gracious, rococo little doll who chatters and giggles all afternoon with that infuriating mixture of brightness and inanity that females have long monopolized. She pretends to be engaged to another, but folds into the little gauleiter's arms nonetheless and allows herself to be kissed before agreeing that she is not engaged at all. 'So that's Jutta Lehmann,' he muses, captivated: 'This spotless, gracious girl.'[46] He wallows in feelings of spurious guilt, knowing that sooner or later he must sacrifice her too on the altar of his Mission.[47] He lies awake, thinking of her tiny hand waving as he drives away, the tears in her eyes when he leaves for his own family fold at Christmas. She is silent on his return and he sees her as 'a child, a lover, a comrade.' He is lucky to possess her, he decides. 'She's a good listener. She sits as quiet as a mouse just listening.'[48] One day she comes in floods of tears because she thinks he's leaving; the next the sweet little schemer turns up with a basket of things for his apartment like a coffee machine and silverware, so that he can stay home of an evening. But he realizes that she is 'pure' and must stay that way. By mid-January 1929 he is back, in soul and body, in Weimar with Anka.[49]

Her husband Mumme is now ingratiating and servile to the gauleiter; Goebbels despises him. She comes on January 19 to his Weimar hotel and they sit talking until two-thirty A.M. on upturned crates at the railroad station. He decides that Anka loves him. 'And I?' he asks his diary: 'I love her, uh, quite differently.'[50]

THE NAZI PARTY nationwide now numbered over one hundred thousand members. Its leaders met at Weimar on January 20, 1929 to discuss the coming year. Young Heinrich Himmler, Hitler's bespectacled deputy propaganda chief, reported on his efforts to develop their movie and press propaganda.[51] The only decisions that Goebbels recorded in Weimar were that the S.A. was to be more firmly anchored to the political leadership, and that the party was to adhere henceforth slavishly to the legal paths to power. 'Take note, Berlin!' noted Goebbels.[52]

Hitler had every reason to counsel restraint. Confronted with the growing Nazi and communist lawlessness in Prussia, Albert Grzesinski had appealed to the Reich minister of the interior, Severing, for a permanent nationwide ban on these parties and their paramilitary formations. The terms imposed on defeated Germany by the peace treaty of 1921 provided adequate legal grounds.[53]

Goebbels reluctantly bowed to Hitler's dictate. Issue No. 32 of *Angriff* portrayed a communist Red Front streetfighter and his Nazi counterpart, both bandaged and bleeding, shaking hands over the crumpled body of a Jew. 'The Day of Realization,' Schweitzer's prophetic caricature was captioned: 'The Dawn of the Third Reich.'[54]

Since January 5, 1929 his newspaper had twelve pages.[55] Meanwhile he methodically built up the infrastructure of the gau. It helped that he had a brand-new limousine, a bright-blue open seven-seater landau built by Opel. Its license tag was IA-53398 – Goebbels claimed that a German idealist living in Argentina had just donated it to the gau.[56] The big car gave the crippled gauleiter power, authority, and mobility. Taking his burly escort with him he used it to tour the sections in red-hot areas like Prenzlauer Berg, Friedrichshain, Alexander Platz, and Kreuzberg.[57] Muchow was doing fine work on the factory floor, establishing cells in big plants like Knorr Brake at Lichterfelde. Too late the marxists woke up to this danger. Goebbels' schools of speaking and politics were also improving. Once he even let Gregor Strasser address a course.[58] Standards here were often higher than in the Reichstag where, as Goebbels himself put it, listening to long boring speakers was like being a pianist and having to hear some lout grinding away on a magnificent grand piano.[59]

Great though his conceit about his own oratory was, Goebbels conceded that Hitler's was better. In fact their styles were different. Hitler's speeches were predictable and repetitious; Goebbels' were more analytical, executed with a thrilling elocution and clarity. Albert Krebs later stated that his Nazis in Hamburg often debated which was better; those who opted for Goebbels sometimes indicated that he would make a better party leader too.[60] The two men were in equal demand all over Germany. 'We lead real gypsy lives,' Hitler had commiserated with him a few days after Weimar.[61]

On character, however, Goebbels found serious fault with Hitler at this time, a tendency to let things slide. He felt that the Führer should get his other men boning up already on their later duties. ('My task,' he already knew in 1929, 'is to be Propaganda and Public Enlightenment.')[62] Only Alfred Rosenberg towered above the 'beerhall' milieu of Hitler's Munich cronies.

BACK IN Berlin after Weimar, Goebbels is subjected to a scene by Tamara. He feels sorry for her, but she has lost the submissive 'Asian' quality he valued before in her. What else is he looking for? It is not sex. Later the 'sweet chatterbox' Jutta Lehmann, still one week shy of eighteen, turns up and keeps him 'tempestuous' company – *stürmisch*, evidently another diary buzzword – until eleven P.M. 'How Jutta will weep,' he notes, almost sadistically, 'when the time comes for us to part!'[63] He is addicted to the company of teenage girls, but prefers them perhaps to bare anything except their intellects. When Kütemeyer's widow turns out to have opinions of her own, he shrieks in his diary, 'For God's sake let's keep women out of politics.'[64]

In fact, he hates most if not all of the human race except for Jutta and Anka, both of whom know how to mother him.[65] He yearns for Anka, the forbidden passion of his life. On February 25, 1929 he takes a sheet of Reichstag notepaper and tries to set up another tryst: 'It would be glorious if you could come to Berlin for a few days. On Friday March 8 there is an important and sensational session in the Reichstag, and on Sunday the tenth my new drama [*Blood Seed*] is being premiered at the Wallner Theater. It's sold out already.' He signs off as ULEX, just as in the old days.[66]

> MARCH 9, 1929. Anka phones. She's coming this afternoon for two days' visit. . . In the afternoon worked at home. Frightful news: Communists have stabbed two S.A. men to death in Schleswig-Holstein [Hermann Schmidt and Otto Streib]. The first storm-cones! Blood seed, from which the new Reich shall grow.

Anka arrives, looking the picture of a cultured lady. He shows her over the Reichstag, then takes her to a patriotic movie starring the swashbuckling Emil Jannings with a powerful plot about a man giving his life for his people. In the Rheingold bar afterwards she yet again pours out her heart about her unhappy marriage, until two A.M.

They sit side by side at Sunday's premiere of his play, which events in Schleswig-Holstein have suddenly rendered so topical. Over a meal at Kempinski's he has one unexpected difference with Anka, on the Jewish problem: now it is she who does not grasp it. Privately he reflects on the happiness that might have been. 'But,' he adds, priggishly distorting history, 'I had to choose: her, or something greater, my Mission.' Then, 'Leave-taking! Farewell,' he writes, slipping effortlessly into the role of scriptwriter again. 'She smiles.'[67]

His private life is becoming more dishonest. While he writes, and his teenaged Jutta cooks for him, he is agonizing over the married Anka returning to her worthless Georg. A few days later his diary encodes him as gossiping with 'the Gypsy' – Anneliese Haegert, another 'darling child.' 'Most women are boring,' he concludes, 'particularly the good lookers. But I suppose it's enough that they do look good.'[68]

After he sees Anka again at Weimar on March 19, her husband comes to fetch her. It is the first time Goebbels has seen Mumme, and she seems ashamed of him. 'That is her husband?' sympathizes Goebbels. 'Oh, Anka!'

Georg Mumme civilly invites him to lunch the next day at their little household at No. 14 Johann-Albrecht Strasse; Goebbels has so often tried to visualize their home. Her baby Christian is a stubborn little boy; seeing the child hurts Goebbels more than he expects. 'That was some situation you snared me in,' he reproaches her in a letter. 'I felt like a fifth wheel on the wagon.' Later he invites her to join the gau's Easter outing to the Harz mountains ('The car's at the doctor's,' he writes with a levity that belies his nervousness, 'but will be discharged at the weekend.') He adds that she must of course invite her Georg along too. 'Pity you can't see from the letter how I stammer out those words.'[69]

Goebbels has the dull but comforting sensation that perhaps he can never marry, because there are so many women that he is fond of.[70]

MARCH 24, 1929. Afternoon at home. Anneliese Haegert is coming round. How am I to meet her? Anka, sweet woman!

Evidently he comes clean about Anka because the Gypsy leaves in tears. Women, he ruminates, have only one real use – as moles planted inside hostile agencies like police headquarters or the League of Human Rights.[71]

On the Easter outing Anka arrives wearing a costly leather coat, of the same gray-green hue as her eyes. She has brought Georg Mumme along but pointedly ignores him throughout, although he continues to sing the gauleiter's praises to her. Goebbels finds him insufferable: Mumme gulps down his beer and cracks painfully pointless jokes; but it is Georg who shares Anka's bed each night and not the gauleiter. 'Thus,' writes Goebbels, 'vengeance exacts a belated, but infinitely crueler, revenge.' Georg utters not a murmur of protest as Goebbels squeezes into the back seat next to Anka and, Goebbels silently asks himself, staring at the husband, why should he? 'Don't I have a greater right to this woman than you, you ignoramus?'

In ancient Goslar, Georg tactfully lets them stroll off together like lovers and he returns that evening reeking of lust and liquor. Goebbels spends another sleepless night elsewhere under the same roof.

At daybreak they drive off through the rain, snow, and ice. Beneath the warming travel rug Goebbels feels Anka's hand seeking his. Unseen, she slips onto his finger the ring her widowed mother gave her.[72]

10: A Rather Obstinate Gentleman

H E HAD THE UNEASY feeling that he was leading a charmed life. He wrote to Anka that he would actually welcome some setback, preferably a minor one, to help break the spell. 'I have liquidated everything ugly from the past,' he wrote, referring perhaps to *Michael* and *Blood Seed*, 'and can now contemplate the future with greater fortitude.'[1]

One ugly item from the past still haunted him: The catholic charity in Cologne now instructed lawyers in Berlin to extract from him the four hundred marks still unpaid from his student loan twelve years before. The lawyers served a writ.[2] The court awarded judgment in default on April 6, 1929. A few days later the bailiffs called and glued their traditional paper cuckoo to his radio set, the only item of value in his apartment. Still he did not pay up. 'We are evidently dealing,' the lawyers reported to Cologne, 'with a rather obstinate gentleman. . . It is to be hoped that this spokesman of the National Socialist party will fight shy of declaring bankruptcy.'[3] The charity calmly ordered the lawyers to have him bankrupted. On May 16 the bailiffs removed his beloved radio – with his piano, the only instrument he had wherewith to amuse his girlfriends – and sent it to be auctioned.[4] When he appealed, the catholics claimed they acted repressively only when there was evidence of a 'ruthless' attitude on the debtor's part. Not until February 1930 would he make the final payment, closing the ledgers on a rather puzzling episode.

True, he had weightier matters on his mind. 'Sunday morning,' he jotted on April 15. 'We march, right into the communist districts. I stand in the thick of the melee and am recognized. Our men march unflinching through the catcalls and whistles of the Reds.'[5] He was planning ahead for the Nuremberg rally in August and for an open-air rally in Berlin in September as a prelude to the important November municipal elections.

Constantly expanding his horizons, on May 10 he launched a National Socialist League of Schoolchildren at a jamboree of one thousand eager girls and boys. Cash was always a problem, however.[6] He pleaded with *Angriff* not to court a renewed prohibition. Finding in one issue a blatant libel on their foreign minister Gustav Stresemann, he himself ordered all unsold copies recalled – not that he was loath to wound the statesman. 'This plenipotentiary of German democracy,' he called him, 'somewhat fat, jaundice-hued, perspiring, his little tricky eyes bedded carefully in cushions of fat, a smooth, rectangular forehead topped by an enormous expanse of bald head, there he stands, in the midst of his beloved Jews.[7]

SUDDENLY THERE is Xenia. Her name means 'friendly stranger'; she is another teenaged girl, and Goebbels risks a first letter to her just after writing to Anka.[8] Xenia von Engelhardt's unexpected visit to Dr Goebbels is the start of a platonic friendship, which endures almost to the end of his bachelor days. She wangles her way past the sentinels posted on his heart by the usual wiles, pouring out her woes about her unfaithful boyfriend, laughing, blushing, and instinctively gauging his needs.[9] Once she stages a scene and turns on her heel; then stalks back and spends a night with him which he describes as *glückdurchbebt*, quaking with happiness. By May 4 they have captured each other, each presuming victory. They take in a Greta Garbo movie (another 'divine woman,' sighs Goebbels). After another tiff, Xenia storms off, returns, knocks on his door. He does not open – he is reading the Sunday papers and, yet again, Moeller van den Bruck's *The Third Reich*. That afternoon they go for a row, and make up again. 'And then,' records Goebbels, selecting his words carefully, 'comes a long, blessed night, filled with silence. Xenia is all modesty and sacrifice.'[10]

Back at his lodgings he finds a letter from the eternal temptress, Anka. She hopes to see him at Weimar. 'Poor Anka,' he notes, 'but she wants it no other way.' When he reaches Weimar Anka realizes that Xenia was coming between them, and bursts into tears. He returns to Berlin early. Here Xenia phones him, fearful on account of Weimar and Anka, as the smug gauleiter records.[11] Back in Berlin, vacillating between the two women, he writes, 'I love Xenia a lot, because she is so young and *unberührt* [sexually innocent] and all self sacrifice and goodness. Anka is too scatterbrained.'[12] A letter comes from Anka with her photograph. He writes back proposing that he return to Weimar on Sunday week? 'But then we'll probably have to hang around with G. all day and can't talk about the things we're interested in.'

At this instant in his complex epistolic devotions, Xenia arrives. Goebbels concludes his letter to Anka with a hurried evasion: 'Sorry can't write much today. . . I'm about to fly to Dortmund.' But just as he is, in fact, dining at his lodgings with Xenia, the phone rings. A voice announces, 'Hitler here.' Hitler is in Berlin. Unable to conceal his joy, Goebbels dashes off the last line of the letter to Anka: 'Life is beautiful, O Queen! Yours, ULEX,' and, abandoning Xenia, he hurries off to Hitler. There is no doubting his order of priorities now.[13]

GOEBBELS sat with Hitler and Hess that night until two A.M. Hitler asked if he would take over the *Reichspropagandaleitung*, propaganda at national level, traveling down to Munich every fortnight for this duty, with a second home there. Goebbels was uncertain, and Hitler tried to tempt him. 'After the party rally,' the gauleiter noted, 'we shall all motor down to Italy for study purposes. . . I am to get a new Mercedes just for this.' The question was left unresolved[14] and in July Hitler again failed to lure Goebbels down to Munich to this end.[15]

In Berlin, he felt he was somebody. His S.A. was growing fast. On May 26, at Frankfurt-on-Oder, he took the salute at a parade of two thousand S.A. men and heard the bands play a stirring new march with words written by Horst Wessel, *Die Fahne hoch!* (Hold the Flag High). Later it would become a second national anthem.

He itched to use the S.A. to seize power, although Hitler had told him, 'We must now learn to wait and above all avoid a ban.'[16] Hitler had good reason to fear a ban. The communists had begun violent disturbances in Berlin; in fighting after they threw up barricades on May Day, nine people were killed and one thousand arrested.[17] To Goebbels' disappointment Grzesinski banned his main opponent, the militant Red Front. In the resulting debate demanded by the communists on June 8 Goebbels spoke for forty minutes using language that differed little from theirs. The essence of the government's policy must be foreign, not domestic policy. 'They brandish the palm frond abroad,' he scoffed, 'and the police truncheon at home. They are skulking pacifists abroad, but bloodthirsty militarists at home, determined to choke any nationalist resistance at birth. . . They sign slave-diktats abroad and enact a Law for the Protection of the Republic at home!' Recalling that it was Severing who had banned Hitler from speaking, Goebbels mocked: 'Every Jew, international pacifist, and traitor has the right of free speech but not a German soldier four times wounded on the battlefield, on the pretext that he is a foreigner.'

The Nazi party had, he recalled, been dissolved in Berlin, although it had erected no barricades. 'We just tossed a lush out of a public meeting after boxing his ears.' The Reichstag itself had annulled Gregor Strasser's immunity because he had dared to call the Republic a 'moneybags-colony.' Countless civil servants had been disciplined for joining the National Socialists.

Goebbels teasingly added that he had no intention of mentioning the private affairs of the Prussian minister of the interior – 'Whether or not for instance Mr Grzesinski travels with his "lovely wife" to Vienna and it turns out the lady's not his "lovely wife" at all' – such things were purely a question of taste.[18] Nor would he dwell upon the fact that their police president had been chief carnival clown of Mainz before the war ('Don't get me wrong. We're not complaining that he was chief carnival clown. Merely that he still is.'). As for Dr Weiss ('whom we must not call Isidor'), he had now sued Goebbels and his men twenty-eight times for calling him a Jew. 'So this police chief has himself recognized how demeaning it is to be a Jew, and he considers it a libel to be properly identified by what we would call his religion or what he would call his race.' 'The time will come,' he shrilled in his peroration, 'when it will not be our party which brings this system crashing down, but the people itself.'[19]

Once more that month, June 1929, he addressed the Reichstag, on the suffocating Law for the Protection of the Republic. After blandly reading out, to loud protests, a letter written by 'the Jewish mega-swindler' Julius Barmat to the former chancellor Heinrich Bauer promising him 'another thousand or fifteen hundred U.S. dollars' if needed, Goebbels snapped that in forty years their former Kaiser had not had so many people charged with *lèse-majesté* as often as Prussia's prime minister Otto Braun had wielded the hated law. He hurled this parting shot at the protesters: 'Once we have [the absolute majority] in the Reich, we shan't need a Law for the Protection of the Republic. We'll hang the lot of you!'[20] He happily noted afterward: 'The Reds foam with rage.'[21] The Reichstag adjourned for the summer amid satisfying scenes of tumult.

THE STAGE was gradually filling with the characters who would dominate this, already the last one-third of Joseph Goebbels' life. He knew young Heinrich Himmler, Hitler's deputy chief of propaganda, as 'a small, fine man, good natured but perhaps a bit indecisive; a Strasser product.'[22] On Hermann Göring he was ambivalent: he had got to know the overweight, bemedalled aviator better after sharing a platform with him in communist-dominated Friedrichshain in May. Göring bragged of having known Mussolini intimately while in Italian exile (in fact they had not met).[23] Partying with his eleven fellow Reichstag deputies at Göring's luxurious apartment in Badensche Strasse, the gauleiter envied his style of life. Six weeks later he recorded that Göring was 'as thick as two planks and lazy as a tortoise,' but it was the former air force captain who introduced Goebbels to Berlin's high society.[24]

The princes, dukes, and counts foregathered in the Göring apartment, and Goebbels gradually acquired a proclivity for having blue-blooded men around him too. His opinions on the Baltic-born Alfred Rosenberg, cold, arrogant, and unapproachable, varied sharply; he feared that Rosenberg's opaque treatise, *The Myth of the Twentieth Century*, would cause friction with the church.[25]

Surprisingly, he also disapproved of Julius Streicher's 'Jew mania.' 'This naked anti-semitism,' he recorded, 'is too primitive. The Jew can't be blamed for everything. We are as much to blame as anybody, and until we accept that we'll never find our way.'[26] But by 1930 he had a soft spot even for Streicher, probably because Hitler did too. 'I like him a lot,' he noted, 'he's a real [*knorke*] guy!'[27]

Hitler towered over them all; but the picture of him, still only forty and unmarried, that is presented by the early Goebbels Diaries is an unfamiliar one – the Great Cunctator, taking refuge in the comforting milieu of his beer-bench pals in Munich, squandering the party's money, and forever chasing young women, of whom Geli was, in Goebbels' despairing estimate, only the latest example.[28] But Hitler had an instinctive, engaging manner. Meeting Goebbels' mother for the first time, Hitler remarked: 'She's just like my own.'[29]

THE summer of 1929, a real tar-boiler in Berlin, sees Dr Goebbels still fighting shy of sexual relations. He observes his caricaturist Hans Schweitzer, whose drawing pen is the scourge of the highest officers of the Republic, living in mortal terror of his new wife. True, in her temporary absences Schweitzer briefly flutters his clipped wings, but she always returns wielding the clippers afresh.[30] Goebbels prefers to shuffle the pack – Xenia, Jutta, Anneliese, and occasionally a glimpse of Anka in Weimar. The kindly and submissive Xenia, now on school vacation, tries in vain to dominate him: She sulks for hours, then capitulates and returns for a night which the gauleiter mechanically logs as *selig*, 'blessed,' though with no supporting details. He serenades her on the piano, but has no intention of letting any woman capture him.[31] He has witnessed too Tonak's fate, totally ensnared by 'the hysterical females' of the Nazi Women's Order ('now the silly lad's gone and got engaged'). So Xenia runs the whole gamut of female trickery from flouncing and huffs to affectionate letters, in vain.[32] 'She is too easygoing and fluttery,' he reports to his diary. 'I don't think it'll last much longer.'[33] Setting off on vacation that July to Prerow, on a Baltic peninsula, he takes his secretary Josephine von Behr and does not invite Xenia, despite her tearful entreaties.

Too late, on July 5, Anka phones from Weimar – she has a sudden chance to visit Berlin for several days. Has the Great Moment finally arrived? Goebbels responds: 'I have thought about it all night. I can't stay in Berlin; I would never get away from work. . . I can't cancel Prerow, and I'm fed up with Berlin.'[34] He suggests an alternative plan: That Anka come to a town fifty miles from Berlin and he will come over and spend one or two days with her there. He even spells out the train times and connections. But at Prerow his little fantasy is dashed. She telegraphs that she cannot come.

> How about this plan [Goebbels then suggests]. I'll come down for a week to Weimar. Can you get me that room in your building again? I hope it won't be too expensive, as I want to go to England in August and to Italy in September. [In fact he undertakes neither foreign trip]. . . Is it okay by you and Georg if I come on Saturday [July 20]? You'll have to leave me to myself a bit as I've a new book in my pen. And don't tell anyone I'm coming to Weimar.

He begs her to cable her agreement – 'Otherwise I may go up to Sweden for a week.'[35]

The book is his drama *The Wanderer*, which he has begun to rework at Prerow. Walking along the rain-soaked beaches he contemplates the placid, gray-green Baltic and reflects how different it is from the wind-whipped North Sea – the one a gentle mistress, the other a diabolical old maid.[36] The Great Moment in any young man's life is, it seems, drawing nigh.

But there is an unscheduled interlude. At a seaside concert he sits next to Erika Chelius, daughter of a local forester, aged 23. Not good-looking, he concedes, but provocative.[37] Is the chase on again? She presses a posy of flowers into his hand and for several days goes out with him and Josephine. Together they all go on a moonlight sail, and Erika talks and flirts and asks bright questions. He suddenly realizes that it is the young Anka that she reminds him of.[38]

Back in Berlin, Xenia comes round for the evening; then it is on to Weimar for the great, week-long adventure with Anka. Georg Mumme carries their self-invited guest's baggage to the apartment just above their own in Johann-Albrecht Strasse. 'I am torn many ways,' confesses Goebbels in his diary that night. Something – is it fear? – is clutching at his vitals. He thinks a lot about Erika Chelius, and suddenly misses Prerow after all. But here he is, at last, only one floor above his dream woman. 'Anka,' he writes, 'is waiting downstairs for me.'[39]

One day that week Georg goes off to Leipzig. Anka bustles happily around her old friend, cooking meals and looking after him, but nothing happens. Neither makes a move. The last day comes, July 25, 1929. Dr Mumme has again gone away, and Goebbels and Anka spend a blissful afternoon out together. Even at two A.M. Georg is still not back. Cursing himself, Goebbels is upstairs, standing irresolutely in the middle of his room when he hears a soft tap at the door. He opens: It is Anka, trembling with so far unrequited passion.

'Georg just phoned,' she announces. 'He can't get back tonight.'

Seized by panic, Goebbels firmly closes the door on her. Perhaps he has smelt an ambush; or just possibly he may have been motivated by those loftier emotions which he carefully sets down for posterity in his diary afterward:

No! I cannot abuse the hospitality and trust of Georg. Wretched though he is in my esteem: And though mine be far the greater right to this beloved woman standing before me in all her wondrous loveliness: Anka must leave the room.

I am trembling in every limb. I lie awake for a long, long time. But this morning I shall be able to look Georg squarely in the eye.[40]

Their paths cross briefly at Weimar station – Goebbels and Mumme. 'Fare thee well, the both of you,' he writes. 'I'll have to leave you to your wretchedness and nothingness. . . Greater missions await.'[41]

11: *The Nightmare*

JOSEPH GOEBBELS' OBSESSIVE devotion to Hitler was illustrated by an incident in September 1929. He was about to speak at Breslau when a telegram signed 'Rosenberg' arrived: ADOLF HITLER KILLED IN ACCIDENT. Goebbels swayed on his feet and nearly fainted. The telegram, a fake, left him a sobbing, nervous wreck. 'Only now,' he wrote afterward, 'do I realize what Hitler means to me and to the movement: Everything! Everything!'[1]

The latter part of the year was dominated by the final illness of his father and his campaign against the new Young Plan for the payment of reparations.[2] He embarked on the latter unwillingly, as it had been initiated by their 'reactionary' rivals the Stahlhelm and the D.N.V.P. (German National People's Party), who were demanding a referendum (*Volksbegehren*); but Hitler gave him no choice. Visiting Berlin on July 4 the Führer told him he was meeting Alfred Hugenberg, chairman of the Deutschnationale Volkspartei (D.N.V.P.), to discuss a joint campaign against the iniquitous diktat of Versailles and the Young Plan.

The prospect of Hitler among these moth-eaten reactionaries alarmed the radical Goebbels.[3] In Nuremberg on the eve of the annual party rally, however, Hitler invited him to dine in his suite with him and Geli – 'a pretty child,' noticed Goebbels again, and managed to get close to him in the group photographs later. He addressed the rally on propaganda and politics.[4]

With their great fireworks displays, concerts by the S.A.'s massed bands and torchlight marches, the famous Nuremberg rallies were beginning to take shape – though Goebbels could not help noticing with vexation the Stahlhelm dignitaries lined up on Hitler's platform. Three chartered trains had brought his men from Berlin. Erika Chelius stepped out of the first. The Berlin stormtroopers marched snappily into the city center with Horst Wessel at the head of his *Sturm*.[5] The S.A. contingent from the Palatinate wore white shirts; the French occupation authorities had banned the brown. 'The time will come,' Hitler promised them to cheers, 'when we'll have the shirts off the French!'

There was one episode with the S.A. that forewarned of trouble to come with them. Hitler was in mid-speech when the heavy doors burst open. Several hundred communists had arrived from Berlin under the leadership of Max Höltz, bent on staging a blood bath. The S.A. dealt with them roughly and, their

*Pg 46-48, The Shadows of Power; by James Perloff.
(Western Islands)

84

bloodlust aroused, rampaged through the streets of Nuremberg afterwards leaving two dead and many injured. Hitler sent a chalk-faced Goebbels out by car to call the stormtroopers to order. Horst Wessel showed particular bravery in reining in his young toughs. Walter Stennes, his S.A. commander, later said that the Brownshirts would have taken over the city there and then had he and their national commander Franz von Pfeffer not headed off the catastrophe.[6]

ON THE EVENING after the riot Erika Chelius joins Goebbels, brimming with coy aspirations. She mentions that she has a twin sister: Double-delight! To Goebbels' dismay Xenia von Engelhardt also suddenly appears, furious at his romantic foray to Weimar. Hoping no doubt to escape her, he drives with Erika over to picturesque Rothenburg. Downstairs the next morning he finds the importunate Xenia again. But as suddenly as this tearful apparition appears, it melts away.[7] Back in Berlin he broods all day on the fair sex. 'Women!' he exclaims. 'Women are to blame for almost everything.'[8]

For Anka, of course, he will always make an exception. Twice after the two A.M. Weimar fiasco, which must have wounded her deeply, he writes to her and cannot understand why she makes no reply. Twice he asks chattily if she has the 'time and inclination' to see him on his way through Weimar.

Again no reply. 'How lazy you are at writing!' he chides her.[9]

'Here in Berlin all hell is loose,' he adds. And in a sense it is, because Erika and her twin Traute have come to drive him out to their forest home. He takes the 'insufferably jealous' Josephine von Behr along too. On September 29 he writes again to Anka. 'The Reichstag is meeting on important matters,' he explains, and suggests she ask Georg's permission to come to Berlin. 'You'd get to see all sorts of things.'[10]

She makes an excuse – she is not well. Goebbels apologizes that he cannot come to Weimar because of his parliamentary duties. 'It is just frightful,' he continues, writing from the Reichstag. 'In the long run one has to dispense with every friendship for the good of the cause.' He might be able, he adds, to fit in Weimar on Sunday. 'But ... I've also got to go home as my father is gravely ill.' 'Fare well!' he concludes. 'The division bell is ringing. It's showtime.'[11]

None of these letters has been published before. He makes no mention of them in his diary. Anka has defeated him.

NOTIONS OF nationalism had stirred only infrequently in his diaries until now. In October 1928 he had thrilled at the majestic airship *Graf Zeppelin* cruising over Berlin on her 112-hour flight to New Jersey; four weeks later, he and Schweitzer had watched the newsreel report on the voyage, furious at the unpatriotic jeers from an audience who only a few minutes later fiercely applauded a Soviet movie.[12] In August 1929 he copied down the inscription on the Brandenburg Gate – 'To all the World War dead' – and made the acid comment that they had forgotten to add: ' – except the German.' The idea of taking over national propaganda began to appeal to him.[13]

Staying at Anka's house he had read Erich Maria Remarque's classic anti-war book, *All Quiet on the Western Front*. He had found it a mean-spirited and even seditious work, and ventured the prediction: 'Two years from now nobody will talk about this book any more.'[14] Nature documentaries like *With Amundsen to the North Pole*, or the mountaineering movie starring the delectable Leni Riefenstahl, enthralled him.[15] He fully recognized the subtle persuasive power of the cinema. At the advertising exhibition in Berlin he lingered at the movie section, and a few days later he took his editor Dagobert Dürr to see the latest sensation, a talking movie. He dismissed the production, The Singing Fool, as kitsch, but the technological advance itself impressed him. 'Here lies the future,' he wrote, 'and we should be wrong to dismiss all this as American gimmickry. Join it! Beat it!'[16] He wanted to use sound films for propaganda. 'Here,' he repeated in November 1929, 'lies a gigantic future, particularly for us orators. The more the movement grows, the more we must exploit technology.'[17]

In the approach to the city elections that month he was already using new techniques. He had posed for a propaganda film in his office. Their amateurish movie *Struggle for Berlin* and two documentaries on the Nuremberg rally were already circulating. Taking control of their propaganda in Berlin, he composed twenty placards. In the evenings he held training courses to ensure that all candidates emphasized their 'socialist' policies. After a bloc meeting in October he noted with approval that all his fellow Reichstag deputies had come down firmly against the right wing.[18]

With himself at their head, constantly aware of his own dwarflike shortcomings, he led the S.A. and its battle standards on violent marches through the communist strongholds of Berlin.[19] He hammered into his S.A. that attack was the only sure defense against being overwhelmed by the communists. Gatecrashing a communist rally in Charlottenburg on August 25 he demanded permission to speak and, when this was refused, turned 150 of his toughs loose on the audience.[20] A few days later Horst Wessel's No. 5 Sturm launched a violent attack on the communist headquarters in a Berlin *Kiez* ('hood'), injuring several Reds.[21] It was open war. Goebbels called the Reds 'roaring, raging sub-humans,' and the women worst of all – 'They scream, they shriek, they bare themselves to us quite shamelessly.' The communists referred to him as 'Goebbels the workers' assassin.'[22]

Police chief 'Isidor' Weiss too went onto the counter-attack. Gregor Strasser, his immunity revoked, was sentenced to six months' jail.[23] In September Weiss seized one entire issue of *Angriff*, charging it with incitement to treason. *Angriff* developed an iconoclastic style of its own, making fun of people's names and lampooning the Central-Verein, the pompous Jewish Central Board which had protested at a spate of Nazi attacks on 'harmless passers-by,' by calling it henceforth the 'Central-Board of Harmless Passers-By.'[24] To Goebbels' discomfiture, the 'Judenpresse' struck back by printing every truly seditious word he had said (and many he had not), trying to get the party banned again.[25] But there was no going back.

His courage, or bravado, was nearly his undoing. One Sunday in September 1929 he took two thousand S.A. marchers into proletarian Neukölln. He expected blood to flow, and it was nearly his own. Standing in his open car he took the salute at Wiener Strasse, then ordered Tonak to drive on and park near the Görlitz station. Here a burly communist called Hans Krause shouted, 'It's Goebbels, the assassin of the workers! Let him have it!' 'Before my very eyes,' recorded Goebbels, 'there appear blackjacks, knives, and knuckle-dusters. . . A communist hurls himself at me. A shot rings out.'

The shots were answered from his car, a pistol loaded with blanks.

His chauffeur was injured yet again. 'I staunch Tonak's bleeding. He accelerates away, bouncing the car off street signs and curbstones. A hail of rocks follows us, and more shots are fired.'[26] Tonak got them to a police station, but the police arrested them both for using a firearm. It was seven P.M. before they were released.

The ill-conceived campaign for a referendum on the Young Plan, which would ask voters among other things to approve the incarceration of any minister guilty of 'enslaving' the German people, occupied him throughout that month.[27] He wrote privately however that nothing was to be achieved by parliamentary means: 'The revolution must march.'[28] By midday on November 2 it was plain that the Nazis and D.N.V.P. combined had collected signatures from more than the requisite ten percent of the electorate, some 4,135,000 names. The government however blocked the referendum and the campaign collapsed.[29]

Goebbels' next campaign was for the communal elections in Prussia. He ordered every man and implement into the fray. 'Our Doctor,' wrote one, 'was everywhere.'[30] He spoke in Berlin and in other cities too. At Weimar he met Anka for five minutes in November; she suddenly kissed him with tears in her eyes.[31] But these women were now history – he was impressed by the sudden firmness of his own resolve.[32]

His headquarters was like a warehouse, with bales of printed propaganda being moved in and out. Fighting on a shoestring the Nazis could not match their rivals' expenditure, but Goebbels' campaign was not without effect. While in May 1928 thirty-nine thousand Berliners had voted the Nazi ticket, on November 17, 1929, his campaign attracted 132,097 votes – or 5·8 percent of the total. Twice during the night he gleefully phoned Hitler. There would now be twenty-three National Socialist deputies in Prussia, with Goebbels at their head.

'The next task,' he declared the day after the election: 'Our own daily paper.'[33] The problem of financing this leap forward had troubled him all year. *Angriff*'s street sales were soaring. He hoped to go daily with it from January 1930. But they would need at least eight thousand new subscribers and massive extra capital. Swallowing his pride he asked Elsbeth Zander to get the Women's Order to raise the forty thousand marks, and five thousand new subscribers too.[34] After he addressed a giggling meeting of six hundred women on November 7 they collected 4,500 marks on the spot. Police agents learned that Helene Bechstein had donated five thousand. As another woman, of the old Russian Potempa family, handed over five thousand marks Goebbels could not help noticing her pretty twin daughters.[35]

Party headquarters in Munich was unenthusiastic about his publishing plans. His politics were still radically different from Hitler's. For a while Rosenberg talked of bringing out a Berlin edition of his stupendously boring *VB*, with *Angriff* as a local supplement. But the latter's war chest was expanding. A Mr Heidenreich donated ten thousand marks, 'trusting,' as he said, 'in our victory.' By early January the Women's Order had amassed twenty-six thousand marks and two thousand new subscribers' names.[36]

THREE days after the November 1929 election Goebbels had traveled down to Munich for planning talks on *Angriff*. After an evening of speeches he stayed up talking with Karl Kaufmann, Göring, and Wilhelm Kube, another gauleiter. They shared his view of Hitler's beer-hall milieu. Hitler again promised to relinquish control of national propaganda to Goebbels, if he would spend more of his time in Munich. Goebbels was appreciative but critical: 'I am not overlooking his failings,' he wrote privately about Hitler. 'He's too soft and he works too little.' 'I suspect,' he continued primly in his diary, 'that he indulges in too much womanizing too.' Lying awake pondering these failings in his adopted father-figure, Goebbels charitably concluded that Hitler was different and that he had a right therefore to be judged on a different scale. 'Hitler the Myth must stand, like a *rocher de bronze*.'[37]

In Rheydt, he was losing his real father. The Goebbels family doctor pronounced the old man's condition as beyond hope. Ashen and gaunt, his face streaked by tears of pain, his father had lain on a sofa in their spotlessly tidy kitchen when he last saw him at Rheydt, surrounded by his family. ('There we are,' Paul Joseph had soliloquized in his diary, 'the Goebbels family: Of diverse character everyone of us, but all of the same blood. Soft as children, and hard as nails.')[38]

He wrote a long last letter to the pious old man and traveled to Rheydt again. A living skeleton, whimpering with pain, his father asked only that they all pray for him.[39] On December 7 he died. What person does not suffer pangs of remorse upon a parent's death?

'Without his children,' Goebbels reflected, 'and all alone, he crossed to the wilderness of Nirvana.'[40] Tonak chauffeured the Goebbels brothers up to the church where the body of their father lay surrounded by flickering candles; helpless tears trickling down his cheeks, Joseph stroked the waxy hands and face of the man who would now never know to what heights his own sacrifices had propelled his son.

A letter of condolence came from Anka. 'It will be my endeavor,' he solemnly replied, 'to equal my late father's fanaticism and devotion to a cause, with the difference that his was for his family, whereas mine shall be for my people and fatherland.' 'I should be glad,' he mechanically concluded, 'to hear again from you soon.'[41]

In Rheydt he had run into Else Janke. She pinked, turned pale, and asked if he ever thought of her.

'What should I reply?' he reflected, and answered with a lie.

All of these events unsettled him. A week before Christmas he had a grotesque nightmare. He dreamed he was back at school being pursued along echoing corridors by rabbis from eastern Galicia. The Jews were chanting as they ran, screaming *Hate, Hate, Hate!* He always kept a few limping strides ahead of them, and answered with the same taunt. In his dream it seemed as though the pursuit lasted for hours, but they never caught up with him.[42]

12: *Hold the Flag High*

WITH ONLY FIVE DEAD BY THE END of 1929 Berlin had as yet few Nazi martyrs.[1] But the war in the streets was intensifying. Sometimes Goebbels found somebody in the headquarters' kitchen being treated for stab injuries; bullet wounds increased.[2] As he was visiting Edmund Behnke, an S.A. man slowly dying from the original Pharus Rooms brawl, another man was brought in with a slashed forehead.[3] On November 4 communists murdered Gerhard Weber; on December 14 a communist gunned down Walter Fischer during a raid on an S.A. office. Capitalizing on these martyrs, Goebbels organized ever larger funerals. At Fischer's he spoke alongside Göring, Prince August-Wilhelm, and Horst Wessel.[4] Spending Christmas with his now widowed mother he heard that their opponents had slit the throat of yet another S.A. man, the bookbinder Fritz Radloff, and New Year's Eve found him at a rainsoaked cemetery burying Radloff too.

No murder really fired the imagination of the party so much as that, when his time came, of young Horst Wessel himself. Goebbels had considered him one of his most promising apostles, although still only twenty-two.[5] But he was a marked man. Wessel's No. 5 Sturm had angered the communist high command by recruiting freely from their ranks. More recently, according to Stennes, he had fallen in with bad company. He dropped out of his law studies and was working as a laborer.[6] Perhaps this was no more than youthful rebellion – his late father had been an evangelical pastor and freemason. Against his mother's wishes he had moved into a sleazy attic room at No. 62 Grosse Frankfurter Strasse with his girlfriend Erna Jänichen, whom he had rescued from the streets.[7]

That December his brother Werner had frozen to death in the mountains; Goebbels buried him with a torchlight parade routed provocatively past the communists' Karl Liebknecht building. On the evening of January 14 the enemy squared accounts with Horst: a dozen communists and Jews beset his lodgings; the carpenter Albrecht Höhler, Salomon Epstein, and another man raced upstairs and hammered on his door. When Wessel, inside with Erna and another girl, opened up, Höhler shouted 'Hands up!' and discharged a nine-millimeter Parabellum pistol into his face, blowing away his jaw.

Seizing papers and a gun from Wessel's locked cupboard (his disaffected landlady, widow of a communist, had obliged them with the keys) the attackers escaped; Höhler kicked the prostrate Wessel as he ran out, yelling, 'You know what that's for!' The communist headquarters put a well-oiled escape plan into action for Höhler, providing refuges in two Jewish households and then funds and a forged passport to flee to Prague.[8]

Horst Wessel clung to life in the hospital for weeks. Goebbels visited him often; he mused that this was the stuff of a real Dostoyevsky novel – 'The Idiot, the Workers, the Harlot, the Bourgeois Family.'[9]

Once Wessel croaked, 'We must go on!'[10]

Foolishly returning to Berlin, Höhler was arrested and confessed.[11] The aftermath was a textbook example of the brilliant disinformation techniques used by Goebbels' opponents. The defense lawyer hired by the communists, Löwenthal, started a whispering campaign to smear Wessel as Erna's pimp.[12] Thus he could portray Höhler's motives as purely personal. The 'Judenpresse' seized on this tidbit. Communist playwright Bertolt Brecht mocked, 'In the search for a fitting hero who really personified the movement, the National Socialists opted, after considerable deliberation, for a pimp.' Goebbels gritted his teeth and fought back: he now had the one real martyr the movement needed. On February 7 he had the Horst Wessel anthem, *Die Fahne hoch!*, 'Hold the Flag High,' sung by massed choirs at the end of a Sport Palace rally. Visiting the hospital he urged the young man not to give up the fight to live, but he died sixteen days later. 'Thou shalt live on with us,' wrote Goebbels mawkishly after visiting the death bed, 'and shalt partake in our victory.'[13]

He ordained a colossal funeral parade for March 1, and Hitler himself promised to attend. Fearing major disturbances Dr Weiss banned it, allowing only ten cars in the cortege and a ceremony confined to the walled Nikolai cemetery itself. Police officers confiscated the flag draping the coffin. Communists, out in force along the route, snatched the wreaths from the horse-drawn hearse and sang the 'Internationale'.[14] At the cemetery Goebbels found a large slogan painted on the wall: 'A FINAL HEIL HITLER TO WESSEL THE PIMP!' He swallowed his fury. As the coffin sank into the ground a thousand throats defiantly roared the anthem that bore its murdered composer's name. In ten years, Goebbels prophesied to the S.A. men parading within the cemetery walls, in one of the finest speeches he ever delivered, that anthem would be sung by every schoolchild, by every factory worker, and by every marching soldier in Germany.[15] A barrage of rocks came flying over the wall from the jeering mob outside. 'They rampage,' recorded Goebbels upon his return home: 'And we win.'[16]

HITLER had missed the funeral; he had decided to spend the weekend at his Obersalzberg cottage with Geli instead. Goebbels took this very hard. He felt he had got to know Hitler better, and deprecated his indolent, undependable, indecisive personality.[17] He believed that Göring shared this view. 'He [Hitler] works too little,' wrote Goebbels, 'and then the women, the *women*!' How many promises Hitler had now given him and broken: to attend the Horst

Wessel funeral; to break with Otto Strasser; to enable *Angriff* to appear as a daily newspaper; and to appoint him Reich propaganda director – these were only some of them.[18]

Delayed by obstructionism from Munich Goebbels had failed to upgrade *Angriff* as planned to a daily newspaper in January 1930.[19] That month the Strassers announced that they would publish a daily in Berlin, *National Sozialist*, from March 1. Since it would flaunt the party's swastika emblem it would be a lethal stab in the back for Goebbels. He protested to Hitler.[20] Characteristically, Hitler did not even reply. 'He lacks the courage to take decisions,' Goebbels deduced.[21] Finally Munich phoned, inviting him down to talk it over with Hitler. Goebbels set off determined to threaten resignation.[22] Hitler however claimed to know nothing of the Strassers' newspaper plan; he feigned a convincing rage about Otto's 'disloyalty,' a rather smaller rage about his brother Gregor, and, with the beloved Geli at his side, comforted the gauleiter, saying he would publish *VB* in Berlin. 'That puts Strasser up against the wall,' wrote Goebbels maliciously, 'just where, he wanted to put me.'[23] He returned to Berlin appeased. In fact, Hitler's subsequent announcement of his plan seemed even to disavow Goebbels.[24] There were howls of glee from Berlin's organized Jewish community and particularly from their *Central-Verein Zeitung*.

An open breach with Munich threatened. Hitler had promised to squelch Otto Strasser's plans to publish his daily newspaper; the Strasser brothers continued however to announce it as coming.[25] No sooner had Hitler persuaded the *VB* to publish an item on Goebbels' behalf than the Strassers talked their Führer round again.[26] Their new daily newspaper hit the streets on March 1, the day of Horst Wessel's funeral. Hitler's capitulation to the Strassers was evidently one reason why he dared not show his face in Goebbels' city.

Immediately after the ceremony Goebbels phoned him and drafted another letter threatening resignation. He sent Göring down to Bavaria carrying this ultimatum. Hitler offered still more promises to be conveyed back to Goebbels.[27] He repeated in particular the offer to make Goebbels Reich propaganda director ('for the umpteenth time!' commented Goebbels sarcastically, learning of this). His faith in Hitler was cooling.[28]

SEVERAL times his diary carried signs that the Nazis were gaining support in Berlin's regular police force.[29] Half of them were former army officers. While Dr Bernhard Weiss seemed secure in office, to Goebbels' delight his political superior Albert Grzesinski was suddenly obliged to resign – on the day of the Horst Wessel funeral – because of his marital irregularities. 'That,' Goebbels triumphed, 'is one swine down.'[30]

He had relied hitherto on his parliamentary immunity to protect him. On February 11, 1930 the Reichstag took the first steps to revoke his immunity in three cases. 'I'll probably be spending the next years in the clink,' he gloomily reflected.[31] His benefactress, the dowager Viktoria von Dirksen, asked Prince August-Wilhelm to contact the lawyer Count Rüdiger von der Goltz. Goltz, an imposing figure who had lost a leg in the war, would act for Goebbels, three years his junior, in many of the coming court battles. They met over dinner at the Dirksen home in Margarethen Strasse. When Goebbels boasted that his Nazis were willing to die for their ideals, one guest, Baron Freytag von Loringhoven, murmured, 'I am sure some might be prepared to die for the D.N.V.P. cause.'

'Indeed,' mocked Goebbels, 'but only of old age!'[32]

The most serious allegation was that of high treason, and on March 10 the Reichstag revoked his immunity on that charge. Meanwhile despite its crippling financial provisions the government passed the Young Plan into law and President von Hindenburg signed it. Anticipating violent opposition, the government revived the hated Law for the Protection of the Republic. Goebbels led the parliamentary protest on March 13.[33]

Rounding on Carl Severing, the minister of the interior, he evoked laughter when he recalled that it was Gustav Noske, a predecessor, who had once said, 'Even an ass can rule by state of emergency.'[34] And that was precisely what this new law was. 'It is no coincidence,' he shrilled, 'that the Law for the Protection of the Republic is being given its second reading precisely one day after the Young Law is enacted.' 'You yourself point out that in the course of the Young Plan economic hardships are inevitable, and that two or three millions will become permanently unemployed in Germany.' This, he said, revealed the law in its true light – 'A law against the unemployed. . . . You promised Freedom, Beauty and, Dignity.'

Several times the Speaker reprimanded him. 'Marxism,' declared Goebbels, 'tried before the war to destroy an honest state with dishonest means. We want to get rid of a dishonest state with honest means.' There were screams of fury. He was ordered to sit down, and the Social Democrats cheered.

The new law was certainly repressive. It was designed to choke even the parliamentary opposition: under it, any prison sentence rendered a person unfit for public office: Dr Weiss's police were empowered to dissolve any political association and to confiscate its entire assets. The crisis however continued, and Dr Heinrich Brüning became chancellor.

Loss of immunity therefore threatened Goebbels with far-reaching consequences. Apart from the old allegation of high treason the files which the police now avidly dusted off concerned a ragbag of misdemeanors, many of them centering on his efforts to puncture Dr Weiss's pride and vanity.[35] Weiss was publicly considered the 'uncrowned king' of Berlin, and in Weimar Germany as in many authoritarian states the offense of *lèse-majesté* was taken dreadfully seriously. Worse, on October 20 *Angriff* had referred to the then Prussian minister of the interior as 'Comrade Grzesinski, born in the House of Cohn.' The court summons in this latter case survives in the archives, a cheaply printed form folded into an envelope and stamped 'MOABIT CRIMINAL COURT.'[36] More summonses seemed to arrive by every mail – on April 14 he counted nine, including the one alleging high treason. 'A fine show this is going to be,' he wrote in his diary. Several times he simply refused to testify, and the hearings ended with the judge in a deeply satisfying fury.[37]

The most delicate case against Goebbels involved the president; a recent article and caricature in *Angriff* had asked 'Is Hindenburg still alive?'[38] The writ from the Field Marshal disturbed him, and he cursed the editorial staff of *Angriff* for saddling him with this case.[39] Hindenburg's personal prestige was very great, even though by modern standards of journalism the article was quite tame. It had appealed to Hindenburg to invoke his presidential powers to block the ruinous Young Plan:

> But even the remaining personal admirers and friends of Hindenburg [the article had said] entertain few illusions about any activity to be expected from him in this direction. Here as in every other similar situation Mr von Hindenburg will do whatever his Jewish and marxist advisers ask of him.'

Goebbels was all for pleading justification (Ritter von Epp had provided him with 'annihilating material' about the field marshal).[40] Goltz discouraged this. Goebbels drafted his own defense speech and looked forward to the court hearing set down for the last day of May 1930. On the eve of the trial however Goltz brought him the unwelcome news that two of the three judges were Jewish. He challenged them right away, but his motion for recusal was denied. 'Then,' he recorded immodestly in his diary, 'I speak: ninety minutes and I am in tip-top form. The whole court is deeply impressed. The prosecutor demands nine months' prison. Goltz speaks, very effective.'[41]

After a two-hour recess the judges announced their verdict – a trifling fine of eight hundred marks. Their judgment all but exonerated Goebbels, who wrote, 'I could have yelped with joy.' Only the cartoon was considered libelous inasmuch as it portrayed one arm of Hindenburg's presidential throne as a Jewish-nosed, Star-of-David-wearing gargoyle. No longer mentioning that the judges who had served him so fairly were themselves Jewish, Dr Goebbels recorded in his diary only the wonderful propaganda effect of this 'victory.' The news even made the far-away columns of the *New York Times*.[42]

Lunching during the long recess with Hermann Göring, Goebbels noticed that the aviator was by no means comfortable with his attack on the old field marshal. His attitude to Göring was now one of scorn tinged with envy. Relying on his war record Göring had established himself firmly in Berlin's society; still lacking home comforts of his own, Goebbels often spent his evenings with Hermann and Carin and one or other of the Nazi princes.[43] His own principles had begun to fray from exposure to the corrupt, blue-blood-loving Göring. He must have realized that Göring could only finance his lifestyle with hefty bribes from the aviation industry, precisely the kind of behavior that Goebbels thundered against when detected in Jews like the financiers Max Sklarek or Julius Barmat. In March Göring grandly offered to procure a new car for Goebbels; this offer proved as empty as the apartment he had promised earlier.[44]

When Easter came in 1930 Göring invited him along to visit his Swedish in-laws. They made a memorable couple – the swaggering aviator and the diminutive figure limping at his side. It was Dr Goebbels' first trip overseas. Every time he awoke the train seemed to be passing a boulder strewn landscape. The Swedes themselves made up for it. He lusted greedily after the statuesque blonde women, and concluded that they were superior to their menfolk. The Swedish men were doormats, from their monarch downward, 'German on the outside,' he wrote, 'half-Jews within.'[45] When he left the Görings he decided that Carin was 'on the verge of' tears and added, using his coded doublespeak, 'She is fond of me' (meaning, he was of her); and more meaningfully, 'I revere her like a mother.' Hermann Göring, he decided, was a good sport.[46]

Hitler's birthday came during the absence. Goebbels did not write his customary eulogy. He was still aggrieved about the Strassers. By mid-March sales of the Strassers' new daily *National Sozialist* in Berlin were soaring, and both *Angriff* and *Völkischer Beobachter* were in difficulties. Reluctant to carry out his threat of resigning, Goebbels wrote: 'Munich, and that includes the chief, has run out of credit with me.' He added, 'Hitler hides away, he takes no decisions. . . . He just lets things drift.'[47] His office manager Franz Wilke returned from Munich with more empty Hitler promises.[48] Himmler came and assured Goebbels that Hitler really wanted him as Reich propaganda director. Goebbels had heard that before.[49] He had brooded for months on Hitler and his broken promises. 'He doesn't dare make a move against Strasser,' he noted. 'What's going to happen later when he has to act the dictator in Germany?'[50] When Hitler suddenly surfaced in Berlin for a conference with Hugenberg and the D.N.V.P. on ways of bringing the government crisis to a head, Goebbels tackled him, taking along Göring for moral support. He frankly accused the Führer of letting things drift. A second meeting with Hitler left Goebbels with the impression that he was losing his nerve. In the event, Hugenberg's party refused to join Hitler in forcing a vote of confidence.[51]

The government's crisis peaked on April 12. Brüning just survived, his majority reduced to seven. On April 14, his majority slumped still further to three; but again he survived. Hitler, who had hurried to Berlin, returned to Munich. None of their opponents wanted an election from which only the Nazis and communists were likely to profit.

AS THE DEPRESSION bit deeper Hitler's party had begun to expand. It ended 1930 with 389,000 registered members. Dr Goebbels doubled his gau's membership, although the wealthier districts were still sparsely represented: the huge West End Ortsgruppe (local) extending from Schloss Strasse to Pichelsdorf and from the grimy Siemensstadt industrial suburb to Halensee still yielded only forty-five members.

Late in April 1930 Goebbels learned while in Munich that Hitler had at last reprimanded Gregor Strasser. The Führer confirmed that he had issued an ultimatum to Strasser to drop either his newspaper in Berlin or the Organization

Department in Munich. Since everybody now had their eyes on Reichstag seats, Hitler had regained his influence. 'Thank goodness,' wrote Goebbels. 'Everybody is right behind him. Strasser . . . sits there like guilt personified. Hitler has strung him up – courteous to the last rung of the scaffold.' Then came the moment that Goebbels had badgered for. Hitler announced – 'amidst,' if Goebbels is to be believed, 'a breathless hush' – his appointment as the party's national chief of propaganda.[52] With it went the rank of Reichsleiter, making him one of a very select body indeed. Goebbels saw Strasser go pale. Afterward, the whole bunch except for Himmler came round to Goebbels' side.

The Berlin gau headquarters now had about thirty on its payroll, including Muchow, who was in charge of perfecting the factory cell-system. Goebbels had twice been able to raise their pay.[53] He began looking round for larger premises, perhaps even an entire building.[54] Cleverly mollifying him, the party's national headquarters purchased for him a brand new open Mercedes with a supercharged engine. He was still a big-car enthusiast like all the top Nazis.[55]

His own modest budget was quite strained. His brother Konrad's business had folded, leaving Hans and Joseph as providers for their mother. 'I want to look after Mother as best I can,' wrote Goebbels. 'Good old Mom, she deserves an old age free of worries.'[56] The glittering Mercedes soaked up his income, however. It was an essential mobile display of might and rank, with some of the attributes of a tank as well. One night after his S.A. men had killed three communists he was driving with six Brownshirts to a parade when he was recognized by his enemies – 'My heart missed a beat' he recorded, 'but our magnificent Supercharger rampaged triumphantly through the howling mob.'[57]

His disenchantment with his Führer continued. Horst Wessel's mother complained that Hitler had not written even one line of sympathy. Privately Goebbels blamed Hitler's waywardness on his 'womanizing.'[58] Two days after the new Mercedes arrived, Hitler came back to Berlin to speak at the Sport Palace. He again brought his young niece Geli. Goebbels again pleaded with him to kill off the rival newspaper *National Sozialist*. From the Berlin gauleiter's new offices Hitler phoned Otto Strasser and forbade him to sell the newspaper that evening.[59] But Otto proved more slippery than that. True, he undertook to sell off the newspaper to Hitler's publisher Max Amann and to cease publication from the twentieth; but he broke both promises. On May 21 Hitler returned to Berlin for a showdown. This time even Gregor disowned his brother Otto. Hitler threatened open war against them.[60]

Goebbels returned to the fold. In Munich Hitler enthusiastically showed him his plans for the Brown House, the party's new national headquarters. It seemed rather over-opulent even to Goebbels.[61]

WHEREAS the departed Social Democratic chancellor Heinrich Müller – unlovingly described by Goebbels as having 'a badly rusted voice well oiled by slime' – had ruled by the truncheon, Brüning's two years in office would be marked by emergency laws and prohibitions. On April 1 Hanover banned the

activities of the Hitler Youth. On June 5 Bavaria banned political uniforms –
in theory those of all parties, in practice only of the Nazis. On June 11, as
Goebbels had anticipated, Prussia's new minister of the interior Dr Heinrich
Waentig banned the S.A.'s brown shirts, and two weeks later Prussia forbade
its civil servants to join the Hitler party. Attired in white shirts with beer-
bottle rings as badges, one thousand of Stennes' S.A. men marched through
Charlottenburg that evening and Friedrichshain two days later. The police
had to adopt ludicrous tactics to enforce the bans.[62] Goebbels no longer feared
them. He had their measure. 'The real enemy,' he recognized, 'is at our rear' –
meaning the Strasser faction.[63]

The Strassers' newspaper continued to appear, spiced with cruel remarks
about Goebbels and his cult of personality. Several section heads (Kreisleiter)
declared for Otto Strasser. Goebbels blamed Hitler and his procrastination, and
meeting him in Leipzig he told him so. Hitler again promised to take action.[64]
Sick with worry, Goebbels wrote: 'Hitler's got to act – he's got to. Or there'll
be a catastrophe.' He found out which of his men were traitors, and lodged
complaints with the Party's powerful arbitration committee, particularly about
Eugen Mossakowsky, editor of the *N.S. Pressekonferenz* and two section heads.
Mossakowsky had done something unforgivable: at gauleiter conferences in
Berlin and Brandenburg he had accused Goebbels of lying about his heroism
during the Ruhr struggle and of forging documents to make his entry into
the party seem earlier than it was. These were sore points for Goebbels. Hitler
told Göring that he would authorize the Strassers' expulsion on Monday the
twenty-third, and personally confirmed this to Goebbels while electioneering
at Plauen in Saxony on June 21.[65]

Again however he did not act. When Goebbels phoned him he said he
preferred to wait. 'Typical Hitler,' wrote Goebbels. 'Rampant at Plauen, and
procrastinating here.'[66] With Hitler's permission however he expelled the
mutinous small fry like Mossakowsky. Mossakowsky preempted his expulsion
by issuing a statement through the wire services repeating all the lies, and
several cruel truths, about Goebbels before resigning.[67]

Gregor Strasser saw the storm signals and assured Goebbels he had broken
with his brother Otto. Goebbels trusted none of them. 'If only we had acted
in February!' he wailed. The entropy inside his organization increased. There
were disturbing reports from Neukölln of scuffles between rival S.A. factions.
Hitler ('the familiar old Hitler . . . the eternal procrastinator!') kept a low
profile. Göring told Goebbels that he too was shattered by Hitler's disloyalty.
But the very next day, June 30, he phoned Goebbels: victory was theirs. Hitler
had now written a powerful open letter excoriating both Strasser brothers.
Gregor laid down the editorship of his newspaper and survived; Otto was
expelled from the party. As Hitler's bluntly phrased letter was read out at
a Berlin party meeting there were shouts from the floor of 'String 'em up!'
Three disgruntled *Angriff* employees left the hall, but that was all. The meeting
ended with a spectacular vote of confidence in Hitler and Goebbels. Goebbels

persuaded the Führer to decree that Kampf Verlag was an enemy of the party. With that, Otto Strasser's goose was cooked.[68]

ONE PROBLEM which remained for Dr Goebbels that summer was the law courts. Dr Weiss was determined to see him serve his two months in jail. On May 13 the prosecutors confidentially asked the Reichstag if it was still formally in session.[69] On Goltz's advice Goebbels persuaded Dr Leonardo Conti, the gau's medical officer, to sign a sick note. That would give him four weeks' grace. The prosecutor's office demanded an independent examination. The mailman brought to Goebbels' Württembergische Strasse lodgings a new summons, for libeling Albert Grzesinski (by calling him 'Cohn'); it was returned to the courthouse with a note, 'Gone away,' and 'no forwarding requested.'[70]

His relations with women have come to a similar impasse. Visiting Anka in January 1930 he has failed to detect that she is four months pregnant by yet another man. Returning to Weimar in June he checks into the Elephant hotel and sends her tulips and a card. 'Can I call round?' it reads.[71]

A half-cocked but still platonic episode begins in June when Lucie Kammer, a young shorthand secretary ('still a pure child') with a much older, unloved, and now mortally ill husband comes to the gauleiter with her marital problems; he rapidly grasps that she loves him.[72]

A few days later he decides that Princess zu Wied loves him too; at the Görings he meets the Baroness Erika von Paleske and records that 'Ika' (because there is already another Erika in his ménage) also loves him. His phone jangles all day – Charlotte, Xenia, Lucie – 'Always the same,' he whimpers in his diary. 'I am a victim.' Women are a plague upon him. 'But they are an incredible stimulation to work,' he confesses. What he fears is losing his liberty. He writes about Ika that August, 'She comes on too strong. . . Thank goodness we were sitting out in the open.'[73]

He is vacationing – or hiding – at Erika's house in the forest when word comes on July 18, 1930 that Brüning's government is in difficulties. Tonak rushes him back to the Reichstag building in the Mercedes Supercharger. Goebbels romanticizes that his one vote may seal Brüning's fate. In fact Brüning dissolves the Reichstag. As the communist deputies roar the 'Internationale,' Goebbels slips out of the building, naked to the law, even his residual parliamentary immunity annulled.

13: *His Week in Court*

S O FAR DR GOEBBELS HAD HAD to face no real challenge as gauleiter. But, as the new Reichstag election of September 14, 1930 approached, the rift between his gau's officers and the impoverished and disgruntled fistfighters of the Berlin S.A. came to a head. Most of the S.A. men were unemployed. They saw no signs that Hitler intended to allow them any tangible reward for their bravery. Battered and bruised, they watched bitterly as the party squandered considerable sums on the Brown House, its national headquarters, in Munich.[1] Recognizing this, Hitler had ordered the gauleiters to enforce a twenty-pfennig monthly levy on each party member to support their local S.A. men; Goebbels sympathized with them. He ordered an additional ten-pfennig levy in Berlin – the S.A. *Groschen* as it was known.[2] 'We shall reach our goals only on the basis of the S.A.,' he asserted at one confidential meeting.[3]

The S.A. however wanted to get at the pork-barrel now, and they were not prepared to wait. The result would be the first full-scale S.A. mutiny, during the heat of the summer in Berlin.

Captain Walter Stennes, the ex-army officer who as supreme S.A. commander (Osaf) 'Ost' commanded twenty-five thousand of these disaffected men east of the river Elbe, shared many of Dr Goebbels' political views. He had dubbed the gauleiter the Nazis' Joseph Stalin, responsible for preserving the purity of the movement's ideals.[4] Both deprecated Hitler's legalistic approach to power. Though not as radically left-wing as the gauleiter, Stennes was like him an activist and revolutionary.

Goebbels was torn between instinct and logic. Captain Stennes and the S.A. represented manpower and muscle-but Hitler and Munich held promise of power, office, and ever bigger automobiles. Late in July Hitler called a secret conference to decide the official list of Nazi candidates. Goebbels was amused to see how tame Strasser and the other fractious big-shots suddenly became. They finally agreed a list of one hundred names (though not in their wildest dreams did they expect to win so many seats).[5]

The list brought the problems with the S.A. to a head. Stennes sent to the national supreme S.A. commander, Franz von Pfeffer, a letter asking for safe Reichstag seats for three S.A. men.[6] But Hitler was opposed to allowing the S.A. any more political clout than it already had. On August 1 Stennes mentioned in his diary reports from his subordinate commanders that relations between the S.A. and Munich were becoming intolerable. He invited his boss, Pfeffer, to Berlin at once. Meanwhile on the second his S.A. commanders reiterated their demands for Reichstag seats. The next day Pfeffer revealed that Hitler was on the contrary talking of cutting the S.A. back to what they could afford.

Financial prudence did not commend itself to the Brownshirt rednecks. 'This shows,' reported Stennes' chief of staff, 'that the objectives of the Reich director [*i.e.*, Pfeffer in Munich] are no longer those of old.' This was true. Hitler intended to attain power by strictly legal means. In Munich Goebbels, now Reich propaganda director, briefed his deputy Himmler on the broad outlines of the election campaign, then returned to Berlin. Nationwide over the next two months the glaring red and black Nazi election posters would invade telegraph poles, billboards, and newspapers.[7]

He printed millions of leaflets to be sold to Nazis at one pfennig each. Sleepless with work and worry, his nerves tautened, frayed, and snapped. At the beginning of August 1930 one thousand of his officials – so rapidly was the party now expanding – packed into a pre-election conference. From tram conductor to princess, every rank of society was active in the party's campaign.[8] In this election battle Goebbels would organize twenty thousand meetings up and down the country; in Berlin he would stage twenty-four mass meetings on the last two days alone.

The ruling Social Democrats tried to bury Goebbels with court actions. The Hindenburg case was revived along with the ancient charges of high treason. Seven more summonses arrived, accusing Goebbels of having libeled the Prussian prime minister Dr Otto Braun,[9] Albert Grzesinski, municipal officials, and the entire Jewish community.[10] Fearing summary imprisonment he stockpiled a batch of articles for *Angriff*; on August 3 he was notified of ten more court dates ('with the gentlemen of *Angriff* to blame for most of them').[11]

While the S.A. built up an ugly steam-head in his rear, Goebbels was fighting a nationwide election campaign and preparing half a dozen trial defenses. Thus the S.A. could hardly have chosen a less propitious moment to strike. Stennes, a sheaf of resignation letters from his commanders in his pocket, wrote to Pfeffer that his S.A. had a right to a hearing from Hitler. He got no reply. He then tackled Goebbels and threatened to withdraw his S.A. commanders – the Berlin S.A. would then shrink from fifteen thousand to perhaps three thousand, he predicted. Goebbels exploded; Hitler described the S.A.'s actions to Pfeffer as 'mutiny and conspiracy.' Believing that Stennes' clumsy intrigues were at the bottom of the S.A.'s unrest, Goebbels tackled the top S.A. commanders in Berlin like Bruno Wetzel; he too spoke of mutiny, comfortable in the knowledge that he had Hitler behind him.[12] A few days later Stennes took an S.A. delegation down to Munich, where he demanded to see Hitler. For two days they waited in the lobby. Loyal S.S. men barred the way. Goebbels, worried, discussed the gathering crisis with Göring. 'I don't trust Stennes at all,' he warned his diary. 'So let's keep an eye on him!'[13]

HIS WEEK in court arrived on Tuesday August 12, beginning with the Otto Braun libel action in Hanover. The Hindenburg appeal was set down for Thursday in Berlin.[14] President Hindenburg let it be known that he would drop the case if they could agree on a joint statement; they could not.

On the twelfth he and his lawyer Goltz took the morning train to Hanover. An eager crowd of Nazis met them at the station along with the local gauleiter Bernhard Rust and his S.A. commander Viktor Lutze, one of the few who were refusing to truckle to Stennes. The rowdy procession swept the one-legged Goltz and his lame client along to the courthouse. The charge was that Goebbels had accused Braun of taking bribes from 'Galician spivs.' Three police agents swore on oath that he had said this; supported by witnesses, Goebbels admitted having accused Bauer, the former Social Democrat Reich chancellor, of taking bribes. The prosecutor demanded nine months' prison, arguing that if Goebbels had libeled Hindenburg he was quite capable of having libeled the prime minister.

Goltz pointed out that even the Jewish arch-swindler Julius had been sentenced to only eleven months, with half remitted. Goebbels was acquitted and awarded his costs. Instead of a jail term he had won huge publicity. Burly S.A. men chaired him out of the courtroom, singing the Horst Wessel anthem; he went off to carouse with Lutze, their commander.[15]

One down, three to go. On Thursday the fourteenth the court heard his appeal in the Hindenburg case. The prosecutor again demanded a nine-month prison sentence. Goltz however read out a letter from Hindenburg – the president himself wanted to withdraw the original complaint. As that was not possible, he now considered the matter closed and had 'no further interest' in punishing Dr Goebbels.[16]

The public prosecutor snapped that he, and not Hindenburg, represented the state in this courtroom. The judge disagreed; he too acquitted Dr Goebbels, finding that his statements had been made in the public interest. Goebbels could see that the newspapermen were stunned by this renewed victory.[17]

Still a free man he prepared for the third day in the courthouse at Moabit on Friday the fifteenth. The plaintiffs here were the Reich government and ex-chancellor Hermann Müller, charging that in *Angriff* in December 1929 he had labeled the Social Democrats a bunch of hired traitors.

The elderly judge Dr Toelke invited him to justify the words, and Goebbels did so with relish, emphasizing how the Social Democrats had signed away Germany's birthright in the postwar treaties while deceiving their own people. Goltz told of how the Social Democrat governments of Saxony, Thuringia, and Prussia had sabotaged the government's postwar struggle for the Ruhr, how Saxony's prime minister had betrayed government secrets to France, how the Social Democrats had thwarted attempts to rescue Schlageter from execution, and how their Philipp Scheidemann had betrayed details of the Reichswehr's violations of Versailles.

Judge Toelke was aghast. 'If we are to hear *evidence* for all these claims,' he stammered, ' – well, *I* have two months from nine A.M. to six P.M., but –'

'Dr Goebbels,' interrupted Goltz, 'has stated openly what millions think. He wants to justify his allegations. He is at the court's disposal. *We have the time!*'

Goebbels had already brought a platoon of military witnesses into court, but the judge refused to allow them. Goltz solemnly picked up his crutch and hobbled out. The prosecutor asked for a six-month sentence on Goebbels. The court reserved its judgment, and moved on without a break to the Grzesinski libel action.[18]

That Saturday, August 16, Goebbels expected to go to prison. Instead the court stipulated modest fines of six hundred and four hundred marks for libeling the government and Müller, and four hundred for Grzesinski. This was cheap publicity indeed.

'These demanding court actions are doing my gut no good,' wrote Goebbels. 'It's enough to throw up.'

Three down: the court moved on to the next charge, of incitement to violence, and handed down another petty fine, of three hundred marks.

'Let them give their verdict,' wrote Goebbels grimly on the seventeenth. We shall utter our verdict on September 14' – election day.

He visited his mother at Rheydt. Berlin phoned him there – four more court summonses had arrived. By the time of his return the number had doubled to eight. Braun and Grzesinski had both appealed for stiffer sentences; Goebbels was now also accused of having, in a speech at Prerow in July 1929, called the Reich's war standard 'a Jewish flag, a dirt rag,' and any republic that it stood for a 'Jew republic'[19]

He decided to ignore these fresh trials. Court officials demanded to see him. He refused – he was now planning the biggest Sport Palace meetings of the campaign. 'The courts,' he recorded, 'are now hounding me with summonses. I've got a thick skin. I won't budge.'[20]

BY THE LATE summer of 1930 there were signs that his diaries had begun concealing his true anxiety about the S.A. The incriminating notebooks might have been snatched at any time by communists, the S.A., or the police. Thus the diary avowed that he shared the S.A.'s indignation. In reality he got his office manager Franz Wilke to take precautions against them. This became more urgent as rumors multiplied that Stennes was planning to issue an ultimatum to Munich. Dr Leonardo Conti, the S.A.'s chief physician, warned both Hitler and Goebbels that Stennes was up to no good.[21] At the end of August, realizing that he could not curb his underlings' revolutionary passions, Pfeffer resigned.[22]

Stennes waited until Goebbels was away in Dresden, then called his commanders together. Melitta Wiedemann, features editor of *Angriff*, could see him through the windows one floor below standing in a white cap at the head of a table round which crowded Berlin's S.A. commanders. There were growls of approval as Stennes proposed they go on strike immediately unless Hitler accepted their demands for a bigger slice of the action.[23]

By telephone Goebbels heard from Berlin that the S.A. commanders had collected their ragged regiments (*Standarten*) for a confrontation with both Berlin (Goebbels) and Munich (Hitler). This put at risk the big Sport Palace election meeting on Friday the twenty-ninth. Back in Berlin on Thursday Goebbels found Stennes demanding three Reichstag seats and more funds. Otherwise, in best trades-union jargon, he could not guarantee that his S.A. lads would not break up Goebbels' meeting, an 'unparalleled impertinence' in the gauleiter's view.

It was an ugly situation. Goebbels phoned Munich and advised them to play for time. They could *appear* to yield to Stennes' demands, fight the election, then take revenge on him. Hitler however said he did not propose to yield anything. Goebbels swooned with rage: Hitler had lost touch with reality – fifteen thousand S.A. in Berlin were threatening violence against him and his embattled headquarters. He left for Hamburg that evening. In his absence thirty S.A. men appeared at the Hedemann Strasse headquarters with the intention of giving Franz Wilke the kind of head massage in which they specialized. Only the intervention of Stennes himself, according to his diary, prevented a rough-house.

'The S.A. commanders,' he dictated, 'left no doubt that, far from protecting today's Sport Palace meeting of General [Karl] Litzmann, Dr [Wilhelm] Frick, and Dr Goebbels, the S.A. men of the Gau Sturm intended to smash it up.' Stennes ordered them to assemble in a beerhall at Hasenheide instead, to receive special orders from him (which his diary does not specify).

Wilke reacted by moving a reliable S.S. guard unit into the headquarters building. Goebbels discreetly left by car the next morning, Saturday the thirtieth, for Breslau. Stennes ordered his commanders to meet him at Hedemann Strasse. As they were meeting here, they found an S.S. man, Hertel, writing notes on their conference from the locked room next door, 'on orders from above.'[24] An S.A. unit bloodily evicted the S.S. men, though not before one of them, Walter Kern, had alerted the police.[25] Dr Bernhard Weiss sent a massive force round within minutes, who hauled off the S.A. trespassers.

An urgent telegram notified Goebbels in Breslau. He phoned Hitler at Bayreuth; Hitler said he would come to Berlin at once.[26] Back in the capital Goebbels found his headquarters a shambles. There were bloodstains everywhere. Unshaven and baggy-eyed, Hitler, Himmler, and Hess reached Berlin around eleven A.M. and checked into an hotel near Potsdamer Platz.[27]

Hitler asked Wilke for a full report, then toured the city's S.A. units to test morale.[28] He was jeered at some locations. That evening he invited the lesser commanders, and then Berlin's S.A. Oberführer Wetzel, to meet him in Goebbels' apartment. Hitler, Goebbels, Göring, and Himmler were present, but not Stennes. 'The Berlin S.A. commanders,' recalled Himmler, 'trooped into Dr Goebbels' apartment that afternoon and acted in an incredibly rowdy manner toward the Führer. Gangs of S.A. men were chorusing slogans outside in the street. Stennes had probably staged the whole thing.' For two hours they bandied allegations and counter-allegations. Rudolf Hess mentioned the odd fact that Stennes had a gun permit issued by the head of the political police, Wündisch, and implied that he was a police agent (a belief which Goebbels came to share).[29] Hitler ruled that Stennes would have to go. In the middle of the night however a Herculean figure, Richard Harwardt, probably the toughest man in the Berlin Sturmabteilung (S.A.), came clattering upstairs into Goebbels' apartment, flung a salute, and roared: 'Adolf, don't get tough with your own S.A.!'[30]

Urged by Harwardt to give Stennes himself a hearing, Hitler reluctantly agreed. It lasted until six A.M., when Hitler sent for all the S.A. commanders once more and declared that he was going to cut their Brown army rigorously in size.

This was getting nowhere. Goebbels left to snatch an hour's sleep – he had to be in court for yet another libel action that morning (he refused to offer any defense, was sentenced to prison; appealed).[31] Exhausted and almost asleep on his feet he pleaded with Hitler once again to promise the S.A. whatever they demanded.[32] Winning the election must come first.

It was now Monday September 1. According to Goebbels' diary, at four P.M. Hitler took the decision he had urged: Stennes should stay. But he would dismiss Pfeffer as supreme commander, despite his resignation, and take over the S.A. himself (with the notorious Ernst Röhm as his chief of staff).[33] A letter went to Stennes, and Stennes pledged loyalty. Taking selected S.S. men as an escort, Hitler spoke in the Veterans' Building to 'his' entire Berlin S.A., promising to meet Stennes' fundamental demands. Police observers reported that Hitler, his voice cracking, appealed for unswerving loyalty: 'Let us pray in this hour that nothing can divide us, and that God will help us against the Devil!' screamed Hitler. 'Almighty Lord, bless our fight!' – and the roars of Heil, so the police reported, had died away as the audience noticed their Führer's hands folded seemingly in prayer.[34] The Görings threw a little reception at Badensche Strasse afterwards. Stennes was not invited. The whole reconciliation had been a charade, as Goebbels had recommended to Hitler. This became plain from remarks made by the top Nazis at the reception.[35] 'Everything shipshape,' wrote Goebbels later that day. 'That's the end of the Stennes putsch.'[36] They would, he added, be drawing the necessary conclusions after the election. The campaign resumed.

GERMANY HAD NEVER seen a battle like this. Over the last two weeks the Nazis staged hundreds of dramatic meetings – in the open air, in halls, by night, in marquees, by torchlight. Goebbels willingly spoke side by side with Gregor Strasser.[37] His headquarters printed tens of millions of leaflets. The streets were carpeted with them. Sixty truckloads of Nazis careered around the capital tossing out pamphlets; Goebbels clambered from truck to truck, haranguing pedestrians through an amplifier and whipping on his men. The posters clearly betrayed his own handiwork. One contrasted unlovely photographs of all their thick-lensed oppressors – pride of place being given to Dr Weiss – with majestic studio portraits of the top eleven Nazis. As for his own likeness, Goebbels placed this right next to Hitler's.[38]

Unemployment had been two million as the year opened. It would reach 4,380,000 as the year ended. 'Out with this rabble!' cried Goebbels in *Angriff*. He hoped for a quarter of a million Nazi voters in Berlin. When Hitler came to the Sport Palace on September 10, one hundred thousand people applied for tickets. The photos show him with clenched fists raised, orating into a box microphone some three feet in front of him (in Hermann Schäfer, Goebbels had now gained one of Europe's finest public-address system technicians).[39] 'With fanaticism like this,' wrote Goebbels afterward, 'a nation can and will rouse itself again.' He attributed the public curiosity to the S.A. mutiny. 'The S.A. must give up all political ambitions,' he wrote after discussing the problem over supper with Hitler and Göring (now the party's liaison to the S.A.).[40] All three – Hitler, Goebbels, and Stennes – were to be seen amiably sharing a meal the next day.[41] On the final electioneering day, the twelfth, the little gauleiter spoke at seven meetings – motoring in his Mercedes Supercharger from hall to hall, flanked by motorcycle outriders.

'Keep calm!' he admonished himself. He had rented the Sport Palace for election night itself, September 14, 1930. By mid-evening the cavernous hall was rocking with cheers as the first results came in. Hitler had banked on winning fifty seats, or eighty at most. As midnight approached, the Nazis had already won 103.[42] Exultant young men jogged around the hall with Goebbels on their shoulders. The final tally was 6,406,397 votes, entitling the Nazis to 107 seats. Suddenly the Nazis were the strongest party in Germany after the Social Democrats. This was democracy with a vengeance. The communists however had also increased their share, from 10·6 to 13·1 percent. (In Berlin the Nazis, with over 360,000 votes, had won 12·8 percent of the vote.) 'Hot months lie ahead,' predicted Goebbels. 'The communists have gained too.'[43]

HE IS IN GRAVE danger of arrest. A month will pass before the Reichstag convenes and he is immune again.

He needs to empty his fevered brain, and for this purpose female company is ideal. He flirts with Xenia ('the best of all'), he escorts Carin Göring, he accompanies the delightful Potempa twins, or phones Charlotte, and he gets to know not only the Weimar architect Professor Paul Schultze-Naumburg but his lovely wife as well, and decides as often as he needs to that they are all madly in love with him.[44]

Horrified by the Nazis' election victories, Dr Weiss's police show him no mercy. Five days after the election baton-wielding police fling Goebbels down the steps of a police station as he protests at their treatment of an S.A. man brought in for questioning.[45] The courts set down five new cases for – surely no coincidence – Monday October 13, the very afternoon that the Reichstag is due to swear him in. The police are ordered to bring him in by force if need be. He takes refuge out at Erika's forest cottage, armed with a dispensation from his doctor. He hunkers down in the back of the Potempas' car to go to Weimar where Hitler speaks in the National Theater, with Göring following as a somewhat implausible decoy in the Supercharger. 'What wizard fellows these fliers are!' enthuses Goebbels, changing his mind yet again.

He drives back from Thuringia that Sunday night in the Schultze-Naumburgs' car, squeezed enjoyably between the professor's comely wife and her stepdaughter Babette; he sleeps at the Schultze-Naumburgs' and it is just as well, for Dr Weiss's police are meanwhile ransacking his lodgings in Würt-tembergische Strasse and lying in wait for him.

October 13 comes. He lies doggo all morning writing up his diary. 'In three hours I am immune again, thank God!' As Berlin's Nazis go on an orgy of destruction through the West End, smashing the windows of Jewish-owned stores on the Potsdamer Platz and in Kurfürstendamm – an inspired move by the gauleiter to distract 'Isidor' – he is driven at breakneck speed over to the Reichstag.

'Portal zwei!' he shouts. Plainclothes detectives see him hobbling frantically up the long flight of steps to Door Two, wearing a light raincoat buttoned tightly to his neck, and grab at him just as he lurches through the great doors. The gau official Hanno Konopath and a Reichstag flunky get a firm grip on him and bundle him inside.[46]

They have torn off his coat. Beneath it for the first time he is wearing the forbidden uniform of the Nazi party. He is once more immune, and he can do and say as he likes.

14: A Blonde in the Archives

AFTER ALL THE OTHER deputies had taken their seats the Nazis marched in. Like Dr Goebbels, all were wearing the forbidden brown shirt. A cacophony of insults greeted them. Five days later Chancellor Brüning set out his economic program. To packed benches the bullheaded, broad-shouldered Gregor Strasser delivered one of the best speeches of his life. Even Goebbels was impressed. 'The House pays the closest attention,' he wrote with more than a soupçon of envy. 'Thus he's back again, firmly in the saddle.'[1] The Nazis called repeatedly for votes of no confidence in Brüning. The Reichstag was then adjourned until early December.

Goebbels was bored with it already. The fight had been the fun. 'The toxic haze of parliaments is not the right air for me,' he decided. 'I can't breathe there.' Back at his lodgings he revived himself with whiffs of the Lieder of Brahms and Wolff, to which he provided his own piano accompaniment.[2]

With the political wind in Germany now beginning to blow Brown, the highest police officials faced an ugly option: to smash the Nazis or to join them. The first alternative entailed facing the risk that the Nazis would gain power. Increasingly the middle-ranking officers decided that Germany's future lay with Goebbels and Hitler. According to Berlin's *Acht-Uhr Abendblatt* at least one senior police officer had been seen cheering the Nazis on during the riots of October 13, 1930 and singing a Nazi song. Albert Grzesinski wrote to Prussia's prime minister Braun that evening, protesting against this 'deliberate' breakdown of police authority.[3] 'In grave times like these,' he wrote, 'what counts is being tough – tough as nails.' If Schutzpolizei commander Heimannsberg himself proved guilty then he too must go. 'If' wrote Grzesinski, getting to his real point, 'Comrade Zörgiebel [Berlin's police president] stands up for both these officers, we must not spare him either.' Braun agreed; he dismissed Waentig as minister of the interior as well as Zörgiebel, appointing Grzesinski in the latter's place. 'It's going to be some winter,' commented a wry Goebbels in his diary. 'But if these bastards think they can get us down with terror and persecution they've got another think coming.'[4]

The mood at Alexander Platz, the brownstone police headquarters in Berlin, was jubilant. Dr Weiss personally welcomed back his fellow socialist Grzesinski at a little police ceremony. 'When we heard it was you,' said the oily Dr Weiss, the real power behind the scenes, 'we all cheered.'[5]

He had turned thirty-three. That month he recorded his first radio broadcast, debating international art with the renowned left-wing stage director Erwin Piscator. A new friend, Arnolt Bronnen, arranged both this interview and another two days later on neutrality in broadcasting and the cowardice of governments.[6] Fritz Prang, his old schoolfriend, had given him a splendid radio and he sat up late marveling at the sounds coming from Rome or Copenhagen. Preferring the aristocracy to carry his bags for him, he had taken on the upright young Count Karl-Hubert Schimmelmann as his private secretary.[7]

His party headquarters in Hedemann Strasse was turning into a fortress. From the reception area one door to the right led to the quarters of the increasingly ill-humored S.A., the other to the left to his gau headquarters. Uniformed men stood guard on each door. Visitors were taken through a locked and guarded doorway at the end of a short passage, past a long suite of rooms separated by shoulder-high glass partitions, to a side chamber off which more locked doors concealed three large rooms; in the very last of these sat the gauleiter, Dr Goebbels, in an otherwise empty room at a desk a full ten yards from the door. He could reach this room via a side staircase directly from the yard door where his new Mercedes delivered him each day.

He installed the editorial offices of *Angriff* on the first floor of this building. From November 1, 1930 it appeared as a daily. Its masthead now read, 'Berlin's German evening paper.' Months of wearying negotiations with Max Amann had preceded this innovation. Goebbels mistrusted the party's publisher, but in September a deal had been worked out giving Franz Eher Verlag 60 percent of the stock in *Angriff* and the gau 40 percent. Goebbels retained editorial control.[8]

The new rotary presses had been assembled at the printers, Süsserott & Co. That afternoon, November 1, Dr Goebbels found the printers' yard crowded with his *Angriff* salesmen all wearing smart uniforms with the newspaper's name picked out in silver on their red cap-bands. The presses glistened with chrome and oil like a locomotive at a station. He gave a signal to start the presses rolling. Everybody saluted, and Horst Wessel's anthem echoed until drowned by the whirring and clanking machinery.

Now a daily, the newspaper differed little from its predecessor except in topicality. Goebbels demanded relentless personal attacks on Dr Weiss, and the editor Dr Lippert complied. On November 3 the robust headline read 'BERNHARD WEISS ALLOCATES NIGHTCLUB CONCESSIONS: HIS BROTHER GETS THE BRIBES.' The story dealt with Weiss's murky dealings with his criminal brother Conrad and an unrelated Jewish night-club owner called Taube Weiss. On the sixth, as his headlines rhetorically asked 'BERNHARD WEISS TO RESIGN?', Goebbels privately rejoiced in his diary: 'Isidor is being destroyed.' On November 8 *Angriff* reported that a communist had punched Zörgiebel in the face: 'Sometimes,' the newspaper editorialized, 'though not often, the acts of the communists are not entirely unwelcome to us.'[9] For this licentious remark Grzesinski banned *Angriff* for one week.[10] Goebbels was livid; his newspaper would be banned on fifteen more occasions before August 1932, for periods ranging from three days to six weeks. Grzesinski, bolder than his predecessor, banned several Goebbels meetings too. Rumors abounded that he would soon ban the party as well. Goebbels doubted the police would really try that now.

Later in November the Sport Palace audience was treated to a double bill as he and Göring harangued them. 'I make short work of the Social Democrats,' recorded Goebbels. 'The giant arena thunders with rage, hatred, and screams of revenge. . . How much further can this be pushed?'[11] He envied Göring his easy access to wealth and high society. Already however a perceptible frost was settling over their relations. On October 9 he had written of Göring, 'He is a true comrade – but not devoid of ambition.' The day after the Reichstag had reconvened he commented privately, 'I rather fear that Fatso Gregor [Strasser] and Fatso Göring may shortly hit it off together.'[12] Admittedly the aviator had introduced him to several useful contacts like Fritz Thyssen, the steel baron; the former airman Erich Niemann, head of Mannesmann Steel, and Wilhelm Tengelmann (Ruhr Coal). They would inject badly needed funds into the party in Berlin.[13] But Hitler had now appointed Göring his personal viceroy in Berlin. This was bound to lead to friction with the gauleiter. As a Reichsleiter Goebbels in fact ranked somewhat higher than Göring in the party, and a hardier tone of mordant criticism crept into the diary entries.[14] Viktoria von Dirksen revealed confidentially to him that Göring was still having problems beating the recurring morphine addiction inflicted on him by Austrian doctors in 1923. Having already made observations about the aviator's evident corruption, he made a note to keep an eye on him.[15]

ENTERING HIS HEADQUARTERS one day in November 1930 Goebbels sees a platinum blonde coming down the steps.

'*Donnerwetter*, Schimmel!' he exclaims to his private secretary. 'Who was that?'

The blonde is working in his press-clippings section. The next day he sends for her, to work on his confidential archives. She turns out to be wealthy, married, and twenty-nine – much older than his usual preference. She rates another diary mention on the fourteenth, helping to sort out early photographs.[16]

Thus he has finally met the woman he will marry. Other females will flit across his stage as, aged thirty-three, he belatedly approaches manhood. (He has detected the first gray hairs.) There is his former secretary, the 'wondrous, goodly, attractive, and affectionate' Ilse Stahl, who stays over one evening until six A.M.; 'and,' he writes, 'wholly sexually innocent, at that.'[17] She blushes the next day and he scribbles her a note, 'Phone me at seven.' But that evening he has a visit from another, the blonde actress Hella Koch, who is already married.[18] His roaming eye alights on Olga Förster, the fiancée of his new friend the broadcaster Arnolt Bronnen. Olga, another petite actress, visits him alone a few days later and tries a much worn female ploy – she is engaged, she sighs, but does not really love her Arnolt. 'But me,' records Goebbels smugly, 'she likes a lot.' He thinks of her that evening as he addresses the gau's Women's Order – the women all 'well behaved' and the girls all 'spotless.'[19] He invites Bronnen and his Olga to the movies and she visits him again the next day. She wheels out every available weapon in the arsenal of female seduction.[20]

He is a sitting duck. He is nest-building for the new apartment that he and Xenia have found at Steglitz – No. 11 Am Bäkequell. He browses the furniture stores, determined to create a drawing room to rival Carin Göring's.[21] His female admirers often come to see his performance in the Reichstag. And perform at last he does: on December 6 the 'touching' and 'devoted' Olga Förster comes round. 'She loves me madly,' he resumes afterwards, to which he adds a nonchalant parenthesis: '(1, 2).' Five days later Olga comes again – as indeed does Goebbels, not once, twice, but thrice: '(3, 4, 5).'[22] A week later she marries her Arnolt Bronnen and that is that. 'No regrets,' writes Goebbels; not once, but twice[23] – although it does pain him when a gossip columnist gets hold of the story and phones him about rumors that Olga's new husband has Jewish blood; Bronnen assures Goebbels it is not so.[24]

For two months after his seduction Goebbels' private life is a flurry of former girlfriends. He has some catching up to do. He treats them, one hopes, more kindly than he writes of them in his diary. Helping move to Steglitz, Ilse is crowned by a falling equestrian bronze and her head bleeds profusely. 'She yammers on all evening,' he writes heartlessly. 'I am quite reactionary,' he confesses to the Bronnens. 'Having, and raising, children is a job for life. My mother is the woman I most revere . . . so close to life. Today women want a say in everything, they just don't want children any more. They call it emancipation.'[25]

IN DECEMBER 1930 Goebbels staged his most effective propaganda demonstration yet, against the Ufa film version of *All Quiet on the Western Front*. The movie was pacifist and anti-German (its author had already emigrated). In one scene, German soldiers were depicted haggling with a dying comrade whose legs had been shot away, over who should inherit his new boots. At its first public showing on the fifth, Goebbels' S.A. men emptied the cinema with stink bombs and live mice.[26] The Nazis found Berlin's police, many of them ex-army officers, in broad sympathy with them. *Angriff* reported laconically that their Doctor had been present 'for informational purposes,' and planned to see the rest of the movie for informational purposes 'on Sunday evening.' His men took the hint and trashed the movie theater while thousands of cheering Berliners looked on. The management cancelled the next performance after that. Even Mosse's Berliner Tageblatt dared not to criticize, because this time the gauleiter had the people behind him.[27] On the seventh the movie theater tried again. Goebbels staged another 'spontaneous' riot.[28] He called for further protests the next night. The police cordoned off entire districts. This time, he estimated, forty thousand Berliners turned out to protest against the movie;

opposing newspapers put the figure at six thousand.[29] Under pressure from Grzesinski the Prussian minister of the interior Severing banned all open-air demonstrations.[30] On the eleventh the Reichstag itself debated the situation. Goebbels was evicted from the building, but the victory was his. At four P.M. the Brüning government ordered the objectionable movie withdrawn from distribution 'because of the danger to Germany's image abroad,' then adjourned until February 3, 1931.[31]

'WE ARE GOING to be on the verge of power soon,' assessed Goebbels on December 2, 1930. 'But what then? A tricky question.' He mistrusted the alliance that Hitler was forming. Strasser warned the Nazi Reichstag bloc that they were making too much headway in bourgeois circles and that this would taint the party's image ('Bravo, Strasser,' observed Goebbels to himself). At a function at the Görings' afterward he had a long talk with Strasser, trying to find common ground with this impressive politician. 'I want to bury the hatchet,' wrote Goebbels, 'and I think he does too.'[32]

He celebrated a pagan Christmas with the S.A. around a Yuletide bonfire at Schönerlinde. But he spent Christmas Eve with the Görings, who had less time for such pagan rites. Carin gave him a fine porcelain bowl, decorated with white mice. Her husband's morphine addiction caused him real concern, and he mentioned it to Hitler. Hitler said he would take Göring under his wing.[33]

Turning to grand strategy Goebbels warned that their party was in danger of losing momentum – it was approaching freezing point, as he put it. 'We must start a crescendo of operations.' And he did: in July the *Red* Flag had challenged him to a public debate, knowing full well that for him to accept would be to invite arrest. His immunity restored, he now challenged both the Social Democrats and the communists to debate before a working-class audience at Friedrichshain.

A thousand communists turned up on January 22, 1931. Their ace propagandist Walter Ulbricht spoke for nearly an hour; the communists then pitched into their rivals with chair legs and broken bottles; while Goebbels and his Nazis held their ground, in Goebbels' narrative, Ulbricht fled 'whimpering' to the S.A. stewards for protection, before leaving the hall with his jacket over his head. 'They banked on brawn instead of brain,' mocked Goebbels in *Angriff*, 'then found that where they had arms, our S.A. men didn't exactly have liverwursts dangling at their sides.' There were over one hundred injured including his chauffeur Kunisch and Olga Bronnen, who was taken to hospital with concussion.[34]

A QUAVERING voice phones him in the small hours, after the riot: Olga, calling from the hospital. Goebbels remains callous and aloof.[35] Ilse Hess writes, chiding him for his attitude to women and holding up Carin Göring as a shining example of feminine supportiveness. Goebbels replies evasively, promising to look the Hesses up more often in 1931. He plans to spend three days every fortnight down in Munich then. 'Unfortunately my sister won't be able to come either to Munich or Berlin,' his letter continues. 'She has to keep my mother company – she's feeling very lonely since my father died.'[36] For the first time since he was at university he has not gone home for Christmas, guiltily suggesting in his diary that he must spare his mother the risk.[37]

He moves into middle-class Steglitz on the first day of 1931. It is a well-appointed two-room apartment. Meanwhile one woman has by her beauty and sheer force of personality crowded out her juniors – Magda Quandt, the platinum blonde working in his private archives, which consist of press clippings from all over the world. There is a perfumed classiness about her. She finds herself drawn toward this Savonarola who has set all Berlin by the ears. Late in January his diary records that she is bringing her work on the archives round to his new Steglitz apartment. 'Knowledge is power,' he explains to Magda, gesturing toward the clippings files.[38]

She reminds him inevitably of a younger, classier Anka. The other girls' names gradually fade from the diary's pages. Charlotte stalks around with a face like thunder.

When Magda visits him again, Goebbels finds himself wishing that she were in love with him.[39]

Two weeks later, the wish becomes father of the deed.

15: *Maria Magdalena Quandt*

MAGDA QUANDT WAS LATER the object of much malicious tittle-tattle. 'She was first married to a crook,' sneered Prince Otto von Bismarck, a German diplomat, 'and earned money through prostitution. Later she became Goebbels' friend, but this did not prevent her from going to bed with many of the habitués of the party meetings at the Sport Palace. . . Now she goes around looking for men, and when she does not suffice there is also her sister-in-law [Ello Quandt], who is another whore.'[1]

None of this was true. Magda had been born in Berlin on November 11, 1901. She believed her father was Oskar Ritschel, an engineer and inventor, of strict catholic upbringing. Her mother Auguste Behrend was twenty-two, an unmarried servant girl of the evangelical-lutheran faith working for a family in Berlin's upmarket Bülow Strasse.[2] In fact she later gave this street as Magda's birthplace, while her birth certificate puts it in a working class suburb at No. 25 Katzler Strasse.[3] Auguste was in Goebbels' words a frightful person;[4] she was probably never married to Ritschel.

In later years she was curiously vague about their divorce, stating that it was when Magda was 'about three' – the word 'about' seems to cast doubt upon the precision of the matrimony itself.[5] It is unlikely that a man of Ritschel's standing would have married a servant girl.[6] In a codicil to his will he mentioned his first wife Hedwig, but no others.[7] To Goebbels, Ritschel was always a *Schubiak* (a scoundrel) and 'wretched prig.'[8]

Since Ritschel was living in Belgium, Auguste chose the infant's names herself – Johanna Maria Magdalena, or Magda for short. Ritschel arranged for the girl to be raised from 1906 in an Ursuline boarding school at Tildonk in Belgium. Auguste visited her behind these forbidding and often chilly walls with Friedländer, her Jewish boyfriend whom she had (perhaps) married in 1908.[9] Upset by the draftiness of Magda's dormitories her mother transferred her to another Ursuline boarding school, Virgo Fidelis, at Vilvoorde.

Her placid existence was interrupted by the Great War. The expatriates in Brussels were shipped home to Germany in evil-smelling cattle trucks. It took six days for the Friedländer family – they had all adopted his name – to reach Berlin. In a refugee camp an East Prussian woman, a Mrs Kowalsky, read Magda's palm. 'You will one day be a Queen of Life,' she pronounced. 'But the ending is fearful.' Magda, always a romantic, often retold this prophecy. She dramatized it sometimes, making the fortune-teller a gypsy, and having her appear mysteriously aboard the refugee train. Friedländer became manager (or perhaps only an employee) of the four-star Eden hotel in Berlin.[10] Their milieu was Jewish: Magda's first real friend was Lisa Arlosorov, whose parents were Ukrainian Jews living in Wilmersdorf. Ritschel paid for his daughter to attend Berlin's Kollmorgen Lycée and sent her three hundred marks as monthly pocket money.[11] Friedländer, the German Jew, faded from the picture and history is not entirely sure what became of him.[*]

In the autumn of 1919 Magda Friedländer matriculated and was found a place at the exclusive ladies' college run by Frau Else Holzhausen in Klaustor Promenade in Goslar. Even at nineteen she was a girl of considerable presence. Traveling down to Goslar on February 18, 1920 she shared the reserved compartment of a Dr Günther Quandt, a prematurely balding, wealthy entrepreneur just twice her age.[12] His first wife had died in a 'flu epidemic two years before, leaving him with two sons, Hellmut and Herbert; he related all this to Magda during the train journey. Strongly taken by this teenage girl with the foreign allure, he visited the college more than once, claiming to be her uncle, and took the matron and Magda out for rides in his open landau.[13]

She dropped out of college, and phoned him instead; one thing led to another, and she invited her mother out to his lakeside villa at Babelsberg, outside Berlin. Events moved rapidly toward matrimony. As a first step Quandt required her birth certificate to be amended so that she was declared the *legitimate* daughter of Ritschel, to expunge the undesirable name Friedländer.[14] Ritschel lodged the necessary application in mid-1920.[15] As a second step, Quandt required his bride to embrace the protestant faith. They were married on January 4, 1921 at Ritschel's parental house in Godesberg. After the honeymoon, said her mother later, Magda rushed into her arms wailing, 'How could you have let me marry him!'[16] But as their first and only child Harald was born just ten months later the matrimonial ardor evidently flickered just long enough.[17]

Günther Quandt was old for his age. Escorting her to concerts or the theater he usually fell asleep behind the *Berliner Börsenzeitung*. The boardroom was his true world. Once when she, with girlish pride, produced her meticulous household accounts he absent-mindedly signed them in red ink, 'Seen and approved. Günther Quandt.' She rapidly tired of his company. Even when he went on business trips to exotic locations like Egypt or Palestine she was reluctant to go with him. He wrote her regularly from abroad, she replied only once.[18]

She began a furtive relationship with his eldest son Hellmut. Sexually unfulfilled, the twenty-three-year-old Magda was fatally attracted to this gifted and delicate young man, then aged only eighteen. Her husband found it wise to send young Hellmut to complete his studies in London and Paris. After an operation for appendicitis in Paris, complications set in and Hellmut died tragically in her arms in 1927. Heartbroken, she accompanied her husband on a

---

[*] Probably he died in Buchenwald in 1939. See APPENDIX, page 696ff.

six-month tour of the Americas, taking their big red Maybach car everywhere they went. Standing next to the balding, blazered, bow-tied millionaire Quandt this bored, blue-eyed blonde was a star attraction in high society on both sides of the border. Something intimate evidently passed between Magda and the former President Herbert Hoover's nephew, because he came to Berlin after her estrangement from Quandt and pleaded with her to marry him.[19]

Back in Berlin, Quandt settled down and purchased a roomy winter home in Charlottenburg, while keeping on their new villa at Neu Babelsberg for the summer. Magda took refuge from her boredom in books – buying a ten-volume Buddhist catechism one day in Leipzig – and wafted from store to store, from one empty social event to the next until she could stand it no longer.[20] In the summer of 1929 she embarked on an affair with a thirty-year old law student, a Jew.[21] She pleaded in vain with Quandt to release her. Hoping to catch him in some infidelity, she had him watched, but equally in vain. The student was a perfect and attentive lover, plying her with flowers, and she accompanied him on a trip to the Hotel Dreesen at Godesberg. This time however Quandt had hired the detectives; after reading their report, he threw her out.

Penniless and unemployed Magda returned to her mother while she negotiated a settlement with Quandt. Ello Quandt, her sister-in-law, advised her to blackmail her aging husband about a bundle of papers she had found.[22] It proved unnecessary, however. He remained a perfect gentleman, agreed to a divorce, and willingly accepted the fiction that he had contributed to the breakdown of the marriage. 'Do we not all,' he would write, 'at times assume the blame, when in fact we are not in the wrong?'[23] Until she should remarry he granted her custody of their son, a lavish four-thousand-mark monthly allowance, and fifty thousand marks to purchase a house. She leased a seven-room luxury apartment at No. 2 Reichskanzler Platz in west Berlin.

There could be no question of marrying her unemployed student lover – marriage to anybody would cut off her alimony cornucopia. So she lived, loved, and traveled around as her law student's paramour while privately planning her future – without him. Drinking heavily one evening at the Nordic Ring club she met the Hohenzollern Prince August-Wilhelm (Goebbels' comrade, 'Auwi,' who had now joined the S.A. with a suitably high rank). The prince suggested that the party needed people like her. She heard Goebbels speak soon after; fascinated, she enrolled at the Nazi party's minuscule West End branch run by the young engine-driver's son Karl Hanke. Her Party membership dated from September 1, 1930.[24] She found herself taking charge of the local Women's Order. From there she gravitated to headquarters at No. 10 Hedemann Strasse. With her above-average education she was appointed secretary to Dr Hans Meinshausen, Goebbels' deputy as gauleiter.[25]

Goebbels, it must be said, had little going for him at this time. He was a cripple; his total monthly salary was one-eighth of Magda's monthly alimony; but she heard him speak again, and she passed him once as he came limping up the steps. 'I thought I might almost catch fire,' she told her mother excitedly,

'under this man's searching, almost devouring, gaze.'[26] She told Ello Quandt
that to judge by his suit Goebbels was obviously in need of, well, mothering.
A few weeks later it struck Günther Quandt, who still frequently met her, that
she talked of nothing but the Nazis. 'At first I thought it was just a passing fad
for the oratorical gift of Dr Goebbels,' he wrote. Her law-student lover also
noticed, and flared that she seemed to be losing her head to that clubfooted
loudmouth. 'You're mad,' she snapped. 'I could never love Goebbels!'

GOEBBELS HAD OTHER preoccupations right now. At the end of January 1931
an S.A. man had gunned down the Berlin communist Max Schirmer; four
days later Nazis shot dead the communist Otto Grüneberg in a Charlottenburg
street fight.[27] On February 4 police chief Grzesinski banned *Angriff* for two
weeks. Goebbels was also down with 'flu. What sickened him even more than
this was how close to the communists he found his position really was. After
one Reichstag interruption on the fifth a Social Democrat rounded on him
with the stinging rejoinder, 'That is from a gentleman . . . fully aware that
Messrs Hitler, Frick, Jung, etc., have been to the Ruhr several times to explain
their National Socialist program to the gentleman of heavy industry and to
demonstrate that they have nothing to fear from the National Socialist brand
of socialism.'

A few days later the government revoked the immunity of three hundred
deputies, including all the Nazis. Goebbels alone had eight criminal cases
pending. He recommended to his colleagues that rather than just becoming
'poorly paid extras' they should walk out *en masse*. Their salaries would stop,
but the tactics were undeniably sound. The move would demonstrate to voters
that the Nazis dissociated themselves from the government's rule by emergency
decree.

On February 10 the Nazis marched in, remained standing while their
bloc leader Franz Stöhr read out the tough declaration which Goebbels had
formulated, then marched out again. After that, one hundred police officers
raided Hedemann Strasse and searched the building. Goebbels' Lustgarten rally
of the fifteenth was banned on the usual pretext ('danger to peace and quiet').

'Your peace and quiet,' swore Goebbels in his diary, 'will be endangered soon
enough.'[28]

IT HAS BEEN a tense and angry week for Dr Goebbels in the Reichstag. At its
end Magda Quandt comes round to see him in his new, luxurious Steglitz
apartment. He finds himself captivated by this woman. Her dress is subtle,
her whole posture is that of a person who now knows where she is going.[29] It
is a Saturday – February 14, 1931 – and Goebbels enters certain code phrases,
circumlocutions, into his diary which show that this visit is not for mere
archival gossip: 'And stays for a very long time,' he carefully records. And,
'How are you, my queen?' The answer follows: '(1)'. Magda has seduced him,
after Olga only the second girl in his life to do so. Sunday finds him in a trance,

or 'replete with satiated happiness,' as he writes. Magda writes him a fond note the next day.[30]

Magda Quandt returns to her elegant leased apartment and servants, and Dr Goebbels goes over to Dortmund where twenty thousand people are waiting to hear him. In Hamburg he speaks to twelve thousand.[31] His mind is on her. When he speaks at Weimar, Anka's Weimar, he takes Magda with him. He phones Anka, speaks tersely with her, and decides that he can't stand her whining and her 'lack of discipline' any longer. Now that he has Magda he can afford to be standoffish.

He takes Magda to the automobile show in Berlin. She wants to buy a new car, but can't make up her mind. Does she buy him one? Suddenly he has a new Opel (it has been stolen already by March 9).[32] They have the usual rows. Magda writes a farewell note. Goebbels has seen it all before – 'the same old melody!' he writes, amused. He can handle it. She comes round for a 'very formal' talk and flounces out as though to leave. Goebbels holds the door open for her. 'You are so hard,' she murmurs, and relents.[33] She visits several times during March 1931, chats, laughs, makes music with him, meals for him, and – occasionally – love. On the ninth he adds '(2, 3)' to his score, and five days later '(4, 5)'.[34]

But mysteries abound. She is often sick; she does not yet invite him back to her own fine apartment in Reichskanzler Platz. Sometimes she is inexplicably away, or does not answer her phone. Jealousy wells up within him. At this time the adventure probably means very little to her; but not to him.[35] Goebbels convinces himself that he has drawn a historic line under his philanderings. 'I'm going to stop the womanizing,' he writes secretly on March 15, 'and favor just the one.'

IN HAMBURG the gauleiter Karl Kaufmann had once remarked to Goebbels that Brüning for one considered Göring mad.[36] Göring had certainly been unbalanced by Carin's near fatal illness during January 1931. After visiting her sickbed Goebbels wrote that he revered her, a word he had used before only for his mother.[37] He was alarmed by Göring's character regression, probably a result of his addiction. 'We've got to get him into a mental clinic in time,' he wrote despairingly. 'He mustn't go to the dogs like this.'[38] Hitler promised to tackle Göring about the morphine. But the aviator's behavior worsened to outright megalomania. 'He alternates,' observed Goebbels in February 1931, 'between imagining he's Reich chancellor and imagining he's defense minister. . . Today he's just ludicrous.[39]

After both men spoke at Essen to an audience of sixteen thousand, including the industrialists Krupp and Thyssen, Göring accompanied him back to Berlin but refused to discuss his drug problem. The gauleiter's remarks about him took on a bitter edge. After they had both addressed some twenty-five thousand people in Frankfurt, Goebbels wrote that Göring had spoken the 'usual crap.'[40] One Sunday he again tackled Göring about the addiction; the aviator's spluttered denials were too thin to be plausible to Goebbels.[41] They separated that evening 'half friends again,' as Goebbels noted, in which was implicit that they were now half enemies.[42]

ON MARCH 6, 1931 the gauleiter addressed another huge meeting at the Sport Palace. His audience greeted Grzesinski's two police observers with roars of 'Out!' lasting several minutes, and Goebbels heaped his own special kind of ridicule on them. On the following day *Angriff* repeated his words verbatim.[43] Seeking public sympathy, on the thirteenth he staged a stupid bomb plot: having ordered the S.A. man Eduard Weiss to open all mail addressed to him at headquarters he arranged for a crude homemade device to be delivered to him there.[44]

Although there is no doubt about Goebbels' authorship of the attack, he lied to his own diary about it.[45] More court actions crowded in on him – eight altogether during March.[46] On March 14 the Reichstag decided that he could be arrested after all. The courts declared Severing's ban on the Brownshirt uniform in Prussia unconstitutional.[47] On the fifteenth Grzesinski nevertheless repeated the ban, and he imposed a speaking prohibition on Goebbels in Berlin, in revenge for the Sport Palace episode. He instructed his police to prevent the gauleiter from speaking to transport workers in Hasenheide the next night.[48] Hitting back, *Angriff* instructed Berlin's Nazis to wear their uniforms and to sue Grzesinski if he ordered any arrests. The next day, two Nazis gunned down a communist deputy in Hamburg. The press called for a general ban on the party, and the speaking ban on Goebbels was extended to the whole of Prussia.[49]

After that Brüning's emergency decrees could no longer contain the rising discontent. Goebbels arrived at one huge Königsberg rally to find that he had been banned from even entering the hall, where twelve thousand had gathered to hear him.

Thousands of cheering East Prussians escorted him and Prince August-Wilhelm back to the railroad station, carrying the little Doctor shoulder-high up to the platform. As he climbed onto a bench, a police major ordered truncheons drawn and thirty of his officers waded in, laying out both Goebbels and the prince.[50] The incident was widely reported abroad.[51]

Magda Quandt visited the injured gauleiter upon his return to Berlin, and her accomplishments in bed that night ('6, 7') made up for his bruises. In his diary he passed over the irritable letters from Hella Koch, from Erika, and from Charlotte almost without comment. 'I now love just one,' he wrote.[52]

When Hitler now invited him down to the Obersalzberg for Easter, Goebbels surprisingly turned him down.[53] His notes had recently contained several disparaging references to that 'damned party home,' the Brown House; to Hitler's coffeehouse mentality and milieu; and to the Führer's softness and 'fanatical compromising' nature.[54] He spent Easter with Magda instead, and added two more notches to the score, '(8, 9)': Nine times in six weeks.[55] It was not, perhaps, enough to justify the jack-rabbit reputation which posterity would endow him with, and which he had carefully encouraged.

ON MARCH 26, the Reichstag adjourned for nearly seven months. Two days later Brüning issued an emergency decree allowing his government to ban any meetings, and to censor the leaflets and posters of any party. 'And Brüning is Göring's friend!' commented Goebbels sarcastically. He did not mind the ban on speaking. At the big Sport Palace meeting on March 27 a recording of his latest speech was played. But he did fear a ban on his newspaper, which was now printing eighty thousand twelve-page copies a day.[56] The supreme court declared Grzesinski's latest ban illegal. Meanwhile Hitler appealed to all his followers to avoid being provoked into illegal actions.[57]

This was particularly addressed to the S.A. The taut relationship between them and the party overhung Goebbels throughout that spring. He was torn between loyalty to Hitler, and his gratitude to these long-suffering streetfighters. In Munich Hitler had confided to him in October 1930 that he was gradually going to reconstruct the S.A. and recover total control of it.[58] But Goebbels found it hard not to sympathize with the criticisms of Munich voiced by his Berlin S.A. men. Their plight was unenviable: two-thirds of them were unemployed, including their Oberführer Bruno Wetzel.[59] While in Breslau one S.A. *Sturm* could not go on parade in the snow because they had no boots, they heard of the opulence of Hitler's new headquarters in Munich and of elite new S.S. units being raised which were no longer subordinate to the S.A. as they should have been.[60]

Both Walter Stennes, the supreme S.A. commander in eastern Germany including Berlin, and his subordinate commanders were already deeply concerned about Munich's 'wretched waffling about legality' and Hitler's persistent wooing of the bourgeois parties. When Hitler now demanded that the S.A. membership cough up another four thousand marks for a painting to go in his study, they were baffled.[61]

At the end of November 1930 Hitler had revealed to his party lieutenants his latest plans for the S.A. He was now their commander, with the pallid, flabby Ernst Röhm as his chief of staff. Goebbels had vaguely known Röhm since 1924 and had read his memoirs, *A Traitor's Story*.[62] After Röhm's return from Bolivia he had entered in his diary, 'He's nice to me and I like him. An open, upright soldier type.' Two weeks later he added, 'He's a dear fellow, but no match for Stennes.'[63] Stennes however noticed only that Röhm was a blatant homosexual, who made few friends other than other notorious homosexuals like Karl Ernst and his lover Paul Röhrbein.[64] Stennes had nothing but contempt for Röhm and his unmanly ways.[65]

Dr Goebbels deduced that Hitler intended to phase out the regional S.A. commanders like Stennes. He suspected that Stennes was plotting to set up a revolutionary Free Corps – 'proof,' he felt, 'how naïve these fellows are about politics.'[66] But Goebbels was even more naïve. He solemnly tipped off Röhm in

January 1931 that Röhrbein was a homosexual, and noted afterward that Röhm was 'very concerned.'[67] Only six weeks later did he learn the truth about Röhm from Stennes. 'Disgusting!' he expostulated in his diary – his own sexuality being at last a matter of record. 'Here too Hitler is paying too little attention. The party must not be allowed to become a paradise for poofters.'[68]

Fearing Stennes' growing influence meanwhile, Hitler removed several S.A. regions (North Saxony, East Prussia, Danzig, and Mecklenburg) from his control. Stennes sent a long letter of complaint to Röhm, causing Goebbels to wonder if Stennes was not biting off more than he could chew.[69] Röhm personally came to Berlin and there was a furious row with Stennes which ended with a categorical refusal by the S.A. commander to swear obedience to Röhm.[70]

This put Goebbels in a dilemma. Not only did he need the S.A. stormtroopers, they provided much of the staff of *Angriff* too. In Munich on March 23 Ernst Röhm told him he was going to get rid of critics like Captain Stennes.[71] Goebbels was horrified and urged both Hitler and Röhm not to do it. But Hitler's loyalty was to Röhm, his old and intimate friend. In his diary, Goebbels began writing alibis: 'If there's got to be a clean break,' he recorded on March 25, 'then I'm with Hitler.' At the same time he told Stennes' men that he was with *them*.[72] He had no choice but to equivocate. The Berlin S.A. was approaching flashpoint. All their hatreds were mirrored in the sarcastic samizdat newsletters which now began to circulate in Berlin. One dated March 20 referred mockingly to 'our own Aryan son Dr Goebbels, whom race-experts have branded an Israelite,' and described cruelly how he had left one meeting early via a back door 'on account of his aching paw.'[73]

This S.A. crisis came to a head in the last week of March 1931. Karl Hanke, the young and virile commander of Goebbels' West End district, told him of rumors that Röhm was about to dismiss Stennes. Fearing this would bring his empire tumbling down, Goebbels said he would fight tooth and claw to prevent it. Stennes had gone to Pomerania that Tuesday, March 31, ostensibly to cool down S.A. hotheads.[74] In his absence, a telegram arrived in Berlin ordering all his senior officers to Weimar for a meeting with Hitler. It was clear that he was about to dismiss Stennes. According to police Intelligence, he also intended to relieve Goebbels as gauleiter.[75] Goebbels had already left to speak in Dresden; from there he drove straight on to Weimar, to see Hitler. This may be the occasion which Elsa Bruckmann later related, when Hitler had planned to sack Goebbels for disloyalty – whereupon the gauleiter threw himself whining at his feet in a most unworthy manner.[76] On balance Hitler decided to keep Goebbels, but nothing could save Stennes.

Wetzel, the Berlin S.A. commander, had already received a phone call at around 8:30 P.M. reporting that Röhm had ordered Stennes' dismissal.[77] Wetzel's men decided to defy Hitler's summons to Weimar. At four A.M. Kurt Daluege, the regional S.S. chief (S.S. Oberführer Ost) typed an urgent warning to Röhm, reporting that since midnight these local S.A. commanders had been meeting in secret cabal in Berlin, and that mutiny was once again in the air. Daluege in fact suspected that Stennes was acting in cahoots with the government, because the mutineers had learned – perhaps through government wiretaps – of Hitler's intentions. 'Jahn has told them,' reported Daluege to Röhm, referring to Stennes' chief of staff, 'that Stennes is to be dismissed by our Führer at a meeting in Weimar at midday today April 1.' The mutineers, he added, had decided to defy Hitler and send a delegation to *Goebbels* in Weimar to win him over for 'an independent freedom movement.'[78]

Things were thus in an unholy mess. It was now April 1, 1931. At about four-thirty A.M. Stennes arrived back in Berlin from Pomerania. A few hours later he was wakened with news that the papers were reporting he had been dismissed. He discounted the story and went back to sleep. Meanwhile his commanders in Berlin went on the rampage, mutinied, and seized Goebbels' gau headquarters and the *Angriff* editorial offices in the Hedemann Strasse building.

Thus the second 'Stennes putsch' began. Perhaps this is a misnomer. Stennes himself was still largely in the dark. At two-thirty P.M. he received, first a registered letter from Röhm dismissing him, then orders from Hitler to go to Weimar.[79] But the fat was already in the fire. This time the S.A.'s political actions met with active support from both Goebbels' staff and the *Angriff*'s employees. Dr Ludwig Weissauer published a statement in the newspaper backing Stennes. Whatever Goebbels' private feelings, however, he knew which side his bread was buttered. He wrote unhesitatingly in his diary, 'I stand loyal to Hitler. . . The S.A. must come into line.' He applied for a court order to evict the S.A. trespassers from the building. Stennes was still floundering. He sent this telegram to Hitler in Weimar: 'IS RÖHM'S DISMISSAL ORDER VALID, I.E., BACKED BY YOU? SIGNED STENNES.' Hitler responded ambiguously: 'YOU ARE NOT TO ASK QUESTIONS BUT HAVING RECEIVED A PROPER ORDER ARE TO REPORT TO WEIMAR AT ONCE WITH THE COMMANDERS AS LISTED. SIGNED ADOLF HITLER.'

By now Daluege was also in Weimar. Hitler gave Goebbels sweeping powers to smash the putsch in Berlin, 'regardless of consequences,' and to dismiss the disruptive elements regardless of rank or office in the party. 'You have my backing,' he wrote in this document, 'whatever you do.'[80] At that evening's public meeting in Weimar both Goebbels and Daluege swore undying loyalty to Hitler.[81] In Berlin meanwhile Stennes had printed thousands of handbills announcing that Goebbels was sacked as gauleiter for 'breach of faith' and replaced by Wetzel; the handbill once more rubbed in the Brown House scandal.[82] Ignoring frantic appeals from his headquarters to return to Berlin, Goebbels went south to Munich, sharing a railroad compartment with Hitler.

Hitler was undoubtedly shaken by these events. The next day's bourgeois press crowed over his embarrassment. In an article in the *VB* he vigorously attacked Stennes for his treachery.[83] Goebbels now wondered which dark powers might have bribed Stennes and Weissauer to act as they had. The party later obtained copies of urgent Berlin police instructions ordering police officers not to seize Stennes' handbills announcing his takeover.[84] Hitler signed an authorization for Goebbels to act 'ruthlessly' in purging his Berlin gau. 'Better no National Socialist movement at all,' this read, 'than a party in disarray, without discipline or obedience.'[85] It was time for backbiting all round. Hearing that Göring had pleaded with Hitler to give these powers to him, Goebbels noted: 'I'll never forgive Göring. . . He's a mound of frozen crap.'[86] Acting from Munich headquarters, he issued appeals for loyalty and sacked the mutinous S.A. men. Stennes took perhaps two hundred others with him, and began a brief flirtation with Dr Otto Strasser.

WORRIED and ill Goebbels finally slunk back to Berlin on Wednesday April 8, 1931. Paul Schultz, who had replaced Stennes, assured him that the Berlin S.A. now stood behind him. Goebbels' five district commanders confirmed that evening that not one party official had defected, only S.A. men.[87] Addressing his officials on the tenth he explained why he had put so much distance between himself and Berlin during the crisis. During a battlefield crisis, he said, the generals did not go into the mutinous trenches either.[88] 'Of course the whole Jewish press is shrieking with glee,' he realized privately, and confined himself to bed with a thermometer for company.[89]

16: *The Stranger and the Shadow*

THE THERMOMETER'S MERCURY THREAD has climbed to 40°C. Goebbels is ill, but Magda phones only once, saying she's at the Quandt estate in Mecklenburg.[1] He struggles out of bed on the Friday April 10, 1931, to speak to two thousand party officials. On Saturday he learns that she is back in Berlin; she does not contact him. Ilse and Olga fuss around the invalid. He is too weak to resist. On Sunday he phones Magda's home. She is not there; later however she phones him, and admits that she has been seeing off a young lover – but he has brought things to a head and fired a revolver at her. She tells Goebbels she is injured (in fact the Jewish law student's bullet has struck the door frame next to her. 'If you had really aimed at me and hit me,' she scoffs, 'I might have been impressed. I find your behavior ridiculous').[2]

Too late Goebbels realizes how much he loves her. Must he always be lonely? These and other thoughts lay siege to him. He spends Sunday pining for her and writing a gripping description of his jealous delirium. Perhaps thirty times he telephones her home, but nobody answers. He glares at the phone, willing it to ring. Staying home on Monday the thirteenth he at last reaches her by phone.

They drive out to a remote forest house at Pichelsdorf. She pours out her heart about the grief her crazed ex-lover has caused her. She answers his reproaches with floods of tears, the last resort of feminine culpability; but she wishes to spend Saturday with the other man, to say farewell. She refuses Goebbels' ultimatum to spend that Saturday with him. 'Thus it is over,' writes Goebbels. Unconsciously scriptwriting again, he adds: 'She exits weeping.'[3]

ON THE TWELFTH he had returned to gau headquarters for the first time since the putsch. Everybody was very kind to him and the S.A. stood smartly to attention. But there were problems. The account books showed that *Angriff* was deep in debt.[4] He instructed Hans Hinkel, Weissauer's successor, to cut back its size from twelve to eight pages.[5] His deputy Mainshausen warned that Göring was double-crossing them. Goebbels needed few warnings on that score.[6]

The next morning he was back in court, charged with having said in a speech at the Veterans' Building in 1929, 'We don't speak of corruption in Berlin or bolshevism at City Hall. No! We just say Isidor Weiss, and that says it all.'[7] He was fined two hundred marks on one count, fifteen hundred marks for having picked on Weiss 'because of his Jewish origins;' still running a high fever, he limped out. He suspected traitors every-where. 'Keep on marching' he penned into his diary. 'Don't look back!'[8] There seemed no end to the court actions. On the seventeenth he was fined two thousand marks, then five hundred, and finally one hundred more for contempt of court. More summonses were heaped onto his desk.[9] He resolved to take revenge on all the Isidors of this world when the time came.

A severe depression seized him, a mental crisis which he acknowledged only when he deemed that it had passed.[10] Magda's shenanigans had triggered it. There was a 'shadow' still lurking around her apartment. Apparently she had had a stormier past than the comparatively innocent Dr Goebbels had suspected. Insane with jealousy, he trusted nobody. The word *spies* surfaced more often in his diary. He searched for them at his headquarters, he even suspected Hinkel; his political life seemed more arduous than ever, a constant round of strange hotel beds briefly sighted at three A.M., of six A.M. railroad platforms for the return to Berlin, of persecution, court hearings, prohibitions, and the constant fear of violence or even assassination.[11]

Grzesinski enforced a new three-month ban on Goebbels speaking – which sometimes meant listening to the pompous and vapid Hermann Göring standing in for him. Hitler now entrusted the aviator Göring with important missions abroad. In May 1931 he visited Rome and returned with a signed photograph of Mussolini for the Führer. 'Jack of all trades,' sniffed Goebbels, meaning master of none.[12]

Eight more court appearances faced him late that April. 'Maddening,' he recorded. 'But I'm not going to lose my nerve.'[13] At Itzehoe near Hamburg he faced a four-month prison sentence but was acquitted.[14] Squirming under Grzesinski's speaking ban, on April 25 he reluctantly signed an undertaking not to make fun of the police observers assigned to his meetings any more.[15] Another hearing was scheduled at Moabit for April 27. He notified the court however that he could not miss an important Nazi meeting in Munich. But the Berlin courts had issued a bench warrant after his non-appearance. As he was eating at the Rose Garden hotel three detectives arrested him and escorted him to the night train to Berlin. 'So much for immunity!' he fumed. 'With a Barmat, a Sklarek and a Kutisker,' declared *Angriff* that morning, referring to the Jewish racketeers, 'they didn't go to such lengths. But then they weren't the elected representatives of sixty thousand *Germans* – just major embezzlers!'[16]

Press photographers crowded the platform as the train arrived back in Berlin. 'The Judenpresse is howling with joy,' Goebbels noted. In Room 664 at the Moabit courthouse (*Angriff* helpfully told its readers where the eight new cases were to be heard) the world's press awaited him.[17] He told the judges what he thought of them, then sat down and refused to speak another word. He was given a month's suspended jail sentence, and heavy fines. Choking with rage he lodged an appeal.[18]

To his lawyer he snarled, indicating the prosecutor Dr Stenig, 'Let's make a note of that man for later.'[19]

May brought still more cases.[20] But daylight was filtering into this long dark tunnel of police harassment. On June 12 he was again acquitted. 'The courts,' he gloated, 'are getting a whiff of things to come' – a reference to the growing likelihood that Brüning's days in office were numbered. 'Then it's our turn.'[21]

KEEPING A TRYST with Magda at the five-star Kaiserhof hotel, he recognizes that the other man, the 'shadow,' is still coming between them.[22] Fretting, he spends his evenings alone at Steglitz fingering his piano keyboard, leafing idly through a book, or fitfully dozing. He phones countless times without reaching her. After one colossal Sport Palace gathering she invites him back to her own luxurious apartment for the first time. The 'shadow' has gone. Her elegant suite of seven rooms includes a music room, and quarters for her guests and servants. He decides that the worst is over between them. His diary soon finds him making plans for the future with her: and he is no longer keeping score.[23]

Shadows flit in and out from his own past. Magda remains a vexatious enigma still, often inexplicably unpunctual for their dates. Once she tells him that 'a stranger' has warned her that Dr Goebbels is a Jew, and has shown her an original letter 'stolen from the gau headquarters files' written a decade earlier by Goebbels to Director Cohnen, a family friend at Mönchen Gladbach. Cohnen was the gauleiter's *real* father, suggests the stranger, who also mentions Peter Simons, the husband of Goebbels' maternal aunt Anna. 'This is what I have to put up with,' winces Goebbels, puzzling over the stranger's identity.[24] (The 'stolen' document is probably a product of Magda's own feline snooping around while working in his personal archives, but this evidently does not occur to him.)

The two spend Whitsun on her ex-husband's estate, Severin in Mecklenburg; Günther Quandt's manager, a leading local Nazi, lets them in. Alone at last they iron out their remaining differences. Sometimes she still wounds him with an ill-considered word, but the wound soon heals.[25] He longs for a hearth and home. He begins talking about setting up a matrimonial home when victory is theirs; this is comfortingly vague, and she goes along with that.[26] After he returns to Berlin – alone, as she has asked to stay on for another day in this country idyll – he writes, 'When we have conquered the Reich we shall become man and wife.'[27] In fact Magda probably entertained little real ambition to harness her uxorial ambitions to such an uncertain chariot. He writes her a real love letter – the first such essay in ten years.[28] Visiting her to give her a clock a few days later, he is thunderstruck to find the Shadow still living there; Magda tells him that since the student will not budge, she is moving out and will have the police evict the trespasser.[29] As a sop to Goebbels, she agrees he shall have the right to walk young Harald to the Herder school across the square.

After speaking at Erfurt Goebbels meets Anka Stalherm and breaks the news about Magda to her. He is pleased to see that Anka goes to pieces. She wants not to believe him, thinks she can hook him back even now. But it is too late – 'I am with Magda,' he vows to his diary, 'and shall stay with her.'[30] When his latest book *Struggle for Berlin* appears later in the year, he will have it mailed to Anka with a typed note ('Dear Party member . . .') signed by his secretary.[31]

THE POLICE LIFTED the speaking ban on May 1, 1931; and how the thousands cheered when he rose at the Sport Palace that evening. But the ban had hurt. His gau was in debt.[32] He decided on a two-month plan to double membership. By mid-June 1931 it had risen to about twenty thousand.[33]

Angriff too was entering troubled times. On May 4 the editor Dagobert Dürr had finally begun serving his two-month sentence for libeling Dr Weiss. Each visit in jail was a reminder to Goebbels of the volcano rim around which he himself was dancing.[34]

He found he had much more in common with the ordinary S.A. men than with the party's self-important aristocracy. 'We are still a worker's party,' he wrote. Göring irritated him the most. At a rally in Saxony he cold-shouldered the former aviator. 'He's sick,' he felt. 'Looks a wreck.'[35] 'He really does go creeping up Hitler's ass,' he added crudely. 'Were he not so fat he might succeed, too.' In Munich for a leadership conference on June 9 however he found himself arguing alone against this 'disgusting . . . big-mouthed slob.' 'I have few friends in the party,' he realized, yet again. 'Virtually just Hitler.'[36]

AS THE RECESSION bit deeper, the central parties in the government flailed at the parties on the left and right. On June 16 Brüning enacted an emergency press decree. Berlin's police chief Grzesinski boasted, 'My powers have been augmented just as I desired.' The next fourteen days would see the prohibition of *Angriff*, the *VB*, and a string of other papers, Nazi and bourgeois alike. The press protested vigorously. When the *Frankfurter Post* was banned, the rival *Frankfurter Zeitung* bravely reprinted the offending sentences for its readers to judge.[37] *Angriff* reappeared on the nineteenth.

Hitler himself started spending more time in Berlin. Police agents sighted him with Goebbels at the Kaiserhof on May 9.[38] Jealous of their intimacy, Goebbels' rivals continued to spread rumors of his imminent resignation. He published a defiant denial.[39] That same evening he staged the gau's annual general meeting at the Sport Palace – the first time that any party had dared to hire the huge arena for such a purpose. He blamed Himmler, who had taken over leadership of the S.S. from Erhard Heiden, for the rumors; he found that the S.S. was now spying on his headquarters and demanded, visiting Munich on July 2, that they desist. After speaking to forty thousand at Dresden's cycle-racetrack[40] he set off on a month's seaside vacation; he took Magda – 'she is a lady, a woman, and a lover' – and a secretary Ilsa Bettge, whose role was less clearly defined.

With Goebbels temporarily absent, on August 1 Hitler appointed the virtually unknown journalist Dr Otto Dietrich as chief of his new Press Office. Dietrich, six weeks older than Goebbels, had got to know Hitler only recently, while working for the *Rheinisch-Westfälische Zeitung*. Goebbels loathed all journalists; but for Dietrich he would reserve a very special fury until the end.[41]

THAT JULY HE SPENDS five weeks with Magda in a cottage on the cliffs at Sankt Peter listening to storm rains pounding the roof while the gray-white waves of the North Sea lash the rocks below. He makes love to her, he plays the piano, and he begins a new book, *The Struggle for Berlin*, dictating a new chapter every day or so.

Unemployment has passed the five-million mark. Brüning's miseries are music to Goebbels' ears. He bickers sometimes with Magda, probing remorselessly into the darker crannies of her past. He dredges up noisome episodes, which he attributes to her wayward manner and tries to forget.[42] The more she teases him with stories of past lovers, the more helplessly jealous he becomes. It seems that some of these old flames are not extinguished even now.[43]

No matter how loving Magda is, he cannot forget that before him she loved another. 'She has loved too much,' he writes, 'and keeps telling me only the half of it. And I lie awake until the small hours lashed by jealousy.'[44] Driven by these powerful emotional engines he has completed three hundred pages of the manuscript when he returns to Berlin: he truly loves Magda, but a shadow still darkens the horizon.

IMPORTANT NEW FACES met him at his gau headquarters. The dynamic, heavily built, square-jawed Karl Hanke, aged twenty-seven, was his new chief of organization.[45] He had a dry, ironic manner that belied his tough, no-nonsense attitude. Berlin's new propaganda chief was Karoly Kampmann; determined to force back the rising Munich tide of bourgeois *Reaktion* – best translated by the word 'diehards' – Goebbels ordered Kampmann to concentrate his efforts on recruiting new members from Berlin's factory floors.[46] Millions of leaflets and stickers were printed with the new slogan, 'Into the factories!'[47] That was the only place, Goebbels would write, where the workers could be won over – and he intended to gain ten thousand new members in the next three months.[48] In consequence of this shift of emphasis to the factory floor, the regular pace of his public propaganda slowed down that autumn; in October, his gau would stage only 125 public meetings.[49]

DURING 1931 the political violence worsened. Since May 1930 there had been twenty-nine political murders in Berlin alone – including twelve communists, six Nazis, one Stahlhelm member, two Social Democrats, and four policemen.[50] In July 1931 Ernst Röhm put a new man in charge of Berlin's S.A., the thirty-four-year-old aristocrat Count Wolf Heinrich von Helldorff. Helldorff had joined the party only in August 1930; Goebbels, meeting him a month later, had not liked him at the time. A whiff of perfume caught his nostrils, and he

wondered if Helldorff were a poofter like the rest. He had since then tackled
Hitler about Röhm's homosexuality, about which a Munich newspaper had
made headlines in June.[51] Goebbels concluded that Helldorff's appointment
was a backdoor affair with Röhm and his bisexual adjutant Karl Ernst. 'The
future of the S.A. looks grim to me,' wrote Goebbels. '§175 [the clause of the
penal code on homosexuality] casts its shadow right across it.'[52]

Yet he soon came round to liking, even adoring, Helldorff, forming an
enduring friendship with the scoundrel which, in the words of the Spanish
proverb, tells us much about Goebbels himself. Born on October 14, 1896, the
arrogant, wastrel son of a blue-blooded landowner, Helldorff was a thoroughly
nasty piece of work, a bully, a Jew-baiter, and a murderer. Police records showed
one warrant against him in 1922 for manslaughter, and another for carrying an
unlicensed weapon.[53] During the Stennes revolt he had sided with the insurgents,
saying 'Hitler is a traitor.'[54] None of this appeared to bother Goebbels. Early
in September 1931 he briefed Helldorff and his chief of staff Karl Ernst to stage
an operation – ostensibly a demonstration by the unemployed – to rough up
Jews along Kurfürstendamm on their New Year's day, Yom Kippur.[55] On the
chosen day, September 12, Helldorff cruised up and down the boulevard in
his green Opel, according to police reports, directing his stormtroopers, who
were disguised as ordinary passers-by, to set on anybody who looked like a
Jew.[56] The police however had been tipped off – one disgruntled S.A. man in
Potsdam said later that it was odd that the police learned what had happened
at a secret briefing attended *only* by Goebbels, Helldorff, and Ernst[57] – and
arrested Helldorff with Ernst, another member of his staff Heini Gewehr, and
thirty-four other S.A. men.[58] (More likely the informer was Goebbels' own
secretary Ilse Stahl.)[59]

The police docket six days later described Helldorff's private life as messy –
he was swamped with unpaid bills, currently separated from his wife, and not
on speaking terms with his family, and he had all but bankrupted his family
estate at Wolmirstedt. The court sentenced him to six months in prison as
ringleader of the riot but he did not serve one day.[60] At Helldorff's appeal in
January Goebbels stood by his new friend, screamed at the prosecutor Dr
Stenig, outrageously insulted the court, demanded that the chief of police
produce his informant as a witness, and flatly refused to testify otherwise,
bringing about the collapse of the prosecution case and earning a fine of five
hundred marks for contempt.

Helldorff's sentence was reduced to a piffling fine of one hundred marks.[61]
(His lawyer was Roland Freisler, whom he would meet again under different
circumstances after July 20, 1944.) Helldorff's streetfighters were less fortunate:
they received prison sentences of up to two years for affray.[62] This inequality
widened the breach between Goebbels and the S.A. men, and that winter saw
several intemperate leaflets circulating in Berlin claiming that he and Helldorff
had left them in the lurch.[63]

His attitude toward the S.A. officers became ambivalent. He began sniping against Röhm.[64] But he kept up his support for the 'army's' rank and file. On September 11, 1931 – the day before the Kurfürstendamm riot – he resorted to his old propaganda tricks at a Sport Palace fund-raiser for the S.A. clinic, at which he presented six recent S.A. casualties.

On Goebbels' instructions [wrote one of the six] we were given brand-new white hospital gowns and the staff at the party clinic began to bandage us. One of us who just had a bad headache was given a gigantic turban bandage. Another . . . who had been kicked in the stomach was given a large and totally pointless bandage around his abdomen. As we entered the Sport Palace it was announced that we were the 'victims of political terrorism.' The resulting applause was deafening.[65]

Still ruling by emergency decree, on October 6 Chancellor Brüning empowered the police to shut down 'dens of activities hostile to the state.' Grzesinski and Weiss immediately sent in their police to evict the S.A. and S.S. from the hostels that Goebbels had set up for them in Berlin, tossing the beds and furniture into the street. Hundreds of Nazis, already unemployed, now became homeless too. The steam-head of hatred slowly built up pressure.

To the authorities' distress Adolf Hitler now moved his political headquarters away from Munich – where a personal tragedy, the suicide of his niece Geli in his apartment, had deeply shocked him – to Berlin. Burying for ever the womanizing, indolent, procrastinating Hitler of old, he retained a suite of rooms in the Kaiserhof hotel, within leering distance of the Reich chancellery. Here he held court with his henchmen like Röhm, Hess, and Julius Schaub. Grzesinski and Weiss were shocked by their government's lack of dignity in tolerating this; their agents learned that Hitler was meeting millionaire businessmen including even Günther Quandt at the Kaiserhof, and that they were pouring money into the Nazi coffers having accepted that Brüning was not going to rescue Germany.[66]

THE LOCALS JOSTLE and vie with each other for Hitler's ear. Göring, his political attaché in Berlin, is also overshadowed by tragedy, as his wife Carin has now contracted her final illness and returned to Stockholm with no hope of recovering. Goebbels tries to buy from the prosecutor's office the documents incriminating Röhm. Röhm, stung by Goebbels' campaign against him, tells Hitler that all Berlin is gossiping about Goebbels' affair with the former Mrs Quandt.[67] But this backfires on Röhm, as Goebbels now often hangs around the lobby of the Kaiserhof with Magda taking tea. Once they send young Harald Quandt, now nearly ten, upstairs to see the Führer wearing the little blue uniform Magda has sewn for him. Harald gives Hitler the appropriate salute and says that he feels twice as strong when wearing a uniform. Goebbels invites Hitler downstairs to meet Magda – 'the divorced wife of the industrialist you saw earlier,' he adds. A stickler for etiquette, Hitler asks Göring whether there is any reason why he should not be seen with Magda. 'No,' admits Göring, 'but you can't be too careful with a "Madame Pompadour."' The name means nothing to Hitler, and he does not grasp that Magda is in a relationship with his propaganda chief.[68]

Thus the three points of an extraordinary triangle converge – Hitler, Magda, and Goebbels. Over tea Magda, not quite thirty, and the freshly bereaved Hitler, twelve years her senior, feast their eyes on each other. To Hitler she looks uncannily like Geli;[69] while Magda, imbued by this time with Nazi lore, feels she is in the presence of a demi-god. Hours later, in his upstairs suite, Hitler remarks to his henchmen that in Geli he believed he had found something almost divine. 'I thought these feelings were dead and buried,' he adds. 'But today these same feelings have suddenly overwhelmed me again.'

For an instant he seems to have fantasized about Magda; she told her mother that he had made cautious and discreet advances to her.[70] His reverie lasts however only a few hours. After midnight he learns that Magda has casually invited Schaub, the S.S. commander Sepp Dietrich, and his chauffeur back to her apartment for drinks; Dr Goebbels then shows up there, letting himself in with a key, and declares stiffly that he is somewhat surprised to find them there at such a late hour. Hitler is clearly astonished to hear this from them: Goebbels, that limping little runt, has won this Germanic beauty? He pulls a wry face and tries to laugh off his disappointment. 'It was just a brief relapse,' he confesses to an aide.[71]

Carin Göring died early on October 17. Hitler took this fresh personal loss hard and again spoke wistfully to the Nazi economics adviser Dr Otto Wagener about Magda Quandt. 'This woman,' he mused, 'might yet play a role in my life. . . . She could become a second Geli for me. It's a pity,' he continued, thinking out loud, 'that she is not married.' He was worried about appearances. Wagener took the hint, and we have his probably reliable account of what followed.

That day, October 17, and the next Hitler and Goebbels were both due to attend a rally by the S.A. at Brunswick. Wagener invited Magda to go in his large 100-horsepower Horch.[72] On the drive over, Wagener stopped for a picnic and put an unusual proposition to her: Hitler, he said, was a rare genius who needed a woman's gentle influence; she must be able to help the Führer to find himself as a human being – somebody to accompany him to the opera, and to entertain him to tea with the finest porcelain. 'This woman could be you.'

'But I would have to be married to somebody,' she pointed out.

'Correct,' he said, and mentioned Goebbels. Magda was hesitant. 'But for Adolf Hitler,' she bravely announced, 'I am willing to do anything.' She promised to keep Wagener informed.

It seems to have been an unusual bargain all round. Magda later told her sister-in-law Ello Quandt that Goebbels attached one condition to their marriage, if he was *quasi* to share her with Hitler, namely that he be allowed extra-marital adventures; a man of his vitality needed this emotional leeway, he argued.[73] Early in November she phoned Wagener to say that they would both be coming to Munich a few days later: 'I have come to keep my promise.' Over lunch with Hitler they announced their engagement and he attended their little hotel celebration afterwards. 'The mood was so carefree,' recalled Wagener, 'that I had the feeling that three people had at last found happiness.'

THE REICHSTAG was due to reconvene after its seven-month recess on October 13, 1931. On the tenth President von Hindenburg sent for Hitler to size him up. He was not impressed. On the following day, in an attempt to concert their opposition, Hitler chaired a meeting with the bourgeois opposition leaders at Bad Harzburg. The upshot was the formation of a 'Harzburg Front' against Brüning. On the fourteenth the Nazis reentered the Reichstag, but only briefly because two days later they walked out again.

By the end of the year there were 5,660,000 registered unemployed – a desperate people turning to the Nazis for their salvation, and a regime determined to stay in office by hook or by crook. On December 8 Brüning issued still more emergency decrees, banning political uniforms and prohibiting all political assemblies until the new year. Two days later Hitler held court again at the Kaiserhof with Röhm, Hess, Ernst 'Putzi' Hanfstaengl, and Schaub; the next day police headquarters learned that Hitler was conferring all morning with the Ruhr steel millionaires Albert Vögler and Fritz Thyssen, and planned to hold a press conference with American journalists. Grzesinski pleaded with Severing to ban at least the press conference as an 'illegal assembly,' or failing that to deport Hitler from Prussia as *persona non grata*: the Berlin police could then forcibly put him on the midday train to Munich. President von Hindenburg however disapproved – another sign that the Nazis were coming in from the cold.

HITLER HAD BEGUN visiting Magda Quandt's apartment on Reichskanzler Platz more often than Göring's. Both Goebbels and Gregor Strasser welcomed this – the Görings, said Strasser, had always had a houseful of fortune-hunters hoping to meet the Führer. ('I myself get on quite well with Goebbels,' Strasser told Wagener.) With Carin now dead, Göring moved permanently into the Kaiserhof. Fleeing from the political atmosphere there, Hitler became a still more frequent visitor to Magda's household. She served her home-baked pastries to Hitler and fussed over him, while he relaxed and expatiated upon the cretins who claimed to admire the degenerate modern works of art. 'Dr Goebbels,' he said casually, 'I want you to think over how we're to stop this rot when we take over and you're in charge of all government propaganda.'

The Goebbels wedding was fixed for December 19, 1931. As a divorcee and convert to protestantism, Magda could not marry under the rites of the catholic church. Goebbels' plea to the bishop of Berlin for a waiver was denied. Marrying as a protestant, he would be excommunicated. 'He thereupon saw no further reason to pay their church tax,' said Hitler years later, mocking the church's hypocrisy. 'But the church informed him that excommunication . . . did not affect the obligation to pay up as before.'[74]

Hitler acted as one witness, and General von Epp as the other. Since a Berlin wedding was out of the question – the communists would have raised mayhem – it was solemnized at Severin, the Quandt estate in Mecklenburg. Quandt did not hear about this until afterwards; he stopped paying alimony forthwith.[75] The village notary of Goldenbow performed the legal ceremony, then Dr Wenzel, a pastor from Berlin, officiated at the protestant ceremony in the chapel at nearby Frauenmark; a swastika banner draped the altar.[76]

Magda's mother came, but not her father, who disapproved of Goebbels; she had stitched together a little brown S.A. uniform for her son Harald to wear as a pageboy. 'We accept the obligation to bring up our children in the evangelical-lutheran faith,' the couple affirmed.[77]

As for Joseph Goebbels, if Magda had looked closely, she would have seen that her new husband was wearing a Gold tiepin shaped like a wolf's head – a gift, he had once told a friend, from a girl he had become very fond of at university.[78]

17: *The Man of Tomorrow*

LEAVING MAGDA ALONE, Dr Goebbels spent Christmas Eve 1931 with the S.A. Nationwide, the party now had over eight hundred thousand members. Two years later he published a popular edition of his diaries for the coming months entitled *From the Kaiserhof to the Reich Chancellery.* The book would sell half a million copies by 1939.[1]

Textual comparison with the handwritten original, which has survived on Nazi microfiches in Moscow,[2] shows that Goebbels edited them less severely than his critics believed. There are the usual exaggerations. The diary's twenty thousand people listening to him speak in Leipzig become '30,000' in *Kaiserhof.*[3] His meetings are always 'overflowing,' and with the right class of people, 'almost all artisans;'[4] 'virtually only workers' in Essen, and a Sport Palace 'brimming with workers' in Berlin.[5] 'He who has the working man,' he pronounces, 'has the people.' He learns more, so he writes, from a sleeping-car conductor than from far more august gentlemen.[6] The published diary also treats President von Hindenburg with far greater respect ('this venerable figure' and 'the grand old man')[7] than does the original handwritten text.

As for Hitler, the image that Goebbels offers readers of his book is of a clear-thinking, resolute, pragmatic Führer who never hesitates unless for tactical advantage. 'He has the tougher nerves and the greater staying power,' writes Goebbels in his book.[8] Banished from the printed page is the image of Hitler Cunctator, the prevaricating Munich coffeeshop demagogue familiar from the handwritten diaries of previous years. 'The Führer is the best raconteur I know,' he writes.[9] 'Wonderful,' he writes of Hitler's final appointment as chancellor, 'how simple the Führer is in his greatness, and how great in his simplicity.'[10]

In editing *Kaiserhof* he has however settled a few old scores. Gregor Strasser lurks through his apparently clairvoyant essay as a sinister figure unrecognizable as the man of bonhomie and talent of whom Goebbels has in fact written so recently in the diary. 'There is one man in the organization trusted by nobody,' he thunders in *Kaiserhof.* 'And this man's name is Gregor Strasser!'[11] Unlike the real man, the book's Strasser is a boring and ineffective speaker, 'the one of our number whom our opponents most love – which tells strongly against him.'[12] Hermann Göring too is barely recognizable. Gone are the references to his morphine addiction; no longer a 'mound of frozen crap,' Göring is a massive and powerful speaker against defense minister Wilhelm

* *Sounds like Karl Marx. "Workers of the world, unite."*

133

Groener.[13] In one handwritten entry he has called Göring an arch prig
(*urpampig*); the published entry reads, 'I find myself agreeing with Goering
[*sic*] on all fundamental and tactical issues'.[14] The difference is that by 1934,
the year of publication, Göring has become a very dangerous man indeed to
cross.

The published diary represents its author, Goebbels, as the one comrade
whom Hitler trusts and regularly consults: Two men sitting like spiders in
the center of the Kaiserhof web, watching as their pawns move to topple first
Groener, then Brüning himself in the late spring of 1932.[15] There is no trace in it
of the depression that laid the gauleiter low the year before, and only the most
antiseptic glimpses of his private life.[16] The book records the gau's crippling
financial plight,[17] but suppresses any reference to the excesses which the private
diary reveals – for instance his craze for the latest automobiles. On May 22
the diary notes, 'The gentlemen from Mercedes come to beg forgiveness. I am
to get new coachwork [for the Opel Nuremberg] and a new Mercedes open
tourer. Now, that's talking!'[18]

The published text also casts a discreet veil over Hitler's private life. On the
anniversary of Geli's suicide, Hitler tearfully visits her grave in Vienna.[19] In
Kaiserhof however he is shown only as driving there for 'a private visit.' There is
more: The real diary shows that contrary to popular belief Miss Eva Braun, the
blonde laboratory assistant of Hitler's photographer, did not step straight into
Geli's shoes, but that a Miss Weinrich briefly claimed Hitler's attentions first.
'So that's Hitler's pet,' notes Goebbels. 'Poor taste. Glum girl. Moist hands.
Brr!' He finds her lunching with Hitler at the Osteria restaurant the next day.
'Pig stupid,' Goebbels decides, before allowing more charitably: 'How great
Hitler's longing for a woman must be!' He wondered what his chief saw in this
little flibbertigibbet – he ought to find a more respectable lady friend.[20]

There is not even a hint of this in the published *Kaiserhof* of course.

NINETEEN thirty-two would be a year of elections – one presidential, two
Reichstag, and five provincial. In most the National Socialists would increase
their vote. Goebbels brought the national propaganda directorate permanently
to Berlin from March 1, and campaigned tirelessly. He now had a vast following
in the capital. The regime could no longer ignore the Nazis. Brüning actually
invited Hitler for talks about extending Hindenburg's term of office.[21] After
discussing it with his partners in the Harzburg Front, Hitler published his
refusal in the *Völkischer Beobachter*, insisting on a new presidential election.[22]

To Brüning's embarrassment, deputy police chief 'Isidor' Weiss chose this
moment to ban Angriff for the tenth time in a year, for inciting contempt of
the Jews – in 1932 there were 172,672 Jews among Berlin's 4,024,165 population.[23]
On January 8 he shut down a meeting at the Sport Palace just as Goebbels had
begun speaking to fifteen thousand people, for inciting contempt of Weiss in
particular.[24] Enraged by Goebbels' behavior in court two weeks later during
the Helldorff appeal hearing – he had demanded that the police informant

testify in open court – Weiss slapped a fresh three-week gag on the gauleiter.[25] Weiss also telexed to every provincial governor in Germany: 'National Socialist deputy Dr Göbbels [*sic*] forbidden to speak here. Meetings only under proviso that G is not speaker, POLICE PRESIDENT BERLIN.'[26]

At the next few meetings organizers read out messages from Goebbels, until the police banned these too. The fight continued. On legal advice – and by now Goebbels was surrounded by eager lawyers willing to help – he deeded his personal library to a third person in case Weiss seized it on the pretext that it served the purposes of spreading revolution.

The tide of political violence was rising. Eighty-six Nazis were murdered during 1932; in twelve months Goebbels alone lost seven men, and the police seldom caught the murderers.

The killing of fifteen-year-old Herbert Norkus was particularly nasty. He and five pals had been distributing leaflets early one Sunday morning when they were overwhelmed by communists. The body of Norkus, son of a working-class Nazi from Plötzensee, was found in the entrance hall of No. 4 Zwingli Strasse, where he had bled to death from six stab wounds. Goebbels personally inspected the scene with its twenty-yard trail of dried blood and the one bloody handprint on the whitewashed wall. After going on to the morgue he wrote these words in his newspaper: 'There in the bleak gray twilight a yellowing childish face stares with half-open, empty eyes. The delicate features have been trampled to a bloody pulp.'[27] The next day he buried the artist Professor Ernst Schwarz, an S.A. officer gunned down in a communist ambush a week before.[28]

ONE evening Dr Goebbels returned home excited, limped up and down chain-smoking for a while, then told Magda he had had a splendid idea. 'Hitler himself must stand for president,' he said. Hitler however proved unexpectedly difficult to persuade: He wanted the opposition to come out with their candidates before making up his own mind. Still delaying his decision, on February 9 Hitler reviewed fifteen thousand of Röhm's stormtroopers in the Sport Palace. Goebbels enthused, 'Chief of Staff Röhm has pulled off a miracle.' This embarrassing laudatio appeared only in the first edition of *Kaiserhof*, and was struck out of all editions published after June 1934.[29]

Police chief Grzesinski gagged at the prospect of Hitler, his arch enemy, becoming president. This centurion of social democracy made little pretense of impartiality: 'How shameful it is,' he declared in Leipzig, 'that millions of Germans are trotting along behind a foreigner. . . How shameful that this foreigner, Hitler, not only conducts serious talks with the government on foreign affairs, but is able to speak to foreign press representatives about Germany's future and about Germany's foreign interests without somebody seeing him off with a dog-whip.'[30]

Dr Goebbels made hay with that remark.[31] In *Angriff* he pointed out how often Grzesinski had banned Nazis for precisely the same kind of incitement to violence.[32] 'Let's see,' he crowed in *Kaiserhof*, published when he already knew the answer, 'which of us gets seen off with a dog-whip out of Germany.'[33]

Hindenburg announced on February 15 that he intended to stand again. Taking Hitler's decision for granted, Goebbels began designing election posters with punchy slogans like *Schluss jetzt!* – 'Time's up!'[34] Hitler was still undecided. Goebbels decided to present him with a *fait accompli*, subjecting him to the pressure of public acclaim. To a cheering Sport Palace audience on February 22, Goebbels simply announced that Hitler would stand for president.[35] Hitler's Headquarters in Munich was horrified and issued an immediate embargo to the party newspaper, forbidding them to print Goebbels' announcement.[36] Hitler had no choice but to agree to stand. Writing in *Kaiserhof* two years later Goebbels claimed that Hitler had phoned him after the meeting to express his delight that the announcement had gone down so well.[37]

Whatever the truth of this self-serving statement, on February 23, speaking in a Reichstag building surrounded by riot police, Groener announced the election date as March 13. After that, speaking on behalf of the Nazis, Dr Goebbels launched into an hour-long assault on Dr Brüning, seated stony faced and with arms folded near him. In one year, he said, the police had banned *Angriff* twelve times; eight times the courts had ruled these bans illegal. 'The *Illustrierter Beobachter*,' he said, 'the picture magazine of the National Socialist movement, has today been banned until March 13 – *i.e.*, for the whole of the election period.' In the last three months twenty-four S.A. men had been murdered ('Probably by other Nazis,' yelled a Social Democrat) and now their police chief was talking of whipping Hitler out of Germany. No foreign power, he declared, was willing to sign treaties with Brüning – 'Because they know, Mr Reich Chancellor, that you are the Man of Yesteryear, and that the Man of Tomorrow is coming.'

To a barrage of abuse from the left, Goebbels doggedly waded into Hindenburg's reputation. '*Lauded by the Berlin gutter press, fêted by the Party of Deserters –*' he declaimed, flinging out a demagogic arm toward the social democrat benches. The rest of his words were lost in the howl of outrage that his taunt provoked.[38] Furiously clanging his bell the Speaker called for silence. 'Dr Goebbels,' he charged, 'you have named one of the parties present in this House the "Party of Deserters". . .'

The Social Democrats screeched at Goebbels, 'Who deserted? Where were *you*?' One of them shouted, 'You weren't at the front for even one day!' Amid mounting hubbub the communist bloc leader Ernst Torgler mocked, 'Let war veteran Goebbels speak.' But the Social Democrats were now hysterical. 'We were at the front!' '*He* was the dodger!' 'Withdraw!' 'Behold Goebbels, the political cripple!'

Barely pausing to draw breath Goebbels continued: 'The Jews of the Berlin gutter press have held the field marshal on high. These are the same Jews and Social Democrats [shouts of 'Sit down!' and 'Time's up!'] who dumped buckets of mockery and scorn on the field marshal in 1925.'

'Sit down! Sit down!' roared the Social Democrats.

'We're not going to be insulted by dodgers!'

The Speaker capitulated, and ordered Goebbels out of the chamber. Gregor Strasser leaped to his defense, pointing out that the gauleiter had not accused any particular party by name. 'When he said "Party of Deserters" only the Social Democrats felt the hat fitted!'[39]

Returning to the attack the next day Goebbels complained that the illegal and unjust bans on *Angriff* had cost the newspaper 180,000 marks already. As for the opposition's specious allegations that he had just slandered Hindenburg as a 'deserter,' he retaliated by reading out devastating passages from press clippings in his confidential archives, reporting what the Social Democrat organ *Vorwärts*, the *Berliner Morgenzeitung*, the *Berliner Morgenpost*, and Carl Severing himself had written about the field marshal during the previous presidential election campaign. In a brutal closing tirade he offered a string of definitions for the Nazi word *System*, ending with this one: 'Where criticizing the Republic lands you in jail, but slandering and belittling the entire German people is rewarded by the highest distinctions!' He cried, 'That is why in the three weeks now beginning, one battle-cry will sound throughout Germany: Time's up, Away with the System . . . the System that Brüning and his Cabinet represent!' As screams of abuse erupted from the left, Goebbels taunted them: 'Well may you laugh and scoff. Events will prove us right. We shall meet again, on March the thirteenth, at Philippi.'[40]

Waging an election campaign of dubious probity Brüning's officials confiscated the *Völkischer Beobachter* and banned *Angriff* yet again, for inciting contempt of the Republic. But the Nazis had poster power. Kampmann, now Goebbels' gau propaganda chief, plastered the circular Litfass advertisement pillars on street corners with huge placards: S.A. men stood guard on each site, and Nazi speakers harangued the crowds that gathered around them.[41] Outsized pictorial posters like Schweitzer's 'A Man Breaks his Chains' adorned the façades of prominent buildings such as the Café Josty on Potsdamer Platz. Goebbels recorded on discs a short speech, cleverly structured so that its real propaganda message was not at first evident, and manufactured fifty thousand cardboard copies of this little recording costing only three pfennigs each for Nazis to mail to their marxist opponents.[42] In 1930 he had seen an inspiring film of Mussolini speaking; The Herold film company now produced a ten-minute movie of Goebbels speaking, to be shown each night in town squares throughout Germany.[43] Somebody – in the Reichstag the taunt was always 'Thyssen!' – must have topped up Goebbels' funds because he would spend two hundred thousand marks on propaganda for this presidential campaign.[44]

With *Angriff* already banned, the government now banned the rest of his posters and leaflets.[45] Goebbels' demands that Hitler be allowed broadcasting time like Hindenburg were refused.[46] On March 9, with four days to go, he addressed eighty thousand people in Berlin's Lustgarten park. The press published doctored photographs to suggest only a sparse attendance.[47] Two days later Grzesinski sent police to raid his headquarters again. The next day

Goebbels addressed an election-eve rally at the Sport Palace.[48] After that he gathered his officials at his apartment to await the first results. By ten P.M. it was clear that, while eleven million votes had been cast for Hitler, Hindenburg was far ahead – indeed, only one hundred thousand votes short of an absolute majority.[49] Goebbels, overcoming his dejection, issued these guidelines to all gauleiters that same Sunday: 'The N.S.D.A.P. has won an unparalleled victory in the first election round. In one and a half years the Party has succeeded in almost doubling its vote.'

Their task now would be to win 25 million more voters for the runoff. Goebbels ordered the Nazi gauleiters to concentrate their scarce resources on the most promising sections of those who had not voted for them. Thus they must tell the bourgeois voters what to expect if Hindenburg was re-elected: The stopping of pensions, huge tax burdens, and renewed inflation, as well as further territorial encroachments by Poland and Lithuania, and civil war with the communists.[50]

Refusing even to look at the gloating headlines of the 'Judenpresse' that Monday morning, Goebbels flew down to Munich with Kampmann for a campaign conference with Hitler. The second round would be held on April 10. Tossing more dirty-trick spanners into the Nazi works, Brüning ordered virtually simultaneous provincial elections for Prussia, Anhalt, Württemberg, and Bavaria. He also decreed an electioneering moratorium until after Easter. 'We're fighting a war,' snarled Goebbels, 'but there's to be no shooting for three weeks!' Carl Severing joined in the spanner-tossing, arresting scores of Goebbels' Berlin officials on mostly trumped-up charges, while Grzesinski and Weiss had their police search for evidence that would justify an outright ban on the S.A.[51]

Goebbels responded with innovative electioneering techniques as soon as the brief but unequal battle was rejoined. He had originally planned to issue four pictorial and sixteen text posters to be released day by day from March 22 onward.[52] The moratorium knocked that plan on the head. Hitler again appealed to the radio stations to allow him air time; but again Brüning permitted only Hindenburg to get near the microphone.[53] The campaign got dirty on both sides. Hitler's opponents distributed leaflets in old people's homes warning that he would take away their pensions and insist on compulsory euthanasia at sixty; other election 'lies' against which Goebbels warned the other gauleiters in a circular were that the Nazis would bring war, inflation, expropriation, destruction of the unions, dissolution of the civil service, disemancipation of women, forced labor, civil war, and the renunciation of all claims to the South Tyrol, West Prussia, and Alsace-Lorraine.[54] (With the passage of time, about three quarters of these 'lies' would come true.)

In the same circular Goebbels suggested that Hindenburg was benefiting from the emotional female vote ('fear of war') and from civil servants' anxieties about their future. The gauleiters had to concentrate on this 'Hindenburg front' – they must ask the butchers, bakers, and innkeepers why they had voted for the field marshal, and then tailor their own propaganda accordingly. (This field-operational analysis would become a hallmark of Goebbels' propaganda strategy.) He suggested they send groups of girl members into the old folks' homes to read to them, and the bands of the S.A. and S.S. to serenade them. He hatched a secret plan to triple the print-run of all Nazi newspapers for election week, the additional copies being sent free to all Hindenburg voters. The *Völkischer Beobachter* alone should send out 800,000 free copies each day.

As for Hitler, Goebbels brought in air power: Flying from city to city in his own plane D–1720 Hitler would address three or four huge meetings a day in twenty-one cities beginning on April 3, tackling a new enemy 'lie' each day. Goebbels printed four pictorial posters, targeting the farming community, city dwellers, women, and vested interests.[55] A glossy photogravure magazine illustrated with pictures of the Führer would round off his campaign package. True, its title, *Flamethrower*, was unlikely to attract the female fear-of-war vote – but he still had a lot to learn about them.

Then the election got dirtier. The government banned Goebbels' free-newspaper stunt. Infuriatingly, their opponents obtained details of Hitler's lavish Kaiserhof expenses.[56] Goebbels called the bill a forgery.[57] He retaliated by claiming to have annihilating material on Severing's 'womanizing,' but declared that, after consulting with the Führer, they would not release it. In fact neither he nor Hitler was in a strong position to scold their opponents on this score.

The moratorium ended on Sunday April 3. While Hitler set out by plane, Goebbels spoke three times that day at Wiesbaden, then at Frankfurt. On the fourth he and Hitler addressed 150,000 people in the Berlin Lustgarten, then *fifty thousand* more in Potsdam. In Goebbels' absence police chief Grzesinski suddenly ordered the gau Headquarters in Hedemann Strasse padlocked, and banned the election posters that Goebbels had designed for the upcoming Prussian campaign.[58]

VOTING WAS ON April 10, 1932. Though again failing to defeat Hindenburg, Hitler now clearly emerged as a statesman of equivalent stature. His vote increased to 13,418,547 (Hindenburg won with 19,359,983 votes). The Nazi vote in Berlin had grown by two hundred thousand, attracting thirty-one percent of the vote in the capital as compared with 36·8 percent nationwide. The communists won only 3,706,759. Seen in this light, Goebbels should have been delighted; but in the privacy of his apartment he made no secret of his disappointment. According to her mother, Magda chose this moment to reveal that she was four months pregnant. Any elation at this was tempered by the announcement that the defense minister Groener had banned the S.A. and S.S. nationwide and ordered their immediate dissolution.[59]

Polling in Prussia, the next round of elections, would be on April 24. Goebbels now directed his propaganda venom at Otto Braun and Carl Severing, and their police minions Grzesinski and 'Isidor' Weiss.[60] He devised more new techniques, including loudspeaker trucks illegally broadcasting the Horst Wessel anthem. One stunt tickled the fancy of the international press: His posters cheekily announced a public debate with Chancellor Brüning in the Sport Palace. In fact he had obtained recordings of a recent Brüning speech in Königsberg, from which he played extracts to his audience, together with his own devastating replies. Brüning's humorless response was to sue Goebbels for infringing the copyright in his intellectual property.[61]

After dropping dark hints in *Angriff* that he had some dirt on Severing, he detected a softening in *Vorwärts'* line. Struggling with 'flu and a 40°C fever he addressed a hundred thousand people in the Lustgarten. On election eve one of his S.A. men was shot dead with a bullet between the eyes. The next day saw every swastika flag in Prussia draped in mourning.

These were the Goebbels methods, and thanks to them the Nazi party increased its numbers in the Prussian parliament from six seats to 162; with 38·3 percent of the votes they were the strongest party. In Bavaria meanwhile the Nazis had swollen from nine seats to forty-three, in Württemberg from one to fifty-one, and in Anhalt from one to fifteen.

In Anhalt Germany's first Nazi prime minister was appointed. Elsewhere, Brüning's allies were still strong enough to form a coalition against the Nazis and stay in power.

'We've got to get into power sooner or later,' wrote Goebbels in understandable frustration at this outcome. 'Otherwise all these election victories will be the death of us.'[62]

18: *Follow that Man*

FOR THE NEXT FEW MONTHS Hitler would spend more time in Berlin than in Munich, wheeling and dealing in tandem with Göring in a persistent effort to cover the last hundred yards to power. Goebbels did what he could to undermine Hitler's trust in Göring. When the aviator started an affair with blonde actress Emmy Sonnemann, a married woman, he lost no time in telling Hitler.[1]

In consequence, Hitler spent more time with the Goebbelses. In any case, he was almost pathological about being recognized in the capital. He would hide his face when the lights came on in movie theaters; one evening, the Goebbelses were out when Hitler returned to Reichskanzler Platz and he had to wait outside. He asked Darré to stand between him and the street. 'Hitler remained standing,' said Darré, 'in the corner of the doorway with his face turned toward the house until Dr Goebbels got back.'[2]

The Center party wooed Hitler the most persistently, stating as their only condition that he must accept a junior role. There were those, Gregor Strasser among them, who felt strongly that half a loaf was better than no bread. But Goebbels insisted that they hold out for absolute power. 'Either – or,' he wrote: 'Power, or opposition.'[3]

His published diary contains only hints at the part in fact played by Franz von Papen and General Kurt von Schleicher in bringing about the demise of the System. Missing from *Kaiserhof* too is the juicy scandal caused when a Munich newspaper published Röhm's homosexual love-letters.[4] Goebbels was not alone in his perplexity at Hitler's indulgence of such perversions.[5]

BY 1932 Goebbels' fame was spreading beyond Germany's frontiers. The distinguished American journalist H. R. Knickerbocker, writing from Berlin for the New York *Evening Post*, singled him out as the 'greatest master of public management' that Europe had ever known. To Goebbels, he wrote, went all the credit for Hitler's election successes. 'He is the best journalist in the party, and the best orator.' His billboards were masterpieces of election psychology.[6]

Goebbels had lost his appeal against the two month sentence for libeling Dr Weiss, and a pro forma warrant had been issued on February 11; on the twentieth Dr Bernhard Weiss was informed that the sentence could be enforced as soon as Goebbels lost his immunity.[7]

Meanwhile, on April 25 supreme court officials from Leipzig served another forty-page indictment on Goebbels, this time for high treason. This document too he shrugged off.[8]

The maneuvering between the Nazis and a camarilla of army officers, jointly and severally eager for power, had begun. Goebbels' diaries show that Hitler had entrusted the backstage negotiations to Röhm, Göring, and Frick, while General von Schleicher operated through his colleague Werner Count von Alvensleben, whom Goebbels identified only in the unpublished version of his diary.[9] As the regime's position weakened in May 1932 Hitler and Goebbels, who had been conferring in Munich, hurried back to Berlin. A minister resigned and Hitler, living in the Kaiserhof or with the Goebbelses, again launched into negotiations with Schleicher's and Hindenburg's emissaries. Power seemed so near to the Nazi leaders, and yet so unattainable. When the Reichstag belatedly resumed, Göring and Strasser spearheaded the attack on Brüning's ruinous financial policies. Brüning survived the Nazi motion of no confidence, this time by 286 votes to 259. The gap was narrowing all the time.

The next day, May 12, saw scandalous scenes in the Reichstag. After Nazi deputies roughed up an opponent, Dr Bernhard Weiss and his police officers stormed in and arrested several of them. Goebbels was thrilled at 'Isidor's' blunder in violating the sovereignty of their parliament. The entire press echoed him. Groener resigned as defense minister. The police arrested Strasser that night on his train heading back to Munich, and Weiss issued yet another libel writ against Goebbels for insulting him as a Jew.[10] Clinging grimly to the tattered remnants of his office, Brüning still refused to resign, instead adjourning the Reichstag until June. Hitler was determined to force a new election, so that his party could bring its now massive voting strength to bear.

For all his public triumphs, Goebbels' finances at this time were on a knife-edge. Angriff was having to pay off his costs in one libel action by monthly installments of twenty marks. His lawyer managed to get the balance of 598 marks annulled.[11] His accountant declared a tax demand of 564 marks for 1931 to be totally beyond his means, and asked if he could pay one hundred marks a month; Goebbels indignantly penciled in the margin, 'Pay – from what?'[12] Magda's handsome alimony payments from Quandt had ended of course with her new marriage.

Goebbels evidently refused however to touch the colossal funds that he raised for the election campaigns. After his private diary recorded on May 22 a visit from some gentlemen from Mercedes, the gau headquarters was suddenly awash with funds. Magda, now in her fifth month of pregnancy, rented a little cottage in the middle of an orchard at Caputh, near Potsdam, on Lake Schwielow. In this idyllic setting they spent their summer nights while frogs bleeped and swallows flitted through their open bedroom windows.[13]

AFTER Dr Brüning resigned on May 30, 1932, the clever, foxy career politician Franz von Papen was appointed interim chancellor. The election was set down for the last day of July. Goebbels called his staff out to a council of war.[14]

Once again it was Goebbels who masterminded the nationwide campaign, from Hitler's fifty-city aerial tour of Germany right down to the tiniest personal details like obtaining the names of eight Berlin Nazis in prison and in hospital and dividing between them the latest meager royalty check from his book *The Unknown S.A. Man* 'as a small token,' he wrote them, 'of recognition.'[15]

He did not intend to allow 'Isidor' to disrupt this campaign and started a drive to get him and Grzesinski sacked. Papen had appointed a bumbling weakling, Baron von Gayl, as minister of the interior. Hitler easily persuaded him to lift the eight-week-old ban on the S.A. and S.S. and Goebbels publicly called on Gayl to 'get rid of Messrs Grzesinski and Weiss' as well.[16] Under Nazi pressure Papen repealed virtually all the bans. A Nazi was appointed Speaker of the Prussian parliament: At his diktat, this body set up a formal commission of inquiry into Weiss's activities. 'Revenge is a repast best served up cold,' wrote Goebbels yet again. Weiss responded by banning *Angriff* for five days.[17]

A month remained before the election day. This time the Nazis enjoyed limited access to the air waves.[18] Goebbels scripted a broadcast on 'National character as a basis for national culture.' It was stripped of its venom however by the radio censors before he could broadcast it.[19] The final list of Nazi candidates for Berlin and Potsdam again poorly justified the claim to be a workers' party: Of the forty-one local names, six were office workers, five businessmen, two former police officers, and among the rest a civil servant, teacher, bookseller, pharmacist, tailor, librarian, and bank clerk; only five were truly working class.[20] All of these candidates, including Goebbels himself, had to sign a five-point declaration for Hitler's personal files, of which the first two points read as follows:

1. I swear that I have no links or relations with the Jews;
2. I swear that I hold no directorships in banks or other corporations.[21]

With the irksome ban on the S.A. lifted by the obliging Franz von Papen, the Brownshirt armies marched again. For two hours twenty thousand marched past Goebbels and Strasser in Dessau on July 3.

As he arrived in Hagen on the twelfth the communists ambushed his car. Clutching a pistol, he signaled his chauffeur to put his foot down and plow through the mob. After that the left signaled his car's number ahead to every town. In Mönchen-Gladbach the communists passed out leaflets stating that he was not to escape alive; no idle threat, because the tide of violence was in full flood.[22] Only a few days earlier he had buried S.A. Scharführer Helmut Köster of No. 24 Sturm; ten thousand people had packed the graveyard.

In Wedding the communists gunned down S.A. man Hans Steinberg. In the fifty days up to July 20 Prussia saw 461 political clashes, resulting in eighty-two deaths on all sides; in the last two weeks of the campaign alone, thirty-two Nazis were killed. On July 17 communist gunmen opened fire on a marching S.A. column in Altona, near Hamburg, leaving nineteen dead and sixty injured.[23]

SUDDENLY EVERYTHING tilted in the Nazis' favor. General von Schleicher agreed to back a putsch against Prussia. Meeting with Göring, Röhm, and Goebbels in Cottbus two days after the Altona bloodbath Hitler announced to them that they were going to appoint a 'commissar for the interior' in Prussia; Carl Severing, the incumbent minister of the interior, huffed that he would yield only to *force majeure*. 'A touch on the wrist sufficed,' mocked Goebbels in *Kaiserhof*.[24] Severing's humiliation was followed by President von Hindenburg signing a decree appointing Papen himself as Reich commissar in Prussia, displacing the leftist prime minister Otto Braun. When Braun squealed, Hindenburg – on Schleicher's advice – called in the army. At 11:20 A.M. on July 20 General Gerd von Rundstedt, the garrison commander, phoned police chief Grzesinski with word that he was imposing a state of emergency: His orders were to replace Grzesinski with the police chief of Essen. Dr Bernhard Weiss was to be summarily dismissed as well. The army sent in its officers at five-thirty P.M. to arrest Grzesinski and Weiss.[25] As they were driven away from their police headquarters at Alexander Platz in an army Mercedes, Weiss had no time even to gather up his bowler hat and pince-nez.[26]

The sheer suddenness of it all took Goebbels' breath away. It was the end of an era. The Nazis had Papen eating out of their hand. He appointed 'reliable' police chiefs and civil governors (*Regierungspräsidenten*) throughout Prussia. He banned the newspapers that had been the bane of Goebbels' life such as the *Acht-Uhr Abendblatt*.

All the fetters thus came off in the last eleven days of Nazi campaigning. In the city's Grunewald stadium Karl Hanke organized the biggest open-air rally yet for Hitler. It was a boiling-hot day until evening when the heavens opened and the rains drenched the 120,000 people gathered to hear him. But nobody left – 'A sign,' in Kampmann's view, 'of how the once Red Berlin had come around, thanks to Dr Goebbels' propaganda.' A mighty cheer went up as Goebbels remarked that even these rains had deterred nobody.[27]

He was in Munich when the election results were announced. The Nazis had attracted nearly fourteen million votes, entitling them to 230 seats in the Reichstag. They were now far the largest single party, but once again the Center party, with seventy-six seats, held the balance. Again Goebbels advised Hitler to hold out for absolute power, and shun any compromise. 'Tolerance will be the death of us,' he argued. Vacationing briefly with him at Tegernsee, Hitler agonized over his next step – 'balking,' jotted Goebbels in his diary, 'at the really big decisions.' In *Kaiserhof* he softened this criticism by applying it to the party as a whole, rather than its Führer.

Leaving Goebbels in Bavaria, Hitler set off for Berlin on August 4, 1932 to state his demands to Hindenburg: he wanted to be chancellor, with Frick as minister of the interior, Strasser as minister of labor, Goebbels as minister of public education (meaning propaganda), and Göring as aviation minister.[28] He returned south on the sixth. Up at his Obersalzberg mountain home he predicted to Goebbels that they would be taking office in a week's time, with Hitler as both chancellor and prime minister of Prussia, Strasser as minister of the interior, and Goebbels acting as minister of culture in Prussia and minister of education in the Reich. 'A Cabinet of real men,' approved Goebbels. 'We shall never give up power. They'll have to carry us out feet first. This is going to be a total solution.'

He stayed for the next five days at Hitler's side, nervous in case somebody talked the Führer into making other dispositions. In Berlin the S.A. under their bullying commander Helldorff had already begun jostling for power. While Göring conducted the political negotiations, Ernst Röhm drew his S.A. army up around the capital to exert a visible and unsubtle pressure on the chancellor Papen. Goebbels was bullish about the outcome of the talks, and stayed up until four A.M. one night discussing with Hitler the structure of his new ministry. Hitler promised him he would be running education, films, radio, theater, and propaganda; as if these were not portfolios enough, Goebbels decided to retain his position as the party's gauleiter of Berlin and as Reichsleiter in charge of its national propaganda. (All of these ambitions remained pipedreams, and nothing about them appeared in *Kaiserhof*.)[29] Daimler-Benz's general manager[30] came to talk automobiles, and for a day visions of newer and even bigger cars danced in the Nazi leaders' heads. But then Schleicher's man Alvensleben phoned with news that the regime was still holding out for a horse-trade. Hitler told him that he was not interested in compromises – 'A total solution,' as Goebbels put it, 'or no dice.'[31]

Not all the Nazis agreed with Hitler's unrelenting stance. The regime spread rumors that a split was beginning to show in their ranks, and even that Goebbels and Strasser were in favor of half-measures. Hitler published a communiqué denying it.[32] He left for Berlin with Goebbels. Here unsatisfactory news waited for them: Papen was still flatly against Hitler becoming chancellor; Röhm and Schleicher were trying to talk him round, without much success. Pacing the verandah of the Goebbelses summer house at Caputh, Hitler discussed this turn of events. They agreed that if the Führer accepted the vice-chancellorship that was on offer, this would saddle the Nazi party for all time with a share of the blame for Papen's failure. In the government quarter at midday on August 13 both Schleicher and Papen urged him to accept. Hitler refused, and Goebbels had to back him.[33] Later Hitler took Frick and Röhm over to see the president; he again left empty-handed. Frustrated and angry, the Nazi leaders gathered at Goebbels' apartment. Typewriters rattled out communiqués. The S.A. commanders were straining at the bit, they wanted action. Together with Röhm, Hitler briefed them to toe the line. He departed for Bavaria, leaving Goebbels in Berlin.

It was a totally unexpected impasse. The Nazis were the largest party: They had followed the path of legality until now, yet the System was thwarting them once more. Goebbels consoled his embittered lieutenants and went on vacation to Heiligendamm. The millionaire banker Emil Georg von Stauss of the Deutsche Bank invited him over to his motor yacht.[34] But Goebbels' mind was in a turmoil. He feared that the Nazis' share of the vote had peaked, and might now rapidly decline.

The Reichstag resumed on August 30. Its members elected Hermann Göring as Speaker, a powerful position indeed. Göring invited Hitler, Röhm, and Goebbels up to his luxurious new apartment on Kaiserdamm to discuss tactics.[35] They agreed that at the very next Reichstag session on September 12 they must force an immediate dissolution. The new election would be held on November 6. The party was now in a precarious position, sliding in the polls and with its campaign coffers dangerously low. Goebbels ordered *Angriff* to appear twice daily instead of once. He organized a consumer boycott of opposition newspapers. He had no mercy on them. When a newspaper impugned Magda's honor he sent an S.S. officer to treat the journalist concerned with a riding whip; in best Prussian style, the S.S. man left his visiting card on the bleeding offender.

Magda had given birth to their first child on September 1, 1932. She had hoped for a boy to call Hellmut, to fill the hole left in her heart by her stepson's tragic death in Paris years before. But it was a girl, so 'Hellmut' became Helga. The infant's nocturnal wails kept the household awake. Goebbels, a novice in the art of parenthood, complained unfeelingly and left Magda in tears.[36]

COUNT VON HELLDORFF took the breakdown of negotiations particularly hard. 'He's only tough,' observed Goebbels shrewdly, 'when the going's good.'[37]

He moved his gau headquarters for one last time, to a building in Voss Strasse barely three hundred yards from the Reich chancellery. He had come a long way since the 'opium den' six years before. He began planning ahead, listing whom he would need to take over the radio system. Hitler again flew a whistlestop tour of fifty cities. Goebbels followed in an open plane, his face anesthetized with cold. When his graphic artist Schweitzer ('Mjölnir') showed him his latest poster designs, he felt that his old friend was running out of steam – but then so was everybody.

The Goebbels Diary for the last weeks before the November 1932 election lacked the sense of urgency and intrigue that had characterized it in July and August. Only rarely did anything of the old fun element surface in this campaign. He ordered the marxist districts plastered with stickers reading simply 'VOTE LIST 1 AGAIN' ('without stating which party that is'): The less sophisticated would assume that List 1 was the Reds.[38] He lured the German National People's Party (D.N.V.P.) into accepting a public debate with him: In the hall the opponents provided him with only two hundred tickets, an inconvenience which Goebbels circumvented with the aid of *Angriff*'s printers, who turned out two thousand more. When his opponents arrived, they found his men had taken over most of the hall.[39]

On October 20 he ordered the Jewish problem placed more firmly to the forefront – citing Papen's Jewish adviser Jakob Goldschmidt as a case in point.[40] He also ordered gau officials to start systematic rumors that Hindenburg had already written off Papen. After quoting with perverse relish from the D.N.V.P.'s organ ('Goebbels is a male Rosa Luxemburg – neither a pretty sight; both are of Jewish countenance. He is impelled by the same burning ambition to incite and to lie')[41] he ordered his troops to refrain from similar personal insults. However, disguised as harmless civilians, his officials were to cluster around Nazi poster hoardings singing the party's praises.[42]

Towards the campaign's end there was an odd episode: Goebbels decided that his Nazis were to back a communist-organized Berlin transport strike. It was as though he had lost sight of the Nazi party's larger election horizon. His men had heavily infiltrated the B.V.G., the capital's public transport authority. The transport workers probably had legitimate grievances, and Goebbels had remained at heart a socialist agitator. Kampmann, his propaganda chief, would claim that the strike was actually quite popular.[43] But the public's backing of the Nazi party melted away as all the usual brutish signs of union intimidation appeared, with the pickets this time wearing Nazi armbands. Together the Nazi and communist strikers terrorized strike breakers, ripped up streetcar lines, and wrecked buses. The liberal and rightwing *Deutsche Allgemeine Zeitung* expressed concern about the spread of class-warfare to the extreme right.[44] 'The bourgeois press,' Goebbels would write in *Kaiserhof*, 'invented the lie that I instigated this strike without the Führer's knowledge or consent . . . although I am in hourly phone contact with the Führer.'

This self-defense is to be regarded with as much skepticism as his claim that the Berlin public displayed an 'admirable solidarity' with the strikers. Less hollow rings his excuse that to have withheld support from the strikers would have confounded all their recruiting efforts among the workers. Perhaps Goebbels had seen a chance for the Nazis to seize control of the strike and shortcut the tedious democratic process by expanding it into a full-blooded coup. But the strike backfired badly on their election campaign. Nationwide, two million voters deserted the party, costing them thirty-four of their 230 Reichstag seats. The communists gained strongly.[45] In Berlin, the Nazi vote slumped from 757,000 (or 28·6 percent) in July to 720,000 (or twenty-six percent) now. The bourgeois press gloated over this setback. At his Voss Strasse headquarters the next day he found his party and S.A. officers in ugly mood – 'all ready to strike out again,' he wrote, a clear indication that a coup was still on their mind.[46] Hitler however ordained, 'There will be no negotiating until this regime and the parties backing it have been totally defeated.'[47]

Although the German electorate had confirmed the Nazis as the largest single party, their opponents still clung on to the chancellorship. Count von Alvensleben reported that Papen hoped Hitler would come to terms; Gregor Strasser, it seemed, suddenly agreed with Papen, and for the first time on November 9 Goebbels recorded real venom about him. 'Let's hope that Fatso

Gregor doesn't put his foot in it. He's so disloyal. . . I warn [Hitler] against Strasser.'[48] Hitler however wrote to Papen, still refusing to do a deal.[49] Papen resigned on the sixteenth.[50]

Now Hindenburg again summoned Hitler to Berlin. On the nineteenth, parting the cheering crowds outside the Kaiserhof, Hitler drove over to the presidential palace in a limousine. After a ninety-minute talk, in which he explained his party's program once more to Hindenburg, Hitler assured his henchmen that he still would not accept any compromise. Hindenburg however wanted to revert to parliamentary rule. Hitler wrote him on the twenty-first, then took Goebbels to the opera – Wagner's *Meistersinger* for the *n*th time.[51]

Hindenburg turned Hitler's proposals down. Some of Goebbels' faction urged that the time had come to seize power, at least in Prussia. For a few days Hitler remained at the Kaiserhof as a passive observer while Papen and Schleicher vied with each other for the coveted chancellorship prize. In Weimar on November 30 for the Thuringian election campaign, Goebbels heard from Hitler that Schleicher had made fresh overtures to him. Goebbels attended a three-hour council of war with Hitler, Frick, Göring, and Strasser. Again Strasser was the only one in favor of a compromise – joining a Cabinet under Schleicher, failing which the party seemed to be doomed to the political wilderness in perpetuity.[52] Adamantly seconded by Goebbels, Hitler again refused to consider accepting the vice-chancellorship.[53]

General von Schleicher sent a new intermediary, Lieutenant-Colonel Eugen Ott. The press ached and heaved with curiosity. Hitler stood firm.

'Follow that man!' marveled Goebbels. 'Then we shall triumph.'

Unable to sway Hitler, on December 2 Hindenburg appointed Schleicher as chancellor.[54] Needing to neutralize the Hitler threat, Schleicher began to cultivate Gregor Strasser instead of Hitler. Goebbels learned that they had met on Sunday the fourth, and that Schleicher had offered Strasser the vice-chancellorship which Hitler had spurned, and had hinted at ministerial positions for any other renegade Nazis as well.

The new Reichstag would shortly meet. As Hitler warned the Nazi bloc in harsh terms about any tendency toward compromise, Goebbels saw Strasser's features harden. Two days later, hearing more specific rumors about Strasser's treachery, Hitler took him to task. Strasser picked up his hat and left: Left the room, left politics, and ultimately (nineteen months later) this life. Julius Streicher called out, 'Exit the traitor!' Goebbels limped from group to group of the Nazi deputies, dispensing further details of Strasser's treachery.

At midday on the eighth Hitler received at the Kaiserhof a letter from Strasser resigning all his high party offices on account of the refusal to cut a deal with the new chancellor.[55] Simultaneously Strasser invited all the senior gauleiters – whom Hitler had just appointed as *Landesinspekteure* – to meet him (except Goebbels). Since August, he told them, Hitler had displayed no clear line except for his monotonous demand to be chancellor. 'He has got to realize that in the long run he has no prospect of attaining this target.' He refused to see the party ruined. Nor would he put up any longer with the intriguing by Hitler's entourage. 'I have no desire to fall in behind Göring, Goebbels, Röhm, and the rest.' (According to Hans Frank he described Göring as a brutal egoist who cared nothing for Germany, Goebbels as 'a hobbling devil,' and Röhm as a 'swine.')[56] One gauleiter later reported: 'After the individual participants had overcome their dismay, they went off bewildered – like children who have lost their father.' Gauleiter Rust took word of Strasser's mutinous remarks to Hitler at the Kaiserhof.[57]

At two A.M. Goebbels found Hitler there studying the first edition of the *Tägliche Rundschau*. It headlined Strasser's bid for power. 'If the party falls apart now,' he told Goebbels, 'I'll finish myself off in three minutes!'[58]

The morning's 'Judenpresse' fawned on Strasser, which probably sobered some of his supporters.[59] Only Gottfried Feder had foolishly echoed his complaints.[60] After that day's Reichstag session – it adjourned until mid-January 1933 – Hitler spoke to all the gauleiters in his suite at the Kaiserhof. His speech was a masterpiece of tragic oratory, and probably saved the party from oblivion.[61] If they deserted him now, said Hitler, his life's work no longer had any purpose. 'Apart from this movement and my appointed mission,' he declared, glancing at the portable bust of Geli on the mantelpiece, 'I have nothing now that could detain me on this earth.' He tore apart Strasser's arguments of the day before. Strasser had hinted at the path of illegality. But General Walter von Reichenau, army chief of staff, had warned that the army and police would open fire. Reichenau himself had urged patience – the party, he said, was bound to achieve power legally sooner or later. The whole speech was 'fabulously sure-footed,' in Goebbels' words – 'annihilating for Strasser. . . Spontaneous ovation at the end, everybody gave Hitler his hand. Strasser is isolated. A dead man! I have fought for six years for this.'[62]

Hitler was unquestionably the master, and Strasser only the sorcerer's apprentice. Two months later, events would prove Hitler's strategy correct: this would temper the loyalty of every high party official who had tortured his conscience this day.

Still reluctant to make a final break, Hitler's press office announced that Strasser had only gone on three weeks' leave.[63] Goebbels' newspaper published a more malicious valedictory; he had to disown it the same day.[64] He would continue his feud with Strasser to the bitter end. As for Strasser, he had left for the sunnier climes of Italy; he told friends afterward that Germany was now at the mercy of a congenital liar from Austria and a clubfooted dwarf, of which the latter was the worse. 'He is Satan in a human's image.'[65]

19: 'It's All Fixed!'

W E HAVE JUST COMPLETED,' reported journalist Louis P. Lochner in December 1932 to his daughter, 'one of the hardest months of reporting in my career. . . I tell you,' Lochner added, 'we had no end of excitement.'[1]

Goebbels had inevitably neglected the provincial election in Thuringia and the party's vote there slumped by forty percent. Wakening to the realization that the Nazi party was in danger of electoral extinction, he took immediate action to revitalize the propaganda campaign: Blaming Dr Lippert for the tactless remarks about Strasser, he replaced him as editor of *Angriff* by Kampmann.[2] Hanke told him that the deputy chief of national propaganda, Heinz Franke, had allowed his Munich organization to go to seed. Goebbels replaced him with Wilhelm Haegert, a sound and popular attorney on his own legal staff.[3]

After consultation with Goebbels, on December 15 Hitler drafted a memorandum explaining how the party was to pack more punch into the election battle.[4]

In the first two weeks of Schleicher's chancellorship a quarter-million more Germans had been thrown out of work. On December 15 the general delivered an insipid broadcast on his economic program. Goebbels wrote a caustic commentary in *Angriff* entitled, 'The Program without a Program.' The people were now too weak, he wrote there a few days later, even to clench their fists.[5]

As he toured the gau's Christmas parties at the historic Pharus Rooms and the Veterans' Building, he saw worse scenes of poverty than ever before.[6]

RETURNING HOME immediately after the Strasser brouhaha he has found Magda feeling ill. She is pregnant again. He is still madly in love with her – Magda tells Ello that their honeymoon is going to last ten more years yet.[7] Her husband worries constantly about her as he mounts his new propaganda campaign. His hours grow longer and longer.

Sometimes he creeps in at three A.M.; when Magda weakly scolds him he brings her roses. Her illness will not go away. When, at some of the Christmas parties, he glances at the beautiful society women, Providence immediately raps his knuckles. Magda collapses on Christmas Eve and is borne off in floods of tears with a miscarriage. 'Just perfect,' he curses in his diary. 'Now everybody else has their gifts and fare, let my own Christmas begin!'[8] He and

Harald set up a Christmas tree outside her ward and wheel the whole glittering contraption in.

Then, thrusting aside all the trappings of Christmas, he sketches out for Magda on a white-lacquered clinic stool his plan for the upcoming election campaign in little Lippe. The Nazi party will focus its entire national propaganda machinery on the tiny rural constituency, like a burning glass. None of the other parties is bothering with Lippe's 150,000 voters.[9] He has Hitler alone speak at sixteen meetings there.

Hitler invites the Goebbels family to the Obersalzberg. Leaving Magda in the clinic, Goebbels takes Harald down there on the twenty-eighth but the news from Berlin steadily worsens and he begins to brood upon the unimaginable, a future without Magda. He pays scant attention to the seismic sounds of fresh political upheaval – the renewed billets-doux from Papen and Alvensleben to Hitler. All joy has left the political fray. New Year's Eve brings word of a relapse and of Magda refusing to eat. The first hours of 1933 see him hurrying by sled and car to Munich; as he waits for the overnight train to Berlin the power of prayer returns to him. 'I am nothing without her,' he writes. The clinic tells him by phone that her fever is worsening. She is at death's door. 'Is this how 1933 is to begin? Horrifying! Even so, I shall stand and fight.' The next morning he arrives to find the crisis over. Magda lies there weeping, with intravenous tubes still connected to her arm, but the fever has passed on.[10] Over the next weeks she makes a slow recovery, and Hitler often comes to see her.

FOR AN ANALYSIS of the epoch-making events of January 1933 the handwritten diaries of Dr Goebbels, preserved in Moscow, are an indispensable tool.[11] For a biographer however their content is less revealing than their structure. True, he was preoccupied with Magda's illness; her gynecologist Professor Walter Stoeckel had already written her off, it turned out.[12] As Hitler's and Göring's meetings resumed with Schleicher, Hugenberg, and Papen, Goebbels dutifully recorded them – but only at second or third hand. On January 4 he launched the Lippe campaign: He now discovered rural Germany, speaking in tiny farming villages sometimes of only a few houses and barns surrounded by fields glistening with snow. Meanwhile Hitler and Himmler secretly met Papen at the Cologne home of a young banker friend of the party.[13] Briefing Goebbels on this meeting, Hitler said that the ex-chancellor still claimed Hindenburg's ear and was now willing to offer Hitler the chancellorship in return for the vice-chancellor's office for himself.[14] But much depended on the Nazis winning a convincing victory at Lippe.

Goebbels shuttled between Berlin and Lippe. Leftists had murdered another young Nazi, the tailor's apprentice Walter Wagnitz, on New Year's Day. Goebbels gave him a funeral fit for a prince, parading the coffin for three hours in drizzling rain past a hundred thousand party members and formations of the S.A., S.S., and Hitler Youth.

The figure of Gregor Strasser still haunted the pages of his diary. Unlike

Stennes, the man still enjoyed wide support in the party's ranks. Even Hitler was not as hostile to him as Goebbels would have liked. Indeed, the Führer sent the gauleiter of Saxony to hint to Strasser that he could let bygones be bygones even now.[15]

At Göring's apartment on the tenth, the talk was again only of Strasser. Hindenburg's office told the press that he was thinking of appointing 'a National Socialist' as vice-chancellor, and on the twelfth his Staatssekretär Otto Meissner revealed that Strasser had secretly met the president. The next day Göring told Goebbels that Strasser was about to do the dirty on them; the press too hinted that Strasser was to become vice-chancellor.[16]

The voting in Lippe on January 15, 1933 brought the personal triumph that Hitler therefore badly needed. The party's vote surged forward by twenty percent. Strasser was done for. On the sixteenth Hitler addressed the gauleiters assembled at Weimar for three hours. 'Hitler's victory,' wrote Goebbels, 'is total. We have sweated out the Strasser affair.'[17]

THE REICHSTAG WAS due to meet again at the end of January 1933, but in effect the Nazis were already in control, as Goebbels proved, staging an outrageous provocation a few days before then: The memorial to Horst Wessel was to be dedicated on the twenty-second. He arranged for twenty thousand S.A. men to parade on Bülow Platz right outside the communist party's national headquarters. General von Schleicher pleaded with Hitler not to risk attending. 'He who dares,' advised Goebbels, 'wins!'[18] The Berlin police had to protect the parade with machine-guns, armored cars, and sharpshooters. The Nazi pageantry was blemished only by Mrs Wessel; she repaid Hitler's earlier indifference to her son's death by arriving late and making him wait half an hour.

Hindenburg's slow-witted son Oskar and his secretary Otto Meissner encouraged Hitler to fight on. All were agreed that Schleicher's time was up. For two days rumors flew as Göring and Frick negotiated with the other aspirants to power. On January 27 Schleicher had been reconciled to resigning on Saturday, but he was still campaigning stubbornly against Hitler's taking over.[19] Hitler bargained with Hugenberg about a coalition that evening. But the D.N.V.P. stated unacceptable demands.

Schleicher resigned on Saturday the twenty-eighth. The Reichstag was to resume on the following Tuesday. Goebbels sat at home, nervously playing with the infant Helga, while Göring carried on the bargaining process. On Sunday Goebbels drafted a belligerent leading article, then went over for coffee at the Kaiserhof. As he was nervously chatting with Hitler, Göring burst in and roared: 'It's all fixed!' Papen had agreed to recommend Hitler's appointment as chancellor.

Those present solemnly rose and shook hands all round. Göring added that Frick was to be minister of the interior in the Reich, with himself as his counterpart in Prussia.[20] Hitler announced that he would dissolve the

Reichstag at once. To establish an absolute majority he needed to fight one more election campaign – 'the very last one,' noted Goebbels cynically, 'but we'll pull it off.'

There was one serious snag for Goebbels. Hitler's canny opponents had not allowed his Nazis even now more than three ministerial portfolios. Goebbels had taken a propaganda ministry for granted. Hitler cleverly weaned him off his disappointment, arguing that a government minister of propaganda could hardly direct a necessarily partisan election campaign. He promised Goebbels he would get his ministry – later; they would appoint a straw man to keep the seat warm meanwhile.

At the eleventh hour, that Sunday January 29, 1933, Alvensleben, Schleicher's man, brought rumors of an army putsch being planned by his generals with General von Hammerstein, the army chief of staff. Not for the last time, however, the German army proved incapable of decisive political action.[21]

AT ELEVEN A.M. – it was now January 30, 1933 – President von Hindenburg sent for Hitler and swore him in as chancellor. Goebbels waited at the Kaiserhof. 'The Old Man was quite emotional,' Hitler told him afterwards. 'He's delighted that the nationalist right wing has united at last.' Goebbels phoned Magda with the news.[22]

'Herr Doctor,' Ello Quandt admonished him afterward, 'now the going gets tougher. You've got to show what you and your friends can do.'

His joy evaporated. 'Whatever!' he snapped. 'Now we're in power. And nobody's going to cheat us of that. We know all the tricks!'[23] He ordered Berlin's biggest-ever torchlight parade for that night, changed into uniform, and drove off to the Reich chancellery for the first time in his life.

III: The Reich Minister

20: *The Big Lie*

FOR JOSEPH GOEBBELS the years of poverty and struggle seemed to be over, though he still had no formal government office.

He was now thirty-five, his life already three-quarters spent. 'G.,' wrote one official English visitor at this time, 'has charm and a captivating smile and manner' – surprising, he felt, in one described as the cruelest man in the whole movement. The Englishman detected in Goebbels something of an intensely enthusiastic undergraduate, but also a dangerous fanatic.[1] Franz von Papen was struck by the wide mouth and intelligent eyes. General Werner von Blomberg, Hitler's new defense minister, felt that Goebbels was convinced of his own superiority.[2] Goebbels' staff would find him a disagreeable employer. He rarely showed gratitude, and preferred cruel sarcasm to measured criticism. 'A man with many enemies,' concluded Blomberg, 'Goebbels had no friends at all.'

Wisely, most of his enemies had fled. Albert Grzesinski had escaped to Paris where he was even now composing memoirs in which Dr Goebbels would not fare well at all.[3] Dr Bernhard Weiss had fled to Czechoslovakia. With their departure, Goebbels was at a rather loose end.

'G.,' Alfred Rosenberg would write, 'was a discharger of purulence. Until 1933 he squirted it at Isidor Weiss. With him gone, he began to discharge it over us instead.'[4] The publication in 1934 of his opinionated diaries *Kaiserhof* would infuriate the other top Nazis. 'They used to say that the falsification of history begins after fifty years,' Ribbentrop would snort to his family. 'Wrong – it starts at once!' (Goebbels had not mentioned him.)[5]

Not that the diaries are devoid of inherent usefulness. While the later volumes utilized repeatedly the same stereotype phrases, this very ossification enables us to deduce where perhaps other unwritten events need to be suspected between the lines.

They lauded Magda Goebbels so cloyingly that one suspects that Goebbels' occasional nocturnal *Spazierfahrt* (motor outing) through Berlin was designed to grab more than just the 'breath of fresh air' to which he referred. The diaries portray him at other times as flogging himself to the limits of endurance for the cause. ('Twelve hours non-stop sitting at my desk today,' he writes in July 1933.) But as the years passed the pages filled with unbecoming references to villas, boats, and motor cars – the latter evidently donated by the party's benefactors in the Daimler-Benz company.

Kaiserhof made him briefly a wealthy man. Tax returns among his papers indicate that his literary royalties total 34,376 marks in fiscal 1933, 134,423 in 1934 (the year of *Kaiserhof*), 62,190 in 1935, 63,654 in 1936, and 66,905 the year after that.[6]

He had firmly hitched his star to his Führer (still often referred to as 'Hitler' in the 1933 diary). Over the following years he consolidated their personal relationship, becoming a regular lunch guest at the chancellery, where he delighted the others with his repartee. Far into the night he and Hitler yarned about cars and kings and criminals. 'And how we laughed,' he recorded after one session that summer. 'Until my jawbone ached.'

In September 1933 Hitler turned the first sod to begin work on Germany's autobahn network; Goebbels saw the crowds cheering and weeping.[7] Often the Führer revealed to him his secret plans – to unite and expand the Reich under one central government, but also eventually to create a senate to provide the checks and balances that even a dictatorship would need. After President von Hindenburg's demise, they agreed, Hitler himself should become head of state, with a popular vote to confirm it when that time came.[8]

ON THAT HISTORIC day when Adolf Hitler came to power Goebbels had stood next to him in the chancellery window looking down on his six-hour torchlight parade. One million Berliners surged past them, holding up their children to their new leader, to the thump and blare of brass bands. A radio truck arrived and Goebbels spoke a running commentary; he found that speaking into a radio microphone took some getting used to. 'It is a moving experience,' he ended, 'for me to see how in this city, where we began six years ago with just a handful of people, the entire public has arisen and is marching past below – workers and citizens and farmers and students and soldiers. . . Truly one can say, Germany is awakening.' Only Munich and Stuttgart refused to carry the broadcast.[9]

Chilling news awaited him on his return home at three A.M. that night. Assassins had gunned down his twenty-four year old S.A. officer Hans-Eberhard Maikowski and a police constable.[10] Maikowski, another veteran of the Pharus Rooms battle, had marched at the head of his No. 33 Sturm in that evening's parade. Hitler told Goebbels that he wanted no reprisals. He wanted the Red Terror to 'burn out' first – a phrase which Goebbels subtly changed in *Kaiserhof*, the published text, to 'flare up.' He had six hundred thousand Berliners line the rain-sodden streets of Berlin for the funeral of Maikowski and the policeman. The Berlin S.A.'s scoundrelly commander Count von Helldorff strutted at the head of the parade; he had put all bars off limits to his S.A. as a mark of respect that day, but he himself was sighted that evening in full uniform in a particularly sleazy Kurfürstendamm bar.[11]

Still feeble from her illness, Magda came home on February 1. Goebbels broke it to her that he was not included in Hitler's Cabinet. 'I am being frozen out,' he wrote in his diary. Although Hitler had mentioned a propaganda ministry several times in recent months, he had now given to the tedious and narrow-minded ex-schoolteacher Bernhard Rust the responsibility for culture and higher education in Prussia. Goebbels heard whispers that he was to be fobbed off with the job of radio commissioner. 'They've stood me in the corner,' he recorded privately. 'Fat lot of good Hitler is.'

Hitler did not even plan to take any steps as yet against the press. 'We want to lull them into a sense of security,' mimicked Goebbels. Things got worse. On February 5 Hitler appointed the financial journalist Walther Funk his Staatssekretär for 'press and propaganda.' Meanwhile throughout Prussia Göring appointed reliable new police chiefs, and added to the provisional arrest-lists of communists already prepared by his predecessors; Göring also banned the police force's rubber truncheons. A flurry of bans descended on their enemies – the Social Democrat newspapers like *Vorwärts* and 'all those Jewish organs,' as Goebbels wrote, 'that have been such a pain in our necks.'

The disappointment at being excluded from office gnawed at Goebbels. Never in robust health, he fell ill, his days and nights troubled by feverish fantasies. 'I am tired and disheartened,' he wrote in mid-February 1933. 'I have no aim and no longer take any pleasure in my work.' The party was in power, and he was an outcast! 'The likes of Göring reign supreme,' he observed ironically. When Karl Hanke, his chief aide, now told him not to expect any government funds for the coming election battle, Goebbels scoffed, 'Then let Fatso Göring do without his caviar for once!' (He prudently cut this suggestion out of the published text.) After a week in bed he went to the Sport Palace with Hitler and listened to His Master's guttural Voice intoning against marxism, setting the tenor of the coming final election battle. Hitler actually ended with the word 'Amen!' – a brilliant touch in Goebbels' view.

In the run-up to election eve, which Goebbels proclaimed to be the Day of the Awakening Nation, he developed a propaganda campaign of a depth and breadth surpassing anything before. Partial control of the radio stations ensured that every night his or Hitler's voice was heard. With the Prussian police now in Göring's hands, of course, the going was much easier. But the Jews and communists who had fled to Prague, Paris, and London poured vitriol over the new Hitler government. Irresponsible foreign journalists did the rest.

Even ex-chancellor Brüning, still in Germany, watched in fury as they filed blatantly untrue stories exaggerating the plight of the Jews. 'In the spring of 1933,' Brüning would write, 'foreign correspondents reported that the river Spree was covered with the corpses of murdered Jews.' At that time, he pointed out, hardly any Jews had suffered except for the leaders of the communist party.[12]

This year, 1933, was however the year of the Big Lie. On Monday evening February 27 occurred one of the most controversial episodes of the whole era. Hitler had come to dine with the Goebbels family. Shortly, Goebbels was called away to take a phone call from Hitler's friend Ernst 'Putzi' Hanfstaengl, a well-known prankster. Hanfstaengl shouted excitedly that the Reichstag building was on fire. Since Goebbels had twitted him with a phone call only days before, he ignored the message. Hanfstaengl phoned again, this time to report that he could see flames leaping out of the Reichstag's cupola.[13] Hitler and Goebbels tried to phone the Reichstag; nobody answered – small wonder, because a phone call to the Brandenburg Gate police station confirmed that the Reichstag was on fire. They drove off at top speed down the Charlottenburg Chaussee.

Afterward the world's press clamored that the Nazis themselves had started the blaze. With this author's discovery of the missing Goebbels Diary entries in Moscow, that version is finally laid to rest. He, Hitler, and Göring were equally stunned by the news.

> Hitler summons me to the Kaiserhof [this day's unpublished entry begins]. He's enthusiastic about my [radio] commentaries. Says Munich and Nuremberg were really great. . . Hitler fabulous as always. . .
>
> Back home to work. Much to do. At nine P.M. Hitler and Auwi come over. Music and gossip. Then Hanfstaengl phones: Says the Reichstag's on fire. What a wit! But turns out to be true. Race straight down there with Hitler. The entire building a mass of flames. [We] go in. Göring follows. Papen, whose acquaintance I thus make, is also there. Thirty arson sites. Fires set by the communists. Göring rampant, Hitler raging, Papen clear-headed. The main assembly chamber a picture of devastation. So take action now!. . . To work! Hitler consults with Papen. We meet back at the Kaiserhof. Everybody beaming. This was the last straw. Now we're well away. Culprit caught, a twenty-four-year-old Dutch communist.[14]

'He's being interrogated now,' Göring told them. 'We decided straight away to ban the communist press,' Goebbels related at the subsequent trial, 'and later the Social Democrat press too, and to take the top communist officials into custody.'[15] Göring ordered the S.A. to stand by in case of an all-out communist uprising.

At midnight Hitler and Goebbels hurried over to the *Völkischer Beobachter*'s Berlin office. It took half an hour even to get into the sleeping building, and more time was wasted while printworkers, compositors, and a surly sub-editor were found. There was no sign of Rosenberg himself, the editor. Scouring the proofs of the next day's edition, Hitler finally found the sensational news tucked away in the Berlin in Brief column ('Fire damage to the Reichstag'). 'Man, are you mad?' he shouted at the sub-editor. 'This is an event on a colossal scale!'[16]

> We drove over to the *VB* [Goebbels' diary continues]. It is really badly laid out. Hitler sets to work there straight away. I dictate a new gau poster and a fabulous article. . . [17] During the night all communist party officials are arrested. Entire communist and Social Democrat press banned. Good work done. . .

Over to Hitler at Kaiserhof. He's delighted with my article. It is half-past
five in the morning. . . Two S.A. men shot in Berlin. To sleep at seven. Three
hours. Then straight back to work!

The fire was a godsend to the Nazi radicals. Goebbels was already disquieted
by the speed with which Hitler and even Göring were succumbing to
Hindenburg's bourgeois spell. This lone communist fire-raiser had rescued the
revolution. During the night he sent for the journalist Alfred-Ingemar Berndt
to take down a fiery press release.[18] This announced the sweeping arrests, and
described the Reichstag fire as a communist beacon, a signal for a marxist
insurrection. This was as much a lie as the claim by Jewish and communist
agencies worldwide that the Nazis had staged the fire. Even the authoritative
Manchester Guardian published a dispatch from an anonymous special
correspondent alleging that Hitler, Göring, and Goebbels had foregathered in
Berlin that evening 'awaiting their fire.'[19] The world's press readily copied this
Big Lie, and historians in time adopted it from them.

Neither Hitler nor Goebbels wanted to believe that the mad Dutch
communist Marinus van der Lubbe had acted alone in torching the Reichstag
building. Eight years later Hitler still suspected that the hand of Ernst Torgler,
the communist leader, had been behind it.[20]

THE LAST FOUR DAYS of the election battle saw the scheming, marching, speaking,
singing, bell-ringing, flagwaving climax of Goebbels' career so far. On election
day itself, March 5, 1933 he and Magda escorted Hitler to a Wagner opera, then
sat up late waiting for the returns. Goebbels found them disappointing. True,
the Nazis had won 43·9 percent, but Hitler was still well short of the absolute
majority he craved; in his own Berlin constituency the Nazis had achieved with
31·3 percent the second lowest vote after Cologne-Aachen.

Goebbels however was now free to come into the government. Hitler
announced at his next Cabinet that the new Reichstag would be solemnly
inaugurated at a session in the famous Garrison Church at Potsdam, with
President von Hindenburg in attendance. 'Now,' he added, 'there must come
about a bold operation of propaganda and enlightenment, designed to forestall
any political lethargy. This public enlightenment must emanate from a newly
created central authority.'[21]

Thus Goebbels got his job as Reich minister of propaganda and public
enlightenment – a cumbersome title pressed on him by Hitler.[22] He hated
that word 'propaganda' and went to elaborate lengths over coming years
to cleanse it of its negative hubris.[23] As for the ministry, he already had the
necessary structure in mind – initially seven divisions, controlling the radio,
press, films, propaganda, and the theater as well as a legal department and
a defense department (to defend, that is, against lies). Nobody would ever
deny that Goebbels proved a capable minister, and in this he was aided by his
first Staatssekretär Walther Funk. They made an odd couple – the one now

notoriously heterosexual and seemingly ascetic, the other a homosexual and bon viveur. Funk later called his minister brilliant but devoid of any scruple and cruelly, coldly calculating. His personal conceit led to angry complaints over the years from composer Richard Strauss, conductor Wilhelm Furtwängler, movie star Emil Jannings, and scores of others. 'Goebbels' treatment of female artistes,' reminisced Funk irritably, 'was a great deal friendlier.'[24]

Berlin's Jewish community was stricken by forebodings. Hans Schäffer, still Staatssekretär in the finance ministry and a board-member of the powerful Ullstein newspaper group, wrote in his well-informed diary: 'It's apparently not definite whether Goebbels will also get the press under him. Hitler and Funk are opposed, as he'd become too powerful.'[25] Bella Fromm, forty-three-year-old society columnist on an Ullstein newspaper, noted the club foot and recalled her grandmother's advice: 'Beware of those who are marked.'[26] At a diplomatic reception later that month Goebbels found her at his table and expatiated rudely against all Jews and communists. The Romanian envoy soothingly told him that Jewish though the lovely Bella might be, she was right-wing. 'Even worse,' snapped the new minister.[27]

Initially Schäffer's minister, the conservative Count Schwerin von Krosigk, refused even to provide any funds for what he called 'this [propaganda ministry] nonsense.'[28] On the eleventh the Cabinet debated the new ministry; Hitler justified it as being necessary to prepare public opinion for important government actions – he cited a harmless-sounding agricultural example involving foodstuff policies, then added: 'The importance of all this in time of war must also be stressed. The government would act only after the public-enlightenment phase had run for some time and taken hold.' He would however reserve ultimate control of the press to himself. Only Hugenberg, a major newspaper owner, expressed qualms.[29] Two days later President von Hindenburg signed the decree establishing the propaganda ministry.[30]

Goebbels, Germany's youngest-ever minister, addressed his first ministerial press conference on March 15. 'The Reich government,' he told the world's newspapermen, 'needs more than fifty-two percent of the whole electorate – he had included the voters of the D.N.V.P., which was in coalition with Hitler – 'it needs the whole nation.'[31] Nobody ignored him now. The American ambassador warned his new president, Franklin D. Roosevelt, that Goebbels was a master orator – far superior to Hitler and far cleverer.[32]

TO HOUSE his new ministry Goebbels had been allocated the rambling old Prince-Leopold Palace on Wilhelms Platz, right across from Hitler's chancellery. It was the kind of listed architecture before which civil servants instinctively genuflected. Its great salons had been kept permanently locked, the priceless furniture shrouded in dustsheets. The paneling was dark and musty, the windows narrow and obscured by heavy drapes. A refit was out of the question. The building's custodian, Hofrat (privy councilor) Schwebel, nervously lectured the young new-comer that not even the minister's own office could be changed. Goebbels ignored him. Had there not been a revolution? He recruited builders and decorators from the ranks of his S.A. and they stripped out the offending plaster and stucco overnight. 'You might go to prison for that,' gasped Schwebel.[33]

Goebbels moved in on Wednesday March 22, 1933.

The international Big Lie campaign (as the Nazis saw it) against Hitler's Germany had redoubled in intensity since the election. Disgruntled opponents committed outrages in stolen Nazi uniforms. The Cabinet approved harsh penalties for such impersonations – Goebbels even urged the death penalty.[34] Émigré journalists published lurid reports from Berlin. One said that Hitler had ordered Torgler's ears cut off; another that the body of Hirsch, the editor of *Red Flag*, had been found floating in a canal; a third that Ernst Thälmann had been tortured to death. Enraged by the newspaper dispatches, the international Jewish community started a boycott of German goods.[35] In London, Jewish restaurants refused to serve Germans. Goebbels retaliated by inviting Sefton Delmer, a British newspaperman who had covered the Reichstag blaze, to visit Torgler, Hirsch, and Thälmann in custody.

Offered the front page of the London *Daily Express*, Goebbels challenged the émigrés to name even one Jew who had yet died. 'The Jews living in Germany,' he wrote in his article, 'have held such an enormously large number of powerful posts in the life of the nation that the German element seemed almost completely excluded from the leading positions.' He blamed the Jews for spreading similar atrocity stories during the world war. 'The German nation today has other business to do than to stage blood baths and indulge in Jew baiting.'[36] Berlin wiretaps confirmed that the Hearst Press's Berlin correspondent was the arch culprit.[37]

The upshot of the Jewish campaign overseas was that Goebbels secured from Hitler – or so he claimed – approval to threaten a short, sharp counter-boycott of the Jews. He told his Cabinet colleagues on March 29 that this threat had been extremely effective and that the main Jewish agency in Berlin, the Central-Verein, had promised that the foreign smear campaign would cease. Nevertheless on March 31 he announced a one-day boycott of all Jewish stores. 'Tomorrow,' he said, broadcasting from a mass rally, 'not one German man or woman is to enter a Jewish store.' There would follow a three-day period to assess the impact of the boycott, and it would be repeated if necessary until, as he put it, 'German Jewry has been annihilated.'[38] Raising the boycott at midnight on April 1, he told a cheering throng in the Lustgarten that he could easily reimpose it. 'If it must be resumed,' he threatened, 'we shall crush German Jewry.'[39]

The world's press greeted Goebbels' crude but effective boycott with uproar (while overlooking the Jewish boycott which had triggered it). Speaking to an official British visitor Goebbels quoted in justification the familiar figures on the preponderance of Jews among Germany's lawyers, doctors, and other wealthy professions. As for isolated anti-Jewish outrages reported during

see Chap 4, Who is Israel by Matt Furse.

The New York Times.

All the News That's Fit to Print.

LATE CITY EDITION

WEATHER—Fair and warmer to-day; tomorrow fair and colder.

VOL. LXXXII....No. 27,487.

NEW YORK, TUESDAY, MARCH 28, 1933.

TWO CENTS

Copyright, 1933, by The New York Times Company.

LEHMAN BEER BILL CHANGED TO ALLOW DRINKING AT BARS

Governor Approves Amendment Authorizing Control Board to Permit It.

SENATE PASSAGE PLEDGED

But McGinnies, After Battle, Wins Assembly Majority for the Dunkel Bill.

3.2 WINE CONTROL ASKED

Executive Calls on Commission to Present Measure—Dunkel Bill Changes Benefit Brewers.

By W. A. WARN.

Federal Pay Cut of 15% on April 1 Looms; 4-Year Decline in Living Costs Put at 23%

By The Associated Press.

WASHINGTON, March 27.

ROOSEVELT SAVES MILLIONS BY UNION OF FARM AGENCIES

Orders Farm Board Abolished in Consolidation Under New Credit Administration.

MORGENTHAU "GOVERNOR"

Red Cross Will Take Over Last of Stabilization Wheat and Cotton.

PLAN TO CUT FARM DEBT

Wife of British Labor Leader Bars Dirges at Her Funeral

By The Canadian Press.

LONDON, March 27 — Mrs. George Lansbury, wife of the leader of the British Labor party, who died Thursday, did not want her funeral to be a mournful affair but rather an occasion for thanksgiving to God for a happy life.

55,000 HERE STAGE PROTEST ON HITLER ATTACKS ON JEWS; NAZIS ORDER A NEW BOYCOTT

BAN ON JEWS SPREADS

Hitler's Party Prepares Boycott in Revenge for 'Atrocity Tales.'

VAST PROPAGANDA OPENS

Religious Leaders Send Cables to Clergymen Here Denying Persecution Reports.

STEEL HELMETERS SEIZED

Leaders of Veterans' Society, Which Has a Cabinet Post,

Braun Cabinet of Prussia Out; Lost Its Power Last Summer

Special Cable to THE NEW YORK TIMES.

BERLIN, March 27.—The Prussian Socialist-Centrist Cabinet, which was headed by Otto Braun,

35,000 JAM STREETS OUTSIDE THE GARDEN

Solid Lines of Police Hard Pressed to Keep Overflow

OTHER FAITHS JOIN IN

Crowd Overflowing the Garden Hears Leaders Assail Persecution.

CHEERS PLEA BY SMITH

He Likens Hitlerism to Klan; Calls Upon German People in Name of Humanity.

NO ATTACK ON COUNTRY

Manning, Wise, McConnell and Green Denounce Bigotry—

JAPAN QUITS LEAGUE TO 'INSURE PEACE'

Says Differences as to the Situation in Manchuria Are Now Irreconcilable.

FRIDAY, MARCH 24, 1933

A Daily Express

To-day's Weather: Fair; Mild.

NO. 10,258.

FRIDAY, MARCH 24, 1933.

ONE PENNY.

BUY BRITISH ballito STOCKINGS

St. IVEL CHEESE Aids digestion 2d., 6d. & 8½d. each.

JUDEA DECLARES WAR ON GERMANY
Jews Of All The World Unite In Action

BOYCOTT OF GERMAN GOODS

MASS DEMONSTRATIONS IN MANY DISTRICTS

DRAMATIC ACTION

"Daily Express" Special Political Correspondent.

ALL Israel is uniting in wrath against the Nazi onslaught on the Jews in Germany.

Adolf Hitler, swept into power by an appeal to elemental patriotism, is making history of a kind he least expected. Thinking to unite only the German nation to race consciousness he has roused the whole Jewish people to a national renaissance.

HIGHER WAGES FOR STEEL WORKERS

AN INCREASE OF THREE SHILLINGS A WEEK

BRIGHT SPOT IN A BLACK TOWN

New "Sweep" Bill In The Dail

THE "Daily Express" has sent a special representative on an unusual mission.

MR. MacDONALD EXPLAINS HIS TOUR

"PEACE CAN BE KEPT IN EUROPE"

MR. RAMSAY MACDONALD faced a crowded House of Commons yesterday afternoon when he spoke about his visits to Paris, Geneva, and Rome, and his talks with Signor Mussolini.

LATE NEWS

On March 24, 1933 newspapers around the world announce the beginning of a Jewish international boycott of Germany. A few days later, Dr Goebbels responds with a German boycott of Jewish stores.

the boycott, he claimed that communists disguised in Nazi uniforms had perpetrated them.[40]

He enjoyed the thrill of unbridled power; he fancied that the world's Jews were whimpering with fear.[41] Yet his antisemitism was still broadly tactical, rather than innate. He *needed* the stimulus of a visible enemy. He could still split his sides laughing at the Jewish comedian Otto Wallburg, who would later die in Auschwitz.[42] When Furtwängler, conductor of the Berlin Philharmonic, bravely protested at the discrimination against Otto Klemperer, Bruno Walter, and Max Reinhardt, Goebbels replied: 'We can see no objection to having Leo Blech [another Jew] direct some German masterpiece at the state opera, because no one gets the feeling of any violence done to the national spirit. But it is not necessary that the *majority* of opera conductors should be Jews. . . Those of Jewish blood who have real ability should be free to exercise their art: But they must not call the shots.'[43]

HE ATTENDED virtually every Cabinet that year. Intellectually far above the rest, he easily worsted them in debate. Between them the dialectician Goebbels and the brutal Göring made opposition impossible. 'They attacked every problem,' Vice-Chancellor von Papen recalled, 'with the furious *élan* of the rabble-rouser.'[44] Goebbels' secret diary now bristled with barbed references to Göring's pathological ambition, his pompous megalomania, and his ever gaudier uniforms.[45] He had to fight hard to wrest control of the radio from the aviator's porcine clutches.[46] He found Göring cavorting with his lady friend Emmy (still married to another) at the Berghof in August. Hitler delivered an outspoken speech to his gauleiters about uniforms – 'no names,' wrote Goebbels, stifling a chuckle, 'but everybody knew whom he meant.'[47] Learning that 'Fatso' was demanding the rank of general, Goebbels wrote, 'Why not field marshal and be done with it!'[48]

ON APRIL 25 he returned home to receive the civic dignities that the worthies of his native Rheydt now hastened to bestow upon him. The townsfolk had hung out a sea of flags; the catholic church bells pealed, no doubt equally willingly. He had let it be known that he desired a torchlight parade past his home. His mother stood beside him at an upstairs window. 'For eight years she has been vilified on my account,' he lectured the mayor. 'And she was the only one who understood me.'[49] At his old school he spoke once more from the stage where he had delivered the valediction sixteen years before. Local boy makes good: His career in infamy was only just beginning.

21: *Bonfire of the Books*

IN APRIL 1933 THE REICH CABINET tackled May Day: Should this traditional workers' festival now be proscribed?

'Leave May Day to me,' said Goebbels, and declared it a Nazi national holiday instead – bigger and brasher than anything that had gone before. He rallied a million and a half Berliners on the Tempelhof fields and basked beside the Führer in his open limousine as it majestically rolled through the cheering masses.

'Mein Führer,' he boasted at the microphone, 'I stand before you as the 'spokesman of the greatest multi-million movement that German soil has ever borne!'[1]

An acrid stench filled the Berlin air as Hitler was dining with Auwi on May 10. He heard that an enormous bonfire of books was blazing beneath newsreel floodlights in the opera square, and made a wry comment about Goebbels' revolutionary activism.[2]

In fact Goebbels was not the instigator.[3] The party's student organization had first approached his ministry a month earlier for financial support for this symbolic burning of decadent and anti-German literature. Although they had listed him as principal speaker in a draft program as early as April 10, for several weeks he had kept his distance: He had after all studied under famous Jewish teachers like Waldberg and Gundolf.

It was not until a week before the event that his adjutant finally conveyed to the students his agreement to deliver the main speech.[4] Between the opera and the university they had erected a crisscross log pyre, some twelve feet square and five feet high, on a thick bed of sand. Some streets away, five thousand students assembled in their full regalia and solemnly marched to the square carrying flaming torches, with an S.A. marching band at their head. Forty thousand Berliners packed the square. As the students hove into sight, followed by motorized tumbrels charged with the condemned books and pamphlets, the Berliners' cheering turned into mass hysteria.

'I thought they'd all gone stark raving mad,' wrote Bella Fromm privately, 'particularly the womenfolk.'[5]

The students marched around the bonfire tossing books onto it. Indictments were read over the loudspeakers. As each hated author was named, the cheers rang louder – and not just in Berlin: In every German university city the

166

bonfires blazed that night, on the Königsplatz in Munich, the Römerberg in Frankfurt, and the Castle Square in Breslau.

At midnight the little Doctor himself drove up and mounted the swastika-decked rostrum. Golo Mann, a student witness of the scene, noticed that Goebbels seemed distinctly ill at ease.[6] His brief radio commentary was heard all over Germany. 'The Age of Jewish Intellectualism is over,' he remarked, in a tone that was more reasoned than inflammatory. 'This symbolic fire is blazing now outside many a German university, to show the world that here the intellectual basis of the November Republic is sinking into the ground.' 'If the old men cannot understand what is going on,' he intoned, 'then let them grasp that we young men have gone and done it!'

The ugly bonfires seized the world's headlines. The New York Times devoted a whole page to them, and published the Nazis' list of 160 proscribed authors in full.[7]

Speaking in the Sport Palace the next day Goebbels warned the Jews against continuing their international boycott against Germany. 'We have spared the Jews,' he said, 'but if they think . . . that they can again stroll down the Kurfürstendamm as if nothing at all has happened, let them heed my words as a last warning.' The Jews were guests in Germany, he said, and must behave accordingly.[8]

THAT MONTH, May 1933, Goebbels announced extensive overseas trips to explain the new Germany. He mentioned Danzig, Vienna, Rome, and Chicago (he hoped to be Germany's delegate to Chicago's World's Fair). Reaction was swift. The Danzig Senate banned him from speaking, and the Jews orchestrated massive protests in Chicago.[9] *Home of Univ. of Chicago + Mercentile Exchange!*

Italy posed none of these problems. Goebbels traveled there at the end of May taking not only the Italian-speaking Magda, as Otto Wagener remarked jealously to Bella Fromm, but 'a few of his mistresses who are disguised as his secretaries.'[10] The incumbent ambassador in Rome, Ulrich von Hassell, struck Goebbels as singularly incompetent.[11]

Officially the propaganda minister's purpose was to study the Italian movie industry, but he also engaged in secret talks with the king and Mussolini. He had long admired the Duce as an inspiring orator. 'Mussolini,' he once observed, 'does not like to be photographed smiling. Why should he? To be a statesman takes instinct, circumspection, and a gift for both organization and oratory.'[12]

On parting, Mussolini bade Goebbels assure Hitler that he would go through thick and thin with him.[13]

A MEN'S FASHION magazine publishes a photograph taken in Rome – of Goebbels in gala uniform, with the tongue-in-cheek caption: 'The Society Dress for Storm Troopers.'[14] Magda has similar public relations problems. Commanded by Ullstein's now Nazi-groveling *Berliner Zeitung* to include her in a series on prominent society hostesses, Bella Fromm gags and persuades

Bertolt Brecht to write the piece for her. Magda's secretary politely returns the draft with the directive that 'Frau Reichsminister Goebbels . . . does not desire the public to be told of her interest in Buddhism.' A reference to her playing chess is also to be deleted.[15]

    With the Frau Reichsminister, as the Goebbels Diary hints that spring, the first problems are arising. The honeymoon is over, and his lifestyle is to blame. After one frigid drive to Koblenz, he writes that he has sorted things out with her – 'We were beginning to fall out. . . She really is a sweet and lovely woman.'[16] While omitting this private passage from *Kaiserhof*, he does leave in their subsequent visit to Freiburg with 'its Castle Hill, and old chestnut trees' – surely a little subtle flagwaving to Anka, whom he fondly imagines among the book's millions of readers.

    In his view there is no room for women in politics.[17] To his irritation however Magda becomes a patron of the new National Socialist Welfare organization (N.S.V.), and a few days later she broadcasts on Mother's Day.[18] Goebbels angrily attends her inaugural reception for the N.S.V. at the Kaiserhof. His diary takes note only of the other gorgeous women there.[19] When her millionaire ex-husband is arrested for tax evasion, Goebbels, jealous of their continued clandestine meetings, refuses to intercede; bail is set at four million marks (a million dollars).[20] On May 10 he records tersely, 'Row with Magda.' He has told her while in Italy that they should now add to their little family, and try this time for something more useful, perhaps, than a girl.[21] With the necessary act still unperformed, Magda betakes herself and their infant Helga to the fashionable Baltic resort of Heiligendamm for the summer, leaving the little Doctor to cool his heels and ardor in Berlin for a while. When Goebbels briefly joins her he again brings several females with him: Among them, Bella Fromm learns, is the lovely Hela Strehl, a fashion editor at Scherl Verlag. 'Relations between Hela and Magda Goebbels,' records the journalist, 'are inevitably strained.'[22]

    The Goebbelses' apartment on Reichskanzler Platz is now overcrowded, what with the chauffeur and burly S.S. bodyguards. At the end of June 1933 Hitler assigns Hugenberg's former official residence to them. It is a secluded little villa built in 1835 in an overgrown park and shielded from the street – soon to be renamed Hermann-Göring Strasse – by centuries-old trees. The villa stands next to the American embassy. Goebbels hands the villa's keys to Magda on July 1. She swiftly turns it into a fairy-tale castle, furnishing it with expensive antiques from a store in Nettelbeck Strasse. Two weeks later they can move in. A week after that Director Jakob Werlin of Daimler-Benz brings them a new Mercedes motor car.[23] What more can the modern German minister's heart desire?

HIS PROPAGANDA MINISTRY has a lavish budget from the first day. He had boasted that it was going to cost the taxpayer nothing, and kept his word. It would have an income in fiscal 1933 of 10,737,500 marks (around $2·7m at that time), largely from radio license fees. Its projected expenditure was 13,528,500 marks; the shortfall would be more than matched by the money, put at 4,247,000 marks, consequently saved by the ministry of the interior, the Reich chancellery, and the foreign ministry. For Goebbels himself the ministry's budget provided an annual expense allowance of 4,800 marks plus a net ministerial income of 59,500 marks (around $15,000). The 1933 budget also allowed 25,000 marks for the purchase of two automobiles for Dr Goebbels and Funk, as well as 190,000 marks for setting up provincial propaganda agencies, *Landespropagandaämter* (from 1937, Reich propaganda agencies); of these there would eventually be forty-one. A quarter of a million marks were set aside for enlarging the ministry building by fifty rooms, and eighty thousand marks for expanding its telephone network from seventy-four to 150 extensions.[24] His own instrument had over fifty pushbuttons coded in a kaleidoscope of colors: his ministry would eventually sprawl over fifty-four buildings in Berlin alone.

His corruption aside, he was a model minister. By enforcing economies on the Berlin radio network alone he would save one million marks and use this money for other cultural activities.[25] He regrouped the regional networks under one national radio authority. In his first months of office he replaced the top echelons in broadcasting with trusty Nazis and appointed the self-important and humorless Eugen Hadamovsky as national director.[26] Broadcasting prospered in Nazi Germany as in no other European country at that time.

From four million listeners in 1933 the figure would soar to twenty-nine million in 1934 and ninety-seven million in 1939, with a corresponding leap in his license income. He was thrilled by the technological advances. At the annual radio fair he found himself telephoning with Siam, and with the captain of the liner Bremen on the high seas. People told him that television would follow within months.[27]

A biography is not the place for a full analysis of the ministerial structure which Dr Goebbels created and ran. He changed its organizational chart frequently – an amorphous structure of vertical departments (*Abteilungen*) which split, subdivided, spawned, and coalesced again over the ministry's twelve-year existence. His office was large but not lavishly furnished, boasting only a desk, some bookcases, and a globe.

He had selected tough young Nazis as his lieutenants and their verve, coupled with the bureaucratic skills of the senior civil servants, initially assigned by other ministries, ensured his success. Eighty-two percent of his initial staff came from outside the civil service; they were *Angestellte* (temporary salaried staff), not *Beamte* (permanent civil servants) – an important distinction.[28] Ninety percent were veteran party members. One hundred of his initial 350 staff members had the party's badge in Gold.[29] He preferred revolutionary fervor to bureaucratic ability.[30] He promoted on performance, not age or seniority – Dr Werner Naumann, quick-witted, lean, and ambitious, would become his last Staatssekretär in 1944 at the age of only thirty-four.

At first there was a shambles as his erstwhile desperadoes and bare-knuckle streetfighters learned the ropes of government service. But they soon had the new ministry up and running. Most outstanding among his minions was Karl Hanke, not yet thirty: Bullet-headed, dour, and handsome, he was put in charge of Goebbels' private office (Ministerbüro). Goebbels persuaded the Cabinet to allow Hanke the high civil service rank of Ministerialrat.[31]

Now Goebbels not only chose the game, he laid down the rules. 'Why the complaints?' he boasted to cheering Nazis at the Sport Palace, explaining his new press laws. 'The foxes outsmarted the sheep, and it's only right that the foxes now forbid the sheep to attack them.'[32] That the professions in Germany were regulated was nothing new: There was already a Literary Academy, of which Heinrich Mann was chairman. The Press Association had also existed before Hitler.[33] But within six months Goebbels would force everybody working in the field of German cultural endeavor to toe the party line – from journalism, writing, and publishing right across the spectrum to the opera, theater, and movie.

On August 14 his diary first mentioned a chamber of culture.[34] Concerned by Robert Ley's attempts to force all cultural workers into his monolithic Labor Front, a month earlier Goebbels had written hastily to the Reich chancellery stating that he intended to establish such a chamber himself.[35] He had set out his ideas to harness Germany's creative artistes to the new National Socialist state in a memorandum to Hitler three days later.[36] Hitler gave him the go-ahead on the Obersalzberg on August 24.[37] This awesome governing body would become the umbrella authority for seven sub-chambers, controlling the press (presided over by Nazi press baron Max Amann),[38] literature (Hans Friedrich Blunck), theater (Otto Laubinger), music (Richard Strauss),[39] the graphic arts (Professor Eugen Hönig),[40] movie, and radio (Hadamovsky).[41] The chamber of culture dispensed considerable funds and subsidies, setting up specialist schools, meeting welfare needs, providing legal aid, and conducting professional examinations. Goebbels was its president and Funk vice-president; but the chamber's day-to-day management was in the hands of the ruthless, ambitious and antisemitic Nazi Hans Hinkel, with the equally rabid Nazi lawyer Hans Ernst Schmidt-Leonhardt as his legal adviser. Full Jews could not belong; nor could anybody stripped of German citizenship.[42] Among the chamber's records was later found a blacklist enumerating all those anti-Nazi writers and émigrés whose membership was banned, including Dr Bernhard Weiss, Albert Grzesinski, and 'Nahum Goldmann, eastern Jew, businessman, and agitator.'[43]

The chamber of culture began operations on September 22. Each of its sub-chambers was further divided into *Fachschaften* and *Fachgruppen* – specialist chapels: The stage had forty thousand members, dance six thousand, and light entertainment thirteen thousand. Each sub-chamber was empowered to impose fines of up to one hundred thousand marks. Each such penalty was reviewed by its corresponding ministerial section and by Dr Goebbels himself.

Henceforth, German art was to be pure. The chamber of music prohibited the playing of atonal, 'Jewish,' and Negro music; surrealist art, cubism, and dadaism were among the prohibited genres. At the formal dedication of

the chamber of culture in mid-November in the Berlin Philharmonic Hall
Goebbels declared the old decadent, worm-eaten liberalism finished.[44] In an
analysis of the 'ruling trio' in Nazi Germany, American ambassador William
E. Dodd had no hesitation in nominating Goebbels as Hitler's 'first lieutenant,'
ranking even above Göring. 'While Hitler is a fair orator as German oratory
goes,' stated Dodd, 'Goebbels is a past master. He . . . has combined all the
newspaper, radio, publications, and art activities of Germany into one vast
propaganda machine.'[45]

The Press Law (*Schriftleitergesetz*) enacted on October 4, 1933 abolished the
principle of anonymous journalism.[46] It made journalists and their editors
personally responsible for their writings. Henceforth the proper qualifications
had to be earned either on the shop floor, starting literally as a compositor's
apprentice, or on an approved university course in journalism.[47] The editor
became a *Schriftleiter*, a true German word replacing *Redakteur*, which to
Goebbels' sensitive ear had a Jewish ring. Jews were excluded here too, often
with mortal consequences. 'My dear "Poulette",' wrote Bella Fromm in her
diary, referring to journalist Vera von Huhn, 'has been so upset, as she's not
wholly Aryan, that she's taken an overdose of Veronal. I am at my wit's end.'[48]

GOEBBELS HAD ALWAYS taken a close interest in the movie industry. He moved
swiftly both to expand it and to impose Nazi constraints on its members. In
May 1933 he reached agreement with Dr Ludwig Klitzsch, general manager of the
largest studio, Universum Film AG (Ufa), about setting up a film credit bank
initially financed by the ministry.[49] Once again no Jews were allowed in the
industry, and on October 19 the industry's chamber announced that it would
not pass for exhibition any films on which non-members had worked.[50]

Under his patronage the German movie industry bloomed. Despite, or
perhaps because of, the treasures that he and his ministry had lavished on
them – the inflated salaries, the pensions, and the handouts when they fell
on hard times – its members almost unanimously heaped calumnies on
Goebbels after 1945. Secure in the knowledge that he was dead, they related
bawdy tales of blackmail and rape in the hope of being regarded as the
victims, and not the beneficiaries, of the Nazi reign. Cant and cattiness would
distort the image of a man who was, admittedly, no saint. Only one actress,
the beautiful Lida Baarova, would speak well of him (and still does);[51] others
would spread malicious gossip, charging for example that actress and director
Leni Riefenstahl 'only made the grade by going to bed with Goebbels.' In self-
defense Riefenstahl too talked unfavorably about the minister. 'I always was
in bad standing with him,' she would confide to her captors. 'He was cold and
forbidding toward me. I almost hated him.'[52]

Five years younger than Goebbels, Leni Riefenstahl starred mostly in snow-
capped mountain dramas. By her published account Goebbels, freshly arrived
as gauleiter in Berlin, had hung around the 1926 première of her movie *The
Sacred Mountain* hoping for a glimpse of her; by his own diary's testimony,

he saw her in 1929 starring in the mountaineering movie *Piz Palü*, and found her a 'delightful child.'[53] He probably met her at Magda's society gatherings at Reichskanzler Platz in the autumn of 1932. In her memoirs she relates sharing a train journey to Munich with him in November 1932; he talked for hours of power struggles and homosexuality, before taking her along to see Hitler speak the next day. In his diary, Goebbels wrote of this train journey: 'Long talk with Mr Schnee. . . He traveled to Munich with me and wants to speak with Hitler here. Arrived dead tired.' It is probably not too fanciful to suspect that his 'Mr Snow' was none other than Leni Riefenstahl.[54]

Whatever ardor may have been concealed by the use of the pseudonym faded rapidly thereafter. In her 1987 memoirs she provided a lurid description of Dr Goebbels visiting her late in 1932 and forcing his attentions on her – of him kneeling before her weeping, of her crying out, 'Go, Herr Doctor, go!'[55] On Christmas Eve, so her narrative continues, Goebbels arrived unannounced with two gifts for her – a red leather-bound first edition of *Mein Kampf* and a bronze Goebbels medallion. 'I am so lonely,' he moaned, explaining that Magda had just been rushed to the clinic: 'I fear for her life.'[56]

Human memory of course plays harmless tricks. It suppresses, elides, compresses, and inflates. But there was more. In May 1933, her memoirs relate, Goebbels persuaded her to drive him deep into the Grunewald woods, where he showed her his pistol ('I don't leave home without it') and then made a pass at her as she drove her car in a slippery slalom around the rain-lashed trees; as he put his arm around her waist, the car hit a hummock and slithered to a halt, its wheels spinning. What had he intended? What indeed had she? The vehicle now immobilized, he limped off distraught in one direction, suggesting she head in the other.[57]

The Goebbels Diaries, not always a monument to truthfulness, made no reference to any such undignified episodes. They did however report continued interviews and discussions with 'L. Riefenstahl' of a frequency now difficult to reconcile with the bodice-ripping tenor of her memoirs. She told him on May 16 of her production plans; he suggested a movie on Hitler himself; Leni, 'inspired,' accompanied the Goebbelses to *Madame Butterfly* that evening. A few days later she picnicked with him and Hitler at Heiligendamm.[58] Magda told her privately that she had married Dr Goebbels only so as to be near to Hitler.[59] What of Leni's politics? 'She is the only one of all the stars,' wrote Goebbels that summer, 'who understands us.'[60]

Her name often cropped up in the diary, and in mid-August she spent the night at Heiligendamm with the Goebbelses again.[61] Given all of this it is hard to visualize the further scene which her memoirs now describe – Goebbels invited her over that summer to suggest a movie on the power of the press: He lunged at her breast, she dragged herself free, ran to the door and found a bell: By which she was saved.[62] That September she made her first great movie of the party's annual Nuremberg rally, a masterpiece which would be surpassed only by her second such movie, *Triumph of the Will*.

ALL OF THIS is not to say that Dr Goebbels does not stray from the path of marital fidelity at all. He certainly dallied with Ello Quandt, Magda's unhappily married sister-in-law.[63] Signing autographs at the Berlin S.A.'s sports festival that summer, Goebbels points his pencil at a particular blonde. 'Find out her name,' he whispers to his adjutant. Police headquarters provide the data he needs, and a few days later she is glimpsed traipsing down the red-carpeted marble staircase from the minister's private quarters.[64]

Relations with Magda are strained. She has accepted the post of honorary patron to the Reich Fashion Bureau. It brings her into contact with the Jews of Germany's rag trade. When he orders Magda to resign, she sulks, and refuses to go down to the annual Bayreuth festival with him. 'If Magda doesn't mend her ways,' he grimly records, 'I'll have to draw some conclusions.' Hitler sends his private plane to fetch her. She makes her grand appearance after Act One, and the Führer negotiates a truce between them. A true pal, reflects Goebbels: 'He agrees with me,' he adds, 'women have no place in public life.'[65] After Wagner's *Valkyrie* on July 25 the minister is summoned by phone to visit a Baltic baroness waiting at the festival restaurant. 'A fabulous woman,' sighs Hitler, and explains: 'The bolsheviks nailed her husband to the door of his house.' She has donated her fortune to the party. Now she wants to introduce Dr Goebbels to a friendly princess; the latter alas turns out to be a corpulent and elderly dowager. Since he makes no secret of his lack of interest, the princess declaims to Hitler loud enough for all the room to hear, 'Excuse me, mein Führer, but tell me: What do you think about *adultery*?' Cringing, Goebbels comments in his diary on how unpleasant Bayreuth has become.[66]

On August 1 he exchanges his well-tailored party uniform for a white summer suit and begins a seaside vacation with Magda at Heiligendamm. He likes to nurse his Latin tan – even in winter he uses a sun lamp – but frowns on women who use such artificial aids. Once, sitting in his beach basket, he lectures the scantily clad beauties who swarm around him: 'The German woman does not bleach her hair.' The girls suppress astonished chuckles. He has not detected that his own wife is not a natural blonde. 'Since when have you worn lipstick, my sweetest,' he once asks her. 'Always,' she replies. (He does not believe her.)[67]

Leni Riefenstahl describes one scene which rings very true. At the chancellery one day Hitler commands her to report on progress with her movie on the 1933 rally. She has filmed a few thousand meters of wooden, unconvincing footage of the event, but protests to Hitler that Goebbels and the party, who have their own agenda, have placed every possible obstacle in her way. Humiliated, Goebbels bawls at her afterward: 'If you were a man, I would throw you down the stairs.'[68] Working now at the party's command she completes the editing of this movie, *Victory of Faith*, and is paid a director's fee of twenty thousand marks from ministry funds. The hour-long movie has its premiere at the Ufa Palace on the first day of December 1933, then vanishes for the next sixty years (because it features Ernst Röhm).

THAT SUMMER Dr Goebbels organized an outing of thousands of automobiles along the land corridor through Poland to East Prussia. It was a clever propaganda exercise; the summer drive through Poland to this amputated German province with its rolling farmland where the famous Trakehnen thoroughbred horses were raised and its gaily decorated German towns like Rastenburg and Gumbinnen – names that still had to find their shivering niche in history – was not without effect on the foreign journalists.[69]

Tightening his grip on the press that September he brought all advertising under the control of one advertising council, the *Werberat*. 'All advertising must be true,' his guidelines laid down. More importantly in a country swamped with six thousand different newspaper titles, he enforced the first elements of standardization to enable even the smallest businesses to profit from advertising, using standard-size matrices.[70] Newspapers were also ordered to publish honest circulation figures. These and other commonsense regulations would long outlive Goebbels in modern Germany.

He also limped briefly onto the stage of international diplomacy. The League of Nations disarmament conference was to resume in Geneva, Switzerland, on September 22. Konstantin von Neurath, Hitler's foreign minister, suggested that Goebbels accompany the German delegation to explain and justify his anti-Jewish measures.[71]

On the eve of departure Goebbels told reporters: 'Germany does not want war. Indeed, we are in no condition for one.'[72] Leaving by air from Rüdesheim the next day he pointed out, 'It is the "pacifist" nations which always prepare for the next war.' On the phone, Hitler advised him to deliver a cautious speech, and Goebbels did as he was told. He dressed impeccably in a suit and striped tie just like the others; interpreter Paul Schmidt marveled at the speed with which the Nazi agitator adopted the local argot – within hours of his arrival he was speaking with all the oleaginous ease of a practiced Geneva diplomat.[73]

At the suggestion of Baron Ernst von Weizsäcker, Hitler's envoy to Switzerland and one of the oiliest of them all, Goebbels was invited to meet lawyers and academic dignitaries. A professor of economics questioned the Führer Principle. 'You are probably a reservist,' Goebbels argued. 'If an enemy barrage is beginning, the *Führerprinzip* is your only salvation. We Germans are under that barrage.'[74]

The mood toward him was initially frosty. For various reasons Goebbels decided to address only a press conference and not the general assembly. Although the French urged a boycott, three hundred journalists turned up to hear him in the mirrored salon of the Carlton Palace hotel. Nobody applauded when he rose, and very few when he finished speaking. This was not Nazi Germany.

In his two-hour speech, pronounced in a serious, baritone voice, he reviewed the Nazi 'revolution' and claimed that eighty percent would vote for Hitler in an election now. Justifying the concentration camps which the Nazis had set up, he invited any foreigner to inspect them.

Turning to the Jewish problem, he trotted out the familiar figures about how the Jews dominated the medical and legal professions in Berlin, with similar figures for the press, literature, theater, cinema, stock exchange, and Reichstag. 'By settling the Jewish problem legally,' he argued, 'the German government has opted for the most humane method.' Nobody, he waspishly pointed out, had offered to absorb Germany's Jewish refugees.[75]

A Polish woman journalist challenged him on Nazi Germany's lack of freedom of expression. 'You can't write what you want either,' retorted Goebbels, baring his teeth into a smile. 'But only what your publisher allows.'[76]

The French foreign minister Joseph Paul-Boncour was impressed by the contrast between Goebbels' gleaming eyes and elegant gestures, and his misshapen physique.[77] Baron Kurt von Stutterheim, the *Berliner Tageblatt*'s former London correspondent, told Anthony Eden that Goebbels reminded him of the Irish rebel leaders during the Troubles. 'There is a strong fanatical strain in him.'[78] All in all Baron von Weizsäcker felt that Goebbels had done a good job.[79]

22: Twilight of the Gods and Tally-Ho

ONE DAY THAT SEPTEMBER of 1933 twenty thousand well-drilled schoolchildren formed up in a Berlin stadium into a map of Germany, while clusters of smiling children standing outside represented the lost German provinces of Memel, Danzig, and the Saar. At a given signal Germany's frontiers opened to engulf these communities abroad, and the whole mass melted into a giant swastika. Germany, Goebbels told the youthful audience, wanted peace.[1] At a ceremony marking the 250th anniversary of the first German settlement in America he spoke of a new era of understanding between nations.[2] 'I am calling over the Rhine,' he said at Bad Honnef a few days later, gesturing toward France. We want peace. We are ready to expunge the past.'[3] That October, Hitler took Germany out of the League of Nations. On November 12 after a typical Goebbels propaganda drive ninety-three percent of the German electorate voted their approval.

A campaign of anti-Nazi Big Lies began – many of them uncomfortably close to the truth. In London, the *Saturday Review* published a forged article, attributed to Goebbels, demanding the revision of the east German border at Poland's expense.[4] In France, the *Petit Parisien* reproduced instructions which Goebbels had allegedly issued to his propaganda offices overseas, backing up these territorial claims; these too were a forgery.[5]

Fighting back, Goebbels took up an idea which the party's propaganda office had already mooted as a fund-raising gimmick in 1932, an anti-Comintern, as the counterpart of the Comintern, the Soviet Union's international subversion agency. 'The Moscow Jews,' wrote Dr Eberhard Taubert, head of his anti-communist section, in a later overview explaining Goebbels' tactics, 'had to be defeated with their own weapons.'[6] Taubert's anti-Comintern plugged the seductive line that bolshevism was a Jewish swindle aiming for world domination, and that Hitler was the only remaining obstacle. With the trial of the alleged Reichstag arsonists approaching, Goebbels told Taubert to publish documentation alleging that the communists had been plotting a *coup d'état*; the book, *Armed Uprising*, appeared a week before the Leipzig trial.

The Reichstag fire trial confronted Goebbels with a difficult conundrum. At the beginning of September a left-wing propaganda cell in Paris had published a convincing *Brown Book of the Hitler Terror* accusing him and Göring of burning down the Reichstag, and listing 250 people allegedly murdered by the

Nazis since then. One such alleged victim was Dr Ernst Oberfohren, a D.N.V.P. politician (who had actually taken his own life in May).[7] The book claimed that Goebbels had ordered his murder to silence him. He set his propaganda the task of establishing that Moscow lay behind the blaze. On October 10 the court came from Leipzig to Berlin to hear testimony. Göring testified on November 4, and Dr Goebbels four days later. Magda, with eye-shadow discreetly applied to her beautiful eyes and her blonde Aryan tresses gathered up beneath a black chapeau, as a court observer wrote in his notes that day, applauded vigorously as her husband testified: He did so, the same expert observer noted, in an extraordinarily suggestive manner – thus, when he appended the word *absurd* to a train of thought he did so in such a persuasive manner that no other verdict seemed conceivable.[8] 'As a layman,' Goebbels stated, 'I cannot conceive how just one individual could carry out and execute the preparations for such an arson attack.' He reminded the court how often the communists had lied during the years of struggle – the Pharus Rooms battle, the drowning of Hans Kütemeyer, the defaming of Horst Wessel as a pimp, the Goebbels–Ulbricht debate.

The ultra-civilized word-duel that ensued between Ernst Torgler and Goebbels showed how similar their intellects were, as they bandied rival quotations about the nature of revolutions. His clash with Torgler's fellow defendant the Bulgarian agitator Georgii Dimitroff was less urbane. After one stinging rebuff, Goebbels replied with a quotation from Schopenhauer: 'Every man deserves to be looked at. But he does not deserve to be spoken to!' (The quotation had been recommended to him in a letter tossed into his open Mercedes by an anonymous well-wisher the day before.)[9]

'I shall expect a loyal hearing from the foreign press,' Goebbels said, concluding his personal defense in terms of injured innocence, 'and I hope they will find space in their columns for this detailed rebuttal; because it is not right that the government of a decent, diligent, and honorable people should be smeared before the whole world like this.'[10]

WITH THE DOMESTIC German press he had fewer qualms. His new press law kept the journalists tightly muzzled, although it was not without its positive elements as well. It imposed on journalists a duty to report truthfully and to refrain from writing anything that might 'injure illegally anybody's honor or well-being, or damage his reputation or hold him up to ridicule or contempt.'

Like all such attempts to regiment the liberal professions, ludicrous situations developed. The chamber of literature addressed warning letters to the Brothers Grimm for not having filled in membership forms (they had been dead for eighty years).[11] One Nazi censor banned an advertisement because it showed a girl clutching a bar of soap to a part of her anatomy 'which could not be identified for reasons of decency.'[12]

Operating through Max Winkler, who had a shrewd business brain, Goebbels began to buy up or close down printing and newspaper concerns, beginning with Hugenberg's Verlagsanstalt ('Vera') and Ullstein, the big

Jewish-controlled newspaper publisher in Berlin.[13] The Reich paid 8·5 million marks for Ullstein's stock, including two millions to liquidate Ullstein's debts. Goebbels renamed it Deutscher Verlag, and purged its recalcitrant editors.[14] When Ehm Welk, editor of the Ullstein magazine *Grüne Post*, took too literally Goebbels' invitation to criticize, the minister shut the publication down for three months and removed Welk to one of Göring's new concentration camps.[15]

Through Winkler, Goebbels also squared accounts with the Jewish Mosse publishing empire, whose *Berliner Tageblatt* had been one of his most dedicated enemies. Real-estate speculation had landed the owner Lachmann Mosse in financial difficulties and he had already fled to Paris before Hitler seized power; the sequestrators were more than pleased to sell off the *Tageblatt* to Goebbels after they found that Mosse had plundered his employees' pension funds. Winkler also acquired for him by more or less forceful methods the share capital of the non-Jewish *Börsenzeitung*, the Frankfurt *Generalanzeiger*, and Hugo Stinnes' *Deutsche Allgemeine Zeitung*.[16]

GOEBBELS' MARRIAGE is still faltering. On New Year's Day 1934 he decides that it's all over between them; but he relents because she is pregnant again.[17]

He has all but forgotten Anka Stalherm. At the 1933 Nuremberg rally he spotted her insufferable husband Mumme, now a middle-rank party dignitary.[18] But now they are divorced and Goebbels hears she is going to the dogs – 'Lost!' he records, 'What a comedown!'

On his birthday, greetings come from her; in a typed reply, he mechanically suggests she drop in some time.[19] The magic has gone. Besides, as overlord of Germany's burgeoning movie industry he has legions of willing, supple starlets like Marianne Hoppe[20] and Käthe Dorsch[21] at his beck and call. He will follow the rest of Anka's story with only half an eye. 'Frau Mumme tells me her woes,' he writes years later. 'She is to be pitied. But what can one do?'[22] She remarries; her husband dies in action. Taking pity on her, Goebbels has her appointed editor of the fashion magazine *Dame*. In an editorial she will fondly mention the book of ballads that the minister lovingly inscribed for her as a fellow student at Heidelberg, by Heinrich Heine, a Jew. Furious, Goebbels has her reduced to the ranks as a mere staff writer.[23]

During 1933 he has earned 4,317 marks (about a thousand dollars) from his seven books in print.[24] He is almost pathologically proper in personal money matters. He draws his salaries as minister and gauleiter but claims only his proper expense entitlements, not charging Magda's car or their household overheads against the ministry. His tailoring is equally punctilious. Gone is his clothes' slept-in look. He polishes his shoes himself. He takes delivery of a motor yacht, and belatedly learns how to drive a car as well.[25] 'I'll get the hang of it soon,' he writes confidently in his unpublished diary on April 6. 'It's just the details that still elude me.' At Easter 1934, as the time for Magda's confinement approaches, he rents a secluded, idyllic little property at Cladow on the Wannsee lakeshore.[26] She often accompanies him to lunch with Hitler now, and the Führer is a surprisingly frequent visitor to her in the clinic. Goebbels meanwhile pursues his old ways, inviting Hela Strehl and Petra Fiedler on boating jaunts on the city's lakes and waterways, and taking them back to the cottage for late-night private movie showings.[27] On April 12 after a farewell meal with him, Magda is taken off to the clinic for the birth of their second child. 'Hope it's a boy,' prays Dr Goebbels, only to open the next day's entry with a surly outburst: 'It's a girl and her name's Hilde. At first it brought disappointment, but then joy and happiness. . . Once more the Führer has proven right. It's a little girl.'[28] The unhappy task of breaking the news to Goebbels has fallen to his adjutant, Prince Schaumburg-Lippe. 'If Fate thinks it can play silly pranks on me,' snaps the minister, stalking up and down in irritation, 'it's got another think coming!' He hurries over to the clinic and finds Magda lying flushed but happy surrounded by pillows and flowers.

The rows resume. 'Armed truce with Magda,' Goebbels laconically notes in his diary after one two-day tiff which ends with him going for a little drive-around.[29] Documenting her irritation with him, Magda stays on with Ello at Dresden after he leaves. Out at Cladow on June 2 he plays with Helga, his favorite daughter, but his pleasure is alloyed by the presence of Magda's very plebeian mother. 'I'm cheesed off by all this,' he notes in his diary. 'I'm often very depressed. I've got to work harder.'[30] He falls seriously ill with worry, and there are more almost suffocating rows with Magda – a certain countess is the cause of some of them.[31] On Wednesday June 20 the entire Reich government has been summoned out to Göring's new estate on the Schorf Heath, Carinhall, to witness the solemn reburial – 'with much Twilight of the Gods and Tally-Ho,' as Goebbels sardonically puts it – of Carin Göring's remains, which have been violated by the enemy in Sweden.[32]

Late that evening he is confronted by Magda with an ugly scene – perhaps about the countess. He puts a spin on it in his diary: 'In the evening I learn something awful from Magda. It's midnight, but I drive out to Cladow. Frightful scene. I am quite shattered.' The next day he keeps thinking of Magda: 'I'm fit to burst. Awful mental agonies.' Magda joins him later and dissolves into tears and hysterics. 'Au fond,' he writes, setting the scene for future readers, 'she is good. I bear much of the blame too. A bitter pill to bite. A gray, rainy day today. Deep down, we have separated.' On Friday the twenty-third, a nervous wreck, he has a long, late discussion with the lovely Hela Strehl, then settles his differences with Magda. 'She finds her way back to me. But I am more than a little to blame myself.' History would of course like to know more about these differences: His infidelities? hers? We do not know and cannot speculate: But one lesson is that the Goebbels Diary is becoming more tricky as a source with each year that passes.

POLITICALLY TOO his quagmire deepened. Those who offended the minister joined Ehm Welk in a concentration camp: There was Dr Jacob Wassermann,

the Jewish nephew of the one-time director of the Deutsche Bank, sent to
Oranienburg camp for slandering Goebbels and Magda; there was an engineer
who remarked casually that Goebbels was 'Germany's hoodoo;' there was a
former Stahlhelm official, convicted for insulting Goebbels.[33] 'Anybody may
grumble,' mocked *Angriff* on May 18, 'if he's not afraid of the concentration
camp.' Operating primarily from the safety of Prague, the émigrés around Dr
Bernhard ('Isidor') Weiss orchestrated a raucous outcry about alleged Nazi
atrocities: They claimed that two Jews had died in a pogrom at Gunzenhausen,
and that the former Social Democrat deputy Heilmann was being maltreated
in a concentration camp. The stories were fictional, but fact would inevitably
follow fiction.[34] Ingeniously, the émigrés paraded a live Nazi 'victim' in Prague
for pathologists to see his 'strangulation' marks. The Czech newspapers
headlined this gruesome stunt 'ENTER A HANGED MAN.' (The Gestapo finally
identified the alleged victim as a notorious communist confidence trickster.)[35]
Goebbels reprimanded the Czech envoy, and Prague promised to silence the
émigrés.[36]

Goebbels was aware that even his powers were limited. When a Mrs Ebeling
asked him to get somebody out of prison, he refused. 'I'm not going to burn my
fingers,' he noted privately.[37]

THROUGHOUT THIS TIME he had turned a deaf ear to the growing internal unrest
generated by the inequities of the Nazi revolution. The S.A. were once again
in revolutionary ferment, and he broadly sympathized. But Hitler needed the
regular armed forces more than he needed the S.A., the party's two-million-
strong Brownshirt army. Not caring to offend the stormtroopers he was putting
out ambiguous signals which Goebbels was not alone in misinterpreting.
Hearing Hitler declare to the assembled gauleiters in Berlin in February 1934
that there were still 'fools' around who argued that the revolution was not yet
complete,[38] Goebbels nodded approvingly; he did not realize that Hitler was
talking about the S.A.

To Goebbels, the unseen enemy throughout the first six months of 1934 was
the diehard *Reaktion*, a word which embraced the conservative politicians,
journalists, intellectuals, reserve officers, and the catholic clergy but never, it
must be pointed out, the S.A.[39] 'The *Reaktion*,' he told a working-class audience
in Berlin's Lustgarten, 'are putting on airs right across the country. But if they
imagine we captured these high offices for *them*, or that we're just keeping
them warm for them, they're very much mistaken.'[40]

The young minister found strong support in the now expanding armed
forces. Impressed by an ideological lecture in the defense ministry at the
end of November 1933, the new minister General Werner von Blomberg had
persuaded Goebbels to address officers based at Jüterbog; the official record
shows that his remarks were greeted with 'storms of applause, ending with
a hooray for the minister.'[41] He spoke too to officers at Dresden, Hanover,
Kiel, and Wilhelmshaven.[42] As tensions grew between the army and the S.A.,

particularly in Silesia, Blomberg asked Goebbels to arrange a second tour; but when he spoke in the Silesian capital Breslau on March 15 he insisted on the presence of the local S.A. and S.S. officers as well.[43] His fame spread among the army officers. In April he spoke in Frankfurt-on-Oder and Stettin. General Walther von Brauchitsch, the commanding general in Königsberg, persuaded him to address seven thousand of his officers and men too. To all of these audiences Goebbels explained the party's ideology, the nature of revolutions, the Jewish problem, and the relationship between the party, army, and state.[44]

In all these speeches, slavishly adhering to Hitler's line, he confirmed that only the regular soldier had a 'sovereign right' to bear arms for Germany.[45] But he had nursed his own relations with the S.A. high command as well – ever since the Stennes putsch of 1930. Not for nothing had he appointed an S.A. officer, Schaumburg-Lippe, as his adjutant. For all his professed loathing of the homosexual cliques, he had learned to get along with Ernst Röhm and with S.A. Obergruppenführer Edmund Heines, the police chief in Breslau; indeed, he had testified during the Reichstag fire trial that he had spent a recent election evening with Heines roaring with laughter about the lies about them in the *Brown Book*.[46] Count von Helldorff, now police chief in Potsdam, was a regular cruising companion aboard the Goebbels yacht.[47] On February 24 a glowing Dr Goebbels presided over a Sport Palace display by the Berlin S.A. at which the banners and uniforms of the prohibition era were paraded. 'Is the world to believe,' he intoned in his speech, 'that we have forgotten all of this? That all this was for nothing? No! The Führer knows, as do we all, to whom we owe this Third Reich.'[48]

And why should he not utter sentiments like these? Hitler too was still fraternizing closely with Röhm. He had appointed him to Cabinet rank in December, written cordial New Year's greetings to both Goebbels and Röhm, and shared with both men his innermost thoughts on foreign policy during a train journey to Munich on January 1, 1934. If anything, Goebbels was marginally more critical of Hitler – impatient at his continued lethargy in foreign affairs and Reich reform. 'We're not making any headway at all,' he wrote in March. 'Hitler doesn't want to hurt anybody. But there's no other way.'[49] On the eve of Hitler's birthday in April, however, Goebbels privately prayed: 'God save our Führer. He's everything to us. Happiness, hope, and future.'[50] Goebbels could not overlook Hitler's infatuation with Röhm – perhaps his only protection in the increasingly shark-infested waters of the Third Reich. Goebbels used more old-fashioned methods to win Hitler's affection too: He donated 'a wonderful Bechstein' piano to him for his new official residence[51] and brought him all the latest American movies, particularly those starring John Barrymore.[52] Visiting Dresden for the national theater week at the end of May 1934 with his own new female outside interest, the beautiful dark-blonde Baroness Sigrid von Laffert, Hitler would invite only the Goebbels couple to share dinner with them at the Bellevue hotel, and they stayed up until three A.M. talking politics.[53]

Goebbels had seen nothing wrong in fraternizing with Röhm. When a wrangle had developed that spring between Magda and ex-husband Günther Quandt over the custody of Harald,[54] he canvassed Röhm's backing as well as Hitler's and Göring's, and he noted one evening, 'Röhm makes a magnificent speech about the S.A.'[55] He had obviously still not singled out any one enemy. Late in April he tilted briefly at the catholic church, warning its functionaries in a speech to eighty thousand people in Düsseldorf: 'You gentlemen should not believe that you can deceive us by wearing the mask of piety. We've seen right through you.'[56]

Visiting Hitler with Himmler and Pfeffer on April 27, Goebbels was interested only in securing decisions in his fight against 'sabotage' by the church; he got Hitler to authorize a fight against the opposition Emergency League of Clergymen on Friday May 4.[57] But Hitler's heart was not in it, and when Hindenburg now fell ill he urged Goebbels to go easy on the church, as it would only cost the Nazis public sympathy.[58]

On May 5 however Goebbels noted for the first time in his unpublished diary that the S.A. were causing trouble in Berlin and elsewhere. He felt that they lacked a clear objective.[59] Visiting Hitler on May 17 to discuss movie business, he found himself taken aside to listen to Hitler griping about Röhm and his personnel policies. Hitler mentioned too the homosexual scandals. Puzzled by this shift in emphasis to the S.A., Goebbels noted afterward: 'Disgusting! But why isn't anything done about it?'

Still floundering, he went on to warn Hitler about monarchists. A few days later Count von Helldorff brought him more worries about the S.A. 'Röhm's not doing too well,' wrote Goebbels. 'He's causing too many conflicts. He's not on such good terms with the Führer either.' Goebbels decided – at least for his diary's eyes – to stand by Hitler: 'He is our bulwark. We must not despair.' On May 21, 1934 he mentioned his worries to Magda – 'About the situation and public mood. Neither all that rosy. Magda,' he continued, 'is very shrewd and loyal to me.'[60] Twice in May he had talks with Gruppenführer Karl Ernst, the doomed S.A. commander in Berlin: After running into him on the seventh he noted, 'He *acts* very nice' – the emphasis being on the verb;[61] on the twenty-sixth, after Ernst came to complain about friction with the regular armed forces, Goebbels recorded: 'I don't trust him any longer. He's a bit too friendly.'

In Dresden the S.A. had staged a magnificent march-past for Hitler and Goebbels.[62] But Hitler had already resolved to purge the S.A. leadership. Goebbels saw him on June 1. 'He no longer really trusts the S.A. leadership,' he recorded. We must all be on our guard. Don't start feeling too secure. Be prepared at all times. Nothing escapes the Führer's notice. Even if he doesn't say anything. Röhm [is] the prisoner of the men around him.'[63]

Goebbels opted for neither side. His own position was precarious. Unlike Himmler or Göring, he had no private army; he also had no real friends. While in 1932, at a typical get-together of battle- and bottle-scarred party veterans in Berlin, Count von Helldorff's arrival had been greeted with silence, a 'storm of applause' had welcomed Goebbels as he entered the hall.[64] But his popularity now was substantially less. The Nazi minister of agriculture wrote scathingly of him in private as did Alfred Rosenberg, who noticed how the other gauleiters hated the commercial success of Goebbels' book *Kaiserhof*.[65] Nobody liked his methods. Rosenberg wrote to Hess protesting that Goebbels would not allow him to broadcast, and was muscling into culture, which had been Rosenberg's territory for fourteen years.[66]

On May 1 Hitler upset them both, by appointing the former gauleiter of Hanover, the suffocatingly narrow-minded Bernhard Rust, as minister for science, culture, and public education. Creating such rivalries was precisely the way that Hitler instinctively worked. *Hegelianism !?*

During June these rivals jockeyed for allies. Goebbels made common cause with Göring. He had noted that on New Year's Day Hitler had not written to the general at all ('out with him!' he had gloated).[67] He had also heard Hitler crack jokes at Göring's expense behind his back.[68] But now Hitler advised him to patch up his differences with Göring; he had read the proofs of *Kaiserhof*, and advised Goebbels to tone down one or two passages and insert a paragraph praising the general. 'It will be worth your while,' advised Hitler cynically.[69] Evidently touched by the (published) references in *Kaiserhof*, Göring now wrote a conciliatory letter to Goebbels, offering him his friendship again.

A STIFLING GRAY UNIFORMITY had descended by now on the abashed and apprehensive German press. Acres of space were devoted to the obligatory reporting of Dr Goebbels' aimless and opaque speaking campaign during May 1934 against 'grousers and fault-finders, rumor-mongers and deadbeats, saboteurs and troublemakers.'[70] He flailed against ill-defined enemies in a speech delivered to fifty thousand Silesians at Gleiwitz on June 6, talking of the 'cowardly carpers at their beer tables,' and about 'the heroes who today are too elegant to go marching with an S.A. Sturm themselves, but stand on the curbside registering all their petty misdemeanors and excesses.'[71] Among other specific enemies identified by him were the Center politicians and militant churchmen.

His campaign blundered on toward its climax – coincidentally set for June 30. His speeches still ignored the S.A., on the party's left, and lambasted only the *Reaktion* on the right, the churches, the conservative elite, the exclusive Herrenklub and its principal member the vice-chancellor Baron Franz von Papen. 'The Nazis,' wrote one shrewd American correspondent, seeking to rationalize Goebbels' puzzling campaign, 'know that they cannot stand still. Their movement is like a bicycle – if it stands still it falls.' He deduced that the Goebbels campaign was a smoke screen to cover a gradual cutback in the two million S.A. stormtroopers.[72]

This was close to the mark. By early June Ernst Röhm was fostering talk of a 'second revolution.' Hanfstaengel would comment on how Goebbels had recently declared that the Nazi revolution was by no means over, and that 'reactionaries' would be swept away by the will of the masses.[73] Perhaps

Goebbels was hedging his bets – half conniving with Röhm, as once he had with Captain Stennes in Berlin. According to Otto Strasser, never the most reliable of sources, at some time during June 1934 Goebbels had a private rendezvous with Röhm in his 'local,' the Munich Bratwurstglöckl tavern; Strasser's only evidence for this was however the liquidation of Karl Zehnter, the bar's owner, in the coming purge. Goebbels certainly spoke in Munich's Künstlerhaus on June 4, but his diary makes no mention of Röhm or the tavern.[74] The ubiquitous Bella Fromm also claimed that Goebbels met with Röhm that day.[75] British diplomats went further: They learned late in June that Goebbels had been backing an attack by Röhm on the armed forces clique, hoping that Göring might 'finally be eliminated.' Later however he had backtracked, fearing to jeopardize his relations with Hitler.[76]

ONE SMALL EPISODE during June 1934 showed that Goebbels was still anxious to enlarge his personal reputation. Envious of recent visits by Göring to Italy and the Balkans, Goebbels secured an invitation to stage the first visit by a member of Hitler's cabinet to Poland, although Poland's great game reserves would have made the huntsman Göring the more obvious choice.[77] His diary shows that Hitler was seriously alarmed by the prospect that an 'intransigent' France might invade Germany to prevent further violations of the Versailles treaty; Germany needed to ensure that Poland and Italy stayed out.[78]

Goebbels flew to Poland for two days on the thirteenth to a chorus of protests from that country's socialist and Jewish newspapers (Jews made up one-tenth of Poland's and one-third of Warsaw's population). Lecturing an invited audience including the Polish prime minister, his Cabinet, and many ambassadors, Goebbels reassured them that National Socialism was not for export, and repeated that Germany desired rapprochement.[79] He had consulted Hitler and foreign minister Baron Konstantin von Neurath closely on the text of this speech.[80] Afterward he drove round Warsaw, and saw the Jewish quarter ('stinking and filthy. The eastern Jews. There they are'). He had meetings with Marshal Piłsudski and foreign minister Beck, then flew on to Kraków. At the same time Hitler had been to Venice to meet Mussolini on a similar mission.

Back in Germany Goebbels resumed his round of 'grouser' speeches – in Freiburg ('I get quite nostalgic. Here I lived, loved, and suffered') and Gera.[81] At Gera Hitler confided to him the outcome of his first talks with Mussolini:

1. *Austria*: Out with Dollfuss! New elections under a neutral man of confidence. Influence of Nazis depending on number of votes. Economic issues to be resolved jointly by Rome and Berlin. Both are agreed. Dollfuss will be notified.

2. *Disarmament*: Mussolini fully endorses our position. 'France has gone mad.' He'll back us.

3. *The East*: we must build further on friendship with Poland. (*Vide* my visit). Seek a modus vivendi with Russia.[82]

Hitherto unpublished entries like these give the Goebbels diaries a historical importance that far transcends their narrower biographical value.

ON THEIR RETURN to Berlin that evening Goebbels learned that Vice-Chancellor von Papen had delivered an amazing speech attacking him at Marburg university; Papen also spoke of the public's revulsion at the S.A., expressed veiled support for a monarchy, and sided with those whom Goebbels called the 'whiners and whingers.' 'A genius,' said Papen, in a pointed criticism of Goebbels himself, 'is never created by propaganda.' A transcript of Papen's words reached Goebbels' villa that evening. His adjutant found him in a blue dressing gown and a tantrum, hurling clothes-hangers downstairs. 'I'll teach this scoundrel a lesson,' he was screaming. 'Humiliating me like this!' On Hitler's instructions – or so he claimed in his diary – he ordered the speech suppressed at once. It was almost too late, as his ministry's foreign desk had already released it and the *Frankfurter Zeitung* had already plated it up. Annoyed that a junior minister had suppressed his speech, Vice-Chancellor Papen threatened to resign. Hitler undertook to censure Goebbels.[83]

The Papen speech was a slap in the face for Goebbels. On June 21 he presided over the monthly tea party for the foreign press and listened in delight to the Reichsbank governor Dr Schacht's witty speech; his grin vanished as Papen arrived uninvited, nonchalantly planted himself in Schacht's vacant chair just to his left, and sat nodding affably to the journalists.[84] He repaid Papen at his gau's midsummer festival that night in Neukölln, delivering another speech against the ludicrous armchair critics who had been too weak to seize power themselves.[85] Although he mentioned by name the Crown Prince, whose hand he wrongly suspected behind the Marburg speech, the foreign journalists recognized his real target as Papen. Hitler told him on the twenty-second that he had seen through his vice-chancellor: 'He's caused himself a heap of trouble.'

For the next week Goebbels continued to fulminate about Papen and the Marburg speech – to Ruhr coalminers, to Berlin civil servants, and to his diary. Papen enjoyed every minute of Goebbels' discomfiture. Sunday June 24 found them both at the Hamburg Derby. According to Papen's account, when the more expensive racegoers sighted him, sporting a light gray top hat, there were cheers of 'Heil Marburg!' Goebbels, flush-faced and piqued, flaunted himself before the cheaper galleries; the workers' applause turned to cheers when they sighted Papen however. 'This fellow Papen,' Goebbels told his deputy gauleiter Görlitzer, 'is getting too big for his boots.'[86] Thus Papen's account; Goebbels' unpublished diary puts a very different spin on the episode: 'Derby. One big mess. Public sharply against Papen. Hard put to avoid a scandal. Ambassadors there. Embarrassing scene. At the end together with Papen. Public totally on my side. I walk right into their midst. These ovations! Poor Herrenklub, if it ever comes to the crunch.'[87] Licking his wounds and seeking scapegoats, the next day Goebbels had the entire racecourse management sacked.[88]

On June 22 he had delivered his stock speech against the *Reaktion* to a gigantic audience of two hundred thousand in Halle.[89] He repeated this theme at Duisburg and Essen on the twenty-fourth. 'There are,' he explained at Essen, 'the *reserve officers*, the *intellectuals*, the *journalists*, the *clergymen*. You need a sharp eye to detect this type of person. . . The public has got to see through this clique.'[90] These words caused uproar among those classes thus branded by Goebbels. After the coming bloody events showed that he had been way off-target, he was forced to issue what he called an 'unabridged' text of what he had said, making plain he was referring only to those who *put on the airs* of reserve officers, intellectuals, journalists, and clergymen; he had not been referring to those worthies themselves. He had had no intention of attacking the actual people named, only the renegades whom they had already cast out of their ranks.[91] If all of this verbiage proved anything, it was that Goebbels still had no idea of which of many windmills he was supposed to be tilting at.

HITLER HAD HIS SIGHTS on clearly defined if very different prey. Deferring to the regular army generals, he had decided to decapitate the S.A. On June 22 he summoned Viktor Lutze by plane from Hanover, swore him to secrecy, and told him that the Gestapo had informed him that Röhm was plotting against the 'reactionary' Reichswehr on the pretext that it was conspiring against the Führer and the S.A. He was going to retire Röhm, he said; Lutze, a reliable if colorless S.A. commander, was to stand by for orders.[92]

Goebbels knew nothing of any S.A. 'plot.' His target was still Franz von Papen.[93] 'There is a ferment afoot,' he wrote on June 27. 'The Reichswehr is not quite clean. Führer's too good-natured. Hess has made a good broadcast, against revolution. Siding strongly with Führer, veiled attack on Papen. Latter's calmly carrying on his intrigues. His [Marburg] speech was drafted by E[dgar] Jung.' Compromising letters, Goebbels learned, had been found. 'We must watch out. If things get critical, then hit hard.'[94] Lunching at the chancellery on June 26 he found Hitler on the alert too.[95]

After gossiping with Hitler on Wednesday June 27, Goebbels left for engagements in Kiel. He was still none the wiser. Writing that Friday he would recall vaguely that the situation had deteriorated. 'The Führer must act. Otherwise the *Reaktion*' – which he still did not identify – 'will get out of hand.'[96] In Kiel he found 'universal concern about the *Reaktion*,' and 'embitterment within the Reichswehr.' The public, he felt, was waiting for them to do something. Flanked by his adjutant Schaumburg-Lippe, himself an S.A. Sturmführer, Goebbels delivered his stock 'whinger' speech to eighty thousand people in and outside the North Baltic Hall in Kiel.[97]

Back in Berlin later that Wednesday he again noted that Papen's seditious Marburg speech had been written for him by Jung, whom the Gestapo had now arrested.[98] Later Karl Hanke brought him the latest equally seditious catholic pastoral letter. 'Now,' wrote Goebbels, still wholly misjudging Hitler's intentions, 'let's go for them.'[99]

Hitler had gone to Essen for Gauleiter Terboven's wedding to Ilse Stahl, an old flame of Goebbels. Hitler was on the brink of committing his first mass murder. On Thursday Goebbels took the afternoon off at Cladow. 'Gloomier and gloomier,' he recorded, adding the vague and helpless comment: 'The *Reaktion* is at work everywhere.'

After a cruise with Magda and the children out on the summery lake, he went downtown to speak at Spandau. 'Talked tough and grim,' he said. 'The people understand.'

He drove back out to Cladow. 'How much longer?' he exclaimed in his diary, writing the next day as the uncertainties suddenly began to clear.[100]

23: *Inkpot Hero*

To CONSOLIDATE HIS ABSOLUTE authority, Hitler was about to become a murderer, and Goebbels would finally cast his lot in with him. They suddenly needed each other urgently: Hitler feared that Goebbels might yet rally the S.A. against him – for they were indeed plotting an uprising, though not yet; Goebbels for his part had so many enemies that he felt safe only at his Führer's side.[1]

In Essen strange things were happening that Thursday June 28, 1934. Lutze saw Hitler called away from the wedding feast to the telephone. A clammy atmosphere, an atmosphere of mistrust, descended on the festivities. Lutze felt that people were setting Hitler up.[2] More phone calls came, from Himmler, from the Gestapo, and from Paul Körner in Berlin (Körner presided over Göring's nationwide telephone-tapping monopoly, the Forschungsamt).[3] Hours later, dapper and businesslike, Körner arrived in person, bringing more reports. These indicated that Röhm and the S.A. were planning to stage a putsch at four P.M. on Saturday.[4] Hitler snapped: 'I'm going to make an example of them!'[5] He phoned Röhm's adjutant at Bad Wiessee, and ordered a meeting there at eleven A.M.

With Hitler in the Ruhr, Dr Goebbels felt very vulnerable, but the Führer had not forgotten him. On Friday morning June 29, 1934 he phoned Dr Goebbels from Essen and summoned him to the Hotel Dreesen at Bad Godesberg that evening. ('Thus,' sneered Alfred Rosenberg a few days later, 'he was allowed to join the big boys.')[6]

'So – *it's on!*' Goebbels wrote, probably quoting Hitler's words, though still in the dark about precisely what *it* was.[7] 'In God's name!' he added. 'But anything is better than this awful waiting.'[8] Hitler also ordered his new private secretary, Christa Schroeder, twenty-five, to fly west to Godesberg in Goebbels' plane.

Goebbels, wearing a lightweight white summer coat, was met by the local Nazi gauleiter Grohé at the airfield. 'We've got to act,' agreed Goebbels – whose unpublished diary of these days' grim events has now been obtained by this author from the secret Moscow archives: It shows him taking a detached interest in the massacre, thrilled to be so close to the killing though relieved not to have wielded the murder instruments himself. Goebbels drove to the Hotel Dreesen, followed by Hitler ('he is very grim') at four P.M. Shortly, Viktor Lutze also arrived. Lutze and Goebbels had been friends since the early days in the

Ruhr. Other veteran Nazis gradually crowded onto the hotel terraces. Hitler, noted Goebbels, told him in detail what was going on. To his astonishment he learned that the Führer was about to act the next day, Saturday, not against the conservative *Reaktion*, but against Röhm and his Brownshirt rebels. Not for a moment did he betray his dismay that Hitler was proving more reactionary than the *Reaktion* itself. 'Drawing blood,' recorded Goebbels approvingly: 'Gotta realize that mutiny costs them their neck. I agree with this. If do it you must, then ruthlessly. Proofs that Röhm was conspiring with [the French ambassador] François-Poncet, Schleicher, and Strasser. So, action!'9

Goebbels recalled: 'After reaching his decision the Führer is very calm. We pass the hours in discussions. Nobody must notice a thing. Talk with Lutze, the new [S.A.] chief of staff. He's very good.' For a while they watched a tattoo by the Labor Service. As six hundred torchbearers marked out a fiery swastika on the far bank of the Rhine, they watched the sun set, and waited in Hitler's suite. 'The Führer,' noted Goebbels, 'is tense but very firm. We all keep silent.' Toward midnight there was a phone call from Berlin – both Lutze and Goebbels recorded it in their diaries. 'The rebels are arming themselves,' wrote Goebbels. 'Not a moment to be lost.' Hitler went pale, and announced: 'We're on our way.'10 Goebbels sent a message to Magda to take the children from the Cladow cottage to the safety of their ministerial villa in Berlin; he ordered police protection for them.

It was now June 30, 1934. Shortly before two A.M. their plane took off for Munich. The broad outline of subsequent events that Saturday is well known. Hitler informed Goebbels of his intention to arrest Ernst Röhm and the mutinous S.A. commanders; Goebbels, prudently, decided to say nothing on their behalf. After touching down at Obenwiesenfeld airfield at four A.M., Hitler received further alarming reports from the army and S.S. – Röhm's rivals for power – that in Munich and Berlin S.A. units had been alerted hours before and had ordered a full mobilization for that afternoon.

Panicked by these (probably exaggerated) reports Hitler took his party to the Bavarian ministry of the interior building. Here he stripped two sleepy-eyed S.A. generals of their badges and sent out S.S. squads to pick up other S.A. commanders from their hotels and trains on their arrival. Gripped by paranoia he announced that he proposed to set off at once to arrest Röhm. In three open Mercedes limousines the size of small trucks, provided by Gauleiter Wagner, he and his posse sallied forth at five-thirty A.M. – Hitler, Lutze, and Hess riding in the first car, a bunch of detectives in the second, and Goebbels and one of Wagner's men in the third.

Out at Wiessee Röhm was vacationing in the lakefront Hotel Hanslbauer. He was wakened in his Room 21 by Hitler himself, a loaded pistol gripped in his hand, screaming: 'You are a traitor!' Goebbels and Lutze said nothing as Röhm, ashen-faced, was led away. They found Edmund Heines, aged thirty-six, sharing Room 31 with a youth, which made it easy for Goebbels to draw odious conclusions. ('May I be excused,' he would say in his broadcast the next day, 'from rendering a description of the loathsome and almost nauseating sights that met our eyes.') He wrote in his diary: 'The chief was brilliant. Heines pitiful. With a rent boy. Röhm remained calm. Everything went off very smoothly.' As Heines too was dragged away, he appealed: 'Lutze, I've done nothing! Help me!'

A chartered omnibus took away the arrested S.A. officers. Hitler's limousine convoy followed, making a prudent detour to the south in case the S.A. had summoned help. Safely back at party headquarters in Munich, Hitler ordered the codeword phoned through to Göring in Berlin to trigger the purge in Prussia. Later that morning, addressing a bewildered audience of middle-ranking S.A. officers, he laid it on thick and rotten, about Röhm's murky financial dealings, his opulent headquarters in Berlin, and his treacherous dealings with an unnamed 'foreign power.' To those around him he revealed that some of the arrested men were to be shot. The Gestapo showed Lutze a list of names; Lutze thoughtfully noticed that several were already marked '✠.'

Hitler proposed however to spare Röhm, a former close friend. Hess argued that there was no justice in sparing Röhm if others were to be executed. Lutze, asked his view, evaded clear comment.[11] Röhm's was however the only one not checked on the list of seven names which Hitler handed at five P.M. to Sepp Dietrich, commander of his S.S. bodyguard. The six others faced a firing squad at Munich's Stadelheim prison later that day.

Goebbels' contribution to these shocking events is not recorded. They had been mirrored in Berlin. Operating from Göring's villa, Himmler, Göring, and the army's general Walter von Reichenau had settled many old scores while Blomberg and General Werner von Fritsch looked in from time to time. Franz von Papen had been spared – to Goebbels' annoyance – but he learned that afternoon that Papen's speechwriter Edgar Jung and his senior aides Herbert von Bose and Erich Klausener had been shot in cold blood and that Berlin's S.A. commander Karl Ernst had been shot by firing squad. The orgy of murder had embraced even General Kurt von Schleicher, Hitler's predecessor as chancellor, and Gregor Strasser, once Goebbels' most powerful rival in Berlin.[12] 'Strafgericht,' was his only terse comment: judgment day. At eight P.M. he flew back to Berlin with Hitler. Witnesses said that he looked like death as their Junkers plane landed at Tempelhof airfield two hours later. Göring met them and nonchalantly told Hitler he had somewhat expanded on the original hit list. Hitler was not pleased by this. 'Göring reports that all went to plan in Berlin,' recorded Goebbels. 'Only cock-up: Mrs Schleicher bought it too. Tough, but can't be helped.'[13]

Back at the chancellery, Hitler vanished to take a bath, after which he revealingly told his secretary, 'Now I feel clean as a new-born babe again!'[14]

THE NEXT day, Sunday July 1, 1934 Goebbels found that Hitler's reputation had soared.[15] But over lunch he found the Führer pale and consumed by bitterness. 'Göring tenders his report. Executions almost over. A few still needed. It's tough but necessary. Ernst, Strasser, Senle [Stempfle?], Detten ✠. One final sweep and we're through the worst. It's tough but can't be avoided. For twenty years there must be peace.' He spent the whole afternoon with Hitler. 'I cannot leave him on his own,' reported Goebbels. 'He's suffering badly, but hanging tough. The death sentences are pronounced with the utmost gravity. Around sixty all told.'

Yielding to his more bloodthirsty colleagues' pressure Hitler ordered his friend Ernst Röhm – still in a Munich prison cell – added to the list. 'Twice,' recorded Goebbels, 'Röhm is given twenty minutes alone with a pistol. He doesn't use it and is then shot. With that, it's all over.'

That evening Goebbels broadcast worldwide for twenty minutes his own version of the purge. In the script he placed himself carefully right at the Führer's side throughout – in intimate, unchallengeable proximity. He spared no nasty detail about Röhm & Co. They had brought discredit to 'our S.A.,' indeed: 'They were about to bring the entire party leadership into disrepute by their sordid and disgusting sexual abnormality.' Hitler had lanced the abscess, he said. Nor did he stint his praise for the S.S.[16] 'The Führer was very nice to me and Magda,' observed Goebbels in his diary. 'As was Göring, who was around all day. A stream of fresh news. [Sepp] Dietrich reports on the executions. A bit white about the gills. We're not cut out to be executioners.' On Monday July 2 Hitler told him the final toll of executed was sixty – 'terrible losses,' wrote Goebbels, without explaining the adjective; Hindenburg however had sent a 'fabulous' telegram, congratulating Hitler on having saved Germany. 'For God's sake,' recorded Goebbels, 'let's have an end to the shooting. And the S.A. must not be too humiliated, above all not by the police.'[17] He returned to this theme, his concern about the S.A., several times in his diaries.[18] Relaxing with Count von Helldorff later that evening at the Goebbels villa, Hitler sighted Goebbels' adjutant Prince Schaumburg-Lippe in his S.A. uniform and asked curiously: 'And where did you spend Saturday?' The prince replied that he had been on duty at the ministry. 'You're lucky,' remarked Hitler. 'I doubt I could have spared you otherwise.'[19]

In Cabinet on Tuesday July 3 Hitler explained that firm action had been necessary, and took full responsibility for 'forty-three' executions. General von Blomberg, speaking for all of them, welcomed his action. Goebbels said nothing.[20] Papen arrived halfway through, belatedly released from house arrest – 'quite broken,' observed Goebbels without sympathy, 'pleads for mercy. We all expect him to resign. His men have all been shot. Edgar Jung too. He had it coming to him.' They enacted thirty-two laws that day, all garbage in his view, and a mockery under the circumstances.[21]

He traveled to Kiel and told audiences of gauleiters, naval officers, and sailors what he knew about the Röhm affair – which was not much. Back in Berlin on the sixth, Hitler told of his visit to the ailing president. Hindenburg, recorded Goebbels, had been a real sport. Papen was to stay in office until September 15, and then be turfed out (*abgemeiert*) – 'There must be no suggestion he was one of Röhm's men.'[22] He kept hearing fresh details about the death roll. '[Karl] von Wechmar was shot too,' he wrote indignantly on July 6, referring to the S.A. Brigadeführer in Breslau. 'Terrible! A lot of things happened that did not entirely accord with the Führer's will. Fate! Victims of the revolution! You learn to think little of human life, once it gets lost like that.'[23]

Hitler flew down to the Obersalzberg. In his absence wild rumors swept Berlin and the foreign press. According to one of them Goebbels had ordered five young S.A. men executed in his ministry garden and had directed his staff to watch.[24] Less implausible was the story that Goebbels had had Röhm's villa raided and staged an exhibition of the spoils in his ministry – delicately holding up silk lingerie and perfume sprays for his staff's inspection.

One rumor had Goebbels personally ordering Strasser's murder. The gullible foreign journalists named thirty-nine other victims who were, as Reinhard Heydrich indignantly protested later to Goebbels, still very much alive, including Helldorff, Alvensleben, Manfred von Killinger, Lossow, Seisser, and the widow of Karl Ernst.[25] (Goebbels offered Helldorff command of Berlin's S.A., but warned him to stop putting on airs.) As the foreign press hysteria grew louder, Goebbels noted nervously: 'High time that the Führer speak and announce that the lists of those shot and the heaps of documentary evidence are being checked and will be published. Meanwhile: Turn a deaf ear, and keep our nerve.'[26] Since Hitler delayed speaking, Goebbels broadcast a diatribe against the British, French, and Russian newspaper stories – 'the direst kind of revolver-journalism,' he exploded, drawing on his characteristically inventive vocabulary.[27] Stung by his language, at their next ministerial tea party the normally hard-bitten foreign journalists in Berlin wept into their teacups with rage and, as Louis Lochner put it, nobody minced their language in speaking to Goebbels. 'I don't think he'll invite us to tea hereafter!'[28]

GOEBBELS REJOINED Magda out at their lakeside cottage at Cladow. She was plagued by fears of assassination.[29] Both needed a vacation. Hitler too came out to Cladow several times that week. 'He now sees things quite clearly,' recorded Goebbels cryptically, adding: 'Lutze has become suspicious too.'[30] Did this mean that Hitler now believed that he had been manipulated, as he had, by Göring, Himmler, and the armed forces?[31] On July 7 Goebbels and Helldorff made a Sunday day trip up to Heiligendamm.[32]

On the thirteenth Hitler spoke to the Reichstag about the purge. Goebbels, Göring, Hess, Lutze, and their respective wives gathered round the exhausted Führer that evening and congratulated him.[33] The next day Goebbels and Hitler drove up to Heiligendamm. 'Putzi' Hanfstaengl, who had just returned from America, found them there. 'Hitler,' he wrote years afterwards, 'had a flushed, evil look, as though gorged on the blood of his victims.' It was not a pleasant vacation. The crowds gawked and cheered them wherever they went, and they had to break off their stay.[34] Later that year Magda invited the widows of all the S.A. victims of the purge to bring her their Christmas lists; one widow wrote a touching thank-you: 'The Führer loves justice,' she wrote. 'So he will look after us too.'[35] His conscience troubled, Hitler ordered generous pensions paid to them.

HITLER HAD BEGUN to plot against his neighbor, Austria – he mentioned it at lunch on July 10.[36] Although he would protest his innocence in later years, there is no doubt that he was fully apprised of the coup being prepared by Austrian Nazis under Theo Habicht. Habicht claimed strong Austrian army backing for a plot to replace the dictatorial chancellor Dr Engelbert Dollfuss with Dr Anton Rintelen, a prominent right-wing politician. Goebbels' unpublished diary shows that he considered Habicht a hothead whom Hitler, with characteristic indecisiveness, was hanging on to for far too long. When Habicht brought the latest news on Austria on April 10, Goebbels again decided 'He's obviously not up to the job.'[37] After discussing Austria with Habicht and Haegert two weeks later Goebbels noted: 'We'll be intervening there more strongly now. Otherwise dilettantism rules.'[38] Intervene – but how?

Attending Bayreuth for the annual Wagner festival on Sunday July 22, he found Hitler conferring secretly with Habicht, Rosenberg, General Walter von Reichenau, and the former S.A. commander Franz von Pfeffer. They had decided to stage a coup in Vienna. In his diary Goebbels inked the terse comment: 'Will it come off? I'm very skeptical.'[39] For three days they went their normal ways: Hitler entertained Goebbels and the others by reading from his Landsberg prison notes, and talking of the past; once they all went for a picnic in the forests. Back at the Wagner household, Goebbels had a little scene with Magda, whom he caught 'snooping' through his mail.[40]

The coup was to take place the next day, Wednesday July 25. General Wilhelm Adam, army commander in Bavaria, was ordered to report at nine A.M. on Wednesday morning to Bayreuth, where Hitler boasted to him that the Austrian army was going to overthrow the Dollfuss government that day: Adam was to arm all the Austrian Nazis who had fled to Germany. The army general was also deeply skeptical.[41]

Goebbels was with Hitler as the first reports came in from Vienna. Things were soon going badly wrong just as he had feared: 'Big rumpus. Colossal tension. Awful wait. I'm still skeptical. Pfeffer more optimistic. Habicht too. Wait and see!'

The word was that Theo Habicht's Nazis had seized Dollfuss and his minister of the interior Emil Fey in a scuffle. Hitler put through endless phone calls to Berlin, because lines to Vienna were dead.

At three P.M. Hitler phoned General Adam: 'Everything is going according to plan in Vienna,' he lied. 'The government building is in our hands. Dollfuss has been injured – the rest of the news is confused as yet. I'll phone again.'

He never did; he and Goebbels listened to Wagner's *Rhinegold* that afternoon with only half an ear. Then came uglier news: Dollfuss had been shot dead, and the rebels were pulling out.

'Habicht was all talk,' decided an outraged Goebbels. 'I just manage to suppress a crazy communiqué by Pfeffer.'

Pfeffer and Habicht were very mute after this. Goebbels switched the propaganda ministry over to emergency damage control. The foreign ministry in Berlin blamed the German ambassador in Vienna and recalled him. 'Führer remains quite calm,' observed Goebbels. 'Casting new plans. Dollfuss is out: That's a serious blow to the Austrian regime.' They tore up their remaining Wagner tickets and returned to Berlin the next day.[42]

Mussolini – who had secretly approved the idea of ousting Dollfuss – was infuriated by the murder, and moved his army to the Austrian frontier. The Italian press waded into the Nazis. Goebbels ordered his press to hit back. Hitler was angry that Mussolini had changed his tune. 'It's all over with Italy,' Goebbels decided. 'The same old disloyalty. The Führer has washed his hands of them.'[43] As a blood bath began in Austria, he persuaded Hitler to dismiss the bungling, cynical dilettante Habicht, if not actually shoot him; Papen was sent as special ambassador to Austria. The assassins would be publicly hanged in Vienna.

Meanwhile, on July 27, Hitler spoke to Goebbels about the future: 'He has a prophetic vision,' wrote the minister. 'Germany as master of the world. Job for a century.'[44]

LATE ON JULY 30 word came that President von Hindenburg was dying. Hitler and Goebbels discussed what to do. 'Immediately he dies,' recorded Goebbels, 'R.W. [armed forces] and Cabinet will appoint the Führer as successor. Then Führer will appeal to the public.'[45] The Cabinet agreed this late on August 1; Goebbels co-signed the decree.[46] Early that day Hitler went to take leave of the aged field marshal and he phoned that afternoon as Goebbels was planning the state funeral. He had found Hindenburg still alive – the president had recognized the chancellor, spoken of his gratitude and affection, then mistaken him for the Kaiser and referred to himself as 'your reverent and humble subject'.[47] Goebbels broadcast news of Hindenburg's death on August 2.[48] Listening to the chaplain's endless eulogy at the funeral ceremony in Tannenberg, Goebbels decided: 'No parson will ever speak at my grave.'[49]

Hitler's appointment was to be confirmed by a plebiscite on the nineteenth. Goebbels reveled in controlling the giant new propaganda machine, but found the results disappointing. Some thirty-eight million Germans, just under ninety percent nationwide, with rather less in Berlin, had endorsed Hitler as head of state.[50] The catholics had let them down; the murder of Klausener had alienated many catholics, but Goebbels blamed Rosenberg and his tactless anti-catholic effusions of late.[51] In his imagination Goebbels saw the 'missing ten percent' glaring at him, and for the next three months he dinned into his staff the need to win them over too – all, that is, except the 'anti-social dregs and professional bleaters' who were incurably hostile to the regime anyway.[52]

Broad sections of the S.A. were deeply disaffected by what Hitler had done.

S.A. brigadier Richard Fiedler, Horst Wessel's old comrade in arms, pleaded that the party had got the S.A. all wrong.[53] Goebbels hardened his heart against them. Twice that summer, addressing them in Berlin, he justified the 'radical cure,'[54] the 'purgative'[55] which had been necessary among their leaders. But both he and Hitler were long racked by remorse after the massacre. Hitler suffered from insomnia and a ringing in his ears which he attributed to those killings, and he ordered generous pensions for the purged men's next of kin.[56] Goebbels took up the cause of the S.A. men who had died in earlier years, protesting to Martin Bormann, who ran the party's benevolent fund, that some S.A. men's widows were drawing pensions of only seventeen marks (four dollars) per month, while Geyer's widow had received nothing at all. [57]

His own finances were in better shape. At the end of October 1934 he paid cash for a swanky new five-liter Daimler-Benz tourer.[58] His ministry's budget for fiscal 1934 projected a revenue of 22,341,250 marks from radio license fees, against outgoings of 27,545,300 marks. His own pretax salary and allowances would total 72,900 marks (around $18,000).[59] And why not? He had worked hard that autumn, limping around the country addressing uniformed farmers (seven hundred thousand of them arrayed like soldier-ants on the slopes of the Bückeberg for the Nazi annual harvest festival), uniformed roadbuilders (who serenaded him with their specially composed *Ballad of the Spade*), uniformed Hitler Youth, and uniformed Nazi maidens with blonde pigtails and uniformly glistening eyes.[60]

In Hitler's new Reich everything was uniform, especially the press, and Goebbels knew it. Lecturing journalists in November he mocked at their monotonous output and lack of courage, as though he himself were in no way to blame.[61] Captain Wilhelm Weiss, deputy editor of the *Völkischer Beobachter* and head of the Press Association, would explain later that it was Goebbels' own draconian press laws that had reduced its fifteen thousand journalist members to gibbering servility.[62] The fire had gone out of the media. It needed an identifiable, flesh-and-blood enemy. With the Jews now fled or fleeing, the protestant church emerged slowly to fill the role. One village church had disobeyed Goebbels' order for bells to toll when Hindenburg died. The pastor had told local party officials, 'I don't take orders from Joseph the catholic.'[63] This attitude was symptomatic of the church problem. 'A nation of sixty-six millions,' said Goebbels at Stettin, 'cannot afford twenty-eight different churches.'[64]

Speaking at Trier a few days later he suggested that only National Socialism had a truly Christian program, as witness its Winter Relief fund.[65] He had launched this Winterhilfswerk fund in September 1933; after glowering at the sumptuous farewell repast for guests at Bayreuth that summer he had there and then decided that millions of Germans could easily forego one meal each month and donate the proceeds to a national fund to feed and clothe the poor.[66]

Only the churlish would deny the real benefits that this WHW fund brought to the hungry and unemployed. In the winter of 1933–34 it had raised

358,136,040·71 marks, and helped 16,617,681 needy Germans, almost a quarter of the population.[67] His motives were of course partly political. Émigrés, he warned party officials in Cologne, were banking on the collapse of the regime during the coming winter.[68]

Goebbels had cast his lot permanently with the Führer. Hang together or be hanged separately: The saying is much the same in German. On December 13 his pathological dependence on Hitler was documented again when Hans Frank told him that Hitler believed he might be dying, and caused the Cabinet that same afternoon to pass a law allowing him to name a successor.[69] 'He thus seems to be assuming the worst,' recorded Goebbels, shocked. 'I am very downcast. I go home weighed down with worries. . . We've got to find a good doctor. The Führer must be brought back to good health. The people around the Führer are too lackadaisical.' At Bremerhaven the next evening however he found Hitler looking well. Words failed him, he was so relieved. 'Our Führer! Long, long may he live!'[70]

On the nineteenth Hitler nominated Göring as his successor, but kept it to himself and a few others – not including Goebbels. A few weeks later, discussing how to compensate Göring for taking the Reich reform program away from him, Hitler told Goebbels he was 'thinking' of nominating Göring as his successor. Goebbels could not even bear to think of that sad eventuality. 'Hitler's got to outlive us all,' he pleaded in his diary. 'We need him like our daily bread.'[71] That Christmas Hitler wrote to Goebbels, telling him how dear he and Magda were to him.[72]

WHAT OF GOEBBELS' private life during that turbulent year, 1934? As minister, he is a magnet for Berlin's nouveau-chic society; he is a host to dazzling starlets, and less frequently their male counterparts. His motor yacht cruises the Wannsee with Magda and a glittering array of twittering females of stage and screen in its well, like Renate Müller, Lil Dagover, Jenny Jugo, Gretl Slezak, Maria Andergast, and Magda's sister-in-law Ello, who says she's being dragged through a messy divorce by her husband's cunning Jewish lawyer.

Ello is all eyes and ears. Once that September her friend Maria Strehl makes a bitchy comment in Magda's hearing about Petra Fiedler, another of the minister's friends. 'Female hysteria,' he scoffs guiltily in his diary. The ensuing row with Magda leaves him aggrieved and sleepless for days afterward.[73]

For a while Magda shuts her ears to Ello's gossip, mindful perhaps of her eccentric pre-nuptial bargain with Joseph.

In his official villa their separate bedrooms are divided by an anteroom and bathroom. One night that autumn she hears a door banging in the wind; going to close it, she finds the connecting bathroom inexplicably locked. Toward morning she hears Joseph softly unlocking the door. She makes no scene; she tells Ello, and over breakfast she icily informs his house guest, a certain countess, 'My car will be taking you to the station in half an hour.'[74]

She punishes him in a subtle but cruel way. To see in the New Year, 1935, she drags him down to the Black Forest – on a skiing holiday. She goes off skiing all day, leaving her lame husband with the infants and a nanny at the hotel.

TO KEEP HIM COMPANY Hitler's press chief sent down to the Feldberger Hof hotel a senior journalist, Dr Alfred Detig, with instructions to let him win every hand at cards. Detig's newspaper, the *Deutsche Allgemeine Zeitung,* had just carried a critique by Furtwängler of Goebbels' recent persecution of the composer Hindemith.[75] 'Do you know,' snapped Goebbels arrogantly, 'why we allow the *DAZ* to keep publishing? It's because if you've got a plague of rats you always leave one or two holes open to see which rats peep out. That way you can trash them better.'

He was facing, unfortunately, a man with literally a better hand of cards than his. By lunchtime Detig had taken him to the cleaners. As the gong sounded and Goebbels made to leave, Detig detained him. 'Minister,' he said, holding out his hand, 'gambling debts are always settled on the nose.'

Goebbels forgave him – temporarily. While Magda went off skiing, he took his friends down into Freiburg to see his old university. He refreshed nostalgic memories of Anka and Castle Hill, of Dattler's, and Berlinger's coffeehouse. In one lecture theater he pointed out a limerick he had carved into a bench fifteen years before: 'The maiden and the inkpot / Get their rims wet quite a lot. / What's the source of all that damp? / All that dunking – what a scamp!'

Smirking naughtily he went off to record his New Year's Eve broadcast. Years later, Detig would ponder upon the minister's tortured psyche: For the two hours that they had trailed this little cripple around with them he had taken such pains to convince them that while at university here he had been a real 'Inkpot Hero' too. How much was true, and how much propaganda? As for the Furtwängler incident, Goebbels had Dr Detig arrested by the Gestapo for sedition, and he spent several months in their Munich prison cells.[76]

24: *While Crowds Exult below*

When you drive through Germany today,' Goebbels had said at the end of November 1934, 'you hear the hammering of the machinery and the singing of the sirens, you see the cargo ships once more majestically gliding down the rivers and the heavy-laden freight trains, and you notice how the country lanes are being widened and the new autobahns laid down. . . These are great times that we have created.'[1] Before a different audience he emphasized Germany's 'absolute desire for peace,' a theme to which he returned in his New Year's broadcast – the coming international plebiscite on the disputed Saar territory would allow Germany to arrive at a lasting peace with 'the great French people.'[2]

Hitler had faced the New Year with a collapse of self-confidence. Calling Goebbels back from his Black Forest vacation, he demanded he do something. Foreign newspapers were full of lies about fresh plots against him. Hitler ordered the entire German leadership to hear him speak in the State Opera House on the third. Together, Goebbels and Göring – now thick as thieves again – drafted a declaration of loyalty for Göring to read out to Hitler. It went down well.[3] At one point Hitler threatened to put a bullet in his own brains if his subjects refused to work in harmony.[4] Goebbels was worried by all this. He felt that Hitler was still unwell, and decided to find a doctor for him. 'I think he needs me now,' he told his unpublished diary.

With Magda staying down in the Black Forest, he stayed up until two A.M. after the Hitler speech entertaining Ello Quandt; on the following day, January 4, he took Hitler out to Babelsberg to tour the Ufa studios. For a while he, Hitler, and Streicher strayed around the lavish set built for *Barcarole*, a romantic movie located in Venice at the turn of the century. The top Nazis were all eyes – not for Germany's leading heart-throb Gustav Fröhlich, but for the actress playing opposite him, a Czech girl of twenty, Lida Baarova.[5]

Hitler took an immediate shine to her; he persuaded himself that she looked like Geli Raubal and invited her to tea at the chancellery.[6] She arrived with tear-streaked cheeks. Gustav Fröhlich, her lover in real life as well as on the screen, a jealous and possessive thirty-two-year-old, had instructed her to phone him every fifteen minutes from the Führer's chancellery, and that put paid to any fantasies. Hitler asked Lida why she did not take German citizenship. Her reply was simply, 'Why should I?'[7] Upstairs in his private quarters a few

198

days later, Hitler moped until three A.M. about how lonely and joyless his life now is – 'Without women,' observed Goebbels, 'without love, still filled with memories of Geli.'[8]

DISCUSSING FOREIGN POLICY after that visit to the movie studio on January 4, 1935, Hitler predicted to Goebbels that France would start turning the screw on Germany if and when she lost the Saar. They had a tough year ahead.[9] Goebbels adopted honeyed language. 'In rapprochement lies order,' he lectured, opening the Saar exhibition in Berlin on the sixth. 'in war lies only ruin and destruction. For Europe there can be no third way.'[10]

The historic plebiscite on the future of the Saar would be held one week later. His opponents, a clamoring ragbag of communists, Jews, freemasons, and disgruntled émigrés, were no match for him. His propaganda line was clear – the Saar was tied by blood to the German fatherland. To abide by the international rules, a local *ad hoc* 'German front' had to fight the campaign. Goebbels provided a weekly illustrated magazine, telling the catholic Saar electorate that the bolsheviks were the sworn enemy of God. In neutral Geneva his ministry's anti-Comintern unit set up a religious front, Pro Deo, which formally received the anti-bolshevik exhibition that he had prepared in Berlin and sent it on to the Saar camouflaged with Swiss certificates of origin.[11] In the Saar, the catholic clergy publicized the exhibition from their pulpits. 'The Saarbrücken clerics never guessed whose errands they were running,' wrote Eberhard Taubert.

His opponents warned the Saar, 'A vote for Germany is a vote for Hitler!' This slogan backfired badly, because over 90·5 percent voted just that way. Hitler telephoned Goebbels from Berchtesgaden, saying he sincerely hoped this meant peace with France. Goebbels had all Germany decked out with flags in an instant. That evening, January 15, he took Generals Blomberg and Fritsch back to his villa, and they all phoned Hitler again. Afterward, they all discussed Germany's long-range foreign policy.[12] Word reached London a few days later that Goebbels had said on this occasion that the overwhelming Saar vote virtually obligated Hitler to bring back all the scattered German peoples into the Reich. Goebbels had particularly indicated Memel and Austria. 'We've got everything ready in the propaganda ministry,' he was quoted as saying.[13]

The Saar plebiscite was proof of what could be achieved bloodlessly, by propaganda alone. On Sunday January 20 Hitler again had lengthy confidential discussions with Goebbels, mapping out his next moves: 'First project concerns Britain,' recorded the diarist Goebbels. 'Guard their empire, in return for thirty years' alliance.'[14]

At the time such a deal seemed quite possible. There was a mutual fascination between Britain's old, and Germany's new, rulers. In December 1934 Goebbels and Hitler met Lord Rothermere at the Ribbentrops'. The British newspaper baron was already a convinced admirer of Hitler. 'A real Englishman,' Goebbels described him. 'John Bull. Really wonderful opinions. If only all the

English thought the same way.' Rothermere applauded Hitler's rearmament and demand for colonies, and criticized Versailles and diplomats. Britain's ambassador in Berlin, the hard-drinking Sir Eric Phipps, almost swooned with rage. After Goebbels got to work on him, Rothermere pronounced him 'the greatest propagandist in the world.' 'If you get tired of Germany,' Rothermere boomed, 'I'll engage you at ten times the salary.' 'I'm not for hire,' responded Goebbels, and reported the remarks to Hitler.[15] The Führer threw a glittering party for his lordship on the nineteenth. Magda was the star attraction. From Rothermere's remarks, it was plain he was totally won over to the Nazi cause.[16] Traveling down to Munich on January 25 Hitler repeated to him that the cornerstone of his foreign policy was an alliance with Britain. 'We shall be supreme on the ground, and they at sea, and we'll be equals in the air.' What then? The fact that Hitler talked of wooing Poland – that would now be Göring's task – indicated expansion to the east.[17]

Speaking to eighty-seven thousand Nazi officials on February 24, Goebbels boasted: 'If the great powers . . . now treat Germany as a sovereign nation again, don't think for an instant, my comrades, that this means the world has come to its senses! No, it's thanks to our tenacity, our resolution, and – I shall be blunt – our newfound *Macht*, our power, alone.'[18]

Rosenberg choked on that word *Macht*. He, Rosenberg, was head of the party's office of foreign policy, he complained that this 'saber-rattling' by Goebbels contradicted Hitler's own theme, the desire for peaceful coexistence.[19] Hitler however trusted Goebbels. When Sir John Simon, the British foreign secretary, announced a visit to Berlin Hitler asked Goebbels as well as Ribbentrop to supply a character study on him.[20]

Increasingly sure of himself, the propaganda minister saw no need to curry favor. He dominated Hitler's lunch table with cruel banter and mimicry – imitating Robert Ley or Otto Meissner, then saying with a disarming chuckle: 'But we've got to be kind to poor old Meissner – he did so much to help us into power.'[21] Some found Goebbels infuriating. 'His smirking superficiality gets physically on my nerves,' wrote Darré after one such chancellery luncheon.'[22] At times Goebbels even gunned for Göring – nagging about the new general's indiscreet fling with the actress Emmy Sonnemann until Hitler coerced them into marrying that May, and then the staggering cost of the nuptials to Hitler, before whispering around the diplomatic community that Emmy's Aryan pedigree was debatable.[23]

THE ARMED FORCES, Germany's muscles, were now beginning to show. Goebbels' unpublished diaries, recently discovered in the Moscow archives, narrate Hitler's next crucial decision:

MARCH 16, 1935 (Saturday). On Friday the Führer suddenly returned. Says he wants to proclaim general conscription today . . . [Prime minister Pierre-Étienne] Flandin has spoken against Germany in the chamber; two-year national service accepted in France. Disarmament? We too have to create *faits accomplis.* Hitler is right. I shall fortify him in his intent...

MARCH 18, 1935 (Monday). Discussions all Saturday morning. Führer argues with Blomberg over the number of divisions. Gets his own way: thirty-six. Grand proclamation to the people: Law on rebuilding the armed forces; conscription. To put an end to the haggling, you've got to create *faits accomplis.* The other side aren't going to war over it. As for their curses: Stuff cotton wool in our ears.

Cabinet 1:30 P.M. Führer sets out situation. Very grim. Then reads out the proclamation and law. Powerful emotions seize us all. Blomberg rises to his feet and thanks the Führer. 'Heil Hitler,' for the first time in these rooms. With one law, Versailles is expunged. Historic hour. Frisson of eternity! Gratitude that we are able to witness and take part in this.

'So, once more we are a great power,' concluded Goebbels. At four P.M. that afternoon he broadcast the proclamation over the radio.[24] The foreign press displayed consternation and panic as Germany announced the reintroduction of conscription. Rome and Paris bleated protests. 'Let them curse,' wrote Goebbels smugly; 'we rearm . . . and put on a brave face meanwhile.'[25] Speaking in Danzig, he bragged openly that the Nazis had torn up the treaty of Versailles.

Sir John Simon hurried to Berlin with Anthony Eden, Minister for the League of Nations, to ascertain the German government's intentions. Goebbels attended the banquet thrown in their honor, and found Simon congenial but Eden cold and arrogant, as he had already warned Hitler from his own sources (contradicting Ribbentrop).[26] 'Immediately afterward with the Führer at the Reich chancellery,' narrated Goebbels in his unpublished diary. 'Göring and Blomberg too. Führer reports; he has given the British a few figures: we want an army of half a million, and we've already achieved parity with the British in the air.' (This was bluff.) 'Huge astonishment at that. Führer spoke out against Russia. Has laid a cuckoo's egg which is intended to hatch into Anglo-German entente.'

Eden had silkily suggested that the 'bolshevik world revolution' was a Goebbels fiction, and promptly flew on alone to Moscow, which rather devalued his talks with Hitler.[27] Unabashed, Goebbels printed a special horror-magazine, *The Red Army*, and had it smuggled onto the desks of every delegate to the League of Nations in Geneva.[28]

For a few days Hitler feared that Eden might pull together his own eastern pact, signing up Moscow and Warsaw against Germany.[29] He remarked to Goebbels that he found foreign affairs pure torture. Strolling in the garden on April 3 he told the propaganda minister that he did not believe there would be war. 'If it came it would be frightful. We have no raw materials. We're doing everything to pull through this crisis... We've got no choice but to keep our nerves. Poland has stood fast. No question of [Eden's] eastern pact... Führer says, let's just hope nobody jumps us.'[30] Goebbels was alarmed that irresponsible elements were speaking of war as though it was a bagatelle. Aided by Hitler's adjutants Fritz Wiedemann and Julius Schaub he saw to it that Hitler was left in no doubt; General von Fritsch also instructed his adjutant Major Fritz Hossbach to brief Hitler about their army's true weakness.[31]

Speaking in Frankfurt however Goebbels gloated over the fact that Germany had 'rearmed secretly, cunningly, and unknown to the world outside,' as the British consul reported on April 11. The minister left this diplomat with the unedifying impression that 'a homicidal lunatic, with winks and whispers and sudden shouts, was propounding his dark schemes to a somewhat bovine but gleeful audience.'[32]

Goebbels was beginning to take on the great names in German culture. He forced Wilhelm Furtwängler to eat humble pie and concede publicly the state's right to control art.[33] After Rosenberg had bombarded him with letters for a year complaining that composer Richard Strauss had used the libretto of Stefan Zweig, a Jew, for his latest opera, Goebbels had to dismiss Strauss as president of the chamber of music.[34] He absented himself from the opera's première, and had it taken off the program at Heiligendamm where he was on summer vacation.[35]

He was also increasingly sensitive to criticism. In May 1935 the Gestapo drew his attention to one cabaret, the Catacombs in Luther Strasse. Agents reported the subversive sketches of comedian Werner Finck, but Reinhard Heydrich reminded S.S. chief Heinrich Himmler that their own *Völkischer Beobachter* had only just praised this act, and that Finck had been a star performer at Goebbels' recent film ball. Goebbels sent his own adjutant to spy on Catacombs and a similar establishment, Tingel-Tangel, in Kant Strasse, and closed them down a few days later.[36]

GOEBBELS GETS TO KNOW Magda better; she tells him about her life, much of it like a stage play.[37] Pregnant again, in January 1935 she takes their two children out to Cladow.[38] Late in March he begins a costly five-month reconstruction of his official residence at taxpayers' expense. Only the finest craftsmen are employed.[39] At the same time he carps about the lavishness of the Göring wedding staged on April 10. 'Two events make the world hold its breath,' he mocks in his unpublished diary on the wedding eve: 'The conference at Stresa, and Göring's wedding. The world of reality, and the world of fantasy. Let's hope the fantasy-world one day stands up to the blows dished out to it by the real one.'

It is as though he can see Göring's hour of failure coming. As Berlin goes crazy next day, with thirty thousand troops lining the streets and throngs cheering the wedding couple, Goebbels turns melancholy thoughts back to his own little country wedding at Severin: He is not envious at all, he decides, but happy as can be. Unable to get Carin Göring out of his mind, he accompanies Magda to the nuptials and the following seven-course banquet ('an impressive picture for the starving') through whispering and finger-pointing crowds; the embarrassment is just one more cross he has to bear.[40]

Magda is momentarily quiescent, sunning herself in the Führer's affections. Hitler often comes out to Cladow and goes cruising with the minister across the lake to see Potsdam's trees in blossom, listening absently to Goebbels' litanies against their turbulent priests and their arrogant Jews. Hitler finds it hard to get worked up about the Jews, now that he is in power.[41] At other times the Cladow villa is filled with brainless chatter as Goebbels invites over actresses like Angela Salloker and again the gorgeous Jenny Jugo, currently filming the Elisa Doolittle role in George Bernard Shaw's *Pygmalion*.[42] ✗

Magda Goebbels' family world revolves around her children – Joseph grumbles once that she has forgotten to make Easter a bit nicer for him too.[43] He takes a month-long seaside vacation at Heiligendamm, leaving her in Berlin. Indifferent to her feelings, he invites stage actress Else Elster (Helldorff's mistress) and movie starlet Luise Ullrich to join him.[44] Ever present is Ello Quandt, who arrives with her nubile friend Hela Strehl. 'Both very nice,' Goebbels records circumspectly, 'and clever and good-lookers too.'[45] When Hitler joins this beach party for two days Magda comes too – only to return to Cladow abruptly.[46] Goebbels writes in his diary the words 'fond farewell' but there has in fact been a ghastly scene about which Hela at once advises diarist Bella Fromm: 'She [Hela] has little brains and even less gumption,' records Fromm, 'but all the more charms for Mr Goebbels which she readily displays to him. She went up to Heiligendamm with him, his wife and children and female secretaries – of which two or three are always among his lady friends. From what one hears,' recorded this Jewish gossip-writer, her newspaper outlet now capped, 'Frau Goebbels did not know about it beforehand and departed suddenly after a violent row – not that either Hela or Goebbels were the least upset.'[47]

Goebbels' diary is not surprisingly oblique about these goings on. He returns to Cladow on July 30. The mood is hostile. 'Magda is crying,' he tells his diary. 'I can't help it.' Magda, now very heavily pregnant, puts him through the wringer. Goebbels enters into a discussion of 'this disagreeable topic' and at once regrets it. 'She's never going to change,' he notes mysteriously.[48] A few days later, he tackles her again and she promises to watch her tongue in future, particularly in the presence of Ello, who 'squawks' far too much in his view. The matrimonial tussle continues all summer, his diary seesawing between references to Magda and three-year-old Helga as 'both so sweet,' and entries like: 'Talked things over with Magda. We don't really see eye to eye any more. But things will probably get better after the birth.'[49]

Her confinement lasts for two weeks, while her jealous sister-in-law feeds her details of Joseph's alternative pursuits, *i.e.*, Hela Strehl. He takes Ello sharply to task. 'I rebuked her to her face about her loose tongue and she felt very small,' he writes, and adds the significant conclusion: 'Now it's all over between us. Never mind!'[50] Even at the maternity clinic there is another colossal row with

✗ See pg 46, 196, The Unseen Hand by A. Ralph Epperson, Publius Press, Tuscon AZ, 1985.

Magda about Hela – he blames Ello – but they kiss and make up. A few days later when he takes the unquestionably beautiful Baroness Sigrid von Laffert back home to the now refurbished villa, he finds Magda there – unwilling to stay at the clinic, although her labor begins the next day.[51]

On October 2, 1935, she gives birth to a boy. She calls him Hellmut after her tragic love, Günther Quandt's firstborn son. 'A real Goebbels face!' triumphs Dr Goebbels – as though there might be some doubt.[52] In fact his paternity as the years pass is undeniable – the flattened temples, the receding forehead, and even the hint of an overbite. Hellmut Goebbels grows to a solemn, slow-witted mutt of nine, 136 centimeters (four feet six inches) tall, with no greater recorded ambition than to become a Berlin subway driver, a source of constant worry to his father, who can see how his sisters – eventually there are five of them – are spoiling him.[53]

True, Hellmut's arrival does restore matrimonial peace, but only for three weeks. After a protracted session with actress Jenny Jugo on October 22, 1935, the diary records Goebbels as working late; he is accordingly subjected to an 'endless parlaver [sic]' by Magda, 'who puts to me,' he wearily writes, 'her views on marriage and family.'[54] One Tuesday a month later the same diary glimpses Miss Jugo wailing that one of her lesser films is likely to be canned. On Wednesday he liaises with her. 'Perhaps her movie can still be saved,' he records afterwards.[55]

His lifestyle is decorated, if not enriched, by this chattering throng of women passing through his portals, not all of whom are even pretty. 'A young poetess Käthe Summer,' he remarks to his diary after she leaves, adding the scandalous generalization: 'Why do brainy women all have to be so plain?'[56] Of his own good looks he has no doubt. He willingly allows photographers, artists, and sculptors to portray, paint, and cast his own likeness, 110 pound, five-foot-four frame, immaculately uniformed, for posterity.[57]

Image is everything and Goebbels, the only Nazi leader with a family, works hard on his. It is his daughter Helga who hands Hitler the posy of flowers on his birthday.

Twice in 1935 she is cover girl on illustrated magazines. A week after Hellmut's birth Goebbels speaks at the Harvest thanksgiving festival at Bückeberg near Hamelin. Three hundred thousand farmers' throats roar their congratulations – or so it seems to his diary.[58] Less cordial receptions are not recorded for posterity. He finds himself booed and hissed by Berlin's discarded S.A. veterans, invited to meet him at the Friedrichshain halls, scene of many a pitched battle. He begins jovially, 'I hope I've not blundered into a meeting of émigrés by mistake,' but the whistling only gets worse and he orders the radio microphones switched off.[59]

Shining through his diary's pages is his affection for his eldest daughter Helga. December 1935 finds them both rattling Winter Relief collection boxes for the assembled media outside the Adlon hotel.[60] He dutifully spends Christmas with the family at the Oberhof ski paradise; he does not omit to send gifts to Anka, but increasingly he prefers escorting more exotic women like Hela Strehl, Ello Quandt, and Jenny Jugo to the opera and theater.[61] In January 1936 he makes this note: 'I want to find a role for Miss [Ilse] Stobrowa' – an up-and-coming Berlin actress. These are trivial and no doubt innocent pursuits, but they bring problems in train which he talks over exhaustively with Magda.[62] There is a clue to what kind of problems when he complains to Hitler about Himmler's secret police: 'This loathsome snooping has got to stop,' he writes. 'Above all into one's most private affairs.'

Hitler promises to ask the minister of posts whether any Reich ministers are being wiretapped, against his orders, and to prohibit check-ups on hotel rooms.[63] But it will take more than the Gestapo to stay Goebbels' roving eye. A batch of new secretaries is introduced to him that March. 'One of them,' he adds laconically, 'is usable.'[64]

A LENGTHY mid-life crisis was beginning. One day in 1935 death knocked loudly on his door. At midday on August 20 he heard a rumble from where a subway tunnel was being excavated just outside his villa. Before his eyes the crane and several trees on the far side sank out of sight and the excavation caved in amid blue flashes from short-circuiting cables. Goebbels phoned Hitler and had the site managers arrested. He spent many hours watching the rescue operations and brooding about the nineteen missing workers, trapped 'cold and rigid' below ground. Several of the bodies were laid out in his garden – a sight he would not easily forget.[65]

He asked Göring to look into his own pension rights. Looking at the cracks wrought in his own walls by the cave-in, he had seen the first fissures in his own immortality.[66]

HUGE sums of money were now at his disposal. The ministry's revenues were swollen by the box-office receipts from the opera house in Charlottenburg.[67] He took a firmer hand in the struggling movie industry and particularly in expanding its domestic market. Movie exports had previously covered forty percent of production costs, but now, with the increasingly effective worldwide Jewish boycott, barely seven percent.[68]

He accepted without rancor that American productions were often superior. The Americans had Greta Garbo, and his passion for her had not dimmed. But he now had directors like Leni Riefenstahl – 'A woman,' he gasped, reeling from their latest encounter, 'who knows what she wants!'[69] Her international award-winning documentary of the chilling, spectacular, drum-thumping 1934 Nuremberg rally, *Triumph of the Will*, had been premièred in Munich in March and would go on to become one of the greatest propaganda films of all time.[70] Goebbels set aside 1·5 million marks to finance a Riefenstahl epic on the approaching Olympic Games. The 1936 Games, he decided, should become a showcase for National Socialism.[71]

His propaganda techniques were subtle and oblique. He directed that films were to convey no explicit party message: merely portraying happy family life in Nazi Germany would suffice. Musicals proliferated. 'Operate seemingly without purpose,' he directed Hadamovsky, criticizing the government radio's obtrusive politicking: 'That's far more compelling.'[72]

This being so, his continued indulgence of Julius Streicher, publisher of the crude tabloid *Stürmer*, is hard to understand. The party and Rudolf Hess demanded a ban on the newspaper. But Streicher enjoyed Hitler's personal backing, which gave him immunity from the normal press sanctions – until he published a scurrilous item about Emmy Göring. Then Hitler ordered *Stürmer*'s suspension. 'At last,' rejoiced Goebbels.[73] But after Streicher delivered a particularly crude speech in the Sport Palace that August he decided that he was 'a great guy' after all. The newspaper was frequently 'pure porn,' he agreed, but Streicher himself, gauleiter of Nuremberg, was 'a character and man of principle.'[74]

Stürmer's favorite ploy was to publish items exposing people who had done favors for Jews.[75] If anything redeemed Streicher in Goebbels' eyes, it was this antisemitic crusade: It made him a useful ally at a time when, as the Nazis felt, the Jews were beginning to throw their weight around again. In mid-July 1935 reports reached him at Heiligendamm that Jews had actually staged a demonstration outside a Berlin cinema showing an antisemitic movie. In consequence, Jews had been manhandled in Kurfürstendamm – the foreign press spoke loosely of a pogrom.[76] Hitler had long wanted to replace the capital's police president, Admiral Magnus von Levetzow. Goebbels suggested that his friend Count von Helldorff replace him.

It was a further indication of the decline in his moral probity. By this time the allegations against Helldorff – even within the Nazi party – filled seven pages. His gambling debts ran into the hundreds of thousands; he was in arrears with his rent; he had borrowed heavily from Jews; he smoked expensive cigars; he had bought a heavy Mercedes in which to swan around the countryside with a Mrs von B.; he had been turfed out of the feudal Union Club for dishonorable conduct.

The ugliest allegation concerned the death of the famous Jewish clairvoyant Erik Jan Hanussen (alias Steinschneider): Late in 1932 Hanussen, currying favor with the Nazis, like many Jews at that time, had offered to donate 150 new uniforms, boots, and cash to the Brownshirts, and he had been seen at Hedemann Strasse early in 1933 handing over money to Helldorff. In February 1933 a Berlin gossip columnist reported that Helldorff had attended a Hanussen séance in full uniform along with Marx, Jewish general manager of the Scala strip-club, and the purported Grand Duchess Anastasia.[77]

As the count dodged and weaved to evade bankruptcy action, an arrest warrant was issued but never acted on. In March 1933 he nevertheless became police chief of Potsdam. Frantically covering the tracks of his earlier misdeeds, Helldorff told his then chief of staff Karl Ernst to have the Jew Hanussen liquidated.[78] The Jewish clairvoyant was arrested on March 24, 1933 and found soon after shot in the back of the head. The papers relating to his donations vanished.[79] After Ernst in turn was shot during the Röhm purge a year later police searched his house and found an envelope marked 'Count von Helldorff' behind a cupboard, containing receipts for the money paid over by Hanussen to Helldorff.[80]

Early in 1935 Berlin's deputy S.A. commander discussed this scandal with Dr Goebbels. Goebbels ignored it and on July 18 persuaded Hitler to promote Helldorff to be the new police chief of Berlin. It was an unpopular choice. The very next day S.A. chief Lutze suspended Helldorff from the S.A. and took away his right to wear its uniform. Both Goebbels and Hitler continued to protect him however and a few months later all legal action against him was halted.[81]

What Helldorff had going for him was that, like Streicher, he was a vicious antisemite. Summoning him to Heiligendamm, Goebbels swore that between them they would 'clean up' the capital. It was time, he announced two weeks later, to tell the Jews 'thus far and no further.' In recent months eighteen thousand more Jews had actually poured into Berlin. Speaking in Essen on August 4, he announced threateningly that the Germans had put up with provocations from their Jewish 'guests' for two years.

The émigrés abroad retaliated with fresh horror stories about persecution. The *Manchester Guardian* published a wholly untrue story about East Prussian mills denying flour to Jewish bakers, and about food stores and pharmacists refusing to serve Jews. A Warsaw-based United Jewish Committee against Anti-Jewish Persecution in Germany appealed for world action.[82]

Goebbels plotted his revenge. In his calculus, the Jews and bolsheviks went hand in hand. That August he read with fascination the typescript memoirs which Ernst Torgler had written in a concentration camp.[83] The revelations came at an opportune time, because Goebbels had persuaded Hitler to give the upcoming seventh Nuremberg rally a pronounced anti-communist flavor. Goebbels' great Nuremberg speech, later published as 'Communism with the Mask Off,' was a chilling indictment of the methods of the Moscow Jews, which did not stop short, he again alleged, of deliberate starvation and mass murder. He stated that the Hungarian communist exile Béla Kun (whom he 'unmasked' as Aaron Cohn) had ordered sixty thousand men machine-gunned in the Crimea in one year in the Twenties. Among the 1·8 million liquidated by the bolsheviks in the first five years of their reign had been teachers, doctors, officers, and policemen, and also 815,000 peasants. Who was behind this genocide? The answer, shrilled Goebbels, was the Jews. 'Cooperation with bolshevism,' he concluded, 'is possible neither on a political nor on a philosophical basis.'[84]

FOR THE NEXT NINE YEARS Goebbels was the motor, goading his reluctant Führer into ever more radical actions against the Jews.[85] He sharpened the anti-Jewish provisions of the Reich chamber of culture.[86] Meeting in special session at Nuremberg that September 1935 the Reichstag passed a set of laws circumscribing the rights of Jews and half-Jews in Germany. Goebbels took no

* Famous Rabbi Stephen Wise said "Communism is Judaism."

part in their drafting, but he welcomed these Nuremberg laws.[87] Subsequently he demanded a more rigorous interpretation of them. In April 1936 he would exclude from the chamber of culture even quarter-Jews and those people married to a half-Jew. Eugenie Nikolajeva had one Jewish parent; as a favor, Goebbels secured for her Hitler's permission to perform. Marianne Hoppe had a Jewish fiancé. She promised to dump him. His struggle to aryanize the chamber would continue for four more years.[88]

To Goebbels' ill-concealed irritation, Hitler leaned toward leniency in applying these new laws. On September 17 he heard the Führer telling the gauleiters that 'above all' there must be no excesses against the Jews.[89] A week later he heard Hitler reiterate this point to the gauleiters in Munich's city hall. 'No [persecution?] of "non-Aryans,"' Goebbels scribbled afterward – the word is illegible but the sense is clear – and described Hitler's speech as one long repudiation of Rosenberg and Streicher (both of whom nevertheless loudly applauded).[90] He tried to talk Hitler round one Sunday at the end of September. 'Jewish problem still not resolved even now,' he recorded. 'We debated it for a long time but the Führer still can't make his mind up.'[91]

Sometimes moderate attitudes did surface in Goebbels too. Curiously, he had argued against overdoing the restrictions on marriages where congenital deformities were involved.[92] When over-zealous Nazis erased Jewish names from war memorials his diary displayed real irritation.[93] But such insights were rare.

The murder of Wilhelm Gustloff, the party's representative in Switzerland, by a Jewish medical student in February 1936 at Davos brought to Goebbels' attention a shadowy, well-funded World League against Racism and Antisemitism (LICA) dedicated to attacking Hitler's Germany. After scanning Emil Ludwig's gloating book on the case, Goebbels remarked in his diary: 'It would convert anybody who wasn't one already into an antisemite.' More ominously he added, 'This Jewish plague must be eradicated [*ausradiert*]. Totally. Nothing must be left.'[94]

In LICA he had momentarily found a worthy enemy. He staged a great funeral ceremony in Schwerin, Gustloff's home town, and when Switzerland put the assassin David Frankfurter on trial he pulled whatever strings he could from Berlin; LICA contributed its vice-president Dr Leon Castro as the assassin's lawyer and portrayed the self-confessed murderer as a martyr.[95] Frankfurter stated that he had hoped that Hitler would die of the throat cancer falsely reported in the press, and when this happy event failed to occur he had intended to bump off Göring or Goebbels; denied that opportunity, he had shot Gustloff instead. The court handed down an eighteen-year sentence. 'Now we have to unmask the camarilla behind him,' wrote Goebbels.[96]

Uncomfortably conscious that LICA might have put out a contract on his life too, he warmed toward Julius Streicher again. He decided in one indulgent diary entry that the gauleiter always would be an *enfant terrible*.[97] 'I have been told that the Jews are getting uppity again,' he intoned on his tenth anniversary as Berlin's gauleiter. 'In the past I over-estimated their intelligence. They are neither intelligent nor clever. If they were intelligent they would either disappear or play possum.' The excessively gentle voice in which he pronounced these lines, which were later omitted from the official text, struck his British listeners as being 'the very refinement of cruelty.'[98]

How much more exhilarating it was to mastermind this ancient feud with the Jews than to pursue his humdrum ministerial routine – the receptions for gaggles of giggling maidens in regional costumes, the speeches to international penal experts,[99] the lectures to Wehrmacht officers.[100]

HITLER FREELY DISCUSSED his strategic intentions and timetable with Goebbels. Debating the political situation with Goebbels, Göring, and Ribbentrop on May 14, 1935, two days after Marshal Pilsudski died, taking with him the hopes of a fruitful alliance with Poland, Hitler had predicted that the years 1936 and 1937 would hold particular dangers for Germany. 'Rearm, rearm!' wrote Goebbels afterwards.[101] Mussolini, running into snags in Abyssinia, was warming toward the Nazis again.[102] Even when unable to speak after a throat operation, Hitler still sent for Goebbels and told him of his worries, writing them down on paper for him.[103]

Vacationing in August 1935 with Goebbels at Tegernsee the Führer repeated that his foreign policy was based on an alliance with Britain and an entente cordiale with Poland. 'Meanwhile, expansion in the east,' recorded Goebbels afterward. 'The Baltic states belong to us.' Peering into the future Hitler envisaged Britain fighting Italy over her invasion of Abyssinia and, a few years later, Japan fighting Russia. 'Then our great historic hour will come,' wrote Goebbels, deeply affected. 'We must be ready then. A grandiose prospect.'[104] He foresaw complications for Hitler over his support for Mussolini since this would be treading on Britain's toes; he briefed his editors accordingly, and Hitler also addressed his ministers and generals on the danger that Britain might include Germany in any sanctions against Italy.[105] 'All of this,' Goebbels realized, 'is coming three years too soon for us.'

Although the Nazis' rearmament program was far from complete, Hitler decided early in 1936 to risk a new coup. In violation of the Locarno pact, Paris was negotiating a treaty with Moscow which Hitler deemed to justify him in moving troops back into Germany's Rhineland provinces, demilitarized since the Versailles treaty.

For a while however he bided his time. 'We are trying to overcome our difficulties,' declared Goebbels, speaking in Berlin on January 17, 1936, 'with the cunning of the serpent.' He added in a pointed reference that was withheld from most of the German press, 'If a treaty has become intolerable there are higher laws than those which are written in ink.'[106] Three days later Hitler notified him in strict confidence that he was contemplating reoccupying the Rhineland suddenly, as soon as Italy's war in Abyssinia ended.[107]

Goebbels could scarcely keep the secret. In the Rhineland he spoke threateningly of both the League of Nations and the Jews, and advised Americans to tackle their own 'gangster problems' before meddling in Germany's affairs. If Germany had had just two more army corps in Belgium in the war, he declared, in an extraordinary and again unreported passage, Germany would have won. 'That was a serious blunder,' he added. 'It won't happen the next time.'[108]

A month passed. On February 27, lunching with Goebbels and Göring, Hitler felt it was still premature to go into the Rhineland. But on the very next day the French confirmed their treaty with Moscow. As he would in each of the next three years' crises, Dr Goebbels initially counseled Hitler against over-hasty action. Still grappling with the decision the Führer phoned to invite him to join his private train that night; they argued for hours, and as it pulled into Munich Goebbels was still urging caution.[109]

Hitler however had made up his mind. On Sunday March 1, wrote Goebbels, his expression was 'calm but determined.' Hitler explained his own credo: 'To the bold belongs the world!' Back in his chancellery in Berlin that Monday Hitler unveiled the plan to his commanders-in-chief. On Saturday (because, wrote Goebbels, Saturdays were best) he would proclaim that Germany was reoccupying the Rhineland, but simultaneously he would offer to return to the League of Nations and to sign a non-aggression pact with France. He was taking a calculated risk: France still had the biggest army in Europe. Britain, France, and Italy would all be justified in intervening.

'Nothing ventured, nothing gained,' was Goebbels' attitude, all his former caution thrown to the winds.[110] After lunching with Hitler that Thursday he mockingly referred to the throngs of 'knicker-wetters' in the foreign ministry.[111] In fact the Cabinet, belatedly briefed on Friday, the eve of the operation, loyally backed Hitler. Goebbels sent two planeloads of puzzled journalists into the Rhineland ahead of the marching troops. After Hitler announced his move to cheering Reichstag deputies that Saturday morning, Goebbels could hear the crowds 'exulting' below – a theme that would soon become a commonplace in his chronicle. 'Wiretaps show the world of diplomacy all at sea,' he recorded, adding, 'And the Rhineland a sea of joy.'[112]

It was perhaps the one moment in history when Hitler could have been stopped. His own generals had panicked, but Goebbels urged him to hang tough. 'If we keep our nerve now,' he wrote afterward, 'we've won.'[113]

25: *A Man of Property*

HITLER HAD CALLED AN ELECTION to endorse his action in the Rhineland. The climax was vintage Goebbels. He ordained that fifteen minutes before Hitler broadcast from Krupps' munitions works in Essen, a fitting stage, on March 27, every radio station would transmit the command to Hoist Flags on every building and homestead in Germany, to flutter until the election was over. As Hitler himself stepped to the microphone at four P.M., the Krupps' sirens were to hail 'the beginning of the Führer's great appeal for peace,' joined by the klaxons of every factory, locomotive, barge, and ship. While these sirens sang all traffic was to halt, demonstrating that the entire nation stood behind the Führer and his 'policy of peace.' The election's eve, Saturday March 28, was to see immense demonstrations throughout the country. Ten minutes before eight P.M. the great bells of Cologne's Gothic cathedral would toll, splendidly amplified by radios throughout the country, their clangor fading only as Hitler himself began to speak. After that, decreed Goebbels, the entire nation in unison, sixty-seven million voices, would sing the ancient Netherlands Prayer of Thanksgiving (to which he was particularly attached). Then would come the crucial Goebbels masterstroke – the deft touch which set him apart from all his imitators: Every radio station would fall *silent* for fifteen minutes, marking a reverent end to this, his 1936 campaign.[1]

Thus it came to pass. Two weeks earlier he had written, 'This election just can't go wrong.'[2] (It would have been a miracle if it had, as the ballot papers bore only the names of Hitler and, in suitably smaller print, of Göring, Hess, Goebbels, and Frick; there was no provision whatever for voters to express dissent.)[3] On March 29, a Sunday, 98·6 percent of the voting population streamed into the polling booths, and 98·7 percent of those voted for Hitler – 44,399,000 adult Germans.

A CONCRETE GESTURE of Hitler's gratitude followed.

For some months Goebbels, now a best-selling author, had been wondering if he could afford to buy the summer cottage at Cladow.[4] On one visit to Obersalzberg he had told Max Winkler, his business adviser, that he wanted to provide for his family and was thinking of buying a farm. Winkler advised against it – the minister would only lose money on the land. Besides, what funds had he in mind? Goebbels mentioned this idea to Hitler, who promised to have a word with Goebbels' publisher Max Amann;[5] the minister now raised his sights and inspected a more luxurious redbrick property on Schwanenwerder, a millionaire's peninsula jutting into the Wannsee lake.[6] The villa and its gate lodge in Insel Strasse stood on a gentle wooded incline verging on the bullrush-fringed lakeshore. The property had, it seems, formerly belonged to one of the Barmat brothers, the Jewish embezzlers who had fled to Holland even before Hitler came to power.[7] It was now in the name of the Jewish bank director Oskar Schlitter.[8] Almost ten years earlier, Dr Goebbels and *Angriff* had repeatedly inveighed against 'Schweinenwerder' (Isle of Pigs) as a 'Jew-boys' paradise.'[9] Now he was going to 'out-Jew' them all.

At the climax of the Rhineland election campaign Karl Hanke brought the necessary papers over to Goebbels at Godesberg.[10] Hitler wholeheartedly approved of the purchase. He believed in assisting his best lieutenants to become men of property.[11] The final purchase price was 270,000 marks. The Führer personally phoned Goebbels from Munich guaranteeing that the money would be forthcoming – 'Amann has turned up trumps again,' Goebbels wrote. He moved his family into the Schwanenwerder property just before Easter 1936, and invited his favorite younger sister Maria to stay with them.[12]

How did he eventually finance the deal? Goebbels asked Winkler to discuss the capital value of his private diaries with Amann. Amann accompanied him back to Berlin one day in October and they agreed terms. Goebbels had in mind an outright payment of three million marks for the diaries, but Amann came up with a different proposal: Goebbels should sell all rights to him, for publication twenty years after his death, '250,000 marks immediately and 100,000 marks per annum. That,' Goebbels recorded in a massive understatement, 'is most generous.'[13]

This was undoubtedly the origin of the cash he handed over in November to complete the Schwanenwerder deal: Surviving among Goebbels' papers in 1945 would be found a sheet of paper listing his account with Amann's publishing house, showing that during 1936 they paid him advances totaling 290,000 marks against earnings of a much lower figure, 63,416·31 marks.[14]

MAGDA FURNISHED the guest lodge for her idol, Adolf Hitler. In later years he will often show up unannounced, bringing perhaps Jakob Werlin, general manager of Daimler-Benz, to sample her crème caramel. Hitler's adjutant tips the Goebbels' servants and, later, will surrender to her the food-ration coupons for Hitler's share of the meal.[15]

For most of 1936 Magda Goebbels alternates between a sulky obstinacy and uxorial bliss. She grouses that she never has enough housekeeping money but the ministry's records show that two days before they move in to Schwanenwerder Goebbels has ordered his ministerial and parliamentary salaries paid directly into her bank account.[16]

She resigns herself to his (perhaps imagined) infidelities.[17] Vacationing with her in Switzerland, Mussolini's daughter Edda Ciano philosophizes that an unfaithful spouse is but a trivial annoyance in one's mortal span. Magda begins to go out more alone. One day Goebbels records moodily that the moment Magda returns home he leaves for Schwanenwerder – 'I have no place I can call home when she's there.'[18]

Oppressed by the chains of marriage, he lies out late on the darkening meadow gazing at the stars.[19] He indulges in a large motor launch, and spends many an afternoon lolling about the lake, chatting on its mobile phone to his friends; he buys another boat for Magda and the children.[20] Hanfstaengl describes one ghastly incident at a Goebbels party: As the last guests leave, the crippled minister trips and falls; Magda helps him to his feet. Purple with rage, he seizes her by the throat and forces her sideways to her knees. 'There,' he screams, 'now you see who is the stronger, who is the master!'[21] After one tiff she resorts to tears. 'Sometimes she gets into a state,' he writes helplessly, 'just like all women. Then you've just got to bare your teeth at her.'[22]

His own circle expands. She becomes accustomed to all the other lovelies fluttering around her powerful husband.[23] There is a stream of delectable wannabee-actresses. 'I'll try,' notes Goebbels succinctly after Eva Vanya visits, seeking a role.[24] Anny Ondra, the blonde, cheerful, and naïve wife of boxer Max Schmeling, comes to Schwanenwerder; Goebbels finds Edda Ciano, who also comes, 'frightfully painted, like just about every other Italian woman.'[25] At the Italian embassy's reception for Edda, Bella Fromm notices that Goebbels ventures only the curtest nod in Leni Riefenstahl's direction.[26]

It is the children who hold the Goebbels marriage together in the mid-Thirties. Helga, the apple of Hitler's eye too now, sits on her papa's lap singing lustily as they return from the seaside near Peenemünde that July.[27] 'Grandma is *old*,' she declares solemnly that summer. 'But Papa is – *new*!'[28] As the three children splash around in a new rubber dinghy, his heart aches with parental love.[29] He persuades the Cabinet to approve the death-penalty for child kidnappers. Hitler will say that if little Helga were twenty years older, and he twenty years younger, she would have made the ideal wife for him. An enchanting, precocious, graceful girl she will captivate everybody with remarks that are as genuine as Hitler's are contrived. 'My little heart is thumping,' she squawks in one moment of girlish panic, and her doting father remembers the words in his diary.[30]

AMONG THE CAVALCADES of English ladies passing through Berlin that summer of 1936 is Diana Mitford. Staying with her sister Unity at Schwanenwerder for the Olympic Games, she conveys to Goebbels a plea from Sir Oswald Mosley for secret funds, an upstanding and forceful former minister who has resigned from the British Labour party to set up his own radical movement along fascist lines. (When Mosley had visited Hitler on April 25, 1935, Goebbels noted in his unpublished diary: 'He makes a good impression. A bit brash, which he tries to conceal behind a forced pushiness. Otherwise acceptable however. Of course he's on his best behavior. The Führer has set to work on him. Wonder if he'll ever come to power?')[31] By 1936 Mosley is already receiving substantial secret aid from Mussolini, and now he is boldly asking Hitler for an infusion of one hundred thousand pounds (around half a million dollars).[32] Taking Diana and her sister Unity to see Hitler on June 19, 1936 Dr Goebbels procures (his diary claims) £10,000 for Mosley – less than the asking amount, but still a very substantial contribution given Germany's currency shortages.[33]

Goebbels is dubious about Mosley, and nominates Franz Wrede, of the party's press office, to smuggle the cash over to London.[34] 'Mosley must work harder,' summarizes Goebbels after Wrede reports back to him, 'and be less mercenary.'[35] When Diana returns in August, asking for more, he fobs her off (with Hitler's approval). 'They must learn to help themselves,' he comments, recollecting his own penniless start in Berlin.[36]

As her private sorrows increase, Magda drinks more heavily, and sometimes her eye wanders. It is Rosenberg, of all people, who tips off Goebbels about a certain Lüdecke in her life.[37] At first she cries a lot and denies it when he asks her, leaving him agonizing over whether she's lying. On the first night in August, the day the Berlin Olympiad opens, she admits that she has strayed. 'A great blow to my trust,' he writes, downcast. 'It'll take me a while to get over it.'[38] He spends sleepless nights brooding, and evidently mentions it to Hitler. 'He praises Magda a lot,' he writes after that. 'Finds her bewitching, "the best wife I could ever find."' 'When I speak alone with him,' records the young minister the next day, 'he talks to me like a father.'[39]

Not for the last time, Magda leaves for the White Hart sanitarium in Dresden, playground of the wealthy, leaving her children at Schwanenwerder for the summer. Goebbels barely misses her. He has his hands full with planning the Nuremberg rally; Hitler has flatly rejected his half-hearted suggestion that they skip the rally this year because of the Olympics.[40]

THE OLYMPIC GAMES of 1936 were a sporting and propaganda triumph for Germany. Tourists flooded in.[41] Confounding foreign expectations Hitler ruled that all competitors be treated with equal respect regardless of race or religion, and shook hands with the Negro Gold-medalist Jesse Owens. Goebbels ordered the party to keep a low profile.[42] As Leni Riefenstahl's crews filmed the events, awash with a 1·2 million-mark loan from the ministry, Goebbels found her increasingly tiresome. 'I have had to knock some sense into La Riefenstahl,' he wrote. 'Her behavior is unspeakable! A hysterical woman! Anyway, no man.'[43] Their spat would continue until Hitler lost patience, banged their heads together, ordered Goebbels to accompany him to Riefenstahl's villa in Dahlem, and had a joint photograph printed in every newspaper the next day.[44]

At the end of the games Goebbels staged the most sumptuous all-night party of his life. Benno von Arent's stage designers and craftsmen had labored for weeks to convert Peacock Island, an unspoiled wilderness near Potsdam, into a fairy grotto; thousands of butterfly-shaped lamps graced the trees, and there were three outdoor dance floors, brightly colored marquees, and tables for thousands of guests – among them Gustav Fröhlich and his eye-catching movie-star fiancée Lida Baarova, upon whom Goebbels heaped particular compliments this night; he had again noticed her talents in her latest movie a few weeks earlier.[45]

'Everybody with legs was there,' recorded the little Doctor proudly afterwards, knowing he had outdone Göring at last. He sashayed around in an elegant white suit; Magda, never one to miss a party, had returned from Dresden, and glided at his side in a bright organdy outfit.

'Where the government gets the money from to entertain thus lavishly,' wrote Louis Lochner in a letter home, 'I don't know'[46]

The good times rolled for Dr Goebbels all that summer. He had the new launch, and a new Mercedes 5·4 liter two-seats sports car.[47] He had ordered yet another limousine, an open Horch tourer just like the Führer's.[48] He test-cruised an even classier motor boat.[49] And yet, in the more distant valleys of his mind, it was as if he could already hear a bell tolling – more persistent, more penetrating than the great peal of Cologne. He sat brooding at his desk, drafting his speech for the Nuremberg rally, reading up on the communist reign of terror in Republican Spain. The Reds there had slain priests and nuns, and butchered seven thousand of their enemies in Madrid alone. Might not the same one day come to pass in Berlin?

'Woe betide us in that event,' he wrote thoughtfully in his diary. 'We and our families would all be done for. The best thing then would be to finish yourself off first.'[50]

26: *Femme Fatale*

'Live wild, live fine!' writes Goebbels in September 1936, opening a new diary.[1] He has just embarked upon the most destructive emotional entanglement of his life. He has seen Lida Baarova in her new movie in June, and again at the Peacock Island fête in August, and it may be no coincidence that his new villa on Schwanenwerder is only a stone's throw from her lover Gustav Fröhlich's twelve-roomed mansion, set amid tennis courts and boathouses by the lake. With Magda a fugitive from marriage in her Dresden sanitarium and again broodily pregnant – is 'Lüdecke' perhaps the father?[2] – the young minister soon tires of his latest private secretary Lucie Kammer. He often glances at his glamorous neighbors. When Lida returns one afternoon from the August Olympiad she finds him casually strolling down Insel Strasse with Helga and Hilde. He asks if he may have a look over the Fröhlich mansion. Her lover Gustl innocently obliges, while the little girls and Lida play with Fröhlich's lavish train set.[3]

On August 18, three days after Peacock Island, he invites the young couple out in his launch.[4] Years later Lida will give her own shy account of this picnic cruise. The pretty actress sisters Höpfner, whom Goebbels is also cultivating, have joined them. It is a broiling-hot day, they swim, cruise, and sip tea until her Gustl apologizes that he has an all-night shoot at the studios and can one of the police escort-launches take them ashore?

'I always go everywhere with him,' explains Lida. The words strike a chord in Goebbels – Magda shares none of his interests. He insists jovially that Lida stay. Gustl, visibly annoyed, leaves without her. As the full moon rises, reflected in the still waters of the Wannsee, Goebbels limps over and stands behind Lida at the railing. 'How do you like it here in Germany?' he asks. His melodious, rich voice seems to caress her, she will later say. The bond is forged at this moment.

His rival, Gustav Fröhlich, meanwhile makes a classic mistake: After visiting his estranged spouse, a Jewess who has emigrated to London, he accidentally calls Lida by the wife's name at a tender moment. She flounces back to her own humble lodgings off Kurfürstendamm.

For a while that August Goebbels lets things drift. He takes Magda to Venice. But it is the actress Lilian Harvey with whom he punts along the canals while pregnant Magda stays in the hotel.[5] The hunt is on – he cannot get Lida out of his mind. She is a head and shoulders taller than he is, but she has an arresting Slavonic beauty. Her fresh young face has both childish innocence and womanly guile. Early in September he ascertains that she is resting with her mother at Franzensbad, a spa near Nuremberg. Suddenly he begins looking forward to this year's Nuremberg rally after all. His diary records 'diverse phone calls' on the fifth about the premiere of *Traitors*, her latest movie with Fröhlich – Goebbels is arranging to switch it to Nuremberg; phoning Magda from Nuremberg he pleads with her to stay away at Dresden or Schwanenwerder. Then phoning Lida he invites her over to Nuremberg, reassuring her that fellow actors Irene von Meyendorff and Willy Birgel will be coming too – 'You can't miss out on this!' he says.

His rally speech on September 8 is one of his finest. Towering above the thousands on a lofty pulpit, he forcefully describes the murderous rampage of the bolsheviks in Spain, and the 'pathological and criminal madness' of their Jewish masters in Moscow.[6]

Lida arrives the next day, Saturday September 9. At the Grand Hotel banquet after the premiere he fusses over her, he flirts, and then commands her to accompany him over to Hitler's hotel. Here a female singer softly croons Nico Dostal's latest hit, 'I am so much in love. . . ', and Lida is flustered to hear Dr Goebbels murmur in her ear, '. . . me too!'[7] He has done this so often before, it is second nature to him now. As the party breaks up she plants a harmless kiss on his cheek; he removes the smudge with a pocket handkerchief, solemnly tucks it into his top pocket, and pleads with her to stay over and lunch with him the next day, Sunday. Here he inquires casually if she is still unmarried, and catching an aggrieved undertone in her reply about her lover's reluctance to remarry, he diffidently asks: 'Would you turn me down if I asked to see you again?'

That Sunday afternoon he asks her to stay on, to hear his second great speech. 'Please look at me closely as I speak,' he says, and pulls out that handkerchief. 'I shall dab at my lips with this, as a sign that I am thinking of YOU.'

What twenty-two-year-old female (Lida's birthday has fallen just three days before) is not bowled over by such artful devices? Bedazzled, Lida again puts off returning to her mother at Franzensbad. Goebbels makes no mention whatever of her in his diary of these days. 'A miracle has happened,' is all he writes.[8] After the speech, in a circumlocution that will become familiar to its readers, he carefully records 'a little drive to recuperate;' the next afternoon, Monday, 'some sleep;' and then, without mentioning *whose*, 'departure to Franzensbad.'[9] He sends his adjutant to the railroad station to see Lida off with roses and a photograph inscribed, 'Auf Wiedersehen!' A few days later he certainly sees her again in Nuremberg. 'A visitor from Franzensbad,' he notes, 'about which I am much pleased.'[10] This is the first time that he has passed significant, if camouflaged, comments on a prospective lover in his diary.

Lida Baarova will affect him more profoundly than any other woman since Anka. They will bring to each other great happiness: But the ensuing romance, which is almost entirely platonic, will sweep him to the brink of divorce, self-exile, and even suicide. As for Lida, she will nobly abstain from the general calumny of him after his death. Legions of obscure starlets will claim, without a shred of supporting evidence, that he forced himself upon them. 'It would have left him no time at all for work,' Lida points out.

'Toward me,' she still insists, 'his behavior was impeccable.' It is his courtesy and patience as a suitor that impress her. But does she ever truly love him? Even years later she cannot be sure. 'I loved him in my own way,' she will recollect. 'I was very young and you are very susceptible at that age. . . He loved me so deeply, that I fell in love with love itself.'[11]

AT THIS NUREMBERG rally Hitler announced a four-year plan for Germany. His grand ideas on foreign policy came as no surprise to Goebbels.[12] After sitting in on one conference aboard Hitler's yacht *Grille* at Kiel in May 1936 he had noted down the Führer's prophetic vision of a United States of Europe under a German leadership. 'Years, perhaps even decades of work toward that end,' he commented in his diary. 'But what an end!'[13] Mussolini's victory in Abyssinia had seemingly confirmed one important lesson: that might was right. 'Anything else is nonsense,' concluded Goebbels.[14] Clearly at Hitler's behest he was already gearing up for future hostilities. He established close relations with the Wehrmacht, and had quiet talks with Blomberg about beefing up transmitter powers and mobilizing war reporters.[15] 'The Führer,' he added after another secret meeting with Hitler, Papen, and Ribbentrop, 'sees a conflict coming in the Far East. Japan will thrash Russia. And then our great hour will come. Then we shall have to carve off enough territory to last us a hundred years. Let's hope that we're ready, and that the Führer is still alive.'[16] Anticipating that moment, late in November 1936 Hitler signed a deal with the Japanese. Over dinner with the signatories, Hitler prophetically remarked that it would not bear fruit for another five years. 'He really is taking the long view in foreign policy,' marveled his propaganda minister.[17]

While relations with Göring were strained but stable, a never-ending feud with Alfred Rosenberg had broken out, fueled by Goebbels' doctrinaire plans for a 105-member cultural senate and a seventh sub-chamber of the Reich chamber of culture. Suffice to say that Rosenberg still claimed culture as his own domain.[18] Toward Hess as deputy Führer Goebbels preserved a bemused if antiseptic cordiality; in truth he found Hess bourgeois and probably unbalanced. Hess's businesslike chief of staff Martin Bormann suggested that he had neither imagination nor initiative – and would be proven wrong on both counts five years later.[19] Goebbels had already spotted that it could be dangerous to have Bormann himself as an enemy.[20] Goebbels' early admiration for Ribbentrop had waned during 1935 and expired entirely after he was appointed ambassador in London in August 1936. He then took every opportunity he could to score off him. When agency photos arrived showing Ribbentrop's seventeen-year-old son leaving their Eaton Square house in his

Westminster School uniform of top hat and tails, Goebbels cruelly ensured that they were printed in every Berlin newspaper that Hitler read.[21] Mercy was not a quality in which he excelled.

IT IS MID-SEPTEMBER 1936 before Magda returns from Dresden to Berlin. She works off her rancor on her little husband. 'Magda's changing,' he notes self-righteously. It's sickening!'[22] Seeking affection he turns to Lida Baarova, temporarily ensconced in the Hotel Eden with Fröhlich, to whom she has returned; their respective villas on Schwanenwerder are mothballed for the winter. He obtains an advance print of Fröhlich's latest movie, *City of Anatolia*, and offers to show it to them. The actor swallows the bait and his pride, and brings Lida along. Afterward Goebbels notes that Fröhlich's acting is not all that good; but it is with Fröhlich that Lida nonetheless leaves, bound for Franzensbad.[23]

A grander campaign plan is called for. With some prodding the City of Berlin agrees to give Goebbels for his lifetime a domain in one of its forests on his forthcoming birthday. He has inspected it with Karl Hanke in mid-September; it is near the forest village of Lanke, about twenty miles north-east of the capital. Hanke has selected an idyllic location on a little swan lake, the Bogensee, enveloped by groves of fir, beech, and pine. 'All around, the deepest solitude,' describes Goebbels. 'Hanke has done his stuff well.' With manpower provided by the Labor Service, a two-story woodframed house is rapidly erected on an incline at the water's edge. A tall wire fence will be thrown up around the entire lake to preserve the minister's privacy.[24] (House and fence are still there. The author, visiting it nearly sixty years later, found one rusting hook in a nearby mildewed tree where once a children's swing had hung.)

Later that month he flies to Greece with Magda, taking in the Acropolis and Parthenon ('this noble temple of Nordic art'); he meets prime minister Johannis Metaxas, who professes to like the Germans as much as he loathes the Jews and bolsheviks. Then he returns to Berlin and continues furnishing his love-nest at Lanke, including among its accouterments a special diary – kept just during his visits out here.[25]

He fantasizes about being out here alone with Lida Baarova. He phones her in Prague, where she is visiting her mother, to ask when she will be back. 'Quite soon,' she replies guilelessly. 'Gustl's staying on at Karlsbad.'

He escorts her out frequently in the evenings. On October 5 his diary coyly records 'a little *Spazierfahrt*,' a motor outing, before he returns late to bed.[26]

Appeasing Magda he buys her a costly ring on Hellmut's first birthday. His diary sparkles with occasional flattery of Magda, but it has a dutiful quality.[27] Visiting the gracious spa resort of Baden-Baden (without Magda) in October he is evidently not alone, as witness the unexplained phrases that slip into its pages, like those on the twelfth, when the night ends with 'a big disappointment,' followed by the disembodied remark: 'Did not come down from room any more.' Followed by: 'I am so sad.'[28] At Berlin upon his return he finds Magda livid: 'About nothing – nothing at all.' Undaunted he goes out motoring again that afternoon, and stops at their (deserted) Schwanenwerder villa on the way back. It would be charitable to assume that he was alone, were it not self-evident that his diary has now become the vehicle for half-truths.

On the day before the new house at Lanke is formally handed over to him Magda takes the dour but handsome Hanke out to see it. Goebbels seizes the opportunity to visit Schwanenwerder again, where Lida Baarova is house-sitting the dust-sheeted Fröhlich villa three lots down the road from his own.[29] He phones to invite himself round for tea. Lida points out how improper that would seem; covered with embarrassment, the minister suggests they motor out one day to see Lanke instead.[30] 'You know I have a little house out there now,' he says. 'We can have tea there. It's very pretty.' She helplessly falls in with his suggestion that one day she should motor out along the new autobahn in her little black and white BMW to the Lanke exit, where his chauffeur Alfred Rach will meet her with his new open Horch tourer.[31] 'All Berlin used to speak about his love affairs,' Rach will later reminisce, adding a revealing remark: 'He found that very flattering.'[32]

On his birthday at the end of October he drives out to Lanke. It is an idyll, romantic and tranquil. After that he takes Magda out there on the first day of November. Alone together in the middle of this autumn forest of yellowing leaves, fog, and rain, they spend a quiet day hanging pictures, playing the piano, and singing Schubert's lieder.[33] The next day his heavy Horch limousine returns, splashing through the fresh puddles – 'all alone,' he writes, an untruth which his own diary exposes a few lines later. (He writes, 'We cook ourselves something.') This is the occasion that Lida will later describe, when his manservant Kaiser burns their only provisions, fried potatoes. Of such tiny episodes romantic memories are made. On November 5 the diary finds him out at Lanke once more, 'taking refuge' from 'unpleasantness' at home. 'She is so fickle,' he sighs on Magda's birthday. 'Sometimes good and sometimes horrid. But that's probably just how women are.'[34]

He has less than nine years left of his allotted span, but he has assembled all the baggage that goes with middle life: A beauteous young mistress; a dissatisfied, nagging wife; and three angelic infants who thump around the bare floor above him far into the night. 'It is music to my ears,' writes Dr Goebbels, still aged only thirty-nine.[35]

ONE EVENING IN SEPTEMBER 1936 Magda brought Diana Mitford to dinner at Schwanenwerder. Hearing that Sir Oswald Mosley, leader of the British Union of Fascists, was planning to marry Diana in secret, Magda suggested they do it in Berlin. Goebbels didn't like the idea and harrumphed about it in his diary: Magda was getting too involved, he felt.[36] Hitler and Goebbels agreed that Mosley was not a great man; but Hitler coughed up funds for Diana, according to the diary, when she visited Berlin at the time of the Edward VIII crisis.[37]

The secret wedding went ahead in Magda's drawing room at No. 20

Hermann-Göring Strasse; Magda invited the guests, who included Hitler, out to Schwanenwerder for lunch. The new Lady Mosley gave Goebbels an inside account of the royal scandal. The new king wanted to marry an American woman, already once divorced and still married to another, she said. Goebbels professed dismay at the depths a proud empire could sink to; but this was the king who, as Prince of Wales, had openly praised Hitler's social program and they all – Hitler, Goebbels, and Ribbentrop – agreed to do the decent thing now. As the American and Continental press broke into a raucous hue-and-cry Dr Goebbels, with Hitler's approval, forbade the German media to print one whisper on the scandal. After King Edward abdicated, the Nazi wiretappers heard one British embassy official commenting that the new Duke of Windsor would not easily forget Hitler's restraint.[38]

Their discretion was poorly rewarded. During 1937 and 1938 the anti-Nazi jibes from some elements of the British press multiplied. Ribbentrop told Goebbels that much of it was controlled by the Jews, as were Britain's cinema chains.[39] He suggested they purchase cinemas in London. Goebbels listened sympathetically. His ministry was awash with money, and he did use some secret funds to buy up foreign newspapers as well.[40] Like Hitler he regarded Britain as holding the key to Germany's future. But how to proceed? Mosley was 'spending a fortune and getting nowhere,' he concluded; he had won no seats at all in the municipal elections. 'I think he's a busted flush,' wrote Goebbels after a further panhandling visitation by Lady Mosley in August 1937.[41]

HIS ADMIRATION OF Hitler was now unconditional.[42] The Führer confided in him regularly. In mid-July 1936 he and Magda had spent three days at the Berghof, Hitler's lavish new mountainside domain high above Berchtesgaden. 'We had a long parlaver,' writes Goebbels. 'The three of us – the Führer, Göring, and I. That's always best.'[43] They had all shared the annual Wagner experience at Bayreuth that summer. In October 1936 Hitler had assigned to Goebbels an upstairs room at his own Berghof, a certain sign of his esteem for him.[44]

Knowing Hitler's intentions, Goebbels took a closer interest in their growing armed forces. In early 1937 he spoke for two hours to selected Wehrmacht commanders about propaganda.[45] General von Blomberg attached significant weight to the wartime role of propaganda. In that autumn's maneuvers Goebbels' new propaganda units took part for the first time. There was one uncomfortable detail: Although Berlin went into full blackout, the 'enemy' planes still got through and Goebbels' ministry was adjudged a blazing ruin by the referees. 'Let's hope it's never for real,' he gasped in his diary.[46]

THE GOEBBELS FAMILY spends a few days early in 1937 at Hitler's Berghof again. Before turning in one night, Goebbels speaks for some hours with Magda, now heavily pregnant, about love and marriage. He feels they are drawing closer again, as always 'when nobody comes between us.'[47] After a couple of days he leaves his family there and returns to Berlin. Predatory females cluster around him there.[48] He drives out some frosty nights to the new house at Lanke, explaining to his diary 'nobody is waiting for me in Berlin.'[49]

Magda and Hitler return to the capital together on the twenty-third. All this sets tongues wagging. Gossip queen Bella Fromm, still holding out in Berlin, records privately that Goebbels has been seen hanging around some pretty low dives, and that Magda now has a list of more than thirty women he has slept with.[50] Magda's closeness to Hitler also attracts salacious comment, and after Werner Count von Alvensleben lets slip an incautious remark about her, her children, and her Führer, Goebbels complains to Hitler and has the count, spluttering denials, whisked off to concentration camp.[51] Shortly the police tell Goebbels that his cook Martha has been gossiping too, and she is sacked without notice. 'Let's hope she hasn't done any harm already,' he writes, while entrusting no details to his diary.

It is of relevance to examine his views on divorce and adultery at this time. Hitler takes a more liberal view of divorce than Goebbels.[52] Goebbels instinctively opposes it, although he feels that most party wives are 'too thick to hang on to their husbands.'[53] There are strains of catholic Puritanism in him. When his young sister, still in her twenties, begins dating a divorced movie producer of forty-five, Max Kimmich, he has detectives discreetly check the man's background. 'It's okay,' he writes after hearing their report. 'Maria can fall in love with him.'[54] Preferring double standards to single, he spends nights out at Lanke ('gossiping and lazing'), and days discussing the new laws with Hitler. He proposes that couples be forced to wait a year after filing for divorce – this cooling-off period will save many faltering marriages.[55] But in his diary are many unconscious hints at his own activities. He criticizes theater director Eugen Klopfer for his womanizing: 'The theater is not a free-for-all for girl-snatchers,' he huffs.[56] Even more hypocritically he lectures the incorrigible Walter Grantzow for falling in love with 'some starlet,' and now wanting to dump his wife.[57]

His stand on adultery is no less self-serving. When the minister of the interior Wilhelm Frick, a pettifogging lawyer whom Goebbels detests, proposes with almost Islamic fervor ten-year jail terms for adultery, Goebbels snorts: 'Then let them begin retroactively with Frick.' That night he drives scriptwriter Thea von Harbou (the lovely wife of Fritz Lang) home; and what right have we to doubt that she only 'tells me of her new movie plans'?[58] He tells Hitler that neither divorce nor adultery is any concern of the public prosecutor. Hitler promises that he will shoot down Frick's draconian proposals on adultery.

At the end of 1937, when the question of adultery again comes before the Cabinet, Goebbels is still fighting. 'Finally,' he records, 'we agree: prison sentences only if demanded by the wronged husband and in the public interest.' The same Cabinet session decides that any rape committed by a Jew shall be a capital offense.[59] During these debates, the diaries' entries glimpse Joseph Goebbels driving the two Hopfner sisters out to Lanke in the snow: Then castigating a chastened actress, Marie-Louise Claudius, for indiscreet remarks:

Then assisting the beautiful Brigitte Horney with her foreign-currency problems: Then receiving the no less shapely actress Gina Falckenberg for a script discussion session ('I can help her too').[60]

After a difficult confinement Magda gives birth on February 19, two months prematurely. The gynecologist says that the sickly little newcomer, another girl, is truly *holde*, sweet; and they leave her with this name. 'Just what I wanted,' cries Helga, cradling her baby sister. 'It came down from the clouds!' Magda lies amid her pillows, tired and happy, and her large dreamy eyes fill with tears as her (cuckolded?) husband limps in.[61]

NONE OF THE Goebbels children would be baptized. Goebbels had declared open war on the church. When the devoutly catholic post-office minister, Eltz von Rübenach, turned down Hitler's gift of party membership, made to all the non-party ministers on January 30, 1937, explaining that he could not join a party that oppressed the church, it was Dr Goebbels who indignantly orchestrated his colleagues' demand for Eltz's resignation.[62] Hitler however was one of the few Nazi leaders who still paid the ten percent church levy on their income, and he saw no point in stirring up a hornets' nest.[63] It was not that he admired the churches. He commented to Goebbels that they had imbued modern man with a fear of death that his ancestors had never known.[64]

Hitler was however a pragmatist. Twice in February 1937 he called conferences at the Berghof on the inter-confessional disputes, to which he invited Goebbels along with Frick, Hess, and Himmler.

On the first occasion he explained that the Reich had to avoid needless discord, since he expected a full-scale world war within a few years.[65]

At the second conference he again predicted 'a great world conflict' in five or six years' time. 'Germany,' he told his colleagues, 'will prevail in a coming battle, or no longer survive.' 'What a genius the Führer truly is,' he wrote, setting all this down for posterity.[66]

27: *The Round Table*

H<small>E WAS NOW</small> in his fortieth year. The three years before war broke out in 1939 would show him at his most innovative as minister. He laid the foundations of an imaginative welfare scheme for Germany's elderly stars of stage and screen.[1] He put his ministry's top officials into blue-collar jobs for two months to gain experience in industry.[2] He created the hugely successful traveling exhibition of degenerate works of art confiscated from galleries and museums. Despite Hitler's strictures he initiated a pitiless campaign of legal repression against church officials, and he maintained his very personal vendetta against the Jews. He bought up Germany's biggest movie studios in a determined attempt to take on Hollywood. He consolidated his hold on the printed and broadcast word, though he never truly controlled the newspapers. And all the time he fine-tuned the propaganda weapon for Hitler's coming wars of conquest.

His was the sharpest tongue in town. 'I've got three men,' Hitler would say, 'who just can't stop laughing when they're sitting down together.'[3] He was referring to Hoffmann, Amann, and Goebbels. At the chancellery's round table the propaganda minister, whom he dubbed the 'chief jester' of the Third Reich, usually sat directly opposite him.[4] Only Goebbels had the nerve and wit to interrupt his monologues.[5] Confident of his personal status, he was merciless toward the other guests. 'Well, Tiny,' he would greet Winifred Wagner's oafish daughter Friedelind, 'as fat and dumb and lazy and gluttonous as ever?'[6]

When the malodorous Otto Dietrich remarked that the best ideas always came to him in the bath-tub, Goebbels piped up: 'Then you must have good ideas more often, Dr Dietrich!'[7] Once, Viktoria von Dirksen, outraged by a Goebbels barb, appealed: 'Mein Führer, tell your minister to shut up!' (Hitler lapsed into Viennese dialect, grinned, and directed Goebbels to change the subject.)[8] Magda, the common object of their affections, winced at his cruel wit.[9] After ordering the summary arrest of all astrologers, magnetopaths, and other occultists he would scoff: 'Remarkably enough not one of these clairvoyants foresaw that he was about to be arrested.'[10]

Those of his victims who fought back lived to regret it. Once 'Putzi' Hanfstaengl read out to the round table a Goebbels press announcement praising 'the eternal immortality of the German people.' 'Don't you worry about my style,' snapped Goebbels. 'With my style I have conquered Germany.'

Hanfstaengl retorted that he had always thought the Führer's style had done that.[11] Hitler, put up to it by Goebbels, dispatched Hanfstaengl on a fake 'parachute mission behind the lines to General Franco' in February 1937: Terrified for his life, Hanfstaengl absconded to London.[12]

It was here at this round table that Hitler and Goebbels plotted the special edition of a counterfeit *Völkischer Beobachter* in which their self-important radio chief Eugen Hadamovsky could learn that he had been awarded the Goethe Prize (he had not). They ushered him out onto the balcony to take the plaudits of the Wilhelm Strasse crowds; once out there, he found the street bare.[13]

The two Nazis had each other's measure. Goebbels joked once that President Roosevelt had written inviting him to become propaganda secretary in Washington. 'A tough choice, dear Doctor,' replied Hitler smoothly. 'Let me know how you decide.'[14] Hitler would recall the election meeting at Stettin where Goebbels, replacing him at short notice, found the ticket price slashed from 60 to 25 pfennigs. 'Remember, now,' he would chide Goebbels. 'You're not worth half as much as I.'[15]

Goebbels needed public adulation as a vampire feeds on blood.[16] The British government decided in June 1937 that he was out of favor, and losing influence in the country.[17] Like many small men he was sensitive to criticism, and swooned with rage at foreign caricatures that highlighted his physical deformity. He had a youth who called him a Jesuit catspaw sentenced to three months.[18] The mayor of Halle earned low marks for recommending in an article that promotions depend on physique. Yet the women around Hitler adored him. Hitler's junior secretaries would rush to the windows whenever Goebbels walked by. 'If you only knew what eyes he has,' they enthused to a new colleague, 'and how captivatingly he laughs.'[19]

Hitler would also mention that laugh, telling Streicher after Goebbels had spent a week at the Berghof, 'Anybody who can laugh as loudly as this man, whom Nature has so cruelly afflicted, cannot be all bad.'[20] Streicher told him that Hitler had said he could not get along without Goebbels.[21] The other top Nazis were less easily captivated. Darré wrote of the minister as a 'mongrel apeman.'[22]

At one training course at Vogelsang, the Nazi staff college, the eight hundred district leaders (Kreisleiter) greeted both Goebbels' appearance and his speech with total silence. One participant saw beads of perspiration trickle down his face before he furiously stalked off the stage.[23]

His own self-image was of a family man and Hitler's most universally popular minister.[24] Once that summer he decided that in future he would walk to the ministry. Two adjutants fetched him from the villa in Hermann-Göring Strasse the next morning. None of the thousands of passers-by took any notice, and he never did it again. He preferred staged photo-opportunities, like the annual first day of the Winter Relief collection, when he would face the photographers with his wife and children, all holding collecting boxes. 'What good fortune,' he marveled, 'to be so loved by one's people.'[25]

His postbag might contain a poem couched in *Plattdeutsch* praising the new four year plan; or a letter beginning engagingly, 'As a fanatical female Nazi I make so bold as to –'[26] His fortieth birthday would bring an avalanche of telegrams ('Those from the people,' he confided to his diary, 'are the most touching').[27] The party's illustrated newspaper featured 'Our Doctor, as Berlin's gauleiter is called by his Berliners,' at home, with Helmut and his pony, and Helga with the toy sewing machine given her by Hitler.[28] Goebbels released a short movie to the cinemas, *Pappi's Birthday*, featuring himself arriving in yet another brand new car, a Maybach, at his country estate, where feudal retainers bowed to him, and liveried grooms tended to the children's ponies. Some liked it: One moviegoer penned these lines to Magda: 'How proudly in the cinema / I saw maternity thus blest. / I cast my mind toward the home / where I have built my nest.'[29] Berlin's starving working class however hooted at the screen and Hitler ordered the movie withdrawn immediately.[30]

IGNORING HITLER'S CALL for peace on the church front, Dr Goebbels began a vitriolic campaign against the two main churches that lasted from March until the end of 1937. It began when the Pope issued a pastoral letter critical of Germany on March 21. Goebbels at first persuaded Heydrich not to notify Hitler, arguing that they should merely confiscate the church printing presses which had disseminated it.[31] As a further response, on April 1 – according to Goebbels – Hitler telephoned the authorization to him to stage a series of show trials against the catholic clergy. The Nazi prosecutors had a back-file of several hundred untried sex cases against catholic priests. The catholics, decided Goebbels, had not properly appreciated the Nazis' patience and moderation. 'Now let them find out how merciless we can be.'[32] He sent Berndt to cover a particularly sleazy case in Belgium, the sex murder of a youngster in a monastery, and persuaded the Reich justice ministry to open the first sex trials at Koblenz.[33] He ordered sound recordings made, keeping Hitler closely informed at each stage – or so his diary claimed.[34]

Goebbels honed the stage-management of these political trials to a fine art. The first, of Franciscan monks charged with sexual perversions, began in Koblenz late in April.[35] He followed the propaganda coverage closely. One priest implicated the Bishop of Trier himself. 'That's a real bombshell,' chortled Goebbels, savoring his revenge. 'I've had it all recorded on discs, in case.'[36] He furnished regular summaries of the sordid details to Hitler, who swore to 'smoke out' this 'gang of pederasts.'[37]

From catholic Austria, Ambassador von Papen pleaded with Goebbels to tone down the campaign, fearing an outright ban on German newspapers there. At first the catholic hierarchy maintained a dignified silence.[38] Goebbels hatched further schemes to destroy them – the sequestration of the church's assets, and laws to end priestly celibacy and to prevent anybody younger than twenty-four studying theology ('Thus we'll deprive them of their finest raw material'). Hitler however urged caution.[39]

Just as the Nazi campaign was flagging, Cardinal George Mundelein, archbishop of Chicago, publicly denounced Hitler over the Koblenz trials. Goebbels, retaliating, began the first trials of protestant clergymen on homosexuality charges too. He inaugurated this new campaign in his biggest speech that spring, from the new Deutschland Halle in Berlin on May 28, 1937.[40]

The state, he declared, was responsible for providing the people with bread, raw materials, currency, cannon, and airplanes; the churches had merely to secure Eternal Happiness – surely, he asked to loud guffaws, that task was big enough for them? He argued that the Nazis had set an example in June 1934: 'over sixty people who tried to cultivate this vice [homosexuality] in the party were shot out of hand; on top of this, the party frankly reported to the nation upon this episode.' The bishops had however become accessories, by shielding those guilty of such practices.[41]

Not hesitating to interfere with the legal system, Goebbels dictated stage directions to the public prosecutor at Koblenz, Paul Windhausen, who had the rank of Brigadeführer in the S.A.[42] (To Anglo-Saxon eyes it seems offensive, but in Germany throughout the twentieth century prosecutors and judges have always been the capstans of the government in office.) Case files piled up on his desk as he compiled dossiers with all the revolting details.[43] Up and down the country that summer the angry priests bravely struck back from their pulpits. Police arrested two of Goebbels' most prominent scourges, Pastor Martin Niemöller and Otto Dibelius.[44]

Dibelius was acquitted – Goebbels called it a slap in the face of the state and got straight on the phone to Hitler. Hitler however ordered all such trials halted for the time being.[45] Fearing that his Führer was getting cold feet, Goebbels sent Hanke to the Berghof with the most loathsome dossiers, but in vain.[46] Several times he reverted to the matter, in December 1937 and again in January. But on each occasion Hitler responded that he wanted peace restored on the church front: It was not a battleground of his own choosing.[47]

Without doubt this anti-church campaign damaged Goebbels' reputation both at home and abroad. An open letter, four pages of articulate, closely typed criticism, circulated in Bavaria. It expressed alarm that the propaganda minister was seemingly able to dictate which cases to prosecute and when. Referring to Goebbels' speech to a 'well-briefed party mob' at the Deutschland Halle, the pamphlet scoffed that, far from acting swiftly to shoot its leaders for homosexuality, the Nazis had turned a blind eye on them until Röhm and his consorts had got out of hand. The people were sick of the extravagances of the leaders of the so-called Workers' party, the letter continued, what with their country mansions, limousines, and yachts. All of this touched very raw nerves indeed. Goebbels had the authors, a church worker and a lawyer, arrested.[48]

Corrupted by power he was becoming more autocratic, even dictatorial. He arbitrarily forbade his adjutant to touch alcohol for six months. He punished radio station directors for going on a binge. He ordered a careless bus driver arrested.[49] He took a sterner line at home too – putting little Helga across his knee when she began to fib; and when two-year-old Helmut answered him back, Goebbels paddled the lad too, though reluctantly. 'He doesn't give in,' he noted indulgently. 'Not a bad sign!'[50]

HIS DIARY IS INNOCENT of any consciousness of his own double standards. He expressed horror at Stalin's show trials, although Hitler had not offered his victims even this formality before shooting them in June 1934. He fiercely protected his own Staatssekretär, the podgy Walther Funk, even while prosecuting the clergy. When Hitler forbade further police prying into Funk's sexual perversions, Goebbels breathed into his diary: 'Thank goodness.'[51] Lustful in private, he was starkly puritan in public. 'They can have a thousand nude women if they want,' he pontificated. 'But without those nasty, smutty jokes.' He sent for Trude Hesterberg, one of the Scala's lovelier singers, and lectured her on the indecency of her act. After visiting the Scala, a burlesque theater, he threatened to have it aryanized or even shut down altogether.[52] But he disclaimed any aspirations to act as a chastity-overlord: When Heiner Kurzbein, the (unfortunately named) chief of his ministry's photographic section, suggested they censor some of the more risqué photos of the 1938 film ball, Goebbels would overrule him: 'A dollop of healthy eroticism is not out of place,' he declared, 'and far better normal than abnormal.'[53]

The aryanization of the sub-chambers of the chamber of culture, particularly the chamber of music, would plod on far into 1939.[54] Furtwängler kept butting in, interceding for individual Jews.[55] At his speech to the chamber of culture on November 26, 1937 Goebbels would boast that he had completely eliminated the Jew from the artistic life of Germany: 'Imagine my surprise,' wrote Louis Lochner privately, 'when the next day *Musical American* arrives and I read that *with the approval of the German Government* no other person than Yehudi Menuhin . . . a Jew, has obtained the right to produce the [newly rediscovered] Schumann [violin] concerto in the USA!'[56]

Elsewhere Goebbels enacted police ordinances to exclude the Jews from stage, screen, and concert performances; he also clamped down harder on their publishing houses and bookstores.[57] When Jews in the United States protested, led by Mayor Fiorello La Guardia of New York, Goebbels banned Jewish and Zionist communal activities in Germany for two months.[58] After Nazi hooligans smashed the windows of Jewish stores in Danzig, the international clamor resumed.[59] Goebbels aryanized Germany's remaining Jewish-owned theaters and turfed the last Jews out of Germany's recording industry.[60] To break the Jewish near-monopoly on overseas movie distribution, he arranged with Alfred Hess, Rudolf's brother, to use the party's Foreign Organization, the AO, instead.[61]

In March 1937, using precisely the methods that he had previously branded as Jewish, Goebbels took over the major Ufa film company for the Reich. As a warning to Ufa he had instructed the press to trash its latest production; the movie flopped disastrously, and the company agreed to sell out.[62] 'Today we buy up Ufa,' recorded Goebbels, 'and thus we [the propaganda ministry] are the biggest movie, press, theater, and radio concern in the world.'[63] Dismissing the entire Ufa board, he began to intervene in movie production at every level, dismissing directors, recommending actresses (like the fiery Spaniard, Imperio Argentina), forcing through innovations like color cinematography, and rationalizing screen-test facilities for all three major studios, Ufa, Tobis, and Bavaria.[64] Depriving the distributors of any say in such matters he created instead artistic boards to steer future movie production. Suddenly the movie industry began to surge ahead. Blockbuster films swept the box offices. With a sure touch, Goebbels stopped the production of pure propaganda and party epics, opting for more subtle messages instead – the wholesome family, the life well spent.

Until then the status of the acting profession had been lowly. He changed all that. He converted the old Rathenau villa on Skagerrak Platz into an Artistes' Club. Its lush furnishings, its dimly lit cocktail bar, and its dance floor made it a popular haunt for raffishly dressed actors, actresses with plunging necklines, and strutting officials of the Nazi party. Both Magda and Dr Goebbels often went there – though seldom in each other's company.

ALTHOUGH HE STRIVES to conceal it from his diary, Joseph Goebbels' infatuation with the ravishingly beautiful Czech actress Lida Baarova has grown more hopeless. The 1937 diary mentions her name without special emphasis, but he carelessly spills enough clues around for the researcher to grasp what is happening. 'Strolled in the park and talked with Magda,' he writes dutifully. 'She is so nice and adorable. I have taken her into my heart.' Then, 'I drive on out to Bogensee' – the lake at Lanke on which he now has his isolated little wooden house.[65] It is out here, in the depths of the forest, that somebody is usually waiting for him. These are, it may be recalled, the very days when Hitler's Cabinet is solemnly discussing fierce new laws on divorce and adultery. 'Out to Bogensee in the afternoon,' he writes the next day, having again left Magda in Berlin. 'Some music, reading, and writing.'

That month he takes a special interest in Lida's latest movie, the spy-thriller *Patriots*, being made for Ufa. He reviews the screen-tests, discusses the story line with director Karl Ritter ('It must get a nationalist slant'), and reworks the film-play himself; on January 25, he goes out to Babelsberg to watch shooting begin.[66]

Viewing the first takes, he finds Lida's acting wonderful. 'The farewell and final scene are deeply touching,' he writes.[67] He becomes addicted to re-runs of her earlier movies. After watching her and Gustav Fröhlich in *Barcarole* on February 23 – after seeing the very scene she had been performing when he and Hitler first set eyes on her at the studios – he tells the diary, 'La Ba[a]rova's acting is wonderful, moving, and heart-breaking.' (Fröhlich however is 'a little twirp who can't act.')[68]

A few days earlier all three have been involved in a silly incident outside Fröhlich's villa on Schwanenwerder. With Magda in the maternity clinic since February 2, Goebbels is often lonely in the evenings. Twice that month he drives out to his own empty villa on the peninsula (the lakeside house at Lanke is being aired).[69] Early on one of these evenings Lida arrives at Gustav's villa; later, hearing a limousine, she steps out into the snow to greet her lover but finds Goebbels inside instead with his chauffeur Alfred Rach at the wheel.

'Hello!' exclaims the minister. 'What brings you out in the middle of the night?'

She puts one foot on the running board and explains, 'I'm waiting for Gustl. He's got a premiere.'

Even as they exchange these brief pleasantries, Fröhlich himself drives up. He leaps out, white with rage, and grabs Lida's arm, perhaps even slapping her. 'Well, Herr Minister,' he snaps, assuming that she has just stepped out of the limousine. 'Now we know where we stand!'

Goebbels acts astonished. 'What was that about?' he asks Lida.

The actress stammers apologies for her lover. When Fröhlich lets himself into his villa, he finds Lida's handbag already there and realizes his mistake.[70] Fröhlich phones an abject apology to Goebbels. The minister records only one further meeting with him, in May 1937 – ostensibly they chat about casting and taxation problems, and they trade society gossip. 'Frö[h]lich,' he mocks in his diary, 'is of consummate stupidity.'[71] A few weeks later he makes a note to look for a different man to play opposite Lida.[72]

Soliciting Lida more persistently, Goebbels often phones her at home. She has no objections. Once, he hears her doorbell ring and the phone being snatched from her; then Fröhlich screaming into the mouthpiece, 'Who is that?' The minister can hear the betrayed lover raging at her, 'It's Goebbels, isn't it? I knew it! How long has this been going on? We're through! Our love is dead – we are standing at its graveside.' Up to this point, in fact, no intimacies have passed between her and the minister.[73]

She moves out, renting a fine villa, No. 14 Taubert Strasse, in the Grunewald. Initially he keeps his interest in her a close secret. Hoping to see her privately, he once directs her to prepare dinner for ten at her Grunewald home, and to join him seemingly unexpectedly that evening in a box at the Scala where she is to invite him and his entourage back home for dinner. Play-acting, Goebbels looks completely surprised. 'Gentlemen,' he says, 'shall we accept?' All do so with alacrity, except for Hanke, who comes along in bad grace. Goebbels never visits her Grunewald villa alone.[74]

Lida Baarova moves out of Fröhlich's life, and Goebbels gives her the key to the barrier on the back road to the Lanke villa. Emotionally she becomes his slave – and he hers. They spend days together at Lanke, with him playing the piano, and her dozing on a sofa or reading. Their relationship is almost platonic. For a year sex hardly comes into it – and then only for weeks rather than months. She does not even notice that he wears a leg-brace.

They sleep in different rooms – his valet Kaiser tiptoes in each morning at five A.M. to wake her, as they both have early starts back to Berlin.[75] If Goebbels cannot get away from the ministry, he commands her to be at the other end of an open phone line: From time to time he picks up the earpiece just to hear her breathing. Sometimes she drives into Voss Strasse and walks past, for him to adore her from his window across the street.[76] Once, out at Lanke, he commands her to show him how she will recognize him if things ever go wrong and they meet only in Heaven; she walks a few yards, turns round, and, a consummate actress, plays the little cameo role to perfection.[77]

Throughout 1937 the affair warms up, while he consequently neglects Magda. The doctors have warned him after Holde's birth that his wife must not get pregnant for two more years. 'I'll see to that,' promises Goebbels, and whiles away the afternoon with yet another movie actress with professional problems ('I believe I can help her').[78] Two or three days later he helps another actress to the best of his ability, noting afterwards. 'She's a good sort.'[79] Having meanwhile met the young sculptress Barbara von Kalckreuth in a train, he sits for her in his snow-decked villa at Lanke and she gets twenty more diary entries over the next three years.[80] He sits for famous sculptor Arno Breker too; Breker rates only three mentions over the same period, one of them a terse: 'Never again.'[81]

On visits to Magda at the clinic her jealous tirades drive their relationship almost to destruction.[82] His diary celebrates her homecoming on March 23 most touchingly. 'She is my One and Only. When she's not there, house and home lie empty and desolate.'[83] With Magda home again, he fills Schwanenwerder with friends from the movie industry like the Veit Harlans, the Willy Birgels, the Höpfner sisters, and Lida Baarova. 'Magda is again the most beautiful of all,' he writes, helplessly caught between the two women. 'Women are a plague on us all,' he reflects in April.[84] In July he discusses his wife's indifferent health with Ilse Hess, who writes to Magda: 'Your husband told me that he's worried about you, and that you ought to have a pause to recuperate before getting down to the next five offspring you've promised the Führer and the Third Reich.'[85]

Caring little for the needs of his own Berliners, but at their expense, he sequestrates still more of the forest terrain surrounding his villa at Lanke. Labor Service gangs clear paths and erect boardwalks through 'my forest,' as he brazenly terms it, and begin laying down a private beach with a little jetty.[86] Officials import swans and wild duck to the lake.[87] On Hanke's advice he commissions Hitler's young architect Albert Speer to redesign his official residence in Hermann-Göring Strasse.[88] As he watches the newly imported deer stealing across his lawn at Lanke, he is becoming more detached than ever from the ordinary Berliners to whom he owes so much, yet Hitler still does nothing against this blatant corruption.

Goebbels proudly shows Hitler the new Baarova movie *Patriots* and hastens out to Lanke afterward to tell her that it has delighted him. Twice that May Hitler comes over to Schwanenwerder to cruise aboard the Goebbels yacht, surrounded by the latest handsome women in the minister's life. And once, as they again cruise alone among the blossoms of Potsdam, Hitler unburdens himself to Goebbels about his secret, innermost ambition – to undo for ever the humiliation done to Germany by the Peace of Westphalia which had concluded the Thirty Years' War in 1648 greatly to her disadvantage.[89]

ENCOURAGED BY THESE CONFIDENCES, Goebbels publicly stated his views on foreign affairs. Speaking in Berlin on February 12, 1937 of the new Czech alliance with Moscow he warned, 'Let the world take note that Germany is a great power.' London bridled.[90] He got on well with the new British ambassador, Sir Nevile Henderson, and both men hoped that if Britain's new prime minister Neville Chamberlain could only rein in the 'Jewish press clamor' there was a real chance of rapprochement, despite all the gaucheries that the new Nazi ambassador Ribbentrop was committing in London.[91]

Hitler had no firm plan of action mapped out as yet. Like Goebbels he believed in the Goddess of Good Fortune – in seizing opportunities as they arose.[92] Goebbels had however begun preparing his ministry for war: At Hitler's instigation he had started to build a cable radio system (*Drahtfunk*) which would free transmitter capacity for a propaganda war while rendering the German listening public impervious to enemy radio propaganda.[93] He issued contracts for five powerful one-megawatt transmitters.[94]

By this time, though without perceptible immediate cause, he had become concerned about his own safety. He underwent pistol training,[95] and in December 1937 he called off at the last minute a private trip to Egypt which he had been planning for three months – one phone call from Rudolf Hess, warning of possible risks, sufficed. 'On occasions,' reported the British embassy, 'he has shown a certain nervousness about his own skin.'[96]

Political events in Central Europe were slowly building up their own head of steam. At the end of July 1937 Goebbels staged a spectacular choral festival at Breslau. Among the thirty thousand Germans from overseas was a large contingent from Austria. The Austrians chanted Goebbels' latest slogan, 'Ein Reich – ein Volk!' There were emotional scenes in the main square as the massed choirs marched past. Newsreel cameras whirred.

The spectacle remained engraved on the memory of every member of Hitler's staff. 'For a quarter of an hour the procession halts,' wrote Goebbels, 'the people just standing still, singing, laughing, weeping.' Everybody knew what Hitler was thinking at that moment, he said later. When – it was now no longer a question of if – they went marching into Austria, hardly a shot would be fired. He showed Hitler the newsreels two days later, but Hitler ordered him not to release them to avoid reprisals against Austrians seen cheering.[97]

On the day after Breslau, Hitler visited Schwanenwerder – Goebbels' sister was celebrating her engagement – and again took him into his confidence. He planned to make a 'clean sweep' in Austria. 'Let's hope we all live to see that day,' wrote Goebbels.

He daydreamed about the Führer's triumphal entry into Vienna. After that, he mused, it would be Czechoslovakia's turn.[98] At the Nuremberg rally in September the Austrian contingent again staged an emotional scene. Here Hitler assured Goebbels: 'Austria will be dealt with one day by force.'[99]

'DR GOEBBELS DOES THESE things well,' remarked one British official dryly, after reading his fifty-page speech at Nuremberg, yet another attack on bolshevism and the Jews.[100] In Russia, said Goebbels, Stalin had murdered forty-two thousand priests; in Spain, his agents had already killed seventeen thousand priests and monks by February; yet the world resounded with squawks of horror if one Jew in Germany had his ears deservedly boxed. The Jew, he said, was a parasite, 'the destroyer of culture . . . the ferment of decomposition.' Hitler's line again varied only marginally from Goebbels'. The Führer had nominated Professor Ernst Sauerbruch as joint winner of the new National Prize, despite objections from Goebbels that the surgeon was a 'vassal of the Jews.' To circumvent criticism Goebbels now asked the surgeon at least to join the party. Sauerbruch politely declined.[101]

Opinion was divided about Goebbels' relationship with Hitler. Which was the evil genius, and which the spellbound princeling? George Ward Price, the perceptive *Daily* Mail journalist, was emphatic that Goebbels was more dangerous even than Himmler, because he committed Hitler to courses of action by presenting him with *faits accomplis*.[102] (The 1932 presidential election, the trials of the priests, the 1938 pogroms against the Jews, and 'total war' speech are all cases in point.)

Only rarely did Hitler actually apply the brake: In November for instance he phoned Goebbels to back off on their colonial demands.[103] When Goebbels initiated a raucous campaign against the Czech government, alleging maltreatment of their German ethnic minority, first the Sudeten German leader Konrad Henlein and then Hitler asked him to slow down.[104] Over lunch at the chancellery the Führer reminded him that Germany could not do anything about it yet.

'The Czechs,' sulked Goebbels, 'are crazy. They are surrounded by a hundred million enemies whose land and people they have usurped. *Na, prost!*' he exclaimed, ironically toasting them. Before lunch ended Hitler had again told him to downplay both the colonial and the church problems. 'We must keep our propaganda powder dry,' agreed Goebbels.[105]

THAT AFTERNOON HOWEVER, in Goebbels' absence, Hitler called a secret Cabinet-level meeting at which he revealed to his foreign minister and his commanders-in-chief his intention to launch a war of territorial conquest, beginning with a 'lightning attack' on Czechoslovakia during 1938.[106]

Winning over Britain in the meanwhile, without offending Mussolini, would be a challenge.[107] Here Goebbels was a greater hindrance than Ribbentrop. Although Ambassador Henderson respected Goebbels, his principal officials believed that the minister was trying to whip up anti-British sentiment.[108] This was not true. While mocking the hypocrisy of the English, he echoed Hitler's regrets that they were losing their empire. He blamed this on the foolish statesmanship of Eden (the new British foreign secretary), and compared him unfavorably with Lord Halifax, the Lord Privy Seal, who was visiting Germany for Göring's international hunting exhibition.[109]

Goebbels took tea with Halifax, this aristocratic English statesman, this 'very calm, collected, and clever' Cabinet minister, and pleaded with him to rein in Britain's unruly, sensation-hungry editors.[110] He drew attention to his own newspapers' restraint during the British abdication crisis. 'I had expected to dislike him [Goebbels] intensely,' confessed Halifax in his own private diary, '– but didn't. I suppose it must be some moral defect in me, but the fact remains.'[111]

28: *Something about March*

ONCE IN 1937 HARALD QUANDT, now sixteen, tiptoes into his step-father's study at Schwanenwerder and finds him writing in a diary. He sees three other diaries on the desk. Consumed by curiosity, in 1938 he picks the lock, rummages around, and finds one of the notebooks; to his disappointment however the handwriting is illegible.[1]

Joseph Goebbels has now filled sixteen such books, and he has begun a seventeenth, as usual with a motto: 'Don't look back, keep marching on!' This 1938 volume will cover 476 closely written pages.*

Probably he himself no longer knows why he is writing a diary. Few diarists do. It would take a psychiatrist to explain the narcissistic self-pity, the recurring proclamations of dire physical exhaustion, and the broad hints at Magda's infidelities (which were clearly not intended for publication in this form.) The text is often stupefyingly banal, and he no longer reveals *all* to the diary that was once his 'dear therapeutic conscience.'[2] Thus the new 1938 volume will draw a veil across his politically subversive views, as well as his own familial misdemeanors. The 1938 diary tells us of his profound misgivings about Hitler's brinkmanship only *after* the Munich agreement has removed the threat of war; and we hear nothing of Lida Baarova at all.

THE FIRST WEEKS OF 1938 had brought an important reorganization of his ministry, originating in Hjalmar Schacht's replacement as minister of economics by Goebbels' Staatssekretär Walther Funk, a move which Goebbels himself had suggested.[3] Funk had been the government's press spokesman, and Hitler appointed the party's press chief Otto Dietrich to the vacant position. 'I've just promoted you to Staatssekretär,' Hitler called out to Dietrich as he walked past. 'Minister Goebbels hasn't signed it yet, but he will – you can bank on that.'[4] Goebbels moved swiftly – his dislike for Dietrich was by now notorious – and divided up Funk's old functions, promoting his trusted chief aide Karl Hanke to senior Staatssekretär along with Dietrich.[5] To Hanke's

* Transcribed and annotated by the author on behalf of Arnoldo Mondadori Editore, Milan, this previously unknown Goebbels diary, February 11 to October 26, 1938, is published as *Der unbekannte Dr. Goebbels. Die geheimen Tagebücher 1938* by Focal Point, London, 1995.

old post as personal assistant Goebbels appointed at his recommendation on December 6, 1937 Dr Werner Naumann, the former chief of propaganda in Breslau.[6]

At the time, Naumann was only twenty-eight. Tall, slim, and athletic, he was a fanatical believer in National Socialism with the accent, where Goebbels too placed it, on the latter word. At seventeen he had already been concerned about the prevailing social injustices in Germany. A young man had invited him to a Nazi discussion evening and he had fallen in with them at once, joining the party late in 1928; in Berlin he had befriended Horst Wessel, and worked on Goebbels' propaganda staff in Berlin in 1929. Voluble and hard-working, self-assured but moody, Naumann would become Goebbels' closest confidant, outlasting all the others, and in the final days succeeding him as minister.[7] His party record had in fact one serious flaw: In 1933 he had become commander of No. 9 S.A. Brigade in Stettin, and at the time of the Röhm putsch he was an S.A. Standartenführer.

After trying unsuccessfully to flee on that day, he was relieved of his command, and imprisoned for eight weeks accused of having known of the plot. 'Naumann,' his successor Friedrich spitefully reported, 'a §175er [homosexual], was introduced to Pomerania by Heines. He got No. 9 Brigade, Stettin, immediately. Heydebreck and Naumann were close friends.'[8] (The S.A. commanders Heines, Heydebreck, and Spreti – all of them his friends – were shot.) Accused too of homosexuality and of permitting financial irregularities in his brigade Naumann had been expelled from the S.A., and then from the party on December 3, 1934. He had returned to university in 1935, studied oriental languages, and gained a doctorate in politics before being rehabilitated in 1936 when the principal accusations against him proved unfounded.

In his little speech introducing Hanke and Dietrich to their respective staffs, Goebbels made clear that Dietrich would have no say in the ministry, and that his preferred confidant was Hanke.[9] His faith in Hanke, this handsome, dynamic Silesian, was unspoken and implicit. Hanke gained automatic in-and-out access to Hitler's chancellery.[10] He was privy to Goebbels' tax affairs,[11] he had introduced him to the architect Albert Speer, he would undertake delicate missions for him.[12] Goebbels gave him the keys to his private dispatch box – an act of trust which ultimately led to his undoing, because Hanke became an even firmer friend and adviser of Magda too.

From now until 1945 Otto Dietrich was a thorn in Goebbels' flesh. He claimed to be not the subordinate of Reich minister Goebbels, as Staatssekretär, but his equal as Reichsleiter, with only Hitler having the authority to arbitrate between them; and since he was attached to Hitler's personal staff he – and not Goebbels – effectively controlled the essential political news output of the daily press. Nor was Goebbels' ministry later able to attach its own man to Hitler's headquarters as Ribbentrop, Rosenberg, and Göring had for example attached Hewel, Koeppen, Bodenschatz, and the military adjutants. The minister swore later that Dietrich was not even a real Reichsleiter – he had had a tailor run up a fantasy uniform for him as 'Reichspressechef' to which he had stitched the same badges of rank as a Reichsleiter; Hitler, said Goebbels, had good-naturedly allowed Dietrich his conceit.[13] There is a ring of authenticity about the story.

AS A STORM RUMBLES and lashes the little lake at Lanke in August 1937 Goebbels finds it too melancholy there and drives back to Berlin where he sends for Lida's movie *Patriots* once more.[14] He and Magda are drifting apart. As in 1936, she stays away from the 1937 Nuremberg rally. Unhappy at the multiplying rumors of her husband's behavior, she accusingly sends him a copy of the communist *Red Flag* which contains the latest scandal. Goebbels splutters, 'A pack of bloody lies,' and buys her off with a silver coffee service.[15] Despite all her doctor's warnings she has become pregnant again. Professor Walter Stoeckel, her gynecologist, urges her to withdraw entirely from social life and to rest out at Schwanenwerder.[16]

Goebbels spends more and more time out at Lanke, although Lida is not always there. Now approaching the apogee of her career, she often films in Prague as well as in Babelsberg.[17] For whatever the reason, Goebbels spends much of his time away from Magda and the children. His diary makes no explicit comment on this, but notes the days when he is with his home and family.[18] No matter how late he arrives when visiting Schwanenwerder, he wraps his toddlers in blankets and shows them the latest movie. They become his best critics. He records Helga's cute praise for Mussolini, paying a state visit to Berlin: 'The other Führer's quite nice too!' she says.[19]

There is no doubt about his own favorite movie star. In October 1937 he reads a movie treatment of Dostoyevsky's novel *The Gambler*. The lead role goes to Lida Baarova. She signs up with the Tobis studios to play Rosalinde in a movie version of *Die Fledermaus*. Simultaneously she makes a successful stage debut in Berlin, taking the title role in Hermann Bahr's *Josephine* in December. Goebbels rapturously leads the applause, and is enchanted all over again by his Liduschka's performance.[20] 'I have never loved another woman as much as you,' he confesses to her.

The raise in his ministerial salary has resolved some problems, but invited others.[21] Magda has inspected a tempting neighboring lot at Schwanenwerder, Nos. 12/14 Insel Strasse. It is owned by a Jew, Samuel Goldschmidt, director of the Goldschmidt-Rothschild bank.[22] Goebbels' friend Dr Lippert, erstwhile editor of *Angriff* and now mayor of Berlin, forces Goldschmidt to sell it to the city for only 117,500 marks; after the sale Goebbels emerges as the real purchaser.[23] He will rebuild this art deco building, converting its stables into a private cinema and the house into what he calls his *Burg* (citadel) – another refuge from Magda and her tantrums. Sometimes he will withdraw to his citadel with a guest, explaining to Magda with a heartless wink that he wants to play the latest records to her.[24] Thus all seems set in December 1937 for a *ménage à trois* – as soon as Lida is ready. On the eleventh he drives out to

Schwanenwerder, talks things over with Magda, and decides to move next door 'to get some peace.'[25] They have been married for six years. 'We are all so happy,' he hypocritically informs his diary. 'The children are playing all around us. I am sitting in my new home in the next-door house. Deep snow lies round about. Slept in.'[26]

Often that January of 1938 he drives out to Lanke where his villa is embedded in snow so deep that his new Maybach barely gets through. Is Lida out there? We don't know. Occasionally he drives into Berlin to see his family, to play some music, and deliberately lose a few hands of Black Peter to Helga before driving off to spend the night at Lanke or his ministry.[27] In his ministry too he is installing a little boudoir, so that he can devote more time to his work there; it is a tastefully furnished bachelor apartment with a bedroom, a bathroom, and an array of bell-pushes to inform his staff when he does not wish to be disturbed.[28]

Simultaneously work will begin on the reconstruction of his official residence. On January 16 Hitler gives the go-ahead. The Goebbelses spend hours more or less happily poring over Professor Baumgarten's plaster model and blueprints; the funds are requisitioned, and on April 27 the wreckers and bricklayers move in. 'I say my farewells to these rooms I have loved so much,' writes Goebbels with false pathos: 'It really hurts. I clear things out and pack, and find manuscripts from my childhood that seem pretty ridiculous today. . . So adieu, dear home! Now let the pickaxes swing.'[29]

There is one snag. Lida Baarova wants to be no part of his planned *ménage*. Fearing that she is trapped, she momentarily goes to England to talk with the talent scouts that Metro-Goldwyn-Mayer have sent over from Hollywood. Gustav Fröhlich persuades her to show them his photos too. Robert Taylor and Maureen O'Sullivan plead with her to leave Berlin. Nothing comes of it, but at the next gala gathering of the movie world in the Kroll opera house in Berlin, Goebbels will warn darkly that the German movie industry is not a haven for Hollywood's cast-offs. 'If anybody else leaves for Hollywood,' he declares, 'they'll find they can't get back into Germany when they fail.'[30] Miss Baarova interprets this threat as directed against her. But Goebbels has others in his sights too, like Luise Ullrich, another popular star who has designs on Hollywood.[31]

Bulky with her new unborn child, Magda is stuck out at Schwanenwerder. She is hoping for another boy, to be called Hartmann or Harder.[32] She seldom has enough funds for the household running costs and property taxes.[33] The purchase of the second property has strained their resources; early in 1938 Goebbels moves his mother in with Magda and there are always shoals of other house-guests. His visits to Schwanenwerder are punctuated by acrimonious scenes. The more he promotes his family-man image in the media however, the less time he actually seems to spend with them.[34]

HIS ONLY CLOSE FAMILY was now one man, Adolf Hitler. More than once in January 1938 the Führer had long private consultations with Goebbels, on affairs well outside his fief – asking for example whom he should now appoint to the German embassies in Rome, Paris, and Bucharest (Goebbels portentously started a card index for key future appointments).[35] When Hitler decided to replace his foreign minister he informed Goebbels two weeks before breaking it to the victim, Neurath.[36] Goebbels frankly warned him that Ribbentrop, the suggested successor, was a 'zero.'[37] When it came to naming their latest new battleship (the *Bismarck*) Hitler again consulted Goebbels.[38] During the major scandal now almost upon them, the Blomberg–Fritsch scandal, Hitler and Goebbels would be closeted together for hours on end. Surprisingly, Goebbels would recommend the ultra-conservative chief of general staff, General Ludwig Beck, against the radical Nazi Walter von Reichenau to succeed Fritsch as the army's commander-in-chief.[39]

THE BROAD OUTLINES of the Field Marshal Blomberg scandal are now well known. On December 14 the war minister, nearly sixty, had unblushingly revealed to Goebbels his intention of marrying a young girl of common stock. Seemingly not appreciating quite how common this twenty-four-year-old's stock had been, Goebbels wished him luck.[40] Both Hitler and Göring officiated as witnesses at the field marshal's hasty wedding on January 12 (the girl had told him she was pregnant).

The crisis burst upon them soon after. At Hitler's lunch table on the twenty-fifth Goebbels detected a certain tension in the air. Aided by an unusually jovial Göring he tried to cheer Hitler up, but it was already too late.[41] Helldorff, now police chief of Berlin, told his friend Goebbels that Blomberg's bride had a criminal record for peddling pornographic photographs featuring herself. He showed Goebbels the police dossier – it was 'hair raising.' Obviously Blomberg had landed Hitler and Göring in a hideous position. Goebbels was speechless with rage at the injury the field marshal had done to his idol. Twice he hinted that any honorable officer should shoot himself.[42] But Blomberg merely resigned as war minister on the pretext of ill-health, and left on a world tour with his bride (who turned out not to be pregnant after all).

This was just the start of Hitler's problems. Who should succeed Blomberg? Göring? General von Fritsch? Himmler now charged that the latter, though the obvious candidate, had once been blackmailed as a closet homosexual. This scandalized Hitler. Since the Röhm affair, his eyes glazed at the slightest mention of homosexuality. Goebbels suggested that Hitler himself take over Blomberg's position, thus becoming supreme commander in one step.[43] Fritsch did not however stand aside without a fight. He denied the allegation of homosexuality, on his word as an officer, and he did not even crack under the Gestapo's grilling.[44]

'It's one man's word against another,' perceived Goebbels, fascinated by Hitler's dilemma: 'That of a homosexual blackmailer against that of the army's commander-in-chief.' But Hitler no longer trusted Fritsch, and there was the rub. Innocent or guilty, the general was doomed even though he refused, to

Himmler's dismay, to confess.[45] 'Heydrich has conducted several all-night interrogations,' recorded Goebbels equally perplexed. 'Fritsch is taking it all on the chin, but standing up to him.'[46]

Goebbels' problems as propaganda minister were also beginning as juicy rumors washed around Berlin. He spent sleepless nights, he even saw Hitler in tears with worry.[47] He promised to keep the lid firmly on things. He suggested that it would help if Hitler chose now to carry out a reshuffle of both his Cabinet and armed forces. 'The damage that one woman can do!' gasped Goebbels, as the hit lists were drawn up. 'And that *kind* of woman too!'[48]

Hitler announced his reshuffle to his ministers at eight P.M. on February 5, 1938. Goebbels' diary provides the only detailed record of this, the last formal Cabinet meeting ever held.[49] Struggling to do justice to both Blomberg and Fritsch and choking with emotion, Hitler spoke of the personal tragedies that had obliged them to resign. He announced that he himself would take over as supreme commander (as Goebbels had suggested). For a few days the world's press seethed with fierce but ill-informed speculation – what Goebbels called 'horror stories.'[50] He directed his rough-and-ready lieutenant Berndt to scatter dust in the eyes of the press corps in Berlin.[51] 'He had the nerve to tell us,' recorded an American journalist, 'that Blomberg's resignation was due solely to reasons of health (yet he was healthy enough to marry!).'[52]

To an equally skeptical Dutch pressman Berndt tactlessly flared, 'What would you say if our newspapers were to state that the baby just born to your royal family isn't really [Crown Princess] Juliana's baby!'[53] Unimpressed, the foreign journalists churned out still more 'horror stories.' So Goebbels told Berndt to go the whole hog and plant rumors that Hitler intended invading France. The newshounds went yelping off after that scent instead. It all provided an interesting example of news-management. 'Anything is better than the truth,' reflected the propaganda minister, in a departure from his norm.[54]

LAYING A SECOND SMOKESCREEN Hitler briefly[55] – as he imagined – and unexpectedly turned to Austria. He summoned Austria's chancellor Dr Kurt Schuschnigg to the Berghof on February 12. No formal record was taken of Hitler's blustering, ranting threats but he boasted with some relish to Goebbels afterward of how he had talked 'pretty tough' with Schuschnigg on a list of demands, and had threatened to get satisfaction by force ('guns speak louder than words').[56] 'It was not just an ultimatum,' summarized Goebbels. 'It was a threat of war. Schuschnigg was shattered.'[57] Under a secret protocol agreed between them Austria guaranteed to model her foreign and military policy on Germany's, and to call a truce in the press war; Schuschnigg was also to appoint the Austrian lawyer Arthur Seyss-Inquart (described by Goebbels as 'our man') as minister of the interior. In return Hitler agreed to refrain from interfering in Austria's domestic affairs.[58]

Four days after the Berghof meeting, Schuschnigg's Cabinet agreed to Hitler's diktats. 'The world's press rages,' observed Goebbels, 'and speaks – not entirely unjustly – of rape.'[59] Hitler formally thanked Schuschnigg in the Reichstag on the twentieth. In private he added that he envisaged cutting a similar deal with Prague when the time came, although he warned Goebbels that the Czech president Edouard Beneš was a far more deadly opponent, 'a crafty, squinty-eyed little rat.'[60]

For all his other sins, Hitler did adhere to the Berghof agreement. When two Austrian Nazi leaders visiting Munich on February 25 still talked of staging a coup, he forbade them to return.[61] Schuschnigg was less scrupulous. After the newly re-emancipated Nazis staged big demonstrations in Graz and Vienna, he called out the army against them in violation of the agreement. Goebbels directed the German press to hold its tongue.[62]

He had other things on his mind – principally the trial of Pastor Niemöller, arrested seven months earlier on sedition charges.[63] As the still overly conservative ministry of justice set aside a full two weeks for a public trial, all Goebbels' hatreds boiled over. 'Lawyers are all mentally defective,' he had written the year before.[64] He pleaded for a two- or three-day trial *in camera*, followed by Niemöller's swift and permanent removal from public view. Hitler himself had ruled that Niemöller was never to be turned loose again.[65]

Was that not an edict simple enough for even the most pettifogging lawyer to understand? When the trial began on February 7, however, the court refused to impose reporting restrictions and allowed the pastor an entire day to reminisce about his career.[66] Goebbels persuaded the court to go into closed session. At this Niemöller's lawyers walked out.[67]

These were the kind of tactics that Goebbels himself had used against the catspaw courts of the Weimar regime, and now, used against him, they stung. When a brave civil servant, Ernst Brandenburg, testified for the pastor, Goebbels had him dismissed from the party.[68]

On March 2 the judges handed down a derisory sentence on Niemöller, allowing his immediate discharge. Exploding with wrath, Goebbels released only the briefest press notice.[69] Hitler directed Himmler to have the pastor removed by a back door from the courthouse and taken straight to Oranienburg concentration camp. 'He won't be set free again,' triumphed Goebbels.[70]

HIMMLER'S ORGANS DID have their uses. Mostly however Goebbels gave a wide berth to the Reichsführer now. 'His entire being breathes sterility,' he decided. 'He is a little man without an ounce of style. Ignore.'[71] When Reinhard Heydrich, Himmler's executive chief, started sniping at Taubert, the minister fired off a terse rebuke. The police, he noted, might poke their nose in elsewhere, 'but not here!'[72]

Once, Helldorff warned him against his personal assistant Fritz Ehrhardt, pointing out that he also held the rank of Hauptsturmführer (captain) in Himmler's security service, the S.D. 'When I became police chief of Berlin,' explained Helldorff, 'I removed from my staff every S.S. officer who was working for the S.D. I advise you to do the same.'[73]

Goebbels' doubt about whether Himmler had any code of ethics was soon resolved. After Helldorff revealed something of the Gestapo's spying techniques, Goebbels exclaimed in his diary, 'We're heading toward a world of informers and sneaks.'[74] Helldorff, Hanke, and Lutze told Goebbels that everybody was now surrounded by a vast network of Gestapo informers. All this informing – which seemed particularly to worry him – was not only stupid but despicable. 'It just begets cowardice, terror, and hypocrisy,' he felt. 'I just can't believe it all,' he wrote on March 1. 'The [Gestapo] methods in the fight against Fritsch are not very honorable.'

The case exposed Himmler in all his treachery. The general had demanded a court martial to clear his name. The pre-trial investigation threw a most unsavory light on Gestapo methods. 'They can prove hardly anything against him,' wrote Goebbels. 'They should never have dragged in the Führer.'[75] Hitler expressed to him serious concern about the investigation. Goebbels learned that it was not going at all smoothly.[76] Goltz, now acting for the general, had established beyond doubt that the Gestapo had cynically framed his client using the dossier on a different man, an army captain Frisch.

This really was a horror story, and it all came out when the court martial, which had been convened on March 10 and immediately adjourned (as we shall see), was resumed on the seventeenth. Goebbels wrote: 'The entire thing seems to be based on mistaken identity. Very nasty,' he wrote, adding with unconcealed satisfaction, 'above all for Himmler. . . The Führer's quite annoyed.'[77] Fritsch was acquitted. Hitler sent him a handwritten apology and handsomely exonerated him in a speech to his generals.[78] Goebbels was delighted, both for Fritsch's sake and because it was 'a terrible put-down for Himmler.'[79]

THE FRITSCH TRIAL had been held over from March 10, 1938 by dramatic new developments.

In the last few days Hitler and Goebbels had paid remarkably little attention to Austria; their private conversations had gyrated around Czechoslovakia instead. 'The Führer is pleased to see Prague being so intransigent,' Goebbels had recorded. 'All the more surely will she be torn to pieces one day.'[80] When Schuschnigg on March 9 broadcast his plan to hold a referendum on the Berghof agreement, Goebbels, diverted by a farewell party at the ministry for Funk, rated it merely a 'rotten trick.'[81] Hitler however had seen his golden opportunity. He summoned Goebbels out of a meeting with editors later that evening: Over at the chancellery the minister found Göring called in too. By staging his 'stupid and crass plebiscite,' Hitler snorted, Schuschnigg was trying to outsmart them. Goebbels was fired by Hitler's enthusiasm for action. He suggested they send a thousand planes over Austria to drop leaflets, then 'actively intervene.'[82]

His newly found 1938 diary makes clear how closely he consulted with Hitler over the next hours and days. In deliberations that would last until five A.M.

on Thursday the tenth Hitler mapped out his 'very drastic' plans to Goebbels and the Austrian general Edmund von Glaise-Horstenau. The latter, a Nazi, had been foisted on Schuschnigg's Cabinet by the Berghof agreement. He paled at the possible consequences of a German invasion, but not Hitler. 'He believes the hour has come,' wrote Goebbels. 'Just wants to sleep on it. Says that Italy and Britain won't do anything. . . That the risk isn't as great as it was when we occupied the Rhineland.' Only France's reaction was unpredictable. After dozing for two hours, however, Goebbels awoke to the news that France's prime minister had resigned over unrelated domestic issues. That clinched it. 'Tally-ho,' he whooped. 'The imponderables are melting away.'

Called over to the chancellery again that Thursday (the tenth) he found a hunched Führer, now brooding over maps. They had two days before Schuschnigg's proposed referendum.

Goebbels suggested this scenario: the two tame Austrian Nazis, Seyss-Inquart and Glaise-Horstenau, should stipulate that the referendum be based on the 1935 Saar referendum statute. Schuschnigg would of course refuse. The two Nazis would resign on Friday. On Saturday the Luftwaffe would send six to eight hundred planes to drop leaflets calling on the Austrian people to arise. 'The people do so. And on Sunday we march in.'

S.A. Obergruppenführer Hermann Reschny, who had four thousand embittered Austrian 'legionnaires' (exiled Nazis) standing by, predicted that Schuschnigg's troops would open fire. But now there was no stopping Hitler. 'There has always been something about March,' mused Goebbels, setting his printing presses rolling. 'It has been the Führer's lucky month so far.'

At midnight Hitler sent for him again. He was speeding things up. The Wehrmacht would invade Austria on Saturday, not Sunday, and push straight through to Vienna. He himself would follow. 'In eight days' – this was Goebbels' sober estimate, with all the bloodshed that it implied – 'Austria will be ours.'

The few remaining hours saw him at his best. At his desk until four A.M., he dictated leaflets, placards, and circulars and arranged with Heydrich for a police guard on the printing works – nobody was to be allowed out until the tanks began to move.[83]

Once, Magda came briefly with the children to see their absentee father. At eight A.M. on Friday Hitler reviewed the leaflets. As the hours ticked away, Hitler, Göring, and Goebbels put their heads together, hatching plans on how to effect the actual Anschluss, political union with Austria. 'The Führer must be popularly elected as [Austria's] federal president as well,' was Goebbels' idea, 'and thereafter bring about the Anschluss little by little.' To legalize the invasion Seyss-Inquart would have to send a telegram from Vienna appealing for Wehrmacht troops. Hitler, Goebbels, and Göring dictated a suitable text. 'It arrives here soon after,' wrote Goebbels, somewhat prematurely, 'and thus we have the legitimation we need.'[84]

The German troops rolled into Austria on Saturday March 12. Leaving Göring and Goebbels in Berlin, Hitler set off to follow them. Not a shot was fired.

The Austrians' overwhelming reception of the 'invaders' stunned even Goebbels. Tears streaming down his cheeks he sat up until three A.M. listening to the radio broadcasts of the emotional scenes. Again and again the music of Horst Wessel's hymn blared forth. Hitler and the rump Austrian Cabinet decided on Anschluss forthwith, which settled that problem. Thereafter things moved at breakneck speed. The Jewish-controlled newspapers in Vienna were banned – the Jews themselves were already routed, stampeding toward those few frontiers that still opened for them ('Where to?' commented Goebbels maliciously. 'As Wandering Jews into Nothingness.')[85] Together with Lida Baarova and her bosom friend Hilde Körber, Goebbels sat glued to the radio in Veit Harlan's house on the afternoon of March 14 listening to the excited commentary as Hitler entered Vienna.[86] The forlorn British and French protests tailed away, blotted out by the totally unexpected sounds of jubilation from Austria.

To consolidate his masterstroke, Hitler called a joint Austrian–German referendum for April 10. Goebbels established a Reich Propaganda Amt (agency) in Vienna, shipped fifty thousand cheap Volks radios there to facilitate the referendum campaign, and prepared an epic reception for Hitler's return to Berlin. This was not easy because, at Berndt's request – he had deputized for Goebbels in Austria – the propaganda minister had just sacrificed Berlin's entire stock of flags and banners for Hitler's entry to Vienna.[87] But when the Führer landed back in Berlin at five P.M. on the sixteenth Goebbels outdid himself. He and Göring sat proudly in the Führer's open car as it slowly drove through the cheering millions to the chancellery.[88]

The speed of events was now almost frightening. Unrolling maps, Hitler discussed with Goebbels and chief engineer Fritz Todt the new autobahns for Austria, and the rebuilding of his native city, Linz.[89] 'Astounding, the fresh plans he is already hatching,' wrote Goebbels – and it is clear that it was not just bricks and concrete that both men had in mind.[90]

FOR A FEW DAYS, after Warsaw had issued a short-fused ultimatum to Lithuania over disputed territories, Hitler stood by to claw back Memel – it is now Klaip da – a little strip of once-German territory annexed years before by Lithuania.[91] Nothing came of it.

The next major victim was to be Czechoslovakia. Goebbels had long known that this was so.[92] After the chief of the Czech general staff had boasted of how their fortifications would allow time for their allies to act, Goebbels pityingly commented: 'Poor fool!'[93] Several times he delivered to Prague's envoy in Berlin, Dr Vojtech Mastný, lofty homilies on the follies of allowing German émigrés to slander Hitler from the false sanctuary of Prague.[94] He knew all Hitler's plans. On March 19 the Führer invited him upstairs to his little study in the Reich chancellery, laid out a map of central Europe, and plotted their next moves, each man egging the other on. Germany would tackle Czechoslovakia next, Hitler confirmed. 'We'll share that with the Poles and Hungarians,' recorded Goebbels afterwards: 'And without further ado.' ('We are a boa constrictor, still digesting,' he added, as though apologizing to the diary for the necessary delay.) Then, the two men agreed, Germany would strike north-east into the Baltic countries, and west into Alsace and Lorraine. 'Just let France wallow deeper and deeper into her crisis,' he wrote. 'Let there be no false sentimentality.' How he admired Hitler. 'How stirring it is when he says his one desire is to live to see with his own eyes this great German, Teutonic Reich.'[95]

Hearing that Göring, now a field marshal, had incautiously reassured Mastný about the sanctity of Czechoslovakia's frontier, Goebbels was distraught. 'Guaranteeing their frontiers! That's right out of line.'[96] A few days later, on March 24, Hitler repeated his innermost intentions to Goebbels and his new foreign minister Ribbentrop. 'The Führer declares,' recorded Goebbels, 'that he wants to adjust our frontier with France one day, but not that with Italy. He particularly does *not* want to reach the Adriatic. Our ocean lies to the north and east. A country cannot throw its weight in two directions at once. If it does, it will split in two.'[97]

His diary reveals the cynical instructions which Hitler now issued to the Sudeten German leader Konrad Henlein: 'Keep demanding more than Prague can deliver. That will set the ball rolling.'[98]

Thus the time-bomb began to tick beneath the Czechs. 'They haven't the foggiest notion of whom the bell is tolling for,' Goebbels chortled. And he repeated: 'Poor fools!'[99]

HE HAD PRINTED seven trainloads of propaganda material to persuade the voters, and his well-tempered election machinery began to hum. Only the actual ballot form proposed by Frick to endorse the Anschluss upset him. 'People can vote either Yes or No at will,' he observed. 'We didn't have that the last time' – in March 1936.[100] Hitler promised to look into it, but the final ballot still had space for a No vote.

Late in March 1938 the two men opened their separate campaigns, speaking in dozens of cities until their throats were sore and their vocal chords ached, and phoning each other each night to bandy details of their rhetorical triumphs. Goebbels spoke in Hanover, Dresden, and Vienna. 'To those who ask, "Why another plebiscite?",' he roared in Vienna's Nordwestbahnhalle, decorated with huge swastika banners, 'we reply that we must put the world face to face with such an overwhelming vote as to close its mouth.'[101] At Breslau, to ensure a capacity audience, his ministry announced that his speech would not be broadcast (but it was).[102]

Soon the first results began to come in – Germans overseas casting their votes aboard German passenger liners in harbor gave Hitler ninety-nine percent backing.[103] The main ballot was to be on April 10, 1938. On the morning before that – proclaimed by Goebbels as the Day of the Grossdeutsches Reich – he took Hitler to Vienna's city hall for another brilliantly stage-managed pageant.

As twenty thousand carrier pigeons fluttered up into the bitingly cold skies, as sirens wailed, and as the Luftwaffe's squadrons thundered over the rooftops, Hitler stepped out onto the balcony.[104] Vienna went wild. After supper, the crowds began to chant – no doubt wholly spontaneously – 'Dearest Führer, please won't you / bring our Doctor out there too!'

Not doubting the outcome of the vote, Hitler told Goebbels he was planning to put Schuschnigg on trial. He would of course commute any death sentence that resulted. ('Pity,' observed Goebbels. 'What has to be, has to be!')[105]

The next morning, as their train back to Berlin passed through Leipzig, Hitler mused out loud about the Jewish problem. He planned, he said, to ship them all off to, say, Madagascar – the first recorded reference by him to this scheme. Madagascar of course was a French possession, but an hour later he reiterated that one day he was going to settle France's hash too. 'His life's burning ambition,' realized Goebbels.[106]

They arrived back in Berlin at one-thirty P.M. It was now election day. Magda was waiting. The cameras whirred as their children handed over posies of flowers to Hitler, and they cast their own votes at a booth on the station concourse.

The voting results revealed a unanimity of almost embarrassing proportions in support of Hitler's new Grossdeutsches Reich. In Austria 99·75 percent of all voters had cast their ballots for Hitler; in Germany, 99·08 percent (Saxony had let them down). From Paris, London, and Prague a shocked silence greeted this extraordinary display of democracy running amok.[107]

'Germany,' commented Goebbels, 'has conquered an entire nation with the ballot box.'[108]

29: *The Gambler*

T HAT ANSCHLUSS VOTE was the crowning achievement of his first five
years as minister, but already he was preoccupied with other things. On
March 18, 1938 Hitler signed a decree setting up a new movie academy,
which would offer courses on movie history, propaganda, and audience-
analysis – a subject close to his heart.[1]

He was also preparing his onslaught on Junk Art *(entartete Kunst)*. In June
1937 he had been shown some sorry examples of what at that time he called
'artistic bolshevism,' and he had begun planning a mocking exhibition. At
first the mortified and effete world of art connoisseurs had given him little
encouragement.[2] Speer had offered to help him stage the exhibition but later
even he balked and changed his mind.[3] On June 29, 1937 Hitler authorized
Goebbels to confiscate all such works in all museums to stage an exhibition.
Goebbels immediately instructed Professor Adolf Ziegler, a radical professor
of art in Munich, to 'select and secure all works of German decadent art and
sculpture since 1910 in German Reich, provincial, or municipal possession' for
the purposes of the exhibition.[4] It opened in Munich in July 1937. 'The "Junk
Art" exhibition is a gigantic success,' recorded Goebbels on the twenty-fourth,
'and a deadly blow. The Führer stands fast at my side against all enmities.' Hess,
Rosenberg, Speer, and other Nazis all had favorite artists they tried to protect,
but Goebbels was merciless; the next day he phoned Ziegler to purge all the
museums – 'It will take three months, then we're clean.'[5] The concentrated
effect of so much that was grotesque and avant-garde was stunning. Although
only six of the 112 exhibits were by Jews, Hitler pinned the blame on them in
his introduction to the catalogue: 'Jewry has been able,' he wrote, 'largely by
exploiting its position in the press, to obscure all normal ideas of the nature
and function of art.' Using methods well proven in the years of struggle,
Goebbels hired actors to circulate among the crowds feigning disgust at the
works on display.

Professor Ziegler told Goebbels that the Weimar government had forked out
six million Gold marks to purchase this Junk Art.[6] With Hitler's approval, and
over the objections of Rust and Rosenberg, Goebbels drafted a law formally
confiscating all such works without compensation.[7] The Reich sold them off
to less discerning nations and used the foreign currency to purchase real Old
Masters.[8] Seen eventually by three million people, the junk art exhibition

would visit thirteen cities in Germany and Austria, exhibiting works by Otto Dix, Emil Nolde, and Oskar Kokoschka. A typical item was Kirchner's *Self-Portrait as a Soldier*, showing him holding up a bloodied stump instead of a hand ('an insult to German heroes,' read the exhibition's tag). Georg Grosz's similar indictments of war were branded a deliberate sabotage of national defense.

THE GLORIOUS REUNIFICATION of Germany and Austria has mellowed Goebbels and his platinum blonde wife. Foreign diplomats often speculate on his replacement however, and rumors about his personal life abound.[9] But often it is just like old times for them. He spends several Sundays out at Schwanenwerder with her. For a few days she has to go to the clinic – her heart is playing up again as the final weeks of this, her seventh pregnancy, begin to tell on her. 'I soon comfort her,' he records.[10] Perhaps this is the occasion when he confesses that he does not find it easy to remain faithful, except now because Magda is pregnant.[11] Magda blissfully repeats these lines to her venomous sister-in-law Ello and adds, starry-eyed, 'Joseph and I are now just as close to one another as ever.'

He is probably telling the truth. Lida Baarova is being difficult. He visits Lanke twice in April, but alone; he plays the piano, sleeps, walks, indulges in some pistol practice, then repeats in his diary, 'I am all alone out here.'[12] On May 2 he leaves Magda to accompany Hitler on his state visit to Italy. 'I give her a Gold medallion bearing my likeness,' he records. 'The dear thing cries at our parting.'[13]

AS THEY WAITED for their limousines at the chancellery Hitler told him that he hoped to conclude a firm alliance with Mussolini which would keep Italy out of the anti-German front that London and Paris were brewing.[14]

There is little point in dwelling on their week-long visit to Italy. Goebbels' newly discovered diary confirms anew the Nazis' contempt for monarchies. All were grimly agreed: 'Never again a monarchy!'[15] The king of Italy treated Hitler's ministers like shoeshine boys, in Goebbels' words. 'This entire pack of royal toadies: Shoot the lot! They make you sick. They treat us as parvenus! . . . Here's a tiny clique of princes who seem to think Europe belongs to them.'[16] As for the Italian people, Goebbels observed that they seemed easily enthused. 'But only the future can show whether they will stand fast when push comes to shove.'[17]

Mussolini's study, Goebbels afterward found, was oppressively large, furnished with just one monolithic desk and a globe. In two long secret meetings with the Italian dictator on May 4, Hitler told him in confidence of his plans in the east.[18] So far, so good, he indicated to Goebbels later that day: he had thanked the Duce for helping him get Austria, and promised to repay the favor. 'Over Czechoslovakia,' noted Goebbels, 'Mussolini has given us a totally free hand.' (Hitler had hinted in a secret letter to the Duce just before the Anschluss that he was going to deal with the Czechs next.) The final outcome was, as Goebbels put it, a military alliance of sorts – though not one on paper as Hitler would have hoped.[19]

The Führer rewarded Mussolini immediately. At their final banquet he ceremonially guaranteed their existing frontier, thus writing off the South Tyrol for ever. 'But it is correct,' conceded Goebbels lamely, as their train headed back north through Italy. 'And things won't work out otherwise.'[20] Through the train windows Goebbels fancied he could see clusters of weeping South Tyroleans whom his Führer had just betrayed.[21] In Florence Mussolini took his leave of Hitler with the words: 'There is no power on earth that can drive us apart.'[22]

WHILE ON BOARD the Italian flagship *Conte Cavour* Hitler has handed a signal form to Goebbels. Magda has given birth to yet another girl at two P.M. that day, May 5. 'Since today is our Navy Day,' Mussolini pompously suggests, 'You might name her "Marina".' Goebbels merely grins. He will decide at first to call the infant Hertha, but shortly opts for Hedda instead – Magda's mother has just seen a fine performance of *Hedda Gabler*.[23]

A week passes before he is back in Berlin and sets eyes on his fourth daughter. Magda has had a difficult confinement. 'What women go through for children!' he sympathizes in his diary, and drives straight out to spend the next two nights at Lanke.[24] Perhaps her delivery has released him from his self-imposed constraints. Whatever; at his lakeside villa he plays music, reads, and relaxes, then lazes, reads some more, takes out the motor launch, basks in the sun, and enjoys 'some music and parlaver,' so he is evidently not alone. By thought association his next diary entry mentions his spouse – 'Magda is okay.'[25]

The next five weeks probably destroy any illusions that Magda may have cherished. True, Goebbels writes about making plans with her for the future, but it is not certain that that future actually *includes* her.[26] There are bitter rows between them. Over the next five weeks he registers eleven 'parlavers' with her[27] – and unequal bouts they must have been, conducted between Goebbels with all his rhetorical skills and his less sophisticated wife, with her Belgian convent accent still clinging thickly to her vowels and consonants. Probably Lida Baarova is the cause, because he has been out to Lanke again twice in mid-May before fetching mother and baby Hedda home from the maternity clinic on the seventeenth – and he goes out there again on May 20. His infatuation with Lida is now at its zenith. He spends so many hours on the phone to her that Göring's wiretappers have to assign extra staff to monitoring her line (because she is a Czech and thus a potential enemy alien).[28] The Gestapo is also involved. He meets Lida at Hilde Körber's villa in Grunewald, No. 1a Lassen Strasse; but she too is a Czech, and her nine-year-old son Thomas will remember Goebbels sending him to keep a look-out for Gestapo cars from the window.[29] Eventually Hitler mentions this to Goebbels and suggests he break off the affair – but it is only this security aspect that bothers him.[30]

On the day after Goebbels once more visits Lanke in mid-June, he, Magda, and his sister all 'talk things over' in a little pub in Berlin's West End.[31] Only twice in all those weeks does he escort Magda to public functions, in Charlottenburg (the diary logs another row that night), and Vienna: On their way back from Vienna, he sets her down in Dresden, where she is to take a cure lasting several weeks at her regular clinic. 'A heartfelt farewell,' writes Goebbels, and drives straight out to Lanke again.[32] That summer one of the two swans on their little lake died. 'It's an omen,' says Lida. 'It's all over.'[33]

Magda puts up with all this only for so long. Once in his absence she spends an evening with Hitler and hints at these problems. Embarrassed, the Führer refuses to listen. Magda sniffs afterward to Ello, 'Once a corporal, always a corporal!'[34] While she is away in Dresden, Goebbels resolves to choose once and for all between her and Lida. It is not an easy choice. He spends a week that July out at Lanke, evidently alone. He decides not to allow anybody to visit.[35] Once after strolling through the rain-soaked woods he writes the exclamation 'Melancholy!' in his diary.[36]

Visiting Schwanenwerder and the children, he takes the girls out for boat trips a couple of times, but unforecast storm-clouds are threatening his love life.[37] He is sleeping badly, his head in a whirl. On July 8, 1938, his diary suddenly erupts without warning: 'I've got such worries. They're fit to burst my heart.'[38]

Goebbels invites Karl Hanke to talk sense into her. Hanke, over two years her junior, pampers Magda and teaches her how to ride; she blossoms in his company. But by no means is he blindly loyal to his minister. For Hanke, it is *Tristan and Isolde*. He sees Magda as a dreadfully wronged woman. A man of unquestionable courage, he becomes her knight in shining armor. Sexually there is probably nothing between them – she is far above this engine-driver's son in social station.[39] But she instinctively sees that with his unrestricted access to her husband's private mail Hanke may become a useful ally. He promises to keep his eyes open. Goebbels' problems are only just beginning.

HE OFTEN SPOKE with Hitler about the future. Seeking ways to thwart any restoration of the monarchy, Hitler had hinted in Cabinet early in 1937 at the creation of a constitutional senate to elect his successor when the time came.[40] Germany must remain a Führer state, he told Goebbels after their visit to Italy.[41] 'The Senate,' predicted Goebbels in June 1938, 'will soon be nominated and convened. It will be incumbent on it to elect each Führer.' Three hours after that the S.A., S.S., and armed forces would swear allegiance to him.[42] (No such elective senate was ever appointed however, as the turbulent events of that summer eventually led directly to war.)

Many of Goebbels' measures were already predicated on a coming war.[43] Meeting his new military liaison officer, Bruno Wentscher, at the end of July he drew heavily on quotations from Hitler's *Mein Kampf* to back his views. 'We soon see eye to eye,' he wrote.[44] Beginning with Breslau, Goebbels erected thousands of loudspeakers in city streets so that he could address the multitudes at the flick of a switch. There was to be no escape from his relentless propaganda. He ordered German radio to extend its broadcasting hours until three A.M. to discourage Hitler's subjects from listening to foreign stations – a prospect that would soon became almost an obsession in Goebbels. Meanwhile he labored to increase movie receipts. Although he had not been able to prevent some resounding flops like Karl Ritter's *Capriccio* – Hitler called it 'premium-grade crap,' while Goebbels found it 'trivial, boring, frivolous, and devoid of style'[45] – there were some box-office hits like *The Holm Murder Case*, filmed with police assistance, and Riefenstahl's now complete two-part movie of the Olympics, a stunning work of cinematic art which premièred on Hitler's birthday in Berlin.[46] Goebbels proudly appeared at that première with Lida Baarova, not Magda, at his side.[47]

Benevolent and brutal alike, he was adopting the airs of a Renaissance patron. He paid Riefenstahl a one-hundred-thousand-mark bonus from his secret funds.[48] He pruned the excessive salaries paid to some movie stars and doubled or even trebled others.[49] The world of music too trembled at his whim. Should the singing of Schubert's or Schumann's lieder be allowed at Viennese music festivals (the words were by Jews)? Goebbels decided that they should.[50] After hearing Richard Strauss conduct in Düsseldorf, he nodded to the great composer, as a hint that he was *persona grata* again ('He has now done penance enough').[51] In August 1938 an author annoyed him: Goebbels had him incarcerated in a concentration camp, and brought back before him a month later. 'A final warning! . . . One more transgression and he's for the high jump. Now we both know that.'[52]

OTHER CAPITALS FOLLOWED Berlin's example in evicting the Jews from cultural life. Rome fired Jews from teaching posts. Warsaw enacted anti-Jewish nationality laws. In Bucharest the short-lived prime minister Octavian Goga forbade Jews to hire young female domestic staff.[53] 'The Jews,' applauded Goebbels, 'are fleeing in every direction. But nobody wants to let them in. Where to dump this scum?' He felt that he had the people behind him in hounding the Jews. 'You've got to knock out a few front teeth,' he reasoned, 'then talk.'[54] He had squelched earlier plans by Streicher to plaster Jewish businesses with garish placards naming people caught shopping there.[55] But he ordered that Jews be excluded from bidding for public works contracts in March 1938.[56] And talking with Hitler he argued that the Jews and the ethnic Czechs should be squeezed out of Vienna – 'That way we shall be solving the housing shortage too.'[57] That a wave of suicides swept through the despairing Viennese Jews left him unmoved. 'It used to be the Germans killing themselves,' he recorded. 'Now the boot's on the other foot.'[58]

Inspired by Vienna's example, he planned with Count von Helldorff, Berlin's police chief, a concerted effort to evict the Jews from the Reich capital. They outlined to Hitler in April various ways of harassing them, including restricting them to designated swimming pools, cinemas, and eating places, and identifying Jewish shops and businesses as such.[59] 'We'll put an end to Berlin's image as a happy hunting ground for Jews,' Goebbels privately swore. 'Madagascar would be the best place for them.' Hitler, who was less keen, asked them to wait until after his state visit to Italy in May. Helldorff arrested the first three hundred Jews on a pretext early in June; but then he went on leave and to Goebbels' dismay his legal staff released them all, apart from a handful with known criminal records.[60] (Helldorff's antisemitism was only skin-deep; a few weeks later Heydrich learned to his disgust that Helldorff had a Jewish dentist.)[61] Recalling the count from leave, Goebbels explained that the object was to hound the Jews out of Berlin.[62] He also spoke directly to audiences of police officers, expounding this policy. Hitler meanwhile had left Berlin to summer in Bavaria.

To coordinate the persecution with Goebbels' gau headquarters, on June 13 Helldorff set up a special Jewish section (*Dezernat*).[63] Over the next few days, in a copybook harassment operation, the Berlin police rounded up 1,122 criminal, 445 'anti-social,' and seventy-seven foreign Jews found without proper papers; sixty-six were imprisoned, 1,029 were thrown into concentration camps, the rest detained for days in police cells. Helldorff imposed steep fines on those found to have been disregarding Nazi price-fixing laws. Meanwhile his police seized 250 Jewish-owned automobiles pending safety tests; he also demanded that Jews give up their adopted German names, particularly those that implied aristocratic birth.[64] There were inevitably distressing scenes, some photographed by British newspapermen; Goebbels had their films confiscated.[65] Meanwhile Nazi hooligans placarded shops wherever their owners were Jews. As the uglier side of human nature came to the fore, even Helldorff asked Goebbels to call a halt, saying that 'unsavory elements' were getting out of hand, under the party's mantle.

It seems that Goebbels had under-estimated the gusto with which the Berlin *lumpenproletariat* would wade into the city's Jews if given half a chance. Belatedly he tried to apply the brakes.[66] In the light of later events his diary entry of June 22, 1938 deserves quoting:

The Jewish problem in Berlin has now become complicated. Probably at Helldorff's instigation the party smeared graffiti all over the Jewish shops. . . There has been some looting too. Gypsies and other underworld elements have moved in on it. I have had them all thrown into concentration camps. Helldorff did precisely the reverse of what I ordered: I had said that the police were to act within the law, with the party just standing by as onlookers. The opposite happened. I summon all the party authorities and issue new orders. There are to be no illegal acts.

'Anyway,' he reflected, 'this type of rough justice does have its blessings. The Jews have been given one hell of a fright and they'll probably think twice now before regarding Berlin as their Eldorado.'[67]

Göring was pained by the antisemitic excesses of June 1938, but Goebbels was unrepentant: 'The fight against the Jews goes on, with legal means, right to the last rung of the gallows.'[68] Although his handwritten diary and Helldorff's report leave no doubt that he had personally instigated the anti-Jewish drive of June 1938, he added a highly deceitful entry reading: 'Operation Jew has now died down. A police major and a Kreisleiter were to blame. . . I take firm action to prevent a recurrence.'[69] He also righteously directed Helldorff to investigate reports that Jews were being manhandled at Sachsenhausen concentration camp.[70]

Discomfited by the unfavorable foreign press reactions, Ribbentrop buttonholed him at the Kaiserhof hotel. Goebbels promised to tread more softly.[71] A few days later, at Bayreuth, he carefully recorded that the Führer 'endorsed' (billigt) his Berlin operation. 'It is immaterial what the foreign press writes,' added Goebbels. 'The main thing is to squeeze out the Jews. Ten years from now they must all have been removed from Germany. But for the time being we intend to keep the Jews here – as pawns.'[72]

DURING MARCH 1938 Hitler had laid plans to seize the whole of Czechoslovakia using the problems of the German minority as a pretext. He had directed the Sudeten German leader Henlein to state impossible demands. In April Henlein had warned Goebbels about the strength of the Czech fortifications.[73] Hitler told Goebbels to invite twenty thousand Sudeten Germans to the Breslau gymnastics display that summer.[74] On May 2, Goebbels had directed his newspapers to start the propaganda campaign, pouring oil on the already flickering flames.[75] Ribbentrop, alarmed, complained to both Hitler and Goebbels, but neither cared. 'Ribbentrop's a typical groveler,' scoffed Goebbels, enjoying every moment of his newfound strategic importance.[76] The first blood flowed as Czech gendarmes shot dead two Sudeten Germans on May 21 near Eger. In the ensuing uproar, Prague mobilized troops, while London and Paris taunted Hitler for inactivity: He bided his time down at the Berghof. Then, claiming the Führer's backing, Goebbels let the full press campaign rip, noting triumphantly: 'Ribbentrop is on the verge of tears.'[77] The foreign minister immediately persuaded Hitler that their press must pull back, leaving an outraged Goebbels with more than a slight feeling of nausea. Hitler well knew that his Wehrmacht would not be ready to attack Czechoslovakia until October.

Goebbels was among those at lunch with Hitler in Berlin on May 27. He noted merely that Hitler had returned for military consultations.[78] He did not mince his words about Ribbentrop. 'Either we publish no more news at all on border violations,' he recorded, claiming once more that Hitler backed him, 'or we take countermeasures.' He saw Hitler pacing up and down and pondering. ('We have to leave him alone. He is brooding on a decision. That often takes some time.')[79] The next day Hitler announced to his generals and ministers that it was his 'unshakable intention' to smash Czechoslovakia.[80]

Less tense now that he had made up his mind, over lunch on the last day of May 1938 Hitler gave Goebbels a thumbnail sketch of the Czechs, calling them 'impertinent, mendacious, devout, and servile.'

'Spot on!' agreed Goebbels.[81]

Hitler said they should give Prague no respite at all that summer. Goebbels went further, pouring more oil on the flames, although the public soon tired.[82] A clammy feeling spread that war was inevitable.[83] Even Goebbels was not immune to this apprehension, writing one day: 'We shall have to be on guard, otherwise we'll slither into a catastrophe – one which nobody wants but which comes along all the same.' When the embassy in London reported that the British did intend to put up a fight, Goebbels recorded further misgivings.[84] Other ministers began to share their fears with him. 'The Führer,' he however concluded, brightening, 'knows what he wants. So far he has always hit upon the right moment to act.'[85]

WHILE GERMANY EDGES toward war during the summer of 1938, Goebbels' personal life also teeters on the brink. Magda, thirty-six, has left on June 20, blubbering, for her regular clinic in Dresden. Karl Hanke is in love with her. And Goebbels is thinking of leaving her for a *Czech* movie actress of twenty-three, Lida Baarova.

Unaware of the rumors, Hitler insists that both Goebbelses attend the opening of the new Künstlerhaus (House of Artists) in Munich on July 8, a glittering social occasion with five hundred guests in medals and evening dress. Goebbels' diary is non-committal: 'Magda accompanies me for the first time in quite a while. The Führer is very nice to both of us. . . Magda is radiant.'[86] Over the next two days they attend two more functions together.[87] From what Magda tells Speer, however, her husband has been badgering her incessantly since collecting her from Dresden: 'He is using the children to blackmail me,' she says. 'He is threatening to take them away from me.'[88] Dr Goebbels returns his wife to the Dresden clinic on the way back to Berlin.

Two more weeks of this conspicuous separation follow. He often visits the children at Schwanenwerder and sometimes sleeps there. He previews two new films in his private cinema there including Lida's latest, *The Gambler*. He records in his diary a kind of even-handed alibi: 'One barely knows which of the two films to favor.' Playing safe, he enters both of them in the Venice film festival.[89]

Scarcely has Magda returned when he leaves for Heidelberg and Austria. Once, she yammers at him on the telephone.[90] As the gorgeous annual Wagner festival begins at Bayreuth, Hitler again commands them to appear together. Dr Goebbels flies down separately on July 24. For his love-smitten aide Hanke it is pure torment to see Magda sharing a bedroom with Goebbels in the new wing of the Wagner household. Of all choices, that evening's offering is *Tristan and Isolde*. Wagner's romantic opera relates the ecstasy of a love which can face even death. Dramatic though the libretto is, neither Hitler nor Goebbels will forget the tragic scenes that accompany it in the auditorium. The Führer and his lady, the voluminous and matronly Englishwoman Winifred Wagner, sit in the large central box flanked by Joseph Goebbels and a loudly sobbing Magda; Albert Speer, summoned to Bayreuth by his distraught friend Hanke, is to Magda's left. During the intermission she slumps with head bowed, loudly weeping, in the salon while Hitler and his white-faced propaganda minister affect not to notice. In his diary Goebbels comments stiffly only on the Wagner – 'What music, and what acoustics! Incomparable!' – and passes over in silence the no less memorable performance of his spouse.[91]

The diary does hint at a row the next day. 'We find ourselves again,' he records however, blandly adding: 'We have been apart so long.'[92] They lunch and dine again with Hitler, Winifred Wagner, and Speer. Hanke, excluded from these occasions, is frantic. By Speer's account, he has enlightened Hitler that morning about what is going on. The Führer sends for Goebbels – the diary shows them talking until three A.M. – and bluntly suggests that he leave Bayreuth forthwith.

It is an appalling turning point in the two men's relations. After only three hours' sleep, Dr Goebbels flies back to Berlin with his tail between his legs, leaving Magda and Hanke in Bayreuth.[93] 'She is so nice and affectionate to me,' he tells his disbelieving diary. The next day she goes – no doubt not alone – to see *Tristan* again. 'That would be too much for me,' observes Goebbels dourly, and drives out to Lanke.[94] While Magda stays on at Bayreuth, he orders a second preview of *The Gambler* at Schwanenwerder, probably for Lida's benefit, and luxuriates in unopposed access to the children.[95] Little Holde, now seventeen months, has come toddling across the tarmac at Tempelhof to greet him. Helga, nearly six, is graceful and ladylike. Hilde is a little moppet, and Hellmut, alas, a stubborn little ne'er-do-well.[96]

Their father conveys all this to his diary, but its pages are becoming increasingly a vehicle for deception. 'A long discussion with Magda,' it records. 'She is very sweet and kind to me. I do love her very much. It's so good to own a person who belongs to one body and soul.'[97] The next day he gives her a beautiful amethyst ring. Later he phones Lida Baarova, calling himself Müller as usual, and announces: 'Liduschka, I have told my wife everything. She knows that I love you and cannot live without you.'[98] On the day after that, August 4, he phones again to say that Magda wants to talk things over with her. 'She's being very sensible about it. . . It will be all right.'[99] Panicking and feeling suddenly trapped, Lida drives over from the studios to Schwanenwerder after the day's filming. Magda receives her swaying gently on her feet, with more than one tot of cognac inside her, and challenges her to reveal her intentions. Lida blurts out, however, 'I want to leave Germany!' She pleads with Magda for help.

'No,' responds Magda tipsily, 'you must not leave! He needs us both. He is a genius. It is our duty to live for him.' Filling Lida's glass, and addressing her as *du*, she lays down a few ground rules. 'I don't want any carrying-on in here,' she says motioning unsteadily around her villa. The two lovebirds can live in the house next door, the citadel. 'What happens elsewhere doesn't bother me.' Nor, she adds as an afterthought, must Lida have any children by Goebbels.

Young Lida is stunned by all this. 'I'm too young,' she protests, indignation momentarily displacing tact. 'I have all my life ahead of me.' She is conscious that, as a Czech, her career is at the minister's mercy – he can order her deportation instantly. Often she has driven home from Lanke in floods of tears, rendered distraught by the hopelessness of her position.[100]

Dr Goebbels walks in, eyes gleaming. He bestows upon Lida a diamond brooch. 'Are we all set?' he asks.

In his diary he records only 'an important talk,' adding: 'It is of great importance to me. I am glad we're all set now.'[101] It makes no mention of Lida at all. It paints an idyllic picture of the next days, as the minister cruises with unidentified friends – six times in one week – on the sun-dappled waters of the Wannsee.[102]

While the temperature in Berlin climbs, they chat, they laze in the sun, they visit Peacock Island for picnics, and they swim around in the lake's warm waters. Once Magda comes splashing alongside Lida and asks, 'Are you happy now?' Lida swims gracefully away from her. But things are already coming unstuck. Goebbels logs another long spat with Magda. 'Things are not entirely clarified. . . ' he grimly records. 'The last months have pretty well worn me down.'[103]

The rows multiply.[104] On one trip he and a scantily clad Lida have adjacent deck chairs on the foredeck overlooked by Magda from aloft. Ello Quandt sees the tears behind Magda's dark glasses and Magda blurts out the unnatural arrangement which her husband is proposing.[105] That Saturday, the thirteenth, they all cruise to Lake Tegel in a violent summer rainstorm. After a visit to Peacock Island, Goebbels invites them back to watch a movie. Most of them elect to see Anny Ondra's latest, but Goebbels, grinning, proposes *The Gambler* instead.[106] It is another little dig at Magda. When the lights come on, Lida turns round and sees Magda and Hanke holding hands in the back row.[107]

As the rain beats down, Magda begins to fight back. That night she assigns Ello to share Lida's bedroom in the citadel, pleading a full house as an excuse.[108] The Czech actress snaps at Goebbels, 'I shan't be coming again. I don't like being spied on!' That Sunday, August 14, after consulting with the poisonous Ello, Magda tells her husband to get out – she's going to sue for divorce.

On Monday, a tropical heatwave returns. 'I'm glad to get away!' he grouches in his diary. Perspiring through his thin white suit, Goebbels drives back to Berlin. Now the heat is on in every sense. As Hitler returns to Berlin that evening, Hanke secures an immediate audience for Magda.[109] She complains that a young Czech actress has invaded her marriage. People at her studios, she says, have heard Lida boasting, 'It is I who shall decide when they divorce!'[110] Hitler knows who Baarova is. He has just seen *The Gambler* (the only movie this week on which he has passed no comment).[111] But he will not hear of divorce in the Reich's 'happiest family.'

He sends for Goebbels. The minister's stock is beginning a decline from which it will take six years to recover. 'I then have a very long and grave conversation with him,' records Goebbels, without being more specific. 'It shakes me to the core. I am deeply moved by it. The Führer is like a father to me. I am so grateful to him. I take grim decisions. But they are final.'[112] Goebbels is hoist by his own petard; trapped by the 'family image' that he has himself created.

He telephones Lida Baarova immediately afterward at her rented Grunewald villa. She will never forget his words. 'My wife is a devil!' he exclaims. 'She's just been over to the Führer and told him everything. She has persuaded him that you're the evil one. I've had to give my word of honor that I won't ever see you again.' 'I love you,' he croaks between sobs. 'I cannot live without you.' He phones her best friend, the actress Hilde Körber, to go over and console Lida. Afterward he drives off aimlessly into the summer evening, half enjoying the suffering he has to endure. Not since Anka Stalherm has he experienced such a delicious torment to his soul.

'I am living as though in a trance,' he writes the next day, analyzing his own emotions. 'Life is so cruel and harsh. . . But one's duty must come first.' After a 'very long and very doleful' farewell phone call (it is, of course, to Lida), he soliloquizes: 'I remain firm, though my heart bids fair to burst. Now let my new life begin. Harsh and cruel, but subservient only to my duty. My youth is now over.'[113]

30: *Duty put on Hold*

I T WAS TO GOEBBELS that Hitler subsequently gave the credit for the bloodless victory over Czechoslovakia in 1938.[1] The propaganda ministry artfully developed the theme that Czechoslovakia was Moscow's 'aircraft carrier' in the heart of Europe. Taubert's anti-Comintern unit published a book, *Europe Betrayed*, to hammer home this line.[2] Later Goebbels flooded the media with Czech atrocity stories concocted by Berndt with the aid of address books, maps, and telephone directories.[3] The Nazi newspapers along the frontier with Czechoslovakia supplied further raw material.

This did lead to local difficulties. Konrad Henlein's press chief Franz Höller objected to one particular story about Czech attacks on Sudeten Germans, pointing out that this was his own village, and it enjoyed particularly good ethnic relations.[4]

'Tell me,' retorted Goebbels, grinning, 'how big is your village?' Höller told him. 'Right,' said Goebbels, grinning evilly. 'So three hundred people know we are lying. But the rest of the world still has to find out!'[5]

For Czechoslovakia the clock was already ticking. On the day of Magda's lachrymose performance at Bayreuth late in July 1938 Hitler had predicted that he would have to use force. 'Prague won't come to terms,' Goebbels wrote afterward.[6] But Hitler's fortifications against France, the West Wall, were still incomplete. This, wrote Goebbels, was why Hitler had just sent an adjutant to London for informal talks with the new foreign secretary Lord Halifax – 'he had to play for time.' 'Of course,' he continued, 'our Berlin generals are all shitting their pants again. . . The Führer wants to avoid actual war. That's why he's preparing for it with everything we've got.'[7]

War psychosis gradually permeated Europe's capitals, including Berlin. Addressing the gauleiters, Göring argued against panicking. Goebbels, listening in his capacity as gauleiter of Berlin, wondered uneasily whether the German people would stand for a long war. They would have to rely on rapid surprise tactics. He could see Hitler's mind constantly turned to Britain – how dearly he would like to be on good terms with her – and to the south-east. 'We don't want these peoples,' Hitler commented later in August, discussing Hungary, Romania, and Czechoslovakia. 'Just their land.'[8]

HIS FAMILY LIFE momentarily a shambles, Goebbels throws himself into his other tasks. For the four weeks until the Sudeten crisis peaks in mid-September he wallows in self-pity. He has barely eaten since that dreadful rainy Sunday, August 14. He lies awake, hollow-eyed, takes sedatives to sleep. 'If only the sun would not shine. If only the day were not so bright and radiant! I draw the curtains and try to work.'[9] A second man-to-man talk with Hitler leaves him badly shaken. 'I cannot think of any way out, almost,' he writes, the casual *almost* being a clue that this dramatic baring of feelings is largely sham. Indeed, each such heartrending passage is followed by humdrum details of ministerial routine. Using Hilde Körber as a conduit he explains that his decision (not to see Lida any more) is 'unalterable.'[10]

That evening he has a long, unforgettable, totally humiliating talk with Magda. 'She is so hardhearted and cruel,' is all he writes. 'I have nobody to help me. Nor do I want anybody. One must drink the full draught from this bitter chalice. And shrink back cravenly before nothing. I am presently suffering the worst time of my life. With [Minister of Posts] Ohnesorge,' he continues, without even dipping his pen, 'I have discussed details of our share of the reduced radio license fee. . .'[11]

What a feast a psychiatrist can dish up from such passages, written in Goebbels' refuge at Lanke as the wind sighs and the rainstorms spatter his lake. 'I go to bed early. . . Loneliness!' He flees to his mother and bewails: 'Ello has behaved despicably. But what else was one to expect of her?'[12] His mother falls ill with worry. Back at the ministry on Thursday, Hilde Körber 'comes with more sob stuff' – the German *weint mir etwas vor* is just as deprecating in tone. He again visits the hardhearted and cruel Magda, and curses in his diary: 'I've never seen her like this before.' He swears that he has now stopped seeing Lida. They agree on a truce until the end of September. 'Much can happen until then,' he reflects miserably. 'Both for better and for worse. . . Let time pass, the universal healer.'[13]

There are some awkward moments. During the important five-day state visit by Admiral Nicholas von Horthy, the Hungarian regent – another of Czecho-slovakia's predatory neighbors – Hitler orders Joseph Goebbels and Magda to appear together at the state reception on the twenty-fourth and at the gala performance of *Lohengrin* the next night.

The photos show her sitting stiffly at her wayward husband's side. 'If only I could drop into an everlasting sleep,' writes Goebbels, still drinking deeply from that chalice, 'and never wake again!' After the farewell banquet in Charlottenburg castle, Magda snarls at him. '*Das alte Lied*,' he records with a wounded sigh: the same old melody. He stays up late talking with his trusty Karl Hanke, then decides on a little midnight motor excursion after all.[14]

He prepares a trial separation from his family. After seeing them briefly at Schwanenwerder on August 27, he spends a crestfallen night out at Lanke, then drops into the Scala strip club with a few friends. He decides to spend two weeks away from Berlin. Magda's nerves are in tatters too. Before leaving Berlin he phones her but finds her more impossible now than ever.[15] He wonders who is putting her up to this and resolves not to phone her again until many more weeks have passed.[16]

THE WAR CLOUDS now conjured up by Hitler over Europe were thus almost a welcome diversion. Several times the diary shows him debating privately with his senior staff whether there would be war – 'the one big topic now.'[17] Through a British mediator, Prague had offered conciliatory terms to the Sudeten Germans, but this only embarrassed Hitler. 'The problem now,' observed Goebbels, 'is how the Führer can create a suitable situation to strike.'

Much depended on whether Britain would then declare war. Goebbels' man in London, the fainthearted Fitz Randolph, lamely telegraphed that nobody could tell.[18] Goebbels' gut feeling was that Britain was merely bluffing. He ordered that her threats should not be reflected in his ministry's monitoring reports, the so-called 'Blue Telegrams,' lest they frighten Ribbentrop's diplomats. He studied Britain's nerve-war tactics with all the analytical detachment of a master propagandist. 'The whole London scenario is well thought-out,' he wrote approvingly. 'Cabinet meetings, Henderson recalled to London, "prepared for grave steps," and so forth. The old one-two. But it doesn't wash with us any more.'[19]

On the last day of August he flew down to the Berghof with Karl Hanke, evidently on his own initiative.[20] While waiting to see his Führer he was briefed by Göring's aide Karl Bodenschatz on the progress being made with their own fortifications; the best month to attack Czechoslovakia, said the colonel, would be October. Otto Dietrich pulled a face and asked, 'What will Britain do?' Hitler, joining them, was reassuring. He delivered a little lecture about Bismarck's courage when it came to taking action. Goebbels afterward trudged downhill to the guest-house – it did not escape him that Hitler no longer housed him in the Berghof itself. He was frantic about this mark of his slipping prestige, but he sensed too the clammy fear of war that was spreading across all Germany.[21] Using Helga's sixth birthday as a pretext he put through a call to Magda. She was as hardhearted as ever.[22]

The next day Hitler told them that the gap in Germany's western defenses was now all but closed. 'Britain will hold back,' he predicted, 'because she does not have the armed might. Paris will do what London does. The whole affair must unroll at top speed. For high stakes you've got to run big risks.'[23] Goebbels could not get that word *risks* out of his mind. Hitler's talk with Henlein turned to finding a suitable pretext to invade. That afternoon, September 2, Hitler delivered another little pep talk to them all – Goebbels, Henlein, Ribbentrop, Bodenschatz, Bormann, Speer, and Hoffmann – on 'keeping one's nerve.' Goebbels passed the message on to Hanke and Dietrich, who were beginning to waver.[24]

For all Goebbels' atrocity propaganda, there was none of the public enthusiasm for war that had marked August 1914. Berndt made this clear to him.[25] Funk was pessimistic too.[26] France noisily called up her reservists and

Goebbels had to remind himself that they were already fighting a war – of nerves.[27] When Czech police bludgeoned more local German officials, he turned the entire German press loose again to help Henlein in his assigned task of bringing the crisis to boiling point.[28]

The Times of London suddenly sided with Hitler, recommending that the Sudeten territories be formally restored to Germany.[29] On the ninth the British ambassador adopted a similar line in private as the annual Nuremberg rally began. Goebbels concluded from this that Britain did not want war.[30] But others like Neurath, the former foreign minister upon whom Hitler occasionally relied as an elder statesman for advice, still preferred waiting another year. 'Waiting,' scoffed Goebbels. 'That's what they all say when they don't want to act at all.' Hitler's ambassadors in London and Paris warned that both Britain and France would march. 'We must just stick to the Führer,' retorted Goebbels, almost piously. 'He commands, we obey. . . I trust in him as I do in God.' But even as he wrote these lines, the nagging private fears returned: 'Just one question gnaws away at me, day and night: what's it to be, war or peace?' Smiling enigmatically, Henderson assured him that France was honor-bound to aid Czechoslovakia, and then Britain could not stand aside.[31]

At the Nuremberg rally, Goebbels branded Prague a 'hotbed of the bolshevik conspiracy against Europe.'[32] But it was in Hitler's closing speech that the world first heard of his determination to go to war. The Sudeten Germans, he declared, were not alone. As they marched out together, Hitler whispered to Goebbels, 'Let's see what happens now.'[33]

'Things are panning out just as we wanted,' triumphed Goebbels as the world's press betrayed the first signs of panic. The death toll began to rise – 'over *fifty* in one village,' he recorded, carelessly confusing his own propaganda with fact. Addressing his editors he called for tough nerves and perseverance.

Then came the totally unexpected. The elderly British prime minister Neville Chamberlain offered to visit Hitler the next day.[34] Still hoping for a military showdown which would give him all of Czechoslovakia, Hitler had little option but to agree. For a moment Prague faltered, and relaxed her pressure. 'Nevertheless,' observed the cynical propaganda minister, 'we make a splash about "Czech terror." Things have got to be brought up to boiling point.'[35] Chamberlain met Hitler at the Berghof on September 15. At first Goebbels learned nothing except that the prime minister had asked for a further meeting at Bad Godesberg. While awaiting word from Hitler, Goebbels addressed a steadying lecture to five hundred gau officials in Berlin.[36] Hitler invited him down to the Obersalzberg for a briefing.

He flew down on the seventeenth, taking Hanke, Fritzsche (press section), and Hadamovsky (radio) with him. Hitler lunched alone with him and then invited him aloft to the newly built Eagle's Nest, along with Himmler and the favored British journalist Ward Price.[37] The Eagle's Nest was a teahouse built by Bormann's engineers on top of the Kehlstein, reached by an amazing lift inside the mountain. Here Hitler described Chamberlain to these listeners as an 'ice-cool,' calculating Englishman. He had not minced his language. London might fear a world war, he had boasted, but he was prepared to accept that risk.

The English prime minister, he said, had undertaken to persuade his Cabinet and the French to endorse a plebiscite in the disputed territories. This did not suit Hitler's purpose at all; but he expected Prague to hold out, which would leave the way open for the total solution he preferred. It was a war of nerves. Goebbels predicted that Prague would buckle under this pressure. Hitler disagreed. 'In 1948,' he said, 'it will be just three hundred years since the Peace of Münster [Westphalia]. We've got to liquidate that peace treaty by then.' Praising Goebbels' propaganda effort so far, he added: 'We've half won the war already.'[38]

The Czech president Beneš, abandoned by Chamberlain, conducted frantic telephone conversations with his legation in London. 'Despair is the only word,' recorded Goebbels smugly, reading the wiretaps which Hitler showed him. 'He [Beneš] just murmurs, "Yes, yes."'[39] Capitalizing on London's sudden helpfulness, Hitler upped the ante. He sketched a new map showing still greater territorial demands, ready for when he next met Chamberlain. With Goebbels limping at his side, he strutted up and down the Berghof terrace beneath a clear canopy of stars.

Goebbels issued fresh instructions to Berndt to create the necessary frontier incidents. Hitler mobilized Czechoslovakia's other neighbors: The cowardly Hungarians made no move, but the Poles were more obliging.[40] They had already hinted that they would entertain Hitler's demand for the return of Danzig, and in gratitude Hitler dictated to their ambassador what Poland might now demand with his blessing from Czechoslovakia.[41] According to what he told Goebbels, as they set off together with Ribbentrop by train for Godesberg, the Polish ambassador had 'promised' force against Czechoslovakia.[42] Goebbels still predicted that the Czechs would ultimately cave in. Hitler however told him that he was poised to strike on September 28 – just one week's time.[43]

Goebbels attended both days of the Hitler–Chamberlain conferences at Godesberg. The first on September 22 began at four P.M. and lasted for three hours. Hitler's new sketch-map shocked the Englishman. But Hitler reminded him that the frontiers would look somewhat worse if he eventually had to use force. (The main thing, realized Goebbels, listening to them haggling, was to get behind the formidable Czech mountain fortifications.) Chamberlain said he would have to consult, and they all adjourned, Hitler and Goebbels to a city launch that chugged up the Rhine into the gentle autumn evening. The next morning Chamberlain sent over a letter to Hitler. The Nazi wiretaps on the British and Czech international phone lines left no doubt now that Beneš was playing for time. Word came shortly that Beneš had mobilized. Undeterred, Hitler handed new demands to Chamberlain.

There was a lot of play-acting on both sides. At that evening's crisis session, Chamberlain rose haughtily to his feet and threatened to walk out.[44] Goebbels did not know what to make of it all. His private alarm deepened. War hysteria was seeping into the German press.[45] Flying back to Berlin with Hitler, he found a mood there wavering between noisy jingoism and grim 'determination' – for want of a more gloomy word which he could safely enter in his diary. The wiretaps showed Beneš digging his heels in. Would he give way? The question dominated Hitler's lunch table. 'The Führer thinks not,' recorded Goebbels. 'I say he will.' Hitler again said that he would attack on or after the twenty-eighth. 'That gives the Führer five days,' calculated Goebbels, adding: 'He fixed these dates way back on May 28.' He somberly agreed that the radical solution was the best. Ribbentrop predicted that nobody would lift a finger to help Prague. For once Goebbels found himself agreeing with him, but he still did not want war.[46]

Hitler proved right and Goebbels wrong: Beneš rejected Hitler's territorial demands outright. Goebbels again had to lecture his editors on steadfastness, and stepped up the propaganda war still further.

The unwitting party faithful might cheer but others – intellectuals, generals, and even ministers – began bombarding Hitler with warnings.[47] Goebbels heard Himmler complaining about the uselessness of the older generals. Hitler gave the Czechs until two P.M. on the twenty-eighth to agree to his terms. Goebbels mechanically told Berndt to stir up discord between Beneš and his people using clandestine transmitters based in Vienna .[48]

This war of nerves reached its climax on the twenty-seventh, when Hitler received Chamberlain's dapper emissary Sir Horace Wilson. He told Goebbels later that he had screamed at the Englishman, accusing him of evasions.[49] 'The Führer,' summarized an admiring Goebbels, 'believes in his mission with the sureness of a sleepwalker. Not for one moment does his hand tremble. A great genius in our midst. . . One has to serve him with profound devotion. He is more true, more simple, more farsighted than any German statesman that has gone before.'[50]

The German public was spared these insights. War panic now gripped its heart. That evening Hitler ordered a mechanized division to rumble through the capital. He sat watching from the darkened foyer of the chancellery as the armor rattled past, while Goebbels mingled unseen with the crowds.[51] 'The public,' he wrote anxiously afterward, 'is filled with a profound worry. They know that we're coming into the last lap now.'

As the deadline for Hitler's ultimatum approached, Goebbels decided to head him off. The British and French ambassadors got to Hitler first, bringing fragrant fresh proposals. Ribbentrop was furious that war might be averted. 'He nurtures a blind hatred of Britain,' decided Goebbels. 'Göring, Neurath, and I urge Hitler to accept. . . You can't get into what may well turn into a world war over procedural issues. Göring . . . totally shares my viewpoint and gives Ribbentrop a piece of his mind.' 'Mein Führer,' he blurted out over lunch in Hitler's chancellery on the twenty-eighth, 'if you think that the German public is thirsting for war, you are wrong. They watch its approach with a leaden sense of apathy.'[52]

In that instant Hitler changed his mind. According to Ribbentrop's Staatssekretär Ernst von Weizsäcker it was primarily Goebbels who persuaded Hitler to back off from war at this, the eleventh hour.[53] Perhaps Hitler even welcomed his moderating influence. He immediately approved suggestions for a four-power conference to take place in Munich the next day. Goebbels saw the likely outcome thus: 'We take the Sudeten territories peacefully; the Grand Solution remains wide open, and we gird ourselves for future contingencies.' He was due to address half a million people in the Lustgarten that evening. He prudently decided not to reveal anything of the morrow's certain victory. 'Nothing would be more improper,' he explained to his staff after that historic luncheon, 'than to announce Chamberlain's coming. That would unleash incredible public scenes of jubilation; and then the British would realize the truth – that all our belligerence is just bluster.'[54]

Remaining in Berlin, he warned his editors not to let their campaign about 'Czech terror' flag either. Soon Hanke, sent to Munich as his observer, reported that Mussolini, Chamberlain, and the French premier Edouard Daladier had agreed to Hitler's demands. Czechoslovakia should hand over the disputed territories in the first ten days of October. 'So that's all we get for the time being,' noted Goebbels. 'Under the circumstances,' he added, hiding his relief, 'we are unable to realize our grand plan' – seizing all of Czechoslovakia.[55]

Hitler had dramatically increased the Reich's international prestige. In a stinging rebuff to Beneš, the four powers had not even invited the Czechs to the Munich conference. 'And now,' triumphed Goebbels in his unpublished diary, 'let us rearm, rearm, and rearm!' Once more he ordered his gau to prepare a hero's welcome for the Führer at the Anhalt railroad station.[56]

He had other causes to rejoice. 'Ribbentrop fell flat on his face,' he wrote. 'Göring is livid with him. Calls him a pompous prima donna.' He had already commented during June on the foreign minister's pathological hatred of the English – a relic of the treatment meted out to him as ambassador by the British establishment.[57] 'The Führer,' Goebbels had added in September 'is in for a big surprise with him'[58].

Back in Berlin, Hitler told his lunch guests about the famous 'piece of paper,' the Anglo-German declaration that Chamberlain had sprung on him afterward for signature. He did not believe that the British meant to honor it, he said. Chamberlain was a fox. 'He tackles each issue ice-cool,' he reiterated. 'We're really going to have watch out for these British.'[59] Over dinner the next day he again revealed his unshakeable resolve to destroy Czechoslovakia, as Goebbels recalled his words. He doggedly argued that London and Paris would not have intervened. Goebbels continued to differ on that score.[60]

A few days later however, with the Sudeten region now in German hands, Hitler personally inspected the Czech fortifications. He now realized that it was fortunate that there had not been any fighting. 'We would have shed a lot of blood,' he privately admitted. It was a good thing, Goebbels decided, that things had turned out the way they had.[61]

31: *The Real Chum*

O<small>N THE DAY OF HITLER'S TRIUMPH</small> in Munich an ugly revelation awaits Goebbels in Berlin. Given the evasions of his diary in matters matrimonial, however, we cannot properly speculate on what it is. Suffice to say that police chief Helldorff visits him late that day and Goebbels then records: 'A sad and difficult day for me personally.' He adds philosophically, 'If it isn't one thing it's another.'[1]

Four painful weeks have already passed since he last visited Schwanenwerder and saw his children. 'Papa has been naughty,' Magda cruelly tells them. 'He's not allowed to come here any more.'[2]

She herself has begun drinking heavily and hitting the night spots – a world of chrome, black leather, and subdued lights. She frequents cabarets where the stand-up comics make fun of her own husband. Admiral Raeder's adjutant is drinking in one such club when Magda utters a boozy invitation to him to share her bar-stool. After a flurry of indiscretions about her marital problems, she invites the navy captain and his pals back to her home.[3] Five years later, when Goebbels snarls in his famous total war speech about 'the nightclub crowd who loll around in stylish bars,' Magda – seated in the front row – has no doubt whatever who is meant by that.[4]

Joseph Goebbels thought he had friends, as Lida Baarova would sadly remark years later: But he had none. Behind his back Karl Hanke starts the sniggering rumor that in the street confrontation early in 1937 Lida's lover Gustav Fröhlich had actually socked Goebbels. Improbable though it is – given that the minister throws men into concentration camp just for their opinions – the story sweeps Germany and delights foreign capitals.[5] A Munich cabaret artiste guffaws, 'We'd all like to be *fröhlich* sometime!' – the word means *contented* in German. Schacht calls the minister's affairs a public scandal.[6]

Himmler complains to Hitler that he has never liked the Goebbels genus, but has so far kept his views to himself: 'Now he's the most hated man in Germany,' he says. There was a time, he continues, when Goebbels used to sound off against the Jews who sexually coerced their female employees; now the minister is doing the same himself. 'It's obvious,' adds the Reichsführer, 'that they are not doing it for love, but because he's propaganda minister.'[7]

Shocked by all this, Hitler orders a watch kept on Goebbels' former girlfriend Lida Baarova. Gestapo limousines cruise up and down outside her rented villa in Grunewald. But Goebbels, feigning indifference, makes no overt effort to contact her.

During the four dramatic weeks preceding Munich, what he calls his private *misère* has receded into the background. For four more weeks he does not see Magda at all. On the verge of a nervous breakdown he occasionally resorts to subterfuge to see Lida. He directs Hilde Körber to take Lida to the theater, and feasts his eyes upon her from a few rows away. He phones Hilde repeatedly to ask how Lida is. He sees the Nuremberg rally as a welcome distraction from 'dumb thoughts,' evidently meaning suicide, because the next day, after talking a party official out of shooting himself over a silly blunder, he remarks grimly in his diary: 'We all make silly blunders.'[8] He gets his mother to see Magda in Berlin: Because to her alone, ultimately, he is beholden – but it's 'the same old melody.'[9] 'I can expect no quarter,' he writes the next day.[10] After phoning his mother again he gives up. 'In Berlin there's the devil to pay. But I'm immune to all that now.'[11] Deprived now of both Magda's and Lida's company, he risks a 'motor outing' upon his return from Nuremberg to Berlin ('just to get some fresh air,' he pleads in his diary) and then another ten days later, followed by a 'drive through the Grunewald, just to get fresh air' the next day.[12] Lida still lives there, of course. During early October, these motor outings multiply.

While his own Staatssekretär Karl Hanke is now gathering evidence to aid Magda, Goebbels apparently suspects nothing. On October 3 he has a long talk with him about his personal affairs. 'Hanke is very nice about it, a real chum,' he informs his diary. 'I've got one person at least I can talk things over with. I couldn't have gone on like this.'[13] A few days later, after another little motor outing, Goebbels again bends Hanke's ear about his plight. 'He proves very attentive and understanding. He then has a very important conversation and this sets my mind very much at rest.' Evidently Hanke has telephoned Magda, and she 'agrees' to see him. 'I am glad,' repeats Goebbels, 'that I now have at least one person I can speak with. These last few weeks I have often felt so lonesome and deserted. . .'[14]

Lida Baarova is now filming *The Sweetheart* with Willy Fritsch and Grete Weiser. She confides in Grete without realizing that she too is in cahoots with the double-dealing Hanke.[15] When Hanke shows Magda his dossier it contains the names of thirty-six women and stolen copies of his minister's correspondence with them.[16]

Visiting Saarbrücken with Hitler, Goebbels phones Hanke to ask the outcome of his visit to Magda. 'Seems it's all over,' he writes afterward, perplexed. 'Nothing I can do will change that. I've tried my utmost. But if that's how it is, so be it. I feel crushed.'[17] Hanke reports back in person on the tenth. 'Things seem pretty hopeless,' decides the minister, caught up in the drama of his own situation. 'A human tragedy is unfurling with neither blameless nor guilty parties. Fate itself has taken a hand and has spoken.' Oddly, he tells his diary that Hanke has questioned 'all' the parties concerned – a hint at infidelities by Magda? He asks Hanke now to report all these facts, as a neutral chum, to the

Führer.[18] He can no longer keep Hitler out of it. 'I shall neither complain nor whine,' he writes, melodramatically. 'I have no cause for hatred or indignation. I await the Führer's decision and shall obediently comply. . . Things just can't go on like this.'[19]

Hanke in fact sees Hitler the next day at Godesberg, and regales him with salacious details of his own minister's wrongdoings – like how he has kept foreign ambassadors waiting while he entertains his female visitors within. Waiting for word from Godesberg, the craziest of notions race through Goebbels' brain. He cruises the streets 'just taking in fresh air.' At last Hanke phones: Hitler is willing to see Goebbels soon, he says, quietly relishing the moment when, he imagines, he will step into the disgraced minister's shoes. 'At any rate he knows how things stand,' writes Goebbels, confident that he has got in first with his version of affairs.[20] After a sleepless night he goes for another little drive, 'to collect my thoughts.'[21]

FOR GOEBBELS THE suffocating ministerial routine has resumed – the struggle to lever out the Jews,[22] the Sudeten referendum, and the inauguration of the magnificent new theater that a grateful Hitler has donated to the Saar.[23] Ignoring the sunshine outside, he mopes for hours in his darkened ministerial chambers, snapping pencils, and writing endlessly in his diary.[24] His brain gyrates pathologically around his personal miseries. His diary reflects his pain – page after page of self-centered whining tinged with a masochistic delight in every moment of this self-flagellation. Once Magda allows the three older children over to him. They all cry loudly and Helga whispers sweet nothings in his ear. Goebbels is still hungry for their childish chatter when it is time for them to leave. He broods alone that night, crushed by his own solitude, and toying with words. 'Those who love me are not allowed to see me: those who can see me don't love me any more.' He grimly puts his affairs in order and closes his diary.[25]

That Saturday afternoon, October 15, he tells Rach to chauffeur him out to Lanke. He is tired of the world – so he writes – and tired of life itself. He has decided to resort to that most feminine of wiles, the feigned suicide attempt.[26] He swallows two Phanodorm sleeping tablets, washed down with alcohol, and goes to bed. He sleeps around the clock while, he assumes, Rach and the panicking manservant Kaiser try to arouse him. All he is aware of is a stabbing pain near his heart. He thinks he is dying, but – he writes – Heaven is again merciful. Apart from Rach and Kaiser however nobody pays him the slightest attention.[27]

His head throbbing from the barbiturates, Goebbels stays out at Lanke until Tuesday, victim of a monster hangover. 'In the afternoon I drive back in despair to Berlin.' Among the films he previews that evening is *Prussian Love Story*, an episode from the life of Prince Wilhelm of Prussia. Lida Baarova plays the prince's first true love, a Polish-Lithuanian aristocrat, the Princess Elisa Radziwill. Two bitter-sweet hours later the tears are streaming down

Dr Goebbels' cheeks. 'I didn't think it would be so hard for me to see it,' he confesses in the diary.[28]

Worse is to come, far worse: On Wednesday he learns from police chief Helldorff the cruel, humiliating truth about Hanke's disloyalty.[29] Hanke – his old comrade in the fight for Berlin: His protégé: His own Staatssekretär! Meanwhile Magda has taken to Emmy Göring her plaintive tales about her husband, calling him 'the devil in human form.'[30] Helldorff at least is a true friend, he reflects. He sends for Walter Funk on Thursday morning, and Funk offers to see Göring. 'Take Helldorff too,' pleads Goebbels. 'He knows best of all.'[31]

Hitler is away, triumphantly touring the Sudeten region, now called Bohemia once more, and does not return to the Berghof until late on the twentieth.[32] Meanwhile Goebbels ostracizes Hanke. 'He is my cruelest disappointment.' He drives out to Göring's Carinhall estate at noon on October 21, and puts his case to the field marshal; he argues that Magda has turned frigid, and that he is therefore entitled to graze in fresher pastures.[33] Göring listens kindly, even jovially, proposes radical solutions, and undertakes to see the Führer. In private he chortles over Goebbels' discomfiture; but he lectures Emmy that she's got to see that Goebbels does have a point.[34] 'Good ole Göring!' writes Goebbels. 'I've really gotten to like him. We part as true pals.'

Relieved, he takes Helldorff off to Hamburg, where he is to speak. Here there is unpleasant news indeed. Magda has got to Hitler first – she is at this moment taking tea with Hitler up at the Kehlstein teahouse, and she has sent for the eldest children to complete the picture. 'So things are hotting up,' remarks Goebbels.[35] His speech at Hamburg's Hanseatic Hall is as truculent and cynical as ever.[36]

No detail of the odd events that Saturday October 22 eludes the foreign diplomats in Hamburg. Goebbels duly attends the reception at the opera house but is missing from the foundation-stone ceremony of the *Hamburger Abendblatt*, the local party newspaper. Even the British consul-general learns that Dr Goebbels has received 'sudden orders to attend Herr Hitler at Berchtesgaden.'[37] Goebbels calls in Helldorff and Funk, but the latter is nowhere to be found. 'I make up my mind to fight,' Goebbels writes. 'I shall defend my name.'

At the Berghof Hitler receives him at once, speaks of solidarity, *raison d'état*, and the greater common cause. Helldorff, duly called upon by Goebbels to testify, backs him up but on the main issue – evidently Goebbels' proposal that he resign, divorce Magda, and marry Lida – Hitler will not budge. Magda herself is now called in – the first time that Goebbels has seen his estranged wife in two months. She is at first rather aggressive, he notes; but ultimately they both have to submit to Hitler's impatient diktat. He orders a moratorium, a cease-fire. For three months they are to live together, at the end of which he will permit a divorce if both still so desire.[38]

Hitler disapproves of Goebbels' behavior, but he cannot dispense with him – not right now. 'The Führer,' Goebbels records afterward, 'detains me for a long time alone. He confides to me his most profound and innermost secrets. . . He sees a really serious conflict brewing in the none-too-distant future. Probably with Britain, which is steadily preparing for it. We shall have to fight back, and thus will be decided the hegemony over Europe. Everything must be geared to that moment. And thus must take precedence over all personal hopes and desires. What are we individuals compared with the fate of great states and nations?'[39]

With Speer and Eva Braun they all take the brass-walled elevator up to the lofty Kehlstein teahouse to celebrate the Goebbels' shotgun reconciliation. Helga and Hilde smother their father with joyful kisses. Hitler instructs a photographer to capture the reconciliation on camera. The camera cannot lie. Berlin radio broadcasts appeals for Heiner ('Shortleg') Kurzbein – is there to be no end of the minister's humiliation? – to report to the propaganda ministry immediately. As head of the photo section, his services are needed urgently because Hitler has decreed that the Goebbels 'family photo' will appear in every newspaper in Germany.[40] 'It will help to expunge a great deal of the unpleasantness,' agrees Goebbels. But much will remain. Hitler has also bowed to Magda's demand that Lida Baarova withdraw from society and the movie world entirely.[41] Hitler's lady friend Eva Braun, an avid movie fan, writes to Lida coldly severing their friendship.[42]

Leaving Magda behind at the Berghof, Goebbels returns by overnight train to Berlin with Helldorff; he is frantic with fear that he may never regain his esteem in Hitler's eyes. In the morning – it is now October 24 – he sends Helldorff over to break the cruel news to Lida. Calling in his senior staff, he strikes the same heroic pose he has seen Prince Wilhelm adopt in *Prussian Love Story* and declares: 'In the conflict between love and duty I have made the choice that men have made throughout history when faced with their duty to the people.'[43]

Shortly Helldorff returns, badly shaken, with word that Lida, whom he has summoned to police headquarters, is demanding to speak with Dr Goebbels and is threatening to kill herself; a doctor has had to sedate her with morphine in Hilde Körber's villa. Göring phones, invites him out to Carinhall, and promises to back him all down the line on condition that Goebbels drop his claim to be the second personality in the country.[44] 'On the critical issue,' records Goebbels himself tantalizingly, without being more specific, 'he immediately knows a way out.'[45] At 9:30 P.M. he phones Hilde Körber from Carinhall, while Göring listens in, and asks her to put Lida on the line. 'I'm out at my good friend's house,' Goebbels says. She will know who that is. 'He's standing next to me. Liduschka, keep a stiff upper lip, whatever they may do to you. Don't be angry. Stay the way you are.' Distraught and her mind numbed with morphine, the actress is unable to reply. They never speak again.[46]

Lida's torment is just beginning. She is confined to Hilde Körber's villa with her phone tapped and two secret police on the door.[47] She is allowed out on Friday October 28 when her latest movie is premiered at the Gloria Palace on Kurfürstendamm. Goebbels notes, 'The premiere of *The Gambler* went off reasonably well.'[48] There are loud sniggers from the audience at one scene when her father, reproached for squandering their money, snarls: 'Money? Go get more money from your Doctor!' As Lida goes on stage at the end there are shouts: 'Minister's whore!' She calls out to the unseen hecklers, 'How much have you been paid!'[49] Karl Hanke's hired hooligans have done their work well. There are similar scenes at the weekend performances, and on Monday the movie is withdrawn. Her life will become a nightmare from which there is no reveille. Julius Schaub, Hitler's personal adjutant, warns her not to leave Germany – 'Something might happen to you if you try.'[50]

Goebbels tries to pick up the pieces of his life. He tackles the personnel problems of the advertising council and the movie industry, he stiffly discusses with Hanke the wartime use of Germany's radio networks, and he admonishes Helldorff and Funk to keep still tongues in their heads. ('We've got a mole in this office,' he writes, 'somebody blabbing to outsiders. I'm going to smoke him out.')[51]

On October 25, the three months' probationary period begins. That evening Goebbels collects Magda and the children at Tempelhof. He berates her until six A.M.; she listens with set and expressionless features. 'Ghastly things come to light,' he wails in his notes, without saying what. He retires to bed, his fevered brain battened down with Phanodorms, and awakes to finish off this (previously unpublished) volume of the diary without having written the name of Lida Baarova in it once.[52]

As for Hitler, the whole episode leaves him with a bitter sense of betrayal. Rosenberg, Schacht, Hanke, and Himmler tell him of the damage that Goebbels has done by his philandering. One French newspaper prints a publicity photo from *The Gambler* showing Lida Baarova fending off a tuxedo'd villain on whose shoulders they have however imposed the Führer's head.

Goebbels is falling from grace, tumbling head over heels, and he knows it. Sick with worry, he begins work on a palliative, an adoring twenty-five-chapter panegyric entitled *Hitler the Man*.[53]

For the next eight weeks the diary shows him dictating this book and revising it; he even has it proof-printed, and negotiates the sale of rights with Eher Verlag in Germany and the Hearst Corporation in the United States. Hitler however, none too happy about being linked in the public eye with Goebbels, asks to run his eye over it, and in mid-January 1939 he stops its publication 'for the time being.'[54] The book is never seen again.

32: *Broken Glass*

IT IS SURELY AGAINST this fraught and unstable background – the marriage-war with Magda, the sniping from his enemies – that we have to examine the historic episode which follows only a few days later: Kristallnacht, the Night of Broken Glass, November 9–10, 1938.[1] Whose was the evil brain behind this outrage? How far was Hitler himself involved in authorizing or endorsing it? Once again the hitherto unpublished Goebbels Diaries provide clues to what really happened – but they are only *clues*, which need proper interpretation.

As the motto with which he opens the next volume of his unpublished diary shows ('It is suffering alone that makes men of us!') he has spent the last week of October 1938 wallowing in self-pity, unable to sleep without sedatives, wearily reopening the wounds of the past with Magda, talking of 'ways out' and flirting with thoughts of suicide, dosing himself with narcotics, and sleeping around the clock.[2] He admonishes Helldorff once again to keep a still tongue in his head about it all, and he decides to replace yet another adjutant, Diether von Wedel (he 'has betrayed me wherever he could').[3]

When October 29 comes, he not once but twice writes of it as 'the saddest birthday of my life.'[4] Magda wakes him from his drugged sleep and 'frostily' congratulates him; his two eldest girls recite their poems; there are artificially glowing reports in the press and photographs of Hanke speaking the birthday eulogy in the ministry. Not surprisingly he finds something spooky about it all. 'What else really is there left for me to do in this world? I can't see any more jobs for me.'[5] Regardless of Hitler's injunctions, Magda is still carved of ice as November begins.[6] The children neither know nor ask the reasons for the perpetual frostiness of the family meals at Schwanenwerder.[7] He loathes the whole human race and yet again tells his diary so.[8]

'I am glad to get back to work,' he writes on November 3, adding the heartfelt sigh: 'How I wish the past could be forgotten!'

At a beer evening at Weimar during the Book Week, Magda, wearing a fetching strawberry-colored dress with a generous lace décolleté, is the star of the evening while Dr Goebbels chain-smokes endlessly and glowers into his beer.[9] 'It is still not working out,' he writes on the fourth after another late row with her.[10]

GERMAN PROPAGANDA drifted, with no firm hand on the helm. The British embassy, trying to detect a pattern, found it aimless and inconsistent.[11] Goebbels now seemed to be trying to conjure up a British 'bogey' – evidently an echo of Hitler's gloomy review of foreign policy to him while at the Berghof on October 23.

Goebbels had sidelined the party's propaganda directorate (the Reichsprop-agandaleitung, based in Munich) by setting up local offices under his direct ministerial control, and through these channels he often dictated policy to the party itself. His direct and evil influence as gauleiter on the Berlin police has already been noted.

Nationwide, his anti-Jewish campaign gathered momentum. Göring was already purging the Jews from the business sector with a verve paralleled by Goebbels' sweep in the chamber of culture.[12] Count Helldorff liaised closely with Goebbels on the continuing and orchestrated police harassment of the Jews that had begun in June.[13] Moreover Warsaw and Prague were following suit. 'The Jews are being driven from country to country,' observed Goebbels, 'reaping the fruits of their eternal intrigues, hate campaigns, and dirty tricks.'[14] Poland announced steps designed to keep the seventy thousand Polish Jews living abroad from returning; to forestall this ban, on October 28 the German police rounded up fifteen thousand Polish Jews and shunted them back across the border into Poland.[15]

This operation indirectly triggered the events that now followed, although there is some frail evidence that LICA, the Paris-based International League against Antisemitism which had lurked behind the 1936 assassination of Wilhelm Gustloff, also had a hand in them. On November 7 a seventeen-year-old wastrel, a penniless illegal immigrant of Jewish-Polish extraction, pumped several bullets into a German diplomat in Paris, and Goebbels' life suddenly had meaning again.[16] Somehow this lad, Herschel Grynszpan, had found the money to check into an expensive hotel one block away from LICA's headquarters and to purchase the pistol with which he gunned down the German official, Counselor Ernst vom Rath. Even before news of the attack leaked out, LICA's attorney Moro Giafferi arrived to represent him.

At first Goebbels had overlooked the news from Paris. He had risen early on November 6 at Schwanenwerder to go to Fürstenberg to visit an N.S.V. (National Socialist Welfare) home for mothers and infants from Berlin. 'I think Magda's glad to see the back of me,' he wrote, still licking the emotional wounds sustained in the prolonged fray with his wife. Back in Berlin he went out with 'some people' to Erich Carow's Laugh-in, one of the premier cabarets in the city, and laughed himself sick-according to his doubtful diary – at a sketch titled 'Family Idyll.' There is little doubt who was its butt.[17]

On November 7, as he and Helldorff took the morning train to Munich, he ordered the shooting in Paris given only two inches on the *Völkischer Beobachter*'s second page.[18] Far more important was the solemn anniversary of the November 9, 1923 putsch, now a pivot of the Nazi calendar with speeches by Hitler and a midnight swearing-in ceremony for the S.S. Goebbels' diary shows

him conferring on the way down to Munich with his new chef de bureau Dr
Werner Naumann ('a decent chap'), with Minister of the Interior Dr Wilhelm
Frick on Reich reform, and Wilhelm Fanderl, editor of Berlin's *12 Uhr Blatt*.

THEN HOWEVER the condition of the shooting victim Ernst vom Rath took a
turn for the worse. Hitler ordered his immediate promotion – an ominous
sign that he was not expected to live. Otherwise his attitude was one of *laissez-
faire*; Goebbels however saw his chance. As surgeons battled to save the shot
diplomat, he swore to take revenge. He ordered press and radio to blame the
outrage on the 'international criminal Jewish rabble.'[19] *Angriff* published
photographs of Frankfurter, the killer of Gustloff, and of Grynszpan, the Paris
assassin, with pictures of the British politicians Winston Churchill, Clement
Attlee, and Duff Cooper, scurrilously captioned 'Jewish murderers and those
who put them up to it.' The party newspaper *Völkischer Beobachter* published a
whole page on the Paris murder attempt. Summarizing these events, Goebbels
wrote: 'But now [NOVEMBER 8] the German press makes itself heard. And
now we're using plain talk. Major antisemitic demonstrations in Hesse. The
synagogues are burned down. If only one could now give free rein to the
public's outrage!'[20]

On November 8 he conferred with propaganda officials in Munich. According
to his diary the topic was merely the Sudeten gau election campaign, but in the
light of antisemitic outbreaks in Hesse, Anhalt, and Saxony on that day and the
next, it certainly cannot be ruled out that he discussed reprisals for the Paris
outrage too. He then spent the afternoon working on his new Hitler book.
In the evening Hitler spoke in the Bürgerbäu to the party veterans, viciously
attacking Churchill, Eden, and Duff Cooper until tears of laughter streamed
down every cheek. 'He's rendering these three unfit for government office,'
wrote Goebbels, explaining Hitler's intent, 'and a good job too.' Afterward he
invited Hitler to his regular cafe, the Cafe Hoch on the Marienplatz, facing the
city hall. Until three A.M. they talked about horses, the Romanian monarchy,
punishments for reckless driving, and their future plans for Germany's screen
and stage. After that Goebbels carried on working back in his hotel, tired but
unable to sleep.[21]

The diary for the next day, the ninth, 'a gray November day,' opened with
the traditional march to the Feldherrnhalle watched by immense crowds. 'The
condition of the diplomat Rath shot by the Jew in Paris,' he noted, 'is still very
grave. The German press opens up with a will.' Helldorff sent instructions
to Berlin to disarm all the Jews. 'They've got a few things coming their way,'
commented Goebbels. He resumed work on his Hitler manuscript, finding
it a delight. More reports came in of demonstrations against the Jews, this
time in Kassel and Dessau, with synagogues being set on fire and businesses
demolished. Later that afternoon Goebbels learned that Rath had died of his
gunshot wounds. 'Enough is enough,' he wrote. At five P.M. the official press
agency released the news.[22]

Events that evening, November 9, are crucial to the history of what followed. As Goebbels and Hitler set out to attend the Nazi reception in the old city hall, they learned that the police were intervening against anti-Jewish demonstrators in Munich. Hitler remarked that the police should not crack down too harshly under the circumstances.[23] 'Colossal activity,' the Goebbels diary entry reports, then claims: 'I brief the Führer on the affair. He decides: Allow the demonstrations to continue. Hold back the police. The Jews must be given a taste of the public anger for a change.' Deciding, so he wrote, that this policy was right and proper, Goebbels issued his own instructions immediately to the police and party.[24] These instructions are confirmed by at least one gauleiter who recalled that an urgent telegram signed by 'Hanke' (as Staatssekretär) went to all forty-two of Goebbels' local propaganda agencies[25] transmitting instructions directly, over the heads of local gauleiters, to the district propaganda directors – who were party officials – to orchestrate outrages against Jewish properties in conjunction with the local S.A. units acting in plain clothes.[26] It was already very similar to what Goebbels had organized in Berlin that summer. He had consulted neither the party's gauleiters nor Lutze, the S.A. chief of staff, before issuing these instructions.

Hitler subsequently left the dinner at the old city hall around nine P.M. according to other sources.[27] Gauleiter Rudolf Jordan now told Goebbels of widespread anti-Jewish violence in Magdeburg.[28] According to Bormann's adjutant Heim, Goebbels seemed taken aback by this: things were getting out of hand and the carefully propagated image of German law and order was taking a battering.[29] Deciding to make a virtue out of necessity, at about nine-thirty he limped up to the podium, signaled for silence, and announced the death of the German diplomat and the spreading anti-Jewish incidents; he described the latter as evidence of a 'spontaneous' public outrage. The local British consulate learned that he also said that Jews were now fair game, and that 'the S.A. could do anything to them short of looting and plundering.'[30] He would not be surprised, another witness heard him say, 'if things got worse during the night.' The same witness saw Lutze however warn his old friend Goebbels that his S.A. men would keep well out of any pogrom.[31] Goebbels himself recorded that after issuing his instructions he had made a brief speech to the Party leaders, greeted by storms of applause. 'Everybody makes a beeline for the telephones,' his diary entry reads. 'Now the public will take action.'

Several people who heard Goebbels' firebrand speech were uncomfortable. Karl Hederich, one of his department heads, felt that it conflicted with the tenor of Hitler's speech.[32]

A few gau officials get cold feet [wrote Goebbels in his hitherto unpublished diary] but I keep pulling everybody together.[33] We must not allow this cowardly murder to go unpunished. Let things run their course. The Stosstrupp 'Hitler' [a shock-troop unit named after the Führer] sallies forth at once to deal with Munich. And things happen right away. A synagogue is smashed to smithereens. I try to save it from the flames, but fail.* Meanwhile I discuss financial issues with [the party treasurer Franz Xaver] Schwarz, the Jewish problem with [Julius] Streicher, and foreign policy with Ribbentrop: He too is of the opinion that we can now pull in the rest of Czechoslovakia by neutral methods. We just have to box cunning. [Czech foreign minister František] Chvalkovský wants it. As for the others, we don't know.

Over to [Munich] gau headquarters with [Gauleiter Adolf] Wagner. I now issue a detailed circular setting out what may be done [against the Jews] and what not. Wagner gets cold feet and trembles for his [i.e., Munich's] Jewish shops.[34] But I won't be deterred. Meanwhile the Stosstrupp goes about its business. And with no half measures. I direct [Werner] Wächter [director of the RPA, propaganda agency, in] Berlin to see that the synagogue in Fasanen Strasse is smashed. He just keeps saying, 'Honored to comply.'

It was by now midnight. Goebbels attended Himmler's impressive S.S. swearing-in ceremony at the Feldherrnhalle. Hitler spoke to these new officers, then went back to his apartment. Goebbels, leaving for his hotel, saw the skies flickering red. According to his diary – written up next morning – he hurried over to gau headquarters, where nobody could tell him what was happening, then directed fire brigades to douse the fires so far as necessary to protect neighboring buildings. 'The Stosstrupp has wrought terrible damage,' he wrote.

With many conflicting orders on the wires, a brutal confusion reigned all over Germany. At 3:30 A.M. the S.A. commander of Marburg ordered his men to burn down the local synagogue (despite Lutze's misgivings).[35] Every synagogue in Darmstadt was destroyed despite orders to the contrary from Mannheim's S.A. Gruppenführer Herbert Lust, still in Munich. The synagogues in Bayreuth, Bamberg, and Reutlingen were also torched.[36]

THERE SEEMS LITTLE DOUBT about Goebbels' sole personal guilt, that he was not just made the scapegoat for others even higher. In the subsequent internal inquiry, the party's Supreme Court headed by Walter Buch – admittedly no friend of his – determined that the propaganda minister had issued 'oral instructions' which had 'probably been understood by every party official present to mean that the party was not to appear publicly as the originator of the demonstration, but that it was in fact to take over its organization and execution.'[37] After hearing these instructions, repeated at first hand by a party official in Munich and so similar to Goebbels' orders to Helldorff in June, the commander of one S.A. Gruppe had telephoned orders to his headquarters in Kiel at 11:20 P.M. in the following terms: A Jew had fired the first shot; now the Jews must pay. There were 'totally superfluous' Jewish shops and synagogues

---

* This sentence is surely blatant window-dressing by Goebbels for posterity, given what we know.

in Friedrichsstadt, Kiel, and Lübeck waiting to be destroyed; the local police were to be tipped off first. 'There is to be no looting,' the message continued (significantly confirming the British consulate's version). 'Nobody is to be roughed up. Foreign Jews are not to be touched. Meet any resistance with firearms. The *Aktion* is to be carried out in plain clothes and must be finished by five A.M.'[38] Once again the similarities with Goebbels' own secret narrative of his orders for the anti-Jewish outrages in Berlin in June 1938 are worth remarking upon.

The pogrom was soon out of control. Only three of the twenty-eight S.A. *Gruppen* received actual orders to stage demonstrations.[39] Fired by five years of Nazi oratory however the mob needed little encouragement. From all over the Reich the reports began to come in: First fifty, then seventy-five synagogues on fire. By dawn on November the tenth, 191 of the country's fourteen hundred synagogues had been destroyed; about 7,500 of the one hundred thousand Jewish shops had had their windows smashed. Thirty-six of the country's half-million Jews had been murdered, and hundreds more badly beaten.[40] 'The Führer,' claimed Goebbels in the diary, 'has directed that twenty or thirty thousand Jews are to be arrested immediately. That'll do it. Let them now see that our patience is exhausted.'

> Wagner is still a bit half-hearted. But I don't let up. Wächter reports back to me, the order has been carried out.[41] We go with [Julius] Schaub to the Artistes' Club to await further bulletins. In Berlin five synagogues are ablaze, then fifteen. Now the people's fury is aroused. This night it is impossible to do anything else against it. Not that I want to. Let it rip.
>
> Schaub is on top form. His old *Stosstrupp* past comes flooding back.
>
> As I drive back to the hotel there is the sound of breaking glass. Bravo! Bravo! Like gigantic old kilns the synagogues are blazing. There is no danger to German property.
>
> Nothing else in particular has to be done. I try to sleep for a few hours.

As he wrote these heartless lines the next morning, the overnight reports came in. 'As was to be expected. The entire nation is in uproar. This is one dead man who is costing the Jews dear. Our darling Jews will think twice in future before simply gunning down German diplomats.' And that, he wrote, concluding this extraordinary, unrepentant diary entry, was the object of the exercise.[42]

WHAT OF HIMMLER and Hitler? Both were totally unaware of what Goebbels had done until the synagogue next to Munich's Four Seasons Hotel was set on fire around one A.M. Heydrich, Himmler's national chief of police, was relaxing down in the hotel bar; he told Karl Wolff to contact Himmler – who was at Hitler's apartment at Prinz-Regenten Platz, about to go on leave – then telexed instructions to all police authorities to restore law and order, protect Jews and Jewish properly, and halt any ongoing incidents.[43] The hotel management telephoned the adjutants at Hitler's apartment building, and thus he too learned that something was going on.[44] He sent for the local police chief, Friedrich von Eberstein. Eberstein found him livid with rage.[45]

According to Luftwaffe adjutant Nicolaus von Below, Hitler phoned Goebbels. 'What's going on?' he snapped, and: 'Find out!'

According to Julius Schaub, the most intimate of his aides, Hitler 'made a terrible scene with Goebbels' and left no doubt about the damage done abroad to Germany's name. He sent Schaub and his colleagues out into the streets to stop the looting (thus Schaub's postwar version).[46] Philipp Bouhler, head of the Führer's private chancellery, told one of Goebbels' senior officials that Hitler utterly condemned the pogrom and intended to dismiss Goebbels.[47] Fritz Wiedemann, another of Hitler's adjutants, saw Goebbels spending much of that night of November 9–10 'telephoning . . . to halt the most violent excesses.'[48] At 2:56 A.M. Rudolf Hess's staff also began cabling, telephoning, and radioing instructions to gauleiters and police authorities around the nation to halt the damage to property.[49] But twenty thousand Jews were already being loaded onto trucks and transported to the concentration camps at Dachau, Buchenwald, and Oranienburg. Hitler made no attempt to halt this inhumanity. He stood by, and thus he too deserved the odium that now fell on all Germany.

Goebbels had anticipated neither Hitler's fury nor, probably, such an uncontrollable, chaotic orgy of destruction. Not surprisingly he made no reference to this unwelcome turn of events in his diary. But perhaps this, rather than Lida Baarova, was the reason why he would write this *mea culpa* to Hitler six years later: 'In the twenty years that I have been with you, particularly in 1938 and 1939, I have occasioned you much private grief.'[50] Ribbentrop relates that when he tackled Hitler about the damage Goebbels had done, Hitler rejoined that this was true, but he could not let the propaganda minister go – not when he was just about to need him again.[51]

As more ugly bulletins rained down on him the next morning, November 10, 1938, Goebbels went to see Hitler to discuss 'what to do next' – there is surely an involuntary hint of apprehension in the phrase.[52] Georg Wilhelm Müller of his ministry had meanwhile reported to him about the conflagrations in Berlin. Goebbels told his diary only, 'A good thing too,' but he immediately composed an ordinance calling a halt to 'operations' (*Aktionen*), and at ten A.M. he broadcast a live appeal for order over the Deutschland-Sender. While it spoke of the 'justifiable and comprehensible' public indignation at the Ernst vom Rath murder, it strictly forbade all further action against the Jews; it was repeated at hourly intervals and printed in next day's party newspapers.[53] The Jewish question, the item stated, would be resolved only by due process of law.

Later that morning Goebbels directed that press and radio were to play down the damage – a few windows had been smashed and synagogues had caught fire, but otherwise, the news items were to suggest, 'the public's understandable indignation was its spontaneous answer to the murder of the embassy counselor.' 'Enough is enough,' the propaganda minister commented in his diary. 'If we let it continue, there's a danger that the mob will take over. In the whole country the synagogues have been burned down.' He repeated yet again, with grim and vengeful satisfaction, 'Jewry is having to pay dear for this dead man.'[54]

He made his report (on 'what to do next') to Hitler in the Osteria, the Führer's favorite Italian restaurant, and was careful to record this – perhaps slanted – note in his diary, which stands alone, and in flagrant contradiction to the evidence of Hitler's entire immediate entourage: 'He is in agreement with everything. His views are quite radical and aggressive. The *Aktion* itself went off without a hitch. A hundred dead. But no German property damaged.' Each of these five sentences was untrue, as will be seen. Goebbels continued: 'With minor alterations the Führer authorizes my decree re breaking off the *Aktionen*. I issue it immediately through the press. The Führer wants to proceed to very harsh measures against the Jews. They must repair their shops themselves. The insurance companies will pay them nothing. Then the Führer wants Jewish businesses gradually expropriated and their owners compensated with paper which we can [illegible word: repudiate?] at any time. Meanwhile people are starting with their own *Aktionen*. I issue appropriate secret decrees. We're waiting to see the repercussions abroad. For the time being there is silence there. But the hullabaloo will come.'

Despite the toughing-it-out tone of these entries, there are more than enough hints that Goebbels was deeply concerned by the extent of the pogrom and its effect on foreign opinion; and that he had hastily thrown everything into reverse. He hoped, he wrote, that the *Judenaktion* was over for the time being – 'Provided there aren't any sequels,' he added with ill-concealed nervousness. But his troubles were just beginning.

> I speak on the phone with Heyderich [*sic.* Heydrich]. The police bulletin from the entire Reich conforms with my own information. Order has been restored everywhere. Only in Bremen have there been ugly excesses. But they submerge from view in the overall Aktion. I arrange with Heyderich how the party and police are to cooperate on this. Work on until evening. Reports come in from Berlin about really serious antisemitic outbreaks there. The public has taken over. But now there really must be an end to it. I have appropriate directives issued to the police and party.

Signing as the party's national director of propaganda, Goebbels issued a confidential 'communiqué' to all gau propaganda officials (printed opposite). It specifically alluded to his earlier orders (which are missing from the archives): 'I refer,' it began, 'to my today's announcement re ending the anti-Jewish demos and *Aktionen*.'

> Together with the police, all gau headquarters are to take all due steps to make good the demolished Jewish shops in the shortest possible time at the expense of their Jewish owners.

Nationalsozialistische Deutsche Arbeiterpartei

Gauleitung Bayerische Ostmark

Gaugeschäftsstelle:
Bayreuth, Maxstraße 2
Fernsprecher Nummer 1002, 1003, 1005, 1026
Postscheckkonto Amt Nürnberg Nr. 29497

Tageszeitung des Gaues: „Bayerische Ostmark", 33 Ausgaben
Geschäftsstelle und Hauptschriftleitung aller Zeitungen:
Gauverlag Bayerische Ostmark Gmb.H., Bayreuth, Blumenstraße 22
Telefon Nummer 1292, 1293, 1294, 1295

Der Gaupropagandaleiter	Schnellbrief	Bayreuth, den 10.11.1938.

34.

Zeichen, Datum und Gegenstand bei
Antwort anzugeben!
Ihr Zeichen:
Gegenstand:

Streng vertraulich !
=============================

An alle Kreisleiter und Kreispropagandaleiter

des Gaues Bayerische Ostmark .

Von nachstehender Bekanntmachung des Reichspropagandaleiters
Pg. Dr. Goebbels bitte ich Kenntnis zu nehmen.

streng vertraulich!

Heil Hitler !

Im Auftrag:

Krüger

Gauhauptstellenleiter.

"Ich verweise auf meine heutige Bekanntmachung betreffs
Beendigung der antijüdischen Kundgebungen und Aktionen,
die auch bereits durch Presse und Rundfunk veröffentlicht
worden ist. Die Gauleitungen haben zusammen mit der Polizei
entsprechende Maßnahmen zu treffen, daß die demolierten
Judengeschäfte in kürzester Zeit auf Kosten ihrer jüdischen
Inhaber wieder in Ordnung gebracht werden.
Es steht eine Verordnung zu erwarten, nach der die Schäden,
die bei den antijüdischen Aktionen entstanden sind, nicht
von den Versicherungen getragen werden, sondern von den be-
troffenen Juden selbst. Weiterhin werden in kurzer Frist
noch eine Reihe von Maßnahmen gegen die Juden auf dem Ge-
setzes- oder Verordnungswege durchgeführt werden. Über diese
werde ich Sie rechtzeitig unterrichten.
Die antijüdischen Aktionen müssen mit derselben Schnellig-
keit, mit der sie entstanden sind, nunmehr eingestellt werden. Sie haben den ihnen gewünschten und erwarteten Zweck
erfüllt. Sollte sich durch Vorgänge im Judentum des In- oder
Auslandes eine neue Lage ergeben, so wird rechtzeitig Mit-
teilung ergehen.   Heil Hitler !
                              gez.Dr. G o e b b e l s

On November 10, 1938 Goebbels issued 'in strict confidence' an urgent circular
telegram to all gau propaganda chiefs halting the *Aktionen* against the Jews which he
himself had ordered the day before (YIVO ARCHIVES, NEW YORK)

He gave notice that a government ordinance would follow voiding the liability of insurance companies to pay out on Jewish claims. 'Moreover a series of measures will shortly be enacted against the Jews. . .' Most significant was the document's last paragraph: 'The anti-Jewish *Aktionen* must now be called off with the same rapidity with which they were launched. They have served their desired and anticipated purpose.'[55] It is worth remarking that Goebbels felt comfortable issuing *orders* both to other gauleiters and to police.[56]

That evening Hitler received four hundred leading pressmen in the Führer Building and delivered an extraordinary secret speech to them. He made no mention of the pogrom, and no secret of his admiration for Dr Goebbels' *propaganda* triumphs.[57] Goebbels sat up until midnight listening to Hitler debating with the journalists, then 'had to' leave, as he put it, for Berlin. The foreign radio stations were now full of the pogrom. Things were getting out of hand. 'I assume full authority for Berlin,' he wrote. 'At such times of crisis, one man must take charge.'[58] Hitler stayed in Munich, perhaps keeping as much distance as possible from Dr Goebbels.

WERNER NAUMANN, who traveled back to Berlin with the minister, would state that Goebbels fulminated with suppressed anger against the extent of the pogrom and issued a public dressing down to his deputies Görlitzer (in the Berlin gau) and Wächter (in the Reichspropagandaleitung, the party's propaganda headquarters) for the synagogue fires when they met him on the railroad platform early on November 11.[59] Given the content of Goebbels' diary – as he and Wächter knew, he himself had ordered the synagogues destroyed – this scene displays nothing but his utter cynicism.

He drove straight out to Schwanenwerder for Magda's birthday. The broken glass had been swept away, the shattered store fronts were already boarded up. 'In Berlin,' he recorded, 'everything has remained calm during the night.' With further breathtaking cynicism he took the credit with his radio broadcast. 'The Jews,' he added, 'ought to be downright grateful to me.'[60]

Rattled by the mounting global outrage over the pogrom, he called one hundred and fifty foreign journalists into his ministry at two-thirty P.M. The atmosphere was icy. 'Explained the whole thing to them,' he told his diary. But the journalists found him pasty, haggard, and ill at ease. 'You can't blame me for what happened,' he said. 'Why, I was in Munich. . .'[61] He claimed that the Reich frowned upon such 'spontaneous' demonstrations – but that the wrath of the people this time had been too great to contain, and that the police could scarcely open fire on crowds with whom they sympathized. Shrugging off any personal responsibility he scoffed: 'If I, Dr Goebbels, had organized the demonstration, the result would have been very different.' To his listeners he seemed unconvincing, self-contradictory, and confused.[62] (A few days later the foreign press corps howled with glee when Louis Lochner told a departing colleague, 'I think you will agree that our efficient secretary managed to organize a very fine *spontaneous* demonstration for you.')[63]

Still unashamed, Goebbels and Hans Hinkel, head of the Jewish desk at his ministry, drafted petty and repressive ordinances denying Jews access to all places of public entertainment henceforth. 'This takes the whole question a great step forward,' he congratulated himself.

WHILE FOREIGN MINISTER von Ribbentrop earned grudging praise for his handling of the protests abroad,[64] Dr Goebbels found himself a pariah in official Berlin. He had to seize and suppress all the foreign newspapers for several days.[65] Lutze entered in his diary: 'Much wailing provoked abroad, but even at home opinions sharply diverge.'[66] Rosenberg, who detected Goebbels' hand and no other behind the pogrom, shrewdly put the cost to the German economy at roughly two years' Winter Relief.[67]

Goebbels however would brag that he had proved that the Jews could be eliminated from the economy, whatever Funk said to the contrary.[68] 'Goebbels,' wrote one German diplomat, 'has seldom found less credibility than for his claim that a "spontaneous outburst of public rage" led to the violence.' Hess confirmed that in his view Goebbels was alone to blame.[69] Hess ordered the Gestapo and the party's courts to delve into the origins of the night's violence and turn the culprits over to the public prosecutors.[70] A top Nazi official advised Hess that there was 'nationwide antipathy to Goebbels.'[71] Heydrich also blamed him. Himmler was furious that Goebbels had issued orders to his police force.[72] 'The order was given by the Propaganda Directorate [R.P.L., i.e., Goebbels wearing his party hat],' minuted Himmler privately, 'and I suspect that Goebbels, in his craving for power, which I noticed long ago, and also in his empty-headedness, started this action just at a time when the foreign political situation is very grave. . . When I asked the Führer about it, I had the impression that he did not know anything about these events.'[73] Many of Goebbels' colleagues wondered if he might be going mad. 'Is Goebbels losing touch with reality?' speculated one minister.[74]

Rosenberg's damage estimate, a hundred million marks, was well short of the true cost of Goebbels' folly. The reality was that German insurance companies would have to pay out for the senseless damage, since most of the destroyed buildings were German-owned; even the plundered stocks were often German-owned, and merely sold by the Jews on commission. On November 11 Göring told all the other gauleiters that he would not tolerate any recurrences. He praised Karl Kaufmann and the others who had abstained from the public violence, and said he was going to insist that Hitler get rid of Goebbels.[75]

At a Cabinet-level conference held the next morning at the air ministry building, Field Marshal Göring roared at Goebbels: 'What the Public needs is a bit more *Enlightenment*!' – an allusion to Goebbels' full title.[76] Repairing the plate-glass windows alone would cost Germany nearly five million marks in scarce foreign currency.[77] Goebbels afterward recorded, 'Heated arguments about the situation. I hold out for a radical viewpoint. Funk a bit weak and wobbly.' They agreed to levy a billion-mark ($250 million) collective fine on the Jewish community for vom Rath's murder, and to take the remaining steps necessary to exclude the Jews from the German economy.[78] With once again less than total honesty Goebbels' diary continued, 'I am cooperating splendidly with Göring. He's going to crack down on them too. The radical line has won.' After drafting a strongly worded communiqué he commented for the *n*th time, 'This is one corpse that's going to cost the Jews a packet.'[79]

He was unrepentant. Interviewed by Reuters chief correspondent Gordon Young that day he dismissed the pogrom as Germany's internal affair. As for the billion-mark fine, he said that the Jews' assets in Germany alone were eight times that figure. Future harmony would depend on their accepting their status in the Reich – 'namely that of a foreign race whom we recognize to be antagonistic to the German people.'[80]

Göring's criticism had sunk in. Visiting working-class Wedding on the thirteenth, Goebbels warned the proletariat in stern language to abstain from further *Aktionen* which would henceforth only damage their own economy.[81] The wider damage had however already been done. Washington recalled the American ambassador.[82] Foreign diplomats reported that Goebbels now outranked both Ribbentrop and Himmler in unpopularity.[83] This was not his own view. After rattling a Winter Relief collecting box outside the Hotel Adlon he recorded for posterity, 'I am very happy that the public loves me so much.'[84]

LATE ON NOVEMBER 15, 1938 Hitler finally returned to Berlin.[85] 'He's in fine fettle,' found Goebbels. 'Sharply against the Jews. Thoroughly endorses my, and our, policies.'[86] (A revealing self-correction – because crossing out the original possessive adjective, my, would have been too obvious.)

All speculation among his fellow ministers about Goebbels' future was however now dispelled: In a public display of support Hitler escorted him to the formal reopening of the rebuilt Schiller Theater that evening, invited Goebbels and Magda to share his box, and stayed the night at Schwanenwerder with them.[87] They all talked until nearly three A.M. (Goebbels then blarneyed for five more hours with Magda). Hitler stayed over at their villa all the next day, conferring with his generals and ministers about the threat that Prague still posed.[88]

Thus the public were to believe that Goebbels still enjoyed Hitler's favor. He resumed work on 'Hitler the Man,' his doomed biography. For an hour or two Hitler frolicked with the Goebbels children. 'All great plans are forged in one's youth,' he told their chastened but grateful father before leaving for Rath's state funeral in Düsseldorf, 'because you still have an imagination then.'

'I found that too,' remarked Goebbels in his diary.[89]

For a while, he believed himself immortal again.

33: On the Verge

NINETEEN THIRTY-EIGHT HAS BEEN a traumatic year for Dr Goebbels. As the New Year, 1939, is rung in, he writes: 'I'd rather go hang myself.'[1] 'I have gained many gray hairs over the last year,' he will add a few weeks later.[2]

Denied marital comforts by Magda for months on end, he allows masculine frustration to overwhelm ministerial prudence. He invites a Miss U. to his study, offers routine pleasantries about her latest movie, presses a check for several thousand marks upon her, and invites her out one day – she assumes to a movie. His car picks her up after dark near the Kroll Opera house. Miss U. nervously has her fiancé follow, but Goebbels' supercharged Mercedes soon shakes him off. Rach drives them out to Lanke. A cold buffet is waiting inside the villa. Seeing the piano, she mentions that she can play. He says that two can play, but when it appears that he has a different tune in mind she fends him off vigorously. Goebbels snaps: 'You must know whom you're dealing with. I'm one of the dozen most important men in Europe!' He drives her back to Berlin in a cold fury, and instructs Rach to halt before the end of the autobahn. 'The lady is alighting here,' he instructs.[3] This victim immediately places herself at Magda's disposal.[4]

By early December 1938 the three-month probationary period is already forgotten. Magda tells her father, now a wealthy industrialist in Duisburg, that she has decided to leave Goebbels for good – perhaps even to emigrate. Her father welcomes her decision. Referring to the 'prevailing tense circumstances,' he assures her: 'Given recent events I agree more than ever with the decisions you tell me of. Be of good heart, my child. Your father has now grown even larger and more independent and you will always find with him, whether at home or abroad, a secure and financially adequate refuge for yourself and your children.'[5]

Goebbels is almost inured to these agonies. After speaking with Magda ('the same old melody') he falls seriously ill.[6] Stomach X-rays reveal no organic disorder. The doctors diagnose nervous complications. He takes to his bed, and for the first time in fifteen years he writes no diary for two weeks.[7] Professor Sauerbruch orders him into the La Charité hospital. Suspecting him of malingering, Magda makes a beeline for the Führer with fresh complaints about his behavior. When she visits the hospital it is just to bespatter him with more matrimonial bile. It is a fair assumption that there is a link between these reproaches and the anonymous large bouquet that arrives for him. On his discharge he spends a lonesome Christmas at his citadel; his family are next door – they leave him lying there alone the whole evening. When Staatssekretär Hanke visits on official business, it is a frosty affair. A sympathetic letter from Funk cheers him up. Funk is one of the few people he can depend on. Funk, and the Führer. Hitler invites him down to the Obersalzberg. Before leaving, Dr Goebbels tries one more approach to Magda, but she launches into more 'speculations,' and he rushes off yelping. 'I don't know her any more,' he laments.[8]

On Hitler's mountain, Goebbels finds he is once again relegated to the guesthouse. 'I live here in splendid isolation,' he writes, making a virtue out of his humiliation. Hitler invites him up to the Berghof for some blunt talking. 'I shall pass over the details here,' writes Goebbels bleakly. The plain speaking continues for four hours the next day. When Hitler leaves for Berlin, Goebbels stays on at the Obersalzberg to convalesce. He is at breaking point. 'From Berlin' – he writes Berlin but means Magda – 'I hear not a word. Not that I want to anyway.'[9] 'It's just that I can't sleep at night. Then comes the anger, and the rage, and the hate.'[10]

Max Amann breaks to him the bad news that Hitler has forbidden publication of Goebbels' biography of him. Accustomed only to censoring others, Goebbels finds it a bitter blow.[11] Later he will concede that Hitler was right, the manuscript was just a hasty pot-boiler.[12] Returning to Berlin on Thursday January 17, 1939 he realizes: 'I am on the verge of a nervous breakdown.'[13] Seeing Hitler at midday he talks about everything other than what's really on his mind. The next afternoon he ventures out to Schwanenwerder, ostensibly to see the children; he stays at the citadel. By the next day he and Magda have reached an unusual agreement, brokered by Hitler.[14] Goebbels will sign a document binding him to one year's good behavior. Magda agrees to remain outwardly his wife meanwhile, after which she can divorce him if she wishes. He may appear at Schwanenwerder only by prior invitation.[15] (It is precisely the kind of matrimonial truce that Goebbels himself had proposed during the divorce-law discussions in Cabinet two years before.)[16] Hitler offers to act as guarantor.

For two hours the two men stroll around Speer's new chancellery building, talking this irksome affair over. To allow it to consume so much of his time Hitler must have had a monumental patience, or a real and enduring fondness for Magda. Her draft of the agreement seems very businesslike. Hitler runs his eye over it and suggests a few minor changes. They all sign it at Schwanenwerder on January 22 – the only peace treaty to which Hitler will ever set his name.[17] 'The best thing will be for you to live like a monk,' he tells the minister. 'And you, madam, should live like a nun.' 'Mein Führer, I have been living like a nun for a year already,' she retorts. Goebbels persuades Hitler to write a certain letter to her – it has not survived – and hopes the affair is closed.[18] It has obscured his entire horizon for months.

Their strained marriage is the whisper of all Germany. Scandalized travelers say he has twenty-three illegitimate children.[19] Foreign newspapers report that he has been dismissed, and that he is to answer charges before a Nazi tribunal about his private life. They remark on his absence from a dinner for foreign journalists.[20] 'Aggravation upon aggravation,' records Goebbels. 'And I've got to swallow hard.' 'There's no end to the rumors and scuttlebutt,' he adds the next day. 'I'm suffering agonies.'[21] An official informs Hanke that even the charwomen are talking about the minister in the 'most contemptuous' terms.[22] Himmler tells Rosenberg at this time that Magda has complained of 'dozens' of infidelities by her husband. 'The women are now lining up to dictate affidavits – both for Mrs G. and for the Gestapo – on how he coerced them,' says Himmler. 'I've handed some of these statements to the Führer.' Unusually well-informed, Himmler adds that in October Magda has given her husband three months to come to heel; in January the time is up.[23]

It has taxed even Hitler's powers of persuasion to induce Magda to return to the conjugal home, reports one major fleeing Germany, to British officers.[24] Grimly, she fulfills her new contractual obligations. The photographers capture pictures of her at the press ball, sitting blank-faced and embittered at her unloved husband's side.[25]

'GOEBBELS,' COMMENTED ROSENBERG with satisfaction on February 6, 'has no friends. Even his hirelings curse him.' Some Nazis felt that he had harmed their movement by his personal behavior and the crudity of his propaganda. One Hitler Youth leader remarked that 'nobody' approved of his anti-Jewish measures.[26] He had regimented and punished, censored and sanitized the media to the consistency of a bland brown pudding, then criticized their lack of individuality. The newsreels were uniformly dull, featuring their beloved Führer so often that even he complained.[27] Lively, thinking newspapers were suppressed, while Streicher's loathsome organ Der Stürmer appeared unmolested.[28] Even popular writers like Hans Grimm were called before Goebbels to be screamed at, for not ending letters with 'Heil Hitler' and for not attending the Weimar literary convention. 'If you don't toe the line I'll break you,' shouted Goebbels, 'whatever the wailing from abroad. Just as I broke Furtwängler. I throw writers like you into concentration camp for four months – and the next time after that they never get out again.'[29]

He censored the latest dance steps, and found nothing absurd in erecting enamel plates in dance halls reading 'Jazz dancing forbidden.'[30] Just once he professed to see the funny side of foreign caricatures of himself.[31] More often he reacted viciously. He took the usual steps to neutralize the acid of political satire. Oblivious of how ludicrous he seemed, he entered pompously in his diary: 'Cranked up the prohibition machinery against the Kabarett der Komiker.'[32] He expelled five of its comedians from the chamber of culture, while announcing a joke contest to prove that the Reich had not lost its sense of humor.[33] In March 1939 he paid a surprise visit to the cabaret, found it packed and totally non-political. 'So it works. You only need a firm hand to get your own way.'[34]

Power had corroded his sense of proportion. He had become more corrupt than the most gluttonous Jewish magnates of his popular invective. At taxpayers' expense he was yet again remodeling his official residence. It was scheduled for completion by July 15, 1939. Its household staff of eighteen would be paid for from his ministry's secret fund.[35] He had installed a private apartment in his ministry. He had the sole use for life of the lakeside villa on the Bogensee at Lanke. He owned outright two luxury properties on the exclusive Schwanenwerder lakeshore. At the nadir of his nervous breakdown in January 1939 he still found the strength to order work to begin on a palatial mansion on the far side of the Bogensee, fencing off a total of 3,200 hectares (eight thousand acres) of woodland in one of Berlin's favorite beauty spots.[36]

Together with Hanke, whose sins he had evidently forgiven, Goebbels paced off the new site and observed incongruously in his diary, 'At least I'll have one place to call home.'[37] His private architect Hugo Bartels promised to have this new refuge ready for his birthday in October 1939. By May, 129 men were laboring on this new Haus am Bogensee. Even after the war broke out construction would continue at the same pace. A letter from Bartels hints at some of the amenities that Goebbels was installing – including a wine cellar and unheard of luxuries like an air-conditioned beer cellar and a refrigerated pastry-cooling table.[38] 'It's going to be beautiful,' he wrote after working on the blueprints, 'but unfortunately a bit expensive. It's laid out on a generous scale, and meant to last a lifetime.'[39] The Haus am Bogensee would ultimately have a small guesthouse, a private cinema, and five bedrooms, including separate rooms for Goebbels and Magda. The architects had provided air conditioning, a disappearing bar, and a large picture window which sank with a faint whir into the floor at the touch of a brass button.[40] The inventory of furnishings would fill twenty-eight pages of single-spaced typescript.

The average Berliner probably knew none of this. To ingratiate himself with them he put on his old trench-coat on November 28, 1938, and made heavily publicized visits to slum-dwellings while reporters took down every word for publication in *Angriff* two days later. 'Heil Hitler, Mrs B – !' he exclaimed. 'Might I look at your apartment for a moment?' 'This man is to have a new apartment, Wächter! Take this down. . .' He allocated two million marks to slum clearance from the fine levied on the Jews.[41]

In a raucous speech to Berlin propaganda workers on November 22 he claimed proof that the Jews had planned the Gustloff and Rath murders long in advance; and, as for the alleged plundering during the pogrom, the reality had been different: Markgraf, the famous jewelers, had not been plundered at all, he said, but had concealed their stock in a nearby hotel 'for safety.' (The next day he told the same story to Hitler, who laughed out loud.)[42] When a British member of parliament suggested resettling Germany's Jews in Britain, Goebbels maliciously applauded: 'I expect it will be a great satisfaction for the British people to assist the much respected Jews from their tremendous financial resources.' That was the problem, he noted: everybody wanted to help the Jews out – but nobody wanted them.⁴³

At a secret ministerial conference a few weeks later, the stenographic record quotes him as saying:

> It is immaterial how the Jewish problem is actually solved, perhaps by denoting some region of the globe later on for the creation of a Jewish state. But it is remarkable that the states whose public opinion is in favor of the Jews all refuse to accept our Jews from us. They say they are magnificent pioneers of culture, and geniuses in economics, diplomacy, philosophy, and poetry, yet the moment we try to press one of these geniuses upon them, they clamp down their frontiers: 'No, no! We don't want them!' I think it must be unique in the history of the world, people turning down geniuses.⁴⁴

Goebbels set up an institute to research the Jewish problem and flood the media with pseudo-scientific articles.⁴⁵ 'We're gradually crowding the Jews together,' he recorded. 'This will release space for the German workers.'⁴⁶

LENI RIEFENSTAHL, RETURNING from Hollywood, confirmed that the Jews were everywhere there.⁴⁷ Although he secretly enjoyed watching American movies like Walt Disney's *Snow White* with his family, he forbade their general release both to save foreign currency and to get his own back for the American–Jewish boycott of Germany's films.⁴⁸ He assiduously pandered to Hitler's lowbrow movie tastes, giving him eighteen Mickey Mouse cartoons for Christmas 1937.⁴⁹ The Führer demanded a copy of the Sherlock Holmes thriller *The Hound of the Baskervilles* as a permanent loan to his movie library.⁵⁰ His obiter dicta on films had the force of law even for Goebbels. *Tarzan* was bad, *Woman at the Wheel* was very bad; and he walked right out of *Madame Dubarry*.⁵¹ Goebbels intervened at every level of movie production, personally editing *In the Name of the People* and the latest Veit Harlan movie *Immortal Heart*, and ordering key scenes of *Hotel Sacher* shot again.⁵² He put sound financial brains in charge of the major studios, with capable artistic directors like Emil Jannings at Ufa, Ewald von Demandowsky at Tobis, Hans Schweikart at Bavaria, Karl Hartl at Tobis-Sascha, and Alfred Greven, a world-war fighter pilot, at Terra.⁵³ (It was around Greven that his next major personal crisis would revolve.)

UPSET BY THE ESTRANGEMENT from Magda and preoccupied with the financial crisis that he had inflicted on himself by his extravagant new plans for Lanke, Goebbels brooded far into the spring of 1939.

Max Amann had invited him to write an article each week for the *Völkischer Beobachter*. Putting on his eyeglasses, he dictated an effortless diatribe against the United States.⁵⁴ Brilliantly composed and elegantly argued, these articles would flow forth like a river of strychnine over the next five years. Usually he hit upon their titles before actually writing the contents.⁵⁵ The articles betrayed his newfound mistrust of the British, in line with Hitler's reluctant acceptance that war with Britain was now inevitable.[56] He did not doubt, he wrote, that the British would defend their way of life to the utmost – they would fight to the last Frenchman, the last Russian, and the last American, if need be.[57]

NEITHER HE NOR HITLER knew for sure what to do next. Opening the Sudeten election campaign at Reichenberg on November 19, 1938 Goebbels, mimicking Hitler's favorite argument, had said, 'When one has the feeling that the time is ripe, that the Goddess of History is descending on Earth, and that the hem of her mantle is touching mankind, then responsible men must have the courage to grasp the hem and not let go.'[58] For a few days in December the possibility of wresting Memel, Germany's ancient port on the Baltic, from Lithuanian control again surfaced.[59] Goebbels damped down speculation. Addressing the Reichstag at the end of January Hitler warned the international Jewish community against provoking a new world war.[60] He told Goebbels that he planned to think over his next moves at the Berghof.

'Perhaps,' speculated Goebbels, 'it's the Czechs' turn again.'[61] Going straight for the Ukraine next would require Polish complicity. At lunch two days later Hitler was still preoccupied with foreign policy decisions. 'He is hatching new plans again,' observed Goebbels. 'A real Napoleon!'[62] The propaganda minister headlined his next article, 'Is war in sight?' In it he fulminated against the British *News Chronicle* – he shortly expelled its Berlin correspondent Ian Colvin. He railed at the communists in New York, at *The Times*' correspondent in Washington, at President Roosevelt, and at the BBC's German service. Germany, he insisted, desired nothing but peace.[63]

Goebbels tried hard to restore his damaged image over the coming year. On the other side of town, Magda let down her hair, modernized her hairstyle, wore make-up, partied, and drank.[64] Goebbels importuned her by phone to join him at the occasional official function, but she rarely did. Early in March he noted without comment that she was busy getting ready for a trip to Italy.[65] Albert Speer had invited her, traveling under an assumed name, to join several other couples including Hitler's surgeon Karl Brandt, touring southern Italy and Sicily, and they left Berlin on the evening of March 9.

THE VERY NEXT DAY the Nazis' months of subversion in Slovakia paid off. For weeks since Munich Hitler's agents had been fomenting discord there. Slovakia declared herself independent from Prague. On the tenth Prague sent in troops to arrest the Slovak prime minister Father Tiso. This was the opportunity Hitler wanted, to 'solve the problem we left half-solved in October,' as Goebbels put it. Springing into action Hitler sent for Goebbels at midday and for Ribbentrop and Keitel soon after. He told them he had decided to march into the rest of the hybrid Czech state on Wednesday the fifteenth and seize Prague. 'Our frontier must extend to the Carpathians,' Goebbels penned into his hitherto unpublished diaries: 'The Ides of March.'

We fix all the details already. We are after all well versed in this now. I recall Berndt and Bömer [domestic and foreign press department heads] from leave. . . We're all very pleased, even Ribbentrop. The Führer shouts with joy. This is going to be a pushover. We'll start broadcasting Slovakian bulletins from our [black] Vienna transmitter. I'll turn the volume up over the next three days to full blast. . . In the afternoon I work out the battle plan on my own. I think it's going to be another masterpiece of strategy and diplomacy.

Late in the afternoon over to the Führer again. We infer from one report that before its arrest the Tiso regime appealed in despair to the German government. The actual text can always be obtained later. The Führer says, and rightly so, that you can't make history with lawyers. You've got to have heart, head, and courage – just what lawyers lack. In the evening, at my suggestion, the Führer visits the People's Theater to put up a façade.

Afterward he sat sipping tea with Hitler until four A.M. in the Artistes' Club – 'We have our alibi,' wrote Goebbels, ignoring the word's criminal connotations. Upsetting Hitler's cynical plot, Tiso refused to sign the appeal for German help that Hitler had sent him. The steam was going out of the plan.[66] Next day Berndt reported in, and Goebbels jokingly appointed the thickset, burly Nazi propagandist his 'Reich Rumor-monger.' It was the Sudeten crisis all over again.

That evening, March 11, he viewed several films, including *The Sweetheart*, starring Lida Baarova, a 'wonderful, poetic and moving love story' which deeply upset him; he drove out to Lanke to sleep it off amid the snow and ice of a winter that had suddenly arrived.[67] (He had not seen Lida since, so the story goes, she had abruptly materialized before him, mischievously disguised in a wig, at a Winter Relief collection.[68]) The news during the night from Bratislava, Slovakia's capital, was distressingly calm. With the activists in jail, the momentum had gone. 'The attempt to whip things up with our S.S. has only partly succeeded. It looks as if Slovakia's not playing along,' noted Goebbels in disappointment. Moreover Prague too was refusing to be provoked this time.

'So we're going to make history there ourselves,' noted Goebbels. He discussed the psychological aspects with Hitler at midday on the twelfth; they decided to keep the crisis out of the editorials, the press must wear an impenetrable mask until Wednesday, the day itself. 'If only we had . . . an appeal for aid or military intervention,' lamented Goebbels. 'That would make it all so simple.'

All day long the messengers scurried between his ministry and Hitler's chancellery, while the Berlin public had not an inkling of what was brewing.[69] That night, after another 'alibi' visit to an operetta, Goebbels and Hitler stayed up until three A.M. talking foreign policy. Ribbentrop, recorded Goebbels afterward, 'takes the view that there's bound to be a conflict with Britain later. The Führer is preparing for it, but he does not consider it inevitable. . . There is a heated argument.'[70]

Still the foreign press acted as though nothing was happening. Early next morning, Monday March 13, Hitler sent for Goebbels to agree on leaflets for the invasion of Prague. While Goebbels, back at his ministry, drafted the wording – 'any resistance will be bloodily put down' – his children came for half an hour to rumster around, a family idyll, on the irony of which he himself commented.

That afternoon Germany's newspapers suddenly opened fire, roaring with one voice a broadside of rage at Prague. 'Berndt . . . is the best man for such jobs,' Goebbels recognized. 'Now the cat is out of the bag.' London and Paris expressed disinterest in Prague's fate.

Over to the Führer in the evening. He has received Tiso. Explained to him that Slovakia's historic hour has come. If they don't act they'll be swallowed up by Hungary. He is to think it over and go back to Bratislava. No revolutions, it must all be constitutional and above board. Not that we expect very much from him. But that doesn't matter now.

The Führer goes over his plan once more. Within five days the whole operation will be over. On the first day we'll already be in Prague. Our planes within two hours in fact. I think we'll pull it off without significant bloodshed. And then the Führer intends to take a lengthy political breather. Amen! I can't believe it, it's too good to be true.[71]

The next morning, March 14, Tiso persuaded his Slovak parliament to declare independence from Prague, but 'not, as at first reported, with an appeal to Berlin for aid.' The Slovaks wanted no German troops. 'Our press,' wrote Goebbels, 'rampages just like last September.' London and Paris still kept well out: 'Once bitten, twice shy!' was his assessment. He had printed twenty-five million leaflets overnight. At midday Hitler discussed with him the new statute for Bohemia and Moravia, as Prague's territories would be styled. ('We order that the name Czechoslovakia is not to be used any more,' noted Goebbels, ordering swift research to back up Germany's historic claim to these regions. 'We shall speak of Bohemia and Moravia as ancient German territories.')

They would be left largely to govern themselves. 'The Czechs will not be germanized, but will enjoy the protection of the Reich's military, foreign, and economic policies.' Hitler told him the Wehrmacht would cross the frontier at six A.M. No sooner had Goebbels predicted that the Czechs would come cap in hand than they did just that. Emil Hácha, Beneš' successor, arranged to come by special train to Berlin immediately. 'Meanwhile we have the first troops move into Czech territory. So Hácha can see what's what.' S.S. units stealthily crossed into Moravian Ostrau and Witkowitz, to prevent the Poles seizing the steel mills there; resistance in two places was quickly broken. Hácha arrived with his foreign minister from Prague that evening. 'The Führer,' recorded his admiring propaganda minister, 'has them wait until midnight, slowly and surely wearing them out. That's what they did with us at Versailles. The tried and tested methods of political tactics.'

The tension mounts as we all wait for the outcome of their talks. . . Once, Hácha collapses in a faint, then they surrender all down the line. They accept more than we ever dreamed possible. And unconditionally. Order their own troops not to offer any resistance.

Hitler dictated a proclamation, which Goebbels himself read out over the microphones to a sleeping Germany at six A.M.[72] When the minister awoke three hours later Hitler had already left to join his troops. In his pocket he carried the new statute for Bohemia and Moravia, and for the Protectorate that he was to establish over this supine neighbor. By evening the entire region had been occupied, a masterpiece of military organization, as Goebbels himself noted.

That evening, as Hitler took up residence in the Czech Hradčany castle, Goebbels felt suddenly very lonely: 'I feel a longing for human beings.' He went over to filmstar Zarah Leander's little birthday party for distraction.[73] On March 16 he issued a significant edict: 'The use of the term "Grossdeutsches Reich" is not desired. This term is reserved for later eventualities.' He began to plan an Easter journey across the Balkans and Greece. That evening he went out for another little drive – after all, Magda was a thousand miles away.

WHILE MAGDA HAD GALLIVANTED off for six weeks late on March 9, 1939 Goebbels enjoyed unrestricted access to their children. Sometimes he brought them into his ministry and let them tumble around his study.[74] Still pursuing Magda, his Staatssekretär Hanke meanwhile addressed love letters to her at every station of her journey.

Late on Tuesday the twenty-first, Goebbels again escorted his Führer to the theater on his return to Berlin. This time they had to camouflage their next move, a crude ultimatum which Ribbentrop was at that moment issuing to Lithuania over Memel.

'These petty crooks of Versailles,' wrote Goebbels with a chuckle, 'are now having to hand back their loot.'

As they waited for word from Lithuania, Hitler outlined his next plans to Goebbels – first he would take that respite, to regain people's confidence; and then he would raise the question of Germany's former colonies. 'Always the old one-two,' marveled Goebbels. At six-thirty A.M. Lithuania agreed to relinquish Memel at once to Germany. It all seemed so easy: Goebbels realized that this was a dangerous notion that he would soon have to counteract.[75]

Yes, as months went there definitely was something about March. After staging a triumphal entry into Memel aboard the battle-cruiser *Deutschland* on March 23, Hitler talked in confidence with Goebbels again. 'What a week that was,' wrote Goebbels. Could Hitler pull off the hat-trick and recover Danzig too – the former German port that the League of Nations had unwisely placed under partial Polish control after the world war? 'He's going to try out a little pressure on the Poles,' wrote Goebbels, 'and he hopes they'll respond to that.

But we're going to have to swallow the bitter pill and guarantee Poland's other frontiers. It will all be decided very soon.'[76]

RIBBENTROP PLAYED THEIR opening gambit. He told the Polish ambassador Josef Lipski that Hitler's offer of a deal at Slovakia's expense was still open, provided that Danzig was returned to Germany. On the twenty-fifth Hitler reassured General von Brauchitsch, his new army commander, that he did not intend to use force against Poland.[77] He really did expect a deal, and the navy drafted plans for Hitler to enter Danzig in triumph aboard the *Deutschland* in a few days' time.[78] This time however it was not going to be a walkover. Puzzled, Hitler said over lunch that Poland was still making up her mind. 'We're cranking up the pressure,' wrote Goebbels – impatiently, because both men were planning their vacations, Goebbels in the Mediterranean and Hitler in Bavaria.

Still Poland would not play ball. Reports soon reached Hitler that Warsaw had partially mobilized. Ambassador Lipski arrived back on the twenty-sixth and brusquely warned Ribbentrop that if Hitler still demanded Danzig it would mean war. 'The Polacks,' observed Goebbels in disgust, 'will always be our natural enemies, however keen in the past they have been, out of pure self-interest, to do us the odd favor.'

He set out by train, taking a private secretary and three senior colleagues on the first leg of his vacation.[79]

34: *Put Poland on Page Two*

S EEN IN RETROSPECT, those last days of March 1939 were the cradle of the coming war, but Dr Goebbels' diary betrayed no awareness of the solemnity of the hour. Seeking relief from his matrimonial *douleurs*, he was off, visiting Budapest, Athens, and Rhodes.[1] In Budapest he was received by the prime minister, foreign minister, and minister of education.[2] In Athens, though formally the guest of the mayor, he again visited Prime Minister Metaxas. The Greeks informed the British that Goebbels had told Metaxas that Hitler was not planning any further move 'for the moment.'[3] In Athens, he learned belatedly that Poland was still holding out over Danzig. 'If the fat hits the fire the Führer will recall me,' he decided, and traveled on.[4] In Rhodes he read that Chamberlain had guaranteed Poland against any aggression.* Several more British guarantees followed to other states on Germany's periphery. 'Britain on the path of virtue,' Goebbels scoffed. 'What a hoot!'[5] He flew on to Egypt, shadowed by British agents wherever he went.[6]

Egypt impressed him. 'Seldom in my life,' he wrote, seeing the Sphinx for the first time, 'has a sight so moved me. Normally one feels cheated. Here, reality surpasses what one had imagined.'[7] He told the German community that he had not come with pots of Gold for propaganda. Germany, he said, again faithfully representing Hitler's policies, had no interest in the Mediterranean, and was 'now fully occupied' digesting the territories she had recently acquired.[8] At this range, it seemed only a small fly in the ointment that Warsaw and London had signed a formal pact. 'One day, perhaps,' he mused, 'Poland will have to pay very dear for this.' Czechoslovakia had, after all, made the same mistake.[9]

After a brief stopover in Turkey[11] he landed back at Tempelhof on April 14 and swapped travel anecdotes with Magda, who had returned from her own travels, at Schwanenwerder that evening. As for foreign affairs he told the diary nothing. Metaxas had speculated that Goebbels was somewhat out of favor.'[12]

---

* Except, it turned out, aggression by the Soviet Union; a secret addendum made this clear. It was Ian Colvin of the *News Chronicle*, whom Goebbels expelled a few days later, who tilted the balance to war by telling Chamberlain, untruthfully, on March 29 that Hitler had already drawn up plans to destroy Poland. However the contingency plan (Hitler's Case WHITE) was now activated as a *result* of the British guarantee.[10]

293

Hitler was certainly in little hurry to take him further into his confidence; four days passed before they next met.

On April 18, after gathering with his family and Magda for his mother's seventieth birthday ('she's the one fixture in this stormy life of mine') Goebbels was among those dining with Hitler. Göring was also there, bronzed and fit from a vacation at San Remo; he would recall Hitler revealing at this dinner his determination to solve the Danzig question by force if necessary. Goebbels noted in his diary only the words, 'We talked politics a bit.'[13]

He was swamped in the preparations for Hitler's grandiose fiftieth-birthday parade. On the evening of the nineteenth he broadcast a special birthday tribute, then went immediately afterward over to the chancellery to join the leading party officials assembled in the ceremonial rooms overlooking Hermann-Göring Strasse. Hitler appeared an hour late, white-faced, as though he had received bad news. Speaking softly and deliberately, he indicated that he had just had a medical check-up; building on that remark, he added that he could not say how many years he still had in which to achieve his life's ambition.[14] He spoke specifically of the grave risks that he was prepared now to take.[15]

More recently retrieved fragments of Goebbels' hitherto unpublished diary throw further shafts of light on the development of Hitler's plans.

'England wants to mend her fences with us again,' Goebbels wrote after lunch with Hitler on the twenty-third. 'Chamberlain has already put out feelers to us. With France we won't have too much difficulty. And Poland is none too comfortable in its policy toward us. But for the time being the Führer doesn't want to repeat his former offer to them on Danzig and the autobahn through the Corridor,' a reference to his offer to settle for an extra-territorial freeway across the Polish territories to East Prussia.[16]

Over the next two weeks Hitler briefed him about Case WHITE (war with Poland, 'if need be'). About the events of May 1 Goebbels wrote: 'The Poles are agitating violently against us. The Führer welcomes it. For the time being we are not to hit back, but to take note. Warsaw will end up one day in the same boat as Prague.'[17] Two days later he ordered all editors to go easy on the Soviet Union 'until further notice.'[18] His next *Völkischer Beobachter* leader article was widely seen as flinging down the gauntlet to Poland.[19]

Presumably with his Führer's approval Goebbels now made Britain his prime target. Speaking without notes in Cologne on May 19 he blasphemed against the democracies, calling them 'old whores' turned sanctimonious nuns in their old age. 'For one like myself,' reported a local British diplomat, 'who had not heard Goebbels before, the power of his voice was a revelation, coming as it does from such a puny body.'[20] The Italian foreign minister came to Berlin to sign a military pact with Germany. At the dinner for Count Ciano Hitler told Goebbels that he had fought twenty years for this.[21]

Preparing Germany for a possible war, Goebbels speeded up work on the cable radio network, to release conventional transmitter capacity; he wrote Hitler a letter urging him to cut the red tape on this project.[22] His ministry was also

ROUGHOUT HIS LIFE Goebbels is acutely aware of his
ny stature and of his club foot. He usually stands
a step for group photographs (*top*, visiting Italy
May 1933) (NATIONAL ARCHIVES, WASHINGTON;
AK COLLECTION)

left: Foreign journals like the U.S. magazine *Life* in
arch 1939 pick photos which show his 'deformity'
IFE ARCHIVE)

The handicap is
painfully visible
as he limps behind
Hitler into the
Nuremberg party
rally arena in 1934
(NATIONAL ARCHIVES,
WASHINGTON)

For Ihre freundlichen Glückwünsche zu unserer
Vermählung danken wir Ihnen herzlich.

Dr. Joseph Goebbels
und Frau Magda, geb. Ritschel

Berlin, Weihnachten 1931

A QUIET VILLAGE WEDDING   Just to be near her beloved Führer, Magda Quandt agrees to marry the puny gauleiter of Berlin, Dr Joseph Goebbels. The civil wedding ceremony is solemnized at Severin, in Mecklenburg, on December 19, 1931, with Hitler as witness and with white-shirted S.A. men forming a guard of honor. Magda's son Harald Quandt, proudly wearing the Brownshirt uniform that she has stitched for him, looks on (NATIONAL ARCHIVES, WASHINGTON)

ALL DIE VIOLENTLY   Harald Quandt (seen *right* in 1932) enthusiastically joins his step-father's cause. He will die in a plane crash after the war. His father has killed himself; Hans Frank, behind Goebbels, and Wilhelm Frick, far left, are hanged at Nuremberg; Gregor Strasser (in raincoat), dies on June 30, 1934 (NATIONAL ARCHIVES, WASHINGTON)

MAGDA'S OTHER MAN The depth of the affection between Magda and Hitler is evident over the years; Otto Meissner's wife will even claim that Magda has borne one child to the Führer.

BEST OF FRIENDS Hitler and Ernst Röhm leave the S.A. officers' convention at the Rhine Hotel Dreesen in Bad Godesberg on August 19, 1933. Ten months later, he summons Goebbels to the same hotel and they sally forth together to eliminate Röhm (AUTHOR'S COLLECTION)

QUEER CROWD Homosexuality is always a problem for the Nazis: Röhm's is notorious; Goebbels frets about it; Funk, his Staatssekretär (behind him), gets away with it; General von Fritsch (with monocle) is wrongly accused of it and resigns (NATIONAL ARCHIVES, WASHINGTON)

THE DIPLOMAT In 1933 Dr Goebbels visits Geneva. As interpreter Paul Schmidt shows him and Karl Hanke a document, Goebbels spot society photographer Alfre Eisenstaedt (*above*) lingerir with his Leica, and recogni es him as a Jew – rewardin; the émigré with one of his most iconic photographs (GETTY IMAGES)

AFTERWARDS, Hitler's forei minister Konstantin von Neurath sits next to Goeb bels in the front row with Karl Hanke now holding t paper. For this group phot graph, all behave impeccal (UNITED NATIONS LIBRARY GENEVA)

FEMME FATALE On January 5, 1935 Hitler and Goebbels visit the Ufa film studios at Babelsberg, where cameraman Friedl Behn-Grund is shooting a scene from *Barcarole* with Gustav Fröhlich (*below left*) and the twenty-year-old film star Lida Baarova (*above, and below right*). It is the moment that Goebbels first sets eyes on the young Czech actress (NATIONAL ARCHIVES, WASHINGTON)

Bottom: The author interviews Lida Baarova in Austria in July 1993 (HELSINKIN SANOMAT)

The Retreat

BIRTHDAY GIFT In 1936 the city of Berlin donates to its gauleiter Dr Goebbels a large parcel of land on the secluded Bogensee lake, near Lanke. Here he builds a little love-nest, buried among the trees. In 1938, on the

Among Goebbels' guests
at his hideaway on the
Bogensee: Lida Baarova
(*top*) and her best friend
Hilde Körber, who shortly
marries film star Veit
Harlan (DEUTSCHES
INSTITUT FÜR FILMKUNDE)

t Lanke

r side of the lake, he begins
onstruction of an imposing
ansion, the Haus am Bogensee
ight) complete with immense
ectrically operated windows.
oth houses still stand today
UTHOR'S COLLECTION)

above: Alfred-Ingemar Berndt, Goebbels' chief propaganda executive. He devised the lies needed to justify the Nazi seizure of Czechoslovakia and Poland (WALTER FRENTZ)

below: Captured by a home movie, Goebbels and Hitler attend a gaudy arts festival in Munich in July 1939. His tunic and cap are in private hands today (*left*) (AUTHOR'S COLLECTION)

'Isidor's' Torment

From the moment of his arrival in Berlin in November 1928 Dr Goebbels wages a pitiless war against the city's humourless Jewish police chief, *right*, Dr Bernhard Weiss (BUNDESARCHIV)

Weiss sues him forty times, mostly for calling him 'Isidor.' Nazi caricaturist Mjölnir portrays him as a donkey skating on thin ice. After a judge rules the cartoon defamatory, Goebbels' newspaper announces 'JUDGE AGREES DONKEY DOES LOOK LIKE ISIDOR.'

Deutsche, verteidigt Euch gegen die jüdische Greuelpropaganda, kauft nur bei Deutschen!

Germans defend yourselves against Jewish atrocity propaganda

<u>**buy only at German shops!**</u>

Goebbels retaliates against the international Jewish boycott of German produce by declaring a boycott of Jewish stores in Germany. It lasts for only one Saturday morning (NATIONAL ARCHIVES, WASHINGTON)

er Jude siegt mit der Lüge

IN MASS MEETINGS at the Deutschlandhalle (*above*) in the late fall of 1935 the German public is whippe
to a frenzy against the Jews. Gigantic banners proclaim THE JEW TRIUMPHS WITH THE LIE AND DI
WITH THE TRUTH.

ABOUT THE VIOLENTLY antisemitic Julius Streicher, the Nazi gauleiter of Franconia (*right*), Goebbe
is ambivalent. In his diaries, he praises the gauleiter's courage and commitment, but fears that h
extreme and vulgar brand of antisemitism will alienate public sympathies (NATIONAL ARCHIVE
WASHINGTON)

...stirbt mit der Wahrheit.

A CRAZED Jew assassinates German diploma
Ernst vom Rath (*above*) in Paris in Novemb
1938 and is arrested (*left*). Goebbels issu
orders for *Kristallnacht*, an orgy of violen
against Jewish stores and buildings. For yea
his precise role in this outrage is dispute
Now his diaries provide the proof (NATION
ARCHIVES, WASHINGTON)

ƎITHER S.S. Reichsführer Heinrich Himmler (*left*) nor foreign minister Joachim von Ribbentrop ɑakes any secret of his fury at Goebbels for masterminding the events leading to the *Kristallnacht* (ᵂALTER FRENTZ; NATIONAL ARCHIVES, WASHINGTON)

N NOVEMBER 11, 1938, the day after *Kristallnacht*, Hitler stands by Goebbels and delivers an impas-ɔned speech to editors on the importance of propaganda to the tasks that lie ahead. To Goebbels' ʒht is Nazi publisher Max Amann, who has bought the rights to his diaries (NATIONAL ARCHIVES, ᴀSHINGTON)

The Exodus Begins

IN MID-OCTOBER 1941 Goebbels' officials ship the first trainloads of Jews out of Berlin to 'the east' – first to Lodz and Minsk, then, one thousand at a time, to Riga, capital of Nazi-occupied Latvia (*below*). On November 30, 1941 a trainload of Berlin Jews arrives at this railroad platform in Riga. They are driven a few miles outside Riga, robbed of their possessions, and machine-gunned into pits a few hours later (KLAUS EWALD)

ALBERT SPEER (*top right and above*) tries to conceal his part in the expulsion of Berlin's Jews. His real diaries leave no room for doubt (NATIONAL ARCHIVES, WASHINGTON; WALTER FRENTZ)

WALTHER

A Shotgun Reconciliation

THE PENNY DROPS In October 1938 Dr Goebbels realizes that none other than his own handsome Staatssekretär Karl Hanke (*left*) is cavorting with Magda. Egged on by Hanke, she takes her matrimonial problems to Hitler. After a long, difficult session with Magda and Eva Braun at his new mountain-top teahouse on October 24, 1938 (*below*) Hitler sends for a photographer to record the family's enforced togetherness for posterity.

building some of the biggest transmitters in the world. The new half-megawatt Deutschland-Sender went on the air on May 19; later, it was to be stepped up to five megawatts. Goebbels was also building four high-powered shortwave transmitters near Hamburg. He wanted the world to hear his voice.[23]

He put the cunning and unscrupulous Berndt in charge of this expanding broadcasting network. Berndt had by now, as he himself admitted to Himmler, the unsavory reputation of being in charge of all the dirty tricks necessary in the Nazis' interests – 'subversion of the enemy, creating the starting points for political operations, and so forth.'[24]

His propaganda fictions had paved the way for Munich. In Berndt's place as inland press chief Goebbels appointed Hans Fritzsche, an impressive intellectual with an educated drawl. Both men held high S.S. rank. Both were party veterans, with the kind of radicalism that Goebbels applauded – Berndt would shoot an American airman in cold blood; Fritzsche would turn over to the Gestapo's hangmen a simple Nuremberg fireman who sent him a crude paste-up montage as a one-man protest in 1941.[25]

UNEXPECTEDLY THE LIDA BAAROVA case returns to haunt Goebbels that spring. Fleeing Germany, she has returned to her native Prague, only to find Hitler's troops invading in March and herself trapped again within the Reich's frontiers. She returns to Berlin. Several times in recent weeks Goebbels has asked Hilde Körber about Lida's well-being; he meets Hilde in the woods, terrified of being followed – once he shows her a pistol he is carrying – and sends her over to Lida with messages (Lida never replies). Touched by his concern, Hilde writes little poems to him. Sitting in the dress-circle once, Lida sees him at a distance, but their eyes do not meet. Emil Jannings and others come to plead with Goebbels to allow Lida to film again. He replies, 'It is out of my hands.'[26]

Then Alfred Greven, now general manager of Ufa, secretly signs her up again. Goebbels blurts out to him: 'But Baarova is banned by the Führer!' The movie boss urges him to lift the ban since so much time has elapsed. 'She can be hired as far as I am concerned,' says Goebbels, softening, 'but I don't think it will be possible. I must talk it over with Hanke.'

Hanke however cannot let bygones be bygones. He still has a covetous eye on the minister's sorely wronged spouse. Storming into Greven's office on May 19 he reminds him of the Czech movie star's notorious affair with 'higher circles.'

'Herr Staatssekretär,' retorts Greven, 'what about your own little affair?'[27] It seems that everybody knows about Magda.

Hanke swings a punch at Greven – 'because,' as he writes at once to Himmler, 'he countered my allegations with a blatant untruth.'[28] Hitler orders Hanke to report to him.

Aghast at this new episode, Goebbels writes in his unpublished diary, 'By his unpardonable assault on Greven of Ufa, Hanke has touched off a hideous scandal. I am furious. Was that the intent? One doesn't know whom to trust.

It's left to me now to try and sort things out. Will I ever manage to get clear of all these *Schweinereien*?[29] For days the Greven affair clouds his diary's horizon. 'It's sickening. One rumor after another.'[30] Greven retaliates, writing to him as gauleiter and demanding a full hearing by the party court. 'He's stirring things up against Hanke now.'[31]

On May 17, Mother's Day, the *Berlin Illustrated* publishes a cover portrait of Magda and a family group photo – without Dr Goebbels. Although an operation on Helga's throat brings them momentarily closer together, the matrimonial stand-off continues.[32] He plays with the children and regales them with bedtime stories of Germany's decline and resurgence; his little treasures 'listen with gleaming eyes.'[33]

One day he takes the ministry staff on three boats across the Wannsee to Schwanenwerder to shout a big hallo to Magda and the children.[34] A couple of days later he gives her a new car (followed by one of the first Volkswagens for the children).[35]

Magda has however begun a clean sweep. She sells off the next-door plot, Nos. 12 to 14 Insel Strasse ('the so-called citadel'), which has brought her so much unhappiness, and in June she is on the point of selling her present plot too, to buy an even more beautiful site a few houses further down the road.[36] The house needs total renovation. 'It will probably take a few months to finish,' she writes to her father Oskar Ritschel. 'I'm looking forward to the job ahead as it will distract me from the more or less grim thoughts that my fate, indeterminate as it is, still provokes in me.' She will take the children to Bad Gastein in Austria for the summer, where her father, no admirer of the minister's, can visit them in privacy.[37]

That summer the *Berlin Illustrated* also published comparative photos of Goebbels' study together with the fantasy version crafted by a Hollywood studio for the film *Confessions of a Nazi Spy*. The American studio version showed 'Goebbels' seated behind a ten-foot-wide desk in front of an eleven-foot Hitler painting, with two huge swastikas embossed in the marble floor. In reality the portrait was six foot tall, and of Frederick the Great; a large globe however dominated the room – and his desk did measure ten feet across.[38]

MEANWHILE GOEBBELS METHODICALLY stoked up the propaganda fires over Danzig, releasing the steam in carefully controlled bursts. Via teleprinter and telephone, editors were told what stories to print and how – how much leeway was allowed, how big the headline should be.[39] 'The [Berlin] press,' an American observer would report to Washington that summer, drawing on the experience of the previous year, 'passes through set stages of invective in preparation for each of the major incidents which have so far occurred.' The first stage, he explained, merely set forth in general terms the German point of view. Secondly, there followed attacks on the foreign government in question. Thirdly, the press attack switched to the 'acts of terror' allegedly perpetrated against the German people by these governments. The fourth and final stage of this cycle, he said, was marked by 'lurid tales of German blood being spilled.' This officer pointed out that the process had begun anew in May 1939, with asseverations of Germany's historic right to Danzig.[40]

This analysis was correct. From May onwards Goebbels had lifted the ban on reporting anti-German incidents in Poland, though restricted for the time being to page two.[41] To imprint Danzig's character firmly on the world's mind as a German city, in June Hitler authorized him to deliver a major speech there – 'a trial balloon,' Goebbels confidentially informed his editors, 'to test the international atmosphere on Danzig.'

With the local gauleiter Albert Forster he plotted a 'spontaneous' – how he loved and abused that word – display in Danzig to demonstrate to the foreign journalists traveling in his party the German character of the city and its people.[42] He delivered the speech 'spontaneously' from the balcony of the Danzig state theater through loudspeakers which had no less spontaneously materialized. 'I am standing here on the soil of a German town,' he emphasized, motioning to the architectural icons all around. 'You long to return to the Reich,' he intoned.

The thousands of well-drilled young Nazis chanted in response, 'We want to see Hitler in Danzig!'[43] 'My speech,' Goebbels told his diary with a conspiratorial air, 'looked quite improvised but I had prepared the whole thing in advance.'[44] 'I know,' he said with a careless wink, speaking that evening at the Casino hotel at Zoppot, near Danzig, to the foreign journalists who had accompanied him, 'that some of you are curious whether today's demonstration was truly spontaneous or not.' In fact their Berlin colleagues had received the text in advance, and it had already been typeset for a special Sunday edition of the party's Danzig newspaper the day before.[45]

At this meeting with the journalists Goebbels lamented that there would have been no problem if the British had not butted in with their 'absurd' guarantee to Poland. 'Morally, the right to Danzig is ours,' he argued. 'Just as we had a moral right to everything else we have taken – with the exception,' he added as a disarming afterthought, 'of Bohemia and Moravia. But we had to take those to create a strategic frontier for ourselves.' The British were just bluffing, he suggested. Hitler's nerves would prove the stronger. 'We know for sure that the stupid English are too weak and too cowardly to get in our way.'[46]

On June 20 Hitler summoned him to report on Danzig at the Berghof. He found the Führer sitting in the teahouse, eager to make prognoses:

Poland will offer resistance at first, but upon the first reverse she will pitifully collapse. The Czechs are more realistic. The Poles are quite hysterical and unpredictable.
London will leave Warsaw in the lurch. They're just bluffing. Got too many other worries. . . The Führer says, and he's right, that Britain now has the most rotten government imaginable. There's no question of their helping Warsaw. They led Prague up the garden path as well.

This is proved by the files we have captured in the Czech foreign ministry.

His bellicose speech in Danzig had sounded alarm bells around the world. Ambassador von Hassell was not alone in wondering if it was the prelude to a solution of the Polish problem by brute force.[47] The British ambassador in Berlin heard that Hitler had ordered Goebbels to make the speech 'as [the] result of reports of castration of Germans in Poland.'[48] But even Henderson believed that Goebbels was deliberately minimizing such incidents.

This was true: On June 23 the propaganda ministry ordered reports of Polish atrocities played down.[49] Goebbels forbade any discussion of Danzig as yet.[50] Even kite-flying items on Danzig printed by British newspapers were not to be picked up.[51] He ordered the press to ignore specific belligerent and anti-German speeches by foreign statesmen, as well as foreign press items about German troop movements, induction of reservists, leave cancellations, and British naval maneuvers in the North Sea. He allowed reports about 'incidents in Poland [and] expropriations of German property,' but still subjected them to 'existing layout guidelines.' Page two was still prominent enough.[52]

He did however order to be emphasized all those news items which served to diminish Britain's prestige – her failing encirclement policy, her floundering negotiations with Moscow, her fumbling in Palestine, and her citizens' humiliation at the hands of Japanese troops in the Far East.[53]

He made some exceptions: Lord Londonderry, a personal friend of Göring's, was to be spared, and Britain's military honor was not to be impugned.[54] He drafted a biting attack on Britain's encirclement efforts himself, but ordered his press to go easier on Britain, while still instructing editors not to overlook the twentieth anniversary of Versailles on June 28. 'The German people know only too well what our enemies would do to us if they got us in their power again.' 'So keep hammering it in – hold Britain up to contempt, depict her as baffled, mendacious, jumpy, and impotent.'[55]

After touring the western fortifications Goebbels afterward sought to reassure the gauleiters and generals secretly assembled in a big Aachen hotel. 'Gentlemen,' he told them, 'there will be no war with England. Here is a letter from London which again confirms my opinion.'[56]

The letter seemed to prove that the British were indeed bluffing. 'Believe me, gentlemen,' said Goebbels, folding away the letter, 'We're going to see things develop just like last time. A war of nerves without parallel, I agree, but they'll end up giving in.'[57] Nobody was eager to die for Danzig, that was the German calculation.

Hitler was now shipping troops to East Prussia, bordering Danzig, under camouflage of the approaching anniversary of the battle of Tannenberg. Goebbels asked newspapers to mention the coming anniversary, though 'without special emphasis.'[58]

Goebbels was confident that Hitler would pull it off with just propaganda again. Continuing his delicious feud, he often told Hitler that he had no confidence in Ribbentrop at all, and squabbled with the foreign minister over the management of the visits of Count Ciano and the Yugoslav royal couple.[59] Once, in Vienna, Hitler had described Ribbentrop to Goebbels as bordering on insanity; when Goebbels told his diary that the man's prima-donna vanity got on his nerves he was telling the reader nothing that he had not long gathered already. Hitler even talked of getting rid of Ribbentrop.[60] To Goebbels' rage the London *Daily* Express published an accurate report on their feud.[61] He revived it a few days later, sending Hanke to the Obersalzberg to wring from Hitler a declaration that radio, press, and even press attachés were his sole domain;

Hitler humored his wish. Goebbels told his diary so often that Ribbentrop was demented that there is cause to question his own stability.[62] When Ribbentrop took petty revenge on the press attachés, Goebbels got his own back by regaling Hitler at the Berghof with witticisms about this 'champagne dealer' and this 'would-be Bismarck' until tears of enjoyment ran down the Führer's face.[63] But the foreign ministry kept up its pressure on the press, and even a personal meeting between Ribbentrop and Goebbels, at which they sat facing each other with white knuckles and clenched teeth assuring each other of their desire for cordial relations, brought the matter no further. 'If he's as flexible as this in our foreign policy dealings,' wrote Goebbels, 'God help us.'[64]

Hitler was conducting his own foreign policy that summer. Watching the reports from Moscow, he could see that the British negotiators were in difficulties, but, he told Goebbels, he could not deduce if Stalin was merely playing hard to get, holding out for a better price, or really intended to hold off altogether as Europe went to war, in order to scoop the pool at the end.[65] On June 10 Hitler confessed to Goebbels in Vienna that he was at a loss about what Moscow really wanted.[66] That he did not breathe a word to Goebbels about his secret overtures to Stalin is evident from the costly anti-Soviet movies to which several of Goebbels' movie studios were still heavily committed.[67]

Meanwhile Poland, bolstered by Britain's guarantee, remained intransigent – or insolent, as Hitler and Goebbels saw it.[68] 'Poland,' said Hitler, 'is pursuing a very stupid political foreign policy. She won't be able to keep it up for long.' He mentioned that in August his own West Wall would be ready.[69]

After supping with Hitler on July 4, Goebbels recorded that the Führer agreed with him they should nurture hatred against Britain – the German people must recognize her as their chief obstacle.[70]

DURING JULY 1939 SOME BRITISH citizens took an initiative which caught Goebbels unawares. Commander Stephen King-Hall, a retired naval officer, started mailing to thousands of German addresses cleverly conceived letters attacking the top Nazis. Goebbels went to extraordinary lengths to answer these 'schoolboy essays.' When the first such letter came, he airily told Hitler that he would publish it in his own press – later a standard propaganda tactic – with a suitably juicy reply.[71] His reply argued for example that their author, having served in the Royal Navy, had helped starve to death hundreds of thousands of German women and children during the blockade; it recited every crime committed by the British empire-builders from the slave-trading history of Liverpool to the bombardment of Zanzibar. He also plotted an undefined 'masterpiece' – probably a fake letter in King Hall's name that was so absurd that nobody would believe him any more.[72] 'We've got to work artfully,' he decided, 'but seemingly objectively.' The trouble was that Hitler announced that he wanted to see it first, and when Goebbels set out on July 8 on a prolonged journey to Austria he found Hitler who asked to see him at the Berghof still working on it.[73] 'Then we discuss top policy,' noted Goebbels, adding vaguely: We must wear down the Poles by further warlike preparations. At the decisive moment their nerves will crack. Britain will be worn down by ceaseless propaganda. And that's how we'll go on for the time being. There can scarcely be any doubt about the

A second King-Hall letter turned up, but the Führer was still tinkering with the Goebbels reply to the first.[75] He did not finally release the reply until the fourteenth.[76] Goebbels ordered it printed in every German newspaper, but it was totally ignored by the British and French.[77] He was disappointed; he was sure he had hit home, but on the twentieth he noted that the incorrigible King-Hall was writing yet again.[78]

ALMOST A LANDED GENTLEMEN now, a man of property like Göring, Goebbels is perceptibly less eager to risk war than the haggard, penniless agitator he had been in the late Twenties. He has a wife and family, although he has not seen much of Magda since the spring. She has taken her brood to holiday in the mountains at Bad Gastein on June 28, leaving him disconsolate, guilty, and lonely; alone, he drives out to Lanke to inspect progress on the lakeside mansion.[79] He learns that Hanke has stubbornly increased his emotional pressure on Magda throughout the year, even showing her a little lakeside house he has bought, No. 13 Gustav-Freytag Strasse, in the Grunewald. Reaching a sudden decision after seeing Hitler at the Berghof on July 8, Goebbels leaves at five P.M. and is with Magda and the children at seven. He is determined to force a total reconciliation with her.

'The children, the children!' he writes after reaching Gastein. 'They rejoice and dance, because Papa's arrived.' He jots proud little cameos of them in his diary – Helga points out the local landmarks, Hilde is a little mouse, Hellmut a clown, and Holde a darling little infant. The spectacular Alpine scenery and climate are made for romance. He goes for long walks with Magda, and sits far into the night with her under the starlit skies, drinking in the peaceful sounds of nature, and the steady rushing of the waterfall.[80] He sleeps ten hours and learns that Hitler is *still* tinkering with his reply to King-Hall, but all that is far away. He takes the family over to Zell am See and swaps nostalgic stories with Magda about the years before they came to power. They pore over architectural blueprints, play games with the children, go rambling in the mountains, and trundle back home in a pony cart.[81] When he leaves Gastein the children cling to him with tear-stained faces and he suspects that Magda too is not unmoved.[82]

He phones her on the sixteenth, and she joins him in Munich for the lavish, ornate, spectacular, and rain-soaked pageant of German Art.[83] Evidently she has told him something about her persistent suitor, because on the twentieth he has a 'serious row' with Hanke.[84] He visits his troubled wife again in Gastein and that evening she unbends to him. 'It's just as I thought,' snarls Goebbels in his diary. 'Hanke has turned out to be a first-class rotter. So my mistrust of him has been totally justified.' Magda, he decides, is on the horns of a terrible dilemma, and they talk all night about ways of escape. He stays in bed all the next day while she sits at his bedside talking softly with him. All the pieces are falling into place, and this alone brings him peace of mind.[85] He blames his Staatssekretär for everything, himself for nothing. 'Hanke is the most perfidious traitor I ever saw,' he writes grimly. 'But he's going to get his come-uppance.'[86] Magda agrees to accompany him to Bayreuth – scene of the previous year's opera scandal – on the twenty-fifth.

On July 25 Hanke sends a member of the ministry's staff to see Goebbels, evidently bearing a mixture of threats and entreaties; Goebbels is unimpressed and sends the man, G. W. Müller, back to Berlin with a flea for Hanke's ear.[87]

On the way to Bayreuth Magda, still torn between the two men, faints several times; she is suffering from the nervous strain. At Bayreuth, Goebbels is phoned by Müller – '[He] has performed his job relatively well. A few more impudent threats and sentimentalities.' Magda is in tears, and Goebbels has difficulty calming her down.

Hitler has other problems on his hands. He is buoyant about his foreign policy. He says that the democracies will shrink back, step by step, from the brink of war.[88] Over dinner, he expands on this theme – that Warsaw will crumble if push comes to shove.[89]

The next day, July 26, Magda is again wild-eyed and tearful. 'Every hour,' records Goebbels, 'alarming new bulletins come from [G. W.] Müller, from Speer, from Mama and the devil knows whom else. It's wrong even to pay any attention to them, they just get on your nerves.'[90] He has a long talk with Magda, he wants to help her but knows no way. That afternoon they sit once again through *Tristan and Isolde*, and Magda faints from the strain of it all. 'If only I could help her,' moans Goebbels. 'When shall we ever find a way out of all this misery?'

After supper he goes alone up to his room, unable to join in the general chatter. But when he emerges to fetch Magda, he finds her lying senseless on the staircase outside; he drags her into the room and revives her only with difficulty. Clearly there is something about Bayreuth that brings out the melodrama in some people.

She murmurs only that she has confessed everything to the Führer; now they must stand together. Hitler tells Ribbentrop later that she is not fool enough to exchange 'Frau Reichsminister' for 'Frau Staatssekretär.' But the truth is that in a grim, almost masochistic way she is beholden to Joseph and will remain his until the end.

Folding her in his arms, he says: 'Magda, Hanke is not the man for you.' She promises to telephone her suitor to announce that she and her husband are reconciled.[91] Goebbels witnesses the dialogue, an 'endless, tortured telephone conversation.'[92] How neatly the summer of 1939 has mirrored the excruciating summer of 1938.

The next day Magda's friends – among them the ubiquitous and bitchy Ello – cut her; a salutary lesson in Goebbels' heartless view. As they drive out of Bayreuth, willingly foregoing the leaden, mystic gloom of *Parsifal*, a burden falls from his shoulders. He and Magda have decided to live together again. He has won the last round.[93]

35: *Pact with the Devil*

G OEBBELS RETURNED BRIEFLY to Berlin for the afternoon of July 28, 1939 to open the radio exhibition. The emphasis was on peace; the big attraction was television; the first television sets would soon go on sale.[1] The rebuilding of No. 20 Hermann-Göring Strasse was nearly complete; he hoped to move in on August 15, although he wanted the color scheme changed before then. Karl Hanke stayed out of sight (he went on leave, and eventually joined the army). Goebbels lived in a daze, his faith in human nature finally shattered, or so he claimed.[2] Back in Munich he found Magda awaiting him.[3] Over the next few days they both thawed out. Magda was taken aside more than once by well-meaning critics; but she told them their decision was now final.[4]

Goebbels was still confident that the September Nuremberg rally would go ahead as planned.[5] Among his miscellaneous directives that summer he requested editors to take note that Peru was not a U.S. state; to report murder trials only in local editions;[6] to mention sex cases involving Jews only where they had seduced Aryan women by concealing their race; always to give Jewish defendants their mandatory first names of Israel or Sara; and to report with the utmost delicacy Sir Oswald Mosley's latest mass meeting in Earl's Court ('so the democratic press has no locus to depict him as being in Germany's pay').

Editors were instructed however not to over-praise the dancer Palucca, a half-Jew; not to refer to the World Exhibition, but to the New York Exhibition; not to review books by marxist liberals; not to reveal that the Führer had commuted the death sentence on a certain murderer; not to disclose the visit of seventy American-born Germans ('so as not to compromise their later operations'); not to refer to the 'Third Reich' but to National Socialist Germany; not to reproduce the Führer's article on architecture from the latest issue of *Art in the Third Reich* (a title which violated his own edict); and not to publish candid-camera photographs of the infinitely vain Hermann Göring or his wife.[7]

Intensifying his propaganda attack on Britain, he ordered editors for example to remind readers of the August 1915 incident when the British warship *Baralong* had sunk the Kaiser's submarine U–27, then murdered its survivors one by one.[8]

Analysis of these secret directives shows that over Poland he was still pulling his punches. On August 1 the national press was ordered to display reserve in discussing the Polish army officers infiltrated into Danzig disguised as customs officials.[9] Only on the seventh did the German press agency D.N.B. issue a full statement.[10] His propaganda was now an integral part of the military build-up. Hitler told economics minister Walther Funk, who had been badgering him to reduce the foreign currency allocated to the propaganda ministry, to leave the sum unchanged.[11]

HITLER HAD GONE DOWN to the Berghof after Bayreuth, and Goebbels attended none of his historic conferences during August. He spent the second week of August in Venice with Magda and several colleagues, returning a visit made by his Italian counterpart Dino Alfieri.[12] There survives a letter from Magda's secretary, her childhood friend Wilma Freybe, to Goebbels' adjutant: The Frau Reichsminister had received an invitation to the coming Nuremberg party rally, her first in two years. Did the minister want her to accept?[13] With Alfieri, he worked on an agreement on collaboration between their two countries' media, as well as movie and radio.[14]

Clad in summer whites, he and Magda lazed around in gondolas, scudded across the Adriatic in torpedo boats, visited art galleries, inspected a Venetian glass factory, sunned themselves on the beaches, and generally acted as man and wife again – 'How long it is since I last had that!'[15] Overwhelmed by the Arabian Nights atmosphere of Venice, he took little note of the developing crisis, except for an insolent speech on Danzig by the Polish president ('so it will soon be time').[16] He learned that Ciano was bound for the Berghof ('but it's not time yet').[17]

On August 8, continuing his holiday, he ordered Polish terror incidents still relegated to page two, with Polish threats against Germany promoted to page one.[18] When *Kurier Polski* declaimed 'Germany must be destroyed,' the ministry ordered editors to headline this quotation on their front page.[19] On the eleventh Hitler ordered the volume of the anti-Polish propaganda turned up to eighty percent.[20]

That day Goebbels ordered Polish terrorist incidents moved onto page one. 'The display is not as yet to exceed two columns however. . . Newspapers must take care,' he instructed, explaining the precise propaganda dosage, 'not to exhaust all their arguments and vocabulary prematurely.'[21] Nobody was to mention territorial claims.[22]

On the fifteenth the minister and his wife flew back to Berlin, picking up the foreign newspapers in Munich on the way. He observed with satisfaction that the British and French were in disarray and were relieved by rumors of German peace initiatives.[23] 'It's now time,' he dictated the next day, 'for the German press to abandon its previous reserve.'[24] News items about Polish terror acts were to be well displayed but not splashed so sensationally that people 'might conclude that a decisive event is imminent.'[25]

At six P.M. on August 15 he and his family moved back into his expensively (3.2 million marks, or three-quarters of a million dollars) rebuilt official residence. The old palace had been demolished in June 1938. To the 164 workmen gathered at the topping-out ceremony in January 1939 his office chief, the blindly submissive Werner Naumann, had explained that the 'leading men and ministers from around the world' would be coming to this official residence, hence the luxurious appointments: There was a marble-galleried banqueting hall at ground level; all the rooms, except for the marbled bathrooms, were paneled in costly walnut, mahogany, rosewood, and cherry. Cost-cutting was confined to the servants' quarters, where the eighteen household staff were allowed three primitive Volksempfänger radio sets and one bathtub between them.[26] It was not yet ready, but it was home. Goebbels grimly prayed that the house would bring them both more happiness than they had known over the last year.

After supper he inspected the house, and found a lot to curse his architect Paul Baumgarten for. A stickler for detail, he dictated five pages of complaints: A picture of a church in his study was to be replaced by one of the Führer; and the up-market interior decorators, United Workshops, were to remake his desk, chair, and upholstery in a red that would match the curtains and carpet.[27] He was moreover having serious problems financing the luxurious new mansion taking shape on the other side of the lake at Lanke.[28] Discussing his personal finances with Dr Karl Ott, his chief of administration, he admitted that they were catastrophic: 'I've got to find some way out.'[29]

'The war,' he wrote on August 17, 'is now expected with a degree of fatalism. It would take almost a miracle to avoid it.' Hitler was lurking down at the Berghof, where he had taken the decision to invade Poland early on the twenty-sixth; but he had evidently not yet notified Goebbels, because the latter began drafting the speeches he would deliver at the Nuremberg party rally still scheduled to be held in September.[30]

On August 18 the ministry instructed editors to adopt a typical Goebbels device, namely to personalize their attack; in this case they were to blame the Polish governor of eastern Upper Silesia personally for the 'barbaric terror' wave.[31]

While newspapers were encouraged to carry interviews with German refugees even these were to be 'deliberately understated.'[32] The war of nerves had begun for him quite literally; he spent that night and all next day doubled up in bed with painful stomach cramps (perhaps of emotional origin?) as he brooded on his own financial crisis and his country slithering toward war.[33] During the day a phone call from the Berghof instructed him to turn up the propaganda volume to full blast by Tuesday the twenty-second. 'So the balloon can go up then,' concluded Goebbels, not liking it at all.[34]

The very regimentation of this press coverage produced a ghastly sense of déjà vu in foreign diplomats, as no doubt Hitler intended. The astute American military attaché observed on the twenty-first that, with German blood now flowing, German refugees fleeing, and German families being attacked by brutish Polish mobs, Goebbels had reached the same stage as in the last week of September 1938: Only the place names and the enemy were different.[35]

ALL OF GOEBBELS' PREVIOUS problems paled beside the psychological problem of presenting to his public the totally unexpected news that Hitler and Stalin were doing a deal.

Previous indicators during July had been so minute that a seismograph would not have detected them. On July 8 Hitler had told Goebbels that he no longer expected London and Moscow to reach an agreement. 'That leaves the way open for us,' Goebbels had deduced. 'Stalin doesn't want either a won or a lost war. In either case he'd be history.'[36] He asked editors not to express glee at the stalling of the Anglo-French negotiations in Moscow;[37] not to comment on differences emerging between Moscow and Tokyo;[38] and not to pick up foreign press reports that Poland was making airfields available to the Soviet air force.[39] Newspapers were told to ignore the German–Soviet trade talks.[40] Totally unexpectedly the news came on August 20 that Berlin had signed a new trade agreement with Moscow: 'How times change,' was Goebbels' only comment, cautious enough; he instructed editors to restrict the news to one column on page one, with commentaries only of an economic nature.[41]

At the government press conference on August 21, he proudly noted, he 'poured oil on the flames. But still kept some in reserve.' General Wilhelm Keitel, chief of the High Command, told him that militarily everything was ready for the attack on Poland.

The Germans had almost 1·5 million men under arms. It would take a miracle to avoid war, decided Goebbels. Overwhelmed by his own preparations, he had no time to start constructing his speech for Nuremberg. Studying the wiretap intercepts, he concluded that blind panic was spreading in the enemy camp.[42] That evening Goebbels heard the news of the Nazi–Soviet pact, and that his arch rival Ribbentrop, triumphant, would be signing the historic document two days later, August 23, in Moscow. 'That really is something!' gasped Goebbels. 'That's a whole new ball-game. We're home and dry. Now we can sleep a bit more peacefully again.'[43]

The news totally threw Goebbels; it was like living in an eternal kaleidoscope. No sooner did he think he had seen it all than there was a completely new constellation. War still seemed likely, but with Poland's only viable ally now eliminated the conclusion seemed foregone. Goebbels and his staff threw themselves into the final war preparations. His first press directive the next morning spoke of a 'sensational turning point' in their relations with Russia; then caution prevailed and his next directive, while allowing editors to remark upon the ideological differences separating Berlin and Moscow, forbade them to quote even foreign commentaries on the probable consequences. 'Any observations must be sober and objective in tenor,' his third directive that day added, 'devoid of either triumph or Schadenfreude.'[44]

The next telephone intercepts revealed 'utter despair' in the enemy camp.[45] Out in Lanke, where he and Magda were inspecting building operations, he received a phone call from Hitler in euphoric mood. Goebbels congratulated him on his masterstroke.[46] That day the Führer had summoned his generals in plain clothes to the Berghof to hear his plan to attack Poland in four days' time, and the astonishing news of the coming non-aggression pact with Russia.[47]

Early the next day, August 23, 1939, before flying down to the Berghof, Goebbels reminded editors that their readers would not understand it if they suddenly sprouted 'flowery and jubilant articles' about German–Soviet friendship. Journalists should gradually warm to the pact to camouflage its opportunistic nature.[48]

The Führer [Goebbels told his diary] is in conference with [Sir Nevile] Henderson. He has brought back a letter from Chamberlain: If Poland is attacked, this says, Britain will go to war. The Führer gives Henderson a robust response. Henderson is quite shattered. The Führer dictates a letter of reply to Chamberlain: If London mobilizes, then Germany's mobilization will ensue. A stop will be put to the Polish provocations. This letter's tone is quite adamant. . .

The Führer greets me very cordially. He wants me to be with him over the next few days. In the afternoon he gives me a broad overview of the situation: Poland's plight is desperate. We shall attack her at the first possible opportunity. The Polish state must be smashed just like the Czech. It won't take much effort. More difficult is the question whether the west will intervene. At present one can't say. It depends. London is talking tougher than in September 1938. So we're going to have to box cunning. At present Britain probably doesn't want war. But she can't lose face. . .

Paris is holding back more and dodging the issue. But there too we can't say anything hard and fast. . .

Italy isn't keen but she'll probably go along with us. She's hardly got any choice. Japan has missed the bus. How often the Führer has urged them to join the military alliance, even telling them he'd have to join forces with Moscow otherwise. . . Now Japan is pretty isolated.

Hitler described to Goebbels the deal he had struck with Stalin, with the Baltic states and Poland being split between Berlin and Moscow.[49] 'The question of bolshevism,' noted Goebbels, 'is for the time being of lesser importance.' It was a throwaway line of breathtaking brevity considering all that he had fought against for fifteen years. Hitler speculated that Chamberlain might even resign. On the phone from Moscow, Ribbentrop asked if the Russians might have the Latvian ports of Libau and Windau. 'The Führer approves this,' observed Goebbels. They whiled away the hours watching a movie, until the communiqué finally came through from Moscow. At one A.M. Poland's fate was sealed. They sat up until four A.M. examining the implications.

It was dawn when Goebbels returned to his quarters – still in the humble guesthouse to which Hitler had relegated him.[50] Probably the Führer had by now told him that he had confidently scheduled the attack on Poland to begin at dawn on Saturday the twenty-sixth.

On the twenty-fourth (Thursday) both men agreed that it was surprising that there had been so little echo from the world's press to the Moscow signing. Goebbels lifted the ban on editors speculating on what the new pact would mean for Poland: 'You can indicate that the purpose of this pact is to enable Germany and Russia alone to settle all outstanding problems in the Lebensraum between them, *i.e.*, in eastern Europe.'[51] A second directive that day probably reflected Hitler's decision to strike in two days' time. Editors were now invited to comment on the speed with which the Moscow pact had been signed. 'Newspapers are permitted to display a degree of Schadenfreude, though not in their editorial columns.'[52] Editors were still not to go into specifics; reports about Polish mobilization and atrocities, and about Danzig, were still to take precedence over the new pact.[53]

The Führer and his propaganda minister decided it was high time to fly back to Berlin. During the flight, Hitler was on edge; Goebbels wondered how he kept his nerve in crises like this.[54] That it *was* a crisis became plain when Goebbels read the telegrams: Chamberlain had told the House of Commons that Britain still stood by her promise to Poland. The radio waves were filled with the chatter of panicking commentators – and Goebbels too lay awake for hours that night.[55]

Friday August 25, 1939 dawned, the eve of war – or so Hitler had planned. At two-thirty P.M. the final mobilization against Poland was due to start. At the noon press conference the ministry instructed editors of the next day's newspapers to highlight Polish preparations for attacking Germany, the Polish blockade of Danzig, and Polish acts of terrorism.[56] A lieutenant-colonel briefed Goebbels that the attack was scheduled to begin at 4:30 A.M. the next morning: A swift *coup de main* against Gdynia, Danzig to declare for the Reich, and then an all-out military onslaught against eastern Upper Silesia. At midday Hitler told him to get two declarations ready, one to the people and one to the party. Forster phoned from Danzig – evidently heedless of telephone security – and demanded leaflets for the Polish army and population. Goebbels heard that the British ambassador had gone to see Hitler again, and that Hitler had offered Britain the closest cooperation after Poland had been dealt with. 'Britain doesn't believe us any more,' commented Goebbels. When Hitler said much the same to France's ambassador, the latter replied stiffly that 'on his word as an officer' France would be obliged to fight.

Undeterred, at 3:02 P.M. Hitler issued the secret executive order for Case WHITE, the attack on Poland at dawn. Japan's ambassador briefly saw him after that – a frosty meeting under the circumstances.

THE JAPANESE AMBASSADOR was followed by the Italian, Bernardo Attolico. Embarrassed, he conveyed to Hitler the shocking news that Italy, his new ally, would not join in this war.

'There you have it,' commented Goebbels acidly. 'As I always feared and probably knew too ever since Venice. Italy wants out.'

It was a hideous new situation: Hitler had been banking on Italy's support. He had to cancel all his orders for WHITE. Goebbels rushed out a 'supplemental' directive to his editors revoking the midday directive. The new instructions called for 'press discipline' and 'caution' – editors were to hold back their stories on the Poles' military actions and terrorism.[57] A photographer snapped Hitler and Bormann with Otto Dietrich and Dr Goebbels, all in plain clothes; the propaganda minister was looking at his feet, baffled.[58] 'The Führer,' recorded Goebbels, 'is brooding and thinking things over. It's a hard blow for him. But he'll find a way out, even from this devilish situation. He's always found one before and he'll do so this time too.' As grim-faced army generals dashed this way and that, Goebbels hurried back to his ministry to throw his whole machinery into reverse as well. it took him until midnight; Magda, ashen-faced with worry, came to be with him. Everything depended on maintaining the pressure, he decided: On keeping a stiff upper lip.

So he wrote afterward, recording this eventful day.[59] And that was the directive he issued at next morning's press conference. It adumbrated for the first time 'preventive' German operations, but forbade speculation on dates and deadlines; there must be no talk of 'one minute to twelve,' or 'an attack is expected hourly.' The tame newshounds were thus led briefly back to their kennels.[60]

Not surprisingly the Wehrmacht was in a foul mood – they had been all set to attack. Gauleiter Forster phoned from Danzig, depressed by this unexpected turn of events. Dino Alfieri phoned Goebbels from Rome, asking it if was true that Hitler was to broadcast; Goebbels called the rumor a foreign fabrication.[61]

He too was in two minds – Britain had now ratified her pact with Poland, encouraged evidently by Italy's defection. When the French and British ambassadors both asked to see Hitler, Goebbels clutched at straws – 'Perhaps we'll manage to extricate ourselves from the current sticky situation,' he wrote. 'We've got to be very cunning now.'

The introduction of food rationing confronted him with serious propaganda problems. He harangued Herbert Backe, Darré's Staatssekretär, in the middle of that night about the minuscule fruit and tea rations allowed for, then gave vent to his feelings about the secretiveness of the foreign ministry. The whole world knew, he grumbled, that the British and French ambassadors had been to see Hitler, but Germany's own radio said nothing – which forced German listeners willy-nilly into the arms of the B.B.C.[62] After that he sat up until three A.M. reading further worrying reports on public morale.[63]

The embassy wiretap reports which he read the next day, Sunday August 27, gave cause for cautious optimism; but not the one-page digest on morale that Gutterer had compiled for Hitler from their propaganda agencies throughout the Reich. In short, the whole population was against war. The document, typed out in half-inch characters on the special typewriter used for the short-sighted Führer, was dynamite. Goebbels, aware of his own precarious position, had no desire to hand it over himself. He took Gutterer along with him to Hitler's lunch table, wearing his black S.S. Brigadeführer's uniform. Hitler read the document, purpled with rage, and took Gutterer through into the winter-garden. But Himmler, joining them there, soberly backed the propaganda official: His own Gestapo morale reports painted just the same picture. Both men had reports of anti-war demonstrations in Vienna. Goebbels said nothing.[64]

Later that day Hitler reviewed the whole situation with him. 'It is very grave,' recorded Goebbels, adding the familiar nostrum: 'But the Führer will pull us through. On Poland, our minimum demand is Danzig and a corridor across their corridor. Maximum – that's a matter of record. The Führer can't abandon our minimum demand. And he'll get his way. It's become a matter of honor. Nobody can say what will transpire. The Führer is glad we don't have a monarchy any more. The Italy snag has been declared top state secret. Death penalty for treason.'

Hitler spoke to all the Reichstag deputies at five P.M. in the ambassadors' suite of the chancellery. He appealed for courage, and was rewarded with an ovation. He told them that Danzig and the Corridor were his minimum demands. If war came, he would be in the front line.

'As long as I live,' he said dramatically, 'there is to be no talk of capitulation.' He justified his controversial deal with Stalin as being a pact with the Devil to drive out Beelzebub.[65]

FOR THE NEXT FIVE DAYS Dr Goebbels held the editors like acrobats frozen in mid-leap: In suspended animation until Hitler gave the order for WHITE to proceed. It was not easy. Germany must not lose the initiative. He released to the front pages a welter of stories about visits of ambassadors and exchanges of letters. The wiretaps meanwhile showed a further deterioration in the situation.[66]

The press conference on August 28 was long and difficult. Goebbels still forbade newspapers to play up 'Polish terrorism.' Birger Dahlerus, Göring's secret emissary, had brought word from London that the British might swallow Hitler's minimum demands but they would insist on a guarantee of Poland's frontiers. They could adjourn the issue of colonies until later. A long peace with Britain would follow, which might set Germany at loggerheads with Italy: 'But Rome left us in the lurch,' reflected Goebbels. 'And Moscow would also have to guarantee Poland's frontiers' – which Stalin would never do.

Tipped off by Rome, London must surely have known of Hitler's present predicament. Chamberlain believed he could let Germany stew in her own juice. ('Italy is standing well back,' Goebbels wrote contemptuously. 'Her diplomats promise to fight with us to the last drop of ink.')[67]

Consumed by these anxieties, Goebbels had long worried talks with press chief Otto Dietrich – he too saw the gravity of the hour – and Göring, who was also, as Goebbels put it, pleading for moderation.[68]

A sweltering August heat baked the capital. There were fist-fights outside food stores, as crowds began hoarding for the coming war; a run on the banks began. Lunchtime found Hitler grim and rather worn down.[69]

The postponement of hostilities had dislocated Goebbels' timetable. With the war machine crassly halted, there was nothing to report. He directed the press on August 29 to step up the attack on Poland, although it was both difficult and unpopular. From the frontline areas like the Saar he had reports that the mood was anything but blind jingoism. Hitler suggested to Ambassador Henderson that there be a plebiscite in the Corridor. 'He hopes to detach London from Warsaw after all,' assessed Goebbels, 'and thus to find some pretext for attack.'

Hitler agreed that Britain might invite a Polish negotiator to come to Berlin.

His head throbbing with the round-the-clock load of ministerial duties, Goebbels feared that the arrival of a Polish diplomat might result in a ruinous wave of optimism in Germany.[70] At the press conference on the thirtieth, Goebbels again pleaded for a stiff upper lip: Editors were to reserve their vitriol for Poland and her 'atrocities,' while still holding back the most glaring examples, and going easy on England for a while as London seemed to be softening towards Hitler's demands.[71] But this directive was later overtaken by one announcing Polish mobilization: 'The news . . . is to be given top billing and editorial commentary.'[72] (In a significant sentence, editors were asked *not* to mention a 'frontier incident at Hochlinde near Gleiwitz.' A phony raid there by S.S. men wearing Polish uniforms had gone off at half-cock.)[73]

At midnight Hitler sent for him:

He sets out the situation. The British are still hanging tough. Not a peep out of Poland yet. The Führer thinks there *will* be war. Italy's defection is not all that bad for us, as Italy is the most vulnerable to attack by the Entente powers. The Führer has drafted a memorandum: Danzig to be German, a plebiscite in the Corridor in twelve months' time on the basis of 1918; fifty-one percent of the vote to be decisive. Loser to get a one-kilometer-wide corridor across the Corridor. Minorities problems to be examined by an international commission. When the time is ripe the Führer will toss this document to the world community.[74]

His head reeling from worry, late nights, and overwork, Goebbels found it hard to write up his diary on September 1 – even as Hitler's war began. The situation changed hourly. He recalled having turned the press conference loose on Britain the day before. Karl Bömer had brought over the latest sheaf of embassy wiretaps from Göring's Forschungsamt: They made clear that alarm bells were ringing in Paris and London. The French and British ambassadors had been overheard agreeing to beg their Polish colleague, Lipski, to go on his own initiative to Hitler.

'But he can't be found,' observed Goebbels, 'for hours at a time. Poland is obviously playing for time.'

'Göring is still skeptical,' he recorded. 'The Führer still does not believe Britain will intervene. Nobody can say as yet. The S.S. is given special orders for the coming night' – commando-style operations behind the Polish lines.[75] In the evening the Polish ambassador was heard asking for an audience. But Hitler had ordered an end to the talking, and Lipski was not allowed to see Ribbentrop until too late. When he confessed that Warsaw had given him no instructions, Ribbentrop brusquely ended the meeting.

'So that's that,' noted Goebbels. 'The Führer is now incommunicado.'

They all talked until midnight, watching the hours tick past. Göring saw a slim chance that London might not act. Goebbels was less sanguine. Hitler released the text of his memorandum, they all hung around a map for a while, then Goebbels returned home to Magda, who was waiting for him.[76]

iv: The Propaganda Warrior

36: *War*

U NTIL THE LAST MOMENT, Dr Goebbels hoped that the western powers
were bluffing, but feared that they were not.[1] After Hans Fritzsche had
provided an opinion analysis showing that the British were determined
to fight, Goebbels submitted a thoughtful memorandum to Hitler.[2] At his
press conference that Friday, September 1, after Hitler's historic speech to the
Reichstag, Goebbels was able to use plain talk again – which he called 'a real
blessing.' Be that as it may, he directed editors to avoid using the word *war*
and to adopt instead the formula: 'We are fending off Polish attacks.'[3] On the
morning of the third, his press attaché Moritz von Schirmeister briefed him on
the latest news from Reuters.

Goebbels asked: 'What about Britain?' Schirmeister replied that she had not
declared war yet. 'Now you see!' triumphed the minister. But an hour later
Chamberlain's ultimatum reached them. 'Well, so it did happen,' conceded
Goebbels. Until that moment he had not believed it.[4] He repeated to the editors
the injunction to use the word *war* only sparingly.[5] 'Believe me,' he told Göring,
'we have not done all we have for six years to throw it all away in a war.'

'This will be a war about political ideas,' he wrote in a twenty-five-page
memorandum for Hitler entitled 'Thoughts on the Outbreak of War, 1939.'
He described the German public mood at that moment as being 'grim but
calm.' The disaster of 1918 was fresh in many minds – 'So there is nothing of
the hooray-atmosphere of 1914,' he warned. With each victory, however, their
determination would grow – he himself would see to that. Foreshadowing the
great dispute with Ribbentrop that was beginning, he insisted that the entire
foreign propaganda effort be concentrated in one hand – namely his own.

He saw great propaganda opportunities this time: Unlike 1914, the declarations
of war had come from the enemy; and the British and French were repeatedly
overflying neutral Holland and Belgium, and committing other violations
of international law. 'Britain,' he pointed out to Hitler, 'is governed by the
old men of 1914 who are incapable of thinking straight or logically because of
their hate complexes.' Poisoned by 'Jewish capital,' Britain would fight to the   ← *
last man, he prophesied – the last man, that was, of every other nation but
herself, and particularly the French. Only the foreign propaganda weapon, he
suggested, would defeat Britain. Even bombing would not yield victory, given
the famed tenacity of the British people.[6]

Rothschilds

The diary and other documents provide intrinsic evidence of how low he still lay in Hitler's esteem. The Führer had barely consulted him about his war plans. He saw little of him during the Polish campaign; once he tried to reach Hitler by phone, but was told he was away at the front.[7] Ignoring Goebbels' lengthy memorandum, the Führer awarded all foreign propaganda work to Ribbentrop – a terrible rebuff to his propaganda minister. Hitler had an enduring respect for Ribbentrop which subsequent historians have been unable to explain or share. 'It is totally incomprehensible to me,' Goebbels recorded, hearing of the draft decree. 'It will destroy my entire ministry.'[8] As will be seen, Hitler would thereafter keep from Goebbels vital information, for instance about the sinking of the British liner *Athenia*,[9] about the attempt on his life in November,[10] and, in 1940–41, about his intention to attack the Soviet Union.

HITLER ANNOUNCED THE OPENING of hostilities to the Reichstag on Friday, September 1, 1939. He wore a field-gray tunic adorned with the simple Iron Cross he had won in the world war. Morale in Berlin that day was 'grave but resolute,' the deputy gauleiter reported. Chamberlain threatened war if Hitler did not pull his troops out of Poland. 'Wait and see,' was Goebbels' private comment.[11] He ordered the press to mute its remarks about London and Paris, reserving its full venom for Warsaw.[12] 'The situation has undergone one remarkable change,' he noted. 'Mussolini has intervened and proposes a six-power conference. A ceasefire until then. The Führer says he's not disinclined to go along, once he gets his hands on something worthwhile. Thus all military efforts are concentrated on sealing off the Corridor.'[13]

The civilian minister, Goebbels, had real cause to fear that the military would henceforth command Hitler's undivided attention. Although his diary had frequently displayed genuine admiration for the junior officer corps, he detested the older, knuckle-brained army generals and found words of admiration only for Blomberg and Fritsch.[14] When Polish machine-gun bullets shortly ended Fritsch's life, Goebbels demonstratively attended the state funeral while Keitel, Himmler, and the S.S. generals stayed away.[15]

HIS FEAR THAT WAR would marginalize him proved well founded. He was invited to visit Hitler's field headquarters only twice during the entire Polish campaign.[16] In Hitler's absence, Goebbels' critics became more vociferous. 'The party veterans reject him to a man,' wrote Rosenberg. 'Gauleiters tell me that if the Führer would only dump him, they'd eat him for breakfast.'[17] The tension between Goebbels and his colleagues was evident whenever Göring's ministerial Reich Defense Committee met. Presiding Buddha-like over these Cabinet-style meetings, Göring did nothing to protect Goebbels. 'Goebbels appears to be finished,' wrote one rival happily after seeing the field marshal. 'What a blessing.'[18] That Göring had the upper hand was evident on Day Two, as he unexpectedly ordered most of Goebbels' radio stations to shut down in the evenings so that the enemy air force could not use them as radio beacons.[19]

The conflict of personalities became plain on the very first day of war, September 1, 1939. Goebbels had circulated a proposed law making it a criminal, even capital, offense to listen to foreign radio broadcasts and calling for all radio sets to be turned over to the authorities.[20] He met an immediate storm of protest from other ministers. Justice Minister Gürtner pointed to the damning effect it would have at home and abroad on the credibility of their own propaganda, besides creating an army of petty snoopers and informers.[21] The Göring committee unanimously turned down Goebbels' proposal.[22]

The next day however the minister of the interior Dr Frick persuaded Hitler to accept a ban on listening to foreign political broadcasts, and that evening Goebbels' radio announced the new law.[23] As both Frick and Rudolf Hess pointed out to Hitler, if Goebbels called in everybody's radio sets the people would be unable to hear their Führer, that suggestion – which was surely one of his less intelligent plans – was abandoned. The confiscation was restricted to Jewish-owned radios.[24] Goebbels circularized all party officials that 'under the Reich Defense Committee ordinance of September 1' even they were forbidden to tune in to foreign broadcasts.[25]

On other issues too he found it hard to prevail. He objected that printing the party's eagle on ration cards would link it too closely with rationing. 'I fear, Dr Goebbels,' retorted Darré sarcastically, 'that this is a war which is not going to be won by popularity.'[26]

'The Russian military mission arrives in Berlin,' Goebbels noted on September 3. 'A great advantage for us.' But his jubilation was short-lived, as London dictated an ultimatum to Hitler at nine A.M., timed to expire at eleven. 'Straight over to the Reich chancellery,' he recorded. 'The Führer is indignant and has no intention of accepting the ultimatum. He dictates a biting memorandum in which he justifies this.' Even after listening to Chamberlain's radio declaration of war Goebbels was still asking: 'Will London really go for broke?'

Before departing for the 'eastern front' that evening, Hitler reassured him that he anticipated only a phony war in the west. Goebbels was skeptical: 'Now that Churchill is known to be in the Cabinet [as First Lord of the Admiralty] I find that hard to believe.' Göring too had his doubts, he discovered in a lengthy conversation with the field marshal that night: Economically and militarily, Germany could see it through – but even Göring secretly wondered whether the German people would.[27]

For a few days, Goebbels was overwhelmed by the new problems of directing propaganda in a shooting war. Hearing of the sinking of the passenger liner *Athenia* ('it can't have been us,' he assured his private diary), he dismissed it at once as 'a fresh bluff and propaganda trick by Churchill & Co.' and started 'the denial machine' rolling.[28] When Poland claimed that Nazi troops had destroyed the Madonna of Częstochowa, Goebbels flew American journalist Louis Lochner thither in a bomber to see that it was a lie. He had eight hundred banners erected along the western front proclaiming to the French, 'WE WON'T

SHOOT IF YOU DON'T. WE'VE NO QUARREL WITH YOU!'[29] Leopold Gutterer, one of his most inventive aides, suggested they cascade tons of forged pound notes over Britain – thirty percent of its entire currency. Goebbels liked the idea until it occurred to him that the British might well retaliate in kind.[30] A file of his phone conversations with his Italian counterpart confirms his early tactics. He suggested that the Italians concentrate on driving a wedge between the British and French, reserving their most hostile language for Churchill, Eden, and Chamberlain; he asked that if he issued a denial, the Italian press should give it prominence too.[31]

At air staff headquarters outside Potsdam on the fifth, Göring assured him that they would soon have a strategic breakthrough in Poland. The field marshal expressed outrage at the Italians for their cold feet. Sitting under the trees, the two Nazis quietly discussed Germany's plight if a full-scale world war developed. Churchill's appointment to Chamberlain's Cabinet had shocked them both – but Goebbels hoped the British might still be bluffing.[32] Göring had nothing but contempt for Ribbentrop, blaming him for having been too inflexible in stating German demands. On the seventh Goebbels flew in a bomber to Hitler's eastern headquarters near Gross Born to discuss Ribbentrop's take-over of foreign propaganda:

> The Führer [he recorded] is living in an armored train in the middle of a forest. . . He looks magnificent and is in good humor. He at once sets out the situation. The Poles are in a state of complete military collapse. . . Their situation is hopeless. Our tanks are pushing on without stopping.

When Goebbels moved to touchier matters – the extraordinary decree granting Ribbentrop control of foreign propaganda – Hitler asked him to settle things with the foreign minister directly. Goebbels tried and not surprisingly failed; he found the next day that Hitler had dictated a brief decree defining the two squabbling ministers' areas of responsibility.[33] Although Goebbels was broadly satisfied to find his own ministry left intact, the decree remained a thorn in his flesh for the next four years.[34]

For all his loud mouth, he was not a fighting man. The prospect of a long war unsettled him, and he registered with alarm each statement by Chamberlain warning that Britain was resolved to fight to the finish.[35] He made a brief foray into foreign policy when Dino Alfieri phoned from Rome on the ninth with word that Mussolini proposed that the Italian press ventilate a possible solution whereby the Polish government resigned in favor of ministers willing to make peace; to fight a war in the west, the Duce had added, would be nonsense. 'I treat the matter dilatorily,' Goebbels cautiously recorded, 'then phone the Führer. He is very interested in the offer, but suspects that Mussolini is aiming at a general European peace conference. He therefore asks me to skirt around the subject for the time being; I am to thank Alfieri for any support, but say that I cannot reach the Führer.'[36]

When Alfieri asked the next day what Moscow was doing, Goebbels stated that he had no official word, but 'something was evidently afoot in Russia.'[37] (Stalin's troops invaded eastern Poland three days later 'to protect her minorities,' and arguing that 'because a Polish state no longer existed.')[38] Ribbentrop shortly asked him to desist from further telephone conversations with Alfieri. 'The Führer does not want to tie himself down.'[39]

Hitler phoned him the next evening and asked to see him on the morrow in Upper Silesia. Together again, they agreed that the fall of Warsaw would be a psychological blow to the enemy. Moscow would probably then intervene. Italy seemed passive, even downright hostile. 'Mussolini seems displeased,' Hitler told Goebbels. But he wanted to preserve their friendship, so Goebbels was to keep the channel to Alfieri open. He showed the Führer the script of his forthcoming speech: Hitler asked him to sharpen the attack on Britain's warmongering role. 'Once we've dealt with the east,' recorded Goebbels, 'he wants to take on the west. He has no use for a long war. If there's got to be war, then short and sharp.'

In Warsaw however the Poles put up a protracted and heroic resistance. The city's commandant called the city's population to arms, and told them to 'resort to every means of combat.' On the sixteenth Goebbels warned Rome that the Wehrmacht would therefore issue an ultimatum and bombard Warsaw. 'There will be an avalanche of protests and defamation from London and Paris,' he anticipated. 'We ask for the support of the Italian press and propaganda.'[40] Warsaw held out for eight more days under a ruinous air and artillery bombardment.

Concerned about Germany's image, Goebbels resorted to legalisms and an appeal to baser human instincts. He directed the platoons of Nazi war reporters and newsreel cameramen:

1. Never refer to Warsaw as a city in reports, but always as a fortress.
2. Use much more film footage than hitherto of Jewish types from Warsaw and the entire occupied area including both character-studies and the Jews at forced labor. This material should service to reinforce our antisemitic education drive, both at home and abroad.[41]

Poland was finished. With Hitler back in Berlin, the phony war began and he gradually became more approachable again. Goebbels attended lunch almost every day. On the twenty-seventh he found Hitler optimistic. He hoped the enemy would see reason. 'It depends on London,' Hitler explained at lunch on October 10, 'whether the war goes on.'[42]

Gradually however his hopes of peace faded, and he authorized Goebbels to turn up the heat on Chamberlain. Churchill however seemed the more rewarding target – easier to identify with the English plutocracy. 'He lives in the sixteenth century,' Hitler would agree. 'Totally out of touch with the real needs of his people.'[43] Since Churchill's speeches were at this sorry pass in

Britain's naval fortunes necessarily economical with the truth, ridiculing him
was too great a temptation for Goebbels to resist.[44]

As the propagandist for an as yet undefeated belligerent Goebbels on the
other hand saw no real need to lie. His untruths were still unintentional:
Relying on Luftwaffe claims, he declared as sunk not only the battleship *Royal
Oak* (sunk that October) but also the aircraft carrier *Ark Royal* and the cruiser
Repulse which remained very much afloat.[45] Egged on by Hitler – who unlike
him knew the truth, that one of his own U-boats had indeed sunk the British
liner *Athenia* – Goebbels reverted to the mystery in the third week of October.[46]
'Perhaps,' he noted, 'we'll even succeed in sinking him [Churchill]. That would
be worth more than sinking two battleships.'[47] He wrote a big article accusing
the Englishman of having had the *Athenia* scuttled himself, and broadcast this
libel worldwide, calling him a criminal who should now be called to the bar
of world opinion. 'I'm working flat out to overthrow this man,' he admitted
privately.[48] Churchill retorted that Goebbels' charge was simply laughable. 'He
won't be laughing soon,' snapped Goebbels in the privacy of his diary.[49]

THE PROPAGANDA MINISTRY had rapidly adjusted for war. At eleven each
morning Goebbels held a 'ministerial' conference with his department heads
and their advisors, about thirty to fifty officials all told, in his private office.[50]
At a quarter to noon Hitler's press officer Otto Dietrich or his hard-nosed
deputy Alfred-Ingemar Berndt would hold a further conference elsewhere in
the same building to coordinate Goebbels' decisions with requests submitted
by other ministries. After 1940 this later conference would end with the
dictation to a stenographer of formal *Tagesparolen*, themes for the day which
were read out to the general press conference immediately following at twelve-
fifteen P.M., attended by one or two hundred German journalists (but only
rarely by Goebbels).

About one-third of his men had been drafted into uniform. Karl Hanke,
whom he had not seen since the summer, found himself spirited away to the
Polish front in a panzer lieutenant's uniform. In September 1939 the ministry
employed 9,762 professional orators, and these would address precisely 156,143
political meetings over the first eleven months of war.[51] He would have nearly
three hundred mobile cinemas by the end of 1940. His printing presses spun
off 560,000 poster-sized portraits of Hitler, and millions of leaflets, placards,
banners, and wall-newspapers; eight million copies of the *Slogan of the Week*
wall-newspaper would be printed by the end of 1940, along with war posters
like 'WITH OUR FLAGS IS VICTORY', and, less famously, 'THE ETERNAL JEW and
'STAR OF DAVID.'

Two years earlier, Goebbels had banned one anti-Jewish film as being too
shrill.[52] It was only now, after the war began, that he started work on his own
major antisemitic films. The first, *The Eternal Jew*, was produced by Franz
Hippler and the Party's movie company DFG. Using photo- and movie-
montage techniques that mixed documentary shots filmed in the squalor of

the Warsaw ghetto and sequences from the feature movies of former big name 'Jewish' movie personalities like Max Reinhardt, Ernst Lubitsch, and Charlie Chaplin this hour-long production conveyed an undeniable visual message. From October 1939 the Goebbels Diary reveals him personally supervising the filming, and checking the necessarily unappetizing footage shot in the Polish synagogues and ghettos. 'One recoils involuntarily from the spectacle of so much filth,' reads one entry.[53] His cameramen had filmed the Jewish ritual slaughter of cattle, and Goebbels was undecided whether to use this revolting footage in this movie or in *Jew Süss*, the Terra studios' remake of the 1935 British movie of that name. [54] 'This will be *the* antisemitic movie,' predicted Goebbels after reading Veit Harlan's treatment: a Jew, Süss Oppenheimer, becomes the Duke of Württemberg's crooked financial adviser and tax collector: involves him in swindles on a Maxwellian or even a Madoffian scale: is condemned to death.[55] Replete with scenes of rape and torture this movie, released in 1940, would become one of the most insidious propaganda films of all time.[56]

He had perceptibly relaxed his personal vendetta against the Jews during 1939, only to be goaded into reviving it by one of their less felicitous moves as the Zionist leader Dr Chaim Weizmann formally declared war on their behalf against Nazi Germany in September 1939.[57] Jewish cartoonists abroad poked fun at Goebbels' lame foot, and Jewish radio commentators in England snarled over the airwaves at him when he turned forty-two.[58] A few days later the *Daily Sketch* printed a cartoon showing him with Hitler and Göring, all hanging from gibbets surrounded by skulls. He repaid these hurts in ways that were petty rather than profound, ordering the Nazi newspapers to publish a cartoon showing Chamberlain in slippers and persuading Hitler to reduce the food allowances for Jews and to withhold chocolate from them altogether.[59]

A visit to the Jewish ghetto in Łódź left an indelible imprint on his mind. 'Those are not human beings any longer,' he wrote after leaving his car to inspect it closer. 'Those are animals. So our task isn't a humanitarian, but a surgical one. . . Otherwise one day Europe will succumb to the Jewish pestilence.'[60] Back in Berlin he reported his impressions to Hitler. 'He thoroughly endorses my description of the Jewish problem,' he claimed in his diary. 'The Jews are a waste-product. They are more of a clinical than a social issue.'[61] After visiting the eastern territories again he told Hitler about the unwholesome spectacles he had witnessed there. 'We must outlaw the Jewish danger,' he recorded afterward. 'But it will surface again in a few generations. There's just no antidote.'[62]

There is evidence of how far his diary now veered from the truth. While it noted that Hitler expressed admiration for his latest speech attacking Churchill over the *Athenia*, Rosenberg recorded that Göring had told him that Hitler had remarked sarcastically that 'not even the entire Reichstag' had risen to such heights of rhetoric.[63] There are also other discrepancies, for example about the latest newsreel. 'The Führer,' Goebbels claimed in the diary, 'finds it very good.' But other sources reveal that Hitler found its mind-numbing sequences on a dance group in the opera, Queen Wilhelmina inspecting the Dutch air-raid defenses, and the Hungarian Labor Service insufferably tedious.[64] 'The newsreels are put together without inspiration or depth of interest,' he fulminated over lunch to Goebbels and a beaming Rosenberg in December. 'We have in Germany an entire nation under arms, yet the newsreels take no notice.' Goebbels protested that Karl Ritter was making excellent patriotic movies like *Pour le Mérite*. 'Yes patriotic,' said Hitler, 'but not National Socialist!' They went at it hammer and tongs for twenty minutes before Dr Goebbels lapsed into a stricken silence. 'His appalling arrogance,' gloated Rosenberg, 'is now too much for even the long-suffering Führer to bear.' Goebbels hated being criticized by Hitler. 'But he has the right to criticize,' he loyally noted. 'He is a genius.'[65]

One never knew, after all, who might read the diary's pages.

IN OCTOBER 1939 GOEBBELS' new stately home at Lanke, called the Haus am Bogensee, is complete. Once his stepson Harald comes, now a young paratrooper whose eyes have seen the horrors of war in Poland. On Goebbels' birthday Hitler invites them to tea; the Führer's face is also lined with worry – the war is not proceeding at all as he had planned.[66] Worries about financing Lanke still beset Goebbels.[67] He visits Magda, hospitalized once more with heart problems, and tells her of these irksome difficulties.[68]

'We have such money worries,' he writes.[69] He puts pressure on his budget chief Dr Ott to 'show more initiative' in dealing with the stubborn ministry of finance; this evidently works, because Ott shortly tells him that he has 'sorted out some of the problems in financing the new buildings.'[70] But they are a family again. Goebbels' marital problems seem over; at least the endless rows have faded from the diary's pages. He takes Magda out to Lanke for an afternoon, and they happily arrange the furniture.[71] Once in November they rake over old embers, 'of which,' notes Goebbels, evidently scorched in the process, 'some are anything but agreeable.'[72] Magda enrolls as a Red Cross nurse.[73] Slowly his domestic worries recede.

November 8, 1939 finds him in Munich listening once more to Hitler's speech on the putsch anniversary. From here one year before, Goebbels had launched the Night of Broken Glass. By six P.M. Himmler, Bouhler, Rosenberg, Frank, Ribbentrop, and other dignitaries had joined him in the Bürgerbräu beerhall; this time they were surrounded by field-gray army uniforms. Hitler delivered an hour-long attack on Britain, pronounced that he was ready for five years of war if necessary, then finished abruptly – he had to hurry back to Berlin since his army commanders had asked to see him urgently the next morning about Case YELLOW, the repeatedly postponed western campaign.

Goebbels joined the Führer in his special railroad car. At Nuremberg station he saw a telegram handed to Hitler: a mighty explosion, it said, had ripped through the beerhall just after they left, killing eight and injuring over sixty.[74] Goebbels was agog at his Führer's seemingly miraculous escape. If they had not left early, they would all surely have been killed. He really must be under God's protection, he privately concluded. 'He won't die until his mission is complete.[75] At the ministry he directed all editors to comment along these lines. 'Urgent state business had called him back to Berlin,' the journalists were told. He forbade them to incriminate any specific groups inside Germany like monarchists, the clergy, or Jews.[76] He did not want any repetition of the November 1938 pogrom. London and Paris meanwhile blamed the Nazis themselves – 'As is their wont,' he observed dryly in his diary, with the Reichstag fire allegations in mind.[77]

There was a bizarre sequel. Hitler showed him a letter received a few days before: the writer, an astrologer living in the Black Forest, had cast Hitler's horoscope and regretted to inform him that he was in mortal danger between the seventh and the tenth. 'I'm curious to know what you make of this,' said Hitler.

'Wow!' replied the minister cautiously, knowing Hitler's aversion to the occult: 'Wow!'

Himmler pocketed the letter, promising to look into it.[78]

THAT NIGHT THERE WAS a mini-pogrom, as rampaging Nazis beat up innocents in Berlin. 'I have them shipped off to concentration camps,' recorded Goebbels grandly, but the outrages continued.[79] Goebbels ordered the guards on his ministry reinforced (a sign that *he* at least regarded the assassination attempt as genuine.)[80] Learning only on the fifteenth that Himmler's men had caught 'the first of the assassins' on the Swiss border, he blamed his old foe Otto Strasser; Strasser, it turned out, had fled from Switzerland to England immediately after the bomb blast. 'We are keeping it all secret,' he summarized, 'so as not to tip off the men really behind it.'[81] The hunt for accomplices turned up nothing; but when the government press agency finally announced the assassin's arrest on November 21, Goebbels released news of the capture of two top British agents on the Dutch border at the same time, so that even the dimmest reader would understand the hint.[82]

GOEBBELS SENT FOR THE ASTROLOGER. He was Karl-Ernst Krafft – a pale, slight fellow with spindly hands and deep-set eyes. Goebbels wanted to learn more about his letter to Hitler, though carefully armoring himself with a veneer of skepticism (as recently as November 2 he had directed the party to keep a watchful eye on seers, astrologers, and clairvoyants).[83] At his confidential eleven A.M. conference on November 11 he ordered all astrological publications checked for relevant prophecies. In fact all such publications had long been banned, but he mentioned casually in his diary, 'I'm having a watch kept on astrology. A load of rubbish is talked and printed about it. And yet, strangely enough, it all speaks in our favor.'[84]

'Speaks' is perhaps too strong a word. As Krafft explained, it depended how one *interpreted* the Delphic prophecies, couched in Old French, of Nostradamus (1503–66). Goebbels promptly took him onto the ministry's payroll.[85] With Krafft's help, and with more than a little imagination, they would hijack Nostradamus' ancient prophecies to benefit the Reich. He ordered a new 'translation' of the prophecies suitable for use in propaganda to France, and printed millions of bogus Nostradamus leaflets, with special editions of the selected passages prophesying the downfalls of, respectively, France and Britain.[86] In December he asked to see the astrological calendars for 1940 (and banned the lot the next day).[87]

That winter he turned out millions of propaganda leaflets designed to subvert the French troops. Some asked the French soldiers how they'd like to die for Danzig. Others were shaped like a yellowing autumn leaf, and asked if they intended to die and fade away like this. Two clandestine radio stations started transmissions in French. He supervised their content closely.[88] 'I direct that enemy statesmen are no longer to be portrayed as figures of fun,' he wrote, 'but as cruel, vengeful tyrants. This goes for Chamberlain above all.'[89] He spared the Duke of Windsor from this campaign, as an investment for the future.[90] For Churchill he had both admiration and contempt. 'Riddled with lies and distortions,' he wrote after one Churchill broadcast. 'He's grown really old. But he's a cunning old fox all the same.'[91]

The topics of his ministerial conferences ranged from the ridiculous to the banal, from the supply of shoes, potatoes, diapers, coal, nail varnish, and cosmetics to the chronic shortcomings in the forces' mail.[92] When London published an uncomfortably accurate account of Himmler's concentration camps, Goebbels commissioned a riposte about their forerunners, the British camps in the Boer War, and other colonial 'atrocities.'[93]

He remained obsessed with the 'crime' of listening to foreign broadcasts. Despite draconian sentences it was clear from Gestapo reports that listening was on the increase.[94] British bombers had also started dropping millions of leaflets including a mock *Völkischer Beobachter* wittily called the *Wölkiger Beobachter*, the Cloudy Observer. The first issue declared: 'The revolver-journalist Goebbels and the young hacks scribbling at his behest may have destroyed the proud craft of German journalism but they cannot assuage so easily the thinking man's natural hunger for news.' Its caricatures were apposite – like Hitler reading Karl Marx and Stalin browsing in *Mein Kampf*, and there was a moving obituary of General von Fritsch complete with a black border.[95] Goebbels irritably conceded that the British propaganda was becoming more sophisticated.[96]

His own press policies were still diffuse. He believed that he had lightened up on the press, directing: 'We must allow them a free rein.'[97] But the press directives reflect none of this. After a train crash near Friedrichshafen killed 132 passengers on December 22, and a second rail accident not far away killed fifty more the very next day, he ordered both news items suppressed.[98] He banned press coverage of the murder trials of several Poles for massacring ethnic Germans, as well as reports on the execution of rebellious Czech students, and other steps against their intelligentsia.[99] More enlightened were his bans on the printing of anonymous movie- or book-reviews and, conversely, the names of defendants in minor court actions.[100] Many of these rules still hold in Germany today.

As Christmas 1939 approached, he warned editors not to delve into the ancestry of the Führer, his childhood, or his private life, and he rebuked them for drawing festive parallels between Adolf Hitler and Jesus Christ. 'The Führer does not desire such comparisons,' he said."[101]

37: The Principles of Propaganda

THE WINTER OF 1939–40 wrote its name in the history of Europe with weeks of barbaric blizzards. The canals froze over; deprived of coal, the arms factories slowed down, and power stations dimmed.[1] The radiators in Goebbels' ministerial palace were stone cold. Playhouses and movie theaters closed.[2] The minister discussed with Albert Speer putting even stronger security fencing around Lanke, and gave orders for a two-month renovation of Schwanenwerder as well.[3] The forests around Lanke were blanketed in snow. He took Magda and the children out on sleigh rides until the snow lost its magic for him. Judging from his diary, the chattering children were his only joy. 'Children are at least quite honest,' he wrote. 'They say what they mean. Why can't we?'[4] Visiting his mother at Rheydt he did what he could to help her to make ends meet. 'She brought me through the world war,' he reasoned. 'Now I'm going to see her through this one.' Still plagued with money problems, he persuaded Magda to pass the hat round among their wealthier friends.[5] As Europe froze, Hitler's plans congealed as well. Once, on January 8, 1940, he invited Goebbels around for a cup of real coffee; but he made no attempt to discuss YELLOW, his planned attack on France.[6]

Goebbels boasted to the Führer that their propaganda broadcasts were now going out in twenty-two foreign languages, including Gaelic, Afrikaans, Arabic, Hindustani and a Babel of Balkan tongues, compared with four languages one year before. Their English-language broadcasts targeted the working classes, with an emphasis on the anti-plutocratic character of the war; the *News Chronicle*, Goebbels told Hitler, reported that fifty-four percent of the 'little people' in England admitted tuning in to his propaganda.[7]

He was ill at ease in war. His ministerial functions largely bored him. To the foreign journalists stationed in Berlin he offered both the carrot and the stick. He told Karl Bömer to open up luxurious retreats for these important gentlemen, with no expense spared to mollycoddle them; but he also recommended arresting one from time to time and saddling him with 'interminable court proceedings' as a salutary lesson.[8] He also directed Bömer to ensure that Otto Strasser's autobiography was banned 'in every country in which it is slated to appear.'[9] The book was not flattering about Goebbels.

SEVERAL TIMES DURING those weeks he defined his basic propaganda tenets.

Ordering Fritzsche to continue plugging the *Athenia* mystery, Goebbels lectured him cynically: 'Never lose sight of the fundamental principle of all propaganda, the constant repetition of the most effective arguments.'[10] A month later he reiterated, 'Propaganda means repetition and still more repetition!'[11]

Almost equal in importance came accuracy and promptness. Local people had been dismayed by the press's furtive reporting on the Friedrichshafen rail disaster.[12] Moreover, headlines had to match the story. A Berlin evening newspaper headlined the sinking of 'two British warships,' but they were only patrol boats.[13] As the British air raids began during May 1940, Goebbels ruled that the local press was always to report casualty figures accurately. After those in one Berlin raid were first announced as six dead, then revised to thirty-six, he ordered the press to admit their error. 'The people must not start doubting the credibility of German reporting,' he explained.[14]

In overseas broadcasting he allowed greater objectivity than at home. He released the newsreel record of the last moments of the pocket battleship *Graf Spee* but only for foreign consumption.[15] With the increasing setbacks of 1941 Goebbels' policy of total truth became harder to enforce. When the navy in one day lost its three top submarine aces, Günter Prien, Joachim Schepke, and Otto Kretschmer, he ordered the news suppressed.[16]

He also began to deceive his own diary more systematically, telling it on November 19, 1941 that Ernst Udet had 'died suddenly,' although it is plain from the rest of the entry that he knew that the disaffected Luftwaffe general had died by his own hand.[17]

He saw little point in issuing official denials. 'Denials alone won't work,' he stated when the British started alleging Nazi atrocities in Poland. 'You've got to counter-attack' – but this did not necessarily mean counter-attacking on the same theme.[18] 'Our principle must always be, never hold your tongue: Always say something. If need be, force our enemies to lose themselves in denials instead of spewing out still more lies.'[19] German denials, he ruled, must always be categorical.[20] When an official asked in 1944 for formal denials of Soviet allegations about Nazi atrocities in Majdanek concentration camp, his ministry replied that none would be issued, 'as we shall be totally on the defensive in any discussion of this matter.'[21]

As for lying, Dr Goebbels laid down strict rules about when this was permissible: It was to be used only as a defensive tactic, never to fake successes; official organs like news agencies and radio stations were never to be used to spread lies, and their source was to be immediately camouflaged; and Germany's domestic radio and press channels must never be burdened with them – they were to be propagated only by their overseas broadcasters.[22]

Perhaps his most enduring method was to pick up the enemy's most lethal propaganda ammunition, like a ticking bomb, and fling it back in his face. During the humiliating British retreat to Dunkirk in May 1940, he made devastating use of the British soldiers' ditty about hanging out the washing on the Siegfried Line.[23] For a while Churchill's famous V-for-victory device caused

Goebbels headaches: the B.B.C. hammered it out in Morse code as the opening bar of Beethoven's fifth symphony, and it appeared overnight as graffiti on walls all over occupied Europe. In July 1941 he hit on the solution. 'I'm taking over that letter V for ourselves,' he announced in his diary, delighted at the simplicity of the solution. 'We're going to say it stands for a German victory. Like a dream!'[24] Three years later he would reload that 'V' and fire it back at London, this time standing for *Vergeltung*, revenge.

RIBBENTROP STILL STOOD in his way. On February 17, 1940 the British violated Norwegian neutrality to board an unarmed homebound German fleet auxiliary, the *Altmark*.[25] There were rich propaganda pickings for both sides, but Churchill won the race by five hours because the foreign ministry in Berlin sat on the dispatches.[26] Livid with rage Goebbels ordered his editors to concentrate on the *Altmark* incident. 'Even those newspapers normally accustomed to sparing the nerves of their readers are to use italic and bold typefaces,' he dictated.[27]

The rivalry between the two ministries created odd situations. Goebbels had a large foreign section, with which he pursued his own foreign policy; he even had his own foreign intelligence agency, based in the stock exchange building in Hamburg and drawing information from its own agents all over neutral and occupied Europe.[28] Ribbentrop's foreign ministry had its own sections for press, cultural policies, and propaganda. Since Hitler had his own press chief, Dietrich, three conflicting 'official' viewpoints often appeared in the same editorial office.[29] Goebbels was unable to prevail upon Hitler to remedy this anomalous position. He had yet to outlive the harm done by the Lida Baarova episode.

He now saw Hitler more often over lunch however. On March 1, 1940 Hitler delivered a three-hour monologue to the gauleiters explaining why the weather still precluded any operations in the west. 'The Führer is a genius,' concluded Goebbels afterward. 'He's going to build the first Germanic people's empire.' He went on debating with Hitler until one A.M. that night. Back at Schwanenwerder it took him hours to get to sleep, what with the vivid plans and daydreams.[30] By a decree later that month he was confirmed as a permanent member of the Cabinet-like ministerial Council for Reich Defense along with Himmler, Bouhler, Milch, and Prussian finance minister Johannes Popitz.[31] True, they had no idea what Hitler was planning. But Goebbels' trust in him was complete.

'Big question,' he wrote on April 2, 1940, referring to YELLOW. 'When does it start?'

Like Ribbentrop, Hess, Dietrich, Himmler, and every other top civilian, Goebbels was totally in the dark about Hitler's real next operation, against Scandinavia.[32] He continued to polemicize about the western powers' 'plans to enlarge the war' through the first week in April, while going about his other humdrum business.[33] He inspected a great new German invention, the tape-recorder, and he labored at his propaganda mills.[34] He had established several 'black' transmitters, to carry his subversive messages directly to millions of French and British radio listeners, eroding their confidence in victory and spreading rumor and confusion.[35] His French transmitters were codenamed Concordia and Humanité, the latter being a 'communist' station run by his brilliant broadcasting expert Dr Adolf Raskin.[36] His trump card was the Irish broadcaster William Joyce; although his overstated English accent earned him the unfriendly nickname Lord Haw-Haw, the mocking, intellectual content of his broadcasts gained him millions of English-speaking listeners around the world.[37]

At Gutterer's suggestion Dr Goebbels rocketed over the French lines millions of pornographic postcards: one, a translucent illustrated postcard entitled *Le Tommy, ou est-il resté?* (Where's Tommy?) implied British hanky-panky with the mademoiselles at the rear while the French soldier was valiantly holding the line. The face of the postcard showed trenches, barbed wire, and a bloodstained French soldier; but held up to the light, the hidden picture revealed a nude man in bed with a woman, with a picture of her husband in French uniform on the wall.[38] Other rockets showered the French with familiar glossy black cartons of cigarette paper that bore however the slogan, 'Why die for Danzig?' and with each sheet arguing that Britain had lured the French into this war. Hitler was dubious, reminding Goebbels that leaflet propaganda had not helped the Nazi party into power. But, he conceded, leafleting flights helped to conceal that the Luftwaffe was taking aerial photographs of vital enemy locations.[39]

Goebbels meanwhile had become a personality of world stature. The American magazine *Life* invited him to contribute four articles: He dictated his own terms.[40] His propaganda could boast of many triumphs. In Warsaw the Nazis had captured the entire Polish diplomatic archives; with a little creative editing Goebbels published the documents to illustrate Roosevelt's meddling in European affairs. A French newspaper printed a photograph of Roosevelt's emissary Sumner Welles visiting the French prime minister; behind them was a map of Europe on which the French had already divided up Germany, Italy, and Yugoslavia among their neighbors. Goebbels reissued this provocative map, with a few deft embellishments, for the foreign press.[41] But the world soon had an even more stunning Hitler coup to cope with.

NOT UNTIL LATE ON APRIL 8, 1940 did Hitler send for Goebbels and inform him, during a stroll in the chancellery gardens, that he would be invading Denmark and Norway at dawn the next day. Guns, troops, and ammunition were at that very moment entering Norwegian waters, concealed inside colliers.[42] Asked by an astonished Dr Goebbels how he expected the United States to react to this new operation, Hitler responded that he did not really care. 'Material aid from them cannot come into play for about eight months, and manpower about a year and a half.' This did however make it essential to win the war before 1941 ended. To get them out of the way, Hitler had sent off all the foreign military attachés to inspect Germany's western defenses. Only one, the Norwegian, had declined to go. Goebbels added to the smoke screen by organizing a mass meeting in Berlin that evening.

That Hitler pulled off this masterstroke on April 9, 1940, only hours before Churchill landed his own expeditionary force in Norway bestowed on him an ill-deserved aura of semi-righteousness. At lunch that day he again began bragging about a new Germanic empire. Goebbels warned editors not to mention their paratroop operations.[43]

The German naval losses in the operation were severe. In Oslo Fiord an ancient Norwegian coastal battery torpedoed the cruiser *Blücher* with heavy loss of life. Eberhard Taubert, one of Goebbels' best men, gave him an eyewitness account of this naval disaster ('As *Blücher* went down there was one last infantryman on deck. He saluted, and the survivors stood to attention. A cheer went up for the Führer').[44]

Unexpectedly, the fighting in Norway grew stiffer, particularly at Narvik. When Hans Fritzsche warned that the British were fighting with great courage, Goebbels became quite pensive. 'We're going to have to take them more seriously,' he decided.[45]

38: *Knocking out Front Teeth*

JOSEPH GOEBBELS' LIFE IS ALREADY nine-tenths over. Hilde has just had her first day at school; life's little milestones are flashing past in a blur. His pride and joy are his four daughters. 'What a delight it is to see the clever, pretty little lasses slowly getting bigger,' he writes, unconsciously excluding his slow-witted infant son from his sentiments.[1] Once he finds that Magda has dressed Hellmut in a frilly silk blouse. 'That's not right for a boy,' he snaps at her, sending him off to change. 'We're not the Ribbentrops or Görings. People expect different of us!'[2]

Magda tells him that her father is ill. Goebbels merely sniffs. He lacks any feeling toward old Oskar Ritschel. She goes alone to the hospital in Duisburg.[3] Gradually her father wastes away, losing forty pounds. He has evidently imbibed the evil drafts brewed by his son-in-law. 'Of course it isn't really a war against Britain and France at all,' Ritschel writes afterwards to his daughter, 'but a war between the Judaic and Germanic races; that is the essence of this gigantic struggle.'[4]

MANY DESKS AT GOEBBELS' MINISTRY were empty; half of his staff were away at the wars.[5] Goebbels encouraged this war service, both for the battlefield experience that men like Gunter d'Alquèn would bring back to the ministry and for the ideological stiffening that they brought to the front lines.[6] He sent out regular hectographed letters disbursing the latest ministry gossip, chocolates, and cigarettes to each of his men in uniform.[7] All the ministry's soldiers acquitted themselves well. Hanke fought his way through France as General Erwin Rommel's adjutant; Berndt succeeded him in Africa.[8] Werner Naumann, an officer in Hitler's elite S.S. Leibstandarte, would return with a wound badge and other decorations from the Balkan campaign.[9] Herbert Heiduschke, another Goebbels adjutant, would meet a paratrooper's death in Crete.[10] G. W. Müller would be wounded in the advance on Murmansk in North Russia.[11] Moritz von Schirmeister, Goebbels' press officer since 1938, would not return from the eastern front to his desk until January 1942.[12]

The Norwegian campaign provided another coup for Goebbels, the capture of British documents proving that Churchill had himself, for all his talk about invasions of neutral countries, intended to invade Norway. 'That is a gift from the gods,' wrote a jubilant Goebbels. 'We missed disaster by hours. Churchill was waiting for reports of the English invasion – and the accursed Germans had got there first.'¹³ The incriminating British documents were rushed into print. He ordered the press to follow up with leading articles, and had the captured British officers interviewed on the newfangled tape-recorder lest Churchill deny the story.¹⁴ The British expeditionary force had behaved despicably, Hitler told Goebbels, looting and pillaging everywhere. In contrast to the Polish campaign, however, the Norwegian defenders had not committed one atrocity – 'They are after all a Germanic breed' – and he ordered the immediate release of all Norwegian prisoners by way of recognition.¹⁵

Unlike Goebbels, Hitler had no special animus against the British. While Goebbels broadly defined their war aims as 'victory over the western plutocracies,'¹⁶ he often heard Hitler speak, within the four walls of his chancellery, of his fondness for the British and their empire. 'The Führer's intention,' recorded Goebbels, 'is to administer one knockout punch. Even so, he would be ready to make peace today, on condition that Britain stay out of Europe and give us back our colonies... He does not want at all to crush Britain or to destroy her empire.'¹⁷ Hitler described the English leaders as criminals. 'They could have had peace on the most agreeable of terms,' he privately assured Goebbels. 'Instead they are fighting a war and shattering their empire to the core.'¹⁸ 'We are neither able nor willing to take over their empire,' added Hitler, reverting to this bitter theme. 'There are some people whom you can talk sense into only after you've knocked out their front teeth.'¹⁹

On the evening of May 9 Hitler boarded his train, bound for the western front. Goebbels showed up conspicuously at Göring's side at the première of Mussolini's play *Cavour* in Berlin, then returned to his deserted ministry building. At 5:35 A.M. on May 10 YELLOW began, with Hitler's tanks and airborne troops invading the Low Countries and France. At eight, Goebbels himself broadcast appeals to them not to resist. 'Our entire public must be convinced that Holland and Belgium did violate their neutrality,' he told his staff.²⁰ Learning that Churchill had that same day replaced Chamberlain as Britain's prime minister, Goebbels penned this jubilant comment in his diary: 'Decks cleared for action!'²¹ Churchill launched the air war immediately, with raids on the Ruhr. Elsewhere twenty-four people, mostly children, were killed by bombs in Freiburg; in fact a stray Luftwaffe plane was to blame, but the harrowing stories from Freiburg were grist to Goebbels' mill all the same.²²

He ordered the media to ignore Churchill's new cabinet, except for the effete minister of information Duff Cooper. On Hitler's personal instructions the popular Queen Wilhelmina of the Netherlands was also spared.²³ As the powerful transmitter at Luxemburg fell into German hands Goebbels offered a substantial reward for the return of its missing valves, which had been removed to disable it; it later became one of his mightiest weapons in the radio propaganda war.²⁴

Initially he laid down the principle of total restraint in their reporting: There was to be no sensationalizing of the Wehrmacht's victories.²⁵ Hitler had evidently briefed him on his real secret strategy, later known as the Manstein Plan, because as it began to unfold on May 16 Goebbels noted that their mission now was to dupe the enemy into expecting a rehash of the old Schlieffen Plan.[26] He spread rumors about fresh airborne landings, and took care not to rebut enemy stories about Nazi secret weapons.[27]

Already he was preparing a new recording of massed choirs singing the Netherlands Thanksgiving Prayer, ready for victory.[28] As Hitler's armies began their historic wheel toward the north-west, following the secret plan, Goebbels reflected unabashedly: 'Since 1938 we have conquered seven European countries.'[29] The king of Belgium conceded defeat, and Churchill's voice was heard broadcasting a famous warning that Britain would fight on the beaches. 'He's still insolent,' decided Goebbels, 'but you can hear the perspiration trickling out of every frightened pore.'[30]

He ordered it brought home to the British and the French that it was their governments which had pronounced this war on Germany, and he even commissioned a special England victory fanfare for the German radio.[31] 'They declared this war,' said Hitler, informing Goebbels of his intention of battering the French into submission. 'Now let them whimper for peace.'[32]

GENERAL VON REICHENAU would tell the propaganda ministry's staff, after Hitler had appointed his field marshals, 'The one who really won the French campaign was Goebbels.'[33] There was something in that. As the British expeditionary force fell back in disarray toward the beaches around Dunkirk, Goebbels' black transmitters were softening up the French public and doing all they could to generate among French soldiers, the *poilus*, a feeling that they had been betrayed. He himself wrote many of the scripts for Concordia and Humanité, including a religious service of cunningly pacifist flavor.

His purpose was simple: To spread alarm and despondency among the French. This he did by reporting rumors that Paul Reynaud's regime was fleeing Paris; by urging all French patriots to withdraw their bank savings immediately lest the Nazis confiscated the banks; and by broadcasting meaningless code-phrases to a non-existent French underground; Hitler directed him to talk freely about this fictitious 'Fifth Column.'[34]

His transmitters gave helpful advice to the French on surviving the cholera epidemic (there was none); and how to hoard scarce food supplies. No true Frenchman, they warned, should trust the perfidious English. He spread rumors of peace talks, then claimed a day later that Britain had torpedoed them. Gutterer and Raskin faked the diary of a British soldier describing his sexual exploits among the wives of Paris. Other stations spread word of appalling atrocities, designed to choke the French roads with panic-stricken refugees. He brought to bear the main transmitters of Radio Cologne, Leipzig, and Stuttgart to beam these poisonous messages into enemy territory.[35]

Learning that the turgid communist jargon of Humanité's scripts was turning off its listeners, Goebbels retrieved Wilhelm Kasper and Karl-Loew Albrecht from concentration camp.[36] Together with the former communist leader Ernst Torgler they helped Goebbels to foment unrest among the Paris working class. 'Magnificent,' he congratulated himself. 'Keep tipping oil onto the flames.'[37] Over the half-megawatt Deutschlandsender his broadcasters warned that many of the Jewish refugees from Nazi Germany to France and England were really Hitler agents in disguise.[38] Churchill ordered the immediate internment of over twenty thousand Jewish refugees, a spectacular success for Goebbels' evil tongue.[39] Settling scores with the exiled Otto Strasser and Hermann Rauschning, he had his ministry issue 'official denials' that they too were members of the Nazi Fifth Column. Then he arranged for an anonymous well-wisher's telegram to reach Strasser tipping him off that the game was up.[40]

As this black-propaganda campaign gathered momentum, the roads behind the French lines were choked with panic-stricken refugees. Twice Hitler mentioned to Goebbels how moved he was by the French 'refugee misery' that he had seen.[41] The minister instructed his staff never to tell outsiders of the part their tactics had played – 'Even after the war,' he directed, 'it will be necessary to keep our operations secret.'[42]

He stepped up the pressure on Britain too. William Joyce toured prison camps recruiting English-speakers.[43] Goebbels was in no doubt that Churchill would prove a tougher opponent than Reynaud. 'He will be England's gravedigger,' he prophesied. He warned the media not to speculate on Churchill's parentage without cast-iron evidence.[44] Normal libels would not suffice against this man: Perhaps monster-libels would. He told Joyce to announce that Churchill was planning to torpedo the liner carrying fleeing Americans back to the United States ('I wouldn't put it past the old rogue anyway,' he commented, as though that were justification enough).[45]

In Churchill however Goebbels had met his match. Before his marveling eyes, the 'old rogue' converted the disaster of Dunkirk into a propaganda triumph for England. Churchill's legend of the Little Ships fired the imagination of the world. 'You can't help admiring the brazen effrontery with which they are putting out this monstrous lie,' wrote Goebbels. 'There's no doubt that they've managed to halt the avalanche in public opinion that was developing.'[46] Goebbels was dismayed to hear from d'Alquèn and Hippler that not only were the French troops loyally covering the British retreat, but that whatever the French were saying to the contrary the Tommies were fighting with unexpected bravery. 'The British,' he realized, 'are going to be a tough nut to crack.'[47]

Hitler staged the surrender talks in the forest at Compiègne, the site of Germany's humiliation in 1918. Telephoning Goebbels that evening he described with relish the French delegation's consternation upon finding him there in person.[48]

Broadcasting over the B.B.C., Churchill announced that Britain would fight on alone. 'That idiot is plunging all England into misfortune,' wrote Goebbels. He ordered his black transmitters realigned on England. He did not share his Führer's maudlin affection for the English. He found the early British war movie *The Lion has Wings* so ludicrous that he had it shown to the press corps and public audiences in Berlin for laughs.[49]

Hitler however hesitated. Goebbels could see that he hated the idea of pursuing the defeated British army across the English Channel. In an interview with American journalist Karl von Wiegand the Führer once again insisted, for English listeners' consumption, that he did not desire the destruction of their empire. This conciliatory attitude suited neither Goebbels nor Churchill, who sent his bombers to Berlin on the night of the Compiègne armistice ceremony. Goebbels drove over to see the resulting damage at nearby Babelsberg and admitted at the next morning's press conference that there had been fatalities. When Hitler phoned later that day Goebbels pleaded in vain for retaliatory raids.[50]

The big question, he added, was how now to proceed against Britain. 'The Führer does not really want to press on. But he may well have to. If Churchill stays on, assuredly.' Göring set up a plan for a mass air attack on Britain, but Hitler kept postponing it.[51] The British bombers kept poking at Germany. 'Churchill,' fumed Goebbels at the end of June, 'is just trying to provoke us. But the Führer doesn't intend to respond, yet.'[52]

A telegram from Hitler curtailed his tour of the battlefields in France – he was to report to the interim Führer headquarters in the Black Forest the next day, July 2 1940. There they decided that Hitler should stage a triumphant homecoming to Berlin that Saturday, July 6, and address the Reichstag two days later.[53] Hitler would then offer Britain one last chance. Failing that, he still believed that he could defeat Britain in four weeks.

'The Führer however does not want to destroy the empire,' Goebbels noted, 'because everything it loses will accrue to foreign powers and not to us.'[54] Goebbels was clearly unhappy with Hitler's procrastination: He recorded that it would be a tough decision to sell to the German people, though no doubt the Führer would bring it off. The tenor of his coming speech, Hitler had said, would be magnanimity. What he did not mention to Goebbels was that he had just begun staff studies on a war with the Soviet Union.[55]

Goebbels hated the idea of offering an easy peace to Britain. Dramatic events came to his rescue. Under the armistice terms Hitler had only recently allowed the defeated French nation to retain her powerful battle fleet, though disarmed and under German supervision. Concerned that the Nazis might somehow seize the biggest warships, lying at anchor at Oran (Mers el-Kébir), Churchill ordered them sunk on July 3, the day after Hitler and Goebbels met. Over a thousand French sailors died in the ruthless British naval bombardment.

This incident dominated a quarter of Goebbels' entire domestic propaganda output for the next four days, while the personal abuse leveled at Churchill equaled the savagery first displayed after the *Altmark* incident.[56] Goebbels' private admiration for Churchill rose, as his diary shows. Moreover, the British were still bombing Germany.

Hitler however still restrained his own bomber force.[57] 'The Führer,' the minister marveled, 'has the patience of an angel.' He directed the press to focus their attack on Churchill and his clique alone. This was not easy, as the entire British press was 'chortling with pleasure' about Oran.[58]

BERLIN'S RECEPTION FOR HITLER on Saturday July 6, 1940 was the most spectacular that Goebbels ever staged.[59] He had issued a million swastika flags to the crowds lining the route, and he himself broadcast the excited running commentary as the train bearing the conquering warlord hauled into the station at three P.M. to an accompanying cacophony of church bells, factory sirens, and steam whistles. Once inside the chancellery Goebbels asked Hitler what he had decided. He now learned that the British fleet's assault on the French at Oran had unhinged all of Hitler's plans. 'He had his speech almost complete,' recorded Goebbels, 'when the attack occurred. It has brought about an entirely new situation. Churchill is a raving lunatic who has burned all his boats behind him.' 'Nevertheless,' Hitler lectured him, 'we must be guided not by hatred but by common sense.'[60]

Postponing the speech, Hitler came out to Lanke that Sunday, and played with the Goebbels children. Several times during the coming week Goebbels lunched with him at the chancellery and heard him daydream about his postwar construction plans. He was going to build a superhighway from Carinthia in southern Austria all the way up to Norway's northernmost cape, with a gigantic new naval base near Trondheim like Britain's Singapore. Darré, another lunch guest, recorded, 'They couldn't decide whether to call it Atalantis (Himmler's suggestion), Atlantis (Frank), Northern Light (Ley), or Stella Polaris (Goebbels).[61] But these were castles in the air because, Goebbels noted, Hitler was still unwilling to deliver the final blow against England. Announcing that he was going to retire to the Berghof to think things over, Hitler left for Bavaria that evening.[62]

JUST AS HITLER HANKERED after his peacetime hobby of architecture, so Dr Goebbels dreamed of retiring to a country estate and firing off magisterial newspaper editorials.[63]

With the birth of *Das Reich*, his new national weekly magazine for the intelligentsia, part of this dream came true. He contributed a regular, and highly-paid, leading article which would come to be quoted around the world as a real sensor of Nazi policies. Appearing every Saturday from May 26, 1940, *Das Reich* became the flagship of his journalistic career.[64] It was well designed, its prose was literate, its photographs superb. It was particularly popular with the officer corps.[65] Its circulation hovered around a million – 'a rare publishing success for which I was not entirely blameless,' Goebbels wrote.[66]

The large circulation involved simultaneous printing in several centers, and this in turn meant that his manuscript had to be delivered by the previous Monday. He began drafting it a week ahead, initially with a schoolboy dread, then with growing enthusiasm as it took shape; he devoted inordinate energy to checking dates, facts, and quotations from the Greek and Latin classics, until he was ready to dictate the final draft just before the weekend. Its influence on German morale was unquestionable; it was a weekly shot in the arm – celebrating successes, explaining setbacks, justifying persecutions, promising retaliation, predicting victory. Toward the end, a Goebbels article would present eloquent arguments from antiquity or parables from the party's struggle for power which briefly lightened the lowering darkness of defeat. After reading the Goebbels leader in *Das Reich* on the day before Hitler died an army lieutenant-general in British captivity could only say, 'They [the Nazis] *must* have something up their sleeves!'[67]

While Hitler stayed brooding at the Berghof, his plans upset, Goebbels boosted Berlin's uncertain morale by staging a homecoming parade for one of its infantry divisions. He shrilled words of welcome through loudspeakers, contrasting this scene with those of 1918: 'You soldiers return to find your country just as you left it. At your head stands the same Führer, on your buildings flutters the same flag, your people are still imbued with the same spirit and the same determination.' 'All we need now,' he triumphed in his diary afterward, 'is Britain's capitulation, total victory, and a lasting peace. . . Who can still harbor any doubt of the outcome of this gigantic struggle?'[68] The mere statement of the question suggests that, way down in his own unfathomed depths, Goebbels was himself beginning to doubt.

AS THE INFANTRY MARCHED in Berlin, Gutterer remarked that the same hordes of Jews were to be seen loitering up and down Kurfürstendamm.[69] Goebbels had to admit it was true. The Jewish problem still ran like a poisonous thread through all his waking thoughts. He had told Gutterer in February 1940 to organize raids on Berlin Jews suspected of hoarding foodstuffs.[70] He had no qualms about the murderous treatment that the S.S. were meting out to the Jews, the clergy, and the intelligentsia in Poland.[71]

More than once over the next five years he reflected that for top Nazis like himself there was now no going back: Winning total victory had become literally a matter of life and death for them. In one cryptic diary entry in January 1940 he reminded himself, 'If there *were* any going back, then one would too easily become faint-hearted. . . That goes for our policies in Poland too. We simply must not lose this war.'[72] Like other top Nazis, he was noticeably careful not to spell out what those policies were. When a well-disposed Polish journalist sent him details of certain 'episodes' in Poland, he noted, 'These could be pretty lethal for us at this moment,' and he had the informant taken into custody for a while.[73] A few weeks later he learned that the Russians were disposing of the Jews in their half of Poland 'in their own way.' 'So much the better for us,' was his cryptic comment.[74]

He had no misgivings about euthanasia either. After hearing Philipp Bouhler reporting to Hitler on the ongoing operation to liquidate Germany's hospital population of mental defectives, Goebbels agreed that this was 'so necessary,' but he made a note that the whole thing was secret and running into difficulties.[75] Over lunch a week later he heard Himmler tell Hitler that in some parts of occupied Poland the Jews had set up their own administration and were imposing a cruel regime on their own race. 'That's how the Jews are,' he commented, 'and that's how they'll be for ever more.'[76] Hitler reassured him in June that they would deal swiftly with the Jews after the war.[77] Commenting on the Jews' disrespectful behavior during the infantry parade, Goebbels announced that he had decided, no doubt in his capacity as gauleiter, to pack all Berlin's Jews – he put their number at 62,000 – off to Poland within eight weeks of the cessation of hostilities. The city's police had already developed the necessary plans.[78] Later still, Hitler revealed to him once again his own preferred final solution, to deport all of Europe's Jews after the war to Madagascar, currently a French colony. 'That will become a German protectorate under a German police governor.'[79]

HITLER HAD NOW PUT the finishing touches to his Reichstag speech. He returned to Berlin on July 19, 1940 in high spirits, and outlined its salient points to his lunch guests, including Goebbels. He would issue a short, terse peace offer to Britain without spelling out any precise terms but with the clear implication that this was his last word, and it was now for London to decide.[80] Goebbels hoped that Churchill might even resign. That evening, he told his staff, Britain's fate would be in the balance.[81] He directed all his English-language radio stations to soften up British public opinion.[82] He now had no fewer than five black radio stations, among them the New British Broadcasting Station, which beamed William Joyce's messages to England via three shortwave transmitters; an 'amateur' Radio Caledonia, pumping out Scottish nationalist propaganda; another transmitter aimed at Welsh nationalists; a medium-wave transmitter beaming socialist slogans to the British working class; and Concordia Plan P, which had soothing words for British Christian pacifists, and regularly broadcast prayer services for peace.[83]

All of these megawatts failed to deflect Britain from her purpose. A rude answer to Hitler's peace offer was broadcast almost immediately over the B.B.C. by journalist Sefton Delmer ('one of Putzi Hanfstaengl's discoveries,' as Goebbels caustically labeled him).[84]

To Hitler's consternation the British bombing continued that night. 'For the moment,' recorded Goebbels, seeing him the next day, 'the Führer does not want to accept that that is indeed Britain's response. He is still minded to wait awhile. After all, he appealed to the British people and not to Churchill.'[85] Agreeing that they could afford to wait, Goebbels warned editors not to overstate Britain's rebuff.[86]

So Germany waited. He himself doubted whether Britain really was interested in peace. She would not come to her senses until she had taken the first blows. 'She can't have any idea of what she's in for,' he reflected.

Churchill responded with more bombs, but Lord Halifax broadcast a statement that Goebbels at first mistook for just an unctuous sermon, only to learn the next day that Hitler recognized it as most definitely Britain's final outright rejection of his offer.[87]

Secretly, Goebbels was rather pleased. 'Everybody,' he wrote, meaning himself, 'was afraid that Britain would grasp the hand of peace extended by the Führer.'[88] Hitler told him that he too would 'very soon' start massive bombing raids. 'The big question,' Goebbels detected, 'is *when*. . . Only the Führer can decide that.'[89]

He instructed his black transmitters to start generating panic in Britain, for instance broadcasting official-sounding English guidelines on what to do when the Nazi mass air raids began; to add authenticity, each bulletin was to start with blistering attacks on the top Nazis. Once again his announcers were to counsel the enemy public to withdraw their life savings and to hoard foodstuffs, and to buy jewelry and valuables against inflation.[90]

It was now late July 1940. Göring was now wearing a new uniform, that of Reichsmarschall. Everyone was ready for the blitz to begin – everyone except Hitler.[91]

39: *Breaking Even*

THE SHORT CAMPAIGNING WEEKS of the English summer flitted past unused. Hitler allowed Reichsmarschall Göring's two thousand bombers to tackle only Britain's war industries, shipping, and ports. Dr Goebbels hungered for the day when they would be unleashed on London.

Britain's intransigence dominated his diaries. 'Feelers from here to Britain without result,' he recorded on the first day of August 1940. 'Via Spain as well. London is looking for a catastrophe.'[1]

He began his own war in the air. There was no limit to his evil inspiration. His mischief-making black transmitters went into stage two of their campaign, advising British listeners on how to defend themselves against Nazi poison-gas attacks, and how to make Molotov cocktails (a few days later the same transmitters warned that some designs had been found spontaneously igniting).[2] Listeners were lectured on how to detect the 'Fifth Columnists' in Britain.[3] The transmitters 'denied' rumors that a hundred thousand British army uniforms had fallen into Nazi hands at Dunkirk, then spread word that thousands of agents wearing these uniforms had already been parachuted into Britain.[4] Then they began broadcasting strings of meaningless ciphers to these non-existent Fifth Columnists.[5]

Studying photographs in British society magazines Goebbels devised a particularly cruel scheme to alienate the working class: His transmitters announced that Churchill was providing funds for twenty thousand working-class children to be evacuated to Canada like the privileged children of the rich and influential; families were to take their children to a meeting place in the center of London, on the basis of first-come, first-saved. 'There's going to be some pushing and shoving there,' cackled the minister heartlessly.[6] His 'English' transmitters also ordered all gas masks to be handed in for special filters to be installed.[7] They followed with educational broadcasts for those English listeners who had not yet witnessed German air force *Schrecklichkeit* at first hand.[8] The effect, if any, of this black propaganda on the British population is not known.

In the air war however the British were now taking the initiative, although Göring's bomber bases were much closer to London than the British were to Berlin. Churchill sent his squadrons to Hamburg and announced it had been 'pulverized.'[9] The American press seized upon that word. Goebbels flew two planeloads of neutral journalists to the port to see for themselves that it was undamaged.[10]

He began to feel ill. He felt overworked and undernourished, his nerves were frayed, his eyes swam from scanning the incoming dispatches for any signs that Britain was collapsing.[11] The doctors diagnosed a nervous complaint resulting from overwork and vitamin deficiency.[12] The Gestapo reported gloomily that the German public was keyed up, waiting for Göring's Grand Slam, but that many people secretly feared they were in for a second winter at war.[13]

Hitler returned to Berlin on August 4. He had decided, he explained to Goebbels, to launch sudden and unheralded mass air raids on Britain and he ordered the propaganda barrage to be intensified. Goebbels postponed a trip he had been planning to occupied Norway and turned the barrage up to half-volume.[14] But still Hitler held back his bombers. He explained that the Reichsmarschall was still testing the sinews of Britain's defenses. 'If the losses we sustain are within reason,' wrote Goebbels after seeing Hitler again on the sixth, 'then the operation will proceed. If they are not, then we shall try new ways. Invasion not planned,' he noted almost casually.* 'But we shall hint at it subliminally in our propaganda to confuse the enemy.'

Goebbels briefed only a few of his staff on Hitler's startling disclosure. 'The Führer has still not ordered the air attack on Britain,' he noted after a further visit to him that day. 'He's still rather hesitant.' Anxious to exculpate his vacillating idol in his diary, Goebbels conceded: 'It is a tricky decision.'[15] And it was: Bombing London would finally close the door to peace. Churchill knew this too, and this was one reason why his bombers were trying to provoke Hitler. Goebbels found himself his unwitting ally. 'The people,' he wrote privately, meaning himself, 'are afraid that we're missing the opportune moment.' Over lunch on the eighth Hitler however said that the weather was not good enough.[16]

To Goebbels' dismay Churchill's information machine proved slicker than his, as the battle of Britain began. He did not mind that Churchill inflated his victories, claiming fifty-three Luftwaffe planes shot down when the real total was ten; but the British announced this victory in a rising crescendo of fourteen bulletins issued during the day, while the German High Command was still ponderously releasing one.[17] Goebbels reminded the world that Churchill had frankly confessed to lying his way out of awkward situations in the earlier war.[18]

Hitler still hesitated to bomb London. Goebbels resorted in his diary to his now threadbare palliative: 'The Führer will surely seek out the right moment and then strike accordingly.'[19] Göring decided to launch Eagle Day, the mass

---

* Thereby settling one major historical controversy. This author has long maintained, *e.g.* in *Churchill's War* (London, 1987) and in *Hitler's War* (London, 1991), 311ff, that Hitler never intended to invade Britain and that Operation SEA LION, the invasion plan, was only strategic deception. Conformist historians have been slow to accept this.

attack on southern England, on the thirteenth; but only half the two thousand planes got airborne in bad weather, and London itself was still off limits.[20] Goebbels anticipated that Churchill would soon get to work on the world's tear glands, as he put it, with harrowing photographs of pregnant air-raid victims. He told his ministry to dig out file photographs of, ironically, the Freiburg raid – which Luftwaffe Heinkels had in fact bombed by mistake – and comparable British atrocities in India.

For several more days bad weather continued to thwart Göring. The Gestapo reported that the German public was getting jittery.[21] On the twentieth Churchill famously extolled Britain's young fighter pilots, speaking of how so much had never been owed by so many to so few. Goebbels mechanically dismissed the speech as 'insolent, arrogant, and mendacious,' but he had to admit, as one orator invigilating over another, that it was good stuff. 'He has a seductive style,' he wrote.[22]

Autumn was drawing in. The nights were getting long enough for Churchill to push his bombers as far as Berlin. On the night of August 19–20 a Blenheim bomber was actually shot down over the city. Goebbels announced the incident only in his overseas services. He was confronted by something of a dilemma – how to profit from the raids on Berlin without affording comfort to the enemy.[23] Late on the twenty-fourth a Luftwaffe bomber, sent to attack a Thames-side oil refinery, strayed over the East End of London; there were no casualties, but Churchill ordered a hundred heavy bombers to Berlin the next night.[24] Alone out at Lanke – Magda and the children had left for Schwanenwerder as the new school term began – Goebbels watched Berlin's flak batteries opening up in the distance. Damage was again minimal, but the four-hour alert robbed him of precious sleep and he spent the next night out at Lanke too. Expecting the worst to be over in three weeks, he agreed with Göring that they should close all theaters until then.[25]

The British raids continued. On August 28–29 their bombs killed ten Berliners. At six A.M. the radio revealed to Germany that the British had bombed their capital. Goebbels decided on balance that since he had little to work on, he might as well stay out at Lanke for another night.[26] Hitler, made of sterner stuff, hurried back from Bavaria to the capital and assured Goebbels over lunch on the thirtieth that if only the weather would improve Göring would begin his unrestricted air warfare against Britain. Goebbels reflected that Berlin would then be in for a 'pretty hot time' too. [27]

CHURCHILL, HITLER, AND GOEBBELS were alike in tragically overestimating the strategic capabilities of saturation bombing. Each side believed that its opponents were less brave.

At his confidential morning conference on September 3, 1940 Goebbels admitted that opinion on this differed. 'There is no doubt,' he said, 'that a nation really determined to defend its freedom can be wrestled to the ground only in man-to-man combat.' He doubted however that Britain had that determination. Common sense might yet prevail there. 'We'll have to see how things turn out.'

In fact he cynically hoped that Churchill's raids would get heavier. He needed what he called an alibi, to justify in advance the *Schrecklichkeit* which the Luftwaffe was about to inflict on London. Hitler had ruled out an invasion of Britain as unnecessary. Both men expected a walk-over once the Luftwaffe really got at London. Goebbels began planning ahead with Gutterer for the occupation of London, nominating first his police major Walter Titel, of his war operations staff, and then Dr Friedrich Mahlo, head of his tourism section, as chief of the England task force, and determining which buildings, like the British Broadcasting Corporation, it would need to seize.[28]

While Berlin now prepared for the worst, removing priceless paintings to safety and digging in flak batteries around the city, Hitler and his propaganda minister debated endlessly the central question: Whether bombing alone would force the British to their knees. Goebbels eschewed any opinion, but wondered privately how much longer London had before the onslaught began. Hitler however was awaiting a response to his further peace feelers, extended through Washington, Stockholm and – via Rudolf Hess's aristocratic contacts – Scotland.

As frustrated as Goebbels at Hitler's forbearance in refusing to authorize bombing raids against London, Churchill intensified his raids on Berlin. Finally his methods worked. Inaugurating the second Winter Relief fund Hitler and Goebbels spoke on September 4 in the Sport Palace; and here Hitler threatened that, if the attacks continued, his Luftwaffe would respond. 'I shall rub out their cities!' he rasped into the microphone. To Goebbels' astonishment, the speech had no apparent impact on Whitehall. In retrospect this was not surprising: Like Goebbels at Lanke, Churchill had a country funk-hole at Dytchley in Oxfordshire whither he repaired whenever his Intelligence services alerted him that London was to be the Luftwaffe's target. The prime minister wanted London bombed to bring in the Americans, to take the weight of enemy air attacks off his fighter and radar defenses, and to spite the peace movement that was now seriously threatening his own war leadership. He cheered silently each time his capital was bombed, as indeed did Goebbels each time Berlin was visited by the Royal Air Force.[29]

Meanwhile Reichsmarschall Göring had set off to the Channel coast to command his pompous air armadas against London. He had prepared a three-day saturation bombing of London. September 5 brought ideal bombing weather but Hitler, clutching at hopes of peace, still procrastinated. That night the British bombed Berlin again, killing fifteen people. Lunching with Hitler on the sixth Goebbels found his patience exhausted. 'The Führer,' he recorded, 'is fed up. He clears London for bombing. It is to begin tonight.' Goebbels certainly did not discourage him, and that night what he would call The Blitz began. Mapping out his own tactics in advance he confided to his diary, 'We're expecting the British to launch a major air strike against Berlin tonight [the seventh]. When it comes we'll kick up one hell of a hullabaloo – and then we'll flatten London with day and night raids.' These would go on around the clock for three days. He only hoped that the weather held out.

Sure enough the British bombers returned. Thus Churchill and Hitler both rose to each other's bait – the British bombing by night, the Luftwaffe by day. Göring again sent his bombers over London that afternoon. 'Let's see now how long the nerves of the English can take it,' wrote Goebbels. He directed William Joyce and the black 'English' transmitters to spread panic; and he told the 'straight' media that they were to stick to the official version that the Luftwaffe was only attacking military targets.[30]

On Sunday the eighth, Reuters agency announced that seven hundred Londoners had died the day before.[31] As Hitler visited the Goebbels family at Schwanenwerder on Sunday night, Churchill's bombers threw another modest punch at Berlin. The propaganda minister ordered their overseas services to exaggerate the results wildly to generate fresh alibis for what was to come.[32] The *New York Times* headlines read '1,500 NAZI PLANES BOMB LONDON' on Sunday, and 'MIGHTY NAZI AIR FLEET AGAIN BOMBS LONDON – DOCKS AND PLANTS HIT, FIRES RAGE' on the following day. London, it seemed to Goebbels, was one huge inferno. How long could its citizens take it?

Over lunch on the tenth Hitler, still undecided, again asked the one question that mattered: Would Britain give in? 'The military share my viewpoint,' recorded Goebbels: 'A city of eight million cannot stand this for long... We have wiped the smirk off their lordships' faces. We shall thrash them until they whimper for mercy.'[33]

That night scattered British bombs fell around the Reichstag. Damage was almost non-existent. Annoyed that Churchill's raids were proving so puny, Goebbels ordered his pyrotechnic experts to stage more convincing fires on top of the Brandenburg Gate, Berlin's famous landmark, and then summoned the press photographers – 'to supply,' as he unblushingly told his diary, 'an alibi for our own coming massive raid on the London government quarter.'[34] When a German bomb shortly after damaged one wing of Buckingham Palace in London, Goebbels directed his agencies to claim that there were 'secret military targets' near by.[35] The neutral press duly equated this raid with the British raid on the Reichstag. 'Thus we are not barbarians,' Goebbels congratulated himself. 'We are just two superpowers knocking the living daylights out of each other.'[36]

Hitler too was taken in. Furious about the raid on the Brandenburg Gate and his Reichstag he told Goebbels that he was now going to blast Churchill's ancient parliament to smithereens. Together they listened to the prime minister broadcast that evening. It was an insipid speech in Goebbels' opinion, riddled with vulgar abuse of his beloved Führer. 'Poor fool,' he commented: 'In his impotent fury he flails at a genius, of whose greatness he has not the slightest inkling.'[37] Churchill however was every inch a match for him. Although he too knew from codebreaking that no German invasion was planned, he predicted a date for the event: It was an old but effective propaganda trick, raged

Goebbels – Churchill could then claim a victory when no invasion came.[38] His admiration for Britain's indomitable prime minister grew. 'You can't help respecting him,' he wrote, 'in his bulldog way.'[39]

Despite all Göring's efforts the British air defenses seemed intact. On September 15 the Luftwaffe dropped two hundred tons of bombs on London, and lost forty-three planes in the battle. Churchill coolly inflated that figure to 155. 'Churchill has got to cheat,' Goebbels reasoned, applying his own standards, 'because the devastation in London is so appalling.'[40] The Luftwaffe's losses faced him with a problem however. He had virtuously ruled only ten days earlier that even if the Luftwaffe was worsted on some days, its losses were to be faithfully reported.[41] But now the Luftwaffe's impotence was becoming something of a liability to Germany's image. For a start, all German radio stations now had to shut down at ten P.M. to avoid helping enemy bombers.[42] Unabashed, the obese Reichsmarschall allowed the world's press to report that he had personally flown over the blazing streets of London in a Stuka dive bomber. Goebbels forbade the German press to print the story ('for obvious reasons').[43] He told his black transmitters to remark on the luxury air raid shelters, complete with armchairs and dance floors, installed for London's plutocrats beneath the Grosvenor House hotel.[44]

'Not yet,' was his terse assessment when his department heads asked whether the British capital was entering its death throes.[45]

In mid-September 1940 Hitler still hoped that prolonging this blitz would do the trick. 'If eight million inhabitants go crazy,' he said, 'that can bring about a catastrophe. If we get good weather and can neutralize the enemy air force, then even a small-scale invasion can work wonders.'[46] Over lunch on the twenty-third however Goebbels heard him admit that they were nowhere near achieving air superiority.[47] The Luftwaffe was losing its finest crews, as its losses over southern England mounted. Hitler compared it with a boxing match. After slogging on for round after round, one pugilist might suddenly slump to the canvas.[48] To Goebbels however the London blitz began to reek of uglier examples in history, and Major Rudolf Wodarg, his Luftwaffe liaison officer, put the same fear into words. 'London,' he said, 'is turning into a Verdun of the air.'[49]

GOEBBELS WAS NOT REALLY PREPARED for this situation. He spent October 1940 in the doldrums, becalmed in a silent, unreasoning hatred of Ribbentrop, of Dietrich, of the plutocrats in London, and of the Jews. He was waiting – waiting for the air war to end, waiting for the renovation of No. 20 Hermann-Göring Strasse to be completed, waiting for Magda, yet again, to give birth. 'Mothers in labor are like soldiers on the battlefield,' he decided.[50] The British bombers remorselessly gnawed away at Germany. Often a single nuisance raider triggered a stampede by four and a half million Berliners into their makeshift shelters.[51] Berlin's flak defenses were strengthened. On October 2 a detonation not far from Lanke marked the end of one British bomber. Goebbels saw the flattened pile of twisted metal the next day and the charred remains of the three aviators, and shuddered.[52] The air staff now asked Goebbels not to announce when the British missed their targets. Goebbels was baffled. 'First we give them the run of our air waves,' he commented, referring to the ten P.M. radio curfew, 'and now we are voluntarily to abstain from rebutting their propaganda lies.'[53]

He traveled to France, at Göring's invitation. He took tea in the Edouard Rothschild palace – the château, replete with pheasants, was now a Luftwaffe command post – and relished the irony of the situation.[54]

Fatter than ever and aglitter with medals, Göring showed him round Paris. They swapped pet-hate stories about Ribbentrop; Goebbels noticed how many German uniforms there were as they strolled along the boulevards and enjoyed the sensation their own presence was creating. At the Casino de Paris the crippled gauleiter goggled at the open display of such statuesque nudity. 'We could never put on a show like that in Berlin,' he decided.[55] Visiting Field Marshal Hugo Sperrle, the bulky, monocled Third Air Fleet commander at Deauville, Goebbels decided that like Göring he too was a real comrade, a devil of a fellow, and his men were just *fabelhaft*.[56]

It is worth emphasizing those contemporary words, because in July 1944 he would recall only the sumptuousness of this peacetime international watering hole – how Sperrle had stuffed his face with caviar canapés and roared, 'In fourteen days all life in London will have been extinguished. . . I am telling you. They'll suffocate in their own crap.'

He plied the propaganda minister with agents' reports, one of which spoke of the fine ladies being forced to pee in Hyde Park as London's water mains ran dry. Goebbels voiced skepticism (or so he claimed in 1944) that that would be sufficient inconvenience to bring down a great world empire.[57]

WHILE DR JOSEPH GOEBBELS is staring at naked showgirls in October 1940 in Paris, his wife, pregnant in Berlin with their sixth child, has had to return to the clinic with heart problems.[58] It is mid-November before she is discharged. Her father writes a sad letter to her: Facing renewed surgery, he is obliged to draw up a will; he is leaving to her the estate at Remagen – he does not mention Joseph at all.[59] Magda's life is anything but easy, and for all his attempts at camouflage Goebbels' diary cannot conceal it. A candle still glows dimly in her heart for Karl Hanke. Her son Harald is now a troublesome adolescent; perhaps the paratroops will make a man out of him.[60] Goebbels privately reflects that it could do wonders for his image if Harald should die in action. Of his daughters, his favorite is still Helga.[61] For more mature female company, he invites the Countess Faber-Castell out to Lanke with her husband as soon as Magda has gone; the countess is a captivating twenty-three-year-old whom he has known for many years. She entertains him with chansons and music – 'She is bewitching,' writes Goebbels wistfully.[62]

Once Magda struggles briefly out of bed to rejoin him. 'When you see eye to eye with her,' writes Goebbels, 'she is a regular guy and a real comrade.'[63] It is the kind of praise his diary has lavished only on Göring or Sperrle before. On his forty-third birthday she presents him with a fifth daughter, Heide. His family is now complete.

On Magda's birthday in November 1940 Hitler himself turns up for her little dinner party and they proudly show him over their now finished ministerial mansion at No. 20 Hermann-Göring Strasse. No fewer than 117 construction workers have been laboring on it during these historic weeks.[64] Thick carpets, tapestries, and velvet or silken wall hangings supplied by the exquisite United Workshops of Munich deaden every sound. In the largest salon are seats for 140; the same number can sit at tables in the Blue Gallery, with eighty-two more at the top table. The huge desk in his study has cost 8,417 marks, around two thousand dollars.[65] The globe of the world is modeled on one he has seen in the radio building but – given his waiflike, five-foot-four stature – it is a more low-slung model. In the garden are marble sculptures by Professor Fritz Klimsch and a bronze nude by Arno Breker. All the telephones are white; on his instructions all have had their 'engaged' indicator-lamps removed. He does not want it to be known when he is telephoning.[66]

He has commissioned no less lavish works in the ministry building itself, on Wilhelms Platz. Work is suspended briefly in November as the interior decorators are called away to work on the special luxurious trains of Hitler and Göring. Goebbels orders that there are to be no flushing toilets in the space next to his personal radio studio, to avoid inappropriate noises during his broadcasts to the Greater German Reich.[67]

At the same time nearly two hundred sub-contractors have labored to complete his mansion at Lanke, the Haus am Bogensee (which stands to this day). He has converted the former guardhouse used by his bodyguard Kaiser into a handsome oblong wood cabin fifty feet long and thirty feet wide, as a guesthouse for two families. The architect's file contains his instructions dated August 6, 1940 for incubators and bird-tables to be erected in the surrounding woods.[68] The new gatehouse will cost thirty thousand marks; alterations to the cinema, drawing room, and Magda's private bedroom one hundred thousand; a twenty-five foot by sixty-five foot swimming pool, twenty-four thousand; and a children's wing, 140,000. By the end of October 1940 the grand total cost of work in hand is 2,663,052·58 marks. Mosquito control, road building, and radio equipment will bring the total to three million. Understandably his diary betrays a certain nervousness as the bills mount.[69] Its pages cannot conceal his eighteenth-century tapestries purchased from France and the Low Countries, nor the paintings by Van Dyck, nor the Goya obtained from 'French private property;' but all these are no doubt paid for by the ministry.[70]

Ministers it seems are endemically blind to their own corruption. Through his friend Max Winkler, Dr Goebbels controls the movie industry. Early in November he notes that Winkler has seen Göring and has taken care of the Lanke problem.[71] At about the same time Winkler gives him a 'belated' birthday present of two magnificent black Trakehn geldings, with a matching carriage. No doubt coincidentally Goebbels 'in conjunction with the movie industry' donates to Winkler a garden cottage worth fifty thousand marks upon his birthday.[72] By November 30 checks totaling 2·3 million marks have been paid toward the cost of Lanke. Thus he settled his debts over Lanke and his tax liabilities at one stroke. 'It was high time,' he wrote. 'If I were to die now, I'd just about break even. A fine reward for twenty years' service to the fatherland. My family would be in for quite a shock.'[73]

RETURNING FROM FRANCE, Goebbels had dictated to his staff his belief that London was bluffing.[74] But each side was wallowing in self-deception. Journalist George Ward Price announced that the British raids had now killed 1,700 Berliners; Goebbels told his overseas services to make plain that the real death toll in Berlin so far was seventy-seven.[75] Göring's bombers had killed seven thousand Londoners during September alone. But as Goebbels privately realized, the British were tough: 'They're still holding out.'[76] Touring public shelters in Berlin on the first night of November he found signs that nerves were getting more frayed.[77] Once again he could only hope that Hitler knew what he was doing.

Hitler did know, but again he had not initiated Dr Goebbels. He had decided as early as July 1940 to attack Russia. Even in December Goebbels still regarded Britain as 'our last remaining enemy.'[78]

After their Black Forest conference on July 2, when Hitler had evidently voiced to him his annoyance that Stalin had annexed parts of Romania, Goebbels mused in his diary: 'The Slavs are spreading out right across the Balkans. . . Perhaps we shall have to go to war again later, against the Soviets.'[79] At the end of that month he had warned the gauleiters to squelch any such rumors.[80]

He and Hitler were both intrigued by the newsreel images of the Soviet–Finnish winter war just ended: The Red Army seemed temptingly primitive.[81] 'Bolshevism is World Enemy No. 1,' Goebbels told Hitler. 'We are bound to collide sooner or later.'[82] Hitler agreed, but still he lied to Goebbels, saying that he was transferring army divisions to the east only on a better-safe-than-sorry basis.[83] 'He says quite spontaneously,' recorded Goebbels after Hitler had revealed his contempt for Moscow, 'that he trusts blindly and implicitly in our future.' The time was coming, Goebbels gathered, when old scores with Moscow were to be settled.[84]

To forestall Stalin, Hitler packed German troops into Romania and Finland during September. 'The Führer is determined,' observed Goebbels, 'not to relinquish any more of Europe to Russia.'[85] During October 1940 his diary revealed no hint of the intensive military preparations already afoot.

Learning, to his surprise, that Hitler had invited the Soviet foreign minister Vyacheslav M. Molotov to Berlin, Goebbels saw it only in terms of a slap in the face to Britain.[86] He did not approve of Molotov. He instructed Berlin's S.A. not to provide guards of honor, and he did nothing to mobilize the cheering crowds that Ribbentrop had requested.[87] Hitler invited him to lunch with their Soviet guests on November 13. The Russian foreign minister seemed clever, even artful; his skin was of a waxy, yellow pallor. He listened politely to Goebbels through an interpreter for two hours, but scarcely even grunted in reply. After lunch Goebbels let fly to his private staff his scorn of Molotov, with his 'school janitor's face.' He paced angrily up and down behind his desk, mimicking his own fruitless attempt at making conversation.

'The Soviets,' he snapped, in a dismissive generalization that was to prove fateful for Germany, 'are like their suits. They are cheap, and off-the-peg.'[88]

40: A Few Choice Drops of Poison

H E NO LONGER SPOKE to Ribbentrop. A state of armed truce existed between them. The two ministers insulted each other by proxy and wounded by petty, bureaucratic devices when they could.[1] 'Everybody has their own daydream for when this war is over,' Goebbels would write. 'Mine is: To loaf around and sleep and make music and read fine books; to lie in the sun; not to pick up a newspaper; and to hear nothing whatever about the foreign ministry.'[2] Ribbentrop fired off a ten-page missive at him in February 1940, but Goebbels disdained even to reply, marveling that his old enemy had time for such things, and calling him a megalomaniac.[3] (A sick man,' he assessed later, 'childishly stuck-up and pompous, with little behind the façade.')[4] Ribbentrop then wrote a twelve-page letter demanding that Goebbels turn over all foreign-language broadcasting to his ministry.[5] After Holland surrendered he tried to snatch the powerful Hilversum transmitter from under Goebbels' nose.[6] When Goebbels sent out one of his best propagandists, Werner Wächter – destroyer of the Berlin synagogues – to organize in Paris, open warfare with Ribbentrop was the result.[7] As a direct snub to him, Goebbels set up a Reichspropaganda-Amt 'Ausland' (Abroad) to match those attached to each gau, under Felix Schmidt-Decker.[8] Learning that the *Börsenzeitung* had fêted Ribbentrop as a second Bismarck, Goebbels ordered Fritzsche to ensure ('in Ribbentrop's own interest') that it did not happen again.[9]

In November 1940 there was a ludicrous show-down, and almost a shoot-out, between the two ministries. Pursuant to Hitler's decree of September 8, 1939 Ribbentrop had emplaced liaison units in various propaganda agencies like the Berlin shortwave radio station at No. 77 Kaiserdamm. Goebbels refused to tolerate these 'spies' and ordered them out early in December 1940.[10] Ribbentrop sent them back in, backed by his own fifteen-man S.S. bodyguard, with orders to use force if necessary, and he then sent Goebbels a telegram from his château at Fuschl telling him what he had done. In a paroxysm of rage Goebbels appealed to Himmler.[11] Over the next week he whipped up the entire Reich chancellery into a froth of indignation and Himmler's unit was again evicted, this time for good.[12] Ribbentrop retired to lick his wounds and cast about for revenge.

HITLER HAD LOST the strategic initiative that November of 1940. Göring had given up hope of defeating Britain in the air and taken six weeks' leave. With Milch in command, the Luftwaffe bombers battered away at London, Coventry, and Birmingham.

'When will that *Kreatur* Churchill finally capitulate?' wondered Goebbels. 'Britain can't take this for ever!'[13] Reading up on that country's national character, however, he came across two ominous words, phlegm, and bovine dullness *(Stumpfsinn)*. 'In their shoes,' he cursed, 'any other nation would have collapsed long ago.'[14]

In Hitler's private cinema they watched newsreels of London in flames. 'The British empire is self-destructing,' Hitler said. He now suggested that Britain was banking on Moscow.[15] The war would continue all winter, he added. He would abstain from all bombing over Christmas, in the hope of wrong-footing Churchill who would surely display no such restraint.[16] 'After which,' wrote Goebbels, 'the British shall see reprisal raids until the tears run down their cheeks.'[17]

Italy's belated entry into the war – in mid-June, after France's defeat was assured – presented Goebbels with special problems.[18] Italy had done so little even then that Goebbels had had to inspire rumors that this was at the Führer's specific request.[19] In Greece, Albania, and Africa the Italians let down the Axis badly. Fearing ugly demonstrations from the ordinary Berliners, he had to discourage the Italians from participating in the next street collections for the Red Cross.[20] 'These are fine allies we've got into bed with,' he wrote.[21] As Italy's rapid retreats degenerated into routs, he advised German radio to stop broadcasting Italian 'quick marches.'

Standing beside Hitler in the Borsig munitions works on December 10 he was relieved to hear him say, to loud cheers, that he was not going in for costly prestige victories – a veiled reference to his resolve not to risk an expedition across the English Channel.[22] Hitler repeated this in a secret speech to all his gauleiters, including Goebbels, the next day. Putting a brave face on things, he called the war as good as won. 'Not that he had wanted this war at all' – so Goebbels summarized his remarks – 'and he would still agree to peace on an acceptable basis. Invasion not planned for the time being. Air supremacy necessary first. Hydrophobia. And he is not one for taking risks if things are possible without them. He wants to avoid heavy casualties.' Goebbels also heard Hitler refer briefly on this occasion to the Soviet Union – she was lurking in the wings, but he was undaunted. He was sending more troops to Romania, his only source of oil. 'We're not letting anybody in there,' he promised.[23]

One week later Hitler signed the BARBAROSSA directive, instructing his generals to prepare a short sharp war against the Soviet Union. He dropped not a hint of this to Goebbels for four more months. Lunching at the chancellery, the minister was puzzled to hear Hitler say that he 'hoped' the war would be over in 1941; Hitler again revealed the irrational dread that restrained him from a cross-Channel invasion. 'He's frightened of the water,' Goebbels realized again. 'He says he would undertake it only if he was in the direst straits.'[24]

ON DECEMBER 30, 1940 Goebbels pre-recorded his New Year's Eve broadcast, to avoid having to leave the comfort (and safety) of Lanke on that night.[25] His original script had read:

> People would probably have called me a fool or a dreamer, or anything but a politician worthy of serious consideration, if I had prophesied on New Year's Eve 1939, when I spoke from this very spot to the German people, that at the end of the New Year then just dawning, 1940, the German front line would extend from Kirkenes to the Bay of Biscay . . . that Norway would have been taken under our wing as far as the Arctic Circle, that France would have suffered a total military defeat, and that Britain would be so stricken by the German counter-blockade and by our Luftwaffe's day-and-night reprisal raids on her vitals that, reeling under the hammer blows of the German armed forces, she would be struggling for naked survival and pleading with the rest of the world to help her out – even if only for a few more weeks.

Hitler, censoring his script, scratched out the last word of this lengthy sentence and wrote *months*; he also pedantically corrected Goebbels' errors of grammar and style.

Where, moreover, Goebbels had written that only one thought inspired them, of victory – 'For that we shall work and we shall fight, until our last enemy lies shattered on the ground,' – Hitler changed it to read 'until the onslaught of our last enemy has been repulsed.'

Goebbels' boast, '*Never shall we capitulate – never*,' was scratched out altogether.[26]

THE NEW YEAR opened on a low key. Goebbels found himself further than ever from his old intimate relationship with Hitler. In North Africa, Italy lost both Bardia and Tobruk to the British. His diary makes no mention of Rommel's rescue expedition to Libya until the end of January 1941 or of Rommel himself until three weeks after that; so Hitler had probably not told him of that diversion either.[27]

A new trade pact was signed with Moscow; unaware of the sinister strategic purpose with which Hitler had vested it, Goebbels saw it only as another slap in the face for Churchill.[28] His secret admiration for the British prime minister remained undiminished, particularly after another belligerent speech by him to parliament in December 1940.

He wrote a flaming attack on Churchill for *Das Reich* but ordered the rest of the press to lay off him for fear of creating a dangerous legend around the man.[29] 'Our press is publishing things which absolutely speak *for* the old swine, for instance scurrilous things about his lifestyle which are not at all ludicrous or even contemptible. He has some attractive features,' admitted Goebbels privately, 'which we don't want to underscore in the press. You've either got to hate your enemy or expose him to ridicule.'[30]

When Hitler returned to Berlin on January 28, 1941 he did not at once send for Goebbels. Goebbels told his diary that *he* had prior engagements.[31] The erosion of his influence is plain from a bleak entry ten days later, after Otto Dietrich had once again put his nose out of joint. 'I may now have to appeal to the Führer,' he wrote, 'awkward though that may prove for me right now.'[32] And then there was the war department (O.K.H.): they had borrowed Goebbels' best movie technicians to make their movie *Victory in the West*; now they refused to let him have them back – another indicator of his momentary impotence.[33] For the first time in years he stayed away from the party's foundation ceremony in Munich on February 24; he listened to Hitler's speech on the radio, a peculiar sensation, he admitted, without being more explicit about their estrangement.[34]

ASSUREDLY IT IS MAGDA who is once again causing his problems with Hitler. Goebbels treats her more scandalously than ever. Her father, his life slowly ebbing in Duisburg, sends to Magda and her mother Auguste Behrend a Christmas telegram which studiously omits all mention of Magda's husband. When she visits the city hospital, her dying father has to send her three hundred marks to defray her travel expenses.[35] On April 3, 1941, Magda returns to Duisburg to share her father's last hours on earth. Her sorrow leaves Goebbels stone cold. 'I scarcely know him,' he callously observes in his diary, not caring who may read it later, 'and I shall not be losing anything when he goes.'[36]

What else has caused the friction? A terse line in his diary for December 20, 1940 refers to a 'short parlaver' with Magda – his euphemism for a blazing row – between two air-raid alerts.[37]

The likely cause is as much the reappearance of Karl Hanke, now a bemedalled war hero of thirty-eight, as the arrival at Schwanenwerder early in November of the vivacious young Ursula Quandt, who has just divorced Magda's boring and half-blind stepson Herbert Quandt. Ursula, nearly a generation younger than Magda, 'now looks quite delicious,' as Goebbels candidly observes.[38] His diary mentions her no fewer than thirty-nine times in the next six months.

Over Christmas 1940 Magda finds that he has invited Ursula out to Lanke too, with his young adjutant Herbert Heiduschke, a paratrooper, for the sake of appearances.[39] At the New Year he pulls the same stunt. The threesome are inseparable for the rest of January, even traveling together to Vienna.[40]

Even in the handwritten diaries the clues about his relationships with women are so urbane as to be almost invisible. He records the curious fact that their nanny has 'quite unexpectedly' given birth to a child. 'Nobody,' he informs his diary, 'had the slightest idea. I arrange for the scared creature to be taken care of. She has suffered fear and pain enough.'[41]

'I discussed with Mrs – her future work,' he writes a few weeks later. 'She's expecting a child now.'[42] For a married woman this would not normally excite comment. Seven weeks later, just before BARBAROSSA, he records this episode: 'A baby in a flower-covered perambulator is put into the ministry's entrance hall for me. With an anonymous letter asking me to show an interest in the baby. I shall concern myself with it. I shall first try to find the mother.'[43]*

If Magda has indeed sought comfort with Hanke, it does not last long.[44] Goebbels prevails on Hitler to banish him from Berlin. The Führer splits the administration of Silesia in two: Hanke becomes gauleiter and Oberpräsident of his native Lower Silesia.[45]

Arriving for supper with Hitler on the day after this arrangement is announced, Goebbels finds Hanke there as well. 'I cut him dead,' he records – four words that say it all.[46]

Even now strange events cast a shadow over his family, which the diary cannot entirely conceal. Magda leaves for a five-week cure in Dresden.[47] All six children leave at the same time. Life in Berlin's air-raid shelters and the indifferent diet are blighting their growth, writes Goebbels, and Göring has offered them sanctuary in his villa on the Obersalzberg.[48]

Midst much weeping Goebbels sees his entire family, with baby Heide in her little basket, leave at ten A.M. on February 12, 1941.

True, nearly one thousand trainloads of other children have been evacuated from Berlin, but as Churchill's raids have momentarily declined other parents are clamoring for their return; besides, Lanke, so expensively built, is hardly at greater risk than the Obersalzberg, and the comely young divorcee Ursula Quandt has no qualms about staying out there at Goebbels' forest estate.[49]

He is no stranger to what he calls the sexual problems of men and women forced to live apart.[50] He feigns dismay at being 'all alone' in the big house at No. 20 Hermann-Göring Strasse, but all that empty it is not. 'Chatted Ursula up a teeny bit,' he records, 'then off to bed exhausted.'[51]

From her sanitarium Magda writes him a long letter about her visit to Hitler when she left the children at the Göring villa.[52] Goebbels tells his staff that Hitler, followed by an inquisitive Bormann, has led her aside, asked, 'Has the Doctor come to his senses?', and then silently squeezed her hand.[53]

Goebbels motors out to Lanke for a week to read, to ride through the forest in his splendid new carriage with the 'nice, naïve,' and 'unproblematic' Ursula, and to listen to classical music.[54] At the end of that week another letter comes from Magda, who has had another mild heart attack. 'Now,' he triumphs, 'she is nice and affectionate to me.'[55]

She pleads for him to visit, and he does spend one evening in Dresden (but again with Ursula in tow) listening to her wifely prattle – 'It is all very nice and harmonious,' he records, another of those give-away phrases like the 'Ursula looks gorgeous' that he writes after a stroll around the gardens at No. 20.[56] When Ursula is away for two weeks visiting the children Goebbels entertains the occasional actress like Margit Syms, a Hungarian beauty; 'helped her career a bit,' he notes afterward.[57]

---

* The diary does not mention any of these episodes again. Visiting Buenos Aires in October 1991, the author was informed that an illegitimate son of Goebbels was living there.

Magda returns to Berlin on March 22. She has arranged for their children to be billeted at Bischofswiesen in Salzburg's countryside.[58] At the end of the month both she and Ursula have competition with the arrival of Marina Shalyapin, a good-looking Russian émigrée with fascinating tales of the 1917 bolshevik revolution to tell. The little Doctor spends three weeks flirting with her, especially when Magda goes down to Dessau to say good-bye to Harald, who is off to the Balkan wars.[59] All three women come out to Lanke for Easter – 'A turbulent Easter,' records Goebbels.[60] On the last day of April Magda leaves, taking Ursula with her, to transfer the six children to a large summer house on a lake near Bad Aussee, in the Upper Danube province. 'They are to stay there,' explained Goebbels, 'until the war is over.'[61] Tragically, they did not.

HE FORBADE ALL PROPHECIES about when the war might in fact be over. 'As for Messrs Sperrle and Stumpff,' he said, expressing his fury at two of the Luftwaffe's most indolent commanders, 'they are in for a surprise. The war game isn't child's play after all.'[62]

The present lull in the war, he had privately explained on January 9 to foreign journalists, opening their new press club on Leipziger Platz, was just a 'creative pause.'[63] In fact the 1941 hunting season for Hitler's bombers and submarines had not yet begun.[64]

By February 6 he knew of Hitler's plans to evict the British expeditionary force currently disembarking in Greece.[65] 'It is high time,' he wrote in *Das Reich*, 'for London to begin listening to harsh facts.'[66] He again began to hint at a coming invasion of England.[67]

'Hitherto,' he teased those foreign journalists on March 7, 'we have never set dates. . . Now for the first time in his political career the Führer has mentioned one, namely: "The decision will come this year."'[68] In the privacy of his diary however he admitted it was fraud. 'For England's benefit we're putting on a bit of an act on the subject of invasion,' he explained, 'to get them all worked up and permanently in a state of fright.'[69]

WHEN HITLER RETURNED to Berlin on March 15, 1941 something still kept the two men apart. 'I am far too rushed to see him,' was Dr Goebbels' lame excuse to his diary.[70] He saw him at a distance the next day, speaking at the Memorial Day ceremony. Goebbels was impressed by the confidence he voiced in victory, but it perplexed him that Hitler was still careful not to state clearly that the war would end in 1941.[71]

He was of course still unaware of BARBAROSSA; he still believed, after an exchange of views with General Eugen von Schobert, that the general's Eleventh Army, now stationed on the eastern frontier, was covering Germany's *rear*.[72]

Hitler finally invited him round to the chancellery on the seventeenth. 'We are slowly strangling Britain,' he told Goebbels, describing their now resumed submarine and air attacks. 'One day she'll lie croaking on the ground.'[73] Not above a bit of crude influence-buying, Goebbels on his next visit to Hitler offered him twenty million marks for his social and cultural funds, from the Winter Relief and movie industry purses which he controlled.[74]

At some stage now Hitler did finally brief him on BARBAROSSA. Perhaps it was on March 20, because the next morning Goebbels requested that all Russian journalists be kept under close surveillance.[75] Moreover, hearing of the friendly reception accorded by Moscow to Japan's foreign minister Yosuke Matsuoka on his way to Berlin the minister commented, 'I don't trust the bolsheviks.'[76] After attending Hitler's banquet for the Japanese minister on March 28 Goebbels handwrote this explicit diary entry:

> [After Yugoslavia] the biggest operation will then follow: Against R. It is being meticulously concealed, only a very few are in the know. It will be initiated with massive west-bound troop movements. We divert attention every which way, except to the east. A feint invasion operation is to be prepared against England, then like lightning everything goes back [east], and up and at 'em. The Ukraine is one vast granary.

Psychologically, he admitted, there were obvious drawbacks – for example parallels with the fate of Napoleon's Grand Army. Propaganda would get around that by playing the anti-bolshevik melody. What a challenge! 'We're going to pull off our masterpiece,' he bragged in the diary. 'Great victories lie in store. It all calls for steady nerves and a clear head... It's great to be in on it,' he added; a hint that it still irked him that Hitler had kept him out of the inner circle for so many months.[77]

AS FOR YUGOSLAVIA, on the day that Berlin welcomed Matsuoka, the Belgrade government which had just joined the Axis was overthrown in a bloodless coup funded by the British secret service.[78] To Goebbels, seeing him at the banquet in Matsuoka's honor, Hitler had seemed under a lot of strain. The Führer told him afterwards that he had decided to deal with Yugoslavia at once. For several days anti-German demonstrations rocked Belgrade. Goebbels allowed his newspapers to publish reports on them without any comment other than, as he himself put it, a few choice drops of poison. On April 4 his black transmitters went into action, broadcasting in all the regional dialects, promising everybody autonomy if Yugoslavia were destroyed.[79] He was already choosing the Balkan victory fanfare.[80]

Looking at the clock over dinner on April 5 he revealed to his closest staff that Germany's bomber squadrons were already fueling up for the attack on Belgrade.[81] At one A.M. Hitler sent for him; he wanted company. Three hundred bombers, he said, would smash Belgrade at daybreak, followed by three hundred more the next night. 'We're going to smoke out this nest of Serbian plotters,' noted Goebbels, aping Hitler's language. The Führer said he would prosecute this war without pity. They sat sipping tea until precisely five-twenty, the hour appointed for the attack, then Hitler retired to bed.[82]

'The Führer himself,' Goebbels told his senior staff at eleven o'clock that morning, 'estimates the duration of this whole operation at two months, I myself think it may well be shorter.' As for Moscow's response, Goebbels reassured his staff. 'Russia will think twice before poking her fingers into this blaze,' he suggested. 'She'll stand aside clenching her fists with rage, and watch what happens next. You know the Führer's methods. Today and tonight a judgment is being inflicted on Belgrade on such a scale that for a thousand kilometers all round people will say, "Stand back! Don't get involved!" And that's the object of the exercise.'[83]

Seventeen thousand were killed in the air raids on Belgrade.[84] There was worldwide outrage; when Churchill bombed Berlin on April 10, damaging the university, state library, and state opera house, Goebbels was perversely pleased, because he could use this raid to offset the bombing of Belgrade. The British claimed to have killed three thousand Berliners; he kept quiet – the real total was just fifteen.[85]

Later that month Churchill started dropping big four-thousand-pound bombs on Berlin – 'blockbusters,' they were called. 'That makes the future look pretty bleak,' Goebbels admitted.[86] He remarked to Hitler that if anything the air raids were making their own public even more refractory.[87] Neither paused to consider that the Luftwaffe's raids might be having the same unwanted effect on the English public. After violent raids on Kiel, Goebbels took charge of relief measures himself, since Göring's officials failed; he ordered the evacuation of women and children and the construction of shelters, and rushed furniture and clothing to the blitzed naval base.[88] At Emden he did the same. These were in fact his first overt steps in the drive to become Germany's next dictator.

FOR HITLER'S CONCURRENT campaign in Greece – designed to prevent a Mussolini fiasco there – Goebbels planned a two-tier propaganda policy. For domestic consumption, the British expeditionary force in Greece was to be described as powerful; but abroad it was to be mocked as puny and ineffective.[89] Moreover, since it was in Germany's strategic interest to detain and destroy the British there, Goebbels publicly accused Churchill of planning to do a bunk.[90] 'We have to pillory Churchill as a typical gambler,' he said on April 15, explaining his tactics to his morning conference, 'more at home in the gambling salons of Monte Carlo . . . cynical, ruthless, and brutal, spilling the blood of others so as to spare the blood of the British.'

If the B.B.C. now announced that Churchill was pouring reinforcements into Greece, he said, their response must be: 'Lies, all lies! It's not true, it's just a cowardly fraud perpetrated by Mr Churchill. Our own precise observations clearly prove, we say, that the British are taking to their heels.' And if London's Reuters agency now referred to the British as 'taking up new positions,' then German propaganda must taunt: 'These new positions consist of the troop transports in which the British are planning their getaway.'[91] Soon the world's press was resounding with the insults which he had dictated at conferences like these.

His orthodox propaganda capabilities within Greece were strictly limited. There were only 37,000 radio sets in the entire country.[92] Besides, the Greeks were never Hitler's enemy. Had the British not sent in their troops, Hitler twice told his propaganda minister, he would have happily left his Italian allies to stew in their own juice.[93]

Now, as the Germans drove the British forces once more back toward the coast, Churchill lapsed into a brooding silence. Goebbels heard that he was seeking solace in whisky and cigars. 'Just the kind of opponent we need,' he observed.[94] By the last day of April the British had all left, aboard troop transports bound for Crete and elsewhere.

'First,' wrote Goebbels, 'a short breather, and then the grand slam.'[95]

UNTIL NOW HE HAD kept his knowledge of BARBAROSSA strictly to himself. On April 10, 1941 he secretly directed Dr Taubert to resuscitate the anti-Comintern project.[96] Taubert's eastern department eventually became a huge body with eight hundred employees running the radio, press, movie, and cultural life of all the occupied eastern territories except the Government-General (as occupied Poland was now called), with a vaguely anti-Moscow-centralism, antisemitic line.[97]

That rainy Easter weekend, Goebbels took a few colleagues out to Lanke. 'How do you think,' he suddenly asked, strolling along the boardwalk around the little Bogensee, 'the German people are going to react to a war with Moscow?' Without waiting for the answer he continued: It would be their ministry's most gargantuan propaganda feat ever. For fifteen years they had demonized the Russians. Then Hitler had signed his pact with Stalin. 'If we do another about-face,' he pointed out, 'nobody is ever going to believe us again.'[98]

Goebbels heard a few days later that Stalin, standing on the Moscow railroad platform for Matsuoka's onward journey to Japan, had hugged the German military attaché Krebs and loudly promised eternal friendship.

'Splendid,' commented the minister. 'Stalin evidently doesn't want to make the acquaintance of our panzer divisions either.'[99]

Before leaving Moscow, Matsuoka signed a Japanese–Soviet non-aggression treaty. 'That doesn't suit the Führer one bit,' Goebbels observed. 'Not given the ongoing planning.'[100]

ON THE EVENING OF April 18 the High Command's liaison officer Major Hans-Leo Martin gate-crashed the little birthday party that Goebbels was staging for his mother in Hermann-Göring Strasse, took him aside, and said: 'Herr Reichsminister, I have been instructed to inform you that our Wehrmacht is shortly to attack Russia.'[101] Goebbels' face revealed not a flicker of emotion.

He had neither compunctions nor fears about the operation. He shortly quoted in his diary this facile prediction by Hitler: 'The entire fabric of bolshevism will collapse like a house of cards.'[102]

Summing up the Balkan campaign in the Reichstag a few days later, Hitler spoke for the first time of the possibility that the war would continue into 1942. The public was dismayed. Goebbels however was already discussing the new fanfare for Russia with his radio bosses.[103]

Returning from the Baltic dockyards at Gotenhafen (formerly Gdynia) and Danzig where he had inspected Germany's mighty new battleships *Bismarck* and *Tirpitz*, Hitler again remarked moodily to Goebbels on the damage that Churchill was doing to the British empire, and on Italy's unbroken series of defeats. 'Without them,' he said, 'Pétain would have stayed at our side, Franco might have joined us after all, and Gibraltar would be in our hands. Then Turkey would have been wide open to offers too. It just doesn't bear thinking about.' For a while he day-dreamed on: Suez dropping like a ripe fruit into his hands, England surrendering. No more. 'We have all that to thank our gentleman-allies for.' On balance however, he still felt that Britain had lost the war in May 1940, at the time of Dunkirk.[104]

The moon would soon be full. Goebbels drove out to Lanke for the weekend. The Luftwaffe was out in strength that Saturday May 10, delivering one last thundering night attack on London before regrouping to the east. The Houses of Parliament were seriously damaged. Goebbels took note of all the war news that Sunday evening. 'The day was quiet,' he wrote the next morning, 'without any major sensation.'[105]

He settled down to vet the latest newsreel.

It featured a visit by Hitler's beetle-browed deputy, Rudolf Hess, to the Messerschmitt aircraft factory in Augsburg.

41: *The Malodorous Thing*

THE SENSATION HAD ALREADY happened. On Monday May 12, 1941 the phone rang at Lanke. It was somebody at the Berghof – though not Hitler himself, he was still too shocked to speak – reporting that the deputy Führer, Rudolf Hess, had taken off for Scotland in a Messerschmitt late on Saturday and was now missing, perhaps dead. Hitler was therefore issuing a communiqué speaking of Hess's 'dementia.'[1] 'What a sight for the world,' exclaimed Goebbels in his diary. 'A mentally-defective deputy to the Führer.' He blamed Otto Dietrich for this infelicitous choice of argument. He was furious that Hitler had not asked his advice.[2] The blow to the party's prestige could be fatal. He immediately ordered the Hess item removed from the weekly newsreel.

He hoped that Hess was dead, but he was not. On Tuesday the British revealed that the Nazi leader had landed by parachute. Goebbels told his secret morning conference to keep a stiff upper lip.[3] He had been summoned to see Hitler that afternoon with all the other gauleiters, he said.[4] 'We'll get to the bottom of the affair this afternoon, and I shall dictate more detailed instructions from the Obersalzberg after that,' he added. Meanwhile they were to concentrate on the air war – on anything but Hess.[5]

At the Berghof Hitler showed him two letters that Hess had left behind, mapping out a 'peace program' he had drafted in October.[6] He was going to England to make her plight plain to her, to get the Duke of Hamilton to overthrow the Churchill regime and to bring about peace without any loss of face for Britain. The two letters oozed half-baked occultist theories. 'That's the kind of men we have ruling Germany,' wrote Goebbels perhaps incautiously. 'The whole business is explicable only in the light of his nature-healing and herb-munching foibles.' Perhaps Hitler's communiqué calling Hess 'demented' was not so far off base after all.[7]

Goebbels quailed at the prospect of what the enemy would make of this. He repeatedly said later that he wished he had been in the enemy's shoes. Then he would have published whatever he liked in Hess's name.[8] He described Duff Cooper & Co. – Cooper was Churchill's minister of information – as dimwitted dilettantes.[9]

When Hitler spoke to all the gauleiters that afternoon, May 13, he was visibly shaken.[10] After driving Goebbels back to the local airfield, S.A. chief of staff

Viktor Lutze noted in his diary that the announcement about Hess would surely lead to a leadership crisis, because the public must ask how such sick men could be retained at the highest level; how could he even have been named 'second man' after Hitler, given that he had been hobnobbing with occultists, astrologers, and hypnotists.[11] In an impotent frenzy Goebbels banned all such charlatans.[12] If explaining BARBAROSSA was going to be tricky for Goebbels, explaining the Hess affair seemed impossible.

He found his department heads waiting for him on the tarmac at Tempelhof.[13] 'Any doctor will tell you,' he said, taking them aside, 'that there are crazy people who seem all along to be perfectly normal and lucid.' Hess had deluded himself that he could single-handedly make peace. Goebbels had however persuaded Hitler, he continued, that they should not breathe one more word about it, and he offered to his dubious colleagues this analogy: A society hostess gives a dinner party; just as they all enter the dining room, her darling whippet dumps a sizable doodah on the priceless Persian carpet. What now? Taking her escort's arm, she strides over to the table acting as though the Malodorous Thing does not exist. 'The Malodorous Thing in our case,' he concluded, 'is the befuddled Mr Hess. He no longer exists.'[14]

He repeated this in more clinical language the next morning.[15] 'Remember the Röhm affair,' he said. 'We shot our mouths off on that occasion with the result that the public talked of little else for years.' 'In any case,' he added mysteriously, 'something is about to happen in the military sphere, and this will distract attention from Hess.'[16]

AFTER THE HESS INCIDENT Goebbels spends two days at Bad Aussee. His children are staying nearby with Magda, Ursula Quandt, and his mother. He gives all three ladies presents for Mother's Day.[17]

Back at Lanke, Ello Quandt visits him. She is our source for an episode which, in bald outline, has Magda suffering a nervous breakdown after witnessing a female secretary clambering from the gardens into her husband's study one night. She hysterically tells Ello that she's going to sue for divorce.[19] The only secretary to whom the diary lays clues is the sweetly named Helga Hoenig, and the date is May 27, 1941. Magda is already in a state of nerves because Göring's costly airborne assault on Crete has just begun, casualties among the paratroops are heavy, and she is worried about Harald.[19] Goebbels meticulously informs his diary that he has been sitting up late working on a new book.[20] 'Fräulein Hoenig helps me with this very assiduously.'[21] It is fair to observe that his female staff very rarely rate such a mention in his dispatches; and to speculate that he, the master of all alibis, is creating yet another.

Ello phones Goebbels to advise him to head off Magda. The diary shows that he indeed drives over to Schwanenwerder. 'Magda's heart is playing up. She's got into a state again, what with the worry about Harald.'[22] They have a 'little chat.' He hopes that she will soon get better. He drives back to Lanke alone. Neither has touched upon the window-climbing secretary. 'The crafty fox ran

rings round me again,' Magda tells Ello as her husband drives away. Ello asks
why she puts up with it all.

'Look at me, Ello,' is the reply. 'I'm growing old. These girls are twenty years
younger – and they haven't had seven children.'[23]

ON DISTANT BATTLEFIELDS the gods of war still thundered. From Rommel's
headquarters in North Africa, Alfred-Ingemar Berndt, his new aide, sent
Goebbels dramatic reports about Tobruk.[24] In Munich the sinister Martin
Bormann took over Hess's vacant role as head of the Party chancellery.
Goebbels neither liked nor trusted him, and for years he would deal with him
only at arm's length through Walter Tiessler. When Bormann began a vicious
campaign against the churches, it was Goebbels who told him – through
Tiessler – to lay off.[25]

In Crete the desperate fighting came to an end. Herbert Heiduschke was
already dead and buried at Khania; the death of his young adjutant affected
Goebbels deeply, if his diary is to be believed.[26] Churchill alleged that Hitler's
paratroops had worn New Zealand uniforms. Why not say they were dressed
as postmen, Goebbels scoffed to his department heads. 'They've already had us
in priests', nuns', and Dutchmen's uniforms.'[27] Göring himself telephoned that
Harald was alive; Goebbels promised his stepson later that he would always see
him provided for. 'He always treated me like his own son,' Harald said later.[28]

Endless German troop transports had begun heading east. Rumors were rife,
most of them deliberately planted by Goebbels.[29] There was talk that Stalin and
Hitler were about to meet: That Stalin was to lease the Ukraine to Germany for
ninety-nine years: That another Soviet state visit to Berlin was imminent: That
millions of red flags were already being stitched.[30] Goebbels lifted his wartime
ban on dancing as a hint that the Nazi appetite was momentarily gorged. All
Germany knew of immense troop movements heading west for the invasion
of England – some people had actually seen the troop trains being loaded at
Grunewald station. He briefed his head of broadcasting Dr Glasmeier to select
new England fanfares, he activated English-speaking propaganda companies,
and he held a top-secret conference of department heads on the last day of May
to confide to them that Germany was about to invade England.[31]

About the real truth – BARBAROSSA – he briefed only a tiny handful including
Hadamovsky and Major Titel. He must also have initiated the ministry's
popular Professor Karl Bömer, head of his foreign press department. Bömer
had an alcohol problem however and on May 22 Otto Dietrich phoned
Goebbels with word that at a Bulgarian legation reception a week earlier the
professor had blurted out these words: 'We'll thrash the Russians in four weeks.
Rosenberg is to become governor-general of Russia. I am to become his under-
Staatssekretär.'[32] The Bulgarian envoy had cabled urgently to Sofia asking to
be recalled for consultations. Tipped off by his press chief Dr Paul Schmidt
and by the Forschungsamt codebreakers, Ribbentrop had greedily seized on
this chance of scoring off Goebbels.[33] Hitler announced that he was going to

have the head of 'whichever minister' had betrayed the BARBAROSSA secret to Bömer. He ordered a full-blooded Gestapo inquiry and the luckless professor was thrown into jail.[34] 'That's what comes from boozing,' wrote Goebbels.[35]

He had to save Bömer if only to save his own skin. Witnesses named by Bömer swore that he had been misquoted; somewhat implausibly, the professor claimed not to have known the secret anyway. His minister did what he could, while cautiously telling his diary that Bömer had only himself to blame.[36] 'Ribbentrop,' he also wrote, 'does not play fair. He confuses politics with selling champagne, where the only thing that matters is doing your opponent down.'[37] On Hitler's insistence Bömer was stood before the People's Court on October 18. In an unusual alliance, forged of a mutual enmity to Ribbentrop, both Dietrich and Goebbels testified on Bömer's behalf – the minister declaiming theatrically, 'If you find Bömer guilty, then you must find me guilty too!'[38] Convicted of carelessness rather than treason, Bömer was sentenced to two years in prison.[39] It was further proof how low Goebbels' stock had sunk at Hitler's headquarters.

He could hardly wait for the new war to begin. On June 4 he shared the deadly secret with Leopold Gutterer, his Staatssekretär and trusty amanuensis ('upon whom,' he had written, 'I can impose at will').[40] Since the last week in May he had been feeding 'invasion' rumors to the British, but there was disappointingly little evidence that they were rising to the bait.[41] He wondered if he was being perhaps too subtle, and decided on blunter tactics.[42] With Hitler's approval he drafted for the Berlin *Völkischer Beobachter*'s June 13 edition an article, 'E.g. Crete,' which implied that the airborne assault on that island had been the final dress-rehearsal for the invasion of the British Isles; he then arranged for the Gestapo to seize the entire edition as soon as the embassies and foreign press corps had received their copies. As soon as the wiretappers heard one American correspondent file his story on this sensation to New York, all phone lines out of Germany were cut.[43]

It was one of his most devious stunts.* To the uninitiated, his 'gaffe' looked like the terminal blow to his prestige. News of it spread throughout the government grapevine. He hammed it up all day: He did not attend his morning press conference (instead, backstage, he was trying out new fanfares for BARBAROSSA). Dyed-in-the-wool Nazis like *Reichsfrauenführerin* Gertrud Scholtz-Klink thought it prudent to cancel longstanding appointments with him. 'That's human nature for you,' reflected Goebbels, and he chuckled at these *faiblesses*, while outside his door Helga Hoenig and his other secretaries wept real tears over his apparent disgrace. Only the much maligned Robert Ley showed strength of character, telephoning him to ask if there was anything he could do – an act of true compassion of which Goebbels often spoke later on.[44]

---

* The effectiveness of this costly stunt was arguable. The *New York Times* and others reported the suppression of the *VB* edition carrying his article, but the truth about BARBAROSSA had long been known to Churchill at least, from code-breaking.

Hitler returned to Berlin that day, Friday June 13, 1941. Keeping up pretenses, Goebbels did not walk over to the chancellery for his usual lunch either that day or the next. On Sunday however he was driven in pouring rain to the back entrance in a borrowed car and hidden behind a copy of the *Börsenzeitung*. Schaub saw him and Hitler laughing uproariously over the fake *VB* edition.[45]

Hitler told him that BARBAROSSA would begin on Sunday June 22 with the mightiest artillery bombardment in history. 'The example of Napoleon will not be repeated.' Fortunately Stalin was massing his armies on the frontiers, so Hitler estimated that it would all be over in four months. Goebbels, who set little store by the Russians' fighting strength, estimated even less. 'If ever an operation was a walkover then this is.' As for the pre-attack period, there would this time be no protracted crescendo in the press, but total silence until the day of the sudden onslaught itself.

Goebbels was pleased that Hitler was going ahead with BARBAROSSA. He had abhorred the period of uneasy collaboration with Stalin as a blot on the Nazi escutcheon. He even spoke kindly of Alfred Rosenberg, saying that the coming campaign justified all that he had stood for. 'Right or wrong,' he quoted Hitler as saying, 'we've got to win. . . Once we've pulled it off, who's to question us about how we did it?' Goebbels added, 'We've got so much to answer for, that we've just *got* to win.'

He had begun drafting the leaflets, brochures, and posters ('Adolf Hitler the liberator') for this new crusade weeks before. In top secrecy Taubert's staff had recorded discs, films, and radio broadcasts in the Ukrainian, White Russian, Lithuanian, Latvian, and Estonian tongues as well as in Russian, and in the dialects of countless Caucasian and other tribes.[46] He naturally assumed that Hitler was planning to exploit these peoples' latent hatred of Moscow as he advanced. 'Probably,' wrote Goebbels, 'our soldiers will never have been welcomed with such enthusiasm.'[47]

He learned of Hitler's actual policies on Russia only gradually, at second hand and, as it turned out, imperfectly. Rosenberg was to become minister for the occupied eastern territories with his chief of staff Arno Schickedanz in the Ukraine. Goebbels was uneasy about these two men – they were too doctrinaire.[48] But Rosenberg told Taubert that he planned to dismantle the Soviet Union and restore each constituent republic's liberty, which seemed sound enough.[49]

Goebbels' dummy Task Force England was unobtrusively disbanded. The East Prussian Joachim Paltzo, with Dr Friedrich Mahlo and Adolf Mauer, both of the ministry's tourist office, would direct the real Task Force Russia.[50] Thirty propaganda companies would fan out behind the armies, making propaganda for the first time among the liberated peoples – one *Propagandatrupp* for each city – and they would bring reports back to Germany.

Goebbels' propaganda guidelines to the Soviet Union also bore little comparison with Hitler's later policies. Their enemies, he said, were Stalin and his Jewish backers; German propaganda was not, of course, to be anti-socialist, nor was there to be a reversion to tsarism; since the Red Army was fiercely nationalist there would also be no hint of dismemberment.[51]

He was therefore shocked by the scope of Hitler's plans for the Soviet empire when he saw them. Only the far eastern regions were to be left untouched.[52] He decided that he would have to forget his past feuds with Rosenberg. 'If you handle him right,' he wrote after meeting him on June 14, 'you can get along with him.'[53]

Behind closed doors and under a Gestapo guard, on Wednesday June 18 his ministry began printing three million copies of Hitler's proclamation to the eastern front.[54] To distract attention, Goebbels invited Italian diplomats out to Schwanenwerder for the weekend. On Saturday afternoon Hitler phoned to summon him to the chancellery, and he left his guests in his private cinema watching *Gone with the Wind*.

For three hours he and Hitler paced up and down the long chancellery drawing room, examining the dangers of attacking Russia, this malignant tumor in the east. The Führer felt that there must still be an influential peace faction in England – why had London otherwise systematically played down Hess's mission ever since he landed? For an hour he listened to the different BARBAROSSA fanfares, then approved of Goebbels' own choice – the pompous, brassy opening chords of Franz Liszt's *Les Préludes* with a short added motif from the Horst Wessel anthem. They separated at two-thirty A.M. It was now Sunday June 22, 1941, the anniversary of Napoleon's ill-starred invasion of Russia. 'He has been working on this since July,' wrote Goebbels. 'And now the hour has struck.'

At three-thirty A.M. Hitler's armies and air force fell upon the Soviet Union. Unable to sleep, Goebbels paced his office, watching the minutes pass, listening to the sigh of history. Two hours later, he sat tautly before the microphone in the building's new studio, flanked by Gutterer and Hadamovsky, and heard the BARBAROSSA fanfare heralding Hitler's new campaign blaring from the loudspeakers. He broadcast the Führer's proclamation, then drove out to Schwanenwerder and his abandoned guests. The birds' dawn chorus was in full cry.[55]

42: No Room for Two of Us

GOEBBELS' DIARIES, NOW ALL RETRIEVED from hiding, chronicle Hitler's Russian campaign almost to the last day. Of particular interest is how this crusade, embarked upon in such a froth of misplaced optimism, impinged upon him as minister: How he argued for the adoption of more realistic policies toward the 'liberated' Russians, and how, when all seemed lost, Hitler finally granted to him the powers he craved to mobilize the entire nation. But he was a realist too. He prohibited the publication of maps of the entire Soviet Union, in case readers felt that this time their Führer had bitten off more than he could chew.[1]

He justified BARBAROSSA effortlessly. Churchill came to his aid with a radio broadcast that same Sunday evening, June 22, 1941, pledging unlimited British aid to Moscow. Goebbels argued that they had been conspiring together all along.[2] In an article published four days later he argued that the Soviet Union had been banking on taking over a stricken and war-ravaged Europe. 'In one hand they clutched the treaty with us . . . but in the other they sharpened the blade to plunge into our back.'[3] Two weeks later *Das Reich* published his *pièce justificative*, 'The Veil Falls,' in which he described BARBAROSSA as a war (though not a 'crusade' – he had forbidden the usage of that overworked noun) by civilized people 'against spiritual putrefaction, against the decay of public morality, against the bloody terrorization of mind and body, against criminal policies whose perpetrators sit astride mounds of corpses casting about for whom to select as their next victim.'[4]

For six days Hitler ordered a news blackout. On the seventh he ordered twelve special communiqués broadcast.[5] At hourly intervals from eleven A.M. the same trumpets sounded. Goebbels was livid about this amateurish day-long deluge of fanfares.[6] It allowed the common man to glimpse the workings of high propaganda. Precisely because it destroyed the *illusion*, he had forbidden newspapers to publish behind-the-scenes photographs at movie studios and reprimanded a weekly magazine for portraying the hallowed phonograph disc from which the victory fanfares were played during the battle of France.[7] 'I shall see to it,' he wrote, wrongly blamed for this stunt, 'that this never happens again.'[8]

For Goebbels, image was everything. War newsreels never showed air-raid victims, and he persuaded Hitler to suppress lingering shots of battle-casualties in a movie on the heroism of the medical corps during the battle of Crete.[9] Like more recent governments, he wanted the German public to believe in an antiseptic, almost bloodless war.

He injected his propaganda into the Soviet Union initially by means of three black transmitters disguised as Trotskyite, separatist, and nationalist.[10] Eventually, despite the lack of receivers in the Soviet Union, he would have twenty-two official transmitters as well, broadcasting thirty-four daily bulletins in eighteen different languages.[11] He had persuaded the communists Torgler, Kasper, and Albrecht, at a secret meeting in his ministry in May, to broadcast appeals to the enemy in authentic communist double-speak to overthrow the 'traitor' Stalin and to set up workers' and soldiers' councils (but Goebbels stopped them from calling for street demonstrations, in case nobody showed up).[12] Hoping to use Ernst Thälmann too, he sent him reports on conditions in the Soviet Union; still in a concentration camp, 'Teddy' Thälmann disdained to collaborate (and was eventually shot).[13]

After a few days in shock, Stalin came back fighting with a famous radio broadcast on July 3, 1941, proclaiming a patriotic war.[14] Hitler now authorized Goebbels to unleash his main anti-Soviet propaganda campaign.[15] There was no lack of material. Hearing of atrocities in Lvov, where the retreating Red Army had murdered six hundred Ukrainians, Goebbels rushed twenty journalists there to get eye-witness accounts.[16] There was no need for him to invent horror stories. Hitler's secret police had stormed the Soviet diplomatic buildings in Paris and Berlin, and found some decidedly undiplomatic equipment including sound-proof execution chambers, a poisons laboratory, and electric crematoria for disposing of human remains.[17] 'If a criminal gang comes to power,' dictated Goebbels reading the reports on these gruesome finds submitted by Reinhard Heydrich and Abwehr chief Vice-Admiral Wilhelm Canaris, 'then it will conduct its politics with criminal methods too.' 'There would have been no room for the two of us in Europe in the long run.'[18]

Goebbels called briefly at No. 20 Hermann-Göring Strasse to check progress on the air-raid shelter that Speer was excavating in its gardens. Architect Hugo Bartels said it was consuming enough cement to build three hundred working-class homes.[19] Seven feet thick, its roof and walls would withstand the heaviest British bombs so far.[20]

Worried that one thoughtless bomb might destroy his diaries, Goebbels moved all twenty volumes to safety in the Reichsbank vaults.[21] He finally abandoned writing the diaries in his barely decipherable script, and began dictating them instead each morning to Otte, his high-speed stenographer, from notes compiled during the previous day. Aged thirty-four, Otte performed this task until the end, sometimes having to sleep on a couch next-door until the next torrent of dictation was ready to sweep over him.[22] One single day's entry might run to 144 pages.[23] Relays of secretaries typed each page on fine bond paper in triplicate, triple-spaced and in an outsize typeface; until the primitive glass microfiches containing all 75,000 pages surfaced in Moscow in

1992, where this author was the first historian privileged to use them, only a fragment was believed to have survived.

OTTE'S FIRST TRANSCRIPT was dated July 9, 1941. His minister had just paid a flying visit to the 'Wolf's Lair,' Hitler's new headquarters built in a swampy, mosquito-infested forest in East Prussia.

Hitler boasted that the Germans had already damaged or destroyed two-thirds of Stalin's forces and written off five-sixths of his tanks and planes. 'Our strategy is to take on our enemies one at a time,' Hitler explained. 'Preventive wars are still the best.'

Stalin had probably been banking on seizing Romania that autumn. Bad weather would have stalled Hitler's counter-moves, and he would have lost his only significant petroleum supplies. Goebbels was impressed: 'The Führer rescued the Reich from its fate,' he dictated. Hitler said that after 'rubbing out' Moscow and Leningrad he would advance on the river Volga and the Ural mountains.

A repetition of Napoleon's disaster was impossible. The Nazi forces had motor transport and panzer divisions, which Napoleon had not. Goebbels told his diary that Hitler had asked him to visit the Wolf's Lair more often, every week or so; but five weeks passed before another invitation came.[24]

A week after BARBAROSSA began, Goebbels ran into unexpected problems with Rosenberg. On the day before his visit to headquarters, Hitler had ruled that Rosenberg's East-Ministry, and not Goebbels, should control all propaganda in the east.[25] Goebbels vainly referred to the decree of September 1939 which entrusted to his ministry all 'practical execution' of propaganda.[26] His old rival was trying to become the next tsar, he decided.[27]

As the years passed Rosenberg proved woefully incapable of organizing on an imperial scale, and Goebbels contemptuously referred to his apparatus, the Ostministerium, as the 'Cha-ost' ministry.[28] 'If only we had proceeded more shrewdly in the east,' he would reflect in 1944, 'and if only we had made clear to the peoples there that we were coming not as conquerors but as liberators from bolshevism, the decisive blow against the Soviet Union might have met with success.'[29]

At first as the Wehrmacht advanced the jubilant natives had greeted Hitler's troops with garlands of flowers, making no attempt to adopt the scorched-earth policies demanded by Stalin.[30] Goebbels stressed in his propaganda that their common enemy was their 'Jewish-bolshevik' oppressors.[31] Rosenberg however pursued very different policies.[32] He pronounced all Soviet citizens equally culpable for having tolerated bolshevism, and acted accordingly. Although there were virtually no printing presses or paper, and although 'every nail and pane of glass' had to be imported from Germany, it was Goebbels' task to cover the eastern territories with (Rosenberg's) propaganda. His ministry blocked Rosenberg's plans where it could, but that was not often.[33] 'We managed to prevent the total eradication of the Ukrainian intelligentsia,' reported Dr

Taubert early in 1945. But it was an unequal fight. Rosenberg unhelpfully declared all Soviet citizens 'sub-humans' and wondered why they flocked to the ranks of the partisans. It would take Goebbels a year to get an odious S.S. brochure called *Sub-Humans* withdrawn.[34] He would fight equally hard to have the 'Ost'-badge issued to Russian slave laborers replaced by something smacking less obviously of the badge worn by Jews.[35] Gunter d'Alquèn told him that the Ukrainians who had, as the Germans marched in, joyfully dug up ancient icons which they had concealed for decades, now lived in mortal terror of these new Nazi oppressors.

AS GOEBBELS FLEW DOWN to Salzburg for the Mozart festival he dipped into a one-hundred-page book by an American, entitled *Germany Must Perish!*[36] The author, Theodore N. Kaufman, proposed the 'summary sterilization' of all Germans. 'Germany must perish forever!' wrote Kaufman. 'In fact – not in fancy.' The dust cover carried what seemed to be endorsements from *Time* magazine, the *Washington Post*, and the *New York Times*.[37]

It was an extraordinary book. 'Well,' dictated Goebbels gleefully to Otte, 'this Jew has done a disservice to the enemy. If he had composed this book at my behest he couldn't have done a better job.'[38] He decided to issue one million copies to German soldiers; after initially shelving this on legal grounds, fearing American reprisals against German copyrights, he issued the book with a photograph showing President Roosevelt apparently dictating the contents.[39]

Solutions to the Jewish problem were never far from his mind. In August 1940 he had discussed with Hitler the liquidation by the Soviet N.K.V.D. of the intelligentsia in the Baltic states. Goebbels had thoroughly approved. Without their intelligentsia, he had pointed out, the Baltic states were emasculated.[40] Later that month he and Hitler again agreed that Europe's Jews should all eventually be shipped off to Madagascar.[41] When Goebbels visited Kattowitz in September 1940 the gauleiter Fritz Bracht had confirmed that all the Jews there had been deported.[42]

For Goebbels there were two difficulties: Neither the broad German public nor their Führer shared his satanic antisemitism. He studied Hitler's attitudes carefully during a dinner with Hans Frank, upon whose Polish domain, the Government-General, would fall the task of absorbing the Reich's detritus of unwanted Jews.[43]

The same Hitler who had issued ruthless orders for the execution of the Soviet commissars was by no means as hostile as Goebbels desired toward western Europe's more cultivated Jews. He heard Hitler speak warmly of both the composer Gustav Mahler and the producer Max Reinhardt (Max Goldmann), and concede that in their performances the Jews were often 'not bad.'[44]

The public attitude was the lesser of these two problems. Goebbels got to work on that with the only three antisemitic films that his studios ever produced, *The Rothschilds* (premiered on July 17, 1940), *Jud Süss* (September 24), and *The Eternal Jew*; this third movie contained such distressing scenes of

Jewish ritual slaughter that Goebbels ordered an expurgated version made for the more squeamish members of the public.[45]

His own visceral hatred of the Jews had become more radical since 1940. Physically liquidating them now seemed an increasingly viable solution. If it was possible to liquidate the insane, if Göring's air force was killing the relatively innocent English by the thousand, why should the 'guilt-laden' Jews be spared? Goebbels had discussed the euthanasia project ('the covert liquidation of the mentally ill,' he called it) with Bouhler on January 30, 1941. Bouhler had informed him that they had quietly disposed of eighty thousand so far, with sixty thousand more still to go. 'Hard work, but necessary too,' applauded Goebbels.[46] To counter public disquiet he commissioned from leading movie director Wolfgang Liebeneiner, the Steven Spielberg of the day, a harrowing film on the human freaks whom a compassionate Third Reich was pleased to put out of their misery.[47]

To him the Jews were fair game. Thus when Jewish ringleaders triggered strikes in Nazi-occupied Holland in February 1941 he demanded that 'this Jewish rabble' be hanged.[48] Visiting Posen soon after, he heard from the gauleiter Arthur Greiser of how he was cleansing the surrounding Warthegau. 'There has been all manner of liquidating going on here,' he reported approvingly in his diary, 'particularly of the Jewish garbage.'[49] He saw every justification: had the Jews not declared war on the Reich?[50] He was wont to say that the advantage of the Nazis' being branded worldwide as antisemites was that they could now do with the Jews as they saw fit.[51]

Primarily he wanted to expel all Berlin's Jews. They formed the dangerous nucleus of an enemy intelligentsia. Hans Hinkel, Goebbels' specialist on Jewish affairs, had reported in September 1940 that there were still some seventy-two thousand in the city. The intermediate aim was to deport five hundred a month to the south-east; as soon as the war ended the rest would be sent back to the east.[52] Later that month Hinkel informed Goebbels that about four million Jews still lived in Hitler's present dominions. 'The Madagascar plan, which has now been given the go-ahead, provides for about three and a half million of these to be shipped to Madagascar over approximately eighteen months after the war.'[53]

'Dr Goebbels,' Tiessler told the party chancellery, 'regards every Jew as a counter-propagandist. Henceforth Jews should rent out accommodation only to other Jews.'[54] Albert Speer agreed with him fervently, though for other reasons. According to his figures there were over twenty-three thousand Jewish homes in the city. His official diary* shows that at the beginning of 1941 he had initiated a cold-blooded slum-clearance plan which involved evicting Jewish

---

* I.e., the original diary, not the sanitized and retyped version which Speer artfully deposited in the German federal archives after his release from Spandau prison, and from which is excised all reference to his infamous Hauptabteilung Umsiedlung (Main Rehousing Office) which conducted the evictions.

tenants and cramming them into other already overcrowded Jewish homes.[55] But no matter how many ordinances Goebbels issued, the Jews found ways to circumvent them; and although he repeated to Dr Gutterer in April 1941 a suggestion that the Jews should be forced to wear a distinctive badge, this idea too made slow progress.[56]

The direct expulsion of the Jews from Berlin was not yet practicable. The cleansing of Vienna had been given priority, and the eastern railroad system was overburdened with war transports.[57] Besides, some thirty thousand of Berlin's Jews were working in munitions factories.[58] Goebbels still felt, as he complained to Hitler on March 17, 1941, that his city should not have to house around seventy thousand Jews. He told Gutterer afterward however that the Führer had still not decided that Berlin should be 'freed of its Jews.'[59] Gutterer at once called an inter-ministerial meeting attended by representatives of both Speer and Heydrich. The latter's man, S.S. Sturmbannführer Adolf Eichmann, went over the recent history: Hitler, he explained, had put Heydrich in charge of evacuating the Jews, and Heydrich had recently developed a plan to lodge them all in Poland though Hans Frank was reluctant to absorb any more there. Eichmann reminded the ministry that their manufacturing industry needed every available Jew.[60] Speer's man (probably Dietrich Clahes, chief of his infamous Rehousing Office) explained that Speer wanted the twenty thousand Jewish homes in Berlin emptied as a reserve for air-raid housing losses.[61]

Goebbels discussed this briefly with Hitler on June 19. Hans Frank was visiting too and made no secret of his eagerness to displace his unwanted Jews still further east once Russia was defeated. 'A fitting punishment,' philosophized Goebbels, 'given the way that they have pitted country against country and plotted the war.' 'The Führer,' he routinely added, 'also prophesied all this to the Jews.' Hitler reassured Frank that Poland was envisaged only as a transit camp for Europe's Jews; in due course they would all be deported further east.[62]

Thwarted in his immediate intention, Goebbels pressed on with the plan for Jews to be forced to wear a distinguishing badge in public, explaining that they were getting more uppity with each day that passed. Polish women in Berlin already had to wear a 'P' badge, and Jewish street workers a yellow armband.[63] He directed Taubert to discuss this idea with the Gestapo. In fact Heydrich had first mooted the idea in 1938, but it had been slapped down by Hitler.[64] Late in 1939 the propaganda ministry had independently suggested that Jews should wear some kind of lapel pin to facilitate the new ordinance that they give up their seats in public transport; the idea had been put to Himmler but got no further.[65] The Gestapo's chief, S.S. Brigadeführer Heinrich Müller, told Taubert that Heydrich had made similar proposals ever since 1940. Tiessler asked Bormann if a decision from Hitler was likely soon, and there the matter rested until the summer of 1941.[66]

As Hitler's armies invaded the Baltic states in June and July 1941, expelling their recent Russian conquerors, the natives of those three countries exacted terrible retribution on the Jews who had figured prominently among the murderous commissars. Shortly before Goebbels saw Hitler that August, he learned from d'Alquèn of this bloody sequel, and pitilessly referred once again to Hitler's famous prophecy of January 1939.[67] During that month Speer evicted five thousand more Berlin Jews from their homes.[68] Goebbels applauded, and rhetorically asked his staff what their returning soldiers would think if they found the Jews still living in eight-room homes and for ever whining in public transport.[69] 'I don't want to see the mob taking the Jewish problem into its own hands again like 1938.'[70] 'You only have to imagine,' he dictated to his secretary Otte, 'what the Jews would do with us if they were ever in power.'[71]

SPEER'S AIR-RAID SHELTER for Goebbels was scheduled for completion at the end of August 1941, and high time too. Autumn was approaching and Churchill's bomber squadrons would soon return. Even the Russians had recently sent bombers over Berlin.[72]

Stalin was playing Goebbels at his own game. One evening an enemy voice from Moscow broke into the brief silence before the evening news bulletin and intoned blasphemies against the Führer.[73] The same voice used subsequent pauses to pass sarcastic comments on each preceding item. There seemed to be no adequate counter-measure. Goebbels, who had total control of the radio news, ordered the bulletins read ever faster, and then had to start rumors to explain away this undignified verbal gallop.[74] The enemy voices continued. They must have seemed like an ill omen from the east.

GOEBBELS REPORTED TO HITLER's headquarters on August 18, 1941 for the first time in over five weeks. Hitler was recovering from an attack of marshland dysentery and, Goebbels was malevolently pleased to hear, some kind of attack brought on by a stand-up row with Ribbentrop. In the four hours that they spent strolling through the heavily patrolled woodlands within the compound Hitler admitted that BARBAROSSA had run into difficulties. His experts had credited Stalin with five thousand tanks: He had closer to twenty thousand, and not ten thousand warplanes but twenty.[75] However he put Stalin's losses at three million dead, and he had already taken 1·4 million Soviet prisoners.* Perhaps, continued Hitler, Stalin would ask for peace terms. He would grant them, provided that Stalin's forces were totally disarmed. He had no qualms about letting bolshevism as such survive. He hoped to conclude the campaign by the onset of winter.

Goebbels touched upon the topic of euthanasia.[77] In a recent sermon Count von Galen, bishop of Münster, had threatened to have the 'murderers' prosecuted. While Goebbels felt that Galen should be hanged for sedition, Hitler argued that in general they must avoid all potentially divisive subjects,

---

* At Potsdam Marshal Stalin confided to Churchill in July 1945 that Soviet losses during the war had amounted to five million killed or missing.[76]

like the inter-denominational conflict.[78] Undeterred, Goebbels raised the Jewish problem and showed the Führer Kaufman's book, *Germany must Perish!* Hitler assured him that his sinister prophesy of January 1939 was automatically being fulfilled. 'In the east,' reported Goebbels, dictating this diary passage to his secretary Richard Otte, 'the Jews are having to foot the bill; they have already paid it in part in Germany.' Angered by the Kaufman book, Hitler gave him carte blanche to introduce the badge for the Jews. Goebbels decided that it should be a yellow cloth star with the word *Jude* emblazoned across it.[79]

AS PROPAGANDA MINISTER he kept his finger on the pulse of German public opinion at several vital points. His staff closely analyzed all incoming mail, including anonymous letters; a brutally frank weekly morale report was compiled by Amt III of Himmler's security service; and his own network of forty-two gau-level Propaganda Offices (Reichspropagandaämter) reported each Monday on public morale (*Stimmung*) and behavior (*Haltung*). They in turn drew their information from cells in individual factories and party branches. Dr Immanuel Schäffer, who had to collate this data at the ministry, found a wide measure of agreement between them. Broadly speaking, while behavior remained remarkably stable, public morale fluctuated wildly.[80]

Goebbels feared that in the long term the easy victories of the Wehrmacht during the early weeks of BARBAROSSA had been devastating for morale.[81] He recalled his trusty Alfred-Ingemar Berndt, now an S.S. Oberführer, from North Africa, to take over his central Propaganda Department.[82] Berndt secretly confided to Himmler that his job would be 'to carry the German public through the coming winter.'

'Our propaganda this summer has blundered badly,' he added. 'We've been in the illusions business, we've painted everything too rosy.' Churchill's method, he reminded Himmler, was to paint the situation to his public in the darkest hue possible, but to stress that in the end British arms would be triumphant.[83] British analysts detected a shift in Goebbels propaganda output to a more somber mood.[84]

FIVE MORE WEEKS PASSED before he saw Hitler again. BARBAROSSA had regained its lost momentum. At five P.M. on September 20, 1941 German radio announced the capture of Kiev, capital of the Ukraine. Two million Russian prisoners were now in German hands. As Goebbels and Hadamovsky flew into the Wolf's Lair for lunch on the twenty-third the news was of even greater victories as four Soviet armies, encircled by army groups Center and South, faced destruction.[85] Hitler told them that the worst would be over by mid-October. He would follow through with thrusts toward Kharkov, Stalingrad, and the river Don, to rob Stalin of his coal- and arms-production centers. Leningrad would be starved out, then plowed literally into the ground.[86] Goebbels learned that Hitler was putting Reinhard Heydrich in charge of an increasingly fractious Prague. 'Such situations,' the minister dictated approvingly, 'call for a strong man.'

He found Heydrich here at Hitler's headquarters and thus he was able to coordinate with him their measures against the Jews.[87] The new badge had been gazetted into law two or three weeks earlier, but there had been unforeseen consequences: There was loud public criticism of the Yellow Star, and some Germans were going out of their way to offer Jews seats in crowded public transport. Goebbels was furious, and ordered that they be reminded of Kaufman's slogan that Germany 'must perish forever from this earth.'[88] To rub it in he issued through the party's Reich Propaganda Directorate (RPL) a leaflet headed, 'Whenever you see this badge, remember what the Jew has inflicted upon our nation.'[89]

In Hans Fritzsche's view it was this unexpected sentimentalism of the Berliner that finally decided Goebbels on the rapid and ruthless deportation of the Jews.[90] Dictating his diary on September 23 the propaganda minister noted that this would still have to await the end of BARBAROSSA. 'They are all to be transported ultimately to [regions?] adjacent to the bolshevik [rump territory?]' he dictated.*

Hitler had confirmed to him that little by little all Jews were to be expelled from Berlin, Vienna, and Prague.[91] This conformed with what he had told Himmler. The aim was to evacuate them all by the end of 1941: First to occupied Poland, then, in the spring of 1942, further east into occupied Russia. The first sixty thousand were to be expelled from Berlin, Vienna, and Prague. These Jews, Himmler had thereupon notified Heydrich, would be dumped in the Łódź ghetto.[92] To the distinctly disenchanted Nazi governor of Lodz, Friedrich Uebelhör, Himmler wrote that such was 'the Führer's will.'[93] 'All the Jews are to be removed,' Hitler repeated during lunch on October 6. 'And not just to the Government-General [former Poland] but right on to the east. It is only our pressing need for war transport that stops us doing so right now.'[94]

AT FIVE-THIRTY A.M. ON October 2, 1941, Hitler's armies began TYPHOON, the attempt to capture Moscow. Nearly two thousand tanks moved off in blinding clouds of dust. Again the Führer had kept Goebbels in the dark. At Goebbels' request however he made a flying visit to Berlin to speak at the Sport Palace on the third: His train arrived at 1:10 P.M., and he spoke at five. Goebbels had packed the front rows with combat-injured men, just like in the good old days.[95] Speaking *ex tempore*, Hitler delivered a witty, boisterous oration and the Berlin audience, which was not the usual stuffed-shirt party crowd, roared approval. He boasted that Russia was 'already broken' and 'would never arise again.' Gales of laughter gusted around the vast hall as he mocked Churchill's self-proclaimed victories; deafening applause followed as he pronounced his own. As Goebbels accompanied him back to his special train at seven-thirty, Hitler

---

* The photocopy is only partially decipherable. On orders from the minister of the interior in Bonn the German federal archives on July 1, 1993 refused to allow the author to inspect the original image. See Author's Acknowledgments, page viii.

prophesied that ('provided the weather stays fine') they would have destroyed the Soviet armed forces within the next fourteen days.

For a few days, as a news blackout prevailed, it seemed that he was right. As the first snows drifted down on October 7 General Jodl called it the most crucial day of the campaign.[96] On the eighth he went further, speaking in private to Walther Hewel: 'We have finally and without exaggeration won this war.'[97] Later that day Hitler sent for Otto Dietrich and his young deputy Heinz Lorenz, and dictated to them a written briefing for the press; he also directed General Rudolf Schmundt to give to Dietrich an order of the day announcing that Marshal Timoshenko's armies were trapped. Dietrich drafted a press statement. General Jodl approved the text.[98] 'The Russian armies have been annihilated,' it said in part. And, 'All that remains in Russia is policing work.' Arriving in Berlin the next day, October 9, Dietrich told a press conference that Russia was 'done for.'

The first that Goebbels knew was when he read the afternoon headlines: 'THE GREAT HOUR HAS STRUCK: THE CAMPAIGN IN THE EAST DECIDED!' He limped furiously up and down his home's carpeted corridor.

He phoned Major Martin, his High Command liaison officer. 'Are there any fresh bulletins since this morning?' he snarled.[99]

As fanfares announced the special communiqué, on the eastern front it was now pouring with rain. Agonies of uncertainty beset Goebbels. On the tenth he telephoned Jodl. The general feigned ignorance and dismay and warned that the war would continue all winter.[100] Goebbels sent agents out into the beer halls to sample public opinion. The people had all heard Dietrich say the campaign was 'decided' but understood it as *won*.

Goebbels switched to damage-control. He put it about that Hitler himself had ordered the communiqué solely as a ploy to jolt the Japanese into some kind of action.[101] Taking a dramatically independent line, he tried to defuse the High Command's gaffe. In the *Völkischer Beobachter* he argued that while victory was indeed certain, nobody could say when; then, in *Das Reich*, as the first wintry blizzards began to harass Hitler's mud-soaked and exhausted riflemen, he published an editorial entitled, 'When, or How?'[102] This too, despite the question in the title, talked of Germany's victory as inevitable. 'The chance which the German nation has today is its greatest, but also its last.' The entire nation, he wrote, must make one gigantic effort for victory.

With powerful echoes of Winston Churchill, on whom he was now increasingly modeling his oratory, appealing to Britain in the dark hours of 1940, Dr Goebbels now exhorted: 'Let us therefore go forth and fight, and labor until victory is ours.'

43: *Exodus*

ISGUISED AS 'DR SEDGWICK,' 'Putzi' Hanfstaengl was now well housed in Washington and advising President Roosevelt on his former top Nazi pals. 'Always smile,' was Goebbels' maxim, he said: 'Lie with a smile, deny with a smile, intrigue with a smile.'[1] Goebbels was still smiling. It was noticeable that he barely mentioned the United States in his articles.[2] Neither he nor Hitler was worried by Washington; the Führer considered Japan's powerful Pacific fleet sufficient to hold the Americans in check.[3] When Roosevelt's lend-lease act was passed Goebbels scoffed that this was purely a means for the Americans to inherit Britain's assets when the time came.[4]

Hitler had imposed restrictions on all hostilities with the United States. He eased them marginally in February 1941 although he would not allow Dr Goebbels to take the gloves off in his propaganda, even when Roosevelt ordered the seizure of German merchant ships and their crews.[5] Goebbels gradually stepped up his shortwave propaganda transmissions across the Atlantic.[6] Writing under a pseudonym he published a leader article in the *VB* depicting Roosevelt as the helpless puppet of Jewish advisers.[7] He issued a rare photograph showing the president in full masonic regalia.[8] Visiting Berlin however his Transozean news agency expert in the United States warned him not to bank on the ethnic Germans there – they were either rotten through and through, or simpletons; he advised Goebbels to make the propaganda to America crude and unsophisticated.[9] He prepared a fifteen-minute movie, *A Stroll through America*, portraying Roosevelt with his 'Jewish henchmen,' the strikes and hunger marches, the Negro jazz and jitterbug, and the prevalence of kidnapping – though not mentioning Charles Lindbergh, whose baby's alleged kidnapper was a German. The movie pirated American newsreels, however, and the foreign ministry warned that showing it abroad would invite legal repercussions from the United States.[10]

Germans were not liked in America. When the New York evening paper *P.M.* offered a prize for the wittiest greetings telegram for Goebbels' next birthday. It received literally thousands of entries: 204 entrants had rhymed *forty-four* and *no more*; 198 had a pun about a ·44 revolver.

'May your next lie read, I am alive and well,' wrote one man. 'Hope you get lockjaw and seasick at the same time,' wished another. 'God keep you – but immediately,' pleaded yet a third.[11]

AS HE RECEIVED THE WINNING 'Goebbelsgram' – its text is not known – from New York, the minister began composing his own most venomous leader article ever for *Das Reich*, entitled 'The Jews are to blame!'

His mass expulsion of the Jews from Berlin was beginning. On October 14, 1941 S.S. General Kurt Daluege signed the formal order as national chief of police and the deportations began the next day.[12] Five hundred or a thousand at a time, family by family, the Berlin Jews were rounded up, corralled in the ruined synagogue in Levetzow Strasse and then loaded aboard passenger trains at Grünwald station for freighting to the east.[13] The first train with 1,103 Jews aboard was dispatched on October 18; three more followed on October 24 (1,024 Jews) and 27 (1,009 Jews), and November 1 (1,033).[14] All four were bound for the ghetto at Lodz. Between October 18 and November 2, confirmed Speer's diary, some 4,500 Jews were 'evacuated,' releasing to him and Gauleiter Goebbels one thousand apartments – supposedly for bombed-out Berliners, but the cream of these vacant buildings went to their closest cronies.[15]

Hitler was neither consulted nor informed. Ten days after the forced exodus began, he referred, soliloquizing over supper to Himmler and Heydrich, to the way the Jews had started this war. 'Let nobody tell me,' Hitler added, 'that despite that we can't park them in the marshier parts of Russia!' 'By the way,' he added, 'it's not a bad thing that public rumor attributes to us a plan to exterminate the Jews.' He pointed out however that he had no intention of starting anything at present. 'There's no point in adding to one's difficulties at a time like this!'[16]

What did the 'east' hold for Berlin's Jews? In the Baltic states they were loved least of all.[17] Nor were the other eastern territories healthier destinations.[18] Berlin's fifth trainload, of 1,030 Jews, set out for Minsk on November 14. Of Minsk's 238,000 citizens in 1939 one hundred thousand had been Jews, many of them skilled workers.[19] By December 1941 only eighteen thousand of the original Jews had not fled or been shot. These and the newcomers from Berlin survived if they were fit for work; the rest died or were put to death a few months later. Some 3,500 unemployable Jews of the seven thousand sent there from Berlin, Bremen, Vienna, and Brno 'on the Führer's orders' during November 1941 were liquidated in the last four days of July 1942.[20]

So much for Minsk. The trainload of Berlin's Jews sent to Kaunas in Lithuania on November 17 probably fared no better.[21] Goebbels had visited the country two weeks before. As in the other Baltic states, the Soviet secret police had deported forty thousand Lithuanians to Siberia in 1940.[22]

'The Jews,' Goebbels learned during his visit, 'were mainly active as G.P.U. [secret police] agents and informants, and they are to blame for the deaths of countless Lithuanian nationalists and intellectuals.' When the tide turned in June 1941 and the Russians were driven out, the Lithuanians took revenge on the sixty thousand remaining Jews, liquidating 3,800 in Kaunas alone.[23] Hundreds of the rest, Goebbels learned, were being shot.[24] Touring the ghetto in Vilnius he shuddered at the sight of Jews huddled together, 'frightful shapes you can't even look at, let alone touch.' 'The Jews are like the lice of civilized mankind,' he dictated in another revealing entry the next day. 'They've got to be exterminated somehow . . . Spare them now and you'll fall victim to them later on.' Hobbling awkwardly around this cheerless, snow-covered second city of Lithuania he reached one firm conclusion: 'Here I would not want to be buried.'[25]

On November 27, 1941 Speer reported to Goebbels on his efforts to make good the air-raid damage in Berlin. Their third *Aktion* against the Jews was just beginning.[26] That day a thousand more, the seventh trainload, departed from Berlin, bound this time for Riga, capital of Latvia. All would die three mornings later.

Like Lithuania, Latvia had begun killing its Jews soon after BARBAROSSA began, in revenge for the 33,038 Latvians kidnapped or murdered by the Soviet secret police since June 1940. In July 1941 there had been seventy thousand Jews in Latvia; some thirty thousand, had fled with their Russian benefactors. German Sonderkommandos aided by Latvian auxiliary police, usually relatives of the Russians' victims, had murdered about thirty thousand Jews by October 1941.[27] In October Hitler ordered a big concentration camp built just outside Riga to house the Jews expelled from the Reich and the occupied Czech territories. A site was eventually chosen at Salaspils to house twenty-five thousand Jews from Germany.[28] But construction was delayed, and when they were told to expect these twenty-five thousand to begin arriving on November 10, with another twenty-five thousand bound for Minsk, Rosenberg's officials appealed for a postponement.[29] The army also protested at this needless burden on already scarce railroad capacity.[30]

For this and other reasons, by November 21 only seven thousand of Berlin's seventy-seven thousand Jews had been expelled.[31] At the end of November, Speer's diary records, he booted three thousand more out of their apartments.[32]

Goebbels uttered not the slightest sympathy for these innocent victims of his obsession, although he was well aware that public resistance was growing. He put up subway posters proclaiming 'The Jews are our misfortune,' with texts explaining precisely why.[33]

Cruel mishaps began to occur. Goebbels had denied to movie actor Joachim Gottschalk the role of Leitwein in the new color movie *The Golden City* unless he divorce his Jewish wife or at least force her to emigrate to Switzerland.[34] When the star's colleagues interceded for him, Goebbels screamed at them about the 'sexual serfdom' of simple ex-matelots like Gottschalk; they were, he said, an easy prey for the sexual knavery of Jewesses. Refused the role, Gottschalk killed himself, his wife Meta, and his eight-year-old son Michael that November. Goebbels dictated in his diary: 'We are living in very harsh times and fate is sometimes pitiless toward the individual.'[35] He then gave the screw another heartless twist. Already deprived of their own telephones, he forbade Jews to use public payphones either. In a cynical and not unrelated ruling, he prohibited the use of the word *liquidation* in connection with their 'summary executions in the east.' That word, he said, was to be reserved for the crimes perpetrated by the Soviets.[36]

IT WAS DURING THESE SAME weeks that he dictated his tract entitled 'The Jews are to blame.'[37] He ordered it given the widest circulation on the eastern front.[38]

It appeared in *Das Reich* on November 16, 1941. A few excerpts suffice to illustrate its pernicious thrust. 'The Jews wanted this war,' he argued, 'and now they have it.' They were getting their just desserts. An eye for an eye. All Jews alike, whether languishing in an eastern ghetto or whining for war from New York, were conspiring against Germany. The Yellow Star, he argued, was akin to a 'hygienic prophylactic,' because the most dangerous were those otherwise not recognizable as Jews. To those who might bleat that the Jews were humans too he pointed out that the same could be said of muggers, rapists, and pimps. 'Suddenly one has the impression that all of Berlin's Jews are either darling little babies who wouldn't hurt a fly, or fragile old ladies.' 'Were we to lose this war,' he continued, 'these oh-so-harmless Jewish worthies would suddenly turn into rapacious wolves. . . That's what happened in Bessarabia and the Baltic states after the bolsheviks marched in, and neither the people nor the governments there had had the slightest sympathy for them. For us, in our fight against the Jews, there is no going back.'

The article displayed a far more uncompromising face than Hitler's towards the Jews. When the Führer came to Berlin for Luftwaffe general Ernst Udet's funeral he again instructed Goebbels to pursue a policy against the Jews 'that does not cause us endless difficulties,' and told him to go easy on mixed marriages in future.[39]

Dieter Wisliceny, one of Adolf Eichmann's closest associates, would describe the Goebbels article in *Das Reich* as a watershed in the Final Solution of the Jewish problem.[40] The S.S. took it as a sign from above. Eichmann would admit in his unpublished memoirs, 'It's quite possible that I got orders to direct this or that railroad transport to Riga.'[41]

On the last day of November, on the orders of the local S.S. commander Friedrich Jeckeln, four thousand of Riga's unwanted Jews were trucked five miles down the Dvinsk highway to Skiatowa, plundered, and machine-gunned into two or three pits.[42] According to one army colonel who witnessed it, a trainload of Jews from Berlin – those expelled three days before – arrived in the midst of this *Aktion;* its passengers were taken straight out to the pits and shot.[43] This happened even as Hitler, hundreds of miles away in the Wolf's Lair, was instructing Himmler that these Berlin Jews were not to be liquidated.[44]

ON THE EASTERN FRONT bitter frost suddenly replaced the autumn quagmires. Long freezing nights gripped central Europe. With them came the British bombers. The Goebbels bunker at No. 20 Hermann-Göring Strasse was hung with costly paintings; there were armchairs, a bath, and air conditioning. On

November 13 Goebbels told his adjutant to see to it that a piano was installed.[45] His children were now back, living out in Schwanenwerder with Magda.[46] But the matrimonial strains were also returning. Later in November the diary hears of Goebbels badgering an 'understanding' Hitler about 'a series of personal problems.'[47]

It would be wrong to infer that he had no concern for his non-Jewish fellow Germans. He pestered Speer to provide more shelters.[48] He was the first to question whether the army had made proper provision for the coming winter.[49] The words 'met. report' began to figure on his daily agenda. He had asked the army months before, in August, if he should announce a ski collection; General Jodl had scrawled in red the flippant retort that their troops would have no time for 'winter sports.'[50]

In October Goebbels suggested a public appeal for woolen garments – just in case. The High Command again scornfully turned him down.[51] 'In the winter,' Jodl now said, 'we shall be warmly billeted in Leningrad and Moscow. Leave the worrying to us.' 'If we had put this in hand at the proper time,' Goebbels would write to Hitler three years later, justifying his views, 'it would have taken care of one of the worst problems we faced in the winter of 1941–42.'[52]

The army's quartermaster-general, the formidable General Eduard Wagner, had neglected the problem until mid-October 1941.[53] Over lunch with Hitler he complacently claimed that one-third to one-half of the winter equipment had already reached the eastern front.[54]

He staged at his field headquarters a totally bogus exhibition of this winter equipment, including wooden cabins, trench-heaters, ear muffs, and fur-lined coats and boots, and boldly invited Dr Goebbels to see it for himself. Still suspicious, Dr Goebbels asked him how much was already available. 'Enough to equip every soldier two or three times over,' lied Wagner.[55]

'That's overwhelming,' Goebbels dictated the next day as Hitler and Jodl themselves visited the exhibition. 'They've thought of everything.'[56] Both he and Hitler were thoroughly taken in.[57]

Hitler instructed him to send the exhibition on tour round Berlin, Munich, and Vienna. 'We had already set up the exhibition on Unter den Linden in conjunction with the Christmas Fair,' he would recall later, 'when suddenly the catastrophe overtook us.'[58]

Several times after that he reminded Hitler and Göring of how General Wagner had duped them, but three years passed before Wagner, one of the July 1944 traitors, met his Maker.

AFTER HIS VISIT TO Lithuania, Goebbels witnessed how ruthlessly Hitler dealt with the recalcitrant. At the party anniversary in Munich, Hitler prefaced his secret speech to the gauleiters by having Gauleiter Joseph Wagner of Bochum physically evicted from their midst: His wife had written an imprudent religious letter to a relative. The brown-uniformed audience was stunned by Hitler's little display of brutality. Viktor Lutze took in the clucking and clatter that broke out, as though a fox had just raided a chicken coop.[59] Others like Goebbels felt a frisson of approval for the Orwellian scene.

When they met in Berlin again, on November 29, Hitler's armies had begun to retreat for the first time. Bitterly criticizing Brauchitsch, his army commander-in-chief, Hitler remarked that he had always opposed occupying the larger Soviet cities; he had no interest in capturing even Moscow – it was not worth it, just to stage a victory parade there. But when his offensive resumed in 1942, he promised, he would advance on the Caucasus for the oil, and he would conquer the Crimea, as a colony to be called the East Gothic gau. 'What need,' he asked, 'do we have for colonies on other continents?'[60]

The Russian winter's savagery temporarily put paid to all these dreams. A German reconnaissance battalion reached the outskirts of Moscow in a raging blizzard, but got no further. On December 5 and 6 Stalin's armies opened their counter-offensive. German tank tracks froze to the ground; their guns jammed; their explosives fizzled and squibbed. BARBAROSSA had come to a standstill.

GOEBBELS DID NOT SHARE Hitler's hopes for a timely Japanese intervention. He expected Tokyo to sit this war out.[61] But Ribbentrop secretly encouraged the Japanese to believe that if they declared war on the United States, Hitler would follow suit. When a Reuters communiqué on the night of Sunday December 7 announced that the Japanese had struck at the American Pacific fleet in Hawaii, Hitler telephoned Goebbels and said that he would leave for Berlin by train the following evening.

At first Washington admitted only to having lost two battleships and a carrier at Pearl Harbor, with four more battleships and four cruisers damaged. 'That,' wrote Goebbels with satisfaction, 'is a loss of blood . . . that they'll never make good.' He was thrilled by Japan's infamous act: She had had no real alternative. Acceptance of Washington's 'provocative and insolent' demands would have meant her abdication as a great power. 'The Japanese went ahead quite calmly and deliberately,' he wrote approvingly, 'and did not take any other power into their confidence.'

There could be no doubt whatsoever about Hitler's next move. 'We shall have no choice,' wrote Goebbels, 'but . . . to declare war on the United States.' Now, he gloated, Roosevelt had got his war. 'Of course,' he added, 'what he's got is very different from what he anticipated. He certainly imagined that he could deal with Germany first.' War with the United States had long seemed likely, particularly since the speech by Hitler in Munich a month before.[62] With Japan taking the first step, what Goebbels described in his hitherto unpublished diary as a 'gasp of relief' escaped the German public: The psychological terror, the uncertainty, was over.

A mood of invincibility swept over the Nazi leaders. Hitler remarked that they now had an ally, undefeated in three thousand years.[63] Goebbels listened to Churchill's broadcast and concluded from his delivery that he was drunk. Hearing Roosevelt's address to the Congress he remarked that he had taken care not to provoke Nazi Germany. 'But it is too late for that,' he happily dictated. 'We are now in the fortunate position of being able to pay them back.'[64]

He hurried round to see Hitler immediately after he arrived in Berlin at eleven A.M. on the ninth.

> He is filled with joy at this fortunate turn of events [recorded Goebbels] ... He rightly points out that he always expected this. That's true. . . He always expressed the view that, when the hour struck the appeasers in Tokyo would have nothing left to say. . . .

Hitler told Goebbels that he had known nothing beforehand. 'He was taken completely by surprise and, like myself, at first didn't dare to believe it.' In his estimate the Japanese now controlled the Pacific Ocean. 'The Japanese adopted precisely the right tactics by attacking right away and not getting drawn into lengthy preliminaries.'

'The Führer,' Goebbels recorded, 'is rightly of the opinion that in modern warfare it is wholly out of date, even medieval, to issue an ultimatum. Once you make up your mind to defeat an enemy you should wade right in and not hang around until he's braced himself to take your blows.'

Hitler confirmed to Goebbels that he would declare war on the United States in his forthcoming Reichstag speech, though delaying it by two or three days, hoping to score a Pearl Harbor of his own against the U.S. navy in the Atlantic.

'He has already given our U-boats unrestricted orders to shoot on sight.' Hitler postponed the historic speech one more day, telling Dr Goebbels that he wanted to work over the text with particular care. He planned to attack Roosevelt mercilessly in it – 'Thank goodness we no longer have to show him any consideration,' noted Goebbels.

In Japan, Goebbels summarized the next day in his diary, Germany had at last found a worthy ally, although she could not very well harp on that without hurting Italy's feelings.[65] In the Indian Ocean Japanese aircraft trapped and sank two of Britain's proudest warships, *Prince of Wales* and *Repulse*. At lunchtime Goebbels found Hitler filled with unstinted *Schadenfreude*.[66]

They were now fighting a global war. The implications were immediately thrust upon Goebbels: Tokyo, eight time-zones ahead of Berlin, pleaded for the historic Reichstag session to be held early so that Japanese listeners could hear Hitler live declaring war on America; but if he spoke too early, most American listeners would be denied that pleasure.[67]

Thus the deputies were convened at three P.M. on the eleventh. Everybody knew what was in the air, but Hitler teased them for a while. He revealed that Germany's losses so far in BARBAROSSA were around 160,000 dead, a figure which provoked a perceptible murmur. In a mocking tone he then laid into the 'warmonger' President Roosevelt with a biting irony that had the Kroll opera house rocking with unkind laughter.[68]

At his ministerial conference the next morning Goebbels again warned against encouraging excessive optimism.[69] Over lunch Hitler however expressed confidence that Japan would soon take the Philippines, Hongkong, and Singapore.[70] With less than utter candor he described the Wehrmacht's plight on the eastern front as less dire than might at first seem. There was pain and suffering, he agreed, but he hoped to reach the prescribed defensive lines without serious losses. Not for the last time the unpublished diaries show Hitler and Goebbels infusing each other with fresh courage in the face of a generally darkening situation with, this time, Japan as their rising sun. Goebbels drew upon the history of the party, conjuring up heroic analogies from the early Thirties showing how they had snatched victory from those hours of defeatist darkness before the dawn.[71]

Addressing the gauleiters while still in Berlin Hitler opted for greater candor. He confessed that he had spent sleepless nights worrying whether he was doing the right thing in declaring war on Roosevelt. 'The Führer,' Goebbels reported to his diary, 'is convinced that he would have had to declare war on the Americans sooner or later. . . Now the conflict in the Far East drops into our laps as an added bonus.' He viewed the battle of the Atlantic with greater confidence. Whoever won there would win the war. Hitler predicted to the gauleiters that the western 'plutocracies' would not abandon their Far East possessions, but would fritter away their forces around the world. The present impasse on the Moscow front was, he said, no more than 'an unavoidable hitch.'[72]

Far from the comforts of Berlin, Hitler's soldiers were dying agonizing deaths in the blizzards. The injured froze to death if they were not dragged under cover within minutes. From one of his staff Goebbels received a horrifying letter describing the useless tanks, the munitions, guns, and planes being blown up by retreating troops, and the army reinforcements arriving still wearing their thin Afrika Korps uniforms.[73] Returning by train on December 16 to the Wolf's Lair, Hitler dictated a famous Order of the Day, forbidding his soldiers to yield even one inch of the eastern front. His generals seemed paralyzed by their own plight.

On the same day, the sixteenth, Hitler sent for Goebbels; he confided to him the next day at his headquarters that he had decided to replace all three army group commanders as well – they all had 'stomach problems,' he said: *magenkrank*. It is not plain if he was being sarcastic. He revealed that he was going to take over command from their 'church-going' C-in-C, Field Marshal von Brauchitsch. 'The more pious the general,' agreed Goebbels, whose loathing of the general staff matched Hitler's, 'the more useless he is.'[74]

There is no doubt that in the failure of these generals Goebbels saw his chance of establishing himself higher in Hitler's esteem. Before returning to Berlin he set out his own plan to rescue the eastern armies from freezing to death. He would launch a public appeal for woolen clothing.

At first it seemed so unpretentious as to be almost ludicrous. But he calculated that this *Aktion* would help to take the country's mind off its other grim preoccupations. Hitler was unenthusiastic. He feared that the appeal would damage the Reich's impregnable image. Goebbels however won him round. Back in Berlin he called a joint conference with the High Command, the Post Office, and the transport and other ministries concerned. The bureaucrats expressed immediate doubts that the public would rise to the occasion. The soldiers were downright hostile. Their obstructionism only spurred Goebbels, the crippled civilian, to greater efforts.[75]

The next day, Saturday December 20, the propaganda minister broadcast an appeal that was to go down in history. 'Particularly during these festive days,' he said, 'countless Germans at home will be conscious of the debt that we all owe to our soldiers and above all those at the fighting front.' How could they best express this gratitude? 'The responsible Wehrmacht authorities,' he reassured his listeners, 'have done everything to provide the front with adequate equipment for the winter.' He saw no point in exposing the inefficiency of the war department. Nevertheless, he purred, the front needed winter gear. 'Top-boots, padded or fur-lined if possible; warm woolen clothing; socks, stockings, waist-coats, cardigans, pullovers, and warm (particularly woolen) underwear, vests, under-pants, body belts, chest and, lung protectors, all manner of headgear, ear-muffs, mittens, kneepads – and so the list went on.

On December 27 the collecting *Aktion* began. It was a huge success. The public handed in sixty-seven million items of winter gear: Now the plodding desk-generals – men, snorted Goebbels, who would not have made it above junior adviser in his ministry – refused to shift them.

Goebbels then ordered the party's welfare agencies to hand out this winter gear to the raw riflemen on the railroad stations as their trains passed through Germany en route to the front. Every document testifies to the uplift which this unique *Aktion* provided for home morale, as well as for the eastern front. When Goebbels phoned his Führer on New Year's Day, he basked in the latter's praise.[76] Together he and his Führer had saved the eastern armies. Their generals had finally proved their mediocrity, and the party had shown its mettle. In that respect, Goebbels was heard to say, it was actually a good thing that the war had not ended at Dunkirk.[77]

Over the weeks that followed, the eastern front stabilized. Hitler told him that his elderly field commanders had lost their head. Not for nothing, he said, had he spent four years as an ordinary dogface infantryman. He knew a thing or two about front-line soldiers and their nerves that their generals did not.

'He is more admirable than ever,' dictated Goebbels to Otte for the diary.[78]

44: A Fate Which Beggars All Description

I N NEW YORK AN OLD ENEMY, Albert C. Grzesinski, former police chief in Berlin, proclaimed his intention of overthrowing the Nazis and taking power himself. With enemies like Grzesinski, reflected Goebbels, one barely needed allies.[1] He was not afraid of the Americans. There were limits to what even they could do. 'It isn't easy to raise and equip an army,' he commented, 'as we know only too well.'[2] He ordered anti-American propaganda prepared however, mocking their lack of culture and their grotesque jazz music.[3] He had discussed a Japanese fanfare for announcing the coming Far East victories; a corresponding Italian fanfare was also to be selected 'in case there are any Italian victories.'[4] Foreseeing race problems, he forbade any hint of the phrase Yellow Peril in their domestic propaganda.[5]

He found it difficult now to fault British propaganda. Dietrich had not helped with his premature announcement of victory in October. 'It's a pity,' Goebbels wrote, 'that we have had so many different agencies cutting the ground away beneath our feet with their silliness.'[6] He told his staff that Churchill had done the right thing in promising his people only blood, sweat, and tears. He had learned to allow morale to slump after setbacks; it was easier to restore afterward.[7] He proposed to copy Churchill's methods. He actually asked Backe if planned food-ration cuts could be brought forward.[8] 'The German people,' he said, 'should get in tune with the war situation and not sustain false hopes.'[9] Once he defined it as his classical mission in this war to become 'the architect of the German soul.'[10]

He would willingly have proclaimed total war, the mobilization of all available manpower from the home economy for the war effort, there and then. When his former press officer Moritz von Schirmeister returned from the eastern front in January 1942 he heard Goebbels expatiate several times during meals on the need for the government to implement total war.[11] The media were still showing peacetime-flavored pictures of lavish social functions even now.[12] Putting deeds before words, he replaced three hundred men of his own ministry with women.[13]

Hitler's riflemen had paid winter's cruel price. By late January 1942 they had suffered 1,856 frostbite amputations.[14] Goebbels addressed them all in his first *Das Reich* article of the new year. 'It behooves us to remain tough and composed,' he wrote.[15] Hitler, a stickler for style, disliked that word 'composed,' and decided on the strength of it that Goebbels should not deliver the party's anniversary speech on January 30. 'I know how to preserve the golden mean between reason and rhetoric,' he explained over supper in the minister's absence. 'I'd not have expressed myself like that. In a situation like this, the soldier is not *composed* but *resolute*. When you've been through it yourself you get a feel for these things.'[16]

Characteristically when Goebbels came for lunch the next day Hitler bit his tongue and said nothing of this. They talked of Britain's eclipse in the Far East. In three weeks the Führer expected the Japanese to overrun Singapore. 'Perhaps,' he mused to Dr Goebbels, 'there is a chance here to bring Britain, if not to her senses, at least to reconsider her position.' He had succeeded in stabilizing Germany's own eastern front. For three weeks he had worked round the clock, reviving the spirits of his demoralized generals in endless conferences and telephone arguments – he described these commanders unflatteringly as like inflatable dummies with slow punctures. Goebbels told Hitler that according to Major Martin many officers in the High Command had openly predicted that the Soviet armies would be on East Prussia's frontiers that spring. Hitler angrily told him to get a list of their names.[17] Back in Berlin Goebbels directed the unfortunate major that it was now his duty to draw up this black list. 'There is only one sin,' he said, quoting Friedrich Nietzsche, 'and that is cowardice.'[18] It was perhaps significant that he was now automatically extending his remit far beyond the portals of his own ministry. A day or two later Schirmeister's wife Emmi, invited by Magda to dinner, innocently told of an officer cousin who had plied her in East Prussia with dark rumors that the Russians were coming. Goebbels told her to name that officer too, saying, 'I guarantee he will be shot within twenty-four hours.'[19]

BEFORE LEAVING THE Wolf's Lair on January 19 Dr Goebbels had also touched briefly on the Jewish problem. 'On this,' he noted, unable to hang any meat on the now threadbare phrases, 'the Führer holds without qualification to the existing and proper hard-line view.'[20]

Behind closed doors the Final Solution, in all its heathen criminality, was already undergoing a deadly shift of emphasis. As Goebbels arrived back in Berlin on January 20 Heydrich was holding his first inter-ministerial conference on the topic at Wannsee, a suburb of Berlin.[21] The ambitious, amoral S.S. Obergruppenführer had issued the original invitations back in November, including one to Goebbels' Staatssekretär Gutterer, but Gutterer had never received it and the propaganda ministry was one of several not represented at this conference.[22] The conference was largely window-dressing anyway. Chaos was spreading in the eastern territories as more trainloads of Jewish evacuees arrived there. Hans Frank's Government-General was flatly refusing to accept any more – Frank had exclaimed irritably at one of his Cabinet meetings in Kraków that Berlin was telling them they'd got no use for the Jews either. 'Liquidate them yourselves!' was his retort.[23] Two more batches, of 1,037 and

1,006 Jews, had left Berlin for Riga on January 13 and 19; but the train which left Berlin, also for Riga, on January 25, loaded with 1,051 Jews, was the last batch for two months.[24]

Goebbels heard his Führer recall, in his speech of January 30, the sinister prophecy which he had made exactly three years before that this war would bring the 'destruction of Jewry.'[25] His own evil deportation project temporarily thwarted by the winter transportation crisis, Goebbels devised a string of regulations calculated to hound and harass the Jews as he had in 1938.[26] He ordered one Jew punished for using coffee rations given him by a non-Jew.[27] He forbade Jews to use public transport at all, apart from those still working in the munitions factories.[28] He prohibited Jews from ordering newspapers by mail, from buying them at kiosks, and from having them delivered.[29]

After lunching with Hitler in February Goebbels dictated: 'The Führer once again expresses his ruthless resolve to make a clean sweep of the Jews out of Europe. One can't go getting all sentimental about it. The Jews have richly deserved the catastrophe they are suffering today. . . We have to accelerate this process with a studied ruthlessness and we are thereby doing an invaluable service to a long-suffering mankind, tormented for millennia by the Jews.' Hitler, he claimed, had ordered him to convert those who were still in two minds about this. 'The major prospects opened up by war are recognized by the Führer in all their significance.'

Fueling the raging fires of his own prejudices, Goebbels spent an evening watching *The Dybbuk*, a Polish Yiddish film. 'Its effect is so antisemitic,' he felt, 'that one can only marvel how little the Jews . . . realize what non-Jews find repellent. Watching this movie,' he continued, 'one perceives once more that the Jewish race is the most dangerous on earth, and that one must display neither mercy nor softness toward it.'[30]

IT IS IMPORTANT, reading entries like this, to recall that Goebbels' diary is not above criticism as a source. It was now dictated each morning to a private secretary, and typed out in triplicate by clerks. It is acceptable as evidence against Goebbels, but not necessarily against third parties. A distinction must be drawn therefore between what he admits putting to his Führer, and what he alleges the Führer put to him.

Even now, Hitler was less radical on the Jewish problem than Goebbels, Himmler, Heydrich, and Speer. He was prevaricating; according to Eichmann, he saw the real Final Solution in the Jewish colonization of Madagascar.[31] But Goebbels was powered by the unflickering light of an unwavering, ineradicable antisemitism. Hearing of an outcry in London against Jewish spivs and black marketeers he gloated: 'The Jews are the same all the world over. You either have to slap a Yellow Star on them, or throw them into a concentration camp, or shoot them.'[32] On March 5 he received a report from Heydrich about guerrilla warfare in the occupied east, and blamed this on the Jews too. 'It is therefore understandable,' he dictated to Otte, 'that many of them must pay with their lives for this. Anyway, in my view the more Jews who are liquidated the more consolidated the situation in Europe will be after the war. Let there be no phony sentimentalism about it. The Jews are Europe's misfortune. They must somehow be eliminated otherwise we are in danger of being eliminated by them.'[33]

On the following day he took note of an extensive report prepared by Heydrich's office, probably on the Wannsee conference.[34] There were still eleven million Jews in Europe, he dictated, summarizing the document. 'For the time being they are to be concentrated in the east [until] later; possibly an island like Madagascar can be assigned to them after the war.' 'Undoubtedly there will be a multitude of personal tragedies,' he added airily, 'But this is unavoidable. The situation now is ripe for a final settlement of the Jewish question.'[35]

In a covering letter Heydrich invited Goebbels to a second conference, on March 6. Goebbels sent two of his senior staff.[36] Eichmann talked crudely at this meeting of 'forwarding' the Jews to the east, like so many head of cattle.[37] The ministry of justice handled the report on this new discussion like a hot potato.[38] The Reich Chancellery referred it all to Hitler.[39] Hitler wearily told Hans Lammers that he wanted the solution of the Jewish problem postponed until after the war was over – a ruling that remarkably few historians now seem disposed to quote.[40]

By now the two-month railroad log-jam was over and another train was being loaded with Berlin Jews marked for deportation. What might be their fate? On March 27, the day before this trainload left Berlin, Goebbels dictated an extraordinary, deadpan but spine-chilling entry into his diary which confirmed that he at least was now in little doubt.

> Beginning with Lublin the Jews are now being deported eastward from the Government-General. The procedure is pretty barbaric, and one that beggars description, and there's not much left of the Jews. Broadly speaking one can probably say that sixty percent of them will have to be liquidated [a word whose use he had of course banned], while only forty percent can be put to work.

'The former gauleiter of Vienna,' he continued, referring to S.S. Brigadeführer Odilo Globocnik, S.S. and police chief of the Lublin District, 'who is carrying out this operation, is doing so pretty discreetly and also using a procedure that is not too flagrant.'[41] The Jews had had it coming to them for a long time, he added, and cited yet again Hitler's prophecy of 1939, and the need to eschew all mawkish sentimentality. 'It's a life-and-death struggle between the Aryan race and the Jewish bacillus,' he concluded, adopting Hitler's favorite analogy. 'Here too,' he dictated to his poker-faced stenographer, 'the Führer is the staunch champion and promoter of a radical solution.'[42]

Nowhere do the diary's seventy-five thousand pages refer to an explicit order by Hitler for the murder of the Jews. (Perhaps this is not surprising, but for the sake of completeness it needs saying.) Goebbels instinctively fashioned every phrase of those diaries with both cunning and ambiguity. The documents clearly show Hitler as the uncompromising architect of the callous plan to shunt all Europe's Jews out, if not to Madagascar, then to the east. The Polish ghettos emptied by this process would be replenished with Jews deported from the Reich. 'The Jews,' wrote Goebbels, 'have nothing to laugh about.'[43] They were having to pay dearly for the misdeeds of their brethren in Britain and America: Such was his rationale. On March 28 he stipulated that they were no longer to be listed in telephone directories.[44] Why should they be? They were disappearing from the face of occupied Europe.

HE CAN DECEIVE his diary, dictating touching entries calculated to portray their author to posterity as a caring family man; but he cannot deceive his own mother. Sometimes she is seen haunting the opulent halls and galleries at No. 20 Hermann-Göring Strasse laughing softly to herself as though she cannot believe that the frenetic demon controlling this evil empire is little Jupp, her youngest son, the waiflike cripple she nursed through infancy. She barely speaks to others, and when she does her thick Rhineland dialect comes as a shock to them.[45]

Once again, pleading problems with her heart, Magda leaves him for a month-long cure in Dresden beginning on January 21.[46] Sometimes he goes over to see his favorite sister Maria, or to talk things over with his mother. They tell him home truths about public attitudes.[47] He takes his two eldest daughters and sleepy little Hellmut out to Lanke. It is his first visit there in three months, and the lovely Ursula Quandt stands in for Magda.[48] He lets the children play truant on the pretext that their younger sisters at Schwanenwerder have whooping cough. They spend happy hours sledding in the snow – the same snow which is shrouding Europe and wreaking havoc on his Jewish evacuation timetable.[49] On the last day of April he moves out to Lanke in a vain attempt to cure a bout of eczema, a chronic health problem.[50]

One evening he is visited here by a ghost from the past, Anka Stalherm, now forty-six, editor of *Dame* and without even a trace of gray defiling her blonde hair. Her second husband Rudolf Oswald, thirteen years her junior, has just been killed on the eastern front. She mentions that there are still some (Jewish) Ullstein hold-outs left at her magazine's publisher, Deutscher Verlag. Goebbels promises to clear them out, but all the quivering, painful *tendresse* of their earlier relationship has faded and gone away.[51]

HE BELIEVED THAT the winter's crisis had now passed its lowest point.[52] Morale had been depressed all winter by the epidemics of frostbite and typhus ravaging the armies in the east.[53] In North Africa, Rommel recaptured Benghazi and lunged on toward Tobruk. Goebbels promoted him to a national hero, although the army discouraged all hero-worship of its commanders.[54]

The British prime minister had no such inhibitions. In Churchill, Goebbels recognized that he had met his match. 'A clever speech,' he had written after one Churchill offering a year earlier.[55] After listening to another speech by the prime minister in Birmingham he had enviously written, 'He plays on the tear glands, the old crook.' He scoffed at Churchill's clever evasions.

'Thus we sent to Greece a large part of our Army of the Nile,' he said, mimicking the prime minister, 'to meet our obligations. It transpired by chance that the formations to hand all came from New Zealand and Australia...'

'It's always "*chance*" that finds the British bringing up the rear,' he mocked, spelling out propaganda lines to his staff. '*Chance* that they are always on the retreat. By *chance* they have no share in the bloody casualties. By *chance* it is the French, the Belgians, and the Dutch who have to bear the brunt of our western offensive. By *chance* the Norwegians have to cover the British as they flee Norway. And by *chance* it is the troops of the empire who, since there are no others left, have to do the job now.'[56] Having said all that, however, he warned against denigrating the British soldier; the British might let others bear the brunt of the fighting, but when cornered they fought like wildcats.[57]

He became obsessed with Churchill. In *Das Reich* he referred to him as 'that old whisky soak' but admitted, 'A chronic whisky drinker is more welcome as Britain's prime minister than a teetotaler.'[58] He and Hitler devoured the fond if scurrilous book in which Churchill's private secretary described his drinking habits and his custom of dictating to her in pink silk underwear or even in his bath.[59] With a sure understanding of the public appetite, Goebbels warned his journalists to go easy on these stories and to concentrate more on the prime minister's dysfunctional family circumstances, his dilettante conduct of the war, and his monstrous lies.[60]

One conclusion was inescapable: Though Churchill might be a 'conceited ape,' they had no choice but to tackle this 'lying old swine;' he was 'a bulldog who may yet give us a run for our money.'[61]

'He's going to be a tough nut for us to crack,' he added a few days later. 'Without him, the war would have been over long ago. But *with* him, there's going to be some hard fighting ahead.'[62]

Studying Churchill's book of pre-war speeches, *Step by Step*, he decided that this implacable foe combined a rare amalgam of heroism and animal cunning. 'If he had come to power in 1933,' he frankly assessed, 'we wouldn't be where we are today.'[63] Many times he discussed Churchill with his Führer. 'He will end by reducing the empire to ruin,' predicted Hitler wisely.[64] He said that all his pre-war English visitors, including Neville Chamberlain, had described Churchill as a fool. 'The Führer naturally regrets very much the knocks that the White man is taking in the Far East,' recorded the propaganda minister. 'But these are no fault of ours.'[65]

Those were dramatic days. As Hitler met him for lunch on February 13 three of the mightiest Nazi warships were plowing in broad daylight eastward through the narrow, wintry straits of Dover under Churchill's very nose; it was one of the most audacious naval operations ever staged. At the same time the Japanese were bearing down on Singapore. Goebbels mocked that the same

British who had been unwilling to allow Danzig to return to Germany now seemed happy to give up Singapore.[66] He told his editors to feign regret – and to remind the British that it was they who had wanted this war.[67] As Singapore raised the white flag, Goebbels added that they should remind readers of the coruscating rebukes that Churchill had heaped upon his Belgian, Dutch, and French allies for surrendering in 1940.[68]

His 1942 birthday address to Hitler displayed a worshipfulness of an almost religious fervor. It revived the image of the 'lonely Führer,' to which he added a soupçon of the 'suffering Führer' and a Christ who suffered only for the Germans.[69] Nowhere did the diary reflect this more clearly than after a visit to Hitler's headquarters in March. 'The Führer, thank God,' he routinely began, 'appears to be in good health.' But then, after more in this gushing vein, he dictated: 'Actually that is not the case. In our intimate talk he told me that recently he has not been very well. From time to time he has had to fight off severe attacks of giddiness.' And finally that day, forty pages later, 'The Führer makes an unnerving impression on me this time. I have never seen him so grim as now. I tell him that I, too, am not at all in the best of health. We continued this discussion very intimately, man to man.'[70] He said that Hitler had urged him to visit again soon, but over five weeks would pass before the one *malade-imaginaire* again set eyes on the other.

Using guarded language, Dr Goebbels had put in a word for his imprisoned colleague Karl Bömer. Hitler agreed to Bömer's immediate release and posting to a punishment battalion. Haggard from his ten months in jail, the former department head was brought into the ministry building a few days later; Goebbels gave him money and a food package, and sent him off on four weeks' leave in Bavaria before his posting to the front.[71] Bömer was wounded in action at Kharkov a few weeks later and died in hospital at Kraków. Goebbels and Dietrich jointly signed a defiantly prominent obituary in the party's gazette.[72]

To his Italian colleagues Goebbels expressed only a qualified optimism about the future. He would personally be content if they reached the Caucasus.[73] Hitler had told him that he was setting himself clear but limited objectives for the coming offensives – Leningrad, Moscow, and the Caucasus. In October, he promised, he would call a halt for the winter and perhaps even for good. He did not stint his praise for the Soviet leadership. 'Stalin's brutal hand saved the Russian front,' Goebbels heard Hitler say. 'We shall have to adopt similar methods.'[74]

THE NEXT DAY, March 20, Gutterer brought to him an extraordinary story. He had just lunched at the Kaiserhof with Professor Otto Hahn, who had discovered nuclear fission in 1938; Hahn hinted at the work that he and Professor Werner Heisenberg were doing on the atomic bomb. 'If we had such a weapon,' Hahn said, 'everybody else would throw in the towel right away!' Gutterer brought him straight round to Goebbels at No. 20 Hermann-Göring Strasse. Goebbels asked how long it would take to build such a weapon. Hahn spoke of the autumn of 1945, but added that he was hampered since Rust, the minister of education, had sacked his best physicist Lisa Meissner (she was Jewish); Goebbels loathed Rust, and exploded in fury; he asked if Meissner could be retrieved – he would guarantee that she would be under Hitler's personal protection and be given a fine estate if they developed the bomb. (She was already in England however.)[75] Quoting Otto Hahn, Goebbels told his diary that a tiny device would yield such immense destructive power that 'one is forced to view with dread the shape of this war, and indeed of all future wars, if it drags on much longer.' It was vital, he noted, to keep the German lead in this field.[76]

After a meeting with the atomic scientists in June, Speer reported to Hitler, though in terms of little enthusiasm, and the small German lead was lost.[77]

CONVENTIONAL BOMBING already seemed destructive enough. On Saturday March 28 Churchill's bombers set medieval Lübeck on fire. Gauleiter Kaufmann told Goebbels that it was unlike any raid that had gone before. When Hitler phoned, raging that he had been unable to raise the ministry of the interior by telephone at all, Goebbels asked for full powers to arrange emergency food and clothing for the city.[78] He discovered that most of his fellow ministers went missing on Friday evenings. The war department not only shut down every weekend but took off Wednesday afternoons too, as though it were still peacetime.

A FEW HOURS BEFORE the Lübeck raid, the Jewish exodus from Berlin had resumed after a two-month hiatus.[79] A train left Berlin with 974 Jews that day, March 28, 1942, bound for Travniki. Goebbels now ordered a comprehensive film record made.[80] 'About a thousand a week are now being shipped out to the east,' he dictated. 'The suicide rate among these Jewish evacuees is extremely high,' he added without emotion. 'It's no skin off my nose. The Jews have had it coming to them. . . They ignored our warnings, and now they're paying for it.'[81] Another train left on April 2 with 654 Berlin Jews, and a third with sixty-five, also bound for Travniki, on April 14. There was then another halt. It would not be easy to get rid of the rest, some forty thousand, because under the current regulations only complete families could be deported: if even one member was exempt, so was the whole family.[82] Controversy was rife about what to do with the half-Jews – sterilize them, or deport, with all that that implied? 'There is no doubt,' Goebbels conceded, 'that these do pose a serious obstacle to the radical solution of the Jewish problem.'[83]

The partisan war provided both camouflage and rationale for the massacres. Among the thousands of victims of the partisan fighters was Tonak, Goebbels' trusty former chauffeur. He was gunned down and buried in swamplands west of R'zhev.[84] 'The Jews get short shrift in all the occupied territories,' Goebbels dictated after reading the latest S.D. report on the partisan war. 'Tens of thousands are being wiped out.' He never tired of repeating Hitler's sinister 1939 prophecy, and did so again.[85] From Moscow came reports on a

Jewish congress uttering bloodthirsty threats of retribution once Hitler was overthrown. 'But that cannot be,' dictated Goebbels. 'That must not be, and that shall not be.'[86]

Fears for his own safety were never far from his mind. He saw every living Jew as a potential assassin. Nine-tenths of the assassinations in Paris were being committed by Jews, which was, he conceded, hardly surprising under the circumstances. 'It would be best either to deport the remaining yids from Paris, or to liquidate the lot.'[87]

He was planning an elaborate public trial of the assassin Herschel Grynszpan, who had fallen into Nazi hands in 1940, but the young man's crafty lawyers had now floated the theory that he and his victim Rath had been homosexual lovers.[88] This was potential dynamite for the enemy propaganda. Before Goebbels could stop it, the minister of justice included this infamous allegation in the court papers and, worse, ruled that the trial should allow public discussion of the deportation of the Jews – a development which Goebbels found 'incredibly inept.'[89] Thus the Grynszpan affair turned to ashes in his hands. Leopold Gutterer reviewed the dossier and advised Goebbels to drop the prosecution entirely.[90]

Grynszpan's trial was put on ice; indeed, he survived the war. Gutterer was told he had sat at the back of a postwar Hamburg courtroom in the Fifties when he himself was on trial. This was one of the ultimate ironies of the Final Solution, which the young Jew's five pistol shots in 1938 had helped to unleash.

45: *At any Price*

Touring austria's principal cities in 1942 to celebrate the fourth anniversary of the Anschluss Goebbels launched a new slogan, 'Victory at any price.'[1] A quarter of a million troops had already died in barbarossa. British air raids and reduced food rations were eroding public morale.[2] Goebbels ordered propaganda onslaughts on the enemies within: He listed black marketeering, excessive paperwork, and – an eternal quest – the surliness of public servants like waiters, transport workers, and post office clerks.[3]

Oblivious of the double standards involved, he persuaded Hitler and Bormann to crack down on the sybaritic lifestyle of top Nazis.[4] He then privately authorized the party's acquisition and total renovation of a château in his native Rheydt for his exclusive use.[5] He generously started public collections of textiles and mosquito nets for the eastern front.[6] To the former he contributed a suit, Magda her riding breeches – Karl Hanke had now galloped out of her life – and Harald his Hitler Youth uniform; they also gave raincoats, trenchcoats, and gabardine coats, as well as two silk dresses, a long evening dress, and a nurse's cloak.[7]

Hitler had repeatedly ordered the church problem postponed, like the Jewish problem, until the war was over. Disregarding him, the party's 'radicalinskis,' as Goebbels called them, confiscated several church buildings in Berlin.[8] Hitler reassured him that once this war was over he too would give no quarter to the clergy who were acting in such a 'vile' way while Germany's soldiers were fighting for their lives. The moment his hands were free he would settle this mutinous clergy's hash, once and for all. Goebbels looked forward to this new battle as one of the great ideological conflicts of all time.[9]

Death and destruction continued to come from the heavens over Germany. Goebbels had believed that the Lübeck raid was just a fluke, but he was mistaken. After a puny raid on Cologne led him to remark that that was all the British were now capable of, on April 23 they began a series of four fire raids on Rostock on the Baltic.[10] It seemed that shutting down their evening broadcast had not hampered the British navigators at all. Even so Goebbels was unwilling to resume broadcasts, fearing that Göring would make him a scapegoat for the next catastrophe.[11] Hitler told him that he was ordering reprisal raids against historic British towns like Bath. Goebbels hoped for propaganda profit from wiping out these 'cultural centers, watering holes, and middle-class towns,' or, as he called it, 'Answering terror with terror.'[12]

Sensing that these fire raids had inclined Hitler toward radical solutions, Goebbels felt it a propitious moment to mention the Berlin Jews again. Hitler reiterated his standpoint. 'He wants to force the Jews right out of Europe,' dictated Goebbels. 'The Jews have inflicted such suffering on our continent that the harshest punishment . . . is still too mild.'[13]

FOR MOST OF MAY 1942 he lingered out at Lanke fighting his eczema. Leopold Gutterer chaired the ministerial conferences in his absence. Returning with his affliction still uncured he heard that unknown assassins had maimed Heydrich in Prague. This episode triggered further antisemitic impulses in Goebbels, who was already concerned for his own security (he had years before remarked to German journalists that if there was one word they had to shun as the Devil shunned Holy Water it was surely 'assassination'). It cheered him when his old comrade Kurt Daluege, standing in for the mortally wounded Heydrich in Prague, had a thousand intellectuals shot. 'Assassinations can set a bad example if we don't act ruthlessly against them,' noted Goebbels, and he took harsh action against the remaining Jews in Berlin, ordering the arrest of five hundred and notifying their community that he would have one hundred shot for every Jewish act of sabotage or murder, though his authority to do this seems obscure.[14] 'I have no desire,' he explained in his diary, 'to have a bullet pumped into my belly by some twenty-two-year-old yid from the east. Give me ten Jews in a concentration camp, or under the sod, to one at large any day.'[15]

The fate awaiting the deportees was evidently swift and deadly. Only nine days after one round-up, that on May 27, the Berlin Gestapo was already writing to the tax authorities attaching a list of 'those who have since died' and the assets they had declared.[16] Lunching with Hitler on May 29 Goebbels persuaded him to instruct Speer, now munitions minister, to have Jewish munitions workers replaced by foreigners. That would remove the exemption from deportation on hundreds of Jewish families. Implying that he was well aware of the ultimate fate of the evacuees, Goebbels dictated that he saw a major danger in having forty thousand Jews 'with nothing more to lose' running loose in the Reich capital. He incidentally also advised Hitler to liquidate Berlin's prison population while he could. 'We have lost so many idealists in this war,' echoed Goebbels, thinking of Tonak, 'that we have to exact a like measure from the negative criminal fraternity.'[17] Hitler agreed with him that it would be a mistake to evacuate Jews to Siberia – the spartan life there would turn them into a virulent breed. 'That's why he would prefer them to be settled in Central Africa,' recorded Goebbels. 'There they'll be living in a climate which definitely won't make them tough and resilient.' 'At any rate,' he concluded, 'it's the Führer's aim to rid western Europe of the Jews entirely.'[18]

Too many Jews were already hearing rumors from the B.B.C. and other sources about the fate awaiting them. Goebbels learned in January 1942 that

Germany's radio-monitoring agencies, and particularly the foreign ministry's Seehaus service were distributing their defeatist digests throughout official Berlin; 180 copies were going to Ribbentrop's ministry alone.[19] Hitler gave him immediate powers to prune the lists of recipients. Soon afterward Goebbels was granted high-level access to the top-secret signals-intelligence and intercept digests prepared by Göring's Forschungsamt, the 'brown pages.'[20] Goebbels expressed an interest only in those bearing upon foreign policy; although the Reichsmarschall usually limited distribution of these intercepts on a strictly need-to-know basis, he humored this curiosity, and Goebbels' liaison officer Dr Severitt brought, in his locked dispatch box, sheaves of reports such as on Molotov's secret deals with the British government in May.[21]

STALIN WAS FIGHTING with his back to the wall; he needed the Allies. The pendulum was swinging back in Hitler's favor. The Germans were fighting a big tank battle at Kharkov. The Kerch peninsula was back in their hands. They sank a million tons of Allied shipping during May 1942, and in the following month, Hitler told Goebbels on May 22, they would commission one and a half times as many new submarines as were currently at sea. When Hitler came to Berlin on May 28 to speak at the Sport Palace, he told Goebbels that he now intended to cut off the Caucasus, thus crushing the Soviet Adam's apple.[22]

Over Germany, an unnatural calm prevailed at night. Where were Churchill's bombers? Goebbels suggested to his department heads that the British were bluffing to forestall Stalin's demands for a second front.[23] Hitler attributed the lull to Britain's dismay at his reprisal raids. The lull ended late on Saturday May 30, 1942. The British bombers returned in unprecedented force, attacking Cologne. Goebbels was at first blissfully unaware, and Hitler's adjutant failed to track him down – or any other minister; Hitler reached Gutterer through the ministry switchboard and told him to start relief operations.

Suspecting that Goebbels was illicitly engaged, Gutterer phoned Hermann-Göring Strasse and left a discreet message for him to call him urgently 'whenever he got back.' After directing Hermann Schäfer, their electrical wizard, to take the Reich Motor Convoy (Reichsautozug) from Munich to Cologne with its powerful mobile generators, kitchens, bakeries, and mobile hospital, Gutterer summoned a ten A.M. disaster conference with the other ministries in Goebbels' appropriately named Pompeii Room.[24]

Truly, a disaster had hit Cologne. The gauleiter was calling it the heaviest raid ever. Churchill was talking of a 'thousand-bomber' raid, but the German air staff was suggesting it was by only seventy bombers (of which they claimed to have shot down forty); while Goebbels assumed that Churchill was exaggerating a bit, he felt that seventy was far too low.[25] Massive retaliation was out of the question, as the Luftwaffe had its main weight on the eastern front. Hitler struck at ancient Canterbury, but had only seventy bombers for the purpose. An unseemly propaganda war developed. The American press spoke of an earthquake hitting Cologne, and inflated the casualties – they claimed sixty thousand dead (the real figure was 474).[26] Significantly changing his tactics, Goebbels authorized live radio interviews with survivors like those broadcast by the B.B.C. at the height of the Nazi blitz.[27]

His shortwave broadcasts to North American linked these 'terror raids' to the Jewish problem, accusing Roosevelt's 'propaganda kikes' of 'yiddling' while Cologne burned.[28] He did not underestimate the Americans' propaganda; he particularly feared their seductive theme that the Allies were fighting the Nazis, and not the German people. If the British had struck this chord, he admitted to his staff, it could have been fatal.[29] His best hope was to drive a wedge between London and Washington, as once he had done between London and Paris.[30] In broadcasts to American audiences he portrayed the British as bunglers who existed only at Stalin's caprice; then he told the British to beware the rapacious, empire-stealing Americans. He depicted the United States as disaster-prone and 'too weak' to be of real assistance.[31]

These unsophisticated messages worked. 'One only has to read the [American] newspapers,' Roosevelt was informed, 'or ride in a bus or visit his [*sic*] club, bar, or coffee shop.'[32] Goebbels put it about that their ethnic cousins, the German-Americans in the United States, were being forced to wear yellow armbands: and thus the vicious circle was completed.[33] He coined the phrase Roosevelt's War, and began putting it about that the president was mentally ill, like Woodrow Wilson before him.[34] *Roosevelt had syphilis !*

He now controlled a Radio Free America ostensibly run by 'independent Americans' in Europe. Early in July 1942 Goebbels closed down four of the other ten black transmitters; among those remaining on the air were the New British Broadcasting Station (starring William Joyce), a Voice of Free Arabs, and the Russian-language station directed by ex-communist Albrecht. Goebbels had also set up a Voice of Free India as a vehicle for the Indian nationalist Subhas Chandra Bose, a former mayor of Calcutta whom he interviewed in July.[35] The bamboo rod, he ordered, must become a symbol of British rule in India 'like the police truncheon in the System era [*i.e.*, the Weimar Republic] in Germany.'[36]

As Churchill traveled to Washington, Goebbels asked his editors to comment on the prime minister's habit of fleeing abroad each time things went wrong. 'Tobruk,' he wrote, as Rommel captured the strategic North African port, 'is our revenge for Cologne.' While Britain's drunken dilettante was squandering his bombers on civilian targets, she was losing vital battles elsewhere through lack of air power. 'Churchill is victorious in Parliament,' he mocked after the British prime minister survived another vote of confidence in July 1942: 'But Germany wins the wars.'[37]

This did not however include the guerrilla war. When Heydrich died of his injuries, the Nazis liquidated the Czech village which they alleged had harbored his assassins.[38] The Czechs as a whole had condemned the murder, and when Gauleiter Baldur von Schirach talked loosely of ridding Vienna of its Czech minority Bormann reminded all the gauleiters, including Goebbels, that Hitler had forbidden any such measures.[39] There were other gaffes. In France S.S. Brigadeführer Carl Oberg announced plans to execute all the male kinsfolk of assassins: their women would be sent to hard labor, and their children to orphanages. Goebbels said that Oberg's proposals violated every propaganda principle. The inclusion of women and children was a gift to the enemy, he said; and hostages should always be taken from the same band of the political spectrum as the culprits.[40]

He attributed the ominous growth of partisan warfare in Russia to the absence of any coherent *Ostpolitik*.[41] Earlier in 1942 he had issued guidelines on how to win over all the occupied populations.[42] Russian prisoners were unanimous under Nazi interrogation that they 'preferred to die on their feet than to live on their knees' – a brilliant slogan coined by Stalin himself.[43] To Hitler, Goebbels hinted that they should set up puppet governments in the Ukraine and Baltic states.[44] 'You can't rule Russia from Berlin,' he said, criticizing Rosenberg.[45] He felt the latter was impractical, naïve, and hopeless at organization.[46] He drafted a decree guaranteeing religious freedom to the Russians, and determined to secure Hitler's approval the next time they met.[47] He felt sure that Hitler was being kept in the dark about the partisan war. From all quarters he was urged to take it up with him.[48] He sent Walter Tiessler to point out to Rosenberg once again that their enemy was bolshevism, not Russia as such. Rosenberg ducked the issue, and the infighting went on.[49]

Another problem was that German visitors to Russia, like the archeologists that Rosenberg had recently sent, were finding things there less primitive than Goebbels had painted.[50] The Germans were learning that the Russians too were capable of fighting and dying for a cause. Russian commanders outnumbered in the fighting for Sevastopol had chosen to blow up their entire position rather than surrender. Knowing the German people's weakness for heroic idols, Goebbels suppressed all such reports. 'National Socialism,' he lectured to his staff, 'teaches that bolshevism is not an ideology, but the effluence of sub-human, criminal, and Jewish instincts.'

He could never forget that five million former communist voters lived in their midst: The disease was only in remission; it had not been extinguished. The sewer rat, he said, reverting to customary Nazi imagery, would always prove more hardy than the domestic pet. Thus their reporting must distinguish between the heroism of the German soldier and the animal survival-instinct of the Russians.[51] He wrote an essay on this problem for *Das Reich* and circulated it throughout the party. 'The superior race will triumph over the inferior one,' he asserted, 'no matter what infernal means the latter may use to escape its personal fate.'[52]

BRITAIN'S FORTUNES WERE NOW at their lowest ebb. As Rommel's exhausted Axis armies dug in at El Alamein, Goebbels' propaganda blared promises of independence to the Egyptians. On the high seas Hitler's submarines had sunk seven hundred thousand tons of shipping during June. In the first days of July his submarines and bombers in the Arctic mauled the Russia-bound Anglo-American convoy PQ.17 so badly that the next convoy-run was abandoned.

Stalin, speculated Goebbels, must be furious about Churchill's failure. Perhaps he would one day be willing to come to terms. Germany would certainly not reject any overtures.[53] From his close study of Soviet newsreels he concluded that Stalin was a quiet, dogged type; head and shoulders above the pigmies of the western democracies. 'That man has style,' he said.[54] Moscow's clamor for a Second Front – a British invasion of the Continent – grew throughout July.[55] On the twenty-third Goebbels warned his staff that given Churchill's 'unstable' character an invasion in the west was quite probable.[56] German propaganda had, he pointed out, no interest in provoking such an event; on the contrary, they must do all they could to help Churchill represent his air raids as a viable substitute for a Second Front.[57] He dealt with such an invasion in a *Das Reich* article on August 2, entitled 'Don't even try it.' Its sardonic tone almost violated his own guidelines: 'We extend to the British a hearty invitation to come over,' he taunted. 'We hope they'll bring along a few Americans too. . .'[58]

Churchill hurried to Moscow. Goebbels ordered the Nazi media to dwell on every detail of the prime minister's humiliation – for example, that Stalin did not even bother to meet him at the airport.[59]

Hitler had meanwhile shifted his summer headquarters to Vinnitsa in the Ukraine. In mid-August he asked Goebbels to fly over to discuss the domestic situation 'and foreign policy,' as the minister noted. 'He also intends to give me special powers to take over civil defense.'[60] He had spent several days touring the blitzed cities.[61] As his plane landed at Vinnitsa on August 19 events in France were taking a dramatic turn. At Churchill's behest two brigades of Canadian troops were storming the beaches on either side of Dieppe. It was a disaster. By midday the landing force had been wiped out.[62]

Hitler told Goebbels the next day what had happened. A German Channel convoy had stumbled on the invasion force. 'Thus,' dictated Goebbels in his diary, 'we had the first report that something was afoot out there in the murk and fog as early as 4:28 A.M.' A German submarine chaser had rammed one landing craft, a second German warship had opened fire on the British motor torpedo-boats. After an exchange of fire at point-blank range which left eleven Germans dead and ten missing, the British raid developed into a débâcle. The raiding force lost one destroyer, thirty-three landing craft, 106 planes, and 4,350 men (including 1,179 dead). London claimed that the raid was merely an 'exercise with live ammunition.' Goebbels dismissed this: 'Obviously the British planned to execute a major operation here,' he wrote. 'At very least they tried to bring about a Second Front . . . thereby complying with Stalin's orders. There can be no doubt about that.'

Not even Churchill, he argued, would have sacrificed all those planes, destroyers, and troop transports, not to mention four thousand dead and missing men, for a mere exercise.[63] 'All of a sudden,' he scoffed the next day, 'the British are declaring that everything went just the way it was planned. From the fact that it was all over in nine hours they are now implying that it was in fact only *planned* to last nine hours.'[64] He noted with glee that Churchill had ordered a strict clamp-down on quoting the American newspaper reports on the fiasco. 'The reality is,' he commented, 'that he is the prisoner of the Kremlin. He can no longer conform to the dictates of common sense. He has to act at the Soviet dictate.'[65]

In glorious sunshine he left Hitler's headquarters and drove back to the airfield, past rolling cornfields lush with the new Ukrainian harvest. If only they could transport it all back home, he sighed. The previous day's *Völkischer Beobachter* had carried a foolish article by Erich Koch, the local dictator, boasting of the agricultural riches now flowing to the Reich. As soon as he got back to his ministry, Goebbels warned against propagating such false illusions.[66]

46: The Road to Stalingrad

GERMANY HAD NOW BEEN at war for three years. Her public's brittle morale was troubling Goebbels and he drafted an article on 'The point of war,' reviewing the events since 1939 from a lofty ideological plane.[1] British leaflets were becoming more insidious, particularly one appealing, 'Get rid of Hitler!'[2] The message seemed unthinkable, but within the four walls of No. 20 Hermann-Göring Strasse even Goebbels began to express reservations about some of Hitler's decisions. Once he stepped out through the padded double-doors and into his morning ministerial conference, however, he radiated unswerving loyalty to his Führer.[3]

He had recently issued a circular to journalists discouraging inflated terms like 'unique' or 'historic' to describe their victories, and words like 'warlord' for anybody other than Hitler.[4]

Morale improved as Hitler's armies fanned out to the south and east across the shimmering, dusty Russian steppe, and Goebbels methodically warned the media against overweening optimism.[5] They captured the oil cities of Maykop and Kraznodar; the Russian population rose against them under the influence of Moscow's propaganda but, as the High Command chided Goebbels, with no visible effect from his. Hitler repeatedly warned him to damp down any spreading optimism.[6] He ordered General Friedrich Paulus to advance with the Sixth Army on Stalingrad, a city of two million souls dominating the Volga waterway.

The Russian summer's heat was as savage as the late winter's cold. The temperature soared to near 50°C. On August 8 Goebbels dictated: 'The battle of Stalingrad has begun.'

As Marshal Timoshenko withdrew before Hitler's tank onslaught, Stalin ordered him to stand and fight. Goebbels compared this harshly worded order approvingly with Hitler's order of December 1941. 'You can see,' he dictated, warming once more to the Soviet leader, 'that in Stalin we are dealing with a man of caliber.'[7] Soviet resistance at Stalingrad stiffened, and so did Goebbels' instinctive reluctance to mention the city's name. He had not forgotten Otto Dietrich's blunder of October 1941.

From late in August onward he repeatedly embargoed all reference to the battle. Nobody could say how long it would last. But already Stalingrad was on every tongue, both friend and foe.[8]

FOR A WEEK HE VANISHED from Germany, visiting Venice again for the biennial movie festival.

Before leaving he wrote for *Das Reich* an article entitled 'Don't be so righteous!,' a critique of the Germans' pedantic sense of justice and over-objectivity. 'We're so frightened of doing an injustice to somebody,' he wrote, 'that when in doubt we prefer that the injustice be done to ourselves. . . Hating is something we Germans still have to learn.' Too much objectivity, he concluded, would be the death of them.[9] He repeated this attack in a secret address delivered to about sixty senior Berlin journalists in the ministry's Throne Room on September 23. He warned against harboring any illusions about victory. They must not underestimate their enemy. 'The German public is not as hardy as the British,' he pointed out. Britain had yet to lose a single war. 'The German public,' he repeated, 'suffers from a craving for righteousness and from a craze for objectivity. It keeps looking for the laudable in our enemies.' Their chronic love-affair with Churchill was just one example.[10]* If he were English, he said, he would have kept repeating ever since 1939 that they were fighting Hitler, and not the Germans; he would also have hammered home *ad nauseam* the eight points of the Atlantic Charter. He warned them that their biggest problem in coming months would be the resumption of the British air raids. Single-line references to enemy air activity in the High Command communiqués would no longer suffice. He set up propaganda companies with no other task than to dramatize the coming blitz and the heroism of the people.[11]

IN THIS SECRET SPEECH to Berlin's top journalists, Goebbels was astonishingly frank about the fate of the city's Jews. Justifying the reporting restrictions imposed, he explained that every ill-considered sentence was liable to be reported abroad by the Jews. 'This conduct of the Jews is understandable enough,' he added, according to the transcript. 'In Berlin there are still forty-eight thousand of them.[12] They know with deadly certainty that in the course of this war they will be deported to the east and left to their murderous fate. They can already sense the inexorable tread of physical annihilation and therefore, so long as they live, they inflict damage on the Reich whenever they can.'[13]

Small wonder that the world's Jews mobilized against Nazi Germany. In London, rabbis rallied to the slogan, 'England awake!' Goebbels derided this as a plagiarism of the Nazis' own rallying-call.[14] In Jerusalem, Jews at the Wailing Wall placed an ancient curse on him. 'I have yet to observe any untoward effects,' he noted.[15]

His humor was ill-chosen. The deportations from Berlin had resumed. To silence public disquiet Goebbels ordered the bourgeois press to feature reports on hostile Jewish activities abroad.[16] Trainloads of elderly Jews had begun leaving Berlin in June for Theresienstadt, the model camp for 'old folks.' On

---

* The Germans cheered Churchill when he drove through the ruins of Berlin in 1945, and the city of Aachen later awarded him the Charlemagne prize.

July 11 the first trainload bound for Auschwitz left Berlin with 210 Jews aboard.[17] In mid-August Berlin packed off 1,004 more Jews to Riga, followed by 790 on September 5; on the twenty-sixth 811 would be shipped to Reval. That day he noted that all Jews were to be excluded from fats and meat rations, except those still working in the munitions industry who would receive the heavy-labor supplements.[18] (The actual regulations were even more pitiless than his diary suggested: Meat *and* bread rations were canceled for all Jews other than those married to non-Jews or wounded in World War One; further, no Jews were to receive milk except infants, an interesting detail; any food packets received from abroad were to be deducted from Jews' ration cards; gifts of tea and coffee were to be confiscated and distributed to field hospitals.)[19]

Seventeen thousand Jews working in industry were still exempt from deportation. According to Goebbels' diary, Hitler agreed with his venomous comments on how their intellectuals and economists were everywhere discovering 'indispensable' Jewish skilled workers who just had to be spared.[20] In Goebbels' view, since they now had 240,000 foreign workers in Berlin it should not be too hard to replace the exempt Jews too.[21] Two more trainloads of Jews left Berlin in October 1942 carrying 963 Jews to Riga and 791 more vaguely – and with sinister connotations – simply to 'the east.'

Despite all this the level hardly seemed to decline. He found out that many of Berlin's judges were half-Jews transferred from other cities in the belief that they would stand out less in Berlin. 'Berlin is not a garbage tip,' he exclaimed.[22] In a letter to the new minister of justice Otto Thierack he proposed simply declaring all Jews 'unconditionally disposable' – the word he used, *ausrottbar*, also has ugly connotations – and commended to him 'the concept of annihilation through work.'[23]

Thierack however was unexpectedly unsympathetic. Some, he pointed out, were half-Jews whose sons had already died in this war. 'So long as the Führer won't allow us to address the broader issue of those with Jewish blood, or in-laws,' continued Thierack, 'we can't carry out an *Aktion* confined to the legal system.'[24] At a meeting chaired by Adolf Eichmann that month the civil servants became bogged down in bureaucratic minutiæ.[25] Frustrated, Goebbels said that he was sure that Berlin's Jews were helping the British bomber crews to find their targets (they weren't). He set himself a new target – to rid Berlin of its remaining Jews by March 1943.[26]

Ugly rumors were already circulating abroad, fueled by British propaganda. The *Daily Telegraph* quoted Polish claims that seven thousand of Warsaw's Jews were being killed each day, often in what it called 'gas chambers.' One of Goebbels' worried civil servants telexed a request for information to Hans Frank's press office in Kraków and to the propaganda field office in Warsaw. The reassuring reply spoke of the Jews being used to construct defenses and roads. Be that as it may, in Goebbels' files the original press report, which had merely summarized the British newspaper item, was rubber-stamped *Geheime Reichssache*, top state secret.[27]

How much did Goebbels know? In his surviving files there is plenty that implies a broad general knowledge of the atrocities. Reporting back to him on November 11, his legal expert Dr Hans Schmidt-Leonhardt, whom he had sent to inspect conditions in Hans Frank's Polish dominions, noted that the Warsaw police had deemed it too dangerous to visit the ghetto there; in the Kraków ghetto he had found all the Jews put to work; in Lublin the ghetto had already been cleared away, and there were now bloody disturbances. 'As a *Geheime Reichssache*,' dictated the lawyer, 'Frank related to us the following characteristic recent instance: –' But whatever it was we cannot know, as Goebbels' shocked staff cut off the top-secret balance of the page that is filed in his ministry's records.[28]

In February 1943 Dr Fritz Prause, a senior staff member, briefed Goebbels on the continued terrorist incidents resulting from their occupation policies – the Germans had begun rounding up Poles in cinemas and churches for slave labor. A poster appealing to 'Poles of German origin' had generated speculation about the likely fate of the rest.

'The rumor is spreading,' Prause reported, 'that the same fate now awaits the Poles as has been meted out to the Jews, and there is not a Pole in the Government-General who does not know precisely what has been done to them.' 'One thing is certain,' recommended Dr Prause: 'That the current derogatory slogan "Pole equals Jew" is no longer viable for the Government-General, particularly since the above-mentioned rumors dwell heavily on what is known to have become of the Jews.'[29]

The wave of terrorist attacks continued. In the first quarter of 1943 forty-four Germans were assassinated in Warsaw. In April 1943 a local propaganda official reported to Goebbels that the 'resettlement' operations in Lublin – Nazi officialese for something clearly far worse – had left non-Jewish Poles with the definite impression that after the Jews their turn would come next.

There were only two alternatives open to the Germans, this brave if circumspect official informed Goebbels: Either to assimilate or to liquidate (*ausrotten*) the Poles. 'Even if for biological reasons the adoption of such radical steps as have for instance been necessary against the Jews can be justified before the bar of history, such a solution still seems unworthy of the tradition of the German people, given that large parts of the population affected are still resident within the Reich's frontiers. The plan of that American Jew to sterilize the male population of the German Reich,' the official reminded Dr Goebbels, referring to Theodore Kaufman, 'was rightly pilloried by the entire German press.'[30]

In sum it appears that by 1943 members of Goebbels' staff both in Berlin and in the field appreciated that the likely fate of the deported Jews was one about which they should use only the skimpiest Nazi euphemisms.[31] The camouflage was universal and perfect. Addressing allegations by Dr Stephen F. Wise,* president of the American Jewish Congress, Himmler wrote to Gestapo chief Heinrich Müller that he was not surprised by such rumors, given the high

* Wise stated, "Communism is Judaism."

mortality rate in the camps; he ordered all the cadavers 'of these deceased Jews' cremated or interred.[32] During November and December the London newspapers published more reports. Goebbels' own Transozean service secretly forwarded to Himmler a Reuters report of February 14, 1943 alleging that six thousand Jews were being murdered in Poland every day.[33]

In mid-December 1942 the B.B.C. concentrated for a whole week on these atrocities, announcing that Poland had become a charnel house, that over one-third of Poland's 3,531,000 Jews had been liquidated, and that the German public was turning a blind eye to the killings; the B.B.C. warned the Germans that they and their children's children would be cast out of the community of nations for all time as punishment.[34]

Goebbels noted this with irritation in his diary: The Jews were exploiting every known propaganda technique – pathos, impertinence, and solemnity – to rouse the world against Germany; but the Reich still had more than enough Jewish pawns in its hands. 'The British are the Jews of the Aryan race,' he dictated, weightier arguments evidently failing him.[35]

On December 22 his monitors reported that the B.B.C. had announced that Hitler was planning to complete liquidating the Jews by December 30: 'The Jews are first robbed of their civil rights and their property, then given less to eat than the rest, and finally thrown into concentration camps or deported to unknown destinations.' There were allegations about a camp in Danzig where Jews were executed by electric chair or gas; other propaganda broadcasts spoke of gas chambers and cyanide. Goebbels delegated to the urbane Hans Fritzsche the task of rebutting the stories.[36]

'In the long run,' he wrote, 'I fear we shall not be able to get away with this by hushing it up. We're going to have to answer something if we are not to get gradually pinned down.'

He privately believed that the Allies were actually glad that the Nazis were clearing out the 'Jewish rabble.' Adopting standard tactics, he ordered that no direct response be made to the allegations – they should remind the world about Britain's role in India instead.[37]

OF GREATER WEIGHT in everybody's mind that winter was the unending battle for Stalingrad. It provided fresh ammunition for Goebbels' feud with Otto Dietrich, Hitler's dapper, spineless press chief – two months Goebbels' senior in age, but his equal in Party rank.[38] There was open war between them, waged with scarcely less ferocity than the Sixth Army's battle at Stalingrad. While the Machiavellian Goebbels based in Berlin mapped out broad propaganda strategy, Dietrich, resident at Hitler's headquarters, issued directives *(Parolen)* to the press which often had the opposite effect. Dietrich found it irksome to be excluded from Hitler's formal conferences with Goebbels, and obnoxious that Goebbels regularly invited newspapermen to his morning conferences. The direct telephone lines from Goebbels' desk to his departmental chiefs including the 'German press' department in Room 24 were a thorn in Dietrich's flesh.

He posted Helmut Sündermann, an experienced journalist, permanently into Goebbels' ministry as his deputy; to Goebbels, this smelt of the creation of an independent 'press ministry.'[39] During the summer of 1942 Hitler banged their heads together; he signed a decree ordering the two men to work in harmony; but he also instructed Goebbels to channel all directives to editors through Dietrich in future.[40]

This left the way open for another Dietrich blunder. On September 15 he announced, 'The struggle for Stalingrad is nearing its triumphant conclusion' – an announcement, he said, was imminent. Some newspapers printed special editions. Headlines announced that Stalingrad was in the bag.

Goebbels, more cautiously, warned his staff to strict secrecy. Even he however began his remarks on the eighteenth with the words, 'Now that the capture of Stalingrad is a certainty. . .'[41] Then caution returned and he urged editors to find something other than Stalingrad for their headlines – a wise move, because soon the High Command was talking about 'exceptionally stubborn' fighting for the city.[42]

Goebbels was not encouraged to hear that the *Daily Mail* was calling Stalingrad the decisive battle of the war.[43] Blaming Goebbels for this new gaffe, London mocked that he had been rather faster on the draw than the Wehrmacht.[44] He cursed Dietrich out loud and announced that he would severely punish any editors who blindly issued special editions in future. 'I am, after all, the one with the name to lose,' he said, 'and I have no desire to see this name, which has taken me twenty years to earn, tarnished by thoughtless stunts like this.'[45]

Hitler, like Dietrich, was taken in by his own propaganda. He assured Goebbels that they would capture Stalingrad shortly. He planned to continue the other prong of his eastern campaign, across the Caucasus mountains, all winter, then building a gigantic wide-gauge railroad from Germany to the new eastern territories.

Together they addressed a huge Sport Palace meeting on the thirtieth. Here Goebbels called for the first time for what he described as total war. 'The more total the war the better,' he said. Developing also his new propaganda line of 'strength through fear' he warned of the consequences of bolshevism, but assured this mighty audience that the worst was over. He drew the familiar comparisons with the last months before 1933.[46] Sitting beside Hitler, Goebbels heard him announce: 'We shall be assaulting Stalingrad, and capturing it too – you can bank on that.' And, thundered Hitler into the microphones, 'You can take it from me, nobody is ever going to shift us from that spot.'

Rommel's position in Egypt also seemed impregnable. The field marshal came to Berlin and stayed for several days at Schwanenwerder, marking up his maps for the Führer and regaling Goebbels with stirring tales of the desert and of the armored gladiators who were disputing its command. Goebbels treated him to all the newsreels issued since Tobruk and to his first ever glimpse of a color movie, the lavishly produced *Golden City*.[47]

ALLOWED BACK INTO MAGDA's home at Schwanenwerder for the Rommel visit, Goebbels was happy to see the children again after so long.[48] His new press expert Rudolf Semler found himself wondering sometimes however whether the minister really did love his children.[49] He seldom showed them true affection, noticed Semler, and only rarely saw them now. He refused to lower himself to play trains with little Hellmut; now seven, Hellmut's blue-gray eyes often had a vacant look which did not endear him to his father. With his precocious oldest daughters Helga and Hilde the minister either flirted outrageously or tested their intellect to the point of tears. The others he virtually ignored except for photo-calls. 'Our children have inherited your good looks and my brains,' he chaffed Magda once. 'How awful it would have been the other way around.' (He was a connoisseur of Bernard Shaw, from whom the remark originally came.) *Shaw was member of Socialist British Fabian Society.*

His forty-fifth birthday came. Hitler sent him a handwritten letter. Goebbels signed his reply, 'At your undeviating and loyal service.'[50] The German Newsreel Company's gift to him was a private half-hour feature showing the Goebbels family – the children reciting poetry, riding ponies, chasing a squealing piglet, and greeting their mother or Rommel as their respective limousines drive up. Helga, ten years old now, with finely molded features and braided hair, was more ladylike than ever.[51] 'I want just two children when *I* marry,' she once emphasized. 'Otherwise I won't have a moment to call my own!'[52] Their mother, Magda, was now something of a virago. Most of her earlier femininity had passed to her five daughters – and to Hellmut too. The newsreel camera found him in the classroom of the village school, flunking the answer to a teacher's trick question about mathematics and offering a goofy smile through protruding upper teeth – the only thing he had inherited from his absentee father, who barely featured in the movie himself.

BY THAT TIME, the late autumn of 1942, Hitler's calculus was also going wrong. His armies faced a stalemate in the Caucasus and perhaps even defeat in Stalingrad. Stalingrad became a matter of personal prestige between Germany's Führer and the Soviet leader after whom it had been named.[53] The morale reports from all Goebbels' sources brought mounting evidence of public disquiet.[54] People were openly wondering if Stalingrad was to become a second Verdun. In private, speaking to Major Martin, the minister criticized Hitler's strategic decisions as increasingly unrealistic.[55] With the sudden and unexpected collapse of Rommel's front at El Alamein, Goebbels' own private nightmare began. To the chronic pessimist Hans Fritzsche, returning from a tour of duty on the Stalingrad front, Goebbels admitted, 'You were right.'[56]

He betrayed none of this in public. Speaking on October 21 he scoffed, 'One cannot prosecute a war without iron, oil, or wheat' (Stalin had now lost both the Donetz basin and the Ukraine).[57] Challenging the enemy's insidious theme that Hitler had lost the race because the Americans would shortly intervene he published in *Das Reich* an article entitled, 'For whom is time working?'[58]

He set up a special unit to start a whispering campaign about 'miracle weapons,' both real and imaginary.[59] He felt it necessary to warn all his senior staff not to display pessimism about the future.[60] But each passing week augmented the grounds for pessimism. On the night of November 6 the B.B.C. announced a British victory at El Alamein and the capture of twenty thousand Axis troops, most of them Italians. Goebbels' machinery lapsed into silence.[61] At his eleven o'clock conference on the seventh he suggested that they describe events at Alamein as 'fighting' rather than a 'battle.' With pursed lips he then announced, 'Three large British convoys have left Gibraltar. This fact is a military secret and is to be treated as such.'[62]

The Abwehr, Germany's military Intelligence service, could offer no clue where these convoys were headed.[63] Goebbels feared they were bound for southern France or Italy itself.[64] But as Goebbels set out for the Munich anniversary of the 1923 putsch he heard that the Allied warships were landing tens of thousands of troops in French Morocco and Algeria. At the Brown House in Munich Hitler phoned Paris, Vichy, and Rome; he secretly invited Vichy France to join the war on his side. But as he began his speech at the beerhall he still had no reply.[65]

Though still flawed by over-confident predictions about Stalingrad, it was otherwise a good speech. 'There was a time,' Goebbels heard him say, 'when the Germans laid down their weapons at a quarter to twelve. I never, ever, stop until five past.' His biting witticisms about the 'perfumed dandy' Anthony Eden delighted Goebbels, as did his sinister reference to his 1939 prophecy about the Jews. 'Of those who laughed then,' Hitler mocked, 'countless laugh no longer today.' Then he boasted that Stalingrad was as good as theirs: 'That was what I wanted to capture, and, do you know – modest that we are – we've got it, too! There are only a few more tiny pockets holding out!'

Back at the Brown House afterward he told Goebbels that the French were unlikely to join the German cause. The Allies would certainly not hesitate to do what he had refrained from in 1940, namely bombing Paris. Sure enough, the Vichy French admiral in Algeria, Jean-François Darlan, asked the Americans for an armistice.

Goebbels returned to Berlin late on the ninth. At his Berlin conference the next morning he cajoled his department heads once more to keep a stiff upper lip. It was like a football match, he suggested, developing a new line of debate: The home team had been four-nil until half-time, but now suddenly the visitors had scored a goal.[66] He hoped for dramatic news from Hitler's meeting that day with Pierre Laval, the French prime minister, and directed the press to express 'warm feelings' toward France.[67]

Nothing came of the meeting however and Hitler ordered his troops into the unoccupied half of France. He moved his air force straight into Tunisia, far ahead of the Allied invasion troops. By occupying this 'bastion of North Africa' he expected to gain another six months and perhaps even give Rommel another chance of victory. 'German propaganda,' admitted Goebbels on the twelfth, 'is in for a tough time. Its most important principle must be to put on a resolute and confident face, to show no signs of weakness, and . . . to pull everyone together as did Churchill after Dunkirk.'[68]

BRITISH AIR-RAID DEAD so far totaled forty-three thousand; the corresponding German figure was 10,900.[69] Preparing to turn the tables on Germany, the British government was loudly proclaiming that it was Hitler who had started the bombing of civilians.[70] In Tokyo the Japanese put captured American bomber crews on trial. Goebbels decided against encouraging the lynching of British bomber crews in Germany however; rather grotesquely, he argued that the result would be total lawlessness.[71] Touring the most vulnerable cities in the west he was encouraged to find people there more phlegmatic than the S.D. reports suggested.[72] 'The enemy,' he announced on November 17, 1942 in Wuppertal, scene of many of his earliest political memories, 'has thank God left us in no doubt as to the fate he has in store for us if we ever lose faith in victory.'

With Rommel now in retreat, Goebbels suggested that the Mediterranean was of less importance than 'the war of the lieutenant-commanders,' as he called the U-boat war. A retreat in North Africa was regrettable, he said, but not of pivotal importance. The German forces had sunk a million tons of shipping during September, 750,000 tons in October, and as much again already during November, or so he claimed. As for the British air raids, which had now resumed, he emphasized: 'Mr Churchill cannot wash his hands of the historic guilt for having started this war against innocent civilians.' He promised that the hour of retribution would come.[73]

Two days later the Red Army crashed through the eastern front at Stalingrad, and Hitler's Sixth Army found itself fighting for its life. By November 22, 1942 it was totally surrounded, and Goebbels was facing the most challenging crisis of his career as a propagandist.

47: *Things have not Panned out*

Hᴏᴡ ᴍᴜᴄʜ ʟᴏɴɢᴇʀ,' Dr Goebbels challenged his loyal press officer Schirmeister that autumn, 'do you think this war's going to last?' 'If it goes on like this,' hedged Schirmeister, 'we might end it next year.'

Goebbels looked at him expressionlessly. 'I don't know,' he murmured.[1]

As Germany's fortunes declined, his own would improve. The more the skies darkened, the more the people needed reminding that the darkest hour comes before the dawn; the more Hitler immured himself in his remote headquarters, the more somebody else had to take control at the center.

From December 1942 Goebbels started to cultivate his fellow gauleiters, inviting them round to his ministry.[2] Many of them were veterans of the earliest days of the party. He saw in them an elite upon whom to fall back when the going got tougher. He was apprehensive lest any gauleiter suspect he might be trying to usurp Hitler's powers, let alone those of the roughneck Martin Bormann, their titular head; Bormann took pains to hold Goebbels and all others of superior intelligence at arm's length from his Führer.

Writing in *Das Reich* Goebbels had declared, 'Nations and mankind alike are at their strongest when fighting for survival.'[3] It was to this survival instinct in the Germans that he now appealed. The British recognized the magnetism of his 'strength through fear' propaganda and tried to undermine it by attacking him, calling him the biggest, most ridiculous, and most contemptible of liars. 'Even so,' one British commentator conceded, 'he's the best political brain of the whole Nazi bunch. That's why he's got to be watched.'[4]

To defeat him they resorted to innuendoes broadcast by their Soldatensender Calais transmitter. They broadcast a lurid and wholly fictitious account of Goebbels' Christmas Eve to blacken his name. 'The chief,' noted one of Sefton Delmer's experts afterward, 'has been at the height of his form over the Christmas season.'[5]

That autumn there was a genuine attempt on Goebbels' life. In November a Dr Hans Heinrich Kummerow, a technician with the Löwe radio company in Berlin, confessed to plotting to blow him up with a remote-controlled bomb which he would plant, disguised as an angler, beneath a bridge on Schwanenwerder. Schirmeister attended the trial; he told Goebbels that it had revealed a picture of a 'totally degenerate' intelligentsia. From now on four detectives and a police car escorted Goebbels wherever he went. At Lanke machine-gun nests were emplaced around the house.[6] As a surprise Christmas gift Hitler sent over an armor-plated Mercedes. Goebbels called it an 'armored coffin' but the Führer gave him no choice but to use it.[7]

That Christmas was overshadowed by renewed problems with Magda's health. After another minor heart attack she was again hospitalized at the West End sanitarium. Two blood transfusions led to complications, and Goebbels recorded what were possibly genuine concerns for her life.

Surrounded by their children they celebrated a cheerless wedding anniversary at her bedside. He lamented in his diary, 'It's a shame that I so seldom get to see the children.' Magda struggled out to Lanke for New Year's Eve, and Helga and Heide were allowed to stay up chattering until midnight as a treat.[8] Then it was back to bed for their mother. Belatedly thanking police general Kurt Daluege in January 1943 for the gift of a pheasant, Magda apologized, 'I have been in a sanitarium for some weeks after a heart attack and I'm going to have to stay in for some time.'[9]

The plight of the Sixth Army in Stalingrad worsened beyond relief. Broadcasting his New Year's sermon Goebbels suggested that his listeners compare their situation with that of the year before when the entire army, struggling at Moscow, had been saved by their Führer's sheer willpower alone. During the past summer they had conquered an area twice that of the British Isles, rich in raw materials, in grain, and in industry.

'Now we've got the upper hand,' he suggested. A world war was however once again upon them. 'Across all the seven seas rages the termagant of destruction,' he said, 'a vengeful goddess of history, raising her arm to smite the Anglo-Saxon powers whose ministers so recklessly and needlessly unleashed this war.' Hinting once again at the coming of a more total warfare he sprinkled his oratorical glitter across the entire German people – across the workers, intellectuals, doctors, teachers, civil servants, and even journalists. 'The continents tremble to the roar of our weaponry.' Nobody knew how long this war would last, he allowed. It might well end as suddenly as it had begun. 'Yonder,' he promised, as the last hours of the old year slipped away, 'we can already see the light.'[10]

Nothing could conceal however that Nazi propaganda was now on the defensive. 'It is not known to us,' his ministry cautioned in a secret directive, 'how far the Soviet resources are already exhausted.'[11] He forbade editors to adopt phrases coined by the enemy like 'United Nations' or even 'Allied,' since these were throwbacks to the previous world war and designed to remind the Germans subliminally that they had lost that one too.[12]

Made-in-USA phrases like 'Liberty ships' and 'Flying Fortresses' were also embargoed, as was the phrase 'Fortress Europe.'[13] The latter invoked, he said, the picture of a fortress under siege, complete with the implication that sooner or later it would be overrun.[14] All of which did not prevent him, from time to time, using the phrase 'Fortress Europe' himself.[15]

He was not yet worried by the Americans. Before returning to Rommel's staff in May 1942 Berndt had suggested they draw upon the occult in their propaganda to the Americans. 'Time for Nostradamus once again,' agreed Goebbels.[16] Gienanth, his former press attaché in Washington, sat in on some interrogations of American bomber crews and told Goebbels afterward that they were in a state of shock, weeping with home-sickness and 'ready to carry out any unpatriotic act.' The British were tougher, he said, but equally bereft of political ideals. 'Nearly all of them voice antisemitic remarks,' noted Goebbels optimistically, 'but more from instinct than insight.'[17]

ATTEMPTS AT SUPPLYING the encircled Sixth Army by air were failing. By December 1942 rumors of a Stalingrad crisis were sweeping the country. 'Things have not panned out as we expected,' Goebbels dictated to his diary on the eighteenth. 'It doesn't seem to be as easy to force open the enemy ring round Stalingrad as some of us had thought.'[18] The High Command ordered a news blackout. The army ordered its radio commentator to purvey only optimism.[19]

Some fundamental decisions were called for. Hitler's headquarters slowly bestirred itself. Late in December Martin Bormann finally visited Dr Goebbels to canvass his ideas on total war. Goebbels had been developing these ideas for almost two years. He had published an article about 'total war' in Das Reich on February 17, 1941. 'The German people,' he had written in his diary six months later, 'has a right to a socialist war.'[20] A year later he was convinced that Stalin was squeezing more than Hitler was out of his people. 'A nation that endeavors to fight such a total war,' he had dictated in September 1942, 'has exceptionally dangerous powers of resistance.'[21]

Reporting back from the eastern front later that month his friend and adviser Major Titel spoke of the outrage that 'certain abuses' at home were causing among the troops.[22] Goebbels thereupon put his ideas for 'radicalizing and totalizing' the war to Walther Hewel, Julius Schaub, Alwin-Broder Albrecht, and other long-standing members of Hitler's personal entourage.[23]

If it had worked for Stalin, he argued, then how much better were the prospects in Germany, where there was so much more slack waiting to be taken up. But, while he himself lived a most ascetic existence, those around him did not. Hans Fritzsche for instance was among the elite who liked to indulge in oysters, real coffee, and fine wines at Otto Horcher's gourmet restaurant in Berlin.[24]

Britain had introduced compulsory labor service for women in March. Goebbels had long believed that at least women without families aged up to fifty should work, regardless of their social standing.[25] In December 1942 he stated this to Hitler and added that school-age boys and girls could help man the anti-aircraft guns.[26] But Hitler had complex biological arguments against it, and others close to him like Göring and the manpower commissioner Fritz Sauckel assured him that such crisis measures were not called for.

Goebbels worked hard to promote his belief in total war. In each offensive, he argued, they had lacked the ten percent that mattered. He discussed it separately with Speer, Funk, and Krosigk, but petty jealousies still smoldered between them as well as between Göring, Lammers, and Bormann; each of them had spent years establishing his own power base, and none would willingly cede territory.[27] Speer agreed on the malady. 'In every offensive,' he said to the central planners, 'we lack just ten percent.' He warned of a coming war of attrition if they could not manage that extra effort. 'I spoke with Goebbels recently,' he continued. 'He holds the view that the public is actually waiting to be called upon to make this last supreme effort.'[28] In 1944 however Speer would become one of the most trenchant opponents of Goebbels' total war.

Pride as much as prejudice constrained Hitler from agreeing to total war. Not until the Sixth Army's position in Stalingrad seemed desperate as it was now did he send Bormann to Goebbels' mansion at Lanke on December 28 to explore with him, as Bormann jotted in his pocket notebook, 'a total effort by the German people to increase its war potential.'[29] Bormann flattered Goebbels cleverly, calling him the 'harbinger' of total war and speaking of their Führer's faith in him.[30] The proposals which Goebbels outlined for releasing manpower to war industry and the forces did not however commend themselves even to Bormann: They were rooted in his fiery socialist adolescence; he wanted punitive sacrifices by the 'upper ten thousand' who still acted as though there were no war. 'I am glad,' the minister remarked afterward at dinner, 'that I have always lived in frugal wartime style.'[31]

Despite Bormann's misgivings, Goebbels set to at once, drawing up a plan for all-out war. 'I see my main task in the weeks ahead,' he dictated at Lanke three days after Bormann's visit, 'as being to radicalize our internal management of the war so that there can be no more talk of sparing the home front and spoiling the war.'[32] He closed the next day's entry, the first of 1943, with this philosophy: 'The radical and most total war is the shortest.'[33]

For several days after submitting his proposals he heard nothing. He pressed the Wolf's Lair daily for a decision. Bormann urged Goebbels to be patient, pleading that it was not so simple to draft new regulations. The minister's staff drew up a more detailed outline plan: It included the introduction of labor service for women, cutbacks in the manufacture of consumer goods, the closure of department stores, and the release of two-thirds of all streetcar and railroad conductors. Dr Lammers, the Reich's top civil servant, agreed to call a Cabinet-level conference on January 7. 'I am today firmly convinced,' Goebbels recorded, 'that if we give it all we've got we'll smash the Soviet Union this coming summer.'[34]

As he understood it, the idea was that after Lammers had put their finished plan to Hitler, a triumvirate would implement it with dictatorial powers delegated to them by their over-burdened Führer.[35] The three he had in mind were himself, Lammers, and Bormann. Göring, as president of the defense committee and chief of the Four-Year Plan, had far too much on his plate already. Not that Goebbels gainsaid Göring's authority – in fact he would draft a fulsome letter to him on his fiftieth birthday a few days hence.[36]

There is no doubt that Goebbels, perhaps over-simplifying, saw total war as the ultimate answer to his embattled country's difficulties.[37] 'Total war,' he felt, 'should have been brought in eighteen months ago.'[38] They had the manpower, if only they could drain it off the home front.

Lammers held the promised conference on January 8 – delayed one day by Speer's tardiness. Sauckel at once threw a spanner into the works, declaring himself quite capable of raising the manpower without total war. Funk and Bormann gave only limited backing to Goebbels' plan.[39] Frustrated, Goebbels re-ran Russian newsreels of the siege of Leningrad which showed what people were willing to do if pressed.[40] More conservative than the Goebbels plan, the document which Lammers drafted and Hitler eventually signed spoke of releasing up to 700,000 men to the armed forces; however it provided for a three-man committee to run total war acting only 'in close touch' with Goebbels.[41] He tried for several days to become at least an equal wheel on this unwieldy wagon. Lammers sought in vain to appease him.[42] Goebbels felt slighted; he was sure that 'certain circles' were trying to freeze him out.[43] When he phoned the Wolf's Lair, Lammers rebuked him, insisting that this was what the Führer himself had decided.[44] The whole episode probably recalled to Goebbels his galling omission from Hitler's first cabinet in 1933.[45]

When Hans Lammers presided over the first meeting on January 20, Goebbels rather pathetically called it the Committee of Four in his diary; but he was very much a junior partner.[46] He harangued them all for an hour and dictated mechanically afterward, 'I am still seen and recognized as the driving force.' This however was not true. Within his own four walls he muttered to personal staff that Lammers had 'wet blanketed' his ideas.[47] For the next month he grappled with the bureaucratic red tape with which Lammers deftly packaged each measure that his three-man committee hesitantly approved.

THUS GOEBBELS BEGAN dreaming about a spectacular mass meeting at which he would appeal over their heads to the people, and ask them what they desired. *Vox populi* – the voice of the street: Ugly enough, but the next best thing to a dictatorship of the proletariat.

During these first three weeks of January 1943, meanwhile, the Sixth Army was dying in Stalingrad. The airlift of food and ammunition failed as the airfields were lost, aircraft engines froze, and aircrew morale slumped. Although Hitler continued a news blackout policy, hoping for better times, millions of Germans now suspected that something was going badly wrong. Goebbels promised to persuade Hitler to release the awful news.[48] Colonel Martin reported to Berlin that Hitler seemed to be out of touch with reality.[49] Hitler was not alone in this.

Attending one propaganda ministry meeting, the army's radio commentator General Dittmar was horrified by the superficiality on display. 'Even that clever-dick Hans Fritzsche asked me how close we are to relieving Stalingrad,' he noted.[50] Five more days would pass before the High Command obliquely admitted that the Sixth Army was encircled, and had been for two months.[51]

On January 21 Goebbels dictated that it was time to make a clean breast to the people. 'It should have been done long ago,' he wrote, adding in almost treasonable language: 'But the Führer was against it until now.' Perhaps Stalingrad might yet become a symbol, as the Alcazár of Toledo had been for the nationalists in the Spanish civil war. He announced to his ministerial conference that he was going to see Hitler the next day to demand that they adhere in future to the unvarnished truth – and to total war.[52]

IT WAS MISTY, GRAY, AND DAMP as he arrived at the Wolf's Lair on January 22, 1943. Hitler's jug-eared chief adjutant General Rudolf Schmundt had just returned from the Stalingrad front. He besought Goebbels to force through his total-war plans. When Goebbels protested to Hitler about being frozen out of the Lammers committee, Hitler expressed surprise: 'You yourself had Bormann inform me that you were happy with the role of "harbinger,"' he said, 'and preferred to leave the implementation to the experts.'[53] Strolling around the compound with Goebbels and his Alsatian bitch Blondi, Hitler blamed the coming catastrophe in Stalingrad on Göring and Germany's allies. The Hungarian troops had abandoned their tanks and stormed the empty hospital trains waiting to carry casualties away.[54] There was however one good thing about their allies' failure, he remarked. If at the end of the war Germany stood alone, then the spoils of victory would be hers alone too. He had resigned himself, he said, to the loss of all twenty-two divisions in Stalingrad. The phone rang incessantly as they talked, bringing fresh messages of woe.[55]

Goebbels then told him of his plans for total war. He promised to raise 1·5 to two million soldiers by the coming summer. Hitler winced at the mention of female labor service, but otherwise endorsed everything.[56] 'He would prefer,' dictated Goebbels with probably less than utter candor, 'that I do not join the three-man committee myself – so as not to become bogged down with the minutiæ of this vast program.' Hitler had however authorized him to attend all its meetings and to ensure that all its proposals were 'radical' enough.

The minister further told his diary that Hitler had ordered an internal dictatorship set up with Goebbels as the 'psychological dictator and motive force.' This was somewhat premature, indeed downright untrue. As Himmler was informed a few days later, Goebbels had tried to persuade Hitler to appoint him alone as 'Führer of the Home Front.' 'But he has not succeeded.'[57]

AFTER THIS MEETING Hitler had to see Goebbels in a new light. None of his army generals had ever stood up to him like this. For that matter, none could inspire him the way his propaganda minister did either.[58] When he now asked Goebbels to return as often as possible, it was perhaps no longer a casual pleasantry. As he hoisted himself aboard the Berlin-bound train at Rastenburg,

Goebbels caught sight of young men of the Führer's escort battalion on another platform, mustering for the eastern front. He wondered how many would survive the next twelve months.[59]

The Sixth Army would probably not survive another week. As Goebbels began drafting the inevitable communiqué – choosing his language with the utmost care, because in ages to come Germans would always recall how they had heard of the death of their army in Stalingrad – the mood in official Berlin was already catastrophic. 'For the first time,' noted General Dittmar, 'there is everywhere personal bitterness against the Führer who led us to Stalingrad. . . A searing sense of shame fills us all.'[60] Dittmar heard from Colonel Martin how easily Goebbels had persuaded Hitler to change the tenor of the High Command communiqué to allow greater gravity and more truth after the generals had not dared to ask Hitler themselves. The question was, Martin had said, how to restore Hitler's bruised prestige among the troops.

It was a somber time. Goebbels decreed that January the Thirtieth, tenth anniversary of the Nazi seizure of power, would this year not be a public holiday: No flags, no parades. At eleven A.M. Göring would broadcast to the armed forces from the air ministry. At five P.M. Goebbels would speak from the Sport Palace and read out a proclamation on Hitler's behalf.[61] Briefed by the British embassy in Stockholm, London shortly announced all this – Goebbels was furious that the enemy had somehow learned of his secret plans.[62]

British Intelligence seemed to be better in every way than Hitler's. When Churchill and Roosevelt met in Casablanca, and announced their demand for unconditional surrender, Goebbels at first missed it and then ignored it; his rage was directed at the Abwehr which had confidently *translated* Casablanca as 'The White House' and declared that the Allied meeting was in Washington.[63] On January 27 Goebbels briefed journalists that unconditional surrender was probably Roosevelt's reference to the capitulation of the French generals in Algiers, and even when Churchill announced the demand in the House of Commons Goebbels ignored it, his only comments being on the prime minister's statements about the submarine war and General Eisenhower's appointment as supreme Allied commander.[64] Reviewing thirty different Nazi newspapers, Allied Intelligence officers found their 'unconditional surrender' slogan ignored except for one reference in the *Deutsche Allgemeine Zeitung*.[65]

CFR

Returning to his struggle for total war, Goebbels dictated a blazing article for *Das Reich*.[66] When the Reich *Gazette* published the first ordinances closing down bars, confectioners, and jewelers however, and announcing the call-up of men and women for labor service, the upper age limit for women was set at forty-five, not at fifty.[67] The lackluster Lammers committee also showed a marked reluctance to shut down many businesses. The enemy bombers, Goebbels bitterly pointed out to Hitler eighteen months later, closed most of them down anyway.[68]

Infuriated by the committee's weakness, he decided to go ahead with his plan for a mass meeting to put pressure on Hitler. 'Public opinion,' he noted, 'is always a powerful ally.'[69] He had honed his skills promoting the images of Hitler, Rommel, Speer, and others. The time had now come to promote his own.

NEVER HAD NAZI GERMANY suffered a disaster like the one approaching in Stalingrad. Goebbels ordered the magnificent Hitler posters entitled 'Adolf Hitler is victory' called in and stored away for future use; a tenth-anniversary poster designed by Mjölnir, the top Nazi artist, 'January 30, 1933 – January 30, 1943: one fight, one victory,' was called in and pulped.[70] On the historic thirtieth itself, British Mosquito bombers inflicted on Göring of all people the ultimate indignity of having to broadcast from an air ministry shelter, and an hour later than planned.[71] As Dr Goebbels spoke from the Sport Palace that evening the bombers reappeared; he carried on regardless.[72]

Goebbels had become by default the spokesman for the Reich. He had tried in vain to get Hitler to speak since December.[73] During the coming year in fact Hitler would speak only four times (and Göring only once). As the Führer reminded Goebbels before this speech, it was still proper to compare Germany's situation now with that of 1933. Goebbels had already done this subtly with his Christmas broadcast, bringing in the voices of soldiers in Stalingrad, Lapland, southern France, and the Caucasus – in short from all four corners of Hitler's still vast empire. He now did it again with the radio preamble to his speech of January 30:

This is the Greater German Radio with the German shortwave stations beamed to all parts of the world –

The transmitter groups Bohemia–Moravia with the stations Prague, Brno, and Moravian Ostrau; the stations of the Government-General, Kraków, Warsaw, and Lvóv; the Baltic transmitter group with the chief station Riga and the stations Madona, Gdynia, and Libau; Radio Kaunas with Vilnius, Radio Reval and Dorpat, Radio Minsk with Baranovice.

The transmitter group Ukraine with the chief station Ukraine, the station Vinnitsa and the shortwave station Kiev; the German Europa stations Alps, Bremen, Calais, Danube, Frisians, and Vistula –

and so the list went on, as listeners were reminded that their troops were also in Belgrade, Athens, Salonika, the occupied eastern territories, Norway, Holland, Belgium, Paris, Argenteuil, Bordeaux, Lille, Normandy, Rennes, Bulgaria, Croatia, Romania, Slovakia, and Hungary.[74] The British thought his delivery diffuse and nervous; the Americans considered that he threw in his climax sooner than usual. Twice he was actually heckled. 'The German people want to know,' one voice was picked up shouting, 'won't we be hearing from the Führer?' As he then read out Hitler's proclamation, the radio microphones recorded applause but also another voice shouting, 'Cease! Stop!'[75] Even so, as he finished speaking, no foreign listener could assume that Germany was near collapse – 'And that was the object of the exercise,' he dictated afterward. His audience of Berliners had acted 'with sound political instinct' throughout.

As he climbed into his armor-plated Mercedes, he asked his adjutant what he had thought of it, and back at No. 20 Hermann-Göring Strasse he had his chauffeur Rach read aloud, from Nietzsche's *Will to Power*, the recipe for 'what the masses call a great man.' 'He must be outrageous, jealous, manipulative, designing, flattering, fawning, inflated,' this ran: 'In short all things to all men.' Goebbels unconsciously slipped into his speaking posture, his hands planted on his hips. 'Make no mistake,' he shrilled. 'You can't change the masses. They will always be the same: Dumb, gluttonous, and forgetful.'[76]

IN THIS JANUARY 30, 1943 speech he had made no reference to U-boats, Churchill, Roosevelt, or North Africa; nor for that matter to unconditional surrender. Sixty percent of his speech had dealt with Russia, ten percent with Britain, and only three percent with the United States. He had used the word *total* ten times, and ninety-three different negative words like *danger, inconceivable, strain, difficult, hard, menace, catastrophe, superhuman, trials, misery, anxiety, hopeless, defeat* and *desperate*.[77] Twenty-three times he had referred to 'faith' (*Glaube* and *gläubig*). 'Defeat,' the Americans unkindly concluded, 'drives the Nazi orators into the arms of historical analogies, bombastic heroizations, and empty irrational appeals.'

On the last day of January 1943 Hitler dramatically promoted the doomed Sixth Army's commander Friedrich Paulus to field marshal, thus pressing a pistol into his hand. As a German officer Paulus had no alternative but suicide. 'Fate,' Goebbels argued in his diary, 'has put him in a situation where, now that so many of his men have died in battle, he must forgo fifteen or twenty years of life to achieve immortality.'[78] He asked Fritzsche, who had been with Paulus most recently, for his view. 'Herr Minister,' responded Fritzsche. 'I'd take a bet on it. The field marshal won't surrender.'[79]

That same night Moscow radio announced that Field Marshal Paulus had surrendered and gone, alive, into captivity. Two days later they added the names of thirteen of his generals.

Goebbels was thunderstruck. Having ordered their men to fight to the death, had these generals meekly turned themselves over to the Russians? Hitler phoned. Goebbels called him back and recommended they postpone any comment – they could not be certain one way or the other.[80]

Paulus' surrender made him more determined than ever to take his own life if the time ever came.

He broadcast the prepared communiqué on Stalingrad at four P.M. on the third – it was 'grave, objective, sober, without pathos but also not without warmth' – accompanied by the heroic ceremonial which he had elaborated with Hitler in advance. 'Loyal to its oath of allegiance to the last breath,' the communiqué read, the Sixth Army had 'succumbed to the superior enemy strength and to the disfavor of the circumstances.' Goebbels ordered three days of national mourning.[81]

Three days later at the Wolf's Lair Goebbels was among the gauleiters who heard Hitler's explanation for Stalingrad. 'You are witnessing a catastrophe of unheard-of magnitude,' Hitler began, before again blaming his allies. 'The Russians broke through, the Romanians gave up, the Hungarians didn't even put up a fight.' He estimated their own losses at one hundred thousand dead.[82] It was a setback, he admitted, but by no means fatal.

'Besides,' he said, brightening, 'world history has a deeper meaning, and it does not consist of having the supreme race of Europe finished off by one of the most inferior.'[83]

It was a novel argument, and Goebbels frequently advanced it thereafter.

48: Sin Will Pluck on Sin

A FTER STALINGRAD, JOSEPH GOEBBELS revealed to Schirmeister that if the worse came to the worst he was going to kill himself and his entire family.[1] His contemptuous remarks about Paulus showed that he regarded self-immolation as the prerequisite for entry to Valhalla.[2] Besides, as he often said, for the top Nazis there was no going back; the enemy had often warned that they could expect nothing but the gallows.

This lethal resolve concentrated his mind, and he threw his puny frame into reviving Germany's fortunes with a fervor lacking in those colleagues who had less cause to fear retribution. His days became even longer. He spoke to workers on the tank-assembly lines of the Alkett plant, gauleiters at Posen, army adjutants from every theater of war.

In his view government officials presented a special problem. His own Staatssekretär Gutterer had privately decided months earlier that the war was lost, and hundreds more thought like him. In mid-February 1943 Goebbels addressed the entire government in the chancellery building – a 'somewhat leaden' audience, he found them.[3] 'Goebbels told us,' wrote Ribbentrop's Staatssekretär von Weizsäcker afterward, 'that we're too defeatist – we know too much to have faith, and too little to comprehend.'[4]

Göring's Staatssekretär Milch was more impressed. 'Minister Goebbels,' he told his colleagues afterwards, 'using incredibly apt and clear, convincing language, indicated that the leadership of a state has the obligation during a crisis to keep a stiff upper lip. . . Our people look to us for leadership. They must not gain the impression that we are not taking up this energy which they are offering to us. From thousands if not millions of letters, this want emerges,' added Milch, quoting Goebbels.[5]

Göring, the real culprit, had taken to his bed after Stalingrad.[6] The army's generals, sensing themselves also under attack, pointed out that Goebbels too was supposed to give up several thousand of his ministry's staff toward the promised 800,000 new troops. General von Unruh swooped on Goebbels' office flanked by General Friedrich Olbricht – of whom more later – and several other officers, and called on him to justify his non-fulfillment of his 3,400-man quota. 'From what I was told,' related an S.S. Obersturmbannführer gleefully to Himmler, 'the Reichsminister threw a fit and intimated to General von Unruh that the Wehrmacht would do well to make a clean sweep in Bendler-Strasse [the war ministry] first and see to it that their fat and well-fed majors there are put to sensible work.[7] The row left feelings ruffled everywhere.

On February 12, after a conspiratorial meeting with Speer and Ley, Goebbels decided to go ahead with his Big Meeting idea. Just six days later he would pack the Sport Palace with his trusty Berliners and stage the most important mass meeting of his life; he would deliver to them a white-hot speech on total war, and broadcast it worldwide.[8] He banked on his audience's response to show the out-of-touch bigwigs like Lammers and Bormann which way the wind was blowing. 'The Führer,' he dictated, 'is much more radical than he's generally given credit for – if only we can stop the faint hearts beating a path to his door and pleading for moderation.'[9]

He began dictating the historic total war speech two days later. Over the next days he trimmed and modulated its tone, and even checked passages on foreign policy with Ribbentrop's officials.[10] He was planning to present Hitler with a *fait accompli*. Probably for the first time, he did not even show him the script.[11]

Structured in three parts the speech drew on Goebbels' twenty years of experience as a demagogue. He selected mawkish, abstract phrases that had not failed him before ('I want to speak to you from the depths of my heart, to the depths of your heart'). He conjured with *holy earnest,* with *utter candor,* with *historic missions,* with *devout faith,* and with *solemn and sacred oaths.* He would begin in the third person ('they'), glide imperceptibly up into the oily-familiar second ('*ich frage Euch*') and finally unite orator and listening public into one all-embracing, gigantic, multi-millionfold first-person we ('we all, the children of our nation . . .'). *Heroic, steely, gigantic –* the adjectives were all there, as were the clichés. The speech would take as its starting point the nation's eagerness for total war and follow through with warnings that a bolshevik victory would entail the liquidation of their entire intelligentsia. Specters of 'Jewish liquidation squads,' terrorism, starvation, and anarchy haunted the pages of his script, as did more complex and inbred hatreds too, as he drew an angry picture of an upper class who must now be compelled to 'sully their dainty hands' along with the rest. In short he saw in this appeal for total war his chance to rededicate the party to its former socialist ideals.[12]

On the morning of the big speech, February 18, his ministry telexed the entire text to newspapers, forewarning editors that Dr Goebbels intended to ask the audience ten questions. 'In your front-page makeup,' the newspapers were instructed, 'their response is to be reported as the express will of the entire nation.'[13] While there were no *claqueurs* in the vast auditorium, Goebbels had arranged for the usual canned applause and laughter to be trickled into the loudspeakers to trigger audience response at the proper moments.

The demand for tickets was colossal. Fifteen thousand packed in, just as in the good old days before 1933, ordinary people coming together in a mood of self-doubt.[14] Here in Germany's undoubted hour of crisis they were to rediscover their community of purpose and sense of power. The hall was sparsely decorated. Just one huge banner hung above the podium, reading

'TOTAL WAR: SHORTEST WAR.' As Goebbels skillfully whipped them up, his audience had an overwhelming sense of release. He had deliberately chosen the amplitude, intonation, and rhythm of each passage. The newsreels captured extraordinary scenes of emotion. Within minutes the audience was leaping to its feet, saluting, screaming, and chanting ('Führer command! We obey!'). 'Goebbels' delivery,' wrote one postwar analyst of this famous speech, 'was grave, imploring, moralizing, stern, provocative, mocking, derisive, ironic, and even monotonous as need dictated.' 'Key words, particularly superlatives, were drawn out and accentuated. He paused deliberately before important passages. Embarking on a particular challenge he increased the tempo so that the words came out in a rush, and he leaned closer to the microphone to increase the volume. He was particularly adept at the trick of building on applause by briefly carrying on speaking despite it. He augmented the shouts of assent to his questions by hurling words into the applause like "Is that what you want?" or "Are you willing?"'[15] Over two hundred times his audience interrupted with exclamations, shouts of approval, applause, and laughter; soon they were cheering every sentence, sometimes every phrase. One seasoned journalist later described the audience reaction as a kind of euphoria. 'Even the foreign and neutral journalists were excitedly jumping up and down applauding Goebbels.'[16]

The audience included most of the government and party leadership. The newsreels show the front rows filled with war-wounded, attended by Red Cross nurses, and bemedalled soldiers. Behind them, as Goebbels remarked during the speech, sat Berlin's ordinary munitions workers, doctors, scientists, artists, engineers, architects, teachers, and civil servants ('Of course,' he pointed out, 'the Jews are not represented here.')* Camera operators picked out popular movie stars like Heinrich George – he was seen in close-up cheering, leaping to his feet, and saluting excitedly – and several children in the front rows, including Helga and Hilde Goebbels, allowed their first glimpse of such a mass meeting.[17] Between them sat their mother, who had just been discharged from the clinic.

Addressing this huge multitude Goebbels promised an unvarnished picture of the crisis – he flattered the 'schooled and disciplined German people' that they could be trusted with the truth. He was not going to apportion blame for Stalingrad, he said: The future would show why the sacrifice had not been in vain. Germany and her allies, he said to tactful applause, were the last bulkhead of 'our venerable continent.'[18] Toward the end he hurled at them the ten questions, challenging their belief in victory, their willingness to fight, and their determination to work if need be sixteen hours each day and to 'give all they had for victory.' The orgiastic climax was reached by the question: 'Do you want total war? Do you want war more total, if need be, and more radical than we can even begin to conceive of today?' And then, almost casually, 'Do

---

* This sentence was cut from the published transcript.

The Deadliest of Enemies

[WHE]N GOEBBELS takes a dislike to [some]body – usually a rival in intellect [or po]wer – he carries on the feud with [tire]seless tenacity.

[Above]: The arrogant ex-businessman [Joac]him von Ribbentrop attracts [his] venom from the moment of his [app]ointment, first as ambassador [to t]he Court of Saint James, then [as] Reich foreign minister – a [pos]ition which Goebbels secretly [wan]ts. Venom turns to fury when [Rib]bentrop sends an S.S. unit to [oc]cupy a Berlin radio station.

[Below]: Following his usual tactic of [divi]de and rule, Hitler cunningly [ap]points Otto Dietrich (*below [lef]t*) as press chief. From then [on] Goebbels snipes at Dietrich, [part]icularly after he prematurely [ann]ounces victory over Russia in October 1941.

[It is] however Alfred Rosenberg (*right*) who earns Goebbels' deadliest contempt. The party's chief [ideo]logue claws at Goebbels' cultural empire, and writes scathing commentaries in his diary: 'G. was [a dis]charger of purulence. Until 1933 he squirted it at Isidor Weiss. With him gone, he has begun to [disc]harge it over us instead' (ALL PHOTOS: WALTER FRENTZ)

STICKLER FOR DETAIL At his field headquarters Hitler inspects models of enemy fortifications with F
Marshal Wilhelm Keitel, at left, Chief of the High Command, and an engineer general (WALTER FREM

IN GOOD TIMES AS IN BAD In 1938, as the good times roll, all the Nazis are proud to march at the
side of Adolf Hitler – seen here on October 1, 1938 taking the salute of an honor guard at a Berli
railroad station after his Munich triumph (VOAK / HOFFMANN COLLECTION)

VALKYRIE MYSTERIES On July 20, 1944 a
explodes under Hitler's conference table in
adquarters at Rastenburg.
n the highly decorated commander of the
guards battalion, Major Otto-Ernst Remer
arrives in Goebbels office in Berlin, ordered
plotters to arrest him. Goebbels talks him
– but there are inexplicable features of that

y does he seem so unmoved by the false
of Hitler's death? What has happened to

the pages of his diary for that day? And why does
panzer general Heinz Guderian (*center*) rumble his
tanks into the heart of Berlin? Whose orders is he
awaiting?

When Goebbels arrives at the Wolf's Lair on
July 22 to inspect the damaged table (*top*, with
Julius Schaub, Karl Koller, and Hermann Göring)
Hitler at last puts him in charge of Total War. But
it is Martin Bormann (*right*) who emerges from
the Bomb Plot as the real power behind the scenes
(AUTHOR'S COLLECTION; WALTER FRENTZ)

Behind an unmarked door in Moscow: The missing Goebbels diaries. The author is the first to use t

The Discovery of the Goebbels Diarie

EARLY IN 1992 Dr Elke Fröhlich, Germany's leading authority on the Goebbels diaries (*below right* with Hitler's secretary Christa Schroeder) comes across Collection No. 1477 in the former Soviet secret state archives in Moscow. There are ninety-two boxes

of Agfa photographic plates. She recognizes the writing of Goebbels' private secretary Richard on the boxes (*bottom picture*). She has found th missing Goebbels diaries – the Reichsminister had them filmed on these glass plates as the wa

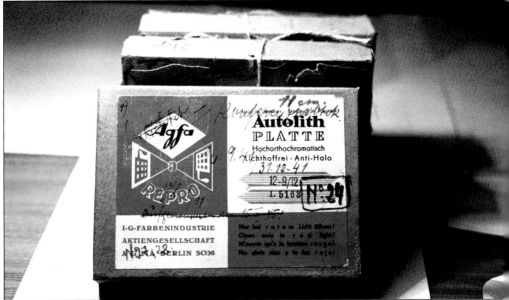

The glass plates give up their secrets.

n Moscow

aws to a close. But her institute denies her
e means to research further. She tips off
e author. In June 1992 he is the first to win
cess to this treasure. On the glass plates he
ds the images of 75,000 pages of diaries.

NDWRITTEN HISTORY Few can read Dr Goebbels' difficult handwriting, even when the enlarged
ginal is as clear as this. On September 4, 1939 he records the day war broke out: '*Gestern: in
r Herrgottsfrühe heraus. London hat um 9ʰ ein Ultimatum bis 11ʰ an uns gerichtet: Schluß der
mpfhandlungen und Zurückziehung der Truppen. Sonst Krieg*' (author's collection)

THE IMAGE THAT Goebbels propagates with millions of picture postcards is not far from the truth. The children are his one consolation in a rapidly darkening scenery. *Far left, top to bottom*: with Harald and the family in 1939; w

The Goebbe

HAPPY FAMILIES Recently discovered origi proof prints of studio portraits of Joseph a Magda Goebbels and their six children. T photographs underline the horror of their tra

da; with Helga and Hedda at Christmas,
above: Magda with her eldest daughter
a, left, and Hedda;
ht: probably the last photograph of the
ster, now visibly weary, with his family.

mily Album

poisoned by their mother's hand in the
ker of the Chancellery in Berlin on May 1, 1945
are them the imagined horrors of survival
post-Hitler Germany.

Geheim!

Rundfunk

(13 B) Sr/Mz.

6. September 1944
Datum:..........................

Sender Moskau:

Erklärung eines kriegsgefangenen deutschen
Generalleutnants über Misshandlungen und
Massenhinrichtungen im Konzentrationslag[...]
Lublin

Der Sender Mosk[...] 5. brachte
am 3.9. um 16[...]olnischer
Sprache folg[...]

"Die Sowjetpresse veröffen[...]e folgende
Erklärung des Deutschen Generals M[...]) +) an das Kom-
mando der Roten Armee:

'Moser, Generalleutnan[...]ger Kommandant der
372. Feldkommandantur in Lubl[...]ng:

Ich ... Moser, ge[...]hre 1880 in Langenroda,
Kreis Roda, diente seit [...]der deutschen Armee. Den
Rang eines Generalmajor[...]h 1935. Generalleutnant wurde ich im Jahre 1942. [...]mpferfolge wurde ich mit
allen in Deutschland [...]ung kommenden Orden ausgezeich-
net. 42 Jahre lang w[...]r ein ehrlicher und anständiger
Soldat; Teilnehmer[...]tkriegen ... und war schwer ver-
wundet. Ich habe [...]d zum Verschweigen der schweren
Verbrechen H i t[...]er zu ihrer Rechtfertigung. Ich
sehe es als me[...]n, die ganze Wahrheit über das sogenannte Vern[...]er zu sagen, das von den Hitleristen
in der Nähe [...]an der (Cholmerstrasse ?) errichtet wurde. Ende N[...]e kam ich nach Lublin mit der Hauptfeld-
kommandan[...]ihr Kommandant. Früher war dort General
V. A l [...](?), der nach drei Wochen weiter nach Osten
zu ein[...]ndantur versetzt wurde. .... dass in Lublin
ein K[...]nslager besteht, das der SD... erklärte, dass
laut[...].... Hauptfeldkommandantur als Vertreter der

+[...]'Krakauer Zeitung' erwähnte am 6.6.44
[...]eneral M o s e r im Zusammenhang mit
[...]Feier in Lublin. 'Reuter' meldete am
[...].44 die Gefangennahme eines Generalleutnants
[...]u s e r - W i l l m a r , Kommandant von
[...]blin.)

- 2 -

[...] R M V P
[...] 1.44

THE SECRET IS OUT
In September 1944 the
Forschungsamt – Hitle[...]
secret telephone and
radio monitoring
agency – picks up a
Moscow broadcast abo[...]
a Nazi 'death camp'
found at Lublin.

Asked by its Kraków
field office for material
to rebut these stories,
Goebbels' ministry
orders silence (YIVO
ARCHIVES, NEW YORK)

1 2. Sep. 19[...]

[...]1, habe ic[...]
[...] vorgelegt
da wir bei einer von uns eingeleiteten abwehrpropagand[...]
aktion restlos in die defensive gedraengt waeren , is[...]
es nicht richtig , eine solche aktion einzuleiten . d[...]
staatssekretaer hat entschieden , dass das thema in den
auslandsdiensten nicht aufgegriffen werden soll.

s t r e n g   v e r t r a u l i c h

im auftrag
gez . dr . schaeffer
+
bi qsl+
krakau meldung nr. 4 erh

you agree that anybody who injures our war effort should be put to death?'[19] The bellow of assent each time was deafening.

He dined that evening with Milch, Paul Körner, Wilhelm Stuckart, Otto Thierack, Ley, and Speer. Somebody remarked that the speech had been a kind of 'silent *coup d'état*' by Goebbels. He quoted this phrase with satisfaction in his diary, while hastening to add that the coup was 'against bureaucracy.'[20]

This speech was his greatest achievement in a lifetime of speaking. Curiously, neither Hitler nor Göring bothered to listen to the broadcast. Hitler was at the front, and Göring had retired to bed at five P.M.[21]

Goebbels however heard it broadcast at eight P.M.; the answers to his ten questions nearly burst the loudspeaker membranes of his radio. For twenty full minutes after his final defiant phrase, 'Arise as one nation, and let the storm burst upon them!' the radio network continued to broadcast the tumult of acclaim. The field agencies of the S.D., briefed to stand by twelve hours earlier, had sent agents to eavesdrop in railroad waiting rooms and cafes; at one A.M. the S.D. regions *(Leitabschnitte)* telexed their collated reports to Himmler's Amt III in Berlin, and this provided the propaganda ministry with a glowing summary two hours later.[22] Goebbels' field offices reported in equally favorable terms.[23] Studying every available newspaper from around the world, he basked in glory. The Forschungsamt, wiretapping the foreign journalists in Berlin, recorded high praise. Only the final S.D. report was critical.[24] Jealous army officers were also less enthusiastic.[25]

No matter, Goebbels was the man of the moment. 'It is beautiful,' he dictated, 'to be the gauleiter of Berlin and to gather around one so many prominent men of party and state.' He decided to do it more often, 'since the central leadership is lacking now, during the Führer's absence from Berlin.'[26] These words reveal that he was setting himself very ambitious goals indeed.

THE FINE WEATHER which now set in displeased Goebbels. For his purposes he needed the winter gloom to linger on.[27] Toward the end of February 1943 the eastern front was stabilized again; he forbade the media to mention it. Their propaganda would forfeit all respect if it bleated about crises each winter, and forgot them in the spring. When the Waffen S.S. shortly retook Kharkov, Goebbels even tried to prevent any special communiqué being issued.[28] 'We got over the first winter crisis relatively well,' he reminded his staff. 'But we only just survived the second. If there's ever a third, I don't want to be propaganda minister.'[29]

The Sport Palace speech was never forgotten. It marked a turning point in Goebbels' career but not in the war effort. 'After Stalingrad,' he reminded Hitler in July 1944, 'I proclaimed total war. . . But it remained only superficial.'[30] He had worked off many private complexes in the speech, and settled many old scores; he had referred to 'a certain social stratum' which was interested only in preserving its almost peacetime lifestyle. National Socialism heeded neither class nor profession. 'It's time to put an end to bourgeois pruderies,' he had

said, and: 'It's time to take off the kid gloves and clench our fists.' His speech
had also referred to the idle classes who 'lolled around in stylish bars' with no
greater concern than the welfare of their stomachs. Not surprisingly, after this
speech the middle class suspected Goebbels of planning to eliminate them,
and Berndt had to issue a discreet denial during May.[31]

Total war remained however a chimera. Goebbels closed down some stores
and restaurants, about half the newspapers, and the Ruhleben racetrack; he
banned manicures, pedicures, and permanent-waves.[32] Even so General von
Unruh reported that they would not meet the new manpower target.[33] What
happened was often a parody of total war. Magda, convalescent and dizzy, was
put to work in the Telefunken factory, but none of the other ministers' wives
followed suit. Goebbels patriotically laid off his domestic staff, including his
treasured chef; Ribbentrop, his arch-enemy, snapped them all up for his own
expanding household.[34]

The inertia produced by easy earlier victories proved impossible to dispel.
Goebbels shut down Rothe's, the exclusive flower shop where Emmy Göring
shopped, but every other luxury flower shop and eating place seemed to have
its protectors. Professor Morell saved the Stadtkrug restaurant in Vienna by a
word in Hitler's ear.[35] Göring pleaded for Horcher's restaurant. After Goebbels
had sent in hired thugs to smash its windows the Reichsmarschall posted two
policemen permanently outside; Goebbels phoned him at the Obersalzberg and
threatened to use his powers as gauleiter; Göring retorted that his Luftwaffe
would in that event take over Horcher's as an exclusive officers' club.[36]

The Reichsmarschall seemed however to be Goebbels' only hope of
neutralizing the incompetent Committee of Three (Lammers, Keitel, and
Bormann). Speer flew down to the Obersalzberg on Sunday February 28 to
suggest that Göring reactivate the moribund Reich Defense Committee. He
phoned Goebbels later that afternoon to come down too and at four P.M. on
Monday Goebbels was driven up the mountain road to Göring's villa. The
Reichsmarschall received him wearing what the propaganda minister wearily
described as a somewhat baroque costume – 'But that's how he is, and you've
got to take him foibles and all.'[37]

They needed Göring's name, his authority, his clout; but no more.

For five hours they wrangled until everybody agreed to let bygones be
bygones – Goebbels dismissed their past differences with a wave of the hand.
Göring bellowed with laughter when he heard of Goebbels' run-in with
Unruh. Cunning as a fox, Goebbels intimated that it was everybody's duty to
rally round the Führer at this time of crisis. But he also left Göring with no
illusions that like him the Reichsmarschall was up to his neck in blood. ('I am
in,' Shakespeare's King Richard III had moaned, 'so far in blood, that sin will
pluck on sin. . .')

'Göring,' dictated Goebbels the next morning, 'is quite clear about what
threatens us all if we go soft in this war . . . Above all we have committed
ourselves so far in the Jewish problem that for us there is no escape any more,

none whatever.' The same would go for Himmler, whom Göring promised to win over too.[38]

With Göring's backing secured, Goebbels took the sleeper back to Berlin that night, March 1, 1943. Churchill's bomber squadrons got there before him and Göring's stock temporarily slipped again. Berlin's death-roll from this one raid topped six hundred.[39] One bomb had fallen two hundred yards from the Goebbels home in Schwanenwerder; he decided to bring his children to No. 20 Hermann-Göring Strasse, where they now had the deep shelter. Many officials, particularly Goebbels' deputy gauleiter, had lost their heads; inadequately drilled in civil defense, thousands had crouched too long in their shelters while buildings which could have been saved burned to the ground. Several plunderers had been caught: They lost their heads too (as Reich Defense Commissioner, Goebbels had the power of life and death in Berlin).[40]

War had a brutalizing effect. Watching rescue operations, S.S. Obersturmbannführer Eichmann found one elderly couple crushed beneath girders, whimpering to be put out of their agony; he told his corporal to oblige.[41] At a wrecked hospital Goebbels looked on as the bodies of patients and nurses were pulled out of the rubble; he too swore revenge, enraged at the thought that 'some Canadian thug' could do this to his city. After the British next hit Essen, the S.D. reported that many people were asking about when Germany would begin hitting back. Speer confided that powerful new secret weapons were in production, and Goebbels began hinting at them in his speeches.

When he arrived at Hitler's headquarters, now at Vinnitsa in the Ukraine, on March 8 he found everybody livid with Göring.[42] For hours the Führer let fly about the Luftwaffe's useless commander-in-chief and his corrupt entourage of high-living World War One cronies – they were all currently shopping for looted art works in Italy.

As Hitler went on to discuss Rosenberg's talents and Goebbels' propaganda offensive against bolshevism,[43] further disastrous news came: British bombers had struck at ancient Nuremberg. Goebbels tried hard to salvage the absent Reichsmarschall's reputation – he phoned Nuremberg and assured Hitler that the damage was less than feared – but in vain. 'Given the prevailing mood,' he dictated to his secretary afterward, 'I consider it inopportune to raise the question of Göring's political leadership with the Führer. Now is not the right time.'

Göring was missing from the next total-war conference that Lammers called in the chancellery on March 16. Goebbels took Speer, Ley, and Funk to see him for three hours on the seventeenth, but he seemed totally out of touch with reality. He was astonished when Goebbels told him that 616 people had died in the latest raid on Berlin.[44] He agreed to ask Hitler's consent for the revival of the Reich Defense Committee.[45] But Hitler was in no mood to listen. He wanted only to hear that the Luftwaffe was hitting back at Britain; when he came to Berlin for Memorial Day Goebbels proposed that they take out London's wealthier suburbs one by one, rather than those of the working class.[46]

Meanwhile Berlin and other cities, particularly in the Ruhr, would just have to bear the onslaught. Many a hardened soldier on home leave soon wished that he was back on the battlefield. Even Count von Helldorff pleaded to be posted to an S.S. unit; Himmler ordered him to stay in Berlin.[47]

'COUNT VON HELLDORFF,' Himmler had been notified in January 1943, 'is very often questioned by Dr Goebbels about the evacuation of the Jews, and about communism and other political affairs in Berlin.'[48]

Talking with Hitler into the small hours of January 22, Goebbels had again badgered him to let him get on with ridding the city of its Jews. It had become an obsession. He devoted twenty-six percent of his speech of January 30 to attacking the Jews.[49] His staff instructed field offices to link them closely to the concept of bolshevism.[50]

So far, seventeen thousand of Berlin's Jews had gone. The trains began heading for Auschwitz, the most brutal of all Himmler's slave-labor camps and the one with the highest mortality rate. Working closely with the S.D., Goebbels planned one final sudden sweep for the night of February 27 when the remaining Jews would be rounded up and held, ready for deportation in trainloads of two thousand at a time.[51]

He set himself the target of evacuating the very last Jews by the end of March. During his total war speech he had called them the incarnation of evil (he had said that neither foreign protests nor crocodile tears would deter Germany from 'the exter –', he began, then checked himself and continued, 'the neutralization of Jewry').

On the day after the speech, February 19, one thousand more Berlin Jews were shipped to Auschwitz. 'Experience goes to show,' he dictated cynically a few days later, 'that a movement, and a party, which have burned their boats fight more ruthlessly than those which still have an avenue of retreat.'[52]

The police bungled their swoop on Berlin's Jews. Goebbels had arranged to use the loyal units of the S.S. Leibstandarte to cordon off factories while police seized their Jewish labor force for deportation.

'Misguided' fellow Germans, wrote Goebbels, had however tipped them off and four thousand slipped through his fingers. 'We'll get our hands on them yet,' he added.[53]

For several days there was chaos, compounded by the horrific air raid of March 1, as the manhunt for missing Jews went on. In the first six days of March five more trains left for Auschwitz (carrying 1,736, 1,758, 1,732, 1,143, and 662 Berlin Jews).

'War is no time to be sentimental,' commented Goebbels.[54] But there was widespread public disquiet at the continuing manhunt, especially after the air raid, and unfortunate scenes outside one Jewish old folks' home where crowds intervened on their behalf: Goebbels professed distress at the tactless timing.[55] He told the S.D. to go easy for a few weeks. After one more transport, of 947 Jews to Auschwitz on March 12, the operation was halted for five weeks.

Widespread damage had however been done. General Dittmar remarked that public concern was growing about Hitler's military leadership, about the air raids, and about the Jewish problem.[56] It did not surprise Goebbels that most of the hate-mail after the total-war speech came from Jews.[57] A significant number of letter writers protested about his picking on the Jews, and some even saw a poetic justice in the air raids on Nazi Germany.[58]

As more than once before, he sought absolution from his Führer. After seeing him on March 8 at Vinnitsa he again noted for the record that Hitler had endorsed his plans to rid Berlin of its Jews. There was much the same diary entry after Hitler phoned him on the fourteenth, and on the twentieth he noted how pleased the Führer, visiting Berlin, had been when he told him that a large part of the Jews had now gone.[59]

The war had, agreed Hitler, enabled them to tackle a number of thorny problems. In mid-April however Goebbels found his city once more seemingly 'overrun' with Jews claiming exemption from deportation. He ordered a thorough screening. 'I am convinced,' he dictated, 'that by ridding Berlin of the Jews I have achieved one of my greatest political goals.'[60]

GOEBBELS' CHRONIC AILMENT, eczema, had returned. He tried to rest out at Lanke. Magda returned to her clinic and remained there, bedridden and despairing, for several weeks.[61] She began drafting her will; once she joined her husband out at Lanke, but he found the melancholy of the Brandenburg landscape getting him down. Morell's assistant Dr Richard Weber gave him a course of the hormone treatment Homoseran and the eczema began to go.[62]

Round-the-clock bombing by the British and Americans had now begun, giving him a headache which no jabs could cure. The British rained fake ration cards on the cities too.[63] True, Germany had still lost only sixteen thousand dead in the raids, but they eroded Nazi prestige and they added to Goebbels' workload as chairman of the inter-departmental committee which directed relief operations.[64] He had accepted this post in January as a stepping stone to power; now it was proving anything but a sinecure.

Among his proposals was one that the most heavily bombed cities be granted the right to wear the Iron Cross in their coat of arms.[65] He also had to suppress inopportune song-hits. The radio band was no longer allowed to play 'I Dance in your Arms right up to the Skies.'[66] Once Fritzsche boasted in a broadcast that despite the latest raids on Essen the Krupps works was still working flat out. The bombers returned, and Goebbels got the blame.[67]

THAT APRIL HE MADE a well-publicized tour of Essen. On the way over, Göring's deputy Milch, who had spent two traumatic weeks on the Stalingrad front, remarked that if *he* had been Paulus he would have disobeyed Hitler and brought the Sixth Army out to safety.[68] Disobey Hitler? Goebbels – for the record – disputed the very notion in his diary, but it clearly gave food for thought. His mother also told him about growing public dissatisfaction with their commanders.[69] Conversely, captured Russian soldiers' letters provided evidence of the enemy's high morale. Stalin's slogan – 'Better to die on your feet than survive on your knees' – had taken root, nurtured by the brutality of the Nazis on Russian soil.[70]

There were thus fundamental problems that Goebbels needed to discuss with Hitler, still recuperating from the winter's strains on the Obersalzberg.

He set off for Berchtesgaden late on April 11, ostensibly for a manpower conference called by Göring with Speer and Ley.[71] The next morning however he learned that Hitler would not see him, pleading lack of time.[72]

Goebbels took this snub very hard; he declared that he would leave at once, and ducked the Göring conference. He dictated a petulant note in his diary that he must have an entire afternoon with the Führer. He masked his injured feelings with a real or imaginary kidney-stone attack. Ley, taken in (again), sent a posy of hand-picked flowers to the train. Morell was summoned to inject morphine; aboard the rattling train Werner Naumann administered two more shots during the night. The minister had the train halted some distance from Berlin's Anhalt station so that nobody would see him alighting, and he took to his bed moaning with pain.[73]

Still sulking, he refused to allow the stockpiled 'Adolf Hitler is victory' posters to go up for the Führer's coming birthday.[74] By the fourteenth the malaise had passed; although an X-ray examination had found nothing, he toyed with taking a cure in Dresden or Karlsbad.[75]

At the end of the month he was still angling for that audience with Hitler, but Bormann kept fobbing him off again. He had a healthy respect for Martin Bormann and he recognized his inherent weakness in his dealings with him. Once over lunch he accurately described him as 'a primitive OGPU type' like the Russians who had escorted Molotov to Berlin in 1940; two days later he warned his staff never to repeat what they heard him say at table.[76]

49: *The Katyn Massacre*

UNTIL THE SPRING OF 1943 two broad streams had carried his propaganda message out to the world, antisemitism and anti-communism.[1] In April 1943 these streams converged in the forest of Katyn, near Smolensk. 'The great surge in antisemitic propaganda,' Fritzsche would testify, 'only really began after Katyn.'[2] After murdering many thousands of Polish officers and intellectuals in the Katyn forest in 1940 Stalin's secret police had planted trees to conceal the graves. Locals had tipped off the Germans in 1942, but it had taken until now for the ground to thaw.

Two months earlier Goebbels had remarked that 'ghosts were coming to life' as other Soviet atrocities in Latvia were revealed.[3] In March 1943 Moscow had begun a serious dispute with the Polish exile government in London over their countries' future common frontier.[4]

It was now that the German troops uncovered at Katyn the mass graves of thousands of Polish prisoners of war, their hands crudely bound with barbed wire, expertly executed by the Russians by bullets in the nape of the neck. The first such grave yielded 4,143 victims.[5] On April 4 an S.S. Unterscharführer reported that they had already found the corpses of a Polish general, senior staff officers, a bishop – and diaries.[6] The letters and diaries in the corpses' pockets had expired, like their authors, in April 1940 when the Russians controlled the region. 'Once again,' dictated Goebbels, 'one sees how the Jews work hand in hand, and what Europe may expect if it ever falls into the hands of the eastern or western denizens of this subversive race.'[7]

Goebbels acted swiftly and shrewdly. He briefed his staff at his April 8 morning conference that he was sending neutral journalists and Polish community leaders with captured British medical officers to witness the opening of further mass graves.[8] Berndt, his finest propagandist, had now returned from Tunisia: Goebbels put him in charge. By April 13 twelve thousand rotting corpses had been exhumed.[9] 'One dare not think what would become of Germany and Europe if this Asiatic-Jewish torrent ever burst upon our country and continent,' wrote Goebbels after seeing the film footage.[10]

He ordered his editors to feature Katyn two or three times each week. Undeniably embarrassed by the discovery, Moscow alternately called the graves 'ancient burial grounds' and blamed the Nazis.[11] Shocked by the revelations, the Polish exile prime minister General Wladyslaw Sikorski appealed to the

International Red Cross to investigate Katyn; Stalin broke off diplomatic relations with him.[12] Goebbels was dizzy with pride at this unexpected triumph of his propaganda. Katyn was suddenly a threat to Churchill's carefully constructed grand coalition. The British prime minister (that 'vassal of the Jews')[13] did as Goebbels himself would have done: He thrice denied all evidence of Soviet culpability for the massacres. When a British plane-crash shortly killed off the inconvenient Polish prime minister Sikorski – the pilot alone survived – Goebbels found still further grist for his pernicious propaganda mills.[14]

The success of the Katyn revelations in a Germany long saturated with anti-Soviet atrocity propaganda was only limited. Editors soon tired of carrying the story. The public profoundly mistrusted the revelations. One reaction cited by the S.D. was that they had no right to get worked up since the Nazis had liquidated far more Poles and Jews than had the Russians.[15] One minor annoyance was when German ammunition was found in some of the graves, probably part of the pre-Barbarossa deliveries to Stalin.[16] When still more Soviet mass graves were found at Vinnitsa, the people commented: 'We also ruthlessly wiped out all opposition elements in the east.'[17]

IN NAZI-OCCUPIED POLAND, the *Generalgouvernement*, the impact of Katyn was equally disappointing.

Goebbels had tried for months to settle his differences with Hans Frank, but the uproar caused by Himmler's anti-Jewish measures rendered all coherent propaganda work impossible.[18] Over lunch on May 9 Hitler and Goebbels agreed that Frank had lost control, but there was nobody fit to replace him.[19] As anti-German incidents multiplied, Frank blamed the S.S.; on May 26 Himmler disclosed to him that he was going to evacuate the last 250,000 Polish Jews regardless.[20] When Goebbels again suggested Frank's replacement in June, Hitler exonerated the Governor-General: 'He has to extract food supplies, prevent the unification of the people, ship out the Jews and yet at the same time accommodate the influx of the Jews from the Reich.'[21]

According to the propaganda minister, Hitler ordered him to link the Jews directly to Katyn.[22]

At the end of April Goebbels composed another major assault on the Jews for *Das Reich*. In this he argued that the Jews had wanted this war. The warmongers in London and Washington were all Jews, as were the Soviet secret police and commissars.[23] 'It is therefore a matter of state security,' he explained, 'for us to take certain steps in our own country.' This was now a race war, in which the Jews aimed at the destruction of the German people. The Jews had always been criminals, he continued: 'The Jews have not enjoyed such remarkable rewards because they are cleverer than non-Jews, but because they operate by a different code of ethics.' Hitler's January 1939 prophecy was ineluctably coming true. 'One day the same punishment will be meted out to Jews worldwide as they are suffering in Germany today.' '*There is no place for sentimental considerations,*' he emphasized. 'When they hatched their plot for the total destruction of the German people they were signing their own death warrant.'[24] Newspapers around the world quoted surprisingly freely from the article, and he took this as proof that many people in every editorial office thought like him.[25]

Despite the apparent implicit admissions in the article, when his press officer showed him foreign allegations about 'Gestapo extermination camps' in Poland, claiming that Jews and others were being gassed and cremated, Goebbels dismissed them as 'sensationalism.'[26] Nevertheless Bormann notified every Reichsleiter and gauleiter including Goebbels in July that Hitler did not want public discussion of any 'overall solution' (*Gesamtlösung*) of the Jewish problem. 'It can however be stated,' Bormann informed them, 'that the Jews are under confinement and being given appropriate employment.'[27]

Goebbels knew different. In the first six months of 1943 fourteen trains had carried 14,620 of his city's Jews to Auschwitz. Over thirty-one thousand Jews had now been expelled from Berlin by the joint efforts of Goebbels, Speer, and the police.[28]

THROUGHOUT THESE MONTHS the Nazi propaganda policies in the eastern territories were chaotic. In occupied Poland there was the usual conflict between rival Nazi agencies. Propaganda was run from Kraków by a capable civil servant, Oberregierungsrat Wilhelm Ohlenbusch, but he was permanently at loggerheads with Hans Frank's press chief Dr Gassner, an Otto Dietrich appointee.[29] Gassner had replaced the once independent Polish press with gutter publications which included pornographic Polish-language magazines whose explicit purpose was to undermine family life and thus destroy Polish society; ✳ conversely Gassner prohibited the importation of the 'healthy' publications produced in Germany under Goebbels' fiat, like *Mother and Child*.[30]

As for the Soviet Union, right up until February 1944 Goebbels bickered with Rosenberg, Bormann, and the tiresome pedant Lammers over jurisdiction.[31] He pleaded for a far-reaching proclamation designed to win over the Russian peoples. He was in no doubt that a slogan that the Germans were fighting the bolsheviks and not the Russian people would significantly aid the propaganda battle.[32] Hitler flatly opposed this: His view was that they could hardly seize the Russian peasants' last cattle at the same time as wooing them for support.[33] Knowing that Hitler and Himmler vehemently opposed it, the German army did not back Goebbels.[34] Several times he resolved to discuss the issue with Hitler, only to lose courage when he faced those steely blue-gray eyes.[35]

So the unproductive bickering with Rosenberg continued.[36] Rosenberg demanded that Goebbels shut down Taubert's eastern propaganda unit. 'It's perfectly obvious,' Goebbels wrote to Hitler, 'that I as propaganda minister should have responsibility for all propaganda throughout the Reich.'[37] The finance ministry cut off all his funds for propaganda work in the east.[38] When Bormann conveyed his protests to the Wolf's Lair, Hitler – after further ·

✳ *PlayBoy, Hustler, Penthouse, even Walt Disney is in Porno movie business !*

delay – agreed that all propaganda *should* be in one hand, and he signed a decree to this effect in August, allowing Goebbels to attach a propaganda field office (*Reichspropaganda-Amt*) to each Nazi governor in the east.[39] But time was already running out: By the time they were in place (and then only in Minsk, Riga, Reval, and Kaunas)[40] it would be February 1944, and the Nazi dominion was coming to an end. Goebbels blamed Rosenberg. 'Now we've missed the bus,' he sourly observed in February 1944.[41]

Their unsettled policies toward the captive lieutenant-general Andrei Vlasov further illustrated this rift at the top. This renegade Russian offered to raise an army of fellow prisoners to overthrow bolshevism in Russia. Goebbels backed him; again Himmler and Hitler did not.[42] When Hitler did grudgingly allow the project to go ahead, it was purely as a dishonest propaganda ploy.[43] Goebbels' radio stations thereupon took up Vlasov's cause. After hearing one such broadcast on his automobile radio in July, Himmler wrote, 'I forbid the S.S. once and for all to fall in, in any way whatsoever, with the entire bolshevik-Vlasov act which the Wehrmacht are staging and which the Führer has so clearly rejected.'[44]

On the very next day the Soviet government established near Moscow the mirror-image of the Vlasov movement – a Free Germany Committee under the communist writer Erich Weinert.[45] Its members were a ragbag of captured German officers, Jews, and other émigrés; its first manifesto was signed by Goebbels' old sparring partners in the Battle for Berlin, Walter Ulbricht and Wilhelm Pieck. Two months later the Russians formed a renegade League of German Officers – primarily those captured at Stalingrad like General Walter von Seydlitz.[46]

Stalingrad had deeply afflicted German morale. The relatives of the one hundred thousand missing German soldiers had been dismayed by Goebbels' revelations about the fate of the Polish prisoners in Soviet hands.[47] The slew of nightly British raids on the Ruhr, coinciding as they did with a drastic cut in the meat ration, further eroded morale. Moreover the German submarine campaign was in disarray as the British introduced new radar devices.[48] Germany was passing through a trough in the waves, said Goebbels; but the waves themselves seemed to be getting ever taller.[49] Women shoppers in Berlin were heard openly cursing this 'damned war.'[50] They inveighed against Göring, and sometimes even against Hitler. Goebbels wished that he could persuade these two to speak up, or at least to pay their respects in a Ruhr city. Limping down Wilhelm Strasse with Dr Naumann after dining with Hitler in May, he spoke pointedly of the need to install a clear political leadership at home.[51]

Speaking alone with Goebbels in his private quarters in the chancellery, Hitler again – allegedly – suggested they whip up more antisemitic propaganda as a smoke screen. Goebbels pointed out that it already accounted for eighty percent of their overseas broadcast output. The virus was already implanted throughout Europe. Antisemitism was steadily rising overseas, and Goebbels was proud to take the credit.[52] Turning to the bombing war, Hitler ruled out copying the Japanese example of executing captured Allied air crews. The Allies would shortly have a hundred thousand more German prisoners, taken in Tunisia, and this probably influenced his decision. He was sick of war, he told Goebbels. He longed to take off his field-gray uniform and become a human being again. He was sick of his generals too: They were all liars, disloyal, reactionary, and hostile to National Socialism.[53] Goebbels will not have disagreed.

THE IMMINENT FINAL LOSS of North Africa faced Goebbels with the problem of explaining how Field Marshal Rommel had been spirited out of Tunisia to safety two months before.[54] Over tea with Goebbels and Berndt, a dispirited and embittered Rommel said that the Italians really were useless as fighters.

Italy was clearly the Allies' next invasion target, with Sicily particularly at risk. Abwehr chief Admiral Canaris however boasted to Goebbels that he had recovered from a corpse washed ashore in Spain a secret letter to General Sir Harold Alexander revealing that the Allies would invade Sardinia.[55] Goebbels – like Hitler – suspected a British plant, and they were right. He did not know what to make of Canaris, this pink-faced and flabby-fingered Abwehr chief. At Colonel Martin's pleading he had first met Canaris a month earlier.[56] Flourishing a sheaf of papers Canaris claimed to have correctly predicted the strength of Soviet armor before BARBAROSSA and the site of the Allied invasion of North-west Africa in November 1942. 'Despite all the assertions,' dictated Goebbels, unconvinced, 'our political and military Intelligence just stinks.'[57]

IN THE MIDDLE of May 1943 the last Axis positions in Tunisia were overrun. As with Stalingrad, Goebbels had prepared an impressive radio ceremony to cushion the bad news. Hitler forbade the broadcast. Goebbels made no secret of his irritation.[58]

To set the loss of North Africa in perspective he wrote a clever leading article entitled 'With sovereign calm.' 'A victory of initially only the barest significance can turn out to be decisive in a war,' he argued, 'while one that has been contested over immense areas and at the cost of many men and much material may soon pale into insignificance.' Let nobody claim, he wrote, that the loss of North Africa was on the same historical plane as Britain's expulsion from Europe at Dunkirk. 'For years,' he scoffed, 'the Allies have committed their entire armed might – to capture what is in effect just barren desert.' 'We have suffered a setback at the periphery,' he conceded, 'but the center of our war effort remains totally undamaged.'[59]

This was an unfortunate turn of phrase, as Churchill was now raining explosives and fire bombs on Hitler's cities night after night. Goebbels pronounced once more that it was the British who had started this bombing of civilians. It was casuistry – true or false, it hardly mattered. Essen, Dortmund, Düsseldorf, and Duisburg were ravaged within days. Sometimes a handful of Mosquito bombers, each armed with a one-ton sting, left a trail of sirens across

Germany that drove twenty-five million Germans into their wet and stinking air-raid shelters.[60] In one daring low-level raid the heavy bombers breached several Ruhr dams.[61] The deluge drowned over a thousand people. Goebbels learned that the British were saying that a Jewish émigré had master-minded this raid.[62] On the evening of May 21 Speer, Ley, and Funk came to see him. They all agreed that the country was in the grip of a 'Göring crisis' – which was an implicit criticism of Hitler too, for tolerating the indolent Reichsmarschall.

In *Das Reich* on May 30 Goebbels lectured his readers on 'The nature of crises.' Was it not Schlieffen, he asked, who had remarked that a battle without a crisis was just a skirmish? Just as a man who survived an illness felt a new urge to live, a nation too must sense 'the healing power of crisis.'[63] And so his silver prose ran on – column after column of clever dialectics. But he could not fool everybody all the time. Still resting at the Berghof, Hitler checked the speech which Goebbels proposed to deliver on June 5. Where the minister had written the words *when victory is ours*, Hitler crossed them out and inked over it, 'when this struggle is over.'[64]

THE SPEECH, TO BERLIN munitions workers, was his first to be devoted to the enemy raids. 'There is only one thought in the mind of the entire German people,' he said, 'and that is to repay the enemy in his own coin.' He spoke of his tour of the Ruhr cities: 2,450 people had been burned alive in Wuppertal on May 29. 'One day,' he promised, 'the hour of retribution will come.' He then launched into a fresh diatribe against the Jews.[65]

Compounding his problems, both he and Magda were ill. Magda had spent several weeks in hospitals undergoing a painful operation on her face; her trigeminal nerve was playing up.[66] The surgeon had botched the operation, and the minister sent her off to the White Hart clinic in Dresden to recuperate.

Infuriatingly, his own eczema had returned. Professor Morell's assistant Dr Weber treated Goebbels with multivitamins, the muscle tonics Tonophosphan and Cortiron, and with injections of Morell's proprietary liver extract; the latter gave the minister three days of excruciating headaches. 'The Reich minister now has so many pockmarks and scars,' Weber advised Morell, 'that injections are virtually impossible.' In mid-July 1943 Dr Weber reverted to his own Homoseran injections. Finally cured, Goebbels gave him two thousand marks, a radio set, and a signed photograph as a reward.[67]

Magda stayed in Dresden until August. Goebbels sent his young and personable chief aide Dr Werner Naumann, who had just turned thirty-four, to join her there on sick-leave.[68] Leaving Hadamovsky or Fritzsche to run the ministerial conferences – the participants hung around outside swapping blasphemous jokes about Hitler and their minister – Goebbels spent Whitsun out at Lanke alone, recovering from the eczema.[69]

With Magda away, some things had not changed. One evening a sentry detected a pretty girl cycling inside the perimeter fence and apprehended her: At which an angry figure limped out of the trees ahead. Volubly cursing the soldier, Goebbels took charge of his young female guest, an actress whom he had invited round for the evening.[70]

As Düsseldorf, Bochum, Oberhausen, Cologne, and Krefeld were devastated by two-thousand-ton bombing raids during June, Goebbels ordered newsreel teams to capture the harrowing scenes for the archives. Dr Gutterer thoughtlessly included some of the footage in one week's newsreel. The screen images of mangled, headless infants and bulldozers tipping bodies into pits were so terrifying that Magda and the children burst into tears at the preview. 'If these pictures have this effect on my National Socialist family,' shrieked Goebbels at his next conference, 'just imagine the utter panic in the public!' 'Whoever let that through understands as much about propaganda as a cow about the quantum theory!'[71] Colonel Martin asked Magda about her husband's callous behavior toward his staff. 'If he talks with the children for longer than a couple of minutes,' she replied with a sigh, 'you can be sure that eventually they will all be in tears. They just can't take his brand of mordant sarcasm.'[72]

Guided by increasingly accurate radar, the enemy's bombers were pulverizing the Ruhr. Goebbels followed them around, speaking in city after city in an undeclared personal campaign for Hitler's succession. He ordered cities to evacuate all non-essential personnel – old people's homes into ancient castles and monasteries, entire schools to provinces remote from the enemy's airfields.[73] Over the next months he issued 157 civil defense circulars covering every aspect of the new warfare from the procurement of excavators for digging mass graves, the escorting or burial of enemy bomber crews, and the use of subway systems for fleeing through firestorms – a new phenomenon in war – to the recovery of the air-raid dead.[74] He ordered static water tanks to be built everywhere. 'In the big conflagrations,' Berndt explained to the gauleiters, 'many people have died even after the All Clear was sounded because they lacked the water to soak their clothing and face-cloths to enable them to breathe.'[75]

Speaking that day at the mass funeral of the Wuppertal air-raid victims Goebbels swore vengeance in their name, and at another rally in the Westphalia Hall at Dortmund, as the wind blew the acrid smell of a burned-out city through the building's windowless sockets, he confided to twenty thousand Ruhr workers that their scientists were working on that revenge even now.[76]

In Stalingrad, he told his staff the next day, wedging his knees nonchalantly against his desk, a quarter of a million soldiers had suffered. But in the Ruhr seven or eight million ordinary people were facing sudden death each night. 'Hats off to them all,' he said. 'Magnificent!' And he snapped a flawless imaginary salute to the unseen heroes.[77]

JUNE 1943 WAS NEARLY OVER. Hitler was about to return to the Wolf's Lair in East Prussia for Operation CITADEL, his tank battle against the Russians at Kursk. Before leaving he called Goebbels down to the Berghof. Comfortably surrounded by his friends and his favorite oil paintings he listened sympathetically to Goebbels' nightmarish descriptions of the air raids and assured him that he was going to speak his mind to the Reichsmarschall the next day. The damage that mattered, he continued, was that to the arms factories; the human casualties were regrettable, but inevitable. He actually welcomed the destruction of the cities; after the war Germany would have fifteen million motor cars, most of them the new Volkswagens, and the fusty and ill-bricked cities of old would never sustain the load.[78] He spoke to Goebbels of their coming 'revenge weapons' – mysterious missiles which would soon rain down on London. He admitted that their U-boats had been thwarted, but soon they would return to their hunting grounds, equipped with noise-making decoys and top-secret torpedoes.[79]

Turning to the eastern front Hitler told him he was going to make 'a few necessary adjustments' to the line which might well cost the Russians several armies. Stalin had nothing to match the new Panther and Tiger tanks. But, he admitted, he had been forced by the winter disasters to abandon his old plans to occupy the Caucasus and march into the Middle East.

If the Italians deserted the Axis, Germany would fight on alone – on Italian soil. 'He no longer trusts them out of his sight,' commented Goebbels afterward. In fact it was because of the Italian factor that he was determined not to get too embroiled at Kursk. After supper that evening he found Hitler quiet and pensive, as they chatted around the open fire. Bormann's teleprinter network reported that the British had delivered another raid on Wuppertal – 2,750 more people had been burned alive.

'When I see the Führer in the middle of the night on the Obersalzberg,' dictated Goebbels to his faithful scribe Otte, 'bowed down by all his cares, my love and veneration of him just grow stronger.'

50: *The First Battle of Berlin*

THE TRUTH,' DEFINED JOSEPH GOEBBELS that summer, 'is whatever helps bring victory.'[1] German propaganda could no longer afford the luxuries of 1940. They would have to lie and deceive to survive. The moral high ground was no longer refuge enough, when the very skies rained phosphorus and death.[2]

If July 1942 had brought victories on every front, July 1943 brought only adversity – in Italy, in Russia, and in the air. Historic air and tank battles raged as Hitler's field marshals staged CITADEL, their classic pincer attack on Kursk. A few days later the Allies invaded Sicily in the Mediterranean, Stalin launched his counter-offensive at Orel, and Hitler called off the CITADEL attack.

More than half the letters addressed to Goebbels' special Berlin post-box now were anonymous, a bad sign. Many asked why Hitler and Göring did not speak or visit the bombing disaster zones – Goebbels had banned the use of 'air war zones' as British propaganda was using the phrase to legalize their raids.[3] Goebbels had no inhibitions about appearing. In Cologne his fellow Rhinelanders greeted him with warmth and he responded in their native dialect. Seeing Cologne's historic High Street in ruins, he remembered Hitler's words; what mayor would have dared to demolish this historic boulevard – now a few British blockbusters had done the job for them.[4]

The night train back to Berlin stopped at Erfurt station, scene of many a tryst with Anka Stalherm. Here he received news that the Allies had landed in Sicily. He muttered unpleasant remarks about 'macaroni eaters.'[5] He did not expect the Italians to hold out for long.

His agents had told him that the German people no longer believed in victory.[6] He half shared that view. Visiting Rechlin, the Luftwaffe's experimental research station, he displayed an uncharacteristic pessimism to the air-force colonels and engineers who met him after dinner. 'The situation does look very fraught,' he admitted, 'and one doesn't really know *which* way things are going to go.'[7]

The time was ripe, he decided, to embark on the biggest movie epic the Reich would ever make: it would be called *Kolberg*, the inspiring story of Gneisenau's historic defense of the Baltic city under Napoleonic siege from 1806 to 1807. 'The movie will fit well into the political and military landscape which we shall probably be facing when it appears,' he observed.[8] Directed by Veit Harlan, the movie cost 8·5 million marks to make, eight times the average. Shooting began late in October 1943 and continued throughout 1944; eventually 187,000 soldiers were conscripted as extras, with six thousand horses in some scenes. The city of ancient Kolberg, rebuilt on a movie set outside Berlin, burned for the cameras as satisfyingly as had 'Atlanta' in *Gone with the Wind*.

During these weeks it seemed that his oratory was all that held Germany together. In mid-July General Schmundt, Hitler's chief adjutant, brought 150 staff officers to hear him. Goebbels spoke in melodious tones for two hours and without notes. 'You could have heard a pin drop,' recalled one major. 'I've seldom seem anyone so polite and charming.' The minister was dressed, he recalled, in gray trousers that were perhaps a shade too light, a double-breasted jacket that was a shade too blue, and a black and white tie that was a little too large. 'He had that dreadful limp too. But one completely overlooked all those faults, and he held one's undivided attention.'[9]

'There is no going back,' Goebbels told these officers. 'We've burned our bridges.' Developing a new theme he said that they had won their victories in the first half too easily. Switching to another line, he talked of how convalescents needed spiritual succor. 'Sometimes a patient owes his life to a nurse who exhorts him at the hour of crisis, "You're just feverish, it'll pass by." Obviously,' continued Goebbels, 'it would be stupid for the doctor to tell the patient how sick he really is.' Perhaps that was a tactless argument, in the circumstances. 'The Soviet Union has also survived exceptional crises,' he added wistfully. 'But at the head of the Soviet Union there is a little clique of very energetic, even brutal leaders with the determination to bring their people through.' Before he ended he warned these officers, 'This passage of arms is decisive. Let nobody think that if we get it wrong this time we can have another shot at it in twenty years' time. It's now or never.'[10]

The passage which his audience most vividly recalled was his analogy between their current strategic position and the moment in the 1936 Olympics when the Japanese marathon winner collapsed after breasting the tape. 'Nobody who saw it,' he said, 'will ever forget that. Why? Because here was an individual making a superhuman effort. . . Over the last five kilometers he perhaps told himself, I don't care if I pass out or have a heart attack – I'm going to hit that tape first!' If, he concluded, like the traitors of November 1918 a nation did not intend to stay the course then it would do better not to begin.

'I think that did the trick,' he said to Lieutenant Wilfried von Oven, his personal assistant, afterward. 'You've got to use a lot of analogies with these people.' He threw back his head and guffawed.

The crisis in public morale could not be so easily laughed off. The British fire raids were sometimes killing thousands every night. Somebody suggested requiring everybody to wear fireproof dogtags to facilitate the identification of corpses. Shades of the Yellow Star! Goebbels shuddered and discarded the idea.[11]

'I am afraid,' he dictated, 'that the British are about to reopen the air war with a massive assault on one German city at their next opportunity.'[12]

THAT WAS THE UNEASY MOOD in Berlin on July 24, 1943 – a broiling-hot Saturday. Desperate for a break, Goebbels took his train down to Dresden. Perhaps Magda had divined that he was bringing her white roses, because she was waiting with Naumann on the platform in a dazzling white summer dress. Lieutenant von Oven watched with voyeurish curiosity as his minister planted a kiss on her lips.

Odd news reports were trickling in from Rome. The Fascist Grand Council there had gone into a secret conclave. The following morning's news was bad. Using new electronic counter-measures to blind the radar defenses, the British bombers had wrecked Hamburg. Hitler had withdrawn the city's heavy flak to Italy only two days before. Two hundred thousand people had lost their homes. The city was still burning. At nine P.M. Goebbels returned to Berlin to direct relief operations. Gutterer told him he had ordered fire brigades into Hamburg from all over northern Germany.

There was worse to come. At No. 20 Hermann-Göring Strasse they found the switchboard alive with blinking lamps. Benito Mussolini had been forced out of office and arrested; Marshal Pietro Badoglio, no friend of Germany, had replaced him. It was stunning news. Goebbels gaped at Gutterer: He ordered Naumann back from Dresden: He sank into a chair in the breakfast niche, and broke the silence finally with an expletive, 'Dreckhammel' – though whether the Duce, Badoglio, the monarchy, or all Italians were the animal so specified remained unclear. 'Finis Italiæ!' he exclaimed after another silence.

The phone rang, Hitler ordering him to catch the five-thirty A.M. flight over to headquarters the next morning. That was something. Goebbels brightened. Sitting at Oven's desk, he mimicked in a faint piping voice the Italian crowds he had seen on the newsreels: 'Duce. . . Duce. . . Duce. . . !' Then he exclaimed, 'So now we're on our own.'[13]

Fascism in Italy had disappeared. Mussolini had been toppled – in fact by just such a senate as Goebbels had been urging upon Hitler since 1933. The Wolf's Lair hosted the next morning a meeting which was the closest to an emergency Cabinet since 1939. From all over occupied Europe the planes flew into Rastenburg, disgorging onto the runway Himmler, Guderian, Göring, Speer, an ailing Ribbentrop, and the naval commander-in-chief Admiral Karl Dönitz. Rumors swept Germany. Some said that Göring had fled or been shot.

Heinz Guderian confided to Goebbels his own misgivings about the war. Goebbels listened attentively (but assured his diary that the general was an 'ardent and unconditional' supporter of their Führer). Both men felt it was time to start parleying with the enemy.[14]

Hitler's eyes however glinted with a sudden determination. He talked about dropping a paratroop division onto Rome to arrest the king and Badoglio. Ribbentrop, shocked at the possible repercussions, and even Goebbels, whose awe of the Catholic Church had never really left him, talked Hitler out of a plan to smoke out the Vatican as well.

Rommel, flown in from Greece, urged that any military operation be carefully thought out. Goebbels sided with Hitler, feeling that they would achieve more with less by striking instantly.[15] With the issue still unresolved, he flew back to Berlin on the twenty-seventh. Gutterer, Martin, and Hadamovsky met him at Tempelhof with his corpulent chief of staff Gerhard Schach. Radiating false confidence he assured them (untruthfully) that Hitler had taken all the necessary decisions: 'Unfortunately I am not at liberty to tell you what they are.'

Goebbels spoke of his puzzlement at Canaris' failure to give any warning of Mussolini's overthrow.[16] 'I am not having anybody "arresting" me,' he said. He stowed a 6·35 millimeter pistol in his desk, and set up an in-house machine-gun company for the protection of the ministry.[17] Against whom? The summer air was clammy, he could hardly breathe, and nobody spoke their true feelings any more.

AS A DISTRACTION from the worsening news he had his two eldest girls, Helga and Hilde, brought into Berlin. That night, July 27–28, over seven hundred British bombers returned to Hamburg and dropped a further 2,312 tons of bombs creating a firestorm, as the entire center, tinder-dry in the summer drought, caught fire. There was no escape from the holocaust. Twice Goebbels phoned his old friend Karl Kaufmann, the Hamburg gauleiter, one of their best: 'We've got fifteen thousand dead,' shouted Kaufmann, his voice cracking. (Richard Otte, taking dictation the next morning, thought that Goebbels might even have said fifty thousand.) He was talking of evacuating the whole city; Goebbels agreed, and ordered all non-essential personnel to leave Hamburg at once.

As Goebbels entered his ministerial conference at eleven A.M. Berlin's sirens sounded. He waited wordlessly for the nerve-wracking wail to die away. From time to time slips of paper were laid before him, but the American squadrons turned away short of Berlin.[18]

Speer said the next day, 'If the raids continue on this scale, three months will see us relieved of many a problem that exercises us today. Things will slide downhill smoothly, irrevocably, and comparatively fast!'[19] The raids did continue. That night the British dropped another 2,277 tons of bombs on Hamburg. Speer told Hitler that if this happened to six more cities the war would be over.[20] 'Things are blacker than Speer paints them,' exclaimed Milch at an air ministry conference. 'If we get just five or six more attacks like these on Hamburg, the German people will just pack up, however great their willpower.'[21] Goebbels however kept his head. On the last night in July he had leaflets issued to every household ordering all children, old people, and non-essential civilians to leave Berlin.[22] When he addressed a panicky meeting of ministers and state-secretaries, with Hitler's sanction, in his ministry on August 2, Milch kept shouting: 'We have lost the war! Finally lost it!'[23]

Subsequently Hitler agreed that Goebbels should brief all the ministers and state-secretaries like this more often, provided that he did so at the chancellery rather than in his own ministry, and provided that he as Führer was consulted each time first.[24]

It was another important step up the ladder of real power. Goebbels had even begun unconsciously prefacing his utterances with the phrase 'if I were Führer,' and venturing criticisms of their *Führung* – *i.e.*, of what their Führer did.[25] He could afford to. Thanks to his air-raid relief work his popularity was steeply rising, while Göring's was in terminal decline. Nothing, remarked Goebbels, was harder to recapture than lost prestige. He had still not made up all the ground he had lost in 1938, he admitted.[26]

RUMORS RAN RIOT THROUGH Berlin's rapidly emptying streets.[27] One had it that 150,000 had died in Hamburg. Goebbels confidentially informed the gauleiters that 18,400 dead had been recovered so far; he asked them to use schoolchildren to spread counter-rumors through their parents.[28] Soon the whisper was that the reprisal bombardment of London had secretly began.[29]

In fact nearly fifty thousand people had died in Hamburg, literally incinerated inside the bunkers, torn apart by explosives, bodily tossed into the flames by the fiery tornadoes.

With Berlin obviously Churchill's next target for such saturation raids, Goebbels forced the pace of evacuation. Fifteen or twenty trains a day carried schoolchildren, infants, mothers, and the elderly eastward to safety.[30] There was opposition from parents and the host provinces, but Goebbels appealed to all the eastern gauleiters to display the proper 'socialist spirit' toward these people, who had often lost all they had.[31]

, He felt himself like the commander of an important battle front. He intended to show the generals how to win. 'In seven years,' he told his staff, 'I earned one title, as Conqueror of Berlin. In seven weeks I intend to add another: Its Defender.'[32] He was in his element. 'Grievous though it was,' he wrote to Hitler afterward, 'I never felt as good as I did during the bombing of Berlin; because all the medal-hunters got cold feet the moment the going got really tough.'[33]

He did not want a blood bath in his city. The evacuation was brought under control as the party and welfare agencies struggled to get the frail and the defenseless out through the railroad stations before the bomber hordes arrived. White-painted arrows appeared at every street corner telling those who remained which way to run if firestorms broke out.[34]

Slit trenches were dug in the streets and parks, water tanks were built, and the remaining art treasures were crated up and trucked out to safety. Removal vans carried Magda's carpets and porcelain out to Lanke, followed two days later by an Aladdin's hoard of antique furniture and silver toilet articles, clocks, engraved cigarette boxes, chandeliers, mirrors, and inkwells along with Gold-rimmed crystal ware, and a huge tapestry.[35]

Fearing that even the white-walled, horseshoe-shaped mansion at Lanke was a landmark for bombers, Goebbels ordered it draped with eight thousand square meters of camouflage netting.[36]

Writing an understated article, 'A word about the air war,' in the newspapers, Goebbels called for a steadfast heart from his Berliners. 'What the British could take in the autumn of 1940 – for which more than one of us admired them at the time – we must now show we too can take,' he declared, and then turned the compliment as deftly as he uttered it: 'But just as Britain turned a new page in the air war after 1940, so too we shall turn a new page now.' The battle of Berlin, he announced, would soon be joined. 'As Berlin's gauleiter, I shall not, of course, be leaving the capital.'[37]

In this defiant spirit he prepared his capital city for its hour of glory. First he investigated whether his own household bunker would withstand the latest enemy bombs. Architect Hugo Bartels replied candidly that the concrete was thick enough for the bombs of 1941, but they had got bigger since then.[38] Bartels also warned that if a firestorm broke out any papers in the safe would be incinerated along with the people in the bunker. During any alert, Goebbels dictated on the sixth, Emil the butler was to take not only the minister's briefcase but also the pistol into the bunker – following Mussolini's arrest, Goebbels intended to be prepared for anything.[39]

Taking his immediate staff, Goebbels flew over to inspect the damage to Hamburg. As their Junkers 52 droned across the first villa-dotted outskirts there was little to be seen. 'You always tend to expect the worst,' said Goebbels, then caught his breath as the plane banked and acres of charred and lifeless ruins unfurled like a black flag from beneath the wing. Gauleiter Kaufmann, a small, spry figure, however impressed him with what he had done. 'I am convinced,' said Goebbels as they flew back, 'that we'd have won the war long ago if it was up to the party rather than the generals.'[40]

WITH THE EVACUATION of two million civilians and almost all children, Berlin was now ready. The nights were long enough for the British to reach the capital city once more.

On August 23, 1943 they came, 625 heavy bombers carrying 1,765 tons of bombs, but what followed was a bomber-massacre. Under Luftwaffe Major Hajo Herrmann, the fighter defenses had developed new tactics using largely visual sightings rather than airborne radar. The British lost fifty-six bombers; 765 Berliners died, and only twenty-seven of these were children. Goebbels took it as a very personal victory. On the last night of the month the enemy tried it again. This time Field Marshal Milch had pots of magnesium blazing around the city and planes laying vapor mists across which the marauding enemy bombers crawled like clumsy insects on a fluorescent table-cloth. Again using Herrmann's new 'Wild Boar' tactics, the Luftwaffe brought in every available fighter squadron, from as far afield as Denmark and central France.[41] Of the 512 heavy bombers which reached Berlin, forty-seven were destroyed. Only thirteen Berliners died, and no children at all. Churchill had difficulty in mounting a third raid at all. On September 3 he sent 295 bombers, all Lancasters; they lost twenty after killing only 346 Berliners (one of them a child). Unable to sustain such losses (126 bombers in three raids, and many more damaged beyond repair) the British called off the attack.[42]

Coming so soon after the holocaust in Hamburg, this unexpected victory gave a palpable boost to Berlin's morale.[43] There were also fringe benefits as thousands of captured British airmen, Churchill's erstwhile elite, were processed through the Dulag Luft interrogation center near Frankfurt. Milch recommended throwing parties for these Englishmen with high-class call-girls – he understood that Goebbels had 'girls on hand for such purposes;' Gutterer agreed, and briefed Milch to ask the prisoners about Lord Haw-Haw, about the bombing atrocities against women and children, about the massacres at Katyn and Vinnitsa, and about the Jews.[44] In January 1944 Goebbels would ask for an ethnic breakdown of captured aircrews, to prove his theory that Churchill was using primarily Canadians and New Zealanders for his 'terror' raids (the answer has not survived in the files).[45]

EARLY ON SEPTEMBER 8, 1943 the telex machines again began to rattle out disquieting rumors about Italy. At five-twenty P.M. Lieutenant von Oven alerted Goebbels that Eisenhower's headquarters had announced that Italy had capitulated. At six P.M. the B.B.C. confirmed it. With difficulty Goebbels got a line to Rome. The embassy there was frankly incredulous as the king and Badoglio were still denying the reports. Shortly the switchboard lamp labeled 'Der Führer' blinked: Hitler gruffly instructed Goebbels to take the night train out to Rastenburg. He had anticipated this treachery all along, forewarned by intercepts of transatlantic phone calls from Churchill to Roosevelt which revealed the Italian plans. He instructed Rommel to invade northern Italy at once. 'You cannot break your word twice in one century,' dictated Dr Goebbels, alluding to Italy's earlier defection in 1915, 'without having a blot on your political escutcheon for ever more.'[46]

A summer downpour drenched Berlin as his train pulled out at nine-twenty P.M. that evening. Since his special saloon coach had been shunted out of Berlin to safety, four regular sleeping compartments had been emptied of their indignant occupants to make room for him. Here on the train he found Professor Hofer, who was to repair the faulty surgery on Magda's jaw.[47] Hofer told him that it was vital to get Hitler to broadcast to the people.

Hitler had spent the whole of the historic previous day flying down to Zaporozh'ye to see Field Marshal Erich von Manstein, then flying back to his headquarters at the Wolf's Lair. He had not retired until five A.M. Despite this and the shocking news about Italy he was poised and optimistic.[48] He sent for Goebbels straight after breakfast and bragged that he was going to wipe the floor with the Italians: He was ready to write off all of Italy south of the Apennines. In Russia too, he would fall back, building an East Wall along the Dniepr river. Finding him in such a realistic mood, Goebbels ventilated the possibility of cutting a deal with Stalin. Hitler however declined – 'And quite right too,' dictated Goebbels prudently afterward to Otte, 'given the crisis in the east.' Hitler seemed more inclined to parley with the west: Surely the British must see reason eventually? Here it was Goebbels who disagreed, although he did ponder whether taking Sicily might satisfy Britain's imperialist appetite. 'Sooner or later,' Goebbels reflected, 'we shall find ourselves having to lean one way or the other.'[49]

For hours that day – the Wolf's Lair diary shows him lunching and dining with Hitler, and taking tea with him until nearly four A.M. – Goebbels pleaded with Hitler to broadcast to the nation. At 6:35 P.M. the next day, September 10, he finally had him before a microphone, speaking a twenty-page script down the ministry's special line to a tape machine in Berlin.

Hitler's broadcast expressed concern about the 'unique injustice' done to Mussolini; but privately he was more callous. Ice-cold pragmatism, he told Goebbels, would dictate his decisions from now on. Now Germany would retrieve the South Tyrol after all, and all of Austria's former dominions as far as Venice. After a special communiqué about Rommel's success in seizing Rome – 'It is,' dictated Goebbels, 'almost like the great advances of 1939 and 1940 all over' – Hitler's speech went out over the airwaves at eight P.M. The Russians were not mentioned. But Hitler did promise *Vergeltung*, revenge for the air raids.

As the days became weeks, Goebbels often expected the bombers to return to Berlin.[50] Once, Beppo Schmid, commanding the night fighter corps, phoned from Holland warning that massed bomber formations were thundering eastward overhead; but their target was Hanover.[51]

Goebbels shifted Magda and the children out to Lanke, where his mother and sister were also living. Their children went by pony cart to the local village school at Wandlitz, leading a Snow White existence with ponies, horses, rabbits, and goats crowding their brief lives.[52] Magda's trigeminal nerve still caused her agony, but Hitler talked her out of an operation, fearing that she would be permanently disfigured.[53] Goebbels delved into Machiavelli, reading his *Thoughts on Politics and War*.[54]

His own literary efforts were complicated by the reversal in Germany's fortunes. Preparing his next anthology of articles and speeches for publication, he now found it prudent to omit several passages where his bolder predictions had been overtaken by events.[55]

51: *The White Suit Bespattered*

ON THE DAY AFTER GOEBBELS' return from the Wolf's Lair, Hitler's special forces liberated Mussolini from his mountain-top prison. Goebbels was initially dismayed, fearing that the Duce's reincarnation would thwart their revanchist ambitions in northern Italy. The communiqué was however a welcome boost to morale.[1]

There was a second boost when Otto Dietrich announced that they were about to throw the American invasion forces back into the sea at Salerno. (They didn't.) Coupled with a spate of recent death sentences and the absence of air raids these announcements had a steadying effect.[2] Goebbels assessed that the low, marked by the Hamburg raids, had been passed.[3] He took stock. Air-raid damage by the end of September 1943 had already cost thirty-two million marks; but the final replacement of damaged cities, factories, roads, and railways would cost about one hundred and twenty millions.[4] Germany had lost 72,000 dead in the air raids; but they had evacuated around 3·9 million civilians to safety.[5] Others were put out of harm's way by more radical means: Goebbels noted with approval that the ministry of justice speeded up the execution of all condemned prisoners to avoid their escape during air raids.[6]

The invasion battle at Salerno had taken a sudden turn for the worse after the Allied warships brought up their big guns. In a barrage of phone calls to the Wolf's Lair Goebbels protested that once again it was he whom the enemy were mocking for one of Dietrich's gaffes.[7] Hitler invited him out to his headquarters and, pacing up and down his map room until 3:40 A.M., he unburdened himself of many a private thought – including his suspicion that Mussolini might actually have been planning to double-cross them in July.[8] He revealed that Admiral Dönitz already had 120 submarines back at sea, equipped with new radar detectors and torpedoes. He also revealed details of new secret weapons to be ready in January, including a high-speed pilotless flying bomb carrying a one-ton warhead and a ballistic missile weighing fourteen tons. Perhaps, he conjectured, all these would bring Britain to her senses.

Goebbels again raised the topic of secretly negotiating with the enemy, pointing out that Germany had never yet won a war on two fronts. Hitler responded that, if only the Russians did not have the upper hand right now, Stalin would still be a more likely prospect than Churchill. Attending Field Marshal Wilhelm Keitel's sixty-first birthday celebration later that evening,

Goebbels noted that Hitler was far less frank to his generals. The Führer said that victory would go to the side which kept its nerve the longest. 'The more strongly the wind howls,' Goebbels dictated in his 144-page diary entry for this day, 'the more obstinately the Führer leans into it.'

Before parting, Goebbels cunningly persuaded Hitler to receive his arch-enemy in the High Command, Major General Hasso von Wedel, chief of Wehrmacht propaganda. He banked on Hitler taking an instant dislike to this pot-bellied, indolent Epicurean. He wished he could cook Otto Dietrich's goose as effectively.[9]

He was confident that he and Hitler were growing together again. At the Wolf's Lair on October 26, 1943 they spent the whole day side by side, from Hitler's first morning stroll until his nocturnal tea party ended at 3:30 A.M. the next day.[10] His rival Rosenberg would see Hitler soon after – for the last time.[11]

THREE DAYS LATER Joseph Goebbels turned forty-six. He ordered the ministry's evening courier limousine to ferry three ladies of his choice out to join his family celebration at Lanke, and to bring a score of foreign movies for their delectation.[12]

His existence at Lanke was almost too idyllic. Each morning S.S. Sturmführer Rach drove him in the large dark unmarked Mercedes into Berlin, taking the Prenzlau highway rather than the more obvious autobahn, with a carload of detectives tailing them behind.[13] They returned between six and seven P.M., and Magda lined up the children with their butler Emil, a forty-six-year-old six-footer, standing behind them in his livery.

To Goebbels it was often too quiet out here. One Sunday he said with a sigh, 'Three days like this in a row and I'd go raving mad.' He needed the pumping adrenaline, the blinking lights on the telephone console, the burden of life-and-death decisions, the Machiavellian intrigue. He probably even needed the hatred of his enemies. He saw them everywhere – not only in Ribbentrop, and Dietrich, and Rosenberg, but in Hans Lammers for example, a member of the *ancien régime* who seemed dangerously interested in becoming Reich chancellor. 'I'll find enough allies,' predicted Goebbels to his diary, 'to put a stop to that.'[14]

The British press dropped strong hints that Berlin's ordeal was about to resume. The Luftwaffe generals assured Goebbels that this time the enemy would lose thirty or forty percent of their planes each night.[15] Goebbels was ready. Speer's engineers had excavated half of Wilhelms Platz next to the Kaiserhof hotel and built a deep underground command post for Goebbels as gauleiter. They had also strengthened 110,000 basements throughout the city to provide rudimentary shelters for three million people, with space for seven hundred thousand more in bunkers in the city center.[16]

The American day-time bombers were also becoming more active at long range, but bloody losses at Schweinfurt and elsewhere still kept them at a respectful distance from Berlin. From the interrogations of captured American aircrews, Goebbels deduced that many were homesick and few had wanted to fight Germany.[17]

The British night bombers were still the greater danger, and not every city was as well prepared as Berlin. Using German émigrés – the very people whom Goebbels had hounded out of Germany – to broadcast confusing orders to the defenses, the British concentrated 444 heavy bombers on Kassel on October 22: 380 planes dropped their bombs within three miles of the aiming point, a colossal concentration which unleashed Germany's second firestorm. Sixty- ✳ five percent of the city was destroyed.[18] Goebbels arrived there on November 5 to investigate the disaster. The local gauleiter Karl Weinrich turned up late at the freight-yard where the minister's train was forced to halt, then drove off downtown in a heated, armored limousine; Goebbels followed in an open-topped Volkswagen with the local police chief at his side.[19]

Much had been done to prepare Kassel for air raids, but not enough: In other cities the gauleiters had ordered basement connecting-walls torn down to provide tunnels of escape in the event of firestorms. Weinrich, the worst type of good-time gauleiter, had done nothing even to evacuate the children.[20] Goebbels harangued the party dignitaries in the still undamaged city hall. 'I expect that you realize, *Mister* Weinrich,' he concluded sarcastically, 'that the *British* can be blamed for only a fraction of the five thousand dead in Kassel – including a thousand children.' (The death toll from the firestorm rose to eight thousand, nearly six thousand of them killed by carbon-monoxide fumes.)[21] Goebbels had Weinrich dismissed immediately from the party and from all his offices.[22]

Hartmann Lauterbacher, the young gauleiter of Hanover who drove them up the autobahn to his city, was all that Weinrich was not. He had prepared his city well, with shelters big enough for thousands, underground command posts, water tanks, and mobile kitchens. In the thick of one raid he had led police and soldiers through the blazing streets to rescue four thousand civilians entombed in a bunker and in danger of asphyxiation.[23]

These latest raids taught Goebbels and his men a lot for Berlin. He issued instructions that bunkers had to have wider exits and be built in open spaces (he withheld from the public the gruesome details of what had happened inside Hamburg's superheated bunkers).[24] On the same date he forbade military honors for the burial of enemy bomber crews, deeming funeral music, graveside salvoes, and official wreaths inappropriate accompaniments for the burial of 'mass-murderers.'[25]

THE RUSSIAN ADVANCE gathered momentum. The Dniepr line was breached. The Red Army retook Katyn. Goebbels resigned himself to Soviet claims that the Nazis had themselves carried out the Katyn massacres. 'In fact,' he conceded, perhaps referring obliquely to the fate of the Jews whom he had expelled, 'that's one problem that's going to cause us a lot of difficulty in future. The Soviets will indubitably take pains to find as many such mass

✳ *Hellstorm: The Death of Nazi Germany, Thomas Goodrich.*
Institute for Historical Review (IHR) Newport Beach, CA.

graves as possible to pin onto us.'²⁶ Putting Nazi officers on trial in Kharkov the Russians alleged that they had used 'gas vans' for exterminations. Tackled by Fritzsche about these allegations, Goebbels promised vaguely to ask Hitler and Himmler about them.²⁷

He certainly asked Hitler more often now about striking another deal with Stalin. He shared Himmler's nervousness about Ribbentrop's 'lack of flexibility' in foreign policy. He clutched at every straw. When Moscow informed Washington that they were insisting on the Polish-Soviet border that Hitler had agreed to in 1939, Goebbels hoped that this was an overture to Berlin.²⁸

AIR RAIDS HAD KILLED ten thousand more Germans during the month of October 1943.²⁹ Over Berlin however the night skies were still silent. After three weeks of quiet, Goebbels mused, one tended to forget all about air raids.³⁰ November brought blankets of low cloud, fog, and drizzle across the city – these probably closed down the enemy bomber airfields too. If the bombers stood down until February or March 1944, Germany's secret weapons should be ready. Ley told Goebbels that the boffins at Peenemünde expected to have them operational by late January; the young professor Wernher von Braun had boasted that his rocket missiles would turn the tide of the war against Britain.³¹

As the nights drew in, Goebbels wondered every evening whether the bombers were coming back. He began to haunt his new two-story command bunker under Wilhelms Platz. From here, thirty feet below ground, he could follow the invading bomber streams and watch as Schach and the men of the S.A. brigade Feldherrnhalle, their uniforms distinguished by red tabs and piping, plotted the damage reports on a Perspex wall map of Berlin.³² Every household now had fire-buckets, syringes, sand boxes, fire-beaters, shovels, sledgehammers, and axes at the ready. Count von Helldorff would be in charge of the fire-fighting. The air-raid wardens had been drilled. Every man in Berlin knew what to do if the firestorms came.

Goebbels had to leave Berlin for three days for the twentieth anniversary of the Munich putsch. He listened with half an ear to General Jodl's lecture to the gauleiters, and with no interest at all to Göring's.³³ For Goebbels, the highlight was a dinner alone with Himmler. They talked about security operations in Berlin.³⁴ The People's Court and military tribunals had crushed some unrest in Berlin caused by the last air raids. Lieutenant-General Paul von Hase, the city's Prussian, monocled commandant, told Goebbels on the fifteenth that he had condemned a dozen officers to death; Goebbels persuaded him to commute some of the sentences.³⁵

Still the bombers had not come. Altogether, Goebbels' evacuation measures had reduced the city's population by some two million, to just over 3,300,000.³⁶

FROM LATE NOVEMBER 1943 the British bomber commander Sir Arthur Harris – 'the mass murderer,' as Goebbels called him – now really did attempt to repeat in Berlin what he had achieved in Hamburg. The city's outline on the radar screens was unmistakable, with its myriads of lakes, canals, and rivers. In sixteen air raids until the spring Harris would hurl over nine thousand heavy-bomber sorties against this sprawling city, with the stated aim of killing as many of its inhabitants as possible, using the most refined tactics that human devilry could devise.[37]

It began late on November 18, 1943. Flanked by special squadrons carrying electronic jamming equipment, approaching stealthily behind showers of aluminum foil while decoy squadrons dropped marker flares and feinted away to the north and south, the leading squadrons of Harris's main bomber force arrived over Berlin late that night. Seen from the ground it was a frightening spectacle as the first waves of Pathfinder Lancasters, four-engined heavy bombers, guided by radar, arrived above the clouds, their engines' roar filling the horizons, and suddenly lit up the night sky with flares, followed by deadly cascades of aerial pyrotechnics colored in red, green, or yellow to indicate the different aiming points for each wave. The searchlight beams probed and flickered, and silent flashes high above the clouds showed that the 'eighty-eights' and the 105-millimeter heavy gun batteries defending Goebbels' city were engaging their first targets.

That first night only fifty or sixty of Harris's bombers ventured all the way into Berlin's airspace. Damage was negligible. The city's morale, astonishingly, soared. It was like wearing a new white suit, said Goebbels, who ought to know: You were terrified of the first mud-splash until it happened – after that you took the rest in your stride.[38]

Four days later, on Sunday November 22, Harris tried again. With Berlin seemingly safe, shrouded in low, rain soaked clouds, Goebbels was speaking in a high school in suburban Steglitz when a slip of paper was handed to him. His face perceptibly paler, he continued but lost his thread. He had uttered only a few more sentences when the sirens started. Nobody who has lived through an air raid will ever forget their sound. A phone call to the Wilhelms-Platz bunker told him that the bombers were already overhead.

With bombs bursting all over the city he raced back to the bunker, his car twice just missing fresh craters. The bunker was filled with the clatter of teleprinters, hobnailed boots, and unattended telephones. Chain-smoking, he watched as S.A. men grease-chalked the first reports onto the Perspex damage-map. The opera and the Schiller Theater were blazing; the Scala burlesque, and the famous Ufa and Gloria Palace movie theaters – where Lida Baarova had been heckled in 1938 – were already gone. The government district was devastated. About twelve hundred Berliners died and two hundred thousand more were left homeless, including both his mother and his mother-in-law – the home they had been sharing in Flensburger Strasse flattened by a two-ton blockbuster bomb.

For the first time in years Goebbels had no time to dictate a diary.[39] The next evening the sirens sounded again. He rode out the attack in the command bunker. Sprays of incendiaries hit the State Theater and the Reichstag building, but both blazes were extinguished. The Kaiserhof hotel – another historic station in his *via dolorosa* – caught fire and collapsed onto the bunker's entrance. Gutterer, on duty at the propaganda ministry, saved that building almost single-handed. Goebbels called in fire brigades from as far away as Hamburg. He appealed to Potsdam for troops to fight the fires.

The army had an emergency plan code-named VALKYRIE; Major-General Hans-Günther von Rost, chief of staff of Third Army district, gave it a dry run and sent in not only infantry but tanks as well; at two A.M. Goebbels angrily phoned Rost's superior, General Kortzfleisch, to order the tanks off the streets before foreign journalists saw them.[40] Goebbels asked what the devil was going on: In July 1944 he would find out.

It was four A.M. before he got back to No. 20 Hermann-Göring Strasse. The house was a sorry sight, its windows smashed but otherwise intact. He went down to the sleeping cabin in his family bunker – its light-paneled walls embellished incongruously with priceless paintings including Rembrandts, Spitzwegs, Rubens', and Giottos also sheltered from the inferno outside.

Magda was already there. 'One of the wildest nights of my life,' he dictated the next morning, referring to the raids. 'But I think we came out on top.' He woke to a searing headache and the smell of burning. There was no power, heating, or water; he could neither wash nor shave. He groped his way out of the bunker by candlelight. Sixty thousand troops, conjured up seemingly from nowhere by the army, were already clearing the streets and railroad tracks. He dictated a proclamation to the Berliners, and since there were no newspapers he had a million copies handed out at communal feeding centers.[41]

His ministry was stone-cold and, like his official residence, windowless. Momentarily disheartened and needing fresh faith, he did what Churchill did – he had his chauffeur Alfred Rach drive him into the worst-hit areas and let the crowds throng round and slap him on the back. He spied one old crone making the sign of the cross over him and chanting a blessing, and he did not even take that amiss. He heard one shout of 'Plutocrat!' as his limousine bumped past, from somebody who may not have recognized him.[42]

Seventy-five percent of the city's labor force turned up for work that day. That was not bad. As dusk fell the sky still glowed red. Beppo Schmid's monitoring posts heard the bombers preparing to take off in England, but bad weather intervened. Goebbels drove out to the totally undamaged Schwanenwerder peninsula: Their house was warm, the phones here and the radio worked, and there was hot water in the bath. This third attack had taken eight hundred lives, and there were now four hundred thousand homeless, but morale was still high.[43] The B.B.C. claimed that up to forty thousand had died in the two latest raids. Goebbels allowed them their cruel belief.

Lunching with him in the badly damaged chancellery building, Lammers told him that Hitler had ordered all the ministries to stay put. Dr Goebbels was to set up an Air War Inspectorate to prepare every city in Germany for a similar ordeal.[44] The early symptoms of another raid again fizzled out that night.

As munitions minister, Albert Speer was more visibly shaken by the raids when he lunched with Goebbels on Thursday the twenty-sixth. It was not just that his ministry had been totally burned out; Berlin housed one-third of the Reich's electrical engineering plants, mainly in Siemens City, the Siemensstadt suburb. He warned Goebbels that their V-weapons would not now be operational until March. 'They keep slipping back,' noted Goebbels.[45]

At first that night, November 26, the British seemed to be making for Frankfurt, but that was a feint and their bomber formations suddenly turned north to Berlin. The Alkett plant and two more of Berlin's finest opera houses were hit. Alkett's, the only assembly plant for the assault gun, produced one-quarter of all tanks other than the Panther and the Tiger, and nearly half of all field artillery. Without hesitation Goebbels ordered Count von Helldorff to save Alkett's. 'Tanks are more vital than operas right now,' he told Schach, and pushed the button on his console to tell Hitler of his decision.[46]

Three more times he phoned Hitler that night. Beppo Schmid reported that they had shot down a hundred of the attacking bombers, and this raid had killed only eight Berliners. Through his propaganda channels Goebbels however spread the whisper around the world that Berlin was finished.[47]

He felt like a hero. The next day he addressed the entire Reich Cabinet. After he had finished telling them of the battle, they gave him a standing ovation. The last time that had happened was in 1933 when Hitler pulled Germany out of the League of Nations. His star was finally in the ascendant. Going behind Ribbentrop's back he began sending regular commentaries on foreign policy to Hitler.[48] He spent all day with the Führer again on December 19.[49]

'I was able to join you at headquarters more frequently than ever this year,' he wrote him afterward. 'These visits have given me far more than you, *mein Führer*, could possibly divine.'[50]

A FIFTH RAID HAD HIT Berlin with over two thousand tons of bombs on December 2. Forty more bombers had been destroyed. Grimly fought and with no quarter given on either side, the battle of Berlin continued all winter. While Goebbels directed the city's civil defense, Magda handled the tide of public queries and complaints. Her files contain harrowing letters from mothers robbed of their children, and from widows of party 'martyrs' – she had looked after their needs ever since 1934; she controlled a small account from which she judiciously dispensed welfare (N.S.V.) funds to those in need, often asking local party agencies to make discreet inquiries first. ('Subject frequents pubs and tobacco stores,' she might be told; or 'Miss A – has seven illegitimate children, not just three as she claims.') Her advice was always tactful. When women asked whether to baptize their infants, Magda, who had baptized none of hers, replied quoting Frederick the Great –'Blessed be each in his own way.' Her replies could be uncompromising too. A Miss Charlotte

Goebel, who had lost everything in the November air raids and wanted only to return to her native – and remote – Danzig was informed: 'In all such cases where blitz victims with employment here have deserted Berlin, Mrs Goebbels has refused any aid whatsoever and they have had to return to their workplace in Berlin.'[51]

Addressing a youth film festival on November 28 Dr Goebbels warned the *britische gentlemen* that they would never score an 'easy, cheap, and totally unmilitary' victory. The British were hoping to win by a war of fire and flame against women and children. 'In the name of the citizens of this capital, and in the name of the entire German people, let me give them this reply. *Never!*' To rising applause he announced: 'In Germany today there is no more urgent demand than that we pay back the criminals on the Thames with added interest for what they have done to us.' Day and night, he promised, this reprisal was being prepared. 'When one day retribution comes, and it's the British people's turn to hurt, then we shall weep not one tear for them.'[52]

A few days later he harangued two score German air attachés seated around a long table at his ministry. Rapping his index finger on the table he taught them about the rift that must come between the Allies, and compared Germany's situation now with the Nazi party's on the eve of power. He brooked no discussion afterward, but silently shook each officer's hand on leaving. 'You had the feeling,' wrote one, 'that Mephistopheles himself had just shaken hands with you.'[53]

Writing in *Das Reich* Goebbels struck an upbeat note. 'When the skies darken and there is scarcely a gleam of light,' he wrote, 'then the people's gaze turns unbidden to the Führer. He is the rock standing in the surging seas of time.'[54]

'ANYTHING IN THE AIR?' Goebbels would now ask Lieutenant von Oven before retiring to bed. If an alert sounded, Oven would let him sleep and dial the minister's extension, 2–4, only after the bombers had reached Mecklenburg. 'About twenty minutes, Herr Minister!' After a while Goebbels would appear in the bunker, immaculately dressed, his tie perfectly knotted.

Göring meanwhile had left for France, sent there by Hitler to prepare revenge raids against London. Before he left, he asked Goebbels to find another word for *catastrophe* – it injured his vanity each time he saw convoys of trucks labeled 'Catastrophe Relief' dashing to the latest bombed city.[55]

At Christmas Goebbels did crack, but only briefly. His adjutants had arranged to show an American movie at Lanke, but Magda had set up her Christmas tree slap in front of the screen. Goebbels threw a tantrum and stormed back to Schwanenwerder, thirty-five miles away. Angry and depressed, he sulked there, glowering into a book of Schopenhauer throughout the festivities.[56]

Reviewing the year in his diary he decided it had been one run of bad luck after another. The British called again, 656 bombers this time laden with death and destruction, if not 'catastrophe' even now. He reached the command bunker just as the flak batteries bellowed into fire. Afterward he drove over to

Neukölln, a working-class district which had been hard hit. The people joked with him, cursed the British, and even shouted 'Heil Hitler' as he left. 'Who ever would have thought that possible of our Neukölln workers,' he exclaimed to Otte.[57]

In fact the Allies now discovered that recently captured German prisoners like those from the battleship *Scharnhorst* had more confidence in victory than ever. 'We must win,' said one, simply, 'and therefore we shall win.' One Viennese-born Luftwaffe lieutenant termed Goebbels' emphasis on 'strength through fear' particularly effective.[58] 'Butcher' Harris, as he liked to be known, had under-estimated the Berliners. His first twelve raids had killed 5,166 people and destroyed one-fifth of the available housing; but shorn of its bureaucracy, Speer's arms output in Berlin was actually increasing.[59]

Visiting the Wolf's Lair in East Prussia, Goebbels found workers again strengthening the bunkers. Sixteen feet of reinforced concrete would henceforth protect Hitler, three times the thickness of the gauleiter's air-raid shelter in Berlin.

52: *When the Going gets Tough*

W E DO NOT KNOW HOW LONG this war will last,' admitted Goebbels in his broadcast on the eve of 1944. 'It would be idle to speculate.'[1] To the party faithful he dictated a new slogan: 'Everything is possible in this war except for one thing – that we ever capitulate.'[2]

On this he and Hitler saw completely eye to eye. During their ten recorded meetings in the course of 1944 they never seriously discussed suing for peace. Goebbels invariably returned to his ministry with his engines recharged by contact with Hitler. To the end of his life he felt totally inferior, even intellectually, to him. 'My dear Naumann,' he would say to his closest aide, 'right now I don't know what the Führer is planning. But I am convinced that he will see us through.'[3]

On this occasion, in the first days of January 1944, they examined a map of London and picked out the most rewarding targets for their rockets and flying bombs. After three undisturbed years, the British were in for a dreadful awakening, Goebbels commented to his staff afterward. 'There's no defense. No warning. Bam! – It just smacks into the unsuspecting city.'[4]

Months would first have to elapse. When Göring launched several conventional raids on London in January, Goebbels forbade newspapers to use the word *Vergeltung* (retribution) or even to adopt tones of triumph or satisfaction.[5]

Responsibility for the civil defense of all of Germany's cities gave him the cachet that he had until now lacked when speaking to high-ranking officers. 'Some of you,' he told three hundred officers assembled for Nazi indoctrination courses in Posen on January 25, 'might well say, a fat lot you people back home know! But, if we disregard for a moment the misery that the enemy's terror raids have inflicted upon us, I am happy about them in one respect: That I can now speak to you, not as a desk-warrior but as the representative of a multi-million-inhabitant city that has been through catastrophes unparalleled by anything that has gone before in history.'[6]

The British were putting out reports, still not denied by him, that up to a million had died in their raids on Berlin.[7] On January 28 Churchill sent 596 bombers to unload 1,954 tons of bombs on the western and south-western suburbs. Reuters agency admitted that the British were trying to burn down whole districts.[8] Among the buildings destroyed this time were the Nollendorf

454

and State theaters.⁹ One hundred thousand more Berliners lost their homes, and forty-six more bombers were shot down. The next raid, on January 30, was the heaviest yet: 489 planes dropped 12,961 tons of bombs. Goebbels surfaced from his bunker to find the doors and windows at Hermann-Göring Strasse blown out. He idly traced a swastika in the mortar dust that covered his desk – then brushed it aside.¹⁰

When he drove around the city a few days later the trams and subways were running again, and eighty-five percent of the labor force was already back at work. At Mariannen-Strasse, where a building had pancaked, he watched rescue operations for a while and spoke with weeping survivors until hope for their families was abandoned. He began to fear that Berlin's morale was indeed cracking.¹¹

Unquestionably, it called for moral fiber – or many protecting feet of concrete – to stay on in Berlin. Goebbels asked Hitler to award the highest medals for bravery to Berlin's top officials Gerhard Schach and police chief Count von Helldorff.¹² He pinned the decorations on these close friends on February 9. 'I have found my colleagues in Berlin to be worth their weight in Gold,' he dictated. 'For the most part they are veterans of the years of struggle, utterly loyal, and willing to go through thick and thin with me.'¹³

On the fifteenth Beppo Schmid warned that the bombers were again heading for Berlin. This time Göring also phoned, to say that he had given the flak artillery a free hand. Goebbels had time to bath and dine before the sirens sounded; 806 bombers bore down on his city. The 2,643 tons of bombs they dropped were widely scattered; one demolished the Hotel Bristol, killing all but eight guests.¹⁴

The city's ordeal was almost over. The British aircrew losses were steadily approaching limits that were unacceptable even to Harris. On February 19, a crystal-clear night, they lost seventy-eight out of 730 bombers raiding Leipzig. Eyes smarting from smoke and fumes, and head aching from 'bunker sickness,' Goebbels again toured the bomb-ravaged streets of his capital. (Hitler made no attempt to emulate him, either now or later.)¹⁵

THE ALLIES MIGHT HAVE the bigger bombs, but the Nazis still believed they had the better cause. Addressing the senior officers' indoctrination course at Posen on January 25, 1944 Goebbels suggested that their ideology compensated for the material supremacy of their adversaries. 'In the heavy raids on the Reich capital,' he told them, 'six hundred thousand lost their homes in two consecutive nights.' Just one such raid in 1918 would have brought the war to an end. 'If I say that at the end of such an ideological conflict there will be only the survivors and the dead,' remarked Goebbels opaquely, 'this should not be taken as meaning that the inevitable outcome will be the utter physical extermination of this or that section of the population.'¹⁶

This Goebbels speech is worth mentioning if only because on the next day Himmler spoke bluntly to the same audience about the fate of Germany's Jews.¹⁷

When he announced that they had totally solved the Jewish problem, most of the officers applauded.[18] 'We were all there in Posen,' recalled one of them, a rear-admiral, 'when That Man told us how he had killed off the Jews. . . I can still recall precisely how he told us: If people ask me, "Why did you have to kill the children too?," then I can only say, "I'm not such a coward that I leave for my children something I can do myself."'[19]

Goebbels was not one of Himmler's audience, but he did learn of a strange episode the very next day at Hitler's headquarters. Unsettled by the pernicious influence of the propaganda spewing forth from Moscow, from the Seydlitz traitors, Hitler tried to inspire these same officers with talk of the coming new secret weapons. 'If the worse comes to the worst,' he then said, 'and if I am ever deserted as supreme commander by my people, then I shall still expect my entire officer corps to muster around me with daggers drawn. . .' At this moment Field Marshal von Manstein, one of Goebbels' bêtes noires, rose and called out: 'And so it will be, mein Führer!'[20]

It was an interpolation of painful ambiguity. Hitler initially took it as a compliment; so, when he read the transcript, did Goebbels.[21] But he shortly realized that it was in reality a 'stupid interruption' designed to provoke.[22] For weeks, fumed Goebbels, Manstein had been demanding permission to retreat before the Soviet onslaught. Between every line was however the field marshal's real message to Corporal Hitler: This is your war, not mine – let's see how your vaunted military genius gets you out of this mess. 'Our generals want defeats,' he exclaimed. 'Not defeat – not even they are as blind as that.'[23]

Defeat still did not seem inevitable, when viewed from No. 20 Hermann-Göring Strasse. Addressing the gauleiters assembled in Munich on February 23, Goebbels reported that despite the thirty to forty percent destruction of Berlin, arms output had actually increased. The flying bomb should begin operations early in April, followed soon after by the rocket missile.[24] 'The Germans are still pinning their hopes on Vergeltung,' dictated Goebbels, worried. 'People are vesting far greater hopes in it than they are actually entitled to.'[25] He again prohibited any official use of the V-word but he promised the gauleiters that there would be reprisal raids.

Over dinner on the twenty-eighth Hitler's adjutant General Schmundt discussed with him their problem-generals. 'They're as thick as thieves,' the general growled. Goebbels suggested that as during the Gregor Strasser crisis of 1932, when the gauleiters had sworn loyalty to Hitler, all their field marshals should sign a loyalty declaration now. It was a good idea. Goebbels dictated a suitable text, and Schmundt left at once to tour every battle front, beginning with the headquarters of Rommel and Rundstedt in France, to collect the field marshals' signatures. Fully aware of his own unpopularity among the generals, Goebbels advised him not to disclose that he was the author of the declaration.[26]

IN AN ARTICLE PUBLISHED in January 1944 entitled 'In ninety days' Goebbels predicted that the Allied invasion would come within that space of time. It was a leaf from Churchill's propaganda book. If nothing happened, he could claim that the Allies had failed. The Americans alone would suffer half a million casualties, the article prophesied. 'On the German side,' he added, 'they will find army commanders confronting them who have already triumphed once in the west, and who tossed the British back across the Channel in a sorry state. . . And above them all stands a Führer who laid France low in six weeks.'[27]

Visiting Hitler's Berghof on March 3, he found that Eva Braun had enlisted the help of her lady friends to distract Hitler from the grimness of fighting a losing war. One eye grotesquely bloodshot from a burst blood vessel, Hitler disclosed that he was soon going to invade Hungary; he asked Goebbels to gear up his propaganda machine accordingly. After disarming Hungary's army, he said, they could tackle her aristocracy and Jewry. As soon as he had smashed the coming Allied invasion, he added, he was going to switch forty divisions to the eastern front. Sooner or later the Allies would have to start talking to him. Meanwhile, he admitted, he had delayed their *Vergeltung* until the second half of April, rather than shoot his bolt too early.

Beefing up the little Doctor's own morale, Hitler portrayed the colossal firepower of the panzer divisions with their new Panther and Tiger tanks. He promised that their fighter planes' heavier armament and new radar would foil the enemy air offensive in the coming winter. Göring was a wash-out, he admitted, but it was their duty to help him. 'He can't stand criticism right now,' Hitler explained. 'You've got to watch your tongue very carefully when you tell him things.' He also forbade Goebbels to attack their Moscow traitors. 'The Führer holds our generals in utter contempt,' noted Goebbels. 'The generals. . . want nothing better than to trip him up.'

Stalin had done well, he reflected, to liquidate his generals early on.

'Only in the Jewish problem have we pursued such a radical policy,' he dictated, taking pride in his own historic accomplishment. 'Rightly so. And today we are the beneficiaries. The Jews are out of harm's way. Yet people told us again and again, before we tackled the Jewish problem, that there was no solution.'[28] Even so there were still six thousand 'privileged' Jews remaining in Berlin and he could not get at them.[29]

With the tail end of 'Butcher' Harris's winter air raids still scorching Berlin, not all its citizens considered it a privilege to remain. The famous conductor Wilhelm Furtwängler was a shining exception. He insisted on staying behind to conduct morale-boosting concerts for the blitz victims and munitions workers. 'We won't forget that after the war,' Hitler promised Goebbels. He ordered a private shelter built for the great conductor. Furtwängler graciously declined and asked that a public shelter be built in a working-class area instead.[30]

RETURNING BY TRAIN from the Obersalzberg to Berlin, Dr Goebbels had good reason to feel that his political come-back from the wilderness was beginning. It was as though he had drunk deeply of a fiery potion, observed Lieutenant von

Oven. Goebbels told his adjutants that Hitler had asked him to return within a week (characteristically, he told his diary that he would try to do so). Standing in the swaying corridor, hands thrust deep into his pockets, he said: 'I'm convinced that if I'd lived a generation earlier I'd have become Reich Chancellor in 1917. In times of danger the cry always goes up for a strong man.' Had not England sent for Churchill in 1940?[31] (There was that comparison again.)

His city's daytime ordeal now began. The Americans always attacked by day. At dawn on March 6 the early-warning radars picked up seven hundred and thirty B-17s and B-24s leaving England, escorted by nearly eight hundred fighter planes. One hundred Luftwaffe fighters engaged them over Dümmer Lake, destroying twenty-three within minutes. Four hundred fighter planes began tearing at the following American formations. Forewarned by telephone, Goebbels stood on the terrace of his lakeside mansion at Lanke, sweeping the pale horizons with binoculars for the attackers.

As the silvery shoals of high-flying bombers passed silently overhead, keeping tight formation, he broke into an ungainly gallop across the lawn to get a better view. He had never seen the British – they still began their lethal business after dusk and left before dawn – but here was the other enemy, crewed by airmen in leather flying-jackets emblazoned with slogans like 'Murder Inc.'[32]

A fighter squadron scrambled from a nearby airbase and zoomed low overhead. He waved to the pilots. He could hear distant cannon-fire as the leading U.S. formations began their bombing runs on the Erkner and Bosch factories. Puffs of smoke hung in the air where the heavy flak shells burst.

One or two B-17s lurched out of station and spiraled earthward spilling smoke and parachutes. Sixty-nine heavies went down this day, with over a hundred more crippled beyond repair. As the fearsome aerial tournament ended, Goebbels' flunkies served lunch. The family came out of the bunker, and while Magda clucked disapprovingly he described to his spellbound youngsters everything he had seen. He told them proudly that their home town was now the most heavily bombed city in the world.[33]

The next American raid, by six hundred bombers on the eighth, killed only forty-nine Germans and twelve foreigners, and left a mere 1,500 homeless.[34] Altogether however the enemy air raids had now killed 116,000 Germans, Goebbels confidentially recorded.[35] He was impatient for the *Vergeltung* to begin. Hitler had ordered Speer to have the V-weapons ready by April 15 but Speer, it seemed, was recovering from depression in a clinic. Goebbels sent Naumann to visit him. Speer pleaded for a further postponement. 'Fourteen days won't bake the cakes any better,' snorted Goebbels; he suspected that Speer was getting cold feet about reprisals.[36]

WHEN GOEBBELS ARRIVED BACK at the Berghof at nine P.M. on March 13, Hitler flattered him by meeting him at the door. Over dinner they debated why the British were still refusing to heed the bolshevik peril. This had been the subject of Goebbels' most recent leader article in *Das Reich*.[37] 'Without doubt,' observed

Goebbels afterward, 'history will see Churchill . . . as the gravedigger of the British empire. With his shortsighted, vindictive policies he has maneuvered Britain into a blind alley, with no way out.'

It snowed heavily all day. Up in Eva Braun's quarters the two men watched the Kodachrome home movies that she had made in 1939 and 1942. The minister noted silently how much Hitler had changed since then. He had become stooped and aging. After lunch the next day he told Goebbels that he longed for the invasion to come so that he could make a clean sweep in the west and then settle Stalin's hash as well. He was even toying with the idea of weakening the west deliberately in order to lure the Allies in. Goebbels did not like that at all.[38] Hearing rumors two weeks later that Hitler was indeed pulling two S.S. divisions out of France, he sent Colonel Martin down to the Berghof to find out, determined not to allow it to happen.[39]

March 1944 brought a decisive downturn in the German public's morale. The failure of the submarine war, the lack of reprisals, and the shrinking Reich frontiers all gave the lie to Goebbels' public assurances.[40] Colonel Martin returned from Berchtesgaden quoting General Jodl as stating that if the Allied invasion succeeded they had lost the war.[41] Tempers in the ministry frayed. After one row, Gutterer snappily advised the minister to recommend a political end to the war before the Reich itself was destroyed.

That afternoon Gutterer reappeared with Dr Hermann Muhs, the former Staatssekretär in the ministry of church affairs, and repeated the treasonable advice. The worst of it was, Goebbels knew they were right. 'Your proposals are out of line,' he retorted, and told them to clear out – 'I don't want to see you again.'[42] Lying, he told Hitler that Gutterer was unwell, and started rumors that he was involved in a newsprint-purchasing scandal.[43] In a little ceremony on Gutterer's birthday he formally replaced him as Staatssekretär by Werner Naumann, a truly meteoric rise for his young bureau chief, who was at that time still only thirty-four.[44]

Premonitions of death occurred to Goebbels. 'I want to be buried in some open space in Berlin,' he decided.[45] The clock was already ticking. He had ordered the cable radio network to provide a running commentary to city dwellers during air raids. Insidious as a Chinese torture, the hollow tick of a radio clock now separated the air-raid bulletins.[46] It got on the strongest nerves and Goebbels replaced it with a melodious four-note jingle which he composed himself.

On April 1, 1944 Hitler appointed him city president of Greater Berlin.[47] He moved the office to the corner of Lietzenburger and Emser Strasse, and – in line with total war – reduced its payroll immediately from six hundred to fifty.[48] Vested already with sweeping powers over life and death as defense commissioner, he authorized other gauleiters to execute looters caught after air raids and to publicize those executions immediately.[49]

On the eve of Hitler's birthday he wrote him a fawning letter and broadcast a eulogy contrasting him with the 'parliamentary mayflies' among their enemies.[50] He closed by predicting, 'He, and not his adversaries, will be the man of the century.' His call to the Berghof at two minutes past midnight was, said Hitler, the first to reach him. Goebbels wished him 'at least thirty' happy returns. As he drove out to Lanke, their Mercedes passed a church with a tattered swastika newly draped from its ruins. 'It's the Furtwängler spirit,' he said. 'When the going gets tough . . . !'[51]

The threat of invasion hung over all the Nazi leaders. Hitler admitted that he slept only three hours a day. His limbs literally trembled when he speculated on the where and when of the invasion.[52] Goebbels too was edgy, though for another reason: He had to compose a leader article for *Das Reich* which events might well overtake before it appeared two weeks later.[53]

That Easter weekend the tides were again just right. But no invasion came. Hitler reassured Goebbels that Rommel had an old score to settle with the British and Americans. 'So let them come!' dictated the minister in his diary. 'I am very pleased with the sovereign calm with which the Führer faces events.'[54] But that very phrase – Hitler's 'sovereign calm' – belied his own deeper misgivings.

The public too was on tenterhooks. 'The letters I am getting,' he recorded on May 13, 'talk almost solely about the invasion. People are not only expecting but looking forward to it. They're only afraid that the enemy may not try.'[55] As April became May, and no invasion came, the S.D. reported that a sense of disappointment was setting in.[56]

Twice in April and again on May 7 and 8 the American bomber squadrons struck at industrial targets in Berlin.[57] A thousand-pound bomb scarred the chancellery, but life otherwise soon returned to normal. Goebbels remarked privately that General Douhet, the much vaunted theorist of air power, had a lot to answer for. 'First it was our airforce generals who thought they could bomb Britain to a pulp, ripe for invasion. Now the strategic-bombing wizards are on the other side.'[58]

Mounds of rubble now choked the center of his city, a breeding grounds for rats which scavenged the flooded cellars for the remains of food or flesh. Typhus cases reached epidemic proportions. Goebbels found himself suffering fierce headaches, and one morning in May a red sore appeared on his face. 'Do you think it might be typhus?' he asked his one-eyed adjutant Günter Schwägermann. A long-distance call was placed to Professor Morell in Bavaria. Morell sent round a specialist, who diagnosed a simple cold-sore.[59]

Recovering out at Lanke with the children, Goebbels watched the frontiers of Hitler's Reich steadily shrinking. The Crimea was lost, and in Italy the Allies broke through at Monte Cassino. Harald Quandt's commanding officer wrote that the young lieutenant was doing well, and the minister sent cigars and cognac down to his stepson's unit.[60]

Magda had serious complications with her neck glands. She saw Morell later in May when she went to spend an evening with Hitler; the doctor insisted she have an operation.[61]

THE AMERICAN AIR FORCE had now begun ground-strafing attacks in Germany.[62] On Sunday May 21, 1944 their fighter planes, flying only a hundred feet up, machine-gunned several people in fields and streets.[63] (Nazi pilots had enjoyed the same sport in their heyday.) On the twenty-third Goebbels secured Hitler's approval for an article encouraging the public to lynch such airmen if they fell into their hands.[64] At midday on May 24 the Americans again bombed Berlin. Coming across a downed American bomber pilot, Second-Lieutenant James G. Dennis, that day Goebbels' propaganda director Alfred-Ingemar Berndt drew his revolver and shot him in cold blood.[65] As Berlin burned, Goebbels began drafting the controversial article. *Not listed in index . (Dennis)*

> It is not provided for in any Article of war [he wrote] that any soldier who commits a heinous crime is exempted from punishment by reason of superior orders, particularly when such orders flagrantly violate every human ethic and every international usage of war.

He quoted from J. M. Spaight's book on air power, *Bombing Vindicated* ('It is not possible to draw a dividing line between the civilian population and the combatants'), and from the *News Chronicle*. 'We are in favor,' the liberal London daily newspaper had written, 'of wiping out every living creature in Germany – man, woman, child, bird, and insect.' The left-wing British novelist H. G. Wells had echoed these words, and even the Archbishop of York had officially described the bombing of civilians as 'the lesser evil.'

Goebbels claimed sanctimoniously to have abstained from citing these words before, lest his public take matters into its own hands and 'do unto the pilots . . . as they have been doing to others.' Such compunctions no longer applied, he now suggested. 'It is asking too much,' he wrote, 'to expect us to use German troops to protect these child-murderers. . . Enough is enough.'

After checking again with Hitler he published the article in the *Völkischer Beobachter*.[66] It provoked outrage – but also apprehension – in London.[67] Ribbentrop had his press chief telephone an angry protest to Goebbels. 'This article,' the propaganda minister retorted, 'was written at the Führer's behest.'[68]

GOEBBELS HAD LOST his awe of the officer caste ever since reading of how the Spartans had borne their diminutive and crippled king Agæsilaus joyously into battle on a shield. That gave him a hero with whom he could identify. After writing the 'lynching' article he traveled down to Sonthofen castle – a Nazi indoctrination center – to speak to front-line generals and admirals.[69] Himmler had already addressed them, once more mentioning his work in killing off the Jews.[70] Wearing a dark-blue suit, he joined Goebbels, wearing the party's brown uniform, and the officers for dinner afterward.[71] The text of Goebbels' own pep talk is not preserved. He did not like having to make one to officers. 'I'm just not in the mood,' he told Oven. 'I've tried telling the Führer we're wasting our time with these people.' But he found himself placed next to the exquisitely named Major-General Hyacinth Count Strachwitz, and this officer, wearing the highest medals for valor, partly restored his faith in the officer-aristocracy.[72]

THE EVACUATION OF THE JEWS from Berlin had dwindled to a trickle, and the Jewish problem had all but vanished from his diary. He had put Berndt in charge of an anti-Jewish propaganda unit.[73] Other top Nazis still wanted to proselytize, taking the anti-Jewish campaign worldwide. Rosenberg suggested reinforcing their antisemitic propaganda among foreign prisoners.[74] Ribbentrop proposed setting up a phony 'Jewish' radio station to discredit all Jews everywhere; Goebbels complained to Hitler that this violated the first law of all propaganda, simplicity.[75]

Hitler's military occupation of Hungary in March had brought more than seven hundred thousand more Jews into the Nazi fold. Goebbels had noted a few days before, 'We'll take care they don't abscond.'[76] Eichmann extracted three hundred thousand for the Nazi war factories, and deported most of the rest to Himmler's camps.[77] Goebbels gloated that, based on his own experience in Berlin, once the Hungarian government had embarked on anti-Jewish policies they would find there was no going back.[78] He advised them to take care to justify their policies in the press.[79]

He did not conceal his cynicism about what he meant by 'justification.' Speaking to two hundred hand-picked German government and business officials in his ministry's Throne Room in June, wearing a sober gray suit and an air of confidentiality, Goebbels reiterated his propaganda canons: Simplicity, constant repetition, and a language capable of holding the intellectuals while not losing the common man.[80] Nazi propaganda, he told this select audience, had only two themes, the dual struggle against bolshevism and the Jews. One day, when the great powers met around the conference table, the question would arise how all this had come about. With one voice, said Goebbels, all must then answer: 'The Jews were to blame!'[81]

53: *The Long-Awaited Day*

To IMPRESS HIS ASCETIC Führer, Goebbels chose this moment in June 1944 to quit smoking (for the umpteenth time). 'A certain nervousness arises,' he dictated on the third. 'Thanks to the constant air raid bulletins.' The Allied bomber forces shortly transferred their attentions to the German synthetic oil refineries. In Italy the battle for Rome had begun. The eastern front was quiet. Nothing had yet happened in France either. One of Rommel's men told Dr Goebbels that the invasion scare was a monstrous Churchillian bluff.[1]

On his way down to the Obersalzberg on June 4 the propaganda minister spoke to fifty thousand people gathered in the ruins of Nuremberg's Adolf-Hitler Platz. 'As for all these Jewish tricks and intimidation attempts,' he shrilled, 'we can only say one thing: We're ready!'[2]

He whiled away the evening with the delectable young Countess Faber-Castell; later, at her husband's castle outside the city, Goebbels listened to her singing, accompanied her on the piano, hummed the tune, or asked for a favorite song like 'A Little Melody shall Join us Forever.'

It was 4:35 A.M. as he boarded the train onward to Munich.[3] Shortly, Lieutenant von Oven brought him the latest telegrams. The United Press reported that Allied troops had entered Rome, greeted by Red flags and communist salutes. 'Onward, Christian soldiers,' commented Goebbels to the lieutenant. 'What good was Rome to us anyway. Just two million more mouths to feed.'

Hitler still expected the invasion to come in Normandy and nowhere else. Field Marshal Rommel however expected the enemy to land between Dieppe and the Somme. 'He has told me,' reported Berndt to Goebbels after touring these defences, 'that if the enemy manages to get ashore it won't be easy to throw them out again.' Rommel was asking for powerful subversive propaganda to be broadcast over Radio Luxembourg to the Allied troops, as in 1940.[4] The French, continued Berndt, were eagerly helping the Nazis and being well paid for it. 'Everywhere there are shouts of Vive Rommel,' he reported. 'The population clusters around and waves to us. They march off to work singing songs.'[5] Rommel, he said, planned to leave France shortly to visit Hitler.[6]

It was June 5 when Goebbels read this report. He believed that the invasion would come in the next five days – or better still not at all.[7] 'I think the Allies have missed the bus,' he said.

Cars ferried them from Salzburg railroad station up to the Obersalzberg. Morell gave him a fortifying injection before the meeting with Hitler.

Hitler revealed that the two V-weapons were ready to open fire, beginning with a salvo of three or four hundred flying bombs against London. Goebbels suggested launching them during London's rush-hour for maximum effect. Like him, Hitler feigned indifference about the fall of Rome. 'The real decision will come in the west,' he said. He blamed their setbacks in Italy on the Allies' air supremacy, but claimed there was little he could do about Reichsmarschall Göring without damaging the authority of the Reich and party.

It was the old story. 'I'm afraid,' dictated Goebbels to Otte afterwards, 'that when the enemy attempt their invasion in the west, their air force may give us precisely the same headaches as we've had in Italy.' Then blind, unreal optimism took over. 'Let's hope the enemy launch their invasion soon, so that we're able to turn the whole war around in the west.'[8]

Thus the eve of the historic Allied invasion of Normandy passed in idle gossip at the Berghof.[9] They talked about Schopenhauer and the art of writing. Goebbels asked, in vain, for the replacement of General Paul von Hase as commandant of Berlin; they had crossed swords recently.[10] He also spoke out for Colonel Martin who had been arrested in a minor corruption scandal. Hitler revealed that he was now toying with suddenly allowing the Russians into Romania, to bring the western powers to their senses. 'He considers Britain done for,' noted Goebbels, 'and is resolved to give her the *coup de grâce* at the slightest opportunity.' He could not resist adding, 'As yet, I cannot quite see how, precisely, he's going to do that.' If he were foreign minister, he knew precisely what he would do to play their enemies off against each other.

Hitler still clung to Ribbentrop, however, calling him an ice-cool tactician however inflexible. When Goebbels criticized Ribbentrop's bloated ministerial apparatus, Hitler replied that he was reluctant to ask the minister to scale it down in case he resigned – a laissez-faire attitude which Goebbels felt disastrous under the circumstances. Strolling back from the tea-house Hitler admitted that he *had* considered replacing Ribbentrop. Surely aware that Goebbels coveted the job for himself, Hitler mentioned however that Rosenberg, of all people, seemed the only possible successor. Goebbels choked. 'That would be out of the frying pan and into the fire!' he exclaimed to Otte, and resigned himself to letting the matter rest.

Relaxing down in Berchtesgaden at ten P.M. he received the first indication, based on radio intercepts, that the Allied invasion of Normandy was beginning.[11] He did not take it seriously at first. Dining at the Berghof later with Hitler and Speer there was still no sense of urgency.[12] They chatted with Eva Braun about theater and movies – her favorite hobbies – then talked round the Berghof fireside of happier times. Goebbels sensed that Hitler was drawing closer to him again. It felt just like the good old days. With an unseasonal thunderstorm lashing the windows, Hitler retired to bed at two A.M. and Goebbels went over to the Bormann's for a while. At two-thirty Goebbels

phoned Semler, his press officer, to bring any telegrams up to his bedroom at
nine o'clock; but at 4:04 A.M. Semler suddenly phoned to say that they were
now getting reports of airborne landings on the Cherbourg peninsula, and an
invasion fleet approaching Normandy.
   'Thank God, at last!' said Goebbels. 'This is the final round.'[13]

HIS AGENCIES BROKE THE NEWS to the world before the British Reuters agency
could do so. At nine-thirty that morning Churchill, 'unable to hold his water,'
as Goebbels put it, announced to the British Parliament that four thousand
ships and eleven thousand planes were taking part: So this clearly was the big
one. Hitler was euphoric. 'The invasion is happening just where we expected
and with exactly the means and methods we've been preparing for,' commented
Goebbels. 'It will be the giddy limit if we can't see them off.'
   At Schloss Klessheim, Goebbels found Ribbentrop in confident mood;
Göring smiling broadly – General Korten, chief of the air staff, was stripping
the Reich of fighter squadrons in a long-prepared operation to switch them
to the invasion front.[14] Himmler was also smiling behind his wire-rimmed
glasses, sure that his S.S. divisions would acquit themselves well. Two first-
class panzer divisions were already rolling into action, and they were expected
to be within range by six P.M. Goebbels noticed that General Jodl was reserved
in his judgment, and decided to speak in their first communiqués only of a
grave and historic struggle. As they left for Berlin at eight P.M., Oven noticed
that his chief was quite thoughtful.
   Goebbels telephoned the Berghof once during the initial invasion battle. The
news was not what he had expected. The panzer divisions had not been able
to counter-attack and the enemy beachhead north of Caën was already fifteen
miles long and three miles deep.[15]
   Within a few days the false euphoria at Hitler's headquarters was dissipated
as the enemy battleships brought their firepower to bear on the defensive
positions far inland. Unable to conceal the breaching of Rommel's 'impregnable'
Atlantic Wall, Goebbels' next article for Das Reich developed the theme that
Stalin alone would profit from the invasion battle, as his enemies tore each
other to pieces in France.[16]
   Morale at home faltered. The public was puzzled that the submarines and
Luftwaffe were failing to crush the invasion.[17] In a cold fury Goebbels watched
the first newsreel takes from Normandy. The telephoto lenses lingered on
beaches where Eisenhower's landing craft seemed to block the entire waterline,
gunwale to gunwale. Mist-shrouded silhouettes of battleships and cruisers
crowded the horizon. Not a German plane was to be seen, and scarcely a flicker
of gunfire. In the reflected glow of a table lamp Goebbels clenched his knuckles
until they were white. 'Mein Gott,' he exclaimed. 'How can the Führer watch
such scenes without sending for the culprits and throttling them with his own
bare hands?'[18] The New York newspapers began to jeer at the conspicuous
absence of the Nazis' vaunted secret weapons.[19]

Late on Monday June 12, Naumann burst in, flushed with excitement. The Berghof had just confirmed that the *Vergeltung* had begun. Goebbels ordered a press clampdown – a prudent measure as the High Command shortly admitted that only ten flying bombs had actually been launched (four of these had crashed on take-off and the 'bombardment' had been halted). On Thursday night however the operation resumed in earnest. Two hundred and forty-four of the pilotless missiles were catapulted, each cruising noisily across southern England with a one-ton warhead aimed at London. This author willingly concedes that nobody who heard the droning approach of those weapons would gainsay their ability to terrify.

At Schwarz van Berk's suggestion Goebbels called this weapon the 'V-1.' That conveyed a hint of more to follow.[20] Although Hitler wanted fanfares, Goebbels allowed only a one-sentence reference in the next communiqué.

That Saturday afternoon however the *Berliner Nachtausgabe* ran a banner headline announcing 'THE DAY FOR WHICH EIGHTY MILLION GERMANS HAVE LONGED IS HERE.' Otto Dietrich had done it again. In a blind fury, Goebbels heard that people were laying odds that the war would be over in a week. He limped up and down clutching the newspaper, scored through and through with his ministerial green pencil.[21] Forced to reverse his policy, he directed Fritzsche to broadcast that evening about the V-weapons; that night his radio stations transmitted eye-witness accounts and recordings of the terrifying organ-like roar as the missiles started out from their bases for central London.[22]

ON JUNE 19, 1944 a Major Otto-Ernst Remer, the tall, lean new commander of the Berlin guards battalion, reported to him. A brand-new Oak Leaves cluster won on the eastern front distinguished his medal bar. They saluted and shook hands – a partnership thus beginning which was to change the course of history one month later.

That day the chief editor of the *Völkischer Beobachter* reported back from the western front. The generals in Normandy, he told Goebbels, had warned him to stand by for disagreeable surprises.[23]

In Goebbels' view a serious crisis was looming. Speaking with him some days earlier General Schmundt had already referred to the Allied beachhead, though still contained, as swelling like a malignant tumor. The time had come, agreed Goebbels, for 'exceptional measures,' which he defined once again as bringing in 'real total war.' Schmundt begged him to make that point at the Berghof.[24] He then persuaded Hitler to agree to discuss this issue with Goebbels.[25] To start the ball rolling the minister drafted a significant article entitled 'Are we waging total war?' Departing from his previous theme that *all* Germans must participate, this urged that power be given in a total war to 'the fanatics.'[26]

Determined to pull no punches, he arrived at the Berghof early on a rainy, gray June 21, 1944. It was not a propitious moment. First, the American army had just cut off the Cherbourg peninsula. Second, only that morning Speer had warned that the air attack on their oil refineries was choking off their oil. Third, General Dietl, also present, now warned that Finland was about to pull out of the war. Fourth, even as they spoke 1,311 American heavy bombers, carrying two thousand tons of bombs and escorted by 1,190 fighter planes, were thundering toward Berlin.[27] Fifth, Hitler told him that he was convinced that a major Soviet offensive was going to begin the next day, the anniversary of BARBAROSSA.

As they talked, the phones rang constantly, and message slips were handed in: Berlin was again blazing. Alone with Hitler after lunch, Goebbels launched into a three-hour debate, pleading for control over total war. They needed a Gneisenau or a Scharnhorst now, he said, not worthless time-serving soldiers like Field Marshal Keitel and General Fromm (both of whom he mentioned by name). Handled properly, the Wehrmacht could squeeze a million extra combat troops out of its bloated 'tail.' Hitler however called Fromm an irreplaceable specialist, and he defended Keitel with much the same stubbornness; true, he heaped contumely on Göring for surrounding himself with sycophants and refusing to hear home truths; but still he would not hear of replacing him. As for putting Goebbels in charge of total war, he rejected that outright. This was still not the right time. He proposed to muddle through as before.

He comforted Goebbels with the meager promise that if, but only if, things got out of hand he would send for him. Hitler was less inclined than ever to hope for a deal with Britain. 'Britain will be totally destroyed in this war,' he again predicted. 'They've had it coming to them.'[28]

Goebbels left at seven P.M. as Berlin, a sea of flames, needed him; he realized that he had achieved nothing. Even as he dictated into his diary the next morning, on June 22, the loyal commentary that 'so far' Hitler's instinct for timing had always proven right, the Soviet summer offensive was beginning – precisely when and where Hitler, against all the sober counsels of his general staff, had predicted. Goebbels watched with impotent anger as Stalin put total war to work. He had mobilized an entire nation, while the luxury-loving Germans were still spared, at their Führer's incomprehensible behest.[29]

Within days this Soviet offensive had demolished the German army group Center. Naumann returned from a three-day tour of the sector; one glance at his map told Goebbels that their eastern front could not fall back much further. 'Bold as brass,' he grimly noted, 'the Soviets are saying that their push is aimed at Berlin.'[30]

Ministering to the needs of posterity, he ordered the horrific air-raid newsreel footage transferred to a secure location.[31] A rash of suicides broke out among the Nazi generals. Even Rommel was in difficulties – 'He has not quite come up to our expectations,' recorded Goebbels on July 4. In the privacy of his bedroom he began smoking cigarettes again; he needed tablets to sleep as well.[32]

WITH BERLIN SWELTERING in a heatwave he took a train through the bomb-flattened south-eastern suburbs to speak in Breslau on July 7. Magda was already in the Silesian capital recovering from the operation on her jaw.

Hanke, the local gauleiter, met Goebbels at the station. Both men had matured in the furnace of war, and put their differences over Magda behind them.[33] Hanke was about to marry the high-society divorcee who had borne him a daughter in December 1943, and Magda had developed a romantic interest in Werner Naumann.[34] Goebbels visited her at the clinic; Professor Stocker had succeeded in extracting the painful nerve without leaving a scar. Husband and wife exchanged a few stiff pleasantries.[35]

Speaking to fifty-three thousand people gathered in and around Breslau's Century Hall Goebbels warned that for Germany it was now or never. There would be no 'next time,' he said. 'If we do not throw them back now, our adversaries will erase Germany and everything German from the face of the globe.' The Allies, he continued, had reduced cities like Berlin, Hamburg, Mannheim, Kassel, Frankfurt, Cologne, and Essen to smoking ruins (Breslau was still out of their range); but they had failed to break the people's morale.[36] He took much the same line in his next article for *Das Reich*: 'The greatest political error that our adversaries have committed in this war is to impose on the Reich a struggle of life and death.'[37]

The Allies listened to his message no less intently than the Silesians. 'Goebbels,' President Roosevelt learned, 'has taken and twisted the slogan of unconditional surrender and made the people feel that the slogan means unconditional annihilation.'[38] 'He also stresses here the theme,' the same source reported, 'which we can expect to have repeated from now on, that bolshevism is on the threshold of Europe.'[39]

WITH GÖRING IN DISGRACE, the undeclared fight for Hitler's succession began. Speer and Goebbels, ostensibly still friends and allies against Göring, jostled each other for control of total war and the supreme authority that would go with it. Leading industrialists told Goebbels that they had investigated the Wehrmacht and found hundreds of thousands of idle troops, just as he had told Hitler. But Speer too had reported this to Hitler; Speer suggested a new total war committee.[40]

Speer thought he had a trump card. After lunch one day he showed to Goebbels Peenemünde's secret movie of the coming rocket missile. The movie left Goebbels breathless. Hitler had told him more details of this fourteen-ton projectile when they last met – it was 'like something out of the imagination of Jules Verne,' he told his staff.[41] In full color the newsreel showed the bomb-proof underground factory where slave laborers were assembling the rocket engines.

At a firing range deep in occupied Poland a special rocket transporter hoisted this V-2 weapon upright onto its fins. Repeated launches filmed from inside the blast-proof control bunker showed the missiles lifting off and gathering speed above the surrounding tree-tops, balanced atop a blinding white flame, and vanishing into the blue sky leaving only jagged vapor trails. Speer told Goebbels that at the height of its trajectory the V-2 was one hundred miles above the surface of their earth. 'If we could show this movie in every movie theater,' exclaimed Goebbels as he hobbled out past the S.S. men guarding the door, 'the most hard-boiled pessimist could no longer doubt our victory.'[42]

They talked until two in the morning. Speer agreed that there were a million men to spare in the economy. He suggested that Hitler would be more receptive now than when Goebbels had last ventured to speak with him. Goebbels however shied away from another marathon debate and decided to set down his views on paper.[43] Interestingly, Speer again decided to get at Hitler first and submitted another paper on total war to Hitler two days later, appropriating many of Goebbels' ideas as his own.[44]

There was little time to lose. Thundering hordes of Russian tanks and men were bearing down on East Prussia. To document his loyalty to that province, Hitler flew back to his Wolf's Lair headquarters on July 16; the army's general staff headquarters, awed by the Russian approach, moved five thousand of its officers in the opposite direction. 'I'd like to turf out every cowardly man jack of them,' snarled Goebbels.[45] The chief of general staff General Zeitzler resigned, pleading a nervous breakdown.[46]

Hitler carried on regardless, unaware that the hand of history was about to be raised against him.

DATED JULY 18, 1944, Goebbels' memorandum on total war, which we shall examine first, was a masterpiece of advocacy. In its final form it was forty-one pages long, and phrased as a personal appeal from one of Hitler's oldest supporters. 'I have stood by you for twenty years now,' he wrote, 'and believe I have always been a staunch companion when the going was roughest.' Events of the last weeks, he said, had proved how thinly their front lines were manned. While his faith in the party was boundless, that in the Wehrmacht was 'badly shaken.' Given the right powers, the gauleiters would be able to raise vast quantities of manpower. He believed that Speer too could release more currently exempted young men from industry to the forces. 'We must act today,' he insisted, 'if we want to see results in three or four months' time.'

Germany needed a firm hand, he argued. In Berlin, each day still brought invitations to official receptions and other functions. Events had rendered Rosenberg's ministry totally redundant. Nobody would miss Ribbentrop's press office either if it was dissolved. During the winter air raids, he recalled, some government agencies vanished for weeks, but nobody had missed them. 'How primitively we worked earlier in the party,' he argued, tugging at Hitler's nostalgia-strings. The Führer himself must now give sufficient authority to 'men of backbone and character' to take charge – men not yet wearied by this war (a sideswipe at Speer, who had returned only in May from his three-month convalescence). Yet another 'committee' such as Speer was proposing would do more harm than good, objected Goebbels. 'I went along with the farce of the "Committee of Three" and would warn most urgently against any revival of it.'

After shamelessly reminding Hitler of his own achievements since 1926, Goebbels urged him to give 'a man of your confidence' the job of coordinating all the others, 'just as we, for example, have been doing highly successfully in the Reich Air-Warfare Inspectorate.' He boldly guaranteed, if given such powers, to raise fifty new divisions within three or four months, while Speer would still get additional manpower for his arms factories. True, the enemy would crow that the Nazis were at their last gasp. But had not Churchill – his hero – called for an all-out effort after Dunkirk? Had not Stalin, when Moscow itself was threatened, cried 'Better to die on your feet than survive on your knees?' In another well-aimed dig at Speer, Rosenberg, and Ribbentrop, all authors of many a verbose memorandum, Goebbels reminded Hitler that this was the first such document he had submitted in twenty years.

With suitable contrition he added:

In the twenty years that I have been with you, particularly in 1938 and 1939, I have occasioned you much private grief. You always responded with a nobility and charity that today still fill me with deep emotion when I think of them.

'But,' he added after these allusions to the Lida Baarova affair and probably the Kristallnacht, 'I believe I have brought no dishonor upon you during this war.'

In battles in Roman times, when all seemed lost, he concluded, the message was: *Res venit ad triarios!* – When the first two ranks fell in battle, he explained, it was up to the third rank, their hardiest warriors, to save the day. 'This hour now seems to have struck for the nation. . .The people wants to do more than we are asking of it. Call in the *triarios* to fulfill the people's wish!'[47]

THE EVENTS OF GOEBBELS' next few days are uncertain and not easy to reconstruct. His diary entries of July 19 to 22 inclusive are missing.[48] Perhaps he never dictated them. Perhaps he did, but later ordered them destroyed. What is certain is that Goebbels' heroic document of July 18, 1944 was set aside by the extraordinary events which rocked Hitler's empire two days later.

There was an odd prelude. On July 19 a news report was telephoned from Berlin to Stockholm that Heinrich Himmler was shortly taking over all military personnel matters, currently the business of Generals Schmundt and Fromm. No sooner had this report reached Stockholm than all telephone lines from Berlin were cut.[49] It is worth recalling that the telephone-monitoring agency was Göring's monopoly.

The next day was no less crowded with the inexplicable: Von Brauchitsch, the retired army C.-in-C., was seen being driven through Berlin in full uniform.[50] It also seems necessary to report here that General Heinz Guderian, Hitler's formidable inspector of tank forces, knew full well what was about to happen and elected to wait outside Berlin.[51] Himmler too kept well away from Berlin until later that day. The behavior even of Albert Speer, a close associate of both generals Fromm and Wagner, also seemed odd in retrospect to Dr Goebbels. For a long time after the Twentieth of July nobody trusted anybody any more.

54: *Valkyrie*

T
HE DAY, JULY 20, 1944, STARTED ROUTINELY. The Goebbels ministry once
again lectured outposts that the word *propaganda* was not to be used
as synonymous with 'lies, duping the public, hypocrisy, and rabble-
rousing.'[1] At nine A.M. the court martial of Colonel Martin, Goebbels' liaison
officer to the Wehrmacht, began; Goebbels' enemies, who were legion, had
rigged the bench to ensure that his man got a stiff sentence for corruption.[2]
After Goebbels had presided over his regular eleven o'clock conference Speer
came over to show to the Cabinet ministers assembled in the theater of the
propaganda ministry some graphs demonstrating how arms output was
increasing.[3] Goebbels rounded off with a few well-chosen words and took
Speer and Funk back to No. 20 Hermann-Göring Strasse for a chat.[4]

At one o'clock the intercom buzzed. 'Herr Minister is wanted by the Führer's
headquarters – Lorenz is on the line.' Heinz Lorenz was Dietrich's deputy at
the Wolf's Lair. He said: 'Herr Minister, there has been an attempt on the life
of the Führer. He has ordered an immediate announcement broadcast that he
is alive and well.' (The radio news was Goebbels' exclusive domain.) Lorenz
dictated the proposed text down the line.[5]

Goebbels – did nothing. He had a direct phone link to the headquarters via
the Winterfeld-Strasse telephone exchange. Not many people were aware of
that – least of all, apparently, those who had just tried to kill Hitler.[6]

Although Lorenz shortly phoned again to stress the urgency, Goebbels
seemed not to grasp that point at all. He chose caution. A plot against their
Führer? 'You've got to soften such a psychological shock,' he explained, and
detailed Hans Fritzsche to draft a well-modulated commentary to that end.[7]

Troubled by a recurring ear-ache, he turned to other business.[8] He dispatched
a telegram of condolences to Leni Riefenstahl on the death of her father, then
withdrew, evidently for his regular nap.[9] Nothing is known about his actions
for several hours.

It is true that soon after the assassin's bomb exploded at his feet at 12:45 P.M.
Hitler had ordered all regular telephone links cut while Himmler and Göring
were called in.[10]

Goebbels had his own secret line; yet he appears to have done nothing more
about the news until five P.M. Did he perhaps speculate on Hitler being dead?[11]
Was he waiting to see which way the cat jumped?

BY MID-AFTERNOON SUSPICION at the Wolf's Lair had narrowed to an army
colonel, Claus Count Schenk von Stauffenberg, Fromm's one-eyed chief of
staff: He had slipped out of Hitler's conference and flown pell-mell back to
Berlin. Upon arrival there he assured Fromm, General Olbricht, and their
fellow plotters that he had seen Hitler dead. The plotters' signals began to go
out at four o'clock, putting into effect the army's Operation VALKYRIE, which
Goebbels had already encountered after that air raid eight months before. The
plotters' scenario was that recalcitrant Nazis had bumped off their beloved
Führer, necessitating martial law. The city commandant General Paul von
Hase ordered Remer's guards battalion to cordon off the government district,
and he detailed other units to seize the radio station and propaganda ministry
and arrest Dr Goebbels as one of the 'plotters.' In fact he was seen as the main
obstacle to any putsch in Berlin.[12]
    When Remer, accustomed to obeying orders, issued them in turn to his
men at Moabit one of them, Lieutenant Hans Hagen, smelt a rat. Formerly a
member of the propaganda ministry and now the Nazi indoctrination officer
attached to Remer's battalion, he obtained permission to ask Goebbels himself
what was up. Arriving at the ministry on a motorbike pillion at five o'clock
he told Regierungsrat Dr Heinrichsdorff, an old friend, that something very
fishy was going on. Heinrichsdorff brought Hagen straight round to No. 20
Hermann-Göring Strasse. Hearing of Remer's unusual orders, to quarantine
the entire government district, Goebbels sprang to his feet. 'That's impossible!'
he exclaimed. Floundering between panic and mistrust he asked Hagen
whether this Major Remer was a loyal national socialist. He sent for Remer,
then phoned the S.S. Leibstandarte, the most Hitler-loyal unit in Germany, at
its barracks in Lichterfelde, and told them to stand by.[13]
    Goebbels' chief of staff Gerhard Schach arrived, puffing.[14] He had received a
telex from Bormann at the Wolf's Lair warning all gauleiters that a full-scale
military putsch was under way.
    At four o'clock the Wolf's Lair had monitored strange orders issuing from
the war department in Bendler Strasse, with the codename VALKYRIE. (At
four-fifteen Keitel had already begun notifying the Wehrmacht districts that
Hitler was alive, that Fromm was dismissed, and that Himmler was replacing
him – exactly as prefigured by the news flash to Stockholm the day before.)
    At five P.M. the plotters in Bendler Strasse were still issuing mutinous signals
to army districts signed by 'Stauffenberg' and 'Witzleben' – a field marshal
whom Hitler had long ago relieved of his duties. Was there no end to the
treachery? Schach told Goebbels he had tried to reach Count von Helldorff,
the police chief, but without success. Suspecting foul play, Goebbels told Police
General Alfred Wünnenberg to stand by to take over, and sent for Speer.
    Speer arrived hatless and more disheveled than usual. Goebbels received
him in his first-floor study and briefed him on what was going on. 'I want
you with me,' he said. 'We've got to act prudently.' Since he hardly consulted
with Speer at all in the hours that followed it is probable that he wanted the

ambitious young man where he could see him.[15] Each time he phoned Hitler later, he sent Speer out of the room.[16] From the window, he could see soldiers taking up position in the street below in full combat gear, slung with machine-guns, ammunition belts, and hand grenades; trucks with more soldiers rattled past toward the Brandenburg Gate. Goebbels pulled his 6·35-millimeter pistol out of his desk and cocked it: 'Just in case.'

One of his staff, sent out on an errand, returned with word that a soldier had prevented him from leaving the building. Goebbels began to wonder what was keeping Remer.

Only now did he telephone the Wolf's Lair. Hitler, still shaken by the bomb blast but stoical, was meeting with Mussolini. Goebbels spoke with Julius Schaub, Hitler's adjutant, but Schaub simultaneously received an incoming call from Hitler's personal adjutant in Berlin, Alwin-Broder Albrecht. Albrecht reported that a detachment of soldiers had just tried to occupy the Reich chancellery.[17] Schaub passed Goebbels' call on to Hitler. 'Mein Führer!' exclaimed Goebbels. 'Has the army gone mad? The guards battalion here is standing guard on my ministry. It's bad for my image, people might think I need military protection.'[18]

Hitler was puzzled by Goebbels' naïveté. He probably could not even hear Goebbels. His ear drums were fractured. 'Doctor,' he croaked into the telephone, 'they've tried to kill me.' His head swimming with pain, he ended the conversation. Around 6:15 P.M. he phoned Goebbels again. 'Where's that radio communiqué?' he asked. It had slipped the minister's attention completely. He explained that he would release it as soon as Fritzsche had drafted a reassuring commentary.

'I want that out now!' shouted Hitler. Goebbels picked up another phone and screamed at Fritzsche. Fritzsche no doubt did the same to his subordinates, because at 6:28 P.M. the German home service was interrupted with the special announcement that an attempt had been made on the Führer's life, but that he had survived.[19]

BY THAT TIME, as ordered, Remer had his cordons in place and General von Hase was taking steps to arrest Goebbels. Remer overheard him briefing Lieutenant-Colonel Hermann Schöne to do so.[20] Hase also sent a colonel to the army bomb-disposal school, commanded by a fellow conspirator, with orders to organize three hundred men into squads which would seize the radio building and propaganda ministry and arrest Goebbels.[21]

At this moment an emissary arrived from Lieutenant Hagen, who had remained with Goebbels, asking Remer to come to see Dr Goebbels at once, as a putsch attempt was under way. Hase naturally forbade Remer to go; equally naturally, Remer was at first less inclined to trust the Machiavelli of Hermann-Göring Strasse than his own commanding officer, but after wrestling with his dilemma he decided to go, while leaving instructions on what to do if Goebbels should detain him. With that decision, the putsch in Berlin was doomed.

At 6:35 P.M. Remer's car drove into Goebbels' forecourt; five minutes later he was brought up to the minister's study.[22] Stiffly at attention, he explained that the Führer had been assassinated.

'I just spoke with the Führer myself a few minutes ago,' Goebbels contradicted him. Then: 'Are you a true National Socialist?'

'Through and through, Herr Minister! But are you loyal to the Führer?'[23]

Goebbels gave his word of honor. Remer was still unconvinced. Might he speak with the Führer himself?

It was about seven P.M. The call was put straight through. Hitler knew Remer personally – he had pinned the Oak Leaves on him only a few weeks earlier. 'Do you recognize my voice?' he said.

'Jawohl, mein Führer!' shouted Remer, stiffening, and slammed his heels together.[24]

'Until the Reichsführer gets there,' said Hitler, 'I am making you personally responsible for crushing any plot against the state's authority.'

Major Martin Korff, commander of a bomb-disposal company, arrived with his squad and told Goebbels he had come to arrest him on Hase's orders. Goebbels and Remer burst out laughing and enlightened the unfortunate major.[25] Korff's comrade Captain Alexander Maître had taken his squad to the propaganda ministry, but promptly placed his men under Remer's command instead. Remer ordered his men to muster in the garden beneath Goebbels' windows, then set off back to the traitorous Hase's headquarters, telling the minister that he would phone every twenty minutes to be on the safe side. Hase however had transferred to the Wehrmacht district headquarters on Hohenzollerndamm.

On General Olbricht's orders a Major Friedrich Jacob with troops from the infantry school at Döberitz had occupied the main radio building in Masuren Allee; Olbricht had ordered Jacob to report back when he seized the building. Instead, he phoned Goebbels. The latter sized up the situation in an instant and told the major to accept orders only from him. 'Nobody broadcasts without my express permission.'[26] Witnessing this exchange Speer marveled at Goebbels' composure. He was 'as cold-blooded as a warlord on a battlefield,' he would say the next day.[27] Hans Fritzsche sent two or three hundred S.S. men over to the radio building under an S.S. Obersturmbannführer.

Together with Jacob they secured the building against the traitors all night and thus enabled a recording of Hitler's speech, made with a sound truck at the Wolf's Lair, to be piped through from East Prussia and transmitted nationwide at one A.M. This dealt a further death blow to the plot.

NOT FOR NOTHING had Goebbels had a company of his senior officials given infantry training after Mussolini's overthrow in 1943.[28] Around seven-thirty P.M. they were ordered to pick up their machine-guns and report to Goebbels' private apartment at No. 20 Hermann-Göring Strasse. Major Remer transferred his command post from Hase's former headquarters to this address as well, a more than symbolic move. Eventually there were about a hundred and fifty soldiers trampling around in Goebbels' garden in the gathering dusk. He went down and spoke briefly to them, illuminated by the light flooding through the open garden door, arousing a fire of holy indignation in these elderly soldiers about the traitors in high places.

Confusion reigned in Berlin even now. When the ministry staff tried to leave their building at about eight-fifteen, the soldiers still detained them. Major Rudi Balzer, Martin's successor, phoned Hase's headquarters; here a Major Baron von Massenbach put him through to a Colonel Fritz Jäger, who said he was just on his way over to the ministry.[29] In fact Hase, making one more attempt to get his man, had ordered Jäger with two units of military police to arrest Goebbels and occupy S.S. Gruppenführer Ernst Kaltenbrunner's Reich Main Security Office; but these units also joined forces with Remer.[30] When a Gestapo official shortly told Major Balzer that the army was staging a coup, he was incredulous, and protested at this peddling of 'unfounded rumors' against the army.

There were unsung heroes in these confusing hours, Hadamovsky later told Goebbels.[31] When Colonel Mertz von Quirnheim had falsely announced at Bendler Strasse that Hitler was dead, a Lieutenant-Colonel Herber, unconvinced, had sallied forth with about fifteen men to No. 20 Hermann-Göring Strasse and armed themselves with machine-guns and grenades; after confirming that Hitler was alive, they burst in on General Olbricht, in conference with Stauffenberg and Quirnheim, and arrested them all after a brief exchange of small-arms fire. There followed an anxious moment as Remer's troops arrived, since Herber had no means of contacting either Hitler or Goebbels to obtain their approval for having arrested these very senior officers.[32]

Remer had ordered Lieutenant-Colonel Rudolf Schlee to contact this loyal unit at the war department building in Bendler Strasse. After hearing Schlee's report, which revealed that the building was nothing less than the traitors' headquarters, Goebbels phoned Hitler and secured authority to smoke them out.[33] He told Schlee to go back and arrest 'every general.' At about nine P.M. he sent a telex to all the gauleiters – he did not state by what authority – reporting for their own information that a 'dilettantish' plot by reactionary army generals had been uncovered. 'Gauleiters are called upon to display extreme vigilance and to ensure that their organization remains effective and intact and that they preserve their freedom of action and movement at all costs. Further directives follow. Heil Hitler. REICHSLEITER DR GOEBBELS.'[34]

At the same time Bormann, the more usual signatory for such directives, telexed to the gauleiters his theory that the 'reactionary criminal vermin' had staged the putsch in conjunction with the traitors in Moscow (he named General von Seydlitz and Count Einsiedel). Had it succeeded, he said, a generals' clique consisting of Fromm, Olbricht, and Hoepner were to have taken power and made peace with Moscow. Bormann followed with a further message at nine-forty, warning that 'a General Beck' was trying to take over the government. 'The erstwhile Field Marshal von Witzleben is posing as the

Führer's successor. Of course no National Socialist gauleiter will allow himself to be duped by, or accept orders from, these criminals. . .'[35]

EVEN NOW DR GOEBBELS' situation was anything but secure. An armored brigade under Colonel Ernest Bolbrinker, one of Rommel's toughest Afrika Corps regimental commanders, had arrived at Fehrbelliner Platz from the armored warfare school at Krampnitz.[36] Another tank unit under Colonel Wolfgang Glaesemer had churned to a halt in the Tiergarten park, only a few hundred yards west of Goebbels' residence. Remer's adjutant Lieutenant Siebert found out that General Guderian, the tank commanders' superior officer, had given them orders to shoot anybody who did not obey his orders. What was he up to? It was common knowledge that Hitler had treated him shabbily in December 1941.[37]

Reiner's predecessor Lieutenant-Colonel Kurt Gehrke offered to go to Fehrbelliner Platz to find out. Not fully trusting any army officers now, Goebbels sent Hadamovsky, his chief of staff in the Reich Propaganda Directorate as well, and even when Gehrke reported that Guderian's officers were 'for the Führer' he was not satisfied and had Remer telephone the Panzer Reserve Brigade at Cottbus to send a battalion of heavy tanks to Berlin in case it came to a firefight with Guderian.[38]

The treacherous General von Hase was still doggedly trying to salvage VALKYRIE from this shambles. He sent an officer over to order Remer to return to him. Major Remer, equipped now with Hitler's personal authority, replied that on the contrary the general was to come to No. 20 Hermann-Göring Strasse. Hase arrived with Schöne and Massenbach. A monocled, upright officer of striking appearance, Hase put on his most affable air and told Remer that General Hermann Reinecke (a loyalist Nazi) had ordered him to seize the Bendler Strasse building. Goebbels intervened and no less affably invited Hase to remain under his roof as his guest. Hase inquired whether the kitchens could provide a meal, and there was a courteous exchange about whether a Rhine wine or a Moselle would complement it better, before Goebbels turned to more pressing business. After a while, Hase asked Remer, 'Major, could you ask the minister whether I can go? My wife is waiting for me.'

At this moment however an S.S. man brought a message in to Goebbels. A search of Hase's office had turned up a rubber stamp reading 'Stauffenberg' and a pad of blank gate-passes. 'I am sorry,' said Goebbels, 'but I must ask you to remain.'[39]

Shortly General von Kortzfleisch, the one-eyed commander of Wehrmacht District III (Berlin), appeared at Goebbels' door. No doubt anxious to establish his credentials he snapped at Hase, 'Well, Mr von Hase! You didn't expect to find *me* here!'

He told Goebbels that earlier that day General Olbricht had placed him under close arrest when he failed to declare for the plotters, and had replaced him with General Baron von Thüngen (the judge on whom Goebbels' enemies had banked at that morning's hearing against Colonel Martin). Kortzfleisch unhesitatingly identified Fromm, Olbricht, and Stauffenberg as the ringleaders.[40]

Goebbels spared him, although there were sound reasons not to. This was an evening when he turned a figurative blind eye to many an officer's shortcomings. Even Guderian's actions seemed ambivalent, but Goebbels thought highly of him and Hitler would shrewdly appoint him to replace Zeitzler the next day. All of the others – including Hase, Witzleben, Thüngen, Schöne – would eventually be hanged.

In fact death was already beginning its harvest. General Fromm had just had his fellow conspirators Olbricht, Quirnheim, and Stauffenberg shot by firing squad in the light of motor headlamps behind the Bendler Strasse building. Fromm hoped he had thus saved his own neck. Brought up to Goebbels' study, the six-foot-two general, until now commander of Germany's reserve army, demanded to be allowed to speak by phone with Hitler. Goebbels ordered his arrest. He believed he was beginning to understand. So this was why the barracks were full of idle troops and tank units. Fromm, Olbricht, & Co. had been cynically holding them back for their VALKYRIE. 'I'll see to it, general,' he told Kortzfleisch, 'that your barracks empty. And that they are refilled. Bank on it!' Inadvertently, the traitors had made total war a near-reality, and his heart sang with joy.

His house overflowed with fearful Reich ministers, Nazi party officials, and no less dejected prisoners. Arriving there after midnight Major Balzer found fifty people milling around upstairs. Somebody asked him to keep an eye on Fromm. Still feigning innocence, Fromm related that after returning from the Wolf's Lair that afternoon Stauffenberg and Olbricht had placed him under arrest. 'The background as described by Fromm was a bit obscure,' reported Balzer, 'and he was very agitated as he regarded his conveyance to Goebbels' home as a kind of arrest.' After ten minutes' questioning by Gestapo chief Kaltenbrunner, Fromm was removed – 'It certainly looked like an arrest to me,' reported Balzer the next day.[41]

Smoking nervously, Goebbels telephoned Magda in Dresden and told her some officers had tried to murder Hitler. She burst into tears. More officers arrived during the night, including General Hermann Reinecke and Colonel-General Stumpff, commanding Luftwaffe forces within the Reich. Göring telephoned an offer of flak units to crush the army revolt. Goebbels turned it down. After midnight Himmler put in a belated appearance. His explanation that he had been 'directing counter-operations from outside Berlin' seemed reasonable enough. In Goebbels' study the Reichsführer expressed relief that Goebbels had used the army itself and not the Waffen S.S. to crush the putsch. There must not be the slightest blemish on the army's name.[42]

It was now July 21. The fated day had passed. At three-forty A.M. Bormann issued a triumphant dispatch. 'The traitors' action can be regarded as at an end.'[43] Around four-thirty A.M. Goebbels emerged from his study and announced, 'Gentlemen, the putsch is over.'[44] He escorted Himmler to his car and shook hands with him. By five his house was almost deserted. He took Naumann, Schwägermann, and Oven back upstairs, pausing on each tread to tell them more tidbits. At the top he briefly shared a little table with a bronze bust of the Führer. 'That was like a purifying thunderstorm,' he said, irreverently propping an elbow on the famous quiff. He lit another cigarette. Months later he would reflect, 'The Twentieth of July was in fact not only the nadir of our war crisis, but Day One of our resurgence.'[45]

WHILE HITLER CALLED all his ministers to the Wolf's Lair on July 21, Goebbels necessarily stayed in Berlin. At his ministerial conference he narrated what had happened, though with cosmetic flourishes. The tanks assembling in Berlin, he averred, were General Guderian's, which 'the Führer had provided for protection.' Kortzfleisch had been magnificent. Hase, he scoffed, had behaved like a fool on his arrest – asking if he 'might telephone his wifey' and might he have a sandwich and a bottle of wine, 'preferably a Moselle.' It was their duty, Goebbels insisted, to ensure that no stain attached to the army's other generals. Himmler, he revealed, had told him that Fromm had kept six hundred thousand soldiers idle in Germany; these would now be released to the fighting front. Thus, this putsch was a real breakthrough toward total war.[46]

Some of his listeners remained unconvinced. Immanuel Schäffer wondered how all this could have escaped Himmler's notice. And what about Göring's wiretappers?[47]

The London press had a field day, with sarcastic references to several of Goebbels' previous utterances. Goebbels instructed his outposts to organize spontaneous open-air demonstrations of the public's happiness and joy.[48]

Inevitably, he claimed that Hitler's 'miraculous escape' was further proof that their Führer was protected by Providence. Otherwise he ordered the putsch glossed over, like the Hess affair. He released no word of the plotters' aims, let alone of the true scale of the conspiracy which had extended from the eastern front to Paris and Vienna.[49] The traitors remained for Goebbels a 'minuscule clique of reactionary officers.'

Despite all his efforts however there was enduring damage to the army; it violated sensibilities that their traitors had been hanged, rather than shot. Officers felt that their entire caste had been impugned.[50] Indeed, the Twentieth of July left residual issues which were still unresolved in Germany scores of years later.

55: *Total War*

CATAPULTED TO THE NAZI EQUIVALENT of stardom for crushing the putsch in Berlin, Dr Goebbels arrived by train in East Prussia on Saturday July 22, 1944. He was determined to speak his mind to Hitler about total war and the need for a major show trial of the plotters.[1] Lieutenant von Oven gave him the latest cables. The British press was bragging about Stauffenberg's English-born wife. Other foreign sources claimed that 'the Jews in the neutral capitals' had known in advance about the bomb plot.[2] Moscow's newspapers were more logical, pointing out that the war would only be won on the battlefields – now barely one hundred miles from the Wolf's Lair. Goebbels saw this as proof that Stalin fully appreciated the hidden strength of ideological mass movements, and that they could talk with him when the time came.[3]

He called first at Hans Lammers' nearby field headquarters. The change in attitude towards him was dramatic. Bormann and Lammers could not have been more friendly. Taking him aside, Keitel admitted that he had wept tears of joy on seeing that their Führer was unscathed. 'A miracle,' agreed Goebbels. The staff conference called by Lammers was soon over. Lammers himself proposed giving Himmler sweeping powers to rationalize the armed forces, and Goebbels the same powers over state and public life. Goebbels was somewhat astonished, but still orated to them for an hour on the need to present a united front to Hitler. 'The Führer,' he said, 'must be relieved of all minutiæ so that he can dedicate himself to his great tasks.' Even Keitel backed him; he freely admitted that the Wehrmacht had manpower to spare.[4] When Speer flourished his own total-war document, Goebbels swatted him like a bothersome insect, casting doubt in particular on the statistics. Lammers agreed to see Hitler the next day to win the agreed powers for Himmler and Goebbels.[5]

Goebbels was flabbergasted by how easy it had been. If Hitler endorsed it, they would have created 'practically a domestic dictatorship' –with Dr Goebbels as the dictator.[6]

He drove round to the Wolf's Lair with Naumann that afternoon beneath a broiling sun. He found Göring snorting about the army generals in Berlin – less for having tried a *coup d'état* than for declaring martial law without consulting him, the lawful successor if Hitler was indeed dead.

HIS HEAD AND LEGS still bandaged and sore from the myriads of splinter-injuries, Hitler limped over from his bunker to greet Dr Goebbels. The spectacle tore at the loyal henchman's heart.[7] Goebbels flung a Nazi salute with exaggerated formality. Hitler responded awkwardly, proffering his left hand. He told Goebbels that his first instinct after the blinding flash and explosion was to check that his eyes, arms, and legs were intact. His stenographer had lost both legs, and Schmundt one eye; Korten had been impaled by a fragment of oak table – all three were mortally injured.

A Berliner, the hut's telephone operator, had first identified Stauffenberg as the murderer. But he had got away – a hidden blessing in fact, as Goebbels reflected, because if he had been stopped they would never have unmasked the traitors in Berlin. Hitler fulminated with rage at 'that masonic lodge,' the general staff. Dr Dietrich was opposing Goebbels' idea of a political show trial, but not Hitler.[8] No buddy-buddy courts martial for them, he grimly said: He would have the culprits stripped of their uniforms and turned over to the People's Court. Judge Roland Freisler would know how to deal with them.

When Hitler revealed that the traitor-generals had planned to arrest all the Reich defense commissioners like Goebbels, it was the minister's turn for indignation. 'What gives some jumped-up general,' he exclaimed, 'the right to treat as gangsters the leading National Socialists who put him in that uniform in the first place!'[9]

Dictating his diary entry afterward, Goebbels spoke with glutinous fervor of his love for the Führer. 'He is the greatest historic genius of our times. With him we shall see victory, or go down heroically.' Even Ribbentrop was nice to him during this visit, although put out by recent Goebbels articles which he felt might create in Tokyo the dangerous impression that Berlin was wooing London. The prospects of doing a deal with Churchill were more than dim, Ribbentrop advised Goebbels.[10]

THE PLOT AND ITS AFTERMATH marked the start of Speer's decline. At dinner with Hitler and Goebbels he was markedly subdued. He had talked with Himmler at midday, but the Reichsführer S.S. was also backing Goebbels.[11] They put their agreed total-war plan to Hitler the next day, July 23. He easily nodded it through. Ribbentrop tried (but failed) to exclude his ministry from the plan's ambit.[12] Lammers authorized Goebbels to call a Cabinet-level meeting on the thirty-first, in the chancellery in Berlin, to introduce his plans.

The total-war decree was published on July 26. 'At the suggestion' of the Reichsmarschall, it read – Göring's vanity being a factor even now – Hitler had appointed Dr Goebbels as Reich plenipotentiary for total mobilization.[13] Goebbels sent a telegram thanking Lammers for the 'loyal manner' in which he had seen things through.[14]

Thus he returned to Berlin as *de facto* the first man after Hitler. Naumann shouted to Lieutenant von Oven, waiting on the platform, 'The Doctor has just won his greatest victory!' Thanks to the traitors, gloated Goebbels over lunch, nobody at headquarters would ever dare to intrigue against him again. On July

26 he broadcast to the nation an account of how he had crushed the putsch. He hinted at new secret weapons and in his next article, entitled 'Going one better,' he developed a new argument that the Reich was now regaining the *technical* superiority which it had lost for a while to the Allies.

In victory he was becomingly magnanimous. Addressing the other ministers in the chancellery on July 31 he invited them to submit ideas voluntarily to him.[15] He proposed to slash his own ministry by thirty or forty percent. His special total-war staff would be limited to just twenty men. Naumann would chair a planning committee, and Gauleiter Wegener an executive committee.[16] Total mobilization could now begin.

His target was to find one million men. One million soldiers: Equals one hundred new divisions: Equals victory. That was his calculus.[17] At ten A.M. the next day Naumann issued the first two ordinances, outlawing token employment (a dodge to evade the labor-draft); and raising the female labor-draft age to fifty.[18]

To make time for his immense new task Goebbels halved his afternoon nap, ate sandwiches at his desk, forfeited his regular evening movie previews, and refused all invitations. Speer was an unwilling ally, but sat in on only the first Goebbels total-war sessions.[19] He agreed to release all draft-exempted men aged between seventeen and thirty-four from his arms factories.[20] This alone would provide eighty thousand men for the armed forces. 'I myself' said Goebbels at this time, 'have only one office with eight people, a few shorthand typists and two colleagues.'[21] He worked all month scaling down his own ministry, shutting its eastern, theater, music, and graphic arts departments and annexing the party's propaganda directorate (the R.P.L.).[22] He closed the training colleges for interpreters, music, and the history of art. He turned over the movie industry's entire rising generation to the Telefunken firm in Berlin for precision labor. He halted his efforts to overtake Hollywood in cartoon production. He scrapped the need for movie tickets, to release the forty-eight workers who printed them. He closed every theater, cabaret, and circus, dissolved some orchestras, and posted a mandatory sixty-hour working week for everyone. He banned all congresses and conventions.[23]

Briefing Hitler, he predicted that he would extract a hundred thousand men from the postal service by cutting red tape and halting junk-mail deliveries; and two hundred thousand more from 'domestic employment.'[24] Only Munich and Berlin would be allowed more than one daily newspaper. To release banking personnel he urged people to pay by cash. He abolished cake-making and closed all restaurants and stores except pharmacies, groceries, and cobblers.[25] He even tried to dissolve the Reich Labor Service.[26] Himmler had to secure a special dispensation to protect his own vital tasks.[27] Goebbels announced the death penalty for anybody caught violating his total war regulations.[28] By these means he expected to raise three hundred thousand men for the front by September 1, 450,000 more by October and a quarter million during November: One million men all told.[29]

AT THE WOLF'S LAIR on August 2, Hitler and Goebbels discussed how to deal with the traitors. The Gestapo investigations were turning up some nasty new details. Even Kluge and Rommel were implicated.[30]

One of those arrested, Major Egbert Hayessen, had incriminated one of Goebbels' oldest friends, Count von Helldorff, in the plot.[31] Goebbels' fury was indescribable.[32] Ignoring Magda's reproaches he and Hitler had personally settled the Berlin police chief's gambling debts and bought him property. Yet even as Goebbels had been decorating him in February for heroism in the air raids, the count had been plotting his and Hitler's downfall. Hitler ordered that Helldorff was to watch each hanging until his own turn came.[33]

Broadcasting that night Goebbels named Carl Goerdeler, the former mayor of Leipzig, as another conspirator and put a million-mark ($250,000) bounty on his head. Among Goerdeler's effects the Gestapo found a draft list of names of future ministers, including both Rommel and Speer.[34] Stauffenberg, wrote Goebbels after reading Kaltenbrunner's investigation reports, had worked for months just setting up the putsch. Squandering immense amounts of scarce gasoline the blue-blooded colonel had motored around, working on one traitor after another, until each ultimately fell in with him, as many had since testified in court. 'A good thing we got rid of Stauffenberg,' noted Goebbels. 'A negative personality with talents like that [is] always extremely dangerous.'[35]

Stauffenberg, it seemed, had been in touch with the traitors in Moscow. Hitler showed Goebbels the latest Soviet propaganda leaflets, signed by German generals.[36] He said that the quartermaster-general Wagner (who had shot himself) had sent ten times more gasoline to sectors without tanks than to those with them.[37]

While both men agreed that they could not publicly excoriate the generals in mid-battle Hitler ordered Goebbels to spare no detail of the other traitors' infamy – for example that they had also planned to kill him by planting a bomb in the knapsacks of three unwitting soldiers demonstrating a new infantry uniform to him.[38] It was not difficult for Goebbels now to persuade him to stage a political show trial rather than court-martial the plotters.

Goebbels and Himmler revealed this decision to the party's gauleiters assembled in Posen the next morning, August 3.[39] In fourteen days, said Goebbels, twenty-two generals of army group Center had deserted to Soviet captivity – and several were already broadcasting from Moscow.[40] Three German armies had been wiped out, he asserted, because the generals in Berlin had devoted less energy to the eastern front than to plotting VALKYRIE; yet he still insisted that it had been only 'a tiny clique' of traitors. 'Those found guilty will be sentenced to death, dressed in convict garb, and hanged regardless of their rank as field marshal or whatever else.'

> How often the Führer pleaded for one more regiment and was told they didn't have one. But if you needed troops in the air-raid areas – in Berlin one day [November 23/24, 1943] they coughed up sixty thousand men! Then

they had them – so you can't help thinking that they weren't sending the troops to the front because they needed them for treachery at home, to put the party down.

Returning briefly from Posen to headquarters to hear Hitler address these gauleiters, Goebbels' train made slow progress as all the routes east were now choked with troop-transports. He allowed himself a contented grin at this visible proof that total war had begun.

ALMOST EVERY WEEK after this he reported to Hitler.[41] The post office patched together for him a secure nationwide conference-network to enable him to address all forty-three gauleiters each noon by loudspeaker telephone. Few of them willingly missed this daily briefing. Hans Frank in Kraków and Kurt Daluege in Prague joined the network, as did Epp in Munich and Kaltenbrunner in Berlin. Only his old enemy Erich Koch disdained it and when the police headquarters in Königsberg was bombed out at the end of August he did not have the link restored.[42]

By now the Red Army had overrun nearly all of Hitler's eastern dominions. The Normandy beachhead had burst, hemorrhaging Allied troops into France. Goebbels warned farmers to prepare for a coming food crisis. After attending a Goebbels Cabinet on August 28, Agriculture Secretary Darré recorded that Goebbels had spoken well: 'We're fighting with our backs to the wall.'[43]

Public sympathy for Dr Goebbels was slipping however. Writing his weekly *Das Reich* article had become a burden.[44] His facile suggestion that the bomb plot had brought them 'one step closer to victory' attracted derision.[45]

There was a growing belief that Germany could no longer win – that her leaders could not have anticipated such a rapid collapse in the west. Kaltenbrunner wrote to Goebbels that the implementation of total war was still taking too long for the public's liking, and that they looked to leading personalities 'and their wives' to set an example.[46]

Taking the hint, Goebbels once more put Magda to work, making war goods at home at Lanke. 'As I'm switchboard girl, manageress, and Jack-of-all-Trades out here,' Magda wrote patiently to a friend, 'you'll always reach me here except for Mondays when I have to turn my work in at the factory!'[47]

Speer began to mutiny as he saw his skilled labor siphoned off into army uniforms. He wrote blistering letters, but with Keitel and Bormann backing Goebbels he had little leverage.[48] He complained privately that Goebbels was violating agreements, not returning calls, and creating *faits accomplis*. He demanded that his name no longer appear in newspaper reports about arms production, since the gauleiters had taken charge. He unloaded a sheaf of protest telegrams onto Goebbels' desk, but the minister remained unmoved.[49] 'You've been asked to give up 150,000 of your fifteen million men,' he reminded Speer. That was just one percent. 'I'd like to see one of *my* department heads tell me he can't produce as much with ninety-nine men as with one hundred. . .

No, Mr Speer, arguments like this won't wash with me!' Speer, he told his staff, was about to find out whom he was up against. 'I can't help wondering why the traitors put his name on their list.'[50]

To Speer's chagrin, on September 1 Goebbels learned that nearly all of the gauleiters had met their August manpower targets. Three hundred thousand men had been called up – thirty new divisions. Despite that, arms production had actually increased. Speer had not a leg to stand on. His vanity punctured beyond repair he none the less flew to the Wolf's Lair to protest about Goebbels. From there he phoned Goebbels, who gave him short shrift, and Speer 'acted all cut up,' as the propaganda minister was pleased to dictate to Otte afterward.[51] He was having his twice-weekly bath that evening when the phone rang – Hitler's S.S. adjutant Otto Günsche, instructing him to take the 8:13 P.M. courier train out to Rastenburg. Speer was calling for a showdown. Its departure delayed until nine o'clock while the minister completed his toilette, the train arrived at Rastenburg twelve hours later.[52] Pre-empting the debate, however, Goebbels sent Hitler a telegram reporting the three hundred thousand new troops. 'I intend,' he dictated on the train, 'to plead with the Führer not to let Speer pick the currants out of my cake.'[53]

THE FÜHRER-BUNKER had been reinforced yet again, but even with twenty-two feet of solid concrete surrounding them they could all hear the rolling thunder of the approaching Russian guns. While Speer glowered, Hitler took Goebbels over to the map table and showed him where he would emplace those three hundred thousand new men. As the two ministers left the bunker their friendship was behind them.[54]

Back in Berlin Goebbels found a minute from Hadamovsky reminding him of Clausewitz's dictum that the most dangerous point for an attacker was when victory seemed in sight: the attacker relaxed his efforts while the defender redoubled his. Clipped to the memo was a British news dispatch: The London *Daily Mail* was bragging, 'Militarily, the war in the west is over.' It was the same blunder that the Germans had made at Moscow in 1941.[55]

The German retreat in France had turned into a rout. Field Marshal von Kluge launched a counter-attack at Avranches, bungled it, and committed suicide.[56] 'The Americans,' noted Goebbels, 'are now showing off to us the same blitzkrieg tactics that we demonstrated to the French and British in 1940.'

Once he sat up with Hitler and his advisers until two A.M. discussing what to do; but Goebbels feared that Hitler was operating in the west with non-existent divisions and useless generals. 'If there were brutal party men in charge of the various sectors things would probably be quite different.'[57]

The Americans crossed the German frontier at Aachen in mid September. The war might be over with dramatic swiftness, in weeks or even days.[58] The day of reckoning suddenly seemed nearer. Goebbels knew that Soviet propaganda was claiming that in three years the Nazis had murdered two million prisoners in Lublin, Poland.[59] He knew too that the Allies considered him a war criminal.[60]

It was likely that top Nazis like him would be shot out of hand. 'It should not be assumed,' Churchill announced in London, 'that the procedure of trial will be necessarily adopted.'[61] During one trial in Rome the mob had lynched a fascist defendant and tossed his corpse into the Tiber.

'These,' Goebbels mused, 'are alarming omens which no thinking man can ignore.'[62] He did not intend to be taken prisoner. Hearing that, like Paulus at Stalingrad, General Hermann Ramcke had surrendered at Brest, Goebbels was baffled at the paratroop general's lack of any sense of immortality.[63] Since the daily commute from Lanke was robbing him of precious hours, Goebbels moved back into No. 20 Hermann-Göring Strasse, while his family stayed out at Lanke. He himself had decided on suicide; but evidently he had no notion yet of killing his children, as he discussed with Max Winkler that autumn what would become of them after his death, adding that his son Hellmut showed few of his daughters' talents and he would like to leave him perhaps a small farm.[64]

Enforcing total war was still an uphill struggle. During September 1944 he ordered teenagers mobilized, and directed women to take over all hairdressing.[65] He had the propaganda companies slashed from fifteen thousand to three thousand men; but the railroad and the foreign ministry declined to make manpower cuts, and Speer stubbornly refused to release the next hundred thousand men from his factories.[66]

He accused Goebbels of organizing a useless people's army. Goebbels called the allegation puerile – 'We don't have any intention of pitting unarmed soldiers against the enemy,' he wrote. After hearing Speer pontificating about his responsibility before history, Goebbels dictated: 'I think we have let this young man get too big for his boots.'[67]

Hitler ruled in his favor every time. When Speer flourished tables of statistics, Goebbels denounced them as lies.[68] The people were still waiting for V–2. 'If we didn't have more such weapons,' they said, 'Dr Goebbels would not have been able to speak so definitely about them.'[69] S.S. Obergruppenführer Hans Kammler told Goebbels that the V–2 missile attack on London had begun on September 8; the rockets were being launched from secret mobile sites in Holland.[70] Churchill however was admitting nothing, so Goebbels dared not commence his V–2 propaganda yet.

With France lost, the Luftwaffe's V–1 pilotless bomb had all but ceased operations. Hitler again considered replacing Göring as commander-in-chief of the Luftwaffe, but again he abandoned the idea.

'It is horrendous,' commented Goebbels, 'the contortions that have to be gone through. . . When the good times rolled, the Führer allowed Göring to get too grand; and now the bad times are here, he's like a ball-and-chain.'[71] The public had no time for either Göring or Ribbentrop, Himmler was told at this time: They thought well only of Hitler, Goebbels, and of course himself, the Reichsführer S.S.[72]

For all his shortcomings however it was Göring who broke it to Goebbels that Harald was missing in action in Italy. Goebbels and Magda decided to keep it from Harald's siblings, who idolized him. He consoled Magda that her son might have been taken prisoner.[73]

SEVERAL TIMES LIEUTENANT von Oven heard Goebbels preface his remarks with the remark, 'If I were foreign minister. . .'[74] He intently followed the Soviet-inspired rumors in the neutral press about Nazi feelers to Moscow and often speculated on Stalin's reasons for refusing to join in the Allied demand for unconditional surrender.[75] The Japanese, he knew, were aghast at recent events like the bomb plot and the military collapse in France, and they too expressed dismay at the lack of flexibility in Ribbentrop's foreign policy. The Japanese ambassador General Hiroshi Oshima urged Naumann to tell Goebbels that Germany must make peace with the Soviets; Japan was even willing to make concessions to that end.[76]

The topic was dynamite, but Goebbels immediately asked both Himmler and Bormann to convey Oshima's message to Hitler. 'We've got to revitalize our foreign policy,' he noted.[77] He was not alone in this view. He found that Dr Ley, rattled that enemy troops had reached German soil, shared his concerns. Ley mentioned that many people hoped to see the propaganda minister replacing Ribbentrop eventually.[78]

The upshot was that Goebbels drafted a twenty-seven-page pitch for Ribbentrop's job – a memorandum for Hitler spelling out brutal home truths on foreign policy.

They had held neither the eastern front nor the Atlantic Wall, he said. They had lost most of their occupied territories. The only positive factor was the disunity among their enemies – redolent of 1932, when clever tactics had ultimately enabled Hitler to outsmart them. 'We did not wait then,' he pointed out, 'for them to approach us: We approached them.' Germany, he reminded Hitler, had never yet won a war on two fronts.

There was however little prospect of negotiating with the western powers, although that would, he conceded, conform with Hitler's own ambitions. 'Even if for instance Churchill secretly desired such a solution,' observed Goebbels, 'which I doubt, he would not in practice be able to implement it as he's hog-tied by domestic politics.' Britain was in a truly tragic situation, he argued: 'For her, even victory will equate to defeat. Not so the Soviet Union,' he continued, reaching the real burden of his memorandum. Stalin had no such inhibitions and the eastern solution would please Tokyo too.

'I cannot conceal,' wrote Goebbels, 'that I do not consider our foreign minister capable of initiating such a development.' He mentioned his ninety-minute row with Ribbentrop in July over his foreign policy articles in *Das Reich*.[79] 'With him,' wrote Goebbels, 'it is prestige *über alles*.'[80]

Goebbels suspected that Hitler would be astonished to see such a brutally frank exposition. He signed it on Friday September 22, sealed it into a large white linen envelope, and sent it off by courier to Hitler's headquarters.[81]

Meanwhile he tried to score off Ribbentrop for one last time, spitefully directing his total-war office to dissolve the foreign ministry's press, propaganda, and cultural departments.

Ribbentrop countered by demanding that Goebbels disband his *foreign* department. Goebbels retorted that he had acted not in his capacity as propaganda minister, but as the Führer's special plenipotentiary for total war: And if Mr Ribbentrop ventured to complain to the Führer then he would tender his resignation and the Führer could whistle for the next seventy divisions.[82]

Perhaps – thus he daydreamed – he would be foreign minister before another week was out. He drove out to Lanke on Saturday morning imagining Hitler opening that white envelope around midday (but he doubted that he would actually find time to read it before evening).[83]

On Sunday Schaub told Naumann that Hitler had 'carefully read' the document, put it away to study again that night, and asked Dr Goebbels to come to the Wolf's Lair in four days' time.[84]

v: The Loyal Henchman

56: The Specter of the Hangman

BEFORE THAT DAY CAME Hitler was taken seriously ill. By Thursday September 28, 1944 it was plain that he had contracted jaundice. Apathetic and weary, he lay in bed for days. His war conferences were cancelled. General Schmundt died of his injuries from the Stauffenberg bomb, but Hitler barely stirred. Goebbels blamed the illness on Professor Morell's neglect, suspecting that the physician had injected so many questionable nostrums that Hitler's own organs had finally rebelled in this way.[1]

From Berlin, he pressed the Führer relentlessly about the foreign-policy document, but only when the Russian assault on East Prussia resumed did Hitler lever himself out of bed and agree to receive him, on Saturday October 14.[2]

Killing time until then Goebbels toured the Rhineland, conferred with the gauleiters, and visited Kluge's successor as C.-in-C. West, Field Marshal Model.[3] The tour increased his disillusionment with Speer. 'You keep falling for his miracle figures,' he told his staff back in Berlin, 'because your heart leaps when you hear of the thousands of tanks and fighter planes we're turning out. But Model says if they get three Tiger tanks it's a red-letter day for them.'[4]

Broadcasting on October 4 Goebbels warned the Allies not to underestimate the powers of a people to resist occupation. He spoke of the 'Morgenthau Plan' devised by President Roosevelt's treasury secretary to destroy Germany's postwar economy; under it, six million Germans would probably die of starvation, and tens of thousands would be shot without trial including Hitler, Göring, Himmler, and Goebbels. Roosevelt and Churchill had just initialed this plan in Québec. Even undistorted, it was a gift for Nazi propaganda. Even other Jews were horrified by it.

In Goebbels' papers is an intercepted letter from a German Jew, a lawyer, in Switzerland, who wrote to Morgenthau that his plan was just 'designed to pitch the vanquished into the swamp of slavery.' 'Where hatred speaks,' warned this émigré, 'revenge answers.'[5] Goebbels exploited the Morgenthau Plan as cynically in 1944 as he had Kaufman's book three years before, telling his propagandists to emphasize constantly the American Jew's premise of 'forty million Germans too many in the world.'[6]

Both the Allies and the Soviets had the same intent, so Goebbels could now suggest in *Das Reich*: 'Namely to truncate the German people by thirty or forty million.'[7]

From Canada, Churchill traveled onward to Moscow. Reading this hopefully as a sign of increasing frictions within the enemy coalition, Goebbels ordered newspapers to abstain from comment. 'I have the utmost respect,' he said in private, 'for this septuagenarian who flies halfway around the world to glue together a crumbling coalition on which his entire war strategy depends.'[8]

HE WOULD BE THE FIRST visitor whom Hitler received after his illness; but the great foreign-policy debate did not take place. Goebbels spent a frustrating Sunday and Monday hanging around the Wolf's Lair, not even invited to share mealtimes with Hitler. The Führer was in bed recovering, but still sickly and feeble.[9] He had neither time nor inclination for a long talk – he granted ten minutes here, an hour there – and he had not even read the Goebbels memorandum. Bormann had given him the gist of it, he said; he flatly refused to replace Ribbentrop, 'a second Bismarck' in his eyes, and that was that.[10]

Returning by train to Berlin, Goebbels sat in silence with his head in his hands. To Oven, he seemed suddenly to have aged.[11] The specter of the hangman loomed dimly ahead.

HITLER HAD HOWEVER confided two decisions to him. The first was his plan to mount a surprise counter-offensive in the west to catch the Allies off balance at their weakest moment – the moment which Clausewitz had prophesied.[12] He briefed his western front commanders a few days later. Goebbels himself was not overly impressed. 'It is strongly to be hoped,' he wrote skeptically, 'that it will succeed.'[13]

Hitler's second major decision was to create a Volkssturm, a people's army of every remaining male between the ages of sixteen and sixty.[14] That was a task that Goebbels could throw himself into. Recruiting posters went up on Thursday October 19. Seventy thousand Berliners volunteered at once, with twenty thousand more on Saturday and thirty-five thousand the next day. In Silesia, Karl Hanke mustered over one hundred thousand men on the castle square in Breslau. Broadcasting nationwide on October 27 Goebbels recalled the words that Clausewitz had used of the Prussian Landsturm, raised to fight Napoleon at Leipzig: 'It shall spread like a bushfire and shall finally smite the territory on which the invader has set foot.'

'We cannot,' said Goebbels, 'be swayed from our resolute and immutable decision . . . to fight until a peace can be attained which will guarantee to our people their right to life, their national independence, and, in a broader sense, the basis of their existence, thus justifying the sacrifices.' This sounded very much like a willingness to discuss terms. 'The Führer,' he continued, 'with whom I spent several days at his headquarters, stands like a rock amid the surging tide.'[15] One of Hitler's adjutants wrote privately that evening, 'Dr Goebbels just spoke. . . It's a treat to hear him every time.'[16]

Not everybody agreed. 'The German people can do without any propaganda stunts,' wrote one army corporal to Ribbentrop's wife after listening to the broadcast. 'We can see things just the way they are.' 'Did you think,' he challenged Mrs von Ribbentrop, 'that we ordinary squaddies don't know about the bestial murders committed particularly by our S.S. in Russia? Where for instance are the 114,000 Jews of Lvov? We were there when they were trucked out of Lvov in 1942 and 1943 and shot not far away.'[17]

The specter looming larger with each news bulletin, Goebbels drove out to Lanke to celebrate his birthday. At midnight Hitler telephoned his greetings, his voice still husky and run down. 'My last weeks have been almost entirely taken up with plotting our revenge,' he said, and Goebbels knew he was alluding to the coming great offensive in the west. Hitler still would not hear of getting rid of Ribbentrop. Disappointed, Goebbels handed the phone to Magda. They spent the evening together, husband and wife, vainly trying not to talk about the war. 'It will never let us out of its clutches,' he dictated the next morning, 'until it's all over.'[18] It was to be his last birthday. Forty-seven and a half years would separate the humble cradle in Rheydt and the unmarked grave in Berlin.

Poisoning the already strained atmosphere, the trials of the bomb-plot traitors in the People's Court continued all autumn. Dr Dietrich had strongly opposed allowing any newspaper coverage of them. Goebbels had overruled him.[19] Hadamovsky went in to observe the first day's proceedings, when Witzleben, Hoepner, and Stieff were tried and sentenced; he praised Judge Freisler as magisterial, National Socialist, and superior.[20] Goebbels had commissioned a movie of the trial and of the hangings.[21] Hitler however forbade its release, fearing a backlash, an 'undesirable debate' about the trial.[22] He ordered the execution footage particularly kept under lock and key. Despite this newspapers reported that the British legation in Switzerland had shown a print to Swiss officers there. Investigations showed that it was a fake furnished by a Mr Saunders, a British secret service agent; it was evidently the origin of several postwar legends about the executions, including rumors that the men were hanged from meat-hooks and took ten hours to die.[23]

The further trials brought many unsavory facts to light about Ribbentrop's diplomats. Goebbels adroitly brought them to Hitler's attention. 'The latest People's Court trials,' he pointed out, 'and reports that foreign service officials are refusing to return to the Reich, have shown that the foreign ministry is riddled with traitors and politically unreliable elements.' Perhaps, he mischievously wondered, the defection of Germany's European allies was the result of their sabotage?[24] Still Hitler refused to let Ribbentrop go.

TRUE TO CLAUSEWITZ'S PROPHECY, the Allies had run out of steam. On the western front they had also outrun their supplies. In the east, Hitler counter-attacked. In East Prussia, towns like Gumbinnen and Nemmendorf were recaptured, revealing the recent atrocities which the Red Army had committed. Göring phoned Goebbels and described the horrific scenes. Oddly, because the result must inevitably be the same scenes of refugee chaos that Goebbels had himself striven to produce in France in 1940, he embodied these atrocity reports in press announcements so lurid that the local population could have no doubt what awaited them if they stayed.[25]

It seems clear that he was interested less in victory now than in his place in posterity. On November 12 the Volkssturm volunteers were sworn in at emotional rallies all over Germany. Goebbels himself took the salute in Berlin, on Wilhelm Platz, that Sunday morning. 'We were home again by noon,' wrote one veteran, who would later die defending Hitler's chancellery. 'This Old Soldier's heart just laughed out loud. So now I'm a full sworn-in Volkssturm man.' He found the minister's speech just *wunderbar*.[26]

The newsreel shows these elderly, bemedalled Berliners marching like a hundred thousand extras in a movie epic: Rank upon rank, proudly keeping step to the thump and blare of the bands, some shouldering ancient flintlock rifles, muskets, and carbines, others bearing more modern weapons that were taken from their hands as soon as they had marched out of camera range. Goebbels promised them better weapons when their time came, and warned them frankly that they might be committed on the main eastern front and not just here in Berlin. His ministry now admonished newspapers not to use the word *durchhalten*, 'hold out,' as it struck unhappy chords in those who had lived through World War One.[27]

History, argued Goebbels in *Das Reich*, would surely not be so unjust as to let Germany lose again.[28] The Allies were war-weary, he said, speaking on November 25. When Churchill now conceded that London had been under V–2 missile attack for five weeks Goebbels used this tardy admission to illustrate the unreliability of British propaganda. 'Millions of people,' he triumphed in *Das Reich*, 'were witnesses of the use of the new German long-range weapon, which is incomparably more destructive than the V–1.'[29]

Hitler left the Wolf's Lair and returned to Berlin for an operation on his throat. Goebbels too felt poorly; he had his chest X-rayed but nothing was found.[30] He called at the chancellery on December 1 and stayed with Hitler until five-thirty A.M. (He would call this one of the most interesting discussions he ever had with the Führer.)

His voice still only a croak, Hitler revealed more about his secret plans for the coming Ardennes offensive. 'When I consider,' marveled Goebbels afterward, 'how sickly and weak he was when I saw him bed-ridden several weeks ago, when he already outlined these same great plans to me . . . then I can only say that a miracle has come over him.'

Hitler's main problem would be to inspire his generals, because they were infected with defeat. Nothing, he said, matched the western front in importance now. If his offensive succeeded they could Dunkirk the British all over again, blame the Americans, and restart their V–1 bombardment of southern England.

As for the V–2, Hitler added meaningfully: 'Mr Churchill had every reason to keep it secret from his public.' With no lack of confidence in the final outcome himself, Hitler mentioned that after the war he was going to give fine estates to his best political and military officers.[31]

IT WAS UNLIKELY THAT Reichsmarschall Göring would qualify. Every night the British destroyed yet another German city.

Hitler expressed uncomprehending sorrow about Göring. How could he still live in such repugnant luxury, wearing his pompous pearl-gray silk uniform? He had advised Göring, he said, to spend less time out at Carinhall surrounded by his assorted aunts, cousins, and sisters-in-law. Göring had even taken to receiving generals in a floor-length dressing gown and furry slippers. Hitler was determined to smash the camarilla of corrupt generals surrounding the Reichsmarschall, and to help his better qualities come to the fore.

In a British fire raid on ancient Heilbronn on December 4, 7,147 people were burned alive; that was the final figure. Göring was powerless to prevent it. At midday on the sixth Goebbels found him out at Carinhall sipping tea surrounded by elderly female relatives and sycophants like Philipp Bouhler (the euthanasia mass-murderer) and Bruno Loerzer, Göring's crony in the Richthofen squadron and former chief of Luftwaffe personnel (Hitler had sacked him). For four hours Göring whined and argued, pleading his innocence of the Luftwaffe's failures. He blamed everybody but himself.[32]

Two days later, at 6:45 P.M. on December 3, 1944, a chauffeur-driven car brought Hitler over to No. 20 Hermann-Göring Strasse to pay what proved to be his last visit to the Goebbels household. The children put on long dresses made from old curtains in 'Uncle Führer's' honor. As he was helped out of his greatcoat, Magda's mother found him a shadow of his former self.[33]

His hands trembled uncontrollably. The children had not seen him for four years. Whereas Helga and Hilde (at twelve and ten, the eldest) had earlier captivated him, now his attention turned to six-year-old Hedda. She had eyes only for Günter Schwägermann, however, her father's one-eyed adjutant: She declared she was going to marry *him*, explaining: *'He* can take his eye out!' Hitler beamed special favors on Hellmut too; two days earlier Goebbels had read out to him his little boy's school essay on 'November 9, 1923' – one of the party's high holy days – and tears of unkind laughter rolled down their cheeks. 'You would never have guessed,' his father had indulgently dictated into his diary, 'that he was the son of a writer.'[34]

Surrounded by paintings which Goebbels had retrieved from the bunker for the occasion, Hitler talked of the devastation in Berlin and his sorrow at the loss of life. But he had done what he could, he sanctimoniously reminded Goebbels, to prevent this kind of barbarism in 1939. Then he chuckled at the rash prophecies the British were uttering about the war's coming end. Things were looking up, he said – an allusion to his new offensive, now only days away.

'Of course,' Goebbels prided himself, 'I understand precisely what he's getting at.'[35]

At eight-thirty P.M. Hitler made his excuses and returned to the chancellery.[36] Werner Naumann, towering over them in his S.S. brigadier's uniform, commented afterward in flattering terms on the astonishing mental and physical health of their Führer. Goebbels registered this without comment in his diary, but he told his former adjutant Prince Schaumburg-Lippe, 'Be glad you didn't see him. The Hitler you once believed in doesn't exist any more.'[37]

MAGDA HAD FALLEN HEAD over heels for Dr Naumann, a more dangerous rival to Goebbels than Hanke ever had been. In charge of the secret project to microfilm the Goebbels Diaries, Naumann had begun dictating passages from them clandestinely to one of his private secretaries, Dorothea von Arnim. He planned to use them to overthrow the minister when the time came.[38] Naumann's own marriage had now completed its seventh year, and was entering the predictable doldrums despite their four children. Like Hanke before him, he regarded Magda as a tragic heroine. Guessing what was going on, Goebbels shortly ordered Naumann to end the relationship. Magda found some solace in her Buddhism and in writing poetry, some of which she sent to Naumann. As the nights lengthened, she spent more time with her husband. Often she found him standing quietly at the bedside of their six sleeping children.[39] Already he and she were nurturing dark plans for their brood.

A week after his visit Hitler left for the western front.

At five-thirty A.M. on Saturday December 16, 1944 his Ardennes offensive began, a last gamble. Artillery barrages drenched the five American infantry divisions holding the target sector. Three German armies backed by 170 bombers, ninety ground-attack planes, and fifteen hundred fighter planes punched at the American lines. Simultaneously V–1s and V–2s rained down on Antwerp, the final goal of his armies. One V–2 killed *two thousand* Allied servicemen in the Rex cinema in Antwerp.

Goebbels, who had joined his family out at Lanke, ordered a total media blackout about the operation, overruling even Hitler, who had wanted a single-sentence, upbeat communiqué. By evening it was plain that Goebbels was right – Eisenhower was still in the dark about what had hit him.[40] Not until Sunday evening did the enemy announce the shocking news that Hitler had managed to launch this audacious operation (although they gave the credit to Field Marshal von Rundstedt).[41] On Monday the eighteenth, Hitler's High Command tersely confirmed it, provoking exultation in Germany's bomb-devastated cities. Goebbels drove out to Lanke again with Magda: Their six children were standing on the steps and sang a welcoming chorus which they had rehearsed all day with their governess.

As Hitler's tanks rolled on it was like the headiest days of 1940; the Allied air forces were virtually grounded by bad weather. Thousands of prisoners were taken, hundreds of tanks destroyed. For Magda too it was a kind of victory: This was their thirteenth wedding anniversary and she had kept her family together, despite everything.

At one A.M. Hitler phoned them from his forward headquarters in western Germany, excitedly predicting that the U.S. First Army was already beaten. Both men agreed that the enemy had not grasped what was happening – Eisenhower was still talking about a localized Nazi push by three or four divisions. Before hanging up Hitler reminisced with Magda about the Goebbels wedding. 'The time since then has gone in a flash,' dictated Goebbels, the specter momentarily forgotten.[42]

By December 21 the Germans had taken twenty-five thousand American prisoners and destroyed 350 tanks. Eisenhower called off all other operations to cope with the emergency. Stalin did nothing to assist his beleaguered Allies. Goebbels still warned against making damaging predictions.[43] This was as well, because on the twenty-third, with Hitler's broad armored blade thrust forty miles deep into the American ribs, the skies cleared and the Allied air forces struck back.

Although history shows that the Nazi offensive was finally halted on the twenty-fourth Goebbels still hoped for a miracle. Using a typewriter to spare his Führer the struggle with his spidery scrawl, he sent him a Christmas message ('even if there's no real Christmas for us') marveling 'that once again, as so oft before, you are leading us out of the dilemma; that you are a lustrous example to us all; that you teach us how mind and will-power overcome matter and corporeality; and that therefore you tower above everybody and everything.'[44]

Even now Goebbels still would not permit any fanfares about Hitler's big offensive. Out at Lanke the children put on their long dresses for Christmas Eve. Snuffing out the candles on the tree that night, after everybody had been given their presents, Magda said to her secretary, 'Next year we'll surely be at peace.'[45] After Christmas Goebbels' sister Maria and his mother left Lanke, and he never saw them again.[46]

HIS NEW YEAR'S EVE BROADCAST to the Reich was an empty panegyric. One propaganda official noted in his diary, 'I can't help it – overall it was a letdown.'[47] Public reaction to Goebbels' next article 'Der Führer,' with its glowing references to Hitler's modesty, his love of peace, and his foresight, was downright hostile. 'He has the Sixth Sense,' Goebbels had written, 'the gift to see what is denied the eyes of other mortals.' A Gestapo agent overheard one less gifted female tartly commenting that this was no doubt why Hitler had consistently picked as his closest friends people like the Italians who had betrayed him the most. 'There's no pulling the wool over his eyes,' Goebbels had written. In that case, grumbled the public, it was hard to understand the bomb plot of the Twentieth of July.[48]

A few days later he went to Hitler's forward headquarters, near Frankfurt, for a two-day Cabinet-level discussion on injecting even more men into the armed forces.[49] On the first day, January 3, 1945, a blazing row developed. Speer objected that it sounded like a *levée en masse*, a people's army, again. He refused to be a part of it. Glaring at him, Goebbels called out: 'Then on your shoulders be the blame before history that we lose this war for the want of a few hundred thousand soldiers!'[50]

He remained alone with Hitler until supper at eight. The Führer was so exhausted by the dispute that his left arm started trembling violently, and Morell had to give him extra injections.[51]

Under the new Goebbels *Aktion*, 240,000 men were promised to the army during the first quarter of 1945; the figure was not even approximately reached.[52] He had bitten off more than he could chew, and he met obstructionism all the way. Ludicrously, Rosenberg still refused to disband his ministry for the occupied eastern territories.[53] The corrupt Nazi upper echelons were interested only in their own well-being.

On January 26 Goebbels drew Hitler's attention to General von Hanneken, who had shipped ham, lard, and furniture from Denmark to Paris, then used the truck to pick up wines and spirits for his own use (instead of urgently needed spare parts); Hanneken's motor launch had consumed a thousand liters of gasoline during July 1944 – a month in painful memory.[54] On March 20, Goebbels pointed out to Hitler that the air force, which had had 172 active generals in 1941, now had 327 generals despite its reduction in size.[55] His campaign against Göring continued unabated, and unavailing to the end.

WHEN HE HAD RETURNED to Berlin from Hitler's headquarters on January 5 the first complete print of the epic movie *Kolberg* had just arrived from Ufa's color laboratories.

Goebbels viewed it privately that evening. Its gigantic battle scenes and the heroic performances by its stars were among the finest ever filmed by the German movie industry. The simultaneous public premières were held on January 30 at the Tauentzien-Palace theater and at Ufa's movie theater on Alexander Platz, directly after the broadcast of what was to prove Hitler's last speech (it lasted only sixteen minutes).

The movie was a stunning success, particularly at the 'Alex' – there were fifteen curtain calls for the stars.[56] It was also shown that day to the troops holding out in Hitler's Atlantic fortress La Rochelle, where a fighter plane had delivered it only hours before. 'The movie is so well suited to our times,' wrote one of Hitler's personal staff, 'that one would almost ascribe clairvoyant powers to those whose brainchild it is – it was conceived as far back as 1942.'[57]

Goebbels also had the movie flown into the besieged fortresses of Breslau and Danzig, and as more copies became available they were sent to embattled Upper Silesia and the bridgeheads of Frankfurt-on-Oder, Neisse, and Königsberg. Copies were also provided for the personal use of Göring, Himmler, Dönitz, and Guderian, who were evidently as much in need of moral sustenance as these fortresses.[58]

57: *Kill off the Prisoners*

IF GOEBBELS NOW REALIZED that the war could not be won he kept this realization to himself. On January 12, 1945 Stalin's great offensive from the Baranov bridgehead on the Vistula began. With his eastern front crumpling, Hitler abandoned his offensive in the Ardennes and returned to Berlin. The Red Army did not halt until it reached the river Oder, just east of Berlin.

From January 24 on, Goebbels visited Hitler's chancellery almost every evening to spend half an hour or an hour alone with Hitler.[1] After their talk on the twenty-eighth, he returned home sunk in thought. 'It is true,' he dictated to Richard Otte for the diary afterward, 'that a great man has to await his great hour, and that there's nothing one can do by way of suggestions that will help him. It's more a matter of instinct than of any logical process. If the Führer should succeed in turning back the tide of events, and I am firmly convinced that the chance will one day come for that, then he will be not the man of the century, but the man of the millennium.'[2]

With large sections of the front now fighting on German soil, propaganda's greatest hour had come, as Goebbels instructed his gau propaganda officials on February 5; ugly reports were coming in of collapsing troop morale. Their propaganda must be firm, realistic, and unhysterical, and not deal in illusions. 'This is not the time for empty phrases,' he said. They had to offer proof that Germany could still triumph. 'Unfortunately it's not possible to speak openly and authoritatively of the weightiest political factor in our favor, namely the problems currently facing the enemy and the friction within the enemy coalition, as any such utterances would damage this promising development.'[3] Goebbels exploited the aftermath of the Ardennes battle to spread rumors, over Radio Arnhem and by breaking into the B.B.C.'s news broadcasts, that the British Field Marshal Montgomery was claiming all the credit for halting Hitler's offensive. It was one of his more successful gambits. The Americans were taken in and Goebbels' English counterpart Brendan Bracken had to make a formal apology to General Eisenhower.[4] *he was CFR.*

Sustaining Hitler's morale became no less important than that of the home front. As the Ardennes operations went into reverse, Goebbels scoured the books for historic parallels. He sent the Führer one such passage from a book on Alexander the Great.[5] During February he began re-reading Thomas Carlyle's ten-volume biography of Frederick the Great, into which he had first dipped fifteen years earlier.[6] Visiting Hitler at the end of the month, he related several chapters of the monarch's life story which, he recorded, greatly moved them both. 'What an example to us all,' he noted early in March. 'And what a solace and comfort in these dark days!'[7] He saw an uncanny parallel between the foppish Hermann Göring and the king's feckless brother, and sent that chapter over to Hitler, underlining the harsh treatment that the king had meted out to his sibling.

THE ENEMY AIR RAIDS CONTINUED with unremitting violence. The Ufa company had compiled a horrifying feature-length documentary on them, but because Ribbentrop had commissioned it Goebbels forbade its release.[8] A feud, after all, was a feud.

In mid-January the propaganda ministry briefed every gauleiter on the latest British bombing tactics: Four to six hundred heavy bombers would attack small cities repeatedly, saturating every square yard with incendiaries and with high-explosive bombs fused to delay detonation long enough for the weapon to penetrate to the crowded basements of even the tallest buildings.[9] The morale problems multiplied. The view became widespread that an occupation of Germany by the Anglo-Americans would not be 'all that bad' if it put an end to the bombing and the strafing attacks. Goebbels circularized the gauleiters on the need to counter this dangerous defeatism by propagating a base hatred of the imperialist and ideologically bankrupt British and Americans. The new line was to be: 'There is no difference between the bolshevik atrocities in East Prussia and the British and American atrocities on the Rhine.' Their enemies' aim, he suggested, was the same – death to all Germans. 'Gangsters at work!' must be the new leitmotif of their propaganda.[10]

At midday on Saturday February 3 over one thousand American B-17 heavy bombers attacked the center of Berlin, dropping 2,265 tons of bombs with the intent of creating maximum casualties and chaos among the refugees thronging into the capital. 'Five thousand-pounders,' wrote one American bombardier, adding in his own patois: 'Shacked [*i.e.*, killed] women and children!'

Although most of the flak artillery had been withdrawn to the Oder front, twenty-one B-17s were destroyed over the city, and ninety-three suffered battle damage.[11] Hitler's chancellery was hit again; fires raged, the streets were festooned in trolley-bus wires, but by late afternoon virtual normality had returned.

Hitler began a troglodyte existence in the bunker beneath his chancellery garden. It was not easy for Goebbels to hobble down the steps into this labyrinth, since the Führer and his staff occupied the remotest rooms at the deepest level, fifty feet beneath the grass and shrubbery. For a time he visited Hitler about every other day.[12]

The Führer's cramped study was tiled in olive green and white, and sparsely furnished – Anton Graff's famous portrait of Frederick the Great on one wall, a faded photograph of Hitler's mother on another, and a sofa upholstered in white and blue being the only accouterments.*

With the Russians now so close, on the last day of January 1945 Goebbels had sent Schwägermann out to Lanke, his lakeside mansion on the Bogensee, to evacuate Magda, their six children and two governesses into the air-raid shelter at Schwanenwerder. The next day he declared Berlin a 'fortress city.' Surrounded by her brood, Magda was in a world of self-delusion. From Berthe the milliner's she purchased a green velvet hat, a black turban, and a brown hat trimmed with fur; she mentioned that 'when things calmed down' she'd like to have a brown hat remodeled.[13]

'The news you'll be hearing isn't rosy,' she wrote to Harald, now in British captivity, on February 10. 'We're all sound in heart and health; but as the whole family belongs together at times like these we've shut down Bogensee and we've all moved back into Berlin. Despite all the air raids our house is still standing and everybody here – including your grandmother and the rest of the family – is well housed. The children find it splendid that there's no school and, thank God, they've noticed nothing of the seriousness of the hour.' 'Papa and I,' she concluded, 'are full of confidence and we're doing our duty as best we can.'[14]

She often thought of her former lover Karl Hanke in Breslau, and once or twice they spoke until telephoning was no longer possible as the Russian armies engulfed and encircled the city; Hanke, a man of undeniable bravery, wrote to his wife that he intended to hold on until help came from outside. 'I can see at any rate,' he said, 'that the Reich will not succumb and that is the main thing.'[15] The gauleiters, Goebbels had often noted, were all cut from a different cloth than the generals. 'You can be sure,' he wrote to Julius Streicher on his sixtieth birthday, 'that right now we are doing everything conceivable to bring this great fight for the destiny of our people to a happy and victorious end.'[16]

ON THE FOLLOWING NIGHT, February 13, the British bombers crowned their orgy of destruction by obliterating the hitherto unscarred capital of Saxony, Dresden. Overcrowded with a million fleeing human beings – refugees, prisoners, evacuees, and children – a city innocent of air-raid shelters, with all of its flak batteries removed to the eastern front and its fighter squadrons grounded for lack of fuel, Dresden became an inferno within minutes. Between sixty and one hundred thousand men, women, and children were choked to death or burned alive in the ensuing firestorms as this and another British raid three hours later engulfed and incinerated the city. British codebreakers read a secret report by the mayor on March 24 that eighty to one hundred thousand were still formally registered as 'missing.' For days after this apocalypse soldiers cremated the victims' bodies five hundred at a time on makeshift pyres in the city center. Tens of thousands more remained interred beneath the ruins.

---

* Of which a bloodstained shred survives in private hands in the United States.

[handwritten note] Apocalypse 1945: The Destruction of Dresden by David Irving (author of this book), Noontide Press, Newport Beach, CA.

On February 14 Goebbels saw Hitler at 7:15 P.M. for three-quarters of an hour. He now demanded that Göring be stood before the People's Court for negligence; but again Hitler weakly refused. Several times afterward Goebbels had fierce arguments with the Führer about Göring and his way of life; both men agreed that the navy's Admiral Dönitz was a shining example, as Raeder had been before him. Goebbels even suggested Dönitz should take over the Luftwaffe. On February 17 he proposed that they formally repudiate the Geneva Convention – why else should Allied pilots feel they could murder, slash, and burn with impunity? They should start executing Allied prisoners: One for each air-raid victim.[17] Hitler told him to draft a proposal.

Two days later, according to one source, the secret twelve-page document was ready in Goebbels' safe.[18] Several people later claimed the credit for preventing the grim plan from being implemented. Ribbentrop's opposition was probably the deciding factor for Hitler.[19] The Führer told Goebbels later, with noticeable regret, that he had allowed Himmler, Keitel, and Bormann to talk him out of it.[20] Fritzsche told interrogators that he delayed the radio announcement until the order was rescinded.[21]

DRESDEN UNMISTAKABLY HERALDED the beginning of the end. As Goebbels contemplated Hitler's stoical attitude to the growing certainty of defeat, comparisons with Frederick the Great again crowded in on him. He put it to Hitler on February 27 that their only aim now must be to set a heroic example to their children's children, in case a similar crisis should ever again beset Germany. Hitler agreed: It was necessary to work for one's people, even if the achievements were only ephemeral.[22]

On the last day of February Goebbels broadcast to the nation for the first time in weeks. He spoke for seventy minutes. 'Seen purely militarily,' he admitted straight away, 'the launching of the successful Soviet offensive from the Baranov bridgehead has sharply changed the general war situation, and not to our advantage.' He was not, he said, going to mince his language about this depressing 'but by no means hopeless' situation. The Soviets had mastered a similar crisis in 1941, and the British in 1940. 'The misfortunes that have beset us are very painful but they are in no way synonymous with the forfeiting of our victory and the consequent dissolution of the Reich and the biological extinction of the German people.'

They had again stabilized an eastern-front, he said, and the territories they had lost would be regained. The indescribable bolshevik atrocities in the east were however 'no products of their fantasy.' 'We would rather die,' he said, echoing Stalin's famous phrase, 'than capitulate.' What was the consequence of the Allies' aerial terrorism? he asked: Just that the Germans hated them even more. He reiterated that they had to believe in victory, 'unless the Goddess of History be just a whore of the enemy.'

Now however he added that if victory be denied them then he would consider life no longer worth living, 'neither for myself, nor for my children, nor for all whom I love and together with whom I have fought for so many years for a better and more noble existence.'

He knew, said Goebbels, that people would ask him how victory could still be theirs. He drew on a familiar analogy. 'Today,' he said, 'we're like the marathon runner who has thirty-five of the forty-two kilometers behind him.'[23]

This, his penultimate broadcast, was a brilliant effort. It met a mixed reception. 'When Goebbels speaks,' said S.S. Oberführer Kurt Meyer that evening in British captivity, 'it really grips you.' 'At any rate,' said an army general, 'he has achieved . . . a people which willingly cooperates with the government.'[24]

Others felt differently. Major-General Bruhn, also in British captivity, called the speech 'the most two-faced, hypocritical exhibition there has ever been,' and Major-General von Felbert agreed: 'What a scoundrel he is. If only I could lay hands on that dirty *beast*, that *swine*. . . this lump of filth, this muckworm!'[25]

'You can't give the people confidence with speeches like that,' remarked Dr Ley to his mistress, adding that Hitler and Goebbels never saw the front line. 'These people have no idea how grave the situation on the fronts actually is. If only one of them would leave his comfortable four walls and visit the fronts!'[26]

Hitler did in fact emerge to inspect the Oder front on the first Saturday in March, but when Goebbels visited him on the fourth Hitler refused even to allow the press to report it. Goebbels found him more depressed than ever, and he was disturbed by the now uncontrollable tremor in Hitler's left hand – the visible proof of the Parkinsonism for which Morell was now treating him.

His sixth sense was however intact. The Führer bitterly pointed out that while his general staff and Himmler, now commanding the army group on the Oder, had expected the Russians to go straight for Berlin, he had anticipated all along that they would first move on Pomerania, to the north-east. He had as usual proved right.

Goebbels wondered why Hitler could not get his own way with his own general staff. When the Führer stressed the need to hold the Rhine, Goebbels could only agree: If the British and Americans once got through into central Germany, there would be no need for them to negotiate with Hitler at all. They talked about the Dresden catastrophe – Hitler's own half-sister Angela Raubal had written him an eye-witness account of the horrors. Goebbels now proudly revealed that Magda and the children would stay with him in Berlin.

The headquarters generals with whom Goebbels spoke were very downcast. 'The atmosphere in the Reich chancellery,' noted the propaganda minister privately, 'is pretty grim. I'd prefer not to go there again because you can't help being infected by the mood.'[27]

Himmler, like Speer before him, was now skulking in bed with nameless disorders in the clinic at Hohenlychen outside Berlin. On March 7, 1945 Goebbels visited him and they warily explored each other's views for two hours and exchanged venomous remarks about Göring and Ribbentrop.

Goebbels said that he had warned Hitler that by hanging on to Göring he was asking for trouble – he hinted at a top-level mutiny; but still Hitler refused to draw the appropriate conclusion. Himmler showed that he believed their only chance lay in doing a deal with the west; Goebbels disagreed – Stalin was far more realistic than the hooligans in London and Washington.[28]

He had evidently given up all hope of a deal with the west. General Dittmar noted on February 27, 'Everybody I speak with in the propaganda ministry is in favor of the western solution. But that too is a leap in the dark.'[29]

GENERAL SCHÖRNER'S TROOPS counter-attacked in Lower Silesia and recaptured Lauban from the Russians. On March 8 Goebbels visited the little market town. Schörner was a popular commander, because he was tough. He told the minister he was hanging deserters in public with a placard round their neck: 'I'm a deserter and refuse to defend German women and children.' This was a general after Goebbels' heart.[30]

While badly damaged by the fighting, Lauban was still better off than any town that had been bombed, reflected Goebbels. Among the paratroops parading to hear him deliver a fiery and wholly improvised speech on its market square he discovered his former department head Willi Haegert – and a sixteen-year-old, Willy Hübner, who had just earned the Iron Cross for bravery.[31] Goebbels saw to it that a picture of himself and Hübner went round the world.

He shuddered as he drove past the burned-out hulks of Soviet tanks, these steely robots with which Stalin was hoping to subjugate all Europe. Back in Görlitz that evening he spoke in the town hall to thousands of soldiers and Volkssturm men. He told them of the children murdered and the women violated by the Russians, and proclaimed à la Ilya Ehrenburg, 'Slay the bolsheviks wherever you find them!'

'This enemy,' he said, 'can be beaten because you've beaten them before! Make them pay dearly in blood for every inch of German soil. We shall fight them in the fields and forests, and in the cities, and in every street and in every building until they have lost so much blood that they're no longer able to fight on.' 'History,' he declared, 'will grant to us the victory, because we alone deserve it.'[32]

Writing in *Das Reich* he said: 'The only thing that matters is for a people to have the nerve to wait for its great hour and then to use it.' The best thing a warring nation could do, he argued, was to think only of war, and then to prosecute it body and soul: 'The most total war is always the most merciful.'[33] These were slogans that all sounded very familiar: They had however lost much of their captivating power.

He saw Hitler again on Sunday evening March 11 and told him about Lauban. Hitler mentioned that Göring had recently visited him to discuss the need to 'clear the air politically' toward the enemy. Hitler had retorted that he'd do better to clear the air, period.

Clutching at straws, Hitler was convinced the enemy coalition was disintegrating. But they could not deal with the British. Churchill, said Hitler, was running amok – he had got it into his head to destroy Germany, regardless of whether he ruined his empire in the process.

In a reversal of his earlier stance Hitler now believed that, if he could inflict a bloody enough reverse on the Russians, the Kremlin might open up toward him: In the resulting separate peace with Russia, he hoped he might still achieve a beneficial partition of Poland, with Hungary and Croatia within the German ægis and freedom to continue operations in the west. Whether he could no longer bear to listen to such fateful illusions, or whether he too was wearying of the war, Goebbels decided that one such talk a week with Hitler, on a Sunday evening, was enough – it was worth any number of regular daily visits.[34]

IT WAS TWELVE YEARS to the day since he had set foot in the propaganda ministry on Wilhelm Strasse for the first time as minister. Schinkel's ornate palace had survived five years of continuous air raids, including some of the heaviest in history. Between eight and nine P.M. on March 13 it was hit by a single 4,000-pound blockbuster bomb dropped by a twin-engined Mosquito plane. Goebbels drove straight over, and found his beloved theater, the Throne Room, the Blue Gallery, and all the other fine architectural features on whose restoration he had lavished so many years of effort, leveled to the ground. For a while the fires which had broken out threatened to touch off five hundred bazooka anti-tank weapons he had stockpiled in the building. The front wing had collapsed, and the blast wave had wrought havoc in Hitler's old chancellery too.[35] 'The worst imaginable augury for the *next* twelve years,' reflected Goebbels, and added some nasty remarks at Göring's expense.

Hitler told him that night that in their latest talks Göring had been 'totally shattered' – 'But what use is that!' exclaimed Goebbels impotently in his diary. Still chewing over past grievances Hitler also showed him the shorthand record of the conferences in which he, unheeded by his generals, had correctly predicted that the Russians were going for Pomerania next. Together they walked over to watch the firefighters quenching the smoldering ruins of the propaganda ministry.[36]

On March 16 Goebbels invited the press round to his residence and lectured them for an hour on the barbarity of the Allies in the west.[37] He now knew that Ribbentrop's peace feelers to Britain had been rebuffed. Goebbels' emotions were mixed, between *Schadenfreude* and apprehension about his own future. He commented on rumors that Himmler had offered the enemy Hitler's head, 'They're demanding more heads than just Hitler's,' he remarked in his diary.[38] Two days later the Americans saturated Berlin's poorer districts with bombs, killing about five hundred people.

Telephoning Goebbels to ask about morale, Hitler mentioned that he had been in conference with his generals until six A.M. That day Kolberg was evacuated, almost without a fight; Goebbels saw to it that it was not mentioned in the High Command communiqué.[39]

One after another all their fortress-cities were captured, except one. On March 20 Gauleiter Karl Hanke sent a dramatic report from Breslau. The city was in ruins, but he and his men were making the Russians pay in blood for every inch.

'Gentlemen, nobody is too good to die for Grossdeutschland,' he had proclaimed, quoting the words of Rommel, his commanding officer in France in 1940: 'Attack!' The experience he had gained in the battle for Berlin before 1933 had served him well, he wrote to Goebbels, and he reflected once more that this was the type of National Socialist who put their army generals to shame.[40] Hanke managed to get through one phone call on March 29 to Goebbels and Magda, and even to send her a gift; she thanked him in terms of touching warmth, praising his courage and telling him that Hitler had recently called him 'the Nettelbeck of this war.'

'Our fondest wishes always go with him,' wrote Magda to Hanke's trustiest friend, 'and I sincerely believe that he will one day get out.'[41] But he did not. Hanke's men fought on until they had only two hundred guns, seven tanks, and eight assault guns left; the city held out until May 6 – by which time Hitler had appointed him Himmler's successor as Reichsführer; Hanke escaped, and was beaten to death by Czechs partisans a few days later.

The army generals meanwhile distinguished themselves by apathy and negligence. The Americans discovered a bridge across the Rhine intact at Remagen and hurled their forces across it. On March 21 Goebbels found Hitler tired and dejected, aged still more by this fresh catastrophe, and kept going only by 'iron will-power.' Morale everywhere in the west was collapsing. Food was running out. Deprived of sleep by the Allied bombers, the population was irritable and hysterical. When Goebbels mechanically mentioned Frederick the Great, Hitler snapped that the Seven Years War was very different from this one. 'I can't get anywhere with him,' noted Goebbels, alarmed, 'even with my analogies from history.' Göring, said Hitler, revealing one cause of his aggravation, had just set off for Bavaria with two trainloads of entourage to visit his wife. Yet he again refused Goebbels' suggestion that the man must go. Goebbels dictated in impotent fury: 'What can I do? All I can do is unremittingly badger the Führer and put my criticisms to him.'

Back home he found No. 20 Hermann-Göring Strasse in darkness: A power cable had been hit in the afternoon's Mosquito raid. Magda had left for Dresden. He felt low and depressed. 'What should I do,' he pondered, 'to implement what I consider to be right?' He felt responsible to the nation, as one of the few people left with Hitler's ear.[42]

In Dresden Magda visited Ello Quandt at the White Hart sanitarium. 'The new weapons will be our salvation,' she encouraged her sister-in-law, then guiltily checked herself: 'No, I'm talking nonsense. There's nothing else. Germany's defeat is only a matter of weeks.'

Ello asked what she intended to do. 'We're all going to die, Ello,' she replied. 'But by our own hand, not the enemy's.' They had been the leaders of the Reich, she explained; they could not duck the responsibility now. '*We* have failed.'[43]

AT THE BACK OF HER HUSBAND's mind were the Russian newsreels of their heroic defense of Leningrad – of civilians collecting the bodies of their soldiers, tossing them into pits, and fighting on.[44] Berlin could and must be defended to the last man. He asked Hitler's permission to convert Berlin's main east-west highway to a landing strip – it would mean dismantling the ceremonial lamp standards and tree-felling in the Tiergarten on either side. Hitler grudgingly said, 'That's okay by me' (but later disallowed the tree-felling).[45] When all this was over, he reasoned, Berliners would still need trees. Goebbels called on the western city of Mönchen-Gladbach to put up a special fight, but that town fell and the neighboring Rheydt, his own home town, surrendered to the Americans in mid-March without a shot being fired.

As these and other grim reports flooded across Goebbels' desk, he wished he could close the window shutters and hide within those four walls for ever: And wrote that wish down in his diary.

58: Death of Another Empress

S O DR GOEBBELS REMAINED in a dying Berlin, a prisoner of his own pride and his own routine, from the moment he strapped on his leg-calipers each morning. In the west General Eisenhower's armies had swept across the Rhine and a pincer operation was about to shut off the Ruhr, the Nazis' last arsenal. The Rhinelanders had seemed almost to welcome the Allies: The civilians saw relief from the air raids, and from the threats of pestilence and starvation. The wording of Goebbels' diaries had become circumspect. 'In fact,' he dictated as April began, 'events in the west seem likely to give the enemy some hope of overwhelming us militarily quite soon.'[1] Lieutenant-Colonel Rudi Balzer brought back from the western front shocking reports of the collapse of morale which confirmed what Field Marshal Kesselring had said a few days earlier.[2] The city of Mannheim had telephoned the approaching Americans offering to surrender.[3] Cologne surrendered in an hour. In Frankfurt German women were embracing the American troops. Townsfolk were openly hanging out the white flag and jeering at their own soldiers.

Goebbels sent in thirty of his finest orators – he had no choice, because the printed media had virtually disappeared. In the south, Hitler's last oil-producing fields in Hungary were about to be overrun. Dictating the diary each morning gave Goebbels little cheer. If only he could get Hitler to broadcast, as Churchill had in 1940 and Stalin in 1941, it would be like a battle won.

The scale of the air war was now such that when nine hundred American heavy bombers attacked Hanover and Berlin he dismissed it as a 'medium-scale' operation. His field office in Hamburg reported that people were commenting scornfully on the swift execution of the German officers who had allowed the Rhine bridge at Remagen to fall into American hands and suggesting quite openly – in letters to which they did not hesitate to append their full names and addresses – that the Reichsmarschall should face a firing squad as well.[4]

THE BRITISH AND AMERICANS had now crossed the Rhine in strength and had flooded into central Germany as far as Würzburg. Hitler suspected treason in the west, and sent for Goebbels at noon on March 27, 1945. For an hour they strolled through the chancellery garden beneath his study window, talking. Goebbels noticed how stooped the man had now become; and that the gardens had been torn up, as reinforcing work on Hitler's subterranean bunker proceeded. Hitler had decided to stay in Berlin, and the mood of the generals around him was already one of despair. Goebbels remarked that they should have repudiated the Geneva Convention when he said: He blamed Speer and Bormann for talking Hitler out of it. They were still half-bourgeois, these men – 'They think, but don't act, as revolutionaries.' Goebbels warned of the collapsing morale in the west, and urged Hitler to broadcast to the nation like Churchill and Stalin in their moment of crisis. Fifteen minutes would do the trick, he said.

GOEBBELS SAW HITLER AGAIN on March 30. A day or two before, he had asked Himmler's security service, the S.D., to scour its files for the old, forbidden horoscopes that had been cast for the birth date of the Republic, November 9, 1918, and the birth date of Hitler's Reich, January 30, 1933.[5] The tracts were on his desk at the ministry on the twenty-ninth. 'Both are in startling agreement,' he furtively informed his diary. 'I can well understand,' he hastened to add, 'that the Führer has prohibited any trafficking in such unverifiable things. Even so it is not without interest to see that both the Republic's horoscope and that of the Führer are prophesying that our military affairs will look up in the latter part of April. In May, June, and July things will go downhill again but hostilities will cease, it seems, in mid-August. God grant,' he dictated cynically, 'that this be so.'

Fearful perhaps lest these pages fall into the wrong hands he added: 'For myself such astrological prophecies are of no account. But I intend to exploit them . . . because in times of crisis people will clutch at the slightest straws.'[6]

Among these people he counted his Führer; but Hitler had slept for only two hours and was in no mood for horoscopes. Just six days ago, Goebbels told him, producing his tattered copy of Carlyle, he had found himself reading the description of the most harrowing days of the Seven Years War.

The great monarch had seen no way out of the imminent defeat; Frederick had set himself a final deadline, and wrote to the Count d'Argenson that if things did not look up by then he would swallow that phial of poison. Three days before that date, continued Goebbels, reading from the book, the Empress Elisabeth of Russia had suddenly died. Her half-witted successor Peter III had offered peace to Frederick, and the House of Brandenburg was saved. Why should they not hope for precisely the same kind of miracle now? Looking up, Goebbels saw tears flooding into Hitler's eyes.[7]

For some days Goebbels had pleaded with Hitler to broadcast a flaming oration to the Reich. But the Führer displayed what was to Goebbels an incomprehensible aversion to facing the microphone now.[8] The S.D. had informed him after his New Year's speech that people felt that it had not said anything new, explained Hitler; now he wanted to wait for good news from the western front before broadcasting again.

That might take some time. The news from there was devastating. The new Me262 jets, upon which he had relied, were scoring notable successes but the mass desertions of his troops could not be ignored. They were, Goebbels suggested, a consequence of Hitler's having rejected his drastic suggestion after the Dresden massacre that they repudiate the Geneva Convention and start executing Allied prisoners. Hitler agreed. Goebbels also criticized their efforts at starting guerrilla warfare. Admittedly, the collapse in the west had come with breathtaking speed, but their Werewolf movement – an attempt to create an underground army of partisans – was a flop.[9] So far only one man, the enemy-appointed mayor of Aachen, had been assassinated.

Goebbels planned to take over 'Werewolf' himself, giving it a newspaper and a radio station, using all the tactics that he had developed in *Angriff* in the early Thirties. He even had a new 'Isidor' in his sights – he was planning the assassination of the newly installed 'Jewish police chief' of American-occupied Cologne as well as Heinrich Vogelsang, a 'former Nazi nincompoop' whom the Americans had appointed the mayor of Rheydt, his home town.[10] The Americans immediately founded 'the first free newspaper' in Rheydt, just to spite Goebbels.[11] Worse, an American army lieutenant held a Passover ceremony for three hundred Jewish soldiers in his parental home in Dahlener Strasse – a Corporal Sidney Talmud of Brooklyn set up a camp stove on the family porch and made pancakes for three hours.[12] This really stuck in Goebbels' craw.

Even now, he complained, the war was still not being fought radically enough. The 'weakling' Otto Dietrich was wet-blanketing his every move. When Goebbels announced that the mayor of Aachen had been 'sentenced by a national tribunal' Dietrich killed the announcement by pointing out that it was untrue.

Hitler needed a Goebbels now, as defender of Berlin, more than a Dietrich. He told Goebbels that Dietrich was sacked.[13] He had just dismissed General Guderian too – the mystery man of the Twentieth of July. Guderian, he said, had lost his nerve again, just as in the battle for Moscow.[14] (This was a signal for Hitler to launch into well-worn reminiscences on how he, single-handed, had saved the entire army that winter of 1941–42 after his generals had thrown their armies into retreat.)

The Führer brooded on the fiasco that Sepp Dietrich had just suffered with his Sixth S.S. Panzer Army in Hungary. He told Goebbels privately that he had come to accept that Himmler had no strategic talents after all. 'Punctilious, but no warlord,' was his assessment. The army's Ferdinand Schörner, whose army group was fighting magnificently in Czechoslovakia, was the only general that Hitler spoke well of – 'one hell of a guy, the type you can blindly *rely* on,' he said, and Goebbels saw tears start into his eyes again.[15]

THEY PARTED, EACH INVIGORATED by the other as so often before. Goebbels did not see his Führer again for two weeks. 'One sometimes has the impression,' he recorded on April 4, 1945, modifying his famous argument of 1943, 'that the struggling German nation is breaking out in a sweat at this, the direst moment of its crisis: And for the layman it is hard to tell whether this is the herald of recovery, or the harbinger of death.'[16]

As the last V–2 rockets were launched at targets in Belgium, the S.S. newspaper *Das Schwarze Korps* adopted the infelicitous line that while Germany now had no hope of avoiding military defeat 'The Idea' must live on.[17] Dr Goebbels inveighed against the 'too clever by half intellectuals' who had penned such defeatist drivel. He issued to the editors of surviving newspapers orders to underscore every act of old-fashioned valor that came to their attention, and print stories about Allied atrocities too – to prove that the British and Americans were no less barbarian than the bolsheviks.

He had persuaded Hitler to authorize the Luftwaffe's first (and last) major kamikaze operation on April 7, 1945.[18] While the fighter-controller radio wavelengths were swamped with female choirs singing the Horst Wessel anthem and voices urging the charioteers to die for Germany, over 180 Me109 fighter pilots took off that day pledged to ram the American bombers. Although seventy-seven Luftwaffe pilots died in the clash over the Steinhuder Meer west of Hanover, only twenty-three bombers were destroyed. Goebbels expressed disappointment at this meager yield of so much individual bravery.[19]

The next day's leader article in *Das Reich* used radical language; even he found, reviewing his own article, that he had 'somewhat abandoned' his previous 'moderation and reserve.' The one slender consolation that he offered was that one way or the other an end was indeed in sight. 'The hour that precedes the sunrise,' he reminded his readers, 'is always the darkest of the night. The stars that have cast their gentle glow have already subsided and the deepest darkness draws in the approaching dawn. None need fear that it will forget to come. The black veil of night will suddenly sink and the sun will soar into the blood-red firmament.'

As it was in nature, he concluded, so it was in the lives of men and nations, particularly in war. 'We are confronted by bloodthirsty and vengeful foes who will put into effect all of their diabolical threats if once they get the chance. Let nobody deceive himself on that score. The one side will decimate the German people by bullets in the nape of the neck and by mass deportations, the other will *ausrotten* by terror and starvation.'[20]

Hunger already stalked the streets. Learning that two hundred housewives had stormed two bakeries in the impoverished suburb of Rangsdorf, Goebbels had two of the ringleaders beheaded that night and ordered the fact announced by wall-poster and via the muted voice of Berlin's cable radio. He hoped to hear no more about mobs storming bakeries after that.[21] He asked his driver if the Berliners would fight to defend their city. Rach answered bluntly, 'They see no point. For them the war's already lost.'[22]

That weekend Magda came back downtown from Schwanenwerder. 'A rather melancholy evening,' Goebbels noted, 'in which one piece of bad news after another came crashing in.' 'We often find ourselves desperately asking where it is all going to end,' he added. They talked over their own rapidly approaching end. Ribbentrop and Göring were both extending feelers to the British via Switzerland, Sweden, and Italy. Unlike the Russians and even the Americans, the British slapped down every such maneuver. 'There is not the slightest opening here,' Goebbels noted. The Russians were allegedly demanding East Prussia as the price of armistice and this was an impossible demand for Hitler.[23] A few days later Goebbels told Rach that the other ministers were leaving – Göring had already sent his wife and child to safety; but, he added, Magda and he had decided to stay.[24]

The Red Army was already overrunning Vienna. Goebbels blamed this on the softness of their gauleiter Schirach. He resolved that the Russians would not have a walkover in Berlin. Volkssturm and Hitler Youth battalions were already drilling at the bridges and streets which they would have to hold. But, Goebbels learned, stocks of gasoline, food, and coal were already running low.

The Americans boasted that they had captured one hundred tons of Gold, the entire German reserves, in a salt-mine in Thuringia. Goebbels recalled that he had opposed Funk's decision to evacuate the treasure from Berlin.[25] The railway board now admitted that they had taken steps to transport the two wagon-loads of this precious metal back to Berlin – but the Easter weekend had intervened.[26]

General Theodore Busse, whose Ninth Army was holding the Oder front, had assured Goebbels that he would hold off the coming Soviet offensive. Goebbels hoped that in the west General Walther Wenck's Twelfth Army would seize the initiative against the exposed American flank in Thuringia. As for the wider outlook, he put the optimistic view to Count von Krosigk that all that mattered now was 'staying on our feet' until the enemy coalition fell apart.[27]

The finance minister argued that it was not enough to wait, and that the Reich could not expect serious results from sending out second-class foreign ministry men – a reference to Ribbentrop's recent abortive peace initiative in Stockholm.[28] 'Goebbels agreed spiritedly,' recorded Krosigk in his diary, 'and confided to me that certain feelers have already been put out.'

Goebbels made no secret that he still coveted Ribbentrop's job, and hinted that Krosigk might put in a word with Hitler. When the count pointed out that he had not seen Hitler for years, Goebbels offered to set up an audience: Krosigk might start with budgetary matters, the Führer would talk sooner or later about the broader situation, 'and that's where you jump in.' Nothing came of it.

ON THE TWELFTH, GOEBBELS paid his regular Thursday visit to the front, the Oder bridgehead at Küstrin, about fifty miles from Berlin, his car loaded with cigarettes and cognac for the men. Like all populist statesmen it thrilled him to descend from the Olympian heights to the levels at which the ordinary man fought, lived, and died. He sat up smoking and drinking with General Busse's staff until midnight had long passed. Busse reassured him that his army would withstand the coming Soviet onslaught. 'We'll stand fast here until the Engländer kicks us up the ass,' he roared.[29]

'If there is any justice in history,' Goebbels declaimed to the officers, 'a turning point must soon come – one like the miracle of the House of Brandenburg in the Seven Years War.'

'Who's the empress who's going to snuff it this time, then?' asked one of the colonels, in a tone just short of sarcasm.

The propaganda minister drove back to Berlin. An air raid was under way. From twenty-five miles away he could see the glittering showers of marker flares and target indicators cascading out of the black, starless skies and the slow, lurid flashes as the blockbusters exploded – 'The darkness before the dawn.' The streets were deserted as he drove up to No. 20 Hermann-Göring Strasse, but there was a knot of people waiting for him on the steps.

A babble of voices greeted him. Somebody thrust a Reuters bulletin into his hands: The American president was dead. Franklin Roosevelt had died at Warm Springs that afternoon.[30]

Goebbels clutched the slip of paper, his polished, receding forehead illuminated by the fires started by a shower of incendiaries on the Hotel Adlon – his gau headquarters now – and the Reich chancellery further down the street. The world swam past him. His eyes glistened, though with Goebbels true tears only rarely came. 'Champagne!' he finally croaked. Was the Nazi sun not now about to soar into a new, blood-red firmament?

'Champagne! Bring out our finest champagne – and put me through to the Führer!'[31]

'Mein Führer,' he shouted down the line. 'It is written in the stars that for us the second half of April will bring the turning point. This is Friday the Thirteenth. The turning point has come.'

59: *The Man of the Century*

A S HE LOOKED AT HIS FAMILY now, Goebbels can have seen them only as actors in a drama, in which he had cast himself in the leading role. Their approaching end inspired no horror in him. Once he had hoped for a peaceful death, a private funeral, and burial in some open space in Berlin. 'I'd prefer to die quite alone somewhere,' he had remarked in 1941, 'and be buried only by those who really love me.'[1] This now seemed an unlikely circumstance. Lord Vansittart of the British Foreign Office had only recently declared that the only issue remaining on war criminals was 'the site of the gallows and the length of the rope.'[2]

In January 1940 when a conversation with Hitler had lightly turned to methods of suicide Goebbels had agreed that the pistol was best.[3] Later he inclined toward cyanide and asked Ley to obtain enough for his entire family.[4] By 1943 he had resolved that suicide *in extremis* was the only way to lasting glory. Had he not expected General Paulus to 'forfeit fifteen or twenty years of his life' to earn a thousand years of immortality?[5]

He told the swashbuckling S.S. Major Otto Skorzeny that he could not figure out why Mussolini had not killed himself after his arrest that July: 'He did not lack the means – we know he had the poison on him. . . Why didn't he swallow it the moment he found himself in captivity and his life's work in ruins?'[6]

'If all our efforts, work, and struggle should lead nowhere,' Goebbels commented a few days later, 'then I should not find it hard to die. In a world where there was no room for my ideals there would be no room for me.'[7] He added weight to his memorandum to Hitler in July 1944 by promising something which his rival Speer never could, the mass suicide of his entire family if they lost the war. 'Each time I am out at Lanke with my six children, then I realize all over again that neither I nor my entire family could, or should, live on into an era that is not our own.'[8]

The more he read the letters of Frederick the Great, the more Dr Goebbels took note that the great monarch was never without his poison capsule during the critical years of the Seven Years War, and that he aspired to be 'buried beneath the batteries of his artillery.'[9] The death of his old friend Eugen Hadamovsky, of which Goebbels learned on March 2, 1945, 'leading his company into action . . . a bullet through the heart,' also affected him deeply.[10] After this, said S.S. Gruppenführer Berger, Goebbels tapped his breast pocket and said: 'I and my whole family will commit suicide.' 'I have the right,' the minister intimated to him, 'not to die alone if I commit suicide, but for a whole lot of my followers to die with me.' The S.S. general contradicted him – he personally had no intention of dying with Goebbels: 'You have had nothing but good out of National Socialism. I have had only worry and work, so I don't feel the same moral obligation.' Goebbels just looked at him blankly.[11]

Magda was at one with him on this matter. She was fatalistic and perhaps even callous about it all. Looking across the room at her at a Berlin society function back in 1933 the French ambassador had remarked, 'I have never in my life come across a woman with such cruel eyes.'[12] Death did not frighten her. After Werner Naumann lit a cigarette for her in March 1945 with a special-agents' lighter, she expressed curiosity about it; Naumann opened it to reveal a poison capsule concealed within, and at her request – in front of Dr Goebbels – gave it to her.[13] Once she had leaned over tipsily to the family's major-domo, Wilhelm Rohrssen, and confided to him how she imagined her family would die. 'We shall all be invited to the Führer's,' she slurred. 'And there we shall drink chocolate. This chocolate will taste good, and it will be our last.' She raised her glass to Rohrssen. 'The Führer will not die without my husband,' she promised.[14] 'We shall all die – even you.' Shortly she would have Joseph to herself, and there would be no contenders.

OF COURSE EVEN AFTER Roosevelt's sudden death the British and Americans did not have one bomber less, nor the Russians fewer tanks; but as Goebbels told Krosigk on the phone that morning, the news would cause a sea-change in morale. 'We can and must see in it the dispensation of an all-powerful history and justice,' he explained.[15]

'Why not just say of God?' rejoined the finance minister. He wrote to Goebbels an hour or two later, arguing that Roosevelt's death was a divine gift – 'but one that we've got to earn.' The president's death removed the last obstacle to dealing with the United States. In this letter Krosigk also sowed the idea in Goebbels' mind that the Americans and the Russians were really making for Prague now, not Berlin.[16]

GOEBBELS' DIARY AS RECORDED on the glass microfiches in Moscow ends with April 12, 1945; the plates also record several hundred pages of shorthand notes, and there is reason to believe that these contain his final diary dictation, which Otte had no more time to transcribe.[17]

Hitler's desk diary shows only one appointment at this time with Goebbels, at midday on April 15.[18] Magda evidently came too – it was a Sunday – because Hitler's pilot Hans Baur saw her stepping in through the back gate just as Hitler was inspecting the outside of the three-storied bunker which Speer had now completed beneath the garden. Hitler was shocked to see her, and offered her Baur's plane to fly down to the Obersalzberg. 'Berlin will be a rat trap!' he said.[19]

'Mein Führer,' she replied, 'my husband is gauleiter of Berlin. Life without my husband would have no purpose for me – nor did I bear my children to have them put on display in the Soviet Union and America as the children of the propaganda minister Goebbels.'

FINIS GERMANIÆ WAS THE SPIRIT of the leading article that Goebbels published that day. The 'bloodthirsty and vengeful' enemy coalition was wasting away; it had 'to triumph swiftly or triumph not at all.' The article displayed a confidence bordering on complacency: 'I know for certain that the Führer will find a way out of the dilemma,' he soothed his readers. The rest was written purely for posterity. 'We have no cause to hang our heads before the enemy,' he wrote. 'What the German people has achieved in this war is already history. No filthy hand of foe shall ever fling aside the crown of laurels that already adorns our nation's brow.' Now, he recommended, was a time for all to fight – 'And what life is too precious to sacrifice *pro patria*!' 'So let each and every one of us swear a private oath, devoid of any pathos, to choose to die rather than accept the yoke of servitude.' They were traversing the final phase of this war, he wrote. 'One cannot humanly conceive of how it can last much longer.'[20]

Indeed it could not. At dawn on the sixteenth Marshal Georgii Konstantinovich Zhukov and Marshal Ivan Stepanovich Koniev threw eighteen Soviet armies at Berlin – not Prague. At night the children looked out of their window and asked why the flashes lighting the horizon produced no rain. Dr Goebbels was in hourly contact with General Busse. He commandeered a fleet of Berlin omnibuses to rush soldiers to the battlefield.[21] To Hitler's anger, Goebbels also sent five of the Volkssturm battalions, although they were supposed only to be used for immediate neighborhood defense.[22]

Goebbels suspected however that this was already the last battle. He asked Lieutenant von Oven to help him burn his private papers – including pictures of parents, yellowing and mounted on thick card, snapshots of the little Joseph in a sailor suit, school reports, a letter of the Rheydt Cotton Trading Association, academic diplomas, and hotel bills. 'Look at this one,' he said, holding up a studio portrait photograph. 'Now there was a woman of perfect beauty!' The portrait, of actress Lida Baarova, joined the others in the flames.[23]

He dedicated to Hitler, on the eve of his birthday, a last brilliant broadcast honoring him as the man whom the German nation had in free elections chosen as their leader. 'If Germany still lives today,' he thundered, 'if Europe and the cultured and civilized Occident have still not been swept away for ever into the fathomless maelstrom that yawns black and ominous before us, then they owe it to him alone. He will be the Man of the Century.' What, he continued, had the enemy to offer? 'Nothing but their superiority in numbers, their brutish mania for destruction, their diabolical rage that masks the chaos of mankind in dissolution. An entire violated continent stands testimony against them. In every country of Europe once flourishing cities and villages have been turned into cratered wastelands.' Now however the final act of this mighty tragedy had begun. 'The chief of the hostile conspiracy has been crushed by Fate, the same Fate which left the Führer on July 20 standing erect and uninjured amid the dead and dying and rubble, so that he might complete his works.' 'Pay heed, ye Germans!' he declared into the microphone. 'Millions of people, in every country on Earth, are looking to this man, wonderingly and perplexed: Does he know a way out of this mighty misfortune that has beset the world? He will show it to the nations.'[24]

The underlying message was vintage Goebbels: Blind, self-sacrificing loyalty to his Führer. A message went to Magda to have the children brought to No. 20 Hermann-Göring Strasse ready to brighten the Führer's birthday the next day. At midnight he went over to the chancellery bunker.

With glazed eyes, red-rimmed from the mortar dust hanging in the air, Hitler spoke to them of his hardening resolve to hold northern Germany and Norway if the Reich should indeed be sliced in two, and to defend the Alps and Bohemia–Moravia. To Dr Ley he hinted that he would move into this southern 'fortress' himself.[25] Goebbels however had already decided to defend Berlin to the last, since the army generals had proven incapable. Ley urged him at least to send his family to safety. Goebbels was obstinate. 'I shall die here, if I have to, and Magda has decided to do likewise.'[26] Not for him the humiliating surrender of a Paulus. 'What does he do, this man who has ordered and exhorted his men to stand and die?' he had said in 1943. 'He trots off into captivity, not forgetting to pack his little suitcase on the way!'[27]

At midday on April 20 there was a small birthday parade. Goebbels followed Hitler up the tower staircase into the garden. The Führer turned up the collar of his gray greatcoat and walked down the line of youngsters, handing out medals to the teenagers who had fought the Russians off with flak guns or bazookas. At four P.M. he went back down into the bunker, never to come out again alive, and Goebbels returned to his residence.

The High Command and war department evacuated Berlin, traveling to Bavaria, leaving skeleton staffs in Berlin. Dr Friedrich-Wilhelm Kritzinger, Lammers' Staatssekretär, broke it to Goebbels that every other ministry had now left for the northern 'fortress'. Infuriated by this news Goebbels demanded to know how he was expected to defend Berlin without them.[28]

Thus his own ministry staff found that they, like their minister, were hemmed into the Reich capital. (Most of the women, around three hundred in all, went into Russian captivity and were not seen again.) When Otto Meissner, Hitler's pettifogging old Staatsminister, phoned later that day from the safety of Mecklenburg to explain that 'the Reich government' had withdrawn from the danger zone 'to preserve its freedom of action' Goebbels snarled at him, 'The Reich government is where the Führer and I are, not where you are! For twelve years I have had the urge to spit in your eye. For twelve years I have suppressed that urge – and today I regret it.'[29] That night Bormann sent a telex down to the Obersalzberg, reading: 'Wolf [Hitler] is staying here, as situation can only be restored by him if at all possible.'

The dawn of Saturday April 21 came with Russian artillery lobbing shells at extreme range into Berlin.[30] White-faced, Goebbels presided over one last eleven o'clock conference at No. 20 Hermann-Göring Strasse, one long tirade against the traitors who had talked Hitler out of actually invading Britain in 1940, who had lost their nerve in Russia, who had failed again in Normandy in June 1944, and who had finally shown their colors on July the Twentieth. When Fritzsche suavely objected, the minister snapped, 'What can I do with men who won't fight even when their womenfolk are being raped?'[31]

Then an evil leer spread over his face, as he paced up and down behind his big desk. 'It's up to the German people,' he murmured softly. They had literally asked for National Socialism. In November 1933, after Hitler quit the League of Nations, 40·5 million Germans had voted for his policies and only 2·1 million against. Hitler had not forced himself on them; and now, God help them. He folded his arms, and almost spat out the final words: 'Well, what were you working with me for, gentlemen? Now they're going to slit your pretty little throats.'[32] According to Werner Naumann, he said: 'Gentleman, we hung together and we'll be hanged together.'[33] He stalked out, pausing only to fling them a Hitler salute.

At noon-fifteen a Russian shell burst only a hundred yards away, shaking the whole structure. Unshaken, Goebbels read out over cable radio the dramatic 'emergency speech' that he had long prepared, pausing only to shake splinters off the pages as another shell burst blew in several panes of glass.

He had intended to send the metal boxes containing the glass-plate microfiches of his diaries into the southern 'fortress' but that road was now closed. That same Saturday afternoon he entrusted to Rudi Balzer his latest diaries and the shorthand notes, and told him to carry them out to the north. Then he told his secretary Otte to bring him all the secret papers from the two ministry safes to the Reich chancellery. 'Go to ground,' he told Otte. 'When Berlin is liberated report back to me again.' Otte rendezvoused at the Adlon with Balzer and they set out in an army staff car for Hamburg. About halfway, for no good reason, the two men halted and buried the precious diary notes in a preserving jar outside Perleberg.[34]*

Goebbels made his final dispositions. His staff was now reduced to Naumann, Heinz Lorenz – the unobjectionable former deputy of Sündermann, who had been dismissed with Otto Dietrich – and perhaps thirty others. He told them that he proposed, when it was all over, to poison his children.[35] In Berlin itself the only newspaper still being printed was an emergency news-sheet, the *Panzer-Bär*. His last leader for *Das Reich* was a shrill call for Germany's women and children to fight from the rear against these insolent invaders who had

---

* Armed with the map drawn by Balzer and aided by a proton magnetometer team from Oxford University, the author searched for this jar in the heavily wooded area in the then communist eastern Germany in 1970, without success. Otte, at the time still a serving West German government official, was unable to accompany us.

wasted entire cities with the cruel air warfare. Some, he wrote, might think nothing of living 'under the knuckles of the Anglo-American banker-Jews,' but the true German would be hurling hand grenades, laying Teller mines, and sniping from rooftops and cellar windows.[36]

AROUND SIX O'CLOCK THE NEXT EVENING, April 22, he received a shocking telephone call from Hitler who asked him, voice breaking, to go over straight away. 'It's all over,' was all that he would say.[37]

In a few brief words Goebbels disbanded the propaganda ministry. He handed out poison capsules to his staff. He told Oven to get Rach and a second driver for Magda and the children. 'We're moving into the Reich chancellery. No. 20 Hermann-Göring Strasse will not be defended. It's to be abandoned. The Volkssturm and S.S. men are to transfer to the chancellery gardens. My staff are to join the troops.' Magda asked if she should pack her toilet articles, and dismissed her children's nanny with the words: 'We're driving over to the Reich chancellery. We've all got to take poison.'[38]

Hitler's midday war conference had broken up, with him on the verge of a nervous breakdown after learning that S.S. Obergruppenführer Felix Steiner had not even begun the counter-attack from the north on which everybody was banking. He had slammed down his bunch of colored pencils and declared that the war was lost. 'But you're very wrong, gentlemen, if you believe that now I'll leave Berlin after all. I'd sooner put a bullet in my brains' – and with that he had pushed through them into his private quarters saying, 'Get me a line to Dr Goebbels.'

They stood aside now as Goebbels limped into Hitler's study. What followed, perhaps his finest speech, was delivered to an audience of only one frightened dictator bent on killing himself within the hour. Setting the ultimate seal on his personal loyalty, he told Hitler that he would move into one of the recently vacated bunker rooms himself at once and bring Magda and the children with him too.[39]

Back outside, Bormann begged him to talk the Führer into flying out while he still could. Goebbels blinked around, his eyes searching out Traudl Junge; he briefed the young, slim secretary to be so kind as to meet his family when they arrived. Taking General Jodl aside, he revealed that Hitler had made up his mind to stand and fight in Berlin. Was there, he asked, no means of preventing the encirclement?

'There's only one way,' replied the general. 'And that's to denude the Elbe front and deploy all our troops in the defense of Berlin. It's just possible then that the Americans won't press their offensive.'[40]

Surprisingly, Hitler agreed to this at once and ordered Keitel and Jodl out of the bunker to take personal command of this historic about-face by Wenck's Twelfth Army.

Moving into Morell's old quarters directly across the gangway from Hitler's rooms and the map room – the quaking physician took one of the last planes out that same night – Goebbels sent out a 'Führer Order' for *Panzer-Bär* to print the next day. 'Anybody who encourages or approves any move that weakens our power to resist is a traitor! He is to be shot out of hand or hanged! This order stands even if his moves are alleged to have been ordered by the gauleiter Reich minister Dr Goebbels or by the Führer himself.'[41] Berlin's cable radio announced that Hitler was staying in Berlin.[42]

That evening Goebbels fetched his family. Rach drove him and Magda, the children followed in a second car. They passed Ribbentrop's car heading in the other direction: He was leaving Berlin for the north.[43] Down in the bunker Magda moved with her children into adjoining rooms, not caring that her matrimonial separation from her husband – whose room was one floor below – thus became obvious to everybody. Traudl Junge took the children to the store-room, where Hitler's birthday presents still lay in a heap, while their mother went to work her magic on the Führer.[44] Later she wrote to Harald that Hitler had told her to flee Berlin. 'But you know your mother,' she wrote, 'we're of the same blood. That was out of the question.'[45] She sent Rohrssen back to pick up a few things at Schwanenwerder, then released him from his duties.[46]

From now on Goebbels directed what was left of the propaganda battle by telephone from the bunker. His old gau headquarters had been converted into an emergency hospital, as had the Adlon and the chancellery's main Voss Strasse bunker, connected by a short tunnel to the Führer bunker. In the Voss bunker surgeons operated in semi-darkness on casualties from the increasingly close battle areas.

The stench in the bunkers was overpowering, but through it all came the laughter and chatter of the six Goebbels children as they collected round their table perched on one of the landings and waited for the two armies that their father and 'Uncle Führer' had promised were coming to rescue them.

Many people offered to take Magda and the children to safety under a Red Cross flag. Shortly before midnight on the twenty-second Professor Karl Gebhardt, head of the Red Cross, knocked on Goebbels' door; Schwägermann, the adjutant, inched it slightly ajar and Gebhardt called out to ask if he should take the children out of the city. Goebbels said sleepily, 'No, we're staying here,' and motioned for Schwägermann to shut the door again.[47]

AT MIDDAY ON APRIL 23 Keitel and Jodl were back. Those two armies were making only slow progress. At 12:40 P.M. Berlin's radio broadcast that Hitler, Goebbels, and his family were still in Berlin.[48] 'The propaganda ministry has been turned into a fortress,' it was announced. 'The staff has been collected into a Volkssturm battalion under Staatssekretär Naumann's command. Even women staff members have been trained to use the Panzerfaust bazooka.'[49] The following day all German shortwave propaganda transmissions to the world ceased.[50]

In the afternoons Hitler went to drink chocolate with the children. His favorite was still the eldest daughter Helga, now twelve. Her long blonde tresses

Hitler's Bunker

1. Hitler's bedroom
2. Hitler's living room
3. Conference room
4. Anteroom to Hitler's quarters
5. Eva Braun's bed-sitting room
6. Heating installation

7. Telephone exchange
8. Martin Bormann's study
9. Dr Joseph Goebbels's study
10. Orderly officers' room

12. Goebbels's bedroom
13. Waiting room
14. Guards' room
15. Observation tower with emergency exit
16. Exit to the Chancellery Garden

11. Room of valet Heinz Linge

The underground bunker beneath Hitler's Berlin Chancellery, based on a rendering by Hanno Ziegler and the original architectural drawings found in the files of Engineer- General Alfred Jacob, the army's expert on fortifications. The plans were compared with original post-war photographs taken in the bunker in July 1945 by U.S. Signal Corps officers (COURTESY *The Military Advisor*).

were demurely plaited – a truly Aryan maiden. She stood 1·58 meters in her socks, and beamed all over her pretty, oval features. When her little brother Hellmut read out his latest essay on 'The Führer's Birthday,' she chirped, 'You pinched that from Pappi!'

'Or Pappi from me!' the eight-year-old retorted, to everybody's delight.

The children told Hitler they were all looking forward to the new soldiers who were going to chase the Russians away.[51]

'We're all waiting for Wenck,' he grimly advised an officer that day.[52]

Doing what they could to lighten the descending gloom, Eva Braun was delicately made up and coifed and wore a different dress each day, while Magda had carefully brushed her own blonde hair and the hairpiece which she had elaborately woven in.

Once she had a young S.S. doctor from the Voss Strasse bunker attend to her teeth; she liked this young man – Helmut Kunz – and found it easy to confide in him as the final days approached.

Hermann Göring, now in safety on the Obersalzberg, began acting as though Hitler were already dead. Hitler ordered his arrest.[53] Traudl Junge glimpsed Goebbels afterward outside the map room, raging about the Reichsmarschall's treason. 'That man never was a true National Socialist,' he exclaimed. 'He just basked in the Führer's reflected glory. He never lived the life of a National Socialist or idealist. It's thanks to him that we are down here now, in this bunker, and about to lose the war.'[54]

Not that either he or Hitler had given up even now. Lorenz's shorthand notes of the remaining bunker conferences show Hitler on April 25 reasoning to Goebbels, 'I can only win a real triumph *here*,' meaning Berlin. 'If I do that – even just a moral victory – then it is at very least a way of saving face or gaining time.'[55]

Unwilling to let anybody rob him of the glamour of sharing Hitler's fast-approaching Götterdämmerung, Goebbels used every argument to keep him in the city. 'In Berlin,' he agreed, 'we can score a world-scale moral victory. Such a victory can be obtained only at the one point on which all the eyes of the world are riveted. The world will not take it half as hard that the Soviets are marching into Brandenburg as if they get Berlin. But if they are thrashed at Berlin that will teach the whole world a lesson.'

'If only!' responded Hitler. 'I hear that the talks between Eden and Molotov have broken down. The Russians are demanding the whole [of Poland]. And that will mean that Britain has lost the war. . . I think,' he added, 'that the time's coming when the rest of them, out of sheer self-preservation, will have to stand up to this insatiable Moloch, this proletarian-bolshevik monster. If I were to duck out like a coward today . . . then National Socialism would be done for and the Reich with it. But if I fight on to victory and hang on to the capital, then maybe hope will spring in British and American breasts that it's possible to stand up to this whole peril, side by side with Nazi Germany, after all. And the only man for the job is me.'

'Leave this city,' emphasized Goebbels in this surreal conversation deep beneath the chancellery, 'and you lose the rest as well.'

Hitler speculated further. Might not the west now turn to him as the only force capable of holding back the bolshevik colossus? 'I would think it one thousand times more craven to finish myself off down on the Obersalzberg than to make a last stand and die in battle here.'

Reverting to his own leitmotif, Goebbels reminded him that the Russians too might yet prefer to strike a bargain with Nazi Germany. 'Once Stalin sees this trend among the western powers resulting from a German victory in Berlin, he may well say to himself, "If I'm not going to get the kind of Europe I had in mind, I'm just throwing the British and Germans into each other's arms. So let's cut a deal with the Germans."' He predicted that Stalin would shortly start a propaganda campaign against the Allies, accusing them of having ravaged Germany's cities with their air raids. 'He is a far better propagandist than the British,' said Goebbels.

Hitler was still pondering his own image in history. 'Better,' he growled, 'to fight honorably to the bitter end than to live on a few months or years in disgrace and dishonor.'

This was very much Goebbels' philosophy; he enlarged on this sepulchral theme, as though it were still an entirely abstract prospect. 'If the worse comes to the worst,' he mused, 'and the Führer dies an honorable death in Berlin, and Europe goes bolshevik, then in five years at most the Führer will have become a legendary figure and National Socialism a mythus sanctified by a last grand finale – and all of its mortal errors that are criticized today will have been expunged at one fell swoop.'

At a war conference later that day he remarked optimistically that the Anglo-American press had already coined the phrase 'Third World War' in uneasy anticipation of the coming clash with Russia. An impregnable Berlin might just be the last straw for the enemy coalition.

LATE ON THE TWENTY-SIXTH Luftwaffe general Robert von Greim arrived as Göring's successor. The renowned aviatrix Hanna Reitsch, who accompanied him, helped Magda with bedtime duties with the children. Once, Hitler came in, took off his own golden party badge and pinned it onto Magda.[56] Goebbels often stood by his children's bedside, gazing at their sleeping forms. In November 1940, during the first British blitz on Berlin, he had seen them all sleeping in each others' arms like this in the cellar at Schwanenwerder – 'all looking as sweet as little angels,' he wrote in that day's diary.[57]

Traudl Junge heard the children through the door, singing in sixfold chorus. 'I went in,' she wrote, 'and found them sitting on their three bunk beds, tightly holding their ears so that the others did not interfere with their three-part song. And there was Hanna Reitsch singing with them and conducting.'[58] 'The children,' wrote Magda two or three days before the end, 'are wonderful. They manage all by themselves in these more than primitive conditions. . .

There's never a word of complaint or the trace of a tear from them. When the bunker trembles under the artillery bombardment the bigger children shield the smaller. Their presence here is a boon to us all, as they even coax a smile from the Führer now and again.'[59]

Philosophizing in their bunker fastness, Hitler and Goebbels waited for those relieving armies. Lorenz heard Goebbels interrupt the war conference on the twenty-seventh, 'Gau headquarters reports that Wenck's group has linked up with our bridgehead at Potsdam.'

'The really crippling thing is,' said Hitler soon after, 'that one doesn't know for certain what is going on.' Phone calls dialed at random established which streets were now in Russian hands.

'God grant that Wenck gets here,' murmured Goebbels.'Just suppose: Wenck gets to Potsdam, and the Soviets are right outside here in Potsdamer Platz!'

'And I'm not in Potsdam,' chimed in Hitler, 'but here in Potsdamer Platz.'

Later that day Soviet tanks flying swastikas broke right through to Wilhelm Platz before being shot to a halt. Hitler, who had once directed army groups of a million soldiers and more, was listening to reports on the placing of individual howitzers and self-propelled guns in the streets above.[60]

For a while he and Goebbels reminisced about the mistakes they now realized they had made in not liquidating their enemies in 1933. That was the hidden snag about being elected legally to office. In Vienna too, in 1938, the sheer peacefulness of the revolution had robbed them of the chance to liquidate all their enemies. Next time, they both resolved in this grotesque conversation, if there ever was a next time, they would not act Mr Nice Guy with their opponents.[61]

SHORTLY BEFORE DINNER Magda collared the S.S. dentist Dr Helmut Kunz and asked him to help when the time came. She led him upstairs to where her children were preparing for bed, and introduced the Sturmbannführer to them, without saying why. Goebbels looked in briefly and said goodnight to the children too. The dentist chatted easily with them all for a while, before returning to his bunker surgery.[62]

On the twenty-eighth, as the bombardment increased, Greim left the bunker. Both the Goebbels parents took the opportunity to write a last letter to Harald in British captivity.[63]

Magda's was defiant. 'Our magnificent ideology is all for naught,' she wrote, 'and with it everything beautiful, admirable, noble, and good that I have come to know in my life. Since there will be nothing to live for in the world that will endure after the Führer and National Socialism, I am taking the children with me. They are too good for the kind of life that will ensue, and a merciful God will understand me for delivering them.' The rest of the letter betrayed a no less hardy fanaticism. 'We have only one aim – to keep faith with the Führer unto death. That we are to be allowed to end our lives together with him is a favor from Fate that we never dared to hope for.'

Dr Goebbels' own farewell letter to his stepson was couched in the same unrepentant vein. 'We are confined to the Reich chancellery's Führer bunker, fighting for our lives and honor. . . I think it unlikely we shall ever meet again.' Justifying the cruel pact that he had agreed with Magda, he continued, 'We do not have to be present in flesh and blood to have an impact on the future of our country. It may well be that you are left alone to continue the family tradition. Germany will survive this terrible war, but only if our people have examples they can look up to for inspiration.' Seized by his own distorted sense of history, he added: 'The lies shall one day come tumbling down, and truth shall triumph over all.' 'Farewell, my dear Harald,' the letter ended.[64]

THAT AFTERNOON THE NEWS AGENCIES announced that Heinrich Himmler had offered to the Allies the unconditional surrender of Germany.[65] It was not true, but to Hitler and Goebbels it now seemed obvious why there was still no news of the relieving armies. They had been betrayed.

The six children came as usual to see 'Uncle Führer' and stroke his Alsatian, Blondi; as they filed back to their room Schwägermann heard them call Eva Braun 'Frau Hitler' in passing, which rather startled him.[66] But Hitler had already revealed to Goebbels and his adjutants his intention to marry the mistress who had shared his isolation for fourteen years.[67] 'At her own wish,' Hitler dictated that night, 'she will meet death with me as my wife.'[68] He asked Goebbels to find an official empowered to solemnize the marriage – no easy charge, given that Russian snipers were now only a few hundred yards away. Presently however a short, slim, fair-haired official of thirty-four wearing the brown party uniform with a Volkssturm armband was brought down into the bunker.[69] Goebbels, Naumann, and Bormann acted as witnesses at the little ceremony in the tiny map room. Goebbels described it to Traudl Junge afterwards as 'very moving.'[70] The official quietly said, 'In the presence of the above-named witnesses I ask you, mein Führer, whether you are willing to take Miss Eva Braun in marriage.' Momentarily forgetful, she began signing with a 'B,' then crossed it out and wrote Eva Hitler instead.[71]

Afterward Hitler invited Goebbels, Magda, and Naumann to an intimate champagne dinner along with a few others.[72] For a while he reminisced about World War One. Fourteen years before, he then recalled, he had been best man at the Goebbels wedding. 'What a contrast!' he wryly observed. 'For me, marriage and death are to be somewhat more closely linked in time.'[73] He confirmed once more that he did not intend to fall into Soviet hands alive. Death would be almost welcome, he said, now that so many had betrayed him.[74]

Hitler went next door to dictate his political testament to Traudl Junge. After a while he called in Goebbels to discuss a new Cabinet. The most important question was who should succeed Hitler as head of state. Himmler had disqualified himself. Göring was in disgrace. For weeks Goebbels had been selflessly canvassing the name of Grand Admiral Dönitz – he was upright, military, and incorruptible.[75] Hitler agreed that the admiral should

be nominated as Reich president and supreme commander. He named the
trusty Dr Goebbels himself as his successor as Reich chancellor, and Bormann
as party minister. Werner Naumann would succeed Goebbels as propaganda
minister.[76] The rest of this document, like a final shuffling of non-existent
armies across long-obsolescent maps, was a global settling of scores. Himmler,
Göring, Speer, and even Ribbentrop – Hitler's 'second Bismarck' – were all
dismissed from office. Probably at Goebbels' recommendation Hitler appointed
Karl Hanke, still holding out in Breslau, as the new Reichsführer S.S.

The testament ended with a final gratuitous outburst against the Jews and
those international statesmen who had sold out to Jewish interests. Hitler
rejoiced that the 'culprits' had paid for their sins, 'albeit by more humane
means than war' – whatever that might mean. He signed at four A.M. and
Goebbels and the others witnessed his signature.

The document had formally commanded Goebbels and his family to leave
Berlin 'to take part in the nation's struggle.' But the minister knew that even as
Reich chancellor his miserable existence would be prolonged only by as many
weeks as would separate his capture and the opening of the gallows trapdoor
beneath his feet. He exclaimed that as defense commissioner for Berlin he
could not in conscience leave. Weeping profusely he rushed next door and
interrupted Traudl Junge's typing of the document to dictate his own defiant
'annex' to it.

'For the first time in my life,' he declaimed, as her pencil flew across the pad, 'I
must categorically refuse to obey an order of the Führer. My wife and children
join me in this refusal.' It was not just that he could not bring himself to desert
the Führer in his hour of need – 'I should appear for the rest of my life as a
dishonorable turncoat and common scoundrel,' with no right to the respect of
his fellow citizens. 'In the delirium of treason which surrounds the Führer in
these most critical days of the war there must be some people at least willing to
abide by him unconditionally until death.' He ended, 'For this reason, together
with my wife and on behalf of my children who are too young to speak for
themselves but would, if old enough, approve this decision unreservedly, I
utter my unalterable decision not to leave the Reich capital even if it falls, and
at the side of the Führer to end a life which will be of no further value to myself
if I cannot spend it in the service of the Führer and next to him.'

By five-thirty A.M. all the documents had been signed. Three couriers slipped
out of the bunker at noon-fifteen, carrying copies to the outside world.

Hitler told Goebbels that he would wait for word that at least one copy had
reached its destination before departing on his own, more distant, journey.
Shortly he was brought a news agency report describing the ugly end of Benito
Mussolini and his mistress, 'hanging from the Standard Oil kiosk in [Milan's]
Piazzale Quindici Martiri.' A dozen of the Duce's staff had been 'shot in the
back' as well.[77]

Hitler handed out cyanide capsules. Goebbels had sent Schwägermann back
to the deserted No. 20 Hermann-Göring Strasse a few days earlier to fetch the

6·35-millimeter pistol with which he intended to kill himself; he kept this and his poison capsule with him all the time.[78] He gave to Heinz Lorenz copies of Hitler's testament and his own annex. 'Make for British- or American-occupied territory,' he briefed him, 'and publish the testaments as and when you think fit for the purpose of the historical record.'[79]

Hitler held three more situation conferences that day. Sharp-shooters of the Russian 301st Guards Division were less than five hundred yards from the barricaded windows of the chancellery. At one-thirty A.M. on April 30, the Soviet High Command ordered heavy artillery to bear on the building. Within minutes the upper floors were ablaze. There were no more conferences. Fifty feet below ground Goebbels heard toward midday that the Russians had broken into the subway system between the ruined Kaiserhof and Potsdamer Platz, and had overrun the Tiergarten bordering on the chancellery.

At lunch time he glimpsed Hitler and Eva going into their private quarters. She was wearing a dark-blue dress with white trimmings. They invited only the two secretaries – but neither Goebbels partner – to join them.

After a while Traudl Junge slipped out to see Magda and smoke a cigarette. Magda was in even more somber mood than Hitler. 'I prefer my children to die rather than survive as the objects of mockery and scandal,' she woodenly said. Around three-thirty P.M. Hitler and Eva emerged for one last time, shook hands wordlessly with Goebbels, and then retired, closing the padded doors behind them. Artur Axmann arrived to request orders for his young tank-killer squads. Goebbels intercepted the one-armed Hitler Youth leader and told him curtly that the Führer was 'seeing no one.'[80]

In the old bunker Traudl Junge found the children waiting restlessly and giggling each time the bunker shook. She busied herself spreading bread and butter until a shot rang out, so close that their giggling stopped.

It echoed through the concrete labyrinth, and Hellmut exclaimed, 'That sounded like a direct hit.'[81]

Otto Günsche went to investigate. He returned to the map room, where Goebbels and the others were waiting. '*Der Führer ist tot,*' he announced.[82]

THUS, IF ONLY BY FIAT of the departed Führer, Joseph Goebbels became the last chancellor of the Third Reich. His brief dominion extended one mile from north to south, from the Weidendamm Bridge to Prinz-Albrecht Strasse, and rather less than that from east to west.

Epilogue: 'Ever at your Side'

R EICH CHANCELLOR JOSEPH GOEBBELS nodded to Otto Günsche, Hitler's broad-shouldered, blond S.S. 'bulldog,' to go ahead. Hitler had commanded Günsche to ensure that he and Eva were truly dead, and then to cremate their remains. They all trooped into Hitler's private sanctum. The sight of their Führer lifeless, the fountainhead until now of their own power and influence, slumped on the sofa with blood oozing from his head and mouth, had a numbing effect on them all. Eva's head rested on his shoulder. Ludwig Stumpfegger, Hitler's wiry young S.S. doctor, stooped briefly and confirmed that they were both dead, which relieved Günsche of a last distasteful duty with which Hitler had also charged him.[1]

While the valet wrapped Hitler's corpse in a blanket and carried it out with Stumpfegger's assistance, Günsche picked up Eva's and followed them to the spiral staircase with Dr Goebbels a few paces behind. Schwägermann reported the scene to Magda. 'He ought not to have done this to us,' she wept.[2]

Upstairs Russian artillery was bracketing the building. Shrapnel was flying around the gardens. Storms of mortar dust and smoke whipped past. The little funeral party unceremoniously tipped the Führer's body into a hollow a few yards from the bunker exit where Goebbels remained, taking shelter. Hitler's corpse lay face upwards with Eva's next to him. A rude gust of wind hoisted her blue dress to reveal her garter-belt. Then, sodden down with the gasoline that Günsche and Hitler's chauffeur slopped out of five jerrycans, the cloth wrapped itself limply round her limbs. Goebbels handed Günsche a match, a lighted rag was tossed onto the bodies, a sheet of flame enveloped the couple, and Bormann, Goebbels, Günsche, and the doctor raised their right arms in a farewell salute.

Goebbels led the way back down into the underground map room. Günsche and Axmann cleaned up in the death chamber. 'Bormann – Burgdorf – Krebs – Mohnke,' Goebbels ordered. 'Please come to an immediate situation conference.' (Wilhelm Burgdorf had succeeded Schmundt; Krebs had replaced Guderian; Wilhelm Mohnke was the citadel's commandant.)

Hitler was dead. The Greatest Warlord of All Times had deserted them. For the last six years Germany had effectively been a Führer state without a Führer. Now Goebbels was Reich chancellor without a Reich. The men clustered round as Goebbels told them of Hitler's testament appointing him.

The main point on his agenda was to secure Moscow's formal recognition for his new government before the Soviet High Command could crush his tiny Reich.[3] Together with Martin Bormann he dictated to secretary Gerda Christian a letter addressed to the Soviet military commander Marshal Zhukov, informing him that the Führer was dead and asking on behalf of the new government for an immediate ceasefire to enable the injured to be evacuated from the chancellery area.[4]

He detailed Krebs, a fluent Russian speaker, to carry this letter to Zhukov's headquarters under a flag of truce.[5] But the preliminaries for this dangerous expedition took longer than planned. Else Krüger recalls that a radio signal went first to the Russian command, then a junior officer went to inquire if they would receive Krebs. It was close to midnight before the general himself set off, accompanied by a colonel, General Weidling's chief of staff, in an armored car flying a white flag.[6]

What was Goebbels' intent? Krebs' remarks to the Soviet officers, of which due record was taken, show that Goebbels had perceived only one hope for his own salvation: If Stalin would cut a deal with him at the expense of his western allies.

For several hours there was no word from Krebs. Goebbels and his men hung around the bunker's lowest level, drinking endless cups of coffee and knocking back tots of schnapps. Goebbels had authorized a mass breakout for that night, and the cooks upstairs had packed all their pots and pans in anticipation; but now that Krebs was still absent the cooks had to unpack and prepare more meals. Upstairs meanwhile a burial party tried in the darkness to complete the cremation work, but the Hitler couple's corpses were only superficially charred. They were buried in a shell crater with the bodies of their two dogs laid out one layer above them, as a decoy. Hitler's Alsatian Blondi had a collar-tag engraved 'IMMER MIT DIR' – ever at your side.[7]

Several efforts were made to persuade the new chancellor even now to spare the lives of his six children. Axmann offered to take them out of Berlin. Goebbels went through the motions of consulting Magda, but returned and said he did not want the children to live to see him branded as a war criminal.[8] Hitler's chauffeur made a similar offer. Goebbels told him that, if Krebs failed, his course was clear.[9] The night passed but General Krebs did not return. Pondering what to do now, Goebbels asked Traudl Junge for a copy of Hitler's testament: But she had destroyed both her own shorthand and the remaining carbon copies.[10]

At seven-forty the next morning – it was now May 1, 1945 – Martin Bormann sent a succinct message to Dönitz in Flensburg, northern Germany: 'Testament in force,' it said. 'I shall join you as rapidly as possible. My advice is to delay publication until then. BORMANN.'[11] At about the same time Goebbels was dressing punctiliously for this day's probable meeting with his Maker, choosing his finest underwear, his light-brown party uniform, dark silk socks, a brown silk necktie clasped with a swastika badge, and the special orthopedic shoes.[12]

The sounds of combat had almost died away – it was the Russian labor day.

TOWARD MID-MORNING THE COLONEL came back from the Russian headquarters, his uniform torn by barbed wire. He reported that General Krebs had been conducted to the Eighth Guards Army command post on the edge of Tempelhof airfield. The commanding officer, General Vassiliy Ivanovich Chuikov, had heard him out; but after conferring by phone with Marshal Zhukov the Russians had refused to discuss anything but unconditional surrender. There could be no talk of a limited armistice. In reply, Krebs had argued, as instructed, that it was in Stalin's interest to recognize the new Goebbels government at once. General Chuikov had repeated the Soviet refusal. Krebs had sent the colonel back to the chancellery with a Soviet signals team to run a field telephone line in to the bunker. But the cable had proved too short by several hundred yards.[13]

With his Führer dead, all the stuffing had gone out of Bormann. The colonel later said that while Bormann was falling apart, he saw no sign of fear in Goebbels. 'Goebbels was calm, clear spoken, and polite. I did notice red blotches in his face – they betrayed his emotions.'

Goebbels asked how long 'Berlin' could hold out.

'Two days, maximum,' replied the colonel. 'Just pockets of resistance after that.'

'Do you think Krebs has any chance of doing a deal?'

'I believe not,' said the colonel, and repeated: 'The Soviets are insisting on total surrender.'

'Never!' exclaimed Goebbels. 'I shall never, never, never give them that.'

Toward eleven A.M. he ordered: 'Fetch Krebs back. I want to hear what he has to say.'

The record shows that Krebs left the Soviet headquarters at 1:08 P.M. It must have been after two o'clock before he arrived in the chancellery bunker. He found officers scurrying hither and thither, many smoking cigarettes and clutching bottles in their hands – unthinkable while their Führer had been alive. Goebbels accused Krebs of having failed to state his terms forcefully enough to the Russians. Instead he had allowed them to take him in with worthless assurances about treating any prisoners according to the conventions.

That was his last official conference. For a while he sauntered up and down, softly whistling two Nazi marching songs.[14] He had given up hope. Krebs' negative report had been the death sentence on the Goebbels family. He authorized the remaining bunker occupants and propaganda ministry staff to stage their mass breakout attempt after dark, around nine P.M. To Dönitz he sent this explicit message at three P.M.:

Führer deceased yesterday at 3:30 P.M. Testament of April 29 confers office of Reich president on you, office of Reich chancellor on Reich minister Dr Goebbels, office of party minister on Reichsleiter Bormann, office of

Reich foreign minister on Reichsleiter Seyss-Inquart. Upon Führer's orders copies of the testament were dispatched to you, to Field Marshal Schörner, and conveyed out of Berlin for public safekeeping. Reichsleiter Bormann will try to get to you today to explain the situation. Manner and time of announcement to public and troops are at your own discretion. Acknowledge receipt. GOEBBELS.[15]

He and Bormann sent an officer to tell the Russians that their terms were refused and to repudiate any assurances that General Krebs might have given them.[16]

Magda phoned her young S.S. dentist friend in the other bunker. 'Time's running out,' she said.

Kunz hurried over, though not bringing any 'medicines' with him yet. He arrived outside the Goebbels' quarters as Axmann was asking, 'Have you decided, Herr Reich minister?' Magda, who also momentarily forgot to refer to her husband as Chancellor, replied: 'The gauleiter of Berlin and his family are staying in Berlin and will die here.'

'Doctor,' said Goebbels in a matter-of-fact way to the dentist. 'I'd be grateful if you would help my wife to put the children to sleep.'[17]

It was about five P.M.[18] Magda had changed into a yellow and brown knitted dress; she had her platinum-blonde hair swept up, and held in place with hairpins and clips. Anxious to get the awful deed behind her she plucked at the dentist's sleeve. 'Our troops are pulling out,' she said. 'The Russians may get in at any moment. We've got to hurry.' She selected a syringe from a cupboard, and handed it to Kunz. 'Morphine,' she explained, and led the way to the other bunker.

'Not to worry,' Magda said brightly to her children, giving each a chocolate. 'The doctor here is going to give you each a little jab that all the other children and soldiers are getting.'[19]

That was all. Choking, she turned and left the room. Rach the chauffeur stepped in briefly to say good-bye to the children: Lying, he told them he was going on a journey. Helga, the eldest, wearing a light-blue nightdress with lace trimmings, would be first. She was old enough to guess what was happening. Hands trembling, the dentist began to inject the narcotics – into Helga, twelve, Hilde, eleven, then nine-year-old Hellmut, who was wearing white pajamas decorated with a turquoise and red flowered pattern, and the three little sisters Holde, Hedda, and Heide, aged eight, seven, and four.[20] It took nearly ten minutes.

'We'll have to wait ten minutes until they're asleep,' the dentist told Magda outside. But there was one hitch – he refused to administer the actual poison himself. She snapped at him to fetch Dr Stumpfegger.[21]

Three or four minutes later the S.S. surgeon found her in the children's room silently watching over her drugged family. Stumpfegger, a family man himself, meticulously laid out six ampoules – each a phial of bluish glass with a red dot in the middle. While Magda gently prized open each mouth, Stumpfegger gingerly crushed the phial with his long, slender fingers and tipped it and its contents in. Young Hellmut still had the wire brace around his upper teeth – they had always protruded just like his father's.[22]

She would have had a heart of ice not to be riven asunder by what she had done. She rushed outside as soon as the sixth child, the youngest, had been dispatched and threw her arms around Günter Schwägermann's neck. The burly six-footer steadied her in his strong arms for a moment. Stumpfegger came out and nodded to her meaningfully. She fainted in their arms.[23] When Rach came in, a few minutes later, he found her closing the dead children's eyes and kissing each one tenderly on the forehead. 'It's so wretched for me,' she said, sobbing loudly. 'It was so painful bringing each one into the world.'[24] They led her downstairs to her husband. 'It's done,' she said. 'The children are dead. Now for ourselves.'

IN THE OTHER BUNKER Günsche and Mohnke briefed the several hundred people who had gathered for the breakout. The women buckled on helmets and side arms too.[25]

At first the new chancellor instructed Rach and Schwägermann to bury the children's, Magda's, and his own bodies properly in the gardens; reluctant to risk lives needlessly in such an effort, the adjutant talked him out of it and promised to see that the bodies were completely cremated.[26] Goebbels told Naumann that he and Magda would kill themselves as soon as the mass breakout began: 'I don't want to survive just to put my signature on a surrender document,' he said.[27] It was 7:55 P.M. when Naumann returned to the ruined ministry building.[28]

For the next half-hour Joseph Goebbels paced restlessly up and down smoking, like a party host discreetly waiting for his last guests to leave. Hitler's remaining staff said their farewells. He pulled a wry grin at Traudl Junge and wished her well. 'You might just make it,' he appraised. He told Hans Baur, the pilot, 'If you should reach Dönitz, tell him of our life down here these last few days.'

At eight-fifteen he called in Schwägermann, as the last squads of men and women, bristling with machine pistols, carbines, and grenades, made their way past to the breakout assembly point in the coal bunker, and told him, 'We've got to hurry now, there's very little time.' He added, 'Schwägermann, this was the worst treachery of all. The generals have betrayed our Führer. It's the end of everything.' Again he implored his adjutant, 'You will burn our bodies – are you capable of that?'

He gave him the silver-framed Hitler portrait that had stood on his desk for nearly twenty years. Magda took the S.S. Hauptsturmführer's hand and said, 'If you ever see Harald again, greet him from us and say that we went honorably to our deaths.'[29]

Schwägermann directed Rach to fetch the gasoline. The stocky, dark-complexioned driver returned with an orderly, probably S.S. Scharführer Ochs, carrying several canisters and a small swastika flag.

Magda turned to her husband. 'Don't let's die down here in the bunker,' she said.

'No, of course not. We'll go up into the garden.'

With a greater sense of history than of the realities of the situation outside, Magda said: 'Not the garden. Wilhelm Platz – that's where you have spent your working life.'

He went to the coat-rack, took his trench coat, adjusted the dark-blue spotted scarf round his neck, carefully pulled on his yellow-leather gloves, and donned his light-gray snap-brimmed fedora. He put the pistol into his pocket, offered Magda his arm. The couple emerged wordlessly from their room and passed Schwägermann and Ochs as though already ghosts.

THE REST CAN ONLY BE PIECED together from the uncertain evidence of the Soviet autopsies.[30] These afford no real clue to who died first or even how. The Russians found the splinters of a poison phial in the right side of Dr Goebbels' jaw. Magda too had swallowed poison. Like Hitler, he had probably also shot himself. Schwägermann certainly heard one shot – others heard two; on Schwägermann's orders Ochs fired two coups *de grâce* into the motionless bodies.[31] The S.S. officers made only cursory attempts to burn the remains. A Walther pistol was found near them a few days later when the Russians tipped the two corpses onto a red and gilt door ripped out of the chancellery building. The corpses were loaded onto a truck and driven away.

THERE WAS ONE FEATURE about the little Doctor, even in death, that caught the Soviet pathologist's attention. His fists were raised, as though spoiling for a fight.[32] Perhaps, somewhere, for Dr Joseph Goebbels the dialectical battle was already beginning anew.

16 apr 2016

Notes to Sources

For a key to abbreviations used, see pages 693–5

Notes to Prologue.

1 Soviet documents on the identification of the cadavers of Goebbels and his family were published by Lev Bezymenski in *Der Tod von Adolf Hitler* (Munich, Berlin, 1982) (hereafter Bezymenski), 48ff and 97ff; Soviet surgeon Lt-Col. Grachow established the children's cause of death as 'toxic carbohemoglobin,' and made no mention of bullet wounds in Joseph or Magda Goebbels; but for political reasons, as Besymenski privately told this author, Soviet Intelligence also suppressed references to the bullet entry in Hitler's head.

2 Testimony of Paul Schmidt at Amtsgericht Berlin-Zehlendorf, Oct 21, 1955 (Institut für Zeitgeschichte, Munich (hereafter IfZ), file F82, Heiber papers); William Henning in *Hamburger Freie Presse*, Nov 5, 1947.

3 Testimony of Fritzsche, Apr 30, 1947 (Hoover Libr., K Frank Korf papers).

4 On May 5, 1945 the British ambassador in Moscow was told that the bodies of Goebbels and family (but not of Hitler) had been found: 'The cause of death was poison' (Tel. 1738 to Foreign Office London (hereafter FO), May 6. Public Record Office (hereafter PRO: currently renamed British 'National Archives') file FO.371/46748); also *Krasnaya Zvyezda*, Moscow, and United Press dispatch in *New York Times* (hereafter *NYT*), May 18, 1945.

5 Former Kommissar of Geheime Feldpolizei Wilhelm Eckold, quoted in 'Zehn ehemalige Generale zurückgekehrt,' in *Frankfurter Allgemeine Zeitung* (hereafter *FAZ*), Jan 9, 1956; he was Goebbels' personal detective 1934–38, 1942–45.

6 Today it is numbered 202 Odenkirchener Strasse.

7 Ralf Georg Reuth, *Goebbels* (Munich, 1990); a solid volume particularly well researched in Reuth's native Berlin archives and the Goebbels papers held by François Genoud in Lausanne (hereafter Reuth).

8 Birth certificate issued by Rheydt-Mitte registrars' office, No. 1017/1897 (IfZ file F82, Heiber papers); under Germany's Data Protection Act such documents are no longer available to historians. Copy of certificate in Landesarchiv Berlin, Rep. 58, item 47, vol. vii. Goebbels' brother Hans listed their father's occupation as Werkmeister (overseer) on his NSDAP (Nazi party) application form (in BDC files); in his handwritten early memoirs (*Erinnerungsblätter*, henceforth EB) Goebbels (JG) himself described his father as a *Handlungsgehilfe* (trade clerk). – The *Erinnerungsblätter* and some diaries (1924–41, incomplete) are transcribed expertly by Dr Elke Fröhlich of the IfZ in *Die Tagebücher von Joseph Goebbels. Sämtliche Fragmente*, four volumes (Munich, 1987); the original manuscript of EB is on microfiche in packet 26, box 2, of the Goebbels collection ('Fond 1477') located by Fröhlich in the former Soviet secret state archives in Moscow early in 1992, a collection of 1,600 glass plates (approximately 75,000 pages) of his diaries and manuscripts, first researched and used by this author. On one microfiche is a 'Tagebuch 1897 – Okt 1923' but this diary is nearly empty. On the 'DNA' of the

family name, see the article 'Der Sippenname "Goebbels"' by Peter Jansen (of Uebach) in *Westdeutscher Beobachter*, Nr. 212, Apr 28, 1939; he found traces of GOBELIN (tapestry) and GODEBERAHT (God-famed) in the name. Also the article 'Geilenkirchener Land. Stammland der Sippe Goebbels,' with photographs of the ancestral Goebbels homes in Uebach, Odenhofen etc., *ibid.*, Oct 26, 1938.

9 In 1923 Goebbels mentioned a 'Rechtsanwalt Joseph' in EB. Dr Josef Joseph published an open letter to JG in Nov 1944 from his exile in the USA. Günter Erckens, *Juden in Mönchengladbach* (Mönchengladbach, 1989), 189f.

10 Conrad was a *Hofverwalter* (farm bailiff) from Gevelsdorf. He had married Gertrud Margarete Rosskamp of Beckrath.

11 The author has adhered more closely to what Goebbels himself wrote in his Jul 1924 EB, 'Von 1897 bis zu meinem ersten Semester 1917 in Bonn,' than to Helmut Heiber or to other secondary sources.

12 Wilfried von Oven, *Mit Goebbels bis zum Ende,* 2 vols. (Buenos Aires, 1949) (hereafter Oven), 241 ('Apr 24, 1944').

13 Diary, Aug 8, 12, 13, 1924. The birth certificate identifies him as *Handlungsgehilfe* (trade clerk).

14 Against which, see *NYT,* Jun 10, 1946: 'Goebbels Never Helped Aged Mother' (an alleged interview of her and Goebbels' sister Maria).

15 Diary, Jul 20, 1924: 'Dat komp op Kreg ut' – That begets war. On the Dutch side of the border river Wurm the Dutch spoke Limburg *platt*, almost identical to the *platt* spoken on the German side.

16 She was born at Uebach on Apr 18, 1869 and died Aug 8, 1953, aged 84. She stated on Mar 25, 1948 that her mother Maria Katharina Odenhausen née Coervers was born in 1824 at Uebach and died in Krefeld, Germany, in 1886; her father (Johann) Michael Odenhausen was born at Uebach and died at München-Gladbach (as it was then spelt) in 1880. All were catholic (Korf papers).

17 Born Aug 8, 1893; joined the NSDAP in Dec 1928, becoming a Kreisleiter; promoted to gau (Nazi party region) publishing chief in 1933, acting as business manager of the Völkischer Verlag in Düsseldorf. In 1935 he became publisher of the *Frankfurter Volksblatt*, then head of the gau publishing house in Hessen-Nassau and manager of the *Rhein-Mainische Zeitung.* From 1932 to 1933 he was in the S.A. reserve. Promoted to Reichsamtsleiter (a medium party rank) in 1936. – Biographical file in the Berlin Document Center and in the National Archives, Washington DC (hereafter NA): Record Group (hereafter RG) 319, XE.246725, Werner Naumann. And *Frankfurter Neue Presse*, Aug 31, 1948.

18 Hans Johann Friedrich Goebbels, born Jan 25, 1895, died Aug 13, 1947; joined NSDAP in 1929 (No. 160,449) and the S.A. in 1931, rising to Oberführer on Nov 9, 1942. In 1931–32 he was Propagandaleiter of an *Ortsgruppe* (local), then of a Kreis (district) and chairman of a Kreis party court (*Uschla*). From 1933 to 1945 he was general manager of the Provincial Fire and Life Insurance Co. of the Rhineland, and permanent deputy president of the provincial Landesversicherungsanstalt Rheinprovinz from 1937. To the dismay of his parents he married a protestant, Hertha Schell, by whom he had a son Lothar (1929) and daughter Eleonore (1935). *Ibid.*

19 Konrad Goebbels died Jun 11, 1949 leaving one daughter. Maria's (deceased) sisters were Maria (died in infancy) and Elisabeth (1901 – 1915): testimony, Mar 25, 1948 (Korf papers). There were also aunts and uncles: his mother's sisters were Anna Simons (1849 – 1939 or 1940), Christine Jansen (1856 – 1939) and Maria Jansen (1862 – 1916); her brothers were

Joseph Odenhausen (died 1902), Peter Odenhausen (1860 – 1915) and Johann Odenhausen (1857 – 1916).

20 In Genoud's papers are Fritz Göbbels's bank statements 1900 – 1920, and a blue account
book in which he recorded every penny spent (Reuth, 14, 17).

21 Writing to Anka Stalherm on Sep 17, 1918 he described poring over old school relics
with Willy Zilles – 'a little picture of my First Communion, a school picture of the
Second Form, a dictation book from the First' (Bundesarchiv Koblenz, hereafter BA]
Goebbels papers, 'Film 1,' NL.118/109); François Genoud, guardian of Goebbels' papers
(and interests) owns a letter from Willy Zilles to JG dated Jan 4–5, 1915.

22 Goebbels manuscript for Else Janke, 1923 (BA file NL.118/126).

23 The late Curt Riess, in *Joseph Goebbels* (Baden-Baden, 1950), states that JG suffered from
a bone-marrow inflammation at age seven, and the foot deformation resulted from
the consequent operation. JG's diary for Aug 21, 1930 records his brother Konrad as
suffering from an unspecified chronic foot complaint. Wilfried von Oven saw that a
Somerset Maugham novel about a youth born with a clubfoot, taunted and bullied in
his childhood, featured prominently in JG's bookshelf in World War Two.

24 Later he would suggest it was a war injury: Party Court, session of Jun 10, 1927 (BDC file,
Goebbels; author's film DI–81)

Notes to Chapter 1.

1 The year is recorded in JG's 1921 handwritten curriculum vitae appended to his doctoral
dissertation (Reuth, 17).

2 An article on Flisges is on fiche in packet 26 of the Goebbels papers (Moscow archives).

3 A one-hour interview of Hompesch's wife taped by Westdeutscher Rundfunk in 1987 is in
Mönchengladbach city archives.

4 JG, 'Der tote Freund,' Apr 1912 (Genoud papers; Reuth, 20).

5 See his school reports 1912–16 in BA file NL.118/113.

6 See JG's eulogy, 'Gerhardi Bartels Manibus!' Dec 6, 1919 (BA file NL.118/120).

7 Fritz Göbbels to Joseph Goebbels, Nov 9, 1919 (facsimile in *Neue Illustrierte*, Jun 6, 1953;
original now in BA file NL.118/112). According to an article, 'Studentenbriefe,' in *Ruhr
Nachrichten*, Dortmund, May 12, 1953, JG left a suitcase filled with snapshots, love letters
(including 115 letters from Anka Stalherm and 'one letter by Joseph Goebbels to Georg
Mumme'), poetry, press clippings, and other early documents with his mother for safekeeping. Worried by a 1943 air raid on Rheydt he phoned his brother Hans to place the
case in safety; Hans deposited it in the lung clinic at Holsterhausen operated by the
Rhineland Insurance Fund of which he was president. In about Feb 1945, according to
Frau Hildegard Meyer, a nurse at that clinic, Hans came to destroy the papers as the
Americans approached; she persuaded him to let her take them. She sold them to the
catholic Wort und Werk GmbH publishing house, according to an article in *Abendzei-
tung*, Aug 31, 1954 (IfZ archives). Alerted by these press items, Swiss lawyer François
Genoud acquired title to JG's writings from the administrator of Goebbels' estate by
contract of Aug 23, 1955, subsequently amended on Oct 21, 1955 and Mar 12, 1956, and he
fought several legal actions against Frau Meyer and others to establish his title to them
in 1956, 1963, and 1964 in Germany. – From court papers in the author's possession.

8 JG, 'Wie kann auch der Nichtkämpfer in diesen Tagen dem Vaterland dienen?', class

paper dated Nov 27, 1914; quoted in 'Joseph Goebbels bewarb sich beim "Judenblatt"' (JG applied for job with 'Jewish rag') in *Westdeutsches Tageblatt*, Jul 7, 1954; these papers from his youth had just been sold in a Berlin auction. They are now in BA file NL.118/117.

9 Now in Genoud's possession.

10 Hans served in 160 Inf. Regt., was in French captivity from Jun 16, 1916 to Jan 22, 1920 (BDC file).

11 Text in BA file NL.118/126.

12 Joseph Goebbels, *Vom Kaiserhof zur Reichskanzlei. Eine historische Darstellung in Tage-buchblättern (vom 1. Januar 1932 bis zum 1. Mai 1933)* (Berlin, 1934): Apr 25, 1933 (hereafter *Kaiserhof*).

13 *Ibid.*, Dec 6, 1930 (Olga Förster).

14 *Ibid.*, Jul 28, 1924.

15 *Ibid.*, Jul 2, 1924.

16 *Ibid.*, Jun 2, 1929.

17 See Kölsch's contribution in *Unitas*, organ of the association of Unitas catholic student fraternities, 57th year, No. 5, June 1917, 227 (BA file NL.118/119).

18 Programm zum Vereinsfest des Bonner Unitas-Vereins, Jun 24, 1917; *Unitas*, Jun and Aug 1917 (IfZ file F82, Heiber papers; and BA file NL.118/119). In September 2003 the University of Bonn boasted in its publicity brochure that Dr Goebbels, like Karl Marx and Konrad Adenauer, had figured among its illustrious alumni.

19 Extracts from twenty-four of these were published in *Echo der Zeit*, Jul 21 and 28, 1952. And see the article 'Ein feiner Vertreter des Dritten Reiches,' by Studienrat Karl Klauck (clerk to the society since 1914) in *Kölnische Volkszeitung*, Jan 31, 1952; also documents in BA file NL.118/113.

20 Hermann Kölsch to JG, Nov 10 and 25, 1917 (Mönchengladbach city archives); Dietz Bering, *Kampf um Namen. Bernhard Weiss gegen Joseph Goebbels* (Stuttgart, 1992) (hereafter Bering), 119.

21 JG's correspondence with Agnes Kölsch is in BA file NL.118/111.

22 Writing to JG on Nov 16, 1917 Mrs Kölsch called herself his Mütterchen (little mother) Number Two (BA file NL.118/111).

23 Diary, Jul 24, 1924; and Mar 20, 1929: Anka's son Christian is 'just like her: blond with blue eyes.'

24 Agnes ('Anka') Stalherm was born on Oct 8, 1895 in Recklinghausen; she died of cancer in 1955, and was buried in an unmarked grave at Horben, above Freiburg. See the curriculum vitæ in Freiburg's Albert Ludwig university archives, 1922, appended to her dissertation, 'Kapitalbedarf und Kapitalbeschaffung in der Industrie nach dem Kriege.' I am indebted to Anka's friend Irene Pranger and Anka's daughter Annette Castendyk for information about this pivotal character on Goebbels' romantic horizon.

25 Undated postcard from Karlheinz Kölsch to Anka in Freiburg (Irene Pranger papers).

26 Anka's daughter volunteered to me (interview, Nov 10, 1991) that her mother told her that she found Goebbels intellectually attractive, but physically not.

27 JG to Anka Stalherm, Jun 15, 1918 (BA file NL.118/109); two letters on this file dated 'Feb 1918' are in fact from Feb 1919.

28 Writing her on Sep 9, 1918 he asks if he may kiss her rosebud lips 'for the first time' (*ibid*).

29 On Jan 26, 1919 he writes her that there is a snapshot of her on Castle Hill meadow on his desk, 'and for Ulex it is as though he must sit down and press a tender kiss on her dear

cheek just like then' (*ibid*).

30 Entitled 'Judas Iscariot. Eine biblische Tragödie in fünf Akten von P J Goebbels,' the 107-page manuscript, written on squared paper in immaculate, legible, copperplate script, is dedicated to Anka Stalherm 'in tiefer Verehrung,' with deep respect (BA file NL.118/127).

31 Agnes Kölsch to JG, Aug 15, 1918 (BA file NL.118/112).

32 JG to Anka, Aug 28, 1918 (BA file NL.118/109). Mrs Castendyk (interviewed, Nov 10, 1991) says Anka's mother regarded JG as an *Emporkömmling* (parvenu).

33 *Cf.* JG to Anka, Sep 9, 1918, 10 A.M.

34 Ditto, Aug 23, 1918.

35 Ditto, Aug 20, 1918.

36 Ditto, Aug 26, 28, 1918.

37 Ditto, Aug 30, 1918.

38 Ditto, Aug 5 and 11, 1918.

39 Ditto, Aug 11, 1918.

40 Anka to JG, Aug 11, 1918.

41 JG to Anka, Aug 26, 1918.

42 Ditto, Aug 30, 1918.

43 Ditto, Sep 2, 1918.

44 Ditto, Sep 3, 1918.

45 Ditto, Sep 8, 1918.

46 Ditto, Sep 9, 1918.

47 JG to Prang, Sep 14, 1918.

48 JG to Anka, Oct 5, 1918.

49 Fritz Göbbels to JG, Nov 14, 1918 (BA file NL.118/113).

50 Ditto, Nov 25, 1918.

51 Anka to JG, Dec 21, 1918.

52 JG memoirs 1924.

53 JG to Anka, Jan 21, 1919 (BA file NL.118/109).

54 Ditto, Jan 25, 1919.

55 Anka to JG, Jan 25, 1919.

56 JG to Anka, Jan 29, Feb 4, 10, 1919.

57 Ditto, Jan 26, 1919.

58 Ditto.

59 Ditto, Jan 27, 1919.

60 Ditto, Jan 29, 1919.

61 Ditto, Feb 24, 1919 (BA file NL.118/109).

62 Diary, Jul 14, 1924.

63 *Ibid.*, Jun 9, 1925.

64 See JG to Anka, Mar 16, 1919 (BA file NL.118/109).

65 JG to Willy Zilles, Jul 26, 1915 (Mönchengladbach city archives; Reuth, 24); JG's essay, 'Wilhelm Raabe,' Mar 7, 1916, is in Genoud's papers.

66 JG to Anka Stalherm, Feb 17, 1919 (BA file NL.118/126).

Notes to Chapter 2.

1 Fritz Göbbels' correspondence with JG is in BA files NL.118/112 and /113.

2 Fragment of a Drama, 'Kampf der Arbeiterklasse,' winter 1919/20 (Genoud papers).

3 'Die Saat. Ein Drama in drei Akten, von Joseph Goebbels.' The cast includes: the worker, his wife, their son; first, second, third workmen; the French lieutenant; a French sentry. 'The setting is somewhere in Germany.' Handwritten MS in BA file NL.118/107.

4 JG to Anka, Mar 4, 1920 (BA file NL.118/110); speaking the *Plattdeutsch* dialect of Rheydt he would have found it easy to learn Dutch.

5 JG, 'Sursum corda!' in *Westdeutsche Landeszeitung*, Nr. 55, Mar 7, 1922 (on film in Mönchengladbach city library; courtesy of Reuth).

6 See JG's correspondence with Geitmann and others in BA file NL.118/112.

7 JG to Anka, Jun 29, 1920 (BA file NL.118/126).

8 The four sheets show no folds. – JG to Anka, undated (BA file NL.118/118).

9 JG, 'Mein Testament,' Rheydt, Oct 1, 1920. Not witnessed; inked on a small page, evidently a flyleaf torn from a book (BA file NL.118/118; a similar version in /113).

10 Flisges to JG, Oct 31, 1920 (BA file NL.118/112).

11 EB, JG's 1924 memoirs.

12 Dr Georg Mumme, born Brunswick Oct 31, 1892, joined NSDAP Feb 1, 1930 (No. 190,196), later headed the Gau legal section of Thuringia and the legal department of the Reichsleitung (NSDAP headquarters) Munich; died in Düsseldorf in 1970 (BDC files).

13 Anka to JG, Nov 24, 1920 (BA file NL.118/126); diary, Aug 7, 1924.

14 Diary, Apr 3, 1929 (BA file NL.118/126).

15 JG, 'Wilhelm von Schütz als Dramatiker. Ein Beitrag zur Geschichte des Dramas der Romantischen Schule,' PhD thesis, 215 pages, Ruprecht-Karl university, Heidelberg, 1921.

16 Diary, Jan 20, 1929: 'I tell [Anka] of the terrible pain I felt at our separation when . . . [Mumme] was so lousy to me and turned up with a lawyer. . . But I believe she was probably not to blame for it.'

17 A copy of the diploma dated Apr 21, 1922 is in BA file NL.118/128.

Notes to Chapter 3.

1 German FO files, Feb 15, 1923, on the Ruhr occupation: Friedrich Ebert foundation archives, Bonn: Carl Severing papers, file 95; execution of Schlageter, *ibid.*, files 99ff.

2 Albert Krebs, *Erinnerungen an die Frühzeit der Partei* (Stuttgart, 1959) (hereafter Krebs), 158. Krebs, no friend of JG's, excused the 'uniform' and remark as a necessary propaganda tactic given the hostile atmosphere of the times. The writer Franz Schauwecker exposed JG's 'military career' later in an open letter.

3 A blue carbon-copy typescript of Goebbels' much revised play, *Michael Voormann. Ein Menschenschicksal in Tagebuchblättern*, dedicated to the memory of Flisges, is in BA file NL.118/127. In it, Michael's mother sends to the mining apprentice Alexander Neumann a copy of *Zarathustra* that had belonged to Michael; Neumann writes to Hertha Holk that he has found one passage lined in red, reading: 'Many die too late, and some too early. Never forget the lesson: Die at the right time!'

4 *NYT*, May 4, 1945.

5 Karl Kaufmann to Otto Strasser, Jun 4, 1927 (BDC: Goebbels file ; author's film DI–81).

6 Müller (editor) to JG, Oct 13, 1922 (BA file NL.118/113).

7 JG, 'Ausschnitte aus der deutschen Literatur der Gegenwart,' Oct 30, 1922 (Genoud papers; *cit.* Reuth, 58).

8 *Kölner Tageblatt* also published two articles by JG in the summer of 1923; a dozen early newspaper articles by JG are preserved in BA file NL.118/113.

9 'Heinrich Kämpfert. Ein Drama in drei Aufzügen' (BA file NL.118/114); completed Feb 12, 1919.

10 'Die die Sonne lieben,' summer 1917 (BA file NL.118/117).

11 'Bin ein fahrender Schüler, ein wüster Gesell. . .' A 32pp. novel handwritten in summer 1917 on squared paper, 'Novelle aus dem Studentenleben von Joseph Goebbels,' dedicated to Kölsch (BA file NL.118/127).

12 'Bei Nacht' (BA file NL.118/118).

13 *Cf.* diary, Mar 8, 1926: 'I weigh just one hundred *Pfund*,' *i.e.*, fifty kilos or about 110 pounds.

14 Diary, Jul 14, 1924; JG's correspondence with Else Janke is in BA file NL.118/110.

15 Diary, Aug 6, 1924.

16 *Ibid.*, Aug 8, 1924.

17 In his diary on Dec 28, 1933 JG would describe another visit to the castle, with 'blissful memories.'

18 On Jul 19, 1924 JG noted, 'Today is one year since Richard was killed at Schliersee'.

19 JG to Else Janke, Sep 22, 1923 (BA file NL.118/110).

20 Fritz Göbbels to JG, Sep 27, 1923 (BA file NL.118/113).

21 JG, 'Schöpferische Kräfte. Richard Flisges, dem toten Freunde!' in *Rheydter Zeitung*, Dec 22, 1923 (BA file NL.118/113; and Moscow archives, Goebbels papers).

22 *Cf.* Diary, Jul 31, 1924.

23 Diary, Oct 17, 1923-Jun 22, 1924 (Moscow archives, Goebbels papers, box 2). The micro-fiches in this box also contain the following segments: Dec 31, 1923 – Mar 11; Mar 13 – Jun 12; Jun 27 – Aug 6, 1924. JG also wrote a 32-page sketch for Else entitled 'From my diary.' This reflected his painful lack of any vocation and his crushing doubts in God and the world. 'I feel the need,' he began, 'to give some account of my life so far.' The best way, he felt, would be to sit in judgment each day upon himself. 'My goal,' he wrote, 'is God. And my greatest joy, the search for Truth.' (BA file NL.118/126); *cf.* Elke Fröhlich (*ed.*), *Die Tagebücher von Joseph Goebbels. Sämtliche Fragmente*, four vols. (Munich, 1987), cv.

24 Diary, Jul 19, 1924.

25 JG, 'Aus meinem Tagebuch,' Jun 1923 (BA file NL.118/126).

26 Else Janke to JG, Nov 4, 1923 (Genoud papers; *cit.* Reuth, 74).

27 Diary, Jul 2, 1924.

28 *Ibid.*, Jul 11, 1924.

29 *Ibid.*, Jul 15, 1924.

30 *Ibid.*, Aug 13, 1924.

31 *Ibid.*, Aug 1, 7, 1924.

32 *Ibid.*, Jul 9, 1924.

33 *Ibid.*, Jul 4, 1924.

34 JG to Rudolf Mosse Verlag (BA file NL.118/113).

35 The papers of Theodor Wolff (1868–1943), chief editor of the *Berliner Tageblatt*, are in BA file NL.207.

36 Diary, Jul 30, 1924.

37 *Ibid.*, Jul 17, 1924.

38 *Rheydter Zeitung* and *Düsseldorfer Nachrichten*. JG's diary for Nov 8, 1928 suggests that he began his career 'as a little country orator' at Hattingen.

39 Boris von Borresholm, *Dr. Goebbels. Nach Aufzeichnungen aus seiner Umgebung* (Berlin, 1949) (hereafter Borresholm), 46ff. It is not clear who the author was.

40 See Manfred Müller, *Den Weg zur Freiheit bahnen! Um Sozialismus und Sozialpolitik: NS-Arbeiteragitator Wilhelm Börger* (Essen, 1993). Börger (not 'Berger,' as Fröhlich has it) was a friend of JG.

41 Diary, Jun 30, 1924. Presumably Rosenberg's diary (Mar 1, 1939) reference to JG's alleged remark to Darré on Feb 25, 1939 that Hitler ought to have told him (JG) 'in 1924' to comport himself differently is a mistake. Hans-Günther Seraphim (ed.), *Das politische Tagebuch Alfred Rosenbergs* (Munich, 1964); the unpublished balance of the Rosenberg diary was last heard of in the private papers of the late Dr Robert M W Kempner, a Frankfurt attorney, but has not turned up in his estate.

42 Diary, Jul 4, 1924.

43 *Ibid.*, Jul 7, 9, 1924.

44 *Ibid.*, Jul 25, 1924.

45 *Ibid.*, Jul 28, 1924.

46 *Ibid.*, Jul 30, 1924.

47 *Ibid.*, Mar 27, 1925.

48 Although Witkowski was often called 'Isidor', *e.g.* in the *Morning Post*, Jun 11, 1922, his real first names were Felix Ernst. His brother was Witting of the National Bank.

49 Diary, Jun 30, Jul 2, 4, 1924; see too Bering, 215, and *Angriff*'s hate-filled obituary, Nov 21, 1927.

50 Diary, Jul 4, 1924.

51 *Briefe aus dem Gefängnis an Karl Liebknecht* (1919); JG diary, Jul 4, 1924.

52 Diary, Aug 25, 1924.

53 *Ibid.*, Aug 20, 1924.

54 *Ibid.*, Aug 22, 1924.

55 W von Ameln, 'Die Stadt Rheydt und die Nationalsozialistische Deutsche Arbeiter-partei,' in *Einwohnerbuch der Stadt Rheydt 1936* (Mönchengladbach city archives).

56 Diary, Jul 2, 1938. 'I receive a secret protocol from the Belgian war ministry on my inter-rogation by Detective Nagel in 1924.' And *cf.* Ameln, 'Die Stadt Rheydt.'

57 *E.g.* in *Rheinische Landeszeitung und Volksparole*, Nr. 239, Sep 1, 1935 (Höffkes collection); JG's police file however states under Feb 1, 1926 he 'fled from the occupied territories because of political machinations.'

58 Diary, Aug 29, 1924.

59 *Ibid.*, Sep 1, 3, 4, 1924.

60 *Völkische Freiheit. Rheinisch-Westfälisches Kampfblatt der Nationalsozialistischen Frei-heitsbewegung für ein völkisch-soziales Deutschland.*

61 Diary, Sep 1, 9, 17, 22, 24, Oct 6, 1924.

62 *Ibid.*, Sep 15, 1924.

63 *Ibid.*, Sep 23, 1924.

64 *Ibid.*, Oct 21, 1925.

65 *Ibid.*, Oct 3, 1924.

66 *Ibid.*, Sep 23, 1924.

Notes to Chapter 4.

1 Diary, Mar 18, 26, Apr 16, 1925.

2 *Ibid.*, Apr 2, May 23, 1925.

3 *Ibid.*, Aug 17, Sep 7, 1925.

4 *Ibid.*, Aug 12, Oct 14, 15, 1925; Aug 17, 1926. JG's original 'Elberfeld diary' (Aug 12, 1925 – Oct 30, 1926) is in the Hoover Library, Stanford, California (Goebbels papers); on microfiches in Moscow archives, Goebbels papers, box 2; published by Helmut Heiber (*ed.*), *Das Tagebuch von Joseph Goebbels 1925/26* (Stuttgart, 1961) (hereafter Heiber); English translation on NA film T84, roll 271, 1116–1222.

5 Diary, Apr 14, 1925.

6 *Ibid.*, Feb 23, 1925.

7 *Ibid.*, Mar 20, 1925.

8 *Ibid.*, Jun 8, Sep 3, 1925. Else survived the war, though her Jewish blood must have caused her problems. JG wrote cryptically (*ibid.*, Jun 25, 1933) after visiting Rheydt: 'I settle the Else problem with [Mother] alone.'

9 *Ibid.*, Apr 18, 1925.

10 *Ibid.*, Apr 22, 1925.

11 Kaufmann to Otto Strasser, Jun 4, 1927 (BDC file, JG).

12 Undated police report in Düsseldorf city archives, *cit.* Reuth, 87.

13 Diary, Mar 26, 1925.

14 JG handwritten letter, Apr 3, 1925, photocopy in NSDAP Hauptarchiv (NA film T581, roll 5; BA file NS.26/136; IfZ film MA.735).

15 *Rheinische Landeszeitung*, Sep 1, 1935.

16 Diary, Mar 26, 28, 1925.

17 *Ibid.*, Mar 18, 26, 30, Apr 7, 28, May 27.

18 *Ibid.*, Apr 16, 1925.

19 *Ibid.*, May 2, 6, 7, 11, 1925.

20 *Ibid.*, May 12, 1925.

21 *Ibid.*, May 19, 1925.

22 *Ibid.*, May 28, 1925.

23 *Ibid.*, Jun 9, 1925.

24 *Ibid.*, May 22, 27; *VB*, May 24, 1925.

25 Diary, Jun 8, 1925.

26 *Ibid.*, Aug 12, 1925. I located the rest of the previously missing diary for Jun 9 – Sep 10, 1925 in box 2 of the Goebbels microfiches in the Moscow archives.

27 Diary, Aug 31, Sep 7, 1925.

28 *Ibid.*, Aug 14–16, 1925.

29 *Ibid.*, Aug 24, 1925. Characteristically JG antedated this in his memory. Speaking at Lutze's state funeral (May 7, 1943), he said: 'I saw him [Lutze] again in the gloomy basements and backyards of Elberfeld, where we founded and together with Karl Kaufmann built up the party in the Ruhr gau between 1923 [*sic*] and 1926... I'll never forget how he escorted us every night when we drove off to the communist meetings in Hattingen, Bochum, Düsseldorf, or Gelsenkirchen.'

30 Diary, Aug 29, 1925.

31 See too JG's note in BA file NL.118/108: 'Jul 25, Hitler Weimar,' and Hinrich Lohse, 'Der Fall Strasser' (IfZ file ZS.265).

32 Diary, Aug 19, 1925.

33 *Ibid.*, Aug 20, 1925.

34 *Ibid.*, Sep 7, 9, 11, 1925.

35 Fobke, 'Report on Founding of the Association of North and West German gaus of the NSDAP,' Göttingen, Sep 11, 1925; publ. by Werner Jochmann, *Nationalsozialismus und Revolution. Ursprung und Geschichte der NSDAP in Hamburg 1922–33*, vol. iii (Hamburg, 1963); NA film T581/44.

36 Diary, Sep 28, 1925.

37 The account in *VB* Oct 7, 1925, did not bear this out, stating that the meeting confirmed Kaufmann, Lutze, and JG as equals in a triumvirate.

38 And *cf.* diary, Jul 6, 1926: 'Somehow, somebody carries me shoulder high into the hall.'

39 For samples see NSDAP Hauptarchiv (NA film T581, roll 52; BA file NS.26/1224).

40 *NS-Briefe*, Oct 15, 1925.

41 *Ibid.*, Nov 15, 1925.

42 Diary, Oct 16, 1925.

43 *Ibid.*, Oct 23, 1925.

44 Letter of Schmitz, Jun 13, 1927 (BDC file, JG).

45 Hanover situation report, Oct 3, 1925 in JG's police file on 'Goebbels, Dr. phil. Paul Josef,' opened on Dec 9, 1925; later placed in the NSDAP Hauptarchiv (NA film T581, roll 52; BA file NS.26/1224) (hereafter: police file), on which see too *NYT*, Sep 29, 1945: with twenty convictions JG's file was thicker than those of Hitler and Göring combined; it was endorsed 'closed' on Feb 13, 1933.

46 JG, *Lenin oder Hitler? Eine Rede gehalten am 19. Februar 1926 im Opernhaus in Königsberg i.Pr.* (Zwickau, 1926).

47 Krebs, 159. His diary and letters are in the archives of the Forschungsstelle für die Geschichte des Nationalsozialismus, Hamburg city archives.

Notes to Chapter 5.

1 Diary, Sep 30, Oct 2, 1925.

2 *Ibid.*, Oct 2, 1925.

3 *Ibid.*, Jan 31, 1926.

4 Diary, Oct 9, 1925; *VB*, Oct 22, 1925.

5 Diary, Oct 26, 1925; Jan 13, 1926. There are entries about payments of 1,500 and 800 marks by Arnold on Mar 21 and 27, 1926.

6 *Ibid.*, Sep 30, 1925.

7 *Ibid.*, Dec 5, 1925.

8 *Ibid.*, Nov 10, 1925.

9 Krebs, 162.

10 Diary, Apr 30, 1926.

11 *Ibid.*, Dec 16, 1925.

12 *Ibid.*, Dec 21, 1925.

13 *Ibid.*, Oct 10, 1925.

14 *Ibid.*, Apr 30; *VB*, Nov 25, 1925, May 5, 1926.

15 Diary, Feb 27, 1926.

16 *Ibid.*, Oct 2, 7, 1925. Carl Severing (1875 – 1952), son of a cigar worker, trades unionist, had been Prussia's minister of the interior since Mar 29, 1920.

17 *Ibid.*, Oct 26; *VB*, Oct 30, 1925. There were forty-nine injured.

18 In notes at the end of his 1927–28 diary JG jotted: 'End of November '25 Hitler. First time Berlin' (BA file NL.118/108).

19 Diary, Nov 6; *cf. VB*, Nov 6, 1925.

20 Diary, Nov 23; *VB*, Nov 25, 1925; *cf.* diary, Nov 21, 1928.

21 *Ibid.*, Nov 23, 1925.

22 *Ibid.*, Jan 25, 1926. On Schlange see Oven, 'Jul 10, 1943,' 39.

23 Diary, Nov 14, 23; *VB*, Nov 29–30, 1925.

24 Diary, Dec 7; *VB*, Dec 13–14, 1925.

25 Richard Wagner, *Über das Dirigieren*. Diary, Jun 27, 1924.

26 Diary, Dec 14, 1925.

27 *Ibid.*, Dec 29, 1925.

28 *Ibid.*, Dec 18, 23, 1925; Jan 6, 1926.

29 *Ibid.*, Jan 8, 1926. The personality studies appeared later as part of JG's *Das Buch Isidor*, which had the sub-title, 'Thirty of this republic's characters.' JG's first published book, *Die Zweite Revolution. Briefe an Zeitgenossen*, appeared Feb 1926.

30 For his fascination with Russia, see *e.g.* diary, Oct 21, 1925.

31 Otto Strasser, *Hitler und ich* (Konstanz, 1948), 116; for several interrogation reports on Otto Strasser and hundreds of postwar telephone and letter intercepts, 1946–59, see NA file RG.319, IRR, G.8172121.

32 Rosenberg diary, Mar 3, 1939.

33 Diary, Feb 11, 1926.

34 *Ibid.*, Feb 15; *cf. VB*, Feb 25, 1926.

35 Krebs, 161.

36 Diary, Feb 22, 1926.

37 JG to Streicher, Feb 18 (BDC file, JG; author's film DI–81). Hitler did not reply; Hess did (diary, Feb 24, 1926).

38 Diary, Mar 13; see JG's article on the South Tyrol in *NS-Briefe*, No. 12, Mar 15, 1926.

39 Diary, Mar 7, 1926.

40 Thus in *VB*, Mar 17, 1926. Kaufmann was still regarded as *primus inter pares*, however, with JG remaining gau manager (*Geschäftsführer*). See the *Rheinische Landeszeitung*, Sep 1, 1935.

41 Report on convention of Rhein-Ruhr gau, Mar 6–7, 1926 (NA film T581, roll 5; BA file NS.26/136).

42 Diary, Apr 13; *VB*, Apr 10, 1926; *cf.* JG's police file.

43 It is in NSDAP Hauptarchiv, NA film T581, roll 54, now BA file NS.26/1290.

44 Diary, Apr 19, 1926. The Württemberg police later (Oct 13) reported to Berlin, 'Goebbels is a man of good education with an unusual talent for speaking. Not on such good terms with Hitler now as earlier' (police file).

45 Minutes of NSDAP annual general meeting, May 22 (NA film T581, roll 52; BA file NS.26/1224). *VB*, May 26; JG diary, May 24, 1926; police file.

46 Diary, Mar 13, Apr 1; *VB*, May 7, 1926.

47 Lutze was commander of the S.A. *Gausturm*; Erich Koch was *Bezirksführer* of the Ruhr's Bergisches Land region.

48 Diary, Jun 12, 1926.

49 *Ibid.*, Jul 12, 15, 23, 1926.

50 *Ibid.*, Jul 23, 1926.

51 *Ibid.*, Jul 15, 1926.

52 *Ibid.*, Jun 16; similar on Jun 17, 1926.

53 *Ibid.*, Jun 21, 1926.

54 *Ibid.*, Feb 22, 1926; she had written him since then (Mar 13).

55 *Ibid.*, Jul 6. He reprinted his speech in *NS-Briefe*, No. 21, Aug 1; see *VB*, Jul 7, 1926.

56 Diary, Jul 23, 24, 1926.

57 *Ibid.*, Jul 25, 1927. In his 'notes on diary for Jun 9, 1925 – Nov 8, 1926' JG recapitulated: 'Jul 23–26 Obersalzberg. Strasser, Hitler, Rust. Decision: Berlin! Jul 30: Pfeffer is to be S.A. supreme commander, me Berlin' (BA file NL.118/108).

58 Diary, Jul 31, Aug 1, 1926.

Notes to Chapter 6.

1 Julek Karl von Engelbrechten, *Eine braune Armee entsteht. Die Geschichte der Berlin-Brandenburger SA.* (Munich, 1937); Martin Broszat, 'Die Anfänge der Berliner NSDAP 1926/27,' in *Vierteljahreshefte für Zeitgeschichte* (quarterly published by IfZ; hereafter *VfZ*), 1960, 85ff; for JG's battle with the Strassers and Kampf Verlag see IfZ file Fa.114.

2 Albert Grzesinski, Berlin's police chief (May 16, 1925 – Oct 6, 1926), boasted in his unpublished memoirs, written in Paris in 1933, 'Im Kampf um die deutsche Republik. Lebensweg eines heute Staatenlosen' (BA file Kl. Erw. 144) that he had installed informers in both the KPD and NSDAP headquarters in Berlin, sometimes 'big shots' (*Prominente*): 'Often only a few hours after decisions were taken in secret conferences, a written report on them lay on my desk.' JG was later warned of this (diary, May 16, 1928).

3 Diary, Aug 21, 26, 1926.

4 *Ibid.*, Sep 3, 10, 1926.

5 Muchow report No. 3, Aug (see note 13 below). See too police file, Aug 26, 1926; and Engelbrechten, *Im Kampf*, 45f.

6 Diary, Aug 28, 1926; JG confirmed in his later notes on diary 1925/26: 'Aug 28: refusal to Hitler *re* Berlin' (BA file NL.118/108).

7 Diary, Sep 8, 1926.

8 *Ibid.*, Sep 11; and see his warm references to her on Oct 17, 1926.

9 *Ibid.*, Sep 17, 1926.

10 JG, *Kampf um Berlin* (Munich, 1932), 24; and see the two-page history of the Berlin gau, Jan 27, 1937 in NSDAP Hauptarchiv (NA film T581, roll 1, BA file NS.26/133; and T581, roll 5, BA file NS.26/5), and *Angriff*'s tenth gau anniversary edition Oct 30, 1936 (BA file NS.26/968; Zentrales Staatsarchiv (ZStA) Potsdam, Rep. 50.01, vol. 1189).

11 Diary, Sep 17, 1926.

12 *Ibid.*, Sep 23, 25, 28, 1926.

13 Reinhold Muchow, Propagandazelle NSDAP, Ortsgruppe Neukölln: situation report No. 1, Jun 1926, NSDAP Hauptarchiv: NA film T581, roll 5; BA file NS.26/133 (hereafter Muchow report). Muchow would die in a foolish shooting accident in 1933.

14 *Dokumente der Zeitgeschichte. Dokumente der Sammlung Rehse* (Munich, 1938) (hereafter *Dokumente*).

15 Diary, Oct 16; Muchow report No. 5, Oct 1926.

16 Schmiedicke to JG, Oct 16, 1926 (BA file Schumacher collection, 199a); see Heiber, 112f.

17 In his notes 1927/28 JG summarized: 'Oct, Potsdam. Mark [Brandenburg] rally. . . Pig-sty Berlin. . . Decision: I'll come' (BA file NL.118/108).

18 Schmiedicke to JG, Oct 28 (BA: Schumacher collection, file 199a).

19 Diary, Oct 18, 1926.

20 Notes on diary (BA file NL.118/108). The hitherto missing diary for Nov 8, 1926 – Jul 21, 1928 is on microfiches in the Moscow archives, Goebbels papers, Fond 1477, box 2.

21 Muchow report No. 1, Jun 1926.

22 Data supplied to the author by the German Federal Office of Statistics.

23 Brüning MS (Syracuse Univ. Libr). A typical government loan was one raised by the merchant banks Lazard Speyer-Ellissen; E Heimann; Lincoln, Menny, Oppenheimer; L Behrens & Sons; M M Warburg & Co.; Veit L Homburger; Salomon Oppenheimer Jr & Co.; J Dreyfus & Co.; Mendelssohn & Co.; Simon Hirschland; Jacob S H Stern, and A Levy (Hoover Institution files).

24 Files on the Kutisker fraud on the Prussian state bank: records of Generalstaatsanwalt bei dem Landgericht Berlin, now in the Landesarchiv Berlin, Rep. 58, item 62; Sklarek's fraud on the Berlin state bank, item 61. I am indebted to Dr R G Reuth for drawing my attention to this source on historic court cases; according to Bering, 283, a Nazi state prosecutor in 1933 decided that these case files, some three thousand of them which would otherwise have been routinely shredded, should be preserved.

25 Dr Bernhard Weiss, born Berlin Jul 30, 1880, died London Jul 29, 1951; member of the Berlin political police since May 1918; their chief from 1920 to 1924, when he was suspended for raiding the Soviet trade mission; social democrat. Subsequently chief of criminal police, then vice police chief after 1927. See his own 160-page book, *Polizei und Politik* (Berlin, 1928; a copy is in the Friedrich Ebert Stiftung, Bonn). This prominent and sorely wronged official emigrated in 1933 via Czechoslovakia to London where his daughter Hilde Baban still lives; he was stripped of German citizenship in 1937 for having allegedly promoted the immigration of eastern Jews into Germany. On this important figure see too *Berlin in Geschichte und Gegenwart. Jahrbuch des Landesarchivs Berlin 1983* (Berlin, 1983); Hsi-Huey Liang, *Die Berliner Polizei in der Weimarer Republik* (Berlin, New York, 1977), 61, 75, 177; and Bernhard J Weiss, *American Education and the European Immigrant 1840–1940* (London/Univ. of Illinois, 1982), and now the scholarly study by *Dietz Bering, Kampf um Namen. Bernhard Weiss gegen Joseph Goebbels* (Stuttgart, 1992), drawing on Weiss's family and official papers. Weiss's own CV is in his files in the ZStA Potsdam, file 21, 344; see too the article, 'He Rules Berlin's Finest,' in *American Hebrew*, Jul 17, 1931, and obituaries in, *e.g., Tagesspiegel*, Jul 31, 1951; *Cronica Israelitica*, Aug 1951.

26 Qualification report 1912 in personnel file on Hptm. Weiss (Bayerisches Hauptstaatsarchiv, Munich, OP 51 391; *cit.* Bering, 41f).

27 See the remarks of his predecessor Ferdinand Friedensburg, *Lebenserinnerungen* (Frankfurt, 1969), 175 (his papers are in BA file NL.114); Bering, 84f.

28 'Der mächtigste Mann in Gross-Berlin / Das ist der Isidor Weiss. / Doch Joseph Goebbels, der "Oberbandit," / der macht ihm die Hölle schon heiss,' etc. Bering, 20; Bering shows that the Berlin communist Otto Steinicke (later a Nazi and editor on Goebbels' *Angriff*) had first dubbed Weiss 'Isidor' in *Rote Fahne*, No. 152, as early as Jul 5, 1923; and see May 16, 1924.

29 Interpol figures, in Deutsches Nachrichten-Büro (hereafter DNB), Jul 20, 1935; and see Kurt Daluege, 'Judenfrage als Grundsatz,' in *Angriff*, Aug 3, 1935 (Hauptamt Ordnungspolizei files, BA file R.19/406); on the criminal demimonde of 1920s Berlin see Paul Weiglin, *Unverwüstliches Berlin. Bilderbuch der Reichshauptstadt seit 1919* (Zürich, 1955) and Walther Kiaulehn, Berlin: *Schicksal einer Weltstadt* (Munich, 1958).

30 Muchow report No. 1.

31 Case against the vendor Zawitalsky, Landesarchiv Berlin, Rep. 58, item 367.

32 Zörgiebel to Landgericht Munich I, Jun 1, 1927 (*ibid*). The editor was acquitted by the Munich courts.

33 Item 24, vol. v, 4; similarly in vol. i, 21, and vol. i, 44.

34 *Angriff*, No. 18, Oct 28, 1927.

35 *Ibid.*, No. 15, Oct 10, 1927; Landesarchiv Berlin, Rep. 58, item 24.

36 His deregistration (*Abmeldung*) with police in Elberfeld was dated Nov 22, 1926: *Angriff*, Oct 30, 1936.

37 Police file.

38 Daluege was born Sep 15, 1897, and hanged by the Czechs on Oct 20, 1946. See his hand-written memoirs on NA film M.1270, roll 3, and in NA: RG.319, file XE.2394.

39 Gau circular No. 1, Berlin, Nov 9, 1926 (NA film T581, roll 5; BA file NS.26/133, and Schumacher collection, file 199a).

40 *Spandauer Volkszeitung*, Nov 15, 1926; *cit.* Reuth, 113.

41 Police file, Dec 26, 1926; Muchow report, Dec 1926; and see JG's references to the League in *NS-Briefe*, No. 31, and diary, Nov 21, 1928.

42 Horst Wessel (Oct 9, 1907-Feb 23, 1930), manuscript, 1929, originally in Staatsbibliothek Berlin, now in the Archiwum Uniwersytetu Jagiellońskiego, Kraków, Ms. Germ. Oct. 761, microfilm No. 5668, 1988. See NSDAP Hauptarchiv file on him, BA file NS.26/1370a, and Thomas Oertel, *Horst Wessel. Untersuchung einer Legende* (Cologne, 1988). Wessel's mother had handed the MS to JG (diary, Mar 24, Apr 26, 1930).

43 Muchow report.

44 Wessel MS, 1929.

45 Muchow report No. 8, Jan 1927; and an anonymous history of the gau by an S.A. man born in 1906 (NA film T581, roll 5; BA file NS.26/133) (hereafter gau history).

46 JG to Otto Strasser, Feb 8, 1927 (BDC file, JG; Heiber, 130ff).

47 Otto Strasser memoirs, *Mein Kampf. Eine politische Autobiographie* (Frankfurt, 1969) and statement, Nov 24, 1959 (IfZ).

48 Muchow report No. 9, Feb 1927; and see Wilfried Bade's account in *Angriff*, Oct 30, 1936.

49 Albert Tonak (1905–1942) joined the NSDAP on Apr 9, 1926 (BDC file, Tonak).

50 *VB*, Mar 10. Detective Inspector Rühl (of Section Ia) reported on Mar 28 that the appeal raised 'big money' for the party: police file. See Heiber, 117ff. The clinic was pictured in the party's *Illustrierter Beobachter*, Mar 15, 1927.

51 Police file.

52 Muchow report No. 9, Feb 1927; JG, *Kampf um Berlin*, 50. The gau's other officials now were: deputy gauleiter, Daluege; manager, Dagobert Dürr; press spokesman, Karl Kern; propaganda director: Werner Studentkowski.

53 Erich Koch, who had it from JG's arch-foe Elsbeth Zander, wrote to Kampf Verlag about this on Jun 13, 1927 (BDC file, JG).

54 Muchow report; and police report, Mar 21, 1927, in Landesarchiv Berlin, Rep. 58, item 302, vol. iv.

55 *Ibid.*, vol. ii, 63.

56 Testimony of Erich Timme, a neutral witness, *ibid.*, 195.

57 Rühl report, Mar 28 (police file); JG had to make a statement on Apr 25, 1927 (*ibid.*).

58 *VB* Mar 24, 1927.

59 Police report in Landesarchiv Berlin, Rep. 58, item 302, vol. i.

60 Muchow report No. 11, Mar 1927, and his special report on this incident (both on NA film T581, roll 5; BA file NS.26/133); also gau history. The Nazis rampaged down Kurfürstendamm, burst into the Romanisches Cafe near the Remembrance church and manhandled Jews; the *Berliner Tageblatt* used the word pogrom for the first time. For twelve volumes of court documents arising from the battle see Landesarchiv Berlin, Rep. 58, item 302.

61 Wessel MS.

62 'The result was,' complained JG in a letter to Hindenburg and Grzesinski on May 6, 1927, 'that our comrade [Kleemann] was besieged in his apartment for several days and had to be liberated by a major police operation' (BA: Schumacher collection, file 199a).

63 Which Hitler denied: *VB*, Jun 25, 1927; for the 'Jewish' character of these newspapers, see Bering, 116.

64 Strasser, *Mein Kampf.*

65 Police file.

66 JG to Dr Eugen Mündler, publ. in *Die Zweite Revolution*.

67 Hess to Ilse Pröhl, Apr 25, 1927; W R Hess, *Rudolf Hess. Briefe 1908 – 1933* (Munich, 1988), 379f. Hitler spoke in the Krupp Saal on Apr 27 to mounting applause. Hess, 380; *Dokumente*, 258.

68 Article in *Berliner Arbeiterzeitung*, Apr 23, 1927; and *Der Nationalsozialist*, No. 17, 1927; in general, JG to Hitler, Jun 5, 1927 and minutes of supreme party court (OPG) session of Jun 10, 1927 (BDC file, JG: author's film DI–81).

69 Koch to JG, Apr 26, 1927 (BDC file, JG); Heiber, 120f.

70 For the history of *Angriff* see Hans Georg Rahm, *Der Angriff 1927–1930. Der national-sozialistische Typ der Kampfzeitung* (Berlin, 1939), based on his PhD thesis; and Carin Kessemeier, *Der Leitartikler Goebbels in den NS-Organen 'Der Angriff' und 'Das Reich'* (Münster, 1967), 51ff.

71 Hans Hinkel, US Seventh Army interrogation, SAIC/28, May 28, 1945 (NA file RG.165, entry 79, box 756).

72 *Vossische Zeitung*, May 5; *Deutsche Allgemeine Zeitung* (hereafter *DAZ*), May 6, 1927; Borresholm, 69ff; police file ; and police report of Jun 20, *op. cit.*

73 Testimony of four detectives, May 5, 1927, in Berlin public prosecutor's files (ZStA Potsdam, Rep. 12B, vol. i, 107). JG was told that Kriegk, assigned to the Clou meeting, had protested: 'I'm not setting one foot in that monkey house' (police report).

74 JG testified that he wanted the journalist to sue him, so as to ascertain his 'real name'. ZStA Potsdam, Rep. 12B, vol. i, 100.

75 *Ibid.*, 107. Writing to Grzesinski on May 6, JG quoted it as: 'Du bist mir auch der rechte germanische Jüngling!' (BA: Schumacher collection, file 199a). *Vossische Zeitung* has it as 'Sie sehen mir gerade aus wie *ein germanischer Jüngling!*'

76 *Germania* and *Berliner Börsen-Courier* of May 5, 1927.

77 The weapons are listed in the public prosecutor's files (ZStA Potsdam, Rep. 12B, Nr. 2); Bering, 97.

78 Pastor Stucke belonged to the Reform Church (after the Church of Nazareth had dismissed him for alcohol problems); it is worth noting that he was prosecuted for blaspheming the Protestant Church in the communist *Rote Fahne* two weeks earlier, Apr 23, 1927 (Landesarchiv Berlin, Rep. 58, item 378).

79 For documents on this dissolution of the Berlin gau see BA: Schumacher collection, file 199a.

80 Landesarchiv Berlin, Rep. 58, items 27 and 385

Notes to Chapter 7.

1 Albert Grzesinski, typescript memoirs (BA file Kl. Erw. 144). See too his published memoirs, *Inside Germany* (New York 1939), translated by Alexander S Lipschitz; and his brochure *Verwaltungsarbeit im neuen Staat* (Berlin, 1928; copy in Friedrich Ebert Stiftung archives).
2 Zörgiebel to JG, May 5, 1927 (BA: Schumacher collection, file 199a).
3 JG to Grzesinski, May 6, 1927 (*ibid*).
4 Stuttgart report, May 18, 1927 (police file).
5 Police file.
6 JG to Berlin-Charlottenburg administrative court (Oberverwaltungsgericht), May 11 (BA: Schumacher collection, file 199a); Zörgiebel to JG, May 23, 1927 (*ibid*).
7 See Hinkel interrogation SAIC/28; and Lippert's reminiscences in *Angriff*, Oct 30, 1936 (BA file NS.26/968).
8 Strasser to Hess, Jun 15, 1927 (BDC file, JG).
9 JG to Hitler, Jun 5, 1927 (*ibid*).
10 JG to Hess, Jun 9, 1927 (*ibid*).
11 Minutes of the meeting (*ibid*).
12 Strasser to Hess, Jun 18, 1927 (*ibid*).
13 Holtz, of the gau *Untersuchungs- und Schlichtungsausschuss* (*Uschla*), to Hitler, Jun 17 (*ibid*).
14 Bruno Heinemann, minute on meeting with JG, Hitler, Hess, Jun 21, 1927 (*ibid*).
15 Police file (NA film T581, roll 52; BA file NS.26/1224). In Aug 1930 the Supreme Court in Leipzig began an investigation of JG's speech as an incitement to treason. JG cited Hermann Esser as a witness in support of the claim that he had not uttered the words alleged. Assize Court Judge Braune to Police headquarters Munich, Aug 13, 21, 1930 and Jan 19, 1931 (*ibid*.), and see Prussian ministry of the interior, minute on the NSDAP, Feb 1932 (BA file R.18/3864; IfZ file ED.4).
16 JG leader in *Angriff*, Oct 5, 1930; and *Kampf um Berlin*, 1934, 136.
17 *VB*, Jul 14, 1927; *cit.* in minutes of Feb 1932.
18 JG, *Der Nazi-Sozi. Fragen und Antworten für den Nationalsozialisten* (Munich, 1927); JG mentions it in his diary as early as Oct 17, 1926.
19 The Prussian ministry of the interior commented (see note 15 above) that the Elberfeld courts had ordered *Der Nazi-Sozi* confiscated on Jan 30, 1928; the case against JG was dropped on Aug 31, 1928 in a general amnesty. See too *Angriff*, Nov 21, 1931.
20 Speech on Sep 14, 1927; *cit.* in Prussian minute of Feb. 1932.
21 Puns on his name: *e.g.* references to 'Edelweiss' in *Angriff*, No. 25, 1927, and to his police as 'Weiss-Guards.'
22 *Angriff*, No. 26, 1930, 'He whose name one may not utter, like the name of the God who is honored and prayed to in the temples of his homeland;' Bering, 275f.
23 Bering, 79ff, denies that Weiss was humorless; this author disagrees.
24 Aug 15, 1927; Apr 8, Jun 18, Oct 29, 1928; Mar 11, May 6, 1929.
25 *Dokumente*, 268.
26 Unpubl. diary, Feb 18, 1928 (Moscow archives, Goebbels papers, Fond 1477, box 2).

27 Eher Verlag to NSDAP Hauptarchiv, Jul 5, 1937 (NA film T581, roll 47; BA file NS.26/968). Documents in the Hauptarchiv dated Feb 27 and Apr 23, 1936 give these quarterly average print figures: III/31, 68,600; IV/31, 58,300; I/32, 68,300; II/32, 107,300; III/32, 108,300; IV/32, 110,600; I/33, 103,500; II/33, 119,300; III/33, 100,600; IV/33, 92,000. JG's diary gives different figures, a circulation of 80,000 (Mar 12, 1931) and 90,000 (Aug 12, 1931).

28 Albertus Magnus Society files. It had taken them until Nov 12, 1927 to find JG, now living at No. 79/II Frege Strasse in Berlin-Friedenau.

29 Krebs, 161.

30 JG to Ilse Pröhl, Nov 16, 1927, unpubl.; on *NS-Briefe* letterhead (Rudolf Hess papers, Hindelang).

31 Diary, Jan 19, 22, 23, Feb 4, 1928; the unpublished diary Jan – Apr 1928 is in the Moscow archives, Goebbels papers, Fond 1477, box 5.

32 *Ibid.*, Feb 18, 1928.

33 *Ibid.*, Mar 16, 1928.

34 Police file.

35 Grzesinski MS; Weiss boasted he had 429,686 fingerprint sets on file: B Weiss, '25 Jahre Kriminalpolizei,' in *Die Polizei* (Berlin, 1928), 212.

36 JG, *Das Buch Isidor: Ein Zeitbild voll Lachen und Hass*; diary, Feb 20, Mar 3, 1928.

37 Diary, Feb 24, 1928.

38 *Ibid.*, Feb 26, 1928.

39 JG to the courts, Mar 12, 1928, Landesarchiv Berlin, Rep. 58, item 24, vol. viii, 8.

40 Diary, Mar 12, 23, 24, 26, Apr 2, 1928; Landesarchiv Berlin, Rep. 58, item 302.

41 Landesarchiv Berlin, Rep. 58, item 24, vol. vii, 16.

42 Diary, Mar 24, 1928.

43 JG to prosecutor, Apr 17, 23, Aug 6, 1928 (Landesarchiv Berlin, Rep. 58, item 24, vol. i).

44 Regierungsdirektor Wündisch to state prosecutor, Apr 23, 1928 (*ibid.*, vol. iv); Bering, 306.

45 Diary, Apr 28, 1928; Landesarchiv Berlin, Rep. 58, item 24.

46 Diary, May 4, 5, 12, 13, 1928.

47 *Angriff*, Sep 9, 1929.

48 Diary, Jun 5; *Berliner Tageblatt*, Jun 4; *Rote Fahne*, Jun 7, 1928; Bering, 77.

49 *Angriff*, Jun 11, 1928; Landesarchiv Berlin, Rep. 58, item 23. Weiss also prosecuted Ernst Schulz, *Angriff*'s printer: *ibid.*, item 28.

50 Diary, Apr 14, 1928.

51 Gau history (BA file NS.26/133).

52 Diary, Apr 16, 20, 1928.

53 *Ibid.*, Apr 17, May 11, 1928.

54 *Ibid.*, Apr 20, 1928.

55 *Ibid.*, Apr 22, 1928.

56 *Ibid.*, May 17, 19, 1928; and Kurt Daluege, 'Zehn Jahre Berliner S.A.,' spring 1935, in his papers, BA file R.19/377 ('Dr. Goebbels mit an unserer Spitze').

57 Diary, Feb 26, Apr 3, 1928. – Born Apr 12, 1895, Stennes was an army officer in Aug 1914, formed the Hacketau Freikorps on Jan 1, 1919, was employed by Berlin police headquarters Jul 19, 1919, was promoted to police captain Jun 12, 1920, resigning Jan 28, 1922; joined NSDAP Dec 20, 1927. See 'Hauptmann Stennes. Ein alter Geheimbündler und Verschwörer,' in *Vorwärts*, Nr. 411, Sep 3, 1930, and *ibid.*, Oct 15, 1929, and *8 Uhr Abendblatt*, Berlin, No. 78, Apr 2, 1931; NSDAP Hauptarchiv file on Stennes (BA file NS.26/1368).

58 Stennes MS and interview, Jul 29, 1968 (IfZ file ZS.1147).

59 Diary, Apr 5, 14, May 10, 16, 1928.

60 Diary, May 22, 1928.

Notes to Chapter 8.

1 *Angriff*, Oct 29, 1928.

2 Police file (NA film T581, roll 52; BA file NS.26/1224).

3 Diary, Jun 20, 1928; case files in Landesarchiv Berlin, Rep. 58, items 58, 302, and Berlin police (Ia) report, Jun 20, 1928 (BDC file, JG); JG accused the police witnesses Bober and Weicker of perjury, and was prosecuted for libel on Dec 15, 1929 (Landesarchiv Berlin, Rep. 58, item 3).

4 Diary, Jun 9, 1928.

5 *Ibid.*, Jun 6, 1928.

6 *Ibid.*, Jun 13, 1928.

7 *Ibid.*

8 *Berliner Arbeiterzeitung*, May 27; in *NS-Briefe*, Jun 15, 1928, Otto Strasser said the proletariat had voted overwhelmingly for the communists, and he blamed those who were 'too clever by half'.

9 On the new headquarters: *ibid.*, Jun 1, 5, 19, 28, Jul 28 1928.

10 See the references to his health in his diary, Apr 19, May 23, Jul 5, Sep 15, Nov 5, 13, 25, 1928.

11 'Ein §175er.' *Ibid.*, Oct 26, 1928.

12 *Ibid.*, Sep 29, Oct 11, 12, 1928.

13 *Ibid.*, Nov 25, 1928.

14 *Ibid.*, Dec 19, 20, 1928; Jan 5, 1929.

15 *Ibid.*, Jan 26, 29, 1929; on Feb 5 he noted that he was measured for a new steel orthopedic caliper.

16 Wessel MS; and JG diary, Jul 13, 14, 1928. Horst Wessel, commander of S.A. Trupp 34, had spent Jan – Jul 1928 in Vienna studying the Nazi youth movement there, which was better organized than that in Germany; he reported back to JG in detail on their methods. See too Richard Fiedler's reminiscences on Wessel in *Angriff*, Oct 30, 1936 (BA file NS.26/968).

17 Diary, Jul 15, 1928. From JG's unpublished diary, Mar 30, 1928 it is plain he was attracted to her: 'Arrive Munich 5 A.M. . . . Then I meet Geli Raubal. She wants to come to Berlin. A darling thing! We've laid plans.' And see diary, Oct 19, 1928.

18 Unpubl. diary, Jan 10, 1928 (microfiche in Moscow archives, Goebbels papers, box 5).

19 JG postcard to Ilse Hess, Jul 9, 1928 (Hess papers, Hindelang); diary, Jul 10, 1928

20 Diary, Apr 16, 1928.

21 *Ibid.*, Jan 19; and Jan 14, 17, 1928.

22 *Ibid.*, Jan 23, Feb 23, 1928.

23 *Ibid.*, Feb 9, 10, 1928.

24 *Ibid.*, Feb 23, 1928.

25 *Ibid.*, Mar 7, 1928; author's interview of Anka's daughter, Annette Castendyk. Her brother Christian Mumme, born Sep 1927, was killed when an American plane strafed his flak position on the Elbe front on Apr 16, 1945.

26 Diary, Mar 9, 13, 1928.

27 *Ibid.*, Mar 23, 24, 1928.

28 *Ibid.*, Mar 30, 1928.

29 *Ibid.*, Apr 10, 1928.

30 *Ibid.*, Apr 12, 1928.

31 *Ibid.*, Apr 22, 1928.

32 *Ibid.*, Apr 17, 1928.

33 *Ibid.*, Apr 25, 1928.

34 *Ibid.*, Apr 27, 1928.

35 *Ibid.*, May 9, 12, 14, Jul 23, 1928.

36 *Ibid.*, May 28, 30, 1928.

37 *Ibid.*, May 30, 1928.

38 Gauorganisationsleiter. See Gerhard Starcke, *NSBO und Deutsche Arbeitsfront* (Berlin, 1934), 198f; JG diary, May 23, Jun 6, 1928.

39 Diary, Aug 7, 1928.

40 *Ibid.*, Aug 10, 1928. On Jul 25, 1924, after watching *Tristan*, JG noted that he had last seen it in Oct 1919 in Frankfurt a. M. with Anka, 'blessed memory.'

41 *Ibid.*, Aug 24, 29, 1928.

42 *Ibid.*, Aug 10, 25, 27, 1928.

43 *Ibid.*, Sep 4, 1928.

44 *Ibid.*, Sep 11, 12, 13, 19, 20, 21, 1928.

45 *Ibid.*, Sep 23, 1928.

46 *Ibid.*, Sep 24, 25, 1928.

47 *Ibid.*, Sep 26, 1928.

48 *Ibid.*, Oct 2, 1928.

49 *Ibid.*, Oct 7, 1928.

50 *Ibid.*, Oct 14, 1928.

51 *Ibid.*, Oct 17, 1928.

Notes to Chapter 9.

1 Diary, Aug 20, 1928.

2 *Ibid.*, Feb 4, 24, 1929.

3 *Ibid.*, Aug 12, 1930. The correct transcription is 'Auwi' – The author disagrees with Dr Fröhlich's 'Anni.' In an entry for Mar 11, 1930 he however scoffed at magnetopaths, and in the unpubl. diary, Jun 22, 1939 he mocks that 'Görlitzer has comically enough become a sucker for astrology.'

4 *Ibid.*, Oct 2, 1930.

5 *Ibid.*, Jul 20, 1928.

6 *Ibid.*, Aug 8, 10, 13, 1928.

7 *Ibid.*, Aug 24, 1928.

8 Under Emil Holtz. Diary, Sep 1, 8, 1928; *Dokumente*, 280f.

9 Diary, Sep 23–25, 1928.

10 Facsimile in *Dokumente*, 285.

11 He was prosecuted for cursing the Republic at this Sport Palace meeting. Case files in Landesarchiv Berlin, Rep. 58, item 697.

12 Diary, Oct 1, 1928.

13 *Ibid.*, Oct 4, 1928.

14 *Ibid.*, Oct 4–6, 9, 11, Nov 2, 1928.

15 *Ibid.*, Nov 5, 1928.

16 Confidential circular, Oct 31, 1928, signing off: 'Mit Hitler Heil!' (Irene Pranger papers).

17 Diary, Oct 21, Nov 4, 1928. Schweitzer 'thinks just as I do.'

18 *Ibid.*, Nov 2, 1928.

19 *Ibid.*, Jan 22, 1929.

20 *Ibid.*, Jun 6, 1929.

21 *Ibid.*, Nov 8, 1928.

22 *Ibid.*, Nov 15, 1928.

23 *Ibid.*, Nov 4, 1928.

24 Public prosecutor, letter of Dec 20, 1928 (police file).

25 *Ibid.*, Nov 13, 15, 16, 1928.

26 *Ibid*, and *VB*, Nov 17, 1928.

27 JG, 'Kütemeyer,' in *Angriff*, Nov 26, 1928.

28 *Dokumente*, 283.

29 Diary, Jun 20, 1929.

30 *Ibid.*, Apr 26, May 30, Jun 11, 1929.

31 *Ibid.*, Jun 18, 1928.

32 *Ibid.*, Dec 3, 1928.

33 *Ibid.*, Jan 31, 1929.

34 *Ibid.*, Feb 15, 1929.

35 *Ibid.*, Apr 26, 1928.

36 *Ibid.*, Jan 3, 1929.

37 *Ibid.*, Jun 30, 1928.

38 *Ibid.*, Feb 3, 8, 9–11, Mar 2, 3, 1929.

39 *Ibid.*, Apr 5, 1929.

40 *Ibid.*, Apr 21, 28, 1929.

41 *Ibid.*, Sep 22, Oct 24, Dec 8, 1928; Feb 5, 6, 9, 1929; premièred on Mar 10, 1929.

42 JG to Ilse Hess, Dec 22, 1928 (Hess papers, Hindelang).

43 Diary, Dec 14, 1928.

44 *Ibid.*, Dec 15, 16, 1928.

45 JG to Anka Stalherm, Dec 16, 1928, handwritten on Reichstag notepaper (Irene Pranger papers).

46 Diary, Dec 18, 1928; she was not eighteen until Jan 26, 1929.

47 *Ibid.*, Dec 20, 1928.

48 *Ibid.*, Dec 22–24, 30, 1928; Jan 3, 1929.

49 *Ibid.*, Jan 4, 6, 7, 1929.

50 *Ibid.*, Jan 20, 1929.

51 *Dokumente*, 291.

52 Diary, Jan 21, 1929.

53 Treaty of Mar 22, 1921, articles 176 and 177; Grzesinski MS (BA file Kl. Erw. 144).

54 In NSDAP Hauptarchiv (NA film T581, roll 26a; BA file NS.26/1768).

55 Diary, Dec 4, 9, 1928; Jan 5, 6, 8, 27, 1929.

56 *Ibid.*, Mar 13, 23, May 15, 16, 1929; police file.

57 *Ibid.*, Feb 26, 1929.

58 *Ibid.*, Apr 17, 1928; Feb 5, 1929.
59 *Ibid.*, Jan 31, Feb 1, 6, 1929.
60 Krebs, 160.
61 Diary, Jan 28, 1929.
62 *Ibid.*, Mar 1, 1929.
63 *Ibid.*, Jan 26, 1929.
64 *Ibid.*, Feb 12, 1929.
65 *Ibid.*, Feb 15, Mar 10, 1929.
66 JG to Anka, Feb 25, 1929 (Irene Pranger papers).
67 Diary, Mar 10–12, 1929.
68 *Ibid.*, Mar 13, 17, 1929.
69 JG to Anka, Mar 20, 1929 (Irene Pranger papers).
70 Diary, Mar 23, 24, 1929.
71 *Ibid.*, Mar 25, 26, 1929.
72 *Ibid.*, Apr 1, 1929.

Notes to Chapter 10.

1 JG to Anka, Apr 9, 1929 (Irene Pranger papers).
2 Papers of the Albertus Magnus Society; and see diary, Mar 21, 1929: 'In the morning a process server comes on embarrassing business.'
3 Lawyers Erwin Plätzer and Carl Bauer to the society, Apr 29, 1929.
4 Diary, May 17, 1929.
5 *Ibid.*, Apr 15, 1929.
6 *Ibid.*, Apr 12, Jun 2, 1929.
7 *Ibid.*, Apr 7, 9, 1929.
8 *Ibid.*, Apr 18, 1929.
9 *Ibid.*, Apr 19, 21, 25, 1929.
10 *Ibid.*, Apr 28, 30, May 5, 6, 13, 17, 20, 1929.
11 Diary, May 25, 26, 1929.
12 *Ibid.*, May 28, 1929.
13 JG to Anka, May 28 (Irene Pranger papers); diary, May 29, 1929.
14 Diary, May 29, 1929. In *Dokumente*, 271, it is wrongly stated that JG was appointed *Reichspropagandaleiter* on Jan 2, 1928 with Himmler as deputy. This is not confirmed by JG's diary.
15 Diary, Jul 5, 1929.
16 *Ibid.*, May 29, 1929.
17 *Ibid.*, May 2, 1929; statement by Carl Severing to Reichstag, Jun 8, 1929, in Reichstag proceedings, 80th session, 2218ff.
18 Grzesinski (MS) lived with a Mrs Daisy Torrens, although not divorced until May 12, 1930; he married her at the end of May.
19 *Cf.* diary, Jun 9, 1929.
20 Reichstag proceedings, 80th session, Jun 25, 1929, 2918ff.
21 Diary, Jun 26, 1929.
22 *Ibid.*, Nov 22, 1929.
23 *Ibid.*, May 3, 4, 1929.

24 *Ibid.*, May 14, Jun 27; and see Sep 2, Nov 8, Dec 21, 1929.

25 *Ibid.*, Feb 20, 1931.

26 *Ibid.*, Jun 29, 1929.

27 *Ibid.*, Nov 8, 1930.

28 *Ibid.*, Oct 28, 1929.

29 Oven, 241, 'Apr 24, 1944.'

30 Diary, Jun 1, 4, 1929.

31 *Ibid.*, Jun 2, 4, 9, 19, 23, 24, 1929.

32 *Ibid.*, Jun 16, 20, 24, 25, 1929.

33 *Ibid.*, Jun 30, 1929.

34 JG to Anka, Jul 6 (Irene Pranger papers); and diary, July 6, 1929.

35 JG to Anka, Jul 8, 1929 (Irene Pranger papers).

36 Diary, Jul 6, 1929.

37 *Ibid.*, Jul 13, 1929. Erika Chelius and her twin sister Waltraud ('Traute') were born July 26, 1906 in Zehdenick, a town in the Oberhavel district north of Berlin. In 1938 she married Karl Wendeborn, bore him one son and died in 1993. A friend loaned her papers and photos to Goebbels-expert Dr Elke Fröhlich at the IfZ, who did not however return them (as of 2010).

38 *Ibid.*, Jul 15, 17, 20, 21, 1929.

39 *Ibid.*, Jul 23, 1929.

40 *Ibid.*, Jul 25, 1929.

41 *Ibid.*, Jul 26, 1929. In Irene Pranger's papers is the snapshot JG sent to Anka, 'With heartfelt greetings and with happy memories of a beautiful week in Weimar. Your ULEX, Jul 30, 1929.'.

Notes to Chapter 11.

1 Diary, Sep 10–12, 1929.

2 *Ibid.*, Aug 24, 1929.

3 *Ibid.*, Jul 12, 1929.

4 *Ibid.*, Aug 2, 1929; *Dokumente*, 299ff; *VB*, Aug 3, 1929.

5 Wessel MS; and gau history (NA film T581, roll 5; BA file NS.26/133).

6 Stennes, statement on Jul 29, 1968 (IfZ file ZS.1147); and Prince Schaumburg-Lippe, *War Hitler ein Diktator?* (Witten, 1976), 57f.

7 Diary, Jul 26, 28, Aug 5, 6, 1929.

8 *Ibid.*, Aug 11, 13, 14, 1929.

9 JG to Anka, Sep 7, 1929 (Irene Pranger papers).

10 JG to Anka, Sep 29, 1929 (*ibid*).

11 JG to Anka, Oct 1, 1929 (*ibid*).

12 Diary, Oct 3, 16, 28, 1929.

13 *Ibid.*, Jul 5, Aug 14, 1929.

14 *Ibid.*, Jul 21, 1929.

15 *Ibid.*, Oct 6, Dec 1, 1929.

16 *Ibid.*, Sep 2, 1929.

17 *Ibid.*, Nov 25, 1929.

18 *Ibid.*, Sep 3–5, Oct 1, 1929.

19 *Ibid.*, Jun 18, 1929: With 1,000 marching farmers' sons, 'I feel like a dwarf.'

20 *Ibid.*, Aug 27–29, 1929.

21 *Angriff*, Sep 9, 1929.

22 *Angriff*, Nov 24, 1929; *cit.* Reuth, 153.

23 Diary, Aug 28: 'The swine. All this will be repaid later.'

24 *Angriff*, 1928, No. 22, 3 and 1929, No. 4, 9; Bering, 236.

25 Diary, Sep 10, 1929.

26 *Ibid.*, Sep 26; see the photo in *Der Montag*, Berlin, Sep 23, 1929, and *Dokumente*, 304.

27 Diary, Sep 19, 20, Oct 5, 1929; and *Der Kampf gegen Young. Eine Sache des deutschen Arbeiters, Rede gehalten am 26. September 1929 im Kriegervereinshaus Berlin* (Berlin, 1929).

28 Diary, Oct 28, 1929.

29 *Ibid*, Oct 31–Nov 3, 5, 29, 30, 1929.

30 Gau history (NA film T581, roll 1; BA file NS.26/133).

31 Diary, Nov 14; hearing (*ibid.*, Nov 22, 1929) that she was involved with another man he had another showdown with Anka and parted without pain: 'It seems I have gotten over Anka.'

32 *Ibid.*, Oct 29, 1929.

33 *Ibid.*, Nov 18, 1929.

34 *Ibid.*, Sep 22, Oct 20, Nov 5, 1929; Franz Eher Verlag to NSDAP Hauptarchiv, Feb 27, 1936 (NA film T581, roll 47; BA file NS.26/968).

35 Diary, Nov 17, 20, 1929; police file.

36 Diary, Nov 20, 22, 23, 1929; Jan 7, 1930.

37 *Ibid.*, Nov 22, 1929.

38 *Ibid.*, Oct 10, 1929.

39 *Ibid.*, Nov 29, 1929.

40 *Ibid.*, Dec 11, 1929.

41 JG to Anka, Dec 14, 1929 (Irene Pranger papers).

42 Diary, Dec 17, 1929.

Notes to Chapter 12.

1 They were Hans Kütemeyer, Nov 17, 1928; Gerhard Weber, Nov 4; Walter Fischer, Dec 14; Werner Dölle, Dec 16, stabbed to death by a Jewish opponent in Kurfürstendamm, and Fritz Radloff, Dec 24, 1929.

2 Diary, Oct 2, 6, Dec 23, 1929.

3 *Ibid.*, Oct 30, 1929.

4 *Ibid.*, Dec 23, 1929.

5 *Ibid.*, Sep 29, 1929.

6 Stennes, Jul 29, 1968 (IfZ file ZS.1147).

7 Report by Berlin police section Ia.III.1, Berlin, Jun 9, 1931 in Wessel's file in NSDAP Hauptarchiv (BA file NS.26/1370a).

8 The case files against 'Ali' Höhler, Else Cohn, Rückert, Kandulski, Junek, Mrs Salm, and the brothers Max, Walter, and Willi Jambrowski (Landesarchiv Berlin, Rep. 58, item 11) were marked for historical preservation but released to the Soviet sector in 1947 and not returned. Höhler, Willi Jambrowski, and seven others were tried on Sep 26, 1930 for manslaughter and given sentences ranging from one to six years. 'There these creatures sit in the dock,' wrote JG (Sep 24, 1930), 'real criminals with an air of injured

innocence... Poor Horst. To die at the hands of [illegible word] pimps like these!' In a subsequent trial from Jun 15, 1934 against the defendants Peter Stoll (seaman), 'Sally' Epstein (Jewish painter), and Hans Ziegler (barber), Epstein and Ziegler were sentenced to death, Stoll to seven and a half years; Höhler (who was abducted from his prison cell in 1933 and lynched by S.A. men) was stated to have 'deceased in the interim' (Landesarchiv Berlin, Rep. 58, item 22; Stoll case files courtesy of R G Reuth). Report on their trial in *Vossische Zeitung*, Sep 23, 24, 1930.

9 Diary, Jan 19, 1930.

10 *Ibid.*, Jan 27, 1930.

11 *Angriff*, Feb 6, 1930.

12 *Rote Fahne*, Jan 15, 1930.

13 Diary, Feb 24, 1930.

14 *Vossische Zeitung*, Mar 2, 1930.

15 *Angriff*, Feb 27, 1930.

16 Diary, Mar 2, 1930; *Dokumente*, 311f.

17 Diary, Jan 13, 1930.

18 *Ibid.*, Jan 20, 31, 1930.

19 *Ibid.*, Jan 16, 17, 1930.

20 *Ibid.*, Jan 24, 1930.

21 *Ibid.*, Jan 29, 1930.

22 *Ibid.*, Jan 30, 1930.

23 *Ibid.*, Jan 31, 1930.

24 *VB*, Feb 5, 1930. On Feb 6 *Angriff* published a statement by JG on the newspaper question designed to reassure his gau members.

25 Diary, Feb 8, 9, 11, 15, 16, 1930.

26 *Ibid.*, Feb 20, 21, 1930.

27 *Ibid.*, Mar 2, 4, 1930.

28 *Ibid.*, Mar 5, 1930.

29 *E.g. ibid.*, Mar 12, 1930.

30 *Ibid.*, Mar 1, 1930; Grzesinski MS.

31 Diary, Feb 11, 1930.

32 *Ibid.*, Feb 21, 1930; Goltz memoirs, MS (BA file Kl. Erw. 653/2), and interrogations (NA file RG.319, IRR, XE.1026; esp. US Seventh Army interrogation SAIC/X/10, Jul 5, 1945). Born Jul 10, 1894, father of ten children, Goltz had been a lawyer in the Stettin county court since 1926.

33 Reichstag proceedings, 141st session, Mar 13, 4442ff; diary, Mar 14, 1930.

34 In the Sport Palace on Feb 7, 1930 he attributed the remark to August Bebel. 'Attacking the present system of government,' the police reported, 'he wound himself up into ever greater ecstasies ... [saying] the opponents of the NSDAP were now laughing on the other side of their face (Justice ministry file, 'Libel actions against Joseph Goebbels Nov 1929-Aug 1931' in Deutsches Zentralarchiv; IfZ film MA.118).

35 Police file, 20f. He was accused of libeling Weiss in issues of *Angriff* dated Oct 29, Nov 26, Dec 10, 1928; Sep 9, 1929; Apr 8, May 1, 1930 (on which, seven volumes of court files are in Landesarchiv Berlin, Rep. 58, item 47); and of libeling him in a speech in the Victoria Park on Mar 23, 1929 (item 39), and in a speech on Sep 20, 1929 at the Veterans' Building printed as *Der Kampf gegen Young. Eine Sache des deutschen Arbeiters* (item 2); for further libel cases resulting from articles in *Angriff*, see item 39.

36 Summons dated May 17, 1930 (ZStA Potsdam, Rep. 90, Go 1, Goebbels, vol. i); for the resulting court case see Landesarchiv Berlin, Rep. 58, item 48.

37 Diary, May 8, 26, 27, 1930.

38 *Angriff*, No. 65, Dec 29, 1929.

39 *Ibid.*, Jan 1, 4, 24, 1930; and see Zezschwitz to (unknown), Apr 20, 1930 on the background to the Hindenburg case (IfZ film MA.744).

40 Diary, May 15, 16, 28, 1930.

41 *Angriff*, Jun 5, 1930.

42 *NYT*, Jun 1, 1930.

43 Diary, Jan 23, 30, Feb 2, 3, 1930.

44 *Ibid.*, Jan 6, 8; Mar 7, 1930.

45 *Ibid.*, Apr 18, 20, 1930.

46 *Ibid.*, Apr 24, 1930.

47 *Ibid.*, Mar 16, 1930.

48 *Ibid.*, Mar 20, 1930.

49 *Ibid.*, Mar 22, 23, 1930.

50 *Ibid.*, Mar 28, 1930; on Mar 29, depressed, he noted, 'No word from Munich.' And the next day, 'All thanks to this stupid Munichery. We're faced by the gravest decisions. And Munich's fast asleep.'

51 *Ibid.*, Apr 1, 2, 5, 1930.

52 *Reichspropagandaleiter.* As late as 1930 the Nazi *Jahrbuch* which had gone to press in Sep 1929 listed Hitler as chairman of the RPL with Himmler as deputy; the last RPL decree countersigned by Himmler was published in *VB* on Apr 5, 1930; the first by JG (as Reichsleiter I) on May 23, 1930. Diary, Apr 28, 1930.

53 Diary, Oct 13, 1929; Apr 9, 1930. – Re Muchow: *ibid.*, Oct 2, 4, 1929; Jan 21, 1930; and see his article, 'Die Strassenzellen-Organisation des Gaues Berlin,' in *VB*, Mar 11, 1930.

54 Diary, Aug 27, Oct 6, 1929; Apr 10, 30; May 2, 1930.

55 *Ibid.*, Apr 30, 1930.

56 *Ibid.*, Apr 16, 1930. JG scraped together 100 marks a month for his mother (diary, May 14, 1930). On Jun 10, 1946 the *New York Times* would report that JG's sister Maria had said, 'We did not see Joseph often, although we lived in Berlin, and I know he never gave mother any money or helped support her.' This seems unjustified. The diaries contain many other references to JG's financial help for his mother, *e.g.* on Jul 13, 1930.

57 Diary, May 18, 1930. The killers of the communist Heimburger claimed self-defense, but there were many arrests. Grzesinski MS.

58 Diary, May 4, 14, 1930.

59 *Ibid.*, May 3, 1930.

60 *Ibid.*, May 22, 1930. Much later Otto Strasser published in *Hitler und ich* (Konstanz, 1948) his own fanciful record of his two talks with Hitler. Postwar American authorities termed him a wastrel, rabid antisemite, and anarchist (NA file RG.319, IRR, G.8172121). This file also contains a 1948 description by Otto Strasser of his May 1930 clash with Hitler. On Otto Strasser see also W Donovan to F D Roosevelt, Jan 20, 1942 (FDR Libr., President's Safe File [hereafter PSF], box 163).

61 Diary, May 24, 1930.

62 *Ibid.*, Jun 11, 12, 15, 17, 1930.

63 *Ibid.*, Jun 12, 1930.

64 *Ibid.*, Jun 14, 17, 1930.

65 *Ibid.*, Jun 18, 21, 1930.

66 *Ibid.*, Jun 25, 1930.

67 *Ibid.*, Jun 29; and Strasser's *Der Nationale Sozialist*, Jul 1, 1930.

68 Diary, Jun 28–30, Jul 1, 2, 5; *Angriff*, Jul 3, 1930. After *Der Nationale Sozialist* reported on Jul 3 that he was still its publisher and director, Gregor Strasser issued a statement through the Telegraphen Union agency sharply disowning the 'circle around Kampf Verlag led by my brother Dr Otto Strasser' and announcing that he had severed ties with the publishing house on Jun 30. 'I still stand loyally behind Adolf Hitler and the NSDAP led by him.' – Hinrich Lohse MS, 'The Strasser Case' (IfZ file ZS.265, 8f); and see Günter Bartsch, *Zwischen drei Stühlen. Otto Strasser, Eine Biographie* (Koblenz, 1990). Otto Strasser later accused JG of ordering 'S.A. Standarte 208' to assassinate him; he was beaten up by several S.A. men in Aug 1930, and claims to have shot two of them (NA file RG.319, IRR, G.8172121).

69 Landesarchiv Berlin, Rep. 58, item 24, vol. iii, 4.

70 Diary, Jun 15, Jul 3, 16, 1930; Moabit criminal court summons to JG, endorsed by the mail carrier on Jul 24, 1930 (ZStA Potsdam, Rep. 90, Go 1, Goebbels, vol. i).

71 Diary, Jan 10–13; JG's visiting card is in Anka's papers, endorsed in her hand on Jun 3, 1930.

72 *Ibid.*, Jun 21, 25, Jul 6, 7, Aug 7, 17, 24. Interrogated on Feb 3, 1948 Lucie Kammer née Zimpel testified that her husband died in 1930; she had joined the NSDAP in 1927 (Staatsarchiv [StA] Nuremberg, Rep. 502, K.19; NA file RG.260, OMGUS files, box 15).

73 Diary, Jul 12–15, Aug 3, 7, 1930.

Notes to Chapter 13.

1 [Lieutenant of the Reserve Walter Jahn], 'How it came to the Stennes putsch!,' typescript in NSDAP archives, IfZ file Fa.88/83 (hereafter Jahn). Jahn, the anonymous author, was Stennes' chief of staff. Stennes testified (letter to Prof. Helmut Krausnick, Nov 12, 1956, IfZ file ZS.1147) that the document was written for internal S.A. Ilse; in fact it was published (with the sub-title 'Adolf Hitler largely to blame') in consecutive issues of the organ of the Stennes faction (the NSKD), *Wahrheit der Woche* from No. 7, Oct 10, 1931 onward (BA file NS.26/325).

2 JG's police file, Apr 5, 1930, 10 (NA film T581, roll 52; BA file NS.26/1224).

3 Jahn.

4 Diary, Nov 5, 1929.

5 Diary, Jul 28, 1930.

6 Stennes MS, Jul 29, 1968 (IfZ file ZS.1147, vol. ii).

7 Diary, Jul 21, 23, 29, 1930.

8 *E.g.* Princess zu Wied. Diary, Aug 4, 1930.

9 When addressing the NSDAP section at Hanover on Sep 5, 1929.

10 Diary, Jul 29, 1930; police file.

11 *Ibid.*, Aug 4, 1930.

12 *Ibid.*, Aug 8, 12, 13, 1930; and Jahn.

13 *Ibid.*, Aug 24, 1930.

14 *Ibid.*, Aug 9, 1930; Goltz MS (BA file Kl. Erw. 653/2).

15 Diary, Aug 13; Goltz MS; *Angriff*, No. 65, Aug 14, 1930.

16 The letter read: 'From a declaration made to me by Dr Goebbels I infer that he had no intention of defaming me personally with the remarks that are the substance of the action against him, but was merely acting in his own political interests. I would withdraw my complaint of Dec 31, 1929 against Dr Goebbels if that were possible at this stage. As it is not in law possible, I have to content myself with the declaration that I regard the matter as closed and have no further interest in punishing Dr Goebbels.'

17 Court transcript in ZStA Potsdam, files of justice ministry (IfZ film MA.118); diary, Aug 14–15; Goltz MS; *Angriff*, Aug 17, 1930.

18 Court transcript (*loc. cit.*) and case files in Landesarchiv Berlin, Rep. 58, item 25; *Angriff*, Aug 17, 1930.

19 JG was also prosecuted for inciting disrespect for the Reich flag in the *NSDAP Mitteilungsblatt* Aug 1930 (Landesarchiv Berlin, Rep. 58, item 8).

20 Diary, Aug 21, 23, 26, 1930.

21 See Dr Conti's letter to ('Osaf') Pfeffer, Sep 8, 1930, in Stennes' papers, NSDAP archives (BA file NS.26/325); on the background of Pfeffer's resignation as Osaf and the first Stennes putsch see Himmler's *aide-mémoire* of May 24, 1941 (NA film T175, roll 123, 8772ff).

22 Himmler (*loc. cit.*) recalled that Pfeffer resigned a few days before the Berlin mutiny, and dismissed Pfeffer's alternative version. 'Pfeffer could no longer exorcise the spirits he had summoned up, and had to admit his incompetence to the Führer.' *Dokumente* (p. 341) agrees, reporting that Pfeffer resigned on Aug 29 'for political reasons,' and that Hitler took over on Sep 2. JG's diary states that Hitler dismissed Pfeffer on the afternoon of Sep 1, *i.e.*, afterward.

23 Wiedemann, in conversation with Fritz Tobias, Jun 1973 (Tobias archives).

24 The Berlin police headquarters dossier states: 'On the night of Aug 30–31, 1930 [Stennes] issued the written order to S.A. men to occupy the Greater Berlin Gau Headquarters. . .' NSDAP archives (BA file NS.26/1368).

25 Hitler had promised to expel anybody carrying firearms; the Prussian ministry of the interior reported in Feb 1932 that between Feb and Sep 1930, despite fifteen trials of NSDAP members for firearms offenses, not one had been expelled; there were seventy-one more such cases by Jul 1931, again without expulsions (BA file R.18/3864).

26 Himmler (*loc. cit.*): 'Upon receiving this alarming news [by phone from Bouhler to Hess] the Führer ordered an immediate departure for Berlin although we had slept hardly at all the last few nights.' They had only just arrived in Bayreuth at 1:30 A.M. Aug 31.

27 Diary, Sep 1, 1930. Wiedemann has Hitler and Hess staying at her apartment.

28 *Ibid.*, Sep 3; *VB*, No. 210, Sep 4, 1930.

29 Thus in JG's broadcast on Jul 26, 1944: 'In Aug 1930 a hireling of the Prussian ministry of the interior staged a revolt.'

30 Borresholm, 71f.

31 *NYT*, Sep 2, 1930.

32 Göring seems to have disapproved. According to Stennes' chief of staff Jahn, Göring told Wetzel on Dec 31, 1930 that he now saw the grave injustice done to Stennes, and that he 'would see an end put to the ugly double-game being played by a certain gauleiter and would not hesitate to have Himmler deposed as Reichsführer SS.'

33 Röhm was still in Bolivian army service; Dr h. c. Otto Wagener continued as chief of staff until Jan 5, 1931.

34 Report by Berlin Landeskriminalpolizeiamt, Sep 16, 1930 (Bremen city archives, 4.65, vol. v); *cit.* Reuth, 173.

35 Wiedemann.

36 Diary, Sep 1, 1930. Stennes was in no doubt about Goebbels' two-faced role (IfZ file Zs.1147).

37 Darré diary, Sep 3, 1930 (BA: Darré papers, vol. 65a).

38 *Dokumente*, 333, 335; diary, Sep 7, 9, 1930. In *Berliner Illustrierte Zeitung* his photo was captioned 'Paul J Goebbels,' leading to mocking suggestions by Otto Strasser's *Berliner Arbeiter-Zeitung* on Nov 2, 1930 that the 'Joseph' concealed Jewish origins. His opponents called him 'Goebbeles' – the '-les' suffix being typically Jewish.

39 Author's interview of Leopold Gutterer.

40 Diary, Sep 11, 1930.

41 *Ibid.*, Sep 12, 1930; on Sep 21 he recorded a cordial encounter with Stennes, and believed he could get on with him in future.

42 On Jan 4, 1932 disgruntled S.A. men would point out in a duplicated circular that the Nazis' 107 Reichstag deputies included thirty-three estate owners, manufacturers, and businessmen; thirty-one senior civil servants; nineteen lawyers, doctors, and other Prof. essionals; nine former officers, eight salaried staff, and seven ('yes, seven!') workers. Files of No. 8 S.A. Standarte in NSDAP archives (BA file NS.26/322).

43 Diary, Sep 16, 1930.

44 *Ibid.*, Sep 24, Oct 1, 9, 1930.

45 *Ibid.*, Sep 20, 1930; *Angriff* published on Jun 1, 1931 an appeal for eyewitnesses, resulting in a letter from Lili and Erna Ernst (Hoover Libr., Goebbels papers, box 2); for Dr Weiss's prosecution of JG for libeling police officials this day, Sep 19, 1930 see Landesarchiv Berlin, Rep. 58, item 5.

46 Diary, Oct 13–14; *Vossische Zeitung*, Oct 14, 1930. The *Berliner Illustrierte Zeitung* published on Oct 28, 1937 a photograph of his dash.

Notes to Chapter 14.

1 Diary, Oct 18, 1930; and see Lohse, 'The Strasser Case' (IfZ, and Karl Höffkes papers, Oberhausen).

2 Diary, Oct 16, 17, 22, 1930.

3 Grzesinski to Braun, Oct 13, 1930 (BA file Kl. Erw. 144).

4 Diary, Oct 23, 1930.

5 Grzesinski MS.

6 *Ibid.*, Oct 21, 23, 1930. Bronnen, born Aug 19, 1895, was an Austrian playwright – famous for his 1920 play *Vatermord* (Patricide) – currently producing the Berlin Radio Hour program. After flirting with communism, he had recently joined the Nazis; after the war he made common cause with the East German regime and died in East Berlin. Told that Bronnen was half-Jewish, JG refused to believe it (*ibid.*, Oct 4, 1930).

7 *Ibid.*, Sep 14, 20, 1930.

8 *Ibid.*, Sep 23, 26, Oct 9, Nov 2; *Angriff*, Nov 3, 1930; Eher Verlag to NSDAP archives, Feb 27, 1936 (NA film T581, roll 47; BA file NS.26/968).

9 *Angriff*, Nov 8, 1930. JG was prosecuted for this editorial under the Law for the Protection of the Republic (Landesarchiv Berlin, Rep. 58, item 13).

10 Grzesinski to *Angriff*, Nov 11; JG diary, Nov 12, 1930; Eher Verlag to NSDAP archives, Jan 7, 1937 (NA film T581, roll 47; BA file NS.26/968).

11 *Ibid.*, Nov 22, 1930.

12 *Ibid.*, Oct 15, 1930.

13 *Ibid.*, Aug 24, Jan 1, 6, 1931.

14 *Ibid.*, Jan 3, 1931.

15 *Ibid.*, Jan 4, 11, 13, 22, 1931.

16 *Ibid.*, Nov 7, 14, 1930.

17 *Ibid.*, Nov 7, 1930. A Nov 15, 1931 memo identifies her as a possible police informer (BA file NS.26/325). – JG's unpubl. diary, Jun 25, 1934, describes a late night with Ilse Stahl – a 'patentes Mädel' (tip-top girl) – and her fiancé Gauleiter Josef Terboven. They married a week later. JG went off Ilse soon after. 'She's all powder and paint,' he wrote on Dec 13, 1935. 'I'm glad to get away.' 'Mrs Terboven,' he noted on Jan 15, 1936, 'brings the latest scuttlebutt. She's changed very much for the worse.' Josef and Ilse Terboven blew themselves up in May 1945.

18 Diary, Nov 9, 1930; he scores with Hella later (*ibid.*, Jan 16, 1931).

19 *Ibid.*, Nov 21, 1930.

20 *Ibid.*, Dec 1, 3, 1930.

21 *Ibid.*, Nov 19, 27, 1930.

22 *Ibid.*, Dec 12, 1920.

23 'Schwamm drüber.' *Ibid.*, Dec 17, 1920.

24 *Ibid.*, Dec 19, 20, 24, 1930.

25 *Ibid.*, Jan 19, 1931.

26 *Ibid.*, Dec 5, 1930. 'In the evening we "take a look" at [the film].' This was typical of JG's caution in writing up his diary.

27 *Ibid.*, Dec 7, 1930. Police chief Grzesinski (memoirs) was frantic; to him, the film was 'politically one of the most valuable in recent years.' He blamed Brüning for the police defeat. 'A huge Nazi demonstration near Nollendorfplatz, at which Goebbels ranted and raged, gave the government an external pretext for caving in.' He himself had planned to ban all demonstrations next day. (BA file Kl. Erw. 144).

28 Diary, Dec 9–12, 1930.

29 *E.g. Vossische Zeitung*, Dec 12, 1930.

30 See Severing's file on the ban (Friedrich Ebert foundation, Severing papers, folder 176).

31 For the transcript of the film censorship board's deliberations on Dec 11, 1930 see BA file Kl. Erw. 457. Universum Film GmbH (Ufa) was represented by the lawyer Dr Frankfurter. On behalf of the ministry of defense Lt-Cdr. von Baumbach described as 'extremely repellent' the scenes of panicking, screaming, and weeping volunteers under artillery bombardment, their animal-like behavior, and their wrangling over their dying comrade's new boots.

32 Diary, Dec 4, 1930.

33 *Ibid.*, Jan 18, 1931.

34 *Ibid.*, Jan 23, 24; *Angriff*, Jan 25, 1931. On Ulbricht's early career see NA file RG.319, IRR, XE.188374.

35 Diary, Jan 24, 1931.

36 JG to Ilse Hess, Nov 24, 1930 (Hess papers).

37 Diary, Dec 12, 1930.

38 Otto Wagener, MS (IfZ archives); Henry A Turner, *Hitler aus nächster Nahe: Aufzeich-*

nungen eines Vertrauten 1929–1932, 377.

39 Diary, Feb 1; on Jan 28, 1931 he writes: 'She is a very beautiful woman.'

Notes to Chapter 15.

1 Bismarck, a counselor at the German embassy in Rome, was quoted in Count Ciano's diary, Oct 17, 1941. – The bitchy Bella Fromm included similar canards about 'Magda Goebbels, divorced Quandt, née Nothing at All' in her diary, mid-Dec 1932: Magda, wrote this Jewish Berlin gossip columnist, had been brought up after World War One by the Nachmanns, a family of Berlin Jews, and had met Quandt at the Ullstein publishing house. 'So she struck real lucky with the Jews.' (Boston Univ. Libr., Special MS Division, Fromm papers, box 1.) Hans Hinkel stated in Jun 1969 he had 'got to know' her before JG (IfZ file ZS.1878).

2 She was born Oct 31, 1879; Alexander Hubert Theodor Wilhelm Oskar Ritschel died in Duisburg, Apr 4, 1941.

3 Birth certificate No. 101/1901, No. 4 Registry Office Kreuzberg, Berlin (IfZ file F82, Heiber papers).

4 Diary, Jan 26, 1933.

5 Auguste Behrend, 'My daughter Magda Goebbels,' a series in *Schwäbische Illustrierte*, Stuttgart (hereafter Behrend), Nos. 8–13; here No. 13, Mar 29, 1952.

6 Heiber is also dubious about Auguste Behrend's marriage, though inclined to accept it. In the Jul 1931 amendment of Magda's birth certificate, referred to later, there is mention of Ritschel only as her father, and not as Behrend's divorced husband.

7 Ritschel, supplementary testament, Apr 3, 1941 (ZStA Potsdam, Rep. 90, Go 2, Magda Goebbels, letters); it benefited Ritschel's two brothers Gustav and Wilhelm, paying off the latter's debts.

8 Diary, Jul 24, 1931.

9 According to Ulrich Reimann, *Goebbels*, Magda's stepfather Friedländer was with Auguste Behrend from 1904 – 1920. I only later found a source which furnished him with a first name, Richard. See *e.g.* the series by 'Jürgen Peters and Hans Roos' (Dr Erich Ebermayer and Dr Hans-Otto Meissner), 'Magda Goebbels,' in *Revue*, Munich (hereafter Ebermayer and Meissner), No. 8, Feb 22, 1952. Since Behrend does not specify any dates of marriage or divorce this may have been an equally loose arrangement. Prof. Klaus Herrmann kindly searched the voluminous *Sigilla Veri* on this author's behalf, but a Friedländer matching Magda's stepfather was not listed; the register of the 1930 Jewish community in Berlin might be more productive. See our APPENDIX, page 696ff.

10 Ebermayer and Meissner, *ibid.*, state that he acquired a small cigar store.

11 Behrend, No. 8.

12 Quandt was born at Pritzwalk (Prignitz) on Jul 28, 1881; he had a brother Werner. Before his first wife Antoine, née Ewald, died in 1918 she bore him two sons – Hellmut, and Herbert, born Jun 22, 1918 at Pritzwalk. For more on Günther Quandt see NA: RG.226, OSS reports, No. 106, 145, Dec 1, 1944.

13 See Quandt's own version of all this in his privately published memoirs, edited by Herbert and Harald Quandt (Mensch & Arbeit Verlag, Munich, 1961).

14 Magda's Jewish background was frequently bowdlerized, *e.g.* by Sir George Ogilvie-Forbes of the British embassy in a telegram to Anthony Eden on Jan 6, 1938: 'He [JG] is married

to the former (divorced) rather pretty wife of a rich Jew . . .' (PRO file FO.371/21671).

15 Amendment to birth register approved by minister of justice on Jul 15, 1920; Magda was 'declared legitimate. . . at her father's request' (IfZ file F.82, Heiber papers).

16 Behrend, No. 10.

17 Harald Quandt was born in Berlin-Charlottenburg on Nov 1, 1921. Under interrogation by K Frank Korf on Apr 4, 1948 he stated he last saw his grandmother 'Auguste Friedländer, divorced Ritschel,' in Berlin in Jan 1944 (Korf papers).

18 Quandt memoirs.

19 Hans-Otto Meissner, *Magda Goebbels, ein Lebensbild* (Munich, 1978); based to a perilous degree on the testimony of the late Ello Quandt.

20 Her interest in Buddhism, which became profound, came from Ritschel. Ebermayer and Meissner, No. 8, Feb 22, 1952.

21 According to the late Curt Riess (*Das war mein Leben. Erinnerungen*, Munich, 1986, 326) this was Viktor Chaim Arlosorov, born in the Ukraine in 1899. See our APPENDIX, page 696ff.

22 Eleonore Quandt, born at Eisenberg on Sep 28, 1899, had married Günther's brother Werner. Lying about her age she told Magda they were the same age; Ello was two years older. Like many others she joined the NSDAP on May 1, 1932 (BDC file).

23 Quandt memoirs.

24 BDC file, Magda Quandt.

25 Hinkel MS.

26 Behrend, No. 13, Mar 29, 1952.

27 *Rote Fahne*, Jan 30; Berliner Tageblatt, Feb 2, 1931.

28 Diary, Feb 13, 1931.

29 Wagener MS.

30 Diary, Feb 15–16, 1931.

31 *Ibid.*, Feb 18–22, 1931.

32 *Ibid.*, Feb 26, Mar 10, 1931.

33 *Ibid.*, Feb 26–27, 1931.

34 *Ibid.*, Mar 10, 15, 1931.

35 *Ibid.*, Mar 11, 13, 1931.

36 *Ibid.*, Feb 22, 1931.

37 *Ibid.*, Jan 29, Feb 19, 1931.

38 *Ibid.*, Feb 20, 1931.

39 *Ibid.*, Feb 22, 1931.

40 *Ibid.*, Mar 1, 8, 1931.

41 *Ibid.*, Mar 15–16, 1931.

42 *Ibid.*, Mar 16; on Mar 28 JG described Göring as a man 'sick with megalomania.' *Angriff* articles on Feb 19 and 26, 1931 had praised Stennes as a brave soldier and Free Corps veteran.

43 *Angriff*, No. 47, Mar 7, 1931; police file (author's film DI–81).

44 *Vossische Zeitung*, Mar 14, 17. – Grzesinski noted on Mar 27: 'The suspicion cannot altogether be ruled out that the attack on Dr Goebbels was staged by the NSDAP itself for publicity purposes' (Landesarchiv Berlin, Rep. 58, item 509). Eduard Weiss came clean with a sworn affidavit published in Stennes' new newspaper *Arbeiter, Bauern, Soldaten*, May 4; which JG assured his diary, May 6, 1931, were just 'Stennes' lies.'

45 Diary, Mar 14, 1931.

46 *Ibid.*, Mar 3, 13, 1931.

47 *Ibid.*, Mar 14, 1931.

48 *Ibid.*, Mar 15; *Angriff*, No. 54, Mar 16, 1931.

49 Diary, May 17–19, 1931.

50 Hans Grimm to Goltz (BA file Kl. Erw. 653/2, pages 192ff); JG diary, Mar 21, 1931, and *Angriff* No. 59 of the same date.

51 *NYT*, Mar 22, 1931.

52 Diary, Mar 22, 1931.

53 *Ibid.*, Mar 25, 1931.

54 *Ibid.*, Feb 26, Mar 6, 1931.

55 *Ibid.*, Mar 26, 1931.

56 *Ibid.*, Mar 13, 27, 1931. He learned that Grzesinski had three police officials whose daily task was to check each new *Angriff* for sufficient cause to ban it.

57 *VB*, Apr 1, 1931.

58 Diary, Oct 9, 1930.

59 Jahn.

60 See the duplicated circular to S.A. comrades, Feb 25, 1931 in the file of No. 8 S.A. Standarte in NSDAP archives (BA file NS.26/322). 'Do Hitler and Röhm think we're stupid enough not to notice what's going on?'

61 Jahn. – A further duplicated circular of Jul 25, 1931 scurrilously mentioned Röhm's prosecution for homosexual offenses in 1925 and the cost of the Brown House where the staircase alone had cost 30,000 marks and the sixty ornate chairs for the Senate Chamber 180,000 marks. 'But Hitler is frightened of Dr Goebbels and daren't do anything against him, in case he starts a revolt because he knows what's going on' (BA file NS.26/322).

62 Diary, Oct 10, 1928.

63 *Ibid.*, Nov 12, 27, 1930.

64 There were frequent references to Röhm's perversion in the underground S.A. circulars (BA file NS.26/322), *e.g.* a spoof advert from Röhm on Jun 30, 1931: 'Wanted, first-class riding breeches with zip flies in perfect working order for uniforms of my palace guard! Size 175 – !' On Röhrbein and Ernst, see Fischer to Hitler, Nov 1, 1932 (BDC file, Helldorff).

65 See Stennes to Röhm, Feb 28, 1931, cited by Jahn; copy in Stennes papers, NSDAP archives (BA file NS.26/325).

66 Diary, Nov 28, 30, 1930.

67 *Ibid.*, Jan 15, 1931.

68 *Ibid.*, Feb 27, 1931.

69 Stennes to Röhm, Feb 28, 1931 (see note 65 above); JG diary, Mar 4, 1931.

70 Jahn. – And see the well-informed report No. 9, on the second Stennes putsch, circulated by the Berlin Landeskriminalpolizei, May 1, 1931 (BA file NS.26/1368; Schumacher collection, file 278).

71 Jahn.

72 *Ibid.*

73 BA file NS.26/322.

74 Diary, Mar 29, 1931. In the Stennes papers is a petition beginning, 'We the undersigned S.A. commanders of Pomerania hereby declare . . . ' etc. (BA file NS.26/325).

75 Landeskriminalpolizei report.

76 Ulrich von Hassell diary, Jul 11, 1942: in *Vom andern Deutschland. Aus den nachgelassen*

Tagebüchern 1938–1944 (Frankfurt, 1964).

77 Jahn.

78 Daluege to Röhm, Apr 1, 1931 (BA file NS.26/325).

79 Jahn, and Stennes MS (IfZ file ZS.1147).

80 Published in *Vossische Zeitung*, Apr 3, 1941.

81 Diary, Apr 2, 1941.

82 *Extrablatt an Nationalsozialisten* (IfZ, Alfred Conn papers).

83 *VB*, Apr 4, 1931.

84 Police order, Apr 2, 1931 (BA file NS.26/325).

85 Hitler to JG, Apr 3, 1941; Borresholm, 76.

86 Diary, Apr 4, 1931.

87 Diary, Apr 9, 1941. Stennes claimed 1,500 supporters in Berlin, but the police noted that only 600 attended his meeting in late Apr 1931.

88 Report No. 9 by the Berlin Landeskriminalpolizei, May 1, 1931 (BA file NS.26/1368; Schumacher collection, file 278).

89 Diary, Apr 10, 1931

Notes to Chapter 16.

1 Diary, Apr 9, 11, 1931.

2 Meissner, *Magda Goebbels*; JG diary, Apr 12, 1941.

3 Diary, Apr 14, 1931.

4 *Ibid.*, Apr 14, 1941; Schickedanz to Amann, Mar 19 and Oct 27, 1931 (Rosenberg files, NA film T484, roll 78, 0109–113).

5 Diary, Apr 21, 25, 1931. Hinkel does not mention his work for *Angriff* in postwar interrogations.

6 *Ibid.*, Apr 14, 18, 29, 1931.

7 Police report on JG's speech of Sep 26, 1929, in Landesarchiv Berlin, Rep. 58, item 2.

8 Diary, Apr 15–16, 1931.

9 *Ibid.*, Apr 18, 1931; Landesarchiv Berlin, Rep. 58, item 23, vol. iii.

10 Diary, Jun 17, 1931.

11 *Ibid.*, Apr 18, 1931.

12 *Ibid.*, Apr 20, May 9, 1931.

13 *Ibid.*, Apr 25, 1931.

14 *Ibid.*, Apr 25, 1931; police file (author's film DI–81).

15 Police file, May 22, 1931. This appears to have become a common police requirement; see the similar declaration signed by JG on Oct 1, 1931 in Hoover Libr. files, NSDAP papers, box 1.

16 *Angriff*, Apr 28, 1931.

17 *NYT*, Apr 28, 1931.

18 Diary, Apr 30; the appeal failed (diary, Jun 2–3, 1931).

19 Memo on file in Landesarchiv Berlin, Rep. 58, item 39, vol. iv.

20 Diary, May 12, 1931; Landesarchiv Berlin, Rep. 58, item 24, vol. iv. For a file of JG correspondence with his lawyer Otto Kamecke see ZStA Potsdam, Rep. 90 Go 1, vol. ii.

21 *Ibid.*, Jun 13, 1931.

22 *Ibid.*, Apr 18, 1931.

23 *Ibid.*, Apr 19–21, 25, 1931.

24 *Ibid.*, May 18, 1931.

25 *Ibid.*, May 26, 1931.

26 *Ibid.*, May 27, 1931.

27 *Ibid.*, May 31, 1931.

28 *Ibid.*, Jun 5–6, 1931.

29 *Ibid.*, Jun 13–14, 1931.

30 *Ibid.*, Jun 11, 1931.

31 Schimmelmann to Anka Stalherm, Dec 17, 1931 (Irene Pranger papers).

32 Diary, May 2, 1931.

33 *Ibid.*, May 3, 8, 10, 12, 19, Jun 16, 1931.

34 *Ibid.*, May 20, 1931.

35 *Ibid.*, Jun 8, 1931.

36 *Ibid.*, Jun 10, 1931.

37 Goltz MS (BA file Kl. Erw. 653/2).

38 Police file, May 29, 1931.

39 *Angriff*, Jun 30, 1931.

40 In Feb 1945 this very oval would be RAF Bomber Command's aiming point in a raid that would kill two to three times more people than were in his audience.

41 *Dokumente*; for Dietrich's career see *Münchner Neueste Nachrichten* (hereafter *MNN*), Jul 30, 1941 (ND: NG–3787); CSDIC (WEA) BAOR report PIR.8, Sep 10, 1945 (NA: RG.319, IRR, XE.003812); defense documents in Nuremberg StA, Rep. 501; and interrogations (*ibid.*, Rep. 502).

42 Diary, Jul 17, 1931.

43 *Ibid.*, Jul 24, 1931.

44 *Ibid.*, Jul 27; and see Jul 31, 1931.

45 Gauorganisationsleiter. Born in Lauban, Silesia, on Aug 24, 1903, the son of an engine driver and four generations of blacksmiths, Karl-August Hanke would become JG's right-hand man, and then Staatssekretär until 1941.

46 Gaupropagandaleiter. See his lengthy MS dated May 1, 1938 in NSDAP archives (NA film T581, roll 47; BA files NS.26/546 and /133).

47 *Hinein in die Betriebe.* His opponents scoffed in one samizdat circular to disgruntled S.A. men, dated Sep 15, 1931, 'If the little clubfoot Joseph, known as Goebbels the Horsewhip, waffles about socialism over the next few months he's thinking of the reply he gave to the question "How do you stand on socialism!" – "Socialism is just a means to an end!"' Files of No. 8 S.A. Standarte in NSDAP archives (BA file NS.26/322).

48 *Kaiserhof*, Jan 6, 1932.

49 Compared with 523 in Saxony, 297 in Silesia, 187 in Brandenburg, 180 in Mecklenburg-Lübeck, and 128 in Württemberg. NSDAP archives (BA file NS.26/1290).

50 Figures announced by Rudolf Diehls, consultant to the police department of the Prussian ministry of the interior, on Nov 13, 1931 in Prussian state council; the police had confiscated 618 firearms, 1,380 knives and coshes, and 12,000 rounds of ammunition. Grzesinski MS.

51 *Münchner Post*, Jun 23; diary, May 17, Jun 24, 30. Maj. Giuseppe Renzetti, Mussolini's agent in Berlin, told JG that Italy took a very dim view of Röhm. JG's opponents in the gau expressed disgust that Hitler not only 'tolerated these homosexuals in high places, but spent so much time hobnobbing with big business. 'Ours must be the first "worker's

party" to set out its ideas in confidential discussions with the captains of industry,' they mocked in a circular of Nov 19, 1931, after Hitler met 400 top businessmen in October. (BA file NS.26/322).

52 Diary, Aug 6, 1931.

53 BDC file, Helldorff. That is, incidentally, how *he* signed his name, not 'Helldorf,' but the second 'f' was sometimes reduced to a deceptive squiggle.

54 S.A. Standartenführer Gottlieb Rösner to Lutze, Jan 24, 1935 (BDC file, Helldorff).

55 Police report of Feb 9, 1932 (author's film DI–81). A letter from Grzesinski to the court dated Oct 5, 1931 states that at a conference with several S.A. Standartenführer three days before they had been drilled as to what evidence to give. Landesarchiv Berlin, Rep. 58, item 20, vol. i.

56 Thus the indictment in the trial of those arrested. Landesarchiv Berlin, Rep. 58, item 20, vol. i.

57 Fischer to Hitler, Nov 1, 1932 (BDC file, Helldorff). He accused Helldorff himself (who was arrested and imprisoned after the riot) of tipping off the police. 'When the orders were given out only Dr Goebbels, [Karl] Ernst and Helldorff were present, but the police still found out' (BDC file, Helldorff). JG's police file, Feb 9, 1932, confirms that a 'police agent' at gau headquarters overheard him and Helldorff plotting the riot.

58 Police report.

59 A memo in Nazi party archives dated Nov 15, 1931 reports: 'Miss Stahl, Dr Goebbels' secretary, has the closest relations with officers of the police, whom she always introduces as her relatives. In fact Miss Stahl is said to report everything that goes on in Hedemann Strasse to these officers' (BA file NS.26/325).

60 Phipps to FO, Feb 22, 1933: Documents on British Foreign Policy, 2nd series, vol. iv, 425.

61 Landesarchiv Berlin, Rep. 58, item 20, vol. vii.

62 *Ibid.*

63 Leaflet in *Ibid.*, vol. iii.

64 See NA film T581, roll 4 for indignant reports of Hanns-Günther von Obernitz on this.

65 Circular, Oct 12, 1931 (BA file NS.26/322); similar in *Rote Fahne*.

66 Grzesinski MS.

67 Obernitz, report Dec 21, 1931 (NA film T581, roll 4; BA file NS.26/87).

68 Dr Otto Wagener MS (IfZ file ED.60); and see his recollections in IfZ file ZS.1732 (partially published by Henry A Turner as *Hitler aus nächster Nahe. Aufzeichnungen eines Vertrauten 1929 – 1932* [Frankfurt, 1978]) For Röhm's intervention, see NA film T581, roll 4; BA file NS.26/87.

69 So he told Henriette von Schirach (author's interview).

70 Behrend, No. 14, Apr 5, 1952.

71 Wagener MS.

72 The date is uncertain. According to the Quandt memoirs, Magda invited him to the foyer of the Kaiserhof in Jul 1931 and told him JG had asked her to marry him.

73 Ebermayer (who interviewed Ello Quandt) and Meissner, No. 12, Mar 22, 1952.

74 Hitler's Table Talk.

75 Quandt memoirs.

76 Copy of the marriage certificate, dated Aug 31, 1975, in Heiber papers (IfZ file F82).

77 The eighteen guests included Hitler, his adjutants Wilhelm Brückner and Julius Schaub, Ritter von Epp, JG's mother and sister, Karl Hanke, Walter Grantzow; Viktoria von Dirksen; Magda's schoolfriend Lola Umbreit. A malicious report reached the Berlin

police headquarters three days later (evidently from the later S.A. Obergruppenführer Hanns-Günther von Obernitz) that JG only married for appearances, 'to mask his homosexual inclinations – they say he didn't marry the woman but her son,' *i.e.*, Harald (NA film T581, roll 4).

78 Borresholm, 82.

Notes to Chapter 17.

1 *National Union Catalog* pre-1956 Imprints, 317ff. JG, *Vom Kaiserhof zur Reichskanzlei. Eine historische Darstellung in Tagebuchblättern (vom 1. Januar 1932 bis zum 1. Mai 1933)* (Berlin, 1934).

2 JG's 'Tagebuch für Ferien und Reisen,' May 22, 1932–Dec 17, 1935, is in box 1 of the Moscow archives (Goebbels papers, Fond 1477); the missing diaries for the Kaiserhof period are on a dozen microfiches in box 4, his original manuscripts of the Era of Struggle ('Kampfzeit') around 1930 will be found in box 3 – vol. i on twenty-one, and vol. ii on fifteen microfiches.

3 Diary, Jun 8; *Kaiserhof,* Jun 7, 1932.

4 *Kaiserhof,* Jan 4, 1932.

5 *Ibid.,* Jan 9, 24, 1932; when JG speaks at the Reichstag, it too is 'overflowing' (Mar 23, 1932).

6 *Ibid.,* Jan 9, 1932.

7 *Ibid.,* Jan 7, 1932.

8 *Ibid.,* Jan 12, 1932; see *e.g.* Jan 6, and May 28, 1932.

9 *Ibid.,* Jan 19, 1932.

10 Jan 30, 1933.

11 *Ibid.,* Jan 6, 1932.

12 *Ibid.,* May 10, 18, 19, 1932.

13 *Ibid.,* May 10, 1932.

14 Diary, Jun 14; *Kaiserhof,* Jun 14, 1932. The unpubl. diary of Apr 11, 1934 shows that Hitler advised JG to flatter Göring in the book (Moscow archives).

15 *Kaiserhof,* May 4, 19, 1932.

16 *Ibid.,* Jan 22, 1932 records his indignation when the press speculates on his family life.

17 *Ibid.,* Jan 5, 1932. Yet according to a note by Staatssekretär Hermann Pünder, chief of the Reich Chancellery, dated Apr 16, 1932, the party was receiving substantial protection-racket payments ('Terror-Abwehrprämien') from the Jewish businessmen Oskar Tietz (owner of the Hermann Tietz superstore) and Schapiro of the Sport Palace (*Akten der Reichskanzlei. Weimarer Republik*, vol. iii, [Boppard, 1990] No. 722, p. 2455).

18 Diary, May 22, and see Jun 8, 11, 12, 1932.

19 *Ibid.,* Sep 19, 1932.

20 *Ibid.,* Oct 5, 1932.

21 *Kaiserhof,* Jan 7, 1932. Hindenburg had taken office on May 5, 1925; the constitution limited his term to seven years.

22 *VB*, Jan 19, 1932.

23 According to the *Statistisches Jahrbuch der Stadt Berlin*, 8th year, 1932, p. 8; published by Berlin city statistical office.

24 *Kaiserhof,* Jan 8, 1932; police dossier, report dated Jan 13, 1932.

25 Weiss to JG, Jan 25; *Angriff*, Jan 26, 1932.

26 Police circular No. 71 to all Regierungspräsidenten, Jan 28, 1932 (BDC, JG; author's film DI–81).

27 *Angriff*, No. 17, Jan 26, 1932. For the trial of the murderers Stolt *et al.*, see Landesarchiv Berlin, Rep. 58, item 9 (10 vols.).

28 *Kaiserhof*, Jan 26, 1932; for the trial of the murderers Adam *et al.*, see Landesarchiv Berlin, Rep. 58, item 37 (22 vols.).

29 *Ibid.*, Feb 12, 1932.

30 Text in *Leipziger Volkszeitung*, Feb 8; and see Grzesinski MS and *Angriff*, No. 31, Feb 11, 1932.

31 JG referred to the dog-whip several times in the Reichstag during Feb 1932, as did Hitler on Mar 23, 1933: 'They even offered to drive me out of Germany with a dog-whip [Storms of jeers from the National Socialist benches].'

32 Thus JG was prosecuted for incitement to violence in a funeral eulogy on Jul 25, 1932 (Landesarchiv Berlin, Rep. 58, item 759).

33 *Kaiserhof*, Feb 10, 1932.

34 Police file, Feb 20; *Berliner Lokalanzeiger*, No. 86, Feb 20; *Kaiserhof*, Feb 20, 1932.

35 According to *Vossische Zeitung*, Feb 23, JG said he was 'authorized' to tell them of Hitler's decision to stand. The speech was published as *Schluss jetzt! Das deutsche Volk wählt Hitler! Rede im Berliner Sportpalast am 22. Februar 1932* (Franz Eher Nachf. Verlag, Munich, 1932). On Apr 4, the 'Opposition within the NSDAP' circulated a pamphlet blaming JG for the *fait accompli*. 'Without being authorized to do so he proclaimed in the Sport Palace at the end of February, "Hitler will be our Reich President."' After remarking yet again on JG's Jewish appearance the pamphlet suggested that JG intended to Prof.it either way, whether Hitler won or lost. (BA file NS.26/322).

36 Krebs, 167. In conversation with Krebs in May 1932 Hitler exonerated JG by saying that he had been speaking to a huge audience. See too Krebs' diary, Sep 19, 1930 – May 30, 1932 in the Hamburg archives.

37 *Kaiserhof*, Feb 22, 1932.

38 See Reichstag proceedings, 58th session, Feb 24, 1932, 2270, and *Angriff*, Mar 5, 1932, for the controversy about his precise words.

39 Reichstag proceedings, 57th session, Feb 23, 1932, 2245ff.

40 Reichstag proceedings, 59th session, Feb 25, 1932, 2346ff.

41 Historical essay by Kampmann as Gaupropagandaleiter May 13, 1938 (NA films T581, rolls 5 and 546; BA files NS.26/133 and /546); JG's drafts of the posters and leaflets for the Mar 13, 1932 election are in NSDAP archives (BA file NS.26/287).

42 *Kaiserhof*, Feb 29, 1932.

43 Diary, Oct 31, 1930; *Kaiserhof*, Feb 29, Mar 3, 1932. The JG film was directed by Häussler. JG to all gauleiters, Mar 13, 1932 (NSDAP archives, NA film T581, roll 29; BA file NS.26/546).

44 *Kaiserhof*, Mar 6, 1932.

45 *Ibid.*, Mar 2, 5, 1932.

46 Papers of Deutsche Welle GmbH, Mar 1932 (BA file R.55/1273).

47 Diary, Mar 9, 1932.

48 *Kaiserhof*, Mar 12, 1932. This glowed with false praise for Göring's oratory.

49 Hindenburg won 18,651,497 votes, Hitler 11,339,446, the communist Ernst Thälmann 4,983,341, and the DNVP's Duesterberg 2,557,729. In the still predominantly Red capital, the Nazis gained 22·9 percent – well below their national average of 30·1 percent.

50 JG to all gauleiters, Mar 13, 1932 (NA film T581, roll 29; BA file NS.26/546).

51 *Kaiserhof,* Mar 14–17, 1932.

52 'A rain of blows on the defeatists' (*Kaiserhof,* Mar 19); JG's drafts of the posters and leaflets (BA file NS.26/287).

53 Hitler to Westdeutscher Rundfunk, Mar 17, 1932 (BA file NS.26/564).

54 JG to all gauleiters, Mar 23, 1932. NSDAP archives (NA film T581, roll 29; BA file NS.26/546).

55 Drafts of his posters for the Apr 10, 1932 election are in BA file NS.26/287; similar files of his Reich election directorate are in file NS.26/290.

56 *Die Welt am Montag,* No. 14, Apr 4, 1932 suggested that Hitler had forfeited the right to be leader of a workers' party, as the Kaiserhof had billed him for 4,408 marks for ten days' food and accommodation in luxury suites on the first floor; *Kaiserhof,* Apr 2, 1932.

57 In *VB,* No. 97, Apr 6, and in *Angriff,* No. 64, 66, and 68 of Apr 4, 6, 8. He claimed Hitler's suite was on the fourth floor. *Die Welt* sued Hitler and JG for libel, producing the original bill. *MNN,* No. 122, May 30, 1932 (BA file NS.26/1932).

58 Severing papers (Friedrich Ebert foundation, Bonn, file 189).

59 Grzesinski alleged in his memoirs that his political police (Ia) raided a Nazi gau office in Pomerania and found compelling evidence of high treason, automatic weapons, and plans by Hitler to stage a putsch if prevented from taking office after an anticipated election victory. See *Märkische Volkszeitung,* Mar 20, 1932; for the Hagen police head-quarters' copy of Groener's telegram transmitting the ban to all police authorities see NA film T81, roll 90.

60 Leaflet drafts by JG are in BA file NS.26/286.

61 *Kaiserhof,* Apr 15–16, 1932; Kampmann MS; *NYT,* Apr 16, 1932, p. 4; Goltz MS.

62 *Kaiserhof,* Apr 24, 1932.

Notes to Chapter 18.

1 Göring had first seen Emmy in the spring of 1932 on the Weimar stage, and sent her a telegram from Capri in May.

2 Quoted by Erwin Giesing in USFET MISC report OI SR/36, 'Adolf Hitler. A Composite Picture,' Mar 12, 1947 (NA file RG.407, entry 427, box 1954F).

3 Diary, Jun 13, 1932.

4 For the prosecution of Röhm for homosexual offenses since 1925 see Landesarchiv Berlin, Rep. 58, item 517; a case against Berlin editors for publishing Munich court documents against Röhm is *ibid.,* item 710.

5 See *e.g.* Konstantin Hierl to Hitler, Mar 24, 1932 (Hoover Libr., NSDAP papers, box 2).

6 H R Knickerbocker MS, 'Nazi Germany' (Syracuse Univ., George Arents Research Libr., Dorothy Thompson papers, box 2); for JG's letter to Knickerbocker, Mar 8, 1932 (Columbia Univ., New York, Rare Book and MS Libr., Knickerbocker Papers).

7 Landesarchiv Berlin, Rep. 58, vol. iii.

8 *Kaiserhof,* Apr 26–30, 1932.

9 Diary, May 25; *Kaiserhof,* May 24, 1932.

10 Lohse MS; *Kaiserhof,* May 12, 1932. Case files on JG's antisemitic libels against Weiss on May 12 are in Landesarchiv Berlin, Rep. 58, item 721.

11 JG's secretariat to lawyer Dr Otto Kamecke, Sep 2, 1932 (ZStA Potsdam, Rep 90, Go 1,

vol. ii).

12 Tax accountant Paul Schüler to JG, Jan 2, 1933 (Hoover Libr., JG papers, box 2).

13 Diary, May 22–23, 1932. Not all was idyllic; the diary on May 24 has Magda 'irritating' JG, but on May 30 'she is clever and pretty.'

14 Kampmann MS, May 13, 1938.

15 JG to Otto Born *et al.*, Jun 9, 1932 (NSDAP archives. NA film T581, roll 11a, BA file NS.26/1224).

16 *Angriff,* Jun 14, 1932; Grzesinski MS.

17 *Kaiserhof,* Jun 24–25; diary, Jul 2, 1932.

18 BA file R.55/1280.

19 Diary, Jul 6; *Kaiserhof,* Jul 10, 18, 1932. For JG's broadcast script, with Gayl's handwritten cuts, see BA file R.55/1273.

20 Gau Gross-Berlin, candidates' list, Jul 4, 1932 (NSDAP archives, NA film T581, roll 29, BA file NS.26/546).

21 JG, declaration, Berlin, Jul 6, 1932 (original in Princeton Univ., Seeley Mudd Libr., Adolf Hitler collection); for the one signed by Gauleiter Herbert Albrecht, Jul 5, 1932, see his BDC file.

22 The Neuer Deutscher Verlag was prosecuted for publishing Goebbels' picture with the caption: 'How'd it be, aside from murdering the workers, to bump off Superman Goebbels too!' (Landesarchiv Berlin, Rep. 58, item 705).

23 See the report in *Hamburger Volkszeitung,* Jul 16–17, 1932, and the Severing papers, folder 192, in the Friedrich Ebert foundation. *Dokumente*; Grzesinski MS; *Kaiserhof,* Jul 17, 1932.

24 For Severing's dismissal see folders 193–6 and 317–22 of his papers in the Friedrich Ebert foundation in Bonn; for his intercession on Dr Weiss's behalf, folder 50.

25 Grzesinski MS.

26 Captured by the Nazis, they were put on display in 1936. *Angriff,* Oct 30, 1936.

27 Kampmann MS.

28 Milch diary, Aug 1932 (author's film DI–59); for correspondence on these negotiations see BA file NS.51/14.

29 Diary, Aug 8–11, 1932.

30 The 'Wirtin' in Fröhlich's transcription of the diary, Aug 10, should read 'Werlin' – Jakob Werlin.

31 Diary, Aug 11, 1932.

32 Press release, Aug 12, 1932.

33 Papers and correspondence on Hitler's talks with Papen, Aug 13, 1932, are in Party chancellery files, NA film T120, roll 2621, E381901ff; BA file NS.51/14.

34 Diary, Aug 15–18, 1932.

35 *Kaiserhof,* Aug 30–31, 1932; Milch diary, Aug 31, Sep 8, 1932 (author's film DI–59).

36 Diary, Sep 19, 1932.

37 *Ibid.*

38 RPL, circular to gauleiters, Oct 17, 1932 (BA file NS.26/263).

39 *Ibid.*, Oct 19; and *Angriff,* Oct 20, 1932.

40 RPL, circular to gauleiters, Oct 20, 1932.

41 *Unsere Nation*, No. 18, Sep 15, and No. 19, Oct 1, 1932.

42 RPL, circular to gauleiters, Oct 27, 1932.

43 Kampmann MS.

44 *DAZ*, Nov 3, 1932.

45 Leopold Gutterer, MS, 28 (Niedersächsisches Landesarchiv, Wolfenbüttel: file 250 N.317).

46 Diary, Nov 8, 1932.

47 *Angriff*, No. 230, Nov 7, 1932.

48 Diary, Nov 9; *Kaiserhof,* Nov 8, 1932.

49 Hitler to Papen, Nov 16, 1932 (NA film T120, roll 2621).

50 See note by Reichstag deputy Dr Hans Eugen Fabricius on this resignation, Nov 17, 1932 (BA file NS.26/4).

51 Hitler to Hindenburg, Nov 21 (NA film T120, roll 2621).

52 Lohse MS.

53 Diary, Dec 1, 1932.

54 For remarks by Schleicher and Ott on why they accepted, at defense ministry conferences Dec 13–15, 1932, see General Liebmann's papers in IfZ file ED.1, pp. 257ff; also Dr Otto Meissner's MS, 'Der Weg der Regierung,' Sep 22, 1945 (US State Dept files).

55 Diary, Dec 9, 1932; according to Wagener (IfZ, ZS.1732), Funk's former secretary once told him that Goebbels had helped Strasser dictate the letter in Funk's apartment. There is no confirmation of this odd detail in the diary.

56 Hans Frank, *Im Angesicht des Galgens. Deutung Hitlers und seiner Zeit auf Grund eigener Erlebnisse und Erkenntnisse* (Munich, 1953), 108. Frank wrote this MS in Nuremberg prison, and Justice Robert H Jackson retrieved it.

57 Lohse MS.

58 Diary, Dec 9, 1932.

59 *Vossische Zeitung*, Dec 9, 10, 1932.

60 Diary, Dec 10; Feder subsequently published a cringing declaration of loyalty in *Angriff,* No. 258, Dec 10, 1932.

61 Based on Lohse's MS.

62 Diary, Dec 10, 1932.

63 *VB*, Dec 9, 1932.

64 *Angriff*, No. 257, Dec 9, 1932.

65 Quoted by Heiber, 104.

Notes to Chapter 19.

1 Lochner to daughter Betty, Dec 11, 1932 (State Historical Society of Wisconsin, Lochner Papers, box 47, copy in FDR Libr., Toland papers).

2 Diary, Dec 11, 1932.

3 Haegert and other propaganda ministry personnel are briefly characterized in CSDIC (UK) Paper 80, 'Reich Ministry for Public Enlightenment and Propaganda, by Dr Richard Arnhold, pers. Referent of Prof. Bömer (PRO file WO.208/4174 and NA file RG. 165, entry 79, box 766).

4 Adolf Hitler, 'Memorandum on the internal reasons for the directives on enhancing the movement's striking power' (NA file T120, roll 2621).

5 *Angriff*, No. 267, Dec 21, 1932; *Dokumente*, 418.

6 Diary, Dec 23, 1932.

7 Ebermayer and Meissner, No. 23, Jun 7, 1952.

8 Diary, Dec 24, 1932.

9 *Ibid.*, Dec 26, 1932; Behrend, No. 19, May 10, 1952; JG to Hitler, Jul 18, 1944 (BA file NL.118/107).

10 Diary, Jan 2, 1933.

11 The microfiches are in Fond 1477.

12 Diary, Jan 13; *Kaiserhof*, Jan 12, 1933. See 'Stationen eines Arztes. Operieren bei Sauer-bruch, Kinderkriegen bei Stoeckel,' in *FAZ Magazin*, May 8, 1987, 52ff.

13 Kurt Baron von Schröder, born Nov 24, 1889; later SS Brigadeführer. See his personnel file in BA NS.48/73. Diary, Jan 6–7, 1933.

14 Diary, Jan 10, 1933.

15 Lohse MS.

16 Diary, Jan 14, 1933: 'That sounds like a traitor to me. I always saw it coming. Hitler is very dismayed.'

17 *Ibid.*, Jan 17, 1933; Lohse MS.

18 *Ibid.*, Jan 22; *Kaiserhof*, Jan 22, 1933.

19 Diary, Jan 23–27, 1933.

20 In the diary, Jan 30, 1933 JG writes that Hugenberg was to be economics minister. Fröhlich has 'Krisenminister,' perhaps a misreading.

21 Diary, Jan 30, 1933.

22 *Ibid.*, Jan 30–31; and diary of Count Lutz Schwerin von Krosigk, Jan 30, 1933.

23 Ebermayer and Meissner, No. 16, Apr 19, 1952.

Notes to Chapter 20.

1 Extracts from the diary of Sir Walter Layton, Apr 3, 1933 (PRO file FO.371/16722).

2 Interrogation, SAIC/FIR/46, Sep 13, 1946 (NA file RG.407, entry 427, box 1945i).

3 Grzesinski MS. – See too Jürgen Wetzel, 'Monarchie gegen Hitler. Aus der Korrespondenz Otto Brauns mit Albert Grzesinski 1934 bis 1936,' in *Der Bär von Berlin, Jahrbuch des Vereins für die Geschichte Berlins*, 1977, 7–14.

4 Rosenberg diary, Mar 1, 1939.

5 Interview of Rudolf von Ribbentrop, Jul 20, 1989.

6 Goebbels papers (Hoover Libr).

7 Diary, Sep 24, 1933.

8 *Ibid.*, Aug 25, 1933.

9 Text of the broadcast in Joseph Wulf's documentation, *Presse und Funk im Dritten Reich* (Frankfurt, 1983), 284ff.

10 *Ibid.*, Feb 1; *Kaiserhof*, Jan 31; gau history (NA film T581, roll 5; BA file NS.26/133); *Angriff*, Jan 31 – Feb 6, 1933. Maikowski, born in Charlottenburg Feb 28, 1908, had joined the Berlin S.A. in 1926 and been stabbed by communists in Dec 1927; after shooting a communist in 1931 he fled to Venice, was arrested Oct 1932, and was released only in December (NSDAP archives, Maikowski papers; BA file NS.26/323). For the trial of Schuckar *et al.*, murderers of Maikowski and police constable Zauritz, see Landesarchiv Berlin, Rep. 58, item 30.

11 Report by Eberhard Assmann, Sep 20, 1934 (BDC file, Helldorff).

12 Unpublished Brüning typescript in Dorothy Thompson papers (Syracuse Univ. Libr).

13 See JG's testimony of Nov 8, in *Vossische Zeitung*, Nov 9, 1933. Heinrich Hoffmann, who

was also present, confirms this in *Hitler Was my Friend* (London, 1955), 71ff, as does Hanfstaengl in his 1970 interview with John Toland (FDR Libr).

14 Diary, Feb 28, 1933; on the microfiche for Feb 16 – May 1, 1933 (Moscow archives, Goebbels papers, box 4).

15 JG's testimony, Reichstag arson trial, Nov 8, 1933, 6ff; transcript provided by Tobias archives.

16 Oven, 'Jul 27, 1943'; and Table Talk, Aug 21, 1942 (Heim, 356f).

17 The leading article was published in *Angriff*, Feb 28, 1933. Communism, JG argued, must now be wiped out so thoroughly that not even the name survived; Hindenburg must give Hitler the powers to do so.

18 SS Oberführer Alfred-Ingemar Berndt, born in Bromberg 1905. His ancestors for six hundred years had been farmers near Thorn and in the Warthe region; after the Poles re-annexed these regions in 1919 and 1920 and seized the estates he and his family were expelled. Berndt had been sacked by Wolff's Telegraph Agency – forerunner of the Nazi DNB agency – in Dec 1932 and became Otto Dietrich's adjutant in Feb 1933; from Apr 1, 1936 he was deputy press chief, and headed the government's press office; he served as an infantry NCO Jul–Aug 1939, as ADC to Rommel in North Africa from Feb 1, 1941, then returned to take over JG's press division on Sep 5, 1941. In Jan 1945 he was given a Panzer IV company in Hungary, where he died in action (BDC file, Berndt; and see Berndt to Himmler, Jul 11, 1944: NA film T175, roll 33).

19 *Manchester Guardian*, Apr 27; *cf. NYT,* Apr 28, 1933. The *NYT* obituary of JG on May 3, 1945 stated, 'It was he who conceived the spectacle of the Reichstag fire.'

20 Diary, Apr 9, 1941. In general see Fritz Tobias, *Der Reichstagsbrand* (Rastatt, 1962); and the critique by Martin Broszat on the controversy in *VfZ* , No. 3, 1960, 275ff.

21 Cabinet, Mar 7, 1933 (BA file R43I/1460).

22 JG had preferred 'Reichsminister of culture and public enlightenment.' Lammers memo, May 9, 1934 (BA file R.43II/1149).

23 He issued repeated directives insisting that the word 'propaganda' be used only in a positive sense; and that it be called 'agitation' when conducted by the enemy. *E.g.* directive of Jul 28, 1937 in Brammer collection, BA file ZSg.101/10; RMVP directive, Nov 8, 1940 (BA file R.55/1410); confidential briefing, Feb 9, 1942 in Oberheitmann collection, BA file ZSg. 109/28; RMVP circular in files of Propaganda-Staffel North-West, Jul 24, 1944 (Hoover Libr., Lerner papers).

24 Interrogation at CCPWE No. 32, report DI–32, Jul 16, 1945 (NA file RG.407, entry 427, box 1954q).

25 Schäffer diary, Mar 8, 1933 (BA file Kl. Erw. 614/17c; IfZ file ED.93, vol. 24a).

26 Fromm diary, Mar 15, 1933 (Fromm papers, box 1). Bella Steuermann-Fromm was a childhood friend of Ludwig III of Bavaria. She fled to the USA in 1938 with, she claimed, only $3.96 (but brought out her entire furniture including a grand piano!). Hanfstaengl described her as an unappetizing and malodorous creature. 'This frump,' he wrote on Jun 23, 1944 to his son, 'was one of those semi-ladies whose mere entrance sufficed to tell me that the company concerned had begun to become what one might call "mixed"' (NA file RG.219, X–7141141, Hanfstaengl).

27 Fromm diary, Mar 29; and see 'bf's' column in the *Berliner Zeitung*, Mar 30, 1933.

28 Gutterer affidavit, Jul 6, 1948 (IfZ file ZS.490).

29 Cabinet, Mar 11, 1933 5 P.M. (BA file R43I/1460 and /1149).

30 *Reichsgesetzblatt* (Reich Law Gazette, hereafter *RGBl.*), 1933, I, 104. An addendum of Jun

30, 1933 (*ibid.*, 440) stipulated that the ministry would perform 'all tasks of spiritual influence on the nation, of publicizing the state, culture, and economy at home and abroad, and administering all bodies serving those functions.' In general, see Z A B Zeman, *Nazi Propaganda* (London, 1964), 'Ernest Kohn Bramsted,' *Goebbels and National Socialist Propaganda 1925–1945* (Michigan State Univ. Press, 1965), and Wolfram Werner, *Zur Geschichte des Reichsministeriums für Volksaufklärung und Propaganda und zur Überlieferung* (Koblenz, 1979).

31 *Kaiserhof,* Mar 15; *NYT,* Mar 20, 1933.

32 William E Dodd to FDR, Mar 27, 1933 (FDR Libr., PSF file 45, Germany, Dodd).

33 Borresholm, 94f; *Kaiserhof,* Mar 11, 1933. There are detailed floor plans in a 70pp. survey (PW paper 80) on the propaganda ministry by Dr Richard Arnhold; and see his PW paper 108, 'Party Control of Propaganda,' a 19pp. analysis of the Reichspropagandaleitung and its associated agencies (PRO file WO.208/4174). On the ministry's later organization and personalities see interrogation SAIC/CIR/4 of Hinkel, Immanuel Schäffer, Martin Schönicke, Rolf Hoffmann, Eugen Maier, Karl Cerff, Paul ('Presse') Schmidt, Jul 10, 1945 (NA file RG.332, entry ETO Mis-Y, Sect., box 116), and PWB/SAIC/22 of Hoffmann, Jul 12, 1945 (*ibid.*); also Special Interrogation Report on Otto Dietrich, CSDIC /WEA, SIR.2, Oct 16, 1945 (NA file RG.332, entry ETO Mis-Y, Sect., box 16).

34 Cabinet, Mar 20, 1933 (BA file R43I/1460).

35 *Sunday Express,* London, Mar 26, 1933; its main Mar 24 headline had read 'JUDEA DECLARES WAR ON GERMANY;' *NYT,* passim.

36 *Sunday Express,* Mar 26, 1933.

37 Cabinet, Mar 29, 4:15 P.M. (BA file R43I/1460); and see *Kaiserhof,* Mar 27, and his press conference reported in *NYT,* Mar 28, 1933.

38 Reported thus in *NYT,* Apr 1, 1933.

39 *NYT,* Apr 2; *Kaiserhof,* Apr 1, 1933. For a sample leaflet protesting against Jewish 'atrocity propaganda' see file G–127 in the archives of the Yivo Institute for Jewish Research in New York, Record Group 215 (hereafter Yivo).

40 Sir Eric Layton diary, Apr 3, 1933 (PRO file FO.371/16722). JG used to state that seventy-five percent of Berlin's lawyers were Jews. Writing to him on Nov 30, 1936 Heydrich gave detailed figures. 'Before March 1933 altogether 3,890 lawyers were active in Berlin. Of these 1,998 (51·36 percent) were Jews. Since the new admission regulations the overall number of Berlin lawyers has sunk to 3,095. Of these 1,203 (38·87 percent) are Jews.' (ZStA Potsdam, Rep. 50.01, propaganda ministry: Diewerge papers, vol. 994).

41 *Kaiserhof,* Mar 27, 1933.

42 Diary, May 16, 1933.

43 JG to Furtwängler, quoted in *NYT,* Apr 16, 1933.

44 Franz von Papen, *Der Wahrheit eine Gasse* (Munich, 1952), 289ff.

45 Diary, May 12, 25, Jul 22; uniforms: Jun 15, 20, Jul 27, 1933.

46 *Ibid.*, Jun 20, 21, 24, 1933.

47 *Ibid.*, Aug 6–7, 1933.

48 *Ibid.*, Aug 23 ('Hope Fatso departs soon') and Sep 2, 1933. JG's rivalry with Göring occasioned much scandalized comment among diplomats in Berlin. *Cf.* Basil C Newton to Orme Sargent (FO), Sep 29, and Eric Phipps to Sir John Simon, Oct 25, 1933 (PRO file FO.371/16728).

49 Borresholm, 92f.

Notes to Chapter 21.

1 Borresholm, 96f; *Kaiserhof,* Apr 28, 30; diary, May 2, 1933.

2 Testimony of Otto Wagener, Feb 5, 1960 (IfZ file ZS.1732).

3 His diary, May 11, seems to make clear it was the Nazi students themselves.

4 Gerhard Sauder, 'Der Germanist Goebbels als Redner bei der Berliner Bücherver-brennung,' in Haarmann, Huder, Siebenhaar (eds.), *'Das war ein Vorspiel nur. . . '* *Bücherverbrennung Deutschland 1933,* Schriftenreihe der Akademie der Künste (Berlin, 1985), 56ff; Reuth, 286.

5 Bella Fromm diary, May 11, 1933 (Fromm papers, box 16).

6 In Conversation with Pierre Bertraux and Brigitte Bermann-Fischer, in *Das war ein Vorspiel nur. . . ,* 230; Reuth, 286.

7 *NYT,* May 11; KB, May 12, 1933: 'Execution of the People's Will.'

8 *NYT,* May 12, 1933.

9 *Ibid.,* Apr 2, May 7, 11, 1933.

10 Fromm diary May 31, 1933.

11 His unpublished diary of Apr 22, 1934 shows he later assessed Hassell as 'quite clever'; on May 25, 1935 he found, 'Hassell . . . sees things very clearly.'

12 Diary, Jun 7, 1928. On Aug 29, 1928, agitated by the South Tyrol question, JG noted: 'Italians are all swine. Except for Mussolini.' After reading the Duce's memoirs JG commented (Jan 19, 1930), 'Magnificent, this Mussolini! My great contemporary model.'

13 *Ibid.,* Jun 4, 1933.

14 *NYT,* Jul 9, 1933.

15 Fromm MS (published in New York as *Blood & Banquets* in 1942), Fromm papers, box 2.

16 Diary, Apr 14, 1933.

17 See his speech at the opening of the exhibition on women, quoted by Knickerbocker (Syracuse Univ., Thompson papers, box 2).

18 Magda Goebbels broadcast, May 14, 1933: *Die deutsche Mutter* (Heilbronn, 1933) 20pp.; JG diary, May 15, 1933.

19 Diary, May 10, 1933.

20 *Ibid.,* May 5, 7, Jun 14, 1933; Magda's mother wrote, 'The very thought that somebody might think he could be influenced through his relatives used to get his goat' (Behrend, No. 17, Apr 26, 1952).

21 Diary, Jun 6, 1933.

22 Fromm MS (Fromm papers, box 61); JG diary, Jun 11, 18, 1933.

23 Diary, Jul 24, 1933.

24 Reichsministerium für Volksaufklärung und Propaganda (hereafter RMVP) budget for fiscal 1933 (ZStA Potsdam, Rep. 50.01, vol. 1059); JG diary, Jun 10, 1933.

25 Blind to his own shortcomings, JG referred (diary, Aug 12, 1933) to German broadcasting as a 'hotbed of corruption' that needed cleansing.

26 Diary, Jul 9, 1933. See Hadamovsky's article on early broadcasting in *Angriff,* Oct 30, 1936.

27 Diary, Aug 19, 1933.

28 *Ibid.,* Jun 11, 1933. For RMVP personnel, jurisdiction, and filing systems see Yivo file G–106; telephone directories 1939–43, G–107, and a list of senior ministry officials, G–108. These show that the RMVP had 956 employees on Apr 1, 1939, 1,356 on Apr 1, 1940, and

1,902 on Apr 1, 1941.

29 Georg Wilhelm Müller, *Das Reichsministerium für Volksaufklärung und Propaganda* (Berlin 1940), 10.

30 On Jul 10, 1934 he discussed with Funk 'how to cast our ministry in an even more national-socialist mold. And particularly the Reich chamber of culture. Ever more tightly to the party' (Unpubl. diary, Jul 11, 1934).

31 Diary, Jun 27, 1933; interrogation of Fritzsche, Sep 17, 1946 (StA Nuremberg, F86). Hanke had been JG's Gauorganisationsleiter, then *pers. Referent* (special assistant), then Adjutant.

32 Much the same on Nov 8: 'If our opponents afforded us the parliamentary means to get rid of them, that was their affair. But that's no reason for us to make the same mistake.' *Frankfurter Zeitung*, No. 804, Nov 10, 1933.

33 Reichsverband der deutschen Presse; for some of its records under the RMVP, see NA films T70, rolls 127–33. See CSDIC (WEA) BAOR report PIR.8, Otto Dietrich interrogation, Sep 9, 1945 (NA file RG.219, XE.003812).

34 Diary, Aug 14; ten days later Hitler authorized a bill on the chamber of culture (*ibid.,* Aug 25, 1933). See the interrogation of Alfred Frauenfeld and Hans Hinkel on the Reichskulturkammer, SAIC/27, May 27, 1945 (NA: RG.165, entry 79, box 756).

35 JG to Lammers, Jul 13, 1933 (BA file R.43II/1244).

36 'Basic thoughts on the establishment of a Reich Chamber of Culture,' Jul 1933 (BA file R.43II/1241).

37 Diary, Aug 25, 1933.

38 Reichspressekammer. See *e.g.* War Dept. Historical Branch (Lt-Col. Oron J Hale) interrogation of Amann, Aug 22, 1945 (NA file RG.332, entry Mis-Y, Sect., box 116); and Dietrich interrogation.

39 Diary, Jul 24, 1933: 'An odd feeling – to sit in front of this great musician.'

40 Reichskammer der bildenden Künste. On which see the 51pp. CSDIC (UK) document PW paper 50 by Erich Mai, a leading member (PRO file WO.208/4174).

41 Reichsrundfunkkammer. See OSS R&A report No. 2100, 'News Distribution System of Germany,' Apr 25, 1944 (USAMHI, Carlisle, Pennsylvania: Donovan papers, box 35c).

42 Membership of a chamber was restricted to pure Aryans, 'second-grade half-Jews,' and Aryans married to 'first-grade half-Jews.' For the questionnaire used by the chamber of music, with elaborate questions on candidates' racial origins, see Yivo file G–54; similarly for the film chamber, file G–55.

43 Dated Jul 1936. USFET report DE.496/DIS.202 (Hoover Libr., Lerner papers).

44 *Rede des Reichsministers Dr. Goebbels bei der Eröffnung der Reichskulturkammer am 15. November 1933* (Frankfurt, 1933).

45 Dodd to FDR, Nov 27, 1933 (FDR Libr., PSF box 45, Germany, Dodd); *cf.* William E Dodd, *Ambassador William E Dodd's Diary, 1933 – 1938* (New York, 1941), 90f.

46 Dr H E Schmidt-Leonhardt, *Das Schriftleitergesetz vom 4. Oktober 1933 mit den einschlägigen Bestimmungen, erläutert von Dr H Schmidt-Leonhardt und Dr P Gast* (Berlin, 1944); and the CSDIC (WEA) BAOR interrogation of Otto Dietrich. – For the preparation of the press law and its implementation see the papers of Prof. Alfred Herrmann (BA files Kl. Erw. 368/13–14).

47 See among other sources CSDIC (UK) PW paper 8, compiled by four prisoners of limited (local press) horizon, but very illuminating on the RMVP control of editors (PRO file WO.208/4174); and the interrogation of Werner Stephan, Dietrich's PA Oct 29, 1947 (NA

file RG.260, OMGUS files, 53–3/7, box 15).

48 Fromm diary, Nov 25, 1933 (Fromm papers, box 1).

49 Diary Mar 29, May 7, 1933.

50 *Jahrbuch der Reichsfilmkammer* (Berlin, 1937), 194; Hinkel interrogation, SAIC/29, May 28, 1945 (NA file RG.165, entry 79, box 756).

51 When interviewed by the author on Jul 14, 1993; and before that in a TV interview for Westdeutscher Rundfunk in May 1991.

52 US Seventh Army interrogation PWB/SAIC/3 of Riefenstahl, May 30, 1945 (NA file RG.332, entry ETO, Mis-Y, Sect., box 116).

53 Leni Riefenstahl, *Memoiren* (Munich, 1987) (hereafter Riefenstahl) 181; JG diary, Dec 1, 1929 (he went with Erika Chelius).

54 Diary, Nov 8, 1932; under interrogation (see above), perhaps naturally, she stated that her first meeting with Hitler was after he came to power, which might be what JG refers to (diary) on Jun 14, 1933: she had been to see Hitler, and 'will now start work on her film.'

55 Riefenstahl, 186ff, and interview with this author, Jul 15, 1989. The only related diary entry is on Dec 11, 1932, when General Italo Balbo is entertained at Hermann Göring's and both Magda and Leni flirt madly with the dashing Italian aviator.

56 There is no reference to a visit to Riefenstahl in the Christmas Eve diary, which shows JG with Harald or visiting Magda at the clinic. She ventilated none of these allegations to her American interrogators in 1945.

57 Riefenstahl, 199f.

58 Diary, May 17, 26, 1933.

59 Riefenstahl, 201.

60 Diary, Jun 12, 1933.

61 *Ibid.*, Jun 16, 20, Jul 4, 9, 18, Aug 14, 16–17, 1933.

62 Riefenstahl, 202ff.

63 So she told Hans-Otto Meissner (interview with the author, Apr 22, 1990).

64 Borresholm.

65 Diary, Jul 22; *NYT*, Jul 20, 25; Fromm diary, Apr 11, 1933.

66 Borresholm, 99f; JG diary, Jul 26 ('An evening with princely personages. In a word, a gang of scoundrels'); and see Aug 5, 1933.

67 Behrend, No. 20, May 17, 1952; his problems with Magda are temporarily over. 'How happy we both are,' he writes on Sep 2, 1933, 'she is my only darling.'

68 Riefenstahl interrogation, and interview, Jul 15, 1989; see JG's reference to her as *fährig* in his unpubl. diary, Aug 26, 1934.

69 *NYT*, Aug 29; letter Louis Lochner to Betty, Nov 12, 1933 (Lochner papers, box 47).

70 *NYT*, Sep 13, Nov 24, 1933.

71 Cabinet meeting, Sep 12, 4:30 P.M. (BA file R.43I/1465); *cf. NYT*, Sep 15, 1933.

72 *NYT*, Sep 24, 25, 1933.

73 Paul Schmidt, *Statist auf diplomatischer Bühne 1923–45* (Bonn, 1949). See *La Suisse*, Sep 25, 26; JG diary, Sep 28; and the report by G Motta, chief of the political department, to the Conseil Nationale, Berne, Sep 27, 1933, publ. in *Documents Diplomatiques Suisses* (Berne, 1982), 835ff.

74 Professor Carl F Burckhardt, *Meine Danziger Mission 1937 – 1939* (Stuttgart, 1960), 51ff.

75 The full text of JG's speech of Sep 28 is in Lord Tyrell's telegram No. 226 to FO (PRO file FO.371/17367 and /16728); see too *NYT* and *La Suisse* of Sep 29, and *Tribune de Genève*, Sep 29–30, 1933.

76 Borresholm, 111f.

77 Paul-Boncour to Daladier, Sep 29, 1933, in *Documents Diplomatiques Français 1932–1939* (1st series) vol. iv, No. 259.

78 Eden, minute, Sep 26, 1933 (PRO file FO.371/17368).

79 Weizsäcker, private letter of Oct 1 (Leonidas E Hill (ed.), *Die Weizsäcker-Papiere, 1933 – 1950* (Berlin, 1974), 76); on Oct 6, 1933 Weizsäcker wrote that he was 'well satisfied' with JG's visit.

Notes to Chapter 22.

1 Basil Newton to Sir John Simon, Sep 13, 1933 (PRO file FO.371/16728).

2 *NYT*, Oct 9, 1933.

3 Phipps to FO, No. 224, Oct 16, 1933 (PRO file FO.371/17368).

4 The forged article was entitled, 'Germany's Aim: She Wants More Territory.' See *NYT*, Nov 18, 19, 22, 1933.

5 *NYT*, Nov 18, 1933.

6 'Querschnitt durch die Tatigkeit des Arbeitsgebiets Dr Taubert (Antibolschewismus) des RMVP bis zum 31.12.1944' (Yivo, file GPA–14) (Taubert report). For records of Anti-Comintern see BA files R55/70, 207, 369, 373, 374–6, 730.

7 Diary, May 8, 1933; at the Reichstag fire trial an incriminating memorandum allegedly by Oberfohren was produced. JG commented (transcript, p. 23), 'Why pick as the author of such a document a dead man who can't defend himself any more?'

8 Trial observations of Prof. Justus Hedemann, a Jena lawyer (BA file Kl. Erw. 433).

9 Court record; Borresholm, 122.

10 Court record, Nov 8, p. 114; *cf. Vossische Zeitung*, Nov 9, 1933. At the press desk was Louis Lochner – see his descriptive letter to Betty, Nov 12, 1933 (Lochner papers, box 47).

11 Borresholm, 118f.

12 DNB release, Jan 27, 1934: 'Dr Goebbels favors saying yes to life and joy'; *NYT*, Jan 27, 1934.

13 Ullstein's *Morgenpost* sold 4–5m daily, *Berliner Illustrierte Zeitung* 1m, *Grüne Post* 400,000, *Berliner Zeitung* 100,000, *Berliner Allgemeine Zeitung* 80,000, and *Vossische Zeitung* 60,000.

14 Unpubl. diary, May 11, 1934. Interrogations of Amann: Nuremberg, Sep 30, 1947 (IfZ file ZS.809) and Jan 10, 1948 (NA file RG.260, box 15); by Frank Korf, May 1, 1948 (Hoover Libr., Korf papers), and CSDIC (UK) PIR.79. And CSDIC (UK) report, SS Obergruppenführer Otto Ohlendorf, 'Notes on Corruption and Corrupted Personalities in Germany,' PW papers 133, Aug 11, 1945 (PRO file WO.208/4174), and CSDIC (WEA) BAOR report FIR.80, appendix Jul 6, 1946: 'Winkler's connection with Party publishing firms' (NA file RG.332, Mis-Y, box 18).

15 Unpubl. diary, Apr 30, May 2, 11: 'The gentlemen from Ullstein. Bluntly told them my opinion. About Jews and suchlike. Ban on *Grüne Post* won't be lifted. They should eliminate the Jews.' *NYT*, May 9, 1934.

16 CSDIC (WEA) BAOR report FIR.80, appendix Jul 6, 1946: 'Winkler's connection with party publishing firms' (NA file RG.332, Mis-Y, box 18).

17 Diary, Jan 2, 1934.

18 *Ibid.*, Sep 1, 1933.

19 JG to 'Frau Dr Mumme,' Nov 3, 1933 (Irene Pranger papers).

20 See JG's unpubl. diary, Mar 20: 'Marianne Hoppe tells me about her new film. I'll help her;' on May 13 he added, 'Talk with Marianne Hoppe. She evidently went shooting her mouth off. Now she's cut down to size.' On Jun 20, 1934, JG notes eloquently: 'Marianne Hoppe: I'm fed up with her.'

21 *Ibid.*, Apr 24, 1934: 'Käthe Dorsch, with whom I discuss film matters. She is very charming.'

22 Diary, Dec 11, 1936.

23 Interview of Irene Pranger, Sep 6, 1990; see the letter written by Deutscher Verlag to Anka Oswald, Apr 20, 1943 (Irene Pranger papers).

24 Eher Verlag to JG, Feb 3, 1933 (ZStA Potsdam, Rep. 90, Go 1, Goebbels, vol. 3).

25 Diary, Mar 25, 31, Apr 4, 6, 13, 1934.

26 Unpubl. diary, Mar 11, 12, 17, 1934.

27 *Ibid.*, Apr 9, 1934.

28 *Ibid.*, Apr 13–14, 1934.

29 *Ibid.*, May 28, 1934.

30 *Ibid.*, Jun 3, 1934.

31 See the reference, *ibid.*, Jun 7, 1934, to a countess with whom he sees the film *Zwischen Heute und Morgen*; he 'parlavers' (as he routinely spells this buzzword) at length with her, finds 'she is very nice.' On Jun 13 he notes meeting Käthe Kruse, 'She is very nice. Drive late through the Grunewald.'

32 JG (*ibid.*, Jun 22, 1934) also called it *eine Art Profanierung*, 'a kind of blasphemy.'

33 *NYT*, May 13, 27, 28; unpubl. diary, May 13, 1934.

34 See the German FO file on the 'Jewish atrocity lies' on NA film T120, roll 4673.

35 A Turkish Jew, Wilhelm Rose, born Aug 18, 1898, who had repeatedly been arrested during the Weimar period for passport forgeries etc., and was arrested and deported on Feb 22, 1934. *Ibid.*

36 Unpubl. diary, Apr 24, 1934.

37 Unpubl. diary, Apr 13, 1934.

38 Gauleiter conference in Berlin, Feb 2, 1934 (BA file NS.26/1290).

39 Thus spake JG in Essen, Jun 24: 'OPEN WAR AGAINST THE REAKTION. DR GOEBBELS SPEAKS OUT AGAINST THE HIDDEN ENEMIES OF STATE.' *National Zeitung*, Essen, Jun 25, 1934.

40 *VB*, Jan 15, 1934.

41 Memo by WIIb, Jan 18, initialed by Fritsch and Reichenau (Reich defense ministry, file H35/29 on JG's lectures: NA film T78, roll 372, 5199f); *VB*, Jan 19, 1934.

42 His speech on all these occasions was the 16pp. 'Wesen und Grundbegriffe des National-sozialismus' (*ibid.*, 5229ff).

43 Unpubl. diary, Mar 16, 1934. 'Spoke to Reichswehr. On top form. General von Kleist very pleasant. I speak two hours.'

44 For JG's speech in Königsberg, May 14, see *ibid.*, 5292ff; and the *Ostpreussische Zeitung* (with photo) and unpubl. diary, both May 15, 1934. He found Brauchitsch 'very nice, but a monarchist like many in the army.' He also spoke in Munich and Münster.

45 *E.g.* NA film T78, roll 372, 5262f.

46 See Willy Münzenberg, *Braunbuch des Hitler-Terrors* (Paris, 1933), 62; and JG's testimony at the Reichstag fire trial, Nov 8, 1933, 28. Afterwards, JG's condemnation of homosexuals became extreme, *e.g.* after Gauleiter Helmuth Brückner, founder of the Nazi party in Silesia, was arrested for homosexual offenses (unpubl. diary, Dec 6, 10, 11, 1934).

47 Diary, Mar 1, 31, 1934.

48 Text of JG's speech in file of No. 8 S.A. Standarte in NSDAP archives (BA file NS.26/322).

49 Unpubl. diary, Mar 17, 1934.

50 *Ibid.*, Apr 20, 1934.

51 *Ibid.*, May 7, 9, 1934.

52 *Ibid.*, May 17, 1934. For an article on JG's interest in American films, see *NYT*, Sep 30, 1945.

53 *Ibid.*, May 28, 1934. Karl von Eberstein, in charge of Hitler's security, reported: 'During the supper Hitler treated the baroness with great distinction, and talked to her almost exclusively.' USFET OI SR/36, May 12, 1947: 'Adolf Hitler. A Composite Picture.' (NA file RG.407, entry 427, box 1954f).

54 Unpubl. diary, Apr 13, 1934.

55 *Ibid.*, Apr 18 and 20, 1934: 'Midday at Führer's re Harald, with Röhm and Göring. Both back me to the hilt. Göring very decent. Talk with Dr Quandt. I stand firm in face of his sentimentalism. He yields. Magda gets her Harald back. She is delighted.'

56 *NYT*, Apr 27; unpubl. diary, Apr 26, 1934.

57 Unpubl. diary, Apr 28, 1934.

58 *Ibid.*, Apr 30, 1934.

59 *Ibid.*, May 5, 1934.

60 *Ibid.*, May 23, 1934.

61 *Ibid.*, May 9, 1934.

62 Diary, May 28, 30, 1934.

63 Unpubl. diary, Jun 3, 1934.

64 Fischer (Potsdam) to Hitler, Nov 1, 1932 (BDC file, Helldorff).

65 Darré diary, Oct 15, Dec 18, 1933; Jan 17, 27, 1934.

66 Rosenberg to Hess, Mar 15 (BA file NS.8/171 and Rosenberg papers, NA film T454, roll 63, 0584ff); JG publ. and unpubl. diaries, Apr 14, 18, 24, 26, Jul 22 ('I can't put up [with Rosenberg] much longer'), Jul 28, Aug 24, 26, 29, 31, Dec 13, 15, 1934.

67 Diary, Jan 2–3 ('feelings running hard against Göring' in the Brown House); *VB*, Jan 2, 1934. In his unpubl. diary of Mar 29, JG noted: 'With the Führer. Things just as they were. He's so nice to me. . . Long time with Führer in the evening. He sets out his foreign policy plans. Great stuff. Our Hitler!'

68 Unpubl. diary, May 26, 1934.

69 *Ibid.*, Apr 11; and see May 7 and 17 ('I'm on good terms with Göring now') 1934.

70 DNB release, May 3, 1934.

71 DNB night release, Jun 6–7; JG unpubl. diary, Jun 7, puts the audience at 80,000. The *NYT* reported on May 19, 1934 that S.A. men had invaded Berlin cafes and restaurants and delivered scorching speeches while comrades prevented customers from leaving.

72 *NYT*, May 13, 1934.

73 Ernst 'Putzi' Hanfstaengel, report on JG for FDR, Jul 16, 1943 (FDR Libr., PSF box 126).

74 NA negatives 242-HLM 1013; unpubl. diary, Jun 5, 1934.

75 Fromm diary, Jun 21: 'That little S.A. man Ulicht told me that, the one on the *Morgenpost* staff;' and *ibid.*, Jun 22, 1934: 'The Schleichers came to dinner with me, and [Major-General Ferdinand von] Bredow [all were victims of the purge eight days later]. . . Of course Papen's Marburg speech was the main topic. We were glad he'd taken a swipe at Goebbels and his endeavors to muzzle public opinion' (Fromm papers, box 2).

76 Orme Sargent to FO, Jun 27 (*i.e.*, written *before* the purge), quoting Glass of the Austrian

News Agency (PRO file FO.371/17707); it is worth noting that, speaking to Gestapo officials on Oct 11 about these events, Himmler referred to rumors in the foreign émigré press, prior to Jun 30, 1934, 'that I was hoping to overthrow Minister Goebbels . . . and that Goebbels no longer had the Führer's confidence' (NA film T175, roll 89, pp. 1536ff).

77 *Czas* (Warsaw), Jun 11, 1934, emphasized this point. Speaking to Polish journalists on May 8 (diary, May 9, and DNB release), JG had talked about the desire for peaceful rapprochement; Józef Piłsudski, the Polish president, and Hitler, he said, both knew what war meant; national socialism was 'not for export.'

78 Diary, May 11, 13 ('Midday with the Führer. He's weighed down with worries. And nobody helps share the load') and May 17, Jun 7, 1934.

79 JG, *Das nationalsozialistische Deutschland als Faktor des europäischen Friedens. Rede vor der Intellektuellen-Union in Warschau, 13. Juni 1934* (Berlin, 1934); DNB special release, Jun 12, 1934; *Westdeutscher Beobachter* ('Our hand is extended') and *DAZ*, Jun 14, 1934. And Sir W Erskine, Warsaw, to Simon, FO, Jun 19, 1934 (PRO file FO.371/17745).

80 Unpubl. diary, Jun 11, 16, 1934.

81 *Ibid.*, Jun 18; according to newspaper reports JG attacked Papen indirectly, referring to Center politicians who made much of their personal friendship with God; but it was the Nazis, he said, who were meanwhile restoring full employment. See *e.g. Gladbach-Rheydter Tageblatt*, Jun 18, 1934.

82 Unpubl. diary, Jun 18; and *cf. ibid.*, Jun 20, 1934.

83 Papen, *Der Wahrheit eine Gasse* (Munich, 1952), 349; Borresholm, 125ff.

84 Phipps to Simon, Jun 22, explaining JG's attack on Papen in his speech that night (PRO file FO.371/17707); Lochner to Betty, Jul 27, 1934 (Lochner papers, box 47.) – JG's diary does not mention the painful episode.

85 *Der Tag* and DNB night release, Jun 22, 1934.

86 Papen memoirs, 310ff; information from the Forschungsstelle für die Geschichte des Nationalsozialismus in Hamburg, May 1991.

87 Unpubl. diary, Jun 25, 1934.

88 *Ibid.*

89 The *Hallischer Nachrichten* put the figure at 225,000; and see *12 Uhr Blatt*, Jun 23, 1934.

90 12 Uhr Blatt, Jun 25 ('Outright fight against the *Reaktion*. Dr Goebbels against the hidden enemies of state'); N*ational Zeitung*, Jun 25 (PRO file FO.371/17707). JG wrote (unpubl. diary, Jun 25, 1934) with satisfaction that everybody took his words as being directed against Papen.

91 DNB press release, *e.g.* in *DAZ*, Jul 8, 1934.

92 'Diary of Viktor Lutze beginning with the ill-starred Jun 30, 1934,' handwritten volume in Friedrich Ebert Foundation archives, partially transcribed by Dr Ulrich Cartarius (hereafter Lutze diary). Publ. in part by *Frankfurter Rundschau*, May 14–16, 1957, and *Hannoversche Presse*, May 17, 1957. It was probably retrospectively written up from early 1936.

93 His London press attaché Dr Fitz Randolph reported to JG (unpubl. diary, Jun 27, 1934) on the damage done there by Papen's speech. 'The Herren-clique,' observed JG, 'cynically make use of foreigners, and hate me most of all.'

94 *Ibid.*, Jun 27, 1934.

95 *Ibid.*

96 Diary, Jun 29, 1934.

97 *Flensburger Nachrichten*, Jun 28; *Hamburger Nachrichten*, Jun 28, 1934 ('Dr Goebbels

settles accounts with the critics and grousers').

98 On Jun 25, 1934. See the dissertation by Karl Martin Grass, *Edgar Jung. Papenkreis und Röhmkrise 1933/34* (Heidelberg Univ., 1966), 242; cited by Heinz Höhne, *Mordsache Röhm* (Hamburg, 1984), 247. Jung's arrest was reported in *Basler Nachrichten*, Jun 30, 1934. See too Sefton Delmer's well-informed account of JG's clash with Papen and Jung in *Daily Express*, Jun 29, 1934.

99 Diary, Jun 29, 1934.

100 *Ibid.*

Notes to Chapter 23.

1 Thus infantry general Röhricht hypothesized that JG had joined Hitler's 'punitive expedition' to Munich primarily to escape the clutches of Himmler and Göring in Berlin (Kurt Dittmar diary, Sep 3, 1945; author's collection, film DI–60).

2 Lutze diary.

3 The nature of the Forschungsamt (FA) reports can only be conjectured. Ministerialrat Walther Seifert, former chief of the FA, wrote to Fritz Tobias on Mar 17, 1977 that both Schleicher and Bredow were wiretapped, though without much success. Milch recalled in a memoir written at Kaufbeuren on Sep 1, 1945 that Göring told him he had sent Körner by plane to Hitler with 'the final bits of evidence against Röhm & Co., probably mostly wiretaps' (Author's collection). Writing to this author on Jun 8, 1989, Klaus von Kitzing of the FA confirmed that their agency had exposed Röhm's plot, as does a BAOR (British Army of the Rhine) report on the FA, Jan 2, 1946 (NA file RG.226, XE.4986). The FA's Dr Gerhard Neuenhoff told this author that their section head Rudolf Popp had himself run the Röhm surveillance.

4 Hitler summarized their purported content to the Cabinet on Jul 3, 1934, 10 A.M. (BA file R.43I/1469); on the specific Forschungsamt intercept(s) concerned, see David Irving, *Das Reich hört mit* (Kiel, 1989).

5 Lutze diary.

6 Rosenberg diary, Jul 7, 1934; his observation of JG's psyche was astute. On Jan 4, 1935 JG would approvingly note (unpubl. diary) a visit to the state opera: 'Entire German leadership. Men only.'

7 He made a virtue of this in his broadcast on Jul 1: 'Once again the Führer acted on his old principle of only telling those who needed to know, and only what and when they needed' (*VB* Jul 1–2, 1934).

8 Diary, Jun 29, 1934. He repeated the phrase, 'So, it's on' (*Also geht es los*) in his unpubl. diary, Jul 1, 1934, recounting Friday's events. Probably he was quoting Hitler.

9 Unpubl. diary, Jul 1, 1934; this author corresponded with the late André François-Poncet, who denied any intrigue with Röhm; nor have French archives yet revealed any such plot. Hanfstaengl recalls one outburst by JG in autumn 1934 over dinner with Hitler in the chancellery, about the monarchists, Potsdam, and the army: 'These people will never change. One should get them together one fine day and mow them down – *reihenweise sollte man sie niederschiessen mit dem Maschinengewehr.*' Report on JG for Pres. Roosevelt, Jul 16, 1943 (FDR Libr., PSF box 126).

10 Fromm diary, Jul 3, citing a hotel employee (Fromm papers, box 2). Lutze diary, and JG broadcast, Jul 1, 1934.

11 Lutze diary.

12 The final death roll was probably eighty-three: NA film, T81, roll 90 (this source says that Klausener 'committed suicide on arrest'); on Strasser's murder see Frau Strasser to Frick, Oct 22, 1934 in Lothar Gruchmann's article in *VfZ*, 1971, 409f. One (unnamed) source, who had been present at Otto Strasser's May 6, 1930 meeting with Hitler, found himself in the next cell to Gregor Strasser as the shot was fired, and personally recognized the murderer: 'Strasser was taken into temporary protective custody on Jun 30, 1934 in the house jail of the Berlin Gestapo, Prinz-Albrecht-Strasse 8, in cell 15. A few hours after his arrival the cell door opened and Gregor was shot down by a personal friend and emissary of Dr Joseph Goebbels, a man named Weiss. . . Hitler completely lost control when he heard but was forced to cover up for Goebbels.' Hitler ordered the widow paid 500 marks per month from police compensation funds. (Memo by Counter-Intelligence Corps region III, Frankfurt, Mar 25, 1948: NA file RG.319, IRR, G8172121, Otto Strasser.) The death was listed as 'suicide' on the Nazi death roll (NA film T81, roll 90). However, the Reich Student-Führer Gustav Scheel told Karl-Heinrich Hederich once when *drunk* that Franz A Six (a student friend since Heidelberg who had however married Scheel's fiancée) had murdered Strasser. Hederich repeated this claim to Dr Werner Hagert (interrogation of Hagert, Sep 5, 1947: NA film M.1019, roll 23); unfortunately Hederich, interrogated Oct 23 and Dec 16, 1947 (*ibid.*, roll 25) was not asked about this.

13 Unpubl. diary, Jul 1, 1934. See the documentation on Schleicher's murder (with proof that his phone was bugged), in *VfZ*, 1953, 71ff.

14 Interview of Hitler's secretary Christa Schroeder, Jun 6, 1976.

15 Unpubl. diary, Jul 1, and 4, 1934: 'The public is right with us. A huge wave of enthusiasm goes through the land. The rebels got public opinion quite wrong.'

16 Broadcast, Jul 1; Phipps to Simon, Jul 2, 1934 (PRO file FO.371/17707).

17 Unpubl. diary, Jul 4, 1934.

18 *Ibid.*, Jul 6: 'S.A. question with Lutze. S.A.'s reputation needs boosting. I send a telegram along these lines to Lutze. The S.A. is to be retained. It's very downcast today;' and see Jul 7, 1934.

19 Schaumburg-Lippe, *War Hitler ein Diktator?*, 46f; JG, unpubl. diary, Jul 4, 1934.

20 BA file R.43I/1469. 'One can now see clearly again,' wrote JG (unpubl. diary, Jul 4, 1934). 'Events came dramatically to a head. The Reich was on the edge of an abyss. The Führer saved it.'

21 Unpubl. diary, Jul 4, 1934.

22 *Ibid.* Jul 6, 1934.

23 *Ibid.*, Jul 14, 1934.

24 Fromm diary, Jul 15, 1934 (Fromm papers, box 2); she identified her source as a ministry employee, 'Max K,' who described JG as being shrewd, unscrupulous, perverse, cynical, moody, and lascivious, driven by hatred of Schacht and the American journalist Dorothy Thompson (the feeling was mutual); and as being involved in desultory love affairs with Maria Stahl and Edith von Coler, subsequently the mistress of Hanns Johst and Darré.

25 Heydrich to JG, Nov 30, 1936 (ZStA Potsdam, Rep. 50.01, Diewerge papers, vol. 994).

26 Unpubl. diary, Jul 7, 1934.

27 JG broadcast, Jul 10, publ. in *Berliner Börsenzeitung* and *The Times*, Jul 11; see JG unpubl. diary, Jul 11, 1934.

28 Lochner to Betty, Jul 22 (Lochner papers, box 47); JG diary, Jui 13, 1934.

29 Renzetti to Mussolini, Jul 14, 1934 (Mussolini papers, NA film T586, roll 419, 9433).

30 Diary, Jul 18, 1934. Lutze deduced that Röhm had been set up by his enemies, and Hitler bamboozled. See Lutze's diary, the testimony of Wilhelm Brückner (IfZ, Irving collection), and an SS officer's report to Himmler on Lutze's later remarks (NA film T175, roll 3, 1892ff).

31 But at Bayreuth on Jul 21 a relaxed Hitler told JG more details about Röhm. 'Terrible! I am horrified,' noted JG in unpubl. diary, Jul 22, 1934.

32 *Ibid.*, Jul 9, 1934.

33 *Ibid.*, Jul 14, 1934.

34 *Ibid.* Ernst Hanfstaengl, 'I was Hitler's Closest Friend,' in *Cosmopolitan*, Mar 1943. – Ebermayer and Meissner, No. 19, May 10, 1952.

35 Magda Goebbels' correspondence with her friend Martha (ZStA Potsdam, Rep. 90, Go 2, Magda Goebbels, vol. 2).

36 Unpubl. diary, Jul 11, 1934.

37 *Ibid.*, Mar 17, Apr 11, 1934. See too *Der 25. Juli 1934 im Bundeskanzleramt in Wien. Forschungsergebnisse und Dokumente* (Vienna, 1965). – The full report of the 'Kommission des Reichsführers SS zur geschichtlichen Feststellung über die Erhebung vom 25. Juli 1934 in Österreich' is in Moscow archives, copies in the US Holocaust Memorial Museum, RG-11.001 M reel 452 and 453.

38 Unpubl. diary, Apr 28, 1934.

39 *Ibid.*, Jul 24, 1934.

40 *Ibid.*, Jul 26: 'Mountains out of molehills.' He was seeing Hela Strehl quite often (*ibid.*, Aug 2, 8) and, in Magda's absence, Ello Quandt ('Long parlaver [*sic*] with Ello. Talks about her [failing] marriage' – Aug 20, 1934).

41 Adam MS (IfZ file ED.109/2); on the Dollfuss murder see Helmuth Auerbach's paper in *VfZ*, 1964, 201ff.

42 Unpubl. diary, Jul 26, 1934.

43 *Ibid.*, Jul 28, 30, 1934. On Jul 28 Hitler told JG he had broken it off with Mussolini, and was going to deal with Yugoslavia instead. On Jul 31 JG noted, after seeing Hitler: 'Italy still being mean. We'll repay her later.' And on Aug 31: 'Discussed Italy question with [Prince] Philipp of Hesse. Mussolini's a puzzle to me.'

44 *Ibid.*, Jul 28, 1934.

45 *Ibid.*, Jul 31, 1934.

46 Cabinet, Aug 1, 1934; unpubl. diary, Aug 2; RGBl., 1934, I, 747; Lammers papers, NA film T580, roll 266.

47 Unpubl. diary, Aug 2, 1934.

48 *Ibid.*; rumors of a Hindenburg 'testament' dictated in his own favor by the wily Papen proved at first unfounded, 'so Papen loses out' (*ibid.*, Jul 31, Aug 4). A few days later the rumors caused Hitler and JG fresh alarm (*ibid.*, Aug 8). The document, published on Aug 15, betrayed Papen's authorship but was innocuous (*ibid.*, Aug 16, 1934).

49 *Ibid.*, Aug 8, 1934.

50 Diary, Aug 22, 1934.

51 Unpubl. diary, *Aug 20, 1934.*

52 *Berliner Morgenpost*, Sep 9, 1934.

53 *Verbiestert.* Unpubl. diary, Jul 4, 1934.

54 *Hamburger Tageblatt*, Aug 26, 1934.

55 *Berliner Lokalanzeiger*, Sep 17, 1934.

56 Dr Carl von Eicken's consultation notes, Aug 1934 (NA film ML.131).

57 JG to Bormann, Aug 17, 1934 (ZStA Potsdam, Rep. 90, Go 1, Goebbels, vol. 3).

58 Daimler Benz to JG, Nov 7, 1934 (ibid).

59 RMVP budget files (ibid., Rep. 50.01, vol. 1059).

60 Farmers, *Rheinisch-Westfälische Zeitung*, Oct 1; Labor Service, *12 Uhr Blatt*, Oct 24; youth, *ibid.*, Nov 2, 1934.

61 *Deutsche Zeitung*, Nov 20, 1934.

62 US interrogation of Weiss, Aug 31, 1945 (NA file RG.332, entry ETO, Mis-Y, Sect., box 116).

63 Note by NSDAP Kreisleitung Bitterfeld, Sep 14, 1934 (ZStA Potsdam, Rep. 50.01, vol. 1175).

64 *DAZ*, Dec 1, 1934.

65 *Ibid.*, Dec 12, 1934. On Jul 2, 1934 (unpubl. diary, Jul 4) he gave Erich Hilgenfeldt, chief of the NSV, directions for the coming Winter Relief: 'It's got to be really big.'

66 Borresholm, 101f.

67 Figures , announced by JG, *Berliner Lokalanzeiger*, Oct 9, 1934.

68 *12 Uhr Blatt*, Oct 15, 1934.

69 Cabinet meeting, Dec 13, 1934, 4:15 P.M. (Lammers papers; NA film T580, roll 266).

70 Unpubl. diary, Dec 15, 1934 (Moscow archives, Goebbels papers, box 5); in January (unpubl. diary Jan 4) he found Hitler still poorly. 'Got to find a good doctor.'

71 *Ibid.*, Feb 4, 1935.

72 Diary, Dec 25, 1934.

73 *Ibid.*, Sep 17, 21, 24, 1934.

74 Behrend, No. 18, May 3, 1952; Ebermayer and Meissner, No. 23, Jun 7, 1952.

75 Wilhelm Furtwängler on Hindemith's opera *Mathis der Maler*, in *DAZ*, Nov 25, 1934; *cf.* Joseph Wulf, *Musik im Dritten Reich* (Frankfurt, 1983), 373ff. A scene in this opera portraying the public burning of heretical writings was evidently the cause of the Nazis' discontent. As recently as Jun 25, 1934 JG had publicly praised Hindemith as one of Germany's up-and-coming musical talents.

76 Described in a 50pp. MS by Detig for Dr Karl Silex, Feb 1970 (in Tobias archives); and see Detig's affidavit, Jul 3, 1948 (StA Nuremberg). – JG diary, Jan 2, 1935.

Notes to Chapter 24.

1 *DAZ*, Dec 1, 1934.

2 *Berliner Lokalanzeiger*, Dec 15, 1934; *Berliner Nachtausgabe*, Jan 2, 1935.

3 Unpubl. diary, Jan 4, 1935. (From the diary volume Oct 23, 1933 – Jun 28, 1935: Moscow archives, Goebbels papers, box 5).

4 Dr Werner Best (IfZ). On Hitler's speech: diaries of Leeb, Milch, and testimonies of Raeder, Fritsch MS, and Adm. Hermann Boehm (IfZ file ZS.12).

5 Unpubl. diary, Jan 6, 1935. 'Interesting visit.' Ludmilla Babkova (stage name Lida Baarova) was born in Prague on Sep 7, 1914. Her recollections, including memoirs in her native Czech, *Sweet Bitterness of Life*, are singularly free of spleen against JG. The author interviewed her in Salzburg, Jul 4, 1993; *cf.* Gustav Fröhlich, *Waren das Zeiten. Mein Film-Heldenleben* (Munich, Berlin, 1983), 362f, and BA file R.55/412.

6 Unpubl. diary, Jan 6, 1935; confirmed by Baarova, interviews; and MI.14 report NOI/108, based on data from an unnamed 'talent scout in the German film world' repeating

very accurately details known, he said, only to Hitler, JG, Sepp Dietrich, Baarova, and himself, Mar 15, 1944 (PRO file WO.208/4462).

7 Author's interview of Lida Baarova, Salzburg, Jul 4, 1993.

8 On Jan 29; unpubl. diary, Jan 31; and very similar *ibid.*, Feb 4, 1935.

9 *Ibid.*, Jan 6, 1935.

10 *Berliner Lokalanzeiger*, Jan 7, 1935.

11 Taubert report.

12 Unpubl. diary, Jan 16, 1935: 'Triumph of Patriotism!'

13 Confidential report by a Capt. Glas in Austria, from Berlin on Jan 18, 1935, forwarded by Wickham Steed to Orme Sargent, FO, Jan 28, 1935 (PRO file FO.371/18824). When *Giornale d'Italia* reported on Feb 8, 1935, 'A Goebbels speech on a plan of operations to return all Germans to the Reich,' specifying particularly Memel and Austria, JG protested in *VB*, Munich, Feb 9, 1935, against this 'poisoning of the wells.' (NA film T81, roll 667, 5251ff). For Glas, see unpubl. diary, Jul 23, 1939.

14 Unpubl. diary, Jan 22, 1935.

15 *Ibid.*, Dec 17, 1934. 'I think I won him. It's worthwhile talking to such people.'

16 *Ibid.*, Dec 21, 1934. The German transcripts of these conferences, captured by the British after the war, are now missing. Some of Rothermere's fulsome correspondence with Hitler is in BA file NS.10/5, and in the Hoover Libr., Hohenlohe papers.

17 Diary, Jan 27. On Jan 20 Hitler had told JG that Poland was standing by Germany; France and Britain were preparing to blackmail Poland (unpubl. diary, Jan 22, 1935).

18 Speech report by Phipps to FO, Feb 25, 1935 (PRO file FO.371/18857). On Jan 22, JG noted: 'Become a Power. Everything else then sorts itself out.'

19 Rosenberg to Hess, Feb 26, 1935 (Rosenberg papers, NA film T454, roll 74, 0704f).

20 Diary, Feb 11, 1935.

21 Fromm diary, Jul 15, 1934 (Fromm papers, box 2).

22 Darré diary, Mar 28, 1935.

23 Phipps to Simon, Mar 22; and to Sargent, May 9 (PRO file FO.371/18879); unpubl. JG diary, Apr 5, 1935: 'A lot of criticism [at Hitler's lunch table] of Göring's marriage pomp. That'll damage us a lot in the people's eyes.'

24 Unpubl. diary, Mar 18, 1935. That evening Hitler told him Phipps had been astonished, but raised no objection; François-Poncet had protested briefly, Cerutti had paled, and 'Lipski was delighted.'

25 Diary, Mar 22, 1935.

26 Unpubl. diary, Mar 25, 1935. Over dinner, after further talks, Hitler told JG that Simon was in a good mood: 'Führer again confirms my characterization of the two.' JG considered the talks a success: 'Now they know what's what. We sit up with the Führer until 4 A.M. and gossip. He's really pleased.'

27 *Ibid.*, Apr 1, 1935. 'Evening . . . Long time with the Führer, together with Göring and Blomberg. . . We must remain steadfast and firm. Don't let them bluff us! But the Führer's got good nerves.'

28 Taubert report.

29 Unpubl. diary, Apr 3, 1935: '[Hitler] has big worries. Ribbentrop brings fresh news. None too cheerful. We've got to watch out like hell.'

30 *Ibid.*, Apr 5, 1935.

31 *Ibid*, Apr 7, 1935.

32 Robert T Smallbones to British embassy, Apr 18, 1935 (PRO file for other views on JG see

Phipps to Sargent, Feb 13, and to Simon, May 4, 1935 (*ibid.*).

33 Diary, Mar 2; *NYT*, Mar 1; unpubl. diary, Apr 11, 1935.

34 JG to Rosenberg, Aug 25, 1934 (BA file NS.8/171); and see Wulf, *Musik*, 194.

35 *NYT*, Jun 12, 24–26; diary, Jul 5, 13, 1935.

36 Gestapo to Stapoleitstelle, Berlin, Dec 27, 1934; Heydrich to Himmler, Apr 16 (BA file R.58/739). *VB*, Mar 29. Unpubl. diary, May 9, 13, 1935.

37 Unpubl. diary, Jan 10, 1935.

38 *Ibid.*, Jan 12, 1935. 'In her second month. . . I hope, I hope it's a boy!'

39 Diary, Mar 22, Aug 1, 15, Sep 8, 1935.

40 Unpubl. diary, Apr 9, 11, 1935.

41 Diary, Apr 29, Sep 19, 25, Oct 1, 1935.

42 *Ibid.*, Apr 15, Aug 1, Sep 4, 1935.

43 *Ibid.*, Apr 21, 23, 1935.

44 *Ibid.*, Jul 3, 1935: 'I console her to the best of my ability.'

45 *Ibid.*, Jul 8, 1935.

46 *Ibid.*, Jul 13, 1935.

47 Fromm diary, Nov 12, 1935 (Fromm papers, box 2).

48 Diary, Aug 3, 1935.

49 *Ibid.*, Jul 25, Aug 9, 15, 27, 31, 1935.

50 *Ibid.*, Sep 25, 1935.

51 *Ibid.*, Oct 3, 1935.

52 *Ibid.*, Oct 5, 1935. Otto Meissner's wife later claimed that the real father was Hitler: *Stars & Stripes*, Oct 9, 1946.

53 Post-mortem on Hellmut Goebbels, May 1945; Behrend, No. 8, Feb 22, 1952; JG diary, Oct 3, 1941 on the need to put Hellmut with other boys. 'Nothing'll come of a boy who grows up surrounded by girls' (BA file NL.118/28).

54 Diary, Oct 24, 1935.

55 *Ibid.*, Nov 21, 1935.

56 *Ibid.*, Oct 26, 1935.

57 *Ibid.*, Oct 24, 1935; and ZStA Potsdam, Rep. 50.01, vol. 748.

58 Diary, Oct 9, 1935.

59 Borresholm, 139.

60 Diary, Dec 9, 11, 1935.

61 JG to Anka, Christmas 1935 (Irene Pranger papers); diary, Jan 1, 9, 1936.

62 Diary, Jan 11, 19, 21, 23, 1936.

63 *Ibid.*, Jan 29, 1936.

64 *Ibid.*, Mar 4, 1936.

65 *Ibid.*, Aug 21–27, 1935; JG's testimony in subsequent court proceedings, 1936 (BA file Kl. Erw. 550); Daluege's final report (BA file R.19/77), and police file (*ibid.*, /406).

66 Diary, Oct 11, 13, 1935; the deaths of Gauleiter Wilhelm Loeper and Ministerialrat Otto Laubinger, head of his Dept VI, Theater, also unsettled him: *Ibid.*, Oct 24, 26, 28, Nov 1, 9, 1935.

67 RMVP budget for fiscal 1935. Revenues were 18·45m marks higher than estimated; increased domestic propaganda and cultural efforts would increase costs to 37,893,650 marks, partly offset by savings from closing down the Pornographic Literature Censorship office. Rebuilding the opera house had cost 2·9m. JG's ministerial salary was 102,840 marks less 21,640 across-the-board cut, or 86,000 net ($21,000). (ZStA Potsdam,

Rep. 50.01, vol. 1059).

68 Julian Petley, *Capital and Culture. German Cinema 1933–45* (London, 1979), 60; Viktoria de Grazia, 'Mass Culture and Sovereignty. The American Challenge to European Cinemas, 1920–1960,' in *Journal of Modern History*, vol. 61, Mar 1989, 53ff.

69 Diary, Oct 15, 1935.

70 Première in Munich's Gloria Palace cinema, Mar 28; Best Film, May 1; major triumph at Venice festival (diary, Aug 27, 1935).

71 Interview with Riefenstahl, Jul 15, 1989. Ufa Filmverleih loaned 300,000 marks to her to make *Triumph*, of which she used 270,000. JG diary, Mar 25 (unpubl.), Aug 17, 21, Oct 3, 10, Nov 7, 1935.

72 Diary, Nov 27, 1935.

73 *Ibid.*, Jul 21, 23, Aug 17, 1935.

74 *Ibid.*, Sep 6, 9, 1935.

75 Interrogation of Hans Fritzsche, Nov 1, 1946 (StA Nuremberg, F86); and Karl Hederich, Jul 9, 1948 (*ibid.*, G15).

76 Diary, Jul 15, 1936; he referred to the demo in a speech at Essen, Aug 4; Newton to Hoare, Aug 6, 1935 (PRO file FO.371/18858).

77 *12 Uhr Blatt*, Feb 17, 1933.

78 Rösner to legal Dept of S.A. Gruppe Berlin-Brandenburg, May 4, 1935, quoting witnesses Oberführer von Arnim and (the late) Karl Ernst. Hanussen's killers were named as the S.A. men Schmidt alias Schweinbacke, Obersturmbannführer Ohst (Ernst's adjutant), and Steinle (BDC file, Helldorff).

79 S.A. Gruppe Berlin-Brandenburg to Röhm, Mar 29, 1933 (BDC file, Helldorff).

80 Rösner minute, Feb 2, 1935; in Helldorff's file (BDC) are receipts for 500 and 1,000 marks signed by him on Feb 9 and Mar 4, and by Stabsführer von Arnim for 400 marks on Mar 4, 1933.

81 Diary, Jul 19, 1935; and BDC file, Helldorff.

82 *Manchester Guardian*, Aug 24, 1935: 'Starving out the Jews.' RMVP to German FO, Sep 9, 1935 (NA film T120, roll 467, 4318).

83 Taubert report. Acquitted at the Reichstag Fire trial, Torgler had been taken into 'protective custody' during which he and fellow communist deputy Maria Reese jointly wrote this manuscript. The book was suppressed (JG diary, Dec 2), but Torgler himself was freed (diary, Dec 23, 1935); Hitler subsequently paid him 800 marks monthly as a consultant provided he did not resume his public career (diary, Dec 25–26, 1937). In 1940 he began working for the RMVP's 'black' transmitters. See BA files R.55/450, 567, and 1289.

84 *Kommunismus ohne Maske* (Munich, 1935); Phipps to Hoare, Sep 16, 1935 (PRO file FO.371/18883).

85 For Hitler's reluctance, see *e.g.* diary, Jun 25, 1936: 'Führer strongly disapproves of work of all the race agencies.'

86 Circular directive by Hinkel to presidents of the sub-chambers, Apr 29, 1936 (BA file R.56V/102).

87 Diary, Sep 17, 1935.

88 *Ibid.*, Oct 1, 5, Nov 1, 7, 15, 1935.

89 *Ibid.*, Sep 19, 1935.

90 *Ibid.*, Sep 25, 1935. The Bundesarchiv would not permit the author to review the missing word. See author's Acknowledgments, page viii.

91 Diary, Oct 1, 1935.

92 *Ibid.*, Oct 19; Cabinet, Oct 18; and see Oct 26, Nov 15, 1935.

93 *Ibid.*, Nov 1, 1935.

94 *Ibid.*, Nov 6, 1935. Emil Ludwig, *Der Mord in Davos* (Amsterdam, 1936), on which see ZStA Potsdam, Rep. 50.01, vol. 998.

95 *Ibid.*, Dec 9–16, 1936. Speaking at Magdeburg in 'impressive language' (Phipps) on the world menace of Jewry, JG stated: 'I regret that the foreign press should display the attitude "it is not the murderer but the murder victim who is guilty"' (Phipps to FO, Feb 22, 1936. PRO file FO.371/19922).

96 Files on the case in ZStA Potsdam, Rep. 50.01, vols. 570, 714–15, 994–7, 999, 1040.

97 Diary Jul 5, 1936.

98 Phipps to FO, Nov 3, 1936 (PRO file FO.371/19924).

99 JG speech to Eleventh International Penal and Prison congress in Berlin, Aug 1935 (*ibid.*, /18880); *NYT,* Aug 28, 1935.

100 JG speech to Wehrmacht academy, 'The Nature of Propaganda' (NA film T78, roll 372, 5312ff).

101 Unpubl. diary, May 15, 1935.

102 *Ibid.*, May 15, 25, 27, 1935.

103 *Ibid.*, May 27, 1935.

104 Diary, Aug 19, 1935. As Italy became more deeply involved in Abyssinia JG longed for Britain to declare war on Italy. 'That's when we'll reap the harvest.'

105 *Ibid.*, Oct 13, 15, 1935.

106 JG speech to the gau, Jan 17 – the *DAZ*, Jan 18, alone printed the missing passage; Phipps to FO, Jan 18 (PRO file FO.371/19922); *The Times*, Jan 18, 1936.

107 Diary, Jan 21, 1936.

108 JG speech in Cologne, Jan 24; British consul-general in Cologne, J E Bell, to Phipps, Jan 27, 29, 1936 (PRO file FO.371/19884).

109 Diary, Feb 29, 1936.

110 *Ibid.*, Mar 2, 1936.

111 *Ibid.*, Mar 6, 1936.

112 *Ibid.*, Mar 8, 1936.

113 *Ibid.*, Mar 17, 1936.

Notes to Chapter 25.

1 JG proclamation, Mar 24, 1936; PRO file FO.371/19884.

2 Diary, Mar 19, 1936.

3 See Phipps to Eden, Mar 31, 1936 (PRO file FO.371/1923).

4 Diary, Feb 17, 1936.

5 Diary, Mar 15, 1936.

6 *Ibid.*, Mar 22, 1936. Recollections differ on how JG financed this deal, *e.g.* Winkler, interrogated by Korf on May 1, 1948. It seems JG merely promised to pay, and completed the deal in Nov 1936. Amann confirmed to Korf, May 4, 1948 that he recalled Hitler saying to him in Thiersch Strasse, Munich that he wanted JG to have a stylish home in Berlin, and that JG needed 300,000 or 370,000 marks to buy a property. 'If I had the money,' said Hitler, 'I'd give it him. Goebbels is one of Eher's best authors.' Amann, no fool, checked

his firm's royalty accounts before advancing the money. His version, and Hitler's role, are independently confirmed by his accountant Joseph Pickel, questioned by Korf on May 13, 1948 (Hoover Libr., Korf papers).

7 *Basler National Zeitung*, Dec 11, 1945. The lot at No. 8–10 Inselstrasse was finally 8,740 square meters in size. A Mr Ludwig of Osnabrück claimed after the war that JG had owed him money for the purchase of the plot. Ludwig and a trustee for Nazi property secured the appointment by the Berlin-Zehlendorf *Amtsgericht* (District Court) of the lawyer Dr Kurt Leyke as administrator on Sep 21, 1954; on Oct 16, 1954 the West Berlin authorities commenced *Wiedergutmachung* (restitution) proceedings against the Goebbels estate and confiscated it. *Tagesspiegel*, Berlin, Nov 24, 1954; and see the papers of Dr Leyke (BA file Kl. Erw. 858).

8 Reuth, 340, citing the Schwanenwerder Land Registry in Schöneberg magistrates' court; the sale was registered on Apr 25, 1935.

9 Hanfstaengel, report on JG for Pres. Roosevelt, Jul 16, 1943 (FDR Libr., PSF box 126).

10 Diary, Mar 29, 1936.

11 *Ibid*, Apr 20, 1936.

12 *Ibid.*, Apr 4, 6, 8, 11, 1936.

13 *Ibid.*, Oct 22, 1936. Winkler and Amann, questioned by Korf, May 1 and 3, 1948, were vague about the details.

14 The real-estate files of the Zehlendorf courthouse confirm that JG paid the whole 270,000 marks in cash; see Korf's interview of JG's conveyancing attorney Dr Alfons Knatsch, Apr 12, 1948. For the 1936 royalty account see the Publisher's Note prefacing Louis P Lochner (ed.), *The Goebbels Diaries* (London, 1948), ix; and Hoover Libr., Goebbels papers, box 2.

15 Diary, Apr 20, 1936; Behrend, No. 17, Apr 26, 1952.

16 JG to Reichshauptkasse, Apr 7, 1936 (ZStA, Potsdam, Rep. 90, Go 1, vol. 3).

17 Diary, May 2, 5, 7, 11, 1936 records their constant rows.

18 *Ibid.*, May 8, 1936.

19 *Ibid.*, Jul 8, 9, 1936.

20 *Ibid.*, Apr 16, May 3, Jun 13, Jul 9, 1936.

21 Ernst Hanfstaengel, report on JG for Pres. Roosevelt, Jul 16, 1943 (FDR Libr. PSF box 126).

22 Diary, Jul 9, 1936.

23 *Ibid.*, Apr 18, 19, 26, May 8, 13, Jun 23, 1936.

24 *Ibid.*, Jul 14, 1936.

25 Ondra: *Ibid.*, May 19, Jun 11; Edda: Jun 8, 9, 1936: 'The Führer does not like painted ladies either.'

26 Fromm diary, Jun 12, 1936 (Fromm papers, box 2; *cf.* MS in box 61).

27 Diary, Jul 2, 1936.

28 *Ibid.*, Jun 25, 1936.

29 *Ibid.*, Jun 16, 1936.

30 *Ibid.*, Feb 2, 1937.

31 Unpubl. diary, Apr 27, 1935 (Moscow archives).

32 Diary, Jun 19, 1936: JG noted that Mosley said he had been promised £60,000 and 'has already received £2,000.' Despite contemporary denials by Sir Oswald, the author found in Italian ambassador Dino Grandi's files the receipts and reports on transfers of substantial cash sums to Mosley in 1936 (Archivio Segreto dello Stato, Rome). While

it must be said there is *no* corresponding evidence in German files, Diana Mosley now admits, 'It is difficult to argue with a diary' (letter to the author, Jan 22, 1994).

33 Diary, Jun 20, 1936.

34 In a self-serving interrogation (6824 DIC[MIS]/M.1169), Otto Dietrich called Wrede 'an arrogant, stupid, fanatic Nazi.'

35 Diary, Jun 24, Jul 29, 1936.

36 *Ibid.*, Aug 6, 7, 1936.

37 Perhaps Hitler's former adviser, the playboy Kurt G Lüdecke; JG also employed a manservant Lüdecke at Lanke – but Magda is unlikely to have crossed the class-barrier. Rosenberg had met JG in the training center of the Party's foreign policy agency (APA) in Berlin-Dahlem on Jul 31, to set aside their differences. (Rosenberg to JG, Aug 28, 1936. Rosenberg papers, NA film, T454, roll 74, 0601ff); JG diary, Aug 1, 1936.

38 Diary, Aug 2, 1936.

39 *Ibid.*, Aug 5, 7, 1936.

40 *Ibid.*, Jul 7, 8, 1936.

41 See BA file R.55/509.

42 Diary, Jun 26, 1936.

43 *Ibid.*, Aug 6, 1936; Cooper C Graham, *Leni Riefenstahl and Olympia* (London, 1986).

44 Schaub MS (IfZ file ED.100/203, Irving collection).

45 Fröhlich, 367; the film was *Stunde der Versuchung* – JG noted (Jun 10, 1936) it was corny, but 'the Baarova woman' acted well.

46 Lochner to children, Aug 1936 (FDR Libr., Toland papers, box 52); *cf.* William E Dodd, *Ambassador Dodd's Diary* , 349f. On JG's two Peacock Island parties see BA file R.55/511, and Gutterer MS (Lower Saxony provincial archives, Wolfenbüttel).

47 Diary, Jun 27, 1936.

48 *Ibid.*, Jul 30; first outing in it, Sep 30, 1936.

49 *Ibid.*, Aug 28, 1936.

50 *Ibid.*, Aug 11, 1936.

Notes to Chapter 26.

1 'Tagebuch für Joseph Goebbels vom 15. September 1936 bis 12. February 1937.' On micro-fiche in Moscow archives, Goebbels papers, box 1.

2 Holde Goebbels was born in Feb 1937 after seven months, *i.e.*, conceived around July 1936. A sickly, quiet child, she was later spurned by her sisters as 'slow-witted and boring.' JG ribbed her mercilessly and often reduced her to tears (Ebermayer and Meissner, No. 20, May 17, 1952).

3 Based primarily on Lida Baarova: interviewed by the author, Jul 4, 1993; by Ota Filip (transcript courtesy of R G Reuth); and by Westdeutscher Rundfunk, May 1991 ('Goebbels through the Eyes of Ufa Star Lida Baarova'). See too the articles in *Die Wochenpost*, Stuttgart, Nov 20, 1949 (IfZ archives) and by Stan Czech (former Ufa employee and historian), in *Heim und Welt*, Hanover, No. 8 *et seq.*, Feb 1950 (hereafter Czech).

4 Diary, Aug 19, 1936.

5 Diary, Sep 1; *cf.* Basil C Newton to Eden, and Wigram to Eden, Aug 1936, in PRO file FO.371/20417.

6 JG, *Der Bolschewismus in Theorie und Praxis* (Berlin, 1936). The speech, based on drafts

from Taubert (diary, Sep 2, 4), ran to 64pp.. Hitler was delighted (diary, Sep 8); 15pp. summary by B C Newton to Eden, Sep 11, 1936 (PRO file FO.371/19948).

7 Baarova interviews; *cf.* JG diary, Sep 10, 1936.

8 Diary, Sep 11, 1936.

9 *Ibid.*, Sep 12, 1936.

10 *Ibid.*, Sep 15, 1936.

11 Westdeutscher Rundfunk interview. For what it is worth, Julius Schaub later insisted that JG's affair with Lida Baarova was the only one he ever had with an actress, and that his reputation resulted from malicious movie star gossip: manuscript in Irving collection (IfZ file ED. 100/202).

12 Diary, May 12: lunch with the Führer, who has 'grandiose plans' on foreign policy. On Nov 30, 1936 JG noted that Hitler was applying his mind to the production of scarce raw materials like copper and iron ore within Germany.

13 *Ibid.*, May 30, 1936.

14 *Ibid.*, May 3, 1936.

15 *Ibid.*, Apr 15; and see Oct 16, 1936.

16 *Ibid.*, Jun 9, 1936.

17 *Ibid.*, Nov 27, 1936.

18 *Ibid.*, Apr 4, 6, 16, May 11, 9, Jun 17, Jul 14, Aug 1, Oct 6, 21; correspondence, Apr 1-Nov 24, 1936 in Rosenberg's files, NA film T454, roll 74, 0580ff; BA file R56/102.

19 Diary, Oct 6, 21, 1936.

20 Unpubl. diary, Apr 5, 1935.

21 Interview of Rudolf von Ribbentrop, Jul 20, 1989.

22 Diary, Sep 18, 19, 1936.

23 *Ibid*, Oct 2, 1936; interviews of Lida Baarova.

24 For JG's Bogensee estate see CSDIC (UK) SIR. 1008, an interrogation of the Lanke forester Kloss, Sep 26, 1944, with his sketch plan; JG diary, Sep 16–18, 29, 30, Oct 4, 12, 23, Nov 13, 1936. – For JG's 1939 staff lists at Lanke see BA file R.55/14.

25 Diary, Sep 27, 1936. 'Tagebuch für Joseph Goebbels am 29. Oktober 1936 bis Dezember 1939 (Haus am Bogensee)' (microfiche in Moscow archives, Goebbels papers, box 1).

26 *Ibid.*, Oct 6, 1936.

27 *Ibid.*, Oct 11, 1936: Magda is 'always the same: friendly, nice, obliging, amiable. I like her best of all.'

28 Who did not come down? The diary (Oct 13, 1936) does not specify.

29 *Ibid.*, Oct 29, 1936.

30 A former Berlin film talent scout told MI.14, British Intelligence, in 1944 that 'the sole inhabitant [at Lanke] is a manservant [Kaiser] who is sent away in the evening when Goebbels entertains. It is here that Goebbels brings women secretly, offering them two alternatives: either to drive back with him to Berlin, or to remain for dinner. . . ' (PRO file WO.208/4462).

31 SS Untersturmführer Alfred Rach, born Feb 8, 1911 in East Prussia, a stocky, blue-eyed ex-fitter with a broad Danzig accent, had been JG's second chauffeur since the beginning of 1933 (BDC file). To him would later fall the grim task of burning his master's corpse.

32 Interviewed in prison by *Pinguin* (Hamburg).

33 Diary, Nov 2, 1936.

34 *Ibid.*, Nov 12, 1936.

35 *Ibid.*, Nov 18, 1936.

36 *Ibid.*, Sep 17, 20, 1936; information from Lady Mosley, Jan 12 and 22, 1994, and see her memoirs *A Life of Contrasts and Loved Ones.* W E D Allen, a former Conservative MP, and Captain Gordon-Cumming were Mosley's witnesses, Diana's sister Unity Mitford and Magda were the bridesmaids.

37 *Ibid.*, Oct 12, Nov 14, 25, Dec 5, 1936.

38 R Likus to Ribbentrop, Dec 17, 1936 (NA film T120, roll 31); Lochner to his children, Dec 10, 1936 (Lochner papers, box 2).

39 Diary, Jan 23, Apr 12, 1937.

40 *Ibid.*, Jan 20, Oct 2, 1937.

41 *Ibid.*, Jan 12, Feb 7, Apr 10, 12, Aug 14, 1937. Lady Mosley does not believe that Hitler provided funds, as the diary suggests; he did however help her to meet Ohnesorge, Eltz's successor as post-office minister, about Sir Oswald's plan for commercial broadcasting; the French government had allowed Capt. L, Plugge, the Conservative MP, to establish Radio Normandy on a similar basis.

42 Diary, Jul 5, 1936.

43 *Ibid.*, Jul 18, 1936.

44 *Ibid.*, Oct 21, 1936.

45 *Ibid.*, Jan 22; text of JG's speech to the Wehrmacht course on the elements of Nazi propaganda, Jan 21, 1937 (BA file R.55/1338).

46 *Ibid.*, Sep 21, 1937. The RMVP subsequently drafted a general plan for propaganda in a hypothetical war, and insisted on independent control of this 'new weapon' (Yivo file G−93).

47 Diary, Jan 4, 5, 1937.

48 Including Erika Dannhoff, who is (diary, Jan 11, 1937) in a good mood and amiable: 'So she's learned her lesson from our last talk.'

49 Diary, Jan 18, 1937.

50 MS of Fromm diary, "Feb 20, 1937' (Fromm papers, box 61).

51 Diary, Mar 4, 8, 11, 25, 1937.

52 *Ibid.*, Feb 3, 1937.

53 *Ibid.*, Feb 11; and see Jan 11, 1937.

54 Günther Rettelsky to JG, Feb 26, 1937, re Max Kimmich, born Nov 4, 1893 in Ulm (ZStA Potsdam, Magda Goebbels papers, Rep. 90 Go 2, vol. 2); diary, Feb 18, 1937.

55 Diary, Feb 3, 4, 1937.

56 *Ibid.*, Mar 2, 4, 1937.

57 *Ibid.*, Mar 18; on Mar 8, 1937 JG had written, 'The old fool! Final fling.'

58 *Ibid.*, Mar 5, 1937.

59 Diary, Dec 10, 1937.

60 *Ibid.*, Mar 11, 13, 15, 18, 1937. According to the talent scout mentioned above, when Falcken-berg refused to become JG's 'one-night mistress' he banned her in Germany; she escaped to Italy and married an Italian (PRO file WO.208/4462). This well-informed source says that the same fate befell Hedda Uhlen, and that when JG had the wife of a Dr Wittmann 'kidnapped' and taken out to Lanke, a scandal ensued.

61 *Ibid.*, Feb 3, 6, 7, 16, 20, 1937.

62 Cabinet, Jan 30, 1937; Milch MS; JG diary, Jan 31, 1937.

63 Karl-Wilhelm Krause, *Zehn Jahre Tag und Nacht. Kammerdiener bei Hitler* (Hamburg, 1949) (hereafter Krause), 52.

64 Diary, Feb 6, 1937.

65 *Ibid.*, Feb 16; Bormann diary, Feb 15, 1937.

66 *Ibid.*, Feb 23; Bormann diary, Feb 22, 1937.

Notes to Chapter 27.

1 Diary, Jan 29, Mar 3, 1937; *passim*, 1938.

2 *Ibid.*, May 5, 15, 1937.

3 Table talk, dinner, Feb 24–25, 1942. Heinrich Heim, *Monologe im Führerhauptquartier 1941–1944* (Munich, 1980), 295; English edition, 1953, 334.

4 Darré diary, Feb 8, 1937, lunch. 'Der Spötter des Dritten Reiches.'

5 Magda told Count Ciano (Ciano diary, May 21, 1939) that dinner with Hitler was stupendously boring.

6 Friedelind Wagner, *Nacht über Bayern* (Munich, 1947).

7 Traudl Junge née Humbs MS (in author's possession) (hereafter Junge MS).

8 Capt. Herbert Friedrichs, interview, Nov 19, 1972, and letter to author, Apr 4, 1989; in his diary, Jan 31, 1938 JG notes one dinner: 'Frau von Dirksen goes yakking on, pure rubbish. I'm furious with her. The Führer is much too indulgent toward her.'

9 Behrend, No. 19, May 10, 1952.

10 Diary, Jun 13, 1941.

11 Hanfstaengl, report on JG for Pres. Roosevelt, Jul 16, 1943 (FDR Libr., PSF box 126).

12 Affidavits by Karl Bodenschatz, Wilhelm Brückner, and others in the Irving collection, IfZ.

13 Interviews of naval adjutant Karl-Jesco von Puttkamer in 1967.

14 Krause, 15ff.

15 *Ibid.*, and Hans-Leo Martin, *Unser Mann bei Goebbels* (Neckargemünd, 1973) (hereafter Hans-Leo Martin).

16 Diary, Feb 24, 1937: 'Greeted everywhere most warmly by the people.'

17 Minute by Stevenson, FO, Jun 15, 1937, citing former diplomat Count Albrecht Bernstorff (PRO file FO. 371/20733); Bernstorff was shot after the July 1944 plot.

18 Diary, Dec 1, 12, 13, 1937. 'One has to make an example of him.'

19 Junge MS.

20 Julius Streicher diary, Nov 13, 1945; by kind permission of Karl Höffkes.

21 Diary, Aug 15, 1937.

22 Darré diary, Feb 22, 1938.

23 This was on Apr 24, 1937. Hans Kehrl, *Krisenmanager im Dritten Reich* (Düsseldorf, 1973) (hereafter Kehrl), 82ff. JG's diary, May 1, 1937 puts a different gloss on it: he had been 'cordially welcomed' everywhere. He then admitted that the 'ill-disciplined' Kreisleiter had all muttered against his speech and he was going to draw the necessary conclusions. 'I tick off [Ley] again about the Vogelsang scandal.' On Jun 13, 1937, he said it was the last time he would make such a speech. 'The Kreisleiter are little demigods,' he wrote on Jan 11, 1938, still furious about the humiliating episode.

24 Diary, Dec 25, 1937: he listens to the broadcast of his conversations with the children, as presents are handed over.

25 *Ibid.*, Dec 5, 1937. The first day of the 1937/8 WHW raised 8·5m marks, 32·5 percent more than the year before.

26 'Material received by the Minister of Propaganda,' Libr. of Congress, film reel 20,

containers 43, 44.

27 Diary, Oct 30, 1937.

28 *Illustrierter Beobachter*, Oct 21, 1937.

29 Kurt Prager to Magda Goebbels, Nov 7, 1937 (Libr. of Congress, film reel 20, containers 43, 44).

30 Kirkpatrick to Strang, FO, Jan 12, 1938 (PRO file FO.371/21660). He traded in the Maybach for a Horch, then a 200hp Mercedes (diary, Oct 26, 1937; Jan 1, Feb 19, 1938); Ogilvie-Forbes to Eden, Jan 4, 1938 (PRO file FO.371/21671). For more detail on the RMVP's cars 1935–43 see BA file R.55/418.

31 Diary, Mar 21, 24, 1937.

32 *Ibid.*, Mar 31, Apr 2, 1937. Hans Günter Hockerts, *Die Sittlichkeitsprozesse gegen katholische Ordensangehörige und Priester 1936/37* (Mainz, 1971).

33 Diary, Apr 4–6, 1937.

34 *Ibid*, Apr 6, 7, 13, 1937.

35 *Ibid*, Apr 26, 29, 1937.

36 *Ibid*, Apr 30, 1937.

37 *Ibid.*, May 1, 1937.

38 *Ibid*, May 4, 1937.

39 *Ibid*, May 12, 13; further church trials that summer, *ibid.*, Jul 1, 4, 1937.

40 *Ibid.*, May 25–26, 1937; this claims that Hitler, cruising with him off Schwanenwerder, gave him tips for the speech.

41 Sir Nevile Henderson to FO, May 29, 1937 (PRO file, FO.371/20727).

42 Diary, Jun 14, 1937.

43 *Ibid*, Jun 3, 4, 1937.

44 *Ibid*, Aug 1, 4, 1937.

45 *Ibid.*, Aug 7, 1937.

46 *Ibid*, Aug 8, 13, 1937.

47 *Ibid*, Dec 22, 1937; Jan 15, 1938.

48 Gestapo Nuremberg to Gestapo Berlin, Sep 23, 1938, with attachments; the open letter circulated in Eichstätt, Oct 3–15, 1937 (NA film T81, roll 184, 3495ff).

49 Diary, Oct 5, 9, 16, 1937.

50 *Ibid*, Aug 11, 12, Oct 27, 1937.

51 *Ibid*, Mar 3, 8, 10, 11; and Dec 31, 1937, further allegations about Funk.

52 *Ibid*, Oct 7, 8, Nov 5, 1937.

53 Unpubl. diary, Mar 7, 1938.

54 Diary, Feb 3, May 5, Jun 4, 30, Sep 21, Oct 9, Dec 3, 1937; Jan 13; unpubl. diary, Mar 16, May 18, Oct 5, 1938; Mar 16, Jun 23, 1939, etc.

55 Diary, Mar 3, 1937.

56 Lochner to his children, Dec 5, 1937 (Lochner papers, box 47).

57 See Yivo files G–58, G–60; and JG diary, Dec 3, 1937.

58 Diary, Mar 6; German foreign ministry circular to all missions, Apr 24, 1937 (NA film T120, roll 4673, 4420).

59 Diary, Oct 26, 1937.

60 *Ibid*, Dec 9, 1937.

61 *Ibid.*, Sep 11, 13, Oct 6, 14, 1937; on the Jewish-organized boycott of German films in the USA see JG's unpubl. diary, Mar 15, 16, 1938.

62 Diary, Mar 5, 6, 8, 9, 10, 12, 1937.

63 *Ibid*, Mar 17, 1937.

64 *Ibid*, Mar 20, 21, Apr 17, Aug 3, 19, 20, 1937.

65 *Ibid*, Jan 2, 1937.

66 *Ibid.*, Jan 10, 13, 17, 26, 1937.

67 *Ibid.*, Feb 14, 1937.

68 *Ibid*, Feb 24, 1937.

69 *Ibid.*, Feb 10 and 18; the flooring at Lanke stank of creosote and was having to be renewed (*ibid.*, Jan 4, 1937).

70 Other writers have assumed this famous incident occurred in 1938; but Fröhlich had sold his villa by Sep 1937 (*cf. ibid.*, Sep 5, 1937). Lida Baarova has stated that it occurred while she was filming *Patrioten*. Filming began late in Jan 1937 (diary, Jan 26), and he showed the film to his family on Apr 20, 1937 (diary). I have preferred to follow her version (see notes to previous chapter) rather than Gustav Fröhlich's.

71 Diary, May 16, 1937.

72 *Ibid*, Jul 27, 1937.

73 Author's interview of Lida Baarova, Salzburg, Jul 4, 1993. 'I had not gone . . . the whole way. *Noch nicht ganz.*'

74 *Ibid.*

75 *Ibid.*

76 Czech; otherwise based on her testimony.

77 Baarova interviews, especially with WDR and with the author.

78 Diary, Feb 25, 1937; the actress was Irene von Meyendorff.

79 *Ibid.*, Feb 28, 1937.

80 *Ibid.*, Feb 2, Mar 3, Apr 3, 13; she may be referred to in the entry of Mar 22, 1937 about a gray Sunday at Lanke: 'But indoors it is warm and comfortable. . . Sat as model. Gossiped. Read until late. Then stayed out at Bogensee. And a long, beneficial sleep.'

81 *Ibid.*, Feb 10, 17, 1937.

82 *Ibid.*, Mar 21, 22, Apr 13, 16, 1937.

83 *Ibid.*, Mar 24, 1937.

84 *Ibid.*, Apr 13, 1937.

85 Ilse Hess to Magda, Jan 21, 1938 (Rudolf Hess papers, Hindelang).

86 Diary, Apr 1, 2, 13, 25, 1937.

87 *Ibid.*, May 15, 1937.

88 *Ibid.*, Apr 17–19, 25; Prof. Paul Baumgarten took over the design work, but Hitler did not at first like his model: *Ibid.*, Aug 24, Oct 7, 17, 1937.

89 *Ibid.*, May 3, 26; Hitler had already spoken of this aim to JG (*ibid.*, Feb 23, 1937); he repeated it a year later (unpubl. diary, Sep 18, 1938).

90 Speech reported by Phipps to FO, Feb 15 (PRO file FO.371/20709); JG diary, Feb 14, 1937.

91 Diary, May 29, 30; on Ribbentrop: Mar 3, May 17, 22, Oct 27, Nov 16, 1937.

92 Thus JG said in Reichenberg, 'When one has the feeling that the time is ripe, the Goddess of History is descending on earth, and the hem of her mantle is touching mankind' (British embassy to FO, Nov 25, 1938: PRO file FO.371/21665).

93 Diary, Feb 5, 13, Mar 4, 12, Apr 22, 23, 30, May 8, 27, Jun 19, 30, 1937. Speaking at lunch on Jul 17, 1942, Hitler blamed JG for the failure to carry out his prewar instructions to set up the cable radio (Picker, Table Talk, 455f).

94 Diary, Feb 13, 1937; the *Drahtfunk* system, first devised in 1934, carried high-frequency radio transmissions over telephone wires to existing radio sets. See OSS R&A Report

No. 2100, May 29, 1944. Ministerialrat Schroeder of the post ministry reported to the Defense Council session of Apr 21, 1937 that cable radio would provide three programs; it would take four or five more years to bring it to all radio subscribers (NA film T77, roll 131, 3465ff).

95 *Ibid.*, Oct 13, 1937.

96 *Ibid.*, Oct 15, 17, Dec 2, 16, 17, 22, 23, 24, 28, 29. Ogilvie-Forbes to FO, Dec 30 (PRO file FO.371/20919); on Dec 7, 1937 the British ambassador in Egypt had expressed puzzlement about why JG and Fritsch should be visiting Egypt at the same time as Himmler was in Libya (FO.371/20919).

97 Borresholm; JG diary, Jul 31, Aug 1, 1937; interviews of Col. von Below, 1967.

98 Diary, Aug 3, 1937.

99 *Ibid.*, Sep 14, 1937.

100 FO minute on Kirkpatrick's report, Sep 10 (PRO file FO.371/20749). That day Henderson sat between Himmler and JG, the two men whom 'he most distrusted,' at Hess's castle for lunch. Henderson to FO, Sep 12, 1937 (FO.371/20722).

101 Diary, Sep 3, 7, 8, 1937. BDIC/FIR/31 interrogation of Sauerbruch, Oct 10, 1945 (NA file RG.332, entry ETO, Mis-Y, Sect., box 22).

102 Minute by Ridsdale, FO, on conversation with *Daily Mail*, Oct 2, 1937 (PRO file FO.371/21176).

103 Diary, Nov 5, 1937; JG had spoken at Bad Segeberg on Oct 10, 1937 about Germany's need for colonies (Ogilvie-Forbes to FO, Oct 11, 1937. PRO file FO.371/20722).

104 Diary, Oct 19, 20, 22, 27, Nov 3, 4, 1937.

105 *Ibid.*, Nov 6, 1937.

106 This was the notorious 'Hossbach conference' of Nov 5, 1937: a partial transcript, ND: 386-PS. *Cf.* Walter Bussmann, in *VfZ*, 1968, 373ff, and General Ludwig Beck's commentary (BA file N.28/4).

107 Diary, Nov 17, 1937.

108 Ogilvie-Forbes to FO, Oct 21, 1937 (PRO file FO.371/20736); on Jan 4, 1938 he described JG as 'small, dark and Jewish in appearance' with one leg crippled (FO.371/21671).

109 Diary, Jan 7, 1938: Eden was a 'danger to Britain' as her foreign secretary.

110 JG had demanded that Low's cruel caricatures of Hitler be suppressed. See Rex Leeper's memo of Dec 9, 1937 (PRO file FO.371/20737).

111 Diary, Nov 22; Henderson, memo on JG's talk with Halifax, Nov 21 (PRO file FO.371/20736); diary of Lord Halifax, Nov 21, 1937 (*ibid.*, and Borthwick Institute, York Univ., Hickleton papers).

Notes to Chapter 28.

1 'The diaries contained a lot of personal material which was not suited for publication without severe editing.' Interrogation of Harald Quandt, Apr 4, 1948 (Hoover Libr., Korf papers).

2 *Mein lieber Gewissensarzt.* Diary, Sep 23, 1925.

3 Diary, Oct 29, 1937. For details see *Nachrichtenblatt des RMVP*, vol. 6, 1938 (BA file R.55/435); and *Berliner Tageblatt, Westdeutscher Beobachter*, etc., Apr 20, 1938.

4 Dietrich affidavit, Oct 1947 (NA film M.1019, roll 13); and interrogations of Hederich, Feb 26 and Mar 1, 1948 (*ibid.*, roll 25).

5 Diary, Dec 1, 1937. Dietrich was Pressechef der NSDAP, Funk Reichspressechef, Hanke Chef des Ministerbüros. See Dietrich's interrogation by CSDIC (WEA) BAOR, report IR.28, Oct 29, 1945 (NA file RG.219, IRR, XE.003812). See too Louis Lochner's letter home, Mar 15, on Dietrich's speech of Mar 7, 1938 (Lochner papers, box 47).

6 Diary, Dec 8, 1937. Naumann was director of JG's Breslau propaganda office (RPA). The author has drawn extensively on Naumann's personnel files in the BDC, and later OSS documentation. See too the manuscript by Dr Jay W Baird of the Dept of History, Miami Univ., Ohio, based on extensive interviews of Naumann taped in 1969/70.

7 Unpubl. diary, Feb 23, 1942: 'He's the most reliable colleague I have!' Naumann was born Jun 16, 1909 in Guhrau; his Nazi party number was 101,399; his SS number 1607. *Schlesische Zeitung*, Aug 27, 1936; May 19, 1937. BDC file, Naumann, and NA file RG.319, IRR, XE.246725, containing especially the British high commission's Jul 1954 report, 'The Naumann Circle. The Study of a Technique in Political Subversion.'

8 Report by S.A. Gruppe Pommern, Jul 27, 1934. During investigations against Gauleiter Helmut Brückner, he claimed to have had an erotic relationship with Naumann: We kissed and slept together.' These were lies, although Naumann admitted to the Breslau Gestapo on Oct 19, 1935 that Brückner had fondled him, 'and perhaps there was a kiss too' after an election victory. In May 1937 Brückner withdrew his testimony. BDC file, Naumann.

9 Affidavit by Karl Hederich, Jul 9, 1948 (StA Nuremberg).

10 Diary, Dec 3, 1937.

11 See Hanke's file of JG's tax affairs in ZStA Potsdam, Rep. 90, Go 1, vol. 2. During fiscal 1937, these show that JG received 25,974 marks from his publisher Eher Verlag.

12 Diary, Feb 12, 1938; Albert Speer, *Erinnerungen* (Berlin, 1969), 35ff.

13 Oven, 'Jun 1944,' 362ff.

14 Diary, Aug 27, 1937.

15 *Ibid.*, Sep 9–10, 1937.

16 *Ibid.*, Sep 23–24, 1937.

17 *Ibid.*, Dec 3, 1937.

18 *E.g. ibid.*, Sep 5, 1937.

19 *Ibid.*, Sep 30, 1937.

20 *Ibid.*, Dec 27, 1937; Czech; interviews of Baarova.

21 Diary, Oct 6, 1937.

22 *Ibid.*, Dec 1, 1937. On Mar 8, 1938 JG noted: 'Helldorff has given the Schwanenwerder Jew who wanted to gazump [diddle] us over the house purchase a going-over. Now it will probably go through easier.' And diary Mar 22, 29, 30, 1938.

23 Reuth, 385f, researching in 1954 files of JG's executor Krech and the Schwanenwerder land register. On Jun 8, 1939 JG sold off part of the new lot to the industrialist Alfred Ludwig of Osnabrück for 180,000 marks. See diary, Mar 24, 30, 1941.

24 Ello Quandt, cited by Ebermayer and Meissner.

25 Diary, Dec 12; there was building work at Lanke (*ibid.*, Dec 21, 1937).

26 *Ibid.*, Dec 19, 1937.

27 *Ibid.*, Jan 6, 1938.

28 *Ibid.*, Jan 12; unpubl. diary Feb 19, Mar 20, 22, Apr 15 (completed), 20, 21, 1938.

29 Diary, Jan 16; unpubl. diary, Feb 13, 27, Mar 29, Apr 3, 22, 26, 27; documents on the plaster model, Jan 31, 1938 (BA file R.43II/1184).

30 This was on Mar 4; unpubl. diary, Mar 5. On Mar 17, 1938 the *Münchner Illustrierter*

Beobachter featured a photo taken at the film ball showing Lida Baarova with Hilde Körber and four other stars.

31 A 'selfish little beast': unpubl. diary, Apr 26, 27, 29, 1938.

32 *Ibid.*, Feb 14, 1938.

33 Letter to Oberregierungsrat G W Muller (of RMVP), Jan 26, 1939: Magda points out she is incapable of paying the taxes for Nos. 12–14 Inselstrasse from her housekeeping money in addition to those for Nos. 8–10 (Hoover Libr., Goebbels papers, box 2).

34 Diary, Jan 20; unpubl. diary, Feb 20, 1938.

35 Diary, Jan 15, 1938. On Feb 8, 1935 JG had recorded in his unpubl. diary a similar private talk with Hitler, on ambassadorial appointments to London and Paris.

36 Diary, Jan 15, 1938.

37 *Ibid.*, Feb 1, 1938.

38 *Ibid.*, Jan 22, 1938.

39 *Ibid.*, Feb 1, 1938.

40 *Ibid.*, Dec 15, 1937; and see Jan 13, 14, 18, 1938.

41 *Ibid.*, Jan 26, 1938.

42 *Ibid.*, Jan 27, 1938.

43 *Ibid.*, Jan 28, 1938.

44 *Ibid.*, Jan 27, 29. The 83pp. transcript of the four-hour grilling on Jan 27, 1938 is on NA film T82, roll 272. The author also used Fritsch's own handwritten record of the scandal, written Feb 1938-Sep 27, 1938 (see IfZ, Irving collection, and BA file N.33).

45 Diary, Jan 30, 1938.

46 *Ibid.*, Jan 31; and see Lutze diary, Jan 30, 1938.

47 Diary, Feb 1, 1938.

48 *Ibid.*, Feb 6, 1938.

49 *Ibid.* See too Fritsch's notes, and the diaries of Milch, Eberhard, and von Leeb.

50 Unpubl. diary, Feb 13, 14, 1938: 'Thank goodness, the world press has still not printed anything of the true background to our "crisis".'

51 Rudolf Likus described Berndt to Ribbentrop on Feb 11, 1938 as a 'tactless fellow' with less manners than a butcher's boy (NA film T120, roll 31, 8876f).

52 Lochner to daughter, Mar 15, 1938 (Lochner papers, box 47).

53 *Ibid.* Juliana had married the German Prince Bernhard von Lippe-Biesterfeld at the end of 1936. At the wedding he had refused to permit the German anthem, speaking in a later declaration of 'foreign national anthems that he no longer desired,' and calling himself somebody who 'is and feels Dutch.' 'A fine patriot,' commented JG, launching a bitter press attack on him with Hitler's blessing (diary, Jan 1, 3, 5, 25, 1937); and see Nigel Law to Orme Sargent, FO, May 16, 1937 (PRO file FO.371/20733).

54 Unpubl. diary, Feb 16, 1938.

55 Goebbels had remarked as recently as Dec 27, 1937 (diary) that a long road still lay ahead to Austria.

56 Unpubl. diary, Feb 16, 1938.

57 *Ibid.*, Feb 21, 1938.

58 *Ibid.*, Feb 13, 1938.

59 *Ibid.*, Feb 17, 1938.

60 *Ibid.*, Feb 16, 1938.

61 *Ibid.*, Feb 26, 1938.

62 *Ibid.*, Mar 1, 1938.

63 Diary, Jul 3, 4, 6, 1937: Niemöller should 'never be turned loose' again.

64 *Ibid.*, Apr 17, 1937. Frick had drafted a new law requiring all civil servants to have law degrees. JG suggested an amendment (Apr 20, 1937): 'Not "only lawyers" may become civil servants, but "even, in exceptional cases, lawyers."'.

65 *Ibid.*, Jan 21, 1938.

66 *Ibid.*, Feb 5, 8, 1938.

67 *Ibid.*, Feb 9; and unpubl. diary, Feb 14, 20, 23, 1938.

68 *Ibid.*, Feb 23, 25, 26, 1938.

69 *Ibid.*, Mar 3: 'That's the clock striking thirteen!' – and Mar 4. See Franz Gürtner's diary, Mar 5, 1938 (BA file R.22/946) and Fritz Wiedemann, *Der Mann, der Feldherr werden wollte* (Velbert, 1964), 149.

70 Unpubl. diary, Mar 3, 1938. Niemöller survived the war after a relatively privileged captivity at Dachau and other camps.

71 Diary, Nov 14, 1937.

72 *Ibid.*, Nov 16, 1937.

73 *Ibid.*, Dec 11, 1937; statement by Ehrhardt to Kurzbein on Apr 22 quoted by Grau to Himmler, Apr 23, 1938 (Tobias archives).

74 Unpubl. diary, Feb 23, 1938.

75 *Ibid.*, Mar 2, 1938.

76 *Ibid.*, Mar 6, 1938.

77 *Ibid.*, Mar 18, 1938.

78 Diary, Jun 15, 1938.

79 *Ibid.*, Aug 12, 13, 1938.

80 Unpubl. diary, Mar 7, 1938.

81 *Ibid.*, Mar 10; JG's glare was fixed on the Czech parliament, where an anti-German debate was raging – 'until one day [our] divisions go marching in.' Party: Milch diary, Mar 9; the *NYT* on Mar 10, 1938 quoted JG as stating at this reception that 'certain journalists of foreign countries . . . stand in the service of secret powers and must fulfil their orders, be these Jewish or Masonic or international-Marxist or capitalistic.'

82 Unpubl. diary, Mar 10. To JG's fury, Daluege's official police magazine *Die deutsche Polizei* revealed 'just about all' their secrets of Mar 10–13 in an article; he had the journal seized and the author arrested (*ibid.*, Apr 3, 4, 1938).

83 *Ibid.*, Mar 11, 1938.

84 *Ibid.* In fact the telegraphed 'invitation' arrived only two days later after the party was over (*ibid.*, Mar 14, 1938). See Seyss-Inquart's MS on the telegram controversy, in his papers (copy in IfZ, Irving collection).

85 Unpubl. diary, Mar 13, 1938.

86 Körber was Harlan's second wife. Veit Harlan, *Im Schatten meiner Filme. Selbstbiographie* (Gütersloh, 1966), 83; and our interview of Thomas Harlan, 1994.

87 Unpubl. diary, Mar 16, 1938.

88 *Ibid.*, Mar 17, 1938: 'This is a chanting, cheering city.'

89 *Ibid.*, Mar 18, 1938.

90 *Ibid.*, Mar 19, 1938.

91 *Ibid.*, and an unpubl. diary of Colonel Alfred Jodl, Apr 1938, transcribed by this author.

92 See JG's unpubl. diary, Mar 10; and Mar 21, 1938: 'They [the Czechs] are too late.'

93 *Ibid.*, Feb 25, 1938.

94 At the Berlin diplomatic reception on Feb 15, 1938, Mastný had spoken with him about a

newspaper truce between their two countries. Subsequently Mastný did urge Prague to curb the anti-German press. See the note on his phone conversation with Krofta, Feb 16, 1938, in Vaclav Král, *Das Abkommen von München 1938* (Prague, 1968), 67f, No. 16.

95 Unpubl. diary, Mar 20, 1938.
96 *Unzeitgemäß*. *Ibid*., Mar 22, 1938.
97 *Ibid*., Mar 25, 1938.
98 *Ibid*., Mar 29, 1938.
99 *Ibid*., Apr 8, 1938.
100 *Ibid*., Mar 22, 1938.
101 See the report in *NYT*, Mar 30, 1938.
102 Monthly report by British vice-consul at Breslau, Mar 31, 1938 (PRO file FO.371/21674).
103 Unpubl. diary, Apr 5, 1938.
104 See the report in *NYT*, Apr 5, 1938.
105 Unpubl. diary, Apr 10, 1938.
106 *Ibid*., Apr 11, 1938.
107 *Ibid*., Apr 12, 1938.
108 *Ibid*., Apr 11. Of 49,403,028 entitled to vote, 49,279,104 had voted, of whom 48,751,857 had voted for Hitler and Anschluss. Analyzed: *Ibid*., Apr 26, 1938.

Notes to Chapter 29.

1 On this decree see OSS R&A report No. 113, Feb 22, 1943 (USAMHI, Donovan papers, box 35c). On the new theater academy see BA file R.55/264.
2 Diary, Jun 5, 1937.
3 *Ibid*., Jun 5–7, 12, 1937.
4 JG to Ziegler, Jun 30, *cit*. Peter-Klaus Schuster, *Die 'Kunststadt' München 1937. Nationalsozialismus und 'entartete Kunst'* (Munich, 1987), 37ff; Reuth, 367; diary, Jun 30, 1937.
5 Diary, Jul 24, 25, Aug 1, 1937.
6 *Ibid*., Sep 1, 1937.
7 *Ibid*., Sep 22, Nov 5, 1937; unpubl. diary, Mar 15, May 17, 1938. The law: diary, Jan 13, 14; unpubl. diary, Feb 12, 14, Mar 15, May 17, 18; diary, Jun 5, 1938.
8 Unpubl. diary, May 18, 16; diary, Jul 29, 1938.
9 See *e.g.* Vaclav Král, *Das Abkommen von München*, 63, No. 9; Prof. Carl Burckhardt's opinion, quoted in Geneva telegram to FO, Jan 27 (PRO file FO.371/21660); and JG unpubl. diary, May 21, 1938.
10 *Ibid*., Mar 14, 21, 24, 1938.
11 Ello Quandt says this was in the last weeks of this pregnancy. Meissner, *Magda Goebbels*, 175f.
12 Unpubl. diary, Apr 13, 14; and see Apr 3, 1938.
13 *Ibid*., May 3, 1938.
14 *Ibid*.
15 *Ibid*., May 5, 1938.
16 *Ibid*., May 6. The nobility, Hitler remarked later, were good only for marrying off to wealthy Jewesses (*ibid*., Jun 16, 1938).
17 *Ibid*., May 4, 1938.
18 *Ibid*., May 5, 1938. Aboard the *Comte di Cavo*ur, Hitler told Mussolini that Germany

would step out along the ancient teutonic road to the east. See Ciano's letter to Ribbentrop, Aug 13, 1939 (Loesch files, NA film T120, roll 610).

19 Unpubl. diary, May 7, 1938.

20 *Ibid.*, May 7–8, 1938.

21 *Ibid.*, May 11, 1938.

22 *Ibid.*, May 12, 1938.

23 *Ibid.*, May 5, 1938; the late Capt. Herbert Friedrichs to the author, Apr 4, 1989; Behrend, No. 19, May 10, 1952.

24 Unpubl. diary, May 12, 1938.

25 Diary, May 13; incorrectly dated May 12, 1938 in E Fröhlich's edition.

26 Unpubl. diary, May 15, 1938.

27 *Ibid.*, May 17, 18, 19, 23, 27, 31; diary, Jun 2, 3, 15, 16, 17, 19, 1938.

28 From a well-informed article by a Forschungsamt official in *Neue Presse*, Coburg, Aug 3, 1946; and see NA file RG.226, file XE.4986.

29 Interview of Thomas Harlan, Jan 13, 1994; Lida Baarova remembers two Gestapo cars shadowing her sometimes.

30 Julius Schaub, MS (IfZ Irving collection, ED. 100/202).

31 Diary, Jun 17, 1938.

32 *Ibid.*, Jun 21, 1938.

33 Author's interview with Lida Baarova, Salzburg, Jul 4, 1993.

34 Meissner, *Magda Goebbels*, 141.

35 Diary, Jun 30, 1938.

36 *Ibid.*, Jul 3, 1938.

37 *Ibid.*, Jul 5, 7, 1938.

38 *Ibid.*, Jul 8, 1938.

39 Hanke told his later wife, the then Baroness Freda née von Fircks, that while he was willing, Magda was not (interview of the late Freda Rössler, Mar 5, 1990).

40 Cabinet, Jan 26; diary, Jan 27, 1937.

41 Unpubl. diary, May 12, 1938.

42 Diary, Jun 16, 1938.

43 *Ibid.*, Aug 13, 1938.

44 *Ibid.*, Jul 30, 1938.

45 Max Wünsche diary, Jun 19 (BA file NS.10/125); JG unpubl. diary, May 1, 3, 1938.

46 Unpubl. diary, Apr 21, 1938; program, BA file NS.10/44.

47 Guest list in Graham, *Leni Riefenstahl and Olympia*, 186ff.

48 Unpubl. diary, Apr 22, 23, 1938.

49 Diary, Aug 13, 1938.

50 Unpubl. diary, Apr 5, 1938.

51 *Ibid.*, May 29, 1938: 'He is happy when I speak a few friendly words to him.'

52 The author was Ernst Wiechert. Diary, Aug 4, 30; unpubl. diary, Sep 11, 1938.

53 Diary, Jan 6, 1938.

54 Unpubl. diary, Feb 12, 1938.

55 *Ibid.*, Mar 6; he was aware how many top Nazis' wives went shopping in Jewish stores, including Emmy Göring. 'Women sometimes can't distinguish between them.' Apr 22, 1938.

56 Yivo file G–61.

57 Unpubl. diary, Mar 20, 1938.

58 *Ibid.*, Mar 23; he used the same turn of phrase in his Vienna speech of Mar 29, 1938.

59 Unpubl. diary, Apr 23; and Helldorff's report to JG on his anti-Jewish operations, Jun 20, 1938 (Princeton Univ., Seeley Mudd Libr., Adolf Hitler collection, box 2). For the SD Hauptamt file on Goebbels' instigation of these outrages, see: 'Berichte und Meldungen zur Judenaktion, Berlin, Juni 1938' in Moscow special archives, fond 500 opis 1 folder 645 (USHMM RSHA films 8 and 9).

60 Diary, Jun 2, 3, 1938.

61 Dr Julius Dresel. See Heydrich to Himmler, Jul 22; Himmler to Helldorff, Jul 30, 1938 (BDC file, Helldorff).

62 Diary, Jun 4, 1938.

63 Under Regierungsassessor Brümmel.

64 Helldorff's report; JG diary, Jun 19, 1938: 'Helldorff is now taking radical steps on the Jewish Problem. The party is helping him in this. . . The police have understood my instructions.' See the United Press report from Berlin, on NA film T120, roll 4357, 5162ff.

65 Lochner to family, Jul 10, 1938 (Lochner papers, box 47). He and his wife witnessed 'orgies of window smearing' on Kurfürstendamm.

66 Diary, Jun 21, 1938.

67 *Ibid.*, Jun 22; Henderson to FO, Jun 22, 1938 (PRO file FO.371/21663). Three thousand Jews had actually moved into Berlin in the last three months, he shrilled. 'They must not behave as if there had never been a national socialist revolution.' *DAZ*, Jun 23, 1938: 'Goebbels über die Auseinandersetzung mit den Juden. Eine Rede bei der Berliner Sonnwendfeier' (BA, Schumacher collection, file 115).

68 Diary, Jun 21, 1938.

69 *Ibid.*, Jun 24, 1938.

70 *Ibid.*, Aug 5, 8, 1938. 'I don't want that'.

71 *Ibid.*, Jul 6, 1938; see Joachim von Ribbentrop, *Zwischen London und Moskau* (Leoni, 1953), 275.

72 Diary, Jul 24; on July 26 Helldorff handed him a report on steps so far taken against Berlin's Jews, and on Aug 3 about subsequent operations: 'They are proceeding to plan' (diary).

73 Unpubl. diary, Apr 15, 1938.

74 *Ibid.*, Apr 23, 1938.

75 *Ibid.*, May 3, 1935. On May 21 he wrote, 'Poor Prague, we'll be seeing soon to you.'

76 *Ibid.*, May 22, 24, 1938.

77 *Ibid.*, May 25, 1938.

78 *Ibid.*, May 28, 1938.

79 *Ibid.*, May 29; the *NYT* noted, May 28, 1938, 'As if by order, the German press ceased abruptly its blasts against Czechoslovakia.'

80 Unpubl. diary, May 30, 1938.

81 *Ibid.*, Jun 1, 1938.

82 *Ibid.*, Jun 3, 4, 1938.

83 Diary, Jul 16, 17, 1938.

84 *Ibid.*, Jul 17; JG, Hitler, and Ribbentrop had all assured Ambassador von Dirksen of their desire for an understanding with Britain. Henderson to Cadogan, May 2, 1938 (PRO file FO.800/269).

85 Diary, Jul 19, 1938.

86 *Ibid.*, Jul 9; Max Wünsche diary, Jul 8, 1938 (BA file NS.10/125).

87 Diary, Jul 10, 11; Wünsche diary, Jul 9, 10, 1938.

88 Author's interview with Speer, May 20, 1968; see Speer, *Inside the Third Reich* (New York, 1970), 218f.

89 Diary, Jul 16, 17, 1938.

90 *Ibid.*, Jul 23, 1938.

91 *Ibid.*, Jul 25; Wünsche diary, Jul 24, 1938. Author's interview of Speer; Speer's memoirs put this episode in July 1939. Wünsche's diary leaves no doubt that it was 1938.

92 Diary, Jul 26; see Wünsche diary, Jul 25, 1938.

93 Diary, Jul 26, 1938.

94 *Ibid.*, Jul y 27, 1938.

95 *Ibid.*, Jul 28; Magda phoned twice from Bayreuth. Diary, Jul 29, 30. There is one unexplained diary entry, Jul 29, 1938: 'The Bronnen affair comes up again. I now squash it for good.' Arnolt Bronnen, by now Programmleiter at Berlin's radio and television station, was a (part-Jewish?) radio official with whose fiancée Olga JG had had his first true sexual encounter years earlier.

96 *Ibid.*, Jul 30, 1938.

97 *Ibid.*, Aug 3, 1938.

98 What follows is based on Lida's various recollections. The amethyst ring is the key to the chronology. *Ibid.*, Aug 4, 1938: 'I give Magda a beautiful ring. We have a long discussion.'

99 Baarova interviews.

100 Author's interview of Lida Baarova, Salzburg, Jul 4, 1993. 'I wanted to get out of the whole thing.'

101 Diary, Aug 5, 1938.

102 *Ibid.*, Aug 6–9, 12, 14, 1938.

103 *Ibid.*, Aug 5, 1938.

104 *Ibid.*, Aug 9, 10, 12, 1938.

105 Ebermayer and Meissner, No. 22, May 31, 1952; see diary, Aug 12, 1938: 'A long parlaver [*sic*] with Magda and Auntie Ello.'

106 *Ibid.*, Aug 14, 1938.

107 Baarova interviews.

108 Diary, Aug 15, 1938: 'Rain, rain, rain. And the whole house full of guests.'

109 *Ibid.*, Aug 16, 1938.

110 Behrend, No. 18, May 3, 1952.

111 Bahls (Hitler's adjutant) to RMVP, Aug 16, 1938 (BA file NS. 10/45).

112 Diary, Aug 16, 1938.

113 *Ibid.*

Notes to Chapter 30.

1 Hitler's secret speech to Nazi editors, Nov 10, 1938 (BA file NS.11/28).

2 Taubert report.

3 Berndt was chief of JG's press department (Abteilung Presse). On his role in fabricating these atrocity stories see the testimony of Schirmeister on Jun 28, 1946 (IMT, xvii, 262), and the Nuremberg interrogation of Heinz Lorenz, Dec 3, 1947 (IfZ file ZS.266).

4 See JG diary, Aug 30, 1938: 'Henlein's propaganda minister Höller reports to me from Prague. . . ' On Höller see *VB*, Oct 13, 1938, p. 2.

5 From the memoirs of JG's press officer (*Pressereferent*): published anonymously by E G
  Schoor as 'Ein enger Mitarbeiter des Reichspropagandaministers erzählt,' copyright
  Hermann Laatzen Verlag, Hamburg, in *Nord-West-Illustrierte*, in 1949 (IfZ archives)
  (hereafter *Pressereferent* memoirs). The author was Moritz von Schirmeister, as both
  the memoirs and he misdate a certain episode as Jul 20, 1939 (*cf.* interrogation, May 6,
  1946, NA film M.1270, roll 19). Schirmeister, an SS Hauptsturmführer, entered the party
  on Oct 1, 1931, and was JG's *Pressereferent* from Jul 1, 1938 to Jul 1, 1943.

6 Diary, Jul 25, 1938.

7 *Ibid.*, but see Aug 17, 1938: Dietrich told JG that Hitler had intended nothing special with
  this visit, merely to reassure Britain.

8 *Ibid.*, Aug 22, 1938.

9 *Ibid.*, Aug 17, 1938.

10 *Ibid.*

11 *Ibid.*, Aug 18, 1938.

12 *Ibid.*, Aug 19, 1938.

13 *Ibid.*, Aug 21, 1938. He repeats the adjectives *hard-hearted* and *cruel* in the diary on Aug
   17, 18, 19, 20, 1938.

14 *Ibid.*, Aug 27, 1938.

15 *Ibid.*, Sep 1, 1938.

16 Unpubl. diary, Sep 2; he does not see the children again until Oct 14, 1938.

17 Diary, Aug 28, 30; unpubl. diary, Sep 2, 1938.

18 Diary, Aug 30; JG (*ibid.*, Sep 16, 1938) called this attaché '*der alte Hosenscheißer.*'

19 *Ibid.*, Aug 31, 1938.

20 *Ibid.*, Sep 1; Wünsche diary, Aug 31, 1938.

21 And see too diary, Aug 28, 1938.

22 Unpubl. diary, Sep 2, 1938.

23 *Ibid.*; Wünsche diary, Sep 1, 1938.

24 Unpubl. diary, Sep 3; Wünsche diary, Sep 2; *NYT*, Sep 2, 1938.

25 Unpubl. diary, Sep 5, 1938.

26 *Ibid.*, Sep 6, 1938.

27 *Ibid.*, Sep 6, 7, 1938.

28 *Ibid.*, Sep 8, 1938.

29 *Ibid.*, Sep 9, 1938.

30 *Ibid.*, Sep 10, 1938.

31 *Ibid.*, Sep 11, 1938.

32 See Ogilvie-Forbes to FO, Sep 14, 1938 (PRO file FO.371/21760); and unpubl. diary, Sep 11,
   12, 1938.

33 *Ibid.*, Sep 14, 1938.

34 *Ibid.*, Sep 15, 1938.

35 *Ibid.*, Sep 18, 1938.

36 *Ibid.*, Sep 16, 17, 1938.

37 *Ibid.*, Sep 18; Wünsche and Bormann diaries, Sep 17, 1938.

38 Unpubl. diary, Sep 18; and again on Sep 19, 1938.

39 *Ibid.*, Sep 20, 1938. Hitler gave a file of these Beneš wiretaps to the British (PRO file
   FO.371/21742). See Irving, *Das Reich hört mit*, appendix. Interrogation of Legationsrat
   Emil Rasche (NA file RG.226, XE.4986); and Hitler's remarks to the editors on Nov 10,
   1938 (BA file NS.11/28).

40 JG was incandescent about Hungary's 'shameless' weakness, cowardice, and greed: see his unpubl. diary, entries of Sep 21, 22, 26, 27, Oct 6, 9, 15, 16, 18, 20, 24, and Nov 4, 1938.

41 Transcript of Hitler's meeting with Lipski, Sep 20; and unpubl. JG diary, Sep 21, 1938.

42 *Ibid.*, Sep 22, 1938:.

43 *Ibid.*, Sep 23, 1938.

44 *Ibid.*, Sep 24, 1938.

45 *Ibid.*

46 *Ibid.*, Sep 26, 1938.

47 In JG's own circle he noted warnings from Funk, Hanke, and Krosigk (*ibid.*, Sep 22); Helldorff (Sep 14); the editors (Sep 15); and that Fritz Wiedemann was to be sacked for having lost his nerve (Oct 24, 1938).

48 *Ibid.*, Sep 28, 1938. JG had originally planned to seal all German radio receivers to immunize the public from enemy propaganda; Keitel dissuaded him.

49 *Ibid.*, Sep 28, Oct 2, 1938.

50 *Ibid.*, Sep 28. He had used the 'sleepwalker' simile before, *ibid.*, Sep 11, 1938.

51 Wiedemann, 176.

52 *In stummer Obstruktion. Ibid.*, 176. JG's unpubl. diary, Sep 29 and especially Oct 2, 1939. See too Klaus-Jürgen Müller, *Das deutsche Heer und Hitler* (Stuttgart, 1969), 373, n.136.

53 Private letter from Weizsäcker's wife Marianne to his mother, Sep 30. This states that he gave JG the main credit, after Göring, over the last few days for averting war. In his diary Weizsäcker wrote on Oct 9, 1938 that JG made his remarks 'in front of everybody and out loud to the Führer,' which he reiterated in his Oct 1939 survey of historical events.

54 *Pressereferent* memoirs. Precisely confirmed by JG's unpubl. diary, Sep 29, 1938.

55 Unpubl. diary, Sep 30, 1938.

56 *Ibid.*, Oct 1, 1938.

57 *Ibid.*, Jun 3, 1938.

58 *Ibid.*, Sep 5, 1938.

59 *Ibid.*, Oct 2, 1938.

60 *Ibid.*, Oct 3, 1938.

61 *Ibid.*, Oct 10; Hanke echoed this view. 'Capturing the fortifications would have cost us rivers of blood' (*ibid.*, Oct 12, 1938).

Notes to Chapter 31.

1 Unpubl. diary, Oct 1, 1938.

2 Czech.

3 Capt. Herbert Friedrichs to the author, Apr 4, 1989.

4 *Der Amüsierpöbel, der sich nachts von Bar zu Bar wälzt.*

5 Mussolini remarks to Count Ciano that JG was wrong to allow his face to be slapped. Ciano diary, Feb 13, 1939.

6 Hassell diary, Jan 22, 1939; his source was Ufa's Dr Oswald Lehnich.

7 Rosenberg diary, Feb 6, 1939, 80f; quoting Himmler.

8 Unpubl. diary, Sep 5, 6, 1938.

9 *Ibid.*, Sep 7, 1938.

10 *Ibid.*, Sep 10, 1938.

11 *Ibid.*, Sep 12, 1938.

12 *Ibid.*, Sep 14, 25, 26, 1938.

13 *Ibid.*, Oct 4, 1938. Of course, JG may have known all along, and inserted this passage to make his ultimate betrayal by Hanke sound even more horrid.

14 *Ibid.*, Oct 9, 1938.

15 Confirmed by Baarova, interviews; and the anonymous report NOI/108, a CSDIC interrogation of her manager, 'Mar 15, 1944,' in MI.14 dossier on JG (PRO file WO.208/4462).

16 Other sources speak of twenty-eight names; *Life*, Mar 20, 1939, states that three divorce attorneys turned Magda down, fearing the risk.

17 Unpubl. diary, Oct 10, 1938.

18 *Ibid.*, Oct 11, 1938.

19 *Ibid.*, Oct 12, 1938.

20 *Ibid.*, Oct 13, 1938.

21 *Ibid.*, Oct 14, 1938.

22 *Ibid.*, Oct 12, 1938: 'Helldorff reports on the state of the anti-Jewish operation in Berlin. This is going to plan. And the Jews are now gradually pulling out.'

23 *Ibid.*, Oct 7, 1938.

24 *Ibid.*, Oct 15, 1938.

25 *Ibid.*

26 *Ibid.*, Oct 16, 1938. Eva Braun won back Hitler by this dubious means in May 1935. She faked a suicidal diary entry, left it lying open, and took some aspirins. See Irving, *The War Path* (London, 1978), 110f.

27 Diary, Oct 18, 1938. According to Max Winkler's slightly different version of the episode, JG sent Rach to Magda with farewell letters addressed to her and his mother. Magda followed Rach back to Lanke, threw herself across what she took to be JG's lifeless form, and besought him to come back to life; JG obliged. (Interrogation, May 1, 1948, Hoover Libr., Korf papers).

28 Unpubl. diary, Oct 19, 1938.

29 *Ibid.*, Oct 20, 1938.

30 Emmy, quoted by Olga Rigele, Göring's sister (Hassell diary, Jan 26, 1939); Olga spoke contemptuously of JG's seduction of young actresses dependent on his ministry.

31 Unpubl. diary, Oct 21, 1938.

32 Bormann diary, Oct 19, 20, 1938.

33 Unpubl. diary, Oct 21, 1938: 'Göring acts like a real comrade. Fair, decent, noble, cordial.'

34 Rigele in Hassell diary.

35 Unpubl. diary, Oct 22; Bormann diary, Oct 21, 1938.

36 Ogilvie-Forbes to FO, Oct 22 (PRO file FO.371/21708); reports in *Hamburger Nachrichten* – its photo shows a very po-faced Goebbels – *DAZ*, and *Börsenzeitung*, Oct 22, 1938.

37 L L Robinson to Ogilvie-Forbes, Oct 25 (PRO file FO.371/21665); and British embassy, Berlin, to FO, Oct 26, 1938 (*ibid.*, /21791).

38 Unpubl. diary, Oct 24, 1938; and Lida Baarova, who was briefed by Helldorff on what happened.

39 Unpubl. diary, Oct 24; Bormann diary, Oct 23, 1938 (note his exclamation mark: 'Führer goes up to Kehlstein house with the Goebbels Family!').

40 This immediately became known abroad. *E.g. Life*, Mar 20, 1939. Different versions of the family photo were published in *e.g. VB, DAZ*, Oct 25–26, 1938. – See too Werner Stephan, *Goebbels – Dämon einer Diktatur* (Stuttgart, 1949; hereafter: Stephan), also

Czech. Sending a copy of the photo to the FO, the British embassy commented on Oct 26, 1938 that JG's matrimonial affairs 'have for long been the subject of much delighted gossip in Berlin.' It (and *Life*) reported the rumors that Fröhlich had beaten up JG, then 'surrendered to Himmler and [said] what about it,' and stated that Magda had cited 'twenty-five' co-respondents (PRO file FO.371/21791).

41 Helldorff told this to her: Author's interview, Salzburg, Jul 4, 1993. JG unpubl. diary, Oct 24, 1938.

42 *I.e.*, withdrawing the *du*. MI.14 report (PRO file WO.208/4462).

43 Stephan; Czech; well confirmed in unpubl. diary, Oct 25, 1938. Julius Schaub (MS) claims it was *he* who broke the news to Lida.

44 Ogilvie-Forbes to Lord Halifax, Nov 3, 1938 (PRO file FO.371/21791); he probably had this from Göring himself.

45 Unpubl. diary, Oct 25, 1938.

46 Author's interview of Lida Baarova, Salzburg, Jul 4, 1993.

47 *Life*, Mar 20, 1939.

48 Unpubl. diary, Oct 29, 1938. He added, 'It was uninterrupted torment.'

49 Rudolf Likus to Ribbentrop, Nov 3 (NA film T120, roll 31, 9042); Stephan wrongly identifies the film as *Preußische Liebesgeschichte*. Writing to the FO on Nov 3, 1938 Ogilvie-Forbes stated: 'Certain remarks [in the script] . . . made her an all too tempting target for public derision and interruptions unflattering to herself and to Dr Goebbels.' See too the detailed account of this incident in *Life*, Mar 20, 1939. Author's interview with Baarova, Jul 4, 1993.

50 Baarova. – She does flee to Prague. When Hitler invades she moves to Rome. She will make half a dozen movies there before the Allied invasion halts her career again. Hounded by Magda Goebbels, Hanke, Himmler, the Gestapo, the American CIC, and finally the Czech communists – her twenty-three-year-old actress sister Zola throws herself out of a window to her death – this talented actress ekes out a postwar living in Austrian exile as a waitress in a greasy-spoon cafe.

51 Unpubl. diary, Oct 26, 1938. It was perhaps Oberregierungsrat Dr Curt Thomalla, who would be found dead in a gas-filled room with his lifeless secretary in Mar 1939. 'He left behind letters containing a full confession' (Diary, Jan 4, 1939); Ebermayer and Meissner, No. 21, May 24, 1952.

52 Unpubl. diary, Oct 26, 1938. 'Thus concludes this book. It covers the most awful period of my life. I am still in the midst of the crisis. Will I ever get over it? That's written in the stars.'

53 Diary, Nov 2, 1938: begins work on MS; unpubl. diary, Nov 7: 'I begin thinking about my new book. I'll soon begin writing it. It's got to be really magnificent.' Nov 10: 'It's real fun.' Nov 15, 'at least one worthwhile task'; 21, dictates four chapters; 24, talks with Baur; Dec 4, Hitler wants to see it when finished; 12, 100 pages finished; 14, 15, 16, completion; 16, talks with Hearst; 30, galley proofs.

54 *Ibid.*, Jan 17, 1939. Rudolf Semler reports that there were two proof copies.

Notes to Chapter 32.

1 Goebbels himself admitted two months later that he had been on the verge of a nervous breakdown: diary, Jan 17, 1939.

2 Unpubl. diary, Oct 27, 29, 1938. The unpubl. fragments of JG's diary from Oct 26, 1938 to Oct 8, 1939 are in the Moscow archives, Goebbels papers, box 1.

3 *Ibid.*, Oct 27, 1938.

4 *Ibid.*, Oct 29, 30, 1938.

5 *Ibid.*, Oct 30, 1938: 'I spend midday in leaden solitude. Can any man bear and endure all that?' *VB*, Oct 29, 30, 1938.

6 Unpubl. diary., Oct 31, 1938.

7 Diary, Nov 3, 4, 1938.

8 *Ibid.*, Oct 29, 1938.

9 Behrend, No. 17, Apr 26, 1952. Unpubl. diary, Oct 31; report on JG's Weimar speech in *VB*, Oct 30, 31, 1938.

10 Diary, Nov 4, 1938.

11 Ogilvie-Forbes to Halifax, Oct 24 (PRO file FO.371/21658); and see Henderson's report on JG's speech at Marienfelde, Oct 13, 1938 (*ibid.*, /21655).

12 In the report on the 31st session of Göring's Defense Council on Oct 14, 1938, two pages were devoted the de-Jewing (*Entjudung*) of the economy (NA film T77, roll 131, 3295ff).

13 Unpubl. diary, Oct 12, 1938: 'It proceeds according to plan.'

14 *Ibid.*, Oct 13, 15 (Prague was now cracking down on émigrés, Jews, and communists, 'a nation is beginning to awake'), and 16, 1938.

15 *Star*, London, Oct 28, 1938: 'Nazis swoop on Polish Jews.' For existing literature, written before JG's diaries became available, see Helmut Heiber, 'Der Fall Grünspan,' in *VfZ*, 1957, 154–72; Hermann Graml, *Der 9. November 1938* (Bonn, 1958). For immense SD files on the assassin, *Kristallnacht*, and its origins, see the Moscow special archives: fond 500 opis 1 folders 602, 622A, 630, 631, 635, etc. (USHMM reels 8 and 9).

16 The Polish Jew Herschel Feibel Grynszpan (Grünspan) had run away from home in Germany in 1936 and drifted around Paris until Feb 1938 when his passport expired and the French ordered him out; he stayed on, lived underground. His parents were among the 15,000 Polish Jews hounded out of Germany in Oct 1938. – See F J Kaul, *Der Fall des Herschel Grynszpan* (East Berlin, 1965), which exploits the ZStA Potsdam files.

17 Unpubl. diary, Nov 7 (Moscow archives, photocopies only, Goebbels papers). – On Fürstenberg, see *VB*, Nov 7. And yet only on Oct 27, 1938 JG had noted: 'I have Schäffer [Willi Schaeffers] warned by Hanke. He's making political jokes again in the Comedians' Cabaret.'

18 *VB*, Nov 8, 1938: 'Jewish raid on German embassy in Paris.'

19 JG directive cited in Günther Gillessen, 'Reichskristallnacht,' anniversary supplement to *FAZ*, Nov 5, 1988.

20 The word with which JG prefaces most diary entries, *gestern* (yesterday), is missing. This suggests that JG in fact wrote it up on the tenth, with minor resulting anachronisms.

21 Unpubl. diary, Nov 9, 1938. I am grateful to Ingrid Weckert for her input on problems in its transcription.

22 It is thus unlikely that Hitler learned of the trouble brewing only after 7 P.M. at the evening's reception, with a messenger whispering it into his ear and him passing it on to JG – the version favored by Professor Hermann Graml, *Reichskristallnacht. Antisemitismus und Judenverfolgung im Dritten Reich* (Munich, 1988), 17ff, and adopted by Reuth, 395.

23 Statement by former S.A. Gruppenführer Max Jüttner (IfZ file ZS.243).

24 Unpubl. diary, Nov 10, 1938.

25 The Reichspropagandaämter. The source of this is a 1950 MS by Gauleiter Albert Hoffmann (BA file Kl. Erw. 954/II).

26 According to Brandenburg's gauleiter Emil Stürtz, speaking to his subordinate Kreisleiter and Gauamtsleiter afterward. Kehrl, 141f.

27 Testimony of Friedrich Eberstein, IMT, xx, 320.

28 Jordan to Weckert, quoted by her to the author, May 26, 1978.

29 Heinrich Heim statement, Oct 1, 1952 (IfZ file ZS.243).

30 British Consulate in Munich to embassy in Berlin, Nov 11, 1938 (PRO file FO.371/21637).

31 The witness was S.A. Gruppenführer Max Jüttner (IfZ file ZS.243). In his unpubl. diary Lutze enters merely: 'On the night of Nov 9–10, 1938 reprisals for the murder of v[om] Rath in Paris. Jews' shops are shut down.'

32 Interrogation of Hederich, Nuremberg, Apr 16, 1947 (NA film M.1019, roll 25). Ludwig Schneider of the Party's Supreme Court (OPG) confirmed this to him.

33 Carl Röver (Bremen), Jakob Sprenger (Frankfurt), Karl Kaufmann (Hamburg), and (surprisingly) Julius Streicher (Nuremberg), refused to have anything to do with it. See Graml, 33. – Streicher claimed to have had a blazing row with his police chief S.A. Gruppenführer von Obernitz and dissociated himself from the destruction of Nuremberg's synagogue. (Witness-application for Fritz Herrwarth, Streicher defense, Jan 24, 1946: NA file RG.260, OMGUS files, box 117).

34 According to testimony by Eugen Maier, one of Otto Dietrich's staff, on Dec 10, 1947, he subsequently learned that this *Aktion* had been 'initiated and launched' on this occasion by JG and Wagner (StA Nuremberg, G15). JG's diary appears to clear Wagner. See too the testimony of Dietrich's aide Heinz Lorenz, Dec 1947 (NA film M.1019, roll 43).

35 US First Army interrogation of S.A. Sturmführer Hans Stech, Apr 18–19, 1945 (NA file RG.407, entry 427, box 1945R).

36 British consulate report.

37 Report of Party Court to Göring, Feb 13, 1939 (ND: 3063-PS).

38 Report by S.A. Gruppe Nordmark, Kiel, on the *Aktion* of Nov 9/10, 1938 (BDC file 240/1). Kiel learned only that 'an unidentified official from the NSDAP headquarters (Reichsleitung)' had uttered these orders at a Munich meeting. At 11:55 P.M. the Gestapo headquarters in Berlin also issued an 'igniting' signal (ND: 374-PS), as did Eberstein at 2:10 A.M. to his police commanders at Nuremberg, Augsburg, etc. (BDC file 240/1 and ND: 374-PS).

39 Ingrid Weckert.

40 First report by Heydrich to Göring (ND: 3058-PS; USA–508).

41 *I.e.,* to destroy the biggest synagogue, at No. 79 Fasanenstrasse. Leopold Gutterer, telephoned with the news, saved the life of the caretaker who had been dragged out of his home and beaten up. Gutterer MS, 80f (Lower Saxony state archives, Wolfenbüttel.) – Nine of Berlin's remaining twelve synagogues were destroyed that night. H G Sellenthin, *Geschichte der Juden in Berlin und des Gebäudes Fasanenstraße 79/80* (Berlin, 1959) (hereafter Sellenthin).

42 Unpubl. diary, Nov 10, 1938.

43 ND: 3052-PS (error for 3051-PS?); but this clashes with Karl Wolff's statement in IfZ file ZS.317 and many taped interviews placing Himmler in Hitler's apartment at this time. The Reichsführer-SS was about to depart on one month's leave.

44 Author's interview of Col. Nicolaus von Below, May 18, 1968.

45 Testimony of Wilhelm Brückner (IfZ, Irving collection).

46 Schaub's unpubl. memoirs, in the author's collection (IfZ, ED.100/202); this of course contrasts starkly with JG's version of Schaub's activities.

47 Hederich interrogation. He was head of JG's *Abteilung Schrifttum* (literature department).

48 Fritz Wiedemann, handwritten MS, Feb 1939 (Libr. of Congress, Wiedemann papers, box 604).

49 ND: 3063-PS; repeated as circular 174, BDC file 240/I. At 3:45 A.M. the Berlin Gestapo headquarters reversed its previous order (Groscurth papers).

50 JG to Hitler, Jul 18, 1944 (BA file NL.118/107).

51 Ribbentrop, *Zwischen London und Moskau* (Leoni, 1953).

52 Unpubl. diary, Nov 10, 1938.

53 The recordings are in the Frankfurt radio archives (Ingrid Weckert); see the summary in PRO file FO.371/21637. The *VB*, Nov 11, 1938 also published the local gau's proclamation of twenty mass meetings in Munich that night to demonstrate against the Jews, to be addressed by Adolf Wagner and twenty others. The British consul reported, 'I hear that there is strong opposition to tonight's meetings from the Gestapo' (PRO file FO.371/21637).

54 Unpubl. diary, Nov 11, 1938.

55 JG, Schnellbrief, quoted in order of Gau headquarters, Bavarian Ostmark, Nov 10, 1938 (Yivo file G–198).

56 This was noted by Ogilvie-Forbes to FO, Nov 11, 1938 (PRO file FO.371/21637).

57 Unpubl. diary, Nov 11; *VB*, Nov 11, 1938; and Bruno Werner, *Die Galeere* (Frankfurt, 1949), 157. The shorthand record of Hitler's speech of Nov 10 is in BA file NS.11/28; see a different transcript with commentary by Wilhelm Treue in *VfZ*, 1958, 175ff, and the summary by Rudolf Likus, NA film T120, roll 31, 9044ff; for those present, see the Hoffmann negatives NA albums 242-HLB.3555–7, 3564.

58 Unpubl. diary, Nov 11, 1938.

59 Cited by Weckert. Wächter was promoted to the RPL (JG diary, Jan 3, 1941), headed its propaganda staff in 1942, and has been missing since 1945.

60 Diary, Nov 12, 1938.

61 *Time*, Mar 20, 1939. For German press coverage of this conference, see *DAZ*, Nov 12, 1938.

62 Likus to Ribbentrop, Nov 11 (NA film T120, roll 31, 9049); see too the FO's summary of events in PRO file FO.371/21637. Goebbels, mocked Ogilvie-Forbes to FO on Nov 12, 1938, maintained in his interview that Grynszpan 'must have' been taught to shoot: but 'he missed with three shots out of five at point-blank range!'

63 Lochner to his children, Jan 1, 1939 (Lochner papers, box 47).

64 Likus to Ribbentrop, Nov 11, 1938.

65 Ogilvie-Forbes to FO, Nov 14, 1938 (PRO file FO.371/21637).

66 Lutze diary, Nov 9–10, 1938.

67 Rosenberg diary, Feb 1939; and see his remarks to Georg Leibbrandt, quoted in interview with John Toland, Sep 6, 1971 (FDR Libr., Toland papers, box 52).

68 Testimony of Schirmeister and Fritzsche, Jun 28, 1946, IMT, xvii, 190f and 235ff.

69 Hassell diary, Nov 25, Dec 29, 1938; for Hess's condemnation of JG's actions that night see the Nuremberg interrogation of his secretary Ingeborg Sperr.

70 Communication of S.A. Supreme headquarters, Dec 19, 1938 (BDC file 240/11).

71 Unsigned letter to Hess, probably from Kurt Daluege, Dec 12, 1938 (BDC file, JG; author's

film DI–81).

72 Heydrich, speaking to Nazi politics course (Napola); quoted in Groscurth diary, Dec 29, 1938.

73 Himmler memorandum, cited by Raul Hilberg, *The Destruction of the European Jews* (New York, 1973).

74 Darré diary, Jun 2, 1939; there are signs that Goebbels was indeed feeling the strain, *e.g.* his diary of Nov 19, 1938 begins: 'I'm so ill and so tired. I must slow down my pace of work a bit.'

75 Kehrl, 142; Burckhardt, *Meine Danziger Mission*; and see Göring's witness summons for Gauleiter Dr Ueberreither (NA file RG.260, shipping list 74–3/7, box 117).

76 A partial stenogram is ND: 1816–PS; Ernst Woermann's two-page telephone summary for Ribbentrop is on NA film T120, roll 722, 1681ff. – General Wenninger, Luftwaffe attaché in London, told British Intelligence on Nov 21, 1938 'that Göring could not bear Goebbels and that there was bitter enmity between them' (PRO file FO.371/21665).

77 Opening the Reich Defense Council session in the air ministry building on Nov 18, Göring said in JG's presence: 'The plate-glass windows smashed during the demonstration against the Jews have not only inflicted a loss on the nation's wealth but necessitated the expenditure of four to five million marks in foreign currency... The Führer has therefore expressly ordered that from this moment on all destruction of assets is categorically forbidden!' (NA film T120, roll 131; summary 3088ff, verbatim 3157ff.); *cf.* JG unpubl. diary, Nov 19, 1938 – he did not mention Göring's rebuke.

78 Ogilvie-Forbes, reporting to the FO on Nov 13, lists Frick, JG, Gürtner, Krosigk, Funk as present, with Göring in the chair (PRO file FO.371/21637). On the economic measures against 50,000 Jews in the professions, see his telegram of Nov 16, 1938.

79 Diary, Nov 13, 1938.

80 The text is in PRO file FO.371/21637; see JG diary, Nov 13, 15; *The Times*, Nov 15. The interview was published with omissions in Germany on Nov 15 (Ogilvie-Forbes to FO, Nov 14, 15, 1938: FO.371/21637).

81 Diary, Nov 14; since Göring was now aryanizing all the Jewish businesses, he said, it would no longer be possible to get back at them by damaging their shops or businesses. *DAZ*, Nov 14: 'Goebbels: the Jewish Question will be Finally Solved.' See Ogilvie-Forbes to FO, Nov 14, 1938 (see note 80 above).

82 Diary, Nov 20, 1938.

83 Memo from W W Astor, Nov 9; British consulate in Vienna to Ogilvie-Forbes, Nov 25; memo by Capt. J McLaren, Nov 29; minute by W Ridsdale, Dec 6, 1938 (PRO file FO.371/21665).

84 Diary, Dec 4, 1938.

85 Wünsche diary, Nov 15, 1938 (BA file NS.10/125). Still further evidence of the unreliability of the 'diary' of Major Gerhard Engel, forged by him after the war and published by the Institut für Zeitgeschichte in Munich: this 'diary' has Hitler and JG 'convincingly explaining' the point of the *Aktion* to Hitler's lunch table at the Berlin chancellery four days before, on Nov 11, 1938. Reuth and other historians have fallen for the forgery, because of the IfZ imprimatur.

86 Diary, Nov 17, 1938.

87 Wünsche diary, Nov 15; JG diary, Nov 17. Kirkpatrick to FO, Nov 18. 'In order to put an end to them [rumors that JG was divorced] . . . Hitler made an appearance two days ago in the same theater sitting in the same box with Dr Goebbels and Frau Goebbels' (PRO file

FO.371/21655). And see C Burckhardt to League of Nations, Dec 2, 1938 (FO.371/21804).

88 Diaries of Wünsche and Eberhard (IfZ, Irving collection), Nov 16; author's interview of Gerhard Engel, Apr 5, 1971.

89 Diary, Nov 17, 1938.

Notes to Chapter 33.

1 Diary, Jan 1, 1939.

2 *Ibid.*, Jan 19, 1939.

3 Borresholm, 143ff; the episode was in the autumn of 1938.

4 Meissner, *Magda Goebbels*, 172. Possibly Hedda Uhlen or the young film actress Anneliese Uhlig. She had screen-tested for the film *Stimme aus dem Äther* (unpubl. JG diary, Jun 11, 1938).

5 Handwritten letter from H O [Oskar] Ritschel, director of the Magno Works, Duisburg, Dec 3 (Magda Goebbels papers, ZStA Potsdam, Rep. 90, Go 2, vol. 3); he mentions a major Norwegian industrialist who has invited him and Magda as guests. JG's diary talks on Dec 3, 1938 of 'many personal agonies. But I'm almost inured to them.'

6 Diary, Dec 8–9, 12; the newspapers reported he was suffering from acute intestinal influenza. *NYT*, Dec 23, 1938.

7 On Dec 30, 1938 he wrote it up in retrospect. He noted (*ibid.*, Dec 20, 1939) that the wedding anniversary then was somewhat nicer than in 1938: 'That was awful. This time we can all celebrate together again.' The *NYT* reported on Dec 31, 1938 that he had recovered enough to make his New Year's address.

8 Diary, Jan 1, 4, 1939.

9 *Ibid.*, Jan 8, 1939.

10 *Ibid.*, Jan 11, 1939.

11 *Ibid.*, Jan 17, 1939.

12 *Ibid.*, Feb 6, 8, 1939.

13 *Ibid.*, Jan 17, 1939.

14 *Ibid.*, Jan 18–20, 1939.

15 See Ebermayer and Meissner, No. 24, Jun 14, 1952.

16 Diary, Feb 4, 1937.

17 *Ibid.*, Jan 23, 1939.

18 *Ibid.*, Jan 25, 1939; the letter has not survived.

19 Letter from a Mr Flood, Mar 15, 1939 (PRO file FO.371/23007).

20 *Nieuwe Rotterdamsche Courant* published on Jan 22 in an article 'De Positie van Goebbels' rumors that the party court under Major Buch had considered JG's future; *NYT*, Jan 1, 21, 26, 1939.

21 Diary, Jan 27, 28, 1939.

22 The official was Gotthard Urban, Rosenberg's most senior political adviser. Rosenberg diary, Feb 6, 1939.

23 *Ibid.* As for the Goebbels manuscript on the Führer, 'Hitler won't let him publish it,' predicted Himmler. On Jun 14, 1939 JG noted (unpubl. diary), 'Amann now wants at last to publish my book about the Führer. But only the Führer himself can decide. I'd be happy to.'

24 Interview between Home Office ARP department and Major Otto Schwink, Feb 23, 1939

(PRO file FO.371/22965).

25 JG writes in his diary, 'Let's gloss over that.' The photo, published *inter alia* in *NYT*, Jan 30, and *Westfälische Landeszeitung*, Jan 31, 1939, shows Magda next to JG in a box, with Hanke and Capt. Wilhelm Weiss (editor of the *VB*).

26 British consul in Dresden, political report, Feb 28, 1939 (PRO file FO.371/22965).

27 Führer's adjutant to RMVP, Jun 2, 1938 (BA file NS.10/44).

28 See interrogation of Fritzsche, Nov 1, 1946. In May 1939 RMVP complained that *Stürmer* had mentioned the Czechs despite official policy to ignore them (Yivo files G–41; G–42, G–43).

29 Diary, Nov 11, 1938; Hassell diary, Jan 17, 1939.

30 Diary, Feb 1, Mar 22, 1939.

31 On Oct 22, 1939 he wrote (*ibid.*) that he could laugh himself sick about the 'wonderful' British caricatures of himself. On Nov 17, 1939 however he furiously noted (*ibid.*) that the *Daily Sketch* had published a cartoon depicting himself, Göring, and Hitler on the gallows: 'But it won't be long before we're paying them back'.

32 Diary, Jan 31, Feb 1, 3; *NYT*, Feb 4, 5, 1939.

33 JG's article in *VB*, Feb 4, was called: 'Do we still have a sense of humor?' – *NYT*, editorial Feb 7; contest ends, Mar 9, 1939.

34 Unpubl. diary, Mar 18, 1939.

35 JG's office to Dept Ib of RMVP, Apr 1, 1939 (BA file R.55/945).

36 Diary, Jan 26, 29, 1939; Rosenberg diary.

37 Diary, Jan 29, 1939.

38 Bartels to JG, Aug 1 (ZStA Potsdam, Rep. 50.01, RMVP, vol. 759); diary, Feb 3, 4, 7, 1939. The refrigeration company warned that JG would have to authorize them to downgrade vital military contracts if he was to get these items on time.

39 Unpubl. diary, Mar 18; on Jun 20, 1939 (*ibid.*) he records further money worries about Lanke, and Amann, faced by tax problems, is refusing to bail him out. 'But I'll find a way out.'

40 Phone book, Haus am Bogensee (BA file R.55/1402); and author's visit to the site. The window still operates.

41 *Angriff*, Nov 30; diary, Dec 17, 1938.

42 Diary, Nov 24, 1938.

43 Ogilvie-Forbes to FO, Nov 23, 1938 (PRO file FO.371/21665); diary, Nov 18, Dec 8, 1938.

44 Dr Paul Schmidt, chief of German FO press section, to Woermann, undated minute, endorsed: '*Morgenbespr.*' (morning conference), Mar 20 [1939?], on NA film T120, roll 1434, D578256f.

45 Heinrich Hansen (Dietrich's press officer) affidavit, Jul 10, 1948 (StA Nuremberg, G15).

46 Diary, Dec 8, 1938.

47 *Ibid.*, Feb 5, 1939; author's interview, Jul 1989.

48 Behrend, No. 19, May 10, 1952; JG diary, Jan 26, Feb 5, 11, 1939.

49 Diary, Dec 22, 1937.

50 Darges to Wünsche, Jun 27, 1939 (BA file NS.10/49).

51 Bahls to RMVP, Apr 24, 1939 (*ibid.*).

52 Diary, Jan 25, 27, 1939.

53 *Ibid.*, Jan 11, 28, Feb 8, 9, 14, 1939.

54 *Ibid.*, Jan 22; JG's article, 'What does America really want?' was also featured in *Hamburger Tageblatt*, *Berliner Tageblatt*, *Frankfurter Zeitung*, and several other newspapers. On Feb

28, 1939 the British consul in Dresden confirmed that by identifying Roosevelt with the influential Jews around him JG had scored quite a propaganda hit.

55 Diary, Jan 3, Feb 6, 1939.

56 *Ibid.*, Nov 5, 12, 1938, Mar 23, 1939.

57 *Ibid.*, Mar 20, 1939.

58 British embassy Berlin to FO, Nov 25 (PRO file FO.371/21665); diary, Nov 20, 1938.

59 Diary, Dec 14, 15, 1938.

60 *VB*, Jan 31, 1939.

61 Diary, Feb 1, 1939.

62 *Ibid.*, Feb 3, 1939.

63 *VB*, Feb 25; reproduced by other newspapers, *e.g. Frankfurter Zeitung*, Feb 26. Writing to the FO, Feb 28, 1939, Henderson urged that Downing Street exercise a moderating influence on newspapers like the *News Chronicle* 'in the interests of appeasement generally' (PRO file FO.371/22966).

64 Ebermayer and Meissner, No. 24, Jun 14, 1952.

65 Diary, Mar 4; unpubl. diary, Mar 5, 10, 1939 (Moscow archives, Goebbels papers, box 1).

66 Unpubl. diary, Mar 11, 1939.

67 *Ibid.*, Mar 12, 1939.

68 CSDIC interrogation of Baarova's manager, 'Mar 15, 1944,' in MI.14 dossier on JG (PRO file WO.208/4462). He had smuggled her back to Germany.

69 Unpubl. diary, Mar 13, 1939.

70 *Ibid.*

71 *Ibid.*, Mar 14, 1939.

72 *Ibid.*, Mar 15, 1939.

73 *Ibid.*, Mar 16, 1939.

74 Diary, Mar 19, 25, 28, 1939.

75 *Ibid.*, Mar 23, 1939.

76 *Ibid.*, Mar 25, 1939.

77 Curt von Siewert, minute on Hitler's meeting with Brauchitsch (ND: R–100).

78 Admiral Erich Raeder's papers.

79 Diary, Mar 28, 1939.

Notes to Chapter 34.

1 Ogilvie-Forbes to FO, Mar 28, 1939 (PRO file FO.371/23006).

2 Diary, Mar 28, 29, Apr 1; Sir G Knox to Halifax, Mar 27, 31, 1939 (PRO file FO.371/23006).

3 Sir Sydney Waterlow to FO, Mar 31 (PRO file FO.371/23006); he stated that JG was accompanied by RMVP officials G W Müller, von Wiesenhof (*sic.* Franz von Weyssenhoff), and Knock (Willi Knoche). And see E M B Ingram to Waterlow, Apr 6, 1939 (*ibid.*, /23007).

4 Diary, Apr 1, 1939.

5 *Ibid.*, Apr 4, 1939.

6 Sir Miles Lampson to FO, Apr 4, 1939 (PRO file FO.371/23006).

7 Diary, Apr 8, 1939.

8 Lampson to FO, Apr 29, 1939 (PRO file FO.371/23007). And see B Vernier, *La Politique islamique de l'Allemagne* (Paris, 1939), 38f, and Lukasz Hirszowicz, *The Third Reich and the Arab East* (London, 1966), 18.

9 Diary, Apr 10, 1939.

10 See the diaries of Bormann; Eberhard; and Major Wilhelm Deyhle, Jodl's staff officer (ND: 1796-PS); also a letter from Col. Eduard Wagner to his wife, Mar 30 and Apr 1 (in which latter he wrote *gestern bei der Führerentscheidung. . .* ' – 'yesterday, when the Führer reached his decision. . . ').

11 Sir H Knatchbull-Hugessen to FO, Apr 21, 1939 (PRO file FO.371/23007).

12 Waterlow to FO, Apr 6, 1939 (PRO file FO.371/23006).

13 US State Dept interrogation of Göring, Nov 6–7, 1945 (author's film DI–34); JG's diary, Apr 19, 1939.

14 Gutterer MS and interview, Jun 30, 1993; JG diary, Apr 20, 1939; the RMVP program in BA file NS.10/127 times this reception at 8 P.M.

15 Karl-Heinz Hederich, interrogation, Dec 17, 1947 (NA film M.1019, roll 25).

16 Unpubl. diary, Apr 24, 1939.

17 *Ibid.*, May 2, 1939.

18 Diary, May 3; press directive, May 5, 1939 in Brammer collection (BA file ZSg.101).

19 Unpubl. diary, May 6, 1939.

20 E G Cable, British consul-general in Cologne, to British embassy in Berlin, May 23 (PRO file FO.371/22989); diary, May 19; *VB*, May 18 and 22, and *DAZ* and *Westdeutscher Beobachter*, May 20, 21, 1939.

21 Unpubl. diary, May 23; Ribbentrop had endless rows with JG afterward over his humiliation at the signing (he had been placed in a rear row). And *ibid.*, Jun 1, 2, 1939.

22 *Ibid.*, May 12, 1939.

23 Report to Reich Defense Council, Jun 5, 1939 (NA film T77, roll 131, 3043f). In addition five one-megawatt transmitters were to be ready later in 1939. Over eight months from May 1941 the RMVP would also take sixteen mobile transmitters into service. For the ministry's mobilization preparations in Jun 1939 see ZStA Potsdam, Rep. 50.01, RMVP, vol. 874.

24 Berndt to Himmler, Jul 11, 1944 (NA film T175, roll 33, 1405).

25 See the analysis by Gabi Frautschi, Aug 21, 1947 in NA file RG.260, shipping list 53–3/7, box 15.

26 Author's interview of Lida Baarova, Salzburg, Jul 4, 1993.

27 CSDIC interrogation of Baarova's manager, 'Mar 15, 1944,' in MI.14 dossier on JG (PRO file WO.208/4462).

28 Hanke to Himmler, May 20, 1939 (BDC file, Hanke). Greven denied this – he said he had lunged at Hanke, whom two burly SS men had saved.

29 Unpubl. diary, May 20, 1939.

30 *Ibid.*, May 23, 25, 1939.

31 *Ibid.*, May 26, Jun 4, 1939.

32 *Ibid.*, Jun 2, 7, 8, 1939.

33 *Ibid.*, May 11, 1939.

34 *Ibid.*, Jun 17, 1939.

35 *Ibid.*, Jun 22, 1939.

36 *Ibid.*, Jun 14, 1939: 'I've at last sold my house. I'm glad to be shot of that burden.'

37 Magda Goebbels to Ritschel, Jun 16 (ZStA Potsdam, Rep. 90, Go 2, vol. 3); JG unpubl. diary, Jun 17, 1939: 'Long discussion with Magda. House selling and buying. The Führer also wants to buy into Schwanenwerder. That would be nice.'

38 *Berliner Illustrierte*, Aug 3, 1939.

39 See the four files of confidential press circulars issued by RPA Berlin, Jun 1 – Dec 30, 1939 in Fritzsche's papers in the Hoover Libr., MS division (accession XX185–9.13), box 4. For an analysis of the press directives, see Walter Hagemann, *Publizistik im Dritten Reich. Ein Beitrag zur Methode der Massenführung* (Hamburg, 1948). For BA files of press conferences from various sources, see ZSg.101 (Karl Brammer); ZSg.102 (Fritz Sänger); ZSg.110 (Gottfried Traub); ZSg.115 (Fritz Nadler); ZSg.109 (Theo Oberheitmann); ZSg.116 (DNB).

40 Comments of Major Percy C Black, acting US military attaché, Berlin, on current events, Report No. 28, Aug 21, 1939 (FDR Libr., Harry L Hopkins papers, box 187, vol. vii).

41 RPA (Reichspropagandaamt) Frankfurt, *Vertrauliche Nachrichten* (hereafter RPA Frankfurt, confidential briefing), Jul 20 and Aug 5, 1939. These and 'special briefings' are published in Helmut Sündermann, *Tagesparolen. Deutsche Presseweisungen 1939–1945. Hitlers Propaganda und Kriegsführung* (Leoni, 1973) (hereafter Sündermann), 20ff. More such items, 1941–43, are in Yivo file G–105. See BA files, ZSg.109, Oberheitmann Material (also ND: NG–3800), and Brammer material (ND: NG–3070).

42 Unpubl. diary, Jun 16, 1939.

43 Dispatches by Shepherd, British consul-general in Danzig, to Halifax, Jun 19 and 21, 1939 (PRO file FO.371/23021).

44 Unpubl. diary, Jun 18, 1939.

45 *Pressereferent* memoirs. And *Danziger Vorposten*, Jun 18, 1939.

46 A verbatim text reached London on Jun 21, 1939 (PRO file FO.371/23020); unpubl. diary, Jun 19, 1939: 'I receive the foreign press and lay it on the line to them.'

47 Hassell diary, Jun 20, 1939.

48 Henderson to FO, Jun 19, 1939 (PRO file FO.371/23020).

49 RPA Berlin, press circulars in the Fritzsche papers, Hoover Libr., MS division, box 4.

50 RPA Berlin, press circular, Jun 30, Jul 1; unpubl. diary, Jul 2, 1939.

51 RPA Berlin, press circular, Jul 1, 1939, commenting on articles in *Daily Mail* and *Le Jour*.

52 *Ibid.*, Jun 3, Jul 20; RPA Frankfurt, special briefing, Jul 1, and confidential briefing, Jul 3, 14, 1939.

53 RPA Berlin, press circular, Jun 24, 27, Jul 1; JG had to drop the Japanese atrocity stories so as not to irritate Tokyo – 'So no more stories about Englishmen being stripped naked' (*ibid.*, Jun 27, 1939).

54 *Ibid.*, Jun 20, 28, 1939. When the RPL published a wall-newspaper, *Die Parole der Woche*, depicting British soldiers killing Palestinians demonstrating against 'Jewish rule,' the OKW objected to attacks on British soldiers who were merely 'obeying orders' (Yivo, file G–52).

55 RPA Berlin, press circular, Jun 27; unpubl. diary, Jun 29, 30, 1939.

56 Interrogation of Schirmeister, May 6, 1946 (NA film M.1270, roll 19); JG unpubl. diary, Jun 27, 1939; Gutterer interview, Jun 30, 1993.

57 *Pressereferent* memoirs. The letter had evidently been drafted by Hans Schwarz van Berk, one of JG's top tacticians. The unpubl. diary, Jun 30, Jul 7, 1939, seems to bear this out.

58 RPA Berlin, press circular, Jun 19, 28, 1939.

59 Unpubl. diary, Jun 2, 4, 12, 1939.

60 *Ibid.*, Jun 12, 13, 1939.

61 *Ibid.*, Jun 25, 1939.

62 *Ibid.*, Jun 16, 17, 18, 20, 1939.

63 *Ibid.*, Jun 21, 1939.

64 *Ibid.*, Jul 6, 8, 1939. 'But at least we both made the effort to restore human relations between us.'

65 *Ibid.*, Jun 2, 3, 11, 1939.

66 *Ibid.*, Jun 23, 1939.

67 *Ibid.*, Oct 29, 1939.

68 Unpubl. diary, Jun 24, 1939

69 *Ibid.*, Jun 11, 1939.

70 *Ibid.*, Jul 5, 1939.

71 *Ibid.*, Jul 5, 1939. For the text of the four King-Hall letters see *Living Age*, Sep 12–16; *Berliner Börsenzeitung*, Jul 16; *MNN*, Jul 17, 1939.

72 Oven, 'Feb 27, 1944,' 240f.

73 Unpubl. diary, Jul 6, 8, 1939.

74 *Ibid.*, Jul 9, 1939.

75 *Ibid.*, Jul 12, 1939.

76 *Ibid.*, Jul 13; printed in *Angriff*, Jul 14, under the headlines 'GOEBBELS REPLY TO BRITAIN. GOEBBELS RIPS MASK OFF KING-HALL. LORD HALIFAX AND THE BRITISH PROPAGANDA BUREAU'S LETTERS,' and in *VB*, Jul 19, 1939.

77 Henderson to FO, Jul 17 and 18, and Sir P Ramsay (Copenhagen) to FO, Jul 14 (PRO file FO.371/22990); *VB*, Jul 14, 1939.

78 Unpubl. diary, Jul 16, 17, 18, 25, 1939.

79 *Ibid*, Jul 4, 1939.

80 *Ibid.*, Jul 9, 1939.

81 *Ibid.*, Jul 10, 11, 1939: 'The Führer is still working over my answer to Britain.'

82 *Ibid.*, Jul 12, 1939.

83 *Ibid.*, Jul 17; RMVP program for Jul 14, 15, 1939 (BA file NS.10/126).

84 Unpubl. diary, Jul 21, 1939.

85 *Ibid.*, Jul 23, 1939.

86 *Ibid.*, Jul 24, 1939.

87 *Ibid.*, Jul 25, 26, 1939.

88 *Ibid.*, Jul 18, 21, 1939.

89 *Ibid.*, Jul 26, 1939.

90 *Ibid.*, Jul 27, 1939.

91 Ebermayer and Meissner, No. 24, Jun 14, 1952, wrongly set the dialogue in Salzburg.

92 Unpubl. diary, Jul 27, 1939.

93 *Ibid.*, Jul 28; the diary mentions the 'decision' several times later, *e.g.*, Jul 30 ('Frau [Helga] Bouhler. She is really happy about our decision') and Aug 1, 5, 1939.

Notes to Chapter 35.

1 Leopold Gutterer had a working television set in his apartment throughout the coming war (interview).

2 Unpubl. diary, Aug 4, 1939.

3 *Ibid.*, Jul 29, 1939.

4 *Ibid.*, Aug 1, 5, 1939.

5 See the hectographed list of 'what to wear to the party rally,' attached to a letter of Aug 8, 1939 (Hoover Libr., Goebbels papers, box 2).

6 Ministerial conference (see note 59 of next chapter), Feb 2; diary, Feb 3, 1940.

7 RPA Berlin, press circular, Jun 3, 9, 20, 23, 27, 28, 30, Jul 1, 8, 10, 12, 13, 17, 31, 1939.

8 *Ibid.*, Aug 2, 1939.

9 *Ibid.*, Aug 1, 2, 1939.

10 *Ibid.*, Aug 7, 1939.

11 At 265,000 marks per month. Brückner to Funk, Aug 18 (BA file NS.10/38); and unpubl. diary, Jun 2, 16, 17, Aug 19, 1939.

12 RPA Berlin, press circular, Aug 10; *VB*, Aug 12, 1939.

13 Freybe to Waldegg, Aug 10, 1939 (Hoover Libr., Goebbels papers, box 2).

14 Unpubl. diary, Aug 9, 10, 1939.

15 *Ibid.*, Aug 13; *Frankfurter Zeitung* and *DAZ*, Aug 9, 1939.

16 Unpubl. diary, Aug 10, 1939.

17 *Ibid.*, Aug 11, 1939.

18 RPA Frankfurt, confidential briefing, Aug 8, 1939.

19 RPA Frankfurt, special briefing, Aug 10, 1939.

20 *Ibid.*, Aug 12, 1939.

21 RPA Berlin, press circular, Aug 11, 1939.

22 RPA Frankfurt, confidential briefing, Aug 14, 1939.

23 RPA Berlin, press circular, Aug 16, 1939.

24 *Ibid.*, Aug 16, 1939.

25 RPA Frankfurt, confidential briefing, Aug 17, 1939.

26 For JG's 1939 domestic staff see BA file R.55/945.

27 Details, correspondence, estimates, and inventories in BA files R.55/421, /423, /1360.

28 Unpubl. diary, Aug 17, 18; and see Jul 3, 1939. On No. 20 Hermann-Göring-Strasse see BA files R.55/421, /423, /430, /1360.

29 Unpubl. diary, Aug 19, 1939.

30 *Ibid.*, Aug 17, 19, 1939.

31 RPA Frankfurt, confidential briefing, Aug 18, 1939. 'In propaganda it has always proved very effective to personalize a political issue.'

32 *Ibid.*

33 Unpubl. diary, Aug 19, 20, 1939.

34 *Ibid.*, Aug 20, 1939.

35 Major Percy C Black (see note 40 of previous chapter).

36 Unpubl. diary, Jul 9, 1939.

37 RPA Frankfurt, special briefing, Jul 12, 1939.

38 RPA Frankfurt, confidential briefing, Jul 27, 1939.

39 *Ibid.*, Aug 7, 1939.

40 RPA Berlin, press circular, Aug 5, 1939.

41 Unpubl. diary, Aug 21; RPA Frankfurt, special briefing, Aug 21, 1939.

42 Unpubl. diary, Aug 22, 1939; the Forschungsamt 'intercepts' will be found in David Irving, *Breach of Security* (London, 1968), 92ff; and *Das Reich hört mit*.

43 Unpubl. diary, Aug 22, 1939.

44 RPA Frankfurt, confidential briefing, Aug 22, 1939, in Oberheitmann collection (BA file ZSg.109).

45 Unpubl. diary, Aug 23, 1939.

46 *Ibid.*

47 Louis Lochner, who obtained Canaris's report on the meeting from General Beck, knew

more than JG; see his interrogation, Jul 25, 1945 (NA film M.1270, roll 12) and *What about Germany?*

48 RPA Frankfurt, confidential briefing, Aug 23, 1939.

49 The London *Daily Express* revealed that the pact had a secret clause relating to the partition of these states (Hans 'Johnny' von Herwarth, a traitor in Hitler's Moscow embassy, had leaked the text). JG issued a denial: RPA press circular, Aug 26, 1939.

50 Unpubl. diary, Aug 24, 1939.

51 RPA Frankfurt, confidential briefing, Aug 24, 1939.

52 RPA Berlin, press circular, Aug 24, 1939, No. 192/39.

53 *Ibid.*, Aug 25, 1939.

54 Unpubl. diary, Aug 25, 1939.

55 *Ibid.*, Aug 25, 1939.

56 RPA Frankfurt, confidential briefing, Aug 25, 1939.

57 *Ibid.*, 1. Ergänzung.

58 Photo in Eva Braun collection, NA file RG.242-EB.

59 Unpubl. diary, Aug 26, 1939.

60 RPA Frankfurt, confidential briefing, Aug 26, 1939.

61 Ettore Slocovich, Alfieri message to JG, Aug 26, 1939, 12:30 P.M. See PWB report No. 6, Documents found in the Italian Ministry of Popular Culture, item No. 6: telephone conversations between Alfieri or Slocovich and JG, Aug–Sep 1939; *cf.* PRO file FO.371/43877. The originals are in Mussolini's files, NA film T586, roll 415, 6577ff. JG noted (unpubl. diary, Aug 27, 1939): 'Alfieri phones. He wants to pump me. But I act dumb.'

62 Backe to his wife, Aug 1939 (Ursula Backe papers).

63 *Ibid.*, Aug 27, 1939.

64 Gutterer MS, and interview, Jun 30, 1933; JG diary, Aug 28, 1939.

65 Bormann diary, Aug 27; diary of F W Krüger, Aug 27 (Hoover Libr., Krüger papers); and the diaries of General Franz Halder and Lt-Col. Helmuth Groscurth, Aug 28, 1939.

66 Unpubl. diary, Aug 28, 1939.

67 *Ibid.*, Aug 30, 1939.

68 *Ibid.*, on Aug 30, 1939 JG had a further talk with Dietrich – 'He sees the situation quite clearly. He loathes Ribbentrop.'

69 *Ibid.*, Aug 29, 1939.

70 *Ibid.*, Aug 30, 1939.

71 *Ibid.*, Aug 31; and RPA Frankfurt, confidential briefing, Aug 30, 1939.

72 RPA Frankfurt, special briefing, Aug 30, 1939.

73 RPA Berlin, press circular, Aug 30, 1939, No. 198a/39.

74 Unpubl. diary, Aug 31, 1939.

75 *Ibid.*, Sep 1, 1939. JG added later, 'Polish attack on the Gleiwitz transmitter. We make a big thing of this.' In fact the attack was by SS men wearing Polish uniforms.

76 *Ibid.*

Notes to Chapter 36.

1 Testimony of Schirmeister, IMT, xvii, 258f, 275f.

2 Testimony of Fritzsche, *ibid.*, 161.

3 RPA Frankfurt, confidential briefing, Sep 1, No. 197/39 (Oberheitmann collection, BA file ZSg.109/5); JG unpubl. diary, Sep 2, 1939.

4 Interrogation of Schirmeister, May 6, 1946 (NA film M.1270, roll 19).

5 RPA Frankfurt, confidential briefing, Sep 3, 1939.

6 JG, 25pp. memo for Hitler, 'Gedanken zum Kriegsbeginn 1939' (BA file NS.10/37). Later (diary, Nov 4, 1939) JG himself would decide not to accept any memoranda longer than 3pp.

7 Note for Italian minister of popular culture on phone call to JG, Sep 10, 1939 (NA film T586, roll 415, 6583ff).

8 Unpubl. diary, Sep 7; Hitler's draft ordinance (*Verfügung*) of Sep 3 is publ. in *ADAP(D)*, vii, No. 574. On Sep 9, 1939 JG recorded, 'There's still no end to Ribbentrop's mischief.'

9 Hitler had known since Sep 27 that a *German* submarine was responsible for the sinking, but he did not tell JG; Heinz Lorenz confirmed this under interrogation, Dec 3, 1947, part ii (NA film M.1019, roll 43).

10 Hitler did not tell JG that the assassin Georg Elser had already been caught on Nov 9 and interrogated.

11 Unpubl. diary, Sep 2, 1939.

12 *Ibid.*, Sep 3, 1939.

13 *Ibid.*

14 On Blomberg, see *ibid.*, Dec 2, 1944; on Fritsch, Jun 14, 1938.

15 Groscurth diary, Sep 29; in unpubl. diary, Sep 24, 1939 JG noted: 'Fritsch died a magnificent death. His body had to be recovered by shock-troops. He was right up front. A true soldier!'

16 JG visited Führer's headquarters on Sep 7 (Führer's headquarters war diary, Sep 7; IfZ film MA.272, 0627); and Sep 14: Bormann diary and JG's phone conv. with Alfieri that day (NA film T586, roll 415, 6577ff).

17 Rosenberg diary, Sep 29, 1939.

18 Darré diary, Sep 9, 1939 (transcript in BA: Darré papers, vol. 65a).

19 Unpubl. diary, Sep 3, 1939.

20 See JG to Lammers, Sep 1, 1939 ('No objections have been raised') and other documents in NA film T120, roll 2474, E255273ff; the Mar 1936 – Jul 1941 file on listening to enemy broadcasts in ZStA Potsdam, Rep. 50.01, RMVP, vol. 630; and C F Latour's paper in *VfZ* 1963, 418ff.

21 Gürtner to Lammers, Sep 1, 1939 (NA film T120, roll 2474, E.255277f).

22 Lammers minute, Sep 1, 1939 (*ibid.*, E.255279).

23 *Ibid.*, Sep 2 ('that's great: we have smitten this weapon from the enemy's hand'); Groscurth, official diary, Sep 8. On Sep 3 (unpubl. diary) JG noted, 'Big row over the decree on foreign radio stations. Göring, Frick, and Gürtner don't want to go as far as I.' The law was gazetted in the *RGBl.* on Sep 7, 1939.

24 Hess to members of the Cabinet, Sep 3 (NA film T120, roll 2474, E255295ff); Heydrich, *Schnellbrief* of Sep 16, 1939 (Hoover Libr., Lerner papers, file DE.460/DIS.202).

25 JG circular to all gauleiters and gau propaganda directors, Sep 10, 1939 (NA film T581/16; BA file NS.26/291).

26 Darré diary, Sep 6; and see the entry for Sep 20, 1939.

27 Unpubl. diary, Sep 4, 1939.

28 *Ibid.*, Sep 5, 7; JG assured Alfieri late on Sep 4, 1939 that since there were no U-boats nearby, Mr Churchill must have ordered the *Athenia*, with its many American passen-

gers, sunk to propel the USA into the war (NA film T586, roll 415, 6577).

29 Unpubl. diary, Sep 5, 1939.

30 *Ibid.*, Sep 6, 1939.

31 Note for Alfieri, Sep 9, 8:30 P.M. (pp. 6577ff).

32 Unpubl. diary, Sep 6, 1939.

33 Führer decree of Sep 8 on Foreign Propaganda, ND: NG.3259 and ADAP(D), viii, No. 31; and see foreign ministry (Habicht) to Keitel, Nov 29, 1939 (OKW files, NA film T77, roll 64, 7860f).

34 Unpubl. diary, Sep 9, 1939.

35 *E.g., ibid.*, Sep 14, 15, 1939.

36 *Ibid.*, Sep 10, 1939.

37 Note for Italian minister of popular culture on phone call to JG, Sep 10 (NA film T586, roll 415, 6583ff); unpubl. diary, Sep 11, 1939. 'Then I brief the Führer and Ribbentrop on our conversation. They want to wait and see. Question what Russia's up to now.'

38 Unpubl. diary, Sep 17, 1939: 'The justification is very original,' commented JG.'

39 *Ibid.*, Sep 13, 1939.

40 Note for Italian minister of popular culture on phone call to JG, Sep 16, 8 P.M. (NA film T586, roll 415, 6586f).

41 JG, *Propaganda Parole*, Oct 2, 1939, in OKW secret propaganda files (NA film T77, roll 964, 7332).

42 Diary, Oct 11, 13, 1939.

43 *Ibid.*, Dec 12, 1939.

44 *Ibid.*, Oct 18, 1939.

45 *Ibid.*, Oct 14, 17, 1939.

46 *Ibid.* Oct 15, 18, 1939.

47 *Ibid.*, Oct 20, 1939.

48 *Ibid.*, Oct 23; *VB*, Oct 21, 1939.

49 Diary, Oct 28, 1939.

50 On this routine, see the interrogations of *inter alia* Helmut Sündermann, Oct 15; Werner Stephan, Oct 29; Fritzsche, Oct 7; Dietrich, Oct 14 and 17; and Gutterer, Dec 18, 1947 (NA: RG.260, list 53–3/7, box 15).

51 *Kreis-, Gau-, Stoßtrupp-, and Reichsredner.* See the RPL report, 'Die Propagandaarbeit der Partei im Kriege,' winter 1940–41 (NSDAP archives, NA film T581, roll 16).

52 Diary, Nov 5, 1937.

53 *Ibid.*, Oct 17, 24, Nov 2, 3, 9, 11, 12, 18, 19, 28, Dec 18, 1939.

54 Harlan, *Im Schatten meiner Filme*, 111f.

55 Diary, Dec 15, 30, 1939.

56 H Parlo *et al.*, *Jud Süss. Historisches und juristisches Material zum Fall Veit Harlan* (Hamburg, 1949).

57 *Sunday Express*, Sep 3, 1939, p. 1.

58 Diary, Oct 31, 1939.

59 *Daily Sketch*, London, Nov 9; diary, Nov 17, 19. Ministerkonferenz, Nov 19, 1939. The transcripts of these ministerial conferences, now on the original microfiches in Moscow archives, were also held on microfilm in ZStA Potsdam; Willi Boelcke, a former ZStA official, fled to West Germany taking microfilms with him, and published them as *Kriegspropaganda 1939–1941. Geheime Ministerkonferenzen im Reichspropagandaministerium* (Stuttgart, 1966), and *Wollt Ihr den totalen Krieg? Die geheimen Goebbels-Konferenzen*

1939–1943 (Stuttgart, 1967). Whether from Boelcke or the original files, they are cited hereafter as MinConf. – See too Karl-Dietrich Abel, *Presselenkung im NS*-Staat (Berlin, 1968), and Fritz Sänger, *Politik der Täuschungen. Mißbrauch der Presse im Dritten Reich. Weisungen, Informationen, Notizen* (Vienna, 1975).

60 Diary, Nov 2. And see *Westdeutscher Beobachter,* Nov 1; *DAZ,* Nov 2; *NYT,* Nov 3; and picture in *Illustrierter Beobachter,* Nov 9, 1939.

61 Diary, Nov 3, 1939.

62 *Ibid.,* Dec 5, 1939.

63 Rosenberg diary, Nov 11, Dec 3; for JG's speech see *DAZ,* and *Berliner Börsenzeitung,* Oct 23, 1939.

64 Diary, Nov 2; RMVP (Hippler) to Schaub, Nov 1, and reply (BA file NS.10/46); *cf.* Rosenberg diary, Dec 8, 1939.

65 Rosenberg diary, Dec 11; JG diary, Dec 12, 1939.

66 *Ibid.,* Oct 27, 30, 1939.

67 See the architect's file, Oct 1939, in ZStA Potsdam, Rep. 50.01, RMVP, vol. 1032; and diary, Oct 15, 21, 22, 28, 1939.

68 Diary, Oct 18–26, 1939.

69 *Ibid.,* Nov 10, 1939.

70 Diary, Dec 6, 9, 1939.

71 *Ibid.,* Nov 5, 1939.

72 *Ibid.,* Nov 8, 1939.

73 *Ibid.,* Dec 4, 1939; and letter from Magda's secretary to ration card office, Jan 9, 1940 (ZStA Potsdam, Rep. 90, Go 2, vol. 2).

74 See Himmler files, NA film T175, roll 473, 4786; and BA file NS.10/126.

75 Diary, Nov 9, 1939.

76 RPA Berlin, press circular, Nov 9, 1939 (Hoover Libr., Fritzsche papers, box 4); on Nov 10, a further circular directed journalists to blame '*world* Jews and not the Jewish community in Germany.'

77 Diary, Nov 10, 11; RPA Berlin, press circular, Nov 22, 1939.

78 Borresholm, 146ff.

79 Diary, Nov 11, 12, 1939.

80 MinConf., Nov 10, 1939.

81 Diary, Nov 13, 14, 15; MinConf., Nov 11, 13; RPA Berlin, press circular, Nov 11; *cf. NYT,* Nov 13, 1939. The murderer Georg Elser, aged thirty-six, a Swabian watch-maker, had been caught a few hours after the bomb blast: see BA files NS.20/65 and R.22/3100; he appeared to have acted alone.

82 RPA Berlin, press circular, Nov 21; news of the capture had been embargoed on the tenth (*ibid.*).

83 MinConf., Nov 2, 22, 25, 1939; Boelcke, *Kriegspropaganda,* 229.

84 MinConf., Nov 11, 13, 1939.

85 Borresholm, 146ff.

86 Karl Loog, *Die Weissagungen des Nostradamus. Erstmalige Auffindung des Chiffreschlüssels und Enthüllung der Prophezeihungen über Europas Zukunft und Frankreichs Glück und Niedergang 1555–2200* (Pfullingen, 1940). And Bruno Winkler, *Englands Aufstieg und Niedergang nach den Prophezeiungen des großen französischen Sehers der Jahre 1555 und 1558* (Leipzig, 1940). Diary, Dec 5, 14; MinConf., Dec 5, 1939. He sent a copy of the Nostradamus brochure to Hitler's adjutant Albert Bormann, estranged brother of Martin, on

Sep 10, 1940 (Princeton Univ. Libr., Hitler collection).

87 MinConf., Dec 11, 12, 1939.

88 Diary, Dec 13, 14, 17. MinConf., Oct 28, 1939; Feb 27, 1940.

89 Diary, Dec 17, 1939.

90 RPA Berlin, press circular, Dec 11, 1939 (Hoover Libr., Fritzsche papers, box 4). For a further collection of RPA Berlin special press circulars Oct 1939 – Jul 1940 see ZStA Potsdam, Rep. 50.01, RMVP, vol. 1041.

91 Diary, Dec 20, 1939.

92 MinConf., Oct 28, 1939; Apr 20, 24, 1940.

93 Diary, Nov 3; MinConf., Nov 2, 3, 11, 1939.

94 MinConf., Nov 17, 18, Dec 19, 20, 1939; Jan 11, 1940. Diary, Dec 14, 15, 17, 19, 1939; Jan 9, 10, 1940. He directed Fritzsche to publish fresh sentences every two or three weeks as a deterrent (MinConf., Apr 19, 1940).

95 For the first *WB* see the SD morale reports called 'Meldungen aus dem Reich,' Nov 22 (NA film T175, roll 258, 0299f and 0317) (hereafter Meldungen); and OKW propaganda files, Dec 2, 1939, NA film T77, roll 964, 7987ff. For the second, third, and fourth *WB* and other leaflets including *Fliegende Blätter Nr. 1* and *Englands Kriegsziel – Englands Friedensziel*, see Meldungen, Dec 6, 29, 1939, and Jan 12, 1940 (0396f, 0535f, 0538f).

96 MinConf., Dec 9, 11, 1939.

97 Diary, Dec 5, 1939.

98 RPA Berlin, press circulars, Dec 23, 26, 1939; Meldung, Jan 5; MinConf., Jan 9, 1940.

99 RPA Berlin, press circular, Nov 17, 18, 1939.

100 *Ibid.*, Nov 21, 23, Dec 18, 1939. In Mar 1942 he informed the magazine *Kirchenmusik* that even reviewers of church singing had to sign their full names (Yivo file G–17).

101 RPA Berlin, press circular, Dec 16, 28, 1939

Notes to Chapter 37.

1 Diary, Jan 24, 25, 1940.

2 *Ibid.*, Feb 2, 3, 1940.

3 *Ibid.*, Jan 17, Mar 10, 1940.

4 *Ibid.*, Feb 10, 1940.

5 *Ibid.*, Feb 17, 22, 23, 1940.

6 *Ibid.*, Jan 9, 1940.

7 JG to Hitler, Jan 10; Hitler read it Jan 29: Lammers to JG, Jan 29, 1940 (Reich chancellery files, NA film T120, roll 3198, E530667ff).

8 MinConf., Jan 5, Feb 6, 1940. A second foreign press club was opened on Jan 10, 1941. 'Dr Goebbels delivered the speech of welcome,' reported Louis Lochner on Jan 26, 'and turned the club rooms over to us. They are beautifully appointed and there are plenty of telephone lines, typewriters, newspapers, and news bulletins available' (FDR Libr., Toland papers, box 52).

9 MinConf., Mar 1, 1940.

10 *Ibid.*, Jan 2; diary Jan 3; for similar remarks see *VB*, Apr 6, text publ. by H A Jacobsen, *Der Zweite Weltkrieg* (Frankfurt, 1965), 180f.; and diary, Aug 2, 1940.

11 MinConf., Feb 8, 1940.

12 Meldung, Jan 5; MinConf., Jan 9, 1940.

13 MinConf., Jan 13, 1940.

14 *Ibid.*, May 18, 20, Dec 23, 1940; Feb 7, 1941.

15 *Ibid.*, Jan 17, 31, Mar 7, 1940.

16 *Ibid.*, Apr 10, May 11, 25, 1941.

17 Unpubl. diary, Nov 19, 1941.

18 MinConf., Jan 27, 1940.

19 *Ibid.*, Apr 12, 1940.

20 *Ibid.*, May 9, 1940.

21 Minutes by Dr Immanuel Schäffer, Sep 7, and by Werner Naumann, Sep 12, 1944 (Yivo file Occ–E2–68).

22 MinConf., Apr 13, 1940.

23 *Ibid.*, May 25, 1940.

24 Diary, Jul 8, 1941.

25 *Ibid.*, Feb 19, 20, 1940.

26 Directive No. 368 from RMVP press conf., Feb 18, 1940 (BA, Brammer files).

27 Press conf., Feb 19, 1940; Boelcke, *Kriegspropaganda*, 289.

28 This 'Aufklärungsausschuss Hamburg,' run by a Dr Johannsen with Staatsrat Dr Helferich, had agents in Budapest, Ankara, Stockholm, Sofia, Bratislava, Madrid, and (Bertram de Colonna) Lisbon; see SAIC report CIR.4 on the organization of the RMVP and RPL, Jul 19, 1945 (NA: RG.332, entry ETO Mis-Y, Sect., box 116). Some of the agency's files are in BA Militärarchiv (BA–MA): RW.49 (in records of the Abwehr's Bremen field office) with a supplementary collection in Hamburg city archives. For its finances see BA files R.55/381, /382, and /383 (with a note on its origins, Dec 1, 1939); duties, /1338; organization, /1425, and ZStA Potsdam, Rep. 50.01, RMVP, vols. 994, 995. Yivo, and BA file R.55/1425. Unpubl. diary, May 1, 1942.

29 Rosenberg diary, May 8, 1940.

30 Diary, Mar 2, 1940.

31 Lammers, decree of Mar 1940 (NA film T84, roll 175, 4957).

32 Affidavit by Karl-Jesco von Puttkamer, May 25, 1948 (StA Nuremberg, G15).

33 Diary, Apr 6, 7, 8, 1940.

34 Diary, Apr 16, 1940.

35 *Ibid.*, Jan 17, Mar 5, 1940.

36 *Ibid.*, Jan 3, 4, 20, 23, Feb 10, 1940. For Humanité's broadcasts May 1 to Jun 24, 1940 see Ortwin Buchbinder, *Geheimsender gegen Frankreich* (Bonn, 1984).

37 Diary, Jan 5, 6, Mar 14, 1940.

38 *Ibid.*, Feb 13, Mar 12, 15, 1940; Gutterer MS, 84f, and interview. The French retaliated with their own porno-leaflets (MinConf., Feb 17, 1940).

39 Diary, Mar 27, 28, Apr 25, 26, May 8, 1940.

40 MinConf., Apr 4; *Life*, Aug 5, 19, Sep 23, Dec 30, 1940.

41 *L'Illustration*, Paris, Mar 16, 1940. Bernd Martin, *Friedensinitiativen und Machtpolitik im Zweiten Weltkrieg, 1939–1942* (Düsseldorf, 1974), 220; Reuth, 442f.

42 Diary, Apr 9; Lt-Col. Hasso von Wedel, chief of Wehrmacht propaganda, handed him Keitel's directive on the operation (WESERÜBUNG) on Apr 9, 1940 (ZStA Potsdam, Rep. 50.01, RMVP, vol. 878). Wedel, a passionate and amply proportioned gourmet cook, became JG's *bête noire*. Wedel's papers are in BA–MA, RW.4 and see his memoirs, *Die Propagandatruppen* (Neckargemünd, 1962).

43 Diary, Apr 10; MinConf., Apr 9, 1940.

44 Diary, Apr 18, 1940.

45 *Ibid.*, Apr 30, 1940. In fact the French Alpine chasseurs and some Norwegian units fought with conspicuous gallantry; the English bravely, but less so.

Notes to Chapter 38.

1 Diary, Apr 29, 1940.

2 Behrend, No. 9, Mar 1, 1952.

3 *Ibid.*, Apr 16, 22, 1940.

4 Ritschel to Magda, Jul 7, 1940; in a file of their correspondence (ZStA Potsdam, Rep. 90, Go 2, vol. 3).

5 Diary, Apr 4, 1940.

6 *Ibid.*, Aug 11, 1941.

7 JG, letters to colleagues in the field, Jan 24, Aug 10, Sep 3, Oct 23, 1940 (ZStA Potsdam, Rep. 50.01, RMVP, vol. 765).

8 Diary, Feb 1, 1940: Berndt had joined the colors on Jan 31, 1940. And BDC file, Berndt.

9 Diary, Apr 29, May 21, 1941.

10 *Ibid.*, May 13, 1940; Feb 20, Apr 21, May 21, 25, Jun 6, 8, 10, 12–15, 1941.

11 *Ibid.*, Jul 4, 1941.

12 Wilfried von Oven, *Mit Goebbels bis zum Ende* (republished as *Finale Furioso*, in Tübingen in 1974), 22ff. Oven's 'diary' was evidently written up only after the war (it was first published in Buenos Aires in 1949). His dates are often late (*e.g.* Mussolini's overthrow, Italy's capitulation); he writes on 'Nov 25, 1943' without even mentioning the colossal air raid two days before on Berlin; Speer has 'recently' taken over air armament on 'Feb 2, 1944' (in fact in Jun 1944). Some parts, *e.g.* JG's views on Gauleiter Weinrich and the entry of Jun 5–6, 1944 seem derived from Rudolf Semler (whose 'diary' had been published in London in 1947 – see note 49 of chapter entitled 'The Road to Stalingrad'). There are syntactical oddities: *e.g.* 'Jul 27, 1944,' which begins 'yesterday afternoon' and proceeds (p. 438f) to 'on the next morning': why not 'today'? – However Oven probably did use contemporary notes: his reference to JG phoning Morell on 'May 7, 1944' is supported by Morell's diary of May 8, 1944; his references to air raids on Mar 6 and May 7 and 8, 1944 are accurate, and on 'Sep 3, 1944' he correctly gives the departure time of the courier train to Rastenburg as 8:13 P.M. (see the corresponding itinerary in ZStA Potsdam, Rep. 50.01, vol. 956).

13 Diary, Apr 25, 1940.

14 *Ibid.*, Apr 28; MinConf., Apr 29, 30, May 3, 19. See too Jodl diary, Apr 23–27; naval staff war diary, Apr 27; and Eduard Wagner's letter of May 7. The German White Book No. 4, *Dokumente zur englisch-französischen Kriegsausweitung* (Berlin, 1940) was issued on Apr 27, 1940.

15 Diary, May 8, 9, 1940.

16 Speech to 500 Reich orators, *VB*, Feb 14, 1940.

17 Diary, Apr 21; and, again quoting Hitler, Apr 25, 1940: 'There is no need for Britain to lose her overseas possessions.'

18 *Ibid.*, May 5, 1940.

19 *Ibid.*, May 7, 1940.

20 MinConf., May 10, 1940.

21 Diary, May 11, 1940: 'Klare Fronten!'

22 *Ibid.*, May 11, 12, 13, 16, 1940.

23 MinConf., May 13, 14; diary, May 15, 17, 1940.

24 MinConf., May 14–16, 1940.

25 Diary, May 11, 1940.

26 *Ibid.*, May 16, 1940.

27 *Ibid.*, May 13, 14, 1940.

28 *Ibid.*, May 16, 17, 1940.

29 *Ibid.*, May 19, 1940.

30 *Ibid.*, May 29, 1940.

31 MinConf., May 14, 17, 21; diary, May 30, 1940.

32 Diary, Jun 15, 1940.

33 Gutterer MS, 83.

34 MinConf., 17, 20–22, 25, 29, 1940.

35 *Ibid.*, May 23, 24, 25, 31, Jun 11, 1940.

36 On Albrecht see US Intelligence files (NA file RG.319, IRR, file XE.131670) and his interrogation, Nuremberg, Jan 27, 1948 (NA film M.1019, roll 2). Born in Weingarten, Württemberg, Nov 8, 1897, he had joined the Spartacus League in Dec 1918, served in Russia from Apr 1924 to Dec 1935, been sentenced to death there in 1934, returned to Germany, and turned his back on Moscow in Mar 1938 after the Soviet execution of twenty-two commissars. He wrote the book *Der verratene Sozialismus.*

37 Diary, May 22, 30, Jun 1, 2, 8, 10, 1940. For JG's subsequent relations with Torgler see BA files R.55/567 and /1289.

38 Diary, May 28; MinConf., May 17, 1940.

39 David Cesarani and Tony Kushner (eds.) *The Internment of Aliens in Twentieth Century Britain* (London, 1993).

40 MinConf., Jun 9; for the dangerous – and still widely quoted – Rauschning book *Gespräche mit Hitler* see diary, Feb 13, 14, Mar 14, 1940.

41 Diary, Jun 6, Jul 8, 1940.

42 MinConf., Jun 7, Jul 7, 1940.

43 *Ibid.*, Jun 22, 1940.

44 Diary, May 17, Jun 3, 1940.

45 *Ibid.*, May 28, 1940.

46 *Ibid.*, Jun 3, 1940.

47 *Ibid.*, Jun 2, 3, 1940.

48 *Ibid.*, Jun 18, 21–23, 1940. Goebbels listened to the secret recordings of the peace negotiations.

49 MinConf., May 27; according to William Shirer, *Berlin Diary,* (New York, 1941), it was shown to the press on Jun 10, 1940.

50 Diary, Jun 23, 1940; he correctly deduced that Churchill had ordered these raids only to provoke Germany to counter-attacks which would dispel the British public's growing war-weariness.

51 *Ibid.*, Jun 27, 1940.

52 *Ibid.*, Jun 29, 1940.

53 For JG's preparations for the homecoming and speech see ZStA Potsdam, Rep. 50.01, RMVP, vol. 7.

54 *Ibid.*, Jul 3; Bormann diary, Jul 2. Other sources confirm that Hitler had at this time no

desire to destroy the British Empire: *e.g.* naval staff war diary, Jun 17, quoting Jodl; the Weizsäcker diary, *passim*; and a private letter by Hitler's secretary Christa Schroeder dated Jun 25, 1940 (IfZ, Irving collection).

55 See *e.g.* Halder's diary, Jul 2, 3, and comments under interrogation; Major Hasso von Etzdorf, diary, Jul 10, 1940; Bernd von Lossberg, private letter of Sep 7, 1956 (IfZ, Irving collection); Jodl's speech to the gauleiters on Nov 7, 1943 (ND: 172-L).

56 British analysis of German propaganda output, Jul 1–16, 1940 (PRO file FO.898/30).

57 Diary, Jul 5, 1940.

58 *Ibid.*, Jul 6, 1940.

59 RMVP program for the Führer's return from the battlefield in BA file NS.10/26.

60 Diary, Jul 7, 1940.

61 Darré diary, Jul 8, 1940 (BA, Darré papers, vol. 65a).

62 Diary, Jul 9; Bormann diary, Jul 8, 1940.

63 G Sander, 'Unbekanntes über Goebbels Rolle im Krieg', *Unser Land Illustrierte*, a well-informed supplement to *Deutsche Bauernzeitung* (Cologne-Deutz), Oct 16, 1949 (IfZ archives; hereafter Sander); Rudolf Semler, *Goebbels: The Man Next to Hitler* (London, 1947) (hereafter Semler), diary, 'Jul 24, 1941.'

64 Diary, Mar 6, Jun 7, Dec 6, 1940; Hans Dieter Müller (ed.), *Facsimile Querschnitt durch Das Reich* (Munich, 1964), and 'Das Reich. Porträt einer Wochenzeitung,' in *Der Spiegel*, Aug 19, 1964, 32ff.

65 See *e.g.* the remarks by a captured German bomber navigator on Feb 18, 1941: 'The best magazine is *Das Reich*. It costs thirty pfennigs. It's got all sorts of interesting things about politics, economics, art, and the armed forces.' CSDIC (UK) report SRA.1360 (PRO file WO.208/4123).

66 Diary, Feb 26, 1941.

67 Conversation between Lt-Gen. Lindner, air-raid protection section, Reich air ministry, and Lt-Gen. Veith, military governor of Brunswick, Apr 29, 1945. CSDIC (UK) report SRGG.1149 (PRO file WO.208/4169).

68 Diary, Jul 19, 1940; some were unimpressed. Milch wrote in his diary, '6 P.M. entry of a Berlin division before Fromm, Goebbels. Awful.' (author's film DI–59).

69 MinConf., Jul 19, 1940.

70 *Ibid.*, Feb 8, 1940.

71 Canaris memo, Sep 12, 1939 (IWM file AL.1933); RSHA department heads conferences Sep 1939 (NA film T175/239); Heydrich memo of May 1941 (*VfZ*, 1963, 197ff); David Irving, *Hitler's War* (London, 1991), 222ff.

72 Diary, Jan 16, 1940.

73 The journalist was Wladyslaw Studnicki. Diary, Feb 9, 13, 21, 23, Jul 26, 1940.

74 His informant was Gauleiter Arthur Greiser. Diary, Mar 13, 1940.

75 *Ibid.*, May 1, 1940; Jan 31, 1941. Bouhler, as chief of the Führer's private chancellery, had found himself in charge of the infamous 'T4-*Aktion.*'

76 *Ibid.*, May 9; on Jul 4, 1940, Hans Frank, governor-general of Poland, reported to JG. 'Jewish problem almost beyond solution,' the latter noted. *Ibid.*, Jul 5, 1940.

77 *Ibid.*, Jun 6; MinConf., Jul 19, 1940.

78 MinConf., Jul 19; and see diary, Jul 23, 1940. Jewish population statistics were chronically vague. In Sep 1940 Hinkel would report that there were still 71,800 Jews in Berlin; the plan was to expel 60,000 in the first four weeks after the war, and the rest four weeks later.

79 Diary, Jul 26; he had seen Hitler on his return from Bayreuth at midday on Jul 24, 1940.

80 *Ibid.*, Jul 20; for Hitler's speech see *Verhandlungen des Reichstags*, vol. 460, 65ff.

81 MinConf., Jul 19, 1940.

82 Diary, Jul 22, 1940.

83 MinConf., Jul 20, 1940; Boelcke, *Kriegspropaganda*, 421.

84 Sefton Delmer, *Die Deutschen und ich*, 420ff; JG diary, Apr 3, 1941.

85 Diary, Jul 21, 1940.

86 MinConf., Jul 22, 1940: 'Given their totally different, insular mentality it is just inconceivable to the English that the offer made in the Führer's speech was not mere bluff but meant in dead earnest.'

87 Diary, Jul 23–24, 1940.

88 *Ibid.*, Jul 24, 1940.

89 *Ibid.*, Jul 25, 1940.

90 MinConf., Jul 24, 1940.

91 Diary, Jul 26, 1940: 'The Führer's still pondering on it.'

Notes to Chapter 39.

1 Diary, Aug 1, 1940.

2 MinConf., Aug 5, 1940.

3 Diary, Aug 8, 1940.

4 MinConf., Aug 8, 1940.

5 Diary, Aug 18, 1940.

6 *Ibid.*, Aug 3, 8, 9; MinConf., Aug 8, 1940.

7 MinConf., Aug 10, 1940.

8 *Ibid.*, Aug 17, 1940.

9 Diary, Aug 2–3, 1940.

10 MinConf., Aug 3; diary, Aug 4; Louis Lochner, letter, Aug 9, 1940 (FDR Libr., Toland papers, box 52).

11 Diary, Aug 1, 21, 1940.

12 *Ibid.*, Sep 26, Oct 2, 4, 1940.

13 *Ibid.*, Aug 4; *cf.* Meldung, Aug 15, 1940 (NA film T175, roll 259, 2178f).

14 Diary, Aug 5, 6, 1940.

15 *Ibid.*, Aug 7, 1940.

16 *Ibid.*, Aug 9, 1940.

17 MinConf., Aug 9, 10; diary, Aug 10–13, 1940.

18 *Ibid.*, Aug 12, 1940.

19 Diary, Aug 13, 1940.

20 *Ibid.*, Aug 14, 1940.

21 *Ibid.*, Aug 23, 1940. On the nineteenth JG noted, 'It makes you sick!'

22 *Ibid.*, Aug 21, 22, 1940.

23 See the Political Warfare Executive (PWE) study, Development of German Propaganda, Aug 1940, p. 9 (PRO file FO.898/30).

24 Churchill's telephoned directive to Bomber Command of Aug 25 is in Air Ministry papers, PRO file AIR.14/775; the *VB* headline on Aug 27 read, 'London dresses up attack

on Berlin as a "reprisal".'

25 Diary, Aug 26, 27, 1940.

26 *Ibid.*, Aug 29, 30, 1940.

27 *Ibid.*, Aug 31, 1940.

28 Titel had organized Goebbels' biggest Berlin events, like the May Day rally of 1933: it was his task to ensure that the columns of marchers converged simultaneously on the stadiums, that they were not too wide for the bridges en route, etc.

29 For the reports to JG on Churchill's air raids on Berlin Sep–Dec 1940, see ZStA Potsdam, Rep. 50.01, RMVP, vol. 896.

30 MinConf., Sep 8, 1940.

31 The real figure was bad enough, 360.

32 Diary, Sep 10; on Sep 11, 1940 he added: 'We're hyping up the raid on Berlin; reverse of hitherto.'

33 *Ibid.*, Sep 11, 1940.

34 MinConf., Sep 11; diary, Sep 12; on Sep 18, 1940 he confirmed: 'After all, we invented the blazing Brandenburg Gate too.' Fake 1940 photos of smoke drifting past St Paul's Cathedral in London are still in use.

35 MinConf., Sep 15, 1940.

36 Diary, Sep 13, 1940.

37 *Ibid.*, Sep 12, 1940.

38 *Ibid.*, Sep 14, 1940.

39 *Ibid.*, Sep 15, 1940.

40 *Ibid.*, Sep 17, 1940.

41 MinConf., Sep 6, 1940.

42 Diary, Sep 15; as Berndt pointed out, this benefited only the BBC. *Ibid.*, Oct 5; MinConf., Oct 7. On Nov 11, JG's diary noted the 'colossal propaganda damage.' Hadamovsky put the RMVP case to Hitler, without success; see diary, Nov 16, and MinConf., Nov 25, 1940.

43 MinConf., Sep 17; diary, Sep 18, 1940.

44 MinConf. and diary, Sep 17; in general, see the PWE fortnightly survey, Development of German Propaganda, Sep 16–30, 1940 (PRO file FO.898/30).

45 MinConf., Sep 20, 1940.

46 Milch diary, Sep 14 (author's film DI–59); and diaries of Halder, OKW WFSt, and naval staff, Sep 14, 1940.

47 Diary, Sep 24, 1940.

48 *Ibid.*, Sep 25; JG used the boxing analogy in his article in *VB*, Dec 28, 1940.

49 Oven, 'Jul 6, 1944,' 380f.

50 Diary, Sep 26, 1940.

51 *Ibid.*, Oct 2, 3, 1940.

52 *Ibid.*, Oct 3, 4, 1940.

53 MinConf., Oct 9; diary, Oct 5, 1940.

54 Diary, Oct 18; diary of General Hoffmann von Waldau, Oct 16, 1940 (author's film DI–75b).

55 Diary, Oct 19, 1940.

56 *Ibid.*, Oct 20, 1940: 'Göring is running a tight ship.'

57 Oven, 'Jul 6, 1944,' 380f: 'I returned from this visit to Deauville with the worst possible impressions.' And see the May 6, 1946 interrogation of Schirmeister, who accompanied

JG to France (NA film M.1270, roll 19).

58 Diary, Aug 3, Sep 18, 24, 25; Freybe to Mrs Weinhold, Oct 15, 1940 (ZStA Potsdam, Rep. 90, Go 2, vol. 3).

59 Ritschel to Magda, Oct 16; Magda to Ritschel, telegram, Dec 4, 1940 (ZStA Potsdam, Rep. 90, Go 2, vol. 3).

60 Diary, Jul 21, Oct 13, 1940.

61 *Ibid.*, Jul 24, 1940.

62 *Ibid.*, Sep 29, 1940; and *cf.* Nov 19, 1941, and Oven, 230.

63 Diary, Oct 15, 1940.

64 Note by Schweitzer, Nov 13, 1940 (ZStA Potsdam, Rep. 50.01, RMVP, vol. 5).

65 Diary, Oct 29; and Bartels, note on desk cost, Nov 12, 1940 (ZStA Potsdam, Rep. 50.01, RMVP, vol. 5).

66 Bartels, note on the desk's cost, Nov 12, 1940 (ZStA Potsdam, Rep. 50.01, RMVP, vol. 5); and Behrend, No. 19, May 10, 1952.

67 Note by Ministerialrat Christian Spieler, Oct 31, 1940 (ZStA Potsdam, Rep. 50.01, RMVP, vol. 5).

68 Naumann to adjutants, Aug 6, 1940 (ZStA Potsdam, Rep. 50.01, RMVP, vol. 759).

69 Diary, Nov 2, 1940.

70 *Ibid.*, Nov 26, 1940; Apr 17, Jun 8, 13, 1941. 'My ministry is gradually turning into a major art collection.'

71 *Ibid.*, Nov 2, 5, 23, 1940.

72 Speer to Bartels, Sep 9, 1940 (ZStA Potsdam, Rep. 50.01, RMVP, vol. 5).

73 Diary, Dec 5, 1940; *cf.* Jan 12, 1941.

74 MinConf., Oct 20, 1940.

75 *Ibid.*, Oct 9; and see *ibid.*, Oct 24, 1940: London was claiming to have killed 2,871 Berliners in the latest raids; the real figure was twelve.

76 Diary, Nov 1, 1941.

77 *Ibid.*, Nov 2, 1940.

78 Speech on occasion of 50th Family Favorites concert (*Wunschkonzert*), Dec 1, 1940 (publ. in *Zeit ohne Beispiel*, 331f; and see our chapter, 'The Malodorous Thing,' note 20, below).

79 Diary, Jul 5, 1940.

80 *Ibid.*, Jul 30, 1940.

81 *Ibid.*, Aug 5, 10, 16, 1940.

82 *Ibid.*, Aug 9, 1940.

83 *Ibid.*, Aug 15, 1940.

84 *Ibid.*, Aug 16, 24, 1940.

85 *Ibid.*, Sep 14, 19, 1940.

86 *Ibid.*, Nov 10, 1940.

87 *Ibid.*, Nov 11, 12, 1940.

88 Sander; and see JG's *Tagesparole* (message for the day), Nov 14, 1940, cited in Boelcke, *Kriegspropaganda*, 566.

Notes to Chapter 40.

1 JG took spiteful disciplinary action against three of Ribbentrop's pet journalists: press conf. of Oct 24, 1940 (BA files, Brammer collection; ND: NG–3870).

2 Diary, Dec 4, 1940.

3 *Ibid.*, Feb 6, 7, 16, 1940.

4 *Ibid.*, Oct 16, 1940.

5 *Ibid.*, Mar 30; *cf.* Jun 6, 1940.

6 *Ibid.*, May 17, 1940.

7 *Ibid.*, Jun 16, Aug 4, 1940.

8 JG circular, Sep 2 (Reich chancellery files, ND: NG–4189); diary, Oct 9, 23, Nov 5, Dec 13, 1940.

9 MinConf., Oct 22; diary Oct 23, 1940. Hitler often compared Ribbentrop with Bismarck: *cf.* Likus report, Nov 13, 1938 (AA files, Serial 43, 29044ff).

10 Diary, Dec 2; Glasmeier to JG, Dec 2, 1940; and letter from Richard Schulze-Kossens to Reinhard Spitzy, Nov 2, 1986 (author's collection).

11 Ribbentrop to JG, Nov 30, and reply, Dec 2 (author's collection); JG diary, Dec 2–5, 1940.

12 Diary, Dec 6–7, 1940.

13 *Ibid.*, Nov 20, 1940.

14 *Ibid.*, Nov 26, 1940.

15 *Cf.* diary of Field Marshal von Bock (C-in-C East), Dec 3, 1940 (BA–MA, Bock papers).

16 Confirmed by Milch diary, Dec 26, 1940: 'From morning of Dec 24–26 no raids on Britain on Führer's orders' (author's film DI–59).

17 Diary, Dec 4; similar words on Dec 5, 1940.

18 'German home morale and neutralizing Italian defeat,' in PWE Analysis of German Propaganda, Dec 1–16, 1940 (PRO file FO.898/30); MinConf., Jun 23, 1940.

19 MinConf., Jun 16, 1940.

20 *Ibid.*, Jul 15, 1940.

21 Diary, Sep 11, and *cf. ibid.*, Sep 13, 1940.

22 Diary, Dec 11, 1940.

23 *Ibid.*, Dec 12, 1940.

24 *Ibid.*, Dec 22, 1940.

25 *Ibid.*, Dec 31, 1940.

26 Script of JG's broadcast, amended by Hitler, in the files of his adjutants (BA file NS.10/37). Hitler also asked JG to shelve an article which he had written attacking the legal profession (diary, Jan 12, 1941).

27 Diary, Jan 30, Feb 22, 1941.

28 *Ibid.*, Jan 12, 1941.

29 JG, 'Winston Churchill,' in *Das Reich*, Feb 5. *Cf.* MinConf., Dec 22; and diary, Dec 22, 1940; Jan 5, 6, 1941.

30 Diary, Jan 26, 1941.

31 *Ibid.*, Jan 29, 1941.

32 *Ibid.*, Feb 14, 1941.

33 *Ibid.*, Feb 18, 21, 1941. For the planning of the film *Die Feuertaufe* (Baptism of Fire) and a film on the Wehrmacht against England, see JG to Brauchitsch, May 9, reply, May 20, 1940 (NA film T78, roll 295, 4501ff).

34 Diary, Feb 25, 1941.

35 Ritschel to Magda, Dec 26, 1940, Jan 28, 1941 (ZStA Potsdam, Rep. 90 Go 2, vol. 3); diary, Jan 6, 7, 8, 1941.

36 Diary, Apr 4, 5, 1941.

37 *Ibid.*, Dec 22, 1940.

38 *Ibid.*, Nov 5; *cf.* Nov 10, 1940 for his unconcealed delight.

39 *Ibid.*, Dec 27, 1940. Regierungsrat Heiduschke had joined the Fallschirmjäger (para-troops) in May 1940, but JG had retrieved him on Oct 1, 1940 as his adjutant. See *ibid.*, May 13, Oct 2, 31, 1940.

40 *Ibid.*, Jan 3, 18, 1941.

41 *Ibid.*, Jan 29, 1941.

42 *Ibid.*, Apr 24, 1941.

43 *Ibid.*, Jun 17, 1941. 'To show an interest in the child': *mich des Kindes anzunehmen.*

44 See the MS by Rittmeister Dr Wilhelm Scheidt (IfZ, Irving collection).

45 Diary, Jan 29, 1941; *cf.* Hanke's biography in Das Reich Mar 11, 1945, and JG diary, May 5, 1940: Hanke was with Rommel's division, but 'is heading for Silesia later.'

46 Diary, Jan 30. On Feb 9 Hess spoke in Breslau at Hanke's induction as gauleiter (*ibid.*, Feb 10, 1941).

47 *Ibid.*, Jan 25, Feb 3, 13, 1941.

48 *Ibid.*, Feb 8, 1941.

49 *Ibid.*, Mar 25, 1941; JG's New Year's broadcast, 1940/41.

50 Diary, Apr 4, 1941.

51 *Ibid.*, Feb 8, 11, 13, 14, 1941.

52 *Ibid.*, Feb 14–16, 1941.

53 Sander; JG diary, Feb 18, 1941.

54 Diary, Feb 16, 17, 21, 24, 1941.

55 *Ibid.*, Feb 21, 23, 26, 1941.

56 *Ibid.*, Mar 3, 1941.

57 *Ibid.*, Mar 16, 17, 1941.

58 *Ibid.*, Mar 15, 17, 18, 23, 1941.

59 *Ibid.*, Mar 29, Apr 11, 20, 21, 1941.

60 *Ibid.*, Apr 14, 1941.

61 *Ibid.*, May 1–3. Linz Irkonsky had provided the summer house (*ibid.*, Apr 2, 1941).

62 Sander.

63 JG used the same phrase in his domestic propaganda: PWE Report on Axis Propaganda and Strategic Intentions, No. 25, Jan 6–12, 1941 (PRO file FO.898/30); diary, Jan 10, 1941.

64 Diary, Feb 1, 4, 1941.

65 *Ibid.*, Feb 7, 1941.

66 *Das* Reich, Mar 7, 1941.

67 MinConf., Mar 14, 1941.

68 Undated transcript and Reuters rewrite dated Mar 10 of JG's speech of Mar 7 in PRO file FO.371/26518; PWE Report on Axis Propaganda and Strategic Intentions, No. 33, Mar 3–9 (PRO file FO.898/30); diary, Mar 8, 1941.

69 Diary, Mar 11, 1941.

70 *Ibid.*, Mar 16, 1941.

71 *Ibid.*, Mar 17, 1941.

72 *Ibid.*, Mar 3, 1941.

73 *Ibid.*, Mar 18, 1941.

74 *Ibid.*, Mar 21, 1941.

75 MinConf., Mar 21, 1941.

76 Diary, Mar 25, 1941.

77 *Ibid.*, Mar 29. He added that there were already 300,000 troops in Norway. 'Moscow

won't have anything to laugh about when the balloon goes up.' On Mar 30, 1941 he noted that the SD Meldung reported reservations in the public's mood toward Russia; people seemed to have a premonition. 'But this summer will see this problem solved too.'

78 Diary, Mar 28, 1941.
79 *Ibid.*, Apr 4–6, 1941.
80 *Ibid.*, Apr 6, 1941.
81 Semler, 'Apr 5, 1941.'
82 Diary, Apr 6, 1941.
83 Shorthand transcript of MinConf., Apr 6, 1941.
84 Lt-Col. Erwin Lahousen diary (author's film DI–43).
85 MinConf., Apr 10; diary, Apr 11, 1941.
86 *Ibid.*, Apr 20, 21, 1941.
87 *Ibid.*, Apr 1, 1941.
88 MinConf., Apr 17; diary, Apr 17–19, 23, 1941.
89 MinConf., Apr 7, 1941.
90 Diary, Apr 13, 1941.
91 Shorthand record of MinConf., Apr 15; diary, Apr 16, 1941.
92 Diary, Apr 17, 1941.
93 *Ibid.*, Apr 8, 9, 1941.
94 *Ibid.*, Apr 24, 1941.
95 *Ibid.*
96 E Taubert, 'Der antisowjetische Apparat des deutschen Propagandaministeriums' (BA file Kl. Erw. 617).
97 Interrogation of Fritzsche, Nov 1, 1946 in OMGUS files (NA: RG.250, shipping list 53–3/7, box 16).
98 Sander; JG did not visit Lanke between Feb 22 and Apr 11, 1941 (diary).
99 Diary, Apr 14, 1941. Semler's account of the Apr 12 Krebs incident, dated 'Apr 1, 1941,' must be discounted.
100 Diary, Apr 15, 1941.
101 Hans-Leo Martin, 115; JG diary, Apr 19, 1941.
102 Diary, May 1, 7; *cf.* Walther Hewel diary, May 1941 (author's film DI-75).
103 Diary, May 5, 8, 9, 1941.
104 *Ibid.*, May 9, 1941.
105 *Ibid.*, May 12, 1941

Notes to Chapter 41.

1 For Berlin's announcement of May 14, 1941 see BA, Schumacher collection, file 236; and PRO files PREM.3/219/4 and INF. 1/912.
2 Semler, 'May 14, 1941.'
3 And again: JG diary, May 14, 1941.
4 *Ibid.*, May 13, 1941.
5 MinConf., May 13; diary, May 14, 1941.
6 MinConf., May 15, 1941.
7 Diary, May 14, 1941.
8 Shorthand record of MinConf., May 15, 1941. Sander quotes him as saying, 'Hess should

have fallen into *my* hands!'

9 Diary, May 14, 16, 1941; in fact Churchill had expressly forbidden any exploitation of the Hess affair.

10 In his memo of May 21 (IWM file AL.2525) Hans Frank said he had never seen him so distressed since the death of Geli Raubal. And see Frank diary May 13, 19, and conference, May 20, 1941; the interrogation of Ernst Bohle, Aug 5/8, 1945; Hewel diary, May 13, 1941.

11 Lutze diary, May 13, 14, 1941; he added, 'my views on Hess have been known for years.'

12 Diary, May 16; circular by Tiessler to the party (Gauringleiter), Jun 24, 1941 (NA film T581, roll 16; BA file NS.26/291). See the RPL file on combating occultism, containing correspondence with Bormann's chancellery and JG's views, Jun–Jul 1943 (BA file NS.18/211).

13 Diary, May 14, 1941.

14 Sander.

15 MinConf., May 14; diary, May 15, 1941.

16 Shorthand record of MinConf., May 15, 1941.

17 Diary, May 19, 1941.

18 Ebermayer and Meissner, *op. cit.*, Revue, Nos. 24–25, May 1952; their source is Ello Quandt.

19 Diary, May 24, 25, Jun 1, 1941.

20 The book was his anthology, *Die Zeit ohne Beispiel. Reden und Aufsätze aus den Jahren 1939/40/41* (Munich, 1941).

21 Diary, May 28, 1941; the entry concludes, 'To bed late, tired, and quite sad' – the latter possibly because of the day's sinking of *Bismarck*.

22 Diary, May 31, 1941: 'particularly since the report of German prisoners being mutilated.'

23 Ebermayer and Meissner, No. 25, Jun 21, 1952.

24 Diary, May 20, 1941.

25 *Ibid.*, May 22, 1941. Tiessler headed the Hauptamt Reichsring in the RPL. For his personal papers see BA file NS.18/5; career to 1934: NS.18/251. His 1941–43 submissions to JG are in file NS.18/194. His MS memoirs are in IfZ files. He died in 1984.

26 Diary, May 21, Jun 9, 10, 12, 13, 1941.

27 MinConf., May 21. In fact Abwehr special forces did wear Polish uniforms in 1939 and Dutch uniforms in 1940.

28 Interrogation by Frank Korf, Apr 4, 1948 (Hoover Libr., Korf papers).

29 Diary, May 25. For the BARBAROSSA deception plans (SHARK, MERCURY) see naval staff war diary May 12, 16, 1941.

30 *Ibid.*, Jun 6, 7, 14; Semler, 'Jun 1, 1941.'

31 Diary, Jun 1, 1941. Semler dates this conference 'Jun 5,' as does Borresholm. Schirmeister (IMT, xvii, 277) testifies that it was in May.

32 Memo for Dr Schlegelberger, ministry of justice, BA file R.22/4087; Borresholm, 157.

33 On the Bömer affair see the interrogation of Paul K ('Presse') Schmidt, Jul 28, 1947 and his affidavit of Dec 1947 (NA film M.1019, roll 64); and of Rolf Hoffmann, PWB/SAIC/22, Jul 12, 1945 (NA file RG.332, entry ETO, Mis-Y, Sect., box 116).

34 Hewel diary, May 25; JG diary, May 26, 1941.

35 Diary, May 23, 31; JG warned his MinConf., May 26, 1941, on the perils of alcohol and bragging.

36 Diary, May 26, 27, 1941.

37 *Ibid.*, May 27, 1941.

38 Schmidt; and Heinz Lorenz, testimony of Dec 3, 1947 (ND: NG–4321; and IfZ, file ZS.266). JG said (diary, Jun 13, 14, 27) he would plead for Bömer, but only after BARBAROSSA; in fact on Aug 13 he recorded that he had submitted a memo on Bömer's behalf to the public prosecutor and hoped for his release.

39 Diary, May 30, 1941. Bormann to party treasurer Schwarz, Feb 22, 1942 (BDC file, Bömer). Bömer had been press chief in Rosenberg's Aussenpolitisches Amt, 1934–38.

40 Diary, Jun 5, May 28, 1941.

41 Ibid., May 23, 1941.

42 Ibid., Jun 11, 1941.

43 Ibid., Jun 15. On this ploy see ibid., Jun 7, 11, 12, 1941, and Werner Stephan's interrogation of Oct 29, 1947 (NA film M.1019, roll 71). Borresholm, 152f ('May 24'), the OKW WFSt war diary ('Jun 16') and Semler ('Jun 8, 1941') all give the wrong dates.

44 Diary, Jun 15, 1941; Oven, 'Oct 29, 1944,' 507f; Sander.

45 Diary, Jun 14, 1941; Schaub MS (IfZ, Irving collection).

46 Taubert report (Yivo file, G-PA–14).

47 Diary, May 1, 1941.

48 Ibid., May 23, 1941; he added that Koch was to get the Ukraine, and Lohse the Baltic states.

49 Ibid., May 24, 1941.

50 Ibid., Jun 12, 1941.

51 Ibid., Jun 7, 1941.

52 Ibid., Jun 8, 1941.

53 Ibid., Jun 15. That day, Jun 14, JG wrote to Rosenberg to urge the centralization of all eastern propaganda within the RMVP (Rosenberg files, IfZ film MA.803, 277f). On Jun 18, 1941 he noted that Rosenberg also expected a rapid Soviet collapse. For their later squabbles about jurisdiction over propaganda in the eastern territories see Rosenberg's papers, especially BA file R.6/11.

54 Diary, Jun 19, 1941.

55 Ibid., Jun 22, 1941. He issued a photograph of himself broadcasting the proclamation (picture archives, Süddeutscher Verlag). See Hewel and Bormann diaries, Jun 22 (author's films DI–75 and DI–19); and the diary of General Kurt Dittmar, the war department's radio commentator, who said JG's broadcast 'sounded convincing,' but added: 'Less attractive are the consequences, particularly the shooting of [Soviet] commissars. . . We obey unwillingly and with considerable misgivings on this point' (author's film DI–60)

Notes to Chapter 42.

1 Diary, Jun 25, 1941.

2 Ibid., Jun 24, 1941.

3 JG in VB, Jun 26, 1941.

4 JG in Das Reich, Jul 6, 1941.

5 Capt. Wolf Junge MS (IfZ, Irving collection), 231; Semler, 'Jun 30, 1941.'

6 Diary, Jun 30, Jul 3, 5, 6, 1941.

7 MinConf., Jun 9, 1940.

8 Diary, Jun 30, 1941; in Aug 1941 JG had a 'very heated argument' with the Führer's headquar-

ters, which in all seriousness again proposed to broadcast five special communiqués at hourly intervals with the same 'odious consequences' as on Jun 29. Unpubl. diary, Aug 10–12. (For the unpubl. diary of Aug 13–20, 1941 see NA film T84, roll 267.)

9 Unpubl. diary, Nov 22, 1941: 'Let's postpone that until the war's over.'

10 Diary, Jun 30, 1941.

11 Unpubl. diary, Aug 16, 1941; annex to JG's letter to Hitler, May 23, 1943 (BA file R.55/799).

12 Diary, Jul 3; Semler, 'Jul 5, 1941.'

13 Unpubl. diary, Nov 7, 1941.

14 For a Soviet leaflet with the German text see BA file NS.26/vorl. 1194.

15 Diary, Jul 5, 1941.

16 *Ibid.*, Jul 5, 6; unpubl. diary, Aug 13, 1941.

17 Heydrich, report, Jul 2; Chef d. SiPo u. SD, 'Durchsuchung sowjetrussischer Botschaft,' Jul 23 (Hewel Vorlagen beim Führer); Lahousen, report on official trip to Paris, Jul 7–10 (IWM file AL.1933); Ambassador Karl Ritter, memo of Jul 20, 1941 (Pol. Archiv AA: Ritter, Russland, vol. 1, on NA film, T120, roll 764, 8996ff); see Irving, *Hitler's War*, 344f.

18 Unpubl. diary fragment, Aug [10–12?], 1941.

19 Diary, Jun 5, 13, Jul 8; unpubl. diary, Aug 13, 1941; Semler, 'Apr 9, 1943.'

20 H C Bartels to JG, Aug 3, 1943 (ZStA Potsdam, Rep. 50.01, RMVP, vol. 4).

21 Diary, Mar 29, 30, 1941.

22 Author's interview of Richard Otte, Mar 31, 1971; and see *Daily Mail*, London, Jul 9, and *General-Anzeiger*, Bonn, Jul 11, 1992. On Mar 12, 1946 Leo Barten of USFET MISC wrote to Capt. Smith (G–2) that Otte, then living near Minden, 'had sole custody of all the personal documents and manuscripts of Goebbels;' on which see also USFET MISC SIR interrogation of Schwägermann, Jun 20, 1946 (Trevor-Roper papers, author's film DI–36).

23 Diary, Sep 23, 1943.

24 *Ibid.*, Jul 9, 1941.

25 Ritter, memo, Jul 14, 1941 (Pol. Archiv AA, Serial 1386; NA film T120, roll 764, 359006); Luther, note of Jul 8, 1941 (*ibid.*, 359008f).

26 Schmidt-Leonhardt to JG, Oct 19, 1942 (BA file R.55/799).

27 Diary, Jun 29. On Jul 3, 1941 however JG noted, 'Rosenberg's stopped making a fuss. He's leaving the propaganda up to us entirely.'

28 So JG said to Göring. Unpubl. diary, Mar 21, 1942 (NA film T84, roll 261).

29 Diary, Feb 5, 1944.

30 *Ibid.*, Jul 13; Semler, 'Sep 24, 1941.'

31 Hadamovsky's report from headquarters, cited in diary, Aug 1, 1941.

32 See *e.g.* the notes by S.A. Standartenführer Werner Koeppen, Rosenberg's *persönlicher Referent*, on Hitler's table talk with him, especially Sep 18 (NA film T84, roll 387, 0770) and Sep 22, 1941 (*ibid.*, 0784f).

33 For Rosenberg's papers on propaganda in the eastern territories see BA file R.6/192; for Goebbels', BA files R.55/799 and /1436.

34 Interrogation of d'Alquèn, Feb 16, 1948 (NA film M.1019, roll 2).

35 Taubert report; and JG diary, Mar 16, 1942.

36 For JG's propaganda issue of this book with a German commentary see BA file NS.26/42; a 12pp. extract by the Reichsring of RMVP is on NA film T81, roll 672, 0606ff. See the SD *Meldung* of Jul 31 for the public's reactions to these extracts (NA film T175, roll 261, 4438ff) and Oct 2, 1941 (*ibid.*, 4918ff).

37 Theodore N Kaufman, *Germany Must Perish!* (Newark, NJ, 1941), 7; reprinted as facsimile by Faksimile Verlag, Bremen, 1985.

38 Unpubl. diary, Aug 3, 1941. Adolf Eichmann wrote in his notes in 1956 or 1957, 'Kaufman's plan for the complete *Ausrottung* of the German people was known to us at the time when the first order was given for the physical destruction of the Jews' (original typescript in the author's possession).

39 See the OSS R&A report No. 695, Jan 14, 1943: 'The Use of Professor Renner's article by Axis propagandists' (USAMHI, Carlisle, Donovan papers, box 35c).

40 Diary, Aug 9; on Aug 29, 1940 he added, 'The Russians ran wild in Kaunas. Anybody who looked a cut above the rest was bumped off.'

41 *Ibid.*, Aug 17, 23, 1940. On the Madagascar plan as a solution of the Jewish problem see note of Jul 2, 1940 (ND: NG–5764).

42 Diary, Sep 2, 1940.

43 *Ibid.*, Nov 5 ('and later on we'll push the Jews out of this region too'). For Hans Frank's version, see his diary, conf. with department heads, Nov 6, 1940.

44 Diary, Dec 22, 1940.

45 MinConf., Apr 26, Jul 8, 15, Sep 12, 24; diary, Sep 25; SD *Meldung*, Nov 28, 1940 (NA film T175, roll 260, 2860f).

46 Diary, Jan 31, 1941. Heydrich had disassociated himself from Bouhler's euthanasia *Aktion* in a letter to the ministry of justice, Nov 1, 1940 (BA file R.22/5021).

47 Diary, Feb 14, Jun 21, 1941.

48 MinConf., Feb 26, 27, Mar 4, 7; diary Feb 27, Mar 1, 1941.

49 Diary, Mar 19, 1941.

50 See *e.g.* MinConf., Mar 23, 26; *VB*, May 24, 1941.

51 *Die Zeit ohne Beispiel*, 319f.

52 MinConf., Sep 6; here he stated 71,800 Jews, but in MinConf., Sep 17, 1940 he stated with perhaps greater precision that 72,327 Jews were in Berlin.

53 *Ibid.*, Sep 17, 1940; testimony of Schirmeister, IMT, xvii, 276.

54 Tiessler, submission to party chancellery, Mar 7, 1941 (NA film T81, roll 676, 5597); *cf.* JG diary, Jun 10, 1941.

55 (Genuine) Speer chronicle, report of Jan 1 to Apr 15, 1941, 21, cited in Matthias Schmidt, *Das Ende eines Mythos* (Munich, 1982), 182f. Speer was general buildings inspector (*Generalbauinspekteur*) for Berlin.

56 MinConf., Apr 21; diary, Apr 22, 1941.

57 Lammers to Schirach (ND: 1950–PS).

58 Diary, Mar 22, 1941. 'Who'd have thought that possible earlier?'

59 *Judenfrei.* 'Bü.,' Reichsring Abt. IIg, note on evacuation of Jews from Berlin, Mar 20, 1941 (NA film T81, roll 676, 5604f); diary, Mar 18, 1941.

60 For documents on Eichmann's organization of a 'central émigré agency' (*Umwandererzentralstelle*) in Posen in Apr 1940 and events thereafter see SS Sturmbannführer Höppner to Eichmann, Sep 3, 1941 (Polish War Crimes Commission archives, courtesy of Dr Gerald Fleming): this speaks of the need to be clear whether the 'undesirable elements' were to survive or 'be totally wiped out' (a memorandum dated Sep 2, 1941); evidently no firm decision had been taken by then.

61 On Apr 16 the genuine Speer chronicle had recorded that Hitler had demanded that 1,000 homes be made available to Germans who had lost theirs in the big air raid. On May 31, 1941 the chronicle records, 'As a result of the Jewish eviction *Aktion* 940 homes were

made available.'

62 Diary, Jun 20; Hans Frank diary, Jul 17, 1941.

63 Note by Tiessler, Apr 21 (NA film T81, roll 676, 5642); MinConf., Apr. 21; diary, Apr 22, 1941.

64 SS Oberführer Dr Werner Best to Taubert, Dec 1939, *cit.* in NA film T81, roll 676, 5596.

65 'Pf.' (Abt. II of RPL), note of Dec 5, 1939: *Ibid.*

66 Taubert to Tiessler, Apr 22 (*ibid.*, 5641); Tiessler to deputy Führer's staff, Apr 25 (*ibid.*, 5638); the result was a briefing note drafted by Gutterer for JG's next visit to Hitler, Aug 17, 1941, entitled Tagging the Jews (*ibid.*, 5739–56).

67 Diary, Aug 11, 1941.

68 (Genuine) Speer chronicle, 1941, 65f.

69 Tiessler circular to party officers, Jul 4, 1941 (NA film T581, roll 16; BA file NS.26/291).

70 Unpubl. diary, Aug 15, 1941.

71 *Ibid.*, Aug 20, 1941.

72 *Ibid.*, Aug 8, 13, 1941.

73 *Ibid.*, Aug 17, 1941.

74 *Propaganda Parole* No. 11, Sep 21, 1942 (NA film T81, roll 672, 0666f); see Himmler to JG, Aug 11, 1943, complaining about how these voices disturbed him by breaking into his car radio (NA film T120, roll 2474, E255436).

75 According to the chief engineer of a Soviet air fleet quoted by Bodenschatz on Oct 6, 1941 Stalin had 12,000 operational war planes when BARBAROSSA began (NA film T84, roll 387, 0796).

76 Record of a private talk between Churchill and Stalin at dinner on Jul 18, 1945 at Potsdam (PRO file PREM.3/430/8, 11).

77 He had brought a print of Liebeneiner's pro-euthanasia film *I accuse* to Hitler's head-quarters. Diary, Aug 15; Hewel diary, Aug 21, 1941.

78 Unpubl. diary, Aug 14, 18; *cf.* Bormann memo, Aug 13 (ND: 3702-PS). On Nov 21 JG again raised the Galen affair. Hitler told him to leave Galen unmolested until the war was over (unpubl. diary, Nov 22); *cf. ibid.*, Nov 29, 1941, and Bormann circular, Apr 26, 1943 (NA film T175, roll 68, 1860).

79 Heydrich however told Martin Luther of the foreign ministry's Abt. Inland II that JG had received from Hitler at the Wolf's Lair the decision that 'the badge will take the form of a white-and-yellow armband.' Luther note for Ribbentrop, Aug 22 (Pol. Archiv AA, Serial 4841H, E247688); Stuckart express letter, Aug 26 (*ibid.*, E247716). Ernst von Weizsäcker maintained in a minute of Sep 15 that his ministry was not consulted beforehand (NA film T120, roll 722, 321630). On Aug 20 JG noted, 'I took up the fight against the Jews in Berlin in 1926 and it is my ambition not to rest until the last Jew has left Berlin.' On which see Tiessler's circular to gau propaganda officers, Aug 21, referred to in his circular of Oct 8, 1941 (NA film T581, roll 16; BA file NS.26/291).

80 U.S. Seventh Army: PWB report SAIC/16, Jun 6, 1945, on Dr Immanuel Schäffer (NA file RG.332, entry ETO, Mis-Y, Sect., box 116); and author's correspondence with Schäffer.

81 Diary, Sep 16, 1941.

82 Diary, Sep 9, 1941.

83 Berndt to Himmler, Sep 11, 1941 (NA film T175, roll 33, 4467f).

84 PWE progress report for week ending Sep 13, 1941 (PRO file FO.898/67). The Propaganda Research Section of the PWE/PWI Political Intelligence Dept (PID) of the British FO issued fortnightly reports 1939–42 with statistical analyses of the shifting theme patterns

displayed by broadcasts, press, and Transozean, in an attempt to gain clues to developing Nazi policies (PRO file FO.898/30).

85 Koeppen report, Sep 23 (NA film T84, roll 387, 0786); Bormann diary, Sep 23; JG diary, Sep 24, 1941.

86 Koeppen report, Sep 10; Wolfram von Richthofen diary, Sep 12; JG diary, Nov 30, 1941.

87 Police ordinance on Tagging the Jews, Sep 1, 1941: *RGBl.*, 1941, I, 547; and Heydrich, regulations on above, BDC file 240/II, 167ff. Diary, Sep 24, and Tiessler note, Sep 24, 1941 (NA film T81, roll 676, 5682).

88 Tiessler circular No. 127/41, Oct 8, 1941 to all gau propaganda chiefs (NA film T581, roll 16; BA file NS.26/291); Kaufman, *Germany Must Perish!*, 83. Similar problems arose in Holland: See unpubl. diary, May 21, 1942 (NA film T84, roll 262).

89 Photocopy in Yivo file G–156.

90 Fritzsche, interrogation, Nov 1, 1946 (NA film, M.1019, roll 19; StA Nuremberg, F86) and NA file RG.260, OMGUS, box 16; *cf.* SD Meldung, Oct 9, 1941 (NA film T175, roll 261, 4963ff).

91 Diary, Sep 24, 1941. Berlin, he noted, would be first.

92 Himmler to Greiser, Heydrich, *et al.*, Sep 18 (NA film T175, roll 54, 8695); JG noted on Sep 24, 1941 that he hoped the deportation would be achieved 'during the course of this same year.'

93 Himmler to SS Gruppenführer Uebelhör, Oct 10 (NA film T175, roll 54, 8662f); *cf.* Heydrich to Himmler, Oct 19, 1941 (*ibid.*, 8645f).

94 Koeppen, note on lunch talk, Oct 6, 1941 (NA film, T84, roll 387, 0800).

95 Diary, Oct 4; Koeppen note, Oct 3, 4; Hewel diary, Oct 3, 1941.

96 Hewel diary, Oct 7, 1941.

97 *Ibid.*, Oct 8, 1941.

98 Dietrich interrogation, Oct 8, 1947 (NA film M.1019, roll 13); Werner Stephan said Dietrich told him Keitel was the source: interrogation, Oct 29, 1947, and affidavit, Nov 1947 (*ibid.*, roll 71). CSDIC (WEA) BAOR report FIR.28, Oct 29, 1945: 'Otto Dietrich' (NA file RG.219, IRR, XE.003812).

99 Sander. JG diary, Oct 10, 11; Semler 'Oct 9;' *VB*, Oct 10, 1941.

100 Diary, Oct 11, 1941.

101 Stephan interrogation (NA film M.1019, roll 71); Semler, 'Oct 11, 1941.'

102 *VB*, Oct 24; *Das Reich*, Nov 9. The latter was circulated by the Sonderdienst of RPL on Nov 4; broadcast on Nov 8, 1941 by Deutschland-Sender (BBC monitoring report, in PRO file FO.371/30928).

Notes to Chapter 43.

1 Hanfstaengl, report on JG for Pres. Roosevelt, Jul 16, 1943 (FDR Libr., PSF box 126, file 'Source S.'); and see memo by 2nd Lieut. Albert F Neumann, Jul 15, 1942 on Hanfstaengl in NA file RG.219, IRR, XE.7141141.

2 Minute by Frank Roberts, FO, Nov 8, 1941 (PRO file FO.371/30928).

3 Diary, Feb 1; MinConf., Feb 5; SD Meldung, Feb 7, 1941.

4 Diary, Mar 10, 1941.

5 *Ibid.*, Feb 21, Apr 1, 2, 5; MinConf., Apr 1, 5, 1941.

6 Diary, Feb 21, 22, 28, Mar 8, 1941.

7 JG, 'So will Roosevelt das USA-Volk kriegsreif machen,' *VB*, May 29; diary, May 29, 1941.

8 Diary, Jul 24, 1941.

9 Briefing by Dr Zapf, in unpubl. JG diary, Aug 13; and *cf.* briefing by Schmitz (Reichsbahn office New York), *ibid.*, Aug 16, 1941. For a similar briefing by Gienanth, JG's press attaché in Washington, see note 17 of chapter titled 'Things Have not Panned Out.'

10 JG to Weizsäcker, Nov 18, 1941 (ND: NG–4742).

11 *PM*, New York, Oct 28, 1941. 'Goebbelsgram contest nears end. . . ' (FDR Libr., PSF box 44, Germany 1940–41).

12 Heydrich to Luther, Nov 29 (Pol. Archiv AA, Abt. Inl. II geh., file Serial 1513; NA film T120, roll 780, 372043f); *cf.* Himmler's phone conversation with Heydrich, Oct 18, 1941: 'No overseas emigration of Jews' (NA film T84, roll. 25). The next day Heydrich wrote to Himmler, 'In daily transports of a thousand apiece, 20,000 Jews and 5,000 gypsies are being sent to the Lodz ghetto between Oct 15 and Nov 8' (NA film T175, roll 54, 8645).

13 Hildegard Henschel, 'Gemeindearbeit und Evakuierung von Berlin,' Oct. 16, 1941 – Jun 16, 1943, in *Zeitschrift für die Geschichte der Juden*, vol. ix, 1972, 34ff. Of the 82,457 Jews registered in Berlin on May 17, 1939, only 5,100 remained on April 1, 1945; 10,351 had been buried in the Jewish cemetery, the Gestapo had deported 50,535. See the tables in Sellenthin, 83.

14 (Genuine) Speer chronicle, 1941, 85; Matthias Schmidt, *Das Ende eines Mythos*, 186, 188.

15 (Genuine) Speer chronicle, 1941; Speer to Otto Wetzel, Reichstag deputy, Apr 21, 1942 (BA file R.3/1605).

16 Heinrich Heim, note on Hitler's (dinner) table talk, Oct 25 (Genoud papers). *Ad hoc* liquidations of Russian Jews had begun on a substantial scale, but Himmler, who had witnessed shootings at Kiev only days earlier, evidently said nothing. On the liquidations, see the report by Canaris or Lahousen, 'Observations made on a trip to the operational area,' Berlin, Oct 23, 1941 (IWM file AL.1933; ND: NOKW.3147).

17 Thus Dr Franz Walther Stahlecker, commander of *Einsatzgruppe* A, reported secretly, 'In the three Baltic states . . . the Jews gained the upper hand only after the bolshevik takeover,' thus 'all influential government positions [in Riga] rapidly fell into the hands of the Jews' (ND: 2273-PS). The original reports by Stahlecker are in the Moscow special archives: fond 500, opis 4, folders 91 and 93; on USHMM microfilms 14 and 15.

18 According to Dieter Wisliceny, writing in Bratislava, Nov 18, 1946, Eichmann had chosen the destinations on the premise that since Hitler's 'Commissar Order' was in force there it would facilitate liquidating the Jews (IfZ file F71/8).

19 Stahlecker report.

20 Wilhelm Kube, governor-general of White Russia, report to Himmler, Jul 31, 1942.

21 A report by SS Standartenführer Jäger on the activities of a unit of Einsatzkommando 3 states that 2,934 Jewish 'Umsiedler' (evacuees) from Berlin, Munich, and Frankfurt/Main were killed in Kaunas on Nov 25, 1941 (document courtesy of Gerald Fleming, from Riga state archives).

22 Stahlecker report. This claims that the deportation was based on preparatory work by the Jews. There had been over 150,000 Jews in Lithuania in 1940. On the role of Lithuanian Jews in the NKVD 1940–41 and the resulting anti-Jewish pogroms in Kaunas and elsewhere after Jun 22, 1941, see the frank essay by Aleksandras Shtromas, Professor of political science and a Lithuanian Jew himself, in *The World & I* (Washington, DC, 1992), 572ff.

23 Stahlecker (who may have been exaggerating) stated, 'Altogether 136,421 people were liquidated in many separate operations' in Lithuania.

24 Diary, Nov 2, 1941: briefing by Lt-Col. Zehnpfennig, district commandant of Vilnius. The Soviet secret police, he said, had rounded up the local businessmen one morning in 1940 and shot them. On Jul 5, 1941 Field Marshal von Leeb reported on the Lithuanians' revenge against the Jews to Hitler's headquarters; Schmundt told him not to intervene (Army Group North war diary, NA film T311, roll 53). See Hitler's talk with Marshal Kvaternik on Jul 22, and the diary of Otto Bräutigam, Jul 11, 1941: 'While we turn a blind eye, the Lithuanian auxiliary police are carrying out numerous pogroms against the Jews' (author's film DI–97). SS Standartenführer Jäger (see note 21 above) states that in Vilnius from Aug 12 – Sep 1, 1941, 425 Jews and 19 Jewesses were killed, and that in a *Sonderaktion* (special operation) on Sep 2, 864 more Jews, 2,019 Jewesses, and 817 Jewish children were killed 'because Jews had opened fire on German soldiers.'

25 Diary, Nov 2, 1941.

26 (Genuine) Speer chronicle, Nov 27, 1941; it quotes JG as being 'extremely surprised' at the scale of the effort.

27 Stahlecker report.

28 Dr Drechsler, Generalkommissar of Latvia, to Lohse, Oct 20; and unsigned memo, Oct 21, 1941 (Yivo file Occ–E3–29).

29 Memo by Lohse's office, Oct 27; and Regierungsrat Trampedach to Ostministerium, Nov 9, 1941 (Yivo, Occ–E3–30, 32).

30 Army commander, Baltic, to Lohse, Nov 20, 1941 (Yivo file Occ–E3–34).

31 Note by Ministerialdirektor Lutterloh of the ministry of the interior, Nov. 21, 1941 (ND: 4055-PS); however a table, 'Distribution of the Jews as of Nov 15, 1941,' puts 65,000 Jews in Berlin (and 50,000 in Vienna, 11,000 in Frankfurt/Main, 8,100 in Breslau) (NA film T81, roll 676, 5695).

32 (Genuine) Speer chronicle, 1941, 87; Matthias Schmidt, *Das Ende eines Mythos*, 188.

33 MinConf., quoted in Willi Krämer to Tiessler, Oct 25, 1941 (NA film T81, roll 676, 5792).

34 Kristina Söderbaum, *Nichts bleibt immer so* (Munich, 1992) 116, 120f. *The Golden City*, premièred Nov 24, 1942, was one of the wartime movie industry's biggest money-spinners.

35 Diary, Nov 7. The Gottschalk family were buried on Nov 6, 1941 in the Stahnsdorf cemetery. Sellenthin, 87f.

36 Undated *Propaganda Parole* No. 6, signed by Berndt, No. 413/41g (Yivo file G–44); Berndt's signature places it after Sep 9. And see the proclamation by the Jewish Culture Association, Berlin, Nov 14, 1941 (Yivo file G–229).

37 JG, 'Die Juden sind schuld!' in *Das Reich*, Nov 16; cf. *NYT,* Nov 14; broadcast Nov 14, 1941, 6:45 P.M. (PRO file FO.371/26569).

38 OKW Wi.II, Gruppenleiter, circular, Nov 17 (NA film T77, roll 672, 8117ff): the government, it said, had ordered steps to get rid of the Jewish danger 'for all times.' JG wrote in his unpubl. diary Nov 23, 1941, 'My article on the Jews has been applauded particularly by the party membership'; it provided 'the ordinary member' with the arguments he needed.

39 Obviously a reference to the Gottschalk tragedy. Typically, JG began this entry (diary, Nov 22, 1941) with the words, 'On the Jewish problem too the Führer is totally in agreement with my opinions.' Clearly he was *not*.

40 Wisliceny report, Bratislava, Nov 18, 1946 (IfZ file F.71/8). For Wisliceny's interrogations

see NA file RG.319, XE.3283.

41 Eichmann, MS: 'Deportation aus den baltischen Ländern' (Original in the author's possession).

42 Stahlecker states that 'at the beginning of Dec 1941' 27,800 Jews (possibly an exaggeration) were killed in an *Aktion* by the SS and police chief in Riga; and see the report by the army liaison officer to the foreign ministry in Riga, Apr 5, 1943 (NA film T120, roll 780, 372, 208ff). Another report by Einsatzgruppe A (ND: NO–3257) gives the overall total as four thousand Jews from the Riga ghetto 'and from an evacuation transport from the Reich.'

43 Conversation of Lt-Gen. Werner Bruns overheard on Apr 25, 1945, CSDIC (UK) report SRGG.1158 (PRO file WO.208/4169). The two or three pits which he described, each 25 meters long, with the victims forced to lie down with their heads toward the center 'like sardines,' would have held one or two thousand victims each. See too his interrogation on Feb 13, 1948 (NA film M.1019, roll 20), and the interrogations of Rocques and Elke Sirewitz. Sellenthin, 85, reproduces a Transportliste confirming that 3,715 Berlin Jews left for Minsk (Nov 14), Kaunas (Nov 17), and Riga (Nov 27, 1941), and on pp. 86f a letter written in Feb 1942 from some of their relatives, published in the *Neue Volkszeitung*, New York, Apr 25, 1942.

44 This is a reasonable interpretation of Himmler's note on his telephone call from Hitler's 'bunker' to Heydrich at 1:30 P.M., Nov 30, 1941: 'Judentransport aus Berlin. Keine Liquidierung' (NA film T84, roll 25).

45 JG's adjutant to Bartels, Nov 13 (ZStA Potsdam, Rep. 50.01, RMVP, vol. 5); on Dec 8, 1941 JG cancelled the piano's purchase.

46 Unpubl. diary, Nov 30, 1941.

47 *Ibid.*, Nov 22, 1941.

48 *Ibid.*; Speer chronicle, Nov 21, 1941.

49 According to JG, this was after his visit to headquarters on Aug 18, 1941. Boelcke, *Kriegspropaganda*, 195. Semler, writes 'Aug 28, 1941'

50 Lt-Col. Martin showed him this months later. Unpubl. diary, Feb 6, 1942: Martin had handed in his proposal for a ski collection; Jodl had scribbled on it, 'Our troops have no time for winter sports' (NA film T84, roll 260). *Cf.* Sander.

51 JG, speech to gauleiters, Aug 3, 1944 (IfZ file Fa.35/3).

52 JG to Hitler, Jul 18 (BA file NL.118/107); *cf.* Oven, 'Jul 25, 1944,' 434.

53 Eduard Wagner, private letter to his wife, Oct 19, 1941 (BA, Irving collection).

54 Koeppen report on Hitler's table talk, Oct 26 (NA film T84, roll 387, 0830); letter by Wagner, Oct 26, 1941 (BA, Irving collection).

55 JG, speech to gauleiters, Aug 3, 1944 (IfZ file Fa.35/3).

56 Diary, Nov 1; Bormann diary, Nov 1; and letter by Wagner, Nov 1, 1941 (BA, Irving collection).

57 Testimonies of Puttkamer, Mar 21, 1953 (IfZ file ZS.285) and Canstein (ZS.345).

58 JG, speech to the gauleiters, Aug 3, 1944.

59 Lutze diary, Nov 9; JG diary, Nov 10, 1941.

60 *Ibid.*, Nov 30, 1941.

61 Diary, Nov 22, 1941.

62 *Ibid.*, Nov 9, 1941.

63 Hewel diary, Dec 7, 1941.

64 Unpubl. diary, Dec 10, 1941 (Moscow archives, Goebbels papers).

65 *Ibid.*, Dec 10 1941.

66 *Ibid.*, Dec 11, 1941.

67 *Ibid.*

68 Führer's speech in *Verhandlungen des Reichstags*, vol. 460, 93ff; *cf.* diaries of Milch and Schmundt, Dec 11, and unpubl. JG diary, Dec 12, 1941.

69 MinConf., Dec 12, 1941.

70 Ambassador Hiroshi Oshima had confided to JG that Japan would capture Singapore shortly. 'He [Oshima] is already forging plans for a joint [Japanese–German] assault on India. But we're some way short of that yet.'

71 Unpubl. diary, Dec 13, 1941.

72 *Ibid.*, Dec 13; JG had said that such a meeting with the gauleiters was necessary (*ibid.*, Dec 11, 1941).

73 Sander.

74 Diary, Dec 20, 1941.

75 MinConf., Dec 19, 1941.

76 Diary, Jan 2, 1942.

77 Weizsäcker, note, Jan 6, 1942: Hill, *Die Weizsäcker-Papiere*, 284.

78 Diary, Jan 7, 1942.

Notes to Chapter 44.

1 Unpubl. diary, Jan 11, 1942 (NA film T84, roll 267).

2 *Ibid.*, Jan 8, 1942.

3 MinConf., Dec 12, 1941.

4 *Ibid.*, Dec 18, 1941.

5 *Ibid.*, Jan 27 (NA film T84, roll 260); and MinConf., Mar 6, 10, 1942.

6 Unpubl. diary, Jan 9, 1942.

7 MinConf., Dec 7, 11, 1941; for a discussion of JG's tactics after the German winter setbacks see *NYT,* Jan 11, 18 (magazine), 23, Apr 12, 1942.

8 Ursula Backe diary, Dec 29, 1941, recording a phone call from Berndt to Backe.

9 Diary, Dec 12, 1941; Jan 21, 1942.

10 *Ibid.*, Dec 19, 1941.

11 Schirmeister interrogation, May 6, 1946 (NA film M.1270, roll 19); and letter to G Moltmann, 1959, *VfZ*, 1964, 13ff.

12 MinConf., Dec 12, 1941.

13 Diary, Jan 23, 1942. Most of the women vanished into Russian captivity in 1945 and were not seen again. For the diary of one unnamed nineteen-year-old RMVP secretary from Jan 28, 1942 to 1944 see BA file Kl. Erw. 716. On Aug 23, 2011 *Bildzeitung*, Germany, published an interview with JG's by then 100-year-old former secretary Brunhilde Pomsel: 'Ich war die Sekretärin von Joseph Goebbels.'

14 Statistics until Jan 20 in MinConf., Feb 4, 1942.

15 JG, 'Das neue Jahr,' *Das Reich*, Jan 4, 1942; *cf. Das eherne Herz. Reden und Aufsätze* (Munich 1943), 168, and *NYT,* Jan 3, 1942.

16 Heinrich Heim, table talk, Jan 18–19, 1941 (Genoud papers).

17 Partly unpubl. diary, Jan 20, 1942.

18 Unpubl. diary Jan 21, 1942 (NA film T84, roll 260).

19 Behrend, No. 21, May 24, 1952. Schirmeister returned from the eastern front to RMVP Jan 20; see unpubl. diary, Jan 21, 1942.

20 Diary, Jan 20, 1942.

21 Memorandum on the [Wannsee] conference of Jan 20, 1942 in files of Abt. Inland II, geh. (Pol. Archiv AA, Final Solution of the Jewish Problem, Serial 1513; NA film T120, roll 780, 372024ff). Those present included Gauleiter Meyer, Stuckart, Freisler, Bühler, Klopfer, Kritzinger, 'Gestapo' Müller, and Eichmann.

22 Heydrich to Luther *et al.*, Nov 29, 1941 (NA film T120, roll 780, 372043; ND: 709-PS). Author's interview of Gutterer, Sep 13, 1992.

23 Hans Frank diary, Dec 16, 1941.

24 Kempner, 185.

25 *VB*, Munich, Feb 1, 1942.

26 Diary, Jan 21, 1942: the Jews were getting insolent again, particularly in Berlin public transport. 'They'll have to be reined in again; I'm already onto it.'

27 RMVP – ministry of justice, correspondence about Schönwald, Dec 1941 (Yivo file G–72).

28 MinConf., Mar 10, 1942; ordinance of Berlin Jewish Cultural Association on the ban, with effect from May 1, 1942 (Yivo file G–16).

29 Reich chamber of the press, ordinance of Feb 17, 1942 (Yivo file G–57).

30 Unpubl. diary, Feb 18, 1942 (NA film T84, roll 260).

31 Eichmann papers, 1956 (in the author's collection).

32 Unpubl. diary, Mar 6, 1942, p. 16 (NA film T84, roll 260).

33 Diary, Mar 6, 1942.

34 Because when Heydrich sent the Wannsee conference minutes to Luther at the foreign ministry on Feb 26, it was date-stamped Mar 2, 1942 (Pol. Archiv. AA, Serial 1513; NA film T120, roll 780, 372023).

35 Diary, Mar 7, 1942, pp. 17f.

36 They were Oberregierungsrat Pay Carstensen of his propaganda division, and Dr Schmidt-Burgk, of its eastern territories sub-section. Minutes of conference at RSHA, Mar 6, 1942, on final solution of the Jewish problem (Pol. Archiv AA, Serial 1513; NA film T120, roll 780, 371962). Carstensen was killed as a fighter pilot at the end of the year (diary, Dec 15, 1942: NA film T84, roll 262).

37 Interrogations of the Reich chancellery's Gottfried Boley, Sep 14, 15, 1945 (NA film M.1270, roll 2) and Jun 10, 1947 (M.1019, roll 8); and of the party chancellery's Edinger Ancker, Jun 11, 1947 (M.1019, roll 3).

38 Staatssekretär Schlegelberger sent his representative's report to Lammers of the Reich chancellery on Mar 12, and described the decisions taken there as 'for the most part totally impracticable' (ND: 4055-PS; USA Exhibit 923; BA file R.22/52).

39 Interrogation of Reich chancellery's Dr Hans Ficker, Jun 11, 1947 (NA film M.1019, roll 17).

40 Schlegelberger's undated (but spring 1942) minute on Lammers' reference to Hitler's ruling is in BA file R.22/52; although listed in their Staff Evidence Analysis sheet, this page was removed by American officials at Nuremberg from the exhibit cited above. And see Ficker (note 39 above). At about the same time JG noted that Hitler was relentless on the Jewish question: 'The Jews must get out of Europe, if necessary by applying the most brutal means' (unpubl. diary, Mar 20, 1942, NA film T84, roll 261).

41 See Globocnik to Himmler, top secret, Jun 3 (NA film T175, roll 122, 7904) on anti-Jewish

operations in Lublin; and Brack to Himmler, Jun 23, 1942 (ND: NO–205), reporting that on Bouhler's instructions he had made men available for 'special duties' and that pursuant to a further request from Globocnik he had detached still more men for the task. 'Brigadeführer Globocnik holds the view that the entire Jew-*Aktion* should be executed as fast as humanly possible in case it runs into a snag halfway through.' Brack himself argued for keeping back two or three million able-bodied Jews from the ten millions involved. On Globocnik's relationship with Eichmann see Wisliceny (IfZ file F7/18).

42 Diary, Mar 27, 1942, pp. 19–22 (BA file NL.118/42). There is no doubt about these pages' authenticity: the originals are in the Hoover archives' Goebbels collection; the microfilm of them (now NA film T84, roll 261) was made in New York in 1947, and the author also checked the microfiche copy made by the Nazis in 1944, in the Moscow archives where the microfiches have languished since 1945.

43 Diary, Mar 27, 1942.

44 Tiessler, note dated Mar 28, 1942 (NA film T81, roll 676, 5707).

45 Oven, 48.

46 Unpubl. diary, Jan 22, Feb 21, 1942 (NA film T84, roll 260).

47 *Ibid.*, Jan 31, Feb 1, 8, 1942.

48 *Ibid.*, Feb 1, 1942.

49 *Ibid.*, Feb 2, 3, 5, 8, 1942.

50 *Ibid.*, Apr 30, May 1, 5, 8, 17, 1942.

51 *Ibid.*, May 21, 1942 (NA film T84, roll 262). Oswald, age thirty-three, was killed at Cholm in Feb 1942. Annette Castendyk (daughter of Anka Stalherm), interview, Nov 10, 1991, and letter, May 20, 1993.

52 MinConf., Jan 29, 1942.

53 Diary, Jan 27; the High Command listed 4,119 cases of typhus in the eastern armies, causing 685 fatalities (MinConf., Feb 5); the typhus epidemic worsened, with 2,301 new cases in the first ten days of May (unpubl. diary, May 28, 1942).

54 MinConf., Jan 26, 1942; unpubl. diary, Nov 28, 1941.

55 Diary, Feb 11, 1941.

56 MinConf., Apr 24; he wrote similarly in *Das Reich*, May 4, 1941.

57 Diary, May 26, 1941.

58 *Das Reich*, May 4, 1941.

59 Phyllis *Moir, I Was Winston Churchill's Private* Secretary (New York and Toronto, 1941); JG diary, May 3, 1941.

60 MinConf., Feb 19, 1942.

61 Diary, May 7, Jun 13, 1941.

62 *Ibid.*, Jun 18, 1941.

63 *Ibid.*, May 8, 1941.

64 *Ibid.*, May 9, 1941; *cf.* unpubl. diary, Jan 28, 1942: Churchill was a 'classic go-for-broke gambler,' the gravedigger of the empire.

65 Diary, Jan 30, 1942.

66 Unpubl. diary, Feb 14 (NA film T84, roll 267); MinConf., Feb 13, 1942.

67 MinConf., Feb 14, 1942.

68 Diary, Feb 16; MinConf., Feb 16, 1942.

69 Thus OSS-director William B Donovan put it in a memo for Roosevelt, Apr 25, 1942 (FDR Libr., PSF box 165, 'OSS Reports').

70 Diary, Mar 20; Bormann diary, Mar 19, 1942.

71 Unpubl. diary, Mar 21, 26, 1942.

72 NS-Parteikorrespondenz, Aug 25, 1942 (BDC file, Bömer).

73 Ciano diary, Mar 19, 1942.

74 Diary, Mar 20, 1942.

75 Gutterer MS, 98f; and interview, Jun 30, 1993. Speer first heard of the Nazi atomic-bomb project at a conference in the Harnack House in June: see Otto Hahn diary, Jun 4; Milch diary, Jun 5, 1942 (copies in the author's collection); Prof. Werner Heisenberg, in *Naturwissenschaften,* vol. 33 (1947), 325; and interviews of Heisenberg and Karl-Otto Saur. See too David Irving, *The German Atomic Bomb* (New York, 1966) and *The Virus House* (London, 1965); partly superseded by Thomas Power's excellent study, *Heisenberg's War* (London, 1993).

76 Diary, Mar 21, 1942, pp. 25f.

77 Speer's conference with Hitler on Jun 23, 1942 is recorded in IWM file FD.3353/45.

78 MinConf., Mar 30; diary, Mar 31, 1942.

79 Kempner, 185.

80 Diary, Apr 27, 1942 (NA film T84, roll 262).

81 Unpubl. diary, Mar 29, 1942 (NA film T84, roll 261).

82 Diary, May 11, 17, 1942.

83 Unpubl. diary, Apr 19, 1942 (NA film T84, roll 262).

84 Killed on Apr 30, 1942 at Gusevo: Rehbein cavalry brigade, report to SS cavalry brigade, Warsaw, Apr 30, 1942 (BDC file, SS Untersturmführer A Tonak).

85 Unpubl. diary, Apr 29, 1942, p. 10.

86 Diary, May 27, 1942.

87 Unpubl. diary, May 15, 1942.

88 Diary, Jan 24, 1942. ZStA Potsdam, Rep. 50.01, RMVP, vols. 713, 977–993 and 1008, and Heiber's study in *VfZ,* 1957, 134ff.

89 Diary, Apr 3, 5, 14; JG's correspondence with Schlegelberger, Apr 10–15, 1942 (ND: NG–973, NG–1028).

90 Gutterer statements Sep 29 and Nov 2, 1953 (IfZ file ZS.490); Otto Abetz, memo on a talk between Hewel and Bormann, Apr 18 (ND: NG–179); JG diary, May 14, 1942. See Weizsäcker's file on France, vol. 11 (Pol. Archiv AA Serial 110; NA film T120, roll 112, 115113–583)

Notes to Chapter 45.

1 MinConf., Mar 18; Propaganda Slogan No. 22, Mar 23, and note of Mar 24 (NA film T81, roll 672, 0928ff); see Office of War Information (OWI) confidential report No. 6, Jul 25, 1942 (NA file RG.226, entry 16, box 115, file 18962).

2 Propaganda Slogan No. 20, Mar 13, 1942 (NA film T81, roll 672, 0905ff): Germany had to feed 2·5m foreign workers and the occupied territories too now.

3 Diary, Apr 5, 13; MinConf., Apr 12; Propaganda slogan Mar 10 (NA film T81, roll 672, 0918ff) and BA file NS. 18/43; *NYT,* Apr 17, Jun 22, 1942.

4 Führer decree, referred to in JG diary, Mar 28, 1942.

5 Diary, May 2, 23, 1942. Included in the 350,000 marks furnishings were 500 phonograph records and silverware for twenty-four guests (ZStA Potsdam, Rep. 50.01, RMVP, vol.

766).

6 MinConf., Apr 11; diary, Apr 14, 1942.

7 Note for JG, Jun 10, 1942 (Hoover Libr., Goebbels papers, box 2).

8 Unpubl. diary, Mar 11, 1942 (NA film T84, roll 267).

9 *Ibid.*, May 14; *cf.* Mar 16 and May 28, 1942 (NA film T84, roll 267).

10 Diary, Apr 9, 1942.

11 MinConf., Apr 27, 1942.

12 Diary, Apr 24; 163 people died in Rostock, and the port center was seventy percent destroyed. To JG's annoyance the foreign ministry sent Countess (Edda) Ciano and a gaggle of Italian court ladies to visit Rostock (diary, May 4). Foreign ministry official Braun von Stumm coined the phrase 'Bædeker raids,' saying the Germans would now attack any town awarded four stars in the famous guide book to Britain (*ibid.*, May 2–4, 1942).

13 Diary, Apr 27, 1942.

14 Unpubl. diary, Jun 2 (NA film T84, roll 267); at the MinConf., May 26 he announced the arrest of seven Jews for firebombing his anti-Soviet exhibition. *Cf.* MinConf., May 27, 1942.

15 Diary, May 28, 1942. According to *NYT*, 258 Jews were shot at Lichterfelde on that day.

16 Stapo-Leitstelle Berlin to Oberfinanzpräsident, Jun 5, 1942; *cit.* Gerald Reitlinger, *Die Endlösung. Hitlers Versuch der Ausrottung der Juden Europas*, 1939–1945 (Berlin, 1956), 111; Reuth, 502. An Apr 26, 1938 decree had required all Jews to list assets in excess of 5,000 marks to local tax offices and police headquarters. Wolfgang Scheffler, *Judenverfolgung im Dritten Reich 1933–1945* (Berlin, 1960), 27ff. The author is indebted to Prof. Klaus J Herrmann of the Concordia University of Montreal for drawing his attention to the harrowing *Deportiertenkartei* (deportees' card-index) in the Landesarchiv Berlin, which houses the records of 50,535 Jews expropriated and deported from Berlin during this period. These records had previously been held in the property administration (*Vermögensverwaltung*) department of the Senator für Finanzen in Fasanenstrasse, and before that they were kept in Tauentzienstraße. Herrmann's cousin Emma Herrmann and her son Peter were among those deported and systematically robbed of their assets by the Berlin finance authorities.

17 See Hitler's table talk, Apr 29, 1942 (Picker edition).

18 Diary, May 30, 1942 (NA film T84, roll 267); Reuth, note 74, makes a brave attempt to reconcile this entry with a Hitler plan to liquidate the Jews.

19 Diary, Jan 25–27; JG express circular to ministries, Jan 30: 'I have had the circulation of Seehaus material stopped with immediate effect' (Reich chancellery files, NA film T120, roll 2474, E255399). The other agencies were DNB, Transozean, and Johannsen's service in Hamburg (diary, Jan 30, 1942).

20 Unpubl. diary, Apr 6, 1942 (NA film T84, roll 261). Irving, *Breach of Security* and *Das Reich hört mit*; JG unpubl. diary, Sep 25, 1942 (IfZ file ED.83/2; author's film DI–52), recording a visit from the FA's Ministerialdirektor Walther Seifert.

21 Unpubl. diary, May 30, 1942 (NA film T84, roll 267); for Severitt's position see the FA phone directory in NA file RG.319, IRR, XE.4986, and interrogations therein of Peipe and Rebien; his predecessors were Dr Schippert and Klaus von Klitzing.

22 Unpubl. diary, May 30, 1942 (NA film T84, roll 267).

23 MinConf., May 29; diary, May 28, 1942.

24 Gutterer MS, and interview, Jun 30, 1993. In his diary, Jun 1, 1942, JG reported Hitler's

criticism of the other ministers for not having left contact numbers – he did not mention his own absence.

25 Diary, Jun 2 (NA film T84, roll 267); MinConf., Jun 2; on Jun 14, 1942 he pointed out that every conceivable bomber type had been shot down, proof that Churchill had scraped the bottom of the barrel.

26 Diary, Jun 2, 5; *NYT*, Jun 2, 1942 wrote of twenty thousand dead.

27 Memo by William B Donovan to Pres. Roosevelt, No. 596, Jun 1942 (FDR Libr., PSF boxes 165–6, 'OSS'); and see JG, 'Der Luft- und Nervenkrieg,' in *Das Reich*, Jun 14, 1942.

28 Memo by William B Donovan to Pres. Roosevelt, No. 581, Jun 5, 1942 (FDR Libr., PSF boxes 165–6, 'OSS'); and see the PWE analysis of German home propaganda, May 13–20, 1942, No. 528, *ibid.*

29 Diary, Mar 27, 1942.

30 Memo by William B Donovan to Pres. Roosevelt, No. 359, Mar 27, 1942 (FDR Libr., PSF boxes 165–6, 'OSS').

31 Ditto, No. 319, Mar 9, 1942.

32 Ditto, No. 318, Mar 7, 1942.

33 OSS R&A Report No. 21, 'Current German Attitudes and the German War Effort,' Mar 19, 1942 (USAMHI, Donovan papers, box 37a).

34 Memo by William B Donovan to Pres. Roosevelt, No. 563, May 29 (*ibid.*); MinConf., Jun 15, 1942.

35 *Ibid.*, Jul 22; see also *ibid.*, Aug 6, 8, 1942.

36 *Ibid.*, Aug 10, 1942.

37 *Ibid.*, Jul 3, 1942.

38 Diary, Jun 5, 1942.

39 Bormann to JG *et al.*, Jun 8, 1942 (NA film T175, roll 139, 7362f).

40 MinConf., Jul 14, 1942.

41 Diary, May 14, 18; unpubl. diary, May 27, 1942.

42 JG as RPL, guidelines, Feb 15, 1942 (Yivo file Occ. E20).

43 MinConf., Jul 6, 1942.

44 Diary, Feb 24; in general, see the report by Hadamovsky and Taubert on the administration of the east, Sep 17, 1942 (Yivo file Occ. E18).

45 Unpubl. diary, Apr 25, 1942 (NA film T84, roll 261).

46 *Ibid.*, Feb 14; and May 2, 1942.

47 *Ibid.*, May 22, 27, 28, 1942 (NA film T84, roll 267).

48 *Ibid.*, Jun 1, 1942 (NA film T84, roll 267).

49 Diary, Jun 5, 1942.

50 MinConf., Jul 1, 1942.

51 *Ibid.*, Jul 7, 9, 1942.

52 JG, 'Die sogenannte russische Seele,' *Das Reich*, Jul 18; circulated to all Reichsleiter and gauleiters, Jul 14 (NA film T581, roll 16; BA file NS.26/291); and see OWI report No. 6, Jul 6, 1942 (NA film RG.226, entry 16, box 115, 18962).

53 MinConf., Jul 28, 1942.

54 Diary, Jun 5, 1942.

55 MinConf., Jul 15, 16, 18, 21, 22, 1942.

56 *Ibid.*, Jul 23, 1942.

57 *Ibid.*, Jul 8; on Aug 3, 1942 he added, 'In particular avoid comments that the air raids will not decide the war.'

58 JG, 'Auch der Versuch ist strafbar,' *Das Reich*, Aug 2; issued as usual by radio and DNB several days ahead. See 'Goebbels über die Zweite Front,' in *Neue Zürcher Zeitung*, Jul 30, and *NYT*, Jul 30, 1942, p. 3. In his diary on Aug 1, 1942, JG wrote, 'Never has an article of mine attracted such lively interest as this one. It is quoted under banner headlines on the front pages of the entire European press.'

59 MinConf., Aug 18, 22, 1942.

60 Unpubl. diary, Aug 14–15, 1942 (BA file NL.118/125).

61 MinConf., Aug 11, 1942.

62 See MinConf., Aug 19, 1942 (Moscow archives, Goebbels papers).

63 Unpubl. diary, Aug 21, 1942 (Moscow archives, Goebbels papers).

64 *Ibid.*

65 *Ibid.*, Aug 22, 1942.

66 MinConf., Aug 21, 1942

Notes to Chapter 46.

1 'Vom Sinn des Krieges.' Unpubl. diary, Aug 14–15, 1942 (NA film NL.118/125).

2 Memo Wilson to R Leeper, Aug 21, 1942 (PRO file FO.898/67).

3 Hans-Leo Martin, 33f.

4 *Propaganda Parole* No. 33, Jun 2, 1942 (NA film T81, roll 672, 0810ff).

5 MinConf., Aug 15–18; diary, Aug 10, 1942. ,

6 MinConf., Aug 21; unpubl. diary, Aug 20, 1942 (Moscow archives, Goebbels papers).

7 Diary, Aug 9, 1942.

8 MinConf., Aug 17, 22, 23, 24, 1942.

9 JG, 'Seid nicht allzu gerecht!' in *Das Reich*, Sep 6, 1942.

10 Unpubl. diary, Sep 30, 1942, pp. 30f (author's film DI–52; IfZ).

11 JG referred to his secret speech, delivered to Berlin's editors and foreign press corps, *ibid.*, Sep 24; see too *VB*, Sep 25, 1942. The text quoted by the author is a 5pp. copy typed on flimsy 'Flight Post' stationery on an English typewriter (no Umlaut), evidently obtained by Polish Intelligence; it was forwarded by Mr F Savery (of the British embassy to the Polish government in exile) to Frank Roberts of the FO: a 'Mr Wzelaki' (*sic*) mailed it to Savery on Feb 25, 1943 (PRO files FO.371/30928, /34454). The forty-nine-year-old Jan Wszelaki (1894–1965) was deputy secretary-general of the Polish ministry of foreign affairs in exile; see his correspondence with Savery in the Sikorski Institute archives, Kol. 39. – As for the text's authenticity, see JG's similar references to 'exaggerated craze for objectivity' in his speech of Nov 17, 1942, and to the needless 'love of truth' and 'functionalism' of German media reporting, in his secret speech of Jul 17 or 18, 1943 (see *VfZ*, 1971, 83ff).

12 However on Jul 22 he had told the People's Court in a speech that there were 'still 40,000 Jews' in Berlin (report by Crohne in Schlegelberger's files, ND: NG–417); he had quoted the same figure in his diary on May 11, 1942.

13 This is very similar to JG's 'Jews who have nothing to lose' argument (*cf.* diary, May 30, 1942; NA film T84, roll 267). At his MinConf. on Dec 8 JG agreed that the 'maltreatment of the Jews in Poland' was a tricky issue, and too hot really to handle; he also discussed the multiplying British and American allegations about 'atrocities against Jews' in the east in his conferences of Dec 12, 14, 16 ('What must happen is that each side accuses

the other of atrocities; the general hullabaloo will eventually lead to the topic being removed from the agenda'), and Dec 18, 1942.

14 Diary, Dec 14, 1942.

15 *Ibid.*, Dec 18, 1942.

16 MinConf., Aug 13, 1942.

17 Kempner, 185.

18 Unpubl. diary, Sep 27, 1942 (author's film DI–52).

19 *Propaganda Parole* to all gauleiters, No. 12, Oct 2, 1942 (NA film T81, roll 672, 0663f).

20 When Fritz Sauckel proposed leaving the Jewish skilled workers in the Government-General (Poland), Hitler agreed but (Sep 20–22) 'reiterated the importance of pulling the Jews out of the munitions plants in the Reich.' (Hitler–Speer conferences, IWM file FD.3353/45). But Himmler noted on Oct 9, 1942 that he was 'collecting the Jewish so-called munitions workers' in Poland and replacing them with Poles (NA film T175, roll 22, 7359f).

21 Unpubl. diary, Sep 30, 1942.

22 Tiessler, note, Oct 5, 1942 (NA film T81, roll 676, 5851).

23 Thierack note on discussion with JG, Sep 14, 1942, about 'destruction of anti-social lives' through work, especially Jews, Poles, gypsies, Czechs, and miscellaneous Germans (ND: 682-PS; IMT, v, 496f.)

24 Tiessler, note, Oct 31; noted by JG on Nov 5, 1942 (*ibid.*, 5845ff). Thierack notified Bormann, 'the legal system can be of only limited assistance in disposing of the members of this race' (Reitlinger, *Die Endlösung*, 176; Reuth, 507).

25 Note on meeting at RSHA on Final Solution of the Jewish Problem, top secret, Oct 27, 1942 (NA film T120, roll 780, 1943ff).

26 MinConf., Nov 3, 1942.

27 Telex from [Regierungsrat Walter] Koerber [chief of Hauptreferat Schnelldienst in domestic press Dept] to the Generalgouvernement press office, and RPA in Warsaw, No. 65, Sep 7, 1942 (Yivo file Occ–E2–72).

28 Schmidt-Leonhardt's report of Nov 11 is in Yivo file Occ–E2–107. On Nov 15, 1942 Himmler wrote to Lammers about briefing Hitler on 'the developing situation in the *Generalgouvernement*' (NA film T175, roll 122, 7770); deputy gauleiter Albert Hoffmann (Upper Silesia) had briefed JG on the disturbances in the Generalgouvernement earlier (unpubl. diary, Sep 25, 1942).

29 Prause (Gutterer's pers. Referent) report to JG, Feb 15; identical wording in his report of Feb 22, 1943 (Yivo file Occ–E2–12).

30 Klimonski (?) to JG, Apr 10, 1943 (NA film T81, roll 671, 9447f).

31 Note that Otto Dietrich claimed ignorance of the transportation (interrogation, Oct 1, 1947. NA film M.1019, roll 13).

32 Himmler to Müller, Nov 30, 1942 (NA film T175, roll 68, 4325).

33 *The Times*, Nov 24, Dec 4, 7, 21, 1942; SS Sturmbannführer Brandt to Kaltenbrunner, Feb 22, 1943 and shorthand note (NA film T175, roll 68, 4398; and roll 18, 1550).

34 RMVP radio monitoring service, summary on Allied agitation on the Jewish problem in Germany, Dec 18, 1942 (BA file R.55/1270).

35 Unpubl. diary, Dec 17, 19, 1942 (NA film T84, roll 262).

36 RMVP radio monitoring service, summary on Allied 'crusade' to save the Jews, Dec 22, 1942 (BA file R.55/1270).

37 Diary, Dec 8, 1942.

38 On the squabbling between JG and Dietrich, see CSDIC (WEA) BAOR Report PIR.8, Sep
   10, 1945, Otto Dietrich (NA file RG.219, IRR, XE.003812); the numerous interrogations of
   Dietrich in StA Nuremberg, Rep. 502, D36 and lawyer Dr Friedrich Bergold's files (Rep.
   501, LV G B). Kurt Dittmar, interrogation, Nuremberg, Oct 14, 1947 (NA file RG.260,
   box 15); Heinz Lorenz, ND: NG.4331; Hans Fritzsche stated under interrogation, StA
   Nuremberg, Sep 27, 1946, F86, that he quit because of Dietrich's dishonest reporting in
   Oct 1942, and went to the front.

39 Interrogations of Sündermann, NA film M.1019, roll 72; and Nov 10, 1947 (IfZ file ZS.747);
   Max Amann, testimony of Dec 18, 1947 (IfZ file ZS.809); interrogations of Gutterer on
   Oct 24 and Dec 12, 1947 (NA film 1019, roll 23); and of Paul K Schmidt, Oct 28, and Nov 4,
   12, and 14, 1947 (NA film M.1019/64).

40 Hitler's thirteen-point decree was dated Aug 23, 1942. Peter Longerich, 'Joseph Goebbels
   und der totale Krieg,' *VfZ*, 1987, 114.

41 MinConf., Sep 18, 1942.

42 *Ibid.*, Sep 21, 1942.

43 Unpubl. diary, Sep 23, 1942 (author's film, DI–52; original in IfZ).

44 *Ibid.*, Sep 27, 1942.

45 *Ibid.*

46 See the PWE report of Oct 1 on Hitler's and JG's speeches of Sep 30 (PRO file FO.371/30928)
   and FO telegram No. 5908 to Washington, Oct 2 (*ibid.*) and analysis of Oct 19, 1942
   (/30927); also the *NYT* report of Oct 1, and the comment in that newspaper by A O
   McCormick, Oct 19, 1942.

47 Unpubl. diary, Sep 29, 1942.

48 *Ibid.*, Sep 28, 1942.

49 Semler, 'Mar 25, 1941' Dr Rudolf Semler, born in Ulm on Dec 31, 1913, replaced Hallensleben
   as JG's press officer in Jan 1941 (JG diary, Dec 22, 1940; Jan 5, 1941); according to Semler's
   'diary,' he was presented to JG on Dec 31, 1940 and started work two days later. During
   1942 he served in the army, and returned from the Stalingrad front to JG's staff in Nov
   1942. He went missing in 1945. Dr Helge Knudsen of *Berlingske Tidende,* Copenhagen,
   obtained the manuscript of the 'diary' from Semler's wife and brought it to London
   where it was published as Rudolf Semmler [*sic*], *Goebbels – The Man Next to Hitler*
   (London, 1947). In correspondence with this author Knudsen has insisted on the diary's
   authenticity; many misdated entries suggest however that the source should be used
   with caution. *E.g.* the diary describes JG as being with his children on 'Mar 25, 1941:'
   but they had been evacuated to Austria months before (*cf.* JG diary, Mar 23: 'All I miss
   now is the children'). On 'Apr 1, 1941' Semler records Stalin's embrace of Krebs, which
   occurred however eleven days later, on Apr 12 (*cf.* JG diary, Apr 14). On 'Aug 28, 1941'
   Semler refers to a meeting 'yesterday' with Hitler which in fact occurred on Aug 18;
   Semler puts Mussolini's overthrow on 'Jul 21, 1943, ' instead of Jul 25; JG's trip to headquarters on 'Jul 27, 1943' instead of Jul 26; the air raid on Berlin on 'Nov 21, 1943,' instead
   of Nov 22. He describes JG's 'Apr 1944' foreign policy memo to Hitler, which is however
   none other than JG's memo of Sep 22, 1944 (BA file NL.118/106); he puts the false start of
   the V–1 attack on London on 'Jun 9, 1944,' instead of Jun 12/16. This author believes that
   the diary was compiled probably in 1945 from notes or memory.

50 In BA file NL.118/106. See the cartoon series in *NYT,* Oct 25, and the report in *NYT,* Oct
   30, 1942.

51 A copy of the film by the Deutsche Wochenschau Gesellschaft is in the author's posses-

sion.

52 Behrend, No. 8, Feb 23, 1952.

53 See the private letter by Col. Helmuth Groscurth, Oct 4, 1942.

54 The SD reported on Oct 26, 1942 (NA film T175, roll 24, 7888f) that a majority of Germans favored doing a deal with the Soviet Union.

55 Hans-Leo Martin, 34.

56 Fritzsche interrogation, Nov 13, 1947 (StA Nuremberg, F86).

57 In Jan 1944 the OSS threw these words back at him in a leaflet addressed to German troops (USAMHI, Donovan papers, box 37a).

58 *Das Reich*, Oct 25; see the SD report on this, Oct 29, 1942 (NA film T175, roll 264, 7919).

59 MinConf., Oct 24; the first meeting of this Arbeitsstab für Rüstungspropaganda was on Nov 5, 1942 (Boelcke, *Wollt Ihr den totalen Krieg?*, 296).

60 MinConf., Nov 6, 1942.

61 The Italian losses were ninety dead and twenty-three thousand missing (mostly prisoners). JG ordered the German press to ignore the figures (diary, Dec 11, 1942).

62 Borresholm, 167ff.

63 On Oct 31 the naval staff war diary quoted an Abwehr agent report that the Allies were about to land in north-western France. On Nov 7 and 8, 1942 the same diary commented on the Abwehr's failure.

64 Stephan, 287.

65 Diary, Nov 9, 1942.

66 MinConf., Nov 10, 1942.

67 *Ibid.*, Nov 11, 1942.

68 *Ibid.*, Nov 12, 1942.

69 *Ibid.*, Oct 2, 1942.

70 *Ibid.*, Sep 16, 1942.

71 *Ibid.*, Oct 22, 1942.

72 *Ibid.*, Nov 20; SD report, Aug 13, 1942, on JG's visits to Cologne and Düsseldorf (NA film T175, roll 263, 7352ff).

73 PWE discussed JG's Wuppertal speech of Nov 17 in German propaganda analysis dated Nov 20 (PRO file FO.371/30927); *cf. NYT,* Nov 19, 1942.

Notes to Chapter 47.

1 Schirmeister interrogation, May 6, 1946 (NA film M.1270, roll 19).

2 Unpubl. diary, Dec 12, 1942 (NA film T84, roll 262; BA file NL.118/48).

3 *Das Reich*, Sep 25, 1942. Ernst Hanfstaengl quoted this passage in one analysis for the OSS, Dec 21, 1942 (NA file RG.219, IRR, X7141141).

4 Paul Anderson, broadcasting on BBC, Nov 26, 3:30 P.M., cited in RMVP monitoring report, Dec 1, 1942 (BA file R.55/1270).

5 Wilson (PWE) to Rex Leeper, Notes on Propaganda to Germany, Dec 18–24, and Dec 25–31, 1942 (*ibid.*).

6 Unpubl. diary Dec 19; Semler, 'Dec 19, 21, 1942;' BDC file, People's Court: Hans Heinrich Kummerow. He is sometimes identified as the source of the famous Oslo Report, which gave British Intelligence advance notice of his country's most important secret devices.

7 Semler, 'Dec 24, 1942.'

8 Unpubl. diary, Dec 7, 13, 20, 1942; Jan 1, 1943.

9 Magda to Daluege, Jan 11, 1943; from Daluege's papers (BDC file, JG; author's film DI– 81).

10 For the BBC monitoring report on JG's speech of Dec 31, 1942, see PRO file FO.371/34454; for the German people's reaction, see NA film T175, roll 264, 8353ff.

11 *Propaganda Parole* No. 15, Dec 14 (NA film T81, roll 672, 0656f); and see MinConf., Dec 7, 1942.

12 For a report by Herbert Uxküll, United Press correspondent in Stockholm, on JG's propaganda guidelines – *e.g.,* always calling Maxim Litvinov 'Finkelstein,' banning the use of 'Second Front' and 'Russian' – see his dispatch of Jan 15, 1943 in NA file R.226, CRR, entry 16, box 323, file 33393.

13 *Propaganda Parole,* Nov 21, 1942 (NA film T81, roll 672, 0651f).

14 *Propaganda Parole* No. 15, Dec 14, 1942 (*ibid.,* 0659f). Ti[essler] advised Bormann on Jan 6, 1943, 'For the same reason he [JG] now has to insist for the last time that the phrase Fortress Europe disappear once and for all from our vocabulary' (*ibid.,* 0895); and see MinConf., Dec 7, 1942, and Jan 5, 1943, and unpubl. diary, Apr 12, 1943.

15 See unpubl. diary, May 13, 1943 (NA film T84, roll 264).

16 *Ibid.,* May 19, 1942.

17 Diary, Dec 16; Gienanth had briefed JG earlier (unpubl. diary, Jun 3, on NA film T84 roll 267) about the Roosevelts' unpopularity, but also that 'the German people and particularly we Nazis' were hated; he addressed propaganda officials Jul 13–14, 1942 on his impressions of the USA 1937–41 (BA file R.55/606); and see his interrogation of Apr 30, 1946 (NA film M.1270, roll 5).

18 Unpubl. diary, Dec 18, 1942. For the rumors, see Dec 15, and the SD reports of Dec 17 and 21, 1942 (NA film T175, roll 264, 8279ff and 8298ff).

19 Dittmar diary, Dec 21, 1942 (author's film DI–60).

20 Unpubl. diary, Aug 13, 1941 (NA film T84, roll 267).

21 *Ibid.,* Sep 24: a briefing by his former adjutant Günther Wittmütz; and Sep 27, 1942, a similar discussion with Major Ihlefeld.

22 *Ibid.,* Sep 29, 1942.

23 *Ibid.,* Sep 30, 1942.

24 Dittmar records in his diary of Dec 22, 1942 being invited to luncheon at Horcher's with Fritzsche, Luftwaffe general Quade, Transozean's Mr Schneider, and the Berlin correspondent of the Essen *Nationalzeitung.*

25 Unpubl. diary, Mar 8, 1942 (NA film T84, roll 261); already on May 13, 1941 he had noted that Hitler had once more shelved the female labor issue. 'I plead for compulsion. . . The fine ladies won't come of their own volition.' On May 23, 1941 he noted that Hitler had rejected compulsion.

26 *Ibid.,* Dec 17, 1942.

27 Kehrl, 249ff.

28 Minutes of Zentrale Planung, Oct 30, 1942 (Milch Documents, vol. 46, 9014f); *cf.* David Irving, *The Rise and Fall of the Luftwaffe* (London, 1967).

29 Bormann diary, Dec 27–28, 1942 (Libr. of Congress); he returned to the Wolf's Lair on Dec 30, and sat alone with Hitler on Dec 31 until 4:15 A.M. next day; *cf.* JG diary, Jan 5, 1943.

30 Oven, 'Jul 25, 1944', 430f.

31 Semler, 'Dec 28, 1942.'

32 Diary, Dec 31, 1942.

33 *Ibid.*, Jan 1; similarly in MinConf., Jan 5, 1943.

34 MinConf., Jan 4; JG diary, Jan 5; Semler, 'Jan 4.' Sauckel spoke in the same vein about an all-out labor effort in Weimar on Jan 6, 1943 (IMT, xli, 225ff).

35 MinConf., Jan 5, 1943.

36 Draft letter from JG to Göring, Jan 12, 1943, in Hoover Libr., Goebbels papers, box 2: 'I am proud to have stood at your side during the hardest times of our movement, and shall always be glad to place myself at your disposal if called upon for advice or assistance.'

37 See his remarks at the MinConf. on Jan 6, 1943: reported by Tiessler to Bormann that day (NA film T81, roll 672, 0895).

38 Diary, Jan 7, 1943.

39 *Ibid.*, Jan 9; Bormann records (Jan 8, 1943) that JG, Bormann, Funk, Sauckel (with Timm), Speer, and Keitel attended, as well no doubt as Lammers.

40 Diary, Jan 16, and MinConf., Jan 16, 1943.

41 Führer decree on a comprehensive effort of men and women for Reich defense purposes, Jan 13 (BA file R.43II/655; IfZ film MA.470, 4910ff); see Himmler's telephone note on a call on Jan 14 to SS Obersturmbannführer With ('Gen. von Unruh's misgivings about the Führer's decree'); and MinConf., Jan 13–14, 1943.

42 Lammers to JG, Jan 15, 1943 (BA file R.43II/655).

43 Diary, Jan 16, 1943.

44 Semler, 'Jan 18, 1943.'

45 Oven, 'Jul 25, 1944,' 434.

46 Diary, Jan 21, 1943. Lammers had brought in besides JG: Sauckel, Funk, and Gen. Walter von Unruh, the army's Sonderbeauftragter für Überprüfung des zweckmässigen Kriegs-einsatzes (special manpower commissioner).

47 Semler, 'Jan 20, 1943.'

48 Dittmar diary, Jan 7, 1943 (a phone conversation with Col. Martin).

49 Diary, Jan 7, 1943.

50 Dittmar diary, Jan 11, 1943.

51 See *ibid.*, Jan 16; for the public shock at this, see SD report, Jan 25, 1943 (NA film T175, roll 264, 8535f). The communiqué referred to German troops in Stalingrad 'who have been fighting a heroic defensive battle against the enemy attacking from all sides.'

52 Dittmar diary, Jan 21, 1943.

53 So Goebbels later recalled. Oven, 'Jul 25, 1944,' 434.

54 Diary, Jan 23; Semler, 'Jan 24, 1943.'

55 Diary, Jan 23, 1943.

56 Naumann confirmed this to the RMVP department heads on the evening of Jan 23, stating that the Führer was now resolved to implement the total-war measures proposed by JG (MinConf., Jan 24, 1943).

57 SS Obergruppenführer Gottlob Berger to Himmler, Jan 29 (NA film T175, roll 124, 9596); see too MinConf., Jan 24, and naval staff war diary, Jan 24, 1943.

58 See JG's comments on this in MinConf., Jan 24; in his speech to the gauleiters on Feb 7, 1943 Hitler borrowed JG's comparisons with the winter of 1932/33.

59 Diary, Jan 23, 1943.

60 Dittmar diary, Jan 23 (Author's film DI–60); at his conference on Jan 27, 1943, JG referred to similar speeches of Caesar and Frederick the Great. 'The few sentences about the

saga of Stalingrad must be clear, devoid of pathos, and modest, as though hewn from solid rock.'

61 JG to all propaganda agencies, Jan 24, 1943 (NA film T84, roll 24, 1959ff).

62 Mallet (Stockholm) to FO, Jan 28, 1943 (PRO file FO.371/34454); Göring had evidently tipped off his Swedish contact Birger Dahlerus.

63 Diary, Jan 28; Semler, 'Jan 14, 1943.'

64 Press directives in BA, Sänger collection.

65 OSS report, Feb 10, 1943 (NA file RG.226, CRR, entry 16, box 2456, file 28480).

66 JG, 'Die harte Stunde,' in *Das Reich*, Feb 7; public reaction to it in SD report, Feb 11, 1943 (NA film T175, roll 264, 8686f).

67 Regulations on male and female recruiting for Reich defense duties, Jan 27, in *RGBl.*, I, 1943, 67; JG's commentary on this in MinConf., Jan 29, 1943.

68 JG to Hitler, Jul 18, 1944 (BA file NL.118/107); see his diary, Jan 26, 29, 1943.

69 Diary, Jan 28; and see Semler, 'Jan 29, 1943.'

70 Frölich (RPL), circular No. 179 to all gau propaganda officers, Jan 30, 1943 (NA film T81, roll 24, 1960f).

71 Diary, Feb 1, 1943.

72 FO (Bruce-Lockhart) to Cairo and Bowes-Lyon to Washington, Feb 1 (PRO file FO.371/34454). The former considered that Göring spoke effectively to the younger generation, the latter commented that Hitler, Göring, and JG refrained from attacking the USA and harped instead on the bolshevik menace. Dittmar (diary, Jan 30, 1943) rated JG's speech as the better.

73 Diary, Dec 7, 12, 1942.

74 BBC Monitoring Report, transcript of JG's speech, Jan 30, 1943 (PRO file FO.371/34454).

75 US Federal Communications Commission, Foreign Broadcast Intelligence Service, Special Report No. 49, Feb 1, 1943: 'The Nazi anniversary speeches of Jan 30, 1943,' 16pp. (NA file R.226, entry 16, box 234, file 27843).

76 Borresholm, 9.

77 In a useful analysis of the speech's defensive utterances the Americans also found that 27 percent were appeals to nostalgia (past anniversaries, trials, successes), 18 percent were praise of Nazi reconstruction, 14 percent were exculpatory statements about Versailles, Hitler having sought peace, etc., 9 percent were protestations of faith in the Führer and his mission, 9 percent were taunts, 7 percent were admissions ('this is a crisis'), 7 percent were glorification of the troops, 5 percent were quasi-mystical (Providence, etc.), 2 percent were exhortations (must try harder), and 2 percent were promises of future rewards. For the German public's response see SD report, Feb 1, 1943 (NA film T175, roll 264, 8587ff). It is worth commenting that in his MinConf. on Dec 22, 1942 JG had forbidden the use of words like *grave* and *critical* 'since if we use the word *grave* in our propaganda the enemy will make *catastrophic* out of it.'

78 Diary, Feb 1, 1943.

79 Willi Krämer, *Vom Stab Hess zu Dr. Goebbels* (Vlotho, 1979), 210f.

80 MinConf., Feb 1–2; diary, Feb 2; Dittmar wrote on Feb 2, 1943, 'Went at noon to Fritzsche's conf. in propaganda ministry. I've never seen him so upset as today. The Russian report has put the cat among the pigeons... Obviously we can't check if it's true. General indignation that P didn't commit suicide. All well and good, but what do we know of the final dramatic hours?'

81 Diary, Feb 4, 1943. Dittmar: 'Now even the dullest among us can see what's up.' – Hinkel

to JG, Feb 3, 1943 (BA file R.55/1254).

82 Hitler's speech is summarized in Ursula Backe's diary, Feb 8, 1943. The Russian official historians have stated that more than one million Soviet soldiers were killed during the Stalingrad battle, with 13,500 executed for cowardice; these figures seem improbable.

83 Diary, Feb 8, 1943.

Notes to Chapter 48.

1 Schirmeister interrogation, May 6, 1946 (NA film M.1270, roll 19).

2 Unpubl. diary, Feb 1, 1943 (author's film DI–52; IfZ).

3 *Ibid.*, Feb 16, 1943; Gutterer interrogation, Oct 24, 1947 (NA film M.1019, roll 23).

4 Ernst von Weizsäcker to his mother, Feb 21, 1943 (Hill, *Die Weizsäcker-Papiere*, 325).

5 Generalluftzeugmeister conference, Feb 16, 1943 (Milch Documents, vol. 18, 4461, 4481); JG diary, Feb 16, 22 (p. 19); and Milch diary, Feb 15, 1943 (author's film DI–59).

6 Göring diary, Feb 1943 (author's film DI–171).

7 With to Himmler, Feb 11 (NA film T175, roll 124, 9607f); and see too the diary of Col. Gerhard Kühne, chief of staff of the Allgemeines Heeresamt (general army office), Feb 9, 1943: '[JG] felt himself under attack, turned nasty, and went over to the counter-attack. . . ' (IfZ archives).

8 On this speech see in general Helmut Heiber's text in *Goebbels Reden* (Düsseldorf, 1972), vol. ii, 172ff; Willi Boelcke, 'Goebbels und die Kundgebung im Berliner Sportpalast vom 18. Februar 1943,' in *Jahrbuch fir die Geschichte Mittel- und Ostdeutschlands*, 1970, 19; Tiessler's file on the propaganda background of total war in BA file NS.18/26, and above all Günter Moltmann's paper, 'Goebbels Rede zum totalen Krieg am 18. Februar 1943,' in *VfZ*, 1964, 13ff.

9 Diary, Feb 13, 1943.

10 *Ibid.*, Feb 14, 15, 18, 1943.

11 Semler. Hitler had certainly endorsed JG's total-war policies (see MinConf., Feb 8); but although both Werner Stephan and Moritz von Schirmeister told Moltmann in 1959 that they believed JG had first obtained Hitler's approval for the speech, see JG's own diary for Feb 18: it was difficult to contact the Führer as he was at the Werewolf head-quarters – but they 'thought alike.' And Feb 25, 1943: a proclamation by the Führer was very much in line with his speech, 'So there's no danger of my being disowned in any way. . . From this one again sees that it's best to create *faits accomplis*.'

12 Edward L Deuss, 'The Effect of Total Mobilization on German Morale,' Feb 22, 1943 (NA file R.226, entry 16, box 0354, file 35653).

13 BA, Fritz Sänger collection.

14 In his diary on Jun 6, 1943 JG would however write, 'While on Feb 18 it was mainly the party, this time it is Berlin's munitions workers. . .' Walter Hagemann, writing in *Publizistik im Dritten Reich. Ein Beitrag zur Methodik der Massenführung* (Hamburg, 1948) suggested that the audience had been bussed in and instructed how to act. Not so. Hagemann judged that the radio audience found the 'hysterical screaming' of the audience irritating. The Allies were however deeply impressed by the broadcast. See Alexander L George, *Propaganda Analysis. A Study of Inferences Made from Nazi Propaganda in World War II* (Evanston, Illinois, 1959).

15 Moltmann paper.

16 Dr Hans Joachim Kausch, 1962, to Moltmann.

17 Diary, Feb 19, 1943. A photo in the *Hamburger Tageblatt* also showed the popular actors Eugen Klöpfer, Theodor Loos, and Franz Grothe.

18 At his MinConf. on Feb 8, 1943 he directed his staff to keep secret the fact that the 300-mile-wide breach in their front had begun with the failure of a certain ally.

19 For the text of his speech see the newspapers of Feb 19, 1943; and A I Berndt and H von Wedel (eds.) *Deutschland im Kampf*, Nos. 83–4, Berlin, Feb 1943, 80ff; and A I Berndt (ed.), *Das Archiv. Nachschlagewerk für Politik, Wirtschaft, Kultur* (Berlin, 1942–43), 975ff. It was issued as a brochure, *Nun Volk steh' auf und Sturm brich los!*, though belatedly because JG kept altering the title and planned a foreword describing the atmosphere in the Sport Palace (Scheffler to gau propaganda officials, May 28, 1943, on NA film T84, roll 24, 1878). A partial audio recording is in the German radio archives, Frankfurt (No. 53 A 688); a complete recording is in BA, No. 650/1943.

20 Diary, Feb 19; Milch diary, Feb 18 (author's film DI–59) and Speer chronicle, 1943 (IWM file FD.3049/49).

21 Göring diary, Feb 18, 1943 (author's film DI–171).

22 See CSDIC (UK) report SIR.1025, the interrogation of Grenadier Kieburg, an agent of the Gestapo Leitstelle in Posen since Jan 10, 1943 (NA file RG.332, Mis-Y, box 5).

23 Summary of RPA reports, Feb 19, 1943, in BA file R.55/612.

24 Diary, Feb 21; see SD report, Feb 22, 1943 (NA film T175, roll 264, 8775f). Ribbentrop was shown a letter from Oberveterinär Dr Michael which doubted the propaganda effects of the speech. Lammers felt it would be 'unwise' to forward the letter to JG (NA film T120, roll 2474, E.255481).

25 Dittmar diary, Feb 18, 1943: 'Barely satisfactory, very coarse, typical Sport Palace rhetoric. G may well have had his reasons to speak like this, but many of his arguments were too cheap to generate more than frenzy.'

26 Diary, Feb 19, 1943.

27 MinConf., Feb 22, 25; diary, Feb 18, Mar 1, 1943 (NA film T84, roll 263; BA file NL.118/54).

28 MinConf., Mar 12. He had to defend himself against the charge that he dealt in 'targeted pessimism' (*Zweckpessimismus*). FCC Foreign Broadcast Service, Special Report No. 84, 'Nazi Predictions and the Present Propaganda Crisis,' Jun 26, 1943 (NA file RG.226, entry 16, box 0384, 37319).

29 MinConf., Feb 22, 1943.

30 JG to Hitler, Jul 18, 1944 (BA file NL.118/107).

31 Berndt, *Propaganda Parole* No. 55, May 7, 1943: as point 16 of the party program proved, he said, it had always supported a strong middle class (NA film T81, roll 672, 0761f).

32 MinConf., Feb 8; Hitler regarded much of this as over-zealous (diary, May 10, 1943).

33 Diary, Feb 28, 1943.

34 Unpubl. diary, Feb 14, 1943; Oven, 'Jul 25, 1944,' 437.

35 Note scribbled by Morell on Stadtkrug's menu, Feb 10, 1943 (Morell papers, NA film T253, roll 39).

36 Author's interviews of Otto Horcher, and of Speer, Dec 7, 1968; Semler, 'Mar 18, 1943;' Oven, 162.

37 Diary, Mar 1–2, and Speer chronicle, 1943. JG was careful to end his diary account of these three-way dialogues with suitably loyal remarks about their complete solidarity with the Führer.

38 Diary, Mar 2, 1943; the quotation is from Shakespeare, *Richard III*, act IV, scene II.

39 Diary, Mar 7, 10, 12, 1943.

40 MinConf., Mar 10, 1943. Later he regretted the executions as they created the impression that looting was rife. But see too his remarks (diary, Apr 3, 1943) about the death sentence passed on the RPL's Mr Ostholt: 'This sleaze bag deserves only to have his block knocked off.'

41 Eichmann MS, ca. 1956 (BA, Irving collection).

42 Diary, Mar 9, 1943. For further papers on this trip see Hoover Libr., Goebbels papers, box 2.

43 For JG's anti–communist tactics see his MinConf., Feb 12; his *Propaganda Parole* No. 49 of Feb 17 laid down the new theme of 'Victory or Bolshevik Chaos!' (NA film T81, roll 672, 0688ff), and *Parole* No. 50 of Feb 23 (*ibid.*, 0686f) noted the success of this new tactic: Churchill and Eden were warning against allowing JG to drive a wedge between the Allies. See General Dittmar's diary of Mar 1 and MinConf., Mar 10, and the OSS report on JG's foreign press briefing of Mar 15 (see diary, Mar 13–16, 18, 1943) in NA file RG.226, entry 16, box 0290, 31183.

44 Diary, Mar 17; Speer chronicle, 1943.

45 Diary, Mar 18, 1943.

46 *Ibid.*, Mar 20, 1943.

47 Helldorff to Himmler, and reply Jul 8, 1943 (BDC file, Helldorff).

48 SS Obergruppenführer Heissmeyer to Himmler, Jan 14, 1943 (*ibid.*).

49 US FCC, Special Report No. 49, *op. cit.*

50 Wächter, *Propaganda Parole* No. 48, Feb 9, 1943 (NA film T81, roll 672, 0690f).

51 Diary, Feb 18, 1943.

52 *Ibid.*, Mar 1, 1943.

53 *Ibid.*, Mar 11, 1943.

54 Unpubl. diary, Mar 11, 1943.

55 Diary, Mar 6, 1943.

56 Dittmar diary, Mar 8, 1943 (author's film DI–60); JG was away at Führer's headquarters.

57 MinConf., Feb 26, 1943.

58 Semler, 'Aug 16, 1943;' Semler reported that out of 150 letters received in the second week of Aug 1943 sixteen protested at reviving the Jewish problem. 'Antisemitism,' he noted, 'is as unpopular as ever among the mass of the people.'

59 Diary, Mar 9, 15, 20, 1943.

60 *Ibid.*, Apr 18, 1943.

61 *Ibid.*, Mar 3, 5, 7, 8, 10–12, 15, 17, 18, Apr 9, 1943.

62 *Ibid.*, Mar 10, Apr 2, 4, 5; Weber to Morell, Jan 25 (NA film T253, roll R45, 8901) and May 25, 1943 (NA film T253, roll 34, 3460), and interview of Jul 21, 1989.

63 JG circular No. 126 to gauleiters, Mar 17, 1943 (NA film T81, roll 24, 1920).

64 Diary, Jan 16, 21, 1943; Oven, 84.

65 Diary, Jan 21, 1943. Churchill had awarded the George Cross to Malta.

66 MinConf., reported by Tiessler to Bormann, Mar 24, and note, Mar 25, 1943 (NA film T81, roll 671, 9792ff).

67 Diary, Apr 12; SD report, Münster, Apr 21, 1943, in PID report DE.63/DIS.202 of Jul 21, 1945 (Hoover Libr., Lerner papers).

68 Diary, Apr 9–10; Milch diary, Apr 8–10, 1943 (author's film DI–59). For JG's speech in Essen see *e.g. Frankfurter Zeitung*, Apr 11, 1943.

69 Diary, Apr 11, 1943.

70 *Ibid.*, Apr 4, 5, 13, 1943.

71 *Ibid.*, Apr 12; Speer chronicle, 1943.

72 Apart from dinner with Antonescu, Hitler's appointment calendar was in fact wide open (diary of SS Untersturmführer Hans Junge/SS Obersturmführer Heinz Linge, Hoover Libr.)

73 Diary, Apr 13–14, 1943.

74 See his directives on NA film T81, roll 24, 1903, 1906.

75 Diary, Apr 15–16, 24, 30, 1943.

76 Semler, 'Nov 20, 21, 1943.'

Notes to Chapter 49.

1 See unpubl. diary, Apr 3, 1943: 'Both antisemitism and anti-bolshevism are currently our best propaganda weapons' (NA film T84, roll 265).

2 Fritzsche interrogation, Sep 29, 1947 (StA Nuremberg, F86).

3 Diary, Feb 17, 1943.

4 *Ibid.*, Mar 1, 3–6, 20, Apr 1, 1943; for further sources see David Irving, *Accident. The Death of General Sikorski* (London, 1967), which draws on the Polish records of the Sikorski Institute in London.

5 Diary, Apr 9, 1943 (from French files, on NA film T84, roll 272).

6 Telex from Smolensk to RSHA Dept IIIC, Apr 4, 1943; forwarded to Gutterer (BA file R.55/115).

7 *Ibid.*, Apr 16, 1943; the former NKVD officer Petr K Soprunenko, who signed the Katyn death warrant, lives in Moscow as an old-age pensioner (1995). See www.massviolence.org/The-Katyn-Massacres-of-1940.

8 MinConf., Apr 8, 1943 (BA file R.55/115).

9 Diary, Apr 14; Semler, 'Apr 12, 1943.' For MinConfs. and further RMVP documents on Katyn see BA file R.55/115.

10 Unpubl. diary, Apr 16, 1943.

11 *Ibid.*, Apr 17, 1943. On the Soviets' insistence Katyn was added into the indictment at the Nuremberg trials and they executed several German officers after a trial in Leningrad in 1945.

12 *Ibid.*, Apr 17, 28; Dittmar records on Apr 19, 1943 a 'very good Goebbels speech' on Katyn at a conference in the ministry.

13 Unpubl. diary, Apr 9, 1943.

14 Dittmar entered in his Jul 5, 1943 diary: 'To the propaganda ministry. Big event of the day: Polish émigré leader [Władysław] Sikorski killed at Gibraltar – by [British] Secret Service?' (author's film DI–60).

15 SD report No. 377, Apr 19, 1943.

16 JG ordered it kept secret (diary, May 8, 1943).

17 SD report, Jul 26, 1943 (NA film T175, roll 265, 9996ff).

18 Schmidt–Leonhardt report, Nov 11, 1942 (Yivo file Occ–E2–107); the draft of an agreement between JG and Frank was ready on Jan 25, 1943. Report to JG, Apr 10, 1943 (NA film T81, roll 671, 9447ff).

19 Diary, May 10; Hans Junge diary and Bormann diary, May 9, and note of May 11, 1943 (BA, Schumacher collection, 371).

20 Diary, May 22. Himmler to Frank, May 26 (NA film T175, roll 128, 4157ff); see Himmler note, Jun 19 (NA film T175, roll 94, roll 0506f), and the final report of the SS and police chief (HSSuPf) in Galicia, Jun 30, 1943 (Hoover Libr., MS DS.135 G2G37).

21 Unpubl. diary, Jun 25, 1943 (author's film DI–52; IfZ).

22 *Ibid.*, Apr 15, 17, 1943.

23 For the statistics on Jews in the Russian communist party see Korherr to Himmler, Apr 28, 1943 (NA film T175, roll 54, 6439).

24 JG, 'Der Krieg und die Juden,' in *Das Reich*, May 9, previewed in *Frankfurter Zeitung* and other journals on May 8, issued by the RPL to all party orators and propagandists on May 4, and as a special edition by the AO, the party's overseas organization, in Jun 1943 (NA film T81, roll 134, 8933a). See Berndt's *Propaganda Parole* on this, Apr 30, 1943 (NA film T81, roll 672, 0754ff).

25 Diary, May 8; *The Times*, May 8; and *NYT*, May 9, 1943.

26 Semler, 'Jan 10, 1944.'

27 Bormann circular No. 33/43, Jul 11, 1943 (BDC file 238/II); it is pertinent to note that this was classified only *geheim* (secret), not *geheime Reichssache* (top state secret).

28 Actually: 31,283. See the table in Kempner, 186.

29 Heinz Lorenz interrogation, Dec 3, 1947 (IfZ file ZS.266).

30 Fritzsche interrogation, Nov 1, 1946 (StA Nuremberg, F86).

31 See unpubl. diary, Sep 27, 1942; and the JG–Rosenberg correspondence, Feb 1943 – Feb 1944 (Yivo file Occ–E 19); and diary, Apr 6, 16, May 19, 20, 1943.

32 *Ibid.*, Jan 14, 21, Feb 10, 14, 16, Mar 2, 8, 9, and *passim*, 1943.

33 *Ibid.*, Feb 10, 1943.

34 *Ibid.*, Jan 7, Mar 2, Apr 16, 1943.

35 *E.g.*, *ibid.*, Jan 21, 1943.

36 Correspondence in Yivo file Occ–E–12.

37 JG submission to Hitler, May 22 '1942' (read: 1943) (Yivo file Occ–E18–19).

38 Naumann to Bormann, Jun 12, 1943 (Yivo file Occ–E12).

39 Unpubl. diary, Jun 25; Führer decree of Aug 15 (Yivo file Occ–E19; BA file R.55/799); and see Taubert (Leiter Ost), proposal for erection of propaganda apparatus in the eastern region on the basis of the Führer's decision, Aug 21, 1943 (Hoover Libr., Fritzsche papers).

40 Taubert report (Yivo file G-PA–14).

41 Diary, Feb 5, 1944.

42 Himmler to Stuckart, Jul 16, 1943 (NA film T175, roll 33, 2113).

43 Führer conf. with Keitel and Zeitzler, Jun 8 (shorthand record on NA film T78, roll 788, ND: 1386–PS); and see Heinz Danko-Herre (Foreign Armies East) diary (IfZ file ZS.406), and Etzdorf to German foreign ministry, Jun 17, 1943 (Pol. Archiv AA, Etzdorf papers).

44 Himmler to Gunter d'Alquèn, Jul 11, 1943 (BDC file, d'Alquèn).

45 On this committee see Gutterer's files in ZStA Potsdam, Rep. 50.01, vol. 799 and Yivo files Occ–E–FD–1 and 4.

46 On whom see JG's diary, Sep 23–24, 1943 and Feb 5, 1944 ('a swine without a fatherland'). Yivo also has good files of the League's publications (Occ. E-FD–9, 10, and 13).

47 The problem of the prisoners' letters now arriving was dealt with by Wächter and Berndt in *Propaganda Parole* No. 57, May 26, 1943 (NA film T81, roll 672, 0773ff).

48 Unpubl. diary, May 1, 14, 16, 27, 1943.

49 *Ibid.*, May 22, 1943.

50 Dr Immanuel Schäffer, interrogation, PWB report SAIC.16, Jun 6, 1945 (NA file RG.332, entry ETO, Mis-Y, Sect., box 116). See too the FCC Foreign Broadcast Intelligence special report No. 84, Jun 26, 1943: 'Nazi Predictions and the Present Propaganda Crisis' (NA file RG.226, entry 16, box 384, OSS file 37319). The SD also reported on May 28, 1943 that the public were baffled by the war and were growing apathetic (NA film T175, roll 265, 0543ff).

51 Diary, May 7, 1943.

52 Unpubl. diary, Apr 9, 11, 14, 19; diary, May 8, 1943.

53 Unpubl. diary, May 10 (NA film T84, roll 264); Hans Junge diary, May 9, 1943.

54 'That's not going to be easy.' Unpubl. diary, May 9, 10, 11 (NA film T84, roll 264); Rommel diary, May 10 (author's film DI–160), and letter to his wife, May 10, 1943 (NA film T84, roll R274, 1099).

55 Unpubl. diary, May 25, 1943. On the 'corpse' see naval staff archives, PG.33216, and NA film T78, roll 343.

56 Hans-Leo Martin, 142ff; diary, Apr 9, 1943.

57 Unpubl. diary, Apr 11, 16, 1943. The naval staff war diary shows that the Abwehr had got every prediction about TORCH wrong. As for the Soviet armor, see Col. Lahousen's note of Jul 20, 1941 (IWM file AL.1933).

58 Diary, May 14, 22, 1943.

59 JG, 'Mit souveräner Ruhe,' in *Das Reich*, May 23, 1943.

60 Diary, May 16, 17, 1943.

61 See the final report of the SS Führungshauptamt, Jun 10 (NA film T611, roll 16); naval staff war diary, May 20, 22; report by deputy gauleiter Albert Hoffmann, BA file Kl. Erw. 854; Speer chronicle, May 17; Hitler's war conference, May 22, 1943 (Heiber, 238ff); and reports of the operations of the NSV on reel 6 of the microfilm files of the NSDAP archives.

62 Diary, May 19, 20, 1943 (NA film T84, roll 265). There is no truth in the claim: the reference was perhaps to Churchill's advisor Professor Friedrich Lindemann (Lord Cherwell), but he was not Jewish.

63 JG, 'Vom Wesen der Krise,' in *Das Reich*, May 30; diary, May 17, 1943.

64 JG's speech draft for Jun 5 with Hitler's handwritten amendments is in BA file NS.6/129. Hitler also deleted three whole pages referring to North Africa. See the analysis of the speech by the British air ministry Director of Intelligence (Ops), Jun 6, 1943 in NA file RG.226, entry 16, box 417, file 3610.

65 For the public's reaction to this speech, see SD report of Jun 10 (NA film T175, roll 265, 9632ff); to Allied air raids, Jun 28 (9758ff); to rumors of new weapons, Jul 1, 1943 (9750ff).

66 Unpubl. diary, May 21, 22; Sep 10, 1943.

67 Morell–Weber correspondence, Jun, Jul 1943 (Morell papers on NA film, T253, roll R34, 3552ff); Naumann note, and Weber to JG, Sep 22, 1943 (ZStA Potsdam, Rep. 90, Go 1, vol. 3).

68 Unpubl. diary, Jul 25–28, 1943 (NA film T84, roll 265).

69 Oven, 32ff. On Jul 8, 1943 the SD report mentioned that the public was beginning to bandy around spiteful jokes about Hitler and other bigwigs (NA film T175, roll 265, 9821ff).

70 Semler, 'Jun 14, 15, 1943.'

71 Oven, 43, 'Jun 27, 1943.' Gutterer independently recalled the taunt, in interviews of Sep 1992 and Jun 30, 1993.

72 Hans-Leo Martin, 42f.

73 JG circular to gauleiters, Jun 14, 1943 (NA film T81, roll 322, 1076ff).

74 Index of these circulars on NA film T81, roll 322, 1070ff.

75 Berndt, circular to gauleiters, Jun 19, 1943 (NA film T81, roll 322, 1083ff).

76 JG's speech in Wuppertal, 'In vorderster Reihe,' text in *Der steile Aufstieg* (Munich, 1944), 323ff. On Jul 1 the SD reported rumors about the new 'revenge' weapons (NA film T175, roll 265, 9758ff); on Jul 2 Tiessler circularized gau propaganda officials on this point, and reminded them that in the Sport Palace (on Jun 5, 1943) JG had referred to it as a 'scientific race,' *i.e.*, a question of time (NA film T58, roll 16; BA file NS.26/291).

77 Oven, 'Jun 23, 1943.'

78 Unpubl. diary, Jun 25, 1943 (author's film DI–52; IfZ); on Mar 14, 1944 JG noted the same arguments from Hitler. On Apr 27, 1944 however JG noted that the Führer was 'suffering enormously under the heavy losses being inflicted, particularly on our population and on our cultural artifacts.'

79 Unpubl. diary, Jun 25, 1943 (author's film DI–52; IfZ).

Notes to Chapter 50.

1 Oven, 43.

2 For the public's reaction to the 'rain of phosphorus' bombs, see SD report Jul 5, 1943 (NA film T175, roll 265, 9810f).

3 Unpubl. diary, Jul 25 (NA film T84, roll 265); RMVP air war notice No. 13, Jul 27, 1943 (NA film T84, roll 322, 1121f).

4 Semler, 'Jul 10'; Oven, 55, 'Jul 10.' JG's speech of Jul 9 at Heidelberg university was published as *Der geistige Arbeiter im Schicksalskampf des Reiches* (Munich, 1943); see too *NYT,* Jul 10, 1943.

5 Semler, 'Jul 10, 1943.'

6 Diary, Jun 5, 1943.

7 Remark by Col. Pasewaldt (Reich air ministry, technical department) on May 2, 1945: CSDIC (UK) report SRGG.1187 (PRO file WO.208/4169); Milch diary, Jul 15 and 20, 1943 (Author's film DI–59); on the latter date all ministers, state-secretaries and gauleiters were at Rechlin.

8 Diary, Mar 25, Jun 5, 1943. JG to Harlan, Jun 1, 1943; quoted in Söderbaum, 191ff.

9 Remark by Major Baron von Blanckart, Aug 25, 1944, in CSDIC (UK) report SRM.831 (PRO file WO.208/4462). The speech was probably on Jul 18, 1943. Oven, who puts it on 'Jun 28', also records the light gray trousers and navy blue jacket. – There is no corresponding entry in Schmundt's war diary (BA–MA: H.4/12).

10 The RPL discs of JG's speech in the ministry's Throne Room, which internal evidence suggests was held on Jul 17 or 18, were found after the war in the mountains at Rottach on the Tegernsee. See Krausnick, Kotze, *Es spricht der Führer* (Gütersloh, 1966), 369ff and Hildegard von Kotze, 'Goebbels vor Offizieren im Juli 1943,' *VfZ,* 1971, 83ff.

11 RMVP air war notice No. 13, Jul 27, 1943 (NA film T84, roll 322, 1121f).

12 Unpubl. diary, Jul 25, 1943 (NA film T84, roll 265); so the entry was less prophetic than would appear.

13 Oven, 'Jul 27,' 81ff; JG diary, Jul 26, 1943.

14 Diary, Jul 28, 1943: 'More and more urgent are the calls to headquarters that some man

in authority, preferably the Führer himself, should speak out . . . We're doing too much warring and too little jawing. In the present situation, in which our military successes are not all that impressive, it would be a good thing if we polished up the art of politics a bit.'

15 Diary, Jul 27, 1943; describing these deliberations I have also used the diaries of Rommel, Richthofen, the naval staff war diary, and the Führer's naval conferences.

16 For Canaris' faulty intelligence on Italy, see OKW war diary, Jul 30–31, Aug 3, 5; naval staff war diary, Jul 29; Lahousen diary, Jul 29 – Aug 3, 1943.

17 Diary, Jul 28, 1943.

18 *Ibid.*, Jul 29, 1943.

19 Speer at a meeting of Central Planning on Jul 29, 1943 (Milch Documents, vol. 48, 10, 443ff).

20 Speer, 297; *cf.* Milch diary, Jul 31, 1943 (author's film DI–59).

21 Milch at a Generalluftzeugmeister conference on Aug 3 (Milch Documents, vol. 23, 6607f). – The SD's morale report of Aug 2, 1943 analyzed the German public's reaction to the dissolution of fascism in Italy; it referred to an increase in anti-Nazi remarks, the smashing of leading Nazis' windows, and the shock about Hamburg as 'November-feelings' (NA film T175, roll 265, 0045ff).

22 Werner Girbig, *Im Anflug auf die Reichshauptstadt* (Stuttgart, 1977), 69f. – *NYT,* and Anneliese Schmundt diary, Aug 2, 1943.

23 Oven, 'Aug 4,' Speer chronicle, 1943. To this author, Milch denied the episode in 1967. Semler, under 'Jul 26, 1943' attributes similar defeatist sentiments to a non-officer, the minister of the interior Frick. According to an affidavit by the High Command's liaison officer to Dietrich, Martin Sommerfeldt, Jun 4, 1948, JG had him charged with defeatism for stating in the ministry that the war could no longer be won (StA Nuremberg, G15).

24 Lammers to JG, Aug 18, 1943 (Chancellery files, NA film T120, roll 2474, E255432).

25 *Ibid.*, 119; and Semler, 'Aug 7, 1943.'

26 Semler, 'Aug 10, 1943.'

27 Dittmar diary, Aug 2; *Propaganda Parole*, signed by Berndt and Wächter, Aug 10, 1943, about rumor-mongering and the British 'black' transmitter Deutscher Atlantik Sender (NA film T81, roll 672, 0882ff).

28 Circular by Gau Hessen-Nassau, No. 44/43, Aug 10 (NA film, T81, roll 168, 7579f); based on *Propaganda Parole* No. 59, signed Berndt and Wächter, Aug 7, 1943 (NA film T81, roll 672, 0890f).

29 Dittmar diary, Aug 2, 1943.

30 JG circular to Bormann, Speer, Ley, *et al.*, Jul 29 (NA film T84, roll 322, 1123f.) – See SD report of Aug 5, 1943 on the Berliners' reaction to evacuation propaganda (NA film T175, roll 265, 0055ff).

31 JG to all gauleiters, air war notice No. 21, Aug 15 (NA film T84, roll 322, 1147f.); and unpubl. diary, Sep 8, 1943.

32 Oven, 'Aug 22, 1943', 110; and similar in Hildegard Springer, *Es sprach Hans Fritzsche. Nach Gesprächen, Briefen und Dokumenten* (Stuttgart, 1949), 17.

33 JG to Hitler, Jul 18, 1944 (BA file NL.118/107).

34 Circular dated Sep 1943 (NA film T84, roll 322, 1203); and diary, Sep 12, 1943.

35 Note to JG's office, Aug 6, 1943, with a 67-line inventory of items to be evacuated (BA file R.55/1392; and Hoover Libr., JG papers, box 2).

36 Bartels note, Aug 14, 1943 (ZStA Potsdam, Rep. 50.01, vol. 759).

37 Published *inter alia* in *Börsenzeitung*, Aug 4, 1943.

38 Bartels to JG, Aug 3, 1943 (ZStA Potsdam, Rep.50.01, vol. 4).

39 Notice of Aug 6, 1943 (Hoover Libr., JG papers, box 2).

40 Oven, 108f.

41 JG, report on this raid to all gauleiters, Aug 27 (ADI[K] report 158a/1945); Milch conference with Speer, Sep 1 (Milch Documents, vol. 30, 377) and night fighter conf., Aug 31, 1943 (*ibid.*, 206).

42 114 more bombers were damaged including eleven beyond repair: Webster & Frankland, *The Strategic Air Offensive against Germany* (London, 1961), vol. ii, 165*n*.

43 Unpubl. diary, Sep 8, 1943 (NA film T84, roll 265); Dr Immanuel Schäffer, interrogation, PWB report SAIC.16, Jun 6, 1945 (NA file RG.332, entry ETO, Mis-Y, Sect., box 116).

44 Gutterer note on talk with Milch, Sep 1, and letter, Sep 9, 1943 (ZStA Potsdam, Rep.50.01, vol. 935).

45 Schnauff (RMVP) to Frankfurt gau, Jan 20, 1944 (NA film T84, roll 169, 6337).

46 Unpubl. diary, Sep 9, 1943 (NA film T84, roll 265); Oven, 128ff.

47 Unpubl. diary, Sep 10, 1943.

48 See Bormann's letter to his wife, Sep 9, 1943.

49 Diary, Sep 10. When Moscow now upgraded its embassy in Stockholm, JG noted foreign speculation about the Soviet ambassador Madame Kollontai becoming a mediator between Berlin and Moscow. Unpubl. diary, Sep 21, 1943.

50 Diary, Sep 15, 17, 18, 1943.

51 Diary, Sep 28, 1943; Webster & Frankland, vol. ii, 165.

52 Diary, Sep 12, 13, 16, 17, 20, 1943; and note on a meeting about organization at Lanke with Naumann and Schwägermann (Hoover Libr., JG papers, box 2; and BA file R.55/1392).

53 Diary, Sep 16, 18, 23, 1943.

54 *Ibid.*, Sep 15, 1943.

55 Unpubl. diary, Sep 25, 1943 (NA film T84, roll 265); the anthology was *Der steile Aufstieg. Reden und Aufsätze aus den Jahren 1942–1943* (Munich, 1944); on which see the records of the party's censorship bureau (PPK) in ZStA Potsdam, Rep. 62, Ka 1, Kanzlei des Führers, vol. 206.

Notes to Chapter 51.

1 Diary, Sep 13. He explained in *Das Reich*, Sep 19, why 'JG' had published no article after the Duce's overthrow. 'A few spiteful people believed that events . . . had taken his breath away,' he wrote. 'There's probably no need for any further proof now that this was not so.' In his diary on Sep 25, 1943 he added: 'People now understand why I had to hold my tongue for a while.' In fact he had known nothing of the plans to free Mussolini (NA film T84, roll 265).

2 SD report Sep 16, 1943 (NA film T175, roll 265, 0456ff).

3 RPÄ reports summarized in diary, Sep 17; mail analysis, in Sep 18, 1943.

4 Kurt Lange, vice-president of Reichsbank, to JG, Mar 16, 1944. The ministry of the interior had stated that air raids had destroyed 58,500 residential buildings in Hamburg by Nov 1, 1943; Lange gave a figure of 324,351 for the Reich as a whole (ZStA Potsdam, Rep. 50.01, vol. 5).

5 Diary, Sep 17, 1943.

6 *Ibid.*, Sep 14, 1943.

7 Unpubl. diary, Sep 18, 19, 21, 1943 (NA film T84, roll 265).

8 *Ibid.*, Sep 23; Heinz Linge, Hitler's appointments register, Sep 22, 1943 (NA film T84, roll 387).

9 Diary, Sep 23, 1943.

10 Linge, Oct 26, 1943 (NA film T84, roll 387).

11 Rosenberg's note on the meeting, Nov 17 (NA film T120, roll 2474, E255448); Linge, Nov 17, 1943 (NA film T84, roll 387).

12 Note by his adjutant, Oct 29, 1943. The three were Countess 'Sigi' Welczek, the actress Käthe Haack, and her daughter.

13 Interrogation of soldier Kloss, Sep 1, 1944: 'Goebbels' Estate on the Bogensee N[orth of] Berlin' CSDIC (UK) report SIR.1008 (NA file RG.332, Mis-Y, box 5; also RG.165, entry 79, box 773); and see Oven, 171.

14 Diary, Sep 21, 1943.

15 Semler, 'Oct 15, 1943.'

16 Speer chronicle, Nov 4, 1943 (IWM file FD. 3949/49).

17 Diary, Sep 2, 1943.

18 *Ibid.*, Nov 2; and police reports by Prince zu Waldeck, Höherer S.S.- und Polizeiführer, Kassel, Nov 30 and Dec 6, 1943 (IfZ, Irving collection).

19 Diary, Nov 6; Oven, 184f; *VB*, Nov 7, 1943.

20 Gutterer MS, and interview, Jun 30, 1993.

21 Police reports by Prince zu Waldeck, Höherer S.S.- und Polizeiführer, Kassel, Nov 30 and Dec 6, 1943 (IfZ, Irving collection).

22 *Ibid.*; and JG diary, Nov 19, 1943.

23 Diary, Nov 6, 1943.

24 Berndt, air war notice No. 62, Nov 11, 1943 (NA film T84, roll 322, 1254f).

25 Ditto (*ibid.*, 1257ff).

26 Unpubl. diary, Sep 29, 1943.

27 Fritzsche testimony, IMT, xvii, 181 (Jun 28, 1946).

28 Diary, Nov 16, 1943.

29 *Ibid.*

30 Unpubl. diary, Nov 11, 1943.

31 Diary, Nov 4, 1943.

32 Speer chronicle, Nov 4, 1943.

33 Jodl's lecture is printed in OKW war diary, vol. iv, 1534ff.

34 Diary, Nov 8; and Himmler diary, Nov 7 (NA film T84, roll 25). Himmler had telephoned JG's ministry and Bormann several times on Sep 1, 1943, about the gau's planned swoop on defeatists (*ibid.*).

35 Unpubl. diary, Nov 16, 1943 (NA film T84, roll 266).

36 As of Sep 1943. United States Strategic Bombing Survey, *A Brief Study of the Effects of Area Bombing on Berlin* (Washington, DC), No. 39, 12a.

37 Webster & Frankland, vol. ii, 190ff. The average load of each bomber was about 7,500lb.

38 Semler, 'Nov 24;' JG diary, Nov 20, 1943.

39 I rely on Semler, 'Nov 22, 1943,' Speer's chronicle, and other sources.

40 Diary, Nov 24, 1943.

41 *VB*, Nov 24, 1943.

42 Diary, Nov 25, 1943.

43 See SD report, Dec 20, on the Berliners' morale during and after the Nov 1943 raids (NA film T175, roll 265, 1196ff).

44 Diary, Nov 25; the result was a Führer decree of Dec 22, 1943, setting up a Reich Inspec- torate for Civil Defense under JG with Gauleiter Albert Hoffmann as his deputy (BA file, R.43II/669d; IfZ film MA.795, 489off). Hoffmann's papers are in BA. Under BAOR interrogation (032/Case No. 0164) Hoffmann said, 'Goebbels was undoubtedly one of the best National Socialist ministers; sober, precise, and very ambitious . . . [and] remarkably industrious, and was at all times during the day and night at the disposal of the gauleiters or any other important people' (NA file RG.332, entry ETO, Mis-Y, Sect., box 50).

45 Diary, Nov 27, 1943.

46 Unpubl. diary, Nov 28 (NA film T84, roll 266); Oven, 'Dec 20, 1943,' 196.

47 Unpubl. diary, Dec 4, 1943 (NA film T84, roll 266); the British could not get good aerial photos that winter (Webster & Frankland, vol. ii, 264).

48 Diary, Dec 4, 7; on Nov 24, 1943 JG complained to Hitler, 'Despite the directive you have several times issued that matters in dispute were only to be put jointly to you, Reichsminister von Ribbentrop has appealed directly to you, mein Führer, without bringing me in and with inadequate information on this matter' – namely JG's propa- ganda work in occupied France (BA file NL.118/106).

49 Linge diary, Dec 19, 1943 (NA film T84, roll 387).

50 JG to Hitler, Dec 1943 (BA file NL.118/106); Oven, 'Jan 25, 1944,' 208, also draws attention to the increasing frequency of JG's visits to headquarters.

51 ZStA Potsdam, Rep. 90, Go 2, Magda Goebbels correspondence with the public, 1933–45, vol. 2.

52 JG's speech, 'Ganz Deutschland ruft nach Rache!,' in *VB*, Nov 29; translation of the *DAZ* summary in OSS file 52614; see SD report, Dec 3, 1943, for the public's reaction (NA film T175, roll 265, 1057ff).

53 Milch diary, Dec 8, 1943; Maj. Karl von Winterfeld, report dated Aug 24, 1945, in Milch papers (author's film DI–59).

54 JG, 'Die Lehren des Krieges,' in *Das Reich*, Dec 5. 'This,' commented an OSS report from Switzerland on Dec 22, 1943, 'is Goebbels in his mystic strain. There is no cry of victory, but a stress on the uncertainties of war, and the expression of a plaintive hope that will- power will win over material force' (NA file RG.226, file 58658).

55 JG to Keitel, Dec 9, 1943 (Hoover Libr., Lerner papers, file S.115). JG had the offending word *Katastropheneinsatz* changed to *Soforthilfe*.

56 Semler, 'Dec 24, 1943.'

57 Unpubl. diary, Dec 30, 1943 (NA film T84, roll 266).

58 CSDIC (UK) survey dated Feb 24, 1944 of German prisoner-of-war opinion, Nov 1943 – Jan 1944 (NA file RG.165, entry 79, box 765; and RG.332, entry ETO, Mis-Y, Sect., box 11).

59 Webster & Frankland, vol. ii, 267. Kurt Lange, vice-president of the Reichsbank, told JG on Mar 16, 1944 that one-third of Berlin's 200,000 homes had been destroyed or damaged (ZStA Potsdam, Rep. 50.01, vol. 5); for statistics on destruction as of Mar 1944 see Gutter- er's file (ZStA Potsdam, Rep. 50.01, vol. 865).

Notes to Chapter 52.

1 JG speech, Dec 31, 1943. BBC monitoring report, text and commentary (PRO file FO.371/34454); *NYT,* Jan 1; SD report on, Jan 3 (NA film T175, roll 265, 1265ff) and Jan 6, 1944 (*ibid.,* 1286ff).

2 RPL leaflet, weekly slogan of NSDAP, Jan 2–8, 1944 (Yivo file, G–169).

3 Jay W Baird, MS, 'The Memoirs of Goebbels' Deputy, Dr Werner Naumann,' 2 vols. Quoted by Elke Fröhlich of IfZ. In his speech on Hitler's birthday JG said much the same, that Hitler always had an instinct for the right and necessary course of action (*DAZ,* Jan 21, 1944).

4 Oven, 'Jan 5, 1944.'

5 Circular No. 158 to all RPÄ Jan 22, 1944 (NA film T84, roll 169, 6299).

6 JG speech, 'Der Krieg als Weltanschauungskampf,' Jan 25, 1944 (NA film T77, roll 852, 8135ff).

7 Circular No. 202, Jan 27 (NA film T84, roll 169, 6250). In his diary, Feb 10, 1944, JG estimated that Berlin had suffered 10,000 dead and missing from the air war. I am indebted to Dr R G Reuth for the 1944 diary, obtained from ZStA Potsdam files via the IfZ.

8 Dr Scharping, radio slogan, Jan 29, 1944 (NA film T84, roll 169, 6228).

9 Only two days earlier JG had asked the armed forces and party to provide men on standby in his remaining theaters to help fight any fires. JG, air war notice No. 84, Jan 26, 1944 (NA film T84, roll 322, 1287f).

10 Oven, 'Feb 2, 1944,' 229.

11 He quoted the SD report in his diary, Feb 5. For a discussion of his campaign to repair morale, see *NYT,* Feb 6, 1944.

12 JG to Hitler, Feb 4, 1944 (BA file NL.118/106).

13 Diary, Feb 10, 1944.

14 *Ibid.,* Feb 16; the *NYT* reported, falsely, on Mar 13, 1944 that JG had escaped death in the hotel only by minutes.

15 Diary, Feb 23, 24, 1944.

16 JG, 'Der Krieg als Weltanschauungskampf,' Jan 25, 1944 (NA film T77, roll 852, 8135ff).

17 The transcript is not found, but see Himmler's handwritten speech notes for Jan 26, 1944: 'Race struggle. Total solution. Don't let avengers emerge against our children . . .' (NA film T175, roll 94, 4836). The wording was similar in Himmler's speeches of Oct 6, 1943 (BDC file 238/III) and May 5, 1944 (NA film T175, roll 92, 3476ff).

18 So Col. Rudolf-Christoph Baron von Gersdorff recalled in *Soldat im Untergang* (Munich, 1977); Bodo Scheurig quoted the colonel's original MS in *FAZ,* Jul 21, 1993.

19 Remark by Rear-Adm. Engel, CSDIC (UK) report SRGG.1167(C) in PRO file WO.208/4169.

20 Hitler's speech of Jan 27, 1944 is recorded in BA files, Schumacher collection, file 365. *Cf.* Irving, *Hitler's War,* 606; the diaries of the naval staff, Jodl, Maximilian von Weichs (Mar 3, 1944), and Salmuth (Mar 27, 1946); and the remarks of generals von Rothkirch in CSDIC (UK) report SRGG.1135 and Veith, SRGG.1149 (PRO file WO.208/4169). The note in Reuth's edition of the diaries, p. 1981, relies on the inadequate version in Manstein's memoirs, *Verlorene Siege* (Bonn, 1955), 579ff.

21 Diary, Feb 6, 1944.

22 *Ibid.,* Feb 29, 1944.

23 Oven, 'Nov 1943,' 176f.

24 JG, secret speech to the Reichsleiter and gauleiters on the political and military situation, Feb 23, 1944. Printed text on NA film T175, roll 145, 3659ff. Reuth, p.1991, wrongly states that the speech's text is unknown.

25 Diary, Feb 10, 1944.

26 Schmundt collected all the signatures by Mar 10, and the field marshals ceremonially read it out to Hitler at Schloss Klessheim on Mar 19 (diary, Mar 11, 14, 20, 1944); see too the diaries of Schmundt (BA–MA: H.4/12) and Weichs.

27 JG, 'In Neunzig Tagen,' in *Das Reich*, Jan 20; circulated by RPL (NA film T81, roll 69, 6415f); *NYT*, Jan 20; analyzed by the OSS on Mar 4, 1944 (NA file RG.226, entry 16, box 706, file 60777).

28 Diary, Mar 4, 1944.

29 *Ibid.*, Mar 16, 1944.

30 *Ibid.*, Mar 4; Oven, 'Apr 2, 1944,' 268.

31 Oven, 'Mar 16, 1944,' 251, 256.

32 Two photos of such airmen were issued by the DNB agency on Dec 23, 1943 (BA, Oberheitmann collection; ND: NG.3800).

33 Roger Freeman, *The Mighty Eighth* (New York, 1970) (hereafter Freeman), 114f; Oven, 'Mar 8, 1944,' 248ff. By the end of March the US Eighth Air Force had carried out four missions to Berlin: 600 bombers on Mar 8 against Erkner; on Mar 9 four-mile-high clouds over Berlin prevented the mission; on Mar 22, 800 bombers attacked, dropping 40 percent incendiaries.

34 Diary, Mar 11, 1944.

35 *Ibid.*, Mar 14, 1944.

36 *Ibid.*, Mar 9, 1944.

37 The *NYT* interpreted it on Mar 10, 1944 as 'one of the most open appeals to British Conservative circles ever to come out of Berlin.'

38 Diary, Mar 15, 1944.

39 *Ibid.*, Mar 28; Hans-Leo Martin, 148f, gets it wrong, stating that JG wanted to persuade Hitler to send the divisions east. Not so.

40 SD report, Mar 30, 1944 (NA film T175, roll 265, 1858ff); Dr Immanuel Schäffer, interrogation, PWB report SAIC.16, Jun 6, 1945 (NA file RG.332, entry ETO, Mis-Y, Sect., box 116).

41 Hans-Leo Martin, 151.

42 Gutterer MS; Wolfenbüttel; Muhs affidavit (Niedersächsisches Landesarchiv, Wolfenbüttel); and interview of Gutterer, Jun 30, 1993.

43 Diary, Apr 18, 1944. On the scandal, which involved the SS swindler, Oberfähnrich der Reserve, and 'Count' Monti, see Helmuth Rosencrantz, 'Büsum diary,' Jul 1945 (see note 2 to chapter entitled 'Valkyrie') and SS Gruppenführer Ohlendorf, CSDIC (UK) PW paper No. 133, Aug 11, 1945: 'Notes on Corruption and Corrupt Personalities in Germany' (PRO file WO.208/4175).

44 On Apr 25, 1944. Oven, 'Apr 29, 1944;' BDC file, Naumann.

45 Diary, Apr 17, 1944.

46 *Ibid.*, Mar 31; Oven, 'Apr 2, 1944', 266f.

47 *NYT*, Apr 8, 1944.

48 Statement of Oberzahlmeister Olbrich, Feb 5, 1945, in CSDIC (UK) report SIR.1434. JG to Hitler, Jul 18, 1944 (BA file NL.118/107).

49 Circular to gauleiters, Apr 5, 1944 (NA film T581, roll 16; BA file NS.26/291).

50 JG to Hitler, Apr 20, 1944 (BA file NL.118/106); Oven, 'Apr 20, 1944,' 276, cites a different

text. The Bundesarchiv would not permit me to recheck the file. See author's acknowledgments, page viii.

51 Oven, 'Apr 20, 1944,' 276.

52 Morell diary, May 9; JG diary, Apr 18, 1944.

53 Oven, 'Apr 12, 1944,' 272ff.

54 Diary, Apr 18, 1944.

55 *Ibid.*, May 13; his RPÄ (field agencies) reported that people were actively looking forward to the invasion, though depressed about the ongoing 'air terror' (*ibid.*, May 12, 1944).

56 SD report, May 25 (NA film T175, roll 265, 2049ff, 2052ff) and Jun 1 (2062ff); JG diary, May 16, 1944.

57 Freeman, 136, 140.

58 Oven, 'May 9, 1944.'

59 *Ibid.*, 'May 7;' Morell diary, May 8–9, 1944.

60 Diary, May 18; JG to General Heidrich, Apr 28, 1944 (ZStA Potsdam, Rep. 90, Go 1, vol. 3).

61 Morell diary, May 19, 1944.

62 Freeman, 126f, states that the US 8th Fighter Command had flown six strafing missions from Mar 26 – Apr 12, shooting up thirty-six trains.

63 The RMVP announced at a press conf. the next day that lynchings of captured American pilots had been prevented only with difficulty: *NYT*, May 24. The Swedish *Aftonbladet* reported that six American aviators had recently been lynched: Reuters, May 30, 1944 (PRO file FO.371/38995).

64 Diary, May 24, 1944.

65 Brandt to Klopfer, Jul 26, 1944 (NA film T175, roll 33, 1405); Staff Evidence Analysis, Aug 21, 1947, in OMGUS files, NA: RG.260, shipping list 53–3/7, box 15); BDC file, Berndt (his enemies wanted him prosecuted for the act); and note by Keitel, in IMT, v, 20.

66 Diary, May 25; JG article, 'Ein Wort zum feindlichen Luftterror,' *VB*, May 27 and 28/29, 1944; ND: 1676-PS; DNB, May 26; *The Times*, May 27; *NYT*, May 27–29. On May 29, 1944 Berlin radio commented that German police would 'refrain from interfering with German mobs who attempt to lynch American aviators.'

67 For obvious reasons Allied military censorship requested that Goebbels' implicit threat *not* be reported in the British media. Memo, Nash to F K Roberts (FO), May 30; Ottawa to Morley-Scott, Canadian high commissioner in London, May 27, and letter from him to Roberts, May 31; Roberts replied that the British government would not ask Berlin for an explanation unless 'information reaches us that any of our airmen have been lynched.' The FO explained to Ottawa on Jun 1, 1944 that they 'wish to avoid all publicity, as likely to have [an] unsettling effect [on] Allied airmen taking part in operations over Germany.' The British press agreed to suppress all such stories along with the report that six American aviators had been lynched (PRO file FO.371/38995).

68 Paul K Schmidt, interrogation, Nov 4, 1947 (NA film M.1019, roll 64).

69 JG's travel file, 'Trip to Sonthofen (political-ideological course for active front-line army and corps commanders) and briefing stop at Augsburg' is in ZStA Potsdam, Rep. 50.01.

70 Himmler speech, May 24, 1944 (NA film T175, roll 94, 4609ff): The Jewish problem had been, he said, 'solved uncompromisingly – on orders and at the dictate of sound common sense.' He again hinted that Jewish women and children had been killed too.

71 Interrogation of Obergrenadier Sanktjohanser, a waiter at Sonthofen: CSDIC (UK) report SIR.1324 (NA file RG.332, Mis-Y, box 6; RG.165, entry 79, box 775).

72 Oven, 'May 24, 1944,' 315f.

73 Berndt to Hinkel, Nov 9, 1943 (BDC file, Berndt).

74 Rosenberg briefing of Hitler, Nov 17, 1943 (NA film T120, roll 2474, E255448): he suggested distributing half a million copies of his antisemitic fortnightly magazine *Weltdienst* to the foreigners. For correspondence Rosenberg–Hitler–Lammers–JG, Dec 1943 see ND: NG–1062.

75 JG to Ribbentrop, Jan 27 (ZStA Potsdam, Rep. 50.01, vol. 791); Oven, 'Feb 27,' 239f; JG diary, Mar 4, 1944.

76 Diary, Mar 13, 1944; on the Nazis' deportation of the Jews from Hungary, see SS Ober-sturmbannführer Adolf Eichmann's MS (in author's collection).

77 Diary, Apr 22, 1944.

78 *Ibid.*, Apr 27, 1944.

79 *Ibid.*, May 4; a Jun 1944 memorandum by Dr Wolf Meyer-Christian on the treatment of the Jewish problem in the German press is in Yivo file G–117.

80 An OSS report of Jul 10, 1944 (via US naval attaché, Istanbul) stated that JG 'thinks of everyone, and his talks and writing show that he has the welfare of all classes at heart' (NA file RG.226, entry 16, box 0975, report 87179).

81 Hassell diary, Jun 8, 1944. Most of his listeners had been impressed by JG's 'great intellect,' observed Hassell. 'Only a few noticed that when all is said and done it was the speech of a man who had shot his bolt.'

Notes to Chapter 53.

1 Diary, May 25, 1944. 'I can not share that view,' he noted.

2 Speech text in *VB,* Jun 6, 1944; *cf.* Heiber, *Goebbels-Reden*, vol. ii, 323ff.

3 Oven, 322f; JG had also seen her in Feb 1944 (*ibid.*, 'Feb 10, 1944,' 230).

4 Schäffer proposed to JG on May 25, 1944 printing propaganda on the aluminum foil anti-radar strips ('chaff') dropped on Britain (ZStA Potsdam, Rep. 50.01, vol. 813).

5 Berndt to JG, Jun 3; one copy found in Sep 1964 concealed in the Black Lake, Czecho-slovakia (Hoover Libr., TS Germany P96 B531); another in ZStA Potsdam, Rep. 50.01, vol. 816. – JG dismissed Berndt for an indiscretion at this time (diary, Jun 7); Berndt to Himmler, Jul 11 (T175, roll 33, 1405) and notes (1399, 1402), and Aug 2 (BDC file, Berndt). Promoted to SS Brigadeführer on Apr 30, 1943, Berndt joined the 5th SS Pz. Div. Wiking on Jan 19, 1945, and died in action at the end of the war in Hungary.

6 Rommel left for Germany on Jun 4, 1944 to visit his wife (Rommel diary, and David Irving, *Trail of the Fox* [London & New York], 1977, 361).

7 Oven, 'Jun 5, 1944,' 336.

8 Diary, Jun 6, 1944.

9 See Bormann's note on the table talk on Jun 5, 1944 (BA.6/166).

10 JG had first met Hase on Dec 11, 1940, when he adjudged the new city commandant 'a magnificent officer with a very positive attitude toward the party.' By 1941 this honeymoon was over. Hase threatened to place the Frasquita bar off-limits to the troops; JG suggested he ask his permission first (MinConf., Mar 3, 1941).

11 Since Jun 1 the SD had been aware of certain BBC messages whose broadcast would presage the invasion. See Kaltenbrunner's telex to the OKW, Jun 1, and OKW to Foreign Armies West, Jun 2 (NA film T78, roll 451, 6880f); Army Group B war diary, Jun 5 (NA

film T311, roll 3, 2156ff); and Irving, *Hitler's War*, 633. At 9:15 P.M. on Jun 5, 1944 the Fifteenth Army had intercepted the first such BBC messages. Oven, 336f, says he tried to phone JG with news of this.

12 Milch diary, May 7, 1947 (author's film DI–59).

13 Diary, Jun 6; Semler, 'Jun 6,' 127f; and Oven, 'Jun 6, 1944,' 336f.

14 Karl Koller diary, Jun 6, 1944 (author's film DI–17).

15 Diary, Jun 7, 1944.

16 JG in *Das Reich*, Jun 11; OSS report, Jun 16, 1944 (NA file RG.226, entry 16, box 0877, file 76692).

17 Diary, Jun 16, 1944.

18 Oven, 'Jun 13, 1944,' 352f.

19 George Axelsson in *NYT*, Jun 11, 1944.

20 Diary, Jun 17, 1944.

21 Oven, 357f.

22 *NYT*, Jun 18; war diary, 'Flak Regiment 155(W),' Jun 17, 1944.

23 Diary, Jun 20, 1944.

24 *Ibid.*, Jun 14, 1944.

25 *Ibid.*, Jun 16, 1944.

26 JG, 'Führen wir einen totalen Krieg?' in *Das Reich*, Jul 2; diary, Jun 20, 1944.

27 Koller diary, Jun 21, 1944; Freeman, 158. On Jun 26 JG wrote to Hitler recommending the Swords to the Knight's Cross for Emil Beck and Johannes Engel for heroism during the raid (BA file NL.118/106).

28 Diary, Jun 22, 1944.

29 *Ibid.*, Jun 20, 1944: Kaltenbrunner had furnished him with an SD monograph on 'Stalin and total war.'

30 *Ibid.*, Jun 26, 28, 1944.

31 JG, air war notice No. 151, Jul 14, 1944 (NA film T84, roll 322, 1419f).

32 Oven, 'Jul 1, 1944,' 377.

33 As JG himself noted, diary, Jul 8, 1944.

34 Hanke married Freda Baroness von Fircks (formerly married to von Johnston), daughter of a landowner, on Nov 25, 1944 (Dr Bernhard Kortüm to Milch, Mar 6, 1950, in Milch papers; and author's interview with the late Freda Rössler)

35 Ebermayer and Meissner, No. 20, May 17, and No. 25, Jun 21, 1952.

36 JG's speech, 'Das Vaterland ist in Gefahr,' in *VB*, Jul 8, *NYT*, Jul 9, 1944.

37 JG, 'Der Krieg in der Sackgasse,' in *Das Reich*, Jul 9, 1944.

38 W J Donovan to FDR, Jul 15, 1944 (FDR Libr., PSF box 168).

39 Ditto, Jul 12 (*ibid.*); *cf.* Oven, 'Jul 4,' 378, and JG diary, Jul 23, 1944.

40 *Ibid.*, Jul 11; Oven, 390ff. Speer suggested the committee might comprise Himmler, Lammers, Keitel, Sauckel, JG, and himself, but not Bormann. On Jul 6–8 Speer had drawn Hitler's attention to the under-utilized manpower still latent in the domestic economy and the armed forces. Speer's notes, Jul 10, 1944. See too JG's correspondence with von Unruh at this time (ZStA Potsdam, Rep. 50.01, vol. 862).

41 Oven, 'Jun 23,' 368. In *NYT* on Jul 16, 1944, George Axelsson mocked that the current rumor of a twelve-ton rocket 'smacks of Jules Verne.'

42 Oven, 'Jul 11, 1944,' 390.

43 Diary, Jul 11; Speer had received a letter from his chief economist Kehrl, dated Jul 10, 1944, drawing attention to under-utilized manpower in the cities. *Cf.* Peter Longerich,

'Joseph Goebbels und der totale Krieg,' *VfZ*, 1987, 289ff.

44 Speer to Hitler, Jul 12; Speer chronicle, Jul 1944.

45 Diary, Jul 15, 1944.

46 Schmundt suggested Manstein as Zeitzler's successor. Dr Weber confirmed in an interview with the author that he had signed a fake sick-note for Zeitzler to cover his 'retreat.'

47 JG to Hitler, Jul 18, 1944 (BA file NL.118/107); Longerich, writing in 1987, is incorrect in calling this 'an unknown memorandum.' Oven's 'diaries,' published in Buenos Aires, 1950, vol. ii, 89, refer to it, and this author used the actual text in *Hitler's War* (New York and London, 1977), based on the French version on NA film T84, roll 272.

48 They were certainly not filmed: The Nazi microfiche camera-operator assigned a serial number to each glass fiche (plate), and wrote this number also on the top left corner of the first diary page filmed on that plate. For example page 55 of the entry for Sep 10, 1943 is the first page filmed on fiche 118 of 1943, and the page is endorsed *118* and *mikrokopiert* as well (NA film T84, roll 265). In box No. 72 of the Moscow collection ('Fond 1477') are twenty complete fiches, serial numbers 121–127 and 129–140, covering the period from mid-June to Jul 18 and Jul 23–24, 1944 (fiche 128 is for Jul 15); the period Jul 25–31, 1944 is covered on the fiches 141–144 in box No. 73.

49 At 4:55 P.M. on Jul 19; see W J Donovan to FDR, Jul 22, 1944 (FDR Libr., PSF box 168).

50 The page for Jul 20, 1944 is also missing from the Milch diary.

51 He confirmed this to Luftwaffe General Barsewisch, whose MS is in the Irving collection (IfZ). Guderian confirmed to Milch (diary, Oct 28, 1945) that he had known of the bomb plot as early as Jul 18, 1944 (author's film, DI–59).

Notes to Chapter 54.

1 RMVP circular; in files of Propaganda-Staffel north-west, Jul 24, 1944 (Hoover Libr., Lerner papers).

2 Generalrichter Dr Helmuth Rosencrantz, MS ('Büsum diary, Jul 1945'), BAOR Counter-Intelligence Bureau report CIB/INT/B5/2908/1/o/D, Sep 29, 1945 (NA file RG.407, entry 427, box 1954m). Rosencrantz had had the trial delayed from Jul 17 to 20 so that his deputy judge Gen. Baron von Thüngen would be available to try it. Hase attended the morning session. Sentence, announced at 2 P.M., was nine months' prison; JG and Naumann interceded for Martin, and it was reduced to five months' fortress confinement.

3 Speer chronicle, Jul 20; Sündermann, 'Jul 21, 1944,' 62.

4 JG confirmed this in his broadcast of Jul 26.

5 One item concerned an article in the mass circulation *Front und Heimat*, No. 22, Jul 1944, which was considered too flattering about conditions in Soviet-occupied Romania. Hadamovsky to JG, Jul 21, 1944 (ZStA Potsdam, Rep. 62, Re 3, Hadamovsky papers, vol. 1).

6 OCMH interrogation of Gen. Wilhelm Arnold, chief of army signals, Aug 25, 1945 (IfZ, Irving collection). Peter Hoffmann, *Widerstand, Staatsstreich, Attentat* (München, 1969), 852. Dr Richard Arnhold, Bömer's PA, confirmed that the RMVP's domestic and foreign press departments had direct telephone and telex links to Dr Dietrich's office at the Führer's headquarters. PW paper 80 (NA file RG.165, entry 79, box 766).

7 Oven, 'Jul 23, 1944,' 398f. His recollection was that he told Lorenz that JG was asleep,

whereupon Lorenz dictated it to him. And see Oven, 'Der 20.Juli 1944 – erlebt im Hause Goebbels,' in *Verrat und Widerstand im Dritten Reich* (Coburg, 1978), 43.

8 Morell treated the ear-ache (diary, Jul 23, 1944).

9 JG to Leni Riefenstahl-Jacob, Jul 20, 1944, 2 P.M.; he deleted the 'Jacob' and a second, over-fulsome, sentence from the draft (ZStA Potsdam, Rep. 90, Go 1, vol. 3).

10 BAOR interrogation of Col. Nicolaus von Below, Jan 23, 1946 (Trevor-Roper papers, IfZ, Irving collection).

11 On Dec 22, 1944 he wrote to the Führer that 'in a dark hour' he had trembled for Hitler's life (BA file NL.118/106).

12 Otto Ernst Remer's report on the events, Jul 22, 1944, is in BA file EAP.105/32; publ. by Hans-Adolf Jacobsen (ed.), *Spiegelbild einer Verschwörung. Die Opposition gegen Hitler und der Staatsstreich vom 20. Juli 1944 in der SD-Berichterstattung* (Stuttgart, 1984), vol. i, 12ff; cf. Hoffmann, *Widerstand, Staatsstreich, Attentat*, 460f. The author also interviewed Remer.

13 Dr Hans W Hagen's report on Jul 22, dated Oct 16, 1944 (NA film T84, roll 19, 0022ff); *Spiegelbild*, vol. ii, 637ff. – Hans W Hagen, *Zwischen Eid und Befehl* (Munich, 1959). Semler, 132ff.

14 Oven, 398f.

15 Speer's dramatic and self-serving *published* 'memoirs' are based more on secondary works than on his memory; he was not ushered out by JG at midnight, as he claims, but left with Himmler around 4:30 A.M., as Balzer's report makes clear.

16 From his perch at the absent Schwägermann's desk, outside JG's room, Speer tried to reach his friend Fromm without success. He did speak with Olbricht and complained that he and JG were being 'detained' by soldiers; Speer reported only the latter conversation to JG.

17 Albrecht to his wife, Jul 22, 1944 (IfZ, Irving collection).

18 Schaub MS (IfZ, Irving collection).

19 BBC monitoring report; see the FO's printed summary of the putsch in PRO file FO.371/39062.

20 Remer report.

21 Hoffmann suggests the colonel may have been Lt-Col. Walter Horstmann.

22 The times are from Remer's and Hagen's testimonies. For what follows we also have JG's version in his broadcast of Jul 26, text in *Zürcher Zeitung*, Jul 27; *Front und Heimat*, No. 13, Juni [*sic*] (BA file NS.6/28); *VB*, Jul 27, 1944.

23 Remer's loyalty to Hitler endured to the end. Aged eighty-two, he was sentenced in 1994 to two years in prison for doubting the authenticity of the 'gas chambers' at Auschwitz – expressing such doubts is a criminal offense in modern Germany; he was granted political asylum in Spain.

24 Hitler told ENT-specialist Erwin Giesing on Jul 26, 'The loyal chap [Remer] recognized my voice at once on the phone and confirmed my orders to him by repeating them to the letter' (Giesing MS, in IfZ, Irving collection).

25 Maj.-Gen. Helmuth Schwierz, CO of No. 1 Army Bomb Disposal School, Berlin-Lichterfelde, undated report in IfZ, Irving collection. A Capt. Messing from the same school had a similar mission: letter intercept, [Horst] von Buttlar to Herbert Steinert, Mar 27, 1947 ('. . . Messing had orders to arrest Dr Goebbels dead or alive'). CCD report, in NA file RG.407, entry 427, box 1954a.

26 Oven, 'Jul 23, 1944;' Hoffmann, *Widerstand, Staatsstreich, Attentat*, 855; Speer memoirs.

27 Kehrl, 398.

28 Dr Immanuel Schäffer, interrogation, PWB report SAIC.16, Jun 6, 1945 (NA file RG.332, entry ETO, Mis-Y, Sect., box 116).

29 Balzer, liaison officer between OKW/WPr and RMVP, report to chief of WPr (Hasso von Wedel), 'Jun 21' [sic: read Jul 21] 1944 (NA film T84, roll 16, 6614; BA file NS.6/31).

30 Hoffmann, *Widerstand, Staatsstreich, Attentat*, citing Hase's testimony to the People's Court, trial vol. xxxiii , 488ff; and *Spiegelbild einer Verschwörung*, 45.

31 Hadamovsky to JG, Aug 3, 1944 (ZStA Potsdam, Rep. 62, Re 3, vol. 1); he named the lieutenant-colonels Pridun, Herber, von der Heyd[t]e, and Kuban, and suggested that JG receive them together with the panzer colonels Bolbrinker and Glaesemer for drinks one day.

32 Hadamovsky to JG, Aug 1 (ZStA Potsdam, Rep. 62, Re 3, vol. 1); JG referred to this incident in his broadcast of Jul 26, 1944.

33 Remer's report.

34 JG's text is repeated in the KR-FSchr. from Höherer S.S.- und Polizeiführer Stuttgart to Gauleiter Wagner (Karlsruhe), Jul 20, 1944, 9:16 P.M. (Records of the Annexed Territory of Alsace, NA film T81, roll 179, 7965f).

35 Bormann to all gauleiters, Jul 20, 1944, nine P.M. and 9:40 P.M. (Trevor-Roper papers, IfZ, Irving collection).

36 Bearer of the Knight's Cross and a veteran Nazi, Bolbrinker commanded an S.A. brigade in Styria during the failed 1934 putsch in Austria, and had to flee to Germany.

37 Remer stated in his Jul 22, 1944 report: 'I was unsure of Colonel-General Guderian's attitude.'

38 On the role of the Panzer Reserve Brigade at Cottbus, see Peter Hoffmann, *Claus Schenk Graf von Stauffenberg und seine Brüder* (Stuttgart, 1992), 400–7, 421, 432–4. There is evidence, states Hoffmann on p. 421, that upon Mertz von Quirnheim's intervention Guderian had agreed on Jul 19, 1944 to delay the removal of the Krampnitz armor to East Prussia by a few days.

39 Rosencrantz. And see his British interrogation, Nov 16, 1945 (Trevor Roper papers, IfZ, Irving collection).

40 Rosencrantz.

41 Balzer report. Fromm was court-martialed and shot for cowardice in Mar 1945.

42 Himmler also emphasized the delicacy of his position in speeches on Jul 21 and 26, 1944 (NA film T175, roll 93, 3904ff, 4146ff).

43 Bormann to the gauleiters, Jul 21, 1944, 3:40 A.M. (Trevor-Roper papers, IfZ, Irving collection).

44 Balzer report.

45 Diary, Dec 4, 1944.

46 Balzer report. – Himmler's remark does not bear closer scrutiny.

47 Dr Immanuel Schäffer, interrogation, PWB report SAIC.16, Jun 6, 1945 (NA file RG.332, entry ETO, Mis-Y, Sect., box 116).

48 JG circulars to all RPÄ, Jul 21, 12:31 and 2:20 P.M. (Trevor-Roper papers, IfZ, Irving collection). The next day Hitler directed him to organize nationwide rallies to demand an end to the treacheries of the generals and to insist that the Führer punish the guilty so severely that there would never be a repetition (diary, Jul 23). On Jul 22, 1944 JG issued *Propaganda Parole* No. 68 ordering all gauleiters to stage mass meetings (BA file R.55/614).

49 The OSS in Berne (Allen Dulles) reported to FDR on Jan 27, 1945 that Stauffenberg had planned to make peace with the Soviets and establish a workers' and peasants' regime in Germany; the generals had disliked this plan, but Stauffenberg was the only officer willing to risk his life by planting the bomb. One of Dulles' sources who was 'with Helldorff when he heard of the fiasco' (probably the Abwehr traitor Hans-Bernd Gisevius) blamed it on the failure of General Fellgiebel to destroy the communications center at the Wolf's Lair, and on 'the defection of Major Remer at the last minute.' Dulles also reported, Feb 1, 1945, that Stauffenberg favored the *Ostlösung* and was in touch through Stockholm with Seydlitz and the Nationalkomitee Freies Deutschland in Moscow (FDR Libr., PSF box 170). Gisevius confirmed in *Bis zum bitteren Ende* (Darmstadt, 1947), vol. ii, 255f, that he was with Helldorff at police headquarters at 11 A.M. on Jul 20, 1944, but Peter Hoffmann has exposed his canard about Stauffenberg's eastern alignment in the appendix to his *Stauffenberg*, 472–4.

50 Dr Immanuel Schäffer, interrogation, PWB report SAIC.16, Jun 6, 1945 (NA file RG.332, entry ETO, Mis-Y, Sect., box 116). For an RMVP analysis on Jul 24, 1944 summarizing RPÄ reports on the universal public condemnation of the plot, see BA file R.55/601.

Notes to Chapter 55.

1 Sündermann, 'Jul 26, 1944,' 76f.
2 Diary, Jul 23; Oven, 'Jul 25, 1944,' 432ff.
3 Diary, Jul 24, 1944: a fragment of the original pages, pp. 27–52, is also in Hoover Libr., Korf papers, box 1.
4 *Cf.* Lammers to Keitel, Jul 17, 1944 (NA film T175, roll 71, 0772f).
5 Minutes of the staff conference on total war, Jul 22, 1944 (BA file R.43II/664a, 82–91). Those present were JG, Bormann, Keitel, Speer, Funk, Sauckel, Boley, and Dr Fricker of the chancellery. Interrogation of Gottfried Boley, Sep 15, 1945 (NA film M.1270, roll 2).
6 Diary, Jul 23, 1944 (the diary on microfiche resumes after the unexplained four-day break).
7 See JG's speech to the gauleiters on the morning of Aug 3, 1944 (IfZ file Fa.35/3).
8 Sündermann, 'Jul 26, 28, Aug 1, 1944,' 76ff.
9 Diary, Jul 23, 1944.
10 *Ibid.*
11 *Ibid.*
12 Lammers' briefing of Hitler, Jul 23, 1944, with Göring, Keitel, Lammers, Bormann, Funk, Speer, Sauckel, Klopfer, Naumann (BA file R.43II/664a); for the resulting inter-departmental disputes see R.43II/665, /666a, b, c. This was Göring's last visit to headquarters for several weeks.
13 Führer decree on total mobilization, Jul 25, signed Hitler, Göring, Lammers (BA file NL.118/106); published in *RGBl.*, I, 1944, No. 34, 161f; *VB* and *NYT*, Jul 26. The British FO was impressed: 'He [JG] and Himmler between them now seem to hold all the reins of power' (PRO file FO.371/39062). But the Americans were not: 'The crucial question for Germany is combat manpower, and this cannot be provided by decree.' OSS R&A Report No. 2456, 'An Evaluation of the Goebbels Program for Total Mobilization in Germany,' Sep 1, 1944 (USAMHI, Donovan papers, box 35a).
14 JG to Lammers, Jul 27, 1944 (BA file R.43II/664a).

15 Note on a conference held by Lammers, Jul 31 (IfZ, F82, Heiber collection); Milch diary, Jul 31 (author's film DI–59); Sündermann, 'Aug 1, 1944,' 82f.

16 These two committees were coordinated by a secretariat under Regierungspräsident Dr Faust of the ministry of the interior.

17 JG's speech to the gauleiters on the morning of Aug 3, 1944 (IfZ, Fa.35/3).

18 Oven, 'Aug 5,' 445f; *NYT*, Jul 28. And JG, broadcast script, 'The first steps,' Jul 1944 (ZStA Potsdam, Rep. 50.01, vol. 761).

19 As the Speer chronicle, Jul 24, 1944, makes plain.

20 *Ibid.*, Aug 1, 1944.

21 JG's speech to the gauleiters on the morning of Aug 3, 1944 (IfZ file Fa.35/3).

22 Hadamovsky to JG, Aug 31 and Sep 7, 1944 (ZStA Potsdam, Rep. 62, Re 3, vol. 1).

23 *NYT*, Aug 11; diary, Sep 2 ('Berlin's entire stage has now been put to work on munitions'); circular to gauleiters, Aug 3, 1944 (NA film T81, roll 154, 8506).

24 JG, information for Führer, Aug 9 (published in Hans-Adolf Jacobsen, *Dokumente*, No. 144); Sündermann, 'Aug 11, 1944,' 100.

25 *NYT*, Aug 25, 1944.

26 Hierl to JG, Aug 13, 1944 (IfZ film MA.356).

27 Directive by JG and Bormann, Aug 18, 1944 (IfZ film MA.434, 3552ff).

28 *NYT*, Aug 25, 1944.

29 Oven, 'Aug 16, 1944;' the figures are broadly confirmed by JG diary, Sep 2, 1944.

30 Jodl diary, Aug 1, 5 p.m. (author's film DI–84); see the JG diary fragment, Aug 1 (?), 1944, p. 22, published in *Der Spiegel*, Jan 24, 1951, p. 9, and the entry for Aug 31, 1944 on the People's Court trial of Stülpnagel and his liaison officer, Cäsar von Hofacker: 'In all these testimonies Field Marshal Kluge and, in part, even Rommel are gravely implicated.'

31 Kaltenbrunner to Bormann, Jul 24, 1944 (NA film T84, roll 19, 0153, 0159); Helldorff was interrogated by the Gestapo on Jul 27, 1944 (*ibid.*, 0269); his last letter before execution will be found quoted in BA file NS.6/44.

32 Dr Immanuel Schäffer, interrogation, PWB report SAIC.16, Jun 6, 1945 (NA file RG.332, entry ETO, Mis-Y, Sect., box 116).

33 Oven, 'Aug 5,' 448; Giesing MS; Dr Georg Kiessel, 'The Plot of July 20, 1944, and its Origins,' Aug 6, 1946 (Trevor-Roper papers, IfZ, Irving collection); and CSDIC interrogation of SS Hauptsturmführer Otto Prochnow (*ibid.*).

34 Transcripts in Trevor Roper papers (IfZ, Irving collection).

35 Diary, Aug 31, 1944 (fragments).

36 Hadamovsky to JG, Aug 11 (ZStA Potsdam, Rep. 62, Re 3, vol. 1). In Jun 1944 the German officers Seydlitz, Daniels, Schlömer, Lattmann, Lenski, Korfes, etc., had signed a declaration 'to the generals of the German Wehrmacht' (Yivo file Occ–E–FD–6); about fifty captured German generals also signed a 'declaration to the people and Wehrmacht' (*ibid.*, FD–7). Diary, May 18, 1944: The SD had asked JG to discuss the matter in public, but JG declined.

37 See Hitler's conference with Jodl, Jul 31, 1944. Helmut Heiber (ed.), *Hitlers Lagebesprechungen. Die Protokollfragmente seiner militärischen Konferenzen, 1942–1945* (Stuttgart, 1962).

38 JG's speech to the gauleiters on the morning of Aug 3, 1944 (IfZ file Fa.35/3).

39 *Ibid.*; Sündermann, 'Aug 3, 5, 1944,' 87ff.

40 Monitoring reports on broadcasts of the Nationalkomitee Freies Deutschland, Aug

1944 – Jan 1945 are in ZStA Potsdam, Rep. 50.01, vols. 1210 and 1205.

41 *E.g.* Aug 23, 1944 (ZStA Potsdam, Rep.50.01, vol. 956).

42 On this network Aug 1944 – Jan 1945 see ZStA Potsdam, Rep. 50.01, vol. 826; Oven, 'Aug 16,' 460f; and Sündermann, 'Aug 11, 1944,' 100.

43 Darré diary, Aug 28; Milch diary, Aug 28, 1944 (author's film DI–59).

44 Diary, Sep 19, 1944: 'I get a real headache when I try to finish off my twenty pages of typescript. But the public awaits the Friday evening broadcast of my leading article like its daily bread ration.'

45 JG, 'In den Stürmen der Zeit,' in *Das Reich*, Aug 20, 1944.

46 Kaltenbrunner to JG, Aug 26, 1944 (ZStA Potsdam, Rep. 50.01, vol. 1052).

47 Magda Goebbels to Alwin-Broder Albrecht, Nov 18, 1944 (Albrecht papers).

48 Speer chronicle, Aug 11; on Aug 28, 1944 Milch noted after one JG speech at the chancellery, 'Speer doesn't like my conciliatory manner!'

49 Oven, 'Sep 1,' 463ff JG circular to gauleiters, Aug 11; Speer to JG, Aug 31, 1944; Speer chronicle.

50 Oven, 'Sep 1, 1944,' 463ff.

51 Diary, Sep 2 ('*Speer . . . spielt die gekränkte Leberwurst*'); Oven, 'Sep 3, 1944,' 467f.

52 Itinerary, Sep 13, 1944 (ZStA Potsdam, Rep. 50.01, vol. 956).

53 Diary, Sep 2, 1944.

54 Afterwards JG wrote that Speer already regretted his mulish stand on Sep 2. 'He . . . finds now that the party regards him to a degree as an outsider if not indeed as an enemy' (diary, Sep 8, 1944).

55 Hadamovsky to JG, Sep 3 (ZStA Potsdam, Rep. 62, Re 3, vol. 1); JG quoted this dictum to Oven, 'Dec 3, 1944,' 518.

56 On which see Keitel's circular, Aug 31; Bormann's circular, Sep 4; and Hadamovsky to JG, Sep 3 and 14, 1944 (ZStA Potsdam, Rep. 50.01, vol. 863).

57 Diary, Sep 2, 1944.

58 *Ibid.*, Sep 19, 1944.

59 Forschungsamt monitoring report RW.29107, Sep 6; telex from Hauptabteilung Propaganda, Kraków, to Immanuel Schäffer (RMVP), Sep 7, 1944 (Yivo file Occ–E2–68); *Freies Deutschland* (Moscow) No. 37, Sep 10, 1944.

60 JG's name appeared in the preamble to the United Nations War Crimes Commission's first list of major war criminals, who were to be punished 'by joint decision of the Allies,' whatever form that decision might take (PRO file FO.371/51013).

61 Hansard, *House of Commons Debates*, Oct 4; *NYT*, Oct 5, 1944. Churchill showed a memo after Quebec to Stalin urging the execution of the top Nazis without trial; Stalin rejected it.

62 Diary, Sep 20, 1944.

63 *Ibid.*, Sep 23, 1944.

64 Interview of Max Winkler by Frank Korf, May 1, 1948. Korf established that no Goebbels testament was filed with the Amtsgericht either in Berlin-Mitte or in Rheydt, nor did his lawyer Dr Alfons Knetsch know of one. Korf to Harold Lee, US Dept of Justice, May 29, 1948 (Hoover Libr., Korf papers).

65 *NYT*, Sep 8, 9, 1944.

66 Diary, Sep 8, 19, 24; Speer chronicle; Speer to JG, Sep 15; JG briefing for Führer, Sep 25; Speer's comments on this, Sep 26; Speer to Bormann, disowning responsibility for arms production, Oct 1; Speer to Hitler, Oct 3, 1944.

67 Diary, Sep 20, 1944.

68 *Ibid.*, Sep 23, 1944.

69 Kaltenbrunner to JG, Aug 26, 1944 (ZStA Potsdam, Rep. 50.01, vol. 1052).

70 Diary, Sep 24, 1944.

71 *Ibid.*, Sep 23, 1944.

72 Berger to Himmler, Sep 26, 1944 (Hallein files: OMGUS report, Nov 8, 1945: NA file RG.407, entry 427, box 1954k).

73 Diary, Sep 23; Oven, 'Sep 25,' 483. On Nov 17, 1944 they heard that Harald was in British captivity (ZStA Potsdam, Rep. 90, Go 1, vol. 4).

74 Oven, 'Sep 20, 1944,' 479.

75 Diary, Sep 19, 1944.

76 JG was in fact Oshima's last, not first, port of call. Japanese offers to mediate had been reaching Berlin since Aug 25 (see Irving, *Hitler's War*, 685), and on Sep 4 Oshima personally put similar proposals to Hitler (see Ribbentrop to Stahmer, Sep 6, in Pol. Archiv AA, Ritter papers, Serial 1436). See naval staff war diary, Sep 5, 1944 too.

77 Diary, Sep 20, 1944.

78 *Ibid.*, Sep 23, 1944. Ley's mistress Madeleine Wanderer wrote (SAIC.40) that, after Aachen fell to the Americans, he became silent and depressed. 'Goebbels,' Ley said, 'was of the same opinion' (NA file RG.332, box 73).

79 See diary, Jul 23, 1944.

80 JG to Hitler, Sep [22] (BA file NL.118/107); Oven, 'Sep 22,' 479ff; Semler wrongly dates this important memorandum months earlier ('Apr 10, 12, 20; May 2, 1944').

81 Diary, Sep 23–24, 1944.

82 Oven, 'Sep 28, 1944,' 483ff; Steengracht conversation, Jun 27, 1945 CCPWE No. 32, X–P.18 (NA file RG.332, ETO G–2 Sect., box 97).

83 Diary, Sep 24; Oven, 'Sep 22, 1944,' 480ff.

84 Diary, Sep 25, 1944

Notes to Chapter 56.

1 Diary, Oct 7; Oven, 'Oct 2, Nov 11, 1944.'

2 Diary, Oct 12, 1944.

3 *NYT*, Oct 5, 1944.

4 Oven, 'Oct 4, 1944,' 490f. Ohlendorf confirmed to Milch after the war that Speer approved the falsification of arms-production figures (Milch diary, Aug 28, 1945). United States Strategic Bombing Survey report No. 59, *The Defeat of the German Air Force*, 37ff, came to the same conclusion.

5 Letter intercepted by ABP (foreign letter intercept office) from Justizrat Victor Fränkl, Locarno, to H R Morgenthau, Oct 4, 1944 (ZStA Potsdam, Rep 50.01, vol. 796).

6 On which see *VB*, Sep 26, 1944. See PID analysis of JG's usage of the Morgenthau plan, DE.2/DIS.202 (Hoover Libr., Lerner papers); *Der politische Soldat*, No. 14, Oct 1944 quoted the Swiss journal *Vaterland* as predicting a 'field of death from Kiel to Konstanz.' Willi Krämer, circular No. 66, Dec 8, 1944 (NA film T84, roll 169, 6532f).

7 W J Donovan to FDR, Oct 17 and 25, 1944 (FDR Libr., PSF box 169). The controversy was too juicy for even Goebbels' opponents in Moscow to eschew and the next issue of *Freies Deutschland*, No. 9–10, Moscow, Oct/Nov 1944 also polemicized against Morgenthau &

Co., 'the representatives of millions in Gold' (Yivo file Occ–E–FD–2).

8 Oven, 'Oct 11, 1944,' 493.

9 Diary, Dec 2; Heinz Linge, Hitler's appointments register, Oct 15–16, 1944 (NA film T84, roll 387).

10 JG reported the 'Bismarck' remark to Speer. FIAT interrogation of Speer, Jun/Jul 1945, pt. ii, No. 19.

11 Oven, 'Oct 15, 1944,' 500ff.

12 On Oct 29, 1944 (diary) JG would write: 'Of course, the Führer set out this operation in detail to me on my last visit to Führer's headquarters. It's been gone over quite adequately in these pages too.'

13 Diary, Oct 24, 1944.

14 Führer decree on the formation of a German Volkssturm, Sep 25, 1944 (*RGBl.*, 1944, I, 72f).

15 JG broadcast, Oct 27: *MNN*, Oct 28; *NYT*, Oct 28. Donovan to FDR, Nov 1, 1944 (FDR Libr., PSF box 170).

16 Albrecht to his wife, Oct 27 (IfZ, Irving collection); JG diary, Oct 29, 1944.

17 Corporal Felix to Mrs [Anneliese] von Ribbentrop, Nov 11, 1944. Ribbentrop initialed its first page and sent it over to the Gestapo (NA film T120, roll 4673, 4788ff).

18 Diary, Oct 29, 1944.

19 Sündermann, 'Aug 6, 1944,' 93.

20 Hadamovsky to JG, Aug 7, 1944 (ZStA Potsdam, Rep. 62, Re 3, vol. 1); Sündermann, 'Aug 7, 1944,' 97.

21 The film was *Verräter vor dem Volksgericht*. The first part, five acts, ran for 105 minutes; the second, also five acts, also for 105 minutes; a silent reel showing the hanging of Witzleben *et al.* in four acts ran for 20–25 minutes. Their current location is unknown. Reichsfilmintendant (Hinkel) to Naumann, Aug 31, 1944 (BA file R.55/664); and Lindenborn to JG, Jan 17, 1945 (ZStA Potsdam, Rep 50.01, vol. 831).

22 Note by Leiter F (of Hinkel's staff), Oct 21, 1944 (ZStA Potsdam, Rep 50.01, vol. 831). The film shown at the Nuremberg trials, *Proceedings against the Criminals of Jul 20, 1944*, was edited from unreleased Deutsche Wochenschau newsreel footage confiscated by OMGUS at the offices of AFIFA in Berlin-Tempelhof.

23 SS Sturmbannführer Ulenberg (RMVP) to Hinkel, Mar 5 (ZStA Potsdam, Rep. 50.01, vol. 831). *Die Nation*, Feb 14, 1945 published an alleged photo of Witzleben and Hoepner hanging.

24 JG to Hitler, draft, Oct 25 (BA film NL.118/106); diary, Oct 29. He named Dr Hermann Kappner (envoy in Stockholm), Miss Schacht (a niece of Dr Hjalmar Schacht), envoy Dr Zechlin, Consul Schwinner, Dr Wilhelm Klein, and Bruno Fiebinger. He heard (diary, Oct 30, 1944) that Hitler had read the letter out approvingly at his next war conference.

25 Diary, Oct 30, 1944. Taubert however said the material hardened the will to resist and helped 'the worldwide defamation of bolshevism' (Taubert report, Yivo file G–PA–14).

26 Albrecht, private letter to his wife, Nov 12; see too Dittmar's diary, Nov 12; *NYT*, Nov 13; and Donovan to FDR, Nov 15, 1944 (FDR Libr., PSF box 170). For the day's Volkssturm ceremonies see BA file R.55/1287.

27 Willi Krämer, circular, Nov 1944 (NA film T84, roll 169, 6550f).

28 *NYT*, Nov 24, 1944.

29 JG, in *Das Reich*, Dec 2; cited in Donovan to FDR, Dec 4, 1944 (FDR Libr., PSF box 170).

30 Morell diary, Nov 30, 1944.

31 Diary, Dec 2, 1944.

32 *Ibid.*, Dec 7, 1944.

33 Behrend, No. 22, May 31, 1952.

34 Diary, Dec 2, 1944.

35 *Ibid.*, Dec 4, 1944.

36 Heinz Linge, Hitler's appointments register, Dec 3, 1944 (NA film T84, roll 387).

37 Interrogation of Schaumburg-Lippe, Apr 1947, in Kempner, *Das Dritte Reich im Kreuz-verhör*.

38 Stated by Arnim confidentially to Hans Meier, the last office chief of the ministry's Room 24. She died in Russian captivity. *Der Spiegel*, Jan 24, 1951.

39 Ebermayer and Meissner, No. 26, Jun 28, 1952; their source was Ello Quandt.

40 Diary, Dec 17; and see Wächter's circular No. 150, Dec 19, 1944 (NA film T84, roll 169, 6526ff).

41 Diary, Dec 18, 1944.

42 *Ibid.*, Dec 20, 1944.

43 JG circular to all Reichsleiter and gauleiters, Dec 21, 1944 (NA film T120, roll 2474, E255458).

44 JG to Hitler, Dec 22; similar to Göring, Dec 22, and Göring's reply, Dec 27, 1944 (all in BA file NL.118/106).

45 Behrend, No. 22, May 31, 1952.

46 Interrogations of Maria Kimmich *née* Goebbels and Katharina Goebbels *née* Oden-hausen, Mar 25, 1948 (Hoover Libr., Korf papers).

47 Dittmar diary, Dec 31, 1944 (author's film DI–60).

48 SD Leitabschnitt Stuttgart, morale report, Jan 12, 1945. DE.415/DIS.202 (Hoover Libr., Lerner papers).

49 Bormann to his wife, Jan 2 (Genoud papers; Hugh Trevor-Roper (ed.), *The Bormann Letters* [London, 1954], 158); JG's unpublished. Jan 1945 diary is BA file NL.118/124.

50 Speer, *Erinnerungen*, 427. Those attending the main 3:30 P.M. conference were JG, Speer, Keitel, Bormann, Ganzenmüller, Buhle, and Hitler. Heinz Linge, Hitler's appointments register (NA film T84, roll 387).

51 Of glucose and other substances. Morell's diary, Jan 5, 1945, one P.M., specifically refers to these 'strenuous talks' as the cause.

52 On Mar 30, 1945 the general army office (AHA) noted that by Mar 25 only ninety-five thousand men had been forthcoming (NA film T84, roll 174, 3363ff).

53 Diary, Mar 18, 1945.

54 JG to Hitler, Jan 26, 1945 (BA file NL.118/106).

55 Ditto, Mar 20, 1945 (*ibid.*)

56 Hinkel to JG, Jan 4; Oberregierungsrat Bacmeister to JG, Feb 1, 1945 (BA file R.55/664).

57 Albrecht to his wife, Jan 31, 1945 (IfZ, Irving collection).

58 Bacmeister to JG, Feb 25, 1945 (BA file R.55/664).

Notes to Chapter 57.

1 *E.g.* Heinz Linge, Hitler's appointments register, Jan 24, 25, 27, 28, 29, 31, 1945 (NA film T84, roll 387).

2 Diary, Jan 29; Linge, appointments register, Jan 28, 1945 (NA film T84, roll 387).

3 JG, circular *Propaganda Parole*, Feb 5, 1945. DE.53/DIS.202 (Hoover Libr., Lerner papers).

4 Diary, Jan 1945, passim (BA file NL.118/124).

5 By Zdenko von Kraft, *Alexanderzug: vom Menschen zum Mythos* (Berlin, 1940); JG to Hitler, Jan 10, 1945 (NL.118/107). The passage begins: 'Death, said Philippos [the king's doctor], had already been quite close for the king.'

6 Diary, Jan 14, 1930. That would be Thomas Carlyle, *History of Friedrich II of Prussia, called Frederick the Great* (London, 1872), in ten volumes.

7 Diary, Feb 28, Mar 5, 22, 24, 1945. Published as *Joseph Goebbels, Tagebücher 1945: Die letzten Aufzeichnungen 1945* (Hamburg 1977).

8 Ministerialrat Dr Fries (of Hippler's office) to JG, Dec 12, 1944; with note, 'The Minister has refused.' DE.492/DIS.202 (Hoover Libr., Lerner papers).

9 RMVP air war notice No. 178, Jan 18, 1945 (NA film T84, roll 322, 1469ff).

10 JG (as RPL) circular to all gau propaganda officials, Jan 15, 1945. DE.331/DIS.202 (Hoover Libr., Lerner papers).

11 Freeman, 208.

12 Linge, Hitler's appointments register, Feb 2, 5, 7, 11, 12, 14, 1945 (NA film T84, roll 387).

13 Freybe to Salon Berthe, Feb 1, 1945 (ZStA Potsdam, Rep. 90, Go 2, vol. 2).

14 Magda to Harald Quandt, Feb 10, 1945: facsimile in Behrend, No. 8, Feb 23, 1952.

15 Hanke to his wife, Feb 13, 1945 (Hanke papers; by kind permission of the late Freda Rössler).

16 JG to Streicher, Feb 12, 1945 (ZStA Potsdam, Rep. 90 Go 1, vol. 3).

17 Sündermann, 'Feb 17,' 273; interrogation of Steengracht, CCPWE No. 32, DI–19, Jul 2; and by US State Dept, Sep 4, 1945.

18 A news item in *Basler Zeitung*, Feb 19, 1949. This adds that JG abandoned the plan because the BBC revealed details on Feb 22; at the MinConf. he threatened to strangle with his bare hands the culprit (who had deliberately revealed it to a Swedish journalist).

19 Steengracht's remarks of Jul 2, 1945 in CCPWE No. 32, report X–P.21 (PRO file WO.208/3438).

20 Diary, Mar 30, 1945. On this subject see Ribbentrop, 266f; Jodl to Hitler, Feb 21, 1945 (ND: 606-D) and notes, Jan 15, 1946 (Jodl papers); William Scheidt's notes in *Echo der Woche*, Oct 28, 1949; and the testimonies of Helmut Sündermann, Baron Steengracht, and Hitler's stenographer Ludwig Krieger (IfZ, Irving collection). Kaltenbrunner also claimed credit for thwarting JG, in conversation with Dr Hermann Neubacher. USFET MISC CI-RIR/4, Feb 1, 1946 (NA file RG.407, entry 427, box 1954b).

21 *NYT*, Jun 29, 1946.

22 Diary, Feb 28; Heinz Linge, Hitler's appointments register, Feb 27, 1945 (NA film T84, roll 387).

23 JG speech, Feb 28, in *DAZ*, Berlin, and *NYT*, Mar 1; the *Daily Herald*, London, Mar 1, 1945 headlined its report 'Goebbels pledged to die.'

24 *Ibid.*

25 Remarks overheard on Feb 28, 1945. CSDIC (UK) report GRGG.265. Maj.-Gen. Bruhn was heard telling Lt.-Gen. von Schlieben, 'According to what Goebbels said . . . pure murder is going on in the east of Germany, on a large scale. That's the first I've heard of it. . . One must assume that that's *another* lie. . . I suspect him of possessing so devilish a nature that he upholds all those things which appeal to the soul of the people without acknowledging their application to himself.' Bruhn then described what Lt-Gen. Kittel had told him about mass shootings which the Nazis had carried out in the east (PRO

file WO.208/4177).

26 'Robert Ley as described by his mistress,' SAIC.40, Jun 4, 1945 (NA file RG.165, entry 79, box 756).

27 Diary, Mar 5, 1945.

28 *Ibid*, Mar 8, 1945.

29 Dittmar diary, Feb 27. JG at first accepted Dittmar's script, with its hidden appeal to the western powers in general (Mar 22) and the Americans as the strongest partner in particular (Apr 7); on Apr 10, 1945 however he banned it (author's film DI–60).

30 Diary, Mar 12, 1945.

31 Sündermann, 'Mar 10, 1945,' 303.

32 Diary, Mar 9. JG's speech in *Hamburger Zeitung*, Mar 10, *VB* and *NYT*, Mar 11. The European Political Report, Mar 16, 1945, vol. ii, No. 11, commented: 'German propaganda this week devoted an extraordinary amount of newspaper and radio output to lurid tales of Allied atrocities' (USAMHI, Donovan papers, box 37b).

33 JG, 'Der Zeitpunkt, der die Wende bringt,' in *Das Reich*, Mar 11, 1945.

34 Diary, Mar 13, 1945.

35 Albrecht to his wife, Mar 14; there were no casualties (IfZ, Irving collection); Sündermann, 'Mar 14, 1945,' 309.

36 Diary, Mar 14, 1945.

37 Sündermann, 'Mar 16, 1945,' 310f.

38 Diary, Mar 17; *cf.* Sündermann, 'Mar 18, 1945,' 311f.

39 Diary, Mar 19, 1945.

40 *Ibid*, Mar 21, 1945.

41 *Ibid.*, Mar 30. Magda Goebbels to Zeller (for Hanke), Apr 9, 1945 (ZStA Potsdam, Rep. 90, Go 2, vol. 2).

42 Diary, Mar 22, 1945.

43 Ebermayer and Meissner, No. 26, Jun 28, 1952.

44 Naumann testimony, May 18, 1950 (IfZ file ZS.1134).

45 Hitler's war conference, Mar 23 (Heiber, *Hitlers Lagebesprechungen*); JG diary, Mar 27; Sündermann, 'Mar 24, 1945,' 322.

Notes to Chapter 58.

1 Diary, Apr 1, 1945.

2 *Ibid.*, Mar 27, 1945.

3 *Ibid.*, Mar 30, 1945.

4 *Ibid.*, Apr 1, 1945.

5 *Ibid.*, Mar 30. On this episode see too JG's conversation with Schwerin von Krosigk on Apr 9: Krosigk diary, Apr 13, 1945. USFET document DE.443/DIS.202 (Hoover Libr., Lerner papers; and Trevor-Roper papers, IfZ, Irving collection).

6 Diary, Mar 30, 1945.

7 So he told Krosigk; and see *ibid.*, Mar 24, 1945.

8 *Ibid*, Mar 31, 1945.

9 See *ibid.*, Mar 27. As it was set up under SS Obergruppenführer Hans-Adolf Prützmann, JG refused to have anything to do with it. See the interrogation of SS Obergruppenführer Ohlendorf, Jul 7: CSDIC (UK) report, SRGG.1322. The RMVP had set up its own

'Werwolf' Referat (section) under Hitlerjugend Bannführer (colonel) Dietrich, aged thirty-one, a radical Nazi in Berlin. See US Seventh Army report SAIC/CIR/4, 'Propaganda Organization RMVP and RPL,' Jul 10, 1945 (NA file RG.332, entry ETO, Mis-Y, Sect., box 116).

10 Diary, Mar 31; he had begun plotting Vogelsang's assassination by dependable Berlin Nazis soon after Rheydt was captured. *Ibid.*, Mar 11, 1945.

11 *Ibid.*, Mar 11, 1945.

12 *NYT*, Mar 31. "'It is retribution come home,'" said First Lieut. Joseph Shubow of Boston who presided over the service.' And see *NYT*, Mar 2, 18, 1945.

13 *Cf.* Sündermann, 'Mar 30, 1945,' 328ff.

14 On the dismissal of Guderian: Oven, 'Apr 2, 1945,' and the Guderian papers (IfZ, Irving collection).

15 Diary, Mar 31, 1945.

16 *Ibid.*, Apr 4, 1945.

17 *Ibid.*, Apr 8, 1945.

18 For the preparations of this *Totaleinsatz* see the Koller diary (author's film DI–17); the war diary of the Luftwaffe High Command, entries for Mar 18, Apr 3, 6, 7, 1945 (NA film T321, roll 10); and ADI(K) reports 294/1945 and 373/1945.

19 Diary, Apr 9, 1945 (the final published entry).

20 JG, 'Kämpfer für das ewige Reich,' in *Das Reich*, Apr 8, 1945.

21 Diary, Apr 8, 1945.

22 SS Hauptsturmführer Alfred Rach, interview publ. in *Pinguin* (Rowohlt Verlag, Hamburg), May 1949 (in IfZ archives).

23 Diary, Apr 8, 1945.

24 Rach interview.

25 Bormann's diary, Feb 14, shows Funk discussing with Hitler the evacuation of the precious metal from Berlin. Funk told Ohlendorf afterward that Hitler was 'completely mad' (it was the day after Dresden). CSDIC (UK) report SRGG.1322, Jul 7, 1945.

26 Diary, Apr 9, 1945.

27 Conversation on Apr 9. See Krosigk diary, Apr 13, 1945. USFET document DE.443/DIS.202 (Hoover Libr. Lerner papers; and Trevor-Roper papers, IfZ, Irving collection).

28 By Fritz Hesse. Diary, Mar 17, 18; and Oven, 'Apr 2, 1945.'

29 Oven, 'Apr 12, 1945' and the Krosigk diary.

30 DNB quoted at 00:08 A.M. the BBC news item: BBC monitoring report, Apr 13, 1945 (IWM archives).

31 Heinz Lorenz, interview, Mar 22, 1967; Werner Naumann, testimony, May 18, 1950 (IfZ file ZS.274); and see Frau Inge Haberzettel's statement to Leslie Randall in *Evening Standard*, London, Feb 16, 1946 (Trevor-Roper papers, IfZ, Irving collection). She was a member of JG's office.

Notes to Chapter 59.

1 The remark was provoked by the behavior of the congregation who had chattered during the eulogy at Justice Minister Gürtner's state funeral (diary, Feb 2, 1941).

2 Diary, Mar 30, 1945.

3 *Ibid.*, Jan 16, 1940.

4 'Robert Ley as described by his mistress,' SAIC.40, Jun 4, 1945 (NA file RG.165, entry 79, box 756). Ley had obtained seven envelopes with cyanide crystals from Prof. Bockacker, chief of the Labour Front's health department. And see *NYT*, Oct 27, 1945.

5 Diary, Feb 1; and similar on Feb 2, 1943.

6 Oven, 'Oct 3, 1943;' Willy Krämer, 229.

7 Semler, 'Nov 16, 1943.'

8 JG to Hitler, Jul 18, 1944 (BA file NL.118/107).

9 *E.g.* in JG's speech to officers, Jul 17 or 18, 1943: 'You only have to read the correspondence of Frederick the Great and you'll find that, uh, he, uh, rolled that poison phial to and fro in his pocket, and was strongly tempted to drink that draught' (*VfZ*, 1971, 83ff).

10 Diary, Mar 3, 1945.

11 SS Gruppenführer Gottlob Berger, chief of the SS Hauptamt, remarks on Jun 13, 1945, reported in CSDIC (UK) report SRGG.1299C (PRO file WO.208/4170).

12 Bella Fromm diary, May 6, 1933 (Fromm papers, box 1).

13 Naumann interrogation, Nuremberg, Oct 10, 1947 (IfZ file ZS.361).

14 Hausintendant Rohrssen, aged fifty-nine, had trained at the court of first the Kaiser, and then the Duke of Dessau. Leo Barton to Capt. Smith, G–2, USFET MISC, Mar 12, 1946 (Trevor-Roper papers, IfZ, Irving collection); interview with Gault McGowan, in *New York Sun*, Aug 4, 1947 (Hoover Libr., Julius Epstein papers, box 26). The story reappears in Behrend, No. 22, May 31, 1952.

15 Krosigk diary, Apr 13, 1945. USFET document DE.443/DIS.202 (Hoover Libr., Lerner papers; and Trevor-Roper papers, IfZ, Irving collection).

16 Krosigk to JG, Apr 14, 1945, in PID report No. 34 (Hoover Libr., Lerner papers, box 5).

17 By their ignoble allegation on Jul 3, 1992 that I had stolen items from the Moscow microfiche collection, the Munich institute of contemporary history (IfZ) achieved its premature closure before I could put this theory to the test. See Author's acknowledgments, page xi.

18 Hitler's desk diary, Apr 1945, was found in his bunker's ruins by British Intelligence officers in Sep 1945. It is now in the Cabinet Office Historical Section, London (Transcript in IfZ, Irving collection).

19 Baur, lecture, ca. 1950 (IfZ file ZS.683).

20 JG, 'Der Einsatz des eigenen Lebens,' in *Das Reich*, No. 15, Apr 15, 1945.

21 Oven, 'Apr 19, 1945.'

22 Naumann testimony, May 18, 1950 (IfZ file ZS.274).

23 Oven, 'Apr 18, 1945.'

24 BBC Monitoring Report, Apr 19 (IWM archives); DNB text of broadcast in *Hamburger Zeitung*, No. 92, Apr 20, 1945.

25 US Seventh Army interrogation of Dr Robert Ley, SAIC.30, May 29, 1945 (NA file RG.332, Mis-Y, box 73).

26 *Ibid.*, and Else Krüger (Bormann's secretary) MS, 'Die letzten Tage . . . im Führerbunker der Reichskanzlei,' written in British captivity, Itzehoe, Jul 22, 1945 (Trevor-Roper papers, IfZ, Irving collection).

27 Hans-Leo Martin, 157ff.

28 JG told this to Krosigk on Apr 24. Krosigk diary, Apr 24, 1945. USFET document DE.443/DIS.202 (Hoover Libr., Lerner papers; and Trevor-Roper papers, IfZ, Irving collection). Kritzinger's own report on the evacuation of the ministries is in Jodl's papers, captured in Flensburg (British FO Libr.).

29 From an MS of Fritzsche's 'Notes on Hitler's last days' in the papers of Field Marshal Erhard Milch (IfZ, Irving collection).

30 Otto Günsche, Soviet interrogation (IfZ, Irving collection); and see Koller diary, Apr 21, 1945. ADI(K) report 348/1945, Jul 12, 1945 (*ibid.*; and author's film DI–39).

31 Fritzsche (see note 29 above); Oven, 'Apr 21, 1945,' 650f.

32 Borresholm, 187f.

33 Naumann testimony, May 18, 1950 (IfZ file ZS.274). Dr Schultz von Dratzig of the RMVP's personnel Dept committed suicide that same Saturday.

34 Author's interviews of Curt Gasper, who accompanied the 'burial party,' Jul 1, 1970, and Otte, Mar 31, 1971; Otte was also interviewed by the *Generalanzeiger*, Bonn, Jul 11, 1972: he says they met the rest of the RMVP *Prominenz* in Hamburg's five-star Hotel Atlantic.

35 Frau Inge Haberzettel's statement to Leslie Randall in *Evening Standard*, London, Feb 16, 1946 (Trevor-Roper papers, IfZ, Irving collection).

36 JG, 'Widerstand um jeden Preis,' in *Das Reich*, Apr 22, 1945.

37 The events of Apr 22 are based on the diaries of Koller and Jodl, Apr 22–23; memos of Koller and Lieutenant Volck, Apr 25, 1945; interrogations of Keitel, Jodl, Christian, Freytag von Loringhoven, Below, Bernd von Brauchitsch, and the duty stenographers Hagen and Herrgesell; and the written testimonies of Keitel, Günsche, Linge, Else Krüger, and Traudl Junge (IfZ, Irving collection).

38 Oven, 'Apr 22, 1945;' Magda's silver toilet accessories are much sought-after items on the memorabilia auction circuit.

39 British interrogations of Else Krüger, Sep 19, Mar 27, 1946 (Trevor-Roper papers, IfZ, Irving collection).

40 Jodl told Russian interrogators on Jun 18, 1945 that it was plain to JG that he neither could nor should survive the destruction of the Nazi system. *Wehrwissenschaftliche Rundschau*, 1961, 535ff.

41 *Der Panzer-Bär*, Apr 23, 1945.

42 British interrogation of General Eckhard Christian, Oct 15, 1945 (Trevor-Roper papers, IfZ, Irving collection).

43 Rach, interview publ. in *Pinguin* (Rowohlt Verlag, Hamburg), May 1949 (in IfZ archives); and Behrend, No. 22, May 31, 1952.

44 USFET CIC interrogation of Gertrud (Traudl) Junge, Aug 30, 1946 (Trevor-Roper papers, IfZ, Irving collection).

45 Magda to Harald Quandt, Apr 28, 1945. Interrogation report on Hanna Reitsch, AIU/IS/5, British Intelligence Objectives Sub-Committee, Oct 5, 1946 (Trevor-Roper papers, IfZ, Irving collection).

46 Ebermayer and Meissner, No. 26, Jun 28, 1952.

47 Trevor-Roper's interrogation of Gebhardt, Mar 27, 1946 (Trevor-Roper papers, IfZ, Irving collection); and USFET MISC special interrogation of SS Hauptsturmführer Günther Schwägermann, Jun 20, 1946 (*ibid.*; and NA file RG.332, Mis-Y). Ohlendorf confirmed this in CSDIC (UK) interrogation report SRGG.1322, Jul 7, 1945.

48 BBC Monitoring Report, Apr 23 (IWM archives); for Radio Werewolf's similar bulletin see *NYT*, Apr 24, 1945.

49 News bulletin issued by propaganda officer attached to Army Group Vistula, Apr 23, 1945: war diary, annexes (NA film T311, roll 170, 2211).

50 At 9:29 P.M. EST, America. JG had operated more than thirty powerful transmitters, which dominated the shortwave bands for twelve years and twenty-four days; the

broadcasts to the USA were from 6 p.m. to 1:15 am. each night, featuring the antisemitic Robert Best (once a Press Association stringer in Vienna), Douglas Chandler ('Paul Revere') of Baltimore, Jane Anderson, the wisecracking Edward Delaney, and Donald Day. *NYT*, May 6, 1945.

51 Traudl Junge, unpubl. MS (IfZ, Irving collection).

52 Soviet interrogation of SS Sturmbannführer Helmut Kunz, reproduced in Lev Bezymenski, *Der Tod des Adolf Hitler* (Hamburg, 1968). Kunz, born 1910 in Ettingen, Baden, was in May 1945 adjutant of the chief physician of the SS Health Dept. The physical data on JG's children are extracted from the autopsies reproduced in this book.

53 The Göring telegram and Bormann's handwritten responses were found by a US officer, Capt. John Bradin, in the bunker in Jul 1945 (IfZ, Irving collection).

54 Junge, interrogation, Aug 30, 1946, and MS (IfZ, Irving collection).

55 Heinz Lorenz, verbatim shorthand notes on Hitler's final war conferences, first published in *Der Spiegel*, No. 3, Jan 10, 1966. Authenticated by the author's interview of Lorenz; by a letter of Capt. H Searle of British Intelligence to CI War Room, London, Mar 5, 1946; and by CSDIC (WEA) interrogation of Lorenz, Nov 30, 1945 (Trevor-Roper papers, IfZ, Irving collection).

56 Interrogation report on Hanna Reitsch, AIU/IS/5, British Intelligence Objectives Sub-Committee, Oct 5, 1946 (Trevor-Roper papers, IfZ, Irving collection); and Korf's interrogation of Reitsch, Apr 28, 1945 (Hoover Libr., Korf papers).

57 Diary, Nov 2, 1940.

58 Traudl Junge MS.

59 Magda to Harald Quandt, Apr 28, 1945.

60 Judge Michael A Musmanno's interrogation of Gertrud (Traudl) Junge, Jan 26, 1948 (transcript from Musmanno papers in IfZ, Irving collection).

61 Lorenz, conference transcript, Apr 27, 1945.

62 Soviet interrogation of SS Sturmbannführer Helmut Kunz.

63 Harald Quandt, now twenty-three, was held prisoner by the British in Egypt from Nov 4, 1944 to Mar 10, 1947. He was killed after the war in an automobile accident.

64 JG to Harald Quandt, Apr 28, 1945. Interrogation report on Hanna Reitsch, AIU/IS/5, British Intelligence Objectives Sub-committee, Oct 5, 1946 (Trevor-Roper papers, IfZ, Irving collection).

65 BBC Monitoring Report, Apr 28, 1945, 1:55 p.m. (IWM archives).

66 USFET MISC special interrogation of SS Hauptsturmführer Günther Schwägermann, Jun 20, 1946 (NA file RG.332, Mis-Y; and Trevor-Roper papers, IfZ, Irving collection).

67 USFET special interrogation of Gerda Christian, Apr 25, 1946 (Trevor-Roper papers, IfZ, Irving collection; and NA file RG.319, IRR, XE.009487); and BAOR interrogation of Nicolaus von Below, Jan 23, 1946 (*ibid.*; and NA file RG.332, Mis-Y).

68 Adolf Hitler, political testament, Apr 28, 1945 (Hoover Libr., special collection).

69 This was Gau-Inspekteur Walther Wagner. BAOR interrogation of Nicolaus von Below, Jan 23, 1946 (NA file RG.332, Mis-Y; and Trevor-Roper papers, IfZ, Irving collection).

70 USFET CIC interrogation of Gertrud (Traudl) Junge, Aug 30, 1946 (Trevor-Roper papers, IfZ, Irving collection).

71 The original wedding certificate, Apr 29, 1945, is in the Hoover Libr., special collection.

72 British interrogation of Else Krüger, Sep 25, 1945, and USFET interrogation of Gertrud Junge, Aug 30, 1946 (Trevor-Roper papers, IfZ, Irving collection).

73 USFET special interrogation of Gerda Christian, Apr 25, 1946 (Trevor-Roper papers, IfZ,

Irving collection; and NA file RG.319, IRR, XE.009487).

74 USFET CIC interrogation of Gertrud Junge, Aug 30, 1946 (Trevor-Roper papers, IfZ, Irving collection). Gen. Wilhelm Burgdorf wrote to Schörner on Apr 29, 1945 enclosing Hitler's political testament and confirming that 'he wrote it today after the crushing news of the Reichsführer's act of disloyalty.'

75 Diary, Feb 28, Mar 14, 21, 22, 1945.

76 USFET CIC interrogation of Gertrud Junge, Aug 30, 1946 (Trevor-Roper papers, IfZ, Irving collection); and Junge MS.

77 *Cf.* BBC Monitoring Report, Apr 29, 1945 (IWM archives).

78 *Der Spiegel*, Jan 24, 1951.

79 CSDIC (WEA) interrogation of Heinz Lorenz, Nov 30, 1945 (Trevor-Roper papers, IfZ, Irving collection).

80 Walter Rapp, interrogation of Axmann, Oct 16, 1947 (Trevor-Roper papers, IfZ, Irving collection); author's interview of Axmann, May 7, 1991.

81 USFET CIC interrogation of Gertrud Junge, Aug 30, 1946 (Trevor-Roper papers, IfZ, Irving collection); and Junge MS.

82 Author's interview of Otto Günsche, Mar 20, 1967; report by headquarters tailor Willi Müller, Nov 9, 1945 (NA file RG.319, IRR, XE.009487).

Notes to Epilogue.

1 Author's interview of Günsche, and letter, Oct 16, 1968; and statement by Erich Kempka, chauffeur, on Hitler's last days, Berchtesgaden, Jun 20, 1945 (Pennsylvania Univ. Libr., No. 46M–15).

2 USFET MISC special interrogation of SS Hauptsturmführer Günter Schwägermann, Jun 20, 1946 (NA file RG.332, Mis-Y; and Trevor-Roper papers, IfZ, Irving collection).

3 Interrogation of Axmann, Apr 27, 1948 (Hoover Libr., Korf papers).

4 USFET special interrogation of Gerda Christian, Apr 25, 1946 (Trevor-Roper papers, IfZ, Irving collection; and NA file RG.319, IRR, XE.009487).

5 The Krebs–Chuikov–JG negotiations are well researched in Erich Kuby, *Die Russen in Berlin 1945* (Munich, 1965); *Der Spiegel*, No. 24, 1965; there is further detail on them in Bezymenski, *op. cit.* On Krebs, formally Chef der Führungsgruppe des Generalstabs des Heeres, see CSDIC (UK) report SIR.1593, Apr 1, 1945. On May 12, 1945 'Franz' stated that 'Pfiffi' Krebs spoke fluent Russian and 'has been received by Stalin personally umpteen times' (CSDIC (UK) report, GRGG.292).

6 British interrogations of Else Krüger Sep 19, 1945 and Mar 27, 1946 (Trevor-Roper papers, IfZ, Irving collection).

7 Statement by Erich Kempka, chauffeur, on Hitler's last days, Berchtesgaden, Jun 20, 1945 (Pennsylvania Univ. Libr., No. 46M–15); SS Brigadeführer Johann Rattenhuber, chief of Hitler's security, told Hugh Trevor-Roper on Oct 30, 1955 that SS Sturmbannführer Franz Schädle had buried the bodies of Hitler and Eva Braun (IfZ file ZS.637). Schädle, injured in one foot, killed himself soon after.

8 Axmann.

9 Kempka.

10 USFET CIC interrogation of Gertrud Junge, Aug 30, 1946 (Trevor-Roper papers, IfZ, Irving collection).

11 Originals and code-strips of these telegrams are in BA file R.62/8, and see NA film T77,

roll 867. *Cf.* Walther Lüdde-Neurath, *Regierung Dönitz. Die letzten Tage des Dritten Reiches* (Göttingen, 1964), 130.

12 The clothing was listed in the Soviet autopsy report on JG, May 9, 1945; Bezymenski, 111ff.

13 Else Krüger, cited by Associated Press, Jun 1, 1946, and British interrogations of Sep 19, 1945 and Mar 27, 1946 (Trevor-Roper papers, IfZ, Irving collection); USFET special interrogation of Gerda Christian, Apr 25, 1946 (*ibid.*; and NA file RG.319, IRR, XE.009487).

14 Interview of Axmann, May 7, 1991.

15 JG to Dönitz, May 1, 1945, received 3:18 P.M. Dönitz's file copy is in BA file R.62/8, and see PRO file FO.371/46914.

16 British interrogations of Else Krüger Sep 19, 1945 and Mar 27, 1946 (Trevor-Roper papers, IfZ, Irving collection); and statement of General Antonov, commanding 301st Guards division, publ. in *Der Spiegel*, No. 24, 1965.

17 Soviet interrogation of SS Sturmbannführer Helmut Kunz, May 7, 1945. Hans Bauer, in *Ich flog Mächtige der Erde* (Kempten, 1956), 273, wrote that Magda had told him she had selected a dentist to give her children the fatal injections.

18 At the time that Gerda Christian left, 5 P.M., the children were dead but JG still alive.

19 Soviet interrogation of SS Sturmbannführer Helmut Kunz.

20 Bezymenski published the autopsy reports (with details of the night-dresses, etc.).

21 In his first interrogation Kunz was less specific than in his second (on May 19) about Stumpfegger's role as the actual killer, not wanting to incriminate him; Stumpfegger had however killed himself on May 2, 1945 (the next day). An indirect version of Kunz's testimony was given by Soviet colonel Ivan Klimenko, who interrogated him, in *Der Spiegel*, No. 19, May 5, 1965.

22 Autopsy report on Hellmut.

23 Heinz Linge, interrogated at Hamburg magistrates' court, May 31, 1956 (IfZ file F82, Heiber papers).

24 SS Hauptsturmführer Alfred Rach, interview publ. in *Pinguin* (Rowohlt Verlag, Hamburg) May 1949 (in IfZ archives).

25 Statement by Erich Kempka, chauffeur, on Hitler's last days, Berchtesgaden, Jun 20, 1945 (Pennsylvania Univ. Libr., No. 46M–15); USFET CIC interrogation of Gertrud Junge, Aug 30, 1946 (Trevor-Roper papers, IfZ, Irving collection); and USFET special interrogation of Gerda Christian, Apr 25, 1946 (*ibid.*; and NA file RG.319, IRR, XE.009487).

26 USFET MISC special interrogation of SS Hauptsturmführer Günther Schwägermann, Jun 20, 1946 (NA file RG.332, Mis-Y; and Trevor-Roper papers, IfZ, Irving collection).

27 Korf interrogation of Axmann, Apr 27 (Hoover Libr., Korf papers); and Nuremberg interrogation of Naumann, Oct 10, 1947 (IfZ file ZS.361).

28 Fritzsche is certain about the time. Interrogation of Sep 17, 1946 (StA. Nuremberg, F86).

29 USFET MISC special interrogation of SS Hauptsturmführer Günther Schwägermann, Jun 20, 1946 (NA file RG.332, Mis-Y; and Trevor-Roper papers, IfZ, Irving collection); and testimony of Feb 16, 1948 (IfZ file F82, Heiber papers).

30 Bezymenski later admitted to this author that he had faked parts of the autopsies which he published, *inter alia* to conceal that Hitler *had* shot himself.

31 The photos of JG's corpse being viewed by Klimenko appear to show a bullet wound in the right neck. Schwägermann told Kempka (*Ich habe Adolf Hitler verbrannt* [Munich, 1948], 127) that JG shot himself, and Magda took poison.

32 In fact, this is known to pathologists as the 'pugilist' position, common in fire victims in

consequence of the shrinking and tautening of muscles in the heat.

Abbreviations used in Notes

AA	*Auswärtiges Amt*: Reich foreign ministry
ADI(K)	British Air Ministry's Assistant Directorate of Intelligence: interrogation and captured documents section
AL	File numbers assigned by CO Enemy Documents Sections; documents now in IWM
ARP	Air Raid Precautions
BA	Bundesarchiv: German federal archives
BAOR	British Army on the Rhine
BDC	Berlin Document Center (of U.S. Mission, Berlin)
–C	A Nuremberg Document Series (*e.g.* 100–C)
CAB	Cabinet File (in the PRO)
CCPWE	U.S. Army Interrogation series (now in NA)
CIC	Counter Intelligence Corps of the U.S. Army
CIR	Consolidated Interrogation Report (U.S. Army)
CO	Cabinet Office file
CSDIC	Combined Services Detailed Interrogation Center
D–	A Nuremberg document series
DAZ	*Deutsche Allgemeine Zeitung*
DBFP	Documents on British Foreign Policy
DDI	*Documenti Diplomatici Italiani*
DGFP	Documents on German Foreign Policy
DI–	Film in author's personal microfilm collection (see page ix)
DIC	Detailed Interrogation Center (see CSDIC)
DIS	Detailed Interrogation Summary (US Army)
DNB	Deutsches Nachrichten-Büro
EC–	A Nuremberg Document series
ED–	*Einzeldokument*, an IfZ document series
F–	An IfZ document series
FA	*Forschungsamt*: literally Research Office: Göring's wiretap agency
FAZ	*Frankfurter Allgemeine Zeitung*
FCC	Federal Communications Commission
FD–	Foreign Documents, a British series of unpublished captured documents, held by the IWM
FDR	Franklin D Roosevelt

FIR	Final Interrogation Report (U.S. Army Interrogation)
FO	Foreign Office, London
FRUS	Foreign Relations of the United States
G–	A file in the Yivo archives, New York
GB–	British documentary exhibit at Nuremberg
GRGG	CSDIC document series
II H–	German army file, in BA, Freiburg
IfZ	Institut fur Zeitgeschichte: Institute of Contemporary History, Munich
IIR	Interim Interrogation Report (U.S. Army interrogation)
IMT	International Military Tribunal: Trial of the Major German War Criminals at Nuremberg
IWM	Imperial War Museum, London
JG	Joseph Goebbels
Kl. Erw.	*Kleine Erwerbung*, a minor accession by BA Koblenz
L–	A Nuremberg document series
46–M	Interrogations at Berchtesgaden, 1945, now in the library of the University of Pennsylvania
MA–	IfZ microfilm series
MD	Milch Documents, original RLM files now restituted by the British government to BA, Freiburg; microfilms of which are available from the NA and the IWM
MGFA	*Militärgeschichtliches Forschungsamt*: German defense ministry historical research section in Freiburg
MI	Military Intelligence branch (British)
MISC	Military Intelligence Service Center (U.S. Army interrogations)
ML–	NA microfilm service
MNN	*Münchner Neueste Nachrichten*
MS	Unpublished manuscript or typescript
NL	*Nachlass*, the papers of a German personage, now held by BA
NA	U.S. National Archives, Washington, DC; now at College Park, Maryland
ND	Nuremberg Document
NG–	A Nuremberg document series
NO–	A Nuremberg document series
NOKW–	A Nuremberg document series
NS	Collection of Nazi documents in BA Koblenz; e.g. NS.10
NSDAP	*Nationalsozialistische Deutsche Arbeiterpartei*
NYT	*New York Times*
OCMH	Office of the Chief of Military History, Washington, DC
OKW	*Oberkommando der Wehrmacht*
OMGUS	Office of Military Government of the United States
O.Qu.	*Oberquartiermeister*, Quartermaster
OWI	Office of War Information

OSS	Office of Strategic Services
PG	Files of German admiralty, now held by BA Freiburg
PID	Political Intelligence Division of the FO
PRO	Public Record Office, London (now U.K. "National Archives")
–PS	A Nuremberg document series
PSF	President's Safe File, in FDR Library
PWE	Political Warfare Executive
R–	A Nuremberg document series (*e.g.* R–100)
RG	Record Group
RGBl.	*Reichsgesetzblatt*
RLM	*Reichsluftfahrtministerium*: Reich air ministry
RIR	Reinterrogation Report (U.S. Army)
RMVP	Reichsministerium für Volksaufklärung und Propaganda: propaganda ministry
RPA	*Reichspropagandaamt*
RPL	*Reichspropagandaleitung*
RSHA	*Reichssicherheitshauptamt*
SA	*Sturmabteilung*
SAIC	U.S. Seventh Army interrogation
SD	*Sicherheitsdienst*
SIR	CSDIC document series
SRGG	CSDIC document series
SS	*Schutzstaffel*
StA	*Staatsarchiv*
T	NA microfilm series, *e.g.* T78 refers to Microcopy T78.
USAMHI	U.S. Army Military History Institute (Carlisle, Pennsylvania)
USFET	U.S. Forces, European Theatre
USSBS	U.S. Strategic Bombing Survey
VB	*Völkischer Beobachter*
VfZ	*Vierteljahrshefte für Zeitgeschichte*, quarterly published by IfZ
X–	OCMH document series, now in NA
X–P	DIC interrogation series (prisoner's conversations recorded by hidden microphones, as at CSDIC)
YIVO	Yivo Archives for Jewish research (New York, NY)
ZS	*Zeugenschrift*: collection by IfZ of written and oral testimonies
ZSg	*Zeitschriftensammlung*: newspaper cuttings collection in BA, Koblenz
ZStA	Staatsarchiv (Potsdam, Germany); former East German archives, whose records have now been taken over by the BA

APPENDIX: *Janke, Arlosorov, and Friedländer*

SINCE THIS BOOK WAS FIRST PUBLISHED in 1996, more details have emerged about three people of Jewish blood whose orbits intersected briefly with that of Joseph Goebbels – an early girlfriend, Else Janke; and one of the earlier lovers of his wife Magda, Victor Arlosorov; and her stepfather, Richard Friedländer.

Else Janke, whom we first met on page 18, was a school teacher and orphan; she taught at a local school in Rheydt, his home town. It was she who found him the job in a bank in Cologne, starting in January 1923. Their friendship lasted from September 1922 until September 1926. Like the private papers of Ilse Stahl, Janke's letters and papers have now surfaced in the American auction market – in Bridgeport, West Virginia, a total of sixty-six pages of letters and three postcards all immaculately penned by Joseph Goebbels and signed a usual by him as 'ULEX.' The first letter concluded with two bars of music; most were lengthy and occasionally included poems too. In fact he sent to Else a thirty-two page exercise book of handwritten poems dedicated to her, and a number of early postcard photographs of himself; the collection also included snapshots of Else with her friends, and one of the couple boating on the Frisian island of Baltrum in 1923 (see our page 19).

She was however half-Jewish, which eventually brought the affair to an end. Else quarreled with him 'about the race question' in 1923, and chided him in a letter: 'I couldn't shake it from my thoughts and really very nearly saw in the problem an obstacle to our continued life together.' She married another in 1933, and it was her son Carl who sold these papers. In documents accompanying them, Carl put a spin on them which should be viewed with a caution appropriate to modern times. According to Carl, it was his mother who broke off the engagement after reading Hitler's *Mein Kampf*, published in 1925–26. 'If my mother had been alive now,' she allegedly told Goebbels, 'You and your guys would have killed her if you ever came to power.' So said Carl, years after the war. Be that as it may, he also claimed that his family used the letters as leverage to keep her family safe.

Else's husband wanted to emigrate to the United States, but she did not. Carl claims that she threatened Goebbels, 'I'll present all your letters to a publisher in America and there will be laughter around the world that a big anti-Semite was engaged to a half-Jewish girl.' For whatever the reason – and it has to be

696

said that Goebbels was not one easily leveraged even in such circumstances, as the Friedländer case below will illustrate – Else retained these letters and the booklet of poems, and told her son about them only later.

The auctioned papers included a photocopy of Else's German Reich identity card in her married name, stamped by a Berlin police official in 1940. Her husband eventually obtained a position with the Reichsfilmkammer, the Reich Movie Chamber, which controlled the film industry in Germany.

AS FOR MAGDA'S FRIEND Lisa Arlosorov (page 114) her brother **Chaim Arlosorov** became quite famous in Zionist history: While attending the Kollmorgen Lycée in Berlin in about 1918, Magda had struck up a friendship with a family of Ukrainian Jewish émigrés, and she started dating Lisa's brother Vitaly, a Zionist fanatic. Born in the Ukraine in 1899, Vitaly was two years older than Magda. She became fascinated with the Jewish religion, sometimes wore a Star of David pendant, and attended a few Zionist meetings. In 1920 however she left Berlin to study in Goslar, the affair ended, and she eventually married the wealthy Günther Quandt in 1921.

Vitaly Arlosorov adopted the name Victor in Germany. He emigrated to Palestine in 1924, and as Chaim Arlosorov rose fast in the Zionist movement there. He was their representative during the Zionist honeymoon with the Nazis; their aims were broadly similar. As head of the political directorate of the Jewish Agency in Palestine, and a close friend of the legendary Chaim Weizmann, he conducted the Berlin negotiations with the new Nazi government in 1933. After arriving in Berlin for that purpose in May of that year he had, as he wrote to his sister Lisa, an unexpected *déjà vu*. In a store window he saw a wedding picture of Joseph Goebbels with his new bride, and recognized 'his' Magda. He phoned her to seek an appointment with the new propaganda minister, Joseph Goebbels; Magda however had moved on, and she told him that she did not want to speak to, or even see, him any more. The Berlin negotiations led to the successful Ha'avara Agreement (finalized that August), which permitted rich Jews emigrating to Palestine to transfer a large part of their fortunes to Palestine, using a special banking mechanism.

On June 16, 1933, two days after his return from Nazi Berlin to the more violent political world of Middle-East Zionism, Arlosorov was murdered by two gunmen while walking with his wife on the beach at Tel Aviv. The killers were evidently Revisionist Zionists of the rival Jabotinsky movement.

GOEBBELS HAD NOT become involved with Magda Quandt until 1931, when she started working at the gau archives in Berlin (our page 113). She had been born on November 11, 1901, the illegitimate daughter of the servant girl Auguste Behrend and an engineer, Oscar Ritschel.

Ritschel at first disavowed paternity. Magda's mother started an affair soon after with **Richard Friedländer**, a Jewish leather-goods manufacturer. According to Viktor Reimann's 1976 book *Goebbels: The Man Who Created*

Hitler Auguste stayed with Friedländer from 1904 to 1920. He moved from Belgium to Berlin and latterly worked there as an underpaid waiter. When the wealthy industrialist Günter Quandt married Magda in 1921, he obliged her to enter the protestant Ritschel's name on the marriage certificate as her father rather than the Jewish Friedländer's.

There is no evidence that either Ritschel or Friedländer actually married Magda's mother, and we may suspect from the way that Auguste (the mother) skirted the issue in her tabloid memoirs that she did not.

Very little was at first known about Richard Friedländer after World War II, not even his first name. We asked the late historian Prof. Klaus Herrmann (a Jewish expert at Montreal University) to investigate the Friedländer case in Berlin, and he went through all the Friedländers in the *Sigilla Veri* but drew a blank, finding no trace of him in Berlin Jewish circles before or after the war.

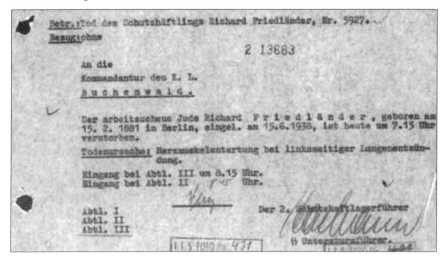

Friedländer did however produce other offspring, and his grandson, Michael Tutsch related in a German ZDF television broadcast in May 2001 that Goebbels had once refused to see his grandfather.

Rather startling facts have more recently emerged about Friedländer. Assuming that there is no confusion over identities, Richard Friedländer, the stepfather of Magda Goebbels, was among the Berlin Jews who were picked up on various pretexts on June 15, 1938, at the start of Goebbels' first pogrom (see page 252). He was imprisoned in Buchenwald concentration camp as a 'work-shy Jew.' There he died a few months later, on February 18, 1939, of pneumonia and heart failure, according to the death certificate reproduced above. There is no hint of this in the Goebbels Diaries.

Index

Boer War, pg 324.

315,

221; criminal activities 46–7, 547(n.24, 29); demonstrations against 273–8; deportation from Hungary 462, 674(n.76); deportation plans 337–8, 369, 374; deportation to east 377, 386–7, 388–9, 392, 402–3; deportees' assets 395, 691 (n.16); discrimination against musicians 165; dominance in movie industry 73; economic measures against 281–2, 615(n.78); enter Berlin 207; eviction from homes 370–2; exclusion from cultural life 228, 251; expelled from Berlin 377, 378, 644(n.13), 645(n.31); forebodings about JG 162; foreign press reports 159, 163; harassment in Berlin 251–3, 606(n.64, 67), 606(n.72); link with Katyn 430, 664(n.23); liquidated in Latvia 378, 379, 646(n.43); liquidated in Lithuania 377–8, 644(n.21), 645(n.23, 24); liquidated in Minsk 377, 644(n.16); Lithuanian, deported to Siberia 377, 644(n.22); manhunt in Berlin 426–7; numbers in German dominions 370; numbers in German professions 163–5, 175, 577(n.40); Nuremburg laws 207–8; Poles repatriated by Nazis 272, 612(n.15); power in Berlin 46; rations 402–3; refugees interned 334; sent to concentration camps 252, 277, 403, 426, 431; skilled workers exempt from deportation 403, 654(n.21); treatment in Poland 337; US boycott of German films 228, 598(n.61); working in industry 371; worldwide condemnation of Nazis 402; yellow star badges 371, 373–4, 642(n.79); *see also* Goebbels, Dr Joseph, antisemitism

Jodl, General 374–5, 380, 646(n.50); defense of Berlin 519, 520, 689(n.40); lecture 448

Jordan, Rudolf 274

journalism, Jews exclusion 171

journalists: international: in Danzig 297, 620(n.46); foreign press club 326, 627(n.8); JG invasion hints 355; reports of SA executions 192

see also newspapers; press

Joyce, William (Lord Haw-Haw) 329, 334, 338, 397

Judas Iscariot (Goebbels) 7, 8, 539(n.30)

Jud Süss movie 369

'Judenpresse' 46, 49, 50; fawn on Strasser 149; reports on Kütemeyer 72; reports of Nazi feuds 52

Jugo, Jenny 204, 205

Juliana, Princess, marriage 240, 602(n.53)

Jung, Edgar 186, 585(n.98); murdered 190, 191

Junge, Gertrud (Traudl) 519, 520, 522, 523, 527; Hitler's testament 525–6, 529

K

Kaiser, JG's manservant 220, 231, 267, 595(n.30)

Kaiserhof hotel, Hitler's court at 131

Kaiserhof diaries 157, 158, 183

Kaltenbrunner, Ernst 475, 482, 483

Kammer, Lucie 98

Kammler, Hans 485

Kampf Verlag publishers 43; anti-JG articles 53; decree against 98

Kampmann, Karoly, 127; 1932 election campaign 137, 138; made *Angriff* editor 150; on transport strike 147

Kasper, Wilhelm 333; broadcasts to Soviets 367

Kassel, air raids 447

Katyn, retaken by Red Army 447

Katyn massacre 429, 663(n.7, 11), 664(n.47); discovery by Germans 429–30; Soviets claim Nazi guilt 447

Kaufman, Theodore 404; *Germany Must Perish* 369, 372–3, 374, 640–1(n.36, 38)

Kaufmann, Karl 18, 26–7, 28, 30, 37, 45, 88, 440, 442; friendship with JG 27–8, 32; sole gauleiter 38

Keitel, General Wilhelm 445, 479; defense of Berlin 519, 520; ready for attack on Poland 306

Kern, Walter 103 .

Kesselring, Field Marshal 508

King-Hall, Commander Stephen, letters 299–300

Klausener, Erich 190, 194

Klimenko, Ivan Isiavich xxi–xxii

Klitzsch, Dr Ludwig 171

Kluge, Field Marshal Günther Hans: implicated in bomb plot 482, 680(n.30); suicide 484

Knickerbocker, H R 141

Knickmann, Ludwig 35

Koch, Erich 27, 38, 57, 400, 483; article on mixed race 53–4

Koch, Hella 109, 563(n.18)

Kolberg movie 437–8, 498

Kölsch, Agnes 6

Kölsch, Hermann 6

Kölsch, Karlheinz (Pille) 6, 10; marriage 68; meets JG at university 5; rival for Anka Stalherm 6–7, 8; thrown out of Unitas 8

Kölsch, Liesel 6

Koniev, Marshal Ivan, battle for Berlin 516

Körber, Hilde 244, 249, 259, 266, 295, 603(n.86)

Korff, Major Martin, ordered to arrest JG 474, 677(n.25)

Körner, Paul, evidence against Röhm 188, 585(n.3)

Kortzfleisch, General Joachim von 476, 477

Krafft, Karl-Ernst 323

Krage, Lene 4–5

Krebs, Albert 31, 75

Conflicting Views
Goebbels: Mastermind of the Third Reich

"THIS IS A REPELLENT book, and not only because of its subject. Irving (*Göring*) has been increasingly under fire for exploiting seemingly indefatigable research to distort history. In the book in hand, he uses enough pejoratives to sustain the illusion of objectivity regarding Hitler's propaganda chief, yet suggests that the admittedly bad man had a cause not entirely bad in itself. Nazi brutality is almost always retaliation for the plots of international Jewry and the criminality of domestic Jews.

"Even the books notoriously burned are 'decadent and anti-German.' The term *Redakteur* (editor) 'to Goebbels' sensitive ear had a Jewish ring.' Protesters in Saarbrücken are 'a clamoring ragbag of communists, Jews, freemasons, and disgruntled émigrés.' There is always, in Irving's own words, a 'Jewish problem' that Goebbels struggles to solve. Much of the book, heavily indebted to the selfserving Goebbels diaries, is in such a vein. . . .

"The real insidiousness of the biography is that its formidable documentation will gain it acceptance as history."
— Anonymous, *Publishers Weekly*, New York

"SILENCING MR IRVING WOULD BE a high price to pay for freedom from the annoyance that he causes us. The fact is that he knows more about National Socialism than most professional scholars in his field, and students of the years 1933–1945 owe more than they are always willing to admit to his energy as a researcher and

to the scope and vigor of his publications. . . There is nothing absolute about historical truth. What we consider as such is only an estimation, based upon what the best available evidence tells us. It must constantly be tested against new information and new interpretations that appear, however implausible they may be, or it will lose its vitality and degenerate into dogma or shibboleth. Such people as David Irving, then, have an indispensable part in the historical enterprise, and we dare not disregard their views."
— Professor Gordon C Craig, *The New York Review of Books*

"IRVING ATTRACTS CREDIBILITY and attention by his indefatigable energy, intelligence and resourcefulness. Compared with most British historians, often a dull, lazy breed, Irving has spent a lifetime ceaselessly criss-crossing the globe to gather eyewitness evidence about World War II."
— Tom Bower, *The Daily Mail*, London

"HE IS THE FIRST to use Goebbels' full diary, 75,000 pages, recently found in Moscow. . . . Irving's trademark research into original manuscripts is uniquely impressive."
— George Stern, *The Literary Review*, London

"THESE DIARIES HAVE long been known in part, but the complete text was only recently identified in the Moscow archives, and Mr Irving is the first writer to use them. For this, and for his archival research generally, he deserves every credit."
— Prof. Hugh Trevor-Roper, *The Sunday Telegraph*, London

"DAVID IRVING KNOWS MORE than anyone alive about the German side of the Second World War. He discovers archives unknown to official historians and turns their contents into densely footnoted narratives that consistently provoke controversy. . . His greatest achievement is *Hitler's War*, which has been described as the 'autobiography the Führer did not write' and is indispensable to anyone seeking to understand the war in the round."
— Sir John Keegan, *The Daily Telegraph*, London

F

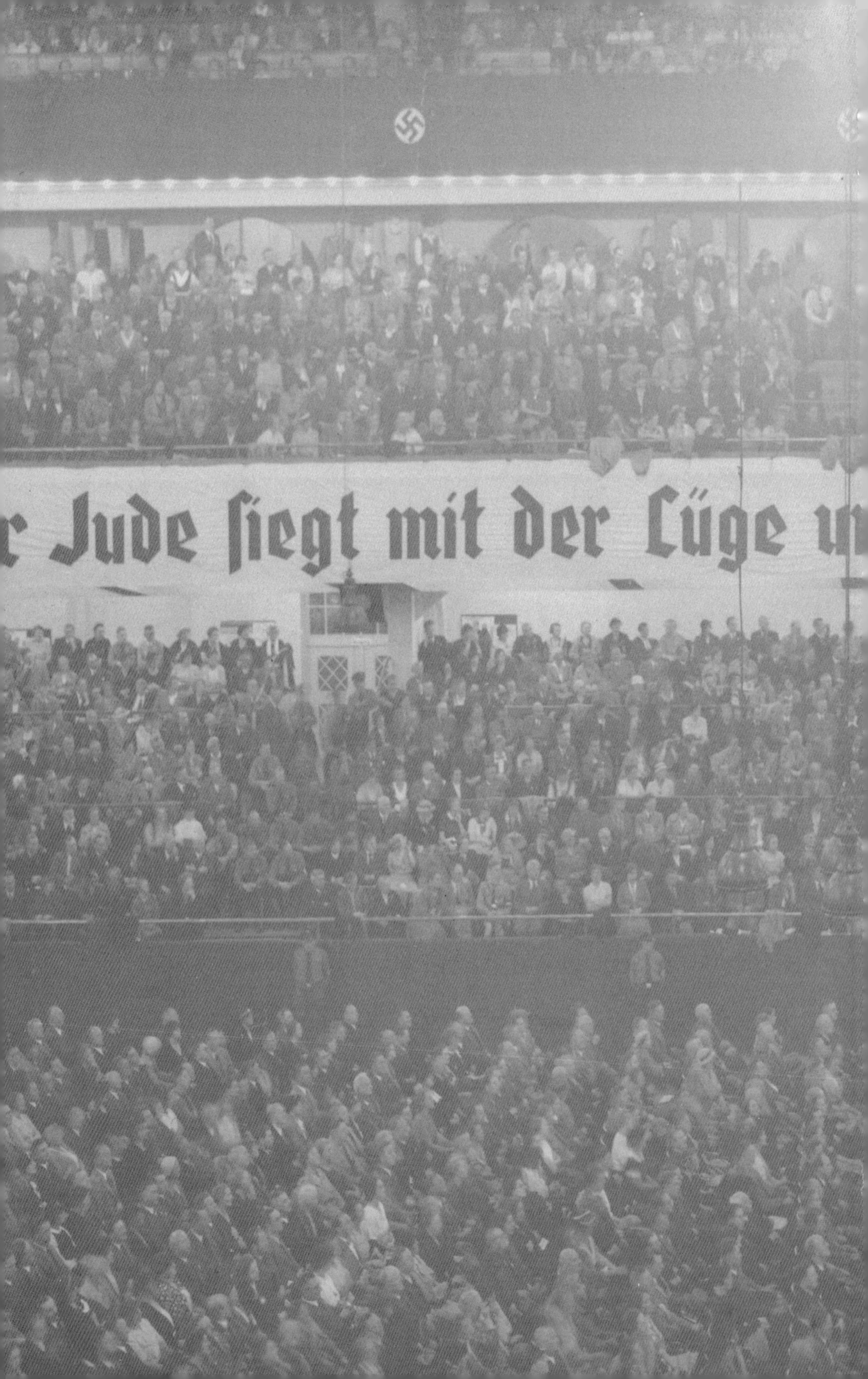
r Jude siegt mit der Lüge u